An Anthology of World Poetry

Edited by Mark Van Doren

IN ENGLISH TRANSLATIONS BY
CHAUCER, SWINBURNE, DOWSON, SYMONS, ROSSETTI,
WALEY, HERRICK, POPE, FRANCIS THOMPSON
E. A. ROBINSON AND OTHERS

Revised and Enlarged Edition

REYNAL & HITCHCOCK
New York

PRINTED AND BOUND BY THE CORNWALL PRESS, INC., FOR
REYNAL & HITCHCOCK, 386 FOURTH AVE., NEW YORK CITY
Printed in the United States of America

TO

THE MEMORY OF

JOHN DRYDEN

POET AND TRANSLATOR

PREFACE

The scope of this anthology is so wide—in time from the thirty-fifth century B.C. to the twentieth century A.D. and in space from China and Japan around through India, Persia, Arabia, Palestine, Egypt, Greece, and Rome to Europe and America—that there is no poet in human history who might not have found a place in it had he ever fallen into the hands of a becoming translator. Not all the poets, of course, are here. The book, big as it is, would have been still bigger had I found more material exactly suited to my purpose, which was to provide a collection revealing those riches of the world's poetry thus far gathered into readable English.

For my purpose was not to "represent" these various poetical literatures. My experience with previous collections which have attempted to do such a thing for "The Poets and Poetry of Europe," "The Poets and Poetry of Greece and Rome," and so on has convinced me that nothing is deadlier than a compilation designed with reference to the originals alone. This is an anthology of the world's best poetry in the best English I could unearth, and when I found no good English at all I left the poet out. Pindar, for instance, is absent from these pages not because I was unwilling to accept his great reputation but because I discovered no English version of him which made him seem great—or even, for that matter, readable. Hence also some apparent oddities in the proportions observed, certain minor poets receiving, it would seem, more than their due of space at the expense of ampler figures let off with very little. I simply went by what I found, preferring, if I had to be representative at all, to represent the present state of English translation in these cases, and considering that there might be some interest in the fact that a minor Frenchman, say, had been given more attention in our language than a major Persian or Russian.

Homer is not here because I decided to exclude parts of long narrative poems, and indeed never—though I broke the rule in a few inconspicuous instances—to offer abridgements. Virgil, Dante, Firdawsi, and Kalidasa appear only through their shorter works; and Goethe, like the Greek tragic dramatists, is represented in his masterpiece solely by lyrics which may be said to stand alone. I might add at this point that I have confined myself to translations in verse. Much good work has been done in prose, but for various reasons I disregarded it.

If the book does after all fairly represent the poetry of the world, and I am sanguine enough to think that it does on a scale not hitherto attempted, the credit goes to a race of translators which runs back at least as far as Chaucer. The index of their names at the end of the volume is almost a list of the best British and American poets, and indeed an interesting comparison might be made between that index and the succession of names to be found under the last three headings in the table of contents, where it will be seen that I have assembled, in order to make good my title, an anthology of original poems in the English language.

That this comparison should be extended to the poetry itself I do not suggest, since I am as much convinced as anybody that translation does not give us what creation gives. Yet I finish the anthology in the faith that it spreads a rich and beautiful feast, and in doing so I must yield to the temptation to point out some of the better and longer things—some of them hitherto not generally accessible—that are here provided. FitzGerald's Omar Khayyam and the Song of Songs take their places as a matter of course; but Lafcadio Hearn's The River of Heaven from the Manyō Shū, E. Powys Mathers's Black Marigolds from Bilhana, Lady Anne Blunt's and Wilfrid Scawen Blunt's Ode from Imr El Kais, Robert Hillyer's twenty-seven prayers from the Egyptian Book of the Dead, Thomas Stanley's Vigil of Venus, and Rossetti's New Life from Dante were not matters of course, and I should be happy if this volume helped to make them as widely known as they deserve to be. I am further tempted to speak of certain famous English poems which will introduce themselves to some readers now for the first time, perhaps, as translations. But I will resist that temptation and leave the pleasure of discovery to those readers.

I trust the volume will be easy to use. Towards that end I have made the table of contents complete and have supplied full indexes. The arrangement is by countries, or rather by languages, and within each section the order of poets is chronological, the name of the translator being given at the end of each poem in parentheses. Occasionally I have prefixed a note to a poet's work in its proper place, not so much to give information about that poet as to suggest his quality and to make him stand out. Further than that there is no apparatus. The poetry is expected to speak for itself. The things which might be said about all these poets are so numerous, and sometimes so difficult to say, that no one I like to think could have said them in the space available.

Horace, Catullus, Heine, Hafiz, Sappho, and others are each rendered by various—perhaps too various—hands. There would have been an advantage in presenting a single poet through a single translator, but on the whole I preferred variety, and I found the comparison of methods an engaging game. As usual, too, I was interested only in what seemed to me the best versions, and was content to take them from as many sources as might be.

I have much courteous assistance to acknowledge in another place, but wish to make particular mention now of the kindness of William Ellery Leonard, Max Eastman, and Allen Tate in giving me unpublished material for my collection. To Ludwig Lewisohn, E. Powys Mathers, Robert Hillyer, Jethro Bithell, Howard Mumford Jones, Ezra Pound, Havelock Ellis, Ford Madox Ford, A. E. Housman, and Louis Untermeyer I am indebted for generous and helpful letters. And to one of my publishers, Mr. Albert Boni, I am under greater obligations than I can well state. The book was his idea long ago; with it in mind he had collected an extensive library which was put entirely at my disposal; and throughout the labor of compilation he was an invaluable advisor.

MARK VAN DOREN.

New York, 1928

PREFACE TO REVISED EDITION

The principal change in this edition of "An Anthology of World Poetry" has been made in the English and American sections, which have been enlarged not only by the addition of new poets but by the addition of new poems from authors previously represented. If the proportions of the book seem thus to be violated, the answer is that a fuller anthology of poems written in the English language has at any rate been provided—an anthology, that is to say, within an anthology; and the matter of proportions can safely be left to those who are wise about such things. As for the other sections, a thorough revision of them may some day be possible; but for the present I prefer to continue collecting translations toward such a revision.

Meanwhile I am assisted at the task by many correspondents who write in to suggest that a certain version of a Latin or a German poem is better than another. It is a pleasure to acknowledge here so much friendly and informed interest in the book; and furthermore to thank the following for corrections of date or text which without their help might never have been made: Alfred R. Bellinger, Henry Seidel Canby, Edward Delavan Perry, George McCracken, Katherine Morse, Edward L. McAdam, Jr., Corliss Lamont, and Donald L. Jacobus. I shall continue to be grateful for suggestions and corrections.

MARK VAN DOREN.

New York, 1936

TABLE OF SECTIONS

	PAGE
CHINESE	1
JAPANESE	35
SANSKRIT	52
ARABIAN	80
PERSIAN	125
HEBREW	162
EGYPTIAN	235
GREEK	252
LATIN	352
ITALIAN	463
SPANISH	616
FRENCH	654
GERMAN	816
SCANDINAVIAN	942
RUSSIAN	994
ENGLISH	1021
IRISH	1272
AMERICAN	1301

CONTENTS

CHINESE

	TRANSLATED BY	PAGE
FROM THE SHI KING (Compiled c. 500 B. C.)		
The Morning Glory	*Helen Waddell*	1
How Goes the Night?	*Helen Waddell*	1
Under the Pondweed	*Helen Waddell*	2
I Wait my Lord	*Helen Waddell*	2
The Pear-Tree	*Allen Upward*	3
Maytime	*L. Cranmer-Byng*	3
You Will Die	*H. A. Giles*	3
Woman	*H. A. Giles*	4
CH'U YÜAN (4th century B. C.)		
The Great Summons	*Arthur Waley*	5
ANONYMOUS (c 124 B. C.)		
Fighting South of the Castle	*Arthur Waley*	10
ANONYMOUS (1st century B. C.)		
Old and New	*Arthur Waley*	11
ANONYMOUS (1st century?)		
Old Poem	*Arthur Waley*	12
ANONYMOUS (1st century?)		
The Song of Lo-Fu	*Arthur Waley*	12
CHANG HĒNG (78-139)		
The Bones of Chuang Tzu	*Arthur Waley*	14
TSO SSŬ (3rd century)		
The Scholar in the Narrow Street	*Arthur Waley*	16
FU HSŪAN (died 278)		
A Gentle Wind	*Arthur Waley*	17
CHAN FANG-SHENG (4th century)		
Sailing Homeward	*Arthur Waley*	18
T'AO CH'IEN (365-427)		
I Built My Hut	*Arthur Waley*	18
Shady, Shady	*Arthur Waley*	19
Once More Fields and Gardens	*Amy Lowell and Florence Ayscough*	19
EMPEROR CH'IEN WĒN-TI (6th century)		
Lo-Yang	*Arthur Waley*	20
LI T'AI-PO (701-762)		
Drinking Alone in the Moonlight	*Amy Lowell and Florence Ayscough*	21
The River-Merchant's Wife: A Letter	*Ezra Pound*	22
Clearing at Dawn	*Arthur Waley*	23
In the Mountains on a Summer Day	*Arthur Waley*	23

	TRANSLATED BY	PAGE
To Tan Ch'iu	*Arthur Waley*	23
TU FU (712-770)		
The Excursion	*Amy Lowell and Florence Ayscough*	24
The Emperor	*E. Powys Mathers*	25
PO CHÜ-I (772-846)		
To Li Chien	*Arthur Waley*	26
Lodging with the Old Man of the Stream	*Arthur Waley*	26
Rejoicing at the Arrival of Ch'en Hsiung	*Arthur Waley*	27
Losing a Slave-girl	*Arthur Waley*	27
On Being Sixty	*Arthur Waley*	28
Remembering Golden Bells	*Arthur Waley*	28
YÜAN CHĒN (779-831)		
The Pitcher	*Arthur Waley*	29
WANG CHIEN (830)		
The South	*Arthur Waley*	30
OU-YANG HSIU (11th century)		
The Cicada	*Arthur Waley*	30
SU TUNG-P'O (1036-1101)		
On the Birth of His Son	*Arthur Waley*	33
LUI CHI (1311-1375)		
A Poet Thinks	*E. Powys Mathers*	33

JAPANESE

FROM THE MANYŌ SHŪ (compiled 8th century)		
Princess Daihaku (7th century)	*Arthur Waley*	35
Hioki no Ko-Okima	*Arthur Waley*	35
Prince Yuhara (7th century)	*Arthur Waley*	35
Okura (660-733)	*Arthur Waley*	36
Hitomaro (c. 700)	*Arthur Waley*	36
The Priest Hakutsu (c. 704)	*Arthur Waley*	37
Akahito (c. 730)	*Arthur Waley*	37
Yakamochi (d. 785)	*Arthur Waley*	38
The Lady of Sakanoye (8th century)	*Arthur Waley*	38
Anonymous	*Arthur Waley*	39
The River of Heaven	*Lafcadio Hearn*	39
FROM THE KOKIN SHŪ (compiled 9th century)		
Ono No Takamura (802-852)	*Arthur Waley*	43
Ono No Komachi (834-880)	*Arthur Waley*	44
Ki No Akimine (9th century)	*Arthur Waley*	44
Mitsune (c. 900)	*Arthur Waley*	44
Ono No Yoshiki (d. 902)	*Arthur Waley*	44
Fujiwara No Toshiyuki (d. 907)	*Arthur Waley*	45
Anonymous	*Arthur Waley*	45
FROM THE SHŪI SHŪ (compiled 10th century)		
Hitomaro (c. 700)	*Arthur Waley*	46

	TRANSLATED BY	PAGE
Tsurayuki (883-946)	Arthur Waley	46
Nakatsukasa (c. 900)	Arthur Waley	46
Onakatomi Yoshinobu (c. 900)	Arthur Waley	46
Kiyowara Fukuyabu (c. 900-930)	Arthur Waley	47
Minamoto No Shigeyuki (d. 1000)	Arthur Waley	47
SAIGYO HŌSHI (1118-1190)		
Seven Poems	Arthur Waley	47
FUJIWARA IETAKA (1158-1237)		
Old Scent of the Plum Tree	E. Powys Mathers	49
FROM THE HYAKU-NIN-ISSHU (13th century)		
Princess Shoku	Curtis Hidden Page	49
Lady Horikawa	Curtis Hidden Page	49
Fujiwara No Michinobu	Curtis Hidden Page	49
Lady Sanuki	Curtis Hidden Page	50
BASHŌ (1644-1694)		
Seven Poems	Curtis Hidden Page	50
SANSKRIT		
FROM THE RIGVEDA (c. 1500 B. C.)		
Indra, the Supreme God	Romesh Dutt	52
Pushan, God of Pasture	Romesh Dutt	55
FROM THE PANCHATANTRA (2nd century B. C. et seq.)		
Kings	Arthur W. Ryder	57
The Penalty of Virtue	Arthur W. Ryder	57
True Friendship	Arthur W. Ryder	58
Fool and False	Arthur W. Ryder	59
Poverty	Arthur W. Ryder	59
AMAROU (1st century)?		
The Drunken Rose	E. Powys Mathers	59
KALIDASA (c. 500)		
The Seasons	Arthur W. Ryder	60
BHARTRIHARI (c. 500)		
Time	Paul Elmer More	65
Peace	Paul Elmer More	66
BILHANA (11th century)		
Black Marigolds	E. Powys Mathers	66
JAYADEVA (12th century)		
From the Gītā Gōvinda		
Hymn to Vishnu	Sir Edwin Arnold	77
ARABIAN		
FROM THE MU'ALLAQĀT (compiled 8th century)		
IMR EL KAIS (6th century)		
Ode	Lady Anne Blunt and Wilfrid Scawen Blunt	80
ANTARA (6th century)		
Abla	E. Powys Mathers	86
IBN KOLTHŪM (6th century)		
Pour Us Wine	E. Powys Mathers	87

CONTENTS

	TRANSLATED BY	PAGE
From the Mufaddaliyat (compiled 8th century)		
Alqamah (6th century)		
His Camel	Sir Charles Lyall	88
Al-Aswad Son of Ya'fur (6th century)		
Old Age	Sir Charles Lyall	89
Salamah Son of Jandal (6th century)		
Gone is Youth	Sir Charles Lyall	90
Khansá (7th century)		
Tears	R. A. Nicholson	93
Ta' Abbata Sharra (7th century)		
Ever Watchful	W. G. Palgrave	93
Omar b. Abi Rabi'a (d. 720)		
The Damsel	W. G. Palgrave	94
Abd-ar-Rahman I. (8th century)		
The Palm Tree	J. B. Trend	94
From the Hamâsah (compiled 9th century)		
Hittân, Son of Al-Mu'alla of Tayyi		
His Children	Sir Charles Lyall	95
Abu 'l-'Ala al-Ma'arrí (973-1057)		
Aweary Am I	R. A. Nicholson	96
Ibn Darrâj al-Andalûsi (11th century)		
The Wing of Separation	J. B. Trend	96
Ibn Zaydūn (1003-1071)		
Cordova	H. A. R. Gibb	97
Mu'tamid, King of Seville		
The Fountain	Dulcie L. Smith	98
Thy Garden	Dulcie L. Smith	98
Tears of the World	Dulcie L. Smith	98
Woo Not the World	Dulcie L. Smith	99
I Traveled with Them	J. B. Trend	99
Ibn Ál-Arabi (1165-1240)		
Ode	R. A. Nicholson	99
Ode	R. A. Nicholson	100
Bahā ad-dīn Zuhayr (d. 1258)		
On a Blind Girl	E. H. Palmer	100
From the Thousand and One Nights (13th century?)		
Dates	E. Powys Mathers	101
Birds	E. Powys Mathers	101
The Song of the Narcissus	E. Powys Mathers	102
Psalm of Battle	E. Powys Mathers	103
To Lighten My Darkness	E. Powys Mathers	103
Haroun's Favorite Song	E. Powys Mathers	104
Love	E. Powys Mathers	104
The Sleeper	E. Powys Mathers	104
Tell Him, O Night	E. Powys Mathers	105
Death	E. Powys Mathers	105
Laments	E. Powys Mathers	105
Abu Nowas for the Barmacides	E. Powys Mathers	105
The Wazir Dandan for Prince Sharkan	E. Powys Mathers	105
Her Rival for Aziza	E. Powys Mathers	106

	TRANSLATED BY	PAGE
Haroun Al-Rachid for Heart's-Life	*E. Powys Mathers*	106
Tumadir Al-Khansa for Her Brother	*E. Powys Mathers*	106
Inscriptions at the City of Brass	*E. Powys Mathers*	109
FROM THE ARABIC		
The Camel-Rider	*Wilfrid Scawen Blunt*	112
The Desolate City	*Wilfrid Scawen Blunt*	115
The Grief of Love	*Wilfrid Scawen Blunt*	118
The Love Secret	*Wilfrid Scawen Blunt*	119
The Days of Our Youth	*Wilfrid Scawen Blunt*	121

PERSIAN

ZOROASTER (7th century B. C.)?		
From the Sacred Book	*A. V. Williams Jackson*	125
FIRDAWSI (935-1025)		
Alas for Youth	*R. A. Nicholson*	125
OMAR KHAYYÁM (d. 1123)		
The Rubáiyát	*Edward FitzGerald*	126
JALÁLU'DDÍN RŪMÍ (1207-1273)		
A Beauty That All Night Long	*R. A. Nicholson*	143
SA'DI (d. 1291)		
FROM THE GULISTAN		
He Hath No Parallel	*L. Cranmer-Byng*	144
The Gift of Speech	*L. Cranmer-Byng*	144
On the Deception of Appearances	*L. Cranmer-Byng*	144
Friendship	*L. Cranmer-Byng*	144
Take the Crust	*L. Cranmer-Byng*	145
Mesnevi	*L. Cranmer-Byng*	145
Love's Last Resource	*L. Cranmer-Byng*	145
Alas!	*L. Cranmer-Byng*	145
Courage	*Sir Edwin Arnold*	145
Help	*Sir Edwin Arnold*	146
The Sooth-sayer	*Sir Edwin Arnold*	146
Wealth	*Sir Edwin Arnold*	146
FROM THE BUSTAN		
The Dancer	*Sir Edwin Arnold*	146
The Great Physician	*Sir Edwin Arnold*	147
Ode	*R. A. Nicholson*	147
HAFIZ (d. 1389)		
A Persian Song of Hafiz	*Sir William Jones*	148
Odes		
1.	*Richard Le Gallienne*	150
2.	*Richard Le Gallienne*	151
3.	*Richard Le Gallienne*	152
4.	*Richard Le Gallienne*	153
5.	*Gertrude Lowthian Bell*	153

	TRANSLATED BY	PAGE
Odes		
6.	*Gertrude Lowthian Bell*	154
7.	*Gertrude Lowthian Bell*	155
8.	*Gertrude Lowthian Bell*	156
9.	*Gertrude Lowthian Bell*	157
10.	*Gertrude Lowthian Bell*	159
11.	*John Hindley*	159
12.	*Ralph Waldo Emerson*	160
13.	*Ralph Waldo Emerson*	160

HEBREW

FROM THE OLD TESTAMENT (10th-1st centuries B. C.)		
The Song of Deborah and Barak	*King James Version*	162
Hannah's Song of Thanksgiving	*King James Version*	164
David's Lament for Saul and Jonathan	*King James Version*	165
From the Book of Psalms	*King James Version*	166
From the Book of Job	*King James Version*	180
From Ecclesiastes	*King James Version*	190
The Song of Songs	*King James Version*	191
From Isaiah	*King James Version*	200
From Jeremiah	*King James Version*	202
From Zechariah	*King James Version*	204
SOLOMON IBN GABIROL (1021-1058)		
The Royal Crown	*Israel Zangwill*	206
JUDAH HA-LEVI (d. 1140)		
To Zion	*Maurice Samuel*	210
Parting	*Nina Salaman*	211
CHAIM NACHMAN BIALIK (1873-)		
The Mathmid	*Maurice Samuel*	213
From "Songs of the People"	*Maurice Samuel*	217
Night	*Maurice Samuel*	220
The Dead of the Wilderness	*Maurice Samuel*	222
YEHOASH (SOLOMON BLOOMGARDEN) (1870-1926)		
An Old Song (Yiddish)	*Marie Syrkin*	234

EGYPTIAN

FROM THE BOOK OF THE DEAD (3500 B. C. et seq.)		
The Dead Man Ariseth and Singeth a Hymn to the Sun	*Robert Hillyer*	235
He Singeth a Hymn to Osiris, the Lord of Eternity	*Robert Hillyer*	236
He Asketh Absolution of God	*Robert Hillyer*	237
He Holdeth Fast to the Memory of His Identity	*Robert Hillyer*	238
He Approacheth the Hall of Judgment	*Robert Hillyer*	238
He Is Declared True of Word	*Robert Hillyer*	239
He Cometh Forth Into the Day	*Robert Hillyer*	240

	TRANSLATED BY	PAGE
He Biddeth Osiris to Arise From the Dead	*Robert Hillyer*	240
He Maketh Himself One with Osiris	*Robert Hillyer*	241
He Maketh Himself One with the God Ra	*Robert Hillyer*	241
He Maketh Himself One with the Only God, Whose Limbs are the Many Gods	*Robert Hillyer*	242
He Walketh by Day	*Robert Hillyer*	243
He Defendeth His Heart Against the Destroyer	*Robert Hillyer*	243
He Establisheth His Triumph	*Robert Hillyer*	244
He Entereth the House of the Goddess Hathor	*Robert Hillyer*	244
He Embarketh in the Boat of Ra	*Robert Hillyer*	244
He Commandeth a Fair Wind	*Robert Hillyer*	245
He Knoweth the Souls of the West	*Robert Hillyer*	245
He Knoweth the Souls of the East	*Robert Hillyer*	246
He Overcometh the Serpent of Evil in the Name of Ra	*Robert Hillyer*	246
He Is Like the Lotus	*Robert Hillyer*	247
He Is Like the Serpent Saka	*Robert Hillyer*	247
He Prayeth for Ink and Palette That He May Write	*Robert Hillyer*	248
He Kindleth a Fire	*Robert Hillyer*	248
He Singeth in the Underworld	*Robert Hillyer*	248
The Other World	*Robert Hillyer*	249
Adoration of the Disk by King Akhnaten and Princess Nefer Neferiu Aten	*Robert Hillyer*	250

GREEK

HOMERIC HYMNS (7th century B. C.?)		
Hymn to Earth the Mother of All	*Percy Bysshe Shelley*	252
Hymn to Selene	*Percy Bysshe Shelley*	253
Hymn to Athena	*Percy Bysshe Shelley*	254
Hymn to Castor and Pollux	*Percy Bysshe Shelley*	254
ALCMAN (c. 680 B. C.)		
Fragment	*Thomas Campbell*	255
MIMNERMUS (620 B. C.)		
Youth and Age	*J. A. Symonds, M.D.*	255
ALCÆUS (610 B. C.)		
Let Us Drink	*John Hermann Merivale*	256
The Storm	*John Hermann Merivale*	256
SAPPHO (610 B. C.)		
Ode to Aphrodite	*William Ellery Leonard*	257

	TRANSLATED BY	PAGE
Ode to Anactoria	*William Ellery Leonard*	258
Farewell to Anactoria	*Allen Tate*	258
Fragments		
Hesperus the Bringer	*Lord Byron*	259
One Girl	*D. G. Rossetti*	259
Mother, I Cannot Mind My Wheel	*Walter Savage Landor*	260
The Dust of Timas	*Edwin Arlington Robinson*	260
Round About Me	*William Ellery Leonard*	260
Love	*William Ellery Leonard*	261
Full Moon	*William Ellery Leonard*	261
Alone	*William Ellery Leonard*	261
Forever Dead	*William Ellery Leonard*	261
THEOGNIS (540 B. C.)		
Enjoyment	*John Hookham Frere*	261
Hope	*John Hookham Frere*	262
Poverty	*John Hookham Frere*	262
ANACREON AND ANACREONTICS (6th century B. C. et seq.)		
The Wounded Cupid	*Robert Herrick*	263
The Cheat of Cupid	*Robert Herrick*	263
Love	*Abraham Cowley*	265
The Grasshopper	*Abraham Cowley*	265
Age	*Abraham Cowley*	266
The Epicure	*Abraham Cowley*	267
Beauty	*Thomas Stanley*	267
Roses	*Thomas Stanley*	268
The Combat	*Thomas Stanley*	268
The Swallow	*Thomas Stanley*	269
All Things Drink	*Thomas Stanley*	269
The Picture	*Thomas Stanley*	269
Spring	*Thomas Stanley*	270
Old I Am	*Thomas Stanley*	271
Youthful Age	*Thomas Stanley*	271
The Wish	*Thomas Stanley*	271
The Cup	*John Oldham*	272
Anacreon's Dove	*Samuel Johnson*	273
SIMONIDES OF CEOS (480 B. C.)		
Thermopylæ	*William Lisle Bowles*	274
BACCHYLIDES (450 B. C.)		
Peace on Earth	*John Addington Symonds*	274
ÆSCHYLUS (525-456 B. C.)		
Chorus from Agamemnon	*Sir Gilbert Murray*	275
Chorus from The Seven Against Thebes	*A. E. Housman*	275
SOPHOCLES (495-406 B. C.)		
Chorus from Œdipus Coloneus	*A. E. Housman*	276
Chorus from Ajax	*Winthrop Mackworth Praed*	277
EURIPIDES (480-406 B. C.)		
Chorus from Alcestis	*A. E. Housman*	279
Choruses from the Cyclops	*Percy Bysshe Shelley*	280
Chorus from the Bacchai	*Sir Gilbert Murray*	281

	TRANSLATED BY	PAGE
Chorus from Hippolytus—O, for the Wings of a Dove	*Sir Gilbert Murray*	282
Chorus from Hippolytus—No More, O My Spirit	*"H. D."*	283
Chorus from Iphigeneia in Aulis	*"H. D."*	284
ARISTOPHANES (444-380 B. C.)		
Chorus of Birds	*Algernon Charles Swinburne*	285
Song of the Clouds	*Oscar Wilde*	287
THEOCRITUS (3rd century B. C.)		
The Death of Daphnis	*Charles Stuart Calverley*	288
The Incantation	*Charles Stuart Calverley*	293
The Herdsmen	*Charles Stuart Calverley*	298
Harvest-Home	*Charles Stuart Calverley*	301
The Fishermen	*Charles Stuart Calverley*	306
The Flute of Daphnis	*Edward Cracroft Lefroy*	308
A Sacred Grove	*Edward Cracroft Lefroy*	308
A Sylvan Revel	*Edward Cracroft Lefroy*	309
Thyrsis	*Edward Cracroft Lefroy*	309
Cleonicos	*Edward Cracroft Lefroy*	310
The Epitaph of Eusthenes	*Edward Cracroft Lefroy*	310
The Monument of Cleita	*Edward Cracroft Lefroy*	311
The Grave of Hipponax	*Edward Cracroft Lefroy*	311
The Cyclops	*Elizabeth Barrett Browning*	312
BION (3rd century B. C.)		
Lament for Adonis	*John Addington Symonds*	315
A Dream of Venus	*Leigh Hunt*	320
MOSCHUS (3rd century B. C.)		
Lament for Bion	*George Chapman*	321
Love's Lesson	*Ernest Myers*	325
The Craft of a Keeper of Sheep	*Ernest Myers*	325
The Ocean	*Percy Bysshe Shelley*	325
Cupid Turned Plowman	*Matthew Prior*	326
"ÆSOP'S FABLES" (3rd century?)		
The Vine and the Goat	*William Ellery Leonard*	326
The Shepherd-Boy and the Wolf	*William Ellery Leonard*	327
The Ass in the Lion's Skin	*William Ellery Leonard*	327
The Mountain in Labor	*William Ellery Leonard*	327
The Swan and the Goose	*William Ellery Leonard*	328
FROM THE GREEK ANTHOLOGY (490 B. C.-1000 A. D.)		
AGATHIAS		
Rhodanthe	*Andrew Lang*	329
Not Such Your Burden	*William M. Hardinge*	329
Plutarch	*John Dryden*	329
ANONYMOUS		
Spirit of Plato	*Percy Bysshe Shelley*	330
Epitaph on Achilles	*William M. Hardinge*	330
This Stone	*Goldwin Smith*	330
Dion of Tarsus	*Alma Strettell*	330
Riches	*William Cowper*	330

	TRANSLATED BY	PAGE
Grapes	*Alma Strettell*	331
The Tomb of Diogenes	*John Addington Symonds*	331
The Lion Over the Tomb of Leonidas	*Walter Leaf*	331
Not of Itself But Thee	*Richard Garnett*	331
Nature's Travail	*Goldwin Smith*	331
ANTIPATER		
Erinna	*A. J. Butler*	332
Aristeides	*Charles Whibley*	332
Pindar	*John Addington Symonds*	332
Undying Thirst	*Robert Bland*	333
ANYTES		
A Shepherd's Gift	*John William Burgon*	333
ARCHIAS OF BYZANTIUM		
Sea Dirge	*Andrew Lang*	333
ASCLEPIADES		
Eumares	*Richard Garnett*	334
CALLIMACHUS		
Heraclitus	*William Cory*	334
Timon's Epitaph	*William Shakespeare*	334
His Son	*G. B. Grundy*	334
Saon of Acanthus	*J. A. Symonds, M.D.*	335
Sopolis	*William M. Hardinge*	335
Crethis	*Richard Garnett*	335
To Archinus	*F. A. Wright*	335
CARPHYLLIDES		
A Happy Man	*Edwin Arlington Robinson*	336
CRINAGORAS		
Epitaph on an Infant	*John William Burgon*	336
DIOTIMUS		
Without the Herdsman	*John William Burgon*	337
ERINNA		
Baucis	*Richard Garnett*	337
GLAUCUS		
An Inscription by the Sea	*Edwin Arlington Robinson*	337
ISIDORUS		
On a Fowler	*William Cowper*	338
LEONIDAS OF ALEXANDRIA		
Menodotis	*Richard Garnett*	338
LEONIDAS OF TARENTUM		
The Fisherman	*Andrew Lang*	338
The Spinning Woman	*Andrew Lang*	339
The Tomb of Crethon	*John Hermann Merivale*	339
Cleitagoras	*William M. Hardinge*	339
The Last Journey	*Charles Merivale*	340
Philocles	*F. A. Wright*	340
LUCIANUS		
Artificial Beauty	*William Cowper*	340
LUCILLIUS		
On An Old Woman	*William Cowper*	341
Treasure	*William Cowper*	341

	TRANSLATED BY	PAGE
MARCUS ARGENTARIUS		
The Old Story	*Edwin Arlington Robinson*	341
MELEAGER		
Upon a Maid That Died the Day She Was Married	*Robert Herrick*	342
O Gentle Ships	*Andrew Lang*	342
Of His Death	*Andrew Lang*	342
In the Spring	*Andrew Lang*	343
Love at the Door	*J. A. Symonds, M.D.*	343
The Little Love-God	*Walter Headlam*	344
Of Himself	*Richard Garnett*	345
Lost Desire	*William M. Hardinge*	345
Spring	*William M. Hardinge*	345
A Garland for Heliodora	*Christopher North*	346
NICARCHUS		
The Raven	*Edwin Arlington Robinson*	347
NICIAS		
The Fountain at the Tomb	*Charles Merivale*	347
PALLADAS		
Vanity of Vanities	*William M. Hardinge*	347
PAULUS SILENTIARIUS		
No Matter	*William Cowper*	348
United	*W. H. D. Rouse*	348
PLATO		
A Farewell	*Matthew Prior*	348
Morning and Evening Star	*Percy Bysshe Shelley*	348
On Alexis	*Thomas Stanley*	349
On Archæanassa	*Thomas Stanley*	349
Love Sleeping	*Thomas Stanley*	349
On a Seal	*Thomas Stanley*	349
Farewell	*Charles Whibley*	349
POSIDIPPUS		
Doricha	*Edwin Arlington Robinson*	350
RUFINUS		
The Lover's Posy	*W. H. D. Rouse*	350
SIMMIAS OF THEBES		
To Prote	*J. A. Symonds, M.D.*	351
SIMONIDES		
On Two Brothers	*W. H. D. Rouse*	351

LATIN

TITUS LUCRETIUS CARUS (95-52 B. C.)		
Address to Venus	*Edmund Spenser*	352
Beyond Religion	*William Ellery Leonard*	353
No Single Thing Abides	*W. H. Mallock*	354
Suave mari Magno	*W. H. Mallock*	358
Against the Fear of Death	*John Dryden*	361
CAIUS VALERIUS CATULLUS (87-57 B. C.)		
My Sweetest Lesbia	*Thomas Campion*	363
To Celia	*Ben Jonson*	363

CONTENTS

	TRANSLATED BY	PAGE
The Death of Lesbia's Bird	*S. T. Coleridge*	364
Lesbia Railing	*Jonathan Swift*	364
True or False	*Walter Savage Landor*	365
To Himself	*William Ellery Leonard*	365
Sappho	*William Ellery Leonard*	366
Hymn to Diana	*R. C. Jebb*	366
On the Burial of His Brother	*Aubrey Beardsley*	367
Sirmio	*Charles Stuart Calverley*	367
Love and Death	*H. W. Garrod*	368
To Varus	*Walter Savage Landor*	368
A Fib Detected	*John Hookham Frere*	369
The Yacht	*John Hookham Frere*	370
Acme and Septimius	*Abraham Cowley*	371
PUBLIUS VERGILIUS MARO (70-19 B. C.)		
The Shepherd's Gratitude	*Charles Stuart Calverley*	373
The Messiah	*John Dryden*	376
Corydon and Thyrsis	*John Dryden*	378
Lycidas and Mœris	*John Dryden*	381
The Georgics: Prelude	*John Dryden*	384
QUINTUS HORATIUS FLACCUS (65-8 B. C.)		
To the Ship in Which Virgil Sailed to Athens	*John Dryden*	386
To Thaliarchus	*John Dryden*	387
To Mæcenas	*John Dryden*	389
Country Life	*John Dryden*	392
The Immortality of Verse	*Alexander Pope*	394
To Fuscus Aristus	*Abraham Cowley*	395
The Profane	*Abraham Cowley*	397
To Licinius	*William Cowper*	399
Persian Fopperies	*William Cowper*	400
To Venus	*Ben Jonson*	400
To Pyrrha	*John Milton*	402
To Sally	*John Quincy Adams*	402
To An Ambitious Friend	*Matthew Arnold*	403
The Ship of State	*William Ewart Gladstone*	405
Extremum Tanain	*Austin Dobson*	405
Albi, ne Doreas	*Austin Dobson*	406
To Chloë	*Austin Dobson*	406
To Phidyle	*Austin Dobson*	407
To the Fountain of Bandusia	*Eugene Field*	407
Ad Leuconoen	*F. P. Adams*	408
Ad Xanthiam Phoceum	*F. P. Adams*	409
Invocation	*Louis Untermeyer*	410
Holiday	*Louis Untermeyer*	410
Revenge!	*Louis Untermeyer*	411
The Pine Tree for Diana	*Louis Untermeyer*	412
ALBIUS TIBULLUS (54-18 B. C.)		
A Pastoral Elegy	*Sir Charles Abraham Elton*	413
SEXTUS AURELIUS PROPERTIUS (51-? B. C.)		
When Thou Must Home	*Thomas Campion*	416
Ah Woe Is Me	*F. A. Wright*	416
Hylas	*F. A. Wright*	418

	TRANSLATED BY	PAGE
Revenge to Come	*Kirby Flower Smith*	419
PUBLIUS OVIDIUS NASO (43 B. C.-18 A. D.)		
A Captive of Love	*Christopher Marlowe*	420
Lente, lente	*Kirby Flower Smith*	422
The Complaisant Swain	*F. A. Wright*	423
Winter at Tomi	*F. A. Wright*	424
FROM THE METAMORPHOSES		
Magic	*William Shakespeare*	425
Baucis and Philemon	*John Dryden*	425
PHAEDRUS (1st century)		
The Purpose of Fable-Writing	*Christopher Smart*	430
Æsop at Play	*Christopher Smart*	431
The Dog in the River	*Christopher Smart*	431
The Man and the Weasel	*Christopher Smart*	432
PETRONIUS ARBITER (1st century)		
Encouragement to Exile	*Howard Mumford Jones*	432
The Malady of Love is Nerves	*Howard Mumford Jones*	433
We Are Such Stuff as Dreams	*Howard Mumford Jones*	433
AULUS PERSIUS FLACCUS (34-62)		
Prologue to the First Satire	*John Dryden*	434
MARCUS VALERIUS MARTIALIS (40-104)		
Non amo te	*Tom Brown*	435
Near Neighbors	*Jonathan Swift*	435
Procrastination	*Abraham Cowley*	436
Verses on Blenheim	*Jonathan Swift*	436
Inviting a Friend to Supper	*Ben Jonson*	436
To His Book	*Robert Herrick*	438
Post-obits and the Poets	*Lord Byron*	438
Bought Locks	*Sir John Harington*	438
Critics	*Sir John Harington*	438
Quits	*Matthew Prior*	438
Temperament	*Joseph Addison*	439
A Hinted Wish	*Francis Lewis*	439
To Cloe	*Thomas Moore*	439
What Makes a Happy Life	*Goldwin Smith*	439
On the Death of a Young and Favorite Slave	*Goldwin Smith*	440
Erotion	*Kirby Flower Smith*	440
Sextus the Usurer	*Kirby Flower Smith*	441
Country Pleasures	*F. A. Wright*	441
DECIMUS JUNIUS JUVENALIS (60-140)		
Celestial Wisdom	*Samuel Johnson*	442
PUBLIUS PAPINIUS STATIUS (61-96)		
Sleep	*W. H. Fyfe*	443
THE EMPEROR HADRIAN (76-138)		
The Dying Christian to His Soul	*Alexander Pope*	443
ANONYMOUS (3rd century?)		
The Vigil of Venus	*Thomas Stanley*	444
DECIMUS MAGNUS AUSONIUS (310-395)		
Idyll of the Rose	*John Addington Symonds*	449
To His Wife	*Terrot Reaveley Glover*	451

	TRANSLATED BY	PAGE
CLAUDIUS CLAUDIANUS (c. 400)		
The Old Man of Verona	*Abraham Cowley*	451
The Lonely Isle	*Howard Mumford Jones*...	452
Epitaph	*Howard Mumford Jones*...	452
SIDONIUS APOLLINARIS (5th century)		
Invitation to the Dance	*Howard Mumford Jones*...	453
MEDIEVAL LATIN STUDENTS' SONGS (12th-13th centuries)		
A Song of the Open Road ..	*John Addington Symonds*..	454
A Pastoral	*John Addington Symonds*..	456
There's No Lust Like to Poetry	*John Addington Symonds*..	456
LATIN HYMNS		
Veni Creator Spiritus	*John Dryden*	457
The Te Deum	*John Dryden?*	458
Hymn for St. John's Eve ...	*John Dryden?*	459
Dies Irae	*Richard Crashaw*	460

ITALIAN

CIULLO D'ALCAMO (c. 1175)		
Dialogue: Lover and Lady ..	*D. G. Rossetti*..........	463
FOLCACHIERO DE' FOLCACHIERI (c. 1175)		
Canzone: He Speaks of His Condition	*D. G. Rossetti*..........	470
ST. FRANCIS OF ASSISI (1182-1226)		
Cantica: Our Lord Christ ...	*D. G. Rossetti*..........	471
GUIDO GUINICELLI (13th century)		
Sonnet: He Will Praise His Lady	*D. G. Rossetti*..........	472
Sonnet: Of Moderation and Tolerance	*D. G. Rossetti*..........	472
Canzone: He Perceives His Rashness in Love	*D. G. Rossetti*..........	473
Canzone: Of the Gentle Heart	*D. G. Rossetti*..........	474
GUERZO DI MONTECANTI (13th century)		
Sonnet: He Is Out of Heart with His Time	*D. G. Rossetti*..........	476
JACOPO DA LENTINO (13th century)		
Sonnet: Of His Lady in Heaven	*D. G. Rossetti*..........	477
Sonnet: Of His Lady's Face .	*D. G. Rossetti*..........	477
Canzonetta: Of His Lady, and of His Making Her Likeness	*D. G. Rossetti*..........	478
Canzonetta: He Will Neither Boast nor Lament to His Lady	*D. G. Rossetti*..........	479
GIACOMINO PUGLIESI (13th century)		
Canzonetta: Of His Lady in Absence	*D. G. Rossetti*..........	481
Canzone: Of His Dead Lady .	*D. G. Rossetti*..........	482

	TRANSLATED BY	PAGE
BARTOLOMEO DI SANT' ANGELO (13th century)		
Sonnet: He Jests Concerning His Poverty	*D. G. Rossetti*	484
FOLGORE DA SAN GEMINIANO (13th century)		
Twelve Sonnets	*D. G. Rossetti*	485
Sonnet: Of Virtue	*D. G. Rossetti*	491
On Knighthood	*John Addington Symonds*	491
GUIDO DELLE COLONNE (13th century)		
Canzone: To Love and To His Lady	*D. G. Rossetti*	492
PIER MORONELLI DI FIORENZA (13th century)		
Canzonetta: A Bitter Song to His Lady	*D. G. Rossetti*	494
PRINZIVALLE DORIA (13th century)		
Canzone: Of His Love	*D. G. Rossetti*	496
RUSTICO DI FILIPPO (1200?-1270)		
Sonnet: Of the Making of Master Messerin	*D. G. Rossetti*	498
NICCOLÒ DEGLI ALBIZZI (13th century)		
Prolonged Sonnet	*D. G. Rossetti*	498
GUIDO CAVALCANTI (1250-1301)		
Sonnet: To Dante Alighieri	*D. G. Rossetti*	499
Sonnet: To His Lady Joan, of Florence	*D. G. Rossetti*	500
Sonnet: He Compares All Things with His Lady	*D. G. Rossetti*	500
Sonnet: A Rapture Concerning His Lady	*D. G. Rossetti*	501
Ballata: Of His Lady Among Other Ladies	*D. G. Rossetti*	501
Sonnet: Of the Eyes of a Certain Mandetta	*D. G. Rossetti*	502
Ballata: He Reveals His Increasing Love for Mandetta	*D. G. Rossetti*	502
Sonnet: To Dante Alighieri	*D. G. Rossetti*	503
Sonnet: To Dante Alighieri	*D. G. Rossetti*	503
Sonnet: On the Detection of a False Friend	*D. G. Rossetti*	504
Sonnet: He Speaks of a Third Love of His	*D. G. Rossetti*	504
Ballata: Of a Continual Death in Love	*D. G. Rossetti*	505
Sonnet: To a Friend Who Does Not Pity His Love	*D. G. Rossetti*	505
Sonnet: Of His Pain from a New Love	*D. G. Rossetti*	506
To Dante	*Percy Bysshe Shelley*	506
Ballata: Concerning a Shepherd-Maid	*D. G. Rossetti*	507
Sonnet: Of An Ill-favored Lady	*D. G. Rossetti*	508
Ballata: In Exile at Sarzana	*D. G. Rossetti*	508

CONTENTS

	TRANSLATED BY	PAGE
FRANCESCO DA BARBERINO (1264-1348)		
A Virgin Declares Her Beauties	*D. G. Rossetti*	509
Of Caution	*D. G. Rossetti*	510
DANTE ALIGHIERI (1265-1321)		
FROM LA VITA NUOVA		
To every heart which the sweet pain doth move	*D. G. Rossetti*	511
All ye that pass along Love's trodden way	*D. G. Rossetti*	511
Weep, Lovers, sith Love's very self doth weep	*D. G. Rossetti*	512
Death, always cruel, Pity's foe in chief	*D. G. Rossetti*	513
A day agone, as I rode sullenly	*D. G. Rossetti*	513
Song, 'tis my will that thou do seek out Love	*D. G. Rossetti*	514
All my thoughts always speak to me of Love	*D. G. Rossetti*	515
Even as the others mock, thou mockest me	*D. G. Rossetti*	515
The thoughts are broken in my memory	*D. G. Rossetti*	516
At whiles (yea oftentimes) I muse over	*D. G. Rossetti*	516
Ladies that have intelligence in love	*D. G. Rossetti*	517
Love and the gentle heart are one same thing	*D. G. Rossetti*	519
My lady carries love within her eyes	*D. G. Rossetti*	519
You that thus wear a modest countenance	*D. G. Rossetti*	519
Canst thou indeed be he that still would sing	*D. G. Rossetti*	520
A very pitiful lady, very young	*D. G. Rossetti*	520
I felt a spirit of love begin to stir	*D. G. Rossetti*	522
My lady looks so gentle and so pure	*D. G. Rossetti*	523
For certain he hath seen all perfectness	*D. G. Rossetti*	523
Love hath so long possessed me for his own	*D. G. Rossetti*	524
The eyes that weep for pity of the heart	*D. G. Rossetti*	524
Stay now with me, and listen to my sighs	*D. G. Rossetti*	526
Whatever while the thought comes over me	*D. G. Rossetti*	527

	TRANSLATED BY	PAGE
That lady of all gentle memories	*D. G. Rossetti*	527
Mine eyes beheld the blessed pity spring	*D. G. Rossetti*	528
Love's pallor and the semblance of deep ruth	*D. G. Rossetti*	528
The very bitter weeping that ye made	*D. G. Rossetti*	529
A gentle thought there is will often start	*D. G. Rossetti*	529
Woe's me! by dint of all these sighs that come	*D. G. Rossetti*	530
Ye pilgrim-folk, advancing pensively	*D. G. Rossetti*	530
Beyond the sphere which spreads to widest space	*D. G. Rossetti*	530
Sonnet: To Guido Cavalcanti	*Percy Bysshe Shelley*	531
Sonnet: To Brunetto Latini	*D. G. Rossetti*	531
Sonnet: Of Beatrice de' Portinari	*D. G. Rossetti*	532
Sonnet: To Certain Ladies	*D. G. Rossetti*	532
Sonnet: To the Same Ladies; with Their Answer	*D. G. Rossetti*	533
Ballata: He Will Gaze Upon Beatrice	*D. G. Rossetti*	533
Canzone: He Beseeches Death for the Life of Beatrice	*D. G. Rossetti*	534
Sonnet: On the 9th of June 1290	*D. G. Rossetti*	536
Sonnet: Of Beauty and Duty	*D. G. Rossetti*	537
Sestina: Of the Lady Pietra degli Scrovigni	*D. G. Rossetti*	537
Sonnet: To the Lady Pietra degli Scrovigni	*D. G. Rossetti*	538
CINO DA PISTOIA (1270-1336)		
Sonnet: To Dante Alighieri	*D. G. Rossetti*	539
Sonnet: To Dante Alighieri	*D. G. Rossetti*	540
Madrigal	*D. G. Rossetti*	540
Sonnet: To Love, in Great Bitterness	*D. G. Rossetti*	541
Sonnet: Death Is Not Without But Within Him	*D. G. Rossetti*	541
Sonnet: A Trance of Love	*D. G. Rossetti*	542
Sonnet: Of the Grave of Selvaggia	*D. G. Rossetti*	542
Canzone: His Lament for Selvaggia	*D. G. Rossetti*	543
DANTE DA MAIANO (c. 1300)		
Sonnet: To Dante Alighieri	*D. G. Rossetti*	543
Sonnet: He Craves Interpreting of a Dream	*D. G. Rossetti*	544

 CONTENTS

	TRANSLATED BY	PAGE
CECCO ANGIOLIERI, DA SIENA (c. 1300)		
Sonnet: To Dante Alighieri ..	*D. G. Rossetti*	544
Sonnet: He Will Not Be Too Deeply in Love	*D. G. Rossetti*	545
Sonnet: Of Love in Men and Devils	*D. G. Rossetti*	545
Sonnet: Of Love, in Honor of His Mistress Becchina	*D. G. Rossetti*	546
Sonnet: Of Becchina's, the Shoemaker's Daughter	*D. G. Rossetti*	546
Sonnet: Of the 20th of June 1291	*D. G. Rossetti*	547
Sonnet: Of Becchina in a Rage	*D. G. Rossetti*	547
Sonnet: In absence from Becchina	*D. G. Rossetti*	548
Sonnet: He Rails Against Dante	*D. G. Rossetti*	548
Sonnet: Of All He Would Do	*D. G. Rossetti*	549
Sonnet: He Is Past All Help.	*D. G. Rossetti*	549
Sonnet: Of Why He is Unhanged	*D. G. Rossetti*	550
Sonnet: Of Why He Would Be a Scullion	*D. G. Rossetti*	550
Sonnet: He Argues His Case with Death	*D. G. Rossetti*	551
Sonnet: To Dante Alighieri ..	*D. G. Rossetti*	551
SIMONE DALL'ANTELLA (c. 1300)		
Prolonged Sonnet	*D. G. Rossetti*	552
GIOVANNI QUIRINO (c. 1300)		
Sonnet: To Dante Alighieri ..	*D. G. Rossetti*	553
FRANCESCO PETRARCA (1304-1374)		
Visions	*Edmund Spenser*	553
The Song of Troylus	*Geoffrey Chaucer*	556
Summer is Come	*The Earl of Surrey*	557
A Complaint by Night	*The Earl of Surrey*	558
Complaint of a Lover Rebuked	*The Earl of Surrey*	558
Love's Fidelity	*The Earl of Surrey*	559
Love's Inconsistency	*Sir Thomas Wyatt*	559
The Heart on the Hill	*C. B. Cayley*	559
Signs of Love	*C. B. Cayley*	560
If It Be Destined	*Edward FitzGerald*	560
GIOVANNI BOCCACCIO (1313-1375)		
Sonnets	*D. G. Rossetti*	561
FAZIO DEGLI UBERTI (1326-1360)		
Canzone: His Portrait of His Lady	*D. G. Rossetti*	564
Of England, and of Its Marvels	*D. G. Rossetti*	567
FRANCO SACCHETTI (1335-1400?)		
Ballata: His Talk with Certain Peasant-girls	*D. G. Rossetti*	569
Catch	*D. G. Rossetti*	570

	TRANSLATED BY	PAGE
ANONYMOUS (14th century)		
Sonnet: A Lady Laments for Her Lost Lover	*D. G. Rossetti*	571
Ballata: One Speaks of the Beginning of His Love	*D. G. Rossetti*	572
Ballata: Of True and False Singing	*D. G. Rossetti*	572
ANGELO POLIZIANO (1454-1494)		
Three Ballate	*John Addington Symonds*	573
LORENZO DE' MEDICI (1448-1492)		
Two Lyrics	*John Addington Symonds*	576
NICCOLO MACHIAVELLI (1469-1527)		
Opportunity	*James Elroy Flecker*	578
MICHELANGELO BUONARROTI (1475-1564)		
The Doom of Beauty	*John Addington Symonds*	579
Celestial Love	*John Addington Symonds*	580
Love, the Light-giver	*John Addington Symonds*	580
Love's Entreaty	*John Addington Symonds*	581
On the Brink of Death	*John Addington Symonds*	581
A Prayer for Purification	*John Addington Symonds*	582
The Transfiguration of Beauty	*John Addington Symonds*	582
The Garland and the Girdle	*John Addington Symonds*	583
Joy May Kill	*John Addington Symonds*	583
Love's Justification	*William Wordsworth*	584
To the Supreme Being	*William Wordsworth*	584
To Vittoria Colonna	*H. W. Longfellow*	585
Dante	*H. W. Longfellow*	585
Three Poems	*George Santayana*	586
GIOVANNI DELLA CASA (1503-1556)		
To Sleep	*John Addington Symonds*	587
GIOVANNI BATTISTA GUARINI (1537-1612)		
From Il Pastor Fido	*Sir Richard Fanshawe*	587
Claim to Love	*Thomas Stanley*	589
Spring	*Leigh Hunt*	590
TORQUATO TASSO (1544-1595)		
The Golden Age	*Leigh Hunt*	590
To His Mistress in Absence	*Thomas Stanley*	592
Love	*John Hermann Merivale*	593
GIORDANO BRUNO (1548-1600)		
The Philosophic Flight	*John Addington Symonds*	593
GABRIELLO CHIABRERA (1562-1637)		
Epitaphs	*William Wordsworth*	594
TOMASSO CAMPANELLA (1568-1639)		
The People	*John Addington Symonds*	599
GIAMBATTISTA MARINI (1569-1625)		
Fading Beauty	*Samuel Daniel*	600
FRANCISCO REDI (1626-1698)		
From Bacchus in Tuscany	*Leigh Hunt*	602
The Creation of My Lady	*Sir Edmund Gosse*	605
VINCENZO FILICAJA (1642-1707)		
Italy	*Lord Byron*	605

	TRANSLATED BY	PAGE
VITTORIO ALFIERI (1749-1803)		
To Dante	*Lorna De' Lucchi*	606
JACOPO VITTORELLI (1749-1803)		
On a Nun	*Lord Byron*	606
GIACOMO LEOPARDI (1798-1837)		
To Italy	*Romilda Rendel*	607
A sè stesso	*Lorna De' Lucchi*	610
L'Infinito	*Lorna De' Lucchi*	610
GIOSUÈ CARDUCCI (1836-1907)		
Snowfall	*Romilda Rendel*	611
Petrarch	*William Dudley Foulke*	611
Primo Vere	*John Bailey*	612
POPULAR SONGS OF TUSCANY	*John Addington Symonds*	613

SPANISH

JUAN RUIZ DE HITA (c. 1343)		
Praise of Little Women	*H. W. Longfellow*	616
JUAN II OF CASTILE (1405-1454)		
Cancion	*George Ticknor*	618
DIEGO DE SALDAÑA (15th century)		
Eyes So Tristful	*H. W. Longfellow*	619
ANONYMOUS (15th century)		
Villancico	*Thomas Walsh*	619
CRISTOBAL DE CASTILLEJO (1490-1550)		
Some Day, Some Day	*H. W. Longfellow*	620
ANONYMOUS (16th century?)		
The Siesta	*William Cullen Bryant*	620
OLD SPANISH BALLADS (16th century?)		
Gentle River, Gentle River	*Thomas Percy*	621
Abenamar, Abenamar	*Robert Southey*	623
The Song of the Galley	*John Gibson Lockhart*	624
The Lamentation for Celin	*John Gibson Lockhart*	625
The Death of Don Pedro	*John Gibson Lockhart*	628
GIL VICENTE (16th century)		
Song	*H. W. Longfellow*	629
SISTER MARCELA DE CARPIO DE SAN FELIX (16th century)		
Amor Mysticus	*John Hay*	629
SAINT TERESA (1515-1582)		
Lines Written in Her Breviary	*H. W. Longfellow*	631
If, Lord, Thy Love For Me is Strong	*Arthur Symons*	631
Let Mine Eyes See Thee	*Arthur Symons*	632
To-day a Shepherd	*Arthur Symons*	632
Shepherd, Shepherd, Hark	*Arthur Symons*	633
LUIS VAZ DE CAMOENS (1524-1580)		
On the Death of Catarina de Attayda	*R. F. Burton*	634
On Revisiting Cintra	*Richard Garnett*	634
Babylon and Sion (Goa and Lisbon)	*Richard Garnett*	635

	TRANSLATED BY	PAGE
Sonnet: Leave Me	*Richard Garnett*	635
Sonnet: Time and the Mortal	*Richard Garnett*	636
FRA LUIS DE LEON (1528-1591)		
The Life of the Blessed	*William Cullen Bryant*....	636
MIGUEL DE CERVANTES (1547-1616)		
Sonnet: When I Was Marked for Suffering	*Sir Edmund Gosse*	638
SAINT JOHN OF THE CROSS (1549-1591)		
The Obscure Night of the Soul	*Arthur Symons*	638
O Flame of Living Love	*Arthur Symons*	640
LUIS DE GÓNGORA (1561-1627)		
The Rosemary Spray	*E. Churton*	640
The Rose of Life	*Sir Richard Fanshawe*	641
Let Me Go Warm	*H. W. Longfellow*.......	642
LOPE DE VEGA (1562-1635)		
A Song of the Virgin Mother	*Ezra Pound*	643
To-morrow	*H. W. Longfellow*.......	644
FRANCISCO DE QUEVEDO Y VILLEGAS (1580-1645)		
Sonnet: Death Warnings....	*John Masefield*	645
PEDRO CALDERON DE LA BARCA (1600-1681)		
The Dream Called Life.....	*Edward FitzGerald*	645
From Life is a Dream	*Arthur Symons*	646
GUSTAVO ADOLFO BECQUER (1836-1870)		
They Closed Her Eyes......	*John Masefield*	647
ANTONIO MACHADO (1879-)		
Poems	*John Dos Passos*	650
SPANISH FOLK SONGS......	*Havelock Ellis*	652

FRENCH

FROM THE PROVENCAL		
GUILLAUME DE POITIERS (11th century)		
Behold the Meads........	*Harriet Waters Preston*....	654
MARCABRUN (12th century)		
At the Fountain.........	*Harriet Waters Preston*....	654
BERNARD DE VENTADOUR (12th century)		
No Marvel Is It........	*Harriet Waters Preston*...	656
ARNAUT DANIEL		
Mot Eran Dous Miei Cossir	*Harriet Waters Preston*....	657
Bel M'es Quan Lo Vens M'alena	*Harriet Waters Preston*....	658
BERTRAN DE BORN (12th century)		
Song of Battle.........	*Ezra Pound*	659
PEIRE VIDAL (12th century)		
Song of Breath.........	*Ezra Pound*	660
ANONYMOUS (12th century?)		
Alba Innominata	*Ezra Pound*	660
MARIE DE FRANCE (13th century)		
Song from Chartivel	*Arthur O'Shaughnessy*	661
Would I Might Go Far Over Sea	*Arthur O'Shaughnessy*...	663

CONTENTS

	TRANSLATED BY	PAGE
THE VIDAME DE CHARTRES (13th century?)		
April	*Algernon Charles Swinburne*	663
JEAN FROISSART (1337-1404)		
Rondel	*H. W. Longfellow*	665
CHARLES D'ORLEANS (1391-1465)		
Rondel	*Andrew Lang*	666
Spring	*Andrew Lang*	666
Alons au bois	*W. E. Henley*	667
Dieu qu'il la fait	*Ezra Pound*	667
ANONYMOUS		
John of Tours	*D. G. Rossetti*	668
My Father's Close	*D. G. Rossetti*	669
Ballade de Marguerite	*Oscar Wilde*	670
The Dole of the King's Daughter	*Oscar Wilde*	672
Medieval Norman Songs	*John Addington Symonds*	673
BALLADS		
The Three Captains	*Andrew Lang*	680
The Bridge of Death	*Andrew Lang*	682
Le Père Sévère	*Andrew Lang*	683
The Milk White Doe	*Andrew Lang*	684
A Lady of High Degree	*Andrew Lang*	686
Lost for a Rose's Sake	*Andrew Lang*	687
FRANÇOIS VILLON (1431-1489)		
Ballad of the Gibbet	*Andrew Lang*	688
Rondel	*Andrew Lang*	689
Arbor Amoris	*Andrew Lang*	690
No., I am not as others are	*Arthur Symons*	691
Villon's Straight Tip to All Cross Coves	*W. E. Henley*	692
The Ballad of Dead Ladies	*D. G. Rossetti*	693
To Death, of his Lady	*D. G. Rossetti*	694
His Mother's Service to Our Lady	*D. G. Rossetti*	694
The Complaint of the Fair Armoress	*Algernon Charles Swinburne*	695
A Double Ballad of Good Counsel	*Algernon Charles Swinburne*	698
Fragment of Death	*Algernon Charles Swinburne*	699
Ballad of the Lords of Old Time	*Algernon Charles Swinburne*	700
Ballad of the Women of Paris	*Algernon Charles Swinburne*	701
Ballad Written for a Bridegroom	*Algernon Charles Swinburne*	702
Ballad against the Enemies of France	*Algernon Charles Swinburne*	703
The Dispute of the Heart and Body of François Villon	*Algernon Charles Swinburne*	704
Epistle in Form of a Ballad to his Friends	*Algernon Charles Swinburne*	705
MELLIN DE SAINT-GELAIS (1491-1558)		
The Sonnet of the Mountain	*Austin Dobson*	706

	TRANSLATED BY	PAGE
CLEMENT MAROT (1495-1544)		
The Posy Ring	*Ford Madox Ford*	707
A Love-lesson	*Leigh Hunt*	707
Madame d'Albert's Laugh	*Leigh Hunt*	708
Friar Lubin	*H. W. Longfellow*	708
JACQUES TAHUREAU (1527-1555)		
Shadows of his Lady	*Andrew Lang*	709
Moonlight	*Andrew Lang*	709
JEAN PASSERAT (1534-1602)		
Love in May	*Andrew Lang*	710
PIERRE DE RONSARD (1524-1585)		
Fragment of a Sonnet	*John Keats*	711
Roses	*Andrew Lang*	712
The Rose	*Andrew Lang*	712
To the Moon	*Andrew Lang*	713
To his young Mistress	*Andrew Lang*	713
Deadly Kisses	*Andrew Lang*	714
Of his Lady's Old Age	*Andrew Lang*	714
On his Lady's Waking	*Andrew Lang*	715
His Lady's Death	*Andrew Lang*	715
His Lady's Tomb	*Andrew Lang*	716
And Lightly, Like the Flowers	*W. E. Henley*	716
The Paradox of Time	*Austin Dobson*	717
The Revenge	*Thomas Stanley*	718
JOACHIM DU BELLAY (1525-1560)		
From the Visions	*Edmund Spenser*	718
Hymn to the Winds	*Andrew Lang*	721
A Vow to Heavenly Venus	*Andrew Lang*	721
To his Friend in Elysium	*Andrew Lang*	722
A Sonnet to Heavenly Beauty	*Andrew Lang*	722
Rome	*Ezra Pound*	723
Heureux qui'comme Ulysse	*Gilbert K. Chesterton*	723
LOUISE LABE (1526-1566)		
Povre Ame Amoureuse	*Robert Bridges*	724
REMY BELLEAU (1528-1577)		
April	*Andrew Lang*	724
PHILIPPE DESPORTES (1545-1606)		
Conquest	*Anonymous*	727
THEOPHILE DE VIAU (1591-1626)		
Sleep	*Sir Edmund Gosse*	727
JEAN DE LA FONTAINE (1621-1695)		
The Cock and the Fox	*Elizur Wright*	728
Love and Folly	*William Cullen Bryant*	729
The Hag and the Slavies	*Edward Marsh*	730
The Crow and the Fox	*Edward Marsh*	731
JEAN-BAPTISTE POQUELIN MOLIÈRE (1622-1673)		
To Monsieur de la Mothe le Vayer	*Austin Dobson*	732
ANDRÉ CHÉNIER (1760-1794)		
Elegies	*Arthur Symons*	732

	TRANSLATED BY	PAGE
PIERRE JEAN DE BERANGER (1780-1857)		
The King of Yvetot	*William Toynbee*	734
ALPHONSE MARIE LOUIS DE LAMARTINE (1792-1869)		
The Cedars of Lebanon	*Toru Dutt*	736
ALFRED DE VIGNY (1797-1863)		
The Sound of the Horn	*Wilfrid Thorley*	737
Nature	*Margaret Jourdain*	738
VICTOR HUGO (1802-1885)		
A Sunset	*Francis Thompson*	739
Heard on the Mountain	*Francis Thompson*	741
The Grave and the Rose	*Andrew Lang*	744
The Genesis of Butterflies	*Andrew Lang*	745
More Strong than Time	*Andrew Lang*	745
The Poor Children	*Algernon Charles Swinburne*	746
GÉRARD DE NERVAL (1808-1855)		
An Old Tune	*Andrew Lang*	747
ALFRED DE MUSSET (1810-1857)		
Souvenir	*George Santayana*	748
Juana	*Andrew Lang*	753
THÉOPHILE GAUTIER (1811-1872)		
Art	*George Santayana*	755
Posthumous Coquetry	*Arthur Symons*	757
Clarimonde	*Lafcadio Hearn*	758
Love at Sea	*Algernon Charles Swinburne*	759
LECONTE DE LISLE (1818-1894)		
Hialmar Speaks to the Raven	*James Elroy Flecker*	760
CHARLES BAUDELAIRE (1821-1867)		
Litany to Satan	*James Elroy Flecker*	762
Don Juan in Hell	*James Elroy Flecker*	763
Epilogue	*Arthur Symons*	764
Les Hiboux	*Arthur Symons*	764
Parfum Exotique	*Arthur Symons*	765
Élévation	*Arthur Symons*	765
Correspondences	*Allen Tate*	766
A Carrion	*Allen Tate*	767
Sois Sage O ma Douleur	*Lord Alfred Douglas*	768
La Beauté	*Lord Alfred Douglas*	769
Le Balcon	*Lord Alfred Douglas*	769
Harmonie du Soir	*Lord Alfred Douglas*	770
HENRI MURGER (1822-1861)		
Spring in the Students' Quarter	*Andrew Lang*	771
Old Loves	*Andrew Lang*	772
FRÉDÉRIC MISTRAL (1830-1914)		
The Mares of the Camargue	*George Meredith*	773
The Cocooning	*Harriet Waters Preston*	774
The Leaf-Picking	*Harriet Waters Preston*	775
SULLY PRUDHOMME (1839-1907)		
The Struggle	*Arthur O'Shaughnessy*	775
CATULLE MENDÉS (1841-1909)		
I Go By Road	*Alice Meynell*	776

	TRANSLATED BY	PAGE
STÉPHANE MALLARMÉ (1842-1898)		
L'Après-midi d'un Faune	*Aldous Huxley*	777
Sigh	*Arthur Symons*	780
Sea-wind	*Arthur Symons*	781
Anguish	*Arthur Symons*	781
JOSE-MARIA DE HEREDIA (1842-1905)		
The Flute: A Pastoral	*H. J. C. Grierson*	782
The Laborer	*Wilfrid Thorley*	782
PAUL VERLAINE (1844-1896)		
Il pleut Doucement sur la Ville	*Ernest Dowson*	783
Spleen	*Ernest Dowson*	783
The Sky Is Up Above the Roof	*Ernest Dowson*	784
A Clymene	*Arthur Symons*	784
Fantoches	*Arthur Symons*	785
Pantomime	*Arthur Symons*	786
Cythère	*Arthur Symons*	786
Dans l'Allée	*Arthur Symons*	787
Mandoline	*Arthur Symons*	787
Clair de Lune	*Arthur Symons*	788
A la Promenade	*Arthur Symons*	788
Cortège	*Arthur Symons*	789
En Bateau	*Arthur Symons*	789
Chansons d'Automne	*Arthur Symons*	790
Femme et Chatte	*Arthur Symons*	791
Art Poetique	*Arthur Symons*	791
From Sagesse	*Arthur Symons*	792
TRISTAN CORBIÈRE (1845-1875)		
Epitaph	*Joseph T. Shipley*	794
ARTHUR RIMBAUD (1854-1891)		
Sensation	*Jethro Bithell*	794
The Sleeper of the Valley	*Ludwig Lewisohn*	795
Hunger	*Edgell Rickword*	795
Song of the Highest Tower	*Edgell Rickword*	796
Les Chercheuses de Poux	*T. Sturge Moore*	797
EMILE VERHAEREN (1855-1916)		
The Poor	*Ludwig Lewisohn*	797
ALBERT SAMAIN (1858-1900)		
Pannyra of the Golden Heel	*James Elroy Flecker*	798
From Summer Hours	*Jethro Bithell*	799
REMY DE GOURMONT (1858-1915)		
Hair	*Jethro Bithell*	799
JULES LAFORGUE (1860-1887)		
For the Book of Love	*Jethro Bithell*	800
MAURICE MAETERLINCK (1862-)		
Song	*Jethro Bithell*	801
The Last Words	*Frederick York Powell*	801
HENRI DE REGNIER (1864-)		
Night	*Seumas O'Sullivan*	802
Je ne veux de personne auprès de ma tristesse	*Seumas O'Sullivan*	803

	TRANSLATED BY	PAGE
ANDRÉ SPIRE (1868-)		
Lonely	Jethro Bithell	803
Spring	Jethro Bithell	804
Nudities	Jethro Bithell	804
FRANCIS JAMMES (1868-)		
Amsterdam	Jethro Bithell	805
Prayer to Go to Paradise with the Asses	Jethro Bithell	808
Love	Jethro Bithell	809
The Child Reads an Almanac	Ludwig Lewisohn	809
PAUL FORT (1872-)		
Pan and the Cherries	Jethro Bithell	810
Ballade	Frederick York Powell	810
PAUL VALÉRY (1872-)		
Narcissus	Joseph T. Shipley	811
Helen, the Sad Queen	Joseph T. Shipley	813
CHARLES GUÉRIN (1873-1907)		
Partings	Jethro Bithell	814
CHARLES VILDRAC (1882-)		
After Midnight	Jethro Bithell	814
JULES ROMAINS (1885-)		
Another Spirit Advances	Joseph T. Shipley	815

GERMAN

FROM THE MINNESINGERS		
SIR DIETMAR VON AIST (12th century)		
Parting at Morning	Frank C. Nicholson	816
A Bird Was Singing	Jethro Bithell	816
A Lady Stood	Jethro Bithell	817
SIR HEINRICH VON RUGGE (12th century)		
He That Loves a Rosy Cheek	Jethro Bithell	817
SIR REINMAR VON HAGENAU (12th century)		
As On the Heather	Jethro Bithell	818
A Childish Game	Jethro Bithell	819
SIR HARTMANN VON AUE (12th century)		
None is Happy	Jethro Bithell	820
SIR WALTHER VON DER VOGELWEIDE (13th century)		
There Is a Lady	Jethro Bithell	820
Awake!	Jethro Bithell	821
With a Rod No Man Alive	Jethro Bithell	821
Tandaradei	Ford Madox Ford	822
SIR WOLFRAM VON ESCHENBACH (13th century)		
His Own True Wife	Jethro Bithell	823
SIR NEIDHART VON REUENTAL (13th century)		
On the Mountain	Jethro Bithell	824
SIR ULRICH VON LIECHTENSTEIN (13th century)		
Love, Whose Month Was Ever May	Jethro Bithell	824
SIR REINMAR VON ZWETER (13th century)		
I Came A-riding	Jethro Bithell	825

	TRANSLATED BY	PAGE
ANONYMOUS (13th century)		
Truelove	Jethro Bithell	826
ANONYMOUS (14th century?)		
Serenade	Jethro Bithell	826
ANONYMOUS (16th century)		
Westphalian Song	Samuel Taylor Coleridge	827
A Lovely Rose is Sprung	Margarete Münsterberg	827
MARTIN LUTHER (1483-1546)		
A Mighty Fortress is Our God	F. H. Hedge	828
JOHANN GOTTFRIED VON HERDER (1744-1803)		
Sir Olaf	Elizabeth Craigmyle	829
Esthonian Bridal Song	W. Taylor	831
LUDWIG HEINRICH CHRISTOPH HÖLTY (1748-1776)		
Harvest Song	Charles J. Brooks	831
JOHANN WOLFGANG VON GOETHE (1749-1832)		
The Erl-King	Sir Walter Scott	832
Wanderer's Night-Songs	H. W. Longfellow	833
The Lay of the Captive Count	James Clarence Mangan	834
The Minstrel	James Clarence Mangan	837
The Rose	James Clarence Mangan	838
The King of Thulé	James Clarence Mangan	839
A Voice from the Invisible World	James Clarence Mangan	840
An Irish Lamentation	James Clarence Mangan	840
Prometheus	John S. Dwight	841
To the Parted One	Christopher Pearse Cranch	843
To a Golden Heart, Worn Round His Neck	Margaret Fuller Ossoli	843
Mignon	James Elroy Flecker	844
The Shepherd's Lament	Bayard Taylor	845
FROM FAUST		
Prologue in Heaven	Percy Bysshe Shelley	845
Soldier's Song	Bayard Taylor	846
The Thought Eternal	Ludwig Lewisohn	847
FRIEDRICH VON SCHILLER (1759-1805)		
Thekla's Song	Samuel Taylor Coleridge	847
The Maid of Orleans	James Clarence Mangan	848
The Unrealities	James Clarence Mangan	848
To My Friends	James Clarence Mangan	851
JOHANN GAUDENZ VON SALIS (1762-1834)		
Song of the Silent Land	H. W. Longfellow	852
SIEGFRIED AUGUST MAHLMANN (1771-1826)		
Allah	H. W. Longfellow	853
JOHANN LUDWIG TIECK (1773-1853)		
Autumn Song	James Clarence Mangan	854
JUSTINUS KERNER (1786-1862)		
Home-sickness	James Clarence Mangan	855
LUDWIG UHLAND (1787-1862)		
Spirits Everywhere	James Clarence Mangan	855
Ichabod! the Glory Has Departed	James Clarence Mangan	856
Durand of Blonden	James Clarence Mangan	857

	TRANSLATED BY	PAGE
The Luck of Edenhall	*H. W. Longfellow*	858
The Castle by the Sea	*H. W. Longfellow*	860
In a Lovely Garden Walking	*George MacDonald*	861
A Leaf	*John S. Dwight*	861
The Hostess' Daughter	*Margarete Münsterberg*	862
FRIEDRICH RUECKERT (1789-1866)		
The Ride Round the Parapet	*James Clarence Mangan*	863
Barbarossa	*Elizabeth Craigmyle*	869
WILHELM MÜLLER (1794-1827)		
Whither?	*H. W. Longfellow*	870
HEINRICH HEINE (1799-1856)		
Proem	*Elizabeth Barrett Browning*	871
Ad Finem	*Elizabeth Barrett Browning*	871
Mein Kind, wir waren Kinder	*Elizabeth Barrett Browning*	872
Ich weiss nicht was soll es bedeuten	*Alexander MacMillan*	873
The Sea Hath its Pearls	*H. W. Longfellow*	873
Sag' mir wer einst die Uhren erfund	*Richard Garnett*	874
Warum sind denn die Rosen so blass	*Richard Garnett*	874
Es fällt ein stern herunter	*Richard Garnett*	875
Mir traümte von einem Königskind	*Richard Garnett*	875
Die Rose, die Lilie	*Richard Garnett*	876
Auf meiner Herzliebsten Augelein	*Richard Garnett*	876
Mein Liebchen, wir sassen zusammen	*James Thomson*	876
Es stehen unbeweglich	*James Thomson*	877
Die Lotosblume ängstigt	*James Thomson*	877
Die Welt ist dumm	*James Thomson*	878
Die blauen Veilchen der Augelein	*James Thomson*	878
Ein Fichtenbaum steht einsam	*James Thomson*	878
Mir träumte wieder der alte Traum	*James Thomson*	879
Mein Herz, mein Herz ist traurig	*James Thomson*	879
Der Mond ist aufgegangen	*James Thomson*	880
Sag', wo ist Dein schönes Liebchen	*James Thomson*	880
Wie langsam kriechet sie dahin	*Lord Houghton*	881
Enfant Perdu	*Lord Houghton*	881
Zu fragmentarisch ist Welt und Leben	*Charles G. Leland*	882
Du bist wie eine Blume	*Kate Freiligrath Kroeker*	882
The Message	*Kate Freiligrath Kroeker*	883
To My Mother	*Matilda Dickson*	883
Im Traum sah Ich	*Sir Theodore Martin*	884

	TRANSLATED BY	PAGE
Mädchen mit dem rothen Mündchen	*Sir Theodore Martin*	884
Anno 1829	*Charles Stuart Calverley*	885
The Azra	*John Hay*	885
Dear Maiden	*John Todhunter*	886
I Met by Chance	*John Todhunter*	887
I Wept as I Lay Dreaming	*John Todhunter*	888
I'm Black and Blue	*John Todhunter*	888
We Cared for Each Other	*John Todhunter*	888
Farewell	*John Todhunter*	889
Fresco-Sonnets to Christian Sethe	*John Todhunter*	889
The Voyage	*John Todhunter*	890
The Window-glance	*John Todhunter*	890
From Die Heimkehr	*Ezra Pound*	891
A Maiden Lies in Her Chamber	*Louis Untermeyer*	892
Oh Lovely Fishermaiden	*Louis Untermeyer*	893
Twilight	*Louis Untermeyer*	893
The Coffin	*Louis Untermeyer*	894
The Storm	*Louis Untermeyer*	895
My Songs Are Poisoned	*Louis Untermeyer*	895
When Two are Parted	*Louis Untermeyer*	896
I Love But Thee	*Louis Untermeyer*	896
When Young Hearts Break	*Louis Untermeyer*	896
FROM THE NORTH SEA		
A Night by the Sea	*Howard Mumford Jones*	897
Evening Twilight	*John Todhunter*	899
Epilog	*Louis Untermeyer*	899
EDUARD MÖRICKE (1804-1875)		
Beauty Rohtraut	*George Meredith*	900
ARTHUR FITGER (1840-1909)		
Evening Prayer	*Jethro Bithell*	901
FRIEDRICH WILHELM NIETZSCHE (1844-1900)		
Star Morals	*Ludwig Lewisohn*	902
The Solitary	*Ludwig Lewisohn*	903
DETLEV VON LILIENCRON (1844-1909)		
Who Knows Where	*Ludwig Lewisohn*	904
After the Hunt	*Ludwig Lewisohn*	905
Autumn	*Ludwig Lewisohn*	905
GUSTAV FALKE (1853-1916)		
Strand-Thistle	*Jethro Bithell*	905
God's Harp	*Ludwig Lewisohn*	906
PETER HILLE (1854-1904)		
The Maiden	*Jethro Bithell*	906
Beauty	*Jethro Bithell*	907
RICHARD DEHMEL (1863-1920)		
My Drinking Song	*Ludwig Lewisohn*	908
Before the Storm	*Ludwig Lewisohn*	909
Vigil	*Ludwig Lewisohn*	910
Harvest Song	*Ludwig Lewisohn*	910
The Silent Town	*Jethro Bithell*	911

CONTENTS

	TRANSLATED BY	PAGE
To ——?	*Jethro Bithell*	912
A Trysting	*Jethro Bithell*	912
The Laborer	*Jethro Bithell*	913
Voice in Darkness	*Margarete Münsterberg*	913
CÄSAR FLAISCHLEN (1864-1920)		
Most Quietly at Times	*Jethro Bithell*	914
OTTO JULIUS BIERBAUM (1865-1910)		
Kindly Vision	*Jethro Bithell*	915
Blacksmith Pain	*Jethro Bithell*	915
Jeannette	*Jethro Bithell*	915
Oft in the Silent Night	*Ludwig Lewisohn*	916
STEFAN GEORGE (1868-1933)		
Stanzas Concerning Love	*Ludwig Lewisohn*	918
Invocation and Prelude	*Ludwig Lewisohn*	918
Rapture	*Ludwig Lewisohn*	920
The Lord of the Isle	*Ludwig Lewisohn*	921
From Das Jahr der Seele—No Way Too Long	*Daisy Broicher*	921
PETER BAUM (1869-1916)		
Horror	*Jethro Bithell*	922
Psalms of Love	*Jethro Bithell*	922
ALFRED MOMBERT (1872-)		
Sleeping They Bear Me	*Jethro Bithell*	924
Idyl	*Ludwig Lewisohn*	924
CARL BUSSE (1872-)		
In the Night of the Full Moon	*Jethro Bithell*	925
The Quiet Kingdom	*Ludwig Lewisohn*	925
RICHARD SCHAUKAL (1874-)		
Images	*Ludwig Lewisohn*	925
HUGO VON HOFMANNSTHAL (1874-1929)		
The Two	*Ludwig Lewisohn*	926
A Venetian Night	*Ludwig Lewisohn*	926
Ballad of the Outer Life	*Jethro Bithell*	928
Many Indeed Must Perish in the Keel	*Jethro Bithell*	928
Stanzas on Mutability	*Jethro Bithell*	929
ARNO HOLZ (1863-)		
A Leave-taking	*Jethro Bithell*	930
Roses Red	*Jethro Bithell*	931
Buddha	*William Ellery Leonard*	932
Phantasus	*Ludwig Lewisohn*	933
KARL BULCKE (1875-)		
There is an Old City	*Ludwig Lewisohn*	934
RAINER MARIA RILKE (1875-1926)		
Prayer of the Maidens to Mary	*Jethro Bithell*	934
Abishag	*Jethro Bithell*	935
For, Lord, the Crowded Cities Be	*Ludwig Lewisohn*	936
The Youth Dreams	*Ludwig Lewisohn*	937
The Song of Love	*Ludwig Lewisohn*	937

	TRANSLATED BY	PAGE
Silent Hour	*Jessie Lemont*	938
Presaging	*Jessie Lemont*	938
ERNST HARDT (1876-)		
The Specter	*Jethro Bithell*	939
HERMANN HESSE (1877-)		
Spring Song	*Ludwig Lewisohn*	939
Night	*Ludwig Lewisohn*	940
KARL GUSTAVE VOLLMOELLER (1878-1922)		
Nocturne in G Minor	*Ludwig Lewisohn*	940

SCANDINAVIAN

OLD NORSE		
FROM THE ELDER EDDA (c. 1000)		
Voluspo	*Henry Adams Bellows*	942
The First Lay of Gudrun	*William Morris and Eirikr Magnusson*	951
The Lay of Sigurd	*William Morris and Eirikr Magnusson*	957
Counsels of Sigrdrifa	*William Morris and Eirikr Magnusson*	974
DANISH		
ANONYMOUS (14th-16th centuries)		
Ballads		
The Elected Knight	*H. W. Longfellow*	976
The Mer-man, and Marstig's Daughter	*Robert Jamieson*	978
Elfer Hill	*Robert Jamieson*	979
JOHANNES EVALD (1743-1781)		
King Christian	*H. W. Longfellow*	981
JENS BAGGESEN (1764-1826)		
Childhood	*H. W. Longfellow*	982
ADAM OEHLENSCHLAGER (1779-1850)		
There is a Charming Land	*Robert Hillyer*	983
NORWEGIAN		
HENRIK ARNOLD THAULOV WERGELAND (1808-1845)		
The Wall-Flower	*Sir Edmund Gosse*	984
HENRIK IBSEN (1828-1906)		
In the Orchard	*Sir Edmund Gosse*	985
BJÖRNSTERNE BJÖRNSON (1832-1910)		
Fatherland Song	*William Ellery Leonard*	987
The Boy and the Flute	*Sir Edmund Gosse*	986
SWEDISH		
GUSTAV ROSENHANE (1619-1684)		
Sonnets	*Sir Edmund Gosse*	988
OLOF WEXIONIUS (1656-1690?)		
On the Death of a Pious Lady	*Sir Edmund Gosse*	989
ERIK JOHANN STAGNELIUS (1793-1823)		
Memory	*Sir Edmund Gosse*	989

TRANSLATED BY PAGE

ESAIAS TEGNER (1782-1846)
FROM FRITHIOFS SAGA
Frithiof's Homestead ... *H. W. Longfellow* 990
Frithiof's Farewell ..... *H. W. Longfellow* 992

RUSSIAN

FOLK SONGS
The Plaint of the Wife ..... *W. R. S. Ralston* 994
Sorrow .... *W. R. S. Ralston* 995
Love-Song .... *W. R. S. Ralston* 996
IVAN ANDREEVICH KRILOFF (1768-1844)
The Peasant and the Sheep .. *C. Fillingham Coxwell*.... 997
ALEXANDER SERGEYEVICH PUSHKIN (1799-1837)
Autumn .... *Max Eastman* 998
Message to Siberia .... *Max Eastman* 1000
Work .... *Babette Deutsch and Avrahm Yarmolinsky* 1000
The Prophet .... *Babette Deutsch and Avrahm Yarmolinsky* 1001
FYODOR TYUTCHEV (1803-1873)
As Ocean's Stream .... *Babette Deutsch and Avrahm Yarmolinsky* 1002
NIKOLAY PLATONOVICH OGAREV (1813-1879)
The Road .... *P. E. Matheson* 1002
MIKHAIL YURYEVICH LERMONTOV (1814-1841)
Dagger .... *Max Eastman* 1003
A Sail .... *Max Eastman* 1003
Composed While Under Arrest .... *Max Eastman* 1004
A Thought .... *Max Eastman* 1004
The Mountain .... *Max Eastman* 1005
The Reed .... *J. J. Robbins* 1006
From The Daemon .... *Babette Deutsch and Avrahm Yarmolinsky* 1007
AFANASY AFANASYEVICH FOETH (SHENSHIN) (1820-1892)
Morning Song .... *Max Eastman* 1008
NIKOLAI NEKRASOV (1821-1877)
The Capitals Are Rocked ... *Babette Deutsch and Avrahm Yarmolinsky* 1008
IVAN SAVVICH NIKITIN (1824-1861)
A Night in a Village .... *P. E. Matheson* 1009
FYODOR SOLOGUB (1863-1927)
The Amphora .... *Babette Deutsch and Avrahm Yarmolinsky* 1009
Austere the Music of My Songs .... *Babette Deutsch and Avrahm Yarmolinsky* 1010
VYACHESLAV IVANOV (1866-)
The Holy Rose .... *Babette Deutsch and Avrahm Yarmolinsky* 1010
IVAN BUNIN (1870-)
Flax .... *Babette Deutsch and Avrahm Yarmolinsky* 1011

	TRANSLATED BY	PAGE
VALERY BRYUSOV (1873-1924)		
Radiant Ranks of Seraphim ..	*Babette Deutsch and Avrahm Yarmolinsky...*	1011
ALEXANDER BLOK (1880-1921)		
Russia	*Babette Deutsch and Avrahm Yarmolinsky...*	1012
From The Twelve	*Babette Deutsch and Avrahm Yarmolinsky...*	1013
The Scythians	*Babette Deutsch and Avrahm Yarmolinsky...*	1017
VLADIMIR MAYAKOVSKY (1894-)		
Our March	*Babette Deutsch and Avrahm Yarmolinsky...*	1020

ENGLISH

ANONYMOUS (c. 1250)
Sumer is icumen in 1021
GEOFFREY CHAUCER (1340?-1400)
Balade 1021
Truth 1022
Gentilesse 1023
Lak of Stedfastnesse 1024
ANONYMOUS (16th-17th centuries)
Sir Patrick Spens 1025
The Wife of Usher's Well 1026
Bonny Barbara Allan 1028
Lord Randal 1029
Bonnie George Campbell 1029
The Twa Corbies 1030
The Maid Freed from the Gallows 1031
Sweet William's Ghost 1033
Helen of Kirconnell 1035
EDMUND SPENSER (1552-1599)
Amoretti 1036
Prothalamion 1037
SIR PHILIP SIDNEY (1554-1586)
A Ditty 1042
From Astrophel and Stella 1043
MICHAEL DRAYTON (1563-1631)
From Idea 1044
CHRISTOPHER MARLOWE (1564-1593)
The Passionate Shepherd to His Love 1044
WILLIAM SHAKESPEARE (1564-1616)
From the Sonnets 1045
Songs from the Plays 1056
BEN JONSON (1573-1637)
Hymn to Diana 1061
Song to Celia 1061
Simplex Munditiis 1062
On My First Son 1062
To Penshurst 1063
To William Camden 1065

CONTENTS

PAGE

John Donne (1573-1631)
- Song ... 1066
- Love's Deity ... 1067
- The Funeral ... 1067
- The Good Morrow ... 1068
- Song ... 1069
- The Blossom ... 1070
- A Lecture Upon the Shadow ... 1071
- A Hymn to God the Father ... 1072

Richard Barnefield (1574-1627)
- The Nightingale ... 1073

John Fletcher (1579-1625)
- Aspatia's Song ... 1074

George Wither (1588-1667)
- The Lover's Resolution ... 1074

William Browne (1590?-1645?)
- On the Countess of Pembroke ... 1075

Robert Herrick (1591-1674)
- The Argument of His Book ... 1076
- An Ode for Ben Jonson ... 1076
- To Live Merrily and to Trust to Good Verses ... 1077
- To Daffodils ... 1079
- Upon Julia's Clothes ... 1079
- Sweet Disorder ... 1079
- Grace for a Child ... 1080
- To the Virgins to Make Much of Time ... 1080
- The Mad Maid's Song ... 1081
- To Meadows ... 1082

George Herbert (1593-1633)
- Virtue ... 1082
- Peace ... 1083
- The Collar ... 1084
- Love ... 1085
- The Pulley ... 1086
- The Flower ... 1086

Thomas Carew (1594?-1639)
- Disdain Returned ... 1088
- Ask Me No More ... 1089

James Shirley (1596-1666)
- A Dirge ... 1089

William Davenant (1606-1668)
- Song ... 1090

Edmund Waller (1606-1687)
- Go, Lovely Rose! ... 1091
- On a Girdle ... 1091

John Milton (1608-1674)
- L'Allegro ... 1092
- Il Penseroso ... 1096
- Lycidas ... 1100
- On His Having Arrived at the Age of Twenty-three ... 1105
- To Mr. H. Lawes on His Airs ... 1106
- To Mr. Lawrence ... 1106

PAGE
On His Blindness 1107
On the Late Massacre in Piedmont 1107
SIR JOHN SUCKLING (1609-1642)
Why So Pale and Wan? 1108
The Constant Lover 1108
RICHARD LOVELACE (1618-1658)
To Lucasta, on Going to the Wars 1109
To Althea, from Prison 1109
ANDREW MARVELL (1621-1678)
The Garden 1110
To His Coy Mistress 1112
The Mower to the Glowworms 1114
Bermudas 1114
HENRY VAUGHAN (1622-1695)
The Retreat 1115
Peace 1116
The World 1117
Departed Friends 1119
JOHN DRYDEN (1631-1700)
To the Memory of Mr. Oldham 1120
Song from Marriage à la Mode 1121
Song from Amphitryon 1121
Song from Secret Love 1122
A Song for St. Cecilia's Day 1122
Characters from the Satires 1124
Achitophel 1124
Zimri 1125
Og and Doeg 1126
SIR CHARLES SEDLEY (1639?-1701)
To Celia 1128
MATTHEW PRIOR (1664-1721)
A Better Answer 1129
An Ode 1130
JOSEPH ADDISON (1672-1719)
Hymn 1131
ALEXANDER POPE (1688-1744)
Ode on Solitude 1131
Characters from the Satires 1132
Atticus 1132
Sporus 1133
Wharton 1134
Chloe 1134
HENRY CAREY (1693?-1743)
Sally in Our Alley 1135
WILLIAM SHENSTONE (1714-1763)
Written at an Inn at Henley 1137
THOMAS GRAY (1716-1771)
Elegy Written in a Country Churchyard 1138
The Progress of Poesy 1142
WILLIAM COLLINS (1721-1759)
Ode to Evening 1146
Ode Written in the Beginning of the Year 1746 1147

CONTENTS

PAGE

Oliver Goldsmith (1728-1774)
Song 1148

William Blake (1757-1827)
The Piper 1148
Nurse's Song 1148
On Another's Sorrow 1149
The Little Black Boy 1149
The Clod and the Pebble 1151
The Sick Rose 1152
The Tiger 1152
Ah, Sunflower 1152
The Garden of Love 1153
A Poison Tree 1153
London 1154
From Milton 1154
Eternity 1155

Robert Burns (1759-1796)
Highland Mary 1155
Song: Mary Morison 1156
Ye Flowery Banks 1157
Of A' the Airts 1157
A Red, Red Rose 1158
Flow Gently, Sweet Afton 1158
My Heart's in the Highlands 1159
John Anderson My Jo 1160
Song: Green Grow the Rashes 1160
Tam Glen 1161
Auld Lang Syne 1162
Willie Brewed a Peck o' Maut 1163

William Wordsworth (1770-1850)
Influence of Natural Objects 1163
She Dwelt Among the Untrodden Ways 1164
I Traveled Among Unknown Men 1166
A Slumber Did My Spirit Seal 1166
The Solitary Reaper 1167
London 1802 1167
Composed Upon Westminster Bridge Sept. 3, 1802 1168
It is a Beauteous Evening, Calm and Free 1169
The World Is Too Much With Us 1169
Ode to Duty 1170
Ode: Intimations of Immortality 1170

Sir Walter Scott (1771-1832)
Soldier, Rest! 1172

Samuel Taylor Coleridge (1772-1834)
Kubla Khan 1178

Charles Lamb (1775-1834)
The Old Familiar Faces 1179

Walter Savage Landor (1775-1864)
Rose Aylmer 1181
Past Ruined Ilion 1181
On His Seventy-fifth Birthday 1182
Dirce 1182

PAGE

THOMAS LOVE PEACOCK (1785-1866)
The War-Song of Dinas Vawr 1182
GEORGE GORDON, LORD BYRON (1788-1824)
She Walks in Beauty 1184
Stanzas for Music 1184
So, We'll Go No More A-roving 1185
The Isles of Greece 1185
PERCY BYSSHE SHELLEY (1792-1822)
To—— 1188
The Indian Serenade 1188
To Night 1189
Chorus from Hellas 1190
Ozymandias 1191
Ode to the West Wind 1192
JOHN KEATS (1795-1821)
Ode to a Nightingale 1194
Ode on a Grecian Urn 1197
To Autumn 1198
Robin Hood 1199
Lines on the Mermaid Tavern 1201
La Belle Dame sans Merci 1202
When I Have Fears That I May Cease To Be 1203
JOHN HENRY, CARDINAL NEWMAN (1801-1890)
The Pillar of the Cloud 1204
ALFRED, LORD TENNYSON (1809-1892)
Mariana 1204
Ulysses 1207
Song from Maud 1209
Break, break, break 1211
Songs from The Princess 1212
To Vergil 1213
ROBERT BROWNING (1812-1889)
Home-Thoughts, from Abroad 1214
Home-Thoughts, from the Sea 1215
Meeting at Night 1215
Parting at Morning 1216
Porphyria's Lover 1216
My Last Duchess 1218
The Bishop Orders His Tomb at St. Praxed's Church ... 1219
Caliban Upon Setebos 1223
ARTHUR HUGH CLOUGH (1819-1861)
Where Lies the Land? 1231
Say Not the Struggle Nought Availeth 1231
MATTHEW ARNOLD (1822-1888)
Requiescat 1232
Dover Beach 1232
GEORGE MEREDITH (1828-1909)
Love in the Valley 1234
Lucifer in Starlight 1240
DANTE GABRIEL ROSSETTI (1828-1882)
The Blessed Damozel 1240

CONTENTS

PAGE

CHRISTINA ROSSETTI (1830-1894)
Song 1245
A Birthday 1245
Remember 1246
WILLIAM MORRIS (1834-1896)
An Apology 1246
ALGERNON CHARLES SWINBURNE (1837-1909)
The Garden of Proserpine 1248
Chorus from Atalanta in Calydon 1250
THOMAS HARDY (1840-1928)
Drummer Hodge 1252
Hap 1253
Let Me Enjoy 1253
On An Invitation to the United States 1254
The Roman Road 1254
Near Lanivet, 1872 1255
The Fallow Deer at the Lonely House 1256
GERARD MANLEY HOPKINS (1844-1898)
God's Grandeur 1256
Pied Beauty 1257
Thou Art Indeed Just, Lord 1257
ALICE MEYNELL (1850-1923)
The Shepherdess 1258
FRANCIS THOMPSON (1857-1907)
Arab Love-song 1258
Daisy 1259
ALFRED EDWARD HOUSMAN (1859-1936)
With Rue My Heart Is Laden 1261
White in the Moon 1261
Loveliest of Trees 1262
Far in a Western Brookland 1262
RUDYARD KIPLING (1865-1936)
Recessional 1263
ERNEST DOWSON (1867-1900)
Vitae Summa Brevis Spem nos Vetat Incohare Longam . 1264
Non Sum Qualis Eram Bonae Sub Regno Cynarae 1264
WILLIAM HENRY DAVIES (1870-)
Leisure 1265
WALTER DE LA MARE (1873-)
The Listeners 1265
JOHN MASEFIELD (1878-)
Sonnet 1267
ALDOUS HUXLEY (1894-)
First Philosopher's Song 1267
ROBERT GRAVES (1895-)
Lost Love 1268
Pure Death 1269
The Cool Web 1269
STEPHEN SPENDER (1909-)
The Pylons 1270
New Year 1271

IRISH

FROM THE GAELIC — TRANSLATED BY — PAGE
COLUM-CILLE (6th century)
Farewell to Ireland ...... Douglas Hyde 1272
HUGH O'DONNELL (16th century)
Dark Rosaleen .... James Clarence Mangan . 1273
O'GNIVE (16th century)
The Downfall of the Gael Sir Samuel Ferguson 1275
EGAN O'RAHILLY (18th century)
Lament for Banba .... James Clarence Mangan . 1278
RAFERTY (d. 1835)
I Am Raferty .... Douglas Hyde 1279
ANONYMOUS
A Poem to be Said on Hearing the Birds Sing . Douglas Hyde 1280
THOMAS MOORE (1779-1852)
How Oft Has the Banshee Cried 1280
ANONYMOUS
The Wearin' o' the Green 1281
KATHERINE TYNAN (1861-1931)
The Doves 1282
WILLIAM BUTLER YEATS (1865-)
To An Isle in the Water 1283
When You Are Old 1283
The Everlasting Voices 1284
The Cold Heaven 1284
To a Friend Whose Work Has Come to Nothing 1285
GEORGE WILLIAM RUSSELL ("A.E.") (1867-1935)
A Mountain Wind 1285
A Holy Hill 1286
The Lonely 1286
Immortality 1287
JOHN MILLINGTON SYNGE (1871-1909)
Prelude 1287
In Kerry 1288
MOIRA O'NEILL
Corrymeela 1288
THOMAS MACDONAGH (1878-1916)
John-John 1289
SEUMAS O'SULLIVAN (1878-)
The Starling Lake 1291
PADRAIC PEARSE (1880-1916)
Ideal (translated from the Gaelic by Thomas MacDonagh) 1291
PADRAIC COLUM (1881-)
River-Mates 1292
A Drover 1293
JOSEPH CAMPBELL (1881-)
The Blind Man at the Fair 1294
The Old Woman 1295
JAMES STEPHENS (1882-)
Deirdre 1295

		PAGE
The Daisies		1296
The Goat Paths		1297
James Joyce (1882-)		
I Hear An Army		1298
Joseph Plunkett (1887-1916)		
The Spark		1298
Francis Ledwidge (1891-1917)		
Lament for the Poets: 1916		1300
Ardan Mór		1300

AMERICAN

	TRANSLATED BY	PAGE
From the American Indian		
Love Song (Papago)	*Mary Austin*	1301
Neither Spirit Nor Bird (Shoshone)	*Mary Austin*	1301
Come Not Near My Songs (Shoshone)	*Mary Austin*	1302
Lament of a Man for His Son (Paiute)	*Mary Austin*	1302
The Grass on the Mountain (Paiute)	*Mary Austin*	1303
Hunting-Song (Navaho)	*Natalie Curtis*	1304
Song of the Horse (Navaho)	*Natalie Curtis*	1305
Song of the Rain Chant (Navaho)	*Natalie Curtis*	1305
Korosta Katzina Song (Hopi)	*Natalie Curtis*	1306
Corn-grinding Song (Laguna)	*Natalie Curtis*	1307
The Voice that Beautifies the Land (Navaho)	*Washington Matthews*	1307
Song to the Mountains (Pawnee)	*Alice C. Fletcher*	1308
A Lover's Lament (Tewa)	*H. J. Spinden*	1308
The Coyote and the Locust (Zuñi)	*Frank Cushing*	1309
Ojibwa War Songs	*H. H. Schoolcraft*	1309
Three Songs from the Haida	*Constance Lindsay Skinner*	1310
William Cullen Bryant (1794-1878)		
Thanatopsis		1311
To a Waterfowl		1313
To the Fringed Gentian		1314
Ralph Waldo Emerson (1803-1882)		
The Rhodora		1315
Brahma		1315
Concord Hymn		1316
The Problem		1317
Give all to Love		1319
Each and All		1320
The Informing Spirit		1321
Bacchus		1322

PAGE
Nature 1324
Terminus 1324
HENRY WADSWORTH LONGFELLOW (1807-1882)
My Lost Youth 1325
The Skeleton in Armor 1328
The Rainy Day 1332
Chaucer 1333
Shakespeare 1333
Milton 1334
JOHN GREENLEAF WHITTIER (1807-1892)
The Farewell of a Virginia Slave Mother 1334
Telling the Bees 1336
The Sisters 1338
EDGAR ALLAN POE (1809-1849)
To Helen 1340
Ulalume 1341
Annabel Lee 1343
Israfel 1344
The Conqueror Worm 1346
Eldorado 1347
HENRY DAVID THOREAU (1817-1862)
Smoke 1348
Mist 1348
WALT WHITMAN (1819-1892)
There Was a Child Went Forth 1349
This Compost 1351
I Saw in Louisiana a Live-Oak Growing 1353
A Noiseless, Patient Spider 1354
Out of the Cradle Endlessly Rocking 1354
When Lilacs Last in the Dooryard Bloomed 1361
I Hear America Singing 1370
On the Beach at Night 1370
EMILY DICKINSON (1830-1886)
Success 1372
A Wounded Deer Leaps Highest 1372
Exclusion 1373
Suspense 1373
I Died for Beauty 1373
Because I Could Not Stop for Death 1374
After a Hundred Years 1374
I Had Not Minded Walls 1375
GEORGE SANTAYANA (1863-)
I would I might forget that I am I 1375
As in the Midst of Battle There is Room 1376
EDWIN ARLINGTON ROBINSON (1869-1935)
Luke Havergal 1376
Miniver Cheevy 1377
Mr. Flood's Party 1378
The Sheaves 1380
AMY LOWELL (1874-1925)
Patterns 1380

CONTENTS

PAGE

ROBERT FROST (1875-)
The Runaway ... 1384
An Old Man's Winter Night ... 1384
The Oven Bird ... 1385
The Tuft of Flowers ... 1385
CARL SANDBURG (1878-)
Grass ... 1387
Three Spring Notations on Bipeds ... 1388
NICHOLAS VACHEL LINDSAY (1879-1931)
The Eagle that is Forgotten ... 1389
EZRA POUND (1885-)
The Garden ... 1390
JOHN GOULD FLETCHER (1886-)
Song of the Moderns ... 1390
Last Judgment ... 1391
"H. D." (1886-)
Adonis ... 1392
Oread ... 1393
WILLIAM ROSE BENÉT (1886-)
Eternal Masculine ... 1393
The Woodcutter's Wife ... 1394
ROBINSON JEFFERS (1887-)
Night ... 1396
Continent's End ... 1398
ELINOR WYLIE (1887-1928)
The Eagle and the Mole ... 1399
Address to My Soul ... 1400
THOMAS STEARNS ELIOT (1888-)
The Love Song of J. Alfred Prufrock ... 1401
Morning at the Window ... 1405
The Hippopotamus ... 1406
JOHN CROWE RANSOM (1888-)
Here Lies a Lady ... 1407
Two in August ... 1408
CONRAD AIKEN (1889-)
Discordants ... 1409
Sound of Breaking ... 1409
ARCHIBALD MACLEISH (1892-)
Ars Poetica ... 1410
You, Andrew Marvell ... 1411
EDNA ST. VINCENT MILLAY (1892-)
Sonnet ... 1412
LOUISE BOGAN (1897-)
Medusa ... 1413
The Alchemist ... 1414
ALLEN TATE (1899-)
The Cross ... 1414
Emblems ... 1415
HART CRANE (1899-1932)
Praise for an Urn ... 1416
Repose of Rivers ... 1417

CHINESE

From the Shi King, or Book of Odes

Compiled c. 500 B.C.

The Shi King was compiled by Confucius from earlier collections which had been long existent. It was through the Odes that Confucius taught his own generation to understand the manners and customs and simple feelings of the men of old. These are the natural songs that float upward from the happy valleys and down the sedge-strewn banks of the wandering K'e. They are naive and bright as on their birthday, with that most precious quality of truth and unconscious art which never lets them tarnish or fade.—L. CRANMER-BYNG.

THE MORNING GLORY

THE morning glory climbs above my head,
Pale flowers of white and purple, blue and red.
I am disquieted.

Down in the withered grasses something stirred;
I thought it was his footfall that I heard.
Then a grasshopper chirred.

I climbed the hill just as the new moon showed,
I saw him coming on the southern road.
My heart lays down its load.

(*Helen Waddell*)

HOW GOES THE NIGHT?

How goes the night?
Midnight has still to come.
Down in the court the torch is blazing bright;
I hear far off the throbbing of the drum.

How goes the night?
The night is not yet gone.

I hear the trumpets blowing on the height;
The torch is paling in the coming dawn.

How goes the night?
The night is past and done.
The torch is smoking in the morning light,
The dragon banner floating in the sun.

(Helen Waddell)

UNDER THE PONDWEED

UNDER the pondweed do the great fish go,
In the green darkness where the rushes grow.
The King is in Hao.

Under the pondweed do the great fish lie;
Down in Hao the sunny hours go by.
The king holds revelry.

Under the pondweed do the great fish sleep;
The dragon-flies are drowsy in the heat.
The King is drinking deep.

(Helen Waddell)

I WAIT MY LORD

THE gourd has still its bitter leaves,
And deep the crossing at the ford.
I wait my lord.

The ford is brimming to its banks;
The pheasant cries upon her mate.
My lord is late.

The boatman still keeps beckoning,
And others reach their journey's end.
I wait my friend.

(Helen Waddell)

THE PEAR-TREE

This shade-bestowing pear-tree, thou
Hurt not, nor lay its leafage low;
Beneath it slept the Duke of Shaou.

This shade-bestowing pear-tree, thou
Hurt not, nor break one leafy bough;
Beneath it stayed the Duke of Shaou.

This shade-bestowing pear-tree, thou
Hurt not, nor bend one leafy bough;
Beneath it paused the Duke of Shaou.

(*Allen Upward*)

MAYTIME

Deep in the grass there lies a dead gazelle,
The tall white grass enwraps her where she fell.
With sweet thoughts natural to spring,
A pretty girl goes wandering
With lover that would lead astray.

The little dwarf oaks hide a leafy dell,
Far in the wilds there lies a dead gazelle;
The tall white grass enwraps her where she fell,
And beauty, like a gem, doth fling
Bright radiance through the blinds of spring.
"Ah, gently! do not disarray
My kerchief! gently, pray!
Nor make the watch-dog bark
Under my lattice dark."

(*L. Cranmer-Byng*)

YOU WILL DIE

You have coats and robes,
But you do not trail them;
You have chariots and horses,

But you do not ride them.
By and by you will die,
And another will enjoy them.

You have courtyards and halls,
But they are not sprinkled and swept;
You have bells and drums,
But they are not struck.
By and by you will die,
And another will possess them.

You have wine and food;
Why not play daily on your lute,
That you may enjoy yourself now
And lengthen your days?
By and by you will die,
And another will take your place.

(H. A. Giles)

WOMAN

A CLEVER man builds a city,
A clever woman lays one low;
With all her qualifications, that clever woman
Is but an ill-omened bird.
A woman with a long tongue
Is a flight of steps leading to calamity;
For disorder does not come from heaven,
But is brought about by women.
Among those who cannot be trained or taught
Are women and eunuchs.

(H. A. Giles)

Ch'ü Yüan

Fourth century B.C.

THE GREAT SUMMONS

When Ch'ü Yüan had been exiled from the Court for nine years, he became so despondent that he feared his soul would part from his body, and he would die. It was then that he made the poem called "The Great Summons," calling upon his soul not to leave him.

GREEN Spring receiveth
The vacant earth;
The white sun shineth;
Spring wind provoketh
To burst and burgeon
Each sprout and flower.
In those dark caves where Winter lurketh
Hide not, my Soul!
O Soul come back again! O do not stray!

O Soul come back again and go not east or west, or north or south!
For to the East a mighty water drowneth
Earth's other shore;
Tossed on its waves and heaving with its tides
The hornless Dragon of the Ocean rideth;
Clouds gather low and fogs enfold the sea
And gleaming ice drifts past.
O Soul go not to the East,
To the silent Valley of Sunrise!

O Soul go not to the South
Where mile on mile the earth is burnt away
And poisonous serpents slither through the flames;
Where on precipitous paths or in deep woods
Tigers and leopards prowl,
And water-scorpions wait;
Where the king-python rears his giant head.
O Soul go not to the South
Where the three-footed tortoise spits disease!

O Soul go not to the West
Where level wastes of sand stretch on and on;
And demons rage, swine-headed, hairy-skinned,
With bulging eyes;
Who in wild laughter gnash projecting fangs.
O Soul go not to the West
Where many perils wait!

O Soul go not to the North,
To the Lame Dragon's frozen peaks;
Where trees and grasses dare not grow;
Where the river runs too wide to cross
And too deep to plumb,
And the sky is white with snow
And the cold cuts and kills,
O Soul seek not to fill
The treacherous voids of the North!

O Soul come back to idleness and peace.
In quietude enjoy
The lands of Ching and Ch'u.
There work your will and follow your desire
Till sorrow is forgot,
And carelessness shall bring you length of days.
O Soul come back to joys beyond all telling!

Where thirty cubits high at harvest-time
The corn is stacked;
Where pies are cooked of millet and bearded-maize.
Guests watch the steaming bowls
And sniff the pungency of peppered herbs.
The cunning cook adds slices of bird-flesh,
Pigeon and yellow-heron and black-crane.
They taste the badger-stew.
O Soul come back to feed on foods you love!

Next are brought
Fresh turtle, and sweet chicken cooked in cheese
Pressed by the men of Ch'u.

And pickled sucking-pig
And flesh of whelps floating in liver-sauce
With salad of minced radishes in brine;
All served with that hot spice of southernwood
The land of Wu supplies.
O Soul come back to choose the meats you love!

Roasted daw, steamed widgeon and grilled quail—
On every fowl they fare.
Boiled perch and sparrow broth—in each preserved
The separate flavor that is most its own.
O Soul come back to where such dainties wait!

The four strong liquors are warming at the fire
So that they grate not on the drinker's throat.
How fragrant rise their fumes, how cool their taste!
Such drink is not for louts or serving-men!
And wise distillers from the land of Wu
Blend unfermented spirit with white yeast
And brew the *li* of Ch'u.
O Soul come back and let your yearnings cease!

Reed-organs from the lands of T'ai and Ch'in
And Wei and Chēng
Gladden the feasters, and old songs are sung:
The "Rider's Song" that once
Fu-hsi, the ancient monarch made;
And the harp-songs of Ch'u.
Then after prelude from the flutes of Chao
The ballad-singer's voice rises alone.
O Soul come back to the hollow mulberry-tree!

Eight and eight the dancers sway,
Weaving their steps to the poet's voice
Who speaks his odes and rhapsodies;
They tap their bells and beat their chimes
Rigidly, lest harp and flute

Should mar the measure.
Then rival singers of the Four Domains
Compete in melody, till not a tune
Is left unsung that human voice could sing.
O Soul come back and listen to their songs!

Then women enter whose red lips and dazzling teeth
Seduce the eye;
But meek and virtuous, trained in every art;
Fit sharers of play-time,
So soft their flesh and delicate their bones.
O Soul come back and let them ease your woe!

Then enter other ladies with laughing lips
And sidelong glances under moth eyebrows;
Whose cheeks are fresh and red;
Ladies both great of heart and long of limb,
Whose beauty by sobriety is matched.
Well-padded cheeks and ears with curving rim,
High-arching eyebrows, as with compass drawn,
Great hearts and loving gestures—all are there;
Small waists and necks as slender as the clasp
Of courtiers' brooches.
O Soul come back to those whose tenderness
Drives angry thoughts away!

Last enter those
Whose every action is contrived to please;
Black-painted eyebrows and white-powdered cheeks.
They reek with scent; with their long sleeves they brush
The faces of the feasters whom they pass,
Or pluck the coats of those who will not stay.
O Soul come back to pleasures of the night!

A summer house with spacious rooms
And a high hall with beams stained red;
A little closet in the southern wing
Reached by a private stair.

And round the house a covered way should run
Where horses might be trained.
And sometimes riding, sometimes going afoot
You shall explore, O Soul, the parks of spring;
Your jewelled axles gleaming in the sun
And your yoke inlaid with gold;
Or amid orchises and sandal-trees
Shall walk in the dark woods.
O Soul come back and live for these delights!

Peacocks shall fill your gardens; you shall rear
The roc and phœnix, and red jungle-fowl,
Whose cry at dawn assembles river storks
To join the play of cranes and ibises;
Where the wild-swan all day
Pursues the glint of idle kingfishers.
O Soul come back to watch the birds in flight!

He who has found such manifold delights
Shall feel his cheeks aglow
And the blood-spirit dancing through his limbs.
Stay with me, Soul, and share
The span of days that happiness will bring;
See sons and grandsons serving at the Court
Ennobled and enriched.
O Soul come back and bring prosperity
To house and stock!

The roads that lead to Ch'u
Shall teem with travelers as thick as clouds,
A thousand miles away.
For the Five Orders of Nobility
Shall summon sages to assist the King
And with godlike discrimination choose
The wise in council; by their aid to probe
The hidden discontents of humble men
And help the lonely poor.
O Soul come back and end what we began!

Fields, villages and lanes
Shall throng with happy men;
Good rule protect the people and make known
The King's benevolence to all the land;
Stern discipline prepare
Their natures for the soft caress of Art.
O Soul come back to where the good are praised!

Like the sun shining over the four seas
Shall be the reputation of our King;
His deeds, matched only in Heaven, shall repair
The wrongs endured by every tribe of men—
Northward to Yu and southward to Annam,
To the Sheep's-Gut Mountain and the Eastern Seas.
O Soul come back to where the wise are sought!

Behold the glorious virtues of our King
Triumphant, terrible;
Behold with solemn faces in the Hall
The Three Grand Ministers walk up and down—
None chosen for the post save landed-lords
Or, in default, Knights of the Nine Degrees.
At the first ray of dawn already is hung
The shooting-target, where with bow in hand
And arrows under arm,
Each archer does obeisance to each,
Willing to yield his rights of precedence.
O Soul come back to where men honor still
The name of the Three Kings.

(*Arthur Waley*)

Anonymous

C. 124 B.C.

FIGHTING SOUTH OF THE CASTLE

They fought south of the Castle,
They died north of the wall.
They died in the moors and were not buried.
Their flesh was the food of crows.

"Tell the crows we are not afraid;
We have died in the moors and cannot be buried.
Crows, how can our bodies escape you?"
The waters flowed deep
And the rushes in the pool were dark.
The riders fought and were slain:
Their horses wander neighing.
By the bridge there was a house.
Was it south, was it north?
The harvest was never gathered.
How can we give you your offerings?
You served your Prince faithfully,
Though all in vain.
I think of you, faithful soldiers;
Your service shall not be forgotten.
For in the morning you went out to battle
And at night you did not return.

(*Arthur Waley*)

Anonymous

1st century B.C.

OLD AND NEW

SHE went up the mountain to pluck wild herbs;
She came down the mountain and met her former
husband.
She knelt down and asked her former husband
"What do you find your new wife like?"
"My new wife, although her talk is clever,
Cannot charm me as my old wife could.
In beauty of face there is not much to choose,
But in usefulness they are not at all alike.
My new wife comes in from the road to meet me;
My old wife always came down from her tower.
My new wife is clever at embroidering silk;
My old wife was good at plain sewing.
Of silk embroidery one can do an inch a day;
Of plain sewing, more than five feet.

Putting her silks by the side of your sewing,
I see that the new will not compare with the old."

(*Arthur Waley*)

Anonymous

1st century ?

OLD POEM

COLD, cold the year draws to its end,
The crickets and grasshoppers make a doleful chirping.
The chill wind increases its violence.
My wandering love has no coat to cover him.
He gave his embroidered furs to the Lady of Lo,
But from me his bedfellow he is quite estranged.
Sleeping alone in the depth of the long night
In a dream I thought I saw the light of his face.
My dear one thought of our old joys together,
He came in his chariot and gave me the front reins.
I wanted so to prolong our play and laughter,
To hold his hand and go back with him in his coach.
But, when he had come he would not stay long
Nor stop to go with me to the Inner Chamber.
Truly without the falcon's wings to carry me
How can I rival the flying wind's swiftness?
I go and lean at the gate and think of my grief,
My falling tears wet the double gates.

(*Arthur Waley*)

Anonymous

1st century ?

THE SONG OF LO-FU

THE sun has risen on the eastern brim of the world,
Shines into the high chambers of the house of Ch'in.
In the house of Ch'in is a lovely lady dwelling,
That calls herself the Lady Lo-fu.
This lady loves her silk-worms and mulberry trees;
She's plucking leaves at the southern edge of the town.

With blue thread are the joints of her basket bound;
Of cassia-boughs are the loops of her basket made.
Her soft hair hangs in loose plaits;
The pearl at her ear shines like a dazzling moon.
Of yellow damask is made her shirt beneath;
Of purple damask is made her cloak above.
The passer-by who looks on Lo-fu
Drops his luggage and strokes the hair on his cheek.
The young men when they see Lo-fu
Doff their caps and show their red scarfs.
The laboring plowman thinks no more of his plow,
The hind in the field thinks no more of his hoe.
Wistful and angry each leaves his task
And can only sit gazing at Lo-fu.
The Lord Governor drives his coach from the south;
His five horses suddenly slow their pace.
He's sent his sheriff: "Quickly bring me word
Of what house may this lovely lady be."
"In the house of Ch'in the fair lady dwells;
She calls herself the Lady Lo-fu."
"Oh tell me, sheriff, tell me how old she may be!"
"A score of years she has not yet filled;
To fifteen she has added somewhat more."
The Lord Governor calls to Lo-fu:
"Tell me, lady, will you ride by me or no?"
She stands before him, she gives him answer straight:
"My Lord Governor has not ready wits.
Has he not guessed that just as he has a wife
So too I have my husband dear?
Yonder to eastward a band of horse is riding,
More than a thousand, and my love is at their head."
"By what sign shall I your husband know?"
"His white horse is followed by a black colt,
With blue thread is tied the horse's tail;
With yellow gold is bridled that horse's head.
At his waist he wears a windlass-hilted sword
You could not buy for many pounds of gold.
At fifteen they made him a Governor's clerk;
At twenty they made him a Chamberlain at court.

At thirty he sat at the Emperor's Council Board,
At forty they gave him a city for his very own—
A wholesome man, fair, white and fine;
Soft and silky is the down that grows on his cheek,
Proudly and proudly he walks to the palace gate;
Stately, stately he strides through the palace hall.
In that great hall thousands of courtiers sit,
Yet none but names him the finest man of them all."

(Arthur Waley)

Chang Hēng

78–139

THE BONES OF CHUANG TZU

I, CHANG P'ING-TZU, had traversed the Nine Wilds and seen their wonders,
In the eight continents beheld the ways of Man,
The Sun's procession, the orbit of the Stars,
The surging of the dragon, the soaring of the phœnix in his flight.
In the red desert to the south I sweltered,
And northward waded through the wintry burghs of Yu.
Through the Valley of Darkness to the west I wandered,
And eastward travelled to the Sun's extreme abode,
The stooping Mulberry Tree.

So the seasons sped; weak autumn languished,
A small wind woke the cold.

And now with rearing of rein-horse,
Plunging of the tracer, round I fetched
My high-roofed chariot to westward.
Along the dykes we loitered, past many meadows,
And far away among the dunes and hills.
Suddenly I looked and by the roadside
I saw a man's bones lying in the squelchy earth,
Black rime-frost over him; and I in sorrow spoke
And asked him, saying, "Dead man, how was it?

Fled you with your friend from famine and for the
last grains
Gambled and lost? Was this earth your tomb,
Or did floods carry you from afar? Were you mighty,
were you wise,
Were you foolish and poor? A warrior, or a girl?"
Then a wonder came; for out of the silence a voice—
Thin echo only, in no substance was the Spirit seen—
Mysteriously answered, saying, "I was a man of Sung,
Of the clan of Chuang; Chou was my name.
Beyond the climes of common thought
My reason soared, yet could I not save myself;
For at the last, when the long charter of my years was
told,
I too, for all my magic, by Age was brought
To the Black Hill of Death.
Wherefore, O Master, do you question me?"
Then I answered:
"Let me plead for you upon the Five Hill-tops,
Let me pray for you to the Gods of Heaven and the
Gods of Earth,
That your white bones may arise,
And your limbs be joined anew.
The God of the North shall give me back your ears;
I will scour the Southland for your eyes;
From the sunrise will I wrest your feet.
The West shall yield your heart.
I will set each several organ in its throne;
Each subtle sense will I restore.
Would you not have it so?"
The dead man answered me:
"O Friend, how strange and unacceptable your words!
In death I rest and am at peace; in life, I toiled and
strove.
Is the hardness of the winter stream
Better than the melting of spring?
All pride that the body knew,
Was it not lighter than dust?
What Ch'ao and Hsü despised,

What Po-ch'eng fled,
Shall I desire, whom death
Already has hidden in the Eternal Way—
Where Li Chu cannot see me,
Nor Tzu Yeh hear me,
Where neither Yao nor Shun can praise me,
Nor the tyrants Chieh and Hsin condemn me,
Nor wolf nor tiger harm me,
Lance prick me nor sword wound me?
Of the Primal Spirit is my substance; I am a wave
In the river of Darkness and Light.
The Maker of All Things is my Father and Mother,
Heaven is my bed and earth my cushion,
The thunder and lightning are my drum and fan,
The sun and moon my candle and my torch,
The Milky Way my moat, the stars my jewels.
With Nature am I conjoined;
I have no passion, no desire.
Wash me and I shall be no whiter,
Foul me and I shall yet be clean.
I come not, yet am here;
Hasten not, yet am swift."
The voice stopped, there was silence.
A ghostly light
Faded and expired.
I gazed upon the dead, stared in sorrow and compassion.
Then I called upon my servant that was with me
To tie his silken scarf about those bones
And wrap them in a cloak of somber dust;
While I, as offering to the soul of this dead man,
Poured my hot tears upon the margin of the road.

(*Arthur Waley*)

Tso Ssū

3rd century

THE SCHOLAR IN THE NARROW STREET

FLAP, flap, the captive bird in the cage
Beating its wings against the four corners.

Depressed, depressed the scholar in the narrow street:
Clasping a shadow, he dwells in an empty house.
When he goes out, there is nowhere for him to go:
Bunches and brambles block up his path.
He composes a memorial, but it is rejected and unread,
He is left stranded, like a fish in a dry pond.
Without—he has not a single farthing of salary:
Within—there is not a peck of grain in his larder.
His relations upbraid him for his lack of success:
His friends and callers daily decrease in number.
Su Ch'in used to go preaching in the North
And Li Ssu sent a memorandum to the West.
I once hoped to pluck the fruits of life:
But now alas, they are all withered and dry.
Though one drinks at a river, one cannot drink more
than a bellyful;
Enough is good, but there is no use in satiety.
The bird in a forest can perch but on one bough,
And this should be the wise man's pattern.

(*Arthur Waley*)

Fu Hsüan

Died 278

A GENTLE WIND

A GENTLE wind fans the calm night:
A bright moon shines on the high tower.
A voice whispers, but no one answers when I call:
A shadow stirs, but no one comes when I beckon,
The kitchen-man brings in a dish of lentils:
Wine is there, but I do not fill my cup.
Contentment with poverty is Fortune's best gift:
Riches and Honor are the handmaids of Disaster.
Though gold and gems by the world are sought and
prized,
To me they seem no more than weeds or chaff.

(*Arthur Waley*)

Chan Fang-sheng

4th century

SAILING HOMEWARD

CLIFFS that rise a thousand feet
Without a break,
Lake that stretches a hundred miles
Without a wave.
Sands that are white through all the year,
Without a stain,
Pine-tree woods, winter and summer
Ever-green,
Streams that for ever flow and flow
Without a pause,
Trees that for twenty thousand years
Your vows have kept,
You have suddenly healed the pain of a traveler's heart,
And moved his brush to write a new song.

(Arthur Waley)

T'ao Ch'ien

365–427

I BUILT MY HUT

I BUILT my hut in a zone of human habitation,
Yet near me there sounds no noise of horse or coach.
  Would you know how that is possible?
A heart that is distant creates a wilderness round it.
I pluck chrysanthemums under the eastern hedge,
Then gaze long at the distant summer hills.
The mountain air is fresh at the dusk of day:
The flying birds two by two return.
In these things there lies a deep meaning;
Yet when we would express it, words suddenly fail us.

(Arthur Waley)

SHADY, SHADY

SHADY, shady the wood in front of the Hall:
At midsummer full of calm shadows.
The south wind follows summer's train:
With its eddying puffs it blows open my coat.
I am free from ties and can live a life of retirement.
When I rise from sleep, I play with books and harp.
The lettuce in the garden still grows moist:
Of last year's grain there is always plenty left.
Self-support should maintain strict limits:
More than enough is not what I want.
I grind millet and make good wine:
When the wine is heated, I pour it out for myself.
My little children are playing at my side,
Learning to talk, they babble unformed sounds.
These things have made me happy again
And I forget my lost cap of office.
Distant, distant I gaze at the white clouds:
With a deep yearning I think of the Sages of Antiquity.

(*Arthur Waley*)

ONCE MORE FIELDS AND GARDENS

EVEN as a young man
I was out of tune with ordinary pleasures.
It was my nature to love the rooted hills,
The high hills which look upon the four edges of
Heaven.
What folly to spend one's life like a dropped leaf
Snared under the dust of streets,
But for thirteen years it was so I lived.

The caged bird longs for the fluttering of high leaves.
The fish in the garden pool languishes for the whirled
water
Of meeting streams.
So I desired to clear and seed a patch of the wild South-
ern moor.

And always a countryman at heart,
I have come back to the square enclosures of my fields
And to my walled garden with its quiet paths.

Mine is a little property of ten *mou* or so,
A thatched house of eight or nine rooms.
On the North side, the eaves are overhung
With the thick leaves of elm-trees,
And willow-trees break the strong force of the wind.
On the South, in front of the great hall,
Peach-trees and plum-trees spread a net of branches
Before the distant view.

The village is hazy, hazy,
And mist sucks over the open moor.
A dog barks in the sunken lane which runs through the village.
A cock crows, perched on a clipped mulberry.

There is no dust or clatter
In the courtyard before my house.
My private rooms are quiet,
And calm with the leisure of moonlight through an open door.

For a long time I lived in a cage;
Now I have returned.
For one must return
To fulfill one's nature.

(*Amy Lowell and Florence Ayscough*)

Emperor Ch'ien Wēn-ti

6th century

LO-YANG

A BEAUTIFUL place is the town of Lo-yang:
The big streets are full of spring light.
The lads go driving out with harps in their hands:
The mulberry girls go out to the fields with their baskets.

Golden whips glint at the horses' flanks,
Gauze sleeves brush the green boughs.
Racing dawn, the carriages come home,—
And the girls with their high baskets full of fruit.

(*Arthur Waley*)

Li T'ai-po

701–762

It is permitted to very few to live in the hearts of their countrymen as Li T'ai-po has lived in the hearts of the Chinese. There is no doubt at all that in Li T'ai-po we have one of the world's greatest lyrists.—FLORENCE AYSCOUGH.

DRINKING ALONE IN THE MOONLIGHT

I

A POT of wine among flowers.
I alone, drinking, without a companion.
I lift the cup and invite the bright moon.
My shadow opposite certainly makes us three.
But the moon cannot drink,
And my shadow follows the motions of my body in vain.
For the briefest time are the moon and my shadow my companions.
Oh, be joyful! One must make the most of Spring.
I sing—the moon walks forward rhythmically;
I dance, and my shadow shatters and becomes confused.
In my waking moments, we are happily blended.
When I am drunk, we are divided from one another and scattered.
For a long time I shall be obliged to wander without intention;
But we will keep our appointment by the far-off Cloudy River.

II

If Heaven did not love wine,
There would be no Wine Star in Heaven.
If Earth did not love wine,

There should be no Wine Springs on Earth.
Why then be ashamed before Heaven to love wine.
I have heard that clear wine is like the Sages;
Again it is said that thick wine is like the Virtuous Worthies.
Wherefore it appears that we have swallowed both Sages and Worthies.
Why should we strive to be Gods and Immortals?
Three cups, and one can perfectly understand the Great Tao;
A gallon, and one is in accord with all nature.
Only those in the midst of it can fully comprehend the joys of wine;
I do not proclaim them to the sober.

(*Amy Lowell and Florence Ayscough*)

THE RIVER-MERCHANT'S WIFE: A LETTER

WHILE my hair was still cut straight across my forehead
I played about the front gate, pulling flowers.
You came by on bamboo stilts, playing horse,
You walked about my seat, playing with blue plums.
And we went on living in the village of Chokan:
Two small people, without dislike or suspicion.

At fourteen I married My Lord you.
I never laughed, being bashful.
Lowering my head, I looked at the wall.
Called to, a thousand times, I never looked back.

At fifteen I stopped scowling,
I desired my dust to be mingled with yours
Forever and forever and forever.
Why should I climb the lookout?

At sixteen you departed,
You went into far Ku-to-yen, by the river of swirling eddies,
And you have been gone five months.
The monkeys make sorrowful noise overhead.

You dragged your feet when you went out.
By the gate now, the moss is grown, the different mosses,
Too deep to clear them away!
The leaves fall early this autumn, in wind.
The paired butterflies are already yellow with August
Over the grass in the West garden;
They hurt me. I grow older.
If you are coming down through the narrows of the river
Kiang,
Please let me know beforehand,
And I will come out to meet you
As far as Cho-fu-Sa.

(*Ezra Pound*)

CLEARING AT DAWN

The fields are chill; the sparse rain has stopped;
The colors of Spring teem on every side.
With leaping fish the blue pond is full;
With singing thrushes the green boughs droop.
The flowers of the field have dabbled their powdered
cheeks;
The mountain grasses are bent level at the waist.
By the bamboo stream the last fragment of cloud
Blown by the wind slowly scatters away.

(*Arthur Waley*)

IN THE MOUNTAINS ON A SUMMER DAY

Gently I stir a white feather fan,
With open shirt sitting in a green wood.
I take off my cap and hang it on a jutting stone;
A wind from the pine-tree trickles on my bare head.

(*Arthur Waley*)

TO TAN CH'IU

My friend is lodging high in the Eastern Range,
Dearly loving the beauty of valleys and hills.
At green Spring he lies in the empty woods,
And is still asleep when the sun shines on high.

A pine-tree wind dusts his sleeves and coat;
A pebbly stream cleans his heart and ears.
I envy you, who far from strife and talk
Are high-propped on a pillow of blue cloud.

(*Arthur Waley*)

Tu Fu

712–770

English writers on Chinese literature are fond of announcing that Li T'ai-po is China's greatest poet; the Chinese themselves, however, award this place to Tu Fu. We may put it that Li T'ai-po was the people's poet, and Tu Fu the poet of scholars.—Arthur Waley.

THE EXCURSION

I

How delightful, at sunset, to loosen the boat!
A light wind is slow to raise waves.
Deep in the bamboo grove, the guests linger;
The lotus-flowers are pure and bright in the cool evening air.
The young nobles stir the ice-water;
The Beautiful Ones wash the lotus-roots, whose fibers are like silk threads.
A layer of clouds above our heads is black.
It will certainly rain, which impels me to write this poem.

II

The rain comes, soaking the mats upon which we are sitting.
A hurrying wind strikes the bow of the boat.
The rose-red rouge of the ladies from Yueh is wet;
The Yen beauties are anxious about their kingfisher-eyebrows.
We throw out a rope and draw in to the sloping bank.
We tie the boat to the willow-trees.

We roll up the curtains and watch the floating wave-
    flowers.
Our return is different from our setting out. The wind
    whistles and blows in great gusts.
By the time we reach the shore, it seems as though the
    Fifth Month were Autumn.

(Amy Lowell and Florence Ayscough)

THE EMPEROR

On a throne of new gold the Son of the Sky
    is sitting among his Mandarins. He shines
    with jewels and is like a sun surrounded by stars.

The Mandarins speak gravely of grave things;
    but the Emperor's thought has flown out by
    the open window.

In her pavilion of porcelain the Empress is
    sitting among her women. She is like a bright
    flower among leaves.

She dreams that her beloved stays too long
    at council, and wearily she moves her fan.

A breathing of perfumed air kisses the face
    of the Emperor.

"My beloved moves her fan, and sends me a
    perfume from her lips."

Towards the pavilion of porcelain walks the
    Emperor, shining with his jewels; and leaves his
    grave Mandarins to look at each other in silence.

(E. Powys Mathers)

Po Chü-i

772–846

There is a story that he was in the habit of reading his poems to an old peasant woman and altering any expression which she could not understand. The poems of his contemporaries were mere elegant diversions which enabled the scholar to display his erudition, or the literary juggler his dexterity. No poet in the world can ever have enjoyed greater contemporary popularity than Po.—ARTHUR WALEY.

TO LI CHIEN

THE province I govern is humble and remote;
Yet our festivals follow the Courtly Calendar.
At rise of day we sacrificed to the Wind God,
When darkly, darkly, dawn glimmered in the sky.

Officers followed, horsemen led the way;
They brought us out to the wastes beyond the town,
Where river mists fall heavier than rain,
And the fires on the hill leap higher than the stars.

Suddenly I remembered the early levees at Court
When you and I galloped to the Purple Yard.
As we walked our horses up Dragon Tail Street
We turned our heads and gazed at the Southern Hills.
Since we parted, both of us have been growing old;
And our minds have been vexed by many anxious cares.
Yet even now I fancy my ears are full
Of the sound of jade tinkling on your bridle-straps.

(*Arthur Waley*)

LODGING WITH THE OLD MAN OF THE STREAM

MEN'S hearts love gold and jade;
Men's mouths covet wine and flesh.
Not so the old man of the stream;
He drinks from his gourd and asks nothing more.

South of the stream he cuts firewood and grass;
North of the stream he has built wall and roof.
Yearly he sows a single acre of land;
In spring he drives two yellow calves.
In these things he finds great repose;
Beyond these he has no wish or care.
By chance I met him walking by the water-side;
He took me home and lodged me in his thatched hut.
When I parted from him, to seek market and Court,
This old man asked my rank and pay.
Doubting my tale, he laughed loud and long:
"Privy Councillors do not sleep in barns."

(*Arthur Waley*)

REJOICING AT THE ARRIVAL OF CH'EN HSIUNG

When the yellow bird's note was almost stopped;
And half formed the green plum's fruit;
Sitting and grieving that spring things were over,
I rose and entered the Eastern Garden's gate.
I carried my cup and was dully drinking alone:
Suddenly I heard a knocking sound at the door.
Dwelling secluded, I was glad that someone had come;
How much the more, when I saw it was Ch'en Hsiung!
At ease and leisure,—all day we talked;
Crowding and jostling, the feelings of many years,
How great a thing is a single cup of wine!
For it makes us tell the story of our whole lives.

(*Arthur Waley*)

LOSING A SLAVE-GIRL

Around my garden the little wall is low;
In the bailiff's lodge the lists are seldom checked.
I am ashamed to think we were not always kind;
I regret your labors, that will never be repaid.

The caged bird owes no allegiance;
The wind-tossed flower does not cling to the tree.
. . . . .
Where to-night she lies none can give us news;
Nor any knows, save the bright watching moon.

(*Arthur Waley*)

ON BEING SIXTY

Between thirty and forty, one is distracted by the Five Lusts;
Between seventy and eighty, one is a prey to a hundred diseases.
But from fifty to sixty one is free from all ills;
Calm and still—the heart enjoys rest.
I have put behind me Love and Greed; I have done with Profit and Fame;
I am still short of illness and decay and far from decrepit age.
Strength of limb I still possess to seek the rivers and hills;
Still my heart has spirit enough to listen to flutes and strings.
At leisure I open new wine and taste several cups;
Drunken I recall old poems and sing a whole volume.
Meng-te has asked for a poem and herewith I exhort him
Not to complain of three-score, "the time of obedient ears."

(*Arthur Waley*)

REMEMBERING GOLDEN BELLS

Ruined and ill,—a man of two score;
Pretty and guileless,—a girl of three.
Not a boy,—but still better than nothing:
To soothe one's feeling,—from time to time a kiss!
There came a day,—they suddenly took her from me;
Her soul's shadow wandered I know not where.
And when I remember how just at the time she died
She lisped strange sounds, beginning to learn to talk,

Then I know that the ties of flesh and blood
Only bind us to a load of grief and sorrow.
At last, by thinking of the time before she was born,
By thought and reason I drove the pain away.
Since my heart forgot her, many days have passed
And three times winter has changed to spring.
This morning, for a little, the old grief came back,
Because, in the road, I met her foster-nurse.

(*Arthur Waley*)

Yüan Chēn

779–831

THE PITCHER

I DREAMT I climbed to a high, high plain;
And on the plain I found a deep well.
My throat was dry with climbing and I longed to drink,
And my eyes were eager to look into the cool shaft.
I walked round it; I looked right down;
I saw my image mirrored on the face of the pool.
An earthen pitcher was sinking into the black depths;
There was no rope to pull it to the well-head.
I was strangely troubled lest the pitcher should be lost,
And started wildly running to look for help.
From village to village I scoured that high plain;
The men were gone: the dogs leapt at my throat.
I came back and walked weeping round the well;
Faster and faster the blinding tears flowed—
Till my own sobbing suddenly woke me up;
My room was silent, no one in the house stirred;
The flame of my candle flickered with a green smoke;
The tears I had shed glittered in the candle-light.
A bell sounded; I knew it was the midnight-chime;
I sat up in bed and tried to arrange my thoughts:
The plain in my dream was the graveyard at Ch'ang-an,
Those hundred acres of untilled land.
The soil heavy and the mounds heaped high;
And the dead below them laid in deep troughs.

Deep are the troughs, yet sometimes dead men
Find their way to the world above the grave.
And to-night my love who died long ago
Came into my dream as the pitcher sunk in the well.
That was why the tears suddenly streamed from my
    eyes,
Streamed from my eyes and fell on the collar of my dress.

(*Arthur Waley*)

Wang Chien

830

THE SOUTH

In the southern land many birds sing;
Of towns and cities half are unwalled.
The country markets are thronged by wild tribes;
The mountain-villages bear river-names.
Poisonous mists rise from the damp sands;
Strange fires gleam through the night-rain.
And none passes but the lonely fisher of pearls
Year by year on his way to the South Sea.

(*Arthur Waley*)

Ou-yang Hsiu

11th century

THE CICADA

In the summer of the first year of Chia-yu (A.D. 1056) there was a great flood. By order of the Emperor I went to the Wine Spring Temple to pray for fine weather, when I heard a cicada singing. Upon which subject I wrote this poem:

Hushed was the courtyard of the temple;
Solemn stood I, gazing
At the bright roofs and gables,
The glorious summits of that towering shrine.

Untroubled were my thoughts, intently prayed
My fasting soul, for every wandering sense
Was gathered to its home.
Unmoved I watched the motions of the world,
Saw deep into the nature of ten thousand things.
Suddenly the rain was over, no wind stirred
The morning-calm; round all the sky
Was cloudless blue, and the last thunder rolled.
Then we, to strew sweet-scented herbs upon the floor,
Drew near the colored cloister, by whose side
Some old trees grew amid the grass
Of the deserted court. Here was a thing that cried
Upon a tree-top, sucking the shrill wind
To wail it back in a long whistling note—
That clasping in its arms
A tapering twig perpetually sighed,
Now shrill as flute, now soft as mandolin;
Sometimes a piercing cry
Choked at its very uttering, sometimes a cold tune
Dwindled to silence, then suddenly flowed again,
A single note, wandering in strange keys,
An air, yet fraught
With undertone of hidden harmony.
"What creature can this be?" "Cicada is its name."
"Are you not he, cicada,
Of whom I have heard told you can transform
Your body, magically molding it
To new estate? Are you not he who, born
Upon the dung-heap, coveted the sky,
The clean and open air;
Found wings to mount the wind, yet skyward sailing
Upon a leafy tree-top checked your flight,
Pleased with its trim retreat? Are you not he
Who with the dew for drink, the wind for food,
Grows never old nor languid; who with looped locks
Frames womanish beauty?
Again your voice, cicada!
Not grave; not gay; part Lydian,
Part Dorian your tune that, suddenly begun,

Suddenly ceases.
Long since have I marveled
How of ten thousand creatures there is not one
But has its tune; how, as each season takes its turn,
A hundred new birds sing, each weather wakes
A hundred insects from their sleep.
Now lisp the mango-birds
Like pretty children, prattling at their play.
As shuttle at the sounding loom
The tireless cricket creaks. Beautiful the flexions
Of tongue and trilling throat, how valiantly
They spend themselves to do it!
And even the croakers of the pond,
When they get rain to fill
Their miry, parching puddles, while they sip
New rivulets and browse the soppy earth,
Sing through the live-long night. And like enough
May frogs be passionate; but oh, what seeks
The silent worm in song?
These and a thousand others, little and great,
Too many to name them all,
Myriads of creatures—each after its own shape and kin,
Hold at their season ceaseless tournament of song;
But swiftly, swiftly
Their days run out, time transmutes them, and there is
silence,
Desert-silence where they sang.

Alas, philosophy has taught
That the transcending mind in its strange, level world
Sees not kinds, contraries, classes or degrees.
And if of living things
Man once seemed best, what has he but a knack
Of facile speech, what but a plausible scheme
Of signs and ciphers that perpetuate
His thoughts and phrases? And on these expends
His brooding wits, consumes his vital breath;
One droning out the extremity of his woe,
Another to the wide world publishing

His nobleness of heart!
Thus, though he shares
The brief span of all creatures, yet his song
A hundred ages echoes after him.
But you, cicada,
What know you of this? Only for yourself
You make your music. . . ."
So was I pondering, comparing,
Setting difference by difference, gain by gain,
When suddenly the clouds came back and overhead
The storm blazed and crashed, spilling huge drops
Out of the rumbling sky. . . .
And silent now
Was the cicada's voice.

(*Arthur Waley*)

Su Tung-p'o

1036–1101

ON THE BIRTH OF HIS SON

Families, when a child is born
Want it to be intelligent.
I, through intelligence,
Having wrecked my whole life,
Only hope the baby will prove
Ignorant and stupid.
Then he will crown a tranquil life
By becoming a Cabinet Minister.

(*Arthur Waley*)

Lui Chi

1311–1375

A POET THINKS

The rain is due to fall,
The wind blows softly.

The branches of the cinnamon are moving,
The begonias stir on the green mounds.

Bright are the flying leaves,
The falling flowers are many.

The wind lifted the dry dust,
And he is lifting the wet dust;
Here and there the wind moves everything.

He passes under light gauze
And touches me.

I am alone with the beating of my heart.

There are leagues of sky,
And the water is flowing very fast.

Why do the birds let their feathers
Fall among the clouds?

I would have them carry my letters,
But the sky is long.

The stream flows east
And not one wave comes back with news.

The scented magnolias are shining still,
But always a few are falling.

I close his box on my guitar of jasper
And lay aside my jade flute.

I am alone with the beating of my heart.

Stay with me to-night,
Old songs.

(E. Powys Mathers)

JAPANESE

From the Manyō Shū

Compiled 8th century

Japanese poetry, as an art, may be said to begin with the Manyō Shū ("Ten-thousand-Leaves Collection"). The chief poets of the Manyō were Kakinomoto no Hitomaro and Yamabe no Akahito.—ARTHUR WALEY.

PRINCESS DAIHAKU

7th century

How will you manage
To cross alone
The autumn mountain
Which was so hard to get across
Even when we went the two of us together?

HIOKI NO KO-OKIMA

7th century

ON the shore of Nawa
The smoke of the saltburners,
When evening comes,
Failing to get across,
Trails over the mountain.

PRINCE YUHARA

7th century

WHAT am I to do with my Sister?
Whom, like the Judas-tree
Which grows in the moon,
I may see with my eyes
But not touch with my hands?

OKURA

660–733

Because he is young
And will not know the way to go
Would I could bribe
The messenger of the Underworld
That on his shoulders he might carry him!

HITOMARO

c. 700

1

O boy cutting grass
On that hill,
Do not cut like that!
Just as it is
I want it to be grass for the honorable horse
Of my Lord who is going to deign to come.

2

On the moor of Kasuga
The rising of smoke is visible.
The women surely
Must have plucked lettuces on the spring moor
and must be boiling them.

3

For my Sister's sake
In plucking with my hand
The plum-blossom of the top branch
I have got wet
With the dew of the lower boughs!

4

May the men who are born
From my time onwards
Never, never meet
With a path of love-making
Such as mine has been!

THE PRIEST HAKUTSU

c. 704

O PINE-TREE standing
At the side of the stone house,
When I look at you,
It is like seeing face to face
The men of old time.

AKAHITO

c. 730

1

I WISH I could lend a coat
To my Lord who is about to cross
The hill of Sanu
Through the cold morning-breath
Of the autumn wind.

2

The men of valor
Have gone to the honorable hunt:
The ladies
Are trailing their red petticoats
Over the clean sea-beach.

3

The plum-blossom
Which I thought I would show
To my Brother
Does not seem to be one at all;
It was only that snow had fallen!

YAKAMOCHI

d. 785

I

WHEN evening comes
I will leave the door open beforehand and then
wait
For him who said he would come
To meet me in my dreams.

2

By way of pretext
I said "I will go
And look at
The condition of the bamboo fence";
But it was really to see you!

THE LADY OF SAKANOYE

8th century

I

THE dress that my Brother has put on is thin.
O wind from Sao,
Do not blow hard
Till he reaches home.

2

My heart, thinking
"How beautiful he is"
Is like a swift river
Which though one dams it and dams it,
Will still break through.

3

Unknown love
Is as bitter a thing
As the maiden-lily
Which grows in the thickets
Of the summer moor.

ANONYMOUS

Shall we make love
Indoors
On this night when the moon has begun to shine
Over the rushes
Of Inami Moor?

(Arthur Waley)

THE RIVER OF HEAVEN

He is coming, my long-desired lord, whom I have been waiting to meet here, on the banks of the River of Heaven. . . . The moment of loosening my girdle is nigh.

Over the Rapids of the Everlasting Heaven, floating in his boat, my lord will doubtless deign to come to me this very night.

Though winds and clouds to either bank may freely come or go, between myself and my far-away spouse no message whatever may pass.

To the opposite bank one might easily fling a pebble; yet, being separated from him by the River of Heaven, alas! to hope for a meeting (except in autumn) is utterly useless.

From the day that the autumn wind began to blow (I kept saying to myself), "Ah! when shall we meet?"—but now my beloved, for whom I waited and longed, has come indeed!

Though the waters of the River of Heaven have not greatly risen (yet, to cross) this near stream and to wait upon my lord and lover remains impossible.

Though she is so near that the waving of her (long) sleeves can be distinctly seen, yet there is no way to cross the stream before the season of autumn.

When we were separated, I had seen her for a moment only,—and dimly as one sees a flying midge; now I must vainly long for her as before, until time of our next meeting!

Methinks that Hikoboshi must be rowing his boat to meet his wife,—for a mist (as of oar-spray) is rising over the course of the Heavenly Stream.

While awaiting my lord on the misty shore of the River of Heaven, the skirts of my robe have somehow become wet.

On the River of Heaven, at the place of the august ferry, the sound of the water has become loud: perhaps my long-awaited lord will soon be coming in his boat.

As Tanabata (slumbers) with her long sleeves rolled up, until the reddening of the dawn, do not, O storks of the river-shallows, awaken her by your cries.

(She sees that) a mist is spreading across the River of Heaven. . . . "To-day, to-day," she thinks, "my long-awaited lord will probably come over in his boat."

By the ferry of Yasu, on the River of Heaven, the boat is floating: I pray you tell my beloved that I stand here and wait.

Though I (being a Star-god) can pass freely to and fro, through the great sky,—yet to cross over the River of Heaven, for your sake, was weary work indeed!

From the august Age of the God-of-Eight-Thousand-Spears, she had been my spouse in secret only; yet now, because of my constant longing for her, our relation has become known to man.

From the time when heaven and earth were parted, she has been my own wife;—yet, to be with her, I must always wait till autumn.

With my beloved, of the ruddy-tinted cheeks, this night indeed will I descend into the bed of the River of Heaven, to sleep on a pillow of stone.

When I see the water-grasses of the River of Heaven bend in the autumn wind (I think to myself): "The time (for our meeting) seems to have come."

When I feel in my heart a sudden longing for my husband, then on the River of Heaven the sound of the rowing of the night-boat is heard, and the plash of the oars resounds.

In the night when I am reposing with my (now) far-away spouse, having exchanged jewel-pillows with her, let not the cock crow, even though the day should dawn.

Though for a myriad ages we should remain hand-in-hand and face to face, our exceeding love could never come to an end. (Why then should Heaven deem it necessary to part us?)

The white cloth which Tanabata has woven for my sake, in that dwelling of hers, is now, I think, being made into a robe for me.

Though she be far-away, and hidden from me by five hundred layers of white cloud, still shall I turn my gaze each night toward the dwelling-place of my younger sister (wife).

When autumn comes, and the river-mists spread over the Heavenly Stream, I turn toward the river (and long); and the nights of my longing are many!

But once in the whole year, and only upon the seventh night (of the seventh month), to meet the beloved person—and lo! The day has dawned before our mutual love could express (or "satisfy") itself!

The love-longing of one whole year having ended to-night, every day from to-morrow I must again pine for him as before.

Hikoboshi and Tanabata-tsumé are to meet each other to-night;—ye waves of the River of Heaven, take heed that ye do not rise!

Oh! that white cloud driven by the autumn-wind—can it be the heavenly hire of Tanabata-tsumé?

Because he is my not-often-to-be-met beloved, hasten to row the boat across the River of Heaven ere the night be advanced.

Late in the night, a mist spreads over the River of Heaven; and the sound of the oar of Hikoboshi is heard.

On the River of Heaven a sound of plashing can be distinctly heard: is it the sound of the rippling made by Hikoboshi quickly rowing his boat?

Perhaps this evening shower is but the spray (flung down) from the oar of Hikoboshi, rowing his boat in haste.

From to-morrow, alas! after having put my jewel-bed in order, no longer reposing with my lord, I must sleep alone!

The wind having risen, the waves of the river have become high;—this night cross over in a row-boat, I pray thee, before the hour be late!

Even though the waves of the River of Heaven run high, I must row over quickly, before it becomes late in the night.

Long ago I finished weaving the material; and, this evening, having finished sewing the garment for him—(why must) I still wait for my lord?

Is it that the current of the River of Heaven (has become too) rapid? The jet-black night advances—and Hikoboshi has not come!

Oh, ferryman, make speed across the stream!—my lord is not one who can come and go twice in a year!

On the very day that the autumn-wind began to blow, I set out for the shallows of the River of Heaven;—I pray you, tell my lord that I am waiting here still!

Methinks Tanabata must be coming in her boat; for a cloud is even now passing across the clear face of the moon.

(*Lafcadio Hearn*)

From the Kokin Shū

Compiled 9th century

ONO NO TAKAMURA

802–852

Did I ever think
That decaying
In the loneliness of a barbarian land
I should become a shore-hunter
Tugging at the ropes of fishermen?

ONO NO KOMACHI

834–880

A THING which fades
With no outward sign—
Is the flower
Of the heart of man
In this world!

KI NO AKIMINE

9th century

THE beloved person must I think
Have entered
The summer mountain:
For the cuckoo is singing
With a louder note.

MITSUNE

c. 900

SINCE I heard
Faintly the voice
Of the first wild-goose,
Upon mid sky alone
My thoughts have been fixed.

ONO NO YOSHIKI

d. 902

MY love
Is like the grasses
Hidden in the deep mountain:
Though its abundance increases,
There is none that knows.

FUJIWARA NO TOSHIYUKI

d. 907

Although it is not plainly visible to the
eye
That autumn has come,
I am alarmed
By the noise of the wind!

ANONYMOUS

1

O cuckoo,
Because the villages where you sing
Are so many,
I am estranged from you, even
In the midst of my love!

2

Hoping all the time
That we should meet
In my dreams,—
I spent the whole night
Without being able to sleep.

3

When the dawn comes
With the flicker flicker
Of sunrise,
How sad the helping each other to put on
our clothes!

4

If only, when one heard
That Old Age was coming
One could bolt the door,
Answer "not at home"
And refuse to meet him!

(*Arthur Waley*)

From the Shūi Shū

Compiled 10th century

HITOMARO

c. 700

WHEN,
Halting in front of it, I look
At the reflection which is in the depths
Of my clear mirror,
It gives me the impression of meeting
An unknown old gentleman.

TSURAYUKI

883–946

THE time I went to see my Sister
Whom I loved unendurably,
The winter-night's
River-wind was so cold that
The sanderlings were crying.

NAKATSUKASA

c. 900

IF it were not for the voice
Of the nightingale,
How would the mountain-village
Where the snow is still unmelted
Know the spring?

ONAKATOMI YOSHINOBU

c. 900

THE deer which lives
On the evergreen mountain
Where there are no autumn-leaves
Can know the coming of autumn
Only by its own cry.

KIYOWARA FUKUYABU

c.900–930

Because river-fog
Hiding the mountain-base
Has risen,
The autumn mountain looks as though it
    hung in the sky.

MINAMOTO NO SHIGEYUKI

d. 1000

Winter has at last come
Unmistakably, even to my cottage
In the land of Tsu,
Which lies hidden
Among the rush-leaves.

(*Arthur Waley*)

Saigyo Hōshi

1118–1190

SEVEN POEMS

1

In my boat that goes
Over manifold salt-ways
Towards the open sea
Faintly I hear
The cry of the first wild-goose.

2

Mingling my prayer
With the clang of the bell
Which woke me from my dreams,
Lo, ten times I have recited the
    Honorable Name.

3

Since I am convinced
That Reality is in no way
Real,
How am I to admit
That dreams are dreams?

4

Startled
By a single scream
Of the crane which is reposing
On the surface of the swamp,
All the other birds are crying.

5

Those ships which left
Side by side
The same harbor
Towards an unknown destination
Have rowed away from one another!

6

Like those boats which are returning
Across the open sea of Ashiya
Where the waves run high,
I think that I too shall pass
Scatheless through the storms of life.

7

Although I do not know
At all whether anything
Honorable deigns to be there,
Yet in extreme awe
My tears well forth.

(Arthur Waley)

Fujiwara Ietaka

1158–1237

OLD SCENT OF THE PLUM TREE

Remembering what passed
Under the scent of the plum-tree,
I asked the plum-tree for tidings
Of that other.
Alas . . . the cold moon of spring. . . .

(*E. Powys Mathers*)

From the Hyaku-Nin-Isshu

13th century

PRINCESS SHOKU

I would that even now
My thread of life were broken—
So should my secret vow
Remain unspoken.

LADY HORIKAWA

How can one e'er be sure
If true love will endure?
My thoughts this morning are
As tangled as my hair.

FUJIWARA NO MICHINOBU

The day will soon be gone,
And night come back, I know . . .
Yet how I hate the dawn
That bids me go.

LADY SANUKI

Like a great rock, far out at sea,
Submerged at even the lowest tide,
Unseen, unknown of man—my sleeve
Is never for a moment dried.

(*Curtis Hidden Page*)

Bashō

1644–1694

SEVEN POEMS

1

Quick-falling dew,
Ah, let me cleanse in you
This wretched life.

2

The roadside thistle, eager
To see the travelers pass,
Was eaten by the passing ass!

3

Friend sparrow, do not eat, I pray
The little buzzing flies that play
Among my flowers.

4

A lonely pond in age-old stillness sleeps . . .
Apart, unstirred by sound or motion . . . till
Suddenly into it a lithe frog leaps.

5

Old battle field, fresh with Spring flowers again—
All that is left of the dream
Of twice ten thousand warriors slain.

6

Old men, white-haired, beside the ancestral graves,
All of the household now
Stand lonesome, leaning on their staves.

7

O cricket, from your cheery cry
No one could ever guess
How quickly you must die.

(*Curtis Hidden Page*)

SANSKRIT

From the Rigveda

C. 1500 B.C.

The Rigveda consists of 1,028 hymns, comprising over ten thousand verses. The hymns are generally simple, and betray a childlike and simple faith in the gods, to whom sacrifices are offered and libations of the Soma juice are poured, and who are asked for increase of progeny, cattle, and wealth, and implored to help the Aryans in their still doubtful struggle against the black aborigines of the Punjab.—ROMESH DUTT.

INDRA, THE SUPREME GOD

HIGHEST of Immortals bright,
God of gods by lofty might,
He, before whose prowess high
Tremble earth and upper sky,
He is,—mortals, hear my verse,—
Indra, Lord of Universe!

He, who fixed the staggering earth,
Shaped the mountains at their birth,
Sky's blue vault held up and bent,
Measured out the firmament,
He is,—listen to my verse,—
Indra, Lord of Universe!

He, who quelled the cloud-fiend's might,
Rolled the seven great rivers bright,
Pierced the caverns of the gloom,
Conquered bright kine from its womb,
Lit the lightning's fire of old,
He is Indra, warrior bold!

He, who shaped with cunning hand
Wonders of the sea and land,
Quelled the Aryan's impious foe,

Doomed the Dasa to his woe,
Robbed the bandit in his hold,
He is Indra, hunter bold!

Have you, doubting, questioned me,—
Where is Indra, who is He?
Mortals, in your impious thought
Have you whispered,—He is not!
Jealous God! In vengeance dire
He can smite ye in his ire!

But his ceaseless mercies seek
High and lowly, strong and weak,
Priest who chants his sacred lays,
Worshiper who sings his praise,
Him who on the altar's flame,
Pours libations to his name!

His the kine and steeds of war,
Village home and battle car;
His right arm uplifts the sun,
Opes the ruddy gates of dawn;
His red bolt the dark cloud rends,
Grateful showers for mortal sends!

Host advancing to the fray
Cry to him on battle's day;
And the strong man shouts his fame,
And the lowly lisps his name;
Warrior-chief on battle-car
Prays to Indra, God of war!

We but triumph by his blade,
Nations court his friendly aid;
Moveless hills that heavenward tower
Tremble at his mighty power;
And the world so vast and broad,
Images the mighty God!

Swift his weapons, red and dire,
To the impious speak his ire;
And his favors never rain
On the boastful and the vain;
And his red right hand can smite
Godless Dasas in the fight!

For he slew Sambara bold,
Sheltered in his mountain hold,
In the fortieth autumn-tide;
Slew the dragon in his pride,
Vritra, rain-witholding cloud,
Titan of the inky shroud!

Seven bright rays bedeck his bow,
Seven great rivers from him flow;
Thunder-armed, quick to ire,
He, in vengeance swift and dire,
Laid the proud Rauhina low,
Heaven-aspiring impious foe!

Earth and sky confess his sway,
Trembling hills obeisance pay;
Wielder of the bolt of heaven,
Be to him libations given;—
He accepts this Soma wine,
Listens to this lay of mine!

Brew the Soma fresh and fair,
Pour libations rich and rare,
For he blesses when we pray,
Helps the singer of his lay;—
He accepts this Soma wine,
Listens to this lay of mine!

Mighty Indra, strong and true,
Hymns to thee and gifts are due,
And our priests libations pour
For thy blessings' endless store;
Speak to us,—for thou art near,—
Let our brave sons know no fear!

(*Romesh Dutt*)

PUSHAN, GOD OF PASTURE

Pushan, God of golden day,
Shorten thou the shepherd's way,
Vanquish every foe and stranger,
Free our path from every danger;
Cloud-born Pushan, ever more,
Lead us as you led before!

Smite the wild wolf, fierce and vile,
Lurking in the dark defile,
Smite the robber and the thief,
Stealing forth to take our life;
Cloud-born Pushan, ever more,
Lead us as you led before!

Chase him, Pushan, in thy wrath,
Who infests the lonely path,
Robber with his ruthless heart,
Slayer with his secret dart;
Child of clouds, for ever more,
Lead us as you led before!

Trample with thy heavy tread,
On the darksome man of dread,
On the low and lying knave,
Smooth-tongued double-dealing slave;
Child of clouds, for ever more,
Lead us as you led before!

Thou dost pathless forests know,
Thou canst quell the secret foe,
Thou didst lead our fathers right,
Wonder-worker, orb of light;
Grant from thy unfailing store
Wealth and blessings ever more!

Thou hast treasures manifold,
Glittering weapons, arms of gold;
Foremost of the Sons of Light,
Shepherds' God and Leader bright;
Grant from thy unfailing store
Wealth and blessings ever more!

Lead us through the dark defile
Past pursuers dread and vile,
Lead us over pleasant ways
Sheltered by thy saving grace,
Lead us o'er this trackless shore,
And we follow ever more!

Where the grass is rich and green,
And the pasture's beauteous seen,
And the meadow's soft and sweet,
Lead us, safe from scorching heat,
Blessings on thy servants pour,
And we follow ever more!

Fill our hearts with hope and courage,
Fill our homes with food and forage,
Save us from a cruel fate
Feed us and invigorate;
We are suppliants at thy door,
And we follow ever more!

Heart and voice we lift in praise,
Chant our hymns and pious lays,
From the Bright One, good and gracious,
Ask for food and pasture spacious;
Shepherds' God! Befriend the poor,
And we follow ever more!

(*Romesh Dutt*)

From the Panchatantra

2d century B.C., *et seq.*

KINGS

In sensuous coil
And heartless toil,
In sinuous course
And armored force,
In savage harms
That yield to charms—
In all these things
Are snakes like kings.

Uneven, rough,
And high enough—
Yet low folk roam
Their flanks as home,
And wild things haunt
Them, hungry, gaunt—
In all these things
Are hills like kings.

The things that claw, and the things that gore
Are unreliable things;
And so is a man with a sword in his hand,
And rivers, and women, and kings.

(*Arthur W. Ryder*)

THE PENALTY OF VIRTUE

The fruit-tree's branch by very wealth
Of fruit is bended low;
The peacock's feathered pride compels
A sluggish gait and slow;
The blooded horse that wins his race,
Must like a cow be led:
The good in goodness often find
An enemy to dread.

Where Jumna's waves roll blue
With sands of sapphire hue,
Black serpents have their lair;
And who would hunt them there,
But that a jewel's bright star
From each hood gleams afar?
By virtue rising, all
By that same virtue fall.

The man of virtue commonly
  Is hateful to the king,
While riches to the scamps and fools
  Habitually cling:
The ancient chant 'By virtue great
  Is man' has run to seed;
The world takes rare and little note
  Of any plucky deed.

(*Arthur W. Ryder*)

TRUE FRIENDSHIP

'Tis hard to find in life
A friend, a bow, a wife,
Strong, supple to endure,
In stock and sinew pure,
In time of danger sure.

False friends are common. Yes, but where
True nature links a friendly pair,
The blessing is as rich as rare.

To bitter ends
You trust true friends,
Not wife nor mother,
Not son nor brother.

No long experience alloys
True friendship's sweet and supple joys;
No evil men can steal the treasure;
'Tis death, death only, sets a measure.

(*Arthur W. Ryder*)

FOOL AND FALSE

With the shrewd and upright man
  Seek a friendship rare;
Exercise with shrewd and false
  Superheedful care;
Pity for the upright fool
  Find within your heart;
If a man be fool and false,
  Shun him from the start.

(Arthur W. Ryder)

POVERTY

A beggar to the graveyard hied
And there "Friend corpse, arise," he cried;
"One moment lift my heavy weight
Of poverty; for I of late
Grow weary, and desire instead
Your comfort; you are good and dead."
The corpse was silent. He was sure
'Twas better to be dead than poor.

(Arthur W. Ryder)

Amarou

1st century?

THE DRUNKEN ROSE

Has not the night been as a drunken rose
Without a witness? And the girl of bloom
Has given up all. What little cries of joy!
What wanton words repeated!
But white dawn shows the rose and green pet bird,
The mighty talker and awake all night.
Hark! The old woman comes; he will tell all.
What shall she, fluttering? Snap small rubies off
From the bright ear-rings, facets sharp as steel;

These with the seed-pulp of the passion-fruit,
His sweet prepared breakfast, mingle featly . . .
So, busy jargoner, silent for ever more.

(*E. Powys Mathers*)

Kalidasa

c. 500

Rarely has a man walked the earth who observed the phenomena of living nature as accurately as he. His nature was one of singular balance, equally at home in a splendid court and on a lonely mountain. For something like fifteen hundred years Kalidasa has been more widely read in India than any other author who wrote in Sanskrit.—ARTHUR W. RYDER.

THE SEASONS

SUMMER

PITILESS heat from heaven pours
  By day, but nights are cool;
Continual bathing gently lowers
  The water in the pool;
The evenings bring a charming peace:
  For summer-time is here
When love that never knows surcease,
  Is less imperious, dear.

Yet love can never fall asleep;
  For he is waked to-day
By songs that all their sweetness keep
  And lutes that softly play,
By fans with sandal-water wet
  That bring us drowsy rest,
By strings of pearls that gently fret
  Full many a lovely breast.

The sunbeams like the fires are hot
  That on the altar wake;
The enmity is quite forgot
  Of peacock and of snake;

The peacock spares his ancient foe,
For pluck and hunger fail;
He hides his burning head below
The shadow of his tail.

Beneath the garland of the rays
That leave no corner cool,
The water vanishes in haze
And leaves a muddy pool;
The cobra does not hunt for food
Nor heed the frog at all
Who finds beneath the serpent's hood
A sheltering parasol.

Dear maiden of the graceful song,
To you may summer's power
Bring moonbeams clear and garlands long
And breath of trumpet-flower,
Bring lakes that countless lilies dot,
Refreshing water-sprays,
Sweet friends at evening, and a spot
Cool after burning days.

The Rains

The rain advances like a king
In awful majesty;
Hear, dearest, how his thunders ring
Like royal drums, and see
His lightning-banners wave; a cloud
For elephant he rides,
And finds his welcome from the crowd
Of lovers and of brides.

The clouds, a mighty army, march
With drumlike thundering
And stretch upon the rainbow's arch
The lightning's flashing string;

The cruel arrows of the rain
  Smite them who live, apart
From whom they love, with stinging pain,
  And pierce them to the heart.

The forest seems to show its glee
  In flowering nipa plants;
In waving twigs of many a tree
  Wind-swept, it seems to dance;
Its ketak-blossom's opening sheath
  Is like a smile put on
To greet the rain's reviving breath,
  Now pain and heat are gone.

To you, dear, may the cloudy time
  Bring all that you desire,
Bring every pleasure, perfect, prime,
  To set a bride on fire;
May rain whereby life wakes and shines
  Where there is power of life,
The unchanging friend of clinging vines,
  Shower blessings on my wife.

Autumn

The autumn comes, a maiden fair
  In slenderness and grace,
With nodding rice-stems in her hair
  And lilies in her face.
In flowers of grasses she is clad;
  And as she moves along,
Birds greet her with their cooing glad
  Like bracelets' tinkling song.

A diadem adorns the night
  Of multitudinous stars;
Her silken robe is white moonlight,
  Set free from cloudy bars;

And on her face (the radiant moon)
  Bewitching smiles are shown:
She seems a slender maid, who soon
  Will be a woman grown.

Over the rice-fields, laden plants
  Are shivering to the breeze;
While in his brisk caresses dance
  The blossomed-burdened trees;
He ruffles every lily-pond
  Where blossoms kiss and part,
And stirs with lover's fancies fond
  The young man's eager heart.

Winter

The bloom of tenderer flowers is past
  And lilies droop forlorn,
For winter-time is come at last,
  Rich with its ripened corn;
Yet for the wealth of blossoms lost
  Some hardier flowers appear
That bid defiance to the frost
  Of sterner days, my dear.

The vines, remembering summer, shiver
  In frosty winds, and gain
A fuller life from mere endeavor
  To live through all that pain;
Yet in the struggle and acquist
  They turn as pale and wan
As lonely women who have missed
  Known love, now lost and gone.

Then may these winter days show forth
  To you each known delight,
Bring all that women count as worth
  Pure happiness and bright;

While villages, with bustling cry,
Bring home the ripened corn,
And herons wheel through wintry sky,
Forget sad thoughts forlorn.

Early Spring

Now, dearest, lend a heedful ear
And listen while I sing
Delights to every maiden dear,
The charms of early spring:
When earth is dotted with the heaps
Of corn, when heron-scream
Is rare but sweet, when passion leaps
And paints a livelier dream.

When all must cheerfully applaud
A blazing open fire;
Or if they needs must go abroad,
The sun is their desire;
When everybody hopes to find
The frosty chill allayed
By garments warm, a window-blind
Shut, and a sweet young maid.

Then may the days of early spring
For you be rich and full
With love's proud, soft philandering
And many a candy-pull,
With sweetest rice and sugar-cane:
And may you float above
The absent grieving and the pain
Of separated love.

Spring

A STALWART soldier comes, the spring,
Who bears the bow of Love;
And on that bow, the lustrous string
Is made of bees, that move

With malice as they speed the shaft
  Of blossoming mango-flower
At us, dear, who have never laughed
  At love, nor scorned his power.

Their blossom-burden weights the trees;
  The winds in fragrance move;
The lakes are bright with lotuses,
  The women bright with love;
The days are soft, the evenings clear
  And charming; everything
That moves and lives and blossoms, dear,
  Is sweeter in the spring.

The groves are beautifully bright
  For many and many a mile
With jasmine-flowers that are as white
  As loving woman's smile:
The resolution of a saint
  Might well be tried by this;
Far more, young hearts that fancies paint
  With dreams of loving bliss.

(Arthur W. Ryder)

Bhartrihari

c. 500

In short verses the Hindus excel. Their mastery of form, their play of fancy, their depth and tenderness of feeling, are all exquisite. Of the many who wrote such verses, the greatest is Bhartrihari.—ARTHUR W. RYDER.

TIME

TIME is the root of all this earth;
These creatures, who from Time had birth,
Within his bosom at the end
Shall sleep; Time hath nor enemy nor friend.

All we in one long caravan
Are journeying since the world began;
We know not whither, but we know
Time guideth at the front, and all must go.

Like as the wind upon the field
Bows every herb, and all must yield,
So we beneath Time's passing breath
Bow each in turn,—why tears for birth or death?

(Paul Elmer More)

PEACE

Courage, my Soul! now to the silent wood
Alone we wander, there to seek our food
In the wild fruits, and woo our dreamless sleep
On soft boughs gathered deep.

There loud authority in folly bold,
And tongues that stammer with disease of gold,
And murmur of the windy world shall cease,
Nor echo through our peace.

(Paul Elmer More)

Bilhana

11th century

BLACK MARIGOLDS

(A free interpretation of the Chauraspanchāsika)

Even now
My thought is all of this gold-tinted king's daughter
With garlands tissue and golden buds,
Smoke tangles of her hair, and sleeping or waking
Feet trembling in love, full of pale languor;
My thought is clinging as to a lost learning
Slipped down out of the minds of men,
Laboring to bring her back into my soul.

Even now
If I see in my soul the citron-breasted fair one
Still gold-tinted, her face like our night stars,
Drawing unto her; her body beaten about with flame,

Wounded by the flaring spear of love,
My first of all by reason of her fresh years,
Then is my heart buried alive in snow.

Even now
If my girl with lotus eyes came to me again
Weary with the dear weight of young love,
Again I would give her to these starved twins of arms
And from her mouth drink down the heavy wine,
As a reeling pirate bee in fluttered ease
Steals up the honey from the nenuphar.

Even now
I bring her back, ah, wearied out with love
So that her slim feet could not bear her up;
Curved falls of her hair down on her white cheeks;
In the confusion of her colored vests
Speaking that guarded giving up, and her scented arms
Lay like cool bindweed over against my neck.

Even now
I bring her back to me in her quick shame,
Hiding her bright face at the point of day:
Making her grave eyes move in watered stars,
For love's great sleeplessness wandering all night,
Seeming to sail gently, as that pink bird,
Down the water of love in a harvest of lotus.

Even now
If I saw her lying all wide eyes
And with collyrium the indent of her cheek
Lengthened to the bright ear and her pale side
So suffering the fever of my distance,
Then would my love for her be ropes of flowers, and
night
A black-haired lover on the breasts of day.

Even now
I see the heavy startled hair of this reed-flute player
Who curved her poppy lips to love dances,
Having a youth's face madding like the moon
Lying at her full; limbs ever moving a little in love,
Too slight, too delicate, tired with the small burden
Of bearing love ever on white feet.

Even now
She is present to me on her beds,
Balmed with the exhalation of a flattering musk,
Rich with the curdy essence of santal;
Girl with eyes dazing as the seeded-wine,
Showing as a pair of gentle nut-hatches
Kissing each other with their bills, each hidden
By turns within a little grasping mouth.

Even now
She swims back in the crowning hour of love
All red with wine her lips have given to drink,
Soft round the mouth with camphor and faint blue
Tinted upon the lips, her slight body,
Her great live eyes, the colorings of herself
A clear perfection; sighs of musk outstealing
And powdered wood spice heavy of Cashmir.

Even now
I see her; far face blond like gold
Rich with small lights, and tinted shadows surprised
Over and over all of her; with glittering eyes
All bright for love but very love weary,
As it were the conjuring disk of the moon when Rahu
ceases
With his dark stumbling block to hide her rays.

Even now
She is art-magically present to my soul,
And that one word of strange heart's ease, good-by,
That in the night, in loth moving to go,

And bending over to a golden mouth,
I said softly to the turned away
Tenderly tired hair of this king's daughter.

Even now
My eyes that hurry to see no more are painting, painting
Faces of my lost girl. O golden rings
That tap against cheeks of small magnolia leaves,
O whitest so soft parchment where
My poor divorcèd lips have written excellent
Stanzas of kisses, and will write no more.

Even now
Death sends me the flickering of powdery lids
Over wild eyes and the pity of her slim body
All broken up with the weariness of joy;
The little red flowers of her breasts to be my comfort
Moving above scarves, and for my sorrow
Wet crimson lips that once I marked as mine.

Even now
By a cool noise of waters in the spring
The asoka with young flowers that feign her fingers
And bud in red; and in the green vest pearls kissing
As it were rose leaves in the gardens of God; the shining at night
Of white cheeks in the dark; smiles from light thoughts within,
And her walking as of a swan: these trouble me.

Even now
The pleased intimacy of rough love
Upon the patient glory of her form
Racks me with memory; and her bright dress
As it were yellow flame, which the white hand
Shamefastly gathers in her rising haste,
The slender grace of her departing feet.

Even now
When all my heavy heart is broken up
I seem to see my prison walls breaking
And then a light, and in that light a girl
Her fingers busied about her hair, her cool white arms
Faint rosy at the elbows, raised in the sunlight,
And temperate eyes that wander far away.

Even now
I seem to see my prison walls come close,
Built up of darkness, and against that darkness
A girl no taller than my breast and very tired,
Leaning upon the bed and smiling, feeding
A little bird and lying slender as ash trees,
Sleepily aware as I told of the green
Grapes and the small bright-colored river flowers.

Even now
I see her, as I used, in her white palace
Under black torches throwing cool red light,
Woven with many flowers and tearing the dark.
I see her rising, showing all her face
Defiant timidly, saying clearly:
Now I shall go to sleep, good-night, my ladies.

Even now
Though I am so far separate, a flight of birds
Swinging from side to side over the valley trees,
Passing my prison with their calling and crying,
Bring me to see my girl. For very bird-like
Is her song singing, and the state of a swan
In her light walking, like the shaken wings
Of a black eagle falls her nightly hair.

Even now
I know my princess was happy. I see her stand
Touching her breasts with all her flower-soft fingers,
Looking askance at me with smiling eyes.

There is a god that arms him with a flower
And she was stricken deep. Here, oh die here.
Kiss me and I shall be purer than quick rivers.

Even now
They chatter her weakness through the two bazaars
Who was so strong to love me. And small men
That buy and sell for silver being slaves
Crinkle the fat about their eyes; and yet
No Prince of the Cities of the Sea has taken her,
Leading to his grim bed. Little lonely one,
You clung to me as a garment clings; my girl.

Even now
Only one dawn shall rise for me. The stars
Revolve to-morrow's night and I not heed.
One brief cold watch beside an empty heart
And that is all. This night she rests not well;
Oh, sleep; for there is heaviness for all the world
Except for the death-lighted heart of me.

Even now
My sole concern the slipping of her vests,
Her little breasts the life beyond this life.
One night of disarray in her green hems,
Her golden cloths, outweighs the order of earth,
Making of none effect the tides of the sea.
I have seen her enter the temple meekly and there seem
The flag of flowers that veils the very god.

Even now
I mind the coming and talking of wise men from towers
Where they had thought away their youth. And I, listening,
Found not the salt of the whispers of my girl,
Murmur of confused colors, as we lay near sleep;
Little wise words and little witty words,
Wanton as water, honied with eagerness.

Even now
I call to mind her weariness in the morning
Close lying in my arms, and tiredly smiling
At my disjointed prayer for her small sake.
Now in my morning the weariness of death
Sends me to sleep. Had I made coffins
I might have lived singing to three score.

Even now
The woodcutter and the fisherman turn home,
With on his axe the moon and in his dripping net
Caught yellow moonlight. The purple flame of fires
Calls them to love and sleep. From the hot town
The maker of scant songs for bread wanders
To lie under the clematis with his girl.
The moon shines on her breasts, and I must die.

Even now
I have a need to make up prayers, to speak
My last consideration of the world
To the great thirteen gods, to make my balance
Ere the soul journeys on. I kneel and say:
Father of Light. Leave we it burning still
That I may look at you. *Mother of the Stars,*
Give me your feet to kiss; I love you, dear.

Even now
I seem to see the face of my lost girl
With frightened eyes, like a wood wanderer,
In travail with sorrowful waters, unwept tears
Laboring to be born and fall; when white face turned
And little ears caught at the far murmur,
The pleased snarling of the tumult of dogs
When I was hurried away down the white road.

Even now
When slow rose-yellow moons looked out at night
To guard the sheaves of harvest and mark down
The peach's fall, how calm she was and love worthy.

Glass-colored starlight falling as thin as dew
Was wont to find us at the spirit's starving time
Slow straying in the orchard paths with love.

Even now
Love is a god and Rati the dark his bride;
But once I found their child and she was fairer,
That could so shine. And we were each to each
Wonderful and a presence not yet felt
In any dream. I knew the sunset earth
But as a red gold ring to bear my emerald
Within the little summer of my youth.

Even now
I marvel at the bravery of love,
She, whose two feet might be held in one hand
And all her body on a shield of the guards,
Lashed like a gold panther taken in a pit
Tearfully valiant, when I too was taken;
Bearding her black beard father in his wrath,
Striking the soldiers with white impotent hands.

Even now
I mind that I loved cypress and roses, dear,
The great blue mountains and the small gray hills,
The sounding of the sea. Upon a day
I saw strange eyes and hands like butterflies;
For me at morning larks flew from the thyme
And children came to bathe in little streams.

Even now
Sleep left me all these nights for your white bed
And I am sure you sistered lay with sleep
After much weeping. Piteous little love,
Death is in the garden, time runs down,
The year that simple and unexalted ran till now
Ferments in winy autumn, and I must die.

Even now
I mind our going, full of bewilderment
As who should walk from sleep into great light,
Along the running of the winter river,
A dying sun on the cool hurrying tide
No more by green rushes delayed in dalliance,
With a clear purpose in his flower flecked length
Informed, to reach Nirvana and the sea.

Even now
I love long black eyes that caress like silk,
Ever and ever sad and laughing eyes,
Whose lids make such sweet shadow when they close
It seems another beautiful look of hers.
I love a fresh mouth, ah, a scented mouth,
And curving hair, subtle as a smoke,
And light fingers, and laughter of green gems.

Even now
I mind asking: Where love and how love Rati's
    priestesses?
You can tell me of their washings at moon down
And if that warm basin have silver borders.
Is it so that when they comb their hair
Their fingers, being purple stained, show
Like coral branches in the black sea of their hair?

Even now
I remember that you made answer very softly,
We being one soul, your hand on my hair,
The burning memory rounding your near lips:
I have seen the priestesses of Rati make love at moon fall
And then in a carpeted hall with a bright gold lamp
Lie down carelessly anywhere to sleep.

Even now
I have no surety that she is not Mahadevi
Rose red of Siva, or Kapagata
The willful ripe Companion of the King,

Or Krisna's own Lakshmi, the violet haired.
I am not certain but that dark Brahma
In his high secret purposes
Has sent my soft girl down to make the three worlds
mad
With capering about her scented feet.

Even now
Call not the master painters from all the world,
Their thin black boards, their rose and green and gray,
Their ashes of lapis ultramarine,
Their earth of shadows the umber. Laughing at art
Sunlight upon the body of my bride,
For painting not nor any eyes for ever.
Oh warm tears on the body of my bride.

Even now
I mind when the red crowds were passed and it was
raining
How glad those two that shared the rain with me;
For they talked happily with rich young voices
And at the storm's increase, closer and with content,
Each to the body of the other held
As there were no more severance for ever.

Even now
The stainless fair appearance of the moon
Rolls her gold beauty over an autumn sky
And the stiff anchorite forgets to pray;
How much the sooner I, if her wild mouth
Tasting of the taste of manna came to mine
And kept my soul at balance above a kiss.

Even now
Her mouth carelessly scented as with lotus dust
Is water of love to the great heat of love,
A tirtha very holy, a lover's lake
Utterly sacred. Might I go down to it
But one more time, then should I find a way
To hold my lake for ever and ever more
Sobbing out my life beside the waters.

Even now
I mind that the time of the falling of blossoms started
my dream
Into a wild life, into my girl;
Then was the essence of her beauty spilled
Down on my days so that it fades not,
Fails not, subtle and fresh, in perfuming
That day, and the days, and this the latest day.

Even now
She with young limbs as smooth as flower pollen,
Whose swaying body is laved in the cool
Waters of languor, this dear bright-colored bird,
Walks not, changes not, advances not
Her weary station by the black lake
Of Gone Forever, in whose fountain vase
Balance the water-lilies of my thought.

Even now
Spread we our nets beyond the farthest rims
So surely that they take the feet of dawn
Before you wake and after you are sleeping
Catch up the visible and invisible stars
And web the ports the strongest dreamer dreamed,
Yet is it all one, Vidya, yet is it nothing.

Even now
The night is full of silver straws of rain,
And I will send my soul to see your body
This last poor time. I stand beside our bed;
Your shadowed head lies leaving a bright space
Upon the pillow empty, your sorrowful arm
Holds from your side and clasps not anything.
There is no covering upon you.

Even now
I think your feet seek mine to comfort them.
There is some dream about you even now
Which I'll not hear at waking. Weep not at dawn,

Though day brings wearily your daily loss
And all the light is hateful. Now is it time
To bring my soul away.

Even now
I mind that I went round with men and women,
And underneath their brows, deep in their eyes,
I saw their souls, which go slipping aside
In swarms before the pleasure of my mind;
The world was like a flight of birds, shadow or flame
Which I saw pass above the engraven hills.
Yet was there never one like to my woman.

Even now
Death I take up as consolation.
Nay, were I free as the condor with his wings
Or old kings throned on violet ivory,
Night would not come without beds of green floss
And never a bed without my bright darling.
It is most fit that you strike now, black guards,
And let this fountain out before the dawn.

Even now
I know that I have savored the hot taste of life
Lifting green cups and gold at the great feast.
Just for a small and a forgotten time
I have had full in my eyes from off my girl
The whitest pouring of eternal light.
The heavy knife. As to a gala day.

(*E. Powys Mathers*)

Jayadeva

12th century

FROM THE GĪTĀ GŌVINDA

HYMN TO VISHNU

O THOU that held'st the blessed Veda dry
When all things else beneath the floods were hurled;
Strong Fish-God! Ark of Men! *Jai!* Hari, *jai!*
Hail, Keshav, hail; thou Master of the world!

The round world rested on thy spacious nape;
  Upon thy neck, like a mere mole, it stood:
O thou, that took'st for us the Tortoise-shape,
  Hail, Keshav, Hail! Ruler of wave and wood!

The world upon thy curving tusk sate sure,
  Like the Moon's dark disc in her crescent pale;
O thou who didst for us assume the Boar,
  Immortal Conqueror! hail, Keshav, hail!

When thou thy Giant-Foe didst seize and rend,
  Fierce, fearful, long, and sharp were fang and nail;
Thou who the Lion and the Man didst blend,
  Lord of the Ūniverse, hail, Narsingh, hail!

Wonderful Dwarf!—who with a threefold stride
  Cheated King Bali—where thy footsteps fall
Men's sins, O Wamuna! are set aside:
  O Keshav, hail! thou Help and Hope of all!

The sins of this sad earth thou didst assail,
  The anguish of its creatures thou didst heal;
Freed are we from all terrors by thy toil:
  Hail, Purshuram, hail! Lord of the biting steel!

To thee the fell Ten-Headed yielded life.
  Thou in dread battle laid'st the monster low!
Ah, Rama! dear to Gods and men that strife;
  We praise thee, Master of the matchless bow!

With clouds for garments glorious thou dost fare,
  Veiling thy dazzling majesty and might,
As when Jamuna saw thee with the share,
  A peasant—yet the King of Day and Night.

Merciful-hearted! when thou camest as Boodh—
  Albeit 'twas written in the Scriptures so—
Thou bad'st our altars to be no more imbrued
  With blood of victims: Keshav! bending low—

We praise thee, Wielder of the sweeping sword,
  Brilliant as curving comets in the gloom,
Whose edge shall smite the fierce barbarian horde;
  Hail to thee, Keshav! hail, and hear, and come,

And fill this song of Jayadev with thee,
  And make it wise to teach, strong to redeem,
And sweet to living souls. Thou Mystery!
  Thou Light of Life! Thou Dawn beyond the dream!

Fish! that didst outswim the flood;
Tortoise! whereon earth hath stood;
Boar! who with thy tush held'st high
The world, that mortals might not die;
Lion! who hast giants torn;
Dwarf! who laugh'dst a king to scorn;
Sole Subduer of the Dreaded!
Slayer of the many-headed!
Mighty Ploughman! Teacher tender!
Of thine own the sure Defender!
Under all thy ten disguises
Endless praise to thee arises.

(*Sir Edwin Arnold*)

ARABIAN

From the Mu'allaqát

Compiled 8th century

Imr El Kais

6th century

The ancient poetry of Arabia, immediately before the advent of Mohammed, is the most delightful wild flower of literature the Eastern world can show. The "Seven Golden Odes," or the "Seven Suspended Poems," have come to be considered the classic poems, and have obtained for their authors a special position as the most famous singers of Pagan Arabia.—Wilfrid Scawen Blunt.

ODE

Weep, ah weep love's losing, love's with its dwelling-
place set where the hills divide Dakhúli and Háumali.
Túdiha and Mikrat! There the hearths-stones of her
stand where the South and North winds cross-weave
the sand-furrows.
See the white-doe droppings strewn by the wind on
them, black on her floor forsaken, fine-grain of pep-
percorns.
Here it was I watched her, lading her load-camels,
stood by these thorn-trees weeping tears as of colo-
cynth.
Here my twin-friends waited, called to me camel-borne:
Man! not of grief thou diest. Take thy pain patiently.
Not though tears assuage thee, deem it beseemeth thee
thus for mute stones to wail thee, all thy foes wit-
nesses.
What though fortune flout thee! Thus Om Howéyrith
did, thus did thy Om Rebábi, fooled thee in Másali.
O, where these two tented, sweet was the breath of them,
sweet as of musk their fragrance, sweet as garánfoli.

Mourned I for them long days, wept for the love of them, tears on my bosom raining, tears on my sword-handle.
Yet, was I un-vanquished. Had I not happiness, I at their hands in Dáret, Dáret of Júljuli?

O that day of all days! Slew I my milch-camel, feasted the maidens gayly,—well did they load for me!
Piled they high the meat-strings. All day they pelted me, pelted themselves with fatness, fringes of camel-meat.
Climbed I to her howdah, sat with Onéyzata, while at my raid she chided: Man! Must I walk afoot?
Swayed the howdah wildly, she and I close in it: there! my beast's back is galled now. Slave of Grief, down with thee.
Answered I: Nay, sweet heart, loosen the rein of him. Think not to stay my kisses. Here will I harvest them.
Grieve not for thy camel. Grudge not my croup-riding. Give me—and thee—to taste things sweeter than clove-apples,
Kisses on thy white teeth, teeth, nay the pure petals, even and clean and close-set, wreathing a camomile.
Wooed have I thy equals, maidens and wedded ones. Her, the nursling's mother, did I not win to her?
What though he wailed loudly, babe of the amulets, turned she not half towards him, half of her clasped to me?
Woe is me, the hard heart! How did she mock at me, high on the sand-hill sitting, vowing to leave and go!
Fátima, nay my own love, though thou wouldst break with me, still be thou kind awhile now, leave me not utterly.
Clean art thou mistaken. Love is my malady. Ask me the thing thou choosest. Straight will I execute.
If so be thou findest ought in thy lover wrong, cast from thy back my garments, moult thee my finery.
Woe is me, the hard heart! When did tears trouble thee save for my soul's worse wounding, stricken and near to die?

Fair too was that other, she the veil-hidden one, howdahed how close, how guarded! Yet did she welcome me.

Passed I twixt her tent-ropes,—what though her near-of-kin lay in the dark to slay me, blood-shedders all of them.

Came I at the mid-night, hour when the Pleiades showed as the links of seed-pearls binding the sky's girdle.

Stealing in, I stood there. She had cast off from her every robe but one robe, all but her night-garment.

Tenderly she scolded: What is this stratagem? Speak, on thine oath, thou mad one. Stark is thy lunacy.

Passed we out together, while she drew after us on our twin track to hide it, wise, her embroideries,

Fled beyond the camp-lines. There in security dark in the sand we lay down far from the prying eyes.

By her plaits I wooed her, drew her face near to me, won to her waist how frail-lined, hers of the ankle-rings.

Fair-faced she—no redness-noble of countenance, smooth as of glass her bosom, bare with its necklaces.

Thus are pearls yet virgin, seen through the dark water, clear in the sea-depths gleaming, pure, inaccessible.

Coyly she withdraws her, shows us a cheek, a lip, she a gazelle of Wújra,—yearling the fawn with her.

Roe-like her throat slender, white as an áriel's, sleek to thy lips up-lifted,—pearls are its ornament.

On her shoulders fallen thick lie the locks of her, dark as the dark date-clusters hung from the palm-branches.

See the side-plaits pendent, high on the brows of her, tressed in a knot, the caught ones fast with the fallen ones.

Slim her waist,—a well-cord scarce has its slenderness. Smooth are her legs as reed-stems stripped at a water-head.

The morn through she sleepeth, muck-stream in indolence, hardly at noon hath risen, girded her day dresses.

Soft her touch,—her fingers fluted as water-worms, sleek
as the snakes of Thóbya, tooth-sticks of Ishali.
Lighteneth she night's darkness, ay, as an evening lamp
hung for a sign of guidance lone on a hermitage.
Who but shall desire her, seeing her standing thus, half
in her childhood's short frock, half in her woman's
robe!
Strip thee of youth's fooling, thou in thy manhood's
prime. Yet to her love be faithful,—hold it a robe to
thee.
Many tongues have spoken, warned me of craft in love.
Yet have they failed an answer,—all were thine
enemies.
Dim the frear night broodeth,—veil upon veil let down,
dark as a mad sea raging, tempting the heart of me.
Spake I to Night stoutly, while he, a slow camel, dragged
with his hind-feet halting,—gone the forehand of him.
Night! I cried, thou snail Night, when wilt thou turn
to day? When? Though in sooth day's dawning worse
were than thou to me.
Sluggard Night, what stays thee? Chained hang the
stars of thee fast to the rocks with hempen ropes set
un-moveable.

Water-skins of some folk—ay, with the thong of them
laid on my nága's wither—borne have I joyfully,
Crossed how lone the rain-ways, bare as an ass-belly;
near me the wolf, starved gamester, howled to his
progeny.
Cried I: Wolf, thou wailest. Surely these lives of ours,
thine and my own, go empty, robbed of prosperity.
All we won we leave here. Whoso shall follow us, seed
in our corn-track casting, reap shall he barrenness.

Rode I forth at day-dawn—birds in their nests asleep—
stout on my steed, the sleek-coat, him the game-
vanquisher.
Lo, he chargeth, turneth,—gone is he—all in one, like
to a rock stream-trundled, hurled from its eminence.

Red-bay he,—his loin-cloth chafing the ribs of him.
  Shifts as a rain-stream smoothing stones in a river-bed.
Hard is he,—he snorteth loud in the pride of him, fierce
  as a full pot boiling, bubbling beneath the lid.

Straineth he how stoutly, while, as spent fishes swim,
  tied to his track the fleet ones plow his steps wearily.
See, in scorn he casteth youth from the back of him,
  leaveth the horseman cloakless, naked the hard-ride.
As a sling-stone hand-whirled, so is the might of him,
  loosed from the string that held it, hurled from the
  spliced ribbon.
Lean his flanks, gazelle-like, legs as the ostrich's; he like
  a strong wolf trotteth; lithe as a fox-cub he.
Stout his frame; behind him, look, you shall note of him
  full-filled the hind-leg gap, tail with no twist in it.
Polished, hard his quarters, smooth as the pounding-
  stone used for a bridegroom's spices, grind-slab of
  colocynth.
As the henna juice lies dyed on a beard grown hoar, so
  on his neck the blood-stains mark the game down-
  ridden.
Rushed we on the roe-herd. Sudden, as maids at play
  circling in skirts low-training, forth leaped the does
  of it.
Flashing fled they, jewels, shells set alternately on a
  young gallant's neck-string, his the high pedigreed.
Yet he gained their leaders, far while behind him lay
  bunched in a knot the hindmost, ere they fled scatter-
  wise.
'Twixt the cow and bull herds held he in wrath his road;
  made he of both his booty,—sweatless the neck of
  him.
All that day we roasted, seethed the sweet meat of them,
  row upon row in cauldrons, firelighters all of us.
Nathless home at night-fall, he in the fore-front still.
  Where is the eye shall bind him? How shall it follow
  him?

The night through he watcheth, scorneth him down to
 lay, close, while I sleep, ﬅill saddled, bridled by side
 of me.

Friend, thou seeﬅ the lightning. Mark where it
 wavereth, gleameth like fingers twiﬅed, clasped in
 the cloud-rivers.
Like a lamp new-lighted, so is the flash of it, trimmed
 by a hermit nightly pouring oil-sésame.
Stood I long a watcher, twin-friends how dear with me,
 till in Othéyb it faded, ended in Dáriji.
By its path we judged it: rain over Káttan is; far in
 Sitár it falleth, ﬅreameth in Yáthoboli.
Gathereth gross the flood-head dammed in Kutéyfati.
 Woe to the trees, the branched ones! Woe the kanáh-
 boli!
El Kanáan hath known it, quailed from the lash of it.
 Down from their lairs it driveth hot-foot the ibexes.
Known it too hath Téyma; ﬅandeth no palm of her
 there, nor no house low-founded,—none but her rock-
 buildings.
Stricken ﬅood Thabíra whelmed by the rush of it, like
 an old chief robe-folded, bowed in his ﬅriped mantle.
Nay, but he Mujéymir, tall-peaked at dawn of day,
 showed like a spinﬅer's diﬅaff tossed on the flood-
 water.
Cloud-wrecked lay the valley piled with the load of it,
 high as in sacks the Yemámi heapeth his corn-
 measures.
Seemed it then the song-birds, wine-drunk at sun-rising,
 loud through the valley shouted, maddened with
 spiceries,
While the wild beaﬅ corpses, grouped like great bulbs
 up-torn, cumbered the hollow places, drowned in the
 night-trouble.

(*Lady Anne Blunt and Wilfrid Scawen Blunt*)

Antara

6th century

ABLA

THE poets have muddied all the little fountains.

Yet do not my strong eyes know you, far house?

O dwelling of Abla in the valley of Gawa,
Speak to me, for my camel and I salute you.

My camel is as tall as a tower, and I make him stand
And give my aching heart to the wind of the desert.

O erstwhile dwelling of Abla in the valley of Gawa;
And my tribe in the valleys of Hazn and Samma
And in the valley of Motethalem!

Salute to the old ruins, the lonely ruins
Since Oum El Aythan gathered and went away.

Now is the dwelling of Abla
In a valley of men who roar like lions.
It will be hard to come to you, O daughter of Makhram.

. . . .

Abla is a green rush
That feeds beside the water.

But they have taken her to Oneiza
And my tribe feeds in lazy Ghailam valley.

They fixed the going, and the camels
Waked in the night and evilly prepared.

I was afraid when I saw the camels
Standing ready among the tents
And eating grain to make them swift.

I counted forty-two milk camels,
Black as the wings of a black crow.

White and purple are the lilies of the valley,
But Abla is a branch of flowers.

Who will guide me to the dwelling of Abla?

(E. Powys Mathers)

Ibn Kolthúm

6th century

POUR US WINE

Rise and hold up the curved glass,
And pour us wine of the morning, of El Andar.

Pour wine for us, whose golden color
Is like a water stream kissing flowers of saffron.

Pour us wine to make us generous
And carelessly happy in the old way.

Pour us wine that gives the miser
A sumptuous generosity and disregard.

O Oum-Amr, you have prevented me from the cup
When it should have been moving to the right;
And yet the one of us three that you would not serve
Is not the least worthy.

How many cups have I not emptied at Balbek,
And emptied at Damas and emptied at Cacerin!

More cups! more cups! for death will have his day;
His are we and he ours.

. . .

By herself she is fearless
And gives her arms to the air,
The limbs of a long camel that has not borne.

She gives the air her breasts,
Unfingered ivory.

She gives the air her long self and her curved self,
And hips so round and heavy that they are tired.

All these noble abundances of girlhood
Make the doors divinely narrow and myself insane.

Columns of marble and ivory in the old way,
And anklets chinking in gold and musical bracelets.

Without her I am a she-camel that has lost,
And howls in the sand at night.

Without her I am as sad as an old mother
Hearing of the death of her many sons.

(*E. Powys Mathers*)

From the Mufaddaliyat

Compiled 8th century

Alqamah

6th century

HIS CAMEL

So leave her, and cast care from thy heart with a sturdy mount—a camel that ambles tireless, carrying riders twain;
To Harith, the generous Lord, I drive her unsparing on, with pantings that shake her breast and throb through her ribs and flanks:
A fleet runner whose flesh over sides and where neck meets hump has vanished beneath noon-tide's hot breath and the onward press;
And yet after night's long toil the dawn breaks and finds her fresh as antelope, young and strong, that flees from the hunter's pack:

They crouched by the *artà*-brake, the hunters, and thought to win a safe prey: but she escaped their shafts and pursuing hounds.
So travels my beast, and makes her object a man far off, and little by little gains the way to his bounteous hand.
Yet, thou wast her labor's end—God keep thee from curse, O King! and through all the Desert's sameness sped she, beset with fears.
Towards thee the Pole-stars led, and there where men's feet had passed a track plain to see that wound by cairns over ridges scarred.
There bodies of beasts outworn lay thickly along the road, their bones gleaming white, their hides all shriveled and hard and dry.
I bring her to drink the dregs of cisterns all mire and draff; and if she mislikes it, all the choice is to journey on.

(*Sir Charles Lyall*)

Al-Aswad Son of Ya'fur

6th century

OLD AGE

If now thou seest me a wreck, worn out and minished of sight, and all my limbs without strength to bear my body along,
And I am deaf to the calls of love and lightness of youth, and follow wisdom in meekness, my steps easy to guide—
Time was I went every night, hair combed, to sellers of wine, and squandered lightly my wealth, compliant, easy of mood.
Yea, once I played, and enjoyed the sweetest flavor of youth, my wine the first of the grape, mingled with purest of rain—
Wine bought from one with a twang in his speech, and rings in his ears, a belt girt round him: he brought it forth for good silver coin.

A boy deals it to our guests, girt up, two pearls in his ears, his fingers ruddy, as though stained deep with mulberry juice,
And women white like the moon or statues stately to see, that softly carry around great cups filled full with the wine—
White women, dainty, that shoot the hearts of men with their eyes, fair as a nest full of ostrich eggs betwixt rock and sand.
Kind words they speak, and their limbs are soft and smooth to the touch, their faces bright, and their hearts to lovers gentle and mild.
Low speech they murmur, in tones that bear no secrets abroad: they gain their ends without toil, and need no shouting to win.

(Sir Charles Lyall)

Salāmah Son of Jandal

6th century

GONE IS YOUTH

Gone is Youth, gone with praise—Youth full of marvelous things! gone and that is a race wherein none may overtake.
Fled is it swiftly, and this hoary Eld comes on its track—ah, would that the galloping steeds could reach it and bring it back!
Gone is fair Youth, that time whose gains are fullness of praise: in it was delight for us: no delight is left for the old!
Yea, two days were good—the day of assemblies and moots of the tribe, and the day of journeying through light and darkness to fall on our foes—

The day we pushed on our steeds homewards the way they had gone, with hoofs chipped, jaded and worn by onset again and again;

And the galloping steeds came home with streaks of blood on their breasts, as though their necks were the stones where victims in Rajab are slain;
Yea, each one fleet, when the sweat soaks through the saddle-pad clear of skin, smooth cheeked, bright of hair, a galloper tireless of pace.
Not thin his forelock, nor humped his nose, no weakling of limb: preferred is he in the dealing of milk, well nurtured at home.
Each leg apart in its gallop seems to stream with a rush of speed as though from a bucket of water poured o'er the field.
Up starts he briskly, as starts a shepherd who in his sleep has left his flock to a wolf to harry, and wakes in alarm.
His withers rise to a neck far reaching upwards, below a breast blood-stained, like a stone on which red saffron is ground.
He races the wild asses, brown, green-lipped with the grass: a thousand drop off behind him, easily wins he unspurred.
To how many wretches have these by God's will brought wealth and ease! how many rich have they spoiled and stript of all luxury!
With such as these do men enter battle with confident heart in spite of spear-play: with such, hard pressed, secure is their flight.

Of late Ma'add thought to do us hurt: but cooled was their wrath before our spears, and the stroke of swords not meant but to bruise:
Yea, swords of proof, and the spear-heads furbished bright, set on shafts hard-grained, not hollow, with knots to bind together their length;
Their heads gained glitter from hands of men that fight in the van—no mongrels they, dark of hue, no slinkers puny of build!

The clip made even their shafts, and straight they carry the steel: no crooked stem canst thou see, but polished well-fitted spears;

Blue steel their points, red and straight their slender Indian stems: atop they bear after fight the heads of chieftains slain.

Our men, when battle is joined, ply briskly, skilled in the play, lances like ropes at the well, where many drawers combine.

Both armies led from Ma'add, the men from Upland and Plain, both feel the pain of our spears, and cannot hide it with lies.

For me, I find that the Sons of Sa'd shine before all with warriors first in the fight like firebrands kindled to blaze;

Tamim the stock they uphold in wealth of glory and fame:—whoso bears credit among mankind, he owes it to race.

A people they, when a year of famine presses, their tents bring strength to starvelings, and rest to wandering sons of the Wild.

When bites Calamity, sharp-toothed, cruel, patience is theirs to bear unflinching, and countless men to stand for the lost.

When wind blows chill from the North, we pitch our tents in the dales where drought has left in their bottoms stumps and brushes to burn:

Their paddocks hoary with frost, their brook-beds trampled and bare, their wallowing-grounds nought but dust, rainless, all greenery gone.

When one comes calling to us for help and succor in need, clear is our answer to him—forth start we straight in his cause;

Swiftly we saddle the camels strong and eager to go, and quick we set on our short-haired steeds the gear for the road.

Men say—"Their beasts are kept tethered close to where they are fed: though scant the milk of their camels, spared is it ever for them."

So stand we, great in men's eyes: our ladies ne'er turn aside whenso they travel from Khatt to upland lava plains.

(*Sir Charles Lyall*)

Khansá

7th century

TEARS

Tears, ere thy death, for many a one I shed,
But thine are all my tears since thou art dead.
To comforters I lend my ear apart,
While pain sits ever closer to my heart.

(*R. A. Nicholson*)

Ta'Abbata Sharra

7th century

EVER WATCHFUL

Nor exults he nor complains he; silent bears whate'er befalls him,
Much desiring, much attempting; far the wanderings of his venture.
In one desert noon beholds him; evening finds him in another;
As the wild ass lone he crosses o'er the jagged and headlong ridges.
Swifter than the wind unpausing, onward yet, nor rest nor slackness,
Wild the howling gusts outspeeded in the distance moan and falter,
Light the slumber on his eyelids, yet too heavy all he deems it;
Ever watchful for the moment when to draw the bitter faulchion;
When to plunge it in the heart-blood of the many-mustered foemen.

(*W. G. Palgrave*)

Omar b. Abi Rabi'a

d. 720

THE DAMSEL

Ah for the throes of a heart sorely wounded!
Ah for the eyes that have smit me with madness!
Gently she moved in the calmness of beauty,
Moved as the bough to the light breeze of morning.
Dazzled my eyes as they gazed, till before me
All was a mist and confusion of figures.
Ne'er had I sought her, and ne'er had she sought me;
Fated the love, and the hour, and the meeting!
There I beheld her, as she and her damsels
Paced 'twixt the temple and outer enclosure:
Damsels the fairest, the loveliest, the gentlest,
Passing like slow-wending heifers at evening,
Ever surrounding with courtly observance
Her whom they honor, the peerless of women.
Then to a handmaid, the youngest, she whispered:
" 'Omar is near; let us mar his devotions.
Cross on his path that he needs may observe us;
Give him a signal, my sister, demurely."
"Signals I gave, but he marked not or heeded,"
Answered the damsel, and hasted to meet me.
Ah for that night by the vale of the sand-hills!
Ah for the dawn when in silence we parted!
He who the morn may awake to her kisses
Drinks from the cup of the blessed in heaven!

(*W. G. Palgrave*)

Abd-ar-Rahman I

8th century

THE PALM TREE

In the midst of my garden
Grows a palm-tree;
Born in the West,
Away from the country of palm-trees.

I cried: You are like me,
For you resemble me
In wandering and peregrination,
And the long separation from kith and kin.

You also
Grew up on a foreign soil;
Like me,
You are far from the country of your birth.

May the fertilizing clouds of morning
Water you in exile,
May the beneficent rains besought by the poor
Never forsake you.

(*J. B. Trend*)

From the Hamâsah

Compiled 9th century

Hittân, son of Al-Mu' Allà of Tayyi

HIS CHILDREN

Fortune has brought me down—her wonted way—
from station great and high to low estate;
Fortune has rent away my plenteous store;
of all my wealth honor alone is left.
Fortune has turned my joy to tears; how oft
did Fortune make me laugh with what she gave!
But for these girls, the *kata's* downy brood,
unkindly thrust from door to door as hard—
Far would I roam and wide to seek my bread
in Earth that has no end of breadth and length.
Nay, but our children in our midst, what else
but our hearts are they, walking on the ground?
If but the breeze blow harsh on one of them,
mine eye says no to slumber all night long.

(*Sir Charles Lyall*)

Abu 'L-'Alá Al-Ma'Arrí

973–1057

AWEARY AM I

Aweary am I of living in town and village—
And oh, to be camped alone in a desert region,
Revived by the scent of lavender when I hunger
And scooping into my palm, if I thirst, well-water!
Meseemeth, the Days are dromedaries lean and jaded
That bear on their backs humanity traveling onward;
They shrink not in dread from any portentous nightmare,
Nor quail at the noise of shouting and rush of panic,
But journey along for ever with those they carry,
Until at the last they kneel by the dug-out houses.
No need, when in earth the maid rests covered over,
No need for her locks of hair to be loosed and plaited;
The young man parts from her, and his tears are flowing—
Even thus do the favors flow of disgustful Fortune.

(*R. A. Nicholson*)

Ibn Darrâj Al-Andalûsi

11th century

THE WING OF SEPARATION

The wing of separation
Bore me away;
The fluttering heart was dismayed
And bore away her senses . . .
Had she but seen me,
When my soul was intent on speeding the journey by night,
When my sounding steps
Held converse with the demons of the desert—
When I wandered through the waste
In the shadows of night,

While the roar of the lion was heard
From his lair among the reeds—
When the brilliant Pleiades circled,
Like dark-eyed maidens in the green woods;
And the stars were borne round
Like wine-cups,
Filled by a fair maid
And served by a watchful attendant—
When the Milky Way
Was as the gray hairs of age
Upon the head of gloomy night;
And the ardor of my resolution,
And the piercer of darkness
Were equally terrible;
When the eyelids of the stars
Were closed for weariness—
Ah, then she had known
That fate itself obeyed my will
And that I was worthy of the favor of Ibn Aâmir.

(J. B. Trend)

Ibn Zaydūn

1003–1071

CORDOVA

Still round thy towers descend the fertile rain!
Still sing the doves in every leafy den!
Cordova, fairest home of gallant men,
Where youth my childhood's trinkets snapped in twain
  And noble sires begat me noble, free!

Happy those days, with purer pleasures blest,
Those winding vales we roamed with boyish zest,
White-throated, raven-haired, all mirth and jest.
Chide not the trailing robes, the silken vest,
  The reckless pride of youth—no wantons we.

Say to an age whose joys long since are fled,
Its traces by the lapse of nights now faint and mouldered
(Softly the breeze its evening fragrance shed!
Bright shone its stars o'er the night-traveler's head!):
"Farewell from one whose love still burns for thee!"

(H. A. R. Gibb)

Mu'tamid, King of Seville

1040–1095

For though his sun of power went down so long ago that the West has forgotten the colors of his glory, and though the kingdom for which he gave his blood and his children and the years of his life now bows to other rulers, another faith, yet among a beauty-loving race he still preserves—by reason of those lines which wars have not scattered nor Time effaced—a gentle eminence.—Dulcie L. Smith.

THE FOUNTAIN

The sea hath tempered it; the mighty sun
Polished the blade,
And from the limpid sheath the sword leaps forth;
Man hath not made
A better in Damascus—though for slaughter
Hath steel somewhat advantage over water.

THY GARDEN

My thoughts are as a garden-plot, that knows
No rain but of thy giving, and no rose
Except thy name. I dedicate it thine,
My garden, full of fruits in harvest time.

TEARS OF THE WORLD

Weep for me, friends, for now that I am hence,
Lo, in Time's dust the footprints of my pride!
Lament, strong lions of my great defense,
Shed tears, my young gazelles and dewy-eyed!
Look ye, the cold stars even in the height
Weep, and the clouds lift not their mournful night.

Weep, Wahíd, weep, and Zahi with the towers,
Weep ye for him that shall not come again.
All waters of the earth, all dew and showers
Have tears for Mu'tamid, and the summer rain
That once strewed pearls upon him, is become
A sea-wave full of sand and sound and foam.

WOO NOT THE WORLD

Woo not the world too rashly, for behold,
Beneath the painted silk and broidering,
It is a faithless and inconstant thing.
(Listen to me, Mu'tamid, growing old.)

And we—that dreamed youth's blade would never rust,
Hoped wells from the mirage, roses from the sand—
The riddle of the world shall understand
And put on wisdom with the robe of dust.

(*Dulcie L. Smith*)

I TRAVELED WITH THEM

I TRAVELED with them,
Whilst the robe of night was of one color;
But when it became striped
I stopped to say farewell;
And the morning received those stars from my hand.

(*J. B. Trend*)

Ibn Al-Arabi

1165–1240

ODE

WHO can support the anguish of love?
Who can drain the bitter draught of destiny?

I said in my grief,
In my burning passion:
"O would that he who caused my sickness
Had tended me when I was sick!"

He passed by the house door,
Mocking, hiding himself;
Veiling his head,
And turning away.

His veiling did me no hurt;
I was only hurt by his having turned away from me.

(*R. A. Nicholson*)

ODE

They journeyed,
When the darkness of night
Had let down her curtain;
And I said to her:
"Pity a passionate lover,
Outcast and distraught,
Whom desires eagerly encompass,
And at whom
Speeding arrows are aimed
Wheresoever he bends his course."

She displayed her teeth
And lightning flashed,
And I knew not
Which of the twain rent the gloom.
And I said:
"Is it not enough for him
That I am in his heart,
And that he beholds me at every moment?
Is it not enough?"

(*R. A. Nicholson*)

Bahā Ad-dīn Zuhayr

d. 1258

ON A BLIND GIRL

They called my love a poor blind maid:
I love her more for that, I said;
I love her, for she cannot see
These gray hairs which disfigure me.

We wonder not that wounds are made
By an unsheathed and naked blade;
The marvel is that swords should slay,
While yet within their sheaths they stay.
She is a garden fair, where I
Need fear no guardian's prying eye;
Where, though in beauty blooms the rose,
Narcissuses their eyelids close.

(*E. H. Palmer*)

From the Thousand and One Nights

13th century ?

DATES

We grow to the sound of the wind
Playing his flutes in our hair,

Palm tree daughters,
Brown flesh Bedouin,
Fed with light
By our gold father;

We are loved of the free-tented,
The sons of space, the hall-forgetters,
The wide handed, the bright-sworded
Masters of horses.

Who has rested in the shade of our palms
Shall hear us murmur ever above his sleep.

BIRDS

Wild pigeon of the leaves,
Brother of lovers,
If you have seen an arrow killing
    From far
The mild-eyed deer
    By rills
    Of summer hills,

If you have heard an arrow singing
From far
And then strike sheer
The wings
Of airy things,

Wild pigeon of the leaves,
You are
Brother of lovers.

THE SONG OF THE NARCISSUS

My beauty is not wine to me,
For I have eyes of languor,
And balance like music
And am nobly born.

I consider the flowers,
I talk with the flowers in moonlight.
My beauty gives me a throne among them,
Yet I am a slave.

I am a slave,
The cincture of obedience,
The good servant
Who stands with a straight body
And bowed head.

I bare my neck,
I abide in my pure tent
Pitched on an emerald column;
My robe is gold and silver.

My modesty will excuse the wantoning of my eyes
As I hang my head above the waters.

PSALM OF BATTLE

God is praise and glory;
Therefore glory and praise be unto Him
Who led me by the hand in stony places,
Who gave me a treasure of gold and a throne of gold
And set a sword of victory in my hand!

He covered the earth with the shadow of my kingdom
And fed me when I was a stranger
Among strange peoples;
When I was lowly He accounted me
And He has bound my brow about with triumph.

His enemies fled before my face like cattle;
The Lord breathed upon them and they were not!
Not with the ferment of a generous wine
But with death's evil grape
He has sent them drunken into the darkness.

We died, we died in the battle,
But He has set us upon happy grass
Beside an eternal river of scented honey.

TO LIGHTEN MY DARKNESS

To lighten my darkness,
I look for the red crescent of her lips
And if that comes not
I look for the blue crescent
Of the sword of death.

Oh, joy of friends gathered upon the cool meadow
To drink wine handed by white hands!

Flowers of Spring on the meadow
Between spread slim fingers!

You sit drinking the tulip-colored wine
In the midst of this green earth
With all her waters.

HAROUN'S FAVORITE SONG

An early dew woos the half-opened flowers,
Wind of the south, dear child,
Close clings about their stalks for drunken hours;
And yet your eyes, dear child,
Cool pools which rise, dear child,
High in the mountains of my soul,
These, these
The lips have drunken whole;
And yet your mouth, dear child,
Your mouth, dear child, is envied of the bees.

LOVE

Love was before the light began,
When light is over, love shall be;
O warm hand in the grave, O bridge of truth,
O ivy's tooth
Eating the green heart of the tree
Of man!

THE SLEEPER

Sleeper, the palm-trees drink the breathless noon,
A golden bee sucks at a fainting rose,
Your lips smile in their sleep. Oh, do not move.

Sleeper, oh, do not move the gilded gauze
Which lies about your gold, or you will scare
The sun's gold fire which leaps within your crystal.

Sleeper, oh, do not move; your breasts in sleep,
Allah, they dip and fall like waves at sea;
Your breasts are snow, I breathe them like sea foam,
I taste them like white salt. They dip and fall.

Sleeper, they dip and fall. The smiling stream
Stifles its laugh, the gold bee on the leaf
Dies of much love and rosy drunkenness,
My eyes burn the red grapes upon your breasts.

Sleeper, oh, let them burn, let my heart's flower,
Fed on the rose and santal of your flesh,
Burst like a poppy in this solitude,
In this cool silence.

TELL HIM, O NIGHT

Tell him, O night,
How your black sword has killed my golden days
And your black brush obscured the smooth delight
About my eyes' dim ways.
The breasts of my distress
Are pressed against the thorns of appetite,
Desire my food and my drink sleeplessness;
Tell him, O night.

DEATH

Once he will miss, twice he will miss,
He only chooses one of many hours;
For him nor deep nor hill there is,
But all's one level plain he hunts for flowers.

LAMENTS

Abu Nowas for the Barmacides

Since earth has put you away, O sons of Barmak,
The roads of morning twilight and evening twilight
Are empty. My heart is empty, O sons of Barmak.

The Wazir Dandan for Prince Sharkan

Wise to have gone so early to reward,
Child of the sword;
Wise with a single new-bathed eagle's flight
To have touched the white

Wild roses spread for feet in paradise.
Ah, my son, wise
Soon to have drained the new and bitter cup
Which, once drunk up,
Leads straightway to an old immortal wine
Pressed from God's vine.

Her Rival for Aziza

I PASSED a tomb among green shades
Where seven anemones with down-dropped heads
Wept tears of dew upon the stone beneath.
I questioned underneath my breath
Who the poor dead might be
And a voice answered me. . . .
So now I pray that Allah may be moved
To drop sleep on her eyes because she loved.
She will not care though lovers do not come
To wipe the dust from off a lover's tomb,
She will not care for anything. But I please
To plant some more dew-wet anemones
That they may weep.

Haroun Al-Rachid for Heart's-Life

CHILD, who went gathering the flowers of death,
My heart's not I, I cannot teach my heart;
It cries when I forget.
It has not learnt my art
To forget lips when scented with their breath
Or the red cup, when I am drunken yet.

Tumadir Al-Khansa for her Brother

WEEP! Weep! Weep!
These tears are for my brother,
Henceforth that veil which lies between us,
That recent earth,
Shall not be lifted again.

You have gone down to the bitter water
Which all must taste,
And you went pure, saying:
"Life is a buzz of hornets about a lance point."

But my heart remembers, O son of my father and
mother,
I wither like summer grass,
I shut myself in the tent of consternation.

He is dead, who was the buckler of our tribe
And the foundation of our house,
He has departed in calamity.

He is dead, who was the lighthouse of courageous men,
Who was for the brave
As fires lighted upon the mountains.

He is dead, who rode costly horses,
Shining in his garments.
The hero of the long shoulder belt is dead,
The young man of valiance and beauty breathes no
more;
The right hand of generosity is withered,
And the beardless king of our tribe shall breathe no
more.

He shall be cold beneath his rock.

Say to his mare Alwa
That she must weep
As she runs riderless for ever. . . .

When the red millstone ground the flowers of youth,
You shattered a thousand horses against the squadrons;
High on the groaning flanks of Alwa
You lifted the bright skirts of your silver mail.

You made the lances live,
You shook their beams,
You quenched their beams in red,
O tiger of the double panoply.

White women wandered with disordered veils
And you saved them in the morning.
Your captives were as troops of antelopes
Whose beauty troubles the first drops of rain. . . .

How effortless were your rhymes of combat
Chanted in tumult, O my brother!
They pierced like lances,
Thev live among our hearts for ever.

Let the stars go out,
Let the sun withdraw his rays,
He was our star and sun.

Who now will gather in the strangers at dusk
When the sad North whistles with her winds?
You have laid down and left in the dust, O wanderers,
Him who nourished you with his flocks
And bared his sword for your salvation.
You set him low in the terrible house
Among a few stakes planted,
You threw down boughs of salamah upon him.
He lies among the tombs of our fathers,
Where the days and the years shall pass over him
As they have passed over our fathers.
Your loss is a great distress to me,
Child of the Solamides,
I shall be glad no more. . .

While you have tears, O daughters of the Solamides.
Weep! Weep! Weep!

INSCRIPTIONS AT THE CITY OF BRASS

I

Enter and learn the story of the rulers,
They rested a little in the shadow of my towers
And then they passed.
They were dispersed like those shadows
When the sun goes down;
They were driven like straws
Before the wind of death.

2

The drunkenness of youth has passed like a fever,
And yet I saw many things,
Seeing my glory in the days of my glory.
The feet of my war-horse
Drummed upon the cities of the world,
I sacked great towns like a hot wind
And fell like thunder upon far lands.
The kings of the earth were dragged behind my chariot
And the people of the earth behind my laws;
But now
The drunkenness of youth has passed like a fever,
Like foam upon sand.
Death took me in a net:
My armies warred against him in vain,
My courtiers flattered him in vain.
Listen, O wayfarer, to the words of my death,
For they were not the words of my life:
Save up your soul
And taste the beautiful wine of peace,
For to-morrow the earth shall answer:
He is with me,
My jealous breast holds him for ever.

3

About this table
Sat many hawk-eyed kings
With many one-eyed kings
To bear them company;
But now all sit in the dark and none are able,
None are able to see.

4

In the name of the Eternal,
In the name of the Master of Strength,
In the name of Him who moves not!
Wayfarer in this place,
Look not upon the glass of appearance,
For a breath may shatter it
And illusion is a pit for the feet of men.
I speak of my power:
I had ten thousand horses
Groomed by captive kings,
I had a thousand virgins of royal blood
To serve my pleasure
And a thousand excellent virgins
With moon-colored breasts,
Chosen from all the world.
They brought forth little princes in my chambers
And the little princes were as brave as lions.
I had peculiar treasures
And the West and the East were two heads
Bowing before me.
I thought my power eternal
And the days of my life
Fixed surely in the years;
But a whisper came to me
From Him who dies not.
I called my captains and my strong riders,
Thousands upon thousands
With swords and lances;
I called my tributary kings together

And those who were proud rulers under me,
I opened the boxes of my treasure to them, saying:
"Take hills of gold, mountains of silver,
And give me one more day upon the earth."
But they stood silent,
Looking upon the ground;
So that I died
And death came to sit upon my throne.
I was Kush bin Shadad bin Ad,
Surnamed the Great.

5

O SONS of men,
You add the future to the future
But your sum is spoiled
By the gray cypher of death.
There is a Master
Who breathes upon armies,
Building a narrow and dark house for kings.
These wake above their dust
In a black commonwealth.

6

O SONS of men,
Why do you put your hands before your eyes
And play in this road as if for ever,
Which is a short passing to another place?
Where are the kings
Whose loins jetted empires,
Where are the very strong men,
Masters of Irak?
Where are the lords of Ispahan,
O sons of men?

7

O SONS of men,
You see a stranger upon the road,
You call to him and he does not stop.

He is your life
Walking towards time,
Hurrying to meet the kings of India and China,
Hurrying to greet the sultans of Sina and Nubia,
Who were blown over the mountain crest
By a certain breath,
Even as he.

8

O sons of men,
Lean death perches upon your shoulder
Looking down into your cup of wine,
Looking down on the breasts of your lady.
You are caught in the web of the world
And the spider Nothing waits behind it.
Where are the men with towering hopes?
They have changed places with owls,
Owls who lived in tombs
And now inhabit a palace.

(*E. Powys Mathers*)

From the Arabic

I

THE CAMEL-RIDER

There is no thing in all the world but love,
No jubilant thing of sun or shade worth one sad tear.
Why dost thou ask my lips to fashion songs
Other than this, my song of love to thee?

See where I lie and pluck the thorns of grief,
Dust on my head and fire, as one who mourns his slain.
Are they not slain, my treasures of dear peace?
This their red burial is, sand heaped on sand.

Here came I in the morning of my joys.
Before the dawn was born, through the dark downs I
rode.
The low stars led me on as with a voice,
Stars of the scorpion's tail in the deep South.

Sighing I came, and scattering wide the sand.
No need had I to urge her speed with hand or heel,
The creature I bestrode. She knew my haste,
And knew the road I sought, the road to thee.

Jangling her bells aloud in wantonness,
And sighing soft, she too, her sighs to my soul's sighs.
Behind us the wind followed thick with scents
Of incense blossoms and the dews of night.

The thorn trees caught at us with their crook'd hands;
The hills in blackness hemmed us in and hid the road;
The specters of the desert howled and warned;
I heeded nothing of their words of woe.

Thus till the dawn I sped in my desire,
Breasting the ridges, slope on slope, till morning broke;
And lo! the sun revealed to me no sign,
And lo! the day was widowed of my hope.

Where are the tents of pleasure and dear love,
Set in the Vale of Thyme, where winds in Spring are
fain?
The highways of the valley, where they stood
Strong in their flocks, are there. But where are they?

The plain was dumb, as emptied of all voice;
No bleat of herds, no camels roaring far below
Told of their presence in the pastures void,
Of the waste places which had been their homes.

I climbed down from my watch-tower of the rocks,
To where the tamarisks grow, and the dwarf palms,
alarmed.
I called them with my voice, as the deer calls,
Whose young the wolves have hunted from their place.

I sought them in the foldings of the hill,
In the deep hollows shut with rocks, where no winds blow.
I sought their footsteps under the tall cliffs,
Shut from the storms, where the first lambs are born.

The tamarisk boughs had blossomed in the night,
And the white broom which bees had found, the wild bees' brood.
But no dear signal told me of their life,
No spray was torn in all that world of flowers.

Where are the tents of pleasure and dear love,
For which my soul took ease for its delight in Spring,
The black tents of her people beautiful
Beyond the beauty of the sons of kings?

The wind of war has swept them from their place,
Scattering them wide as quails, whom the hawk's hate pursues;
The terror of the sword importunate
Was at their backs, nor spared them as they flew.

The summer wind has passed upon their fields;
The rain has purged their hearth-stones, and made smooth their floors;
Low in the valley lie their broken spears,
And the white bones which are their tale forlorn.

Where are the sons of Saba in the South,
The men of mirth and pride to whom my songs were sung,
The kinsmen of her soul who is my soul,
The brethren of her beauty whom I love?

She mounted her tall camel in the waste,
Loading it high for flight with her most precious things;
She went forth weeping in the wilderness,
Alone with fear on that far night of ill.

She fled mistrusting, as the wild roe flees,
Turning her eyes behind her, while fear fled before;
No other refuge knew she than her speed,
And the black land that lies where night is born.

Under what canopy of sulphurous heaven,
Dark with the thunderclouds unloosing their mad tongues,
Didst thou lie down aweary of thy burden,
In that dread place of silence thou hadst won?

Close to what shelter of what naked rocks,
Carved with what names of terror of what kings of old,
Near to what monstrous shapes unmerciful,
Watching thy death, didst thou give up thy soul?

Or dost thou live by some forgotten well,
Waiting thy day of ransom to return and smile,
As the birds come when Spring is in the heaven,
And dost thou watch me near while I am blind?

Blind in my tears, because I only weep,
Kindling my soul to fire because I mourn my slain,
My kindred slain, and thee, and my dear peace,
Making their burial thus, sand heaped on sand.

For see, there nothing is in all the world
But only love worth any strife or song or tear.
Ask me not then to sing or fashion songs
Other than this, my song of love to thee.

II

THE DESOLATE CITY

Dark to me is the earth. Dark to me are the heavens.
Where is she that I loved, the woman with eyes like stars?
Desolate are the streets. Desolate is the city,
A city taken by storm, where none are left but the slain!

Sadly I rose at dawn, undid the latch of my shutters,
Thinking to let in light, but I only let in love.
Birds in the boughs were awake; I listened to their chaunting;
Each one sang to his love; only I was alone.

This, I said in my heart, is the hour of life and of pleasure,
Now each creature on earth has his joy, and lives in the sun,
Each in another's eyes finds light, the light of compassion,
This is the moment of pity, this is the moment of love.

Speak, O desolate city! Speak, O silence in sadness!
Where is she that I loved in my strength, that spoke to my soul?
Where are those passionate eyes that appealed to my eyes in passion?
Where is the mouth that kissed me, the breast I laid to my own?

Speak, thou soul of my soul, for rage in my heart is kindled.
Tell me, where didst thou flee on the day of destruction and fear?
See, my arms still enfold thee, enfolding thus all Heaven,
See, my desire is fulfilled in thee, for it fills the Earth.

Thus in my grief I lamented. Then turned I from the window,
Turned to the stair, and the open door, and the empty street,
Crying aloud in my grief, for there was none to chide me,
None to mock at my weakness, none to behold my tears.

Groping I went, as blind. I sought her house, my beloved's.
There I stopped at the silent door, and listened and tried the latch.
Love, I cried, dost thou slumber? This is no hour for slumber,
This is the hour of love, and love I bring in my hand.

I knew the house, with its windows barred, and its leafless fig-tree,
Climbing round by the doorstep the only one in the street;
I knew where my hope had climbed to its goal and there encircled
All that those desolate walls once held, my beloved's heart.

There in my grief she consoled me. She loved me when I loved not.
She put her hand in my hand, and set her lips to my lips.
She told me all her pain and showed me all her trouble.
I, like a fool, scarce heard, hardly returned her kiss.

Love, thy eyes were like torches. They changed as I beheld them.
Love, thy lips were like gems, the seal thou settest on my life.
Love, if I loved not then, behold this hour thy vengeance;
This is the fruit of thy love and thee, the unwise grown wise.

Weeping strangled my voice. I called out, but none answered;
Blindly the windows gazed back at me, dumbly the door;

She whom I love, who loved me, looked not on my yearning,
Gave me no more her hands to kiss, showed me no more her soul.

Therefore the Earth is dark to me, the sunlight blackness,
Therefore I go in tears and alone, by night and day;
Therefore I find no love in Heaven, no light, no beauty,
A Heaven taken by storm, where none are left but the slain!

III

THE GRIEF OF LOVE

Love, I am sick for thee, sick with an absolute grief,
Sick with the thought of thy eyes and lips and bosom.
All the beauty I saw, I see to my heart revealed.
All that I felt I feel to-day for my pain and sorrow.

Love, I would fain forget thee, hide thee in deeper night,
Shut thee where no thought is, in the grave with tears.
Love, I would turn my face to the wall and, if needs be, die;
Death less cruel were than thy eyes which have blinded me.

Since thou art gone from me, glory is gone from my life;
Dumb are the woods and streams, and dumb the voice of my soul;
Dead are the flowers we loved, blackened and sere with blight;
Earth is frost-bound under my foot where our footsteps trod.

Give me back for my sorrow the days of senseless peace,
Days when I thought not of thee, or thought in wisdom;

Let me see thee once more as thou to my folly wert,
  A woman senseless as sounding brass or as tinkling cymbal.

Why didst thou show me thy heart, which I thought not of?
  Why didst thou bare me thy soul, who to me were soulless?
Why didst thou kiss my mouth, when my mouth did mock?
  Why didst thou speak to my lips of love, ere my lips had spoken?

Love, thou hast made me thine, thine, and in my despite,
  Laying thy hand on my heart in the soft Spring weather;
Love, thou hast bought my soul at a price, the price of thine,
  Never again to mock at love, ah, never, never!

IV

THE LOVE SECRET

Love has its secrets, joy has its revealings.
  How shall I speak of that which love has hid?
If my beloved shall return to greet me,
  Deeds shall be done for her none ever did.

My beloved loved me. How shall I reveal it?
  We were alone that morning in the street.
She looked down at the ground, and blushed, and trembled.
  She stopped me with her eyes when these did meet.

"What wouldst thou, sweet one? What wouldst thou with sorrow,
  Thou, the new morning star with me, the night?
What are those flowers thou holdest to thy bosom?
  What are the thoughts thou hidest from my sight?"

"Thine are these flowers," she said, "these foolish roses,
And thine the thoughts, if thus it be thy will.
I hold them close for fear that thou shouldst mock me,
I hold them to my heart for fear of ill."

"Nay, what of ill? 'Tis only age is evil,
Only forgetfulness and grief and pain;
What dost thou know of grief, that thou shouldst fear it?
Mine is the grief who cannot love again."

She raised her eyes, she looked at me in wonder,
"The ache is here," she said, "by night and day;
I cannot teach my heart to bear its burden,
I cannot turn my silence from its way."

"Speak to me child. I am the wise physician,
A man acquainted with all grief can teach;
There is no sorrow but has joy for sister,
No silence but finds counterpart in speech."

My beloved laughed. She saw through my dissembling;
She held to me her hand, that I might kiss
The inside of her hand. 'Twas like a petal
Of her own roses, but more dear than this.

I felt its pulses, like a bird in prison;
"Sweet child," I said, "what wouldst thou I should prove?
I cannot make thee wiser than thy wisdom,
Who knowest all things since thou knowest love."

How shall I tell it? How shall I reveal it?
I led her by the hand, as thus I said,
Back from the street to where it stood, my dwelling,
And closed the door on where it stood, my bed.

Her laughter stopped. "Nay, use not thou unkindly.
Thine is the hand to deal or spare the blame;
I dare not be to thee thus uninvited,
Thou dost not know me, hast not learned my name."

How shall I tell it? How shall I reveal it?
Love in that instant found its latest birth,
"Soul of my soul," I cried, "thy name is Pleasure,
The sweetest thing to love on this sad Earth."

I held her in my arms, I pressed her fastly.
"Ah, if thou lovedst me indeed," she cried.
"I love thee, and I love thee," was my answer,
"My sister, my beloved one, my bride!"

Love has its secrets. Joy has its revealings.
I speak of this which love in vain has hid;
If my beloved shall return to greet me,
Deeds shall be done for her none ever did.

V

THE DAYS OF OUR YOUTH

THESE are the days of our youth, our days of glory and honor.
Pleasure begotten of strength is ours, the sword in our hand.
Wisdom bends to our will, we lead captivity captive,
Kings of our lives and love, receiving gifts from men.

Why do I speak of wisdom? The prize is not for the wisest.
Reason, the dull ox, plows a soil which no joy shall reap.
Folly is fleeter far 'neath the heel of the fearless rider,
Folly the bare-backed steed we bestride, the steed of the plains.

Mine is a lofty ambition, as wide as the world I covet.
Vast is the empire I claim for thee, thou spouse of my soul.
Show me new lands to win, and, by God in heaven, I swear it:
These shall be mine and thine to-night for all time to hold.

Time is our slave and Fortune's. We need not years for fruition.
Here in our hands behold a key which unlocks the world.
Each new day is a life. For us there is no to-morrow.
Love no yesterday knows nor we, but to-day is ours

See, what a wealth I bring thee, what treasure of myrrh and spices!
Every kingdom of Earth have I sacked to procure thee gold.
All the knowledge that fools have learned at the feet of women,
All that the wise have been taught in tears for thy sake I know.

Give thyself up to Love. There is naught divine but madness.
Give thyself up to me Love's priest in his inmost shrine.
Shut thy eyes on the world, sublime in thy abnegation.
Only the wise who have bowed their will shall receive the prize.

Shut thy eyes on the light. I have nobler dreams to read thee,
Here in the shades of this darkened room, than the sun can show.
Is there not light in my eyes to-night more light than the dreamlight?
See it breaks in streams on thy face; it illumes thy soul.

Let me persuade thy weakness. I see thee here with my reason.
Let me convince thee of love with thy lips till thou cease to think.

Let me enfold thee with words more sweet than the prayers of angels,
  Speaking thus with my hand on thy heart till it cease to beat.

Let me assuage thy grief with laughter, thy fear with kisses.
  Let me cajole thy doubts with surprise, thy pride with tears.
Let me outshame the shame of thy face, outblush thy blushes.
  Let me teach thee what Love can dare and yet dream no shame.

Let me uncover thy bosom and prove to thee its glory.
  Let me preach to thee of thyself the live night long.
Let me chant new hymns to thy praise as I kneel and worship,
  Rising still like a god from my knees from eve till morn.

Let me discourse of love with my hands and lips and bosom.
  Let me explain with my limbs the joy that a soul can feel.
Let me unveil to thy bodily sense thy god incarnate
  Taking flesh in a visible form for thy body's need.

Lo, on the mount of Love, the holiest place of holies,
  Incense and prayer and the people's shout and the fires have risen.
Love descends on the feast. He mounts the pyre in silence,
  Victim and priest and god in one, to thy dreams revealed.

There, the rite is accomplished. Whatever Love knows thou knowest.

Sudden the victim staggers and falls. In the dust
it lies.
See the hot blood flows for thy sake, it o'erflows the altar.
Dost thou not feel it stream in thy veins? It still lives
in thee.

These are the days of our youth, the days of our
dominion.
All the rest is a dream of death and a doubtful thing.
Here we at least have lived, for love is all life's wisdom,
Joy of joys for an hour to-day; then away, farewell!

(*Wilfrid Scawen Blunt*)

PERSIAN

Zoroaster

7th century B.C.?

FROM THE SACRED BOOK

This I ask Thee—tell it to me truly, Lord!
Who the Sire was, Father first of Holiness?
Who the pathway for the sun and stars ordained?
Who, through whom is't moon doth wax and wane again?
This and much else do I long, O God, to know.

This I ask Thee—tell it to me truly, Lord!
Who set firmly earth below, and kept the sky
Sure from falling? Who the streams and trees did make?
Who their swiftness to the winds and clouds hath yoked?
Who, O Mazda, was the Founder of Good Thought?

This I ask Thee—tell it to me truly, Lord!
Who, benignant, made the darkness and the light?
Who, benignant, sleep and waking did create?
Who the morning, noon, and evening did decree
As reminders to the wise, of duty's call?

(*A. V. Williams Jackson*)

Firdawsí

935–1025

ALAS FOR YOUTH

Much have I labored, much read o'er
Of Arabic and Persian lore,
Collecting tales unknown and known;
Now two and sixty years are flown.
Regret, and deeper woe of sin,

'Tis all that youth has ended in,
And I with mournful thoughts rehearse
Bu Táhir Khusrawáni's verse:
"I mind me of my youth and sigh,
Alas for youth, for youth gone by!"

(*R. A. Nicholson*)

Omar Khayyám

d. 1123

And this, I think, especially distinguishes Omar from all other Persian poets: That, whereas with them the Poet is lost in his Song, the Man in Allegory and Abstraction; we seem to have the Man—the *Bonhomme*—Omar himself, with all his humors and passions, as frankly before us as if we were really at Table with him, after the Wine had gone round.—EDWARD FITZGERALD.

RUBAIYAT

I

WAKE! For the Sun, who scattered into flight
The Stars before him from the Field of Night,
Drives Night along with them from Heaven, and strikes
The Sultàn's Turret with a Shaft of Light.

II

Before the phantom of False morning died,
Methought a Voice within the Tavern cried,
"When all the Temple is prepared within,
Why nods the drowsy Worshiper outside?"

III

And, as the Cock crew, those who stood before
The Tavern shouted—"Open then the Door!
You know how little while we have to stay,
And, once departed, may return no more."

IV

Now the New Year reviving old Desires,
The thoughtful Soul to Solitude retires,
Where the White Hand of Moses on the Bough
Puts out, and Jesus from the Ground suspires.

V

Iram indeed is gone with all his Rose,
And Jamshyd's Seven-ringed Cup where no one knows;
But still a Ruby kindles in the Vine,
And many a Garden by the Water blows.

VI

And David's lips are lockt; but in divine
High-piping Pehlevì, with "Wine! Wine! Wine!
Red Wine!"—the Nightingale cries to the Rose
That sallow cheek of hers to incarnadine.

VII

Come, fill the Cup, and in the fire of Spring
Your Winter-garment of Repentance fling:
The Bird of Time has but a little way
To flutter—and the Bird is on the Wing.

VIII

Whether at Naishápúr or Babylon,
Whether the Cup with sweet or bitter run,
The Wine of Life keeps oozing drop by drop,
The Leaves of Life keep falling one by one.

IX

Each Morn a thousand Roses brings, you say:
Yes, but where leaves the Rose of Yesterday?
And this first Summer month that brings the Rose
Shall take Jamshyd and Kaikobád away.

X

Well, let it take them! What have we to do
With Kaikobád the Great, or Kaikhosrú?
  Let Zál and Rustum bluster as they will,
Or Hátim call to Supper—heed not you.

XI

With me along the strip of Herbage strown
That just divides the desert from the sown,
  Where name of Slave and Sultán is forgot—
And Peace to Mahmúd on his golden Throne!

XII

A Book of Verses underneath the Bough,
A Jug of Wine, a Loaf of Bread—and Thou
  Beside me singing in the Wilderness—
Oh, Wilderness were Paradise enow!

XIII

Some for the Glories of This World; and some
Sigh for the Prophet's Paradise to come;
  Ah, take the Cash, and let the Credit go,
Nor heed the rumble of a distant Drum!

XIV

Look to the blowing Rose about us—"Lo,
Laughing," she says, "into the world I blow,
  At once the silken tassel of my Purse
Tear, and its Treasure on the Garden throw."

XV

And those who husbanded the Golden Grain,
And those who flung it to the winds like Rain,
  Alike to no such aureate Earth are turned
As, buried once, Men want dug up again.

XVI

The Worldly Hope men set their Hearts upon
Turns Ashes—or it prospers; and anon,
Like Snow upon the Desert's dusty Face,
Lighting a little hour or two—is gone.

XVII

Think, in this battered Caravanserai
Whose Portals are alternate Night and Day,
How Sultán after Sultán with his Pomp
Abode his destined Hour, and went his way.

XVIII

They say the Lion and the Lizard keep
The Courts where Jamshyd gloried and drank deep:
And Bahrám, that great Hunter—the Wild Ass
Stamps o'er his Head, but cannot break his Sleep.

XIX

I sometimes think that never blows so red
The Rose as where some buried Cæsar bled;
That every Hyacinth the Garden wears
Dropt in her Lap from some once lovely Head.

XX

And this reviving Herb whose tender Green
Fledges the River-Lip on which we lean—
Ah, lean upon it lightly! for who knows
From what once lovely Lip it springs unseen!

XXI

Ah, my Belovèd, fill the Cup that clears
To-DAY of past Regrets and future Fears:
To-morrow!—Why, To-morrow I may be
Myself with Yesterday's Seven thousand Years.

XXII

For some we loved, the loveliest and the best
That from his Vintage rolling Time hath prest,
  Have drunk their Cup a Round or two before
And one by one crept silently to rest,

XXIII

And we, that now make merry in the Room
They left, and Summer dresses in new bloom,
  Ourselves must we beneath the Couch of Earth
Descend—ourselves to make a Couch—for whom?

XXIV

Ah, make the most of what we yet may spend,
Before we too into the Dust descend;
  Dust into Dust, and under Dust to lie,
Sans Wine, sans Song, sans Singer, and—sans End!

XXV

Alike for those who for To-DAY prepare,
And those that after some To-MORROW stare,
  A Muezzin from the Tower of Darkness cries,
"Fools! your Reward is neither Here nor There."

XXVI

Why, all the Saints and Sages who discussed
Of the Two Worlds so wisely—they are thrust
  Like foolish Prophets forth; their Words to Scorn
Are scattered, and their Mouths are stopt with Dust.

XXVII

Myself when young did eagerly frequent
Doctor and Saint, and heard great argument
  About it and about: but evermore
Came out by the same door where in I went.

XXVIII

With them the seed of Wisdom did I sow,
And with mine own hand wrought to make it grow;
  And this was all the Harvest that I reaped—
"I came like Water, and like Wind I go."

XXIX

Into this Universe, and *Why* not knowing
Nor *Whence,* like Water willy-nilly flowing;
  And out of it, as Wind along the Waste,
I know not *Whither,* willy-nilly blowing.

XXX

What, without asking, hither hurried *Whence?*
And, without asking, *Whither* hurried hence?
  Oh, many a Cup of this forbidden Wine
Must drown the memory of that insolence!

XXXI

Up from Earth's Center through the Seventh Gate
I rose, and on the Throne of Saturn sate,
  And many a Knot unraveled by the Road;
But not the Master-knot of Human Fate.

XXXII

There was the Door to which I found no Key;
There was the Veil through which I might not see:
  Some little talk awhile of Me and Thee
There was—and then no more of Thee and Me.

XXXIII

Earth could not answer; nor the Seas that mourn
In flowing Purple, of their Lord forlorn;
  Nor rolling Heaven, with all his Signs revealed
And hidden by the sleeve of Night and Morn.

XXXIV

Then of the THEE and ME who works behind
The Veil, I lifted up my hands to find
A Lamp amid the Darkness; and I heard,
As from Without—"THE ME WITHIN THEE BLIND!"

XXXV

Then to the Lip of this poor earthen Urn
I leaned, the Secret of my Life to learn:
And Lip to Lip it murmured—"While you live,
Drink!—for, once dead, you never shall return."

XXXVI

I think the Vessel, that with fugitive
Articulation answered, once did live,
And drink; and Ah! the passive Lip I kissed,
How many Kisses might it take—and give!

XXXVII

For I remember stopping by the way
To watch a Potter thumping his wet Clay:
And with its all-obliterated Tongue
It murmured—"Gently, Brother, gently, pray!"

XXXVIII

And has not such a Story from of Old
Down Man's successive generations rolled
Of such a clod of saturated Earth
Cast by the Maker into Human mold?

XXXIX

And not a drop that from our Cups we throw
For Earth to drink of, but may steal below
To quench the fire of Anguish in some Eye
There hidden—far beneath, and long ago.

XL

As then the Tulip for her morning sup
Of Heavenly Vintage from the soil looks up,
Do you devoutly do the like, till Heaven
To Earth invert you—like an empty Cup.

XLI

Perplext no more with Human or Divine
To-morrow's tangle to the winds resign,
And lose your fingers in the tresses of
The Cypress-slender Minister of Wine.

XLII

And if the Wine you drink, the Lip you press,
End in what All begins and ends in—Yes;
Think then you are TO-DAY what YESTERDAY
You were—TO-MORROW you shall not be less.

XLIII

So when the Angel of the darker Drink
At last shall find you by the river-brink,
And, offering his Cup, invite your Soul
Forth to your Lips to quaff—you shall not shrink.

XLIV

Why, if the Soul can fling the Dust aside,
And naked on the Air of Heaven ride,
Were 't not a Shame—were 't not a Shame for him
In this clay carcase crippled to abide?

XLV

'Tis but a Tent where takes his one day's rest
A Sultán to the realm of Death addrest;
The Sultán rises, and the dark Ferrásh
Strikes, and prepares it for another Guest.

XLVI

And fear not lest Existence closing your
Account and mine, should know the like no more;
The Eternal Sákí from that Bowl has poured
Millions of Bubbles like us, and will pour.

XLVII

When You and I behind the Veil are past,
Oh, but the long, long while the World shall last,
Which of our Coming and Departure heeds
As the Sea's self should heed a pebble-cast.

XLVIII

A Moment's Halt—a momentary taste
Of Being from the Well amid the Waste—
And Lo!—the phantom Caravan has reached
The Nothing it set out from—Oh, make haste!

XLIX

Would you that spangle of Existence spend
About THE SECRET—quick about it, Friend!
A Hair perhaps divides the False and True—
And upon what, prithee, may life depend?

L

A Hair perhaps divides the False and True;
Yes; and a single Alif were the clue—
Could you but find it—to the Treasure-house,
And peradventure to The Master too;

LI

Whose secret Presence, through Creation's veins
Running Quicksilver-like eludes your pains;
Taking all shapes from Máh to Máhi; and
They change and perish all—but He remains;

LII

A moment guessed—then back behind the Fold
Immerst of Darkness round the Drama rolled
  Which, for the Pastime of Eternity,
He doth Himself contrive, enact, behold.

LIII

But if in vain, down on the stubborn floor
Of Earth, and up to Heaven's unopening Door,
  You gaze To-DAY, while You are You—how then
To-MORROW, when You shall be You no more?

LIV

Waste not your Hour, nor in the vain pursuit
Of This and That endeavor and dispute;
  Better be jocund with the fruitful Grape
Than sadden after none, or bitter, Fruit.

LV

You know, my Friends, with what a brave Carouse
I made a Second Marriage in my house;
  Divorced old barren Reason from my Bed,
And took the Daughter of the Vine to Spouse.

LVI

For "Is" and "Is-NOT" though with Rule and Line,
And "UP-AND-DOWN" by Logic I define,
  Of all that one should care to fathom, I
Was never deep in anything but—Wine.

LVII

Ah, but my Computations, People say,
Reduced the Year to better reckoning?—Nay,
  'Twas only striking from the Calendar
Unborn To-morrow, and dead Yesterday.

LVIII

And lately, by the Tavern Door agape,
Came shining through the Dusk an Angel Shape
Bearing a Vessel on his Shoulder; and
He bid me taste of it; and 't was—the Grape!

LIX

The Grape that can with Logic absolute
The Two-and-Seventy jarring Sects confute:
The sovereign Alchemist that in a trice
Life's leaden metal into Gold transmute:

LX

The mighty Mahmúd, Allah-breathing Lord,
That all the misbelieving and black Horde
Of Fears and Sorrows that infest the Soul
Scatters before him with his whirlwind Sword.

LXI

Why, be this Juice the growth of God, who dare
Blaspheme the twisted tendril as a Snare?
A Blessing, we should use it, should we not?
And if a Curse—why, then, Who set it there?

LXII

I must abjure the Balm of Life, I must,
Scared by some After-reckoning ta'en on trust,
Or lured with Hope of some Diviner Drink,
To fill the Cup—when crumbled into Dust!

LXIII

Oh, threats of Hell and Hopes of Paradise!
One thing at least is certain—*This* Life flies;
One thing is certain and the rest is Lies;
The Flower that once has blown for ever dies.

LXIV

Strange, is it not? that of the myriads who
Before us passed the door of Darkness through,
  Not one returns to tell us of the Road,
Which to discover we must travel too.

LXV

The Revelations of Devout and Learned
Who rose before us, and as Prophets burned,
  Are all but Stories, which, awoke from Sleep
They told their comrades, and to Sleep returned.

LXVI

I sent my Soul through the Invisible,
Some letter of that After-life to spell:
  And by and by my Soul returned to me,
And answered "I Myself am Heaven and Hell:"

LXVII

Heaven but the Vision of fulfilled Desire,
And Hell the Shadow from a Soul on fire,
  Cast on the Darkness into which Ourselves,
So late emerged from shall so soon expire.

LXVIII

We are no other than a moving row
Of Magic Shadow-shapes that come and go
  Round with the Sun-illumined Lantern held
In Midnight by the Master of the Show;

LXIX

But helpless Pieces of the Game He plays
Upon this Chequer-board of Nights and Days;
  Hither and thither moves, and checks, and slays,
And one by one back in the Closet lays.

LXX

The Ball no question makes of Ayes and Noes,
But Here or There as strikes the Player goes;
And He that tossed you down into the Field,
He knows about it all—HE knows—HE knows!

LXXI

The Moving Finger writes; and, having writ,
Moves on: nor all your Piety nor Wit
Shall lure it back to cancel half a Line,
Nor all your Tears wash out a Word of it.

LXXII

And that inverted Bowl they call the Sky,
Whereunder crawling cooped we live and die,
Lift not your hands to *It* for help—for It
As impotently moves as you or I.

LXXIII

With Earth's first Clay They did the Last Man knead,
And there of the Last Harvest sowed the Seed:
And the first Morning of Creation wrote
What the Last Dawn of Reckoning shall read.

LXXIV

YESTERDAY *This* Day's Madness did prepare;
TO-MORROW's Silence, Triumph, or Despair:
Drink! for you know not whence you came, nor why:
Drink! for you know not why you go, nor where.

LXXV

I tell you this—When, started from the Goal,
Over the flaming shoulders of the Foal
Of Heaven Parwín and Mushtarí they flung,
In my predestined Plot of Dust and Soul

LXXVI

The Vine had struck a fiber: which about
If clings my Being—let the Dervish flout;
Of my Base metal may be filed a Key,
That shall unlock the Door he howls without.

LXXVII

And this I know: whether the one True Light
Kindle to Love, or Wrath-consume me quite,
One Flash of It within the Tavern caught
Better than in the Temple lost outright.

LXXVIII

What! out of senseless Nothing to provoke
A conscious Something to resent the yoke
Of unpermitted Pleasure, under pain
Of Everlasting Penalties, if broke!

LXXIX

What! from his helpless Creature be repaid
Pure Gold for what he lent him dross-allayed—
Sue for a Debt we never did contract,
And cannot answer—Oh, the sorry trade!

LXXX

Oh Thou, who didst with pitfall and with gin
Beset the Road I was to wander in,
Thou wilt not with Predestined Evil round
Enmesh, and then impute my Fall to Sin!

LXXXI

Oh Thou, who Man of baser Earth didst make,
And even with Paradise devise the Snake:
For all the Sin wherewith the Face of Man
Is blackened—Man's forgiveness give—and take!

* * * * * * * *

LXXXII

As under cover of departing Day
Slunk hunger-stricken Ramazàn away,
Once more within the Potter's house alone
I stood, surrounded by the Shapes of Clay.

LXXXIII

Shapes of all Sorts and Sizes, great and small,
That stood along the floor and by the wall;
And some loquacious Vessels were; and some
Listened perhaps, but never talked at all.

LXXXIV

Said one among them—"Surely not in vain
My substance of the common Earth was ta'en
And to this Figure molded, to be broke,
Or trampled back to shapeless Earth again."

LXXXV

Then said a Second—"Ne'er a peevish Boy
Would break the Bowl from which he drank in joy;
And He that with his hand the Vessel made
Will surely not in after Wrath destroy."

LXXXVI

After a momentary silence spake
Some Vessel of a more ungainly Make:
"They sneer at me for leaning all awry:
What! did the Hand then of the Potter shake?"

LXXXVII

Whereat some one of the loquacious Lot—
I think a Sufti pipkin—waxing hot—
"All this of Pot and Potter—Tell me then,
Who is the Potter, pray, and who the Pot?"

LXXXVIII

"Why," said another, "Some there are who tell
Of one who threatens he will toss to Hell
  The luckless Pots he marred in making—Pish!
He's a Good Fellow, and 'twill all be well."

LXXXIX

"Well," murmured one, "Let whoso make or buy,
My Clay with long Oblivion is gone dry:
  But fill me with the old familiar Juice,
Methinks I might recover by and by."

XC

So while the Vessels one by one were speaking,
The little Moon looked in that all were seeking:
  And then they jogged each other, "Brother! Brother!
Now for the Porter's shoulder-knot a-creaking!"

* * * * * * * *

XCI

Ah, with the Grape my fading Life provide,
And wash the Body whence the Life has died,
  And lay me, shrouded in the living Leaf,
By some not unfrequented Gardenside.

XCII

That even my buried Ashes such a snare
Of Vintage shall fling up into the Air
  As not a True-believer passing by
But shall be overtaken unaware.

XCIII

Indeed the Idols I have loved so long
Have done my credit in this World much wrong:
  Have drowned my Glory in a shallow Cup,
And sold my Reputation for a Song.

XCIV

Indeed, indeed, Repentance oft before
I swore—but was I sober when I swore?
And then and then came Spring, and Rose-in-hand
My thread-bare Penitence apieces tore.

XCV

And much as Wine has played the Infidel,
And robbed me of my Robe of Honor—Well,
I wonder often what the Vintners buy
One half so precious as the stuff they sell.

XCVI

Yet Ah, that Spring should vanish with the Rose!
That Youth's sweet-scented manuscript should close!
The Nightingale that in the branches sang,
Ah whence, and whither flown again, who knows!

XCVII

Would but the Desert of the Fountain yield
One glimpse—if dimly, yet indeed, revealed,
To which the fainting Traveler might spring,
As springs the trampled herbage of the field!

XCVIII

Would but some wingéd Angel ere too late
Arrest the yet unfolded Roll of Fate,
And make the stern Recorder otherwise
Enregister, or quite obliterate!

XCIX

Ah Love! could you and I with Him conspire
To grasp this sorry Scheme of Things Entire,
Would not we shatter it to bits—and then
Re-mold it nearer to the Heart's Desire!

* * * * * * * *

C

Yon rising Moon that looks for us again—
How oft hereafter will she wax and wane;
How oft hereafter rising look for us
Through this same Garden—and for *one* in vain!

CI

And when like her, Oh Sáki, you shall pass
Among the Guests Star-scattered on the Grass,
And in your joyous errand reach the spot
Where I made One—turn down an empty Glass!

(Edward FitzGerald)

Jalālu'ddīn Rūmī

1207–1273

A BEAUTY THAT ALL NIGHT LONG

A BEAUTY that all night long teaches love-tricks to Venus and the moon,
Whose two eyes by their witchery seal up the two eyes of heaven.
Look to your hearts! I, whate'er betide, O Moslems,
Am so mingled with him that no heart is mingled with me.
I was born of his love at the first, I gave him my heart at the last;
When the fruit springs from the bough, on that bough it hangs.
The tip of his curl is saying, "Ho! betake thee to rope-dancing."
The cheek of this candle is saying, "Where is a moth that it may burn?"
For the sake of dancing on that rope, O heart, make haste, become a hoop;
Cast thyself on the flame, when his candle is lit.

Thou wilt never more endure without the flame, when
thou hast known the rapture of burning;
If the water of life should come to thee, it would not
stir thee from the flame.

(*R. A. Nicholson*)

Sa'di

d. 1291

FROM THE GULISTAN

Sadi's favorite mode is a simplicity and tenderness of heart, a delicacy of feeling and judgment, and that exquisitely natural vein in which he relates his many apologues and parables with a sort of sententious and epigrammatic turn.—James Ross.

He Hath No Parallel

Should any ask me on His form to dwell,
Helpless I say,—"He hath no parallel."
The lovers by the loved one all are slain,
No voice can answer from the dead again.

The Gift of Speech

Now, while thou hast the wondrous power of word,
Let every thought in shining grace appear;
To-morrow, when Death's messenger is here,
He will constrain thee to depart unheard.

On the Deception of Appearances

The man that never will declare his thought
Conceals a soul of honor or of sin.
Dost think yon silent jungle holdeth naught?
Perchance a lurking tiger sleeps therein.

Friendship

He is no friend who in thine hour of pride
Brags of his love and calls himself thy kin.
He is a friend who hales his fellow in,
And clangs the door upon the wolf outside.

Take the Crust

My precious life I spent considering
What I should eat in summer, wear in spring.
Vile belly! take the crust! 'tis nobler food
Than all the capons plucked in servitude.

Mesnevi

If livelihood by knowledge were endowed,
None would be poorer than the brainless crowd;
Yet fortune on the fool bestows the prize,
And leaves but themes for wonder to the wise.

The luck of wealth dependeth not on skill,
But only on the aid of Heaven's will:
So it has happened since the world began—
The witless ape outstrips the learned man;
A poet dies of hunger, grief, and cold;
A fool among the ruins findeth gold.

Love's Last Resource

Since nought avails, let me arise and leave,
Though down the way of swords I wounded crawl;
Perchance I shall attain to touch her sleeve,
And surely on her threshold dying fall.

Alas!

She, who could neither rest nor sleep
Ere round her she had scattered hyacinths and roses,
Now with the roses of her face death-strewn reposes,
And o'er her tomb wild brambles creep.

(*L. Cranmer-Byng*)

Courage

Whoever hath washed his hands of living
Utters his mind without misgiving.

In straits which no escape afford
The hand takes hold of the edge of the sword.

Help

Vex no man's secret soul—if that can be—
The path of life hath far too many a thorn!
Help whom thou may'st—for surely unto thee
Sharp need of help will e'er the end be borne.

The Sooth-Sayer

What could he know of sky and stars, or heaven's all-hidden life,
Who did not see in his own house the knave that kissed his wife?

Wealth

He that owns wealth, in mountain, wold, or waste,
Plays master—pitches tent at his own taste;
Whilst he who lacks that which the world commends
Must pace a stranger, e'en in his own lands.

(Sir Edwin Arnold)

FROM THE BUSTAN

The Dancer

I heard how, to the beat of some quick tune,
There rose and danced a Damsel like the moon,
Flower-mouthed and Pâri-faced; and all around her
Neck-stretching Lovers gathered close; but, soon

A flickering lamp-flame caught her skirt, and set
Fire to the flying gauze. Fear did beget
Trouble in that light heart! She cried amain.
Quoth one among her worshipers, "Why fret,

Tulip of Love? Th' extinguished fire hath burned
Only one leaf of thee; but I am turned
To ashes—leaf and stalk, and flower and root—
By lamp-flash of thine eyes!"—"Ah, Soul concerned

"Solely with self!"—she answered, laughing low,
"If thou wert Lover thou hadst not said so.
Who speaks of the Belov'd's woe as not his
Speaks infidelity, true Lovers know!"

The Great Physician

A tumult in a Syrian town had place:
They seized an old man there of wit and grace;
Still in my ear lingers his noble saying,
When, fettered fast, they smote him in the face.

Quotha: "If of all Sultans the Sultàn
Gives not the word for plunder, who else can?
Who, save upon His bidding, would be bold
To do such deeds? Therefore I hold the man

That wrongs me not mine enemy but friend;
God hath appointed him unto this end!
If there fall scorn or honor, gifts or shackles,
'Tis God—not Zayd or Omar—who doth send."

Right, Sheykh! no griefs the wise heart will annoy;
The Great Physician sharp drugs doth employ!
A sick man's not more skillful than his Hâkim;
Take what the Friend gives as a bliss and joy.

(*Sir Edwin Arnold*)

ODE

Until thine hands clasp girdlewise the waist of the Belov'd,
Thou ne'er wilt kiss to heart's desire the mouth of the Belov'd.
Know'st thou what is the life of him the sword of Love hath slain?
To bite an apple from the orchard-cheek of the Belov'd.
Khusrau and Shirin's mighty love is rased and washed away

By tide of turmoil swelling high 'twixt me and the Belov'd.
The champion whom in far war's field no paynim arrow slew,
His blood was shed by bow-like fair eyebrow of the Belov'd.
Gone is mine heart, mine eye weeps blood; and if my faint soul lives,
'Tis only that I may bestow its life on the Belov'd.
Ay, one day I will fling myself beneath his Arab's hoof,
Unless disdain and pride pull in the rein of the Belov'd.
Howbeit in this quest, alas, I never win to joy,
It may be that my name will pass the lips of the Belov'd.
Sith life must once be yielded up, whatever fate befall,
Most sweet to die in Love's abode at the door of the Belov'd!
Surely will I then bear with me this passion to the grave,
And from the grave arise and ask the way to the Belov'd.
All men cry out against the hand of hated enemy,
But Sa'di cried against the unloving heart of the Belov'd.

(*R. A. Nicholson*)

Hafiz

d. 1389

Hafiz is the prince of Persian poets, and in his extraordinary gifts adds to some of the attributes of Pindar, Anacreon, Horace, and Burns the insight of a mystic. —Ralph Waldo Emerson.

A PERSIAN SONG OF HAFIZ

Sweet maid, if thou wouldst charm my sight,
And bid these arms thy neck infold;
That rosy cheek, that lily hand,
Would give thy poet more delight
Than all Bocara's vaunted gold,
Than all the gems of Samarcand.

Boy, let yon liquid ruby flow,
And bid thy pensive heart be glad,
Whate'er the frowning zealots say:
Tell them, their Eden cannot show
A stream so clear as Rocnabad,
A bow'r so sweet as Mosellay.

Oh! when these fair perfidious maids,
Whose eyes our secret haunts infest,
Their dear destructive charms display,
Each glance my tender heart invades,
And robs my wounded soul of rest,
As Tartars seize their destined prey.

In vain with love our bosoms glow:
Can all our tears, can all our sighs,
New luster to those charms impart?
Can cheeks, where living roses blow,
Where Nature spreads her richest dyes,
Require the borrowed gloss of art?

Speak not of fate:—ah! change the theme,
And talk of odors, talk of wine,
Talk of the flow'rs that round us bloom:
'Tis all a cloud, 'tis all a dream;
To love and joy thy thoughts confine,
Nor hope to pierce the sacred gloom.

Beauty has such resistless pow'r,
That ev'n the chaste Egyptian dame
Sighed for the blooming Hebrew boy:
For her how fatal was the hour
When to the banks of Nilus came
A youth so lovely and so coy!

But ah! sweet maid, my counsel hear
(Youth should attend when those advise
Whom long experience renders sage)
While music charms the ravished ear,
While sparkling cups delight our eyes,
Be gay, and scorn the frowns of age.

What cruel answer have I heard?
And yet, by Heav'n, I love thee still
Can aught be cruel from thy lips?
Yet say, how fell that bitter word
From lips which streams of sweetness fill,
Which nought but drops of honey sip?

Go boldly forth, my simple lay,
Whose accents flow with artless ease,
Like orient pearls at random strung;
Thy notes are sweet, the damsels say,
But oh, far sweeter, if they please
The Nymph for whom these notes are sung.

(*Sir William Jones*)

ODES

I

Saki, for God's love, come and fill my glass;
  Wine for a breaking heart, O, Saki, bring!
For this strange love which seemed at first, alas!
  So simple and so innocent a thing,
How difficult, how difficult it is!
    Because the night-wind kissed the scented curl
    On the white brow of a capricious girl,
And, passing, gave me half the stolen kiss,
  Who would have thought one's heart could bleed and
      break
For such a very little thing as this?
  Wine, Saki, wine—red wine, for pity's sake!

O Saki, would to God that I might die!
  Would that this moment I might hear the bell
    That bids the traveler for the road prepare,
  Be the next stopping-place or heaven or hell!
Strange caravan of death—no fears have I
    Of the dark journey, gladly would I dare

The fearful river and the whirling pools;
  Ah! they that dwell upon the other side,
    What know they of the burdens that we bear?
  With lit-up happy faces having died,
    What know they of Love's bitter mystery,
    The love that makes so sad a fool of me?
A fool of HAFIZ!—yea, a fool of fools.

(Richard Le Gallienne)

2

COMRADES, the morning breaks, the sun is up;
  Over her pearly shoulder the shy dawn
  Winds the soft floating mists of silver lawn;
Comrades, the morning cup! the morning cup!

With dew the tulip's cheek is dappled gray,
  And from the ground sweet smells of morning rise,
  The breeze blows softly out of Paradise;
Drink to the morning of another day!

The red rose sits upon her emerald throne,
  The glittering grass about her feet is spread;
  Wine, Saki, bright as fire, as rubies red!
Comrades, the morning cup, ere morn be flown!

What! they have shut the wine-house up again!
  On such a morning closed the tavern door!
  Great Opener of Doors, Thee we implore
Open it for us, for we knock in vain.

It is a wonderful and wicked thing
  They at this season should the tavern close;
  Drink shall we none the less—under the rose;
The Water of Life runs from this little spring.

Sikandar's mirror is this magic cup;
  In it the whole round world reflected lies;
  'T is filled with pictures for anointed eyes;
'T is the World's wisdom thou art drinking up.

Under the red rose drinking the red wine,
  In a red dawn, and kissing her red lips,
  No honey-bee from such a flower sips—
No emperor lives such a life as mine.

Once more, O HAFIZ, dawns the morning cup,
  Another day in which to seek her face!
  Patience! the day will come, in some strange place,
When thy strong hands her veil at last lift up.

(Richard Le Gallienne)

3

The rose is not the rose unless thou see;
Without good wine, spring is not spring for me.

Without thy tulip cheek, the gracious air
Of gardens and of meadows is not fair.

Thy rosy limbs, unless I may embrace,
Lose for my longing eyes full half their grace;

Nor does thy scarlet mouth with honey drip
Unless I taste its honey, lip to lip.

Vainly the cypress in the zephyr sways,
Unless the nightingale be there to praise.

Nothing the mind imagines can be fair,
Except the picture that it makes of her.

Surely good wine is good, and green the end
Of gardens old—but not without the Friend.

HAFIZ, the metal of thy soul is base:
Stamp not upon it the Beloved's face.

(Richard Le Gallienne)

4

A GRIEVOUS folly shames my sixtieth year—
My white head is in love with a green maid;
I kept my heart a secret, but at last
I am betrayed.
Like a mere child I walked into the snare;
My foolish heart followed my foolish eyes;
And yet, when I was young—in ages past—
I was so wise.

If only she who can such wonders do
Could from my cheeks time's calumny erase,
And change the color of my snow-white locks—
Give a young face
To my young heart, and make my old eyes new,
Bidding my outside tell the inward truth!
O 't is a shallow wit wherewith time mocks
An old man's youth!

Ah! it was always so with us who sing!
Children of fancy, we are in the power
Of any dream, and at the bidding we
Of a mere flower;
Yet HAFIZ, though full many a foolish thing
Ensnared thy heart with wonder, never thou
Wert wont imagination's slave to be
As thou art now.

(*Richard Le Gallienne*)

5

WHERE is my ruined life, and where the fame
Of noble deeds?
Look on my long-drawn road, and whence it came,
And where it leads!

Can drunkenness be linked to piety
And good repute?
Where is the preacher's holy monody,
Where is the lute?

From monkish cell and lying garb released,
    Oh heart of mine,
Where is the Tavern fane, the Tavern priest,
    Where is the wine?

Past days of meeting, let the memory
    Of you be sweet!
Where are those glances fled, and where for
    Reproaches meet?

His friend's bright face warms not the enemy
    When love is done—
Where is the extinguished lamp that made night day,
    Where is the sun?

Balm to mine eyes the dust, my head I bow
    Upon thy stair.
Where shall I go, where from thy presence? thou
    Art everywhere.

Look not upon the dimple of her chin,
    Danger lurks there!
Where wilt thou hide, oh trembling heart, fleeing in
    Such mad haste—where?

To steadfastness and patience, friend, ask not
    If Hafiz keep—
Patience and steadfastness I have forgot,
    And where is sleep?

(*Gertrude Lowthian Bell*)

6

The jewel of the secret treasury
Is still the same as once it was; the seal
Upon Love's treasure casket, and the key,
Are still what thieves can neither break nor steal;
Still among lovers loyalty is found,
And therefore faithful eyes still strew the ground
With the same pearls that mine once strewed for thee.

Question the wandering winds and thou shalt know
That from the dusk until the dawn doth break,
My consolation is that still they blow
The perfume of thy curls across my cheek,
A dart from thy bent brows has wounded me—
Ah, come! my heart still waiteth helplessly,
Has waited ever, till thou heal its pain.

If seekers after rubies there were none,
Still to the dark mines where the gems had lain
Would pierce, as he was wont, the radiant sun,
Setting the stones ablaze. Would'st hide the stain
Of my heart's blood? Blood-red the ruby glows
(And whence it came my wounded bosom knows)
Upon thy lips to show what thou hast done.

Let not thy curls waylay my pilgrim soul,
As robbers use, and plunder me no more!
Years join dead years, but thine extortionate rule
Is still the same, merciless as before.
Sing, Hafiz, sing again of eyes that weep!
For still the fountain of our tears is deep
As once it was, and still with tears is full.

(*Gertrude Lowthian Bell*)

7

WIND from the east, oh Lapwing of the day,
I send thee to my Lady, though the way
Is far to Saba, where I bid thee fly;
Lest in the dust thy tameless wings should lie,
Broken with grief, I send thee to thy nest,
Fidelity.

Or far or near there is no halting-place
Upon Love's road—absent, I see thy face,
And in thine ear my wind-blown greetings sound,
North winds and east waft them where they are bound,
Each morn and eve convoys of greeting fair
I send to thee.

Unto mine eyes a stranger, thou that art
A comrade ever-present to my heart,
What whispered prayers and what full meed of praise
I send to thee.

Lest Sorrow's army waste thy heart's domain,
I send my life to bring thee peace again,
Dear life thy ransom! From thy singers learn
How one that longs for thee may weep and burn;
Sonnets and broken words, sweet notes and songs
I send to thee.

Give me the cup! a voice rings in mine ears
Crying: "Bear patiently the bitter years!
For all thine ills, I send thee heavenly grace.
God the Creator mirrored in thy face
Thine eyes shall see, God's image in the glass
I send to thee.

"Hafiz, thy praise alone my comrades sing;
Hasten to us, thou that art sorrowing!
A robe of honor and a harnessed steed
I send to thee."

(*Gertrude Lowthian Bell*)

8

Lady that hast my heart within thy hand,
Thou heed'st me not; and if thou turn thine ear
Unto the wise, thou shalt not understand—
Behold the fault is thine, our words were clear.
For all the tumult in my drunken brain
Praise God, who trieth not His slave in vain;
Nor this world nor the next shall make me fear!

My weary heart eternal silence keeps—
I know not who has slipped into my heart;
Though I am silent, one within me weeps.
My soul shall rend the painted veil apart.

Where art thou, Minstrel! touch thy saddest strings
Till clothed in music such as sorrow sings,
My mournful story from thy zither sweeps.

Lo, not at any time I lent mine ear
To hearken to the glories of the earth;
Only thy beauty to mine eyes was dear.
Sleep has forsaken me, and from the birth
Of night till day I weave bright dreams of thee;
Drunk with a hundred nights of revelry,
Where is the tavern that sets forth such cheer!

My heart, sad hermit, stains the cloister floor
With drops of blood, the sweat of anquish dire;
Ah, wash me clean, and o'er my body pour
Love's generous wine! the worshipers of fire
Have bowed them down and magnified my name,
For in my heart there burns a living flame,
Transpiercing Death's impenetrable door.

What instrument through last night's silence rang?
My life into his lay the minstrel wove,
And filled my brain with the sweet song he sang.
It was the proclamation of thy love
That shook the strings of Life's most secret lyre,
And still my breast heaves with last night's desire,
For countless echoes from that music sprang.

And ever since the time that Hafiz heard
His Lady's voice, as from a rocky hill
Reverberates the softly spoken word,
So echoes of desire his bosom fill.

(*Gertrude Lowthian Bell*)

9

I CEASE not from desire till my desire
Is satisfied; or let my mouth attain
My love's red mouth, or let my soul expire,
Sighed from those lips that sought her lips in vain.

Others may find another love as fair;
Upon the threshold I have laid my head,
The dust shall cover me, still lying there,
When from my body life and love have fled.

My soul is on my lips ready to fly,
But grief beats in my heart and will not cease,
Because not once, not once before I die,
Will her sweet lips give all my longing peace.
My breath is narrowed down to one long sigh
For a red mouth that burns my thoughts like fire:
When will that mouth draw near and make reply
To one whose life is straitened with desire?

When I am dead, open my grave and see
The cloud of smoke that rises round thy feet:
In my dead heart the fire still burns for thee;
Yea, the smoke rises from my winding-sheet!
Ah, come, Beloved! for the meadows wait
Thy coming, and the thorn bears flowers instead
Of thorns, the cypress fruit, and desolate
Bare winter from before thy steps has fled.

Hoping within some garden ground to find
A red rose soft and sweet as thy soft cheek,
Through every meadow blows the western wind,
Through every garden he is fain to seek.
Reveal thy face! that the whole world may be
Bewildered by thy radiant loveliness;
The cry of man and woman comes to thee,
Open thy lips and comfort their distress!

Each curling lock of thy luxuriant hair
Breaks into barbed hooks to catch my heart,
My broken heart is wounded everywhere
With countless wounds from which the red drops start.

Yet when sad lovers meet and tell their sighs,
Not without praise shall Hafiz' name be said,
Not without tears, in those pale companies
Where joy has been forgot and hope has fled.

(Gertrude Lowthian Bell)

10

THE days of Spring are here! the eglantine,
The rose, the tulip from the dust have risen—
And thou, why liest thou beneath the dust?
Like the full clouds of Spring, these eyes of mine
Shall scatter tears upon the grave thy prison,
Till thou too from the earth thine head shalt thrust.

(Gertrude Lowthian Bell)

11

I HAVE borne the anguish of love, which ask me not
to describe:
I have tasted the poison of absence, which ask me not
to relate.

Far through the world have I roved, and at length
I have chosen
A sweet creature (a ravisher of hearts), whose name ask
me not to disclose.

The flowing of my tears bedews her footsteps
In such a manner as ask me not to utter.

On yesternight from her own mouth with my own ears
I heard
Such words as pray ask me not to repeat.

Why dost you bite thy lip at me? What dost thou not
hint (*that I may have told*)?
I have devoured a lip like a ruby: but whose, ask me not
to mention.

Absent from thee, and the sole tenant of my cottage,
I have endured such tortures, as ask me not to enumerate.

Thus am I, HAFIZ, arrived at extremity in the ways of Love,
Which, alas! ask me not to explain.

(John Hindley)

12

I SAID to heaven that glowed above
O hide yon sun-filled zone,
Hide all the stars you boast;
For, in the world of love
And estimation true,
The heaped-up harvest of the moon
Is worth one barley-corn at most,
The Pleiads' sheaf but two.

If my darling should depart,
And search the skies for prouder friends,
God forbid my angry heart
In other love should seek amends.

When the blue horizon's hoop
Me a little pinches here,
Instant to my grave I stoop,
And go find thee in the sphere.

(Ralph Waldo Emerson)

13

OFT have I said, I say it once more,
I, a wanderer, do not stray from myself.
I am a kind of parrot; the mirror is holden to me;
What the Eternal says, I stammering say again.

Give me what you will; I eat thistles as roses,
And according to my food I grow and I give.
Scorn me not, but know I have the pearl,
And am only seeking one to receive it.

(Ralph Waldo Emerson)

HEBREW

From the Old Testament

10th–1st centuries B.C.

THE SONG OF DEBORAH AND BARAK

—JUDGES V.

PRAISE ye the Lord for the avenging of Israel, when the people willingly offered themselves.

Hear, O ye kings; give ear, O ye princes; I, even I, will sing unto the Lord; I will sing praise to the Lord God of Israel.

Lord, when thou wentest out of Seir, when thou marchedst out of the field of Edom, the earth trembled, and the heavens dropped, the clouds also dropped water.

The mountains melted from before the Lord, even that Sinai from before the Lord God of Israel.

In the days of Shamgar the son of Anath, in the days of Jael, the highways were unoccupied, and the travelers walked through byways.

The inhabitants of the villages ceased, they ceased in Israel, until that I Deborah arose, that I arose a mother in Israel.

They chose new gods; then was war in the gates: was there a shield or spear seen among forty thousand in Israel?

My heart is toward the governors of Israel, that offered themselves willingly among the people. Bless ye the Lord.

Speak, ye that ride on white asses, ye that sit in judgment, and walk by the way.

They that are delivered from the noise of archers in the places of drawing water, there shall they rehearse the righteous acts of the Lord, even the righteous acts toward the inhabitants of his villages in Israel: then shall the people of the Lord go down to the gates.

Awake, awake, Deborah: awake, awake, utter a song: arise, Barak, and lead thy captivity captive, thou son of Abinoam.

Then he made him that remaineth have dominion over the nobles among the people: the Lord made me have dominion over the mighty.

Out of Ephraim was there a root of them against Amalek; after thee, Benjamin, among thy people; out of Machir came down governors, and out of Zebulun they that handle the pen of the writer.

And the princes of Issachar were with Deborah; even Issachar, and also Barak: he was sent on foot into the valley. For the divisions of Reuben there were great thoughts of heart.

Why abodest thou among the sheepfolds, to hear the bleatings of the flocks? For the divisions of Reuben there were great searchings of heart.

Gilead abode beyond Jordan: and why did Dan remain in ships? Asher continued on the sea shore, and abode in his breaches.

Zebulun and Naphtali were a people that jeoparded their lives unto the death in the high places of the field.

The kings came and fought, then fought the kings of Canaan in Taanach by the waters of Megiddo; they took no gain of money.

They fought from heaven; the stars in their courses fought against Sisera.

The river of Kishon swept them away, that ancient river, the river Kishon. O my soul, thou hast trodden down strength.

Then were the horsehoofs broken by the means of the prancings, the prancings of their mighty ones.

Curse ye Meroz, said the angel of the Lord, curse ye bitterly the inhabitants thereof; because they came not to the help of the Lord, to the help of the Lord against the mighty.

Blessed above women shall Jael the wife of Heber the Kenite be, blessed shall she be above women in the tent.

He asked water, and she gave him milk; she brought forth butter in a lordly dish.

She put her hand to the nail, and her right hand to the workmen's hammer; and with the hammer she smote Sisera, she smote off his head, when she had pierced and stricken through his temples.

At her feet he bowed, he fell, he lay down: at her feet he bowed, he fell: where he bowed, there he fell down dead.

The mother of Sisera looked out at a window, and cried through the lattice, Why is his chariot so long in coming? why tarry the wheels of his chariots?

Her wise ladies answered her, yea, she returned answer to herself,

Have they not sped? have they not divided the prey; to every man a damsel or two; to Sisera a prey of divers colors, a prey of divers colors of needlework, of divers colors of needlework on both sides, meet for the necks of them that take the spoil?

So let all thine enemies perish, O Lord: but let them that love him be as the sun when he goeth forth in his might.

HANNAH'S SONG OF THANKSGIVING

—I Samuel ii.

My heart rejoiceth in the Lord, mine horn is exalted in the Lord: my mouth is enlarged over mine enemies; because I rejoice in thy salvation.

There is none holy as the Lord: for there is none beside thee: neither is there any rock like our God.

Talk no more so exceeding proudly; let not arrogancy come out of your mouth: for the Lord is a God of knowledge, and by him actions are weighed.

The bows of the mighty men are broken, and they that stumbled are girded with strength.

They that were full have hired out themselves for bread; and they that were hungry ceased: so that the barren hath born seven; and she that hath many children is waxed feeble.

The Lord killeth, and maketh alive: he bringeth down to the grave, and bringeth up.

The Lord maketh poor, and maketh rich: he bringeth low, and lifteth up.

He raiseth up the poor out of the dust, and lifteth up the beggar from the dunghill, to set them among princes, and to make them inherit the throne of glory: for the pillars of the earth are the Lord's and he hath set the world upon them.

He will keep the feet of his saints, and the wicked shall be silent in darkness; for by strength shall no man prevail.

The adversaries of the Lord shall be broken to pieces; out of heaven shall he thunder upon them: the Lord shall judge the ends of the earth; and he shall give strength unto his king, and exalt the horn of his anointed.

DAVID'S LAMENT FOR SAUL AND JONATHAN

—2 Samuel i.

The beauty of Israel is slain upon thy high places: how are the mighty fallen!

Tell it not in Gath, publish it not in the streets of Askelon; lest the daughters of the Philistines rejoice, lest the daughters of the uncircumcised triumph.

Ye mountains of Gilboa, let there be no dew, neither let there be rain, upon you, nor fields of offerings: for there the shield of the mighty is vilely cast away, the shield of Saul, as though he had not been anointed with oil.

From the blood of the slain, from the fat of the mighty, the bow of Jonathan turned not back, and the sword of Saul returned not empty.

Saul and Jonathan were lovely and pleasant in their lives, and in their death they were not divided: they were swifter than eagles, they were stronger than lions.

Ye daughters of Israel, weep over Saul, who clothed

you in scarlet, with other delights, who put on ornaments of gold upon your apparel.

How are the mighty fallen in the midst of the battle! O Jonathan, thou wast slain in thine high places.

I am distressed for thee, my brother Jonathan: very pleasant hast thou been unto me: thy love to me was wonderful, passing the love of women.

How are the mighty fallen, and the weapons of war perished!

THE BOOK OF PSALMS

Psalm 1

Blessed is the man that walketh not in the counsel of the ungodly, nor standeth in the way of sinners, nor sitteth in the seat of the scornful.

But his delight is in the law of the Lord; and in his law doth he meditate day and night.

And he shall be like a tree planted by the rivers of water, that bringeth forth his fruit in his season; his leaf also shall not wither; and whatsoever he doeth shall prosper.

The ungodly are not so; but are like the chaff which the wind driveth away.

Therefore the ungodly shall not stand in the judgment, nor sinners in the congregation of the righteous.

For the Lord knoweth the way of the righteous: but the way of the ungodly shall perish.

Psalm 8

O Lord our Lord, how excellent is thy name in all the earth! who hast set thy glory above the heavens.

Out of the mouth of babes and sucklings hast thou ordained strength because of thine enemies, that thou mightest still the enemy and the avenger.

When I consider thy heavens, the work of thy fingers, the moon and the stars, which thou hast ordained;

What is man, that thou art mindful of him? and the son of man, that thou visitest him?

For thou hast made him a little lower than the angels, and hast crowned him with glory and honor.

Thou madest him to have dominion over the works of thy hands; thou hast put all things under his feet:

All sheep and oxen, yea, and the beasts of the field;

The fowl of the air, and the fish of the sea, and whatsoever passeth through the paths of the seas.

O Lord our Lord, how excellent is thy name in all the earth!

Psalm 19

The heavens declare the glory of God; and the firmament sheweth his handywork.

Day unto day uttereth speech, and night unto night sheweth knowledge.

There is no speech nor language, where their voice is not heard.

Their line is gone out through all the earth, and their words to the end of the world. In them hath he set a tabernacle for the sun,

Which is as a bridegroom coming out of his chamber, and rejoiceth as a strong man to run a race.

His going forth is from the end of the heaven, and his circuit unto the ends of it: and there is nothing hid from the heat thereof.

The law of the Lord is perfect, converting the soul: the testimony of the Lord is sure, making wise the simple.

The statutes of the Lord are right, rejoicing the heart: the commandment of the Lord is pure, enlightening the eyes.

The fear of the Lord is clean, enduring for ever: the judgments of the Lord are true and righteous altogether.

More to be desired are they than gold, yea, than much fine gold: sweeter also than honey and the honeycomb.

Moreover by them is thy servant warned: and in keeping of them there is great reward.

Who can understand his errors? cleanse thou me from secret faults.

Keep back thy servant also from presumptuous sins; let them not have dominion over me: then shall I be upright, and I shall be innocent from the great transgression.

Let the words of my mouth, and the meditation of my heart, be acceptable in thy sight, O Lord, my strength, and my redeemer.

Psalm 23

The Lord is my shepherd; I shall not want.

He maketh me to lie down in green pastures: he leadeth me beside the still waters.

He restoreth my soul: he leadeth me in the paths of righteousness for his name's sake.

Yea, though I walk through the valley of the shadow of death, I will fear no evil: for thou art with me; thy rod and thy staff they comfort me.

Thou preparest a table before me in the presence of mine enemies; thou anointest my head with oil; my cup runneth over.

Surely goodness and mercy shall follow me all the days of my life: and I will dwell in the house of the Lord for ever.

Psalm 24

The earth is the Lord's, and the fullness thereof; the world, and they that dwell therein.

For he hath founded it upon the seas, and established it upon the floods.

Who shall ascend into the hill of the Lord? or who shall stand in his holy place?

He that hath clean hands, and a pure heart; who hath not lifted up his soul unto vanity, nor sworn deceitfully.

He shall receive the blessing from the Lord, and righteousness from the God of his salvation.

This is the generation of them that seek him, that seek thy face, O Jacob.

Lift up your heads, O ye gates; and be ye lift up, ye everlasting doors; and the King of glory shall come in.

Who is this King of glory? The Lord strong and mighty, the Lord mighty in battle.

Lift up your heads, O ye gates; even lift them up, ye everlasting doors; and the King of glory shall come in.

Who is this King of glory? The Lord of hosts, he is the King of glory.

Psalm 29

Give unto the Lord, O ye mighty, give unto the Lord glory and strength.

Give unto the Lord the glory due unto his name; worship the Lord in the beauty of holiness.

The voice of the Lord is upon the waters: the God of glory thundereth: the Lord is upon many waters.

The voice of the Lord is powerful; the voice of the Lord is full of majesty.

The voice of the Lord breaketh the cedars; yea, the Lord breaketh the cedars of Lebanon.

He maketh them also to skip like a calf; Lebanon and Sirion like a young unicorn.

The voice of the Lord divideth the flames of fire.

The voice of the Lord shaketh the wilderness; the Lord shaketh the wilderness of Kadesh.

The voice of the Lord maketh the hinds to calve, and discovereth the forests: and in his temple doth every one speak of his glory.

The Lord sitteth upon the flood; yea, the Lord sitteth King for ever.

The Lord will give strength unto his people; the Lord will bless his people with peace.

Psalm 42

As the hart panteth after the water brooks, so panteth my soul after thee, O God.

My soul thirsteth for God, for the living God: when shall I come and appear before God?

My tears have been my meat day and night, while they continually say unto me, Where is thy God?

When I remember these things, I pour out my soul in me: for I had gone with the multitude, I went with them to the house of God, with the voice of joy and praise, with a multitude that kept holyday.

Why are thou cast down, O my soul? and why art thou disquieted in me? hope thou in God: for I shall yet praise him for the help of his countenance.

O my God, my soul is cast down within me: therefore will I remember thee from the land of Jordan, and of the Hermonites, from the hill Mizar.

Deep calleth unto deep at the noise of thy waterspouts: all thy waves and thy billows are gone over me.

Yet the Lord will command his loving kindness in the daytime, and in the night his song shall be with me, and my prayer unto the God of my life.

I will say unto God my rock, Why hast thou forgotten me? why go I mourning because of the oppression of the enemy?

As with a sword in my bones, mine enemies reproach me; while they say daily unto me, Where is thy God?

Why art thou cast down, O my soul? and why art thou disquieted within me? hope thou in God: for I shall yet praise him, who is the health of my countenance, and my God.

Psalm 46

God is our refuge and strength, a very present help in trouble.

Therefore will not we fear, though the earth be removed, and though the mountains be carried into the midst of the sea;

Though the waters thereof roar and be troubled, though the mountains shake with the swelling thereof.

There is a river, the streams whereof shall make glad

the city of God, the holy place of the tabernacles of the most High.

God is in the midst of her; she shall not be moved: God shall help her, and that right early.

The heathen raged, the kingdoms were moved: he uttered his voice, the earth melted.

The Lord of hosts is with us; the God of Jacob is our refuge.

Come, behold the works of the Lord, what desolations he hath made in the earth.

He maketh wars to cease unto the end of the earth; he breaketh the bow, and cutteth the spear in sunder; he burneth the chariot in the fire.

Be still, and know that I am God: I will be exalted among the heathen, I will be exalted in the earth.

The Lord of hosts is with us; the God of Jacob is our refuge.

Psalm 55

Give ear to my prayer, O God; and hide not thyself from my supplication.

Attend unto me, and hear me: I mourn in my complaint, and make a noise;

Because of the voice of the enemy, because of the oppression of the wicked: for they cast iniquity upon me, and in wrath they hate me.

My heart is sore pained within me: and the terrors of death are fallen upon me.

Fearfulness and trembling are come upon me, and horror hath overwhelmed me.

And I said, Oh that I had wings like a dove! for then would I fly away, and be at rest.

Lo, then would I wander far off, and remain in the wilderness.

I would hasten my escape from the windy storm and tempest.

Destroy, O Lord, and divide their tongues: for I have seen violence and strife in the city.

Day and night they go about it upon the walls thereof: mischief also and sorrow are in the midst of it.

Wickedness is in the midst thereof: deceit and guile depart not from her streets.

For it was not an enemy that reproached me; then I could have borne it: neither was it he that hated me that did magnify himself against me; then I would have hid myself from him:

But it was thou, a man mine equal, my guide, and mine acquaintance.

We took sweet counsel together, and walked unto the house of God in company.

Let death seize upon them, and let them go down quick into hell: for wickedness is in their dwellings, and among them.

As for me, I will call upon God; and the Lord shall save me.

Evening, and morning, and at noon, will I pray, and cry aloud: and he shall hear my voice.

He hath delivered my soul in peace from the battle that was against me: for there were many with me.

God shall hear, and afflict them, even he that abideth of old. Because they have no changes, therefore they fear not God.

He hath put forth his hands against such as be at peace with him: he hath broken his covenant.

The words of his mouth were smoother than butter, but war was in his heart: his words were softer than oil, yet were they drawn swords.

Cast thy burden upon the Lord, and he shall sustain thee: he shall never suffer the righteous to be moved.

But thou, O God, shalt bring them down into the pit of destruction: bloody and deceitful men shall not live out half their days; but I will trust in thee.

Psalm 77

I cried unto God with my voice, even unto God with my voice; and he gave ear unto me.

In the day of my trouble I sought the Lord: my sore ran in the night, and ceased not: my soul refused to be comforted.

I remembered God, and was troubled: I complained, and my spirit was overwhelmed.

Thou holdest mine eyes waking: I am so troubled that I cannot speak.

I have considered the days of old, the years of ancient times.

I call to remembrance my song in the night: I commune with mine own heart: and my spirit made diligent search.

Will the Lord cast off for ever? and will he be favorable no more?

Is his mercy clean gone for ever? doth his promise fail for evermore?

Hath God forgotten to be gracious? hath he in anger shut up his tender mercies?

And I said, This is my infirmity: but I will remember the years of the right hand of the most High.

I will remember the works of the Lord: surely I will remember thy wonders of old.

I will meditate also of all thy work, and talk of thy doings.

Thy way, O God, is in the sanctuary: who is so great a God as our God.

Thou art the God that doest wonders; thou hast declared thy strength among the people.

Thou hast with thine arm redeemed thy people, the sons of Jacob and Joseph.

The waters saw thee, O God, the waters saw thee; they were afraid: the depths also were troubled.

The clouds poured out water: the skies sent out a sound: thine arrows also went abroad.

The voice of thy thunder was in the heaven: the lightnings lightened the world: the earth trembled and shook.

Thy way is in the sea, and thy path in the great waters, and thy footsteps are not known.

Thou leddest thy people like a flock by the hand of Moses and Aaron.

Psalm 90

Lord, thou has been our dwelling place in all generations.

Before the mountains were brought forth, or ever thou hadst formed the earth and the world, even from everlasting to everlasting, thou art God.

Thou turnest man to destruction; and sayest, Return, ye children of men.

For a thousand years in thy sight are but as yesterday when it is past, and as a watch in the night.

Thou carriest them away as with a flood; they are as a sleep: in the morning they are like grass which groweth up.

In the morning it flourisheth, and groweth up; in the evening it is cut down, and withereth.

For we are consumed by thine anger, and by thy wrath are we troubled.

Thou hast set our iniquities before thee, our secret sins in the light of thy countenance.

For all our days are passed away in thy wrath: we spend our years as a tale that is told.

The days of our years are threescore years and ten: and if by reason of strength they be fourscore years, yet is their strength labor and sorrow: for it is soon cut off, and we fly away.

Who knoweth the power of thine anger? even according to thy fear, so is thy wrath.

So teach us to number our days, that we may apply our hearts unto wisdom.

Return, O Lord, how long? and let it repent thee concerning thy servants.

O satisfy us early with thy mercy; that we may rejoice and be glad all our days.

Make us glad according to the days wherein thou hast afflicted us, and the years wherein we have seen evil.

Let thy work appear unto thy servants, and thy glory unto their children.

And let the beauty of the Lord our God be upon us: and establish thou the work of our hands upon us; yea, the work of our hands establish thou it.

Psalm 91

He that dwelleth in the secret place of the most High shall abide under the shadow of the Almighty.

I will say of the Lord, He is my refuge and my fortress: my God; in him will I trust.

Surely he shall deliver thee from the snare of the fowler, and from the noisome pestilence.

He shall cover thee with his feathers, and under his wings shalt thou trust: his truth shall be thy shield and buckler.

Thou shalt not be afraid for the terror by night; nor for the arrow that flieth by day;

Nor for the pestilence that walketh in darkness; nor for the destruction that wasteth at noonday.

A thousand shall fall at thy side, and ten thousand at thy right hand; but it shall not come nigh thee.

Only with thine eyes shalt thou behold and see the reward of the wicked.

Because thou hast made the Lord, which is my refuge, even the most High, thy habitation;

There shall no evil befall thee, neither shall any plague come nigh thy dwelling.

For he shall give his angels charge over thee, to keep thee in all thy ways.

They shall bear thee up in their hands, lest thou dash thy foot against a stone.

Thou shalt tread upon the lion and adder: the young lion and the dragon shalt thou trample under feet.

Because he hath set his love upon me, therefore will I deliver him: I will set him on high, because he hath known my name.

He shall call upon me, and I will answer him: I will be with him in trouble; I will deliver him, and honor him.

With long life will I satisfy him, and shew him my salvation.

Psalm 95

O come let us sing unto the Lord: let us make a joyful noise to the rock of our salvation.

Let us come before his presence with thanksgiving, and make a joyful noise unto him with psalms.

For the Lord is a great God, and a great King above all gods.

In his hand are the deep places of the earth: the strength of the hills is his also.

The sea is his, and he made it: and his hands formed the dry land.

O come, let us worship and bow down: let us kneel before the Lord our maker.

For he is our God; and we are the people of his pasture, and the sheep of his hand. To-day if ye will hear his voice,

Harden not your heart, as in the provocation, and as in the day of temptation in the wilderness:

When your fathers tempted me, proved me, and saw my work.

Forty years long was I grieved with this generation, and said, It is a people that do err in their heart, and they have not known my ways:

Unto whom I swear in my wrath that they should not enter into my rest.

Psalm 103

Bless the Lord, O my soul: and all that is within me, bless his holy name.

Bless the Lord, O my soul, and forget not all his benefits.

Who forgiveth all thine iniquities; who healeth all thy diseases;

Who redeemeth thy life from destruction; who crowneth thee with loving kindness and tender mercies;

Who satisfieth thy mouth with good things; so that thy youth is renewed like the eagle's.

The Lord executeth righteousness and judgment for all that are oppressed.

He made known his ways unto Moses, his acts unto the children of Israel.

The Lord is merciful and gracious, slow to anger, and plenteous in mercy.

He will not always chide: neither will be keep his anger for ever.

He hath not dealt with us after our sins; nor rewarded us according to our iniquities.

For as the heaven is high above the earth, so great is his mercy towards them that fear him.

As far as the east is from the west, so far hath he removed our transgressions from us.

Like as a father pitieth his children, so the Lord pitieth them that fear him.

For he knoweth our frame; he remembereth that we are dust.

As for man, his days are as grass: as a flower of the field, so he flourisheth.

For the wind passeth over it, and it is gone; and the place thereof shall know it no more.

But the mercy of the Lord is from everlasting to everlasting upon them that fear him, and his righteousness unto children's children.

To such as keep his covenant, and to those that remember his commandments to do them.

The Lord hath prepared his throne in the heavens; and his kingdom ruleth over all.

Bless the Lord, ye his angels, that excel in strength, that do his commandments, hearkening unto the voice of his word.

Bless ye the Lord, all ye his hosts; ye ministers of his, that do his pleasure.

Bless the Lord, all his works in all places of his dominion: bless the Lord, O my soul.

Psalm 121

I will lift up mine eyes unto the hills, from whence cometh my help.

My help cometh from the Lord, which made heaven and earth.

He will not suffer thy foot to be moved: he that keepeth thee will not slumber.

Behold, he that keepeth Israel shall neither slumber nor sleep.

The Lord is thy keeper: the Lord is thy shade upon thy right hand.

The sun shall not smite thee by day, nor the moon by night.

The Lord shall preserve thee from all evil: he shall preserve thy soul.

The Lord shall preserve thy going out and thy coming in from this time forth, and even for evermore.

Psalm 133

Behold, how good and how pleasant it is for brethren to dwell together in unity!

It is like the precious ointment upon the head, that ran down upon the beard, even Aaron's beard: that went down to the skirts of his garments;

As the dew of Hermon, and as the dew that descended upon the mountains of Zion: for there the Lord commanded the blessing, even life for evermore.

Psalm 136

O give thanks unto the Lord; for he is good; for his mercy endureth for ever.

O give thanks unto the God of gods: for his mercy endureth for ever.

O give thanks to the Lord of lords: for his mercy endureth for ever.

To him who alone doeth great wonders: for his mercy endureth for ever.

To him that by wisdom made the heavens: for his mercy endureth for ever.

To him that stretched out the earth above the waters: for his mercy endureth for ever.

To him that made great lights: for his mercy endureth for ever:

The sun to rule by day: for his mercy endureth for ever:

The moon and stars to rule by night: for his mercy endureth for ever.

To him that smote Egypt in their firstborn: for his mercy endureth for ever:

And brought out Israel from among them: for his mercy endureth for ever:

With a strong hand, and with a stretched out arm: for his mercy endureth for ever.

To him which divided the Red Sea into parts: for his mercy endureth for ever:

And made Israel to pass through the midst of it: for his mercy endureth for ever:

But overthrew Pharaoh and his hosts in the Red Sea; for his mercy endureth for ever.

To him which led his people through the wilderness: for his mercy endureth for ever.

To him which smote great kings: for his mercy endureth for ever:

And slew famous kings: for his mercy endureth for ever:

Sihon king of the Amorites: for his mercy endureth for ever:

And Og the king of Bashan: for his mercy endureth for ever:

And gave their land for an heritage: for his mercy endureth for ever:

Even an heritage unto Israel his servant: for his mercy endureth for ever.

Who remembered us in our low estate: for his mercy endureth for ever:

And hath redeemed us from our enemies: for his mercy endureth for ever.

Who giveth food to all flesh: for his mercy endureth for ever.

O give thanks unto the God of heaven: for his mercy endureth for ever.

Psalm 137

By the rivers of Babylon, there we sat down, yea, we wept, then we remembered Zion.

We hanged our harps upon the willows in the midst thereof.

For there they that carried us away captive required of us a song; and they that wasted us required of us mirth, saying, Sing us one of the songs of Zion.

How shall we sing the Lord's song in a strange land?

If I forget thee, O Jerusalem, let my right hand forget her cunning.

If I do not remember thee, let my tongue cleave to the roof of my mouth: if I prefer not Jerusalem above my chief joy.

Remember, O Lord, the children of Edom in the day of Jerusalem; who said, Rase it, rase it, even to the foundation thereof.

O daughter of Babylon, who art to be destroyed: happy shall he be, that rewardeth thee as thou hast served us.

Happy shall he be, that taketh and dasheth thy little ones against the stones.

THE BOOK OF JOB

Job's Curse

Let the day perish wherein I was born, and the night in which it was said, There is a man child conceived.

Let that day be darkness; let not God regard it from above, neither let the light shine upon it.

Let darkness and the shadow of death stain it; let

a cloud dwell upon it; let the blackness of the day terrify it.

As for that night, let darkness seize upon it; let it not be joined unto the days of the year, let it not come into the number of the months.

Lo, let that night be solitary, let no joyful voice come therein.

Let them curse it that curse the day, who are ready to raise up their mourning.

Let the stars of the twilight thereof be dark; let it look for light, but have none; neither let it see the dawning of the day:

Because it shut not up the doors of my mother's womb, nor hid sorrow from mine eyes.

Why died I not from the womb? why did I not give up the ghost when I came out of the belly?

Why did the knees prevent me? or why the breasts that I should suck?

For now should I have lain still and been quiet, I should have slept: then had I been at rest.

With kings and counsellors of the earth, which built desolate places for themselves;

Or with princes that had gold, who filled their houses with silver:

Or as an hidden untimely birth I had not been; as infants which never saw light.

There the wicked cease from troubling; and there the weary be at rest.

There the prisoners rest together; they hear not the voice of the oppressor.

The small and great are there; and the servant is free from his master.

Wherefore is light given to him that is in misery, and life unto the bitter in soul;

Which long for death, but it cometh not; and dig for it more than for hid treasures;

Which rejoice exceedingly, and are glad, when they can find the grave?

Why is light given to a man whose way is hid, and whom God hath hedged in?

For my sighing cometh before I eat, and my roarings are poured out like the waters.

For the thing which I greatly feared is come upon me, and that which I was afraid of is come unto me.

I was not in safety, neither had I rest, neither was I quiet; yet trouble came.

Job's Entreaty

Man that is born of a woman is of few days, and full of trouble.

He cometh forth like a flower, and is cut down: he fleeth also as a shadow, and continueth not.

And dost thou open thine eyes upon such an one, and bringest me into judgment with thee?

Who can bring a clean thing out of an unclean? not one.

Seeing his days are determined, the number of his months are with thee, thou hast appointed his bounds that he cannot pass;

Turn from him, that he may rest, till he shall accomplish, as an hireling, his day.

For there is hope of a tree, if it be cut down, that it will sprout again, and that the tender branch thereof will not cease.

Though the root thereof wax old in the earth, and the stock thereof die in the ground;

Yet through the scent of water it will bud, and bring forth boughs like a plant.

But man dieth, and wasteth away: yea, man giveth up the ghost, and where is he?

As the waters fail from the sea, and the flood decayeth and drieth up:

So man lieth down, and riseth not: till the heavens be no more, they shall not awake, nor be raised out of their sleep.

O that thou wouldest hide me in the grave, that thou

wouldest keep me secret, until thy wrath be past, that thou wouldest appoint me a set time, and remember me!

If a man die, shall he live again? all the days of my appointed time will I wait, till my change come.

Thou shalt call, and I will answer thee: thou wilt have a desire to the work of thine hands.

For now thou numberest my steps: dost thou not watch over my sin?

My transgression is sealed up in a bag, and thou sewest up mine iniquity.

And surely the mountain falling cometh to nought, and the rock is removed out of his place.

The waters wear the stones: thou washest away the things which grow out of the dust of the earth: and thou destroyest the hope of man.

Thou prevailest for ever against him, and he passeth: thou changest his countenance, and sendest him away.

His sons come to honor, and he knoweth it not; and they are brought low, but he perceiveth it not of them.

But his flesh upon him shall have pain, and his soul within him shall mourn.

Then the Lord Answered

Who is this that darkeneth counsel by words without knowledge?

Gird up now thy loins like a man; for I will demand of thee, and answer thou me.

Where wast thou when I laid the foundations of the earth? declare, if thou hast understanding.

Who hath laid the measures thereof, if thou knowest? or who hath stretched the line upon it?

Whereupon are the foundations thereof fastened? or who laid the corner stone thereof;

When the morning stars sang together, and all the sons of God shouted for joy?

Or who shut up the sea with doors, when it brake forth, as if it had issued out of the womb?

When I made the cloud the garment thereof, and thick darkness a swaddling band for it,

And brake up for it my decreed place, and set bars and doors,

And said, Hitherto shalt thou come, but no further: and here shall thy proud waves be stayed?

Hast thou commanded the morning since thy days; and caused the dayspring to know his place;

That it might take hold of the ends of the earth, that the wicked might be shaken out of it?

It is turned as clay to the seal; and they stand as a garment.

And from the wicked their light is withholden, and the high arm shall be broken.

Hast thou entered into the springs of the sea? or hast thou walked in the search of the depth?

Have the gates of death been opened unto thee? or hast thou seen the doors of the shadow of death?

Hast thou perceived the breadth of the earth; declare if thou knowest it all.

Where is the way where light dwelleth? and as for darkness, where is the place thereof,

That thou shouldest take it to the bound thereof, and that thou shouldest know the paths to the house thereof?

Knowest thou it, because thou wast then born? or because the number of thy days is great?

Hast thou entered into the treasures of the snow? or hast thou seen the treasures of the hail,

Which I have reserved against the time of trouble, against the day of battle and war?

By what way is the light parted, which scattereth the east wind upon the earth?

Who hath divided a water-course for the overflowing of waters, or a way for the lightning of thunder;

To cause it to rain on the earth, where no man is; on the wilderness, wherein there is no man;

To satisfy the desolate and waste ground; and to cause the bud of the tender herb to spring forth?

Hath the rain a father? or who hath begotten the drops of dew?

Out of whose womb came the ice? and the hoary frost of heaven, who hath gendered it?

The waters are hid as with a stone, and the face of the deep is frozen.

Canst thou bind the sweet influences of Pleiades, or loose the bands of Orion?

Canst thou bring forth Mazzaroth in his season? or canst thou guide Arcturus with his sons?

Knowest thou the ordinances of heaven? canst thou set the dominion thereof in the earth?

Canst thou lift up thy voice to the clouds, that abundance of waters may cover thee?

Canst thou send lightnings, that they may go, and say unto thee, Here we are?

Who hath put wisdom in the inward parts? or who hath given understanding to the heart?

Who can number the clouds in wisdom? or who can stay the bottles of heaven,

When the dust groweth into hardness, and the clods cleave fast together?

Wilt thou hunt the prey for the lion? or fill the appetite of the young lions,

When they couch in their dens, and abide in the covert to lie in wait?

Who provideth for the raven his food? when his young ones cry unto God, they wander for lack of meat.

KNOWEST thou the time when the wild goats of the rock bring forth? or canst thou mark when the hinds do calve?

Canst thou number the months that they fulfill? or knowest thou the time when they bring forth?

They bow themselves, they bring forth their young ones, they cast out their sorrows.

Their young ones are in good liking, they grow up with corn; they go forth, and return not unto them.

Who hath sent out the wild ass free? or who hath loosed the bands of the wild ass?

Whose house I have made the wilderness, and the barren land his dwellings.

He scorneth the multitude of the city, neither regardeth he the crying of the driver.

The range of the mountains is his pasture, and he searcheth after every green thing.

Will the unicorn be willing to serve thee, or abide by the crib?

Canst thou bind the unicorn with his band in the furrow? or will he harrow the valleys after thee?

Wilt thou trust him, because his strength is great? or wilt thou leave thy labor to him?

Wilt thou believe him, that he will bring home thy seed, and gather it into thy barn?

Gavest thou the goodly wings unto the peacocks? or wings and feathers unto the ostrich?

Which leaveth her eggs in the earth, and warmeth them in dust,

And forgetteth that the foot may crush them, or that the wild beast may break them.

She is hardened against her young ones, as though they were not her's: her labor is in vain without fear:

Because God hath deprived her of wisdom, neither hath he imparted to her understanding.

What time she lifteth up herself on high, she scorneth the horse and his rider.

Hast thou given the horse strength? hast thou clothed his neck with thunder?

Canst thou make him afraid as a grasshopper? the glory of his nostrils is terrible.

He paweth in the valley, and rejoiceth in his strength: he goeth on to meet the armed men.

He mocketh at fear, and is not affrighted; neither turneth he back from the sword.

The quiver rattleth against him, the glittering spear and the shield.

He swalloweth the ground with fierceness and rage: neither believeth he that it is the sound of the trumpet.

He saith among the trumpets, Ha, ha; and he smelleth the battle afar off, the thunder of the captains, and the shouting.

Doth the hawk fly by thy wisdom, and stretch her wings toward the south?

Doth the eagle mount up at thy command, and make her nest on high?

She dwelleth and abideth on the rock, upon the crag of the rock, and the strong place.

From thence she seeketh the prey, and her eyes behold afar off.

Her young ones also suck up blood: and where the slain are, there is she.

Out of the Whirlwind

Gird up thy loins now like a man: I will demand of thee, and declare thou unto me.

Wilt thou also disannul my judgment? wilt thou condemn me, that thou mayest be righteous?

Hast thou an arm like God? or canst thou thunder with a voice like him?

Deck thyself now with majesty and excellency; and array thyself with glory and beauty.

Cast abroad the rage of thy wrath: and behold every one that is proud, and abase him.

Look on every one that is proud, and bring him low; and tread down the wicked in their place.

Hide them in the dust together; and bind their faces in secret.

Then will I also confess unto thee that thine own right hand can save thee.

Behold now behemoth, which I made with thee; he eateth grass as an ox.

Lo now, his strength is in his loins, and his force is in the navel of his belly.

He moveth his tail like a cedar: the sinews of his stones are wrapped together.

His bones are as strong pieces of brass; his bones are like bars of iron.

He is the chief of the ways of God: he that made him can make his sword to approach unto him.

Surely the mountains bring him forth food, where all the beasts of the field play.

He lieth under the shady trees, in the covert of the reed, and fens.

The shady trees cover him with their shadow; the willows of the brook compass him about.

Behold he drinketh up a river, and hasteth not: he trusteth that he can draw up Jordan into his mouth.

He taketh it with his eyes: his nose pierceth through snares.

Canst thou draw out leviathan with an hook? or his tongue with a cord which thou lettest down?

Canst thou put an hook into his nose? or bore his jaw through with a thorn?

Will he make many supplications unto thee? will he speak soft words unto thee?

Will he make a covenant with thee? wilt thou take him for a servant for ever?

Wilt thou play with him as with a bird? or wilt thou bind him for thy maidens?

Shall the companions make a banquet of him? shall they part him among the merchants?

Canst thou fill his skin with barbed irons? or his head with fish spears?

Lay thine hand upon him, remember the battle, do no more.

Behold, the hope of him is in vain: shall not one be cast down even at the sight of him?

None is so fierce that dare stir him up: who then is able to stand before me?

Who hath prevented me, that I should repay him? whatsoever is under the whole heaven is mine.

I will not conceal his parts, nor his power, nor his comely proportion.

Who can discover the face of his garment? or who can come to him with his double bridle?

Who can open the doors of his face? his teeth are terrible round about.

His scales are his pride, shut up together as with a close seal.

One is so near to another, that no air can come between them.

They are joined one to another, they stick together, that they cannot be sundered.

By his neesings a light doth shine, and his eyes are like the eyelids of the morning.

Out of his mouth go burning lamps, and sparks of fire leap out.

Out of his nostrils goeth smoke, as out of a seething pot or caldron.

His breath kindleth coals, and a flame goeth out of his mouth.

In his neck remaineth strength and sorrow is turned into joy before him.

The flakes of his flesh are joined together: they are firm in themselves; they cannot be moved.

His heart is as firm as a stone; yea, as hard as a piece of the nether millstone.

When he raiseth up himself, the mighty are afraid; by reason of breakings they purify themselves.

The sword of him that layeth at him cannot hold: the spear, the dart, nor the habergeon.

He esteemeth iron as straw, and brass as rotten wood.

The arrow cannot make him flee: slingstones are turned with him into stubble.

Darts are counted as stubble: he laugheth at the shaking of a spear.

Sharp stones are under him: he spreadeth sharp pointed things upon the mire.

He maketh the deep to boil like a pot: he maketh the sea like a pot of ointment.

He maketh a path to shine after him; one would think the deep to be hoary.

Upon earth there is not his like, who is made without fear.

He beholdeth all high things: he is a king over all the children of pride.

ECCLESIASTES

Cast Thy Bread upon the Waters

Cast thy bread upon the waters: for thou shalt find it after many days.

Give a portion to seven, and also to eight; for thou knowest not what evil shall be upon the earth.

If the clouds be full of rain, they empty themselves upon the earth: and if the tree fall toward the south, or toward the north, in the place where the tree falleth, there it shall be.

He that observeth the wind shall not sow; and he that regardeth the clouds shall not reap.

As thou knowest not what is the way of the spirit, nor how the bones do grow in the womb of her that is with child: even so thou knowest not the works of God who maketh all.

In the morning sow thy seed, and in the evening withhold not thine hand: for thou knowest not whether shall prosper, either this or that, or whether they both shall be alike good.

Remember Now Thy Creator

Remember now thy Creator in the days of thy youth, while the evil days come not, nor the years draw nigh, when thou shalt say, I have no pleasure in them;

While the sun, or the light, or the moon, or the stars, be not darkened, nor the clouds return after the rain:

In the day when the keepers of the house shall tremble, and the strong men shall bow themselves, and the grinders cease because they are few, and those that look out of the windows be darkened,

And the doors shall be shut in the streets, when the sound of the grinding is low, and he shall rise up at the voice of the bird, and all the daughters of music shall be brought low;

Also when they shall be afraid of that which is high, and fears shall be in the way, and the almond tree shall flourish, and the grasshopper shall be a burden, and desire shall fail: because man goeth to his long home, and the mourners go about the streets:

Or ever the silver cord be loosed, or the golden bowl be broken, or the pitcher be broken at the fountain, or the wheel broken at the cistern.

Then shall the dust return to the earth as it was: and the spirit shall return unto God who gave it.

THE SONG OF SONGS

I

LET him kiss me with the kisses of his mouth: for thy love is better than wine.

Because of the savor of thy good ointments thy name is as ointment poured forth, therefore do the virgins love thee.

Draw me, we will run after thee: the king hath brought me into his chambers: we will be glad and rejoice in thee, we will remember thy love more than wine: the upright love thee.

I am black, but comely, O ye daughters of Jerusalem, as the tents of Kedar, as the curtains of Solomon.

Look not upon me, because I am black, because the sun hath looked upon me: my mother's children were angry with me; they made me the keeper of the vineyards; but mine own vineyard have I not kept.

Tell me, O thou whom my soul loveth, where thou feedest, where thou makest thy flock to rest at noon: for why should I be as one that turneth aside by the flocks of thy companions?

If thou know not, O thou fairest among women, gc thy way forth by the footsteps of the flock, and feed thy kids beside the shepherds' tents.

I have compared thee, O my love, to a company of horses in Pharaoh's chariots.

Thy cheeks are comely with rows of jewels, thy neck with chains of gold.

We will make thee borders of gold with studs of silver.

While the king sitteth at his table, my spikenard sendeth forth the smell thereof.

A bundle of myrrh is my well-beloved unto me; he shall lie all night betwixt my breasts.

My beloved is unto me as a cluster of camphire in the vineyards of En-gedi.

Behold, thou art fair, my love; behold, thou art fair; thou hast doves' eyes.

Behold, thou art fair, my beloved, yea, pleasant: also our bed is green.

The beams of our house are cedar, and our rafters of fir.

2

I AM the rose of Sharon, and the lily of the valleys.

As the lily among thorns, so is my love among the daughters.

As the apple tree among the trees of the wood, so is my beloved among the sons. I sat down under his shadow with great delight, and his fruit was sweet to my taste.

He brought me to the banqueting house, and his banner over me was love.

Stay me with flagons, comfort me with apples: for I am sick of love.

His left hand is under my head, and his right hand doth embrace me.

I charge you, O ye daughters of Jerusalem, by the roes, and by the hinds of the field, that ye stir not up, nor awake my love, till he please.

The voice of my beloved! behold, he cometh leaping upon the mountains, skipping upon the hills.

My beloved is like a roe or a young hart: behold, he standeth behind our wall, he looketh forth at the windows, shewing himself through the lattice.

My beloved spake, and said unto me, Rise up, my love, my fair one, and come away.

For, lo, the winter is past, the rain is over and gone;

The flowers appear on the earth; the time of the singing of birds is come, and the voice of the turtle is heard in our land;

The fig tree putteth forth her green figs, and the vines with the tender grape give a good smell. Arise, my love, my fair one, and come away.

O my dove, that art in the clefts of the rock, in the secret places of the stairs, let me see thy countenance, let me hear thy voice; for sweet is thy voice, and thy countenance is comely.

Take us the foxes, the little foxes, that spoil the vines: for our vines have tender grapes.

My beloved is mine, and I am his he feedeth among the lilies.

Until the day break, and the shadows flee away, turn, my beloved, and be thou like a roe or a young hart upon the mountains of Bether.

3

By night on my bed I sought him whom my soul loveth: I sought him, but I found him not.

I will rise now, and go about the city in the streets, and in the broad ways I will seek him whom my soul loveth: I sought him, but I found him not.

The watchmen that go about the city found me: to whom I said, Saw ye him whom my soul loveth?

It was but a little that I passed from them, but I found him whom my soul loveth: I held him, and would not let him go, until I had brought him into my mother's house, and into the chamber of her that conceived me.

I charge you, O ye daughters of Jerusalem, by the roes, and by the hinds of the field, that ye stir not up, nor wake my love, till he please.

Who is this that cometh out of the wilderness like pillars of smoke, perfumed with myrrh and frankincense, with all powders of the merchant?

Behold his bed, which is Solomon's; three score valiant men are about it, of the valiant of Israel.

They all hold swords, being expert in war: every man hath his sword upon his thigh because of fear in the night.

King Solomon made himself a chariot of the wood of Lebanon.

He made the pillars thereof of silver, the bottom thereof of gold, the covering of it of purple, the midst thereof being paved with love, for the daughters of Jerusalem.

Go forth, O ye daughters of Zion, and behold king Solomon with the crown wherewith his mother crowned him in the day of his espousals, and in the day of the gladness of his heart.

4

BEHOLD, thou art fair, my love; behold, thou art fair; thou hast doves' eyes within thy locks: thy hair is as a flock of goats, that appear from mount Gilead.

Thy teeth are like a flock of sheep that are even shorn, which came up from the washing; whereof every one bear twins, and none is barren among them.

Thy lips are like a thread of scarlet, and thy speech is comely: thy temples are like a piece of a pomegranate within thy locks.

Thy neck is like the tower of David builded for an armory, whereon there hang a thousand bucklers, all shields of mighty men.

Thy two breasts are like two young roes that are twins, which feed among the lilies.

Until the day break, and the shadows flee away, I

will get me to the mountains of myrrh, and to the hill of frankincense.

Thou art all fair, my love; there is no spot in thee.

Come with me from Lebanon, my spouse, with me from Lebanon: look from the top of Amana, from the top of Shenir and Hermon, from the lions' dens, from the mountains of the leopards.

Thou hast ravished my heart, my sister, my spouse; thou hast ravished my heart with one of thine eyes, with one chain of thy neck.

How fair is thy love, my sister, my spouse! how much better is thy love than wine! and the smell of thine ointments than all spices!

Thy lips, O my spouse, drop as the honey-comb: honey and milk are under thy tongue; and the smell of thy garments is like the smell of Lebanon.

A garden inclosed is my sister, my spouse; a spring shut up, a fountain sealed.

Thy plants are an orchard of pomegranates, with pleasant fruits; camphire, with spikenard,

Spikenard and saffron; calamus and cinnamon, with all trees of frankincense; myrrh and aloes, with all the chief spices:

A fountain of gardens, a well of living waters, and streams from Lebanon.

Awake, O north wind; and come, thou south; blow upon my garden, that the spices thereof may flow out. Let my beloved come into his garden, and eat his pleasant fruits.

5

I AM come into my garden, my sister, my spouse: I have gathered my myrrh with my spice; I have eaten my honeycomb with my honey; I have drunk my wine with my milk: eat, O friends; drink, yea, drink abundantly, O beloved.

I sleep, but my heart waketh: it is the voice of my

beloved that knocketh, saying, Open to me, my sister, my love, my dove, my undefiled: for my head is filled with dew, and my locks with the drops of the night.

I have put off my coat; how shall I put it on? I have washed my feet; how shall I defile them?

My beloved put in his hand by the hole of the door, and my bowels were moved for him.

I rose up to open to my beloved; and my hands dropped with myrrh, and my fingers with sweet smelling myrrh, upon the handles of the lock.

I opened to my beloved; but my beloved had withdrawn himself, and was gone: my soul failed when he spake: I sought him, but I could not find him; I called him, but he gave me no answer.

The watchmen that went about the city found me, they smote me, they wounded me; the keepers of the walls took away my veil from me.

I charge you, O daughters of Jerusalem, if ye find my beloved, that ye tell him, that I am sick of love.

What is thy beloved more than another beloved, O thou fairest among women? what is thy beloved more than another beloved, that thou dost so charge us?

My beloved is white and ruddy, the chiefest among ten thousand.

His head is as the most fine gold, his locks are bushy, and black as a raven.

His eyes are as the eyes of doves by the rivers of waters, washed with milk, and fitly set.

His cheeks are as a bed of spices, as sweet flowers: his lips like lilies, dropping sweet smelling myrrh.

His hands are as gold rings set with the beryl: his belly is as bright ivory overlaid with sapphires.

His legs are as pillars of marble, set upon sockets of fine gold: his countenance is as Lebanon, excellent as the cedars.

His mouth is most sweet: yea, he is altogether lovely. This is my beloved, and this is my friend, O daughters of Jerusalem.

6

Whither is thy beloved gone, O thou fairest among women? whither is thy beloved turned aside? that we may seek him with thee.

My beloved is gone down into his garden, to the beds of spices, to feed in the gardens, and to gather lilies.

I am my beloved's, and my beloved is mine: he feedeth among the lilies.

Thou art beautiful, O my love, as Tirzah, comely as Jerusalem, terrible as an army with banners.

Turn away thine eyes from me, for they have overcome me: thy hair is as a flock of goats that appear from Gilead.

Thy teeth are as a flock of sheep which go up from the washing, whereof every one beareth twins, and there is not one barren among them.

As a piece of a pomegranate are thy temples within thy locks.

There are threescore queens, and fourscore concubines, and virgins without number.

My dove, my undefiled is but one; she is the only one of her mother, she is the choice one of her that bare her. The daughters saw her, and blessed her; yea, the queens and the concubines, and they praised her.

Who is she that looketh forth as the morning, fair as the moon, clear as the sun, and terrible as an army with banners?

I went down into the garden of nuts to see the fruits of the valley, and to see whether the vine flourished, and the pomegranates budded.

Or ever I was aware, my soul made me like the chariots of Ammi-nadib.

Return, return, O Shulamite; return, return, that we may look upon thee. What will ye see in the Shulamite? As it were the company of two armies.

7

How beautiful are thy feet with shoes, O prince's daughter! the joints of thy thighs are like jewels, the work of the hands of a cunning workman.

Thy navel is like a round goblet, which wanteth not liquor: thy belly is like an heap of wheat set about with lilies.

Thy two breasts are like two young roes that are twins.

Thy neck is as a tower of ivory; thine eyes like the fishpools in Heshbon, by the gate of Bathrabbim: thy nose is as the tower of Lebanon which looketh toward Damascus.

Thine head upon thee is like Carmel, and the hair of thine head like purple; the king is held in the galleries.

How fair and how pleasant are thou, O love, for delights!

This thy stature is like to a palm tree, and thy breasts to clusters of grapes.

I said, I will go up to the palm tree, I will take hold of the boughs thereof: now also thy breasts shall be as clusters of the vine, and the smell of thy nose like apples;

And the roof of thy mouth like the best wine for my beloved, that goeth down sweetly, causing the lips of those that are asleep to speak.

I am my beloved's, and his desire is toward me.

Come, my beloved, let us go forth into the field; let us lodge in the villages.

Let us get up early to the vineyards; let us see if the vine flourish, whether the tender grape appear, and the pomegranates bud forth: there will I give thee my loves.

The mandrakes give a smell, and at our gates are all manner of pleasant fruits, new and old, which I have laid up for thee, O my beloved.

8

O THAT thou wert as my brother, that sucked the breasts of my mother! when I should find thee without, I would kiss thee; yea, I should not be despised.

I would lead thee, and bring thee into my mother's house, who would instruct me: I would cause thee to drink of spiced wine of the juice of my pomegranate.

His left hand should be under my head, and his right hand should embrace me.

I charge you, O daughters of Jerusalem, that ye stir not up, nor awake my love, until he please.

Who is that cometh up from the wilderness, leaning upon her beloved? I raised thee up under the apple tree: there thy mother brought thee forth: there she brought thee forth that bare thee.

Set me as a seal upon thine heart, as a seal upon thine arm: for love is strong as death; jealousy is cruel as the grave: the coals thereof are coals of fire, which hath a most vehement flame.

Many waters cannot quench love, neither can the floods drown it: if a man would give all the substance of his house for love, it would utterly be contemned.

We have a little sister, and she hath no breasts: what shall we do for our sister in the day when she shall be spoken for?

If she be a wall, we will build upon her a palace of silver: and if she be a door, we will inclose her with boards of cedar.

I am a wall, and my breasts like towers: then was I in his eyes as one that found favor.

Solomon had a vineyard at Baalhamon; he let out the vineyard unto keepers; every one for the fruit thereof was to bring a thousand pieces of silver.

My vineyard, which is mine, is before me: thou, O Solomon, must have a thousand, and those that keep the fruit thereof two hundred.

Thou that dwellest in the gardens, the companions hearken to thy voice: cause me to hear it.

Make haste, my beloved, and be thou like to a roe or to a young hart upon the mountains of spices.

ISAIAH

The Messiah

Behold, a virgin shall conceive, and bear a son, and shall call his name Immanuel.

Butter and honey shall he eat, that he may know to refuse the evil, and choose the good.

For before the child shall know to refuse the evil, and choose the good, the land that thou abhorrest shall be forsaken of both her kings.

The Lord shall bring upon thee, and upon thy people, and upon thy father's house, days that have not come, from the day that Ephraim departed from Judah; even the king of Assyria.

And it shall come to pass in that day, that the Lord shall hiss for the fly that is in the uttermost part of the rivers of Egypt, and for the bee that is in the land of Assyria.

And they shall come, and shall rest all of them in the desolate valleys, and in the holes of the rocks, and upon all thorns, and upon all bushes.

In the same day shall the Lord shave with a razor that is hired, namely, by them beyond the river, by the king of Assyria, the head, and the hair of the feet: and it shall also consume the beard.

And it shall come to pass in that day, that a man shall nourish a young cow, and two sheep;

And it shall come to pass, for the abundance of milk that they shall give he shall eat butter: for butter and honey shall every one eat that is left in the land.

And it shall come to pass in that day, that every place shall be, where there were a thousand vines at a thousand silverlings, it shall even be for briers and thorns.

With arrows and with bows shall men come thither; because all the land shall become briers and thorns.

And on all hills that shall be digged with the mattock, there shall not come thither the fear of briers and thorns: but it shall be for the sending forth of oxen, and for the treading of lesser cattle.

THE ROD OF JESSE

AND there shall come forth a rod out of the stem of Jesse, and a Branch shall grow out of his roots:

And the spirit of the Lord shall rest upon him, the spirit of wisdom and understanding, the spirit of counsel and might, the spirit of knowledge and the fear of the Lord;

And shall make him of quick understanding in the fear of the Lord: and he shall not judge after the sight of his eyes, neither reprove after the hearing of his ears:

But with righteousness shall he judge the poor, and reprove with equity for the meek of the earth: and he shall smite the earth with the rod of his mouth, and with the breath of his lips shall he slay the wicked.

And righteousness shall be the girdle of his loins, and faithfulness the girdle of his reins.

The wolf also shall dwell with the lamb, and the leopard shall lie down with the kid; and the calf and the young lion and the fatling together; and a little child shall lead them.

And the cow and the bear shall feed; their young ones shall lie down together: and the lion shall eat straw like the ox.

And the sucking child shall play on the hole of the asp, and the weaned child shall put his hand on the cockatrice' den.

They shall not hurt nor destroy in all my holy mountain: for the earth shall be full of the knowledge of the Lord, as the waters cover the sea.

And in that day there shall be a root of Jesse, which shall stand for an ensign of the people; to it shall the Gentiles seek: and his rest shall be glorious.

Watchman, What of the Night?

He calleth to me out of Seir, Watchman, what of the night? Watchman, what of the night?

The watchman said, The morning cometh, and also the night: if ye will enquire, enquire ye: return, come.

In the forest in Arabia shall ye lodge, O ye traveling companies of Dedanim.

The inhabitants of the land of Tema brought water to him that was thirsty, they prevented with their bread him that fled.

For they fled from the swords, from the drawn sword, and from the bent bow, and from the grievousness of war.

JEREMIAH

The Misery of Jerusalem

How doth the city sit solitary, that was full of people! how is she become as a widow! she that was great among the nations, and princess among the provinces, how is she become tributary!

She weepeth sore in the night, and her tears are on her cheeks: among all her lovers she hath none to comfort her: all her friends have dealt treacherously with her, they are become her enemies.

Judah is gone into capitivity because of affliction, and because of great servitude: she dwelleth among the heathen, she findeth no rest: all her persecutors overtook her between the straits.

The ways of Zion do mourn, because none come to the solemn feasts: all her gates are desolate: her priests sigh, her virgins are afflicted, and she is in bitterness.

Her adversaries are the chief, her enemies prosper; for the Lord hath afflicted her for the multitude of her transgressions: her children are gone into captivity before the enemy.

And from the daughter of Zion all her beauty is departed: her princes are become like harts that find no pasture, and they are gone without strength before the pursuer.

Jerusalem remembered in the days of her affliction and of her miseries all her pleasant things that she had in the days of old, when her people fell into the hand of the enemy, and none did help her: the adversaries saw her, and did mock at her sabbaths.

Jerusalem hath grievously sinned; therefore she is removed: all that honored her despise her, because they have seen her nakedness: yea, she sigheth, and turneth backward.

Her filthiness is in her skirts; she remembereth not her last end; therefore she came down wonderfully; she had no comforter. O Lord, behold my affliction: for the enemy hath magnified himself.

The adversary hath spread out his hand upon all her pleasant things: for she hath seen that the heathen entered into her sanctuary, whom thou didst command that they should not enter into thy congregation.

All her people sigh, they seek bread; they have given their pleasant things for meat to relieve the soul: see, O Lord, and consider; for I am become vile.

Is it nothing to you, all ye that pass by? behold, and see if there be any sorrow like unto my sorrow, which is done unto me, wherewith the Lord hath afflicted me in the day of his fierce anger.

From above hath he sent fire into my bones, and it prevaileth against them: he hath spread a net for my feet, he hath turned me back: he hath made me desolate and faint all the day.

The yoke of my transgressions is bound by his hand: they are wreathed, and come up upon my neck: he hath made my strength to fall, the Lord hath delivered me into their hands, from whom I am not able to rise up.

The Lord hath trodden under foot all my mighty men in the midst of me: he hath called an assembly against me to crush my young men: the Lord hath trodden the virgin, the daughter of Judah, as in a winepress.

For these things I weep; mine eye, mine eye runneth down with water, because the comforter that should relieve my soul is far from me: my children are desolate, because the enemy prevailed.

Zion spread forth her hands, and there is none to comfort her: the Lord hath commanded concerning Jacob, that his adversaries should be round about him: Jerusalem is as a menstruous woman among them.

The Lord is righteous; for I have rebelled against his commandment: hear, I pray you, all people, and behold my sorrow: my virgins and my young men are gone into captivity.

I called for my lovers, but they deceived me: my priests and mine elders gave up the ghost in the city, while they sought their meat to relieve their souls.

Behold, O Lord; for I am in distress: my bowels are troubled; mine heart is turned within me; for I have grievously rebelled: abroad the sword bereaveth, at home there is as death.

They have heard that I sigh: there is none to comfort me: all mine enemies have heard of my trouble; they are glad that thou hast done it; thou wilt bring the day that thou hast called, and they shall be like unto me.

Let all their wickedness come before thee; and do unto them, as thou hast done unto me for all my transgressions: for my sighs are many, and my heart is faint.

ZECHARIAH

Open Thy Doors, O Lebanon

Open thy doors, O Lebanon, that the fire may devour thy cedars.

Howl, fir tree; for the cedar is fallen; because the mighty are spoiled: howl, O ye oaks of Bashan: for the forest of the vintage is come down.

There is a voice of the howling of the shepherds; for

their glory is spoiled: a voice of the roaring of young lions; for the pride of Jordan is spoiled.

Thus saith the Lord my God; Feed the flock of the slaughter;

Whose possessors slay them, and hold themselves not guilty: and they that sell them say, Blessed be the Lord; for I am rich: and their own shepherds pity them not.

For I will not more pity the inhabitants of the land, saith the Lord: but, lo, I will deliver the men every one into his neighbor's hand, and into the hand of his king: and they shall smite the land, and out of their hand I will not deliver them.

And I will feed the flock of slaughter, even you, O poor of the flock. And I took unto me two staves; the one I called Beauty, and the other I called Bands; and I fed the flock.

Three shepherds also I cut off in one month; and my soul loathed them, and their soul also abhorred me.

Then said I, I will not feed you: that that dieth, let it die; and that that is to be cut off, let it be cut off; and let the rest eat every one the flesh of another.

And I took my staff, even Beauty, and cut it asunder, that I might break my covenant which I had made with all the people.

And it was broken in that day: and so the poor of the flock that waited upon me knew that it was the word of the Lord.

And I said unto them, If ye think good, give me my price; and if not forbear. So they weighed for my price thirty pieces of silver.

And the Lord said unto me, Cast it unto the potter: a goodly price that I was prised at of them. And I took the thirty pieces of silver and cast them to the potter in the house of the Lord.

Then I cut asunder mine other staff, even Bands, that I might break the brotherhood between Judah and Israel.

(King James Version)

Solomon Ibn Gabirol

1021–1058

THE ROYAL CROWN

I

Wonderful are thy works, as my soul overwhelmingly knoweth.

Thine, O Lord, are the greatness and the might, the beauty and the triumph and the splendor.

Thine, O Lord, is the Kingdom, and Thou art exalted as head over all.

Thine are the riches and honor. Thine the creatures of the heights and depths.

They bear witness that they perish, while Thou endurest.

Thine is the might in whose mystery our thoughts can find no stay, so far art Thou beyond us. . . .

Thine is the loving-kindness that ruleth over all Thy creatures, and the good treasured up for those who fear Thee.

Thine are the mysteries that transcend understanding and thought. . . .

Thine is the existence from the shadow of whose light every being was created,

Of which we say, in His shadow we live.

Thine are the two worlds between which Thou hast set a boundary,

The first for deeds and the second for reward. . . .

II

Thou art One, the first of every number, and the foundation of every structure.

Thou art One, and at the mystery of Thy Oneness the wise of heart are struck dumb,

For they know not what it is.

Thou art One, and Thy Oneness can neither be increased nor lessened,

It lacketh naught, nor doth aught remain over.

Thou art One, but not like a unit to be grasped or counted,

For number and change cannot reach Thee.

Thou art not to be envisaged, nor to be figured thus and thus. . . .

III

Thou existest, but hearing of ear cannot reach Thee, nor vision of eye,

Nor shall the How have sway over Thee, nor the Wherefore and Whence.

Thou existest, but for Thyself and for none other with Thee.

Thou existest, and before Time began Thou wast,

And without place Thou didst abide.

Thou existest, and Thy secret is hidden and who shall attain to it?

"So deep, so deep, who can discover it?"

IV

Thou livest, but not from any restricted season nor from any known period.

Thou livest, but not through breath and soul, for Thou art soul of the soul.

Thou livest, but not with the life of man, which is like unto vanity and its end the moth and the worm.

Thou livest, and he who layeth hold of Thy secret shall find eternal delight:

"He shall eat and live for ever."

V

Thou are great, and compared with Thy greatness all greatness is humbled and all excess diminished.

Incalculably great is Thy being,

Superber than the starry heaven,
Beyond and above all grandeur,
"And exalted beyond all blessing and praise." . . .

VII

Thou are Light celestial, and the eyes of the pure shall behold Thee,

But the clouds of sin shall veil Thee from the eyes of the sinners.

Thou art Light, hidden in this world but to be revealed in the visible world on high. . . .

VIII

Thou art God, and all things formed are Thy servants and worshipers.

Yet is not Thy glory diminished by reason of those that worship aught beside Thee,

For the yearning of them all is to draw nigh Thee,
But they are like the blind,
Setting their faces forward on the King's highway,
Yet still wandering from the path.
One sinketh into the well of a pit,
And another falleth into a snare,
But all imagine they have reached their desire,
Albeit they have suffered in vain.

But Thy servants are those walking clear-eyed in the straight path,

Turning neither to the right nor the left,
Till they come to the court of the King's palace.

Thou art God, by Thy Godhead sustaining all that hath been formed,

And upholding in Thy Unity all creatures.

Thou art God and there is no distinction betwixt Thy Godhead and Thy Unity, Thy pre-existence and Thy existence,

For 'tis all one mystery,
And although the name of each be different,
"Yet they are all proceeding to one place."

IX

Thou art wise. And wisdom is the fount of life and from Thee it welleth,
And by the side of Thy wisdom all human knowledge turneth to folly.
Thou art wise, more ancient than all primal things,
And wisdom was the nursling at Thy side.
Thou art wise, and Thou hast not learnt from any beside Thee,
Nor acquired wisdom from any save Thyself.
Thou art wise, and from Thy wisdom Thou hast set apart Thy appointed purpose,
Like a craftsman and an artist,
To draw up the films of being from Nothingness
As light is drawn that darteth from the eye:
Without bucket from the fountain of light hath Thy workmen drawn it up,
And without tool hath he wrought. . . .

XXIV

Who shall understand the mysteries of Thy creations?
For Thou hast exalted above the ninth sphere the sphere of intelligence.

It is the Temple confronting us
"The tenth that shall be sacred to the Lord."
It is the Sphere transcending height,
To which conception cannot reach,
And there stands the veiled palanquin of Thy glory.
From the silver of Truth hast Thou cast it,
And of the gold of Reason hast Thou wrought its arms,
And on a pillar of Righteousness set its cushions,
And from Thy power is its existence,
And from and toward Thee its yearning,
"And unto Thee shall be its desire."

(Israel Zangwill)

Judah Ha-Levi

1085–1140

TO ZION

Art thou not hungry for thy children, Zion,—
Thy sons far-scattered through an alien world?
From earth's four corners, over land and sea,
The heavy-hearted remnant of thy flock
Now send thee greeting: "Know that as the dew
Falls daily on the ancient slopes of Hermon,
So daily on the faces of thy children
Tears of vain-longing fall." And as for me,
When I remember thee, the Desolate,
My voice is like the jackal's in the night,
A wailing and a lamentation old;
But when a dream of resurrection wakes—
A momentary glory—then my voice
Breaks like the harp's into a jubilant ringing.
Thy names are on my lips, and in my heart
Restless desire: Beth-El, Mach'nayim, P'niel—
Assemblies once of the elect—on you
The glory of His name was shed, for you
The gates were open flung, and with a light
Neither of sun, moon, stars, your beauty shone.
Where on the dearest of His chosen ones
God poured his spirit, let me pour my heart.
I will pass to Hebron, where the ancient graves
Still wait for me, and wander in the dusk
Of the forests of Carmel. I will go to Gilead
And from Gilead pass to Habarim and Hor,
And stand upon the summit of the mountains
Where once the unforgotten brothers stood
And the light of them was seen throughout the world.
There let me fall to earth and press my lips
Into the dust, and weep thy desolation
Till I am blind, and, blind, still comfort thee.
I would to God that I were turned to dust

So that the wind could scatter me upon thee.
What comfort is in life for me, since now
Thine eagles have become the prey of vultures?
What pleasure in the light of day, since now
Thy lions, dead, are less than living dogs?
Oh, I can weep no more: enough, the cup
Of bitterness is full and overflows.
O Zion, beauty and gladness of the world,
Thine is all love and grace, and unto thee
In love and grace we are for ever chained.
We who in thy happiness were happy
Are broken in thy desolation. Each
In the prison of his exile bows to earth,
And turns him toward thy gates. Scattered and lost,
We will remember till the end of time
The cradle of our childhood, from a thousand seas
Turn back and seek again thy hills and vales.
Glory of Pathros, glory of Shinar,
Compared to the light and truth that streamed from thee
Are dust and vanity: and in all the world
Whom shall I find to liken to thy seers,
Thy princes, thy elect, thy anointed ones?
The kingdoms of the heathen pass like shadows,
Thy glory and thy name endure for ever.
God made His home in thee: well for the man
Who makes God's choice his own, with thee to dwell.
And happy, happy the man who vigil keeps
Until the day break over thee again,
Until thy chosen are returned to thee,
And thy first youth in glory is renewed.

(*Maurice Samuel*)

PARTING

If parting be decreed for the two of us,
Stand yet a little while I gaze upon thy face. . . .

By the life of love, remember the days of thy longing,
As I remember the nights of thy delight.

As thine image passeth into my dreams,
So let me pass, I entreat thee, into thy dreams,
Between me and thee roar the waves of a sea of tears
And I cannot pass over unto thee.
But O, if thy steps should draw nigh to cross—
Then would its waters be divided at the touch of thy foot.
Would that after my death unto mine ears should come
The sound of the golden bells upon thy skirts!
Or shouldst thou be asking how fareth thy beloved, I from the depths of the tomb
Would ask of thy love and thy welfare.
Verily, to the shedding of mine heart's blood
There be two witnesses, thy cheeks and thy lips.
How sayest thou it is not true, since these be my witnesses
For my blood, and that thine hands have shed it?
Why desirest thou my death, whilst I but desire
To add years unto the years of thy life?
Though thou dost rob my slumber in the night of my longing,
Would I not give the sleep of mine eyes unto thy eyelids? . . .
Yea, between the bitter and the sweet standeth my heart—
The gall of parting, and the honey of thy kisses.
After thy words have beaten out my heart into thin plates,
Thine hands have cut it into shreds.
It is the likeness of rubies over pearls
What time I behold thy lips over thy teeth.
The sun is on thy face and thou spreadest out the night
Over his radiance with the clouds of thy locks.
Fine silk and broidered work are the covering of thy body,
But grace and beauty are the covering of thine eyes.
The adornment of maidens is the work of human hands,
But thou—majesty and sweetness are thine adornment. . . .

In the field of the daughters of delight, the sheaves of
 love
Make obeisance unto thy sheaf. . . .
I cannot hear thy voice, but I hear
Upon the secret places of my heart, the sound of thy
 steps.
On the day when thou wilt revive
The victims whom love for thee hath slain—on the
 day when thy dead shall live anew,
Then turn again to my soul to restore it to my body;
 for on the day
Of thy departure, when thou wentest forth, it went out
 after thee.

(Nina Salaman)

Chaim Nachman Bialik

1873–

THE MATHMID

There are abandoned corners of our Exile,
Remote, forgotten cities of Dispersion,
Where still in secret burns our ancient light,
Where God has saved a remnant from disaster.
There, brands that glimmer in a ruin of ashes,
Pent and unhappy souls maintain the vigil—
Spirits grown old beyond the count of time,
Grown old beyond the reckoning of days.
And when thou goest forth alone, at nightfall,
Wandering in one of these, the sacred cities,
When heaven above is quick with breaking stars,
And earth beneath with whispering spirit-winds—
Thine ear will catch the murmur of a voice,
Thine eye will catch the twinkle of a light
Set in a window, and a human form—
A shadow, like the shadow of death—beyond,
A shadow trembling, swaying back and forth,
A voice, an agony, that lifts and falls,

And comes toward thee upon the waves of silence.
Mark well the swaying shadow and the voice:
It is a *Mathmid* in his prison-house,
A prisoner, self-guarded, self-condemned,
Self-sacrificed to study of the Law. . . .

Within these walls, within this prison-house,
Six years have passed above his swaying form:
Within these walls the child became the youth,
The youth became the man, fore-ripened swift,
And swift as these went, swifter yet were gone
The cheek's bloom and the luster of his eyes.
Six years have passed since first he set his face
To the dark corner of the inner walls;
Six years since he has seen, for joyous sunlight,
Gray limestone, lizards and the webs of spiders;
Six years of hunger, years of sleeplessness,
Six years of wasting flesh and falling cheeks—
And all, to him, as if it had not been.
He knows that Jews have studied thus of old,
He knows the fame and glory they have won.

. . . .

Since that dark corner has become his own,
No man, no living thing, has seen his coming,
No man, no living thing, has seen his going.
Not even the rising and the setting suns
Have witnessed his arrival, his return;
The morning-star, black midnight and the moon
Alone knew when he slept and when he rose:
Daylight has never looked upon his ways,
The mid-day sun has never burned his skin.
In the dimmest dawn, "before thou canst distinguish
A white thread from an azure, wolf from dog"—
(Thereby the Jew shall know, the Rabbis say,
The hour for morning-prayer is not yet come)—
In the dimmest dawn, while through the lifeless dark
Ten thousand times ten thousand stars yet shine,

Before the crowing of the cock disturbs
The burghers of the city, sleep-enfolded,
Yea, even before the most elect of faith
Rise to do honor to Creation's Lord:
In that hour, when the world in silence trembles
Before the new awakening of life,
Trembles as if she dreamed the last of dreams,
As if a wandering and secret thought
Made a light stirring in her folded wings—
In that hour from his stolen sleep he starts,
Dresses in darkness and to his corner runs.
Light are his footsteps on the garden path,
Only the winds have heard them passing by,
Only the stars have seen them running swift.

But there are moments when a playful wind
Out of the blue deep like the Tempter comes,
And with a loving hand his earlock fondles,
And whispers to him with dissolving sweetness.
And the boy's eyelids cling to one another,
As if they pleaded with him: "*Brother, brother,*
Have pity on the dark eyes under us;
And we are weary, for with thee we suffer:
A full day we have toiled, a summer day,
And half a summer night: it is enough.
Brother, return and sleep, and we with thee,
Too short thy sleep was to restore our strength. . . ."
But sudden starts the boy, draws his lean hand
Across his eyes, as if temptation sat
Upon his leaden lid: and clear and swift
His footsteps echo from the empty streets.

And then the wind that blows about the garden
Takes up the theme, and gentle is its voice:
"*Green is my cradle, child of happiness,*
Joy in my blossom, ere thine own be withered. . . ."
And left and right of him the flowers and grasses
Speak to him from their dreams, "*We too are sleeping.*"

Even the stars above him take on voices,
And wink: *"We sleep, although our eyes are open."*
The drunken odors of a thousand flowers
Mount to his nostrils in resistless waves:
They break upon his eyes, his lips, his throat.
He bares his breast then to receive the wind,
And lifts his strengthless hands as if in prayer:
"O dear wind, take me, carry me from here,
And find a place for me where I may rest:
For here is only weariness and pain. . . ."
His raised hands bruise against the garden fence,
And tell him he has wandered from the path:
Swift he recalls his vows, recalls his corner,
And turns him from the Tempter's voice, and flees.

In the Yeshivah reigns a sacred silence
Which he, the sacred youth, is first to break;
For there, in the dark corner, wait for him—
Faithful companions since the day he came—
Three friends: his stand, his candle and his Talmud.
As if the moments could not move too swiftly
That lie between him and his trusted friends,
He hastens to his place and takes his stand,
And like a pillar stands from morn till night.
Still standing he will eat his midday crust,
Still standing he will half outwatch the night.
Granite is yielding clay compared with him—
A Jewish boy unto the Torah vowed.

"Oi, omar Rabba, tonu rabonon,
Thus Rabba speaks, and thus our teachers taught,"
(Backward and forward swaying he repeats,
With ceaseless singsong the undying words);
The dawn, the garden, the enchanted fields,
Are gone, are vanished like a driven cloud,
And earth and all her fullness are forgotten. . . .

(Maurice Samuel)

FROM "SONGS OF THE PEOPLE"

I

Two steps from my garden rail
Sleeps my well beneath its pail:
    Every sabbath comes my love
    And I let him drink thereof.

All the world is sleeping now
Like the fruit beneath the bough.
    Father, mother, both are gone
    And my heart wakes here alone.

And the pail awakes with me,
Dripping, dripping, drowsily:
    Drops of gold and crystal clear . . .
    And my love is drawing near.

Hist! I think that something stirred;
Was it he, or but a bird?
    Dearest friend, my lover dear,
    There is no one with me here.

By the trough we sit and speak,
Hand in hand and cheek to cheek;
    Hear this riddle: Can you tell
    Why the pitcher seeks the well?

That you cannot answer, nor
What the pail is weeping for?
    Morn to even, drop by drop,
    Fall its tears and cannot stop.

This then tell me, why my breast
Daylong, nightlong is oppressed.
    Spoke my mother truth in saying
    That your heart from me was straying?

And my lover answered: See,
Enemies have slandered me.
    Ere another year be gone,
    We shall marry, foolish one.

On that golden day of days
Shall the summer be ablaze.
    Fruited branches overhead
    Shall in benediction spread.

Friend and kinsman, young and old
Shall be gathered to behold,
    And with music and with mirth
    They shall come to lead us forth.

And the bridal canopy
In this place shall lifted be.
    I shall slip a ring of gold
    On this finger that I hold.

And pronounce the blessing: "Thee
God makes consecrate to me."
    And my enemies shall there
    Burst with envy and despair.

(*Maurice Samuel*)

2

On a hill there blooms a palm
'Twixt Tigris and Euphrates old,
And among the leafy branches
Sits the phœnix, bird of gold.

Bird of gold, go forth and find me
Him whose bride I am to be:
Search and circle till thou find him,
Bind him, bring him, bird, to me.

If thou hast no thread of scarlet,
Give him greeting without end:
Tell him, golden bird, my spirit
Languishes towards my friend.

Tell him: Now the garden blossoms,
Closed except to his command;
Mid the leaves the golden apple
Waits and trembles for his hand.

Tell him, nightly on my pillow
Wakes the longing without name,
And the whiteness of my body
Burns my couch as with a flame.

If he comes not, hear my secret:
All prepared my coffer stands;
Linen, silk, and twenty singlets
Wrought and knitted by these hands.

And the softest of all feathers
By my mother plucked and stored:
Through the nights she filled the cushions
For her daughter's bridal hoard.

And the bridal veil of silver
Waits to deck me when I marry:
Bride and dowry, both are ready—
Wherefore does the bridegroom tarry?

. . . .

Seethe and whisper, magic potion:
Thus the phœnix makes reply:
"In the night to thy beloved
With my secret will I fly.

"In his dreams I give thy greeting,
In his dreams reveal thy face:
Lo! Upon a broomstick mounted
Unto thee he flies apace.

"And he comes and speaks; 'Behold me,
Oh, my joy, my hope, my pride:
Not with golden gifts or dowry,
But with love become my bride.

" 'Gold and silk I have aplenty—
Fire of youth and ringlets fine:
Both I give thee—swiftly, lightly,
Come to me, beloved mine.' "

. . . .

When the night was dark above me
And the stars with clouds were stilled,
On his quest the phœnix vanished—
And his words are unfulfilled.

And at morn, at noon, at even,
Still I watch the clouds of fire:
"Clouds above me, answer, Wherefore
Comes he not, my heart's desire?"

(Maurice Samuel)

NIGHT

I KNOW that this my crying, like the crying
Of owls on ruins in a wilderness,
Wakes neither consolation nor despair.
I know that these my tears are as a cloud
Of barren waters in a desert land,
That my lament, grown old with many years,
Is strengthless in the stony hearts of men. . . .
Still the unhappy heart in vain laments
And seeks in vain to weep itself to rest.

From my pent prison I put forth my head
And call unto the storm and question it,
And search the clouds and with the gloom confer—
When will the darkness and the tempest pass?

When will the whirlwind die and the clouds scatter
And moon and stars break forth again in light?
I search from heaven to earth, from earth to heaven:
No sign, or answer—only storm and night.

Within the womb God consecrated me
To sickness and to poverty and said:
Go forth and find thy vanished destiny.
And among the ways of life buy air to breathe
And steal with craft a beggar's dole of light,
Carry from door to door thy beggar's pack;
Before the wealthy crook the knees for bread. . . .
But I am weary now with wandering:
Ah, God, my God, how long is yet the road?

From the dark womb, like an uncleanliness,
On a heap of gathered foulness I was cast,
Unwashed from filth, with rags for swaddling-clothes,
My mother stretched to me a withered breast
And stilled me with the bitter milk of madness.
And in my heart a viper made its nest
And sucks my blood to render it in poison.
Where can I hide me from its burning fangs?
God! answer me with either life or death.

In the broad sky the light clouds are unraveled
And stars among them are like single pearls.
The wind moves dreamlike in the tranquil darkness
And in the wind still broods the peace of God.
And a faint whisper, like a secret kiss,
Laden with revelation, stirs the grass,
And sleep that heals and comforts falls on earth—
But not on me, the outcast,—not on me.

In the dead night-time I begin my song,
When two alone awake, my pain and I.
Beneath my skin my bones are turned to dust,
My weak eyes fall, for they have wept too long.

Now my song wakens like a bird at dawn,
Her dewy wings beat rain into my heart
And melt the tear-drops on my frozen eyes. . . .
In vain, in vain, for tears alone I know.

Bring me not rain-drops, but a fount of tears,
Tears that will shake the hearts of men with storm;
Then by the ancient mounds of desolation,
By the ruined Temple, by my fathers' graves,
Where the road passes I will take my stand,
And travelers on the road will pity me,
And charity will waken with their pity.
There let men hear thee, O my song, until
Thy tears are ended and my pain is stilled.

(Maurice Samuel)

THE DEAD OF THE WILDERNESS [1]

Yonder great shadow—that blot on the passionate glare of the desert—
'Tis not an army of lions couched in the sun with their young ones,
'Tis not the pride of the forests of Bashan uprooted and fallen:
Those are the Dead of the Wilderness under the sunlight recumbent.
Hard by their tents are they laid, like children of Anak for stature,
Stretched on the desolate sands like numberless lions in slumber;
Under the might of their limbs the floor of the desert is hollowed.
Armed as for battle they sleep and clad in the armor of giants;
Swords like crags at their heads and spears twixt their shoulders protruding,

[1] The subject of this poem is derived from a Talmudic legend which says that the Jews who left Egypt did not die in the desert, as the Bible tells, but were cast into slumber.—(Tr.)

Sound to their girdle the quiver and firm in the sand is
the lance thrust.

Deep in the earth are their heads sunk, heavy with
tangles neglected,
Matted and monstrous and vast, and uncouth as the
mane of a lion;
Matted and monstrous and vast are their beards like to
tangles of serpents.
Strong are their faces and burnished, and darkened to
bronze are their eyelids,
Targets to arrows of sunlight and rocks to the fury of
tempests.
Hard are their foreheads and grim and changeless up-
turned to the heavens,
Eyes that are cruel and terrible peer through the tangle
of eyebrows.
Cast as of lava upthrown from volcanoes and hardened
their breasts are
Lifted like anvils of iron that wait for the blow of the
hammer;
Yet though the hammer of time beats long and un-
ceasing upon them,
Like to the stone that enfolds it the strength of their
hearts sleeps for ever.
Only, the faces unmoving, the breasts multitudinous,
naked,
Strangely are covered, like ancient memorials, with runes
of the desert
Graven by arrows and swords which the tempests have
tossed and uplifted.
And when the eagle descends in his flight to behold he
shall read there,
Graven on breast and on brow, the tale of unbroken
endurance,
How many arrows and spears these breasts have en-
countered and shattered.

Sunlight and darkness revolve and cycle succeeds unto cycle,
Stormwinds awake and are stilled and the desert turns back to its silence.
Far stand the crags, as amazed in beholding the first things created,
Clothed by the silence with splendor, the proud, the eternally lonely,
Limitless, limitless stretches the wilderness, lifeless and soundless.
Lost to the end of all time is the jubliant voice of the giants,
Laid into stillness for ever the tumult that followed their footsteps;
Where they once trod are now lifted the sandhills and crags of the desert.
Silence has breathed on the mighty and cast into slumber their fierceness.
And the hot winds of the desert eaten their strength and their beauty.

Fierce burns the sun on the blades gigantic and wears them to brightness;
Blinding arrows of sunlight shot at the heads of the lances
Break into myriads of sparks that are dashed on the breasts of the sleepers
Lying there bared to the desolate sunlight for ever and ever.
Dried by the withering east-wind, dust of their bodies is lifted,
Whirled into other lands, scattered under the footsteps of pygmies;
Jackals there nuzzle with unclean snouts in the ruins of heroes.
No one remembers among them the old generation of giants
Fallen and turned into voiceless stone in the sands of the desert. . . .

Sometimes a shadow is born alone on the face of the
desert,
Floats on the sands till it reaches the ranks of the army
of sleepers,
Trembles a moment above them and breaks into circles
of motion,
Suddenly chooses a body outstretched and over it stands
and is moveless;
And the body beneath it is darkened and half of its
neighbor.
Suddenly quivers the air as the pinions stupendous are
folded.
Full with his weight like a meteor descending he falls
on his victim—
One of the eagle-kings, crag-born, crooked of beak and
of talon.
Over the breast of the sleeper a granite-like talon is
lifted;
Yet but an instant and granite on granite will ring in
the stillness;
And in that instant he pauses and stands with his talon
uplifted,
Stilled and rebuked in his pride by the loftier pride of
the sleeper;
Wondering stands, then unfolds the strength of his
pinions and rises,
Beating great waves through the air and screaming in
stretches of sunlight,
Scales untiring the measureless heights and is lost in the
splendor.
Long, long after still flutters, held fast on the point of
a lancehead,
One gray feather that fell unseen and unmarked was
abandoned,
Flutters and strains at the lance-head and fluttering
earthwards is wafted.
Silence returns to the desert and peace to the sleep of
the heroes.

Sometimes when midday is hot and the desert swoons
under the sunlight,
Slides from its fastness a serpent, vast as the beam of a
weaver,
Issues to warm on the sands the glistening rings of his
body.
Now he shrinks on himself, coils himself moveless and
breathless,
Languid with joy in the warmth and bathing in light
as in waters;
Now he wakes and uncoils and stretches his length in
the sunlight,
Opens the width of his jaws and his scales are like net-
work of lightnings,
Spangled and knitted in splendor, a lonely delight in
the desert.
Sudden he starts from his languor, leaps into rigid at-
tention,
Bends and unwinds on the sand, then swiftly he glides
from his station
Over the waste till he reaches the army of sleepers and
stands then,
Lifted one-third in the air, like a column of bright
hieroglyphics,
Raises his crown and outstretches his neck and his eye-
balls green sparkle.
Swaying he broods on the slumbering army from margin
to margin.
Vast is the soundless encampment and countless the dead
it encloses,
Numberless, numberless faces and foreheads exposed to
the heavens.

Then like a flash reawakens the hatred of dead gener-
ations,
Gleams in the start of his eyes like a brand that is
sudden uncovered.
Hatred instinctive and ancient runs through the shud-
dering body.

Trembling he lowers his head and darts with it hither
and thither,
Hangs then suspended an instant and stares in the face of
a sleeper.
Under their hoods are his eyeballs twin centers of
hatred and fury;
Hissing he opens his jaws and the flash of his fangs
is uncovered—
And in that instant he pauses, sinks on the coils of his
body,
Stilled and rebuked in his rage by the bitterer rage of
the sleeper,—
Sinks and uncircles his length and turns from the visage
of granite,
Moves off, a rhythm of waves till his splendor is lost
in the distance.
Silence returns to the desert and peace to the sleep of
the heroes.

Moonlight descends on the waste and sleeps on the
measureless broadness,
Lays on the desert a garment speckled with light and
with shadow.
Pallid the wilderness league after league rolls from dim-
ness to dimness.
Broad at the foot of the towering crags are their shadows
recumbent,
Couched like dragons primeval, things from the dawn
of creation.
Gathered in monstrous conspiracy under the cover of
darkness—
They will arise ere the morning, return to the caverns
they came from.
Mournful the moon from her loneliness looks on the
mystery threefold—
Wilderness, midnight and monsters crept out from the
dawn of creation.
Lapped is the desert in merciless dreams of its old deso-
lation,

Wails in its dreams, and its wailing half-uttered is broken
and stifled.

Sometimes a wandering lion, thewed as with roots of
an oak tree,
Massive and certain of footstep comes down to the army
and stands there,
Raises his head from his shoulders, heavy, magnificent-
crested.
Fitfully gleam the two eyeballs over the enemy army;
Vast is the army outspread and its vastness is utterly
silent;
Dark is the sleep of the heroes, there is not an eyelid
aflutter.
Shadows of lances, like thongs, are close on their bodies
and bind them.
Moonlight is spilled on their faces and rims the black
mass of their eyebrows.
Stonelike in wonder the lion stares at their slumbering
power,
Till from his wonder awaking he shakes with his roaring
the desert,
Startling the mountains and setting the flanks of the
desert atremble.
Far pours the strength of his voice, and the crags in
the distance give answer,
Hither and thither is rolled till it crumbles in frag-
ments of thunder.
Then in a wailing responsive arises the cry of the
jackals,
Mingles with howling of beasts till the night-time is
hideous with voices—
This is the wail of the desert, a desperate protest and
bitter,
Worn with the infinite vigil and weary with long deso-
lation.
Still stands the lion, intent on the tumult his strength has
awakened;

Silent he turns from the dead and is kingly again in
his silence,
Turns and departs like a king and his eyes are like
torches attendant,
Massive and certain of step departs and is lost in the
darkness.
Long is the desert awake and its bitterness will not be
silenced,
Long it moans for its ancient pain and the comfortless
future.
Dawn returns and the desert is weary from moaning,
and slumbers,
Slumbers and yet is awake, and shrinks from the day and
its evil.
Slow dies the moon in her pallor and drops to the rim
of the heavens;
Stealthy the shadows arise from under the crags, and
they are not.
Gaunt stand the rocks to the morning and anger is
written upon them;
Under the wrath of their looks the desert is timid and
trembles,
Strains to answer with anger responsive and fails and
is voiceless,
Stilled by the shattering sun. And silence returns as for
ever.
Deep is the sleep of the heroes . . . and cycle succeeds
unto cycle.

But there are moments when, tortured too long by the
silence eternal,
Wild with unbearable sickness of æons, the desert up-
rises,
Wakens and rages for vengeance against the inhuman
Creator,
Raises a column of sand to ascend to the fastness of
heaven,
Once and for ever to meet Him and shatter the throne
of His glory,

Once for the torture eternal to loose the floods of its
fury,
Sweep his whole world into darkness and bring back the
kingdom of chaos. . . .
Then the Creator is stirred, and His anger envelops the
heavens,
Like a great cover of iron, He bends them to blot out
the desert.
Red from the blast of His breath, the flame of His anger
outbreaking
Wraps the desert in fury and scatters its crags in a
furnace.
Stubborn and bitter the desert responds, and new furies
are loosened,
Rise from the bowels of Hell, and all earth is in fury
confounded.
Seized by the madness that spins like a vehement wheel
in the vastness
Tigers and lions, with manes unlifted and eyeballs
aglitter,
Join in the riot infernal, and howl with the voice of the
tempest,
Lifted and torn by the strength of the tempest like
gossamer insects.
And in that instant—
Wakes the terrible power that slumbered in chains,
Suddenly stirs and arises the old generation of heroes,
Mighty in battle: their eyes are like lightning, like blades
are their faces.
Then flies the hand to the sword.
Sixty myriads of voices—a thunder of heroes—awaken,
Crash through the tempest and tear asunder the rage
of the desert.
Round them in wildness and blindness:
And they cry
"We are the mighty!
The last generation of slaves and the first generation
of freemen!
Alone our hand in its strength

Tore from the pride of our shoulders the yoke of
bondage.
We lifted our heads to the heavens and behold their
broadness was narrow in the pride of our eyes,
So we turned to the desert, we said to the Wilderness:
'Mother!'
Yea, on the tops of the crags, in the thickness of clouds,
With the eagles of heaven we drank from her fountains
of freedom.
And who is lord of us?
Even now, though the God of vengeance has shut the
desert upon us,
A song of strength and revolt has reached us, and we
arise.
To arms! To arms! Form ranks! Forward!
Forward into the heavens and the wrath thereof.
Behold us! We will ascend
With the tempest!
Though the Lord has withdrawn His hand from us,
And the Ark stands moveless in its place,
Still we will ascend—alone!
Even under the eye of His wrath, daring the lightning
of His countenance,
We will carry with storm the citadels of the hills,
And face to face in combat encounter the armed foe!
Listen!
The storm, too, calls unto us—'Courage and daring!'
To arms! To arms! Let the hills be shattered and the
mountains blasted into dust,
Or let our lifeless bodies be heaped in countless cairns.
Forward!
On to the hills!"

. . . .

And in that instant the desert is wild with a fierce
anger—
And who shall conquer it?
In the storm goes up a terrible voice, a mingling of
cries.

It must surely
That the desert is bringing to birth a deed of evil,
A bitter thing, a cruel and a terrible. . . .

Passed is the tempest. The desert is silent, and pure is the silence.
Bright is the broadness of heaven, and marvelous quiet beneath it.
Now from their terror awaking, the caravans trapped in the tempest
Rise from their crouching and call on their God and adore Him and praise Him.
Still in the sand are the sixty myriads of heroes aslumber.
Darkened their faces, for death has brought them to peace with their Maker.
No man knoweth the place of their slumber. The crags of the desert,
Split by the strength of their rising, over them closed in their falling.
Sometimes a rider, in daring adventure his caravan leaving,
Spurs his horse ever onwards and enters the heart of the desert.
Strong is the heart of the rider, and swift is the horse to the spurring.
Riding he flings up his spear in the sunlight, and takes it descending,
Throws it and takes it again, and throws it again and pursues it;
Like to a river of lightning it flashes and dances before him.
Far in the distance a vision appears, and the horse is drawn onwards,
Mounts with its rider a hill the clouds overtopping—and sudden,
Quivering it pauses and looks, then bounds to the rear by its whole length.
Startled the rider uplifts his hand for a shadow and gazes. . . .

Stonelike he stands with his horse, and the terror of God
is upon him.
Then leaps the horse in its strength and, turning, descends like an arrow. . . .
Fast spurs the rider and halts not until, with his caravan
meeting,
Swift he dismounts and tells of the vision he saw in the
stillness.
Marveling listen the Arabs, and wonder is writ on their
faces.
Then speaks the oldest amongst them, a patriarch sprung
from the Prophet,
Answers the tale of the rider: "Blessed be Allah the
True One;
For by the Beard of the Prophet, it was not a vision
thou sawest.
Those are the Dead of the Wilderness thou hast discovered and gazed on.
This was the host of the Lord, a people of valor gigantic,
Older than man can remember—yea, of the first generations,
Stubborn and strong was this people, stiff-necked as the
crags of the desert,
Deaf to the word of their Prophet, and proud with the
God of their fathers.
Therefore He cast sleep upon them, and sealed up their
path with the mountains,
Laid His command on the wilderness for a memorial
eternal. . . .
Allah protect true Believers from touching the hem of
their garments.
Once did a son of the Faithful lay hand on a fringe and
uplift it.
Withered his body became till the fringe was restored to
the sleeper.
These are the sires of the race of the Book. . . ."
Then the speaker is silent,
Wordless the Arabs have heard, and they tremble and
give praise to Allah.

Silent they walk at the side of their camels to weariness laden.
Long is the whiteness that gleams on their hoods to be seen in the distance.
Slow sway the camels their monstrous backs till they fail in the brightness,
Bearing away from the desert one more of its marvelous legends.
Stillness returns as of old. Desolate stretches the desert.

(Maurice Samuel)

Yehoash

(Solomon Bloomgarden)
1870–1926

AN OLD SONG

(Yiddish)

In the blossom-land Japan
Somewhere thus an old song ran

Said a warrior to a smith
"Hammer me a sword forthwith.
Make the blade
Light as wind on water laid.
Make it long
As the wheat at harvest song.
Supple, swift
As a snake, without rift,
Full of lightnings, thousand-eyed!
Smooth as silken cloth and thin
As the web that spiders spin.
And merciless as pain, and cold."
"On the hilt what shall be told?"

"On the sword's hilt, my good man,"
Said the warrior of Japan,
"Trace for me
A running lake, a flock of sheep
And one who sings her child to sleep."

(Marie Syrkin)

EGYPTIAN

From the Book of the Dead

3500 B.C., *et seq.*

Both external detail and central faith of the Egyptian religion are incorporated in the Chapters of Coming Forth by Day, commonly known as the Book of the Dead. About 3500 B.C., when the first Chapter was set down by the scribes, many of the symbols were already so ancient that the men who wrote them were ignorant of their significance. Yet all were retained, because all were holy to the traditional-minded people of the Nile. . . . This race loved life and pleasure with a fierce intensity; all the somber pomp of the ritual of the dead had as its object the prolongation of an existence too delightful to relinquish. It is erroneous to picture the early Egyptians as an austere, funereal people. . . . Their theology, their sacraments, and their conception of the after life are based on a single doctrine: eternal life manifested through eternal living forms.—ROBERT HILLYER.

THE DEAD MAN ARISETH AND SINGETH A HYMN TO THE SUN

HOMAGE to thee, O Ra, at thy tremendous rising!
Thou risest! Thou shinest! the heavens are rolled aside!
Thou art the King of Gods, thou art the All-comprising,
From thee we come, in thee are deified.

Thy priests go forth at dawn; they wash their hearts
  with laughter;
Divine winds move in music across thy golden strings.
At sunset they embrace thee, as every cloudy rafter
Flames with reflected color from thy wings.

Thou sailest over the zenith, and thy heart rejoices;
Thy Morning Boat and Evening Boat with fair winds
  meet together;
Before thy face the goddess Maat exalts her fateful
  Feather,
And at thy name the halls of Anu ring with voices.

O Thou Perfect! Thou Eternal! Thou Only One!
Great Hawk that fliest with the flying Sun!
Between the Turquoise Sycamores that risest, young for ever,
Thine image flashing on the bright celestial river.

Thy rays are on all faces; Thou art inscrutable.
Age after age thy life renews its eager prime.
Time whirls its dust beneath thee; thou art immutable,
Maker of Time, thyself beyond all Time.

Thou passest through the portals that close behind the night,
Gladdening the souls of them that lay in sorrow.
The True of Word, the Quiet Heart, arise to drink thy light;
Thou art To-day and Yesterday; Thou art To-morrow!

Homage to thee, O Ra, who wakest life from slumber!
Thou risest! Thou shinest! Thy radiant face appears!
Millions of years have passed,—we can not count their number,—
Millions of years shall come. Thou art above the years!

HE SINGETH A HYMN TO OSIRIS, THE LORD OF ETERNITY

Glory to Osiris, the Prince of Everlastingness,
Who traveleth through all the million years into Eternity,
Crowned with the North and South, the Lord of gods and men,
Bearing the crook and whip of mercy and of power.

O King of Kings, O Prince of Princes, Lord of Lords,
Through thee the world is green again by virtue of thy Passion;
Thou leadest in thy train what has been and what shall be,
Thy heart shall rest content upon the hidden Mountain.

Thy body is of shining metal, and thy head is azure;
The color of the turquoise plays about thee where thou goest.
All-pervading is thy body, radiant thy countenance,
As the fields and river valleys of the world hereafter.

Grant my spirit strength on earth, and triumph in eternity.
Grant me favorable winds to sail about thy Kingdom.
Grant me wings on which to rise and fly up like the Phœnix.
Grant me welcome freely in the pylons of the gods.

In the House of Coolness, let thy bread be given to me,
The blessed food of them who rise from death with thee, Victorious,
And let there be a home for me amid the happy meadows
Where I may sow and reap those sunny fields of wheat and barley.

HE ASKETH ABSOLUTION OF GOD

O Thou who speedest Time's advancing wing,
Thou dweller in all mysteries of Life,
Thou guardian of every word I speak,—
Behold thou art ashamed of me, thy son;
Thy heart is full of sorrow and of shame,
For that my sins were grievous in the world,
And proud my wickedness and my transgression.
O be at peace with me, O be at peace!
And break the barriers that loom between us!
Let all my sins be washed away, and fall
Forgotten to the right and left of thee.
Yea, do away with all my wickedness,
And put away the shame that fills thy heart,
That thou and I henceforth may be at peace!

HE HOLDETH FAST TO THE MEMORY OF HIS IDENTITY

In the Great House, and in the House of Fire,
On the dark night of counting all the years,
On the dark night when months and years are numbered,—
O let my name be given back to me!

When the Divine One on the Eastern Stairs
Shall cause me to sit down with him in peace,
And every god proclaims his name before me,—
Let me remember then the name I bore!

HE APPROACHETH THE HALL OF JUDGMENT

O my Heart, my Mother, my Heart, my Mother,
The seed of my being, my earthly existence,
O stay with me still in the Hall of the Princes,
In the presence of the God who keepeth the Balance.
And when thou art weighed in the scale with the feather
Of Truth, then render no judgment against me;
Let not the Lords of the Trial cry before me:
He hath wrought Evil and spoken Untruth!

And ye, divine Gods, cloud-enthroned with your scepters,
At the weighing of words, speak me fair to Osiris.
Lift up my cause to the Forty-two Judges,
And let me not die yet again in Amentet.

Behold, O my Heart, if there be not a parting
Between us, our name shall be one with to-morrow,
Yea, Millions-of-Years is the name we have written,
Yea, Millions-of-Years, O my Mother, my Heart!

HE IS DECLARED TRUE OF WORD

THUS saith the great god Thoth,
The judge of Right and Truth,
Unto the Company of Gods
Who sit before Osiris.

"Now verily this heart
Was weighed, and it is pure.
No wickedness was found in him
Whose heart withstood the Balance."

And thus respond the gods
Who sit before Osiris,
"Thy words are true, let him come in
And live in peace for ever.

"Give him a house amid
The everlasting Fields.
Let not Oblivion devour
The soul that is triumphant."

Thus Horus, son of Isis,
Saith to divine Osiris,
"O Father, I have brought to thee
This vindicated spirit.

"His deeds have been adjudged,
His heart weighed in the Balance;
Grant him thy cakes and ale, and grant
Him welcome in thy presence."

Thus saith the living soul,
"Behold, O Lord of lords,
Here to thy presence am I come,
Sinless before Osiris.

"Thou art the Beautiful,
The Prince of all the World,
Thee have I loved, O favor me,
And make me thy Beloved."

HE COMETH FORTH INTO THE DAY

I AM here, I have traversed the Tomb, I behold thee,
Thou who art strong!
I have passed through the Underworld, gazed on Osiris,
Scattered the night.

I have come, I have gazed on my Father, Osiris,
I am his son.
I am the son who loveth his Father,
I am beloved.

I have made me a path through the western horizon,
Even as God.
I have followed his footsteps, and won through his magic
Millions of years.

The Gate between Heaven and Earth standeth open,
Glad is my path.
Hail, every god! every soul! out of darkness
Shineth my light!

Like the Hawk I went in; I come forth like the Phœnix,
Star of the dawn.
In the beautiful world by the bright Lake of Horus,
Riseth the Day.

HE BIDDETH OSIRIS TO ARISE FROM THE DEAD

ARISE up on thy feet, O Quiet Heart!
O Quiet Heart, thy body is made perfect.
Isis among the reeds beside the Nile
And in the dark papyrus swamps bewailed thee,

And sheltered Horus to avenge thy fate.
He hath come forth from secret habitations;
He hath warred mightily against thy foe,
And now he saileth in the boat of Sunrise.
Come forth, O Quiet Heart,—I have avenged thee.

HE MAKETH HIMSELF ONE WITH OSIRIS

I AM the Prince in the Field,
  I am Osiris.
I am Horus and Ra,
  One with Osiris.

I was on guard at his door
  In his birth-chamber.
I was brought forth at his birth;
  I am Osiris.

One with his heart and his strength,
  Ever renewing
My youth with his youth in the place
  Whither he goeth.

Slaying his slayer, I too
  Rise out of darkness;
Thus I take vengeance myself,
  Working his vengeance.

All that is offered to him
  Decketh my altar.
He who hath risen from Death
  Beareth me with him.

HE MAKETH HIMSELF ONE WITH THE GOD RA

I AM the Lord of Light, the self-begotten Youth,
First-born of life primeval, first Name from nameless
  matter.
I am the Prince of Years; my body is Eternity;
My form is Everlastingness that trampleth down the
  darkness.

Call me by name: the Master who dwelleth in the
Vineyard,
The Boy who roameth through the town, the Young
Man in the plain.
Call me by name: the Child who traveleth toward his
Father,
The Child of Light who findeth his Father in the
Evening.

HE MAKETH HIMSELF ONE WITH THE ONLY GOD, WHOSE LIMBS ARE THE MANY GODS

O EVERLASTING Kingdom of the Scepter,
O Resting-place where Ra's bright boat is moored,
O White Crown of the Form which is divine!
I come! I am the Child! I am the Child!
My hair is Nu, my face the disk of Ra,
My eyes are Hathor, and my neck is Isis;—
Each member of my body is a god,
My flesh and bones, the names of Living Gods.
Thoth shelters me, for always, day by day.
I come as Ra, I come as he whose name
Is yet unknown. I come as Yesterday,
As Prophet of the million years to be
For nations and for peoples still untold.
I am the Child who marcheth down the road
Of Yesterday, To-day, and of To-morrow.
I am the One, the Only One, who goeth
Forever round his course through all horizons;
Whose moment is in your bodies, but whose forms
Rest in their temple, secret and unveiled;
Who holdeth you in his hand, but whom no hand
Can ever hold; who knoweth your name and season,
But whom you can not know, nor any mortal;
For whom the days return in constant passing,
Moving in splendor toward the end of time.

Yea, I am He, and shall not die again;
Nor men, nor sainted dead, nor even gods
Shall drag me back from my immortal path!

HE WALKETH BY DAY

I AM Yesterday, To-day and To-morrow,
The Divine Hidden Soul who created the gods,
And who feedeth the blessed.

I am Lord of the Risers from Death,
Whose Forms are the lamps in the House of the Dead,
Whose shrine is the Earth.

When the sky is illumined with crystal,
Then gladden my road and broaden my path
And clothe me in light.

Keep me safe from the Sleeper in Darkness,
When eventide closeth the eyes of the god
And the door by the wall.

In the dawn I have opened the Sycamore;
My Form is the form of all women and men,
My spirit is God.

HE DEFENDETH HIS HEART AGAINST THE DESTROYER

I AM the Pure, the True of Word, Triumphant,
I am the Prince in the Field: I am Osiris.
In his death-chamber I was born with him,
I died with him, and now I rise from death.
My heart hath been adjudged before Osiris,
And none shall carry it away from me.
Yea, this, my heart, hath wept before Osiris,
And supplicated in the Hall of Judgment.
And now I sit victorious in peace,
Upon the Mountain of Eternity.
Stretching my hand, I grasp the southern breeze,
Opening my nostrils, breathe the western wind:

A shining flame, I light the way for Him
Who Opens the portals of the Million Years.
I am the standard of young plants and flowers,
I am the Flower-Bush that blooms for ever.

HE ESTABLISHETH HIS TRIUMPH

Hail, thou who shinest from the Moon
And walketh through the crowded night
Lifting high thy torch!

I also come, a Shining Soul
Standing firm upon my feet
Despite my shadowy foes.

Open wide the Gate of Death
For me who bear the Rod of Gold
Victorious through the Dark!

HE ENTERETH THE HOUSE OF THE GODDESS HATHOR

I am the pure traveler.
Behold thou me! Behold thou me
O Ahi of the threshold.
For lo, I too would follow
Hathor, who is Love.

HE EMBARKETH IN THE BOAT OF RA

Hail, thou Great God in thy Boat,
Let me be thy Sailor!
Grant me speech with mariners
Of Sunrise and of Sunset.
I have traveled to thy port,
O take me in Thy travels;
Make me of thy followers
Among the stars that sleep not.
I have touched no filthy thing,

Nought that is not holy;
Morning Boat and Evening Boat
Feed me from thine altar.
Of white barley is my bread,
And my ale, red barley;
Pure the heart that sings the hymn,
Safe from many travels.
Let me sail with thee, O Ra!
In thy Boat, O Traveler!

HE COMMANDETH A FAIR WIND

Open to me!
 Who are thou? and whither goest thou?
What is thy name?
 My name? Lo, I am one of you.
For I am setting forth to the temple of the gods,
And I sail in a boat named the Assembler of Souls.

HE KNOWETH THE SOULS OF THE WEST

High on the Mountain of Sunrise where standeth the
 Temple of Sebek,
There lieth a serpent of flint and glistening plates of
 metal.
His name is The Dweller in Fire, and he is the foe of
 the Morning,
He stoppeth the Boat of Ra, and wrappeth the Boatman
 in slumber.
But he shall be held in restraint and the Boat of Ra
 sail onward,
Yea, I am the Man who restraineth the Serpent with
 mighty enchantment
And fettereth the foe of the Sunrise till Ra resume the
 horizon.
I, even I, have fettered him, and greeted the Souls of
 the West,
The Lord of the Mountain of Sunset, and Hathor, the
 Lady of Evening.

HE KNOWETH THE SOULS OF THE EAST

I EVEN I know the Eastern Gate of Heaven,
Whence Ra shall come in the Golden Boat of the
Morning,
Sailing before fair winds to the Port of Triumph.

I even I have hoisted the sails of the morning;
I have embarked with Ra by the Turquoise Sycamores,
And I am his sailor for ever in endless travels.

Mine eyes have gazed on the Fields of Peace, whose
ramparts
Are girded with iron, whose harvest is bursting with
plenty;
And there the Souls of the East are the deathless reapers.

I even I have seen the deathless Triumphant,
And the Morning Star who walks divinely among them.
The Fields of Peace have been given to me as my City.

HE OVERCOMETH THE SERPENT OF EVIL IN THE NAME OF RA

Now get thee back, retreat, depart, O Serpent,
Or thou shalt drown deep in the Pool of Sky
In the slaughter place thy father hath ordained.
Behold, my spirit riseth even as Ra,
I am become the Soul of Ra the Terrible,
Yea I have issued from the House of Terror.
Now get thee back, depart; the arrows of Ra
Fly through the shadow; beaming darts of light
Flash at thy head and tear thy bones asunder,
As the roaring clouds lift up on the horizon
With gnashing fires to fetter thee dumb in death,
To fetter thy mouth that thy words be scattered in
silence.

In the Halls of the Mighty I hear the voice of the Gods.
Hail! saith the old god Tem, make strong your faces
O soldiers of Ra, that evil be driven before us.
And there crieth the voice of Seb: Hail! all you Princes,
Make firm the seats of them who sail with the sun,
Now rise you up with your weapons and strike with
lightning.
Hail! saith Hathor the lovely; and loudly responding
The Company of Gods who go round the Pool of
Turquoise:
Hail! we will lift up the Mighty One over his foes.
Let praise be recited before him by you and by us!
O Ra! Thou terrible Light! the heavens are quaking
With the sound of gods on the march, and the Serpent
dieth.

Now get thee back, retreat, depart, O thou Serpent!
Behold I am Ra of the Eastern and Western Skies!

HE IS LIKE THE LOTUS

I AM the pure lotus,
Springing up in splendor
Fed by the breath of Ra.

Rising into sunlight,
Out of soil and darkness,
I blossom in the Field.

HE IS LIKE THE SERPENT SAKA

I AM the Serpent, fat with years,
Who dwelleth in remote domains,
Who day by day dieth and is born,
Even as I die and am born.

HE PRAYETH FOR INK AND PALETTE THAT HE MAY WRITE

HAIL, aged God who lookest on thy Father,
And guardest hidden books of Thoth unopened!
Behold, I am a scribe, and I have copied
Each day the words of beautiful Osiris
Even as Thoth hath done. O therefore grant me
Eternal use of these, my ink and palette;
And every day thou shalt receive my writings,
And thou shalt find that I have written truly.

HE KINDLETH A FIRE

THE Shining Eye of Horus cometh.
In peace it blazeth in the darkness.
And Ra is glad on the horizon
To see its flame consuming Evil.
Against the power of Set I kindle
Fire to shine with Ra, and follow
Adoring in his train for ever
Upon the hands of the Twin Sisters.

In peace the Eye of Horus liveth.

HE SINGETH IN THE UNDERWORLD

PURE is the body on the Earth,
The Spirit in the Field;
Pure are the praises from my mouth
Happy with two-fold joy.

The Serpent dieth in the place
Established by the gods.
Osiris liveth, and his throne
Is set upon the waters.

Thy beauties are a flowing stream
Resting the traveler,
A house of festival, where all
Adore their chosen gods.

Thy beauties are a columned court
With incense burned to Ra.
Thy face is brighter than the hall
Where shineth the full moon.

Thy hair is rippling like the hair
Of women from the East,
And blacker than the doors which guard
The midnight underworld.

Thy face is azure blue, and bright
As lapis lazuli;
The rays of Ra are on thy face.
Thy garments are of gold.

Thine eyebrows are twin goddesses
Who sit enthroned in peace,
And when thy nostrils breathe, the winds
Of heaven bend the grain.

Thine eyes look on the Mount of Dawn;
Thy hands are crystal pools;
Thy knees are sedges where the birds
Sing in their golden nest.

Thy feet are on the happy path;
O thou, the favored one,
Thou bathest in the Lake of God,
And goest on thy way.

THE OTHER WORLD

HERE are cakes for thy body,
Cool water for thy throat,
Sweet breezes for thy nostrils,
And thou art satisfied.

No longer dost thou stumble
Upon thy chosen path,
From thy mind all evil
And darkness fall away.

Here by the river,
Drink and bathe thy limbs,
Or cast thy net, and surely
It shall be filled with fish.

The holy cow of Hapi
Shall give thee of her milk,
The ale of gods triumphant
Shall be thy daily draught.

White linen is thy tunic,
Thy sandals shine with gold;
Victorious thy weapons,
That death come not again.

Now upon the whirlwind
Thou followest thy Prince,
Now thou hast refreshment
Under the leafy tree.

Take wings to climb the zenith,
Or sleep in Fields of Peace;
By day the Sun shall keep thee,
By night the rising Star.

ADORATION OF THE DISK BY KING AKHNATEN AND PRINCESS NEFER NEFERIU ATEN

Thy dawn, O Ra, opens the new horizon,
And every realm that you hast made to live
Is conquered by thy love, as joyous Day
Follows thy footsteps in delightful peace.

And when thou settest, all the world is bleak;
Houses are tombs where blind men lie in death;
Only the lion and the serpent move
Through the black oven of the sightless night.

Dawn in the East again! the lands awake,
And men leap from their slumber with a song;
They bathe their bodies, clothe them with fresh garments,
And lift their hands in happy adoration.

The cattle roam again across the fields;
Birds flutter in the marsh, and lift their wings
Also in adoration, and the flocks
Run with delight through all the pleasant meadows.

Both north and south along the dazzling river
Ships raise their sails and take their course before thee;
And in the ocean, all the deep-sea fish
Swim to the surface to drink in thy light.

For thou art all that lives, the seed of men,
The son within his mother's womb who knows
The comfort of thy presence near, the babe
To whom thou givest words and growing wisdom;

The chick within the egg, whose breath is thine,
Who runneth from its shell, chirping its joy,
And dancing on its small, unsteady legs
To greet the splendor of the rising sun.

Thy heart created all, this teeming earth,
Its people, herds, creatures that go afoot,
Creatures that fly in air, both land and sea,
Thou didst create them all within thy heart.

Men and their fates are thine, in all their stations,
Their many languages, their many colors,
All thine, and we who from the midst of peoples,
Thou madest different, Master of the Choice.

And lo, I find thee also in my heart,
I, Khu en Aten, find thee and adore.
O thou, whose dawn is life, whose setting, death,
In the great dawn, then lift up me, thy son.

(*Robert Hillyer*)

GREEK

Homeric Hymns

7th century B.C. ?

HYMN TO EARTH THE MOTHER OF ALL

O UNIVERSAL Mother, who dost keep
From everlasting thy foundations deep,
Eldest of things, Great Earth, I sing of thee!
All shapes that have their dwelling in the sea,
All things that fly, or on the ground divine
Live, move, and there are nourished—these are thine;
These from thy wealth thou dost sustain; from thee
Fair babes are born, and fruits on every tree
Hang ripe and large, revered Divinity!

The life of mortal men beneath thy sway
Is held; thy power both gives and takes away!
Happy are they whom thy mild favors nourish;
All things unstinted round them grow and flourish;
For them, endures the life-sustaining field
Its load of harvest, and their cattle yield
Large increase, and their house with wealth is filled.
Such honored dwell in cities fair and free,
The homes of lovely women, prosperously;
Their sons exult in youth's new budding gladness,
And their fresh daughters free from care and sadness,
With bloom-inwoven dance and happy song,
On the soft flowers the meadow-grass among,
Leap round them sporting—such delights by thee
Are given, rich Power, revered Divinity.

Mother of gods, thou wife of starry Heaven,
Farewell! be thou propitious, and be given
A happy life for this brief melody,
Nor thou nor other songs shall unremembered be.

(*Percy Bysshe Shelley*)

HYMN TO SELENE

Daughters of Jove, whose voice is melody,
Muses, who know and rule all minstrelsy,
Sing the wide-winged Moon! Around the earth,
From her immortal head in Heaven shot forth,
Far light is scattered—boundless glory springs;
Where'er she spreads her many-beaming wings
The lampless air glows round her golden crown.

But when the Moon divine from Heaven is gone
Under the sea, her beams within abide,
Till, bathing her bright limbs in Ocean's tide,
Clothing her form in garments glittering far,
And having yoked to her immortal car
The beam-invested steeds whose necks on high
Curve back, she drives to a remoter sky
A western Crescent, borne impetuously.
Then is made full the circle of her light,
And as she grows, her beams more bright and bright
Are poured from Heaven, where she is hovering then,
A wonder and a sign to mortal men.

The Son of Saturn with this glorious Power
Mingled in love and sleep—to whom she bore
Pandeia, a bright maid of beauty rare
Among the Gods, whose lives eternal are.

Hail Queen, great Moon, white-armed Divinity,
Fair-haired and favorable! thus with thee
My song beginning, by its music sweet
Shall make immortal many a glorious feat
Of demigods, with lovely lips, so well
Which minstrels, servants of the Muses, tell.

(*Percy Bysshe Shelley*)

HYMN TO ATHENA

I sing the glorious Power with azure eyes,
Athenian Pallas! timeless, chaste, and wise,
Tritogenia, town-preserving Maid,
Revered and mighty; from his awful head
Whom Jove brought forth, in warlike armor dressed,
Golden, all radiant! wonder strange possessed
The everlasting Gods that Shape to see,
Shaking a javelin keen, impetuously
Rush from the crest of Ægis-bearing Jove;
Fearfully Heaven was shaken, and did move
Beneath the might of the Cerulean-eyed;
Earth dreadfully resounded, far and wide;
And, lifted from its depths, the sea swelled high
In purple billows, the tide suddenly
Stood still, and great Hyperion's son long time
Checked his swift steeds, till, where she stood sublime,
Pallas from her immortal shoulders threw
The arms divine; wise Jove rejoiced to view.
Child of the Ægis-bearer, hail to thee,
Nor thine nor others' praise shall unremembered be.

(*Percy Bysshe Shelley*)

HYMN TO CASTOR AND POLLUX

Ye wild-eyed Muses, sing the Twins of Jove,
Whom the fair-ankled Leda, mixt in love
With mighty Saturn's heaven-obscuring Child,
On Taygetus, that lofty mountain wild,
Brought forth in joy, mild Pollux void of blame,
And steed-subduing Castor, heirs of fame.
These are the Powers who earth-born mortals save
And ships, whose flight is swift along the wave,
When wintry tempests o'er the savage sea
Are raging, and the sailors tremblingly
Call on the twins of Jove with prayer and vow,
Gathered in fear upon the lofty prow,

And sacrificed with snow-white lambs, the wind
And the huge billow bursting close behind.
Even then beneath the weltering waters bear
The staggering ship—they suddenly appear,
On yellow wings rushing athwart the sky,
And lull the blasts in mute tranquillity,
And strew the waves on the white ocean's bed,
Fair omen of the voyage; from toil and dread
The sailors rest, rejoicing in the sight,
And plow the quiet sea in safe delight.

(Percy Bysshe Shelley)

Alcman

c. 680 B.C.

FRAGMENT

THE mountain summits sleep, glens, cliffs, and caves
Are silent;—all the black earth's reptile brood,
The bees, the wild beasts of the mountain wood;
In depths beneath the dark red ocean's waves
Its monsters rest; whilst, wrapt in bower and spray,
Each bird is hush'd, that stretch'd its pinions to the day.

(Thomas Campbell)

Mimnermus

620 B.C.

YOUTH AND AGE

AH! fair and lovely bloom the flowers of youth;
On men and maids they beautifully smile:
But soon comes doleful eld, who, void of ruth,
Indifferently afflicts the fair and vile;
Then cares wear out the heart: old eyes forlorn
Scarce reck the very sunshine to behold—
Unloved by youths, of every maid the scorn—
So hard a lot God lays upon the old.

(J. A. Symonds, M.D.)

Alcæus

610 B.C.

LET US DRINK

Why wait we for the torches' lights?
Now let us drink, while day invites,
In mighty flagons hither bring
The deep-red blood of many a vine,
That we may largely quaff, and sing
The praises of the god of wine,
The son of Jove and Semele,
Who gave the jocund wine to be
A sweet oblivion to our woes.
Fill, fill the goblet, one and two;
Let every brimmer, as it flows,
In sportive chase the last pursue.

(John Hermann Merivale)

THE STORM

Jove descends in sleet and snow,
Howls the vexed and angry deep;
Every stream forgets to flow,
Bound in winter's icy sleep,
Ocean wave and forest hoar
To the blast responsive roar.

Drive the tempest from your door,
Blaze on blaze your hearthstone piling,
And unmeasured goblets pour
Brimful, high with nectar smiling.
Then, beneath your poet's head
Be a downy pillow spread.

(John Hermann Merivale)

Sappho

610 B.C.

Judging even from the mutilated fragments fallen within our reach from the broken altar of her sacrifice of song, I for one have always agreed with all Grecian tradition in thinking Sappho to be beyond all question and comparison the very greatest poet that ever lived.—ALGERNON CHARLES SWINBURNE.

ODE TO APHRODITE

DEATHLESS Aphrodite, throned in flowers,
Daughter of Zeus, O terrible enchantress,
With this sorrow, with this anguish, break my spirit,
Lady, not longer!

Hear anew the voice! O hear and listen!
Come, as in that island dawn thou camest,
Billowing in thy yoked car to Sappho
Forth from thy father's

Golden house in pity! . . . I remember:
Fleet and fair thy sparrows drew thee, beating
Fast their wings above the dusky harvests,
Down the pale heavens,

Lighting anon! And thou, O blest and brightest,
Smiling with immortal eyelids, asked me:
"Maiden, what betideth thee? Or wherefore
Callest upon me?

"What is here the longing more than other,
Here in this mad heart? And who the lovely
One beloved thou wouldst lure to loving?
Sappho, who wrongs thee?

"See, if now she flies, she soon must follow;
Yes, if spurning gifts, she soon must offer;
Yes, if loving not, she soon must love thee,
Howso unwilling. . . ."

Come again to me! O now! Release me!
End the great pang! And all my heart desireth
Now of fulfillment, fulfill! O Aphrodite,
Fight by my shoulder!

(*William Ellery Leonard*)

ODE TO ANACTORIA

Peer of the golden gods is he to Sappho,
He, the happy man who sits beside thee,
Heark'ning so divinely close thy lovely
Speech and dear laughter.

This it was that made to flutter wildly
Heart of mine in bosom panting wildly! . . .
Oh! I need to see thee but a little,
When, as at lightning,

Voice within me stumbles, tongue is broken,
Tingles all my flesh with subtle fire,
Ring my ears with waterfalls and thunders,
Eyes are in midnight,

And a sweat bedews me like a shower,
Tremor hunts my body down and seizes,
Till, as one about to die, I linger
Paler than grass is. . . .

(*William Ellery Leonard*)

FAREWELL TO ANACTORIA

Never the tramp of foot or horse,
Nor lusty cries from ships at sea,
Shall I call loveliest on the dark earth—
My heart moves lovingly.

I say that what one loves is best—
The midnight fastness of the heart. . . .
Helen, you filched the beauty of men
With unpitying art!

White Paris from Idean hills
For you the Trojan towers razed—
Who swiftly plowed the black seas
Had on your white arms gazed!

Oh, how loving from afar
Led you to grief, for in your mind
The present was too light, as ever
Among fair womankind. . . .

So, Anactoria, you go away
With what calm carelessness of sorrow!
Your gleaming footstep and your grace,
When comes another morrow,

Much would I rather then behold
Than Lydian cars or infantry.
I ask the lot of blessedness,
Belovèd, in memory.

(*Allen Tate*)

FRAGMENTS

Hesperus the Bringer

O Hesperus, thou bringest all good things—
Home to the weary, to the hungry cheer,
To the young bird the parent's brooding wings,
The welcome stall to the o'erlabored steer;
Whate'er of peace about our hearthstone clings,
Whate'er our household gods protect of dear,
Are gathered round us by thy look of rest;
Thou bring'st the child too to its mother's breast.

(*Lord Byron*)

One Girl

I

Like the sweet apple which reddens upon
the topmost bough,
A-top on the topmost twig,—which the
pluckers forgot, somehow,—

Forget it not, nay, but got it not, for none
could get it till now.

2

Like the wild hyacinth flower which on the
hills is found,
Which the passing feet of the shepherds
for ever tear and wound,
Until the purple blossom is trodden in the
ground.

(*D. G. Rossetti*)

Mother, I Cannot Mind My Wheel

Mother, I cannot mind my wheel;
My fingers ache, my lips are dry;
Oh! if you felt the pain I feel!
But oh, who ever felt as I!

(*Walter Savage Landor*)

The Dust of Timas

This dust was Timas; and they say
That almost on her wedding day
She found her bridal home to be
The dark house of Persephone.

And many maidens, knowing then
That she would not come back again,
Unbound their curls; and all in tears,
They cut them off with sharpened shears.

(*Edwin Arlington Robinson*)

Round About Me

Round about me hum the winds of autumn,
Cool between the apple boughs: and slumber,
Flowing from the quivering leaves to earthward,
Spreads as a river.

Love

Love, like a mountain-wind upon an oak,
Falling upon me, shakes me leaf and bough.

Full Moon

Off in the twilight hung the low full moon,
And all the women stood before it grave,
As round an altar. Thus at holy times
The Cretan damsels dance melodiously
With delicate feet about the sacrifice,
Trampling the tender bloom of the soft grass.

Alone

The moon and seven Pleiades have set;
It is the midnight now; the hours go by;
And still I'm lying in my bed alone.

Forever Dead

Death shall be death forever unto thee,
Lady, with no remembrance of thy name
Then or thereafter; for thou gatherest not
The roses of Pieria, loving gold
Above the Muses. Even in Hades' House
Wander thou shalt unmarked, flitting forlorn
Among the shadowy, averted dead.

(William Ellery Leonard)

Theognis

540 B.C.

ENJOYMENT

Enjoy your time, my soul! another race
Shall shortly fill the world, and take your place
With their own hopes and fears, sorrow and mirth;
I shall be dust the while, and crumbled earth.

But think not of it. Drink the racy wine
Of rich Taygetus, pressed from the vine
Which Theotimus in the sunny glen
(Old Theotimus, loved of gods and men,)
Planted and watered from a plenteous source,
Teaching the wayward stream a better course:
Drink it, and cheer your heart, and banish care,
A load of wine will lighten your despair.

(*John Hookham Frere*)

HOPE

For human nature Hope remains alone
Of all the deities; the rest are flown.
Faith is departed; Truth and Honor dead;
And all the Graces too, my friends, are fled.
The scanty specimens of living worth,
Dwindled to nothing, and extinct on earth.
Yet whilst I live and view the light of heaven,
Since Hope remains and never has been driven
From the distracted world—the single scope
Of my devotion is to worship Hope.
When hecatombs are slain, and altars burn,
When all the deities adored in turn,
Let Hope be present; and with Hope, my friend,
Let every sacrifice commence and end.
Yes, Insolence, Injustice, every crime,
Rapine and Wrong, may prosper for a time;
Yet shall they travel on to swift decay,
Who tread the crooked path and hollow way.

(*John Hookham Frere*)

POVERTY

For noble minds, the worst of miseries,
Worse than old age, or wearisome disease,
Is Poverty. From Poverty to flee,
From some tall precipice into the sea,

It were a fair escape to leap below!
In Poverty, dear Kyrnus, we forego
Freedom in word and deed, body and mind;
Action and thought are fetter'd and confin'd.
Let me then fly, dear Kyrnus, once again!
Wide as the limits of the land and main,
From these entanglements; with these in view,
Death is the lighter evil of the two.

(John Hookham Frere)

Anacreon and Anacreontics

6th century B.C. *et seq.*

THE WOUNDED CUPID

Cupid, as he lay among
Roses, by a bee was stung.
Whereupon in anger flying
To his mother, said, thus crying,
Help! O help! your boy's a-dying.
And why, my pretty lad? said she.
Then blubbering replièd he,
A wingèd snake has bitten me,
Which country people call a bee.
At which she smiled, then with her hairs
And kisses, drying up his tears,
Alas! said she, my wag, if this
Such a pernicious torment is;
Come, tell me then how great's the smart
Of those thou woundest with thy dart!

(Robert Herrick)

THE CHEAT OF CUPID

OR, THE UNGENTLE GUEST

One silent night of late,
  When every creature rested,
Came one unto my gate,
  And knocking, me molested.

Who's that, said I, beats there,
  And troubles thus the sleepy?
Cast off, said he, all fear,
  And let not locks thus keep ye.

For I a boy am, who
  By moonless nights have swervèd;
And all with showers wet through,
  And e'en with cold half starvèd.

I pitiful arose,
  And soon a taper lighted,
And did myself disclose
  Unto the lad benighted.

I saw he had a bow,
  And wings too, which did shiver;
And looking down below,
  I spied he had a quiver.

I to my chimney's shine
  Brought him, as love professes,
And chafed his hands with mine,
  And dried his dropping tresses.

But when he felt him warmed,
  Let's try this bow of ours
And string, if they be harmed,
  Said he, with these late showers.

Forthwith his bow he bent,
  And wedded string and arrow,
And struck me that it went
  Quite through my heart and marrow.

Then laughing loud, he flew
  Away, and thus said, flying,
Adieu, mine host, adieu,
  I'll leave thy heart a-dying.

(*Robert Herrick*)

LOVE

I'LL sing of heroes and of kings,
In mighty numbers, mighty things.
Begin, my Muse!—but lo! the strings
To my great song rebellious prove;
The strings will sound of nought but love.
—I broke them all, and put on new;
—'Tis this, or nothing, now will do.
"These, sure," said I, "will me obey;
These, sure, heroic notes will play."
Straight I began with thundering Jove
And all th' immortal powers; but Love,
Love smil'd; and from my enfeebled lyre
Came gentle airs, such as inspire
Melting love and soft desire.—
Farewell, then, heroes! farewell, kings!
And mighty numbers, mighty things!
Love tunes my heart just to my strings.

(*Abraham Cowley*)

THE GRASSHOPPER

HAPPY insect! what can be
In happiness compar'd to thee?
Fed with nourishment divine,
The dewy morning's gentle wine!
Nature waits upon thee still,
And thy verdant cup does fill;
'Tis filled wherever thou dost tread,
Nature self's thy Ganymede.
Thou dost drink, and dance, and sing;
Happier than the happiest king!
All the fields which thou dost see,
All the plants belong to thee;
All that summer hours produce;

Fertile made with early juice.
Man for thee does sow and plow;
Farmer he, and landlord thou!
Thou dost innocently joy;
Nor does thy luxury destroy;
The shepherd gladly heareth thee,
More harmonious than he.
Thee country-hinds with gladness hear,
Prophet of the ripen'd year!
Thee Phœbus loves, and does inspire;
Phœbus is himself thy sire.
To thee, of all things upon earth,
Life's no longer than thy mirth.
Happy insect, happy, thou
Dost neither age nor winter know;
But, when thou'st drunk, and danc'd and sung
Thy fill, the flowery leaves among,
(Voluptuous and wise withal,
Epicurean animal!)—
Sated with thy summer feast,
Thou retir'st to endless rest.

(*Abraham Cowley*)

AGE

Oft am I by the women told,
"Poor Anacreon! thou grow'st old;
Look! how thy hairs are falling all;
Poor Anacreon, how they fall!"—
Whether I grow old or no,
By the effects I do not know;
But this I know, without being told,
'Tis time to live, if I grow old;
'Tis time short pleasures now to take,
Of little life the best to make,
And manage wisely the last stake.

(*Abraham Cowley*)

THE EPICURE

Underneath this myrtle shade,
On flowery beds supinely laid,
With odorous oils my head o'erflowing,
And around it roses growing,
What should I do but drink away
The heat and troubles of the day?
In this more than kingly state,
Love himself shall on me wait.
Fill to me, Love; nay, fill it up;
And mingled cast into the cup
Wit, and mirth, and noble fires,
Vigorous health, and gay desires.
The wheel of life no less will stay
In a smooth than rugged way:
Since it equally doth flee,
Let the motion pleasant be.
Why do we precious ointments shower?
Nobler wines why do we pour?
Beauteous flowers why do we spread
Upon the monuments of the dead?
Nothing they but dust can show,
Or bones that hasten to be so.
Crown me with roses whilst I live,—
Now your wines and ointments give;
After death I nothing crave,
Let me alive my pleasures have!
All are Stoics in the grave.

(Abraham Cowley)

BEAUTY

Horns to bulls wise Nature lends;
Horses she with hoofs defends;
Hares with nimble feet relieves;
Dreadful teeth to lions gives;
Fishes learn through streams to slide;
Birds through yielding air to glide;

Men with courage she supplies;
But to women these denies.
What then gives she? Beauty, this
Both their arms and armor is:
She, that can this weapon use,
Fire and sword with ease subdues.

(Thomas Stanley)

ROSES

Roses (Love's delight) let's join
To the red-cheek'd God of Wine;
Roses crown us, while we laugh,
And the juice of Autumn quaff!
Roses of all flowers the king,
Roses the fresh pride o' th' Spring,
Joy of every deity.
Love, when with the Graces he
For the ball himself disposes,
Crowns his golden hair with roses.
Circling then with these our brow,
We'll to Bacchus' temple go:
There some willing beauty lead,
And a youthful measure tread.

(Thomas Stanley)

THE COMBAT

Now will I a lover be;
Love himself commanded me.
Full at first of stubborn pride,
To submit my soul denied;
He his quiver takes and bow,
Bids defiance, forth I go,
Arm'd with spear and shield, we meet;
On he charges, I retreat:
Till perceiving in the fight
He had wasted every flight,
Into me, with fury hot,

Like a dart himself he shot,
And my cold heart melts; my shield
Useless, no defense could yield;
For what boots an outward screen
When, alas, the fight's within!

(*Thomas Stanley*)

THE SWALLOW

Chattering swallow! what shall we,
Shall we do to punish thee?
Shall we clip thy wings, or cut
Tereus-like thy shrill tongue out?
Who Rhodantha driv'st away
From my dreams by break of day.

(*Thomas Stanley*)

ALL THINGS DRINK

Fruitful earth drinks up the rain;
Trees from earth drink that again;
The sea drinks the air, the sun
Drinks the sea, and him the moon.
Is it reason then, d'ye think,
I should thirst when all else drink?

(*Thomas Stanley*)

THE PICTURE

Painter, by unmatch'd desert
Master of the Rhodian art,
Come, my absent mistress take,
As I shall describe her: make
First her hair, as black as bright,
And if colors so much right
Can but do her, let it too
Smell of aromatic dew;
Underneath this shade, must thou
Draw her alabaster brow;

Her dark eyebrows so dispose
That they neither part nor close,
But by a divorce so slight
Be disjoin'd, may cheat the sight:
From her kindly killing eye
Make a flash of lightning fly,
Sparkling like Minerva's, yet
Like Cythera's mildly sweet:
Roses in milk swimming seek
For the pattern of her cheek:
In her lip such moving blisses,
As from all may challenge kisses;
Round about her neck (outvying
Parian stone) the Graces flying;
And o'er all her limbs at last
A loose purple mantle cast;
But so ordered that the eye
Some part naked may descry,
An essay by which the rest
That lies hidden, may be guess'd.
So, to life th' hast come so near,
All of her, but voice, is here.

(*Thomas Stanley*)

SPRING

See the Spring herself discloses,
And the Graces gather roses;
See how the becalmed seas
Now their swelling waves appease;
How the duck swims, how the crane
Comes from winter home again;
See how Titan's cheerful ray
Chaseth the dark clouds away;
Now in their new robes of green
Are the plowman's labors seen:
Now the lusty teeming Earth
Springs each hour with a new birth;

Now the olive blooms: the vine
Now doth with plump pendants shine;
And with leaves and blossoms now
Freshly bourgeons every bough.

(Thomas Stanley)

OLD I AM

Old I am, yet can (I think)
Those that younger are out-drink;
When I dance no staff I take,
But a well-fill'd bottle shake:
He that doth in war delight,
Come, and with these arms let's fight;
Fill the cup, let loose a flood
Of the rich grape's luscious blood;
Old I am, and therefore may,
Like Silenus, drink and play.

(Thomas Stanley)

YOUTHFUL AGE

Young men dancing, and the old
Sporting I with joy behold;
But an old man gay and free
Dancing most I love to see;
Age and youth alike he shares,
For his heart belies his hairs.

(Thomas Stanley)

THE WISH

Niobe on Phrygian sands
Turn'd a weeping statue stands,
And the Pandionian Maid
In a swallow's wings array'd;
But a mirror I would be,
To be look'd on still by thee;
Or the gown wherein thou'rt drest,
That I might thy limbs invest;

Or a crystal spring, wherein
Thou might'st bathe thy purer skin;
Or sweet unguents, to anoint
And make supple every joint;
Or a knot, thy breast to deck;
Or a chain, to clasp thy neck;
Or thy shoe I wish to be,
That thou might'st but tread on me.

(*Thomas Stanley*)

THE CUP

Make me a bowl, a mighty bowl,
Large as my capacious soul,
Vast as my thirst is. Let it have
Depth enough to be my grave.
I mean the grave of all my care,
For I intend to bury't there.
Let it of silver fashioned be,
Worthy of wine! worthy of me!
Worthy to adorn the spheres
As that bright Cup among the stars!

Yet draw no shapes of armor there,
No casque nor shield nor sword nor spear,
Nor wars of Thebes nor wars of Troy,
Nor any other martial toy.
For what do I vain armor prize,
Who mind not such rough exercise?
But gentle sieges, softer wars,
Fights that cause no wounds or scars.
I'll have not battles on my plate,
Lest sight of them should brawls create,
Lest that provoke to quarrels too,
Which wine itself enough can do.

(*John Oldham*)

ANACREON'S DOVE

"Lovely courier of the sky,
Whence and whither dost thou fly?
Scattering, as thy pinions play,
Liquid fragrance all the way.
Is it business? Is it love?
Tell me, tell me, gentle Dove."—
"Soft Anacreon's vows I bear,
Vows to Myrtale the fair;
Graced with all that charms the heart,
Blushing nature, smiling art,
Venus, courted by an ode,
On the Bard her Dove bestow'd.
Vested with a master's right,
Now Anacreon rules my flight:
As the letters that you see,
Weighty charge consign'd to me:
Think not yet my service hard,
Joyless task without reward:
Smiling at my master's gates,
Freedom my return awaits:
But the liberal grant in vain
Tempts me to be wild again.
Can a prudent Dove decline
Blissful bondage such as mine?
Over hills and fields to roam,
Fortune's guest without a home;
Under leaves to hide one's head,
Slightly shelter'd, coarsely fed;
Now my better lot bestows
Sweet repast, and soft repose;
Now the generous bowl I sip
As it leaves Anacreon's lip;
Void of care, and free from dread
From his fingers snatch his bread,
Then with luscious plenty gay
Round his chambers dance and play;

Or, from wine as courage springs,
O'er his face expand my wings;
And, when feast and frolic tire,
Drop asleep upon his lyre.
This is all; be quick and go,
More than all thou can'st not know;
Let me now my pinions ply,—
I have chatter'd like a pye."

(*Samuel Johnson*)

Simonides of Ceos

480 B.C.

THERMOPYLÆ

Go tell the Spartans, thou that passeth by,
That here, obedient to their laws, we lie.

(*William Lisle Bowles*)

Bacchylides

450 B.C.

PEACE ON EARTH

To mortal men Peace giveth these good things:
Wealth, and the flowers of honey-throated song;
The flame that springs
On craven altars from fat sheep and kine,
Slain to the gods in heaven; and, all day long,
Games for glad youths, and flutes, and wreaths, and circling wine.
Then in the steely shield swart spiders weave
Their web and dusky woof:
Rust to the pointed spear and sword doth cleave;
The brazen trump sounds no alarms;
Nor is sleep harried from our eyes aloof,
But with sweet rest my bosom warms:
The streets are thronged with lovely men and young,
And hymns in praise of boys like flames to heaven are flung.

(*John Addington Symonds*)

Æschylus

525-456 B.C.

Nothing could equal the sublime emotion with which the Trilogy inspired me, and to the last words of the *Eumenides* I lived in an atmosphere so far removed from the present day that I have never since been really able to reconcile myself with modern literature.—Richard Wagner.

CHORUS FROM AGAMEMNON

Great Fortune is an hungry thing,
And filleth no heart anywhere,
Though men with fingers menacing
Point at the great house, none will dare,
When Fortune knocks, to bar the door
Proclaiming: "Come thou here no more!"
Lo, to this man the Gods have given
Great Ilion in the dust to tread
And home return, emblazed of heaven;
If it is writ, he too shall go
Through blood for blood spilt long ago;
If he too, dying for the dead,
Should crown the deaths of alien years,
What mortal afar off, who hears,
Shall boast him Fortune's Child, and led
Above the eternal tide of tears?

(*Sir Gilbert Murray*)

CHORUS FROM THE SEVEN AGAINST THEBES

Lament for the Two Brothers Slain by Each Other's Hand

Now do our eyes behold
The tidings which were told:
Twin fallen kings, twin perished hopes to mourn,
The slayer, the slain,
The entangled doom forlorn
And ruinous end of twain.

Say, is not sorrow, is not sorrow's sum
  On home and hearthstone come?
  Oh, waft with sighs the sail from shore,
  Oh, smite the bosom, cadencing the oar
That rows beyond the rueful stream for aye
    To the far strand,
    The ship of souls, the dark,
    The unreturning bark
Whereon light never falls nor foot of Day,
Even to the bourne of all, to the unbeholden land.

(*A. E. Housman*)

Sophocles

495-406 B.C.

Who saw life steadily, and saw it whole.—MATTHEW ARNOLD.

CHORUS FROM ŒDIPUS COLONEUS

WHAT man is he that yearneth
  For length unmeasured of days?
Folly mine eye discerneth
  Encompassing all his ways.
For years over-running the measure
  Shall change thee in evil wise:
Grief draweth nigh thee; and pleasure,
  Behold it is hid from thine eyes.
  This to their wage have they
  Which overlive their day.
And He that looseth from labor
  Doth one with other befriend,
  Whom bride nor bridesmen attend,
Song, nor sound of the tabor,
  Death, that maketh an end.

Thy portion esteem I highest,
  Who wast not ever begot;
Thine next, being born who diest
  And straightway again art not.

With follies light as the feather
  Doth Youth to man befall;
Then evils gather together,
  There wants not one of them all—
  Wrath, envy, discord, strife,
  The sword that seeketh life.
And sealing the sum of trouble
  Doth tottering Age draw nigh,
  Whom friends and kinsfolk fly,
Age, upon whom redouble
  All sorrows under the sky.

This man, as me, even so,
Have the evil days overtaken;
And like as a cape sea-shaken
With tempest at earth's last verges
And shock of all winds that blow,
His head the seas of woe,
The thunders of awful surges
Ruining overflow;
Blown from the fall of eve,
  Blown from the dayspring forth,
Blown from the noon in heaven,
  Blown from night and the North.

(*A. E. Housman*)

CHORUS FROM AJAX

Fair Salamis, the billow's roar
  Wanders around thee yet;
And sailors gaze upon thy shore
  Firm in the Ocean set.
Thy son is in a foreign clime
  Where Ida feeds her countless flocks,
  Far from thy dear remembered rocks,
Worn by the waste of time,—

Comfortless, nameless, hopeless,—save
In the dark prospect of the yawning grave.
And Ajax, in his deep distress
Allied to our disgrace,
Hath cherished in his loneliness
The bosom friend's embrace.
Frenzy hath seized thy dearest son,
Who from thy shores in glory came
The first in valor and in fame;
The deeds that he hath done
Seem hostile all to hostile eyes;
The sons of Atreus see them and despise.

Woe to the mother, in her close of day,
Woe to her desolate heart, and temples gray,
When she shall hear
Her loved one's story whispered in her ear!
"Woe, woe!" will be the cry,—
No quiet murmur like the tremulous wail
Of the lone bird, the querulous nightingale,—
But shrieks that fly
Piercing, and wild, and loud, shall mourn the tale;
And she will beat her breast, and rend her hair,
Scattering the silver locks that Time hath left her there.

Oh! when the pride of Græcia's noblest race
Wanders, as now, in darkness and disgrace,
When Reason's day
Sets rayless—joyless—quenched in cold decay,
Better to die, and sleep
The never-waking sleep, than linger on,
And dare to live, when the soul's life is gone:
But thou shalt weep,
Thou wretched father, for thy dearest son,
Thy best beloved, by inward Furies torn,
The deepest, bitterest curse thine ancient house hath borne!

(*Winthrop Mackworth Praed*)

Euripides

480-406 B.C.

Sad Electra's poet—Milton.

CHORUS FROM ALCESTIS

The Strength of Fate

In heaven-high musings and many,
Far-seeking and deep debate,
Of strong things find I not any
That is as the strength of Fate.
Help nor healing is told
In soothsayings uttered of old,
In the Thracian runes, the verses
Engraven of Orpheus' pen;
No balm of virtue to save
Apollo aforetime gave,
Who stayeth with tender mercies
The plagues of the children of men.

She hath not her habitation
In temples that hands have wrought;
Him that bringeth oblation,
Behold, she heedeth him naught.
Be thou not wroth with us more,
O mistress, than heretofore;
For what God willeth soever,
That thou bringest to be;
Thou breakest in sunder the brand
Far forged in the Iron Land;
Thine heart is cruel, and never
Came pity anigh unto thee.

Thee, too, O King, hath she taken
And bound in her tenfold chain;
Yet faint not, neither complain:
The dead thou wilt not awaken
For all thy weeping again.

They perish, whom gods begot;
The night releaseth them not.
Beloved was she that died
And dear shall ever abide,
For this was the queen among women, Admetus, that lay by thy side.

Not as the multitude lowly
Asleep in their sepulchres,
Not as their grave be hers,
But like as the gods held holy,
The worship of wayfarers.
Yea, all that travel the way
Far off shall see it and say,
Lo, erst for her lord she died,
To-day she sitteth enskied;
Hail, lady, be gracious to usward; that alway her honor abide.

(*A. E. Housman*)

CHORUSES FROM THE CYCLOPS

Love Song

One with eyes the fairest
Cometh from his dwelling,
Some one loves thee, rarest,
Bright beyond my telling.
In thy grace thou shinest
Like some nymph divinest,
In her caverns dewy:—
All delights pursue thee,
Soon pied flowers, sweet-breathing,
Shall thy head be wreathing.

Chorus of Satyrs, Driving Their Goats

Where has he of race divine
Wandered in the winding rocks?
Here the air is calm and fine
For the father of the flocks;

Here the grass is soft and sweet,
And the river-eddies meet
In the trough beside the cave,
Bright as in their fountain wave.
Neither here, nor on the dew
  Of the lawny uplands feeding?
Oh, you come!—a stone at you
  Will I throw to mend your breeding;
Get along, you hornèd thing,
Wild, seditious, rambling!
An Iacchic melody
  To the golden Aphrodite
Will I lift, as erst did I
  Seeking her and her delight
With the Mænads, whose white feet
To the music glance and fleet.
Bacchus, O belovèd, where
Shaking wide thy yellow hair,
Wanderest thou alone, afar?
  To the one-eyed Cyclops we,
Who by right thy servants are,
  Minister in misery,
In these wretched goat-skins clad,
  Far from thy delights and thee.

(Percy Bysshe Shelley)

CHORUS FROM THE BACCHAI

The Home of Aphrodite

Where is the home for me?
O Cyprus, set in the sea,
Aphrodite's home in the soft sea-foam,
Would I could wend to thee;
Where the wings of the Loves are furled,
And faint the heart of the world!

Ay, or to Paphos' isle,
Where the rainless meadows smile
With riches rolled from the hundred-fold

Mouths of the far-off Nile,
Streaming beneath the waves
To the roots of the seaward caves!

But a better land is there
Where Olympus cleaves the air,
The high still dell where the Muses dwell,
Fairest of all things fair.
O there is Grace and there is the Heart's desire
And peace to adore thee, thou spirit of Guiding Fire!

(*Sir Gilbert Murray*)

CHORUSES FROM HIPPOLYTUS

O For the Wings of a Dove

Could I take me to some cavern for mine hiding,
  In the hilltops where the Sun scarce hath trod;
Or a cloud make the home of mine abiding,
  As a bird among the bird-droves of God.
Could I wing me to my rest amid the roar
Of the deep Adriatic on the shore
Where the water of Eridanus is clear,
  And Phaeton's sad sisters by his grave
Weep into the river, and each tear
  Gleams a drop of amber, in the wave.

To the strand of the Daughters of the Sunset,
  The Apple-tree, the singing and the gold;
Where the mariner must stay him from his onset,
  And the red wave is tranquil as of old;
    Yea, beyond that pillar of the End
    That Atlas guardeth, would I wend;
Where a voice of living waters never ceaseth
  In God's quiet garden by the sea,
And Earth, the ancient life-giver, increaseth
  Joy among the meadows, like a tree.

(*Sir Gilbert Murray*)

No More, O My Spirit

No more, O my spirit,
are we flawless,
we have seen evil undrempt:
I myself saw it:
the Greek, the most luminous,
the Athenian, the star-like,
banished through his father's hate
to a country far distant.

O sand dunes and sand-stretches
of the Athenian coast,
O mountain-thickets
Where you climbed,
following the wild beasts,
with hounds, delicate of feet,
hunting with the dæmon, Artemis!

No more
will you mount your chariot,
yoked with horses of Enetas,
nor spur forward your steed
toward the stadium at Limnas,
and your chant, ever rapturous,
and the answering lyre-note,
shall cease in the king's house:
far in the forest depth
in the glades where she loves to rest,
Latona's child shall be crownless:
at your flight
the contest of the maidens will cease,
and their love-longing, comfortless.

And because of your fate,
I accept bitter hurt,
and weep:
ai, ai poor mother,
your birth-pangs were fruitless:

I am wroth with these spirits:
alas, Karites, never-separate,
why, why have you sent him forth,
the unfortunate, blameless,
from his palace,
from his own gates?

(*H. D.*)

CHORUS FROM IPHIGENEIA IN AULIS

And Pergamos,
City of the Phrygians,
Ancient Troy
Will be given up to its fate.
They will mark the stone-battlements
And the circle of them
With a bright stain.
They will cast out the dead—
A sight for Priam's queen to lament
And her frightened daughters.

And Helen, child of Zeus,
Will cry aloud for the mate
She has left in that Phrygian town.

May no child of mine,
Nor any child of my child
Ever fashion such a tale
As the Phrygians shall murmur,
As they stoop at their distaffs,
Whispering with Lydians,
Splendid with weight of gold—

"Helen has brought this.
They will tarnish our bright hair.
They will take us as captives
For Helen—born of Zeus
When he sought Leda with bird-wing
And touched her with bird-throat—
If men speak truth.

"But still we lament our state,
The desert of our wide courts,
Even if there is no truth
In the legends cut on ivory
Nor in the poets
Nor the songs."

(*H. D.*)

Aristophanes

444-380 B.C.

The half divine humorist in whose incomparable genius the highest qualities of Rabelais were fused and harmonized with the supremest gifts of Shelley.—ALGERNON CHARLES SWINBURNE.

CHORUS OF BIRDS

COME on then, ye dwellers by Nature in darkness, and
like to the leaves' generations,
That are little of might, that are molded of mire,
unenduring and shadow-like nations,
Poor plumeless ephemerals, comfortless mortals, as
visions of shadows fast fleeing
Lift up your mind unto us that are deathless, and dateless the date of our being;
Us, children of heaven; us, ageless for aye; us, all of
whose thoughts are eternal:
That ye may from henceforth, having heard of us all
things aright as to matters supernal,
Of the being of birds and beginning of Gods and of
streams and the dark beyond reaching,
Trustfully knowing aright, in my name bid Prodicos
pack with his preaching,
It was Chaos, and Night at the first, and the blackness of
darkness, and Hell's broad border,
Earth was not, nor air, neither heaven; when in depths
of the womb of the dark without order
First thing, first born of the black-plumed Night, was a
wind-egg hatcht in her bosom,

Whence timely with seasons revolving again sweet Love
burst out as a blossom,
Gold wings glittering forth of his back, like whirlwinds
gustily turning.
He, after his wedlock with Chaos, whose wings are of
darkness, in Hell broad burning,
For his nestlings begat him the race of us first and up-
raised us to light new-lighted.
And before this was not the race of the Gods, until all
things by Love were united:
And of kind united in kind with communion of Nature
the sky and the sea are
Brought forth and the earth and the race of the Gods
everlasting and blest. So that we are
Far away the most ancient of all things blest! And
that we are of Love's generation
There are manifest manifold signs. We have wings and
with us have the Loves habitation;
And manifold fair young folk that forswore love once,
ere the bloom of them ended
Have the men pursued that pursued and desired them
subdued by the help of us only befriended,
With such bait as a quail, a flamingo, a goose, or a
cock's comb staring and splendid.
All best good things that befall men come from us birds,
as is plain to all reason:
For fist we proclaim and make known to them Spring
and the Winter and Autumn in season;
Bid sow, when the crane starts clanging for Afric in
shrill-voiced emigrant number
And calls to the pilot to hang up his rudder again for
the season and slumber;
And then weave a cloak for Orestes the thief, lest he
strip men of theirs if it freezes.
And again thereafter the kite reappearing announces a
change in the breezes.
And that here is the season for shearing your sheep ot
their spring wool. Then does the swallow

Give you notice to sell your greatcoat and provide something light for the heat that's to follow.
Thus are we as Ammon or Delphoi unto you, Dodona, nay Phoibos Apollo!
For, as first ye come all to get auguries of birds, even such is in all things your carriage,
Be the matter a matter of trade, or of earning your bread, or of any one's marriage.
And all things ye lay to the charge of a bird that belongs to discerning prediction.
Winged fame is a bird, as you reckon; you sneeze and the sign's as a bird for conviction.
All tokens are *birds* with you—sounds, too, and lackeys and donkeys. Then must it not follow
That we are to you all as the manifest Godhead that speaks in prophetic Apollo?

(*Algernon Charles Swinburne*)

SONG OF THE CLOUDS

Cloud-maidens that float on forever,
Dew-sprinkled, fleet bodies, and fair,
Let us rise from our Sire's loud river,
Great Ocean, and soar through the air
To the peaks of the pine-covered mountains where the pines hang as tresses of hair!
Let us seek the watch-towers undaunted,
Where the well-watered cornfields abound,
And through murmurs of rivers nymph-haunted
The songs of the sea-waves resound;
And the sun in the sky never wearies of spreading his radiance around!
Let us cut off the haze
Of the mists from our band,
Till with far-seeing gaze
We may look on the land!
Cloud-maidens that bring the rain-shower,
To the Pallas-loved land let us wing.

To the land of stout heroes and Power,
  Where Kekrops was hero and king,
Where honor and silence is given
  To the mysteries that none may declare,
Where the gifts to the high gods in heaven
  When the house of the gods is laid bare,
Where are lofty-rooft temples and statues well-carven and
    fair;
Where are feasts to the happy immortals
  When the sacred procession draws near,
Where garlands make bright the bright portals
  At all seasons and months of the year;
          And when Spring days are here,
Then we tread to the wine-god a measure
In Bacchanal dance and in pleasure,
  Mid the contests of sweet-singing choirs,
    And the crash of loud lyres!

(*Oscar Wilde*)

Theocritus

3rd century B.C.

That which distinguishes Theocritus from all other poets, both Greek and Latin, and which raises him even above Virgil in his Eclogues, is the inimitable tenderness of his passions, and the natural expression of them in words so becoming of a pastoral. A simplicity shines through all he writes: he shows his art and learning by disguising both.—JOHN DRYDEN.

IDYLL I

THE DEATH OF DAPHNIS

THYRSIS

SWEET are the whispers of yon pine that makes
Low music o'er the spring, and, Goatherd, sweet
Thy piping; second thou to Pan alone.
Is his the horned ram? then thine the goat.
Is his the goat? to thee shall fall the kid;
And toothsome is the flesh of unmilked kids.

GOATHERD

SHEPHERD, thy lay is as the noise of streams
Falling and falling aye from yon tall crag.
If for their meed the Muses claim the ewe,
Be thine the stall-fed lamb; or if they choose
The lamb, take thou the scarce less-valued ewe.

THYRSIS

PRAY by the Nymphs, pray, Goatherd, seat thee here
Against this hill-slope in the tamarisk shade,
And pipe me somewhat, while I guard thy goats.

GOATHERD

I DURST not, Shepherd, O I durst not pipe
At noontide; fearing Pan, who at that hour
Rests from the toils of hunting. Harsh is he;
Wrath at his nostrils aye sits sentinel.
But, Thyrsis, thou canst sing of Daphnis' woes;
High is thy name for woodland minstrelsy:
Then rest we in the shadow of the elm
Fronting Priapus and the Fountain-nymphs.
There, where the oaks are and the Shepherd's seat,
Sing as thou sang'st erewhile, when matched with him
Of Libya, Chromis; and I'll give thee, first,
To milk, ay thrice, a goat—she suckles twins,
Yet ne'ertheless can fill two milkpails full;—
Next, a deep drinking-cup, with sweet wax scoured,
Two-handled, newly-carven, smacking yet
O' the chisel. Ivy reaches up and climbs
About its lip, gilt here and there with sprays
Of woodbine, that enwreathed about it flaunts
Her saffron fruitage. Framed therein appears
A damsel ('tis a miracle of art)
In robe and snood: and suitors at her side
With locks fair-flowing, on her right and left,
Battle with words, that fail to reach her heart.

She, laughing, glances now on this, flings now
Her chance regards on that: they, all for love
Wearied and eye-swoln, find their labor lost.
Carven elsewhere an ancient fisher stands
On the rough rocks: thereto the old man with pains
Drags his great casting-net, as one that toils
Full stoutly: every fiber of his frame
Seems fishing; so about the gray-beard's neck
(In might a youngster yet) the sinews swell.
Hard by the wave-beat sire a vineyard bends
Beneath its graceful load of burnished grapes;
A boy sits on the rude fence watching them.
Near him two foxes: down the rows of grapes
One ranging steals the ripest; one assails
With wiles the poor lad's scrip, to leave him soon
Stranded and supperless. He plaits meanwhile
With ears of corn a right fine cricket-trap,
And fits it on a rush: for vines, for scrip,
Little he cares, enamored of his toy.
The cup is hung all round with lissom briar,
Triumph of Æolian art, a wondrous sight.
It was a ferryman's of Calydon:
A goat it cost me, and a great white cheese.
Ne'er yet my lips came near it, virgin still
It stands. And welcome to such boon art thou,
If for my sake thou'lt sing that lay of lays.
I jest not: lad, sing: no songs thou'lt own
In the dim land where all things are forgot.

THYRSIS

Begin, sweet Maids, begin the woodland song.
The voice of Thyrsis. Ætna's Thyrsis I.
Where were ye, Nymphs, oh where, while Daphnis pined?
In fair Peneus' or in Pindus' glens?
For great Anapus' stream was not your haunt,
Nor Ætna's cliff, nor Acis' sacred rill.
Begin, sweet Maids, begin the woodland song.

O'er him the wolves, the jackals howled o'er him;
The lion in the oak-copse mourned his death.
Begin, sweet Maids, begin the woodland song.
The kine and oxen stood around his feet,
The heifers and the calves wailed all for him.
Begin, sweet Maids, begin the woodland song.
First from the mountain Hermes came, and said,
"Daphnis, who frets thee? Lad, whom lov'st thou so?"
Begin, sweet Maids, begin the woodland song.
Came herdsmen, shepherds came, and goatherds came;
All asked what ailed the lad. Priapus came
And said, "Why pine, poor Daphnis? while the maid
Foots it round every pool and every grove,
(*Begin, sweet Maids, begin the woodland song*)
"O lack-love and perverse, in quest of thee;
Herdsman in name, but goatherd rightlier called.
With eyes that yearn the goatherd marks his kids
Run riot, for he fain would frisk as they:
(*Begin, sweet Maids, begin the woodland song*):
"With eyes that yearn dost thou too mark the laugh
Of maidens, for thou may'st not share their glee."
Still naught the herdsman said: he drained alone
His bitter portion, till the fatal end.
Begin, sweet Maids, begin the woodland song.
Came Aphrodite, smiles on her sweet face,
False smiles, for heavy was her heart, and spake:
"So, Daphnis, thou must try a fall with Love!
But stalwart Love hath won the fall of thee."
Begin, sweet Maids, begin the woodland song.
Then "Ruthless Aphrodite," Daphnis said,
"Accursed Aphrodite, foe to man!
Say'st thou mine hour is come, my sun hath set?
Dead as alive, shall Daphnis work Love woe."
Begin, sweet Maids, begin the woodland song.
"Fly to Mount Ida, where the swain (men say)
And Aphrodite—to Anchises fly:
There are oak-forests; here but galingale,
And bees that make a music round the hives.

Begin, sweet Maids, begin the woodland song.
"Adonis owed his bloom to tending flocks
And smiting hares, and bringing wild beasts down.
Begin, sweet Maids, begin the woodland song.
"Face once more Diomed: tell him 'I have slain
The herdsman Daphnis! now I challenge thee.'
Begin, sweet Maids, begin the woodland song.
"Farewell, wolf, jackal, mountain-prisoned bear!
Ye'll see no more by grove or glade or glen
Your herdsman Daphnis! Arethuse, farewell,
And the bright streams that pour down Thymbris' side.
Begin, sweet Maids, begin the woodland song.
"I am that Daphnis, who lead here my kine,
Bring here to drink my oxen and my calves.
Begin, sweet Maids, begin the woodland song.
"Pan, Pan, oh whether great Lyceum's crags
Thou haunt'st to-day, or mightier Mænalus,
Come to the Sicel isle! Abandon now
Rhium and Helice, and the mountain-cairn
(That e'en gods cherish) of Lycaon's son!
Forget, sweet Maids, forget your woodland song.
"Come, king of song, o'er this my pipe, compact
With wax and honey-breathing, arch thy lip:
For surely I am torn from life by Love.
Forget, sweet Maids, forget your woodland song.
"From thicket now and thorn let violets spring,
Now let white lilies drape the juniper,
And pines grow figs, and nature all go wrong:
For Daphnis dies. Let deer pursue the hounds,
And mountain-owls outsing the nightingale.
Forget, sweet Maids, forget your woodland song."

So spake he, and he never spoke again.
Fain Aphrodite would have raised his head;
But all his thread was spun. So down the stream
Went Daphnis: closed the waters o'er a head
Dear to the Nine, of nymphs not unbeloved.
Now give me goat and cup; that I may milk

The one, and pour the other to the Muse.
Fare ye well, Muses, o'er and o'er farewell!
I'll sing strains lovelier yet in days to be.

Goatherd

Thyrsis, let honey and the honeycomb
Fill thy sweet mouth, and figs of Ægilus:
For ne'er cicala trilled so sweet a song.
Here is the cup; mark, friend, how sweet it smells:
The Hours, thou'lt say, have washed it in their well.
Hither, Cissætha! Thou, go milk her! Kids,
Be steady, or your pranks will rouse the ram.

(Charles Stuart Calverley)

Idyll II

THE INCANTATION

Where are the bay-leaves, Thestylis, and the charms?
Fetch all; with fiery wood the caldron crown;
Let glamour win me back my false lord's heart!
Twelve days the wretch hath not come nigh to me,
Nor made enquiry if I die or live,
Nor clamored (oh unkindness!) at my door.
Sure his swift fancy wanders otherwhere,
The slave of Aphrodite and of Love.
I'm off to Timagetus' wrestling-school
At dawn, that I may see him and denounce
His doings; but I'll charm him now with charms.
So shine out fair, O moon! To thee I sing
My soft low song: to thee and Hecate
The dweller in the shades, at whose approach
E'en the dogs quake, as on she moves through blood
And darkness and the barrows of the slain.
All hail, dread Hecate: companion me
Unto the end, and work me witcheries
Potent as Circe or Medea wrought,
Or Perimede of the golden hair!

Turn, magic wheel, draw homeward him I love.
First we ignite the grain. Nay, pile it on:
Where are thy wits flown, timorous Thestylis?
Shall I be flouted, I, by such as thou?
Pile, and still say, "This pile is of his bones."
Turn, magic wheel, draw homeward him I love.
Delphis racks me: I burn him in these bays,
As, flame-enkindled, they lift up their voice,
Blaze once, and not a trace is left behind:
So waste his flesh to powder in yon fire!
Turn, magic wheel, draw homeward him I love.
E'en as I melt, not uninspired, the wax,
May Mindian Delphis melt this hour with love:
And, swiftly as this brazen wheel whirls round,
May Aphrodite whirl him to my door.
Turn, magic wheel, draw homeward him I love.
Next burn the husks. Hell's adamantine floor
And aught that else stands firm can Artemis move.
Thestylis, the hounds bay up and down the town:
The goddess stands i' the crossroads: sound the gongs.
Turn, magic wheel, draw homeward him I love.
Hushed are the voices of the winds and seas;
But O not hushed the voice of my despair.
He burns my being up, who left me here
No wife, no maiden, in my misery.
Turn, magic wheel, draw homeward him I love.
Thrice I pour out; speak thrice, sweet mistress, thus:
"What face soe'er hangs o'er him be forgot
Clean as, in Dia, Theseus (legends say)
Forgat his Ariadne's locks of love."
Turn, magic wheel, draw homeward him I love.
The coltsfoot grows in Arcady, the weed
That drives the mountain-colts and swift mares wild.
Like them may Delphis rave: so, maniac-wise,
Race from his burnished brethren home to me.
Turn, magic wheel, draw homeward him I love.
He lost this tassel from his robe; which I
Shred thus, and cast it on the raging flames.

Ah baleful Love! why, like the marsh-born leech,
Cling to my flesh, and drain my dark veins dry?
Turn, magic wheel, draw homeward him I love.
From a crushed eft to-morrow he shall drink
Death! But now, Thestylis, take these herbs and smear
That threshold o'er, whereto at heart I cling
Still, still—albeit he thinks scorn of me—
And spit, and say, " 'Tis Delphis' bones I smear."
Turn, magic wheel, draw homeward him I love.
Now all alone, I'll weep a love whence sprung,
When born? Who wrought my sorrow? Anaxo came,
Her basket in her hand, to Artemis' grove.
Bound for the festival, troops of forest beasts
Stood round, and in the midst a lioness.
Bethink thee, mistress Moon, whence came my love.
Theucharidas' slave, my Thracian nurse now dead,
Then my near neighbor, prayed me and implored
To see the pageant: I, the poor doomed thing,
Went with her, trailing a fine silken train,
And gathering round me Clearista's robe.
Bethink thee, mistress Moon, whence came my love.
Now, the mid-highway reached by Lycon's farm,
Delphis and Eudamippus passed me by.
With beards as lustrous as the woodbine's gold
And breasts more sheeny than myself, O Moon,
Fresh from the wrestler's glorious toil they came.
Bethink thee, mistress Moon, whence came my love.
I saw, I raved, smit (weakling) to my heart.
My beauty withered, and I cared no more
For all the pomp; and how I gained my home
I know not: some strange fever wasted me.
Ten nights and days I lay upon my bed.
Bethink thee, mistress Moon, whence came my love.
And wan became my flesh, as 't had been dyed,
And all my hair streamed off, and there was left
But bones and skin. Whose threshold crossed I not,
Or missed what grandam's hut who dealt in charms?
For no light thing was this, and time sped on.

Bethink thee, mistress Moon, whence came my love.
At last I spake the truth to that my maid:
"Seek, an thou canst, some cure for my sore pain.
Alas, I am all the Mindian's! But begone,
And watch by Timagetus' wrestling-school:
There doth he haunt, there soothly take his rest.
Bethink thee, mistress Moon, whence came my love.
"Find him alone: nod softly: say, 'she waits';
And bring him." So I spake: she went her way,
And brought the lustrous-limbed one to my roof.
And I, the instant I beheld him step
Lightfooted o'er the threshold of my door,
(*Bethink thee, mistress Moon, whence came my love,*)
Became all cold like snow, and from my brow
Brake the damp dewdrops: utterance I had none,
Not e'en such utterance as a babe may make
That babbles to its mother in its dreams;
But all my fair frame stiffened into wax.
Bethink thee, mistress Moon, whence came my love.
He bent his pitiless eyes on me; looked down,
And sate down on my couch, and sitting, said:
"Thou hast gained on me, Simætha, (e'en as I
Gained once on young Philinus in the race),
Bidding me hither ere I came unasked.
Bethink thee, mistress Moon, whence came my love.
"For I had come, by Eros I had come,
This night, with comrades twain or maybe more,
The fruitage of the Wine-god in my robe,
And, wound about my brow with ribands red,
The silver leaves so dear to Heracles.
Bethink thee, mistress Moon, whence came my love.
"Had ye said 'Enter,' well; for 'mid my peers
High is my name for goodliness and speed:
I had kissed that sweet mouth once and gone my way.
But had the door been barred, and I thrust out,
With brand and axe would we have stormed ye then.
Bethink thee, mistress Moon, whence came my love.
"Now be my thanks recorded, first to Love,
Next to thee, maiden, who didst pluck me out,

A half-burned helpless creature, from the flames,
And badst me hither. It is Love that lights
A fire more fierce than his of Lipara;
Bethink thee, mistress Moon, whence came my love.
"Scares, mischief-mad, the maiden from her bower,
The bride from her warm couch." He spake: and I,
A willing listener, sat, my hand in his,
Among the cushions, and his cheek touched mine,
Each hotter than its wont, and we discoursed
In soft low language. Need I prate to thee,
Sweet Moon, of all we said and all we did?
Till yesterday he found no fault with me,
Nor I with him. But lo, to-day there came
Philista's mother—hers who flutes to me—
With her Melampo's; just when up the sky
Gallop the mares that chariot rose-limbed Dawn:
And divers tales she brought me, with the rest
How Delphis loved, she knew not rightly whom:
But this she knew; that of the rich wine aye
He poured "to Love"; and at the last had fled,
To line, she deemed, the fair one's hall with flowers.
Such was my visitor's tale, and it was true:
For thrice, nay four times, daily he would stroll
Hither, leave here full oft his Dorian flask:
Now—'tis a fortnight since I saw his face.
Doth he then treasure something sweet elsewhere?
Am I forgot? I'll charm him now with charms.
But let him try me more, and by the Fates
He'll soon be knocking at the gates of hell.
Spells of such power are in this chest of mine,
Learned, lady, from mine host in Palestine.

Lady, farewell: turn ocean-ward thy steeds:
As I have purposed, so shall I fulfill.
Farewell, thou bright-faced Moon! Ye stars, farewell,
That wait upon the car of noiseless Night.

(*Charles Stuart Calverley*)

IDYLL IV

THE HERDSMEN

BATTUS. Who owns these cattle, Corydon? Philondas? Prythee say.

CORYDON. No, Ægon: and he gave them me to tend while he's away.

BATTUS. Dost milk them in the gloaming, when none is nigh to see?

CORYDON. The old man brings the calves to suck, and keeps an eye on me.

BATTUS. And to what region then hath flown the cattle's rightful lord?

CORYDON. Hast thou not heard? With Milo he vanished Elisward.

BATTUS. How! was the wrestler's oil e'er yet so much as seen by him?

CORYDON. Men say he rivals Heracles in lustiness of limb.

BATTUS. I'm Polydeuces' match (or so my mother says) and more.

CORYDON. —So off he started; with a spade, and of these ewes a score.

BATTUS. This Milo will be teaching wolves how they should raven next.

CORYDON. —And by these bellowings his kine proclaim how sore they're vexed.

BATTUS Poor kine! they've found their master a sorry knave indeed.

CORYDON. They're poor enough, I grant you: they have not heart to feed.

BATTUS. Look at that heifer! sure there's naught, save bare bones, left of her.

Pray, does she browse on dewdrops, as does the grasshopper?

CORYDON. Not she, by heaven! She pastures now by Æsarus' glades,

And handfuls fair I pluck her there of young and green grass blades;
Now bounds about Latymnus, that gathering-place of shades.
  Battus. That bull again, the red one, my word but he is lean!
I wish the Sybarite burghers aye may offer to the queen
Of heaven as pitiful a beast: those burghers are so mean!
  Corydon. Yet to the Salt Lake's edges I drive him, I can swear;
Up Physcus, up Neæthus' side—he lacks not victual there,
With dittany and endive and foxglove for his fare.
  Battus. Well, well! I pity Ægon. His cattle, go they must
To rack and ruin, all because vain-glory was his lust.
The pipe that erst he fashioned is doubtless scored with rust?
  Corydon. Nay, by the Nymphs! That pipe he left to me, the self-same day
He made for Pisa: I am too a minstrel in my way:
Well the flute-part in *'Pyrrhus'* and in *'Glauca'* can I play.
I sing too *'Here's to Croton'* and *'Zacynthus O 'tis fair,'*
And *'Eastward to Lacinium:'*—the bruised Milo there
His single self ate eighty loaves; there also did he pull
Down from its mountain dwelling, by one hoof grasped, a bull,
And gave it Amaryllis: the maidens screamed with fright;
As for the owner of the bull he only laughed outright.
  Battus. Sweet Amaryllis! thou alone, though dead, art unforgot.
Dearer than thou, whose light is quenched, my very goats are not.
Oh for the all-unkindly fate that's fallen to my lot!
  Corydon. Cheer up, brave lad! to-morrow may ease thee of thy pain:

Aye for the living are there hopes, past hoping are the slain:
And now Zeus sends us sunshine, and now he sends us rain.

BATTUS. I'm better. Beat those young ones off! E'en now their teeth attack
That olive's shoots, the graceless brutes! back, with your white face, back!

CORYDON. Back to thy hill, Cymætha! Great Pan, how deaf thou art!
I shall be with thee presently, and in the end thou'lt smart.
I warn thee, keep thy distance. Look, up she creeps again!
Oh were my hare-crook in my hand, I'd give it to her then!

BATTUS. For heaven's sake, Corydon, look here! Just now a bramble-spike
Ran, there, into my instep—and oh how deep they strike,
Those lancewood-shafts! A murrain light on that calf, I say!
I got it gaping after her. Canst thou discern it, pray?

CORYDON. Ay, ay; and here I have it, safe in my finger-nails.

BATTUS. Eh! at how slight a matter how tall a warrior quails!

CORYDON. Ne'er range the hill-crest, Battus, all sandal-less and bare;
Because the thistle and the thorn lift aye their plumed heads there.

BATTUS. —Say, Corydon, does that old man we wot of (tell me please!)
Still haunt the dark-browed little girl whom once he used to tease?

CORYDON. Ay my poor boy, that doth he: I saw them yesterday
Down by the byre; and, trust me, loving enough were they.

Battus. Well done, my veteran light-o'-love! In deeming thee mere man,
I wronged the sire: some Satyr he, or an uncouth-limbed Pan.

(Charles Stuart Calverley)

Idyll VII

HARVEST-HOME

Once on a time did Eucritus and I
(With us Amyntas) to the riverside
Steal from the city. For Lycopeus' sons
Were that day busy with the harvest-home,
Antigenes and Phrasidemus, sprung
(If aught thou holdest by the good old names)
By Clytia from great Chalcon—him who erst
Planted one stalwart knee against the rock,
And lo, beneath his foot Burinè's rill
Brake forth, and at its side poplar and elm
Shewed aisles of pleasant shadow, greenly roofed
By tufted leaves. Scarce midway were we now,
Nor yet described the tomb of Brasilas:
When, thanks be to the Muses, there drew near
A wayfarer from Crete, young Lycidas.
The horned herd was his care: a glance might tell
So much: for every inch a herdsman he.
Slung o'er his shoulder was a ruddy hide
Torn from a he-goat, shaggy, tangle-haired,
That reeked of rennet yet: a broad belt clasped
A patched cloak round his breast, and for a staff
A gnarled wild-olive bough his right hand bore.
Soon with a quiet smile he spoke—his eye
Twinkled, and laughter sat upon his lip:
'And whither ploddest thou thy weary way
Beneath the noontide sun, Simichidas?
For now the lizard sleeps upon the wall,
The crested lark folds now his wandering wing.
Dost speed, a bidden guest, to some reveler's board?
Or townward to the treading of the grape?

For lo! recoiling from thy hurrying feet
The pavement-stones ring outright merrily.'
Then I: 'Friend Lycid, all men say that none
Of haymakers or herdsmen is thy match
At piping: and my soul is glad thereat.
Yet, to speak sooth, I think to rival thee.
Now look, this road holds holiday to-day:
For banded brethren solemnize a feast
To richly-dight Demeter, thanking her
For her good gifts: since with no grudging hand
Hath the boon goddess filled the wheaten floors.
So come: the way, the day, is thine as mine:
Try we our woodcraft—each may learn from each.
I am, as thou, a clarion-voice of song;
All hail me chief of minstrels. But I am not,
Heaven knows, o'ercredulous: no, I scarce can yet
(I think) outvie Philetas, nor the bard
Of Samos, champion of Sicilian song.
They are as cicadas challenged by a frog.'

I spake to gain mine ends; and laughing light
He said: 'Accept this club, as thou'rt indeed
A born truth-teller, shaped by heaven's own hand!
I hate your builders who would rear a house
High as Oromedon's mountain-pinnacle:
I hate your song-birds too, whose cuckoo-cry
Struggles (in vain) to match the Chian bard.
But come, we'll sing forthwith, Simichidas,
Our woodland music: and for my part I—
List, comrade, if you like the simple air
I forged among the uplands yesterday.

[*Sings*]

Safe be my true-love convoyed o'er the main
To Mitylené—though the southern blast
Chase the lithe waves, while westward slant the Kids,
Or low above the verge Orion stand—
If from Love's furnace she will rescue me,
For Lycidas is parched with hot desire.

Let halcyons lay the sea-waves and the winds,
Northwind and Westwind, that in shores far-off
Flutters the seaweed—halcyons, of all birds
Whose prey is on the waters, held most dear
By the green Nereids: yea let all things smile
On her to Mitylené voyaging,
And in fair harbor may she ride at last.
I on that day, a chaplet woven of dill
Or rose or simple violet on my brow,
Will draw the wine of Pteleas from the cask
Stretched by the ingle. They shall roast me beans,
And elbow-deep in thyme and asphodel
And quaintly-curling parsley shall be piled
My bed of rushes, where in royal ease
I sit and, thinking of my darling, drain
With steadfast lip the liquor to the dregs.
I'll have a pair of pipers, shepherds both,
This from Acharnæ, from Lycopé that;
And Tityrus shall be near me and shall sing
How the swain Daphnis loved the stranger-maid;
And how he ranged the fells, and how the oaks
(Such oaks as Himera's banks are green withal)
Sang dirges o'er him waning fast away
Like snow on Athos, or on Hæmus high,
Or Rhodopé, or utmost Caucasus.
And he shall sing me how the big chest held
(All through the maniac malice of his lord)
A living goatherd: how the round-faced bees,
Lured from their meadow by the cedar-smell,
Fed him with daintiest flowers, because the Muse
Had made his throat a well-spring of sweet song.
Happy Cometas, this sweet lot was thine!
Thee the chest prisoned, for thee the honey-bees
Toiled, as thou slavedst out the mellowing year:
And oh hadst thou been numbered with the quick
In my day! I had led thy pretty goats
About the hill-side, listening to thy voice:
While thou hadst lain thee down 'neath oak or pine,
Divine Cometas, warbling pleasantly.'

He spake and paused; and thereupon spake I,
'I too, friend Lycid, as I ranged the fells,
Have learned much lore and pleasant from the Nymphs,
Whose fame mayhap hath reached the throne of Zeus.
But this wherewith I'll grace thee ranks the first:
Thou listen, since the Muses like thee well.

[*Sings*]

On me the young Loves sneezed: for hapless I
Am fain of Myrto as the goats of Spring.
But my best friend Aratus inly pines
For one who loves him not. Aristis saw—
(A wondrous seer is he, whose lute and lay
Shrinéd Apollo's self would scarce disdain)—
How love had scorched Aratus to the bone.
O Pan, who hauntest Homolé's fair champagne,
Bring the soft charmer, whosoe'er it be,
Unbid to his sweet arms—so, gracious Pan,
May ne'er thy ribs and shoulderblades be lashed
With squills by young Arcadians, whensoe'er
They are scant of supper! But should this my prayer
Mislike thee, then on nettles mayest thou sleep,
Dinted and sore all over from their claws!
Then mayest thou lodge amid Edonian hills
By Hebrus, in midwinter; there subsist,
The Bear thy neighbor: and, in summer, range
With the far Æthiops 'neath the Blemmyan rocks
Where Nile is no more seen! But O ye Loves,
Whose cheeks are like pink apples, quit your homes
By Hyetis, or Byblis' pleasant rill,
Or fair Dioné's rocky pedestal,
And strike that fair one with your arrows, strike
The ill-starred damsel who disdains my friend.
And lo, what is she but an o'er-ripe pear?
The girls all cry "Her bloom is on the wane."
We'll watch, Aratus, at that porch no more,
Nor waste shoe-leather: let the morning cock

Crow to wake others up to numb despair!
Let Molon, and none else, that ordeal brave:
While we make ease our study, and secure
Some witch, to charm all evil from our door.'

I ceased. He smiling sweetly as before,
Gave me the staff, 'the Muses' parting gift,'
And leftward sloped tow'rd Pyxa. We the while,
Bent us to Phrasydeme's, Eucritus and I,
And baby-faced Amyntas: there we lay
Half-buried in a couch of fragrant reed
And fresh-cut vineleaves, who so glad as we?
A wealth of elm and poplar shook o'erhead;
Hard by, a sacred spring flowed gurgling on
From the Nymphs' grot, and in the somber boughs
The sweet cicada chirped laboriously.
Hid in the thick thorn-bushes far away
The treefrog's note was heard; the crested lark
Sang with the goldfinch; turtles made their moan,
And o'er the fountain hung the gilded bee.
All of rich summer smacked, of autumn all:
Pears at our feet, and apples at our side
Rolled in luxuriance; branches on the ground
Sprawled, overweighed with damsons; while we brushed
From the cask's head the crust of four long years.
Say, ye who dwell upon Parnassian peaks,
Nymphs of Castalia, did old Chiron e'er
Set before Heracles a cup so brave
In Pholus' cavern—did as nectarous draughts
Cause that Anapian shepherd, in whose hand
Rocks were as pebbles, Polypheme the strong,
Featly to foot it o'er the cottage lawns:—
As, ladies, ye bid flow that day for us
All by Demeter's shrine at harvest-home?
Beside whose cornstacks may I oft again
Plant my broad fan: while she stands by and smiles,
Poppies and cornsheaves on each laden arm.

(*Charles Stuart Calverley*)

Idyll XXI

THE FISHERMEN

Want quickens wit: Want's pupils needs must work,
O Diophantus: for the child of toil
Is grudged his very sleep by carking cares:
Or, if he taste the blessedness of night,
Thought for the morrow soon warns slumber off.
  Two ancient fishers once lay side by side
On piled-up sea-wrack in their wattled hut,
Its leafy wall their curtain. Near them lay
The weapons of their trade, basket and rod,
Hooks, weed-encumbered nets, and cords and oars,
And, propped on rollers, an infirm old boat.
Their pillow was a scanty mat, eked out
With caps and garments: such the ways and means,
Such the whole treasury of the fishermen.
They knew no luxuries: owned nor door nor dog;
Their craft their all, their mistress Poverty:
Their only neighbor Ocean, who for aye
Round their lorn hut came floating lazily.
  Ere the moon's chariot was in mid-career,
The fishers girt them for their customed toil,
And banished slumber from unwilling eyes,
And roused their dreamy intellects with speech:—

Asphalion. They say that soon flit summer-nights away,
Because all lingering is the summer day:
Friend, it is false; for dream on dream have I
Dreamed, and the dawn still reddens not the sky.
How? am I wandering? or does night pass slow?

Comrade. Asphalion, scout not the sweet summer so.
'Tis not that willful seasons have gone wrong,
But care maims slumber, and the nights seem long.

A. Didst thou e'er study dreams? For visions fair
I saw last night; and fairly thou should'st share
The wealth I dream of, as the fish I catch.
Now, for sheer sense, I reckon few thy match;
And, for a vision, he whose motherwit
Is his sole tutor best interprets it.
And now we've time the matter to discuss:
For who could labor, lying here (like us)
Pillowed on leaves and neighbored by the deep,
Or sleeping amid thorns no easy sleep?
In rich men's halls the lamps are burning yet;
But fish come alway to the rich man's net.

C. To me the vision of the night relate;
Speak, and reveal the riddle to thy mate.

A. Last evening, as I plied my watery trade,
(Not on an o'erfull stomach—we had made
Betimes a meager meal, as you can vouch)
I fell asleep; and lo! I seemed to crouch
Among the bowlders, and for fish to wait,
Still dangling, rod in hand, my vagrant bait.
A fat fellow caught it: (e'en in sleep I'm bound
To dream of fishing, as of crusts the hound:)
Fast clung he to the hooks; his blood outwelled;
Bent with his struggling was the rod I held:
I tugged and tugged: my efforts made me ache:
'How, with a line thus slight, this monster take?'
Then gently, just to warn him he was caught,
I twitched him once; then slacked and then made taut
My line, for now he offered not to run;
A glance soon showed me all my task was done.
'Twas a gold fish, pure metal every inch,
That I had captured. I began to flinch:
'What if this beauty be the sea-king's joy,
Or azure Amphitrite's treasured toy!'
With care I disengaged him—not to rip
With hasty hook the gilding from his lip:
And with a tow-line landed him, and swore

Never to set my foot on ocean more,
But with my gold live royally ashore.
So I awoke: and, comrade, lend me now
Thy wits, for I am troubled for my vow.

C. Ne'er quake: you're pledged to nothing, for no prize
You gained or gazed on. Dreams are nought but lies.
Yet may this dream bear fruit; if, wide-awake
And not in dreams, you'll fish the neighboring lake.
Fish that are meat you'll there mayhap behold,
Not die of famine, amid dreams of gold.

(*Charles Stuart Calverley*)

Epigram II

THE FLUTE OF DAPHNIS

I am the flute of Daphnis. On this wall
He nailed his tribute to the great god Pan,
What time he grew from boyhood, shapely, tall,
And felt the first deep ardors of a man.
Thro adult veins more swift the song-tide ran,—
A vernal stream whose swollen torrents call
For instant ease in utterance. Then began
That course of triumph reverenced by all.
Him the gods loved, and more than other men
Blest with the flower of beauty, and endowed
His soul of music with the strength of ten.
Now on a festal day I see the crowd
Look fondly at my resting-place, and when
I think whose lips have prest me, I am proud.

Epigram IV

A SACRED GROVE

I know a spot where Love delights to dream,
Because he finds his fancies happen true.
Within its fence no myrtle ever grew
That failed in wealth of flower; no sunny beam

Has used its vantage vainly. You might deem
Yourself a happy plant and blossom too,
Or be a bird and sing as thrushes do,
So sweet in that fair place doth nature seem.
A matted vine invests the rocks above,
And tries to kiss a runlet leaping through
With endless laughter. Hither at noon comes Love,
And woos the god who is not hard to woo,
Taking his answer from the nested dove
That ever hymneth skies forever blue.

Epigram V

A SYLVAN REVEL

What ho! my shepherds, sweet it were
To fill with song this leafy glade.
Bring harp and flute. The gods have made
An hour for music. Daphnis there
Shall give the note with jocund blare
From out his horn. The rest will aid
With fifes and drums, and charm the shade,
And rout the dusky wings of care.
We'll pipe to fox and wolf and bear,
We'll wake the wood with rataplan,
Fetch every beast from every lair,
Make every creature dance who can,
Set every Satyr's hoof in air,
And tickle both the feet of Pan!

Epigram VI

THYRSIS

Sad Thyrsis weeps till his blue eyes are dim,
Because the wolf has torn his pride away,—
The little kid so apt for sport and play,
Which knew his voice and loved to follow him.
Who would not weep that cruel Fate and grim
Should end her pranks on this unhappy day,

And give her tender innocence a prey
For savage jaws to harry limb from limb?
Yet think, O shepherd, how thy tears are vain
To rouse the dead or bring the slain again;
Beyond all hope her body lies, alack!
Devoured she is; no bones of her remain.
The leaping hounds are on the murderer's track,
But will they, can they, bear thy darling back?

Epigram IX

CLEONICOS

Let sailors watch the waning Pleiades,
And keep the shore. This man, made over-bold
By godless pride, and too much greed of gold,
Setting his gains before his health and ease,
Ran up his sails to catch the whistling breeze:
Whose corpse, ere now, the restless waves have rolled
From deep to deep, while all his freight, unsold,
Is tost upon the tumult of the seas.
Such fate had one whose avaricious eyes
Lured him to peril in a mad emprise.
Yea, from the Syrian coast to Thasos bound,
He slipt his anchor with rich merchandise,
While the wet stars were slipping from the skies,
And with the drowning stars untimely drowned.

Epigram XI

THE EPITAPH OF EUSTHENES

A bard is buried here, not strong, but sweet;
A Teacher too, not great, but gently wise;
This modest stone (the burghers thought it meet)
May tell the world where so much virtue lies.
His happy skill it was in mart and street
To scan men's faces with a true surmise,
Follow the spirit to its inmost seat,

And read the soul reflected in the eyes.
No part had he in catholic renown,
Which none but god-inspired poets share;
Not his to trail the philosophic gown,
That only sages of the School may wear;
But his at least to fill an alien town
With friends, who make his tomb their loving care.

Epigram XVIII

THE MONUMENT OF CLEITA

Here Cleita sleeps. You ask her life and race?
Read on, and learn a simple tale and true.
A nurse she was from the far land of Thrace,
Who tended little Medëos while he grew
A healthy, happy child, and did imbue
His nascent mind with godliness and grace;
So fencing him from evil that he knew
No word of what is impious or base.
And when at length, her tale of years all told,
She came to lie in this reposeful spot,
Young Medëos, still a child, but sagely old,
Upreared this monument, that unforgot
The care beyond his recompense of gold
Might live a memory and perish not.

Epigram XXI

THE GRAVE OF HIPPONAX

Here lies a bard, Hippònax—honored name!
Sweet were the songs that won him endless praise,
And yet his life was sweeter than his lays.
Traveler, a question fronts thee: Canst thou claim
Kinship with such in conduct void of blame?
If not, forbear this precinct; go thy ways;
Lest some bright watcher of the tomb should raise
A jealous hand to cover thee with shame.

But if thy soul is free from shade of guilt,
Or, having sinned, hath been at length forgiven
To thee all rights of common kin belong;
Lay down thy weary limbs, and, if thou wilt,
Let slumber wrap them round, nor fear that Heaven
Will suffer any sprite to do thee wrong.

(*Edward Cracroft Lefroy*)

Idyll XI

THE CYCLOPS

And so an easier life our Cyclops drew,
The ancient Polyphemus, who in youth
Loved Galatea while the manhood grew
Adown his cheeks, and darkened round his mouth.
No jot he cared for apples, olives, roses;
Love made him mad; the whole world was neglected,
The very sheep went backward to their closes
From out the fair green pastures, self-directed.
And singing Galatea, thus, he wore
The sunrise down along the weedy shore,
And pined alone, and felt the cruel wound
Beneath his heart, which Cypris' arrow bore,
With a deep pang: but, so, the cure was found;
And, sitting on a lofty rock, he cast
His eyes upon the sea, and sang at last:
"O whitest Galatea, can it be
That thou shouldst spurn me off who love thee so?
More white than curds, my girl. thou art to see,
More meek than lambs, more full of leaping glee
Than kids, and brighter than the early glow
On grapes that swell to ripen,—sour like thee!
Thou comest to me with the fragrant sleep,
And with the fragrant sleep thou goest from me;
Thou fliest . . . fliest as a frightened sheep
Flies the gray wolf!—yet love did overcome me,
So long!—I loved thee, maiden, first of all,
When down the hills (my mother fast beside thee)

I saw thee stray to pluck the summer-fall
  Of hyacinth-bells, and went myself to guide thee;
And since my eyes have seen thee, they can leave thee
  No more, from that day's light! But thou . . . by
    Zeus,
Thou wilt not care for *that,* to let it grieve thee!
  I know thee, fair one, why thou springest loose
From my arm round thee. Why? I tell thee, dear!
  One shaggy eyebrow draws its smudging road
Straight through my ample front, from ear to ear;
  One eye rolls underneath; and yawning, broad,
Flat nostrils feel the bulging lips too near.
Yet . . . ho, ho!—*I,*—whatever I appear,—
  Do feed a thousand oxen! When I have done,
I milk the cows, and drink the milk that's best!
  I lack no cheese, while summer keeps the sun;
And after, in the cold, it's ready prest!
  And then, I know to sing, as there is none
Of all the Cyclops can, . . . a song of thee,
Sweet apple of my soul, on love's fair tree,
And of myself who love thee . . . till the West
Forgets the light, and all but I have rest.
I feed for thee, besides, eleven fair does,
  And all in fawn; and four tame whelps of bears.
Come to me, sweet! thou shalt have all of those
  In change for love! I will not halve the shares.
Leave the blue sea, with pure white arms extended
  To the dry shore; and, in my cave's recess,
Thou shalt be gladder for the noon-light ended;
  For here be laurels, spiral cypresses,
Dark ivy, and a vine whose leaves infold
Most luscious grapes; and here is water cold,
  The wooded Ætna pours down thro the trees
From the white snows, which gods were scarce too bold
  To drink in turn with nectar. Who with these
  Would choose the salt wave of the lukewarm seas?
Nay, look on me! If I am hairy and rough,
  I have an oak's heart in me; there's a fire

In these gray ashes which burns hot enough;
  And, when I burn for *thee,* I grudge the pyre
No fuel . . . not my soul, nor this one eye,—
Most precious thing I have, because thereby
I see thee, fairest! Out, alas! I wish
My mother had borne me finnèd like a fish,
That I might plunge down in the ocean near thee,
  And kiss thy glittering hand between the weeds,
If still thy face were turned; and I would bear thee
  Each lily white, and poppy fair that bleeds
Its red heart down its leaves!—one gift, for hours
  Of summer,—one for winter; since to cheer thee,
I could not bring at once all kinds of flowers.
Even now, girl, now, I fain would learn to swim,
If stranger in a ship sailed nigh, I wis,
  That I may know how sweet a thing it is
To live down with you in the deep and dim!
Come up, O Galatea, from the ocean,
  And, having come, forget again to go!
As I, who sing out here my heart's emotion,
  Could sit forever. Come up from below!
Come, keep my flocks beside me, milk my kine;
  Come, press my cheese, distrain my whey and curd!
Ah, mother! she alone . . . that mother of mine . . .
  Did wrong me sore! I blame her! Not a word
Of kindly intercession did she address
Thine ear with for my sake; and ne'ertheless
  She saw me wasting, wasting, day by day:
  Both head and feet were aching, I will say,
All sick for grief, as I myself was sick.
  O Cyclops, Cyclops! whither hast thou sent
  Thy soul on fluttering wings? If thou wert bent
On turning bowls, or pulling green and thick
  The sprouts to give thy lambkins, thou wouldst make
    thee
  A wiser Cyclops than for what we take thee.
Milk dry the present! Why pursue too quick
That future which is fugitive aright?
Thy Galatea thou shalt haply find,

Or else a maiden fairer and more kind;
For many girls do call me thro the night,
  And, as they call, do laugh out silvery.
  I, too, am something in the world, I see!"

While thus the Cyclops love and lambs did fold,
Ease came with song, he could not buy with gold.

(*Elizabeth Barrett Browning*)

Bion

3rd century B.C.

Idyll I

LAMENT FOR ADONIS

Wail, wail, Ah for Adonis! He is lost to us, lovely Adonis!
Lost is lovely Adonis! The Loves respond with lamenting.

Nay, no longer in robes of purple recline, Aphrodite:
Wake from thy sleep, sad queen, black-stoled, rain blows on thy bosom;
Cry to the listening world, *He is lost to us, lovely Adonis!*
  Wail, wail, Ah for Adonis! The Loves respond with lamenting.

Lovely Adonis is lying, sore hurt in his thigh, on the mountains,
Hurt in his thigh with the tusk, while grief consumes Aphrodite:
Slowly he drops toward death, and the black blood drips from his fair flesh,
Down from his snow-white skin; his eyes wax dull 'neath the eyelids,
Yea and the rose hath failed his lips, and around them the kisses

Die and wither, the kisses that Kupris will not relinquish:
Still, though he lives no longer, a kiss consoles Aphrodite;
But he knows not, Adonis, she kissed him while he was dying.
  Wail, wail, Ah for Adonis! The Loves respond with lamenting.

Cruel, cruel the wound in the thigh that preys on Adonis:
But in her heart Cytherea hath yet worse wounds to afflict her.
Round him his dear hounds bay, they howl in their grief to the heavens;
Nymphs of the woodlands wail: but she, the Queen Aphrodite,
Loosing her locks to the air, roams far and wide through the forest,
Drowned in grief, disheveled, unsandaled, and as she flies onward,
Briars stab at her feet and cull the blood of the goddess.
She with shrill lamentation thro' glen and thro' glade is carried,
Calling her Syrian lord, demanding him back, and demanding.
But where he lies, dark blood wells up and encircles the navel;
Blood from the gushing thighs empurples the breast; and the snow-white
Flank that was once so fair, is now dyed red for Adonis.
  Wail, wail, Ah, Cytherea! The Loves respond with lamenting.

She then hath lost her lord, and with him hath lost her celestial
Beauty; for fair was he, and fair, while he lived, Aphrodite:

Now in his death her beauty hath died. *Ah, Ah,*
Cytherea!
All the mountains lament, and the oaks moan, *Ah for*
Adonis!
Streams as they murmur and flow complain of thy griefs,
Aphrodite:
Yea and the springs on the hills, in the woods, weep
tears for Adonis:
Flowers of the field for woe flush crimson red; and
Cythêra,
Thorough the dells and the glens, shrills loud the dirge
of her anguish:
Woe, woe, Ah, Cytherea! He is lost to us, lovely Adonis!
Echo repeats the groan: *Lost, lost, is lovely Adonis!*
Kupris, who but bewailed thy pangs of a love over-
whelming?

She, when she saw, when she knew the unstanchable
wound of Adonis,
When she beheld the red blood on his pale thigh's
withering blossom,
Spreading her arms full wide, she moaned out: "Stay,
my Adonis!
Stay, ill-fated Adonis! that I once more may approach
thee!
Clasp thee close to my breast, and these lips mingle with
thy lips!
Rouse for a moment, Adonis, and kiss me again for the
last time;
Kiss me as long as the kiss can live on the lips of a
lover;
Till from thy inmost soul to my mouth and down to
my marrow
Thy life-breath shall run, and I quaff the wine of thy
philter,
Draining the draught of thy love: that kiss will I
treasure, Adonis,
E'en as it were thyself; since thou, ill-starred, art de-
parting,

Fleeing me far, O Adonis, to Acheron faring, the sad realm
Ruled by a stern savage king: while I, the unhappy, the luckless,
I live; goddess am I, and I may not follow or find thee.
Persephone, take thou my lord, my lover; I know thee
Stronger far than myself: all fair things drift to thy dwelling.
I meanwhile am accursed, possessed with insatiable sorrow,
Weeping my dead, my Adonis who died, and am shaken and shattered.
Diest thou then, my desired? and desire like a dream hath escaped me.
Widowed is now Cytherea; the Loves in her halls are abandoned;
Perished with thee is my girdle. Ah, why wouldst thou hunt, over-bold one?
Being so beautiful, why wast thou mad to fight with a wild beast?"
Thus then Kupris mourned; and the Loves respond with lamenting:
Wail, wail, Ah for Adonis! He is lost to us, lovely Adonis!
Tears the Paphian shed, drop by drop for the drops of Adonis'
Blood; and on earth each drop, as it fell, grew into a blossom:
Roses sprang from the blood, and the tears gave birth to the wind-flower.
Wail, wail, Ah, Cytherea! He is lost to us, lovely Adonis!

Wail, wail, Ah for Adonis! He is lost to us, lovely Adonis!
Now in the oak-woods cease to lament for thy lord, Aphrodite.
No proper couch is this which the wild leaves strew for Adonis.

Let him thy own bed share, Cytherea, the corpse of
Adonis;
E'en as a corpse he is fair, fair corpse as fallen aslumber.
Now lay him soft to sleep, sleep well in the wool of the
bedclothes,
Where with thee through the night in holy dreams he
commingled,
Stretched on a couch all gold, that yearns for him stark
though he now be.
Shower on him garlands, flowers: all fair things died in
his dying;
Yea, as he faded away, so shrivel and wither the
blossoms.
Syrian spikenard scatter, anoint him with myrrh and
with unguents:
Perish perfumes all, since he, thy perfume, is perished.
Wail, wail, Ah for Adonis! The Loves respond with
lamenting.

Lapped in his purple robes is the delicate form of
Adonis.
Round him weeping Loves complain and moan in their
anguish,
Clipping their locks for Adonis: and one of them treads
on his arrows,
One of them breaks his bow, and one sets heel on the
quiver;
One hath loosed for Adonis the latchet of sandals, and
some bring
Water to pour in an urn; one laves the wound in his
white thigh;
One from behind with his wings keeps fanning dainty
Adonis.
Wail, wail, Ah for Adonis! The Loves respond with
lamenting.

Wail, wail, Ah, Cytherea! The Loves respond with
lamenting.

Every torch at the doors hath been quenched by thy
hand, Hymenæus;
Every bridal wreath hath been torn to shreds; and no
longer,
Hymen, Hymen no more is the song, but a new song
of sorrow,
Woe, woe! and *Ah for Adonis!* resounds in lieu of the
bridesong.
This the Graces are shrilling, the son of Cinyras hymn-
ing,
Lost is lovely Adonis! in loud antiphonal accents.
Woe, woe! sharply repeat, far more than the praises of
Paiôn,
Woe! and *Ah for Adonis!* the Muses who wail for
Adonis,
Chaunt their charms to Adonis.—But he lists not to
their singing;
Not that he wills not to hear, but the Maiden doth not
release him.
Cease from moans, Cytherea, to-day refrain from the
death-songs:
Thou must lament him again, and again shed tears in a
new year.

(*John Addington Symonds*)

A DREAM OF VENUS

I DREAMT I saw great Venus by me stand,
Leading a nodding infant by the hand;
And that she said to me familiarly—
"Take Love, and teach him how to play to me."
She vanisht then. And I, poor fool, must turn
To teach the boy, as if he wished to learn.
I taught him all the pastoral songs I knew
And used to sing; and I informed him, too,
How Pan found out the pipe, Pallas the flute,
Phœbus the lyre, and Mercury the lute.
But not a jot for all my words cared he,
But lo! fell singing his love-songs to me;

And told me of the loves of gods and men,
And of his mother's doings; and so then
I forgot all I taught him for my part,
But what he taught me I learnt all by heart.

(Leigh Hunt)

Moschus

3rd century B.C.

LAMENT FOR BION

Ye mountain valleys, pitifully groan!
Rivers and Dorian springs, for Bion weep!
Ye plants drop tears; ye groves, lamenting moan!
Exhale your life, wan flowers; your blushes deep
In grief, anemones and roses, steep;
In whimpering murmurs, Hyacinth! prolong
The sad, sad woe thy lettered petals keep;
Our minstrel sings no more his friends among—
Sicilian Muses! now begin the doleful song.

Ye nightingales! that mid thick leaves set loose
The gushing gurgle of your sorrow, tell
The fountains of Sicilian Arethuse
That Bion is no more—with Bion fell
The song—the music of the Dorian shell.
Ye swans of Strymon! now your banks along
Your plaintive throats with melting dirges swell
For him, who sang like you the mournful song;
Discourse of Bion's death the Thracian nymphs among—

The Dorian Orpheus, tell them all, is dead.
His herds the song and darling herdsman miss,
And oaks, beneath whose shade he propt his head;
Oblivion's ditty now he sings for Dis;
The melancholy mountain silent is;
His pining cows no longer wish to feed,
But moan for him; Apollo wept, I wis,
For thee, sweet Bion! and in mourning weed
The brotherhood of Fauns, and all the Satyr breed.

The tears by Naiads shed are brimful bourns;
Afflicted Pan thy stifled music rues;
Lorn Echo 'mid her rocks thy silence mourns,
Nor with her mimic tones thy voice renews;
The flowers their bloom, the trees their fruitage lose;
No more their milk the drooping ewes supply;
The bees to press their honey now refuse;
What need to gather it and lay it by,
When thy own honey-lip, my Bion! thine is dry?

Sicilian Muses! lead the doleful chant;
Not so much near the shore the dolphin moans;
Nor so much wails within her rocky haunt
The nightingale; nor on their mountain thrones
The swallows utter such lugubrious tones;
Nor Cëyx such for faithful Halcyon,
Whose song the blue wave, where he perished, owns;
Nor in the valley, neighbor to the sun,
The funeral birds so wail their Memnon's tomb upon—

As these moan, wail, and weep for Bion dead,
The nightingales and swallows, whom he taught,
For him their elegiac sadness shed;
And all the birds contagious sorrow caught;
The sylvan realm was all with grief distraught.
Who, bold of heart, will play on Bion's reed,
Fresh from his lip, yet with his breathing fraught?
For still among the reeds does Echo feed
On Bion's minstrelsy. Pan only may succeed

To Bion's pipe; to him I make the gift;
But, lest he second seem, e'en Pan may fear
The pipe of Bion to his mouth to lift.
For thee sweet Galatea drops the tear,
And thy dear song regrets, which sitting near
She fondly listed; ever did she flee
The Cyclops and his songs—but ah! more dear
Thy song and sight than her own native sea;
On the deserted sands the nymph without her fee

Now sits and weeps, or weeping tends thy herd.
Away with Bion all the muse-gifts flew—
The chirping kisses breathed at every word:
Around thy tomb the Loves their playmate rue;
Thee Cypris loved—more than the kiss she drew,
And breathed upon her dying paramour.
Most musical of rivers! now renew
Thy plaintive murmurs; Meles! now deplore
Another son of song—as thou didst wail of yore

That sweet, sweet mouth of dear Calliope;
The threne, 'tis said, thy waves for Homer spun,
With saddest music filled the refluent sea;
Now melting wail and weep another son!
Both loved of fountains; that of Helicon
Gave Melesigenes his pleasant draught;
But to his Arethuse did Bion run,
And from her urn the glowing rapture quaffed:
Thy elder glory sung how Helen bloomed and laughed;

On Thetis' mighty son his descant ran
And Menelaus; but our Bion chose
Not arms and tears to sing, but Love and Pan;
While browsed his herd, his gushing music rose;
He milked his kine; did pipes of reeds compose;
Taught how to kiss; and fondled in his breast
Young Love, and Cypris pleased. For Bion flows
In every glorious land a grief confest;
Ascra for her own bard, wise Hesiod, less exprest;

Bœotian Hylæ mourned for Pindar less;
Teös regretted less her minstrel hoar,
And Mitylene her sweet poetess;
Nor for Alcæus Lesbos suffered more;
Nor lovely Paros so much did deplore
Her own Archilochus. Breathing her fire
Into her sons of song, from shore to shore
For thee the pastoral Muse attunes her lyre
To woeful utterance of passionate desire.

Sicelidas, the famous Samian star,
And he with smiling eye and radiant face,
Cydonian Lycidas, renowned afar,
Lament thee; where quick Hales runs his race
Philetas wails; Theocritus, the grace
Of Syracuse, thee mourns; nor these among
Am I remiss Ausonian wreaths to place
Around thy tomb; to me doth it belong
To chant for thee, from whom I learnt the Dorian song;

Me with thy minstrel skill as proper heir—
Others thou didst endow with thine estate.
Alas! alas! when in a garden fair
Mallows, crisp dill, and parsley yield to fate,
These with another year regerminate;
But when of mortal life the bloom and crown,
The wise, the good, the valiant, and the great
Succumb to death, in hollow earth shut down,
We sleep, for ever sleep—for ever lie unknown.

Thus art thou squeezed, while frogs may croak at will;
I envy not their croak. Thee poison slew—
How kept it in thy mouth its nature ill?
If thou didst speak, what cruel wretch could brew
The draught? He did of course thy song eschew.
But Justice all o'ertakes. My tears fast flow
For thee, my friend. Could I, like Orpheus true,
Odysseus or Alcides, pass below
To gloomy Tartarus, how quickly would I go!

To see, and hear thee, haply, sing for Dis;
But in the nymph's ear warble evermore,
O dearest friend! thy sweetest harmonies·
For whilom, on her own Etnëan shore,
She sang wild snatches of the Dorian lore.
Nor will thy singing unrewarded be;
Thee to thy mountain-haunts she will restore,
As she gave Orpheus his Eurydice.
Could I charm Dis with songs, I too would sing for thee.

(George Chapman)

Idyll VI
LOVE'S LESSON

Pan loved his neighbor Echo; Echo loved
A gamesome Satyr; he, by her unmoved,
Loved only Lyde; thus through Echo, Pan,
Lyde, and Satyr, Love his circle ran.
Thus all, while their true lovers' hearts they grieved,
Were scorned in turn, and what they gave received.
O all Love's scorners, learn this lesson true;
Be kind to Love, that he be kind to you.

(*Ernest Myers*)

Idyll IX
THE CRAFT OF A KEEPER OF SHEEP

Would that my father had taught me the craft of a keeper of sheep,
For so in the shade of the elm-tree, or under the rocks on the steep
Piping on reeds I had sat, and had lulled my sorrow to sleep.

(*Ernest Myers*)

THE OCEAN

When winds that move not its calm surface sweep
The azure sea, I love the land no more;
The smiles of the serene and tranquil deep
Tempt my unquiet mind.—But when the roar
Of Ocean's gray abyss resounds, and foam
Gathers upon the sea, and vast waves burst,
I turn from the drear aspect to the home
Of earth and its deep woods, where intersperst,
When winds blow loud, pines make sweet melody.
Whose house is some lone bark, whose toil the sea,
Whose prey the wondering fish, an evil lot

Has chosen.—But I my languid limbs will fling
Beneath the plane, where the brook's murmuring
Moves the calm spirit, but disturbs it not.

(*Percy Bysshe Shelley*)

CUPID TURNED PLOWMAN

IMITATED

His lamp, his bow, and quiver laid aside,
A rustic wallet o'er his shoulders tied,
Sly Cupid always on new mischiefs bent,
To the rich field and furrowed tillage went;
Like any plowman toiled the little god,
His tune he whistled, and his wheat he sowed,
Then sat and laughed, and to the skies above
Raising his eye, he thus insulted Jove:
"Lay by your hail, your hurtful storms restrain,
And as I bid you, let it shine or rain;
Else you again beneath my yoke shall bow,
Feel the sharp goad, or draw the servile plow;
What once Europa was, Nannette is now."

(*Matthew Prior*)

"Æsop's Fables"

3rd century?

THE VINE AND THE GOAT

A Goat was nibbling on a Vine,
On glossy leaves and tendrils fine:
"Why wilt thou rend me thus, alas—
And is there then no good in grass?
But when the vintage comes, I'll be,
Thou bearded Goat, revenged on thee—
For at the altar 'twill be mine
To furnish to the priest the wine
Which he with pious lips and eyes
Shall pour o'er thee, thou sacrifice
To Dionysos, god of grapes."

THE SHEPHERD-BOY AND THE WOLF

A Shepherd-boy beside a stream
"The Wolf, the Wolf," was wont to scream,
And when the Villagers appeared,
He'd laugh and call them silly-eared.
A Wolf at last came down the steep—
"The Wolf, the Wolf—my legs, my sheep!"
The creature had a jolly feast,
Quite undisturbed, on boy and beast.

For none believes the liar, forsooth,
Even when the liar speaks the truth.

THE ASS IN THE LION'S SKIN

An Ass put on a Lion's skin and went
About the forest with much merriment,
Scaring the foolish beasts by brooks and rocks,
Till at last he tried to scare the Fox.
But Reynard, hearing from beneath the mane
That raucous voice so petulant and vain,
Remarked, 'O Ass, I too would run away,
But that I know your old familiar bray.'

That's just the way with asses, just the way.

THE MOUNTAIN IN LABOR

A Mountain was in great distress and loud
She roared and rumbled, till there rushed a crowd
Of peasants, kings, and princes, looking at her
And wondering what of all things was the matter,

When mid her pangs there issued from her side
A Mouse—who gave one little squeak and died.
The moral here is learnèd and occult—
The bigger fuss, the smaller the result.

THE SWAN AND THE GOOSE

A RICH man bought a Swan and Goose—
That for song, and this for use.
It chanced his simple-minded cook
One night the Swan for Goose mistook.
But in the dark about to chop
The Swan in two above the crop,
He heard the lyric note, and stayed
The action of the fatal blade.

And thus we see a proper tune
Is sometimes very opportune.

(*William Ellery Leonard*)

The Greek Anthology

490 B.C.-1000 A.D.

The Anthology may from some points of view be regarded as the most valuable relic of antique literature which we possess. Composed of several thousand short poems, written at different times and by a multitude of authors, it is coextensive with the whole current of Greek history, from the splendid period of the Persian war to the decadence of Christianized Byzantium. Perhaps, however, the true secret of their charm is this; that in their couplets, after listening to the choric raptures of triumphant public art, we turn aside to hear the private utterances, the harmoniously modulated whispers of a multitude of Greek poets telling us their inmost thoughts and feelings. The unique melodies of Meleager, the chaste and exquisite delicacy of Callimachus, the clear dry style of Straton, Plato's unearthly subtlety of phrase, Antipater's perfect polish, the good sense of Palladas, the fretful sweetness of Agathias, the purity of Simonides, the gravity of Poseidippus, the pointed grace of Philip, the few but mellow tones of Sappho and Erinna, the tenderness of Simmias, the biting wit of Lucillius, the sunny radiance of Theocritus—all these good things are ours in the Anthology. But beyond these perfumes of the poets known to fame is yet another. Over very many of the sweetest and the strongest of the epigrams is written the pathetic word *ἀδέσποτον*—"without a master." Hail to you, dead poets, unnamed, but dear to the Muses! Surely with Pindar and Anacreon, with Sappho and with Sophocles, the bed of flowers is spread for you in those "black-petalled hollows of Pieria" where you bade Euripides farewell.—JOHN ADDINGTON SYMONDS.

Agathias

RHODANTHE

Weeping and wakeful all the night I lie,
And with the dawn the grace of sleep is near,
But swallows flit about me with their cry,
And banish drowsihead and bring the tear.
Mine eyes must still be weeping, for the dear
Thought of Rhodanthe stirs in memory;
Ye chattering foes have done! it was not I
Who silenced Philomel: go, seek the sheer

Clefts of the hills, and wail for Itylus
Or clamor from the hoopoe's craggy nest,
But let sweet sleep an hour abide with us,
Perchance a dream may come, and we be blest,
A dream may take Rhodanthe piteous,
And bring us to that haven of her breast.

(*Andrew Lang*)

NOT SUCH YOUR BURDEN

Not such your burden, happy youths, as ours—
Poor women-children nurtured daintily—
For ye have comrades when ill-fortune lours,
To hearten you with talk and company;
And ye have games for solace, and may roam
Along the streets and see the painters' shows.
But woe betide us if we stir from home—
And there our thoughts are dull enough, God knows!

(*William M. Hardinge*)

PLUTARCH

Chaeronean Plutarch, to thy deathless praise
Does martial Rome this grateful statue raise;
Because both Greece and she thy fame have shared,
(Their heroes written and their lives compared;)
But thou thyself could'st never write thine own;
Their lives have parallels, but thine has none.

(*John Dryden*)

Anonymous

SPIRIT OF PLATO

Eagle! why soarest thou above that tomb?
To what sublime and star-ypaven home
    Floatest thou?
I am the image of swift Plato's spirit,
Ascending heaven—Athens doth inherit
    His corpse below.

(*Percy Bysshe Shelley*)

EPITAPH ON ACHILLES

This mound the Achæans reared—Achilles' tomb—
    For terror to the Trojans yet to be,
Leans seaward, that his mighty spirit whom
    Sea Thetis bore may hear its dirge of the sea.

(*William M. Hardinge*)

THIS STONE

This stone, beloved Sabinus, on thy grave
    Memorial small of our great love shall be.
I still shall seek thee lost; from Lethe's wave,
    Oh, drink not thou forgetfulness of me.

(*Goldwin Smith*)

DION OF TARSUS

Dion of Tarsus, here I lie, who sixty years have seen.
I was not ever wed, and would my father had not been!

(*Alma Strettell*)

RICHES

Poor in my youth, and in life's later scenes
    Rich to no end, I curse my natal hour,
Who nought enjoyed while young, denied the means:
    And nought when old enjoy'd, denied the power.

(*William Cowper*)

GRAPES

While yet the grapes were green, thou didst refuse me,
When they were ripe, didst proudly pass me by;
But do not grudge me still a single cluster,
Now that the grapes are withering and dry.

(*Alma Strettell*)

THE TOMB OF DIOGENES

'Tell me, good dog, whose tomb you guard so well.'
'The Cynic's.' 'True; but who that Cynic tell.'
'Diogenes, of fair Sinope's race.'
'What? He that in a tub was wont to dwell?'
'Yes: but the stars are now his dwelling-place.'

(*John Addington Symonds*)

THE LION OVER THE TOMB OF LEONIDAS

Of beasts am I, of men was he most brave
Whose bones I guard, bestriding this his grave.

(*Walter Leaf*)

NOT OF ITSELF BUT THEE

I send thee myrrh, not that thou mayest be
By it perfumed, but it perfumed by thee.

(*Richard Garnett*)

NATURE'S TRAVAIL

Long Nature travailed, till at last she bore
Homer: then ceased from bearing evermore.

(*Goldwin Smith*)

Antipater

ERINNA

Though short her strain nor sung with mighty boast;
Yet there the power of song had dwelling room;
So lives her name for ever, nor lies lost
Beneath the shadow of the wings of gloom,
While birds of after days, in countless host,
Slumber and fade forgotten in the tomb.
Better the swan's brief note than thousand cries
Of rooks in springtime blown about the skies.

(*A. J. Butler*)

ARISTEIDES

One heifer and one fleecy sheep
Were Aristeides' scanty store;
With this poor wealth he strove to keep
Grim pinching hunger from his door.
Yet strove in vain: a wolf the one
And labor pains the other slew,
And left the herdsman, all undone,
His loss of livelihood to rue.
Poor wretch! The thong, which lately bound
His wallet, round his neck he tied,
And near his cabin, where the sound
No more was heard of lowing, died.

(*Charles Whibley*)

PINDAR

As the war-trumpet drowns the rustic flute,
So when your lyre is heard all strings are mute:
Not vain the labor of those clustering bees
Who on your infant lips spread honey-dew;
Witness great Pan who hymned your melodies,
Pindar, forgetful of his pipes for you.

(*John Addington Symonds*)

UNDYING THIRST

This rudely sculptured porter-pot
Denotes where sleeps a female sot;
Who passed her life, good easy soul,
In sweetly chirping o'er her bowl.
Not for her friends or children dear
She mourns, but only for her beer.
E'en in the very grave, they say,
She thirsts for drink to wet her clay;
And, faith, she thinks it very wrong
This jug should stand unfilled so long.

(*Robert Bland*)

Anytes

A SHEPHERD'S GIFT

To shaggy Pan, and all the Wood-Nymphs fair,
Fast by the rock this grateful offering stands,
A shepherd's gift—to those who gave him there
Rest, when he fainted in the sultry air;
And reached him sweetest water with their hands.

(*John William Burgon*)

Archias of Byzantium

SEA DIRGE

Crushed by the waves upon the crag was I,
Who still must hear these waves among the dead,
Breaking and brawling on the promontory,
Sleepless; and sleepless is my weary head!
For me did strangers bury on the coast
Within the hateful hearing of the deep,
Nor Death, that lulleth all, can lull my ghost,
One sleepless soul among the souls that sleep!

(*Andrew Lang*)

Asclepiades

EUMARES

Tumultuous sea, whose wrath and foam are spent
So nigh to Eumares' worn monument;
Spare if thou wilt and shatter if thou must,
For nothing shalt thou find but bones and dust.

(*Richard Garnett*)

Callimachus

HERACLITUS

They told me, Heraclitus, they told me you were dead,
They brought me bitter news to hear and bitter tears
to shed.
I wept as I remembered how often you and I
Had tired the sun with talking and sent him down
the sky.

And now that thou art lying, my dear old Carian guest,
A handful of gray ashes, long, long ago at rest,
Still are thy pleasant voices, thy nightingales, awake;
For Death, he taketh all away, but them he cannot take.

(*William Cory*)

TIMON'S EPITAPH

Here lie I, Timon; who, alive, all living men did hate:
Pass by, and curse thy fill; but pass and stay not here
thy gait.

(*William Shakespeare*)

HIS SON

But twelve short years you lived, my son,
Just twelve short years, and then you died:
And now your life's brief course is run,
This grave a father's hopes doth hide.

(*G. B. Grundy*)

SAON OF ACANTHUS

Here lapped in hallowed slumber Saon lies,
Asleep, not dead; a good man never dies.

(J. A. Symonds, M.D.)

SOPOLIS

Now would to God swift ships had ne'er been made!
Then, Sopolis, we had not mourned thy shade—
  Dear son of Diocleides seaward sent!
Now somewhere in deep seas thy corse is tost
Hither and thither—and for whom we lost
  We find thy name and empty monument.

(William M. Hardinge)

CRETHIS

For Crethis' store of tales and pleasant chat
Oft sigh the Samian maidens, missing that
Which cheered their tasks, but she, beyond their call,
Sleeps here the sleep that must be slept by all.

(Richard Garnett)

TO ARCHINUS

If I did come of set intent
Then be thy blame my punishment;
But if by love a capture made
Forgive my hasty serenade.
Wine drew me on, Love thrust behind,
I was not master of my mind.
And when I came I did not cry
My name aloud, my ancestry;
Only my lips thy lintel pressed;
If this be crime, the crime's confessed.

(F. A. Wright)

Carphyllides

A HAPPY MAN

When these graven lines you see,
Traveler, do not pity me;
Though I be among the dead,
Let no mournful word be said.

Children that I leave behind,
And their children, all were kind;
Near to them and to my wife,
I was happy all my life.

My three sons I married right,
And their sons I rocked at night;
Death nor sorrow ever brought
Cause for one unhappy thought.

Now, and with no need of tears,
Here they leave me, full of years,—
Leave me to my quiet rest
In the region of the blest.

(Edwin Arlington Robinson)

Crinagoras

EPITAPH ON AN INFANT

Full oft of old the islands changed their name
And took new titles from some heir of fame;
Then dread not yet the wrath of Gods above,
But change your own and be "The Isles of Love";
For Love's own name and shape the infant bore
Whom late we buried on yon sandy shore.
Break softly there, thou never-weary wave,
And, earth, lie lightly on his little grave.

(John William Burgon)

Diotimus

WITHOUT THE HERDSMAN

Covered with snow, the herd, with none to guide,
Came to the stall adown the mountain side;
For, ah! Therimachus beneath an oak
Slept the long sleep, from which he ne'er awoke,
Sent to his slumber by the lightning's stroke.

(*John William Burgon*)

Erinna

BAUCIS

My funeral-shaft, and marble shapes that dwell
Beside it, and sad urn, receptacle
Of all I am, salute who seek thy tomb,
If from my own, or other cities come;
And say to them, a bride I hither came,
Tenos my country, Baucis was my name.
Say also, this inscription for her friend
Erinna, handmaid of the Muses, penned.

(*Richard Garnett*)

Glaucus

AN INSCRIPTION BY THE SEA

No dust have I to cover me,
  My grave no man may show;
My tomb is this unending sea,
  And I lie far below.
My fate, O stranger, was to drown;
And where it was the ship went down
  Is what the sea-birds know.

(*Edwin Arlington Robinson*)

Isidorus

ON A FOWLER

WITH reeds and bird-lime from the desert air
Eumelus gather'd free, though scanty, fare.
Nor lordly patron's hand he deign'd to kiss:
Thrice thirty years he lived, and to his heirs
His reeds bequeath'd, his bird-lime, and his snares.

(*William Cowper*)

Leonidas of Alexandria

MENODOTIS

MENODOTIS's portrait here is kept;
Most odd it is
How very like to all the world, except
Menodotis.

(*Richard Garnett*)

Leonidas of Tarentum

THE FISHERMAN

THERIS the old, the waves that harvestèd,
More keen than birds that labor in the sea,
With spear and net, by shore and rocky bed
Not with the well-manned galley, labored he;
Him not the Star of Storms, nor sudden sweep
Of wind with all his years hath smitten and bent.
But in his hut of reeds he fell asleep,
As fades a lamp when all the oil is spent:
This tomb nor wife nor children raised, but we
His fellow-toilers, fishers of the sea.

(*Andrew Lang*)

THE SPINNING WOMAN

Morning and evening, sleep she drove away,
Old Platthis,—warding hunger from the door,
And still to wheel and distaff hummed her lay
Hard by the gates of Eld, and bent and hoar;
Plying her loom until the dawn was gray,
The long course of Athene did she tread:
With withered hand by withered knee she spun
Sufficient for the loom of goodly thread,
Till all her work and all her days were done.
And in her eightieth year she saw the wave
Of Acheron,—old Platthis,—kind and brave.

(*Andrew Lang*)

THE TOMB OF CRETHON

I am the tomb of Crethon; here you read
His name; himself is number'd with the dead;
Who once had wealth not less than Gyges' gold;
Who once was rich in stable, stall, and fold;
Who once was blest above all living men—
With lands, how narrow now, how ample then!

(*John Hermann Merivale*)

CLEITAGORAS

Shepherds that on this mountain ridge abide,
Tending your goats and fleecy flocks alway,
A little favor, but most grateful, pay
Cleitagoras, nor be the boon denied!
For sake of mother earth, and by the bride
Of Hades under earth, let sheep, I pray,
Bleat near me, and the shepherd softly play
From the scarred rock across the pasture wide.

Ah! but, in early spring, cull meadowsweet,
Neighbor, and weave a garland for my tomb;
And with ewe's milk be the stone edge bedewed

When the lambs play about their mother's feet.
So shall you honor well the shades, from whom
Are thanks—and from the dead is gratitude.

(William M. Hardinge)

THE LAST JOURNEY

With courage seek the kingdom of the dead;
The path before you lies,
It is not hard to find, nor tread;
No rocks to climb, no lanes to thread;
But broad, and straight, and even still,
And ever gently slopes down-hill;
You cannot miss it, though you shut your eyes.

(Charles Merivale)

PHILOCLES

This noiseless ball and top so round,
This rattle with its lively sound,
These bones with which he loved to play,
Companions of his childhood's day,
To Hermes, if the god they please,
An offering from Philocles.

(F. A. Wright)

Lucianus

ARTIFICIAL BEAUTY

You give your cheeks a rosy stain,
With washes dye your hair,
But paint and washes both are vain
To give a youthful air.

Those wrinkles mock your daily toil;
No labor will efface them;
You wear a mask of smoothest oil,
Yet still with ease we trace them.

An art so fruitless then forsake,
  Which though you much excel in,
You never can contrive to make
  Old Hecuba young Helen.

(*William Cowper*)

Lucillius

ON AN OLD WOMAN

Mycilla dyes her locks, 'tis said,
  But 'tis a foul aspersion;
She buys them black, they therefore need
  No subsequent immersion.

(*William Cowper*)

TREASURE

They call thee rich; I deem thee poor;
Since, if thou darest not use thy store,
But savest only for thine heirs,
The treasure is not thine, but theirs.

(*William Cowper*)

Marcus Argentarius

THE OLD STORY

Like many a one, when you had gold
Love met you smiling, we are told;
But now that all your gold is gone,
Love leaves you hungry and alone.

And women, who have called you more
Sweet names than ever were before,
Will ask another now to tell
What man you are and where you dwell.

Was ever anyone but you
So long in learning what is true?
Must you find only at the end
That who has nothing has no friend?

(*Edwin Arlington Robinson*)

Meleager

UPON A MAID THAT DIED THE DAY SHE WAS MARRIED

That morn which saw me made a bride,
The evening witnessed that I died.
Those holy lights, wherewith they guide
Unto the bed the bashful bride,
Served but as tapers, for to burn,
And light my relics to their urn.
This epitaph, which here you see,
Supplied the epithalamy.

(*Robert Herrick*)

O GENTLE SHIPS

O gentle ships that skim the seas,
And cleave the strait where Hellè fell,
Catch in your sails the northern breeze,
And speed to Cos where she doth dwell,

My love, and see you greet her well!
And if she looks across the blue,
Speak, gentle ships, and tell her true—
"He comes, for Love hath brought him back,
No sailor, on the landward tack."

If thus, O gentle ships, ye do,
Then may ye win the fairest gales,
And swifter speed across the blue,
While Zeus breathes friendly on your sails.

(*Andrew Lang*)

OF HIS DEATH

Ah! Love, my Master, hear me swear
By all the locks of Timo's hair,
By Demo, and that fragrant spell
Wherewith her body doth enchant
Such dreams as drowsy lovers haunt,
By Ilias' mirth delectable.

And by the lamp that sheds his light
On love and lovers all the night,
By those, ah Love, I swear that thou
Hast left me but one breath, and now
Upon my lips it fluttereth,
Yet *this* I'll yield, my latest breath,
Even this, oh Love, for thee to Death!

(*Andrew Lang*)

IN THE SPRING

Now the bright crocus flames, and now
The slim narcissus takes the rain,
And, straying o'er the mountain's brow,
The daffodillies bud again.
The thousand blossoms wax and wane
On wold, and heath, and fragrant bough,
But fairer than the flowers art thou
Than any growth of hill or plain.

Ye gardens cast your leafy crown,
That my love's feet may tread it down,
Like lilies on the lilies set;
My Love, whose lips are softer far
Than drowsy poppy petals are,
And sweeter than the violet!

(*Andrew Lang*)

LOVE AT THE DOOR

Cold blows the winter wind: 't is Love,
Whose sweet eyes swim with honeyed tears,
That bears me to thy doors, my love,
Tossed by the storm of hopes and fears.

Cold blows the blast of aching Love;
But be thou for my wandering sail,
Adrift upon these waves of love,
Safe harbor from the whistling gale!

(*J. A. Symonds, M.D.*)

THE LITTLE LOVE-GOD

I

A PLAGUE is Love, a plague! but yet
what profit shall it prove
again and oft again to fret
and cry: *A plague is Love?*

The boy but laughs to hear such news;
chid with a tongue let loose,
enjoys it; and if I abuse,
he thrives upon abuse.

O hither through the green wave sent,
Cypris I must admire
how thou from that moist element
hast brought to birth a fire!

II

LET him be sold, though still he sleep
upon his mother's breast!
let him be sold! why should I keep
so turbulent a pest?

For wingéd he was born, he leers,
and sharply with his nails
he scratches, and amid his tears
oft laughs the while he wails.

Withal and further, glances keen
he plies, devoid of shame,
a ceaseless babbler, wild, nor e'en
to his own dear mother tame.

An utter monster: on that ground
sold he shall be to-day:
if any trader outward bound
would buy a boy, this way!

But see, in tears beseecheth he:
nay, thee no more I sell:
fear not, with my Zenophile
remain thou here to dwell.

(*Walter Headlam*)

OF HIMSELF

TYRE brought me up, who born in thee had been,
Assyrian Athens, city Gadarene;
My name is Meleager, Eucrates
My sire, my skill with graceful strains to please;
My Syrian lineage do not discommend,
One world have all, one origin, one end;
Stricken in years, I yet can touch the string,
And this unto the tomb, my neighbor, sing;
Salute my garrulous old age, and be
Thine own what now thou honorest in me.

(*Richard Garnett*)

LOST DESIRE

LOVE brought by night a vision to my bed,
One that still wore the vesture of a child
But eighteen years of age—who sweetly smiled
Till of the lovely form false hopes were bred
And keen embraces wild.
Ah! for the lost desire that haunts me yet,
Till mine eyes fail in sleep that finds no more
That fleeting ghost! Oh, lovelorn heart, give o'er—
Cease thy vain dreams of beauty's warmth—forget
The face thou longest for!

(*William M. Hardinge*)

SPRING

Now Winter's winds are banished from the sky,
Gay laughs the blushing face of flowery Spring:
Now lays the land her duskier raiment by
And dons her grass-green vest, for signal why
Young plants may choose themselves appareling.

Now drinking tender dews of generous morn,
The meadows break into their summer smile,
The rose unfolds her leaves: and glad, the while,
In far-off hills the shepherd winds his horn,
And his white brede the goatherd's heart beguile.

Now sail the sailors over billowing seas
While carelss Zephyr fills the canvas fair,
And singing crowds with dances debonair
Praise Dionysus for the grapes' increase—
The berried ivy twisted in their hair.

Forth from the rotting hide now bees are come—
Deft craftsmen working well and warily—
And in the hive they settle, while they ply
Fresh-flowing waxen store, with busy hum,
And small pierced cells for their sweet industry.

Now shrilleth clear each several bird his note,
The Halcyon charms the wave that knows no gale,
About our eaves the swallow tells her tale,
Along the river banks the swan, afloat,
And down the woodland glades the nightingale.

Now tendrils curl and earth bursts forth anew—
Now shepherd's pipe and fleecy flocks are gay—
Now sailors sail, and Bacchus gets his due—
Now wild birds chirp and bees their toil pursue—
Sing, poet, thou—and sing thy best for May!

(*William M. Hardinge*)

A GARLAND FOR HELIODORA

I'LL frame, my Heliodora! a garland for thy hair,
Which thou, in all thy beauty's pride, mayst not disdain
 to wear;
For I with tender myrtles white violets will twine,
White violets, but not so pure as that pure breast of
 thine;

With laughing lilies I will twine narcissus, and the sweet
Crocus shall, in its yellow hue, with purple hyacinth meet.
And I will twine with all the rest, and all the rest above,
Queen of them all, the red red rose, the flower which lovers love.

(*Christopher North*)

Nicarchus

THE RAVEN

The gloom of death is on the raven's wing,
The song of death is in the raven's cries:
But when Demophilus begins to sing,
The raven dies.

(*Edwin Arlington Robinson*)

Nicias

THE FOUNTAIN AT THE TOMB

Stay weary traveler, stay!
Beneath these boughs repose;
A step out of the way
My little fountain flows.
And never quite forget
The monumental urn,
Which Simus here hath set
His buried child to mourn.

(*Charles Merivale*)

Palladas

VANITY OF VANITIES

Naked to earth was I brought—naked to earth I descend.
Why should I labor for naught, seeing how naked the end?

(*William M. Hardinge*)

Paulus Silentiarius

NO MATTER

My name, my country, what are they to thee?
What, whether proud or base my pedigree?
Perhaps I far surpassed all other men;
Perhaps I fell below them all. What then?
Suffice it, stranger, that thou seest a tomb.
Thou knowst its use. It hides—no matter whom.

(*William Cowper*)

UNITED

How long must we two hide the burning gaze,
And look by stealth in one another's eyes?
Let us proclaim our love; and whoso stays
The sweet embrace that lulls all miseries —
The sword's our doctor: best that you and I
Should live together, or together die.

(*W. H. D. Rouse*)

Plato

A FAREWELL

Venus, take my votive glass,
Since I am not what I was:
What from this day I shall be,
Venus, let me ever see.

(*Matthew Prior*)

MORNING AND EVENING STAR

Thou wert the morning star among the living,
Ere thy fair light had fled;
Now, having died, thou art as Hesperus, giving
New splendor to the dead.

(*Percy Bysshe Shelley*)

ON ALEXIS

"Fair is Alexis" I no sooner said
When every one his eyes that way convey'd.
My soul, as when some dog a bone we show
Who snatcheth it—lost we not Phædrus so?

(*Thomas Stanley*)

ON ARCHÆANASSA

To Archæanassa, on whose furrow'd brow
Love sits in triumph, I my service vow.
If her declining graces shine so bright,
What flames felt you who saw her noon of light?

(*Thomas Stanley*)

LOVE SLEEPING

Within the covert of a shady grove
We saw the little red-cheek'd god of Love:
He had nor bow nor quiver: these among
The neighboring trees upon a bow were hung.
Upon a bank of tender rosebuds laid,
He smiling slept; bees with their noise invade
His rest, and on his lips their honey made.

(*Thomas Stanley*)

ON A SEAL

Five oxen, grazing in a flowery mead,
A jasper seal, done to the life, doth hold;
The little herd away long since had fled,
Were't not enclos'd within a pale of gold.

(*Thomas Stanley*)

FAREWELL

Far from the deep roar of the Ægean main,
Here lie we in the midst of Media's plain.
Farewell, great Fatherland! Farewell to thee,
Eubœa's neighbor, Athens! Farewell, Sea!

(*Charles Whibley*)

Posidippus

DORICHA

So now the very bones of you are gone
Where they were dust and ashes long ago;
And there was the last ribbon you tied on
To bind your hair, and that is dust also;
And somewhere there is dust that was of old
A soft and scented garment that you wore—
The same that once till dawn did closely fold
You in with fair Charaxus, fair no more.

But Sappho, and the white leaves of her song,
Will make your name a word for all to learn,
And all to love thereafter, even while
It's but a name; and this will be as long
As there are distant ships that will return
Again to your Naucratis and the Nile.

(*Edwin Arlington Robinson*)

Rufinus

THE LOVER'S POSY

I SEND a garland to my love
Which with my own hands I wove:
Rose and lily here there be
Twined with cool anemone,
White narcissus, dewy wet,
And the purple violet.
Take and bind it on your brow,
Nor be proud, as you are now.
As the flowers bloom and fade,
So must you too, haughty maid.

(*W. H. D. Rouse*)

Simmias of Thebes

TO PROTE

Thou art not dead, my Prote! thou art flown
To a far country better than our own;
Thy home is now an island of the blest;
There 'mid Elysian meadows take thy rest,
Or lightly trip along the flowery glade,
Rich with the asphodels that never fade!
Nor pain, nor cold, nor toil shall vex thee more,
Nor thirst, nor hunger on that happy shore;
Nor longings vain (now that blest life is won)
For such poor days as mortals here drag on;
To thee for aye a blameless life is given
In the pure light of ever-present Heaven.

(J. A. Symonds, M.D.)

Simonides

ON TWO BROTHERS

This earth Pythonax and his brother hides,
Who died before they reached youth's lovely prime.
The tomb their father built them; which abides
For ever, though they lived so short a time.

(W. H. D. Rouse)

LATIN

Titus Lucretius Carus

95-52 B.C.

The distinguishing character of Lucretius (I mean of his soul and genius) is a certain kind of noble pride, and positive assertion of his opinions. . . . From this sublime and daring genius of his it must of necessity come to pass that his thoughts must be masculine, full of argumentation, and that sufficiently warm. From the same fiery temper proceeds the loftiness of his expressions, and the perpetual torrent of his verse, where the barrenness of his subject does not too much constrain the quickness of his fancy. . . . He was so much an atheist that he forgot sometimes to be a poet.—JOHN DRYDEN.

ADDRESS TO VENUS

GREAT Venus, Queene of Beautie and of grace,
The joy of Gods and men, that under skie
Dost fayrest shine, and most adorne thy place;
That with thy smyling looke doest pacifie
The raging seas and makst the stormes to flie:
Thee, Goddess, thee the winds, the clouds do feare;
And when thou spredst thy mantle forth on hie
The waters play, and pleasant lands appear,
And heavens laugh, and all the world shews joyous cheare.

Then doth the daedale earth throw forth to thee
Out of her fruitfull lap abundant flowres;
And then all living wights, soone as they see
The Spring break forth out of his lusty bowres,
They all doe learne to play the Paramours;
First doe the merry birds, thy prety pages,
Privily priked with thy lustful powres,
Chirpe loud to thee out of their leavy cages
And thee their mother call to coole their kindly rages.

Then doe the salvage beasts begin to play
  Their pleasant friskes, and loath their wonted food;
The Lyons rore; the Tygres loudly bray;
  The raging Buls rebellow through the wood,
  And breaking forth dare tempt the deepest flood
    To come where thou doest draw them with desire.
  So all things else, that nourish vitall blood,
    Soone as with fury thou doest them inspire
In generation seeke to quench their inward fire.

So all the world by thee at first was made,
  And dayly yet thou doest the same prepayre:
Ne ought on earth that merry is and glad,
  Ne ought on earth that lovely is and fayre
  But thou the same for pleasure didst prepayre:
    Thou art the root of all that joyous is:
  Great God of men and women, queene of the air,
    Mother of laughter and welspring of blisse,
O graunt that of my love at last I may not misse!

(Edmund Spenser)

BEYOND RELIGION

WHILST human kind
Throughout the lands lay miserably crushed
Before all eyes beneath Religion—who
Would show her head along the region skies,
Glowering on mortals with her hideous face—
A Greek it was who first opposing dared
Raise mortal eyes that terror to withstand,
Whom nor the fame of Gods nor lightning's stroke
Nor threatening thunder of the ominous sky
Abashed; but rather chafed to angry zest
His dauntless heart to be the first to rend
The crossbars at the gates of Nature old.
And thus his will and hardy wisdom won;
And forward thus he fared afar, beyond
The flaming ramparts of the world, until
He wandered the unmeasurable All.

Whence he to us, a conqueror, reports
What things can rise to being, what cannot,
And by what law to each its scope prescribed,
Its boundary stone that clings so deep in Time.
Wherefore religion now is under foot,
And us his victory now exalts to heaven.
  I know how hard it is in Latian verse
To tell the dark discoveries of the Greeks,
Chiefly because our pauper-speech must find
Strange terms to fit the strangeness of the thing;
Yet worth of thine and the expected joy
Of thy sweet friendship do persuade me on
To bear all toil and wake the clear nights through,
Seeking with what of words and what of song
I may at last most gloriously uncloud
For thee the light beyond, wherewith to view
The core of being at the center hid.
And for the rest, summon to judgments true,
Unbusied ears and singleness of mind
Withdrawn from cares; lest these my gifts, arranged
For thee with eager service, thou disdain
Before thou comprehendest: since for thee
I prove the supreme law of Gods and sky,
And the primordial germs of things unfold,
Whence Nature all creates, and multiplies
And fosters all, and whither she resolves
Each in the end when each is overthrown.

(*William Ellery Leonard*)

NO SINGLE THING ABIDES

Sic igitur magni quoque circum moenia mundi
Expugnata dabunt labem putresque ruinas.

I

No single thing abides; but all things flow.
Fragment to fragment clings—the things thus grow
  Until we know and name them. By degrees
They melt, and are no more the things we know.

II

Globed from the atoms falling slow or swift
I see the suns, I see the systems lift
  Their forms; and even the systems and the suns
Shall go back slowly to the eternal drift.

III

Thou too, oh earth—thine empires, lands, and seas—
Least, with thy stars, of all the galaxies,
  Globed from the drift like these, like these thou too
Shalt go. Thou art going, hour by hour, like these.

IV

Nothing abides. Thy seas in delicate haze
Go off; those mooned sands forsake their place;
  And where they are, shall other seas in turn
Mow with their scythes of whiteness other bays.

V

Lo, how the terraced towers, and monstrous round
Of league-long ramparts rise from out the ground,
  With gardens in the clouds. Then all is gone,
And Babylon is a memory and a mound.

VI

Observe this dew-drenched rose of Tyrian grain—
A rose to-day. But you will ask in vain
  To-morrow what it is; and yesterday
It was the dust, the sunshine and the rain.

VII

This bowl of milk, the pitch on yonder jar,
Are strange and far-bound travelers come from far.
  This is a snow-flake that was once a flame—
The flame was once the fragment of a star.

viii

Round, angular, soft, brittle, dry, cold, warm,
Things *are* their qualities: things *are* their form—
And these in combination, even as bees,
Not singly but combined, make up the swarm:

IX

And when the qualities like bees on wing,
Having a moment clustered, cease to cling,
As the thing dies without its qualities,
So die the qualities without the thing.

X

Where is the coolness when no cool winds blow?
Where is the music when the lute lies low?
Are not the redness and the red rose one,
And the snow's whiteness one thing with the snow?

XI

Even so, now mark me, here we reach the goal
Of Science, and in little have the whole—
Even as the redness and the rose are one,
So with the body one thing is the soul.

XII

For, as our limbs and organs all unite
To make our sum of suffering and delight,
And without eyes and ears and touch and tongue,
Were no such things as taste and sound and sight.

XIII

So without these we all in vain shall try
To find the thing that gives them unity—
The thing to which each whispers, "Thou art thou"—
The soul which answers each, "And I am I."

XIV

What! shall the dateless worlds in dust be blown
Back to the unremembered and unknown,
And this frail Thou—this flame of yesterday—
Burn on, forlorn, immortal, and alone?

XV

Did Nature, in the nurseries of the night
Tend it for this—Nature whose heedless might,
Casts, like some shipwrecked sailor, the poor babe,
Naked and bleating on the shores of light?

XVI

What is it there? A cry is all it is.
It knows not if its limbs be yours or his.
Less than that cry the babe was yesterday.
The man to-morrow shall be less than this.

XVII

Tissue by tissue to a soul he grows,
As leaf by leaf the rose becomes the rose.
Tissue from tissue rots; and, as the Sun
Goes from the bubbles when they burst, he goes.

XVIII

Ah, mark those pearls of Sunrise! Fast and free
Upon the waves they are dancing. Souls shall be
Things that outlast their bodies, when each spark
Outlasts its wave, each wave outlasts the sea.

XIX

The seeds that once were we take flight and fly,
Winnowed to earth, or whirled along the sky,
Not lost but disunited. Life lives on.
It is the lives, the lives, the lives, that die.

XX

They go beyond recapture and recall,
Lost in the all-indissoluble All:—
Gone like the rainbow from the fountain's foam,
Gone like the spindrift shuddering down the squall.

XXI

Flakes of the water, on the waters cease!
Soul of the body, melt and sleep like these.
Atoms to atoms—weariness to rest—
Ashes to ashes—hopes and fears to peace!

XXII

Oh Science, lift aloud thy voice that stills
The pulse of fear, and through the conscience thrills—
Thrills through the conscience the news of peace—
How beautiful thy feet are on the hills!

(*W. H. Mallock*)

SUAVE MARI MAGNO

I

WHEN storms blow loud, 't is sweet to watch at ease
From shore, the sailor laboring with the seas:
Because the sense, not that such pains are his,
But that they are not ours, must always please.

II

Sweet for the cragsman, from some high retreat
Watching the plains below where legions meet,
To await the moment when the walls of war
Thunder and clash together. But more sweet,

III

Sweeeter by far on Wisdom's rampired height
To pace serene the porches of the light,
And thence look down—down on the purblind herd
Seeking and never finding in the night

IV

The road to peace—the peace that all might hold,
But yet is missed by young men and by old,
Lost in the strife for palaces and powers,
The axes, and the lictors, and the gold.

V

Oh sightless eyes! Oh hands that toil in vain!
Not such your needs. Your nature's needs are twain,
And only twain: and these are to be free—
Your minds from terror, and your bones from pain.

VI

Unailing limbs, a calm unanxious breast—
Grant Nature these, and she will do the rest.
Nature will bring you, be you rich or poor,
Perhaps not much—at all events her best.

VII

What though no statued youths from wall and wall
Strew light along your midnight festival,
With golden hands, nor beams from Lebanon
Keep the lyre's languor lingering through the hall,

VIII

Yours is the table 'neath the high-whispering trees;
Yours is the lyre of leaf and stream and breeze.
The golden flagon, and the echoing dome—
Lapped in the Spring, what care you then for these?

IX

Sleep is no sweeter on the ivory bed
Than yours on moss; and fever's shafts are sped
As clean through silks damasked for dreaming kings,
As through the hood that wraps the poor man's head.

X

What then, if all the prince's glittering store
Yields to his body not one sense the more,
 Nor any ache or fever of them all
Is barred out by bronze gates or janitor—

XI

What shall the palace, what the proud domain
Do for the mind—vain splendors of the vain?
 How shall these minister to a mind diseased,
Or raze one written trouble from the brain?

XII

Unless you think that conscience with its stings
And misery, fears the outward pomp of things—
 Fears to push swords and sentinels aside,
And sit the assessor of the king of kings.

XIII

The mind! Ay—there's the rub. The root is there
Of that one malady which all men share.
 It gleams between the haggard lids of joy;
It burns a canker in the heart of care.

XIV

Within the gold bowl, when the feast is set,
It lurks. 'T is bitter in the laborer's sweat.
 Feed thou the starving, and thou bring'st it back—
Back to the starving, who alone forget.

XV

Oh you who under silken curtains lie,
And you whose only roof-tree is the sky,
 What is the curse that blights your lives alike?
Not that you hate to live, but fear to die.

XVI

Fear is the poison. Wheresoe'er you go,
Out of the skies above, the clods below,
The sense thrills through you of some pitiless Power
Who scowls at once your father and your foe;

XVII

Who lets his children wander at their whim,
Choosing their road, as though not bound by him:
But all their life is rounded with a shade,
And every road goes down behind the rim;

XVIII

And there behind the rim, the swift, the lame,
At different paces, but their end the same,
Into the dark shall one by one go down,
Where the great furnace shakes its hair of flame.

XIX

Oh ye who cringe and cower before the throne
Of him whose heart is fire, whose hands are stone,
Who shall deliver you from this death in life—
Strike off your chains, and make your souls your own!

(*W. H. Mallock*)

AGAINST THE FEAR OF DEATH

WHAT has this bugbear Death to frighten man,
If souls can die, as well as bodies can?
For, as before our birth we felt no pain,
When Punic arms infested land and main,
When heaven and earth were in confusion hurl'd
For the debated empire of the world,
Which awed with dreadful expectation lay,
Soon to be slaves, uncertain who should sway:
So, when our mortal frame shall be disjoin'd,
The lifeless lump uncoupled from the mind,

From sense of grief and pain we shall be free;
We shall not feel, because we shall not be.
Though earth in seas, and seas in heaven were lost,
We should not move, we only should be toss'd.
Nay, e'en suppose when we have suffered fate
The soul should feel in her divided state,
What's that to us? for we are only we,
While souls and bodies in our frame agree.
Nay, though our atoms should revolve by chance,
And matter leap into the former dance;
Though time our life and motion could restore,
And make our bodies what they were before,
What gain to us would all this bustle bring?
The new-made man would be another thing.
When once an interrupting pause is made,
That individual being is decay'd.
We, who are dead and gone, shall bear no part
In all the pleasures, nor shall feel the smart,
Which to that other mortal shall accrue,
Whom to our matter time shall mold anew.
For backward if you look on that long space
Of ages past, and view the changing face
Of matter, toss'd and variously combin'd
In sundry shapes, 'tis easy for the mind
From thence to infer, that seeds of things have been
In the same order as they now are seen:
Which yet our dark remembrance cannot trace,
Because a pause of life, a gaping space,
Has come betwixt, where memory lies dead,
And all the wandering motions from the sense are fled.
For whosoe'er shall in misfortunes live,
Must be, when those misfortunes shall arrive;
And since the man who is not, feels not woe,
(For death exempts him, and wards off the blow,
Which we, the living, only feel and bear,)
What is there left for us in death to fear?
When once that pause of life has come between
'Tis just the same as we had never been.

(*John Dryden*)

Caius Valerius Catullus

87–57 B.C.

Tenderest of Roman poets nineteen hundred years ago.—
LORD TENNYSON.

MY SWEETEST LESBIA

My sweetest Lesbia, let us live and love,
And though the sager sort our deeds reprove,
Let us not weigh them. Heaven's great lamps do dive
Into their west, and straight again revive,
But, soon as once set is our little light,
Then must we sleep one ever-during night.

If all would lead their lives in love like me,
Then bloody swords and armor should not be;
No drum nor trumpet peaceful sleeps should move,
Unless alarm came from the camp of Love:
But fools do live and waste their little light,
And seek with pain their ever-during night.

When timely death my life and fortune ends,
Let not my hearse be vext with mourning friends,
But let all lovers rich in triumph come
And with sweet pastimes grace my happy tomb:
And, Lesbia, close up thou my little light,
And crown with love my ever-during night.

(*Thomas Campion*)

TO CELIA

Kiss me, sweet: the wary lover
Can your favors keep, and cover,
When the common courting jay
All your bounties will betray.
Kiss again! no creature comes;
Kiss, and score up wealthy sums
On my lips, thus hardly sundered,

While you breathe. First give a hundred,
Then a thousand, then another
Hundred, then unto the other
Add a thousand, and so more;
Till you equal with the store
All the grass that Romney yields,
Or the sands in Chelsea fields,
Or the drops in silver Thames,
Or the stars that gild his streams
In the silent summer-nights,
When youths ply their stolen delights;
That the curious may not know
How to tell 'em as they flow,
And the envious when they find
What their number is, be pined.

(*Ben Jonson*)

THE DEATH OF LESBIA'S BIRD

Pity! mourn in plaintive tone
The lovely starling dead and gone!
  Pity mourns in plaintive tone
The lovely starling dead and gone.
Weep, ye Loves! and Venus! weep
The lovely starling fallen asleep!
Venus sees with tearful eyes—
In her lap the starling lies!
While the Loves all in a ring
Softly stroke the stiffened wing.

(*Samuel Taylor Coleridge*)

LESBIA RAILING

Lesbia forever on me rails.
To talk of me she never fails.
Now, hang me, but for all her art,
I find that I have gained her heart.
My proof is this: I plainly see
The case is just the same with me;
I curse her every hour sincerely,
Yet, hang me, but I love her dearly.

(*Jonathan Swift*)

TRUE OR FALSE

None could ever say that she,
Lesbia! was so loved by me.
Never all the world around
Faith so true as mine was found.
If no longer it endures
(Would it did!) the fault is yours.
I can never think again
Well of you: I try in vain.
But . . . be false . . . do what you will.—
Lesbia! I must love you still.

(*Walter Savage Landor*)

TO HIMSELF

Wretched Catullus, play the fool no more:
The lost is lost, the dead forever dead—
White were the suns that gleamed for you of yore,
When roamed your footsteps where your lady led,
O loved by us as none was loved before:
O then I spoke those playful words so dear
That then my lady loved so well to hear—
White were the suns that gleamed for you of yore.

She wishes them no more; and 'tis for you,
Poor weakling, now to cease to wish them too.
No longer strive to follow what will flee:
No longer live the wretch you've lived to be.
But now with steadfast mind, be calm and bear.
Farewell, my child, Catullus now is strong;
He will not ask nor seek you anywhere
Unbidden more.

But you shall grieve for long,
When none will ask. O what a life is there,
Miscreant woman. Who will come, ah who
Hereafter? Unto whom shall you be fair?

Who now will love? To whom shall you belong?
Whom will you kiss? and bite whose lips!—
But you,
Catullus, still remember to be strong.

(*William Ellery Leonard*)

SAPPHO

Like to a god he seems to me,
O more than god, if that may be,
The man who, seated next to thee,
Gazes, and hears

Thy laugh of love that snatched away
My soul and sense: for on the day
I saw thee, lady, voice could say
Not any word;

But tongue grew stark, and thro my frame
Fed unforeseen a subtle flame,
And rang my ears, and eyes became
Veiled, as in night.

(*William Ellery Leonard*)

HYMN TO DIANA

Diana guardeth our estate,
Girls and boys immaculate:
Boys and maidens pure of stain,
Be Diana our refrain.

O Latonia, pledge of love
Glorious to most glorious Jove,
Near the Delian olive-tree
Latonia gave thy life to thee,

That thou shouldst be forever queen
Of mountains and of forests green;
Of every deep glen's mystery;
Of all streams and their melody:

Women in travail ask their peace
From thee, our Lady of Release:
Thou art the Watcher of the Ways
Thou art the Moon with borrowed rays;

And as thy full or waning tide
Marks how the monthly seasons glide,
Thou, Goddess, sendest wealth of store
To bless the farmer's thrifty floor!

Whatever name delights thine ear,
By that name be thou hallowed here;
And as of old be good to us,
The lineage of Romulus!

(*Richard Claverhouse Jebb*)

ON THE BURIAL OF HIS BROTHER

By ways remote and distant waters sped,
Brother, to thy sad graveside am I come,
That I may give the last gifts to the dead,
And vainly parley with thine ashes dumb;
Since She who now bestows and now denies
Hath ta'en thee, hapless brother, from mine eyes.
But lo! these gifts, the heirlooms of past years,
Are made sad things to grace thy coffin-shell;
Take them, all drenchèd with a brother's tears,
And, brother, for all time, hail and farewell.

(*Aubrey Beardsley*)

SIRMIO

Gem of all isthmuses and isles that lie,
Fresh or salt water's children, in clear lake
Or ampler ocean: with what joy do I
Approach thee, Sirmio! Oh! am I awake,
Or dream that once again my eye beholds
Thee, and has looked its last on Thynian wolds?
Sweetest of sweets to me that pastime seems,

When the mind drops her burden: when—the pain
Of travel past—our own cot we regain,
And nestle on the pillow of our dreams!
'Tis this one thought that cheers us as we roam.
Hail, O fair Sirmio! Joy, thy lord is here!
Joy too, ye waters of the Garda Mere!
And ring out, all ye laughter-peals of home.

(*Charles Stuart Calverley*)

LOVE AND DEATH

Friend, if the mute and shrouded dead
Are touched at all by tears,
By love long fled and friendship sped
And the unreturning years,

O then, to her that early died,
O doubt not, bridegroom, to thy bride
Thy love is sweet and sweeteneth
The very bitterness of death.

(*H. W. Garrod*)

TO VARUS

Suffenus, whom so well you know,
My Varus, as a wit and beau,
Of smart address and smirking smile,
Will write you verses by the mile.
You cannot meet with daintier fare
Than title-page and binding are;
But when you once begin to read
You find it sorry stuff indeed,
And you are ready to cry out
Upon this beau—"O what a lout!"
No man on earth so proud as he
Of his own precious poetry,
Or knows such perfect bliss as when
He takes in hand that nibbled pen.

Have we not all some faults like these?
Are we not all Suffenuses?
In others the defect we find,
But cannot see our sack behind.

(*Walter Savage Landor*)

A FIB DETECTED

Varus, whom I chanced to meet
The other evening in the street,
Engaged me there, upon the spot,
To see a mistress he had got.
She seemed, as far as I can gather,
Lively and smart and handsome rather.
There, as we rested from our walk,
We entered into various talk—
As, how much might Bithynia bring?
And had I found it a good thing?
I answered, as it was the fact,
The province had been stript and sackt;
That there was nothing for the prætors,
And still less for us wretched creatures,
His poor companions and toad-eaters.
"At least," says she, "you bought some fellows
To bear your litter; for they tell us,
Our only good ones come from there."
I chose to give myself an air;
"Why, truly, with my poor estate,
The difference wasn't quite so great
Betwixt a province, good or bad,
That where a purchase could be had,
Eight lusty fellows, straight and tall,
I shouldn't find the wherewithal
To buy them." But it was a lie;
For not a single wretch had I—
No single cripple fit to bear
A broken bedstead or a chair.
She, like a strumpet, pert and knowing,
Said—"Dear Catullus, I am going

To worship at Serapis' shrine—
Do lend me, pray, those slaves of thine."
I answered—"It was idly said,—
They were a purchase Cinna made
(Caius Cinna, my good friend)—
It was the same thing in the end,
Whether a purchase or a loan—
I always used them as my own;
Only the phrase was inexact—
He bought them for himself in fact.
But you have caught the general vice
Of being too correct and nice,
Overcurious and precise;
And seizing with precipitation
The slight neglects of conversation."

(John Hookham Frere)

THE YACHT

Stranger, the bark you see before you says
That in old times and in her early days
She was a lively vessel that could make
The quickest voyages, and overtake
All her competitors with sail or oar;
And she defies the rude Illyrian shore,
And Rhodes with her proud harbor, and the seas
That intersect the scattered Cyclades,
And the Propontic and the Thracian coast,
(Bold as it is) to contradict her boast.
She calls to witness the dark Euxine sea
And mountains that had known her as a tree,
Before her transformation, when she stood
A native of the deep Cytorian wood,
Where all her ancestors had flourished long,
And, with their old traditionary song,
Had whispered her responses to the breeze.
And waked the chorus of her sister trees.

Amastris, from your haven forth she went,
You witnessed her first outset and descent,
Adventuring on an unknown element.
From thence she bore her master safe and free
From danger and alarm through many a sea;
Nor ever once was known to lag behind,
Foremost on every tack, with every wind.
At last, to this fair inland lake, she says
She came to pass the remnant ot her days,
Leaving no debt due to the Deities
For vows preferred in danger on the seas:
Clear of incumbrance, therefore, and all other
Contentious claims, to Castor or his brother
As a free gift and offering she devotes
Herself, as long as she survives and floats.

(John Hookham Frere)

ACME AND SEPTIMIUS

Whilst on Septimius' panting Breast
(Meaning nothing less than Rest)
Acme lean'd her loving head,
Thus the pleas'd Septimius said.

My dearest Acme, if I be
Once alive, and love not thee
With a Passion far above
All that e'er was called Love,
In a Lybian desert may
I become some Lion's prey,
Let him, Acme, let him tear
My Breast, when Acme is not there.

The God of Love who stood to hear him,
(The God of Love was always near him)
Pleas'd and tickl'd with the sound,
Sneez'd aloud, and all around
The little Loves that waited by,
Bow'd and blest the Augurie.

Acme enflam'd with what he said,
Rear'd her gently-bending head,
And her purple mouth with joy
Stretching to the delicious Boy.
Twice (twice could scarce suffice)
She kissed his drunken, rolling eyes.

My little Life, my All (said she)
So may we ever servants be
To this best God, and ne'er retain
Our hated Liberty again,
So may thy passion last for me,
As I a passion have for thee,
Greater and fiercer much than can
Be conceiv'd by Thee a Man.
Into my Marrow is it gone,
Fixed and settled in the Bone,
It reigns not only in my heart,
But runs, like life, through ev'ry part.
She spoke; the God of Love aloud
Sneez'd again, and all the crowd
Of little loves that waited by,
Bow'd and blessed the Augurie.
This good omen thus from heaven
Like a happy signal given,
Their loves and lives (all four) embrace,
And hand in hand run all the race.
To poor Septimius (who did now
Nothing else but Acme grow)
Acme's bosom was alone,
The whole world's Imperial Throne,
And to faithful Acme's mind
Septimius was all human kind.

If the Gods would please to be
But advis'd for once by me,
I'd advise 'em when they spy
Any illustrious piety,

To reward her, if it be she;
To reward him, if it be he;
With such a husband, such a wife,
With Acme's and Septimius' life.

(*Abraham Cowley*)

Publius Vergilius Maro

70-19 B.C.

Thou that singest wheat and woodland, tilth and vineyard, hive and horse and herd;
All the charm of all the Muses often flowering in a lonely word.—LORD TENNYSON.

ECLOGUE I

THE SHEPHERD'S GRATITUDE

MELIBŒUS. Stretched in the shadow of the broad beech, thou
Rehearsest, Tityrus, on the slender pipe
Thy woodland music. We our fatherland
Are leaving, we must shun the fields we love:
While, Tityrus, thou, at ease amid the shade,
Bidd'st answering woods call Amaryllis "fair."
TITYRUS. O Melibœus! 'Tis a god that made
For me this holiday: for god I'll aye
Account him; many a young lamb from my fold
Shall stain his altar. Thanks to him, my kine
Range, as thou seest them: thanks to him, I play
What songs I list upon my shepherd's pipe.
M. For me, I grudge thee not; I marvel much:
So sore a trouble is in all the land.
Lo! feeble *I* am driving hence my goats—
Nay *dragging,* Tityrus, one, and that with pain.
For, yearning here amidst the hazel-stems,
She left her twin kids—on the naked flint
She left them; and I lost my promised flock.
This evil, I remember, oftentimes,
(Had not my wits been wandering) oaks foretold

By heaven's hand smitten: oft the wicked crow
Croaked the same message from the riften holm.
—Yet tell me, Tityrus, of this "God" of thine.
T. The city men call *Rome* my folly deemed
Was e'en like this of ours, where week by week
We shepherds journey with our weanling flocks.
So whelp to dog, so kid (I knew) to dam
Was likest: and I judged great things by small.
But o'er all cities this so lifts her head,
As does o'er osiers lithe the cypress tree.
M. What made thee then so keen to look on Rome?
T. Freedom: who marked, at last, my helpless state:
Now that a whiter beard than that of yore
Fell from my razor; still she marked, and came
(All late) to help me—now that all my thought
Is Amaryllis, Galatea gone.
While Galatea's, I despaired, I own,
Of freedom, and of thrift. Though from my farm
Full many a victim stept, though rich the cheese
Pressed for yon thankless city: still my hand
Returned not, heavy with brass pieces, home.
M. I wondered, Amaryllis, whence that woe,
And those appeals to heav'n: for whom the peach
Hung undisturbed upon the parent tree.
Tityrus was gone! Why, Tityrus, pine and rill,
And all these copses, cried to thee, "Come home!"
T. What could I do? I could not step from out
My bonds; nor meet, save there, with Pow'rs so kind.
There, Melibœus, I beheld that youth
For whom each year twelve days my altars smoke.
Thus answered he my yet unanswered prayer;
"Feed still, my lad, your kine, and yoke your bulls."
M. Happy old man! Thy lands are yet thine own!
Lands broad enough for thee, although bare stones
And marsh choke every field with reedy mud.
Strange pastures shall not vex thy teeming ewes,
Nor neighboring flocks shed o'er them rank disease.
Happy old man! Here, by familiar streams
And holy springs, thou'lt catch the leafy cool.

Here, as of old, yon hedge, thy boundary line,
Its willow-buds a feast for Hybla's bees,
Shall with soft whisperings woo thee to thy sleep.
Here, 'neath the tall cliff, shall the vintager
Sing carols to the winds: while all the time
Thy pets, the stockdoves, and the turtles make
Incessantly their moan from aery elms.
T. Aye, and for this shall slim stags graze in air,
And ocean cast on shore the shrinking fish;
For this, each realm by either wandered o'er,
Parthians shall Arar drink, or Tigris Gauls;
Ere from this memory shall fade that face!
M. And we the while must thirst on Libya's sands,
O'er Scythia roam, and where the Cretan stems
The swift Oaxes; or, with Britons, live
Shut out from all the world. Shall I e'er see,
In far-off years, my fatherland? the turf
That roofs my meager hut? see, wondering last,
Those few scant cornblades that are realms to me?
What! must rude soldiers hold these fallows trim?
That corn barbarians? See what comes of strife,
Poor people—where we sowed, what hands shall reap!
Now, Melibœus, pr'thee graft thy pears,
And range thy vines! Nay on, my she-goats, on,
Once happy flock! For never more must I,
Outstretched in some green hollow, watch you hang
From tufted crags, far up: no carols more
I'll sing: nor, shepherded by me, shall ye
Crop the tart willow and the clover-bloom.
T. Yet here, this one night, thou mayst rest with me,
Thy bed green branches. Chestnuts soft have I
And mealy apples, and our fill of cheese.
Already, see, the far-off chimneys smoke,
And deeper grow the shadows of the hills.

(*Charles Stuart Calverley*)

Eclogue IV

THE MESSIAH

Sicilian Muse, begin a loftier strain!
Tho' lowly shrubs, and trees that shade the plain,
Delight not all; Sicilian Muse, prepare
To make the vocal woods deserve a consul's care.
The last great age, foretold by sacred rhymes,
Renews its finished course: Saturnian times
Roll round again; and mighty years, begun
From their first orb, in radiant circles run.
The base degenerate iron offspring ends;
A golden progeny from heaven descends.
O chaste Lucina, speed the mother's pains,
And haste the glorious birth! thy own Apollo reigns!
The lovely boy, with his auspicious face,
Shall Pollio's consulship and triumph grace;
Majestic months set out with him to their appointed race.
The father banished virtue shall restore,
And crimes shall threat the guilty world no more.
The son shall lead the life of gods, and be
By gods and heroes seen, and gods and heroes see.
The jarring nations he in peace shall bind,
And with paternal virtues rule mankind.
Unbidden Earth shall wreathing ivy bring,
And fragrant herbs (the promises of spring),
As her first offerings to her infant king.
The goats with strutting dugs shall homeward speed,
And lowing herds secure from lions feed.
His cradle shall with rising flowers be crowned:
The serpent's brood shall die; the sacred ground
Shall weeds and poisonous plants refuse to bear;
Each common bush shall Syrian roses wear.
But when heroic verse his youth shall raise,
And form it to hereditary praise,
Unlabored harvests shall the fields adorn,
And clustered grapes shall blush on every thorn;

The knotted oaks shall showers of honey weep,
And thro' the matted grass the liquid gold shall creep.
Yet of old fraud some footsteps shall remain:
The merchant still shall plow the deep for gain;
Great cities shall with walls be compassed round,
And sharpened shares shall vex the fruitful ground;
Another Tiphys shall new seas explore;
Another Argo land the chiefs upon the Iberian shore;
Another Helen other wars create,
And great Achilles urge the Trojan fate.
But when to ripened manhood he shall grow,
The greedy sailor shall the seas forego;
No keel shall cut the waves for foreign ware,
For every soil shall every product bear.
The laboring hind his oxen shall disjoin;
No plow shall hurt the glebe, no pruning hook the vine;
Nor wool shall in dissembled colors shine.
But the luxurious father of the fold,
With native purple, or unborrowed gold,
Beneath his pompous fleece shall proudly sweat;
And under Tyrian robes the lamb shall bleat.
The Fates, when they this happy web have spun,
Shall bless the sacred clew, and bid it smoothly run.
Mature in years, to ready honors move,
O of celestial seed! O foster son of Jove!
See, laboring Nature calls thee to sustain
The nodding frame of heaven, and earth, and main!
See to their base restored, earth, seas, and air;
And joyful ages, from behind, in crowding ranks appear.
To sing thy praise, would Heaven my breath prolong,
Infusing spirits worthy such a song,
Not Thracian Orpheus should transcend my lays,
Nor Linus crowned with never-fading bays;
Tho' each his heavenly parent should inspire;
The Muse instruct the voice, and Phœbus tune the lyre.
Should Pan contend in verse, and thou my theme,
Arcadian judges should their god condemn.
Begin, auspicious boy, to cast about

Thy infant eyes, and, with a smile, thy mother single
out:
Thy mother well deserves that short delight,
The nauseous qualms of ten long months and travel to
requite.
Then smile: the frowning infant's doom is read;
No god shall crown the board, nor goddess bless the bed.

(John Dryden)

Eclogue VII

CORYDON AND THYRSIS

Beneath a holm repaired two jolly swains
(Their sheep and goats together grazed the plains),
Both young Arcadians, both alike inspired
To sing, and answer as the song required.
Daphnis, as umpire, took the middle seat,
And fortune thither led my weary feet;
For, while I fenced my myrtles from the cold,
The father of my flock had wandered from the fold
Of Daphnis I enquired: he, smiling, said:
"Dismiss your fear;" and pointed where he fed;
"And, if no greater cares disturb your mind,
Sit here with us, in covert of the wind.
Your lowing heifers, of their own accord,
At watering time will seek the neighboring ford.
Here wanton Mincius winds along the meads,
And shades his happy banks with bending reeds.
And see, from yon old oak that mates the skies,
How black the clouds of swarming bees arise."
What should I do! Nor was Alcippe nigh,
Nor absent Phyllis could my care supply,
To house, and feed by hand my weaning lambs,
And drain the strutting udders of their dams.
Great was the strife betwixt the singing swains;
And I preferred my pleasure to my gains.
Alternate rhyme the ready champions chose:
These Corydon rehearsed, and Thyrsis those.

Corydon. Ye Muses, ever fair, and ever young,
Assist my numbers, and inspire my song.
With all my Codrus, O inspire my breast!
For Codrus, after Phœbus, sings the best.
Or, if my wishes have presum'd too high,
And stretched their bounds beyond mortality,
The praise of artful numbers I resign,
And hang my pipe upon the sacred pine.

Thyrsis. Arcadian swains, your youthful poet crown
With ivy wreaths; tho' surly Codrus frown:
Or, if he blast my Muse with envious praise,
Then fence my brows with amulets of bays,
Lest his ill arts, or his malicious tongue,
Should poison, or bewitch my growing song.

C. These branches of a stag, this tusky boar
(The first essay of arms untried before)
Young Micon offers, Delia, to thy shrine:
But speed his hunting with thy power divine;
Thy statue then of Parian stone shall stand;
[illegible] legs in buskins with a purple band.

T. This bowl of milk, these cakes (our country
fare),
For thee, Priapus, yearly we prepare,
Because a little garden is thy care;
But, if the falling lambs increase my fold,
Thy marble statue shall be turned to gold.

C. Fair Galatea, with thy silver feet,
O, whiter than the swan, and more than Hybla sweet,
Tall as a poplar, taper as the bole,
Come, charm thy shepherd, and restore my soul!
Come, when my lated sheep at night return,
And crown the silent hours, and stop the rosy morn!

T. May I become as abject in thy sight
As seaweed on the shore, and black as night;
Rough as a bur; deformed like him who chaws
Sardinian herbage to contract his jaws;

Such and so monstrous let thy swain appear,
If one day's absence looks not like a year.
Hence from the field, for shame: the flock deserves
No better feeding while the shepherd starves.

C. Ye mossy springs, inviting easy sleep,
Ye trees, whose leafy shades those mossy fountains keep,
Defend my flock! The summer heats are near,
And blossoms on the swelling vines appear.

T. With happy fires our cheerful hearth is crowned;
And firs for torches in the woods abound:
We fear not more the winds and wintry cold,
Than streams the banks, or wolves the bleating fold.

C. Our woods, with juniper and chestnuts crowned,
With falling fruits and berries paint the ground;
And lavish Nature laughs, and strows her stores around:
But, if Alexis from our mountains fly,
Even running rivers leave their channels dry.

T. Parched are the plains, and frying is the field,
Nor withering vines their juicy vintage yield;
But, if returning Phyllis bless the plain,
The grass revives, the woods are green again,
And Jove descends in showers of kindly rain.

C. The poplar is by great Alcides worn;
The brows of Phœbus his own bays adorn;
The branching vine the jolly Bacchus loves;
The Cyprian queen delights in myrtle groves;
With hazel Phyllis crowns her flowing hair;
And, while she loves that common wreath to wear,
Nor bays, nor myrtle boughs, with hazel shall compare.

T. The towering ash is fairest in the woods;
In gardens pines, and poplars by the floods:
But, if my Lycidas will ease my pains,
And often visit our forsaken plains,
To him the towering ash shall yield in woods,
In gardens pines, and poplars by the floods.

Melibœus. These rhymes I did to memory commend,
When vanquished Thyrsis did in vain contend;
Since when 'tis Corydon among the swains,
Young Corydon without a rival reigns.

(*John Dryden*)

Eclogue IX

LYCIDAS AND MŒRIS

Lycidas

Ho, Mœris! whether on thy way so fast?
This leads to town.

Mœris

O Lycidas, at last
The time is come I never thought to see,
(Strange revolution for my farm and me!)
When the grim captain in a surly tone
Cries out: "Pack up, ye rascals, and be gone."
Kick'd out, we set the best face on 't we could;
And these two kids, t'appease his angry mood,
I bear—of which the Furies give him good!

Lycidas

Your country friends were told another tale;
That, from the sloping mountain to the vale,
And dodder'd oak, and all the banks along,
Menalcas sav'd his fortune with a song.

Mœris

Such was the news, indeed; but songs and rhymes
Prevail as much in these hard iron times,
As would a plump of trembling fowl, that rise
Against an eagle sousing from the skies.
And, had not Phœbus warn'd me, by the croak
Of an old raven from a hollow oak,
To shun debate, Menalcas had been slain,
And Mœris not surviv'd him, to complain.

Lycidas

Now Heav'n defend! Could barb'rous rage induce
The brutal son of Mars t' insult the sacred Muse!
Who then should sing the numphs, or who rehearse
The waters gliding in a smoother verse!
Or Amaryllis praise—that heav'nly lay,
That shorten'd, as we went, our tedious way:
"O Tit'rus, tend my herd, and see them fed;
To morning pastures, evening waters, led;
And 'ware the Libyan ridgil's butting head."

Mœris

Or what unfinish'd he to Varus read;
"Thy name, O Varus, (if the kinder pow'rs
Preserve our plains, and shield the Mantuan tow'rs,
Obnoxious by Cremona's neighb'ring crime,)
The wings of swans, and stronger-pinion'd rhyme,
Shall raise aloft, and soaring bear above,
Th' immortal gift of gratitude to Jove."

Lycidas

Sing on, sing on; for I can ne'er be cloy'd:
So may thy swarms the baleful yew avoid;
So may thy cows their burden'd bags distend,
And trees to goats their willing branches bend.
Mean as I am, yet have the Muses made
Me free, a member of the tuneful trade:
At least the shepherds seem to like my lays;
But I discern their flatt'ry from their praise:
I nor to Cinna's ears, nor Varus', dare aspire,
But gabble, like a goose, amidst the swan-like choir.

Mœris

'Tis what I have been conning in my mind;
Nor are they verses of a vulgar kind.

"Come, Galatea, come, the seas forsake:
What pleasures can the tides with their hoarse murmurs make?
See, on the shore inhabits purple spring,
Where nightingales their love-sick ditty sing:
See, meads with purling streams, with flow'rs the ground,
The grottoes cool, with shady poplars crown'd;
And creeping vines on arbors weav'd around.
Come then, and leave the waves' tumultuous roar;
Let the wild surges vainly beat the shore."

LYCIDAS

Or that sweet song I heard with such delight;
The same you sung alone one starry night
The tune I still retain, but not the words.

MŒRIS

"Why, Daphnis, dost thou search in old records,
To know the seasons when the stars arise?
See, Cæsar's lamp is lighted in the skies:
The star whose rays the blushing grapes adorn,
And swell the kindly ripening ears of corn.
Under this influence, graft the tender shoot:
Thy children's children shall enjoy the fruit."
The rest I have forgot; for cares and time
Change all things, and untune my soul to rhyme.
I could have once sung down a summer's sun;
But now the chime of poetry is done:
My voice grows hoarse; I feel the notes decay,
As if the wolves had seen me first to-day.
But these, and more than I to mind can bring,
Menalcas has not yet forgot to sing.

LYCIDAS

Thy faint excuses but inflame me more:
And now the waves roll silent to the shore;

Hush'd winds the topmoſt branches scarcely bend,
As if thy tuneful song they did attend:
Already we have half our way o'ercome;
Far off I can discern Bianor's tomb.
Here, where the laborer's hands have form'd a bow'r
Of wreathing trees, in singing waſte an hour.
Reſt here thy weary limbs; thy kids lay down:
We've day before us yet to reach the town;
Or if, ere night, the gath'ring clouds we fear,
A song will help the beating ſtorm to bear.
And, that thou may'ſt not be too late abroad,
Sing, and I'll ease thy shoulders of thy load.

Mœris

Cease to requeſt me; let us mind our way:
Another song requires another day.
When good Menalcas comes, if he rejoice,
And find a friend at court, I'll find a voice.

(*John Dryden*)

THE GEORGICS

Prelude

What makes a plenteous harveſt, when to turn
The fruitful soil, and when to sow the corn;
The care of sheep, of oxen, and of kine,
And how to raise on elms the teeming vine;
The birth and genius of the frugal bee,
I sing, Mæcenas, and I sing to thee.
  Ye deities, who fields and plains proteſt,
Who rule the seasons, and the year direſt,
Bacchus and foſtering Ceres, powers divine,
Who gave us corn for maſt, for water, wine;
Ye Fauns, propitious to the rural swains,
Ye nymphs, that haunt the mountains and the plains,
Join in my work, and to my numbers bring
Your needful succor; for your gifts I sing.

And thou, whose trident struck the teeming earth,
And made a passage for the course's birth;
And thou, for whom the Cæan shore sustains
Thy milky herds, that graze the flow'ry plains;
And thou, the shepherds' tutelary god,
Leave, for a while, O Pan, thy loved abode;
And, if Arcadian fleeces be thy care,
From fields and mountains to my song repair.
Inventor, Pallas, of the fattening oil,
Thou founder of the plow, and plowman's toil;
And thou, whose hands the shroud-like cypress rear,
Come, all ye gods and goddesses, that wear
The rural honors, and increase the year:
You, who supply the ground with seeds of grain;
And you, who swell those seeds with kindly rain;
And chiefly thou, whose undetermined state
Is yet the business of the gods' debate,
Whether in after times to be declared
The patron of the world, and Rome's peculiar guard,
Or o'er the fruits and seasons to preside,
And the round circuit of the year to guide—
Powerful of blessings, which thou strewest around,
And with thy goddess-mother's myrtle crowned.
Or wilt thou, Cæsar, choose the watery reign,
To smooth the surges, and correct the main?
Then mariners, in storms, to thee shall pray;
Even utmost Thule shall thy power obey,
And Neptune shall resign the fasces of the sea. . . .
But thou, propitious Cæsar, guide my course,
And to my bold endeavors add thy force:
Pity the poet's and the plowman's cares;
Interest thy greatness in our mean affairs,
And use thyself betimes to hear and grant our prayers.

(*John Dryden*)

Quintus Horatius Flaccus

65-8 B.C.

That which will distinguish his style from all other poets is the elegance of his words, and the numerousness of his verse; there is nothing so delicately turned in the Roman language. There appears in every part of his language a kind of noble and bold purity. There is a secret happiness attends his choice, which in Petronius is called *curiosa felicitas*. But the most distinguishing part of all his character seems to me to be his briskness, his jollity, and his good humor.—JOHN DRYDEN.

TO THE SHIP IN WHICH VIRGIL SAILED TO ATHENS

(ODES, I, 3)

So may the auspicious Queen of Love,
And the twin Stars (the seed of Jove),
And he who rules the raging wind,
To thee, O sacred ship, be kind,
And gentle breezes fill thy sails,
Supplying soft Etesian gales,
As thou, to whom the Muse commends
The best of poets and of friends,
Dost thy committed pledge restore,
And land him safely on the shore;
And save the better part of me
From perishing with him at sea.
Sure he, who first the passage tried,
In harden'd oak his heart did hide,
And ribs of iron arm'd his side!
Or his at least, in hollow wood
Who tempted first the briny flood;
Nor fear'd the winds' contending roar,
Nor billows beating on the shore;
Nor Hyades portending rain;
Nor all the tyrants of the main.
What form of death could him affright
Who, unconcern'd, with steadfast sight,

Could view the surges mounting steep,
And monsters rolling in the deep?
Could through the ranks of ruin go,
With storms above, and rocks below?
In vain did Nature's wise command
Divide the waters from the land,
If daring ships, and men profane,
Invade the inviolable main;
The eternal fences overleap,
And pass at will the boundless deep.
No toil, no hardship can restrain
Ambitious man inured to pain;
The more confin'd, the more he tries,
And at forbidden quarry flies.
Thus bold Prometheus did aspire,
And stole from heaven the reed of fire:
A train of ills, a ghastly crew,
The robber's blazing track pursue;
Fierce Famine, with her meager face,
And fevers of the fiery race,
In swarms the offending wretch surround,
All brooding on the blasted ground;
And limping Death, lash'd on by Fate,
Comes up to shorten half our date.
This made not Dedalus beware,
With borrow'd wings to sail in air:
To hell Alcides forced his way,
Plunged through the lake, and snatch'd the prey.
Nay, scarce the gods, or heavenly climes,
Are safe from our audacious crimes:
We reach at Jove's imperial crown,
And pull the unwilling thunder down.

(*John Dryden*)

TO THALIARCHUS

(Odes, I, 9)

Behold yon mountain's hoary height,
  Made higher with new mounts of snow;

Again behold the winter's weight
 Oppress the laboring woods below:
And streams with icy fetters bound,
Benumb'd and cramp'd to solid ground.

With well-heap'd logs dissolve the cold,
 And feed the genial hearth with fires;
Produce the wine, that makes us bold,
 And sprightly wit of love inspires.
For what hereafter shall betide,
God, if 'tis worth his care, provide.

Let him alone, with what he made,
 To toss and turn the world below:
At his command the storms invade;
 The winds by his commission blow;
Till with a nod he bids them cease,
And then the calm returns, and all is peace.

To-morrow and her works defy,
 Lay hold upon the present hour,
And snatch the pleasures passing by,
 To put them out of Fortune's power.
Nor Love, nor Love's delights, disdain;
Whate'er thou gett'st to-day is gain.

Secure those golden, early joys,
 That youth, unsour'd by sorrow, bears,
Ere withering Time the taste destroys
 With sickness and unwieldly years.
For active sports, for pleasing rest,
This is the time to be possest;
The best is but in season best.

The appointed hour of promis'd bliss,
 The pleasing whisper in the dark,
The half-unwilling, willing kiss,
 The laugh that guides thee to the mark,

When the kind nymph would coyness feign,
And hides but to be found again:
These, these are joys, the gods for youth ordain.

(John Dryden)

TO MÆCENAS

(Odes, III, 29)

Descended of an ancient line,
That long the Tuscan scepter sway'd,
Make haste to meet the generous wine,
Whose piercing is for thee delay'd:
The rosy wreath is made;
And artful hands prepare
The fragrant Syrian oil, that shall perfume thy hair.

When the wine sparkles from afar,
And the well-natur'd friend cries, come away;
Make haste and leave thy business and thy care,
No mortal interest can be worth thy stay.
Leave, for a while, thy costly country seat;
And, to be great indeed, forget
The nauseous pleasures of the great.

Make haste and come:
Come and forsake thy cloying store;
Thy turret that surveys from high
The smoke, and wealth, and noise of Rome,
And all the busy pageantry
That wise men scorn, and fools adore.
Come, give thy soul a loose, and taste the pleasures of
the poor.
Sometimes 'tis grateful for the rich to try
A short vicissitude, and fit of poverty:
A savory dish, a homely treat,
Where all is plain, where all is neat,
Without the stately spacious room,
The Persian carpet, or the Tyrian loom,
Clear up the cloudy foreheads of the great.

The sun is in the Lion mounted high;
  The Syrian star barks from afar,
And with his sultry breath infects the sky;
The ground below is parch'd, the heavens above us fry.
  The shepherd drives his fainting flock
  Beneath the covert of a rock,
And seeks refreshing rivulets nigh:
The sylvans to their shades retire,
Those very shades and streams new shades and streams
      require,
And want a cooling breeze of wind to fan the raging fire.
  Thou, what befits the new Lord Mayor;
  And what the city factions dare,
  And what the Gallic arms will do,
  And what the quiver-bearing foe,
  Art anxiously inquisitive to know:
But God has wisely hid from human sight
  The dark decrees of future fate,
And sown their seeds in depths of night.
  He laughs at all the giddy turns of state,
  Where mortals search too soon, and fear too late.

Enjoy the present smiling hour,
And put it out of Fortune's power;
The tide of business, like the running stream,
  Is sometimes high and sometimes low,
  A quiet ebb or a tempestuous flow,
And always in extreme.

Now with a noiseless gentle course
  It keeps within the middle bed;
  Anon it lifts aloft its head,
And bears down all before it with impetuous force;
  And trunks of trees come rolling down,
  Sheep and their folds together drown:
Both house and homestead into seas are borne,
And rocks are from their old foundations torn,
And woods, made thin with winds, their scatter'd honors
      mourn.

Happy the man, and happy he alone,
He, who can call to-day his own:
He who secure within, can say,
To-morrow do thy worst, for I have lived to-day.
Be fair or foul, or rain or shine,
The joys I have possess'd, in spite of fate, are mine.
Not Heaven itself upon the past has power,
But what has been, has been, and I have had my hour.

Fortune that with malicious joy
  Does man, her slave, oppress,
Proud of her office to destroy,
  Is seldom pleased to bless:
Still various, and inconstant still,
But with an inclination to be ill,
Promotes, degrades, delights in strife,
And makes a lottery of life.
  I can enjoy her while she is kind;
  But when she dances in the wind,
And shakes her wings, and will not stay,
I puff the prostitute away;
  The little or the much she gave, is quietly resign'd:
Content with poverty my soul I arm,
And Virtue, though in rags, will keep me warm.

What is 't to me,
Who never sail in her unfaithful sea,
If storms arise, and clouds grow black;
If the mast split, and threaten wreck?
Then let the greedy merchant fear
  For his ill-gotten gain,
And pray to gods that will not hear
While the debating winds and billows bear
  His wealth unto the main.
For me, secure from Fortune's blows,
Secure of what I cannot lose,
In my small pinnace I can sail,
  Contemning all the blustering roar;

And running with a merry gale,
With friendly stars my safety seek
Within some little winding creek,
And see the storm ashore.

(*John Dryden*)

COUNTRY LIFE

(Epode 2)

How happy in his low degree,
How rich, in humble poverty, is he,
Who leads a quiet country life;
Discharg'd of business, void of strife,
And from the griping scrivener free!
Thus, ere the seeds of vice were sown,
Liv'd men in better ages born,
Who plow'd, with oxen of their own,
Their small paternal field of corn.
Nor trumpets summon him to war,
Nor drums disturb his morning sleep,
Nor knows he merchants' gainful care,
Nor fears the dangers of the deep.
The clamors of contentious law,
And court and state he wisely shuns,
Nor brib'd with hopes, nor dar'd with awe,
To servile salutations runs;
But either to the clasping vine
Does the supporting poplar wed,
Or with his pruning hook disjoin
Unbearing branches from their head,
And grafts more happy in their stead;
Or climbing to a hilly steep,
He views his buds in vales afar,
Or shears his overburden'd sheep,
Or mead for cooling drink prepares
Or virgin honey in the jars,
Or, in the now declining year,
When beauteous Autumn rears his head,
He joys to pull the ripen'd pear,
And clust'ring grapes with purple spread.

Sometimes beneath an ancient oak,
  Or on the matted grass he lies:
No God of Sleep he need invoke;
  The stream, that o'er the pebble flies,
  With gentle slumber crowns his eyes.
The wind, that whistles through the sprays,
  Maintains the concert of the song:
And hidden birds with native lays,
  The golden sleep prolong.
But when the blast of winter blows,
  And hoary frost invests the year,
Into the naked woods he goes,
  And seeks the tusky boar to rear,
  With well-mouth'd hounds and pointed spear!
Or spreads his subtle nets from sight,
  With twinkling glasses, to betray
The larks that in the meshes light,
  Or makes the fearful bear his prey.
Amidst his harmless, easy joys,
  No anxious care invades his health,
Nor love his peace of mind destroys,
  Nor wicked avarice of wealth.
But, if a chaste and pleasing wife,
To ease the business of his life,
Divides with him his household care,
Such as the Sabine matrons were,
Such as the swift Apulian's bride,
  Sunburnt and swarthy though she be,
Will fire for winter nights provide,
  And—without noise—will oversee
  His children and his family:
And order all things till he come,
Sweaty and overlabor'd home;
If she in pens his flocks will fold,
  And then produce her dairy store
With wine to drive away the cold,
  And unbought dainties for the poor;
Not oysters of the Lucrine lake
  My sober appetite would wish,

Nor turbot, or the foreign fish
That rolling tempests overtake,
And hither waft the costly dish.
Not heathpoult, or the rarer bird,
Which Phasis or Ionia yields
More pleasing morsels would afford
Than the fat olives of my fields;
Than shards or mallows for the pot,
That keep the loosened body sound,
Or than the lamb, that falls by lot
To the just guardian of my ground.
Amidst these feasts of happy swains,
The jolly shepherd smiles to see
His flock returning from the plains;
The farmer is as pleas'd as he,
To view his oxen sweating smoke,
Bear on their necks the loosen'd yoke:
To look upon his menial crew,
That sit around his cheerful hearth,
And bodies spent in toil renew
With wholesome food and country mirth.

This Alphius said within himself;
Resolv'd to leave the wicked town,
And live retir'd upon his own,
He call'd his money in:
But the prevailing love of pelf,
Soon split him on the former shelf,—
He put it out again.

(*John Dryden*)

THE IMMORTALITY OF VERSE

(Odes, IV, 9)

Lest you should think that verse shall die,
Which sounds the silver Thames along,
Taught on the wings of truth to fly
Above the reach of vulgar song;

Though daring Milton sits sublime,
  In Spenser native Muses play;
Nor yet shall Waller yield to time,
  Nor pensive Cowley's mortal lay.

Sages and chiefs long since had birth
  Ere Cæsar was, or Newton named;
These raised new empires o'er the earth,
  And those, new heavens and systems framed.

Vain was the chief's, the sage's pride!
  They had no poet, and they died.
In vain they schemed, in vain they bled!
  They had no poet, and are dead.

(*Alexander Pope*)

TO FUSCUS ARISTUS

(Epistles I, 10)

Health from the lover of the country, me,
Health to the lover of the city, thee.
A difference in our souls this only proves;
In all things else, we pair like married doves.
But the warm nest and crowded dove-house thou
Dost like: I loosely fly from bough to bough,
And rivers drink, and all the shining day
Upon fair trees or mossy rocks I play;
In fine, I live and reign, when I retire
From all that you equal with heaven admire;
Like one at last from the priest's service fled,
Loathing the honied cakes, I long for bread.
Would I a house for happiness erect,
Nature alone should be the architect;
She'd build it more convenient than great,
And doubtless in the country choose her seat:
Is there a place doth better helps supply
Against the wounds of winter's cruelty?
Is there an aid that gentlier does assuage
The mad celestial dog's, or lion's rage?

Is it not there that sleep (and only there)
Nor noise without, nor cares within does fear?
Does art through pipes a purer water bring
Than that which Nature strains into a spring?
Can all your tap'stries, or your pictures, show
More beauties than in herbs and flowers do grow?
Fountains and trees our wearied pride do please,
Ev'n in the midst of gilded palaces;
And in your towns that prospect gives delight
Which opens round the country to our sight.
Men to the good from which they rashly fly,
Return at last; and their wild luxury
Does but in vain with those true joys contend,
Which Nature did to mankind recommend.
The man who changes gold for burnish'd brass,
Or small right gems for larger ones of glass,
Is not at length more certain to be made
Ridiculous, and wretched by the trade,
Than he who sells a solid good to buy
The painted goods of pride and vanity.
If thou be wise, no glorious fortune choose,
Which 'tis but pain to keep, yet grief to lose;
For, when we place ev'n trifles in the heart,
With trifles, too, unwillingly we part.
An humble roof, plain bed, and homely board,
More clear untainted pleasures do afford
Than all the tumult of vain greatness brings
To kings, or to the favorites of kings.
The horned deer by Nature arm'd so well,
Did with the horse in common pasture dwell;
And when they fought, the field it always won;
Till the ambitious horse begg'd help of man,
And took the bridle, and thenceforth did reign
Bravely alone, as lord of all the plain.
But never after could he the rider get
From off his back, or from his mouth the bit.
So they, who poverty too much do fear,
T' avoid that weight, a greater burden bear;
That they might power above their equals have,

To cruel masters they themselves enslave.
For gold, their liberty exchang'd we see,
That fairest flower which crowns humanity.
And all this mischief does upon them light,
Only, because they know not how, aright,
That great, but secret, happiness to prize,
That's laid up in a little, for the wise:
That is the best and easiest estate
Which to a man sits close, but not too straight;
'Tis like a shoe, it pinches and it burns,
Too narrow; and too large, it overturns.
My dearest friend! stop thy desires at last,
And cheerfully enjoy the wealth thou hast:
And, if me seeking still for more you see,
Chide and reproach, despise and laugh at me.
Money was made, not to command our will,
But all our lawful pleasures to fulfill:
Shame! woe to us, if we our wealth obey:
The horse doth with the horseman run away.

(*Abraham Cowley*)

THE PROFANE

(Odes, III, 1)

Hence, ye profane! I hate you all;
Both the great vulgar, and the small.
To virgin minds, which yet their native whiteness hold,
Nor yet discolored with the love of gold,
That jaundice of the soul,
(Which makes it look so gilded and so foul,)
To you, ye very few, these truths I tell;
The Muse inspires my song; hark, and observe it well.
We look on men, and wonder at such odds
'Twixt things that were the same by birth;
We look on kings, as giants of the earth,
These giants are but pigmies to the gods.
The humblest bush and proudest oak
Are but of equal proof against the thunder-stroke.

Beauty and strength, and wit, and wealth, and power,
Have their short flourishing hour;
And love to see themselves, and smile,
And joy in their preëminence awhile:
Ev'n so in the same land,
Poor weeds, rich corn, gay flowers, together stand;
Alas! death mows down all with an impartial hand:
And all ye men, whom greatness does so please,
Ye feast, I fear, like Damocles:
If ye your eyes could upwards move,
(But ye, I fear, think nothing is above,)
Ye would perceive by what a little thread
The sword still hangs over your head:
No tide of wine would drown your cares;
No mirth or music over-noise your fears:
The fear of death would you so watchful keep,
As not 't admit the image of it, Sleep.
Sleep is a god too proud to wait in palaces,
And yet so humble too, as not to scorn
The meanest country cottages:
His poppy grows among the corn.
The halcyon Sleep will never build his nest
In any stormy breast.
'Tis not enough that he does find
Clouds and darkness in their mind;
Darkness but half his work will do:
'Tis not enough; he must find quiet too.
The man, who in all wishes he does make
Does only Nature's counsel take,
That wise and happy man will never fear
The evil aspect of the year;
Nor tremble, though two comets should appear;
He does not look in almanacs, to see
Whether he fortunate shall be:
Let Mars and Saturn in the heavens conjoin,
And what they please against the world design,
So Jupiter within him shine.
If of your pleasures and desires no end be found,
God to your cares and fears will set no bound.

What would content you? who can tell?
Ye fear so much to lose what ye have got,
As if ye liked it well:
Ye strive for more, as if ye liked it not.
Go, level hills, and fill up seas,
Spare nought that may your wanton fancy please:
But, trust me, when you have done all this,
Much will be missing still, and much will be amiss.

(*Abraham Cowley*)

TO LICINIUS

(Odes, II, 10)

Receive, dear friend, the truths I teach;
So shalt thou live beyond the reach
Of adverse Fortune's power;
Not always tempt the distant deep,
Nor always timorously creep
Along the treacherous shore.

He that holds fast the golden mean,
And lives contentedly between
The little and the great,
Feels not the wants that pinch the poor,
Nor plagues that haunt the rich man's door,
Embittering all his state.

The tallest pines feel most the power
Of wintry blasts; the loftiest tower
Comes heaviest to the ground;
The bolts that spare the mountain's side,
His cloud-capt eminence divide,
And spread the ruin round.

The well-inform'd philosopher
Rejoices with a wholesome fear,
And hopes, in spite of pain;
If winter bellow from the north,
Soon the sweet spring comes dancing forth,
And Nature laughs again.

What if thine heaven be overcast?
The dark appearance will not last;
Expect a brighter sky.
The god, that strings the silver bow,
Awakes sometimes the Muses too,
And lays his arrows by.

If hindrances obstruct thy way,
Thy magnanimity display,
And let thy strength be seen;
But oh! if Fortune fill thy sail,
With more than a propitious gale,
Take half thy canvas in.

(*William Cowper*)

PERSIAN FOPPERIES

(Odes, I, 38)

Boy, I hate their empty shows,
Persian garlands I detest,
Bring not me the late-blown rose
Lingering after all the rest:

Plainer myrtle pleases me
Thus outstretched beneath my vine,
Myrtle more becoming thee,
Waiting with thy master's wine.

(*William Cowper*)

TO VENUS

(Odes, IV, 1)

Venus, again thou mov'st a war
Long intermitted, pray thee, pray thee spare!
I am not such, as in the reign
Of the good Cynara I was; refrain
Sour mother of sweet Loves, forbear
To bend a man, now at his fiftieth year.

Too stubborn for commands so slack:
  Go where youth's soft entreaties call thee back.
More timely hie thee to the house
  (With thy bright swans) of Paulus Maximus:
There jest and feast, make him thine host
  If a fit liver thou dost seek to toast.
For he's both noble, lovely, young,
  And for the troubled client fills his tongue:
Child of a hundred arts, and far
  Will he display the ensigns of thy war.
And when he, smiling, finds his grace
  With thee 'bove all his rivals' gifts take place,
He'll thee a marble statue make,
  Beneath a sweet-wood roof, near Alba lake;
There shall thy dainty nostril take
  In many a gum, and for thy soft ear's sake
Shall verse be set to harp and lute,
  And Phrygian hau'boy, not without the flute.
There twice a day in sacred lays,
  The youths and tender maids shall sing thy praise!
And in the Salian manner meet
  Thrice 'bout thy altar, with their ivory feet.
Me now, nor girl, nor wanton boy
  Delights, nor credulous hope of mutual joy;
Nor care I now healths to propound
  Or with fresh flowers to girt my temples round.
But why, or why, my Ligurine,
  Flow my thin tears down these pale cheeks of mine?
Or why my well-graced words among,
  With an uncomely silence, fails my tongue?
Hard-hearted, I dream every night
  I hold thee fast! but fled hence with the light,
Whether in Mars his field thou be,
  Or Tiber's winding streams, I follow thee.

(*Ben Jonson*)

TO PYRRHA

(Odes, I, 5)

What slender youth, bedew'd with liquid odors,
Courts thee on roses in some pleasant cave,
Pyrrha? For whom bind'st thou
In wreaths thy golden hair,
Plain in thy neatness? O how oft shall he
Of faith and changed gods complain, and seas
Rough with black winds, and storms
Unwonted shall admire!
Who now enjoys thee credulous, all gold,
Who, always vacant, always amiable
Hopes thee, of flattering gales
Unmindful. Hapless they
To whom thou untried seem'st fair. Me, in my vow'd
Picture, the sacred wall declares to have hung
My dank and dropping weeds
To the stern god of sea.

(*John Milton*)

TO SALLY

(Odes, I, 22)

The man in righteousness arrayed,
A pure and blameless liver,
Needs not the keen Toledo blade,
Nor venom-freighted quiver.
What though he wind his toilsome way
O'er regions wild and weary—
Through Zara's burning desert stray,
Or Asia's jungles dreary:

What though he plow the billowy deep
By lunar light, or solar,
Meet the resistless Simoom's sweep,
Or iceberg circumpolar!

In bog or quagmire deep and dank
  His foot shall never settle;
He mounts the summit of Mont Blanc,
  Or Popocatapetl.

On Chimborazo's breathless height
  He treads o'er burning lava;
Or snuffs the Bohan Upas blight,
  The deathful plant of Java.
Through every peril he shall pass,
  By Virtue's shield protected;
And still by Truth's unerring glass
  His path shall be directed.

Else wherefore was it, Thursday last,
  While strolling down the valley,
Defenseless, musing as I passed
  A canzonet to Sally,
A wolf, with mouth-protruding snout,
  Forth from the thicket bounded—
I clapped my hands and raised a shout—
  He heard—and fled—confounded.

Tangier nor Tunis never bred
  An animal more crabbèd;
Nor Fez, dry-nurse of lions, fed
  A monster half so rabid;
Nor Ararat so fierce a beast
  Has seen since days of Noah;
Nor stronger, eager for a feast,
  The fell constrictor boa.

(*John Quincy Adams*)

TO AN AMBITIOUS FRIEND

(Odes, II, 11)

Omit, omit, my simple friend,
Still to inquire how parties tend,
Or what we fix with foreign powers.

If France and we are really friends,
And what the Russian Czar intends,
Is no concern of ours.

Us not the daily quickening race
Of the invading populace
Shall draw to swell that shouldering herd.
Mourn will we not your closing hour,
Ye imbeciles in present power,
Doomed, pompous, and absurd!

And let us bear, that they debate
Of all the engine-work of state,
Of commerce, laws, and policy,
The secrets of the world's machine,
And what the rights of man may mean,
With readier tongue than we.

Only, that with no finer art
They cloak the troubles of the heart
With pleasant smile, let us take care;
Nor with a lighter hand dispose
Fresh garlands of this dewy rose,
To crown Eugenia's hair.

Of little threads our life is spun,
And he spins ill, who misses one.
But is thy fair Eugenia cold?
Yet Helen had an equal grace,
And Juliet's was as fair a face,
And now their years are told.

The day approaches, when we must
Be crumbling bones and windy dust;
And scorn us as our mistress may,
Her beauty will no better be
Than the poor face she slights in thee,
When dawns that day, that day.

(*Matthew Arnold*)

THE SHIP OF STATE

(Odes, I, 14)

Oh Ship! new billows sweep thee out
Seaward. What wilt thou? Hold the port, be stout:
See'st not thy mast
How rent by stiff Southwestern blast?

Thy side, of rowers how forlorn?
Thine hull, with groaning yards, with rigging torn,
Can ill sustain
The fierce, and ever fiercer main;

Thy gods, no more than sails entire,
From whom yet once thy need might aid require,
Oh Pontic Pine,
The first of woodland stocks is thine,

Yet race and name are but as dust.
Not painted sterns give storm-tost seamen trust;
Unless thou dare
To be the sport of storms, beware.

O fold at best a weary weight,
A yearning care and constant strain of late,
O shun the seas
That gird those glittering Cyclades.

(*William Ewart Gladstone*)

EXTREMUM TANAIN

(Odes, III, 10)

Before thy door too long of late,
O Lyce, I bewail my fate;
Not Don's barbarian maids, I trow,
Would treat their luckless lovers so;
Thou,—thou alone art obstinate.

Hast thou nor eyes nor ears, Ingrate!
Hark! how the NORTH WIND shakes thy gate!
  Look! how the laurels bend with snow
    Before thy doors!

Lay by thy pride,—nor hesitate,
Lest Love and I grow desperate;
  If prayers, if gifts for naught must go,
  If naught my frozen pallor show,—
Beware! . . . I shall not always wait
    Before thy doors!

(Austin Dobson)

ALBI, NE DOREAS

(Odes, I, 33)

Love mocks us all. Then cast aside
These tuneful plaints, my Albius tried
  For heartless Glycera, from thee
  Fled to a younger lover. See,
Low-browed Lycoris burns denied

For Cyrus; he—though goats shall bide
With wolves ere she in him confide—
  Turns, with base suit, to Pholœ:—
    Love mocks us all!

So Venus wills, and joys to guide
'Neath brazen yoke pairs ill-allied
  In form and Mind. So linked she me
  (Whom worthier wooed) to Myrtale,
Fair, but less kind than Hadria's tide:—
    Love mocks us all!

(Austin Dobson)

TO CHLOË

(Odes, I, 23)

You shun me, Chloë, wild and shy,
  As some stray fawn that seeks its mother

Through trackless woods. If spring winds sigh
It vainly strives its fears to smother.

Its trembling knees assail each other
When lizards stir the brambles dry;—
You shun me, Chloë, wild and shy,
As some stray fawn that seeks its mother.

And yet no Libyan lion I,—
No ravening thing to rend another;
Lay by your tears, your tremors dry,
A husband's better than a brother;
Nor shun me, Chloë, wild and shy,
As some stray fawn that seeks its mother.

(*Austin Dobson*)

TO PHIDYLE

(Odes, III, 23)

Incense, and flesh of swine, and this year's grain,
At the new moon, with suppliant hands, bestow,
O rustic Phidyle! So naught shall know
Thy crops of blight, thy vine of Afric bane,
And hale the nurslings of thy flock remain
Through the sick apple-tide. Fit victims grow
'Twixt holm and oak upon the Algid snow,
Or Alban grass, that with their necks must stain
The Pontiff's axe: to thee can scarce avail
Thy modest gods with much slain to assail,
Whom myrtle crowns and rosemary can please.
Lay on the altar a hand pure of fault;
More than rich gifts the Powers it shall appease,
Though pious but with meal and crackling salt.

(*Austin Dobson*)

TO THE FOUNTAIN OF BANDUSIA

(Odes, III, 13)

O fountain of Bandusia!
Whence crystal waters flow,

With garlands gay and wine I'll pay
  The sacrifice I owe;
A sportive kid with budding horns
  I have, whose crimson blood
Anon shall dye and sanctify
  Thy cool and babbling flood.

O fountain of Bandusia!
  The Dog-star's hateful spell
No evil brings into the springs
  That from thy bosom well;
Here oxen, wearied by the plow,
  The roving cattle here
Hasten in quest of certain rest,
  And quaff thy gracious cheer.

O fountain of Bandusia!
  Ennobled shalt thou be,
For I shall sing the joys that spring
  Beneath yon ilex-tree.
Yes, fountain of Bandusia,
  Posterity shall know
The cooling brooks that from thy nooks
  Singing and dancing go.

(*Eugene Field*)

AD LEUCONOEN

(Odes, I, 13)

It is not right for you to know, so do not ask, Leuconoë,
How long a life the gods may give or ever we are gone
  away;
Try not to read the Final Page, the ending colophonian,
Trust not the gypsy's tea-leaves, nor the prophets Baby-
  lonian,
Better to have what is to come enshrouded in obscurity
Than to be certain of the sort and length of our futurity.
Why, even as I monologue on wisdom and longevity
How Time has flown! Spear some of it!
  The longest life is brevity.

(*F. P. Adams*)

AD XANTHIAM PHOCEUM

(Odes, II, 4)

Nay, Xanthias, feel unashamed
  That she you love is but a servant.
Remember, lovers far more famed
  Were just as fervent.

Achilles loved the pretty slave
  Briseïs for her fair complexion;
And to Tecmessa Ajax gave
  His young affection.

Why, Agamemnon at the height
  Of feasting, triumph, and anointment,
Left everything to keep, one night,
  A small appointment.

And are you sure the girl you love—
  This maid on whom you have your heart set
Is lowly—that she is not of
  The Roman smart set?

A maiden modest as is she,
  So full of sweetness and forbearance,
Must be all right; her folks must be
  Delightful parents.

Her arms and face I can commend,
  And, as the writer of a poem,
I fain would compliment, old friend,
  The limbs below 'em.

Nay, be not jealous. Stop your fears.
  My tendencies are far from sporty.
Besides, the number of my years
  Is over forty.

(*F. P. Adams*)

INVOCATION

(Odes, I, 21)

Maidens young and virgins tender,
Sing Diana in her splendor;
Boys at play within the hollow,
Sing the flowing-haired Apollo.

(Ye that, moved by love and duty,
Praise Diana's holy beauty,
Shall be granted joys unceasing
And, perhaps, a mate that's pleasing.)

(And if winning words we hit on,
Phœbus may present the Briton,
Persian, Parthian and the rest, with
All the wars and plagues *we're* blessed with.)

(Louis Untermeyer)

HOLIDAY

(Odes, III, 28)

What celebration should there be? . . .
  Quick, Lyde, bring a jar!
Against a dull sobriety
  We'll wage a lusty war.

The festive sun is setting low,
  The dusk is almost there;
And yet you scarcely move, as though
  We both had time to spare!

Let's pour the wine and sing in turns
  Of Neptune in his lair,
Of mermaids in the water-ferns,
  And of their sea-green hair.

And you, upon your curving lyre,
  Shall spend a tuneful hour,
Singing Diana's darts of fire
  And her benignant power.

Hymns shall arise to Her who sends
  Fresh laughter and delight,
Until our weary singing ends
  In lullabies to-night.

(Louis Untermeyer)

REVENGE!

(ODES, IV, 13)

THE gods have heard me, Lyce,
  The gods have heard my prayer.
Now you, who were so icy,
  Observe with cold despair
  Your thin and snowy hair.

Your cheeks are lined and sunken;
  Your smiles have turned to leers;
But still you sing, a drunken
  Appeal to Love, who hears
  With inattentive ears.

Young Chia, with her fluty
  Caressing voice compels.
Love lives upon her beauty;
  Her cheeks, in which He dwells,
  Are His fresh citadels.

He saw the battered ruin,
  This old and twisted tree;
He marked the scars, and flew in
  Haste that He might not see
  Your torn senility.

No silks, no purple gauzes
  Can hide the lines that last.
Time, with his iron laws, is
  Implacable and fast.
  You cannot cheat the past.

Where now are all your subtle
  Disguises and your fair
Smile like a gleaming shuttle?
  Your shining skin, your rare
  Beauty half-breathless—where?

Only excelled by Cinara,
  Your loveliness ranked high.
You even seemed the winner, a
  Victor as years went by,
  And she was first to die.

But now—the young men lightly
  Laugh at your wrinkled brow.
The torch that burned so brightly
  Is only ashes now;
  A charred and blackened bough.

(Louis Untermeyer)

THE PINE TREE FOR DIANA

(Odes, III, 22)

Oh virgin queen of mountain-side and woodland,
Blessèd protector of young wives in travail,
Who snatchest them from death if thrice they call thee—
    Goddess and guardian;

To thee I dedicate this slender pine-tree;
And each year with a boar's blood I shall bless it—
A youngling boar just dreaming of his first thrust,
    Savage and sidelong.

(Louis Untermeyer)

Albius Tibullus

54-18 B.C.

A PASTORAL ELEGY

LET others pile their yellow ingots high,
And see their cultured acres round them spread;
While hostile borderers draw their anxious eye,
And at the trumpet's blast their sleep is fled!

Me let my poverty to ease resign;
While my bright hearth reflects its blazing cheer;
In season let me plant the pliant vine,
And, with light hand, my swelling apples rear!

Hope, fail not thou! let earth her fruitage yield;
Let the brimmed vat flow red with virgin wine;
For, still, some lone bare stump that marks the field,
Or antique cross-way stone, with flowers I twine,

In pious rite; and, when the year anew
Matures the blossom on the budding spray,
I bear the peasant's God his grateful due;
And firstling fruits upon his altar lay.

Still let thy temple's porch, O Ceres! wear
The spiky garland from my harvest field;
And, midst my orchard, against the birds of air,
His threatening hook let red Priapus wield!

Ye too, once guardians of a rich domain,
Now of poor fields, domestic Gods; be kind!
Then, for unnumbered herds, a calf was slain;
Now to your altars is a lamb consigned!

The mighty victim of a scanty soil,
A lamb alone shall bleed before your shrine;
While round it shout the youthful sons of toil,
"Hail! grant the harvest! grant the generous wine!"

Content with little, I no more would tread
  The lengthening road, but shun the Summer day,
Where some o'erbranching tree might shade my head;
  And watch the murmuring rivulet glide away.

Nor could I blush to wield the rustic prong,
  The lingering oxen goad; or some stray lamb,
Embosomed in my garment, bear along,
  Or kid forgotten by its heedless dam.

Spare my small flocks! ye thieves, and wolves, assail
  The wealthier cotes, that ampler booty hold;
Ne'er for my shepherd due lustrations fail;
  I soothe with milk the Goddess of the fold.

Be present, Deities! nor gifts disdain
  From homely board; nor cups with scorn survey,
Earthen, yet pure; for such the ancient swain
  Formed for himself and shaped of ductile clay.

I envy not my sires their golden heap;
  Their garners' floors with sheafy corn bespread;
Few sheaves suffice: enough, in easy sleep
  To lay my limbs upon the accustomed bed.

How sweet! to hear, without, the howling blast,
  And strain a yielding mistress to my breast!
Or, when the gusty torrent's rush has past,
  Sink, lulled by beating rains, to sheltered rest!

Be this my lot; be his the unenvied store,
  Who the drear storm endures and raging seas;
Ah! perish emeralds and the golden ore,
  If the fond anxious nymph must weep for me.

Messala! range the earth and main, that Rome
  May shine with trophies of the foes that fell;
But me a beauteous nymph enchains at home,
  At her hard door a sleepless sentinel.

I heed not praise, my Delia! while with thee;
  Sloth brand my name, so I thy sight behold;
Let me the oxen yoke; oh, come with me!
  On desert mountains I will feed my fold.

And, while I prest thee in my tender arms,
  Sweet were my slumber on the ragged ground;
What boots the purple couch, if cruel charms
  In wakeful tears the midnight hours have drowned?

Not the soft plume can yield the limbs repose,
  Nor yet the broidered covering soothe to sleep;
Not the calm streamlet that in murmurs flows,
  With sound oblivious o'er the eyelids creep.

Iron is he who might thy form possess,
  Yet flies to arms and thirsts for plunder's gains;
What though his spear Cicilian squadrons press,
  What though his tent be pitcht on conquered plains;

In gold and silver mail conspicuous he
  May stride the steed that, pawing, spurns the sand;
May I my last looks fondly bend on thee,
  And grasp thee with my dying, faltering hand!

And thou wilt weep when, cold, I press the bier,
  That soon shall on the flaming pyre be thrown;
And print the kiss and mingle many a tear;
  Not thine a breast of steel, a heart of stone.

Yes, thou wilt weep! No youths shall thence return
  With tearless eye; no virgin homeward wend;
But thou forbear to violate my urn,
  Spare thy soft cheeks, nor those loose tresses rend.

Now Fate permits; now blend the sweet embrace;
  Death, cowled in darkness, creeps with stealing tread;
Ill suits with sluggish age love's sprightly grace,
  And murmured fondness with a hoary head!

The light amour be mine; the shivered door;
  The midnight fray; ye trumps and standards, hence!
Here is my camp; bleed they who thirst for ore:
  Wealth I despise in easy competence.

(*Sir Charles Abraham Elton*)

Sextus Aurelius Propertius

51-? B.C.

WHEN THOU MUST HOME

When thou must home to shades of underground,
And there arrived, a new admirèd guest,
The beauteous spirits do ingirt thee round,
White Iope, blithe Helen, and the rest,
To hear the stories of thy finished love
From that smooth tongue whose music hell can move;

Then wilt thou speak of banqueting delights,
Of masks and revels which sweet youth did make,
Of tourneys and great challenges of knights,
And all these triumphs for thy beauties' sake:
When thou hast told these honors done to thee,
Then tell, O tell, how thou didst murder me.

(*Thomas Campion*)

AH WOE IS ME

(Elegies, I, 1)

Ah woe is me, of passion naught I knew
  Till Cynthia's glances pierced my poor heart through.
Love ruthless pressed his heel upon my head,
  My eyes cast down, my pride all vanquishèd.
He taught me soon to hate each virgin's face
  And reckless live in folly's fond embrace.
And now my madness burns for all a year,
  While still the anger of the gods I bear.

Milanion, friend, by labors undismayed
  Conquered the scorn of the Iasian maid.
See now he wanders in Parthenian caves,
  And now with shaggy monsters blindly raves,
Now the Arcadian rocks repeat his groans
  As wounded by Hylæus' club he moans.
But so at last he tamed the flying fair;
  Such power in love have loving deeds and prayer.

With me Love lingers still, nor tries his art
  To fly his wonted way, and leave my heart.
Come then ye seers, well skilled the moon to take
  And on your altars expiation make;
Come now, my lady's heart to me incline
  And make her cheeks turn still more pale than mine.
Then I shall know to you the power belongs
  To draw the stars and streams with magic songs.

And you, dear friends, too late my fall to turn,
  Seek me some help; with madness now I burn.
I will endure the steel, the cruel fire,
  If only I may vent my bitter ire.
Take me to distant lands beyond the sea,
  While so no woman knows where I shall be.
Do you remain to whom God has been kind
  And grants a mutual bliss with tranquil mind.

Love haunts my days; he never gives me cease;
  And Venus turns my nights to bitterness.
I warn you —shun this hell: constant remain,
  Nor let your heart range loosely o'er love's plain.
For if too late you give my words belief,
  To you remembrance naught will bring but grief.

(F. A. Wright)

HYLAS

(Elegies, I, 20)

"This warning, Gallus, for thy love I send,
Nor let it from thy heart unheeded fall.
Thou hast a Hylas too, thy fairest friend,
Whom many a wanton nymph would fain enthral
By Anio's stream, or in the forests tall,
Or at the Giant's Causeway cast her spell,
Or on some wandering river. Shun them all,
Remembering what the Minyæ befell,
And listen to the tale which now to thee I tell.

From Pagasæ—so runs the story old—
The Argo sailed to Phasis' distant land,
And passing by the waves that Hellë hold
With gliding keel drew near the Mysian strand,
Where on the quiet shore the hero band,
The voyage done, their limbs did gently lay,
Making them beds of leaves upon the sand.
There Hylas left his knight—ah woe the day!—
And sought the secret streams of fountains far away.

Scarce had he started when the winged twain,
Whom Orithyia by the North Wind bred,
Pursued in haste, his kisses to obtain.
Zetes and Calăis above his head
With downstretched hands in flight alternate sped
To snatch their booty from his cheeks of rose,
While he beneath their wings for refuge fled
And waved a branch to scare his treacherous foes,
And so at last escapes and to the wood-nymphs goes.

Beneath Arganthus' crest there lies a spring,
Wherein to bathe the Thynian nymphs delight.
Above uncared-for dewy apples swing,
And water meadows all around are bright
With scarlet poppies and with lilies white.

Childlike he cared not why he had been sent;
But now would pluck such flowers as pleased his sight
And now in wonder o'er the fountain bent
Enraptured by his beauty's imaged blandishment.

At last, the task remembered, on his arm
He leaned, and in his hands the water took.
At once his beauty did the Naiads charm
Who 'neath the wave their wonted dance forsook,
And, as the lad bent forward, rose to look,
And drew him through the water. Loud he cried
For help. Alcides at his voice awoke,
And from afar with 'Hylas' loud replied;
But only Echo answered from the fountain side.

Long did the hero seek him on the shore,
Vexing his weary feet against the stone
Of cruel mountains: long the pain he bore,
While every lake he searched and hillside lone,
And to untamed Ascanius made his moan.
Ah that his fate may make thee, Gallus, wise!
Guard well thy Hylas now he is thine own;
Nor trust our nymphs with so desired a prize.
For Fortune often mocks the careless lover's eyes."

(*F. A. Wright*)

REVENGE TO COME

(Elegies, III, 25)

I was a joke at dinners; aye, any would-be wit
Might use me for a target, and I must stomach it.
Five years I could be loyal; but now, you'll often mourn,
Biting your nails for anguish, the faith at last outworn,
Nay, weeping will not touch me—I know that trick of old;
You always weep from ambush, I cannot be cajoled.
I shall depart in tears, but my wrongs will check their flow;

Ours was a team well sorted—you could not leave it so.
So now, my mistress' threshold, where oft my tear-drops fell,
And thou, the door I haunted, I bid ye both farewell.
May age afflict you, Cynthia, with ill-dissembled years,
And may you see the wrinkles your fading beauty fears.
And when your glass flings at you the ruin pictured there,
Go curse them, every wrinkle, and every whitening hair.
Be you in turn excluded, and suffer proud disdain,
And all you did to others be done to you again.
So fate shall soon avenge me—my page bids you give ear—
Your beauty waits this ending. Woman, believe—and fear!

(*Kirby Flower Smith*)

Publius Ovidius Naso

43 B.C.-18 A.D

As the soul of Euphorbus was thought to live in Pythagoras, so the sweet witty soul of Ovid lives in mellifluous and honey-tongued Shakespeare.—Francis Meres.

A CAPTIVE OF LOVE

(Elegies, I, 2)

What makes my bed seem hard, seeing it is soft?
Or why slips down the coverlet so oft?
Although the nights be long, I sleep not though
My sides are sore with tumbling to and fro.
Were Love the cause, it's like I should descry him;
Or lies he close, and shoots where none can spy him?
'T was so he struck me with a slender dart;
'T is cruel Love turmoils my captive heart.
Yielding or struggling, do we give him might?
Let's yield: a burden easily borne is light!
I saw a brandisht fire increase in strength;
Which being not shaked, I saw it die at length.
Young oxen newly yoked are beaten more
Than oxen which have drawn the plow before;

And rough jades' mouths with stubborn bits are torn;
But managed horses' heads are lightly borne.
Unwilling lovers Love doth more torment
Than such as in their bondage feel content.
Lo, I confess, I am thy captive, I!
And hold my conquered hands for thee to tie.
What needst thou war? I sue to thee for grace:
With arms to conquer armless men is base!
Yoke Venus' doves, put myrtles on thy hair:
Vulcan will give thee chariots rich and fair.
The people thee applauding, thou shalt stand,
Guiding the harmless pigeons with thy hand:
Young men and women shalt thou lead as thrall;
So will thy triumph seem magnifical:
I, lately caught, will have a new-made wound,
And captive-like be manicled and bound:
Good meaning, shame and such as seek Love's wrack,
Shall follow thee, their hands tied at their back:
Thee all shall fear and worship as a king;
Iö-triumphing shall thy people sing;
Smooth speeches, Fear, and Rage shall by thee ride,
Which troops have always been on Cupid's side:
Thou with these soldiers conquer'st Gods and men;
Take these away, where is thine honor then?
Thy mother shall from Heaven applaud this show,
And on their faces heaps of roses strow:
With beauty of thy wings thy fair hair gilded,
Ride, golden Love, in chariot richly builded.
Unless I err, full many shalt thou burn,
And give wounds infinite at every turn:
In spite of thee, forth will thine arrows fly;
A scorching flame burns all the standers-by.
So having conquered Ind, was Bacchus' hue:
Thee pompous birds, and him two tigers drew.
Then, seeing I grace thy show in following thee,
Forbear to hurt thyself in spoiling me.
Behold thy kinsman Cæsar's prosperous bands,
Who guards the conqueror with his conquering hands.

(*Christopher Marlowe*)

LENTE, LENTE

(Elegies, I, 14)

The old man's fair-haired consort, whose dewy axle-tree
Brings morning to us mortals, now rises from the Sea.
I pray you, stay, Aurora; and to your Memnon's shade
A sacrifice—I vow it —shall every year be made.
'Tis now my love is by me, her lips are mine to kiss,
Her arms are twined about me—is any hour like this?
'Tis cool, and one is sleepy, and from their slender
throats
The little feathered songsters pour forth their liquid
notes.
Now prithee, Rosy Fingers, why take such parlous pains
To hurry? No one wants you! Then stay those dewy
reins.
Ere you arrive, the sailor can watch his stars and keep
His course, nor wander blindly amid the vasty deep;
With you, the weary traveler must rise and hie away,
Must rise the cruel soldier and arm him for the fray;
The hind resumes his mattock and grubs the stubborn
soil,
The slow and patient oxen begin their day of toil;
Schoolboys you cheat of slumber, to go at your com-
mands
Where pedagogues are waiting to smack their tender
hands;
You summon to the courthouse the bailsmen, where
they taste
The pain of paying dearly for one word said in haste.
The lawyers find you hateful, i'faith, and always will;
You wake them every morning to new contention still.
That girls cease toiling sometimes, 'twere surely fair
to ask;
But no, you rouse the spinners each to her daily task.
All else I might put up with; but who was ever known
To make the girls rise early, who had one of his own?

How oft I've prayed that Darkness refuse to give you
place,
How oft, that Stars might brave you, nor flee before
your face;
How oft, I've prayed some whirlwind an axle-tree might
twist,
Or that a courser stumble and stick in some thick mist!
Why hurry, spiteful goddess? I see it now, alack,
Why Memnon was so swarthy—his mother's heart was
black!
I wish poor old Tithonus had power to testify
To what he knows—'twould make you the scandal of
the sky!
Your spouse is old and feeble; that's why you leave
your bower
And mount your hateful chariot at such an early hour!
If Cephalus replaced him, you know you'd clasp him
tight,
And cry out, 'Pray, go slowly, ye coursers of the Night!'
Why pester me, a lover? Your spouse is all but dead;
But did I urge him on you, or ever bid you wed?
How oft, the while he slumbers, our sovereign Lady
Moon—
And she more fair than you are—comes to Endymion!
Jove joined two nights in one; I dare swear the tale is
true,
For Jove was then a lover—and tired of seeing you!
You'd know Aurora heard me—she turned so rosy red;
The day though came no later, in spite of all I said.

(Kirby Flower Smith)

THE COMPLAISANT SWAIN

(Amores, III, 14)

I do not ask—for you are fair—
That you should never have a lover,
But only that I be not there
You to discover.

I am no censor to demand
That you should always virtuous be,
I only ask that you should stand
Upon some decency.

The girl who can her fault deny
Will always at the end be winner;
'Tis she who does for pardon cry
That's held the sinner.

(*F. A. Wright*)

WINTER AT TOMI

(Tristia)

The snow lies deep: nor sun nor melting shower
Serves to abate the winter's icy power.
One fall has scarcely come another's there,
And stays in drifts unmelted all the year.
Fierce and tempestuous is the North-wind's sway;
It levels towers of stone and carries roofs away.

With skins and trousers men keep out the cold;
Naught but their faces can your eyes behold.
Into one mass their hair is frozen tight,
Their beards with hoary rime hang glistening white.
Nor need they jars their liquor to confine,
They do not quaff a cup, they break a bit of wine.

Water is brittle here; you use a spade;
And running streams by frost are solid made.
Even the Danube flows with waves concealed
The dark blue surface into ice congealed.
On foot we go across the unmoving tide
And horses' hoofs ring loud where once their oarsmen plied.

(*F. A. Wright*)

FROM THE METAMORPHOSES

Magic

Ye elves of hills, brooks, standing lakes, and groves,
And ye that on the sands with printless foot
Do chase the ebbing Neptune, and do fly him
When he comes back, you demi-puppets that
By moonshine do the green sour ringlets make,
Whereof the ewe not bites; and you whose pastime
Is to make midnight mushrooms, that rejoice
To hear the solemn curfew; by whose aid,
Weak masters though ye be, I have bedimm'd
The noontide sun, call'd forth the mutinous winds,
And 'twixt the green sea and the azur'd vault
Set roaring war; to the dread rattling thunder
Have I given fire, and rifted Jove's stout oak
With his own bolt; the strong-bas'd promontory
Have I made shake, and by the spurs pluck'd up
The pine and cedar; graves at my command
Have wak'd their sleepers, op'd, and let 'em forth
By my so potent art.

(*William Shakespeare*)

Baucis and Philemon

Then Lelex rose, an old experienced man,
And thus, with sober gravity, began:
"Heaven's power is infinite: earth, air, and sea,
The manufactur'd mass, the making power obey:
By proof to clear your doubt; in Phrygian ground
Two neighboring trees, with walls encompass'd round,
Stand on a moderate rise, with wonder shown;
One a hard oak, a softer linden one:
I saw the place, and them, by Pittheus sent
To Phrygian realms, my grandsire's government.
Not far from thence is seen a lake, the haunt
Of coots, and of the fishing cormorant:
Here Jove with Hermes came; but in disguise

Of mortal men conceal'd their deities;
One laid aside his thunder, one his rod,
And many toilsome steps together trod:
For harbor at a thousand doors they knock'd;
Not one of all the thousand but was lock'd.
At last a hospitable house they found,
A homely shed; the roof, not far from ground,
Was thatch'd, with reeds and straw together bound.
There Baucis and Philemon lived, and there
Had lived long married, and a happy pair:
Now old in love, though little was their store,
Inured to want, their poverty they bore,
Nor aim'd at wealth, professing to be poor.
For master or for servant here to call
Were all alike, where only two were all.
Command was none, where equal love was paid,
Or rather both commanded, both obey'd.
"From lofty roofs the gods repulsed before,
Now stooping, enter'd through the little door:
The man (their hearty welcome first express'd)
A common settle drew for either guest,
Inviting each his weary limbs to rest.
But ere they sat, officious Baucis lays
Two cushions stuff'd with straw, the seat to raise;
Coarse, but the best she had; then rakes the load
Of ashes from the hearth, and spreads abroad
The living coals; and, lest they should expire,
With leaves and bark she feeds her infant fire.
It smokes; and then with trembling breath she blows,
Till in a cheerful baze the flames arose.
With brushwood and with chips she strengthens these
And adds at last the boughs of rotten trees.
The fire thus form'd, she sets the kettle on
(Like burnish'd gold the little seether shone;)
Next took the coleworts which her husband got
From his own ground (a small, well-water'd spot;)
She stripp'd the stalks of all their leaves; the best
She cull'd, and them with handy care she dress'd.
High o'er the hearth a chine of bacon hung;

Good old Philemon seized it with a prong,
And from the sooty rafter drew it down,
Then cut a slice, but scarce enough for one;
Yet a large portion of a little store,
Which for their sakes alone he wish'd were more.
This in the pot he plunged without delay,
To tame the flesh, and drain the salt away.
The time between, before the fire they sat,
And shorten'd the delay by pleasing chat.
"A beam there was, on which a beechen pail
Hung by the handle, on a driven nail:
This fill'd with water, gently warmed, they set
Before their guests; in this they bathed their feet,
And after with clean towels dried their sweat.
This done, the host produced the genial bed,
Sallow the feet, the borders, and the stead,
Which with no costly coverlet they spread,
But coarse old garments; yet such robes as these
They laid alone at feasts on holydays.
The good old housewife, tucking up her gown
The table sets; the invited gods lie down.
The trivet-table of a foot was lame,
A blot which prudent Baucis overcame,
Who thrust beneath the limping leg a sherd;
So was the mended board exactly rear'd:
Then rubb'd it o'er with newly-gather'd mint,
A wholesome herb, that breathed a grateful scent.
Pallas began the feast, where first was seen
The party-color'd olive, black and green:
Autumnal cornels next in order serv'd,
In lees of wine well pickled and preserved.
A garden salad was the third supply,
Of endive, radishes, and succory:
Then curds and cream, the flower of country fare,
And new-laid eggs, which Baucis' busy care
Turn'd by a gentle fire, and roasted rare.
All these in earthenware were served to board,
And, next in place, an earthen pitcher stored
With liquor of the best the cottage could afford.

This was the table's ornament and pride,
With figures wrought: like pages at his side
Stood beechen bowls; and these were shining clean,
Varnish'd with wax without, and lined within.
By this the boiling kettle had prepared,
And to the table sent the smoking lard;
On which with eager appetite they dine,
A sav'ry bit, that serv'd to relish wine;
The wine itself was suiting to the rest,
Still working in the must, and lately press'd.
The second course succeeds like that before,
Plums, apples, nuts; and of their wintry store
Dry figs, and grapes, and wrinkled dates were set
In canisters, to enlarge the little treat:
All these a milkwhite honey-comb surround,
Which in the midst a country banquet crown'd:
But the kind hosts their entertainment grace
With hearty welcome, and an open face:
In all they did, you might discern with ease
A willing mind, and a desire to please.
"Meanwhile the beechen bowls went round, and still,
Though often emptied, were observed to fill:
Fill'd without hands, and, of their own accord,
Ran without feet, and danced about the board.
Devotion seiz'd the pair, to see the feast
With wine, and of no common grape, increased;
And up they held their hands, and fell to pray'r,
Excusing, as they could, their country fare.
"One goose they had ('twas all they could allow,)
A wakeful sentry, and on duty now,
Whom to the gods for sacrifice they vow:
Her with malicious zeal the couple view'd;
She ran for life, and limping they pursued:
Full well the fowl perceived their bad intent,
And would not make her master's compliment;
But persecuted, to the powers she flies,
And close between the legs of Jove she lies:
He with a gracious ear the suppliant heard,
And saved her life; then what he was declared,

And own'd the god. 'The neighborhood,' said he,
'Shall justly perish for impiety:
You stand alone exempted: but obey
With speed, and follow where we lead the way:
Leave these accursed, and to the mountain's height
Ascend, nor once look backward in your flight.'
"They haste, and what their tardy feet denied,
The trusty staff (their better leg) supplied.
An arrow's flight they wanted to the top,
And there secure, but spent with travel, stop;
They turn their now no more forbidden eyes;
Lost in a lake the floated level lies:
A watery desert covers all the plains,
Their cot alone, as in an isle, remains.
Wondering, with weeping eyes, while they deplore
Their neighbor's fate, and country now no more;
Their little shed, scarce large enough for two,
Seems, from the ground increased, in height and bulk to grow.
A stately temple shoots within the skies,
The crotches of their cot in columns rise;
The pavement polish'd marble they behold,
The gates with sculpture graced, the spires and tiles of gold.
"Then thus the sire of gods, with looks serene:
'Speak thy desire, thou only just of men;
And thou, O woman, only worthy found
To be with such a man in marriage bound.'
"Awhile they whisper; then, to Jove address'd,
Philemon thus prefers their joint request:
'We crave to serve before your sacred shrine,
And offer at your altar rites divine:
And since not any action of our life
Has been polluted with domestic strife,
We beg one hour of death, that neither she
With widow's tears may live to bury me,
Nor weeping I, with wither'd arms, may bear
My breathless Baucis to the sepulchre.'
The godheads sign their suit. They run their race,

In the same tenor, all the appointed space:
Then, when their hour was come, while they relate
These past adventures at the temple gate,
Old Baucis is by old Philemon seen
Sprouting with sudden leaves of sprightly green:
Old Baucis look'd where old Philemon stood,
And saw his lengthen'd arms a sprouting wood:
New roots their fasten'd feet begin to bind,
Their bodies stiffen in a rising rind:
Then, ere the bark above their shoulders grew,
They give and take at once their last adieu.
'At once farewell, O faithful spouse,' they said;
At once the encroaching rinds their closing lips invade.
E'en yet, an ancient Tyanæan shows
A spreading oak, that near a linden grows;
The neighborhood confirm the prodigy,
Grave men, not vain of tongue, or like to lie.
I saw myself the garlands of their boughs,
And tablets hung for gifts of granted vows;
And offering fresher up, with pious prayer,
'The good,' said I, 'are God's peculiar care,
And such as honor Heaven, shall heavenly honor share.' "

(*John Dryden*)

Phaedrus

1st century

THE PURPOSE OF FABLE-WRITING

What from the founder Æsop fell,
In neat familiar verse I tell:
Twofold's the genius of the page,
To make you smile and make you sage.
But if the critics we displease,
By wrangling brutes and talking trees,
Let them remember, ere they blame,
We're working neither sin nor shame;
'Tis but a play to form the youth
By fiction, in the cause of truth.

(*Christopher Smart*)

ÆSOP AT PLAY

As Æsop was with boys at play,
And had his nuts as well as they,
A grave Athenian, passing by,
Cast on the sage a scornful eye,
As on a dotard quite bereaved:
Which, when the moralist perceived,
(Rather himself a wit professed
Than the poor subject of a jest)
Into the public way he flung
A bow that he had just unstrung:
"There solve, thou conjurer," he cries,
"The problem, that before thee lies."
The people throng; he racks his brain,
Nor can the thing enjoined explain.
At last he give it up—the seer
Thus then in triumph made it clear:
"As the tough bow exerts its spring,
A constant tension breaks the string;
But if 'tis let at seasons loose,
You may depend upon its use."
Thus recreative sports and play
Are good upon a holiday,
And with more spirit they'll pursue
The studies which they shall renew.

(*Christopher Smart*)

THE DOG IN THE RIVER

The churl that wants another's fare
Deserves at least to lose his share.
As through the stream a Dog conveyed
A piece of meat, he spied his shade
In the clear mirror of the flood,
And thinking it was flesh and blood,
Snapped to deprive him of the treat:—
But mark the glutton's self-defeat,
Missed both another's and his own,
Both shade and substance, beef and bone.

(*Christopher Smart*)

THE MAN AND THE WEASEL

A WEASEL, by a person caught,
And willing to get off, besought
The man to spare. "Be not severe
On him that keeps your pantry clear
Of those intolerable mice."
'This were," says he, "a work of price,
If done entirely for my sage,
And good had been the plea you make:
But since, with all these pains and care.
You seize yourself the dainty fare
On which those vermin used to fall,
And then devour the mice and all,
Urge not a benefit in vain."
This said, the miscreant was slain.
The satire here those chaps will own,
Who, useful to themselves alone,
And bustling for a private end,
Would boast the merit of a friend.

(*Christopher Smart*)

Petronius Arbiter

1st century

ENCOURAGEMENT TO EXILE

LEAVE thine own home, O youth, seek distant shores!
For thee a larger order somewhere shines—
Fear not thy fate! For thee through unknown pines
Under the cold north-wind the Danube pours;
For thee in Egypt the untroubled lands
Wait, and strange men behold the setting sun
Fall down and rise. Greatly be thou as one
Who disembarks, fearless, on alien sands.

(*Howard Mumford Jones*)

THE MALADY OF LOVE IS NERVES

Night's first sweet silence fell, and on my bed
Scarcely I closed defeated eyes in sleep
When fierce Love seized me by the hair, and said,
(Night's bitter vigil he had bade me keep),
"Thou slave," he said, "a thousand amorous girls
Hast thou not loved? And canst thou lie alone?
O hard of heart!" I leaped, and he was gone,
And with my garment in disordered swirls,
And with bare feet I sought his path where none
There was by which to go. And now I run,
Being weary, and to move brings me no peace;
And turning back is bitter, and to stay
Most shames me in the midmost of my way—
And all men's voices slowly sink and cease;
The singing birds, my dogs that, faithful, keep
My house, the roaring streets, to me are still.
Alone of men, I dread my couch, my sleep—
I follow after Love, lord of my will.

(*Howard Mumford Jones*)

WE ARE SUCH STUFF AS DREAMS . . .

Dreams that delude with flying shade men's minds
No airy phantoms are, nor sent by gods
From any shrine of theirs, but each man only
Weaves for himself his dream. And when in sleep,
Conquered, his limbs repose, and quiet comes,
Then the imponderable mind pursues
In darkness the slow circuit of the day.—
If towns have shook before him and sad cities
Under the weight of flames have been down-razed,
Javelins and fleeing armies he beholds,
The funerals of kings and plains wide-watered
With rivers of shed blood. If he's an orator,
Statutes and courts appear before his eyes;
He looks with terror on tribunals thronged

With multitudes. The miser hides his riches
And digs up buried treasure, and the huntsman
Drives through the shaken woods his yelling dogs.
The sailor dreams of shipwreck; from the waves,
Gasping, he takes his vessel, or in death
Seizes on it and sinks. And the adultress
Dreams, and so yields herself. The woman writes
In dreams unto her lover: why, the dog,
Sleeping, believes he follows on the hare!—
So all night long endured, the wounds of day
Doubly are sorrow to the miserable.

(Howard Mumford Jones)

Aulus Persius Flaccus

34-62

PROLOGUE TO THE FIRST SATIRE

I NEVER did on cleft Parnassus dream,
Nor taste the sacred Heliconian stream;
Nor can remember when my brain, inspir'd,
Was by the Muses into madness fir'd.
My share in pale Pyrene I resign,
And claim no part in all the mighty Nine.
Statues, with winding ivy crown'd, belong
To nobler poets, for a nobler song:
Heedless of verse, and hopeless of the crown,
Scarce half a wit, and more than half a clown,
Before the shrine I lay my rugged numbers down.
Who taught the parrot human notes to try,
Or with a voice endued the chatt'ring pie?
'Twas witty want, fierce hunger to appease;
Want taught their masters, and their masters these.
Let gain, that gilded bait, be hung on high;
The hungry witlings have it in their eye:
Pies, crows, and daws, poetic presents bring;
You say they squeak, but they will swear they sing.

(John Dryden)

Marcus Valerius Martialis

40-104

Not altogether a pleasant period, those evil days of Domitian. But after dwelling in the gloom of Tacitus, after being dazzled by the lightning of Juvenal's rhetoric, it is well for us that we can see that age in the broad sunlight of Martial's genius, that we can use the keen and penetrating yet just and kindly eyes of one who saw it as it really was. As he himself said, "his page has the true relish of human life."—KIRBY FLOWER SMITH.

NON AMO TE

I DO not love thee, Doctor Fell,
The reason why I cannot tell;
But this alone I know full well,
I do not love thee, Dr. Fell.

(*Tom Brown*)

NEAR NEIGHBORS

MY neighbor Hunks's house and mine
Are built so near they almost join;
The windows, too, project so much,
That through the casements we may touch.
Nay, I'm so happy, most men think,
To live so near a man of chink,
That they are apt to envy me,
For keeping such good company:
But he's as far from me, I vow,
As London is from good Lord Howe;
For when old Hunks I chance to meet,
Or one or both must quit the street;
Thus he who would not see old Roger,
Must be his neighbor or his lodger.

(*Jonathan Swift*)

PROSCRASTINATION

To-morrow you will live, you always cry;
In what far country does this morrow lie,
That 'tis so mighty long ere it arrive?
Beyond the Indies does this morrow live?
'Tis so far fetched, this morrow, that I fear
'Twill be both very old and very dear.
To-morrow I will live, the fool does say;
To-day itself's too late: the wise lived yesterday.

(*Abraham Cowley*)

VERSES ON BLENHEIM

See, here's the grand approach,
That way is for his grace's coach;
There lies the bridge, and there the clock,
Observe the lion and the cock;
The spacious court, the colonnade,
And mind how wide the hall is made;
The chimneys are so well designed,
They never smoke in any wind:
The galleries contrived for walking,
The windows to retire and talk in;
The council-chamber to debate,
And all the rest are rooms of state.
Thanks, sir, cried I, 'tis very fine,
But where d'ye sleep, or where d'ye dine?
I find by all you have been telling
That 'tis a house, but not a dwelling.

(*Jonathan Swift*)

INVITING A FRIEND TO SUPPER

To-night, grave sir, both my poor house and I
Do equally desire your company.
Not that we think us worthy such a guest,
But that your worth will dignify our feast,

With those that come; whose grace may make that seem
Something, which else could hope for no esteem.
It is the fair acceptance, sir, creates
The entertainment perfect, not the cates.
Yet shall you have, to rectify your palate,
An olive, capers, or some better salad
Ushering the mutton, with a short-legged hen
If we can get her, full of eggs, and then
Lemons, and wine for sauce; to these, a coney
Is not to be despaired of for our money;
And though fowl now be scarce, yet there are clerks,
The sky not falling, think we may have larks.
I'll tell you of more, and lie, so you will come:
Of partridge, pheasant, woodcock, of which some
May yet be there; and godwit if we can,
Knat, rail, and ruff too. Howsoe'er, my man
Shall read a piece of Virgil, Tacitus,
Livy, or of some better book to us,
Of which we'll speak our minds, amidst our meat;
And I'll profess no verses to repeat:
To this if aught appear, which I not know of,
That will the pastry, not my paper, show of.
Digestive cheese and fruit there sure will be,
But that which most doth take my Muse and me,
Is a pure cup of rich Canary wine,
Which is the Mermaid's now, but shall be mine:
Of which had Horace or Anacreon tasted,
Their lives, as do their lines, till now had lasted.
Tobacco, nectar, or the Thespian spring,
Are all but Luther's beer, to this I sing.
Of this we will sup free, but moderately,
And we will have no Pooly or Parrot by;
Nor shall our cups make any guilty men,
But, at our parting, we will be as when
We innocently met. No simple word
That shall be uttered at our mirthful board,
Shall make us sad next morning; or affright
The liberty that we'll enjoy to-night.

(*Ben Jonson*)

TO HIS BOOK

To read my book, the virgin shy
May blush, while Brutus standeth by:
But when he's gone, read through what's writ,
And never stain a cheek for it.

(Robert Herrick)

POST-OBITS AND THE POETS

He unto whom thou art so partial,
Oh, reader! is the well-known Martial,
The Epigrammatist: while living,
Give him the fame thou wouldst be giving;
So shall he hear, and feel, and know it—
Post-obits rarely reach a poet.

(Lord Byron)

BOUGHT LOCKS

The golden hair that Gulla wears
Is hers: who would have thought it?
She swears 'tis hers, and true she swears,
For I know where she bought it.

(Sir John Harington)

CRITICS

The readers and the hearers like my books,
And yet some writers cannot them digest;
But what care I? for when I make a feast,
I would my guests should praise it, not the cooks.

(Sir John Harington)

QUITS

To John I owed great obligation;
But John unhappily thought fit
To publish it to all the nation;
Sure John and I are more than quit.

(Matthew Prior)

TEMPERAMENT

In all thy humors, whether grave or mellow,
Thou'rt such a touchy, testy, pleasant fellow,
Hast so much wit and mirth and spleen about thee,
There is no living with thee nor without thee.

(Joseph Addison)

A HINTED WISH

You told me, Maro, whilst you live
You'd not a single penny give,
But that, whene'er you chanct to die,
You'd leave a handsome legacy:
You must be mad beyond redress,
If my next wish you cannot guess!

(Francis Lewis)

TO CLOE

I could resign that eye of blue
Howe'er its splendor used to thrill me;
And even that cheek of roseate hue,—
To lose it, Cloe, scarce would kill me.

That snowy neck I ne'er should miss,
However much I've raved about it;
And sweetly as that lip can kiss,
I *think* I could exist without it.

In short, so well I've learned to fast,
That, sooth my love, I know not whether
I might not bring myself at last,
To—do without you altogether.

(Thomas Moore)

WHAT MAKES A HAPPY LIFE

What makes a happy life, dear friend,
If thou wouldst briefly learn, attend—
An income left, not earned by toil;

Some acres of a kindly soil;
The pot unfailing on the fire;
No lawsuits, seldom town attire;
Health; strength with grace; a peaceful mind;
Shrewdness with honesty combined;
Plain living; equal friends and free;
Evenings of temperate gayety;
A wife discreet yet blithe and bright;
Sound slumber that lends wings to night.
With all thy heart embrace thy lot,
Wish not for death, and fear it not.

(*Goldwin Smith*)

ON THE DEATH OF A YOUNG AND FAVORITE SLAVE

Dear youth, too early lost, who now art laid
Beneath the turf in green Labicum's glade,
O'er thee no storied urn, no labored bust
I rear to crumble with the crumbling dust;
But tapering box and shadowy vine shall wave,
And grass, with tears bedewed, shall clothe thy grave.
These gifts my sorrowing love to thee shall bring,
Gifts ever fresh and deathless as the Spring.
O when to me the fatal hour shall come,
Mine be as lowly and as green a tomb!

(*Goldwin Smith*)

EROTION

Dear father and dear mother: Let me crave
Your loving kindness there beyond the grave
For my Erotion, the pretty maid
Who bears these lines. Don't let her be afraid!
She's such a little lassie—only six—
To toddle down that pathway to the Styx
All by herself! Black shadows haunt those steeps
And Cerberus the Dread who never sleeps.
May she be comforted, and may she play
About you merry as the livelong day,

And in her childish prattle often tell
Of that old master whom she loved so well.
Oh earth, bear lightly on her! 'Tis her due;
The little girl so lightly bore on you.

(Kirby Flower Smith)

SEXTUS THE USURER

WHENEVER he observes me purchasing
A slave, a cloak, or any such like thing,
Sextus the usurer—a man, you know,
Who's been my friend for twenty years or so—
In fear that I may ask him for a loan,
Thus whispers, to himself, but in a tone
Such as he knows I cannot choose but hear:
"I owe Secundus twenty thousand clear,
I owe Philetus thirty thousand more,
And then there's Phœbus—that's another four—
Besides, there's interest due on each amount,
And not one farthing on my bank account!"
Oh stratagem profound of my old friend!
'Tis hard refusing when you're asked to lend;
But to refuse before you're asked displays
Inventive genius worthy of the bays!

(Kirby Flower Smith)

COUNTRY PLEASURES

DEAR Fronto, famed alike in peace and war,
If you would learn what my chief wishes are,
Know that I crave some acres few to till,
And live at ease as careless as I will.
Why should I always trudge the stony street
And go each morn some haughty lord to greet,
When all the country's spoils are mine to get
Caught in the meshes of a hunting-net?
When I with line could snare the leaping trout
And from the hive press golden honey out,

While Joan my humble board with eggs supplies
Boiled on a fire whose logs she never buys?
May he not love this life who loves not me,
And still in Rome a pale-faced client be!

(*F. A. Wright*)

Decimus Junius Juvenalis

60-140

CELESTIAL WISDOM

(From the Tenth Satire)

Must hapless man, in ignorance sedate,
Roll darkling down the torrent of his fate?
Must no dislike alarm, no wishes rise,
No cries invoke the mercies of the skies?
Inquirer, cease: petitions yet remain,
Which Heaven may hear: nor deem religion vain.
Still raise for good the supplicating voice,
But leave to Heaven the measure and the choice.
Safe in his power, whose eyes discern afar
The secret ambush of a specious prayer,
Implore his aid, in his decisions rest,
Secure, whate'er he gives, he gives the best.
Yet when the sense of sacred presence fires,
And strong devotion to the skies aspires,
Pour forth thy fervors for a healthful mind,
Obedient passions, and a will resigned;
For love, which scarce collective man can fill;
For patience, sovereign o'er transmuted ill;
For faith, that, panting for a happier seat,
Counts death kind Nature's signal of retreat.
These goods for man the laws of Heaven ordain,
These goods he grants, who grants the power to gain;
With these celestial Wisdom calms the mind,
And makes the happiness she does not find.

(*Samuel Johnson*)

Publius Papinius Statius

61-96

SLEEP

WHAT sin was mine, sweet, silent boy-god, Sleep,
Or what, poor sufferer, have I left undone,
That I should lack thy guerdon, I alone?
Quiet are the brawling streams: the shuddering deep
Sinks, and the rounded mountains feign to sleep.
The high seas slumber pillowed on Earth's breast;
All flocks and birds and beasts are stilled in rest,
But my sad eyes their nightly vigil keep. . . .
O! if beneath the night some happier swain,
Entwined in loving arms, refuse thy boon
In wanton happiness,—come hither soon,
Come hither, Sleep. Let happier mortals gain
The full embrace of thy soft angel wing:
But touch me with thy wand, or hovering
Above mine eyelids sweep me with thy train.

(W. H. Fyfe)

The Emperor Hadrian

76–138

THE DYING CHRISTIAN TO HIS SOUL

VITAL spark of heavenly flame!
Quit, oh quit this mortal frame:
Trembling, hoping, lingering, flying,
Oh the pain, the bliss of dying!
Cease, fond Nature, cease thy strife,
And let me languish into life.

Hark! they whisper; Angels say,
Sister Spirit, come away.
What is this absorbs me quite?
Steals my senses, shuts my sight,
Drowns my spirits, draws my breath?
Tell me, my Soul, can this be Death?

The world recedes; it disappears!
Heaven opens on my eyes! my ears
  With sounds seraphic ring:
Lend, lend your wings! I mount! I fly!
O Grave! where is thy Victory?
  O Death! where is thy Sting.

(*Alexander Pope*)

Anonymous

3rd century (?)

THE VIGIL OF VENUS

The ringing phrases turn and return, and expand and interlace and fold in, as though set in motion by a strain of music; the first line perpetually repeating itself through the poem like a thread of gold in the pattern or a phrase in the music. Flower-garlanded and myrtle-shrouded, the Spring worshipers go dancing through the fields that break before them into a sheet of flowers; among them the boy Love goes with his torch and his arrows; the whole land sings with the voices of innumerable birds.—J. W. Mackail.

Love he to-morrow, who loved never;
To-morrow, who hath loved, persever.

The spring appears, in which the earth
Receives a new harmonious birth;
When all things mutual love unites;
When birds perform their nuptial rites;
And fruitful by her watery lover,
Each grove its tresses doth recover.
Love's Queen to-morrow, in the shade,
Which by these verdant trees is made,
Their sprouting tops in wreaths shall bind,
And myrtles into arbors wind;
To-morrow, raised on a high throne,
Dione shall her laws make known.

Love he to-morrow, who loved never;
To-morrow, who hath loved, persever.

Then the round ocean's foaming flood
Immingled with celestial blood,
'Mongst the blue purple of the main,
And horses whom two feet sustain,
Rising Dione did beget
With fruitful waters dropping wet.

Love he to-morrow, who loved never;
To-morrow, who hath loved, persever.

With flowery jewels everywhere
She paints the purple-color'd year;
She, when the rising bud receives
Favonius' breath, thrusts forth the leaves,
The naked roof with these t' adorn;
She the transparent dew o' th' morn,
Which the thick air of night still uses
To leave behind, in rain diffuses;
These tears with orient brightness shine,
Whilst they with trembling weight decline,
Whose every drop, into a small
Clear orb distill'd, sustains its fall.
Pregnant with these the bashful rose
Her purple blushes doth disclose.
The drops of falling dew that are
Shed in calm nights by every star,
She in her humid mantle holds,
And then her virgin leaves unfolds.
I' th' morn, by her command, each maid
With dewy roses is array'd;
Which from Cythera's crimson blood,
From the soft kisses Love bestow'd,
From jewels, from the radiant flame,
And the sun's purple luster, came.
She to her spouse shall married be
To-morrow; not ashamed that he
Should with a single knot untie
Her fiery garment's purple dye.

Love he to-morrow, who loved never;
To-morrow, who hath loved, persever.

The goddess bade the nymphs remove
Unto the shady myrtle grove;
The boy goes with the maids, yet none
Will trust, or think Love tame is grown,
If they perceive that anywhere
He arrows doth about him bear.
Go fearless, nymphs, for Love hath laid
Aside his arms, and tame is made.
His weapons by command resign'd,
Naked to go he is enjoin'd,
Lest he hurt any by his craft,
Either with flame, or bow, or shaft.
But yet take heed, young nymphs, beware
You trust him not, for Cupid's fair,
Lest by his beauty you be harm'd;
Love naked is completely arm'd.

Love he to-morrow, who loved never;
To-morrow, who hath loved, persever.

Fair Venus virgins sends to thee,
Indued with equal modesty:
One only thing we thee desire,
Chaste Delia, for a while retire;
That the wide forest, that the wood,
May be unstain'd with savage blood.
She would with prayers herself attend thee,
But that she knew she could not bend thee;
She would thyself to come have pray'd,
Did these delights beseem a maid.
Now might'st thou see with solemn rites
The Chorus celebrate three nights;
'Mongst troops whom equal pleasure crowns,
To play and sport upon thy downs;
'Mongst garlands made of various flowers,
'Mongst ever-verdant myrtle bowers.
Ceres nor Bacchus absent be,
Nor yet the poet's deity.
All night we wholly must employ

In vigils, and in songs of joy;
None but Dione must bear sway
Amongst the woods; Delia, give way.

Love he to-morrow, who loved never;
To-morrow, who hath loved, persever.

She the tribunal did command
Deck'd with Hyblæan flowers should stand;
She will in judgment sit; the Graces
On either side shall have their places;
Hybla, the flowers pour forth, whate'er
Was brought thee by the welcome year;
Hybla, thy flowery garment spread,
Wide as is Enna's fruitful mead;
Maids of the country here will be;
Maids of the mountain come to see;
Hither resort all such as dwell
Either in grove, or wood, or well.
The wing'd boy's mother every one
Commands in order to sit down;
Charging the virgins that they must
In nothing Love, though naked, trust.

Love he to-morrow, who loved never;
To-morrow, who hath loved, persever.

Let the fresh covert of a shade
Be by these early flowers display'd,
To-morrow (which with sports and play
We keep) was Æther's wedding day;
When first the father of the spring
Did out of clouds the young year bring.
The husband Shower then courts his spouse,
And in her sacred bosom flows,
That all which that vast body bred
By this defluxion may be fed:
Produced within, she all there sways
By a hid spirit, which by ways

Unknown diffused through soul and veins,
All things both governs and sustains.
Piercing through the unsounded sea,
And earth, and highest heaven, she
All places with her power doth fill,
Which through each part she doth distil;
And to the world the mystic ways
Of all production open lays.

Love he to-morrow, who loved never;
To-morrow, who hath loved, persever.

She to the Latins did transfer
The Trojan nephews; and by her
Was the Laurentian virgin won,
And join'd in marriage to her son.
By her assistance did Mars gain
A votaress from Vesta's fane.
To marriage Romulus detray'd
The Sabine women, by her aid,
(Of Romans the wide-spreading stem,)
And in the long descent of them
In whom that offspring was dilated,
Cæsar her nephew she created.

Love he to-morrow, who loved never;
To-morrow, who hath loved, persever.

The fields are fruitful made by pleasure;
The fields are rich in Venus' treasure;
And Love, Dione's son, fame yields
For truth, his birth had in the fields;
As soon as born the field reliev'd him,
Into its bosom first receiv'd him;
She bred him from his infant hours
With the sweet kisses of the flowers.

Love he to-morrow, who loved never;
To-morrow, who hath loved, persever.

See how the bulls their sides distend,
And broom-stalks with the burthen bend;
Now every one doth safely lie
Confined within his marriage tie;
See, with their husbands here are laid
The bleating flocks beneath the shade.
The warbling birds on every tree
The goddess wills not silent be.
The vocal swans on every lake,
With their hoarse voice a harsh sound make;
And Tereus' hapless maid beneath
The poplar's shade her song doth breathe;
Such as might well persuade thee, love
Doth in those trembling accents move;
Not that the sister in those strains
Of the inhuman spouse complains.
We silent are whilst she doth sing,
How long in coming is my spring?
When will the time arrive, that I
May swallow-like my voice untie?
My muse for being silent flies me,
And Phœbus will no longer prize me:
So did Amiclæ once, whilst all
Silence observed, through silence fall.

Love he to-morrow, who loved never;
To-morrow, who hath loved, persever.

(*Thomas Stanley*)

Decimus Magnus Ausonius

310–395

IDYLL OF THE ROSE

'Twas spring, and dawn returning breathed new-born
From saffron skies the bracing chill of morn.
Before day's orient chargers went a breeze,
That whispered: Rise, the sweets of morning seize!
In watered gardens where the cross-paths ran,

Freshness and health I sought ere noon began:
I watched from bending grasses how the rime
In clusters hung, or gemmed the beds of thyme;
How the round beads, on herb and leaf outspread,
Rolled with the weight of dews from heaven's bright
shed.
Saw the rose-gardens in their Pæstan bloom
Hoar 'neath the dawn-star rising through the gloom.
On every bush those separate splendors gleam,
Doomed to be quenched by day's first arrowy beam.
Here might one doubt: doth morn from roses steal
Their redness, or the rose with dawn anneal?
One hue, one dew, one morn makes both serene;
Of star and flower one Venus reigns the queen.
Perchance one scent have they; the star's o'erhead
Far, far exhales, the flower's at hand is shed.
Goddess of star, goddess of rose no less,
The Paphian flings o'er both her crimson dress.
Now had the moment passed wherein the brood
Of clustering buds seemed one twin sisterhood.
This flower, enlaced with leaves, shows naught but
green;
That shoots a roseate streak from forth the screen:
One opes her pyramid and purple spire,
Emerging into plenitude of fire:
Another thrusts her verdant veil aside,
Counting her petals one by one with pride:
Expands her radiant cup of gorgeous hue,
And brings dense hidden veins of gold to view:
She who had burned erewhile, a flower of flame,
Now pales and droops her fainting head with shame:—
So that I mused how swift time steals all worth,
How roses age and wither with their birth;
Yea, while I speak, the flower with crimson crowned
Hath fallen and shed her glories on the ground.
So many births, forms, fates with changes fraught,
One day begins and one day brings to naught!
Grieve we that flowers should have so short a grace,
That Nature shows and steals her gifts apace?

Long as the day, so long the red rose lasts;
Eld following close on youth her beauty blasts:
That flower which Phosphor newly-born had known,
Hesper returning finds a wrinkled crone:
Yet well if, though some brief days past she die,
Her life be lengthened through posterity!
Pluck roses, girl, when flower, when youth is new,
Mindful the while that thus time flies for you.

(John Addington Symonds)

TO HIS WIFE

Be life what it has been, and let us hold,
Dear wife, the names we each gave each of old;
And let not time work change upon us two,
I still your boy, and still my sweetheart you.
What though I outlive Nestor? and what though
You in your turn a Sibyl's years should know?
Ne'er let us know old age or late or soon;
Count not the years, but take of each its boon.

(Terrot Reaveley Glover)

Claudius Claudianus

c. 400

THE OLD MAN OF VERONA

Happy the man, who his whole time doth bound
Within th' inclosure of his little ground.
Happy the man whom the same humble place,
The hereditary cottage of his race,
From his first rising infancy has known,
And by degrees sees gently bending down,
With natural propension, to that earth
Which both preserved his life, and gave him birth.
Him no false distant lights, by fortune set,
Could ever into foolish wanderings get.
He never dangers either saw or feared:
The dreadful storms at sea he never heard.

He never heard the shrill alarms of war,
Or the worse noises of the lawyers' bar.
No change of consuls marks to him the year;
The change of seasons is his calendar.
The cold and heat, winter and summer shows;
Autumn by fruits, and spring by flowers, he knows.
He measures time by landmarks, and has found
For the whole day the dial of his ground.
A neighboring wood, born with himself, he sees,
And loves his old contemporary trees.
He has only heard of near Verona's name,
And knows it, like the Indies, but by fame.
Does with a like concernment notice take
Of the Red sea, and of Benacus' lake.
Thus health and strength he to a third age enjoys,
And sees a long posterity of boys.
About the spacious world let others roam,
The voyage, life, is longest made at home.

(*Abraham Cowley*)

THE LONELY ISLE

Deep in a distant bay, and deeply hidden,
There is an island far away from me
Which lulls the tumbling waves to dreamy quiet;
And there steep cliffs against the water's riot
Stand up, and to their shelter ships are bidden,
Where those curved arms shut in a tranquil sea.

(*Howard Mumford Jones*)

EPITAPH

Fate to beauty still must give
Shortened life and fugitive;
All that's noble, all that's fair
Suddenly to death repair.
Here a lovely woman lies,
Venus in her hair and eyes;
Since with these she must divide
Heaven's envy, here she died.

(*Howard Mumford Jones*)

Sidonius Apollinaris

5th century

INVITATION TO THE DANCE

Spread the board with linen snow,
Bid ivy and the laurel grow
Over it, and with them twine
The green branches of the vine.
Bring great baskets that shall hold
Cytisus and the marigold,
Cassia and starwort bring
And crocuses, till everything,
Couch and sideboard, all shall be
A garland of perfumery.
Then with balsam-perfumed hand
Smooth disheveled locks; and stand
Frankincense about, to rise—
An Arabian sacrifice—
Smoking to the lofty roof.

Next, let darkness be a proof
That our lamps with day may vie,
Glittering from the chamber's sky.
Only in their bowls be spilled
Oil nor grease, but have them filled
With such odorous balm as came
From the east to give them flame.
Then bid loaded servants bring
Viands that shall please a king,
Bowing underneath the weight
Of chased silver rich and great.
Last, in bowl and patera
And in caudron mingle a
Portion of Falernian wine
With due nard, while roses shine
Wreathed about the cup and round
The cup's tripod. We'll confound—
Where the garlands sway in grace

From vase to alabaster vase—
All the measures of the dance;
And our languid limbs shall glance
In a mazy, Mænad play.—
Step and voice shall Bacchus sway,
And in garment let each man
Be a Dionysian!

(Howard Mumford Jones)

Medieval Latin Students' Songs

12th-13th centuries

A SONG OF THE OPEN ROAD

We in our wandering,
Blithesome and squandering,
Tara, tantara, teino!

Eat to satiety,
Drink with propriety;
Tara, tantara, teino!

Laugh till our sides we split,
Rags on our hides we fit;
Tara, tantara, teino!

Jesting eternally,
Quaffing infernally:
Tara, tantara, teino!

Craft's in the bone of us,
Fear 'tis unknown of us:
Tara, tantara, teino!

When we're in neediness,
Thieve we with greediness:
Tara, tantara, teino!

Brother catholical,
Man apostolical,
Tara, tantara, teino!

Say what you will have done,
What you ask 'twill be done!
Tara, tantara, teino!

Folk, fear the toss of the
Horns of philosophy!
Tara, tantara, teino!

Here comes a quadruple
Spoiler and prodigal!
Tara, tantara, teino!

License and vanity
Pamper insanity:
Tara, tantara, teino!

As the Pope bade us do,
Brother to brother's true:
Tara, tantara, teino!

Brother, best friend, adieu!
Now, I must part from you!
Tara, tantara, teino!

When will our meeting be?
Glad shall our greeting be!
Tara, tantara, teino!

Vows valedictory
Now have the victory;
Tara, tantara, teino!

Clasped on each other's breast,
Brother to brother pressed,
Tara, tantara, teino!

(*John Addington Symonds*)

A PASTORAL

There went out in the dawning light
  A little rustic maiden;
Her flock so white, her crook so slight,
  With fleecy new wool laden.

Small is the flock, and there you'll see
  The she-ass and the wether;
This goat's a he, and that's a she,
  The bull-calf and the heifer.

She looked upon the green sward, where
  A student lay at leisure:
"What do you there, young sir, so fair?"
  "Come, play with me, my treasure!"

(John Addington Symonds)

THERE'S NO LUST LIKE TO POETRY

Sweet in goodly fellowship
  Tastes red wine and rare O!
But to kiss a girl's ripe lip
  Is a gift more fair O!
Yet a gift more sweet, more fine,
  Is the lyre of Maro!
While these three good gifts were mine,
  I'd not change with Pharaoh.

Bacchus wakes within my breast
  Love and love's desire,
Venus comes and stirs the blessed
  Rage of Phœbus' fire;
Deathless honor is our due
  From the laureled sire:
Woe should I turn traitor to
  Wine and love and lyre!

Should a tyrant rise and say,
"Give up wine!" I'd do it;
"Love no girls!" I would obey,
Though my heart should rue it.
"Dash thy lyre!" suppose he saith,
Naught should bring me to it;
"Yield thy lyre or die!" my breath,
Dying, should thrill through it!

(*John Addington Symonds*)

Latin Hymns

VENI CREATOR SPIRITUS

Creator Spirit, by whose aid
The world's foundations first were laid,
Come visit ev'ry pious mind;
Come pour thy joys on humankind;
From sin and sorrow set us free,
And make thy temples worthy thee.
O source of uncreated light,
The Father's promis'd Paraclite!
Thrice holy fount, thrice holy fire,
Our hearts with heav'nly love inspire;
Come, and thy sacred unction bring
To sanctify us, while we sing!
Plenteous of grace, descend from high,
Rich in thy sev'nfold energy,
Thou strength of his almighty hand,
Whose pow'r does heav'n and earth command!
Proceeding Spirit, our defense,
Who dost the gifts of tongues dispense,
And crown'st thy gift with eloquence!
Refine and purge our earthy parts;
But, O, inflame and fire our hearts!
Our frailties help, our vice control,
Submit the senses to the soul;
And when rebellious they are grown,

Then lay thy hand, and hold 'em down.
  Chase from our minds th' infernal foe,
And peace, the fruit of love, bestow;
And lest our feet should step astray,
Protect and guide us in the way.
  Make us eternal truths receive,
And practice all that we believe:
Give us thyself, that we may see
The Father and the Son, by thee.
  Immortal honor, endless fame,
Attend th' Almighty Father's name:
The Savior Son be glorified,
Who for lost man's redemption died;
And equal adoration be,
Eternal Paraclete, to thee.

(John Dryden)

THE TE DEUM

THEE, Sovereign God, our grateful accents praise;
We own thee Lord, and bless thy wondrous ways;
To thee, Eternal Father, earth's whole frame,
With loudest trumpets, sounds immortal fame.
Lord God of Hosts! for thee the heavenly powers
With sounding anthems fill the vaulted towers.
Thy Cherubims thrice, Holy, Holy, Holy, cry;
Thrice, Holy, all the Seraphims reply,
And thrice returning echoes endless songs supply.
Both heaven and earth thy majesty display;
They owe their beauty to thy glorious ray.
Thy praises fill the loud apostles' choir;
The train of prophets in the song conspire.
Legions of martyrs in the chorus shine,
And vocal blood with vocal music join.
By these thy church, inspir'd by heavenly art,
Around the world maintains a second part;
And tunes her sweetest notes, O God, to thee,
The Father of unbounded majesty;
The Son, ador'd copartner of thy seat,
And equal everlasting Paraclete.

Thou King of Glory, Christ, of the most high,
Thou coeternal filial Deity;
Thou who, to save the world's impending doom,
Vouchsaf'dst to dwell within a Virgin's womb;
Old tyrant Death disarm'd, before thee flew
The bolts of heaven, and back the foldings drew,
To give access, and make thy faithful way;
From God's right hand thy filial beams display.
Thou art to judge the living and the dead;
Then spare those souls for whom thy veins have bled.
O take us up amongst thy blest above,
To share with them thy everlasting love.
Preserve, O Lord, thy people, and enhance
Thy blessing on thine own inheritance.
For ever raise their hearts, and rule their ways;
Each day we bless thee, and proclaim thy praise:
No age shall fail to celebrate thy name,
No hour neglect thy everlasting fame.
Preserve our souls, O Lord, this day from ill;
Have mercy on us, Lord, have mercy still:
As we have hop'd, do thou reward our pain;
We've hop'd in thee—let not our hope be vain.

(*John Dryden ?*)

HYMN FOR ST. JOHN'S EVE

I

O SYLVAN prophet, whose eternal fame
Echoes from Judah's hills, and Jordan's stream,
The music of our numbers raise,
And tune our voices to thy praise.

II

A messenger from high Olympus came
To bear the tidings of thy life and name;
And told thy sire each prodigy
That Heaven design'd to work in thee.

III

Hearing the news, and doubting in surprise,
His falt'ring speech in fetter'd accent dies;
But Providence, with happy choice,
In thee restor'd thy father's voice.

IV

In the recess of nature's dark abode,
Tho' still inclos'd, yet knewest thou thy God!
Whilst each glad parent told and bless'd
The secrets of each other's breast.

(*John Dryden ?*)

DIES IRAE

Hear'st thou, my soul, what serious things
Both the Psalm and Sibyl sings
Of a sure Judge, from whose sharp ray
The world in flames shall fly away!

O that Fire! before whose face
Heaven and earth shall find no place:
O those Eyes! whose angry light
Must be the day of that dread night.

O that Trump! whose blast shall run
An even round with th' circling Sun,
And urge the murmuring graves to bring
Pale mankind forth to meet his King.

Horror of Nature, Hell, and Death!
When a deep groan from beneath
Shall cry, "We come, we come!" and all
The caves of night answer one call.

O that book! whose leaves so bright
Will set the world in severe light.
O that Judge! whose hand, whose eye
None can endure, yet none can fly.

Ah then, poor soul! what wilt thou say?
And to what patron choose to pray,
When stars themselves shall stagger, and
The most firm foot no more shall stand?

But Thou giv'st leave, dread Lord, that we
Take shelter from Thyself in Thee;
And with the wings of Thine own dove
Fly to Thy scepter of soft love!

Dear [LORD], remember in that day
Who was the cause Thou cam'st this way;
Thy sheep was strayed, and Thou wouldst be
Even lost Thyself in seeking me!

Shall all that labor, all that cost
Of love, and even that loss, be lost?
And this loved soul judged worth no less
Than all that way and weariness?

Just mercy, then, Thy reck'ning be
With my price, and not with me;
'Twas paid at first with too much pain
To be paid twice, or once in vain.

Mercy, my Judge, mercy I cry,
With blushing cheek and bleeding eye;
The conscious colors of my sin
Are red without, and pale within.

O let Thine own soft bowels pay
Thyself, and so discharge that day!
If Sin can sigh, Love can forgive,
O, say the word, my soul shall live!

Those mercies which Thy Mary found,
Or who Thy cross confess'd and crowned,
Hope tells my heart the same loves be
Still alive, and still for me.

Though both my prayers and tears combine,
Both worthless are, for they are mine;
But Thou Thy bounteous self still be,
And show Thou art by saving me.

O when Thy last frown shall proclaim
The flocks of goats to folds of flame,
And all Thy lost sheep found shall be,
Let "Come ye blessed" then call me!

When the dread *"ITE"* shall divide
Those limbs of death from Thy left side,
Let those life-speaking lips command
That I inherit Thy right hand!

O, hear a suppliant heart all crush'd,
And crumbled into contrite dust!
My hope, my fear—my Judge, my Friend!
Take charge of me, and of my end!

(*Richard Crashaw*)

ITALIAN

Ciullo d' Alcamo

c. 1175

DIALOGUE: LOVER AND LADY

He: THOU sweetly-smelling fresh red rose
That near thy summer art,
Of whom each damsel and each dame
Would fain be counterpart;
O! from this fire to draw me forth
Be it in thy good heart:
For night or day there is no rest with me,
Thinking of none, my lady, but of thee.

She: If thou hast set thy thoughts on me,
Thou hast done a foolish thing.
Yea, all the pine-wood of this world
Together might'st thou bring,
And make thee ships, and plow the sea
Therewith for corn-sowing,
Ere any way to win me could be found:
For I am going to shear my locks all round.

He: Lady, before thou shear thy locks
I hope I may be dead:
For I should lose such joy thereby
And gain such grief instead.
Merely to pass and look at thee,
Rose of the garden-bed,
Has comforted me much, once and again.
Oh! if thou wouldst but love, what were it then!

She: Nay, though my heart were prone to love,
I would not grant it leave.
Hark! should my father or his kin
But find thee here this eve,
Thy loving body and lost breath
Our moat may well receive.

Whatever path to come here thou dost know,
By the same path I counsel thee to go.
He: And if thy kinsfolk find me here,
Shall I be drowned then? Marry,
I'll set, for price against my head,
Two thousand agostari.
I think thy father would not do't
For all his lands in Bari.
Long life to the Emperor! Be God's the praise!
Thou hear'st, my beauty, what thy servant says.
She: And am I then to have no peace
Morning or evening?
I have strong coffers of my own
And much good gold therein;
So that if thou couldst offer me
The wealth of Saladin,
And add to that the Soldan's money-hoard,
Thy suit would not be anything toward.
He: I have known many women, love,
Whose thoughts were high and proud,
And yet have been made gentle by
Man's speech not over-loud.
If we but press ye long enough,
At length ye will be bow'd;
For still a woman's weaker than a man.
When the end comes, recall how this began.
She: God grant that I may die before
Any such end do come,—
Before the sight of a chaste maid
Seem to me troublesome!
I marked thee here all yestereve
Lurking about my home,
And now I say, Leave climbing, lest thou fall,
For these they words delight me not at all.
He: How many are the cunning chains
Thou hast wound round my heart!
Only to think upon thy voice
Sometimes I groan apart.

For I did never love a maid
Of this world, as thou art,
So much as I love thee, thou crimson rose.
Thou wilt be mine at last: this my soul knows.
She: If I could think it would be so,
Small pride it were of mine
That all my beauty should be meant
But to make thee to shine.
Sooner than stoop to that, I'd shear
These golden tresses fine,
And make one of some holy sisterhood;
Escaping so thy love, which is not good.
He: If thou unto the cloister fly,
Thou cruel lady and cold,
Unto the cloister I will come
And by the cloister hold;
For such a conquest liketh me
Much better than much gold;
At matins and at vespers I shall be
Still where thou art. Have I not conquered thee?
She: Out and alack! wherefore am I
Tormented in suchwise?
Lord Jesus Christ the Saviour,
In whom my best hope lies,
O give me strength that I may hush
This vain man's blasphemies!
Let him seek through the earth; 'tis long and broad:
He will find fairer damsels, O my God!
He: I have sought through Calabria,
Lombardy, and Tuscany,
Rome, Pisa, Lucca, Genoa,
All between sea and sea:
Yea, even to Babylon I went
And distant Barbary:
But not a woman found I anywhere
Equal to thee, who art indeed most fair.
She: If thou have all this love for me,
Thou canst no better do

Than ask me of my father dear
And my dear mother too:
They willing, to the abbey-church
We will together go,
And, before Advent, thou and I will wed;
After the which, I'll do as thou hast said.

He: These thy conditions, lady mine,
Are altogether nought:
Despite of them, I'll make a net
Wherein thou shalt be caught.
What, wilt thou put on wings to fly?
Nay, but of wax they're wrought,—
They'll let thee fall to earth, not rise with thee:
So, if thou canst, then keep thyself from me.

She: Think not to fright me with thy nets
And suchlike childish gear;
I am safe pent within the walls
Of this strong castle here;
A boy before he is a man
Could give me as much fear.
If suddenly thou get not hence again,
It is my prayer thou mayst be found and slain.

He: Wouldst thou in very truth that I
Were slain, and for thy sake?
Then let them hew me to such mince
As a man's limbs may make!
But meanwhile I shall not stir hence
Till of that fruit I take
Which thou hast in thy garden, ripe enough:
All day and night I thirst to think thereof.

She: None have partaken of that fruit,
Not Counts nor Cavaliers:
Though many have reached up for it,
Barons and great Seigneurs,
They all went hence in wrath because
They could not make it theirs.
Then how canst *thou* think to succeed alone
Who hast not a thousand ounces of thine own?

He: How many nosegays I have sent
Unto thy house, sweet soul!
At least till I am put to proof,
This scorn of thine control.
For if the wind, so fair for thee,
Turn ever and wax foul,
Be sure that thou shalt say when all is done,
"Now is my heart heavy for him that's gone."
She: If by my grief thou couldst be grieved,
God send me a grief soon!
I tell thee that though all my friends
Prayed me as for a boon,
Saying, "Even for the love of us,
Love thou this worthless loon,"
Thou shouldst not have the thing that thou dost hope.
No, verily: not for the realm o' the Pope.
He: Now could I wish that I in truth
Were dead here in thy house:
My soul would get its vengeance then;
Once known, the thing would rouse
A rabble, and they'd point and say,—
"Lo! she that breaks her vows,
And, in her dainty chamber, stabs!" Love, see:
One strikes just thus: it is soon done, pardie!
She: If now thou do not hasten hence,
(My curse companioning,)
That my stout friends will find thee here
Is a most certain thing:
After the which, my gallant sir,
Thy points of reasoning
May chance, I think, to stand thee in small stead,
Thou hast no friend, sweet friend, to bring thee aid.
He: Thou sayst truly, saying that
I have not any friend:
A landless stranger, lady mine,
None but his sword defend.
One year ago, my love began,
And now, is this the end?

Oh! the rich dress thou worest on that day
Since when thou art walking at my side alway!
She: So 'twas my dress enamored thee!
What marvel? I did wear
A cloth of samite silver-flowered,
And gems within my hair.
But one more word; if on Christ's Book
To wed me thou didst swear,
There's nothing now could win me to be thine:
I had rather make my bed in the sea-brine.
He: And if thou make thy bed therein,
Most courteous lady and bland,
I'll follow all among the waves,
Paddling with foot and hand;
Then, when the sea hath done with thee,
I'll seek thee on the sand.
For I will not be conquered in this strife:
I'll wait, but win; or losing, lose my life.
She: For Father, Son, and Holy Ghost,
Three times I cross myself.
Thou art no godless heretic,
Nor Jew, whose God's his pelf:
Even as I know it then, meseems,
Thou needs must know thyself
That woman, when the breath in her doth cease,
Loseth all savor and all loveliness.
He: Woe's me! Perforce it must be said
No craft could then avail:
So that if thou be thus resolved,
I know my suit must fail.
Then have some pity, of thy grace!
Thou may'st, love, very well;
For though thou love not me, my love is such
That 'tis enough for both—yea overmuch.
She: Is it even so? Learn then that I
Do love thee from my heart.
To-morrow, early in the day,
Come here, but now depart.

By thine obedience in this thing
I shall know what thou art,
And if thy love be real or nothing worth;
Do but go now, and I am thine henceforth.
He: Nay, for such promise, my own life,
I will not stir a foot.
I've said, if thou wouldst tear away
My love even from its root,
I have a dagger at my side
Which thou mayst take to do't;
But as for going hence, it will not be.
O hate me not! my heart is burning me.
She: Think'st thou I know not that thy heart
Is hot and burns to death?
Of all that thou or I can say,
But one word succoreth.
Till thou upon the Holy Book
Give me thy bounden faith,
God is my witness that I will not yield:
For with thy sword 'twere better to be kill'd.
He: Then on Christ's Book, borne with me still
To read from and to pray,
(I took it, fairest, in a church,
The priest being gone away,)
I swear that my whole self shall be
Thine always from this day.
And now at once give joy for all my grief,
Lest my soul fly, that's thinner than a leaf.
She: Now that this oath is sworn, sweet lord,
There is no need to speak:
My heart, that was so strong before,
Now feels itself grow weak.
If any of my words were harsh,
Thy pardon: I am meek
Now, and will give thee entrance presently.
It is best so, sith so it was to be.

(*D. G. Rossetti*)

Folcachiero de' Folcachieri
Knight of Siena

c. 1175

CANZONE

He speaks of his Condition through Love

All the whole world is living without war,
  And yet I cannot find out any peace.
    O God! that this should be!
O God! what does the earth sustain me for?
  My life seems made for other lives' ill-ease:
    All men look strange to me;
    Nor are the wood-flowers now
    As once, when up above
    The happy birds in love
Made such sweet verses, going from bough to bough.

And if I come where other gentlemen
  Bear arms, or say of love some joyful thing—
    Then is my grief most sore,
And all my soul turns round upon me then:
  Folk also gaze upon me, whispering,
    Because I am not what I was before.
    I know not what I am.
    I know how wearisome
    My life is now become,
And that the days I pass seem all the same.

I think that I shall die; yea, death begins;
  Though 'tis no set-down sickness that I have,
    Nor are my pains set down.
But to wear raiment seems a burden since
  This came, nor ever any food I crave;
    Not any cure is known
    To me, nor unto whom
    I might commend my case:
    This evil therefore stays
Still where it is, and hope can find no room.

I know that it must certainly be Love:
  No other Lord, being thus set over me,
      Had judged me to this curse;
With such high hand he rules, sitting above
  That of myself he takes two parts in fee,
      Only the third being hers.
      Yet if through service I
      Be justified with God,
      He shall remove this load,
Because my heart with inmost love doth sigh.

Gentle my lady, after I am gone,
  There will not come another, it may be,
      To show thee love like mine:
For nothing can I do, neither have done,
  Except what proves that I belong to thee
      And am a thing of thine.
      Be it not said that I
      Despaired and perished, then;
      But pour thy grace, like rain,
On him who is burned up, yea, visibly.

(*D. G. Rossetti*)

Saint Francis of Assisi

1182-1226

CANTICA

Our Lord Christ: of order

Set Love in order, thou that lovest Me.
  Never was virtue out of order found;
And though I fill thy heart desirously,
  By thine own virtue I must keep My ground:
When to My love thou dost bring charity,
  Even she must come with order girt and gown'd.
      Look how the trees are bound
      To order, bearing fruit;
      And by one thing compute,
In all things earthly, order's grace or gain.

All earthly things I had the making of
 Were numbered and were measured then by Me;
And each was ordered to its end by Love,
 Each kept, through order, clean for ministry.
Charity most of all, when known enough,
 Is of her very nature orderly.
  Lo, now! what heat in thee,
  Soul, can have bred this rout?
  Thou putt'st all order out.
Even this love's heat must be its curb and rein.

(D. G. Rossetti)

Guido Guinicelli

13th century

SONNET

He will praise his Lady

Yea, let me praise my lady whom I love:
 Likening her unto the lily and rose:
 Brighter than morning star her visage glows;
She is beneath even as her Saint above;
She is as the air in summer which God wove
 Of purple and of vermilion glorious;
 As gold and jewels richer than man knows.
Love's self, being love for her, must holier prove.
Ever as she walks she hath a sober grace,
 Making bold men abashed and good men glad;
  If she delight thee not, thy heart must err.
No man dare look on her, his thoughts being base:
 Nay, let me say even more than I have said;—
  No man could think base thoughts who looked on
   her.

(D. G. Rossetti)

SONNET

Of Moderation and Tolerance

He that has grown to wisdom hurries not,
 But thinks and weighs what Reason bids him do

And after thinking he retains his thought
Until as he conceived the fact ensue.
Let no man to o'erweening pride be wrought,
But count his state as Fortune's gift and due.
He is a fool who deems that none has sought
The truth, save he alone, or knows it true.
Many strange birds are on the air abroad,
Nor all are of one flight or of one force,
But each after his kind dissimilar:
To each was portioned of the breath of God,
Who gave them divers instincts from one source.
Then judge not thou thy fellows what they are.

(*D. G. Rossetti*)

CANZONE

He perceives his Rashness in Love, but has no choice

I HOLD him, verily, of mean emprise,
Whose rashness tempts a strength too great to bear;
As I have done, alas! who turned mine eyes
Upon those perilous eyes of the most fair.
Unto her eyes I bow'd;
No need her other beauties in that hour
Should aid them, cold and proud:
As when the vassals of a mighty lord,
What time he needs his power,
Are all girt round him to make strong his sword.

With such exceeding force the stroke was dealt
That by mine eyes its path might not be stay'd;
But deep into the heart it pierced, which felt
The pang of the sharp wound, and waxed afraid;
Then rested in strange wise,
As when some creature utterly outworn
Sinks into bed and lies.
And she the while doth in no manner care,
But goes her way in scorn,
Beholding herself alway proud and fair.

And she may be as proud as she shall please,
For she is still the fairest woman found:
A sun she seems among the rest; and these
Have all their beauties in her splendor drown'd.
In her is every grace,—
Simplicity of wisdom, noble speech,
Accomplished loveliness;
All earthly beauty is her diadem,
This truth my song would teach,—
My lady is of ladies chosen gem.

Love to my lady's service yieldeth me,—
Will I, or will I not, the thing is so,—
Nor other reason can I say or see,
Except that where it lists the wind doth blow.
He rules and gives no sign;
Nor once from her did show of love upbuoy
This passion which is mine.
It is because her virtue's strength and stir
So fill her full of joy
That I am glad to die for love of her.

(D. G. Rossetti)

CANZONE

Of the gentle Heart

WITHIN the gentle heart Love shelters him
As birds within the green shade of the grove.
Before the gentle heart, in nature's scheme,
Love was not, nor the gentle heart ere Love.
For with the sun, at once,
So sprang the light immediately; nor was
Its birth before the sun's.
And Love hath his effect in gentleness
Of very self; even as
Within the middle fire the heat's excess.

The fire of Love comes to the gentle heart
  Like as its virtue to a precious stone;
To which no star its influence can impart
  Till it is made a pure thing by the sun:
    For when the sun hath smit
From out its essence that which there was vile
    The star endoweth it.
And so the heart created by God's breath
    Pure, true, and clean from guile,
A woman, like a star, enamoreth.

In gentle heart Love for like reason is
  For which the lamp's high flame is fanned and bow'd:
Clear, piercing bright, it shines for its own bliss;
  Nor would it burn there else, it is so proud.
    For evil natures meet
With Love as it were water met with fire,
    As cold abhorring heat.
Through gentle heart Love doth a track divine,—
    Like knowing like; the same
As diamond runs through iron in the mine.

The sun strikes full upon the mud all day:
  It remains vile, nor the sun's worth is less.
'By race I am gentle,' the proud man doth say:
  He is the mud, the sun is gentleness.
    Let no man predicate
That aught the name of gentleness should have,
    Even in a king's estate,
Except the heart there be a gentle man's.
    The star-beam lights the wave,—
Heaven holds the star and the star's radiance.

God, in the understanding of high Heaven,
  Burns more than in our sight the living sun:
There to behold His Face unveiled is given;
  And Heaven, whose will is homage paid to One
    Fulfills the things which live

In God, from the beginning excellent.
So should my lady give
That truth which in her eyes is glorified,
On which her heart is bent,
To me whose service waiteth at her side.

My lady, God shall ask, 'What daredst thou?'
(When my soul stands with all her acts review'd;)
'Thou passedst Heaven, into My sight, as now,
To make Me of vain love similitude.
To Me doth praise belong,
And to the Queen of all the realm of grace
Who slayeth fraud and wrong.'
Then may I plead: 'As though from Thee he came,
Love wore an angel's face:
Lord, if I loved her, count it not my shame.'

(*D. G. Rossetti*)

Guerzo di Montecanti

13th century

SONNET

He is out of Heart with his Time

If any man would know the very cause
Which makes me to forget my speech in rhyme,
All the sweet songs I sang in other time,—
I'll tell it in a sonnet's simple clause.
I hourly have beheld how good withdraws
To nothing, and how evil mounts the while:
Until my heart is gnawed as with a file,
Nor aught of this world's worth is what it was.
At last there is no other remedy
But to behold the universal end;
And so upon this hope my thoughts are urged:
To whom, since truth is sunk and dead at sea,
There has no other part or prayer remain'd,
Except of seeing the world's self submerged.

(*D. G. Rossetti*)

Jacopo da Lentino

13th century

SONNET

Of his Lady in Heaven

I HAVE it in my heart to serve God so
That into Paradise I shall repair,—
The holy place through the which everywhere
I have heard say that joy and solace flow.
Without my lady I were loath to go,—
She who has the bright face and the bright hair;
Because if she were absent, I being there,
My pleasure would be less than nought, I know.
Look you, I say not this to such intent
As that I there would deal in any sin:
I only would behold her gracious mien,
And beautiful soft eyes, and lovely face,
That so it should be my complete content
To see my lady joyful in her place.

(*D. G. Rossetti*)

SONNET

Of his Lady's Face

HER face has made my life most proud and glad;
Her face has made my life quite wearisome;
It comforts me when other troubles come,
And amid other joys it strikes me sad.
Truly I think her face can drive me mad;
For now I am too loud, and anon dumb.
There is no second face in Christendom
Has a like power, nor shall have, nor has had.

What man in living face has seen such eyes,
Or such a lovely bending of the head,
Or mouth that opens to so sweet a smile?

In speech, my heart before her faints and dies,
And into Heaven seems to be spirited;
So that I count me blest a certain while.

(D. G. Rossetti)

CANZONETTA

Of his Lady, and of his making her Likeness

My Lady mine, I send
These sighs in joy to thee
Though, loving till the end,
There were no hope for me
That I should speak my love;
And I have loved indeed,
Though, having fearful heed,
It was not spoken of.

Thou art so high and great
That whom I love I fear;
Which thing to circumstate
I have no messenger:
Wherefore to Love I pray,
On whom each lover cries,
That these my tears and sighs
Find unto thee a way.

Well have I wished, when I
At heart with sighs have ach'd,
That there were in each sigh
Spirit and intellect,
The which, where thou dost sit,
Should kneel and sue for aid,
Since I am thus afraid
And have no strength for it.

Thou, lady, killest me,
Yet keepest me in pain,
For thou must surely see
How, fearing, I am fain.

Ah! why not send me still
  Some solace, small and slight,
  So that I should not quite
Despair of thy good will?

Thy grace, all else above,
  Even now while I implore,
Enamoreth my love
  To love thee still the more.
Yet scarce should I know well—
  A greater love to gain,
  Even if a greater pain,
Lady, were possible.

Joy did that day relax
  My grief's continual stress,
When I essayed in wax
  Thy beauty's life-likeness.
Ah! much more beautiful
  Than golden-haired Yseult,—
  Who mak'st all men exult,
Who bring'st all women dule.

And certes without blame
  Thy love might fall to me,
Though it should chance my name
  Were never heard of thee
Yea, for thy love, in fine,
  Lentino gave me birth,
  Who am not nothing worth
If worthy to be thine.

(D. G. Rossetti)

CANZONETTA

He will neither boast nor lament to his Lady

Love will not have me cry
  For grace, as others do;
Nor as they vaunt, that I
  Should vaunt my love to you.

For service, such as all
Can pay, is counted small;
Nor is it much to praise
  The thing which all must know;—
  Such pittance to bestow
On you my love gainsays.

Love lets me not turn shape
  As chance or use may strike;
As one may see an ape
  Counterfeit all alike.
Then, lady, unto you
Be it not mine to sue,
For grace or pitying.
  Many the lovers be
  That of such suit are free,—
It is a common thing.

A gem, the more 'tis rare,
  The more its cost will mount:
And, be it not so fair,
  It is of more account.
So, coming from the East,
The sapphire is increased
In worth, though scarce so bright;
  I therefore seek thy face
  Not to solicit grace,
Being cheapened and made slight.

So is the colosmine
  Now cheapened, which in fame
Was once so brave and fine,
  But now is a mean gem.
So be such prayers for grace
Not heard in any place;
Would they indeed hold fast
  Their worth, be they not said,
  Nor by true lovers made
Before nine years be past.

Lady, sans sigh or groan,
  My longing thou canst see;
Much better am I known
  Than to myself, to thee.
And is there nothing else
That in my heart avails
For love but groan and sigh?
  And wilt thou have it thus,
  This love betwixen us?—
Much rather let me die.

(D. G. Rossetti)

Giacomino Pugliesi

13th century

CANZONETTA

Of his Lady in Absence

THE sweetly-favored face
  She has, and her good cheer,
Have filled me full of grace
  When I have walked with her.
They did upon that day:
  And everything that pass'd
  Comes back from first to last
Now that I am away.

There went from her meek mouth
  A poor low sigh which made
My heart sink down for drouth.
  She stooped, and sobbed, and said,
"Sir, I entreat of you
  Make little tarrying:
  It is not a good thing
To leave one's love and go."

But when I turned about
  Saying, "God keep you well!"
As she look'd up, I thought
  Her lips that were quite pale
Strove much to speak, but she
  Had not half strength enough:
  My own dear graceful love
Would not let go of me.

I am not so far, sweet maid,
  That now the old love's unfelt:
I believe Tristram had
  No such love for Yseult:
And when I see your eyes
  And feel your breath again,
  I shall forget this pain
And my whole heart will rise.

(D. G. Rossetti)

CANZONE

Of his Dead Lady

DEATH, why hast thou made life so hard to bear,
  Taking my lady hence? Hast thou no whit
Of shame? The youngest flower and the most fair
  Thou hast plucked away, and the world wanteth it.
O leaden Death, hast thou no pitying?
Our warm love's very spring
  Thou stopp'st, and endest what was holy and meet;
And of my gladdening
Mak'st a most woeful thing,
And in my heart dost bid the bird not sing
  That sang so sweet.

Once the great joy and solace that I had
  Was more than is with other gentlemen:—
Now is my love gone hence, who made me glad.
  With her that hope I lived in she hath ta'en

And left me nothing but these sighs and tears,—
Nothing of the old years
  That come not back again,
Wherein I was so happy, being hers.
Now to mine eyes her face no more appears,
Nor doth her voice make music in mine ears,
  As it did then.

O God, why hast thou made my grief so deep?
  Why set me in the dark to grope and pine?
Why parted me from her companionship,
  And crushed the hope which was a gift of thine?
To think, dear, that I never any more
Can see thee as before!
  Who is it shuts thee in?
Who hides that smile for which my heart is sore,
And drowns those words that I am longing for,
  Lady of mine?

Where is my lady, and the lovely face
  She had, and the sweet motion when she walk'd?—
Her chaste, mild favor—her so delicate grace—
  Her eyes, her mouth, and the dear way she talk'd?—
Her courteous bending—her most noble air—
The soft fall of her hair? . . .
My lady—she to whom my soul
  A gladness brought!
Now I do never see her anywhere,
And may not, looking in her eyes, gain there
  The blessing which I sought.

So if I had the realm of Hungary,
  With Greece, and all the Almayn even to France,
Or Saint Sophia's treasure-hoard, you see
  All could not give me back her countenance.
For since the day when my dear lady died
From us, (with God being born and glorified,)
  No more pleasaunce

Her image bringeth, seated at my side,
But only tears. Ay me! the strength and pride
  Which it brought once.

Had I my will, beloved, I would say
  To God, unto whose bidding all things bow,
That we were still together night and day:
  Yet be it done as His behests allow.
I do remember that while she remain'd
With me, she often called me her sweet friend;
  But does not now,
Because God drew her towards Him, in the end.
Lady, that peace which none but He can send
  Be thine. Even so.

(D. G. Rossetti)

Bartolomeo di Sant' Angelo

13th century

SONNET

He jests concerning his Poverty

I AM so passing rich in poverty
  That I could furnish forth Paris and Rome,
  Pisa and Padua and Byzantium,
Venice and Lucca, Florence and Forli;
For I possess in actual specie,
  Of nihil and of nothing a great sum;
  And unto this my hoard whole shiploads come,
What between nought and zero, annually.
In gold and precious jewels I have got
  A hundred ciphers' worth, all roundly writ;
    And therewithal am free to feast my friend.
    Because I need not be afraid to spend,
  Nor doubt the safety of my wealth a whit:—
No thief will ever steal thereof, God wot.

(D. G. Rossetti)

Folgore da San Geminiano

13th century

OF THE MONTHS

Twelve Sonnets

Addressed to a Fellowship of Sienese Nobles

DEDICATION

Unto the blithe and lordly Fellowship,
(I know not where, but wheresoe'er, I know,
Lordly and blithe,) be greeting; and thereto,
Dogs, hawks, and a full purse wherein to dip;
Quails struck i' the flight; nags mettled to the whip;
Hart-hounds, hare-hounds, and blood-hounds even so;
And o'er that realm, a crown for Niccolò,
Whose praise in Siena springs from lip to lip.
Tingoccio, Atuin di Togno, and Ancaiàn,
Bartolo and Mugaro and Faënot,
Who well might pass for children of King Ban,
Courteous and valiant more than Lancelot,—
To each, God speed! how worthy every man
To hold high tournament in Camelot.

January

For January I give you vests of skins,
And mighty fires in hall, and torches lit;
Chambers and happy beds with all things fit;
Smooth silken sheets, rough furry counterpanes;
And sweetmeats baked; and one that deftly spins
Warm arras; and Douay cloth, and store of it;
And on this merry manner still to twit
The wind, when most his mastery the wind wins.
Or issuing forth at seasons in the day,
Ye'll fling soft handfuls of the fair white snow
Among the damsels standing round, in play:
And when you all are tired and all aglow,
Indoors again the court shall hold its sway,
And the free Fellowship continue so.

February

In February I give you gallant sport
  Of harts and hinds and great wild boars; and all
  Your company good foresters and tall,
With buskins strong, with jerkins close and short;
And in your leashes, hounds of brave report;
  And from your purses, plenteous money-fall,
  In very spleen of misers' starveling gall,
Who at your generous customs snarl and snort.
At dusk wend homeward, ye and all your folk,
  All laden from the wilds, to your carouse,
    With merriment and songs accompanied:
And so draw wine and let the kitchen smoke;
  And so be till the first watch glorious;
    Then sound sleep to you till the day be wide.

March

In March I give you plenteous fisheries
  Of lamprey and of salmon, eel and trout,
  Dental and dolphin, sturgeon, all the rout
Of fish in all the streams that fill the seas.
With fishermen and fishing-boats at ease,
  Sail-barques and arrow-barques, and galleons stout,
  To bear you, while the season lasts, far out,
And back, through spring, to any port you please.
But with fair mansions see that it be fill'd,
  With everything exactly to your mind,
    And every sort of comfortable folk.
No convent suffer there, nor priestly guild:
  Leave the mad monks to preach after their kind
    Their scanty truth, their lies beyond a joke.

April

I give you meadow-lands in April, fair
  With over-growth of beautiful green grass;
  There among fountains the glad hours shall pass,

And pleasant ladies bring you solace there.
With steeds of Spain and ambling palfreys rare;
  Provençal songs and dances that surpass;
  And quaint French mummings; and through hollow
      brass
A sound of German music on the air.
And gardens ye shall have, that every one
  May lie at ease about the fragrant place;
    And each with fitting reverence shall bow down
    Unto that youth to whom I gave a crown
  Of precious jewels like to those that grace
The Babylonian Kaiser, Prester John.

May

I GIVE you horses for your games in May,
  And all of them well trained unto the course,—
  Each docile, swift, erect, a goodly horse;
With armor on their chests, and bells at play
Between their brows, and pennons fair and gay;
  Fine nets, and housings meet for warriors,
  Emblazoned with the shields ye claim for yours;
Gules, argent, or, all dizzy at noonday.
And spears shall split, and fruit go flying up
In merry counterchange for wreaths that drop
  From balconies and casements far above;
And tender damsels with young men and youths
Shall kiss together on the cheeks and mouths;
  And every day be glad with joyful love.

June

IN June I give you a close-wooded fell,
  With crowns of thicket coiled about its head,
  With thirty villas twelve times turreted,
All girdling round a little citadel;
And in the midst a springhead and fair well
  With thousand conduits branched and shining speed,
  Wounding the garden and the tender mead.

Yet to the freshened grass acceptable.
And lemons, citrons, dates, and oranges,
  And all the fruits whose savor is most rare,
Shall shine within the shadow of your trees:
  And every one shall be a lover there;
Until your life, so filled with courtesies,
  Throughout the world be counted debonair.

July

For July, in Siena, by the willow-tree,
  I give you barrels of white Tuscan wine
  In ice far down your cellars stored supine;
And morn and eve to eat in company
Of those vast jellies dear to you and me;
  Of partridges and youngling pheasants sweet,
  Boiled capons, sovereign kids: and let their treat
Be veal and garlic, with whom these agree.
Let time slip by, till by-and-by, all day;
  And never swelter through the heat at all,
But move at ease at home, sound, cool, and gay;
  And wear sweet-colored robes that lightly fall;
And keep your tables set in fresh array,
  Not coaxing spleen to be your seneschal.

August

For August, be your dwelling thirty towers
  Within an Alpine valley mountainous,
  Where never the sea-wind may vex your nouse,
But clear life separate, like a star, be yours.
There horses shall wait saddled at all hours,
  That ye may mount at morning or at eve:
  On each hand either ridge ye shall perceive,
A mile apart, which soon a good beast scours.
So alway, drawing homewards, ye shall tread
  Your valley parted by a rivulet
    Which day and night shall flow sedate and smooth.
There all through noon ye may possess the shade,
  And there your open purses shall entreat
    The best of Tuscan cheer to feed your youth.

September

And in September, O what keen delight!
Falcons and astors, merlins, sparrowhawks;
Decoy-birds that shall lure your game in flocks;
And hounds with bells: and gauntlets stout and tight;
Wide pouches; crossbows shooting out of sight;
Arblasts and javelins; balls and ball-cases;
All birds the best to fly at; moulting these,
Those reared by hand; with finches mean and slight;
And for their chase, all birds the best to fly;
And each to each of you be lavish still
In gifts; and robbery find no gainsaying;
And if you meet with travelers going by,
Their purses from your purse's flow shall fill;
And avarice be the only outcast thing.

October

Next, for October, to some sheltered coign
Flouting the winds, I'll hope to find you slunk;
Though in bird-shooting (lest all sport be sunk),
Your foot still press the turf, the horse your groin.
At night with sweethearts in the dance you'll join,
And drink the blessed must, and get quite drunk,
There's no such life for any human trunk;
And that's a truth that rings like golden coin!
Then, out of bed again when morning's come,
Let your hands drench your face refreshingly,
And take your physic roast, with flask and knife,
Sounder and snugger you shall feel at home
Than lake-fish, river-fish, or fish at sea,
Inheriting the cream of Christian life.

November

Let baths and wine-butts be November's due,
With thirty mule-loads of broad gold-pieces;
And canopy with silk the streets that freeze;

And keep your drink-horns steadily in view.
Let every trader have his gain of you:
Clareta shall your lamps and torches send,—
Caëta, citron-candies without end;
And each shall drink and help his neighbor too.
And let the cold be great, and the fire grand:
And still for fowls, and pastries sweetly wrought,
For hares and kids, for roast and boiled, be sure
You always have your appetites at hand;
And then let night howl and heaven fall, so nought
Be missed that makes a man's bed-furniture.

December

Last, for December, houses on the plain,
Ground-floors to live in, logs heaped mountain-high,
And carpets stretched, and newest games to try,
And torches lit, and gifts from man to man:
(Your host, a drunkard and a Catalan;)
And whole dead pigs, and cunning cooks to ply
Each throat with tit-bits that shall satisfy;
And wine-butts of Saint Galganus' brave span.
And be your coats well-lined and tightly bound,
And wrap yourselves in cloaks of strength and weight,
With gallant hoods to put your faces through.
And make your game of abject vagabond
Abandoned miserable reprobate
Misers; don't let them have a chance with you.

Conclusion

And now take thought, my sonnet, who is he
That most is full of every gentleness;
And say to him (for thou shalt quickly guess
His name) that all his 'hests are law to me.
For if I held fair Paris town in fee,
And were not called his friend, 'twere surely less.
Ah! had he but the emperor's wealth, my place
Were fitted in his love more steadily

Than is Saint Francis at Assisi. Alway
  Commend him unto me and his,—not least
    To Caian, held so dear in the blithe band.
"Folgore da San Geminiano" (say),
  "Has sent me, charging me to travel fast,
    Because his heart went with you in your hand."

(D. G. Rossetti)

SONNET

Of Virtue

The flower of Virtue is the heart's content;
  And fame is Virtue's fruit that she doth bear;
  And Virtue's vase is fair without and fair
Within; and Virtue's mirror brooks no taint;
And Virtue by her names is sage and saint;
  And Virtue hath a steadfast front and clear;
  And Love is Virtue's constant minister;
And Virtue's gift of gifts is pure descent.
And Virtue dwells with knowledge, and therein
  Her cherished home of rest is real love;
    And Virtue's strength is in a suffering will;
And Virtue's work is life exempt from sin,
  With arms that aid; and in the sum hereof,
    All Virtue is to render good for ill.

(D. G. Rossetti)

ON KNIGHTHOOD

I

This morn a young squire shall be made a knight;
  Whereof he fain would be right worthy found,
  And therefore pledgeth lands and castles round
  To furnish all that fits a man of might.
Meat, bread, and wine he gives to many a wight;
  Capons and pheasants on his board abound,
  Where serving men and pages march around;
  Choice chambers, torches, and wax candle light.

Barbed steeds, a multitude, are in his thought,
  Mailed men at arms and noble company,
  Spears, pennants, housing cloths, bells richly
    wrought;
Musicians following with great barony
  And jesters through the land his state have brought,
  With dames and damsels whereso rideth he.

II

Comes Blithesomeness with mirth and merriment,
  All decked in flowers she seemeth a rose-tree;
  Of linen, silk, cloth, fur, now beareth she
  To the new knight a rich habiliment;
Head-gear and cap and garland flower-besprent,
  So brave they were May-bloom he seemed to be;
  With such a rout, so many and such glee,
  That the floor shook. Then to her work she went;
And stood him on his feet in hose and shoon;
  And purse and gilded girdle neath the fur
  That drapes his goodly limbs, she buckles on;
Then bids the singers and sweet music stir,
  And showeth him to ladies for a boon
  And all who in that following went with her.

(John Addington Symonds)

Guido delle Colonne

13th century

CANZONE

To Love and to his Lady

O Love, who all this while hast urged me on,
  Shaking the reins, with never any rest,—
  Slacken for pity somewhat of thy haste;
I am oppress'd with languor and foredone,—
Having outrun the power of sufferance,—
  Having much more endured than who, through faith
  That his heart holds, makes no account of death.

Love is assuredly a fair mischance,
And well may it be called a happy ill:
  Yet thou, my lady, on this constant sting,
So sharp a thing, have thou some pity still,—
Howbeit a sweet thing too, unless it kill.

O comely-favored, whose soft eyes prevail,
  More fair than is another on this ground,—
  Lift now my mournful heart out of its stound,
Which thus is bound for thee in great travail:
For a high gale a little rain may end.
  Also, my lady, be not angered thou
  That Love should thee enforce, to whom all bow.
There is but little shame to apprehend
If to a higher strength the conquest be;
  And all the more to Love who conquers all.
Why then appal my heart with doubts of thee?
Courage and patience triumph certainly.

I do not say that with such loveliness
  Such pride may not beseem; it suits thee well,
  For in a lovely lady pride may dwell,
Lest homage fail and high esteem grow less:
Yet pride's excess is not a thing to praise.
  Therefore, my lady, let thy harshness gain
  Some touch of pity which may still restrain
Thy hand, ere Death cut short these hours and days.
The sun is very high and full of light,
  And the more bright the higher he doth ride:
So let thy pride, my lady, and thy height,
Stand me in stead and turn to my delight.

Still inmostly I love thee, laboring still
  That others may not know my secret smart.
  Oh! what a pain it is for the grieved heart
To hold apart and not to show its ill!
Yet by no will the face can hide the soul;
  And ever with the eyes the heart has need
  To be in all things willingly agreed.

It were a mighty strength that should control
The heart's fierce beat, and never speak a word:
  It were a mighty strength, I say again,
To hide such pain, and to be sovran lord
Of any heart that had such love to hoard.

For Love can make the wisest turn astray;
  Love, at its most, of measure still has least;
  He is the maddest man who loves the best;
It is Love's jest, to make men's hearts alway
So hot that they by coldness cannot cool.
  The eyes unto the heart bear messages
  Of the beginnings of all pain and ease:
And thou, my lady, in thy hand dost rule
Mine eyes and heart which thou hast made thine own.
  Love rocks my life with tempests on the deep,
Even as a ship round which the winds are blown:
Thou art my pennon that will not go down.

G. Rossetti)

Pier Moronelli di Fiorenza

13th century

CANZONETTA

A Bitter Song to his Lady

O LADY amorous,
Merciless lady,
Full blithely play'd ye
These your beguilings.
So with an urchin
A man makes merry,—
In mirth grows clamorous,
Laughs and rejoices,—
But when his choice is
To fall aweary,
Cheats him with silence.
This is Love's portion:—

In much wayfaring
With many burdens
He loads his servants,
But at the sharing,
The underservice
And overservice
Are alike barren.

As my disaster
Your jest I cherish,
And well may perish.
Even so a falcon
Is sometimes taken
And scantly cautell'd;
Till when his master
At length to loose him,
To train and use him,
Is after all gone,—
The creature's throttled
And will not waken.
Wherefore, my lady,
If you will own me,
O look upon me!
If I'm not thought on,
At least perceive me!
O do not leave me
So much forgotten!

If, lady, truly
You wish my profit,
What follows of it
Though still you say so?—
For all your well-wishes
I still am waiting.
I grow unruly,
And deem at last I'm
Only your pastime.
A child will play so,
Who greatly relishes

Sporting and petting
With a little wild bird:
Unaware he kills it,—
Then turns it, feels it,
Calls it with a mild word,
Is angry after,—
Then again in laughter
Loud is the child heard.

O my delightful
My own, my lady,
Upon the Mayday
Which brought me to you
Was all my haste then
But a fool's venture?
To have my sight full
Of you propitious
Truly my wish was,
And to pursue you
And let love chasten
My heart to the center.
But warming, lady,
May end in burning.
Of all this yearning
What comes, I beg you?
In all your glances
What is't a man sees?—
Fever and ague.

(*D. G. Rossetti*)

Prinzivalle Doria

13th century

CANZONE

Of his Love, with the Figure of a sudden Storm

Even as the day when it is yet at dawning
  Seems mild and kind, being fair to look upon,
While the birds carol underneath their awning
  Of leaves, as if they never would have done;
  Which on a sudden changes, just at noon,

And the broad light is broken into rain
  That stops and comes again;
Even as the traveler, who had held his way
  Hopeful and glad because of the bright weather,
  Forgetteth then his gladness altogether;
Even so am I, through Love, alas the day!

It plainly is through Love that I am so.
  At first, he let me still grow happier
Each day, and made her kindness seem to grow;
  But now he has quite changed her heart in her.
  And I, whose hopes throbbed and were all astir
For times when I should call her mine aloud,
  And in her pride be proud
Who is more fair than gems are, ye may say,
  Having that fairness which holds hearts in rule;—
  I have learnt now to count him but a fool
Who before evening says, A goodly day.

It had been better not to have begun,
  Since, having known my error, 'tis too late.
This thing from which I suffer, thou hast done,
  Lady: canst thou restore me my first state?
  The wound thou gavest canst thou medicate?
Not thou, forsooth: thou hast not any art
  To keep death from my heart.
O lady! where is now my life's full meed
  Of peace,—mine once, and which thou took'st away?
  Surely it cannot now be far from day:
Night is already very long indeed.

The sea is much more beautiful at rest
  Than when the storm is trampling over it.
Wherefore, to see the smile which has so bless'd
  This heart of mine, deem'st thou these eyes unfit?
  There is no maid so lovely, it is writ,
That by such stern unwomanly regard
  Her face may not be marr'd.

I therefore pray of thee, my own soul's wife,
That thou remember me who am forgot.
How shall I stand without thee? Art thou not
The pillar of the building of my life?

(*D. G. Rossetti*)

Rustico di Filippo

1200?-1270

SONNET

Of the Making of Master Messerin

When God had finished Master Messerin,
He really thought it something to have done:
Bird, man, and beast had got a chance in one,
And each felt flattered, it was hoped, therein.
For he is like a goose i' the windpipe thin,
And like a cameleopard high i' the loins;
To which, for manhood, you'll be told, he joins
Some kinds of flesh-hues and a callow chin.
As to his singing, he affects the crow;
As to his learning, beasts in general;
And sets all square by dressing like a man.
God made him, having nothing else to do;
And proved there is not anything at all
He cannot make, if that's a thing He can.

(*D. G. Rossetti*)

Niccolò degli Albizzi

13th century

PROLONGED SONNET

When the Troops were returning from Milan

If you could see, fair brother, how dead beat
The fellows look who come through Rome to-day,—
Black yellow smoke-dried visages,—you'd say
They thought their haste at going all too fleet.

Their empty victual-wagons up the street
  Over the bridge dreadfully sound and sway;
  Their eyes, as hanged men's, turning the wrong way;
And nothing on their backs, or heads, or feet.
One sees the ribs and all the skeletons
  Of their gaunt horses; and a sorry sight
Are the torn saddles, crammed with straw and stones.
  They are ashamed, and march throughout the night;
Stumbling, for hunger, on their marrowbones;
  Like barrels rolling, jolting, in this plight.
Their arms all gone, not even their swords are saved;
And each as silent as a man being shaved.

(D. G. Rossetti)

Guido Cavalcanti

1250-1301

Sonnet

TO DANTE ALIGHIERI

He interprets Dante's Dream, related in the first Sonnet of the Vita Nuova

Unto my thinking, thou beheld'st all worth,
  All joy, as much of good as man may know,
  If thou wert in his power who here below
Is honor's righteous lord throughout this earth.
Where evil dies, even there he has his birth,
  Whose justice out of pity's self doth grow.
  Softly to sleeping persons he will go,
And with no pain to them, their hearts draw forth.
Thy heart he took, as knowing well, alas!
  That Death had claimed thy lady for a prey:
    In fear whereof, he fed her with thy heart.
    But when he seemed in sorrow to depart.
  Sweet was thy dream; for by that sign, I say,
Surely the opposite shall come to pass.

(D. G. Rossetti)

SONNET

To his Lady Joan, of Florence

Flowers hast thou in thyself, and foliage,
  And what is good, and what is glad to see;
The sun is not so bright as thy visàge;
  All is stark naught when one hath looked on thee;
There is not such a beautiful personage
  Anywhere on the green earth verily;
If one fear love, thy bearing sweet and sage
  Comforteth him, and no more fear hath he.
Thy lady friends and maidens ministering
  Are all, for love of thee, much to my taste:
And much I pray them that in everything
  They honor thee even as thou meritest,
And have thee in their gentle harboring:
  Because among them all thou art the best.

(*D. G. Rossetti*)

SONNET

He compares all Things with his Lady, and finds them wanting

Beauty in woman; the high will's decree;
  Fair knighthood armed for manly exercise;
  The pleasant song of birds; love's soft replies;
The strength of rapid ships upon the sea;
The serene air when light begins to be;
  The white snow, without wind that falls and lies;
  Fields of all flower; the place where waters rise;
Silver and gold; azure in jewelry:
Weighed against these the sweet and quiet worth
  Which my dear lady cherishes at heart
    Might seem a little matter to be shown;
  Being truly, over these, as much apart
As the whole heaven is greater than this earth.
    All good to kindred natures cleaveth soon.

(*D. G. Rossetti*)

SONNET

A Rapture concerning his Lady

Who is she coming, whom all gaze upon,
  Who makes the air all tremuious with light,
And at whose side is Love himself? that none
  Dare speak, but each man's sighs are infinite.
  Ah me! how she looks round from left to right,
Let Love discourse: I may not speak thereon.
Lady she seems of such high benison
  As makes all others graceless in men's sight.
The honor which is hers cannot be said;
  To whom are subject all things virtuous,
    While all things beauteous own her deity.
Ne'er was the mind of man so nobly led,
  Nor yet was such redemption granted us
    That we should ever know her perfectly.

(*D. G. Rossetti*)

BALLATA

Of his Lady among other Ladies

With other women I beheld my love;—
  Not that the rest were women to mine eyes,
Who only as her shadows seemed to move.

I do not praise her more than with the truth,
  Nor blame I these if it be rightly read.

But while I speak, a thought I may not soothe
  Says to my senses: 'Soon shall ye be dead,
  If for my sake your tears ye will not shed.'

And then the eyes yield passage, at that thought,
To the heart's weeping, which forgets her not.

(*D. G. Rossetti*)

SONNET

Of the Eyes of a certain Mandetta, of Thoulouse, which resemble those of his Lady Joan, of Florence

A CERTAIN youthful lady in Thoulouse,
Gentle and fair, of cheerful modesty,
Is in her eyes, with such exact degree,
Of likeness unto mine own lady, whose
I am, that through the heart she doth abuse
The soul to sweet desire. It goes from me
To her; yet, fearing, saith not who is she
That of a truth its essence thus subdues.
This lady looks on it with the sweet eyes
Whose glance did erst the wounds of Love anoint
Through its true lady's eyes which are as they.
Then to the heart returns it, full of sighs,
Wounded to death by a sharp arrow's point
Wherewith this lady speeds it on its way.

(*D. G. Rossetti*)

BALLATA

He reveals, in a Dialogue, his increasing Love for Mandetta

BEING in thought of love, I chanced to see
Two youthful damozels.
One sang: 'Our life inhales
All love continually.'

Their aspect was so utterly serene,
So courteous, of such quiet nobleness,
That I said to them: 'Yours, I may well ween,
'Tis of all virtue to unlock the place.
Ah! damozels, do not account him base
Whom thus his wound subdues:
Since I was at Thoulouse,
My heart is dead in me.'

(*D. G. Rossetti*)

SONNET

TO DANTE ALIGHIERI

He reports. in a feigned Vision, the successful Issue of Lapo Gianni's Love

DANTE, a sigh that rose from the heart's core
  Assailed me, while I slumbered, suddenly:
So that I woke o' the instant, fearing sore
  Lest it came thither in Love's company:
Till, turning, I beheld the servitor
  Of Lady Lagia: 'Help me,' so said he,
'O help me, Pity.' Though he said no more,
  So much of Pity's essence entered me,
That I was ware of Love, those shafts he wields
  A-whetting, and preferred the mourner's quest
    To him, who straightway answered on this wise:
'Go tell my servant that the lady yields,
  And that I hold her now at his behest:
    If he believe not, let him note her eyes.'

(*D. G. Rossetti*)

SONNET

TO DANTE ALIGHIERI

He mistrusts the Love of Lapo Gianni

I PRAY thee, Dante, shouldst thou meet with Love
  In any place where Lapo then may be,
  That there thou fail not to mark heedfully
If Love with lover's name that man approve;
If to our Master's will his lady move
  Aright, and if himself show fealty:
  For ofttimes, by ill custom, ye may see
This sort profess the semblance of true love.

Thou know'st that in the court where Love holds sway
A law subsists, that no man who is vile
Can service yield to a lost woman there.
If suffering aught avail the sufferer,
Thou straightway shalt discern our lofty style
Which needs the badge of honor must display.

(*D. G. Rossetti*)

SONNET

On the Detection of a false Friend

Love and the Lady Lagia, Guido and I,
Unto a certain lord are bounden all,
Who has released us—know ye from whose thrall?
Yet I'll not speak, but let the matter die:
Since now these three no more are held thereby,
Who in such homage at his feet did fall
That I myself was not more whimsical,
In him conceiving godship from on high.
Let Love be thanked the first, who first discern'd
The truth; and that wise lady afterward,
Who in fit time took back her heart again;
And Guido next, from worship wholly turn'd;
And I, as he. But if ye have not heard,
I shall not tell how much I loved him then.

(*D. G. Rossetti*)

SONNET

He speaks of a third Love of his

O thou that often hast within thine eyes
A Love who holds three shafts,—know thou from me
That this my sonnet would commend to thee
(Come from afar) a soul in heavy sighs,
Which even by Love's sharp arrow wounded lies.
Twice did the Syrian archer shoot, and he
Now bends his bow the third time, cunningly,
That, thou being here, he wound me in no wise.

Because the soul would quicken at the core
Thereby, which now is near to utter death,
From those two shafts, a triple wound that yield.
The first gives pleasure, yet disquieteth;
And with the second is the longing for
The mighty gladness by the third fulfill'd.

(D. G. Rossetti)

BALLATA

Of a continual Death in Love

THOUGH thou, indeed, hast quite forgotten ruth,
Its steadfast truth my heart abandons not;
But still its thought yields service in good part
To that hard heart in thee.

Alas! who hears believes not I am so.
Yet who can know? of very surety, none.
From Love is won a spirit, in some wise,
Which dies perpetually:

And, when at length in that strange ecstasy
The heavy sigh will start,
There rains upon my heart
A love so pure and fine,
That I say: 'Lady, I am wholly thine.'

(D. G. Rossetti)

SONNET

To a Friena who does not pity his Love

IF I entreat this lady that all grace
Seem not unto her heart an enemy,
Foolish and evil thou declarest me,
And desperate in idle stubbornness.
Whence is such cruel judgment thine, whose face,
To him that looks thereon, professeth thee
Faithful, and wise, and of all courtesy,

And made after the way of gentleness?
Alas! my soul within my heart doth find
Sighs, and its grief by weeping doth enhance,
That, drowned in bitter tears, those sighs depart:
And then there seems a presence in the mind,
As of a lady's thoughtful countenance
Come to behold the death of the poor heart.

(*D. G. Rossetti*)

SONNET

Of his Pain from a new Love

Why from the danger did mine eyes not start,—
Why not become even blind,—ere through my sight
Within my soul thou ever couldst alight
To say: 'Dost thou not hear me in thy heart?'
New torment then, the old torment's counterpart,
Filled me at once with such a sore affright,
That, Lady, lady, (I said,) destroy not quite
Mine eyes and me! O help us where thou art!
Thou hast so left mine eyes, that Love is fain—
Even Love himself—with pity uncontroll'd
To bend above them, weeping for their loss:
Saying: 'If any man feel heavy pain,
This man's more painful heart let him behold:
Death has it in her hand, cut like a cross.'

(*D. G. Rossetti*)

TO DANTE

Returning from its daily quest, my Spirit
Changed thoughts and vile in thee doth weep to find:
It grieves me that thy mild and gentle mind
Those ample virtues which it did inherit,
Has lost. Once thou didst loathe the multitude
Of blind and maddening men: I then loved thee—
I loved thy lofty songs, and that sweet mood
When thou wert faithful to thyself and men.

I dare not now, through thy degraded state,
Own the delight thy strains inspire—in vain
I seek what once thou wert—we cannot meet
As we were wont. Again and yet again
Ponder my words: so the false Spirit shall fly,
And leave to thee thy true integrity.

(*Percy Bysshe Shelley*)

BALLATA

Concerning a Shepherd-maid

WITHIN a copse I met a shepherd-maid,
More fair, I said, than any star to see.

She came with waving tresses pale and bright,
With rosy cheer, and loving eyes of flame,
Guiding the lambs beneath her wand aright.
Her naked feet still had the dews on them,
As, singing like a lover, so she came;
Joyful, and fashioned for all ecstasy.

I greeted her at once, and question made
What escort had she through the woods in spring?
But with soft accents she replied and said
That she was all alone there, wandering;
Moreover: 'Do you know, when the birds sing,
My heart's desire is for a mate,' said she.

While she was telling me this wish of hers,
The birds were all in song throughout the wood.
'Even now then,' said my thought, 'the time recurs,
With mine own longing to assuage her mood.'
And so, in her sweet favor's name, I sued
That she would kiss there and embrace with me.

She took my hand to her with amorous will,
And answered that she gave me all her heart,
And drew me where the leaf is fresh and still,
Where spring the wood-flowers in the shade apart.
And on that day, by Joy's enchanted art,
There Love in very presence seemed to be.

(*D. G. Rossetti*)

SONNET

Of an ill-favored Lady

Just look, Manetto, at that wry-mouth'd minx;
Merely take notice what a wretch it is;
How well contrived in her deformities,
How beastly favored when she scowls and blinks.
Why, with a hood on (if one only thinks)
Or muffle of prim veils and scapularies,—
And set together, on a day like this
Some pretty lady with the odious sphinx;—
Why, then thy sins could hardly have such weight,
Nor thou be so subdued from Love's attack,
Nor so possessed in Melancholy's sway,
But that perforce thy peril must be great
Of laughing till the very heart-strings crack:
Either thou'dst die, or thou must run away.

(*D. G. Rossetti*)

BALLATA

In Exile at Sarzana

Because I think not ever to return,
Ballad, to Tuscany,—
Go therefore thou for me
Straight to my lady's face,
Who, of her noble grace,
Shall show thee courtesy.

Thou seekest her in charge of many sighs,
Full of much grief and of exceeding fear.
But have good heed thou come not to the eyes
Of such as are sworn foes to gentle cheer:
For, certes, if this thing should chance,—from her
Thou then couldst only look
For scorn, and such rebuke
As needs must bring me pain;—
Yea, after death again
Tears and fresh agony.

Surely thou knowest, Ballad, how that Death
  Assails me, till my life is almost sped:
Thou knowest how my heart still travaileth
  Through the sore pangs which in my soul are bred:—
  My body being now so nearly dead,
          It cannot suffer more.
          Then, going, I implore
          That this my soul thou take
          (Nay, do so for my sake,)
          When my heart sets it free.

Ah! Ballad, unto thy dear offices
  I do commend my soul, thus trembling;
That thou mayst lead it, for pure piteousness,
  Even to that lady's presence whom I sing.
  Ah! Ballad, say thou to her, sorrowing,
          Whereso thou meet her then:—
          'This thy poor handmaiden
          Is come, nor will be gone,
          Being parted now from one
          Who served Love painfully.'

Thou also, thou bewildered voice and weak,
  That goest forth in tears from my grieved heart,
Shalt, with my soul and with this ballad, speak
  Of my dead mind, when thou dost hence depart,
  Unto that lady (piteous as thou art!)
          Who is so calm and bright,
          It shall be deep delight
          To feel her presence there.
          And thou, Soul, worship her
          Still in her purity.

(*D. G. Rossetti*)

Francesco da Barberino

1264–1348

A VIRGIN DECLARES HER BEAUTIES

Do not conceive that I shall here recount
All my own beauty: yet I promise you

That you, by what I tell, shall understand
All that befits and that is well to know.

My bosom, which is very softly made,
Of a white even color without stain,
Bears two fair apples, fragrant, sweetly-savored,
Gathered together from the Tree of Life
The which is in the midst of Paradise.
And these no person ever yet has touched;
For out of nurse's and of mother's hands
I was, when God in secret gave them me.
These ere I yield I must know well to whom;
And for that I would not be robbed of them,
I speak not all the virtue that they have;
Yet thus far speaking:—blessed were the man
Who once should touch them, were it but a little;—
See them I say not, for that might not be.
My girdle, clipping pleasure round about,
Over my clear dress even unto my knees
Hangs down with sweet precision tenderly;
And under it Virginity abides.
Faithful and simple and of plain belief
She is, with her fair garland bright like gold;
And very fearful if she overhears
Speech of herself; the wherefore ye perceive
That I speak soft lest she be made ashamed.

Lo! this is she who hath for company
The Son of God and Mother of the Son;
Lo! this is she who sits with many in heaven;
Lo! this is she with whom are few on earth.

(*D. G. Rossetti*)

OF CAUTION

Say, wouldst thou guard thy son,
That sorrow he may shun?
Begin at the beginning
And let him keep from sinning.

Wouldst guard thy house? One door
Make to it, and no more.
Wouldst guard thine orchard-wall?
Be free of fruit to all.

(*D. G. Rossetti*)

Dante Alighieri

1265-1321

FROM LA VITA NUOVA

The narrative of the New Life is quaint, embroidered with conceits, deficient in artistic completeness, but it has the simplicity of youth, the charm of sincerity, the freedom of personal confidence; and so long as there are lovers in the world, and so long as lovers are poets, this first and tenderest love-story of modern literature will be read with appreciation and responsive sympathy.—CHARLES ELIOT NORTON.

1

To every heart which the sweet pain doth move,
And unto which these words may now be brought
For true interpretation and kind thought,
Be greeting in our Lord's name, which is Love.
Of those long hours wherein the stars, above,
Wake and keep watch, the third was almost nought,
When Love was shown me with such terrors fraught
As may not carelessly be spoken of.
He seemed like one who is full of joy, and had
My heart within his hand, and on his arm
My lady, with a mantle round her, slept;
Whom (having wakened her) anon he made
To eat that heart; she ate, as fearing harm.
Then he went out; and as he went, he wept.

2

ALL ye that pass along Love's trodden way,
Pause ye awhile and say
If there be any grief like unto mine:

I pray you that you hearken a short space
Patiently, if my case
  Be not a piteous marvel and a sign.
Love (never, certes, for my worthless part,
But of his own great heart),
  Vouchsafed to me a life so calm and sweet
That oft I heard folk question as I went
What such great gladness meant:—
  They spoke of it behind me in the street.

But now that fearless bearing is all gone
  Which with Love's hoarded wealth was given me;
  Till I am grown to be
So poor that I have dread to think thereon.

And thus it is that I, being like as one
  Who is ashamed and hides his poverty,
  Without seem full of glee,
And let my heart within travail and moan.

3

a

Weep, Lovers, sith Love's very self doth weep,
  And sith the cause for weeping is so great;
  When now so many dames, of such estate
In worth, show with their eyes a grief so deep
For Death the churl has laid his leaden sleep
  Upon a damsel who was fair of late,
  Defacing all our earth should celebrate,—
Yea all save virtue, which the soul doth keep.
Now hearken how much Love did honor her.
  I myself saw him in his proper form
    Bending above the motionless sweet dead,
And often gazing into Heaven; for there
  The soul now sits which when her life was warm
    Dwelt with the joyful beauty that is fled.

b

Death, always cruel, Pity's foe in chief,
Mother who brought forth grief,
Merciless judgment and without appeal!
Since thou alone hast made my heart to feel
This sadness and unweal,
My tongue upbraideth thee without relief.

And now (for I must rid thy name of ruth)
Behoves me speak the truth
Touching thy cruelty and wickedness:
Not that they be not known; but ne'ertheless
I would give hate more stress
With them that feed on love in very sooth.

Out of this world thou hast driven courtesy,
And virtue, dearly prized in womanhood;
And out of youth's gay mood
The lovely lightness is quite gone through thee.

Whom now I mourn, no man shall learn from me
Save by the measure of these praises given.
Whoso deserves not Heaven
May never hope to have her company.

4

A day agone, as I rode sullenly
Upon a certain path that liked me not,
I met Love midway while the air was hot,
Clothed lightly as a wayfarer might be.
And for the cheer he showed, he seemed to me
As one who hath lost lordship he had got;
Advancing tow'rds me full of sorrowful thought,
Bowing his forehead so that none should see.
Then as I went, he called me by my name,
Saying: "I journey since the morn was dim
Thence where I made thy heart to be which now

I needs must bear unto another dame."
Wherewith so much passed into me of him
That he was gone, and I discerned not how.

5

SONG, 'tis my will that thou do seek out Love,
And go with him where my dear lady is;
That so my cause, the which thy harmonies
Do plead, his better speech may clearly prove.

Thou goest, my Song, in such a courteous kind,
That even companionless
Thou mayst rely on thyself anywhere.
And yet, an thou wouldst get thee a safe mind,
First unto Love address
Thy steps; whose aid, mayhap, 'twere ill to spare
Seeing that she to whom thou mak'st thy prayer
Is, as I think, ill-minded unto me,
And that if Love do not companion thee,
Thou'lt have perchance small cheer to tell me of.

With a sweet accent, when thou com'st to her,
Begin thou in these words,
First having craved a gracious audience:
"He who hath sent me as his messenger,
Lady, thus much records,
An thou but suffer him, in his defense.
Love, who comes with me, by thine influence
Can make this man do as it liketh him:
Wherefore, if this fault *is* or doth but *seem*
Do thou conceive: for his heart cannot move."

Say to her also: "Lady, his poor heart
Is so confirmed in faith
That all its thoughts are but of serving thee:
'Twas early thine, and could not swerve apart."
Then, if she wavereth,
Bid her ask Love, who knows if these things be.
And in the end, beg of her modestly

To pardon so much boldness: saying too:—
"If thou declare his death to be thy due,
The thing shall come to pass, as doth behove."

Then pray thou of the Master of all ruth,
Before thou leave her there,
That he befriend my cause and plead it well.
"In guerdon of my sweet rhymes and my truth"
(Entreat him) "stay with her;
Let not the hope of thy poor servant fail;
And if with her thy pleading should prevail,
Let her look on him and give peace to him."
Gentle my Song, if good to thee it seem,
Do this: so worship shall be thine and love.

6

All my thoughts always speak to me of Love,
Yet have between themselves such difference
That while one bids me bow with mind and sense,
A second saith, "Go to: look thou above";
The third one, hoping, yields me joy enough;
And with the last come tears, I scarce know whence:
All of them craving pity in sore suspense,
Trembling with fears that the heart knoweth of.
And thus, being all unsure which path to take,
Wishing to speak I know not what to say,
And lose myself in amorous wanderings:
Until, (my peace with all of them to make,)
Unto mine enemy I needs must pray,
My Lady Pity, for the help she brings.

7

Even as the others mock, thou mockest me;
Not dreaming, noble lady, whence it is
That I am taken with strange semblances,
Seeing thy face which is so fair to see:
For else, compassion would not suffer thee
To grieve my heart with such harsh scoffs as these.
Lo! Love, when thou art present, sits at ease,

And bears his mastership so mightily
That all my troubled senses he thrusts out,
  Sorely tormenting some, and slaying some,
    Till none but he is left and has free range
    To gaze on thee. This makes my face to change
  Into another's; while I stand all dumb,
And hear my senses clamor in their rout.

8

The thoughts are broken in my memory,
  Thou lovely Joy, whene'er I see thy face;
  When thou art near me, Love fills up the space,
Often repeating, "If death irk thee, fly."
My face shows my heart's color, verily,
  Which, fainting, seeks for any leaning-place;
  Till, in the drunken terror of disgrace,
The very stones seem to be shrieking, "Die!"
It were a grievous sin, if one should not
  Strive then to comfort my bewildered mind
    (Though merely with a simple pitying)
For the great anguish which thy scorn has wrought
  In the dead sight o' the eyes grown nearly blind,
    Which look for death as for a blessed thing.

9

At whiles (yea oftentimes) I muse over
  The quality of anguish that is mine
  Through Love: then pity makes my voice to pine,
Saying, "Is any else thus, anywhere?"
Love smiteth me, whose strength is ill to bear;
  So that of all my life is left no sign
  Except one thought; and that, because 'tis thine,
Leaves not the body but abideth there.
And then if I, whom other aid forsook,
  Would aid myself, and innocent of art
    Would fain have sight of thee as a last hope,
No sooner do I lift mine eyes to look
  Than the blood seems as shaken from my heart,
    And all my pulses beat at once and stop.

10

LADIES that have intelligence in love,
Of mine own lady I would speak with you;
Not that I hope to count her praises through,
But telling what I may, to ease my mind.
And I declare that when I speak thereof,
Love sheds such perfect sweetness over me
That if my courage failed not, certainly
To him my listeners must be all resign'd.
Wherefore I will not speak in such large kind
That mine own speech should foil me, which were base;
But only will discourse of her high grace
In these poor words, the best that I can find,
With you alone, dear dames and damozels:
'Twere ill to speak thereof with any else.

An angel, of his blessed knowledge, saith
To God: "Lord, in the world that Thou hast made,
A miracle in action is display'd,
By reason of a soul whose splendors fare
Even hither: and since Heaven requireth
Nought saving her, for her it prayeth Thee,
Thy Saints crying aloud continually."
Yet Pity still defends our earthly share
In that sweet soul; God answering thus the prayer:
"My well-belovèd, suffer that in peace
Your hope remain, while so My pleasure is,
There where one dwells who dreads the loss of her:
And who in Hell unto the doomed shall say,
'I have looked on that for which God's chosen pray.'"

My lady is desired in the high Heaven:
Wherefore, it now behoveth me to tell,
Saying: Let any maid that would be well
Esteemed keep with her: for as she goes by,
Into foul hearts a deathly chill is driven
By Love, that makes ill thought to perish there:

While any who endures to gaze on her
        Must either be ennobled, or else die.
        When one deserving to be raised so high
Is found, 'tis then her power attains its proof,
Making his heart strong for his soul's behoof
        With the full strength of meek humility.
Also this virtue owns she, by God's will:
Who speaks with her can never come to ill.

Love saith concerning her: "How chanceth it
    That flesh, which is of dust, should be thus pure?"
    Then, gazing always, he makes oath: "Forsure,
        This is a creature of God till now unknown."
She hath that paleness of the pearl that's fit
In a fair woman, so much and not more;
She is as high as Nature's skill can soar;
        Beauty is tried by her comparison.
        Whatever her sweet eyes are turned upon,
Spirits of love do issue thence in flame,
Which through their eyes who then may look on them
        Pierce to the heart's deep chamber every one.
And in her smile Love's image you may see;
Whence none can gaze upon her steadfastly.

Dear Song, I know thou wilt hold gentle speech
    With many ladies, when I send thee forth:
    Wherefore (being mindful that thou hadst thy birth
        From Love, and art a modest, simple child,)
Whomso thou meetest, say thou this to each:
"Give me good speed! To her I wend along
In whose much strength my weakness is made strong."
        And if, i' the end, thou wouldst not be beguiled
        Of all thy labor seek not the defiled
And common sort; but rather choose to be
Where man and woman dwell in courtesy.
        So to the road thou shalt be reconciled,
And find the Lady, and with the lady, Love.
Commend thou me to each, as doth behove.

11

Love and the gentle heart are one same thing,
  Even as the wise man in his ditty saith:
  Each, of itself, would be such life in death
As rational soul bereft of reasoning.
'Tis Nature makes them when she loves: a king
  Love is, whose palace where he sojourneth
  Is called the Heart; there draws he quiet breath
At first, with brief or longer slumbering.
Then beauty seen in virtuous womankind
  Will make the eyes desire, and through the heart
    Send the desiring of the eyes again;
Where often it abides so long enshrin'd
  That Love at length out of his sleep will start.
    And women feel the same for worthy men.

12

My lady carries love within her eyes;
  All that she looks on is made pleasanter;
  Upon her path men turn to gaze at her;
He whom she greeteth feels his heart to rise,
And droops his troubled visage, full of sighs,
  And of his evil heart is then aware:
  Hate loves, and pride becomes a worshiper.
O women, help to praise her in somewise.
Humbleness, and the hope that hopeth well,
  By speech of hers into the mind are brought,
    And who beholds is blessèd oftenwhiles.
    The look she hath when she a little smiles
  Cannot be said, nor holden in the thought;
'Tis such a new and gracious miracle.

13

a

You that thus wear a modest countenance
  With lids weigh'd down by the heart's heaviness,
  Whence come you, that among you every face

Appears the same, for its pale troubled glance?
Have you beheld my lady's face, perchance,
  Bow'd with the grief that Love makes full of grace?
  Say now, "This thing is thus;" as my heart says,
Marking your grave and sorrowful advance.
And if indeed you come from where she sighs
  And mourns, may it please you (for his heart's relief)
    To tell how it fares with her unto him
Who knows that you have wept, seeing your eyes,
  And is so grieved with looking on your grief
    That his heart trembles and his sight grows dim?

b

Canst thou indeed be he that still would sing
  Of our dear lady unto none but us?
  For though thy voice confirms that it is thus,
Thy visage might another witness bring.
And wherefore is thy grief so sore a thing
  That grieving thou mak'st others dolorous?
  Hast thou too seen her weep, that thou from us
Canst not conceal thine inward sorrowing?
Nay, leave our woe to us: let us alone:
  'Twere sin if one should strive to soothe our woe,
    For in her weeping we have heard her speak:
Also her look's so full of her heart's moan
  That they who should behold her, looking so,
    Must fall aswoon, feeling all life grow weak.

14

A very pitiful lady, very young,
  Exceeding rich in human sympathies,
    Stood by, what time I clamor'd upon Death
And at the wild words wandering on my tongue
  And at the piteous look within mine eyes
    She was affrighted, that sobs choked her breath.
    So by her weeping where I lay beneath,
Some other gentle ladies came to know
My state, and made her go:

Afterward, bending themselves over me,
One said, "Awaken thee!"
And one, "What thing thy sleep disquieteth?"
With that, my soul woke up from its eclipse,
The while my lady's name rose to my lips:

But utter'd in a voice so sob-broken,
So feeble with the agony of tears,
That I alone might hear it in my heart;
And though that look was on my visage then
Which he who is ashamed so plainly wears,
Love made that I through shame held not apart,
But gazed upon them. And my hue was such
That they look'd at each other and thought of death;
Saying under their breath
Most tenderly, "O let us comfort him:"
Then unto me: "What dream
Was thine, that it hath shaken thee so much?"
And when I was a little comforted,
"This, ladies, was the dream I dreamt," I said.

"I was a-thinking how life fails with us
Suddenly after such a little while;
When Love sobb'd in my heart, which is his home.
Whereby my spirit wax'd so dolorous
That in myself I said, with sick recoil:
'Yea, to my lady too this Death must come.'
And therewithal such a bewilderment
Possess'd me, that I shut mine eyes for peace;
And in my brain did cease
Order of thought, and every healthful thing.
Afterwards, wandering
Amid a swarm of doubts that came and went,
Some certain women's faces hurried by,
And shrieked to me, 'Thou too shalt die, shalt die!'

"Then saw I many broken hinted sights
In the uncertain state I stepp'd into.
Meseem'd to be I know not in what place,

Where ladies through the streets, like mournful lights,
Ran with loose hair, and eyes that frighten'd you,
By their own terror, and a pale amaze:
The while, little by little, as I thought,
The sun ceased, and the stars began to gather,
And each wept at the other;
And birds dropp'd in mid-flight out of the sky;
And earth shook suddenly;
And I was 'ware of one, hoarse and tired out,
Who ask'd of me: 'Hast thou not heard it said? . . .
Thy lady, she that was so fair, is dead.'

"Then lifting up mine eyes, as the tears came,
I saw the Angels, like a rain of manna,
In a long flight flying back Heavenward;
Having a little cloud in front of them,
After the which they went and said, 'Hosanna';
And if they had said more, you should have heard.
Then Love said, 'Now shall all things be made clear:
Come and behold our lady where she lies.'
These 'wildering phantasies.
Then carried me to see my lady dead.
Even as I there was led,
Her ladies with a veil were covering her;
And with her was such very humbleness
That she appeared to say, 'I am at peace.'

15

I FELT a spirit of love begin to stir
Within my heart, long time unfelt till then;
And saw Love coming towards me fair and fain,
(That I scarce knew him for his joyful cheer),
Saying, "Be now indeed my worshiper!"
And in his speech he laugh'd and laugh'd again.
Then, while it was his pleasure to remain,
I chanced to look the way he had drawn near

And saw the Ladies Joan and Beatrice
  Approach me, this the other following,
    One and a second marvel instantly.
And even as now my memory speaketh this,
  Love spake it then: "The first is christen'd Spring;
    The second Love, she is so like to me."

16

My lady looks so gentle and so pure
  When yielding salutation by the way,
  That the tongue trembles and has nought to say,
And the eyes, which fain would see, may not endure.
And still, amid the praise she hears secure,
  She walks with humbleness for her array;
  Seeming a creature sent from Heaven to stay
On earth, and show a miracle made sure.
She is so pleasant in the eyes of men
That through the sight the inmost heart doth gain
  A sweetness which needs proof to know it by:
And from between her lips there seems to move
A soothing essence that is full of love,
  Saying for ever to the spirit, "Sigh!"

17

For certain he hath seen all perfectness
  Who among other ladies hath seen mine:
  They that go with her humbly should combine
To thank their God for such peculiar grace.
So perfect is the beauty of her face
  That it begets in no wise any sign
  Of envy, but draws round her a clear line
Of love, and blessed faith, and gentleness.
Merely the sight of her makes all things bow:
  Not she herself alone is holier
    Than all; but hers, through her, are raised above.
From all her acts such lovely graces flow
  That truly one may never think of her
    Without a passion of exceeding love.

18

Love hath so long possessed me for his own
  And made his lordship so familiar
That he, who at first irked me, is now grown
  Unto my heart as its best secrets are.
  And thus, when he in such sore wise doth mar
My life that all its strength seems gone from it,
  Mine inmost being then feels throughly quit
  Of anguish, and all evil keeps afar.
Love also gathers to such power in me
  That my sighs speak, each one a grievous thing,
  Always soliciting
My lady's salutation piteously.
Whenever she beholds me, it is so,
Who is more sweet than any words can show.

19

The eyes that weep for pity of the heart
  Have wept so long that their grief languisheth,
    And they have no more tears to weep withal:
And now, if I would ease me of a part
  Of what, little by little, leads to death,
    It must be done by speech, or not at all.
    And because often, thinking, I recall
How it was pleasant, ere she went afar,
  To talk of her with you, kind damozels,
  I talk with no one else,
But only with such hearts as women's are.
  And I will say,—still sobbing as speech fails,—
That she hath gone to Heaven suddenly,
And hath left Love below, to mourn with me.

Beatrice is gone up into high Heaven,
  The kingdom where the angels are at peace;
    And lives with them: and to her friends is dead.
Not by the frost of winter was she driven
  Away, like others; nor by summer-heats;
    But through a perfect gentleness, instead.
    For from the lamp of her meek lowlihead

Such an exceeding glory went up hence
  That it woke wonder in the Eternal Sire,
  Until a sweet desire
Entered Him for that lovely excellence,
  So that He bade her to Himself aspire;
Counting this weary and most evil place
Unworthy of a thing so full of grace.

Wonderfully out of the beautiful form
  Soared her clear spirit, waxing glad the while;
    And is in its first home, there where it is.
Who speaks thereof, and feels not the tears warm
  Upon his face, must have become so vile
    As to be dead to all sweet sympathies.
    Out upon him! an abject wretch like this
May not imagine anything of her,—
  He needs no bitter tears for his relief.
  But sighing comes, and grief,
And the desire to find no comforter,
  (Save only Death, who makes all sorrow brief,)
To him who for a while turns in his thought
How she hath been among us, and is not.

With sighs my bosom always laboreth
  In thinking, as I do continually,
    Of her for whom my heart now breaks apace;
And very often when I think of death,
  Such a great inward longing comes to me
    That it will change the color of my face;
    And, if the idea settles in its place,
All my limbs shake as with an ague-fit:
  Till, starting up in wild bewilderment,
  I do become so shent
That I go forth, lest folk misdoubt of it.
  Afterward, calling with a sore lament
On Beatrice, I ask, 'Canst thou be dead?'
And calling on her, I am comforted.

Grief with its tears, and anguish with its sighs,
  Come to me now whene'er I am alone;
    So that I think the sight of me gives pain.
And what my life hath been, that living dies,
  Since for my lady the New Birth's begun,
    I have not any language to explain.
    And so, dear ladies, though my heart were fain,
I scarce could tell indeed how I am thus.
  All joy is with my bitter life at war;
  Yea, I am fallen so far
That all men seem to say, 'Go out from us,'
  Eyeing my cold white lips, how dead they are.
But she, though I be bowed unto the dust,
Watches me; and will guerdon me, I trust.

Weep, pitiful Song of mine, upon thy way,
  To the dames going and the damozels
  For whom and for none else
Thy sisters have made music many a day.
Thou, that art very sad and not as they,
  Go dwell thou with them as a mourner dwells.

20

Stay now with me, and listen to my sighs,
  Ye piteous hearts, as pity bids ye do.
  Mark how they force their way out and press through:
If they be once pent up, the whole life dies.
Seeing that now indeed my weary eyes
  Oftener refuse than I can tell to you
  (Even though my endless grief is ever new,)
To weep and let the smothered anguish rise.

Also in sighing ye shall hear me call
  On her whose blessed presence doth enrich
    The only home that well befitteth her:
And ye shall hear a bitter scorn of all
  Sent from the inmost of my spirit in speech
    That mourns its joy and its joy's minister.

21

WHATEVER while the thought comes over me
That I may not again
Behold that lady whom I mourn for now,
About my heart my mind brings constantly
So much of extreme pain
That I say, Soul of mine, why stayest thou?
Truly the anguish, soul, that we must bow
Beneath, until we win out of this life,
Gives me full oft a fear that trembleth:
So that I call on Death
Even as on Sleep one calleth after strife,
Saying, Come unto me. Life showeth grim
And bare; and if one dies, I envy him,

For ever, among all my sighs which burn,
There is a piteous speech
That clamors upon death continually:
Yea, unto him doth my whole spirit turn
Since first his hand did reach
My lady's life with most foul cruelty.
But from the height of woman's fairness, she,
Going up from us with the joy we had,
Grew perfectly and spiritually fair;
That so she treads even there
A light of Love which makes the Angels glad,
And even unto their subtle minds can bring
A certain awe of profound marveling.

22

THAT lady of all gentle memories
Had lighted on my soul;—whose new abode
Lies now, as it was well ordained of God,
Among the poor in heart, where Mary is.
Love, knowing that dear image to be his,
Woke up within the sick heart sorrow-bow'd,
Unto the sighs which are its weary load

Saying, 'Go forth.' And they went forth, I wis;
Forth went they from my breast that throbbed and ached;
With such a pang as oftentimes will bathe
Mine eyes with tears when I am left alone.
And still those sighs which drew the heaviest breath
Came whispering thus: 'O noble intellect!
It is a year to-day that thou art gone.'

23

Mine eyes beheld the blessed pity spring
Into thy countenance immediately
A while agone, when thou beheldst in me
The sickness only hidden grief can bring;
And then I knew thou wast considering
How abject and forlorn my life must be;
And I became afraid that thou shouldst see
My weeping, and account it a base thing.
Therefore I went out from thee; feeling how
The tears were straightway loosened at my heart
Beneath thine eyes' compassionate control.
And afterwards I said within my soul:
'Lo! with this lady dwells the counterpart
Of the same Love who holds me weeping now.'

24

Love's pallor and the semblance of deep ruth
Were never yet shown forth so perfectly
In any lady's face, chancing to see
Grief's miserable countenance uncouth,
As in thine, lady, they have sprung to soothe,
When in mine anguish thou hast looked on me;
Until sometimes it seems as if, through thee,
My heart might almost wander from its truth.
Yet so it is, I cannot hold mine eyes
From gazing very often upon thine
In the sore hope to shed those tears they keep;

And at such time, thou mak'st the pent tears rise
  Even to the brim, till the eyes waste and pine;
    Yet cannot they, while thou art present, weep.

25

The very bitter weeping that ye made
  So long a time together, eyes of mine,
  Was wont to make the tears of pity shine
In other eyes full oft, as I have said.
But now this thing were scarce rememberèd
  If I, on my part, foully would combine
  With you, and not recall each ancient sign
Of grief, and her for whom your tears were shed.
It is your fickleness that doth betray
  My mind to fears, and makes me tremble thus
    What while a lady greets me with her eyes.
Except by death, we must not any way
  Forget our lady who is gone from us.
    So far doth my heart utter, and then sighs.

26

A gentle thought there is will often start,
  Within my secret self, to speech of thee:
  Also of Love it speaks so tenderly
That much in me consents and takes its part.
'And what is this,' the soul saith to the heart,
  'That cometh thus to comfort thee and me,
  And thence where it would dwell, thus potently
Can drive all other thoughts by its strange art?'
And the heart answers: 'Be no more at strife
  'Twixt doubt and doubt: this is Love's messenger
    And speaketh but his words, from him received;
And all the strength it owns and all the life
  It draweth from the gentle eyes of her
    Who, looking on our grief, hath often grieved.'

27

Woe's me! by dint of all these sighs that come
Forth of my heart, its endless grief to prove,
Mine eyes are conquered, so that even to move
Their lids for greeting is grown troublesome,
They wept so long that now they are grief's home
And count their tears all laughter far above;
They wept till they are circled now by Love
With a red circle in sign of martyrdom.
These musings, and the sighs they bring from me,
Are grown at last so constant and so sore
That love swoons in my spirit with faint breath;
Hearing in those sad sounds continually
The most sweet name that my dead lady bore,
With many grievous words touching her death.

28

Ye prilgrim-folk, advancing pensively
As if in thought of distant things, I pray,
Is your own land indeed so far away—
As by your aspect it would seem to be—
That this our heavy sorrow leaves you free
Though passing through the mournful town midway;
Like unto men that understand to-day
Nothing at all of her great misery?
Yet if ye will but stay, whom I accost,
And listen to my words a little space,
At going ye shall mourn with a loud voice.
It is her Beatrice that she hath lost;
Of whom the least word spoken holds such grace
That men weep hearing it, and have no choice.

29

Beyond the sphere which spreads to widest space
Now soars the sigh that my heart sends above;
A new perception born of grieving Love
Guideth it upward the untrodden ways.

When it hath reached unto the end, and stays,
It sees a lady round whom splendors move
In homage; till, by the great light thereof
Abashed, the pilgrim spirit stands at gaze.
It sees her such, that when it tells me this
Which it hath seen, I understand it not,
It hath a speech so subtile and so fine.
And yet I know its voice within my thought
Often remembereth me of Beatrice:
So that I understand it, ladies mine.

(*D. G. Rossetti*)

SONNET

TO GUIDO CAVALCANTI

GUIDO, I would that Lapo, thou, and I,
Led by some strong enchantment, might ascend
A magic ship, whose charmèd sails should fly
With winds at will, where'er our thoughts might wend,
And that no change, nor any evil chance,
Should mar our joyous voyage; but it might be
That even satiety should still enhance
Between our hearts their strict community,
And that the bounteous wizard then would place
Vanna and Bice and my gentle love,
Companions of our wandering, and would grace
With passionate talk, wherever we might rove,
Our time, and each were as content and free
As I believe that thou and I should be.

(*Percy Bysshe Shelley*)

SONNET

TO BRUNETTO LATINI
Sent with the Vita Nuova

MASTER BRUNETTO, this my little maid
Is come to spend her Easter-tide with you:
Not that she reckons feasting as her due,—

Whose need is hardly to be fed, but read.
Not in a hurry can her sense be weigh'd,
  Nor mid the jests of any noisy crew:
  Ah! and she wants a little coaxing too
Before she'll get into another's head.
But if you do not find her meaning clear,
  You've many Brother Alberts hard at hand,
    Whose wisdom will respond to any call.
Consult with them and do not laugh at her;
  And if she still is hard to understand,
    Apply to Master Janus last of all.

(*D. G. Rossetti*)

SONNET

Of Beatrice de' Portinari, on All Saints' Day

Last All Saints' holy-day, even now gone by,
  I met a gathering of damozels:
  She that came first, as one doth who excels,
Had Love with her, bearing her company:
A flame burned forward through her steadfast eye,
  As when in living fire spirit dwells:
  So, gazing with the boldness which prevails
O'er doubt, I knew an angel visibly.
As she passed on, she bowed her mild approof
  And salutation to all men of worth
Lifting the soul to solemn thoughts aloof.
  In Heaven itself that lady had her birth,
I think, and is with us for our behoof:
  Blessed are they who meet her on the earth.

(*D. G. Rossetti*)

SONNET

To certain Ladies; when Beatrice was lamenting her Father's Death

Whence come you, all of you so sorrowful?
  An it may please you, speak for courtesy.
  I fear for my dear lady's sake, lest she

Have made you to return thus filled with dule.
O gentle ladies, be not hard to school
  In gentleness, but to some pause agree,
  And something of my lady say to me,
For with a little my desire is full.
Howbeit it be a heavy thing to hear:
  For Love now utterly has thrust me forth,
With hand for ever lifted, striking fear.
  See if I be not worn unto the earth;
Yea, and my spirit must fail from me here,
    If, when you speak, your words are of no worth.

(*D. G. Rossetti*)

SONNET

To the same Ladies; with their Answer

Ye ladies, walking past me piteous-eyed,
  Who is the lady that lies prostrate here?
  Can this be even she my heart holds dear?
Nay, if it be so, speak, and nothing hide.
Her very aspect seems itself beside,
  And all her features of such altered cheer
  That to my thinking they do not appear
Hers who makes others seem beatified.

'If thou forget to know our lady thus,
  Whom grief o'ercomes, we wonder in no wise,
For also the same thing befalleth us.
  Yet if thou watch the movement of her eyes,
Of her thou shalt be straightway conscious.
  O weep no more; thou art all wan with sighs.'

(*D. G. Rossetti*)

BALLATA

He will gaze upon Beatrice

Because mine eyes can never have their fill
Of looking at my lady's lovely face,
  I will so fix my gaze
That I may become blessed beholding her.

Even as an angel, up at his great height
Standing amid the light,
Becometh blessed by only seeing God:—
So, though I be a simple earthly wight,
Yet none the less I might,
Beholding her who is my heart's dear load,
Be blessed, and in the spirit soar abroad.
Such power abideth in that gracious one;
Albeit felt of none
Save of him who, desiring, honors her.

(D. G. Rossetti)

CANZONE

He beseeches Death for the Life of Beatrice

DEATH, since I find not one with whom to grieve,
Nor whom this grief of mine may move to tears,
Whereso I be or whitherso I turn:
Since it is thou who in my soul wilt leave
No single joy, but chill'st it with just fears
And makest it in fruitless hopes to burn:
Since thou, Death, and thou only, canst decern
Wealth to my life, or want, at thy free choice:—
It is to thee that I lift up my voice,
Bowing my face that's like a face just dead.
I come to thee, as to one pitying,
In grief for that sweet rest which nought can bring
Again, if thou but once be entered
Into her life whom my heart cherishes
Even as the only portal of its peace.

Death, how most sweet the peace is that thy grace
Can grant to me, and that I pray thee for,
Thou easily mayst know by a sure sign,
If in mine eyes thou look a little space
And read in them the hidden dread they store,—
If upon all thou look which proves me thine.
Since the fear only maketh me to pine
After this sort,—what will mine anguish be

When her eyes close, of dreadful verity,
  In whose light is the light of mine own eyes?
But now I know that thou wouldst have my life
As hers, and joy'st thee in my fruitless strife.
  Yet I do think this which I feel implies
That soon, when I would die to flee from pain,
I shall find none by whom I may be slain.

Death, if indeed thou smite this gentle one
  Whose outward worth but tells the intellect
    How wondrous is the miracle within,—
Thou biddest Virtue rise up and begone,
  Thou dost away with Mercy's best effect,
    Thou spoil'st the mansion of God's sojourning.
    Yea, unto nought her beauty thou dost bring
Which is above all other beauties, even
In so much as befitteth one whom Heaven
  Sent upon earth in token of its own.
Thou dost break through the perfect trust which hath
Been alway her companion in Love's path:
  The light once darkened which was hers alone,
Love needs must say to them he ruleth o'er,
'I have lost the noble banner that I bore.'

Death, have some pity then for all the ill
  Which cannot choose but happen if she die,
    And which will be the sorest ever known.
Slacken the string, if so it be thy will,
  That the sharp arrow leave it not,—thereby
    Sparing her life, which if it flies is flown.
    O Death, for God's sake, be some pity shown!
Restrain within thyself, even at its height,
The cruel wrath which moveth thee to smite
  Her in whom God hath set so much of grace.
Show now some ruth if 'tis a thing thou hast!
I seem to see Heaven's gate, that is shut fast,
  Open, and angels filling all the space
About me,—come to fetch her soul whose laud
Is sung by saints and angels before God.

Song, thou must surely see how fine a thread
 This is that my last hope is holden by,
  And what I should be brought to without her.
Therefore for thy plain speech and lowlihead
 Make thou no pause: but go immediately,
  Knowing thyself for my heart's minister,
  And with that very meek and piteous air
Thou hast, stand up before the face of Death,
To wrench away the bar that prisoneth
 And win unto the place of the good fruit.
And if indeed thou shake by thy soft voice
Death's mortal purpose,—haste thee and rejoice
 Our lady with the issue of thy suit.
So yet awhile our earthly nights and days
Shall keep the blessed spirit that I praise.

(*D. G. Rossetti*)

SONNET

On the 9th of June 1290

Upon a day, came Sorrow in to me,
 Saying, 'I've come to stay with thee a while;'
 And I perceived that she had ushered Bile
And Pain into my house for company.
Wherefore I said, 'Go forth—away with thee!'
 But like a Greek she answered, full of guile,
 And went on arguing in an easy style.
Then, looking, I saw Love come silently,
Habited in black raiment, smooth and new,
 Having a black hat set upon his hair;
And certainly the tears he shed were true.
 So that I asked, 'What ails thee, trifler?'
Answering he said: 'A grief to be gone through;
 For our own lady's dying, brother dear.'

(*D. G. Rossetti*)

SONNET

Of Beauty and Duty

Two ladies to the summit of my mind
  Have clomb, to hold an argument of love.
  The one has wisdom with her from above,
For every noblest virtue well designed:
The other, beauty's tempting power refined
  And the high charm of perfect grace approve:
  And I, as my sweet Master's will doth move,
At feet of both their favors am reclined.
Beauty and Duty in my soul keep strife,
  At question if the heart such course can take
    And 'twixt the two ladies hold its love complete.
    The fount of gentle speech yields answer meet,
  That Beauty may be loved for gladness sake,
And Duty in the lofty ends of life.

(*D. G. Rossetti*)

SESTINA

Of the Lady Pietra degli Scrovigni

To the dim light and the large circle of shade
I have clomb, and to the whitening of the hills,
There where we see no color in the grass.
Natheless my longing loses not its green,
It has so taken root in the hard stone
Which talks and hears as though it were a lady.

Utterly frozen is this youthful lady,
Even as the snow that lies within the shade;
For she is no more moved than is the stone
By the sweet season which makes warm the hills
And alters them afresh from white to green
Covering their sides again with flowers and grass.

When on her hair she sets a crown of grass
The thought has no more room for other lady,
Because she weaves the yellow with the green

So well that Love sits down there in the shade,—
Love who has shut me in among low hills
Faster than between walls of granite-stone.

She is more bright than is a precious stone;
The wound she gives may not be healed with grass:
I therefore have fled far o'er plains and hills
For refuge from so dangerous a lady;
But from her sunshine nothing can give shade,—
Not any hill, nor wall, nor summer-green.

A while ago, I saw her dressed in green,—
So fair, she might have wakened in a stone
This love which I do feel even for her shade;
And therefore, as one woos a graceful lady,
I wooed her in a field that was all grass
Girdled about with very lofty hills.

Yet shall the streams turn back and climb the hills
Before Love's flame in this damp wood and green
Burn, as it burns within a youthful lady,
For my sake, who would sleep away in stone
My life, or feed like beasts upon the grass,
Only to see her garments cast a shade.

How dark soe'er the hills throw out their shade,
Under her summer-green the beautiful lady
Covers it, like a stone cover'd in grass.

(*D. G. Rossetti*)

SONNET

To the Lady Pietra degli Scrovigni

My curse be on the day when first I saw
The brightness in those treacherous eyes of thine,—
The hour when from my heart thou cam'st to draw
My soul away, that both might fail and pine:
My curse be on the skill that smooth'd each line

Of my vain songs,—the music and just law
  Of art, by which it was my dear design
That the whole world should yield thee love and awe.
Yea, let me curse mine own obduracy,
  Which firmly holds what doth itself confound—
    To wit, thy fair perverted face of scorn:
    For whose sake Love is oftentimes forsworn
So that men mock at him: but most at me
  Who would hold fortune's wheel and turn it round.

(D. G. Rossetti)

Cino da Pistoia

1270-1336

Sonnet

TO DANTE ALIGHIERI

He interprets Dante's Dream, related in the first Sonnet of the Vita Nuova

Each lover's longing leads him naturally
  Unto his lady's heart his heart to show;
  And this it is that Love would have thee know
By the strange vision which he sent to thee.
With thy heart therefore, flaming outwardly,
  In humble guise he fed thy lady so,
  Who long had lain in slumber, from all woe
Folded within a mantle silently.
Also, in coming, Love might not repress
  His joy, to yield thee thy desire achieved,
    Whence heart should unto heart true service bring.
But understanding the great lovesickness
  Which in thy lady's bosom was conceived,
    He pitied her, and wept in vanishing.

(D. G. Rossetti)

Sonnet

TO DANTE ALIGHIERI

He conceives of some Compensation in Death

Dante, whenever this thing happeneth,—
That Love's desire is quite bereft of Hope,
(Seeking in vain at ladies' eyes some scope
Of joy, through what the heart for ever saith,)—
I ask thee, can amends be made by Death?
Is such sad pass the last extremity?—
Or may the Soul that never feared to die
Then in another body draw new breath?
Lo! thus it is through her who governs all
Below,—that I, who entered at her door,
Now at her dreadful window must fare forth.
Yea, and I think through her it doth befall
That even ere yet the road is traveled o'er
My bones are weary and life is nothing worth.

(D. G. Rossetti)

MADRIGAL

To his Lady Selvaggia Vergiolesi; likening his Love to a search for Gold

I am all bent to glean the golden ore
Little by little from the river-bed;
Hoping the day to see
When Crœsus shall be conquered in my store.
Therefore, still sifting where the sands are spread,
I labor patiently:
Till, thus intent on this thing and no more,—
If to a vein of silver I were led,
It scarce could gladden me.
And, seeing that no joy's so warm i' the core
As this whereby the heart is comforted
And the desire set free,—

Therefore thy bitter love is still my scope,
  Lady, from whom it is my life's sore theme
More painfully to sift the grains of hope
  Than gold out of that stream.

(*D. G. Rossetti*)

SONNET

To Love, in great Bitterness

O Love, O thou that, for my fealty,
  Only in torment dost thy power employ,
  Give me, for God's sake, something of thy joy,
That I may learn what good there is in thee.
Yea, for, if thou art glad with grieving me,
  Surely my very life thou shalt destroy
  When thou renew'st my pain, because the joy
Must then be wept for with the misery.
He that had never sense of good, nor sight,
  Esteems his ill estate but natural,
    Which so is lightlier borne: his case is mine.
    But, if thou wouldst uplift me for a sign,
  Bidding me drain the curse and know it all,
I must a little taste its opposite.

(*D. G. Rossetti*)

SONNET

Death is not without but within him

This fairest lady, who, as well I wot,
  Found entrance by her beauty to my soul,
  Pierced through mine eyes my heart, which erst was
    whole,
Sorely, yet makes as though she knew it not;
Nay, turns upon me now, to anger wrought;
  Dealing me harshness for my pain's best dole,
  And is so changed by her own wrath's control,

That I go thence, in my distracted thought
Content to die; and, mourning, cry abroad
On Death, as upon one afar from me;
But Death makes answer from within my heart.
Then, hearing her so hard at hand to be,
I do commend my spirit unto God;
Saying to her too, 'Ease and peace thou art.'

(*D. G. Rossetti*)

SONNET

A Trance of Love

VANQUISHED and weary was my soul in me,
And my heart gasped after its much lament,
When sleep at length the painful languor sent.
And, as I slept (and wept incessantly),—
Through the keen fixedness of memory
Which I had cherished ere my tears were spent,
I passed to a new trance of wonderment;
Wherein a visible spirit I could see,
Which caught me up, and bore me to a place
Where my most gentle lady was alone;
And still before us a fire seemed to move,
Out of the which methought there came a moan
Uttering, 'Grace, a little season, grace!
I am of one that hath the wings of Love.'

(*D. G. Rossetti*)

SONNET

Of the Grave of Selvaggia, on the Monte della Sambuca

I WAS upon the high and blessed mound,
And kissed, long worshiping, the stones and grass,
There on the hard stones prostrate, where, alas!
That pure one laid her forehead in the ground.
Then were the springs of gladness sealed and bound,
The day that unto Death's most bitter pass
My sick heart's lady turned her feet, who was
Already in her gracious life renown'd.

So in that place I spake to Love, and cried:
'O sweet my god, I am one whom Death may claim
Hence to be his; for lo! my heart lies here.'
Anon, because my Master lent no ear,
Departing, still I called Selvaggia's name.
So with my moan I left the mountain-side.

(*D. G. Rossetti*)

CANZONE

His Lament for Selvaggia

Ay me, alas! the beautiful bright hair
That shed reflected gold
O'er the green growths on either side of the way:
Ay me! the lovely look, open and fair,
Which my heart's core doth hold
With all else of that best remembered day;
Ay me! the face made gay
With joy that Love confers;
Ay me! that smile of hers
Where whiteness as of snow was visible
Among the roses at all seasons red!
Ay me! and was this well,
O Death, to let me live when she is dead?

(*D. G. Rossetti*)

Dante da Maiano

c. 1300

Sonnet

TO DANTE ALIGHIERI

He interprets Dante Alighieri's Dream, related in the First Sonnet of the Vita Nuova

Of that wherein thou art a questioner
Considering, I make answer briefly thus,
Good friend, in wit but little prosperous:
And from my words the truth thou shalt infer,—

So hearken to thy dream's interpreter.
If, sound of frame, thou soundly canst discuss
In reason,—then, to expel this overplus
Of vapors which hath made thy speech to err,
See that thou lave and purge thy stomach soon.
But if thou art afflicted with disease,
Know that I count it mere delirium.
Thus of my thought I write thee back the sum:
Nor my conclusions can be changed from these
Till to the leech thy water I have shown.

(*D. G. Rossetti*)

SONNET

He craves interpreting of a Dream of his

Thou that art wise, let wisdom minister
Unto my dream, that it be understood.
To wit: A lady, of her body fair,
And whom my heart approves in womanhood,
Bestowed on me a wreath of flowers, fair-hued
And green in leaf, with gentle loving air;
After the which, meseemed I was stark nude
Save for a smock of hers that I did wear.
Whereat, good friend, my courage gat such growth
That to mine arms I took her tenderly:
With no rebuke the beauty laughed unloath,
And as she laughed I kissed continually.
I say no more, for that I pledged mine oath,
And that my mother, who is dead, was by.

(*D. G. Rossetti*)

Cecco Angiolieri, da Siena

c. 1300

Sonnet

TO DANTE ALIGHIERI

On the last Sonnet of the Vita Nuova

Dante Alighieri, Cecco, your good friend
And servant, gives you greeting as his lord,
And prays you for the sake of Love's accord,

(Love being the Master before whom you bend,)
That you will pardon him if he offend,
Even as your gentle heart can well afford.
All that he wants to say is just one word
Which partly chides your sonnet at the end.
For where the measure changes, first you say
You do not understand the gentle speech
A spirit made touching your Beatrice:
And next you tell your ladies how, straightway,
You understand it. Wherefore (look you) each
Of these your words the other's sense denies.

(*D. G. Rossetti*)

SONNET

He will not be too deeply in Love

I AM enamored, and yet not so much
But that I'd do without it easily;
And my own mind thinks all the more of me
That Love has not quite penned me in his hutch.
Enough if for his sake I dance and touch
The lute, and serve his servants cheerfully:
An overdose is worse than none would be:
Love is no lord of mine, I'm proud to vouch.
So let no woman who is born conceive
That I'll be her liege slave, as I see some,
Be she as fair and dainty as she will.
Too much of love makes idiots, I believe:
I like not any fashion that turns glum
The heart, and makes the visage sick and ill.

(*D. G. Rossetti*)

SONNET

Of Love in Men and Devils

THE man who feels not, more or less, somewhat
Of love in all the years his life goes round
Should be denied a grave in holy ground

Except with usurers who will bate no groat;
Nor he himself should count himself a jot
Less wretched than the meanest beggar found.
Also the man who in Love's robe is gown'd
May say that Fortune smiles upon his lot.
Seeing how love has such nobility
That if it entered in the lord of Hell
'Twould rule him more than his fire's ancient [sting;
He should be glorified to eternity,
And all his life be always glad and well
As is a wanton woman in the spring.

(*D. G. Rossetti*)

SONNET

Of Love, in honor of his Mistress Becchina

Whatever good is naturally done
Is born of Love as fruit is born of flower:
By Love all good is brought to its full power:
Yea, Love does more than this; for he finds none
So coarse but from his touch some grace is won,
And the poor wretch is altered in an hour.
So let it be decreed that Death devour
The beast who says that Love's a thing to shun.
A man's just worth the good that he can hold,
And where no love is found, no good is there;
On that there's nothing that I would not stake.
So now, my Sonnet, go as you are told
To lovers and their sweethearts everywhere,
And say I made you for Becchina's sake.

(*D. G. Rossetti*)

SONNET

Of Becchina, the Shoemaker's daughter

Why, if Becchina's heart were diamond,
And all the other parts of her were steel,
As cold to love as snows when they congeal

In lands to which the sun may not get round;
And if her father were a giant crown'd
  And not a donkey born to stitching shoes,
  Or I were but an ass myself;—to use
Such harshness, scarce could to her praise redound.
Yet if she'd only for a minute hear,
  And I could speak if only pretty well,
  I'd let her know that I'm her happiness;
That I'm her life should also be made clear,
  With other things that I've no need to tell;
    And then I feel quite sure she'd answer Yes.

(*D. G. Rossetti*)

SONNET

Of the 20th June 1291

I'm full of everything I do not want,
  And have not that wherein I should find ease;
  For alway till Becchina brings me peace
The heavy heart I bear must toil and pant;
That so all written paper would prove scant
  (Though in its space the Bible you might squeeze,)
  To say how like the flames of furnaces
I burn, remembering what she used to grant.
Because the stars are fewer in heaven's span
  Than all those kisses wherewith I kept tune
    All in an instant (I who now have none!)
Upon her mouth (I and no other man!)
  So sweetly on the twentieth day of June
    In the new year twelve hundred and ninety-one.

(*D. G. Rossetti*)

SONNET

Of Becchina in a Rage

When I behold Becchina in a rage,
  Just like a little lad I trembling stand
  Whose master tells him to hold out his hand.

Had I a lion's heart, the sight would wage
Such war against it, that in that sad stage
I'd wish my birth might never have been plann'd,
And curse the day and hour that I was bann'd
With such a plague for my life's heritage.
Yet even if I should sell me to the Fiend,
I must so manage matters in some way
That for her rage I may not care a fig;
Or else from death I cannot long be screen'd.
So I'll not blink the fact, but plainly say
It's time I got my valor to grow big.

(D. G. Rossetti)

SONNET

In absence from Becchina

My heart's so heavy with a hundred things
That I feel dead a hundred times a-day;
Yet death would be the least of sufferings,
For life's all suffering save what's slept away;
Though even in sleep there is no dream but brings
From dream-land such dull torture as it may.
And yet one moment would pluck out these stings,
If for one moment she were mine to-day
Who gives my heart the anguish that it has.
Each thought that seeks my heart for its abode
Becomes a wan and sorrow-stricken guest:
Sorrow has brought me to so sad a pass
That men look sad to meet me on the road;
Nor any road is mine that leads to rest.

(D. G. Rossetti)

SONNET

He rails against Dante, who had censured his homage to Becchina

Dante Alighieri in Becchina's praise
Won't have me sing and bears him like my lord.
He's but a pinchbeck florin, on my word;

Sugar he seems, but salt's in all his ways;
He looks like wheaten bread, who's bread of maize;
He's but a sty, though like a tower in height;
A falcon, till you find that he's a kite;
Call him a cock!—a hen's more like his case.
Go now to Florence, Sonnet of my own,
And there with dames and maids hold pretty parles,
And say that all he is doth only seem.
And I meanwhile will make him better known
Unto the Court of Provence, good King Charles;
And in this way we'll singe his skin for him.

(D. G. Rossetti)

SONNET

Of all he would do

If I were fire, I'd burn the world away;
If I were wind, I'd turn my storms thereon;
If I were water, I'd soon let it drown;
If I were God, I'd sink it from the day;
If I were Pope, I'd never feel quite gay
Until there was no peace beneath the sun;
If I were Emperor, what would I have done?—
I'd lop men's heads all round in my own way.
If I were Death, I'd look my father up;
If I were life, I'd run away from him;
And treat my mother to like calls and runs.
If I were Cecco (and that's all my hope),
I'd pick the nicest girls to suit my whim,
And other folk should get the ugly ones.

(D. G. Rossetti)

SONNET

He is past all Help

For a thing done, repentance is no good,
Nor to say after, Thus would I have done:
In life, what's left behind is vainly rued;
So let a man get used his heart to shun;

For on his legs he hardly may be stood
  Again, if once his fall be well begun.
But to show wisdom's what I never could;
  So where I itch I scratch now, and all's one.
I'm down, and cannot rise in any way;
  For not a creature of my nearest kin
    Would hold me out a hand that I could reach.
I pray you do not mock at what I say;
  For so my love's good grace may I not win
    If ever sonnet held so true a speech!

(D. G. Rossetti)

SONNET

Of why he is unhanged

Whoever without money is in love
  Had better build a gallows and go hang;
  He dies not once, but oftener feels the pang
Than he who was cast down from Heaven above.
And certes, for my sins it's plain enough,
  If Love's alive on earth, that he's myself,
  Who would not be so cursed with want of pelf
If others paid my proper dues thereof.
Then why am I not hanged by my own hands?
  I answer: for this empty narrow chink
    Of hope;—that I've a father old and rich,
And that if once he dies I'll get his lands;
  And die he must, when the sea's dry, I think.
    Meanwhile God keeps him whole and me i' the ditch.

(D. G. Rossetti)

SONNET

Of why he would be a Scullion

I am so out of love through poverty
  That if I see my mistress in the street
  I hardly can be certain whom I meet,
And of her name do scarce remember me.

Also my courage it has made to be
So cold, that if I suffered some foul cheat
Even from the meanest wretch that one could beat,
Save for the sin I think he should go free.
Ay, and it plays me a still nastier trick:
For, meeting some who erewhile with me took
Delight, I seem to them a roaring fire.
So here's a truth whereat I need not stick;—
That if one could turn scullion to a cook,
It were a thing to which one might aspire.

(*D. G. Rossetti*)

SONNET

He argues his case with Death

GRAMERCY, Death, as you've my love to win,
Just be impartial in your next assault;
And that you may not find yourself in fault,
Whate'er you do, be quick now and begin.
As oft may I be pounded flat and thin
As in Grosseto there are grains of salt,
If now to kill us both you be not call'd,—
Both me and him who sticks so in his skin.
Or better still, look here; for if I'm slain
Alone,—his wealth, it's true, I'll never have,
Yet death is life to one who lives in pain:
But if you only kill Saldagno's knave,
I'm left in Siena (don't you see your gain?)
Like a rich man who's made a galley-slave.

(*D. G. Rossetti*)

SONNET

TO DANTE ALIGHIERI

He writes to Dante, then in exile at Verona, defying him as no better than himself

DANTE ALIGHIERI, if I jest and lie,
You in such lists might run a tilt with me:
I get my dinner, you your supper, free;

And if I bite the fat, you suck the fry;
I shear the cloth and you the teazel ply;
  If I've a strut, who's prouder than you are?
  If I'm foul-mouthed, you're not particular.
And you've turned Lombard, even if Roman I.
So that, 'fore Heaven! if either of us flings
  Much dirt at the other, he must be a fool:
For lack of luck and wit we do these things.
  Yet if you want some lessons at my school,
Just say so, and you'll find the next touch stings—
  For, Dante, I'm the goad and you're the bull.

(D. G. Rossetti)

Simone dall' Antella

c. 1300

PROLONGED SONNET

In the last Days of the Emperor Henry VII

Along the road all shapes must travel by,
  How swiftly, to my thinking, now doth fare
  The wanderer who built his watchtower there
Where wind is torn with wind continually;
Lo! from the world and its dull pain to fly,
  Unto such pinnacle did he repair,
  And of her presence was not made aware,
Whose face, that looks like Peace, is Death's own lie.
Alas, Ambition, thou his enemy,
  Who lurest the poor wanderer on his way,
But never bring'st him where his rest may be,—
  O leave him now, for he is gone astray
Himself out of his very self through thee,
  Till now the broken stems his feet betray,
And, caught with boughs before and boughs behind,
Deep in thy tangled wood he sinks entwin'd.

(D. G. Rossetti)

Giovanni Quirino

c. 1300

SONNET

TO DANTE ALIGHIERI

He commends the work of Dante's Life, then drawing to its close; and deplores his own deficiencies

GLORY to God and to God's Mother chaste,
Dear friend, is all the labor of thy days:
Thou art as he who evermore uplays
That heavenly wealth which the worm cannot waste:
So shalt thou render back with interest
The precious talent given thee by God's grace:
While I, for my part, follow in their ways
Who by the cares of this world are possess'd.
For, as the shadow of the earth doth make
The moon's globe dark, when so she is debarr'd
From the bright rays which lit her in the sky,—
So now, since thou my sun didst me forsake,
(Being distant from me), I grow dull and hard,
Even as a beast of Epicurus' sty.

(*D. G. Rossetti*)

Francesco Petrarca

1304-1374

What he had achieved for the modern world was not merely to bequeath to his Italian imitators masterpieces of lyrical art unrivalled for perfection of workmanship, but also, and far more, to open out for Europe a new sphere of mental activity. Standing within the threshold of the middle ages, he surveyed the kingdom of the modern spirit, and, by his own inexhaustible industry in the field of scholarship, he determined what we call the revival of learning.—J. A. SYMONDS.

VISIONS

I

BEING one day at my window all alone,
So manie strange things happened me to see,

As much it grieveth me to thinke thereon.
  At my right hand a hynde appear'd to mee,
So faire as mote the greatest god delite;
  Two eager dogs did her pursue in chace,
Of which the one was blacke, the other white:
  With deadly force so in their cruell race
They pincht the haunches of that gentle beast,
  That at the last, and in short time, I spide,
Under a rocke, where she alas, opprest,
  Fell to the ground, and there untimely dide.
Cruell death vanquishing so noble beautie
Oft makes me wayle so hard a destenie.

II

After, at sea a tall ship did appeare,
  Made all of heben and white yvorie;
The sailes of golde, of silke the tackle were:
  Milde was the winde, calme seem'd the sea to bee,
The skie eachwhere did show full bright and faire:
  With rich treasures this gay ship fraighted was:
But sudden storme did so turmoyle the aire,
  And tumbled up the sea, that she (alas)
Strake on a rock, that under water lay,
  And perished past all recoverie.
O! how great ruth, and sorrowfull assay,
  Doth vex my spirite with perplexitie,
Thus in a moment to see lost, and drown'd,
So great riches, as like cannot be found.

III

The heavenly branches did I see arise
  Out of the fresh and lustie lawrell tree,
Amidst the young greene wood of paradise;
  Some noble plant I thought my selfe to see:
Such store of birds therein yshrowded were,
  Chaunting in shade their sundrie melodie,
That with their sweetnes I was ravisht nere.
  While on this lawrell fixed was mine eie,

The skie gan everie where to overcast,
  And darkened was the welkin all about,
When sudden flash of heavens fire out brast,
  And rent this royall tree quite by the roote;
Which makes me much and ever to complaine;
For no such shadow shal be had againe.

IV

Within this wood, out of a rocke did rise
  A spring of water, mildly rumbling downe,
Whereto approched not in anie wise
  The homely shepheard, nor the ruder clown;
But manie muses, and the nymphes withall,
  That sweetly in accord did tune their voyce
To the soft sounding of the waters fall;
  That my glad heart thereat did much rejoyce.
But, while herein I tooke my chiefe delight,
  I saw (alas) the gaping earth devoure
The spring, the place, and all cleane out of sight;
  Which yet aggreeves my hart even to this houre,
And wounds my soule with rufull memorie,
To see such pleasures go so suddenly.

V

I saw a phœnix in the wood alone,
  With purple wings, and crest of golden hewe;
Strange bird he was, whereby I thought anone,
  That of some heavenly wight I have the vewe;
Untill he came unto the broken tree,
  And to the spring, that late devoured was.
What say I more? each thing at last we see
  Doth passe away: the phœnix there alas,
Spying the tree destroid, the water dride,
  Himselfe smote with his beake, as in disdain,
And so foorthwith in great despight he dide;
  That yet my heart burnes, in exceeding paine,
For ruth and pitie of so hapless plight:
O! let mine eyes no more see such a sight.

VI

At last so faire a ladie did I spie,
  That thinking yet on her I burne and quake;
On hearbs and flowres she walked pensively,
  Milde, but yet love she proudly did forsake:
White seem'd her robes, yet woven so they were,
  As snow and golde together had been wrought:
Above the wast a darke clowde shrouded her,
  A stinging serpent by the heele her caught;
Wherewith she languisht as the gathered floure;
  And, well assur'd, she mounted up to ioy.
Alas, on earth so nothing doth endure,
  But bitter griefe and sorrowfull annoy:
Which makes their life wretched and miserable,
Tossed with stormes of fortune variable.

VII

When I beheld this fickle trustles state
  Of vaine worlds glorie, flitting too and fro,
And mortall men tossed by troublous fate
  In restles seas of wretchedness and woe;
I wish I might this wearie life forgoe,
  And shortly turne unto my happie rest,
Where my free spirite might not anie moe
  Be vext with sights, that doo her peace molest.
And ye, faire ladie, in whose bounteous brest
  All heavenly grace and vertue shrined is,
When ye these rythmes doo read, and vew the rest,
  Loath this base world, and thinke of heavens blis:
And though ye be the fairest of Gods creatures,
Yet thinke, that Death shall spoyle your godly features.

(*Edmund Spenser*)

THE SONG OF TROYLUS

If no love is, O God, what fele I so?
And if love is, what thinge and whiche is he?
If love be gode, from whennes comth my wo?

If it be wykke, a wonder thynketh me,
Whenne every torment and adversite,
That cometh of him, may to me savory thynke;
For ay thirst I the more that Iche it drynke.
  And if that in myn owne lust I brenne,
From whennes cometh my wailynge and my pleynte?
If harme agree me, whereto pleyne I thenne?
I noot, ne why, unwery, that I feynte.
O quyke deth! O swete harm so queynte!
How may I se in me swiche quantite,
But if that I consente that it so be?
  And if that I consente, I wrongfully
Compleyne ywis; thus possed to and fro,
Al sterelees withinne a boot am I
Amyd the see, betwexen windes two,
That in contrarie standen ever mo.
Allas! what is this wonder maladye?
For hete of cold, for cold of hete I dye.

(*Geoffrey Chaucer*)

SUMMER IS COME

The soote season, that bud and bloom forth brings
With green hath clad the hill, and eke the vale.
The nightingale with feathers new she sings;
The turtle to her mate hath told her tale.
Summer is come, for every spray now springs;
The hart has hung his old head on the pale;
The buck in brake his winter coat he flings;
The fishes flete with new repairèd scale;
The adder all her slough away she slings;
The swift swallow pursueth the flies smale;
The busy bee her honey now she mings.
Winter is worn that was the flowers' bale,
And thus I see among these pleasant things
Each care decays, and yet my sorrow springs!

(*The Earl of Surrey*)

A COMPLAINT BY NIGHT OF THE LOVER NOT BELOVED

Alas, so all things now do hold their peace!
  Heaven and earth disturbèd in no thing;
The beasts, the air, the birds their song do cease,
  The nightès car the stars about doth bring;
Calm is the sea; the waves work less and less:
  So am not I, whom love, alas! doth wring,
Bringing before my face the great increase
  Of my desires, whereat I weep and sing,
In joy and woe, as in a doubtful case.
  For my sweet thoughts sometime do pleasure bring;
But by and by, the cause of my disease
  Gives me a pang that inwardly doth sting,
When that I think what grief it is again
To live and lack the thing should rid my pain.

(*The Earl of Surrey*)

COMPLAINT OF A LOVER REBUKED

Love, that liveth and reigneth in my thought,
  That built his seat within my captive breast,
Clad in the arms wherein with me he fought,
  Oft in my face he doth his banner rest.
She, that me taught to love, and suffer pain:
  My doubtful hope and eke my hot desire
With shamefaced cloak to shadow and restrain;
  Her smiling grace converteth straight to ire,
And coward Love then to the heart apace
  Taketh his flight, whereas he lurks, and plains
His purpose lost, and dare not show his face.
  For my lord's guilt thus faultless bide I pains;
Yet from my lord shall not my foot remove:
Sweet is his death, that takes his end by love.

(*The Earl of Surrey*)

LOVE'S FIDELITY

Set me whereas the sun doth parch the green,
Or where his beams do not dissolve the ice:
In temperate heat, where he is felt and seen;
In presence preſt of people mad or wise;
Set me in high, or yet in low degree;
In longeſt night, or in the shorteſt day;
In cleareſt sky, or where clouds thickeſt be;
In luſty youth, or when my hairs are gray:
Set me in heaven, in earth, or else in hell,
In hill or dale, or in the foaming flood;
Thrall, or at large, alive whereso I dwell,
Sick or in health, in evil fame or good,
Hers will I be; and only with this thought
Content myself although my chance be nought.

(*The Earl of Surrey*)

LOVE'S INCONSISTENCY

I find no peace, and all my war is done;
I fear and hope, I burn and freeze likewise;
I fly above the wind, yet cannot rise;
And nought I have, yet all the world I seize on;
That looseth, nor locketh, holdeth me in prison,
And holds me not, yet can I 'scape no wise;
Nor lets me live, nor die, at my devise,
And yet of death it giveth none occasion.
Without eyes I see, and without tongue I plain;
I wish to perish, yet I ask for health;
I love another, and yet I hate myself;
I feed in sorrow, and laugh in all my pain;
Lo, thus displeaseth me both death and life,
And my delight is causer of my grief.

(*Sir Thomas Wyatt*)

THE HEART ON THE HILL

Thou green and blooming, cool and shaded hill,
Where sits, now songful, now in thought, thy gueſt,

By whom the world's of glory dispossessed,
And heavenly spirits are made credible—
My heart, which quitted me for her (what skill
He showed; and if he come not back, shows best!)
Goes on relating, how that foot hath pressed,
And how those eyes the sward are softening still.
He says, and with a shrug at every pace,
"Oh were that caitiff here a little now,,
Who is so tired of tears and of his lot!"
She smiles, and how unequal is the case,
I being heartless stone, and Eden thou,
Oh hallowed, fortunate, delightsome spot!

(*C. B. Cayley*)

SIGNS OF LOVE

If amorous faith, a heart of guileless ways,
Soft languors, courteously controlled desire,
And virtuous will, kindled with noble fire,
And lengthened wanderings in a lightless maze;
If thoughts, which evermore the brow displays,
Or words that faint and brokenly suspire,
Still checked with fear and shame; if hues no higher
Than the pale violet hath, or love displays;
If holding some one than one's self more dear,
If sorrowing and sighing evermore,
If chewing grief, and rage, and many a cross,
If burning far away, and freezing near,
Are signs that Love consumes me to the core,
Yours, lady, is the fault and mine the loss.

(*C. B. Cayley*)

IF IT BE DESTINED

If it be destined that my Life, from thine
Divided, yet with thine shall linger on
Till, in the later twilight of Decline,
I may behold those Eyes, their luster gone;
When the gold tresses that enrich thy brow
Shall all be faded into silver-gray,

From which the wreaths that well bedeck them now
For many a Summer shall have fall'n away;
Then should I dare to whisper in your ears
The pent-up Passion of so long ago,
That Love which hath survived the wreck of years
Hath little else to pray for, or bestow,
Thou wilt not to the broken heart deny
The boon of one too-late relenting Sigh.

(Edward FitzGerald)

Giovanni Boccaccio

1313-1375

SONNETS

I

To one who had censured his public Exposition of Dante

If Dante mourns, there wheresoe'er he be,
That such high fancies of a soul so proud
Should be laid open to the vulgar crowd,
(As, touching my Discourse, I'm told by thee,)
This were my grievous pain; and certainly
My proper blame should not be disavow'd;
Though hereof somewhat, I declare aloud
Were due to others, not alone to me.
False hopes, true poverty, and therewithal
The blinded judgment of a host of friends,
And their entreaties, made that I did thus.
But of all this there is no gain at all
Unto the thankless souls with whose base ends
Nothing agrees that's great or generous.

II

Inscription for a Portrait of Dante

Dante Alighieri, a dark oracle,
Of wisdom and of art, I am; whose mind
Has to my country such great gifts assign'd

That men account my powers a miracle.
My lofty fancy passed as low as Hell,
  As high as Heaven, secure and unconfin'd;
  And in my noble book doth every kind
Of earthly lore and heavenly doctrine dwell.
Renownéd Florence was my mother,—nay,
  Stepmother unto me her piteous son,
    Through sin of cursed slander's tongue and tooth.
Ravenna sheltered me so cast away;
  My body is with her,—my soul with One
    For whom no envy can make dim the truth.

III

To Dante in Paradise, after Fiammetta's death

Dante, if thou within the sphere of Love,
  As I believe, remain'st contemplating
  Beautiful Beatrice, whom thou didst sing
Erewhile, and so wast drawn to her above;—
Unless from false life true life thee remove
  So far that Love's forgotten, let me bring
  One prayer before thee: for an easy thing
This were, to thee whom I do ask it of.
I know that when all joy doth most abound
  In the third Heaven, my own Fiammetta sees
    The grief which I have borne since she is dead.
O pray her (if mine image be not drown'd
  In Lethe) that her prayers may never cease
    Until I reach her and am comforted.

IV

Of Fiammetta singing

Love steered my course, while yet the sun rode high,
  On Scylla's waters to a myrtle-grove:
  The heaven was still and the sea did not move;
Yet now and then a little breeze went by
Stirring the tops of trees against the sky:

And then I heard a song as glad as love,
So sweet that never yet the like thereof
Was heard in any mortal company.
"A nymph, a goddess, or an angel sings
Unto herself, within this chosen place,
Of ancient loves"; so said I at that sound.
And there my lady, 'mid the shadowings
Of myrtle-trees, 'mid flowers and grassy space,
Singing I saw, with others who sat round.

V

Of his last sight of Fiammetta

Round her red garland and her golden hair
I saw a fire about Fiammetta's head;
Thence to a little cloud I watched it fade,
Than silver or than gold more brightly fair;
And like a pearl that a gold ring doth bear,
Even so an angel sat therein, who sped
Alone and glorious throughout heaven, array'd
In sapphires and in gold that lit the air.
Then I rejoiced as hoping happy things,
Who rather should have then discerned how God
Had haste to make my lady all His own,
Even as it came to pass. And with these stings
Of sorrow, and with life's most weary load
I dwell, who fain would be where she is gone.

VI

Of three Girls and of their Talk

By a clear well, within a little field
Full of green grass and flowers of every hue,
Sat three young girls, relating (as I knew)
Their loves. And each had twined a bough to shield
Her lovely face; and the green leaves did yield
The golden hair their shadow; while the two
Sweet colors mingled, both blown lightly through

With a soft wind for ever stirred and still'd.
After a little while one of them said,
(I heard her,) "Think! If, ere the next hour struck,
Each of our lovers should come here to-day,
Think you that we should fly or feel afraid?"
To whom the others answered, "From such luck
A girl would be a fool to run away."

(*D. G. Rossetti*)

Fazio degli Uberti

1326-1360

CANZONE

His Portrait of his Lady, Angiola of Verona

I LOOK at the crisp golden-threaded hair
Whereof, to thrall my heart, Love twists a net,
Using at times a string of pearls for bait,
And sometimes with a single rose therein.
I look into her eyes which unaware
Through mine own eyes to my heart penetrate;
Their splendor, that is excellently great,
To the sun's radiance seeming near akin,
Yet from herself a sweeter light to win.
So that I, gazing on that lovely one,
Discourse in this wise with my secret thought:—
"Woe's me! why am I not,
Even as my wish, alone with her alone,—
That hair of hers, so heavily uplaid,
To shed down braid by braid,
And make myself two mirrors of her eyes
Within whose light all other glory dies?"

I look at the amorous beautiful mouth,
The spacious forehead which her locks enclose,
The small white teeth, the straight and shapely nose,
And the clear brows of a sweet penciling.

And then the thought within me gains full growth,
Saying, "Be careful that thy glance now goes
Between her lips, red as an open rose,
Quite full of every dear and precious thing;
And liſten to her gracious answering,
Born of the gentle mind that in her dwells,
Which from all things can glean the nobler half.
Look thou when she doth laugh
How much of her laugh is sweeter than aught else."
Thus evermore my spirit makes avow
Touching her mouth; till now
I would give anything that I possess,
Only to hear her mouth say frankly, "Yes."

I look at her white easy neck, so well
From shoulders and from bosom lifted out;
And at her round cleft chin, which beyond doubt
No fancy in the world could have design'd.
And then, with longing grown more voluble,
"Were it not pleasant now," pursues my thought,
"To have that neck within thy two arms caught
And kiss it till the mark were left behind?"
Then, urgently: "The eyelids of thy mind
Open thou: if such loveliness be given
To sight here,—what of that which she doth hide?
Only the wondrous ride
Of sun and planets through the visible heaven
Tells us that there beyond is Paradise.
Thus, if thou fix thine eyes,
Of a truth certainly thou muſt infer
That every earthly joy abides in her."

I look at the large arms, so lithe and round,—
At the hands, which are white and rosy too,—
At the long fingers, clasped and woven through,
Bright with the ring which one of them doth wear.
Then my thought whispers: "Were thy body wound
Within those arms, as loving women's do,

In all thy veins were born a life made new
Which thou couldst find no language to declare.
Behold if any picture can compare
With her just limbs, each fit in shape and size,
Or match her angel's color like a pearl.
She is a gentle girl
To see; yet when it needs, her scorn can rise.
Meek, bashful, and in all things temperate,
Her virtue holds its state;
In whose least act there is that gift express'd
Which of all reverence makes her worthiest."

Soft as a peacock steps she, or as a stork
Straight on herself, taller and statelier:
'Tis a good sight how every limb doth stir
For ever in a womanly sweet way.
"Open thy soul to see God's perfect work,"
(My thought begins afresh,) "and look at her
When with some lady-friend exceeding fair
She bends and mingles arms and locks in play.
Even as all lesser lights vanish away,
When the sun moves, before his dazzling face,
So is this lady brighter than all these.
How should she fail to please,—
Love's self being no more than her loveliness?
In all her ways some beauty springs to view;
All that she loves to do
Tends alway to her honor's single scope;
And only from good deeds she draws her hope."

Song, thou canst surely say, without pretense,
That since the first fair woman ever made,
Not one can have display'd
More power upon all hearts than this one doth;
Because in her are both
Loveliness and the soul's true excellence:—
And yet (woe's me!) is pity absent thence?

(*D. G. Rossetti*)

OF ENGLAND, AND OF ITS MARVELS

Now to Great Britain we must make our way,
Unto which kingdom Brutus gave its name
What time he won it from the giants' rule.
'Tis thought at first its name was Albion,
And Anglia, from a damsel, afterwards.
The island is so great and rich and fair,
It conquers others that in Europe be,
Even as the sun surpasses other stars.
Many and great sheep-pastures bountifully
Nature has set there, and herein more bless'd,
That they can hold themselves secure from wolves.
Black amber also doth the land enrich,
(Whose properties my guide Solinus here
Told me, and how its color comes to it;)

And pearls are found in great abundance too.
The people are as white and comely-faced
As they of Ethiop land are black and foul.
Many hot springs and limpid fountain-heads
We found about this land, and spacious plains,
And divers beasts that dwell within thick woods.
Plentiful orchards too and fertile fields
It has, and castle-forts, and cities fair
With palaces and girth of lofty walls.
And proud wide rivers without any fords
We saw, and flesh, and fish, and crops enough.
Justice is strong throughout those provinces.

Now this I saw not; but so strange a thing
It was to hear, and by all men confirm'd,
That it is fit to note it as I heard;—
To wit, there is a certain islet here
Among the rest, where folk are born with tails,
Short, as are found in stags and such-like beasts.
For this I vouch,—that when a child is freed
From swaddling bands, the mother without stay
Passes elsewhere, and 'scapes the care of it.

I put no faith herein; but it is said
Among them, how such marvelous trees are there
That they grow birds, and this is their sole fruit.

Forty times eighty is the circuit ta'en,
With ten times fifteen, if I do not err,
By our miles reckoning its circumference.
Here every metal may be dug; and here
I found the people to be given to God,
Steadfast, and strong, and restive to constraint.
Nor is this strange, when one considereth;
For courage, beauty, and large-heartedness,
Were there, as it is said, in ancient days.

North Wales, and Orkney, and the banks of Thames,
Land's End and Stonehenge and Northumberland,
I chose with my companion to behold.
We went to London, and I saw the Tower
Where Guenevere her honor did defend,
With the Thames river which runs close to it.
I saw the castle which by force was ta'en
With the three shields by gallant Lancelot,
The second year that he did deeds of arms.
I beheld Camelot despoiled and waste;
And was where one and the other had her birth,
The maids of Corbonek and Astolat.
Also I saw the castle where Geraint
Lay with his Enid; likewise Merlin's stone,
Which for another's love I joyed to see.
I found the tract where is the pine-tree well,
And where of old the knight of the black shield
With weeping and with laughter kept the pass,
What time the pitiless and bitter dwarf
Before Sir Gawaine's eyes discourteously
With many heavy stripes led him away.
I saw the valley which Sir Tristram won
When having slain the giant hand to hand
He set the stranger knights from prison free.
And last I viewed the field, at Salisbury,

Of that great martyrdom which left the world
Empty of honor, valor, and delight.

So, compassing that Island round and round,
I saw and hearkened many things and more
Which might be fair to tell but which I hide.

(*D. G. Rossetti*)

Franco Sacchetti

1335-1400?

BALLATA

His Talk with Certain Peasant-girls

"Ye graceful peasant-girls and mountain-maids,
Whence come ye homeward through these evening shades?"

"We come from where the forest skirts the hill;
 A very little cottage is our home,
Where with our father and our mother still
 We live, and love our life, nor wish to roam.
 Back every evening from the field we come
And bring with us our sheep from pasturing there."

"Where, tell me, is the hamlet of your birth,
 Whose fruitage is the sweetest by so much?
Ye seem to me as creatures worship-worth,
 The shining of your countenance is such.
 No gold about your clothes, coarse to the touch,
Nor silver; yet with such an angel's air!

"I think your beauties might make great complaint
 Of being thus shown over mount and dell;
Because no city is so excellent
 But that your stay therein were honorable.
 In very truth, now, does it like ye well
To live so poorly on the hill-side here?"

"Better it liketh one of us, pardiè,
Behind her flock to seek the pasture-stance,
Far better than it liketh one of ye
To ride unto your curtained rooms and dance.
We seek no riches, neither golden chance
Save wealth of flowers to weave into our hair."

Ballad, if I were now as once I was,
I'd make myself a shepherd on some hill,
And, without telling any one, would pass
Where these girls went, and follow at their will;
And "Mary" and "Martin" we would murmur still,
And I would be for ever where they were.

(D. G. Rossetti)

CATCH

On a Wet Day

As I walk'd thinking through a little grove,
Some girls that gathered flowers came passing me,
Saying, "Look here! look there!" delightedly.
"Oh, here it is!" "What's that?" "A lily, love."
"And there are violets!"
"Further for roses! Oh, the lovely pets—
The darling beauties! Oh, the nasty thorn!
Look here, my hand's all torn!"
"What's that that jumps!" "Oh, don't! it's a grass-hopper!"
"Come run, come run,
Here's bluebells!" "Oh, what fun!"
"Not that way! Stop her!"
"Yes, this way!" "Pluck them, then!"
"Oh, I've found mushrooms! Oh, look here!" "Oh, I'm
Quite sure that further on we'll get wild thyme."

"Oh, we shall stay too long, it's going to rain!
There's lightning, oh there's thunder!"
"Oh, shan't we hear the vesper bell, I wonder?"
"Why, it's not nones, you silly little thing;

And don't you hear the nightingales that sing
Fly away O die away?"
"Oh, I hear something! Hush!"
"Why, where? what is it, then?" "Ah! in that bush!"
So every girl here knocks it, shakes and shocks it,
Till with the stir they make
Out skurries a great snake.
"O Lord! O me! Alack! Ah me! alack!"
They scream, and then all run and scream again,
And then in heavy drops down comes the rain.

Each running at the other in a fright,
Each trying to get before the other, and crying,
And flying, stumbling, tumbling, wrong or right;
One sets her knee
There where her foot should be;
One has her hands and dress
All smothered up with mud in a fine mess;
And one gets trampled on by two or three.
What's gathered is let fall
About the wood and not picked up at all.
The wreaths of flowers are scattered on the ground;
And still as screaming hustling without rest
They run this way and that and round and round,
She thinks herself in luck who runs the best.

I stood quite still to have a perfect view,
And never noticed till I got wet through.

(*D. G. Rossetti*)

Anonymous

14th century

SONNET

A Lady laments for her lost Lover, by similitude of a Falcon

Alas for me, who loved a falcon well!
So well I loved him, I was nearly dead:
Ever at my low call he bent his head,

And ate of mine, not much, but all that fell.
Now he has fled, how high I cannot tell,
Much higher now than ever he has fled,
And is in a fair garden housed and fed;
Another lady, alas! shall love him well.
Oh, my own falcon whom I taught and rear'd!
Sweet bells of shining gold I gave to thee
That in the chase thou shouldst not be afeard.
Now thou hast risen like the risen sea,
Broken thy jesses loose, and disappear'd,
As soon as thou wast skilled in falconry.

(D. G. Rossetti)

BALLATA

One speaks of the Beginning of his Love

This fairest one of all the stars, whose flame,
For ever lit, my inner spirit fills,
Came to me first one day between the hills.

I wondered very much; but God the Lord
Said, "From Our Virtue, lo! this light is pour'd."
So in a dream it seemed that I was led
By a great Master to a garden spread
With lilies underfoot and overhead.

(D. G. Rossetti)

BALLATA

Of True and False Singing

A little wild bird sometimes at my ear
Sings his own verses very clear:
Others sing louder that I do not hear.

For singing loudly is not singing well;
But ever by the song that's soft and low
The master-singer's voice is plain to tell.
Few have it and yet all are masters now,
And each of them can trill out what he calls
His ballads, canzonets, and madrigals.

The world with masters is so covered o'er,
There is no room for pupils any more.

(*D. G. Rossetti*)

Angelo Poliziano

1454-1494

THREE BALLATE

I

I FOUND myself one day all, all alone,
For pastime in a field with blossoms strewn.

I do not think the world a field could show
  With herbs of perfume so surpassing rare;
But when I passed beyond the green hedge-row,
  A thousand flowers around me flourished fair,
  White, pied and crimson, in the summer air;
Among the which I heard a sweet bird's tone.

I found myself one day all, all alone,
For pastime in a field with blossoms strewn.

Her song it was so tender and so clear
  That all the world listened with love; then I
With stealthy feet a-tiptoe drawing near,
  Her golden head and golden wings could spy,
  Her plumes that flashed like rubies neath the sky,
Her crystal beak and throat and bosom's zone.

I found myself one day all, all alone,
For pastime in a field with blossoms strewn.

Fain would I snare her, smit with mighty love;
  But arrow-like she soared, and through the air
Fled to her nest upon the boughs above;
  Wherefore to follow her is all my care,
  For haply I might lure her by some snare
Forth from the woodland wild where she is flown.

I found myself one day all, all alone,
For pastime in a field with blossoms strewn.

Yea, I might spread some net or woven wile;
  But since of singing she doth take such pleasure,
Without or other art or other guile
  I seek to win her with a tuneful measure;
  Therefore in singing spend I all my leisure,
To make by singing this sweet bird my own.

I found myself one day all, all alone,
For pastime in a field with blossoms strewn.

II

He who knows not what thing is Paradise,
Let him look fixedly on Myrrha's eyes.

From Myrrha's eyes there flieth, girt with fire,
  An angel of our lord, a laughing boy,
Who lights in frozen hearts a flaming pyre,
  And with such sweetness doth the soul destroy,
  That while it dies, it murmurs forth its joy:
Oh blessed am I to dwell in Paradise!

He who knows not what thing is Paradise,
Let him look fixedly on Myrrha's eyes.

From Myrrha's eyes a virtue still doth move,
  So swift and with so fierce and strong a flight,
That it is like the lightning of high Jove,
  Riving of iron and adamant the might;
  Nathless the wound doth carry such delight
That he who suffers dwells in Paradise.

He who knows not what thing is Paradise,
Let him look fixedly on Myrrha's eyes.

From Myrrha's eyes a lovely messenger
  Of joy so grave, so virtuous, doth flee,

That all proud souls are bound to bend to her
  So sweet her countenance, it turns the key
  Of hard hearts locked in cold security:
Forth flies the prisoned soul to Paradise.

He who knows not what thing is Paradise,
Let him look fixedly on Myrrha's eyes.

In Myrrha's eyes beauty doth but make her throne,
  And sweetly smile and sweetly speak her mind:
Such grace in her fair eyes a man hath known
  As in the whole wide world he scarce may find:
  Yet if she slay him with a glance too kind,
He lives again beneath her gazing eyes.

He who knows not what thing is Paradise,
Let him look fixedly on Myrrha's eyes.

III

I WENT a roaming, maidens, one bright day,
In a green garden in mid month of May.

Violets and lilies grew on every side
  Mid the green grass, and the young flowers wonderful,
Golden and white and red and azure-eyed;
  Toward which I stretched my hands, eager to pull
  Plenty to make my fair curls beautiful,
To crown my rippling curls with garlands gay.

I went a roaming, maidens, one bright day,
In a green garden in mid month of May.

But when my lap was full of flowers I spied
  Roses at last, roses of every hue;
Therefore I ran to pluck their ruddy pride,
  Because their perfume was so sweet and true
  That all my soul went forth with pleasure new,
With yearning and desire too soft to say.

I went a roaming, maidens, one bright day,
In a green garden in mid month of May.

I gazed and gazed. Hard task it were to tell
  How lovely were the roses in that hour:
One was but peeping from her verdant shell,
  And some were faded, some were scarce in flower:
  Then Love said: Go, pluck from the blooming bower
Those that thou seest ripe upon the spray.

I went a roaming, maidens, one bright day,
In a green garden in mid month of May.

For when the full rose quits her tender sheath,
  When she is sweetest and most fair to see,
Then is the time to place her in thy wreath,
  Before her beauty and her freshness flee.
  Gather ye therefore roses with great glee,
Sweet girls, or e'er their perfume pass away.

I went a roaming, maidens, one bright day,
In a green garden in mid month of May.

(John Addington Symonds)

Lorenzo de' Medici

1448-1492

TWO LYRICS

I

Into a little close of mine I went
  One morning, when the sun with his fresh light
  Was rising all refulgent and unshent.
Rose-trees are planted there in order bright,
  Whereto I turned charmed eyes, and long did stay,
  Taking my fill of that new-found delight.
Red and white roses bloomed upon the spray;
  One opened, leaf by leaf, to greet the morn,

Shyly at first, then in sweet disarray;
Another, yet a youngling, newly born,
Scarce struggled from the bud, and there were some
Whose petals closed them from the air forlorn;
Another fell, and showered the grass with bloom;
Thus I behold the roses dawn and die,
And one short hour their loveliness consume.
But while I watched those languid petals lie
Colorless on cold earth, I could but think
How vain a thing is youthful bravery.
Trees have their time to bloom on winter's brink;
Then the rathe blossoms wither in an hour,
When the brief days of spring towards summer sink
The fruit, as yet unformed, is tart and sour;
Little by little it grows large, and weighs
The strong boughs down with slow persistent power;
Nor without peril can the branches raise
Their burden; now they stagger 'neath the weight
Still growing, and are bent above the ways;
Soon autumn comes, and the ripe, ruddy freight
Is gathered: the glad season will not stay;
Flowers, fruit, and leaves are now all desolate.
Pluck the rose, therefore, maiden, while 'tis May.

II

How can I sing light-souled and fancy-free,
When my loved lord no longer smiles on me?

Dances and songs and merry wakes I leave
To lovers fair, more fortunate and gay;
Since to my heart so many sorrows cleave
That only doleful tears are mine for aye:
Who hath heart's ease, may carol, dance, and play;
While I am fain to weep continually.

How can I sing light-souled and fancy-free,
When my loved lord no longer smiles on me?

I too had heart's ease once, for so Love willed,
When my lord loved me with love strong and great:
But envious fortune my life's music stilled,
And turned to sadness all my gleeful state.
Ah me! Death surely were less desolate
Than thus to live and love-neglected be!

How can I sing light-souled and fancy-free,
When my loved lord no longer smiles on me?

One only comfort soothes my heart's despair,
And mid this sorrow lends my soul some cheer;
Unto my lord I ever yielded fair
Service of faith untainted pure and clear;
If then I die thus guiltless, on my bier
It may be she will shed one tear for me.

How can I sing light-souled and fancy-free,
When my loved lord no longer smiles on me?

(*John Addington Symonds*)

Niccolo Machiavelli

1469-1527

OPPORTUNITY

"But who art thou, with curious beauty graced,
O woman, stamped with some bright heavenly seal?
Why go thy feet on wings, and in such haste?"

"I am that maid whose secret few may steal,
Called Opportunity. I hasten by
Because my feet are treading on a wheel,

"Being more swift to run than birds to fly.
And rightly on my feet my wings I wear,
To blind the sight of those who track and spy;

"Rightly in front I hold my scattered hair
To veil my face, and down my breast to fall,
Lest men should know my name when I am there;

"And leave behind my back no wisp at all
For eager folk to clutch, what time I glide
So near, and turn, and pass beyond recall."

"Tell me; who is that Figure at thy side?"
"Penitence. Mark this well that by degrees
Who lets me go must keep her for his bride.

"And thou hast spent much time in talk with me
Busied with thoughts and fancies vainly grand,
Nor hast remarked, O fool, neither dost see
How lightly I have fled beneath thy hand."

(James Elroy Flecker)

Michelangelo Buonarroti

1475-1564

THE DOOM OF BEAUTY

CHOICE soul, in whom, as in a glass, we see,
  Mirrored in thy pure form and delicate,
  What beauties heaven and nature can create,
  The paragon of all their works to be!
Fair soul, in whom love, pity, piety,
  Have found a home, as from thy outward state
  We clearly read, and are so rare and great
  That they adorn none other like to thee!
Love takes me captive; beauty binds my soul;
  Pity and mercy with their gentle eyes
  Wake in my heart a hope that cannot cheat.
What law, what destiny, what fell control,
  What cruelty, or late or soon, denies
  That death should spare perfection so complete?

(John Addington Symonds)

CELESTIAL LOVE

No mortal thing enthralled these longing eyes
When perfect peace in thy fair face I found;
But far within, where all is holy ground,
My soul felt Love, her comrade of the skies:
For she was born with God in Paradise;
Nor all the shows of beauty shed around
This fair false world her wings to earth have bound:
Unto the Love of Loves aloft she flies.
Nay, things that suffer death, quench not the fire
Of deathless spirits; nor eternity
Serves sordid Time, that withers all things rare.
Not love but lawless impulse is desire:
That slays the soul; our love makes still more fair
Our friends on earth, fairer in death on high.

(*John Addington Symonds*)

LOVE, THE LIGHT-GIVER

With your fair eyes a charming light I see,
For which my own blind eyes would peer in vain;
Stayed by your feet the burden I sustain
Which my lame feet find all too strong for me;
Wingless upon your pinions forth I fly;
Heavenward your spirit stirreth me to strain;
E'en as you will, I blush and blanch again,
Freeze in the sun, burn 'neath a frosty sky.
Your will includes and is the lord of mine;
Life to my thoughts within your heart is given;
My words begin to breathe upon your breath:
Like to the moon am I, that cannot shine
Alone; for lo! our eyes see nought in heaven
Save what the living sun illumineth.

(*John Addington Symonds*)

LOVE'S ENTREATY

Thou knowest, love, I know that thou dost know
That I am here more near to thee to be,
And knowest that I know thou knowest me:
What means it then that we are sundered so?
If they are true, these hopes that from thee flow,
If it is real, this sweet expectancy,
Break down the wall that stands 'twixt me and thee;
For pain in prison pent hath double woe.
Because in thee I love, O my loved lord,
What thou best lovest, be not therefore stern:
Souls burn for souls, spirits to spirits cry!
I seek the splendor in thy fair face stored;
Yet living man that beauty scarce can learn,
And he who fain would find it, first must die.

(*John Addington Symonds*)

ON THE BRINK OF DEATH

Now hath my life across a stormy sea
Like a frail bark reached that wide port where all
Are bidden, ere the final reckoning fall
Of good and evil for eternity.
Now know I well how that fond phantasy
Which made my soul the worshiper and thrall
Of earthly art, is vain; how criminal
Is that which all men seek unwillingly.
Those amorous thoughts which were so lightly dressed,
What are they when the double death is nigh?
The one I know for sure, the other dread.
Painting nor sculpture now can lull to rest
My soul that turns to His great love on high,
Whose arms to clasp us on the cross were spread.

(*John Addington Symonds*)

A PRAYER FOR PURIFICATION

PERCHANCE that I might learn what pity is,
That I might laugh at erring men no more,
Secure in my own strength as heretofore,
My soul hath fallen from her state of bliss:
Nor know I under any flag but this
How fighting I may 'scape those perils sore,
Or how survive the rout and horrid roar
Of adverse hosts, if I thy succor miss.
O flesh! O blood! O cross! O pain extreme!
By you may those foul sins be purified,
Wherein my fathers were, and I was born!
Lo, Thou alone art good: let Thy supreme
Pity my state of evil cleanse and hide—
So near to death, so far from God, forlorn.

(*John Addington Symonds*)

THE TRANSFIGURATION OF BEAUTY

(*A Dialogue with Love*)

NAY, prithee tell me, Love, when I behold
My lady, do mine eyes her beauty see
In truth, or dwells that loveliness in me
Which multiplies her grace a thousandfold?
Thou needs must know; for thou with her of old
Comest to stir my soul's tranquillity;
Yet would I not seek one sigh less, or be
By loss of that loved flame, more simply cold.—
The beauty thou discernest, all is hers;
But grows in radiance as it soars on high,
Through mortal eyes unto the soul above:
'Tis there transfigured; for the soul confers
On what she holds, her own divinity:
And this transfigured beauty wins thy love.

(*John Addington Symonds*)

THE GARLAND AND THE GIRDLE

What joy hath yon glad wreath of flowers that is
Around her golden hair so deftly twined,
Each blossom pressing forward from behind,
As though to be the first her brows to kiss!
The livelong day her dress hath perfect bliss,
That now reveals her breast, now seems to bind:
And that fair woven net of gold refined
Rests on her cheek and throat in happiness!
Yet still more blissful seems to me the band
Gilt at the tips, so sweetly doth it ring
And clasp the bosom that it serves to lace:
Yea, and the belt, to such as understand,
Bound round her waist, saith: Here I'd ever cling.—
What would my arms do in that girdle's place?

(John Addington Symonds)

JOY MAY KILL

Too much good luck no less than misery
May kill a man condemned to mortal pain,
If, lost to hope and chilled in every vein,
A sudden pardon comes to set him free.
Thus thy unwonted kindness shown to me
Amid the gloom where only sad thoughts reign,
With too much rapture bringing light again,
Threatens my life more than that agony.
Good news and bad may bear the self-same knife;
And death may follow both upon their flight;
For hearts that shrink or swell, alike will break.
Let then thy beauty, to preserve my life,
Temper the source of this supreme delight,
Lest joy so poignant slay a soul so weak.

(John Addington Symonds)

LOVE'S JUSTIFICATION

Yes! hope may with my strong desire keep pace,
And I be undeluded, unbetrayed;
For if of our affections none find grace
In sight of Heaven, then wherefore hath God made
The world which we inhabit? Better plea
Love cannot have, than that in loving thee
Glory to that eternal peace is paid,
Who such divinity to thee imparts
As hallows and makes pure all gentle hearts.
His hope is treacherous only whose love dies
With beauty, which is varying every hour:
But, in chaste hearts uninfluenced by the power
Of outward change, there blooms a deathless flower,
That breathes on earth the air of paradise.

(*William Wordsworth*)

TO THE SUPREME BEING

The prayers I make will then be sweet indeed,
If Thou the spirit give by which I pray:
My unassisted heart is barren clay,
Which of its native self can nothing feed:
Of good and pious works Thou art the seed,
Which quickens only where Thou say'st it may;
Unless Thou show to us Thine own true way,
No man can find it: Father! Thou must lead.
Do Thou, then, breathe those thoughts into my mind
By which such virtue may in me be bred
That in Thy holy footsteps I may tread;
The fetters of my tongue do Thou unbind,
That I may have the power to sing of Thee,
And sound Thy praises everlastingly.

(*William Wordsworth*)

TO VITTORIA COLONNA

When the prime mover of my many sighs
Heaven took through death from out her earthly place,
Nature, that never made so fair a face,
Remained ashamed, and tears were in all eyes.
O fate, unheeding my impassioned cries!
O hopes fallacious! O thou spirit of grace,
Where art thou now? Earth holds in its embrace
Thy lovely limbs, thy holy thoughts the skies.
Vainly did cruel death attempt to stay
The rumor of thy virtuous renown,
That Lethe's waters could not wash away!
A thousand leaves, since he hath stricken thee down,
Speak of thee, nor to thee could Heaven convey,
Except through death, a refuge and a crown.

(*H. W. Longfellow*)

DANTE

What should be said of him cannot be said;
By too great splendor is his name attended;
To blame is easier those who him offended,
Than reach the faintest glory round him shed.
This man descended to the doomed and dead
For our instruction; then to God ascended;
Heaven opened wide to him its portals splendid,
Who from his country's, closed against him, fled.
Ungrateful land! To its own prejudice
Nurse of his fortunes; and this showeth well
That the most perfect most of grief shall see.
Among a thousand proofs let one suffice,
That as his exile hath no parallel,
Ne'er walked the earth a greater man than he.

(*H. W. Longfellow*)

THREE POEMS

1

I KNOW not if from uncreated spheres
Some longed-for ray it be that warms my breast,
Or lesser light, in memory expressed,
Of some once lovely face, that reappears,
Or passing rumor ringing in my ears,
Or dreamy vision, once my bosom's guest,
That left behind I know not what unrest,
Haply the reason of these wayward tears.
But what I feel and seek, what leads me on,
Comes not of me; nor can I tell aright
Where shines the hidden star that sheds this light.
Since I beheld thee, sweet and bitter fight
Within me. Resolution have I none.
Can this be, Master, what thine eyes have done?

2

The haven and last refuge of my pain
(A strong and safe defense)
Are tears and supplications, but in vain.
Love sets upon me banded with Disdain,
One armed with pity and one armed with death,
And as death smites me, pity lends me breath.
Else had my soul long since departed thence.
She pineth to remove
Whither her hopes of endless peace abide
And beauty dwelleth without beauty's pride,
There her last bliss to prove.
But still the living fountain of my tears
Wells in the heart when all thy truth appears,
Lest death should vanquish love.

3

Ravished by all that to the eyes is fair,
Yet hungry for the joys that truly bless,

My soul can find no stair
To mount to heaven, save earth's loveliness.
For from the stars above
Descends a glorious light
That lifts our longing to their highest height
And bears the name of love.
Nor is there aught can move
A gentle heart, or purge or make it wise,
But beauty and the starlight of her eyes.

(*George Santayana*)

Giovanni della Casa

1503–1556

TO SLEEP

O Sleep, O tranquil son of noiseless Night,
Of humid, shadowy Night; O dear repose
For wearied men, forgetfulness of woes
Grievous enough the bloom of life to blight!
Succor this heart that hath outworn delight,
And knows no rest; these tired limbs compose;
Fly to me, Sleep; thy dusky vans disclose
Over my languid eyes, then cease thy flight.
Where, where is Silence, that avoids the day?
Where the light dreams, that with a wavering tread
And unsubstantial footing follow thee?
Alas! in vain I call thee; and these gray,
These frigid shades flatter in vain. O bed,
How rough with thorns! O nights, how harsh to me!

(*John Addington Symonds*)

Giovanni Battista Guarini

1537-1612

FROM IL PASTOR FIDO

How I forsook
Elias and Pisa after, and betook
Myself to Argos and Mycenæ, where

An earthly god I worshiped, with what there
I suffered in that hard captivity,
Would be too long for thee to hear, for me
Too sad to utter. Only thus much know;—
I lost my labor, and in sand did sow:
I writ, wept, sung; hot and cold fits I had;
I rid, I stood, I bore, now sad, now glad,
Now high, now low, now in esteem, now scorned;
And as the Delphic iron, which is turned
Now to heroic, now mechanic use,
I feared no danger,—did no pains refuse;
Was all things,—and was nothing; changed my hair,
Condition, custom, thoughts, and life,—but ne'er
Could change my fortune. Then I knew at last,
And panted after, my sweet freedom past.
So, flying smoky Argos, and the great
Storms that attend on greatness, my retreat
I made to Pisa,—my thought's quiet port.

. . . . .

Who would have dreamed 'midst plenty to grow poor;
Or to be less, by toiling to be more?
I thought, by how much more in princes' courts
Men did excel in titles and supports,
So much the more obliging they would be,
The best enamel of nobility.
But now the contrary by proofs I've seen:
Courtiers in name, and courteous in their mien,
They are; but in their actions I could spy
Not the least transient spark of courtesy.
People, in show, smooth as the calmed waves,
Yet cruel as the ocean when it raves:
Men in appearance only did I find,—
Love in the face, but malice in the mind;
With a straight look and tortuous heart, and least
Fidelity where greatest was professed.
That which elsewhere is virtue is vice there:
Plain truth, fair dealing, love unfeigned, sincere
Compassion, faith inviolable, and
An innocence both of the heart and hand,

They count the folly of a soul that's vile
And poor,—a vanity worthy their smile.
To cheat, to lie, deceit and theft to use,
And under show of pity to abuse,
To rise upon the ruins of their brothers,
And seek their own by robbing praise from others,
The virtues are of that perfidious race.
No worth, no valor, no respect of place,
Of age, or law,—bridle of modesty,—
No tie of love or blood, nor memory
Of good received; nothing's so venerable,
Sacred, or just, that is inviolable
By that vast thirst of riches, and desire
Unquenchable of still ascending higher.
Now I, not fearing, since I meant not ill,
And in court-craft not having any skill,
Wearing my thoughts charactered on my brow,
And a glass window in my heart,—judge thou
How open and how fair a mark my heart
Lay to their envy's unsuspected dart.

(*Sir Richard Fanshawe*)

CLAIM TO LOVE

Alas! alas! thou turn'st in vain
  Thy beauteous face away,
Which, like young sorcerers, rais'd a pain
  Above its power to lay.

Love moves not as thou turn'st thy look,
  But here doth firmly rest:
He long ago thine eyes forsook
  To revel in my breast.

Thy power on him why hop'st thou more
  Than his on me should be?
The claim thou lay'st to him is poor
  To that he owns from me.

His substance in my heart excels,
His shadow, in thy sight;
Fire where it burns more truly dwells
Than where it scatters light.

(*Thomas Stanley*)

SPRING

O Spring, thou youthful beauty of the year,
Mother of flowers, bringer of warbling quires,
Of all sweet new green things and new desires,
Thou, Spring, returnest; but, alas! with thee
No more return to me
The calm and happy days these eves were used to see.
Thou, thou returnest, thou,
But with these returns now
Nought else but dread remembrance of the pleasure
I took in my lost treasure.
Thou still, thou still, art the same blithe, sweet thing
Thou ever wast, O Spring;
But I, in whose weak orbs these tears arise,
Am what I was no more, dear to another's eyes.

(*Leigh Hunt*)

Torquato Tasso

1544-1595

FROM AMINTA

THE GOLDEN AGE

O lovely age of gold!
Not that the rivers rolled
With milk, or that the woods wept honeydew;
Not that the ready ground
Produced without a wound,
Or the mild serpent had no tooth that slew;
Not that a cloudless blue
For ever was in sight,
Or that the heaven, which burns

And now is cold by turns,
Looked out in glad and everlasting light;
No, nor that even the insolent ships from far
Brought war to no new lands nor riches worse than
war:

But solely that that vain
And breath-invented pain,
That idol of mistake, that worshiped cheat,
That Honor,—since so called
By vulgar minds appalled,—
Played not the tyrant with our nature yet.
It had not come to fret
The sweet and happy fold
Of gentle human-kind;
Nor did its hard law bind
Souls nursed in freedom; but that law of gold,
That glad and golden law, all free, all fitted,
Which Nature's own hand wrote,—What pleases is
permitted.

Then among streams and flowers
The little winged powers
Went singing carols without torch or bow;
The nymphs and shepherds sat
Mingling with innocent chat
Sports and low whispers; and with whispers low,
Kisses that would not go.
The maiden, budding o'er,
Kept not her bloom uneyed,
Which now a veil must hide,
Nor the crisp apples which her bosom bore;
And oftentimes, in river or in lake,
The lover and his love their merry bath would take.

'Twas thou, thou, Honor, first
That didst deny our thirst
Its drink, and on the fount thy covering set;
Thou bad'st kind eyes withdraw

Into constrained awe,
And keep the secret for their tears to wet;
Thou gather'dst in a net
The tresses from the air,
And mad'st the sports and plays
Turn all to sullen ways,
And putt'st on speech a rein, in steps a care.
Thy work it is,—thou shade, that wilt not move,—
That what was once the gift is now the theft of Love.

Our sorrows and our pains,
These are thy noble gains.
But, O, thou Love's and Nature's masterer,
Thou conqueror of the crowned,
What dost thou on this ground,
Too small a circle for thy mighty sphere?
Go, and make slumber dear
To the renowned and high;
We here, a lowly race,
Can live without thy grace,
After the use of mild antiquity.
Go, let us love; since years
No truce allow, and life soon disappears;
Go, let us love; the daylight dies, is born;
But unto us the light
Dies once for all; and sleep brings on eternal night.

(*Leigh Hunt*)

TO HIS MISTRESS IN ABSENCE

Far from thy dearest self, the scope
Of all my aims,
I waste in secret flames;
And only live because I hope.

O when will Fate restore
The joys, in whose bright fire
My expectation shall expire,
That I may live because I hope no more!

(*Thomas Stanley*)

LOVE

Love, the great master of true eloquence,
Disdain the tribute of a vulgar tongue:
Cold are the words, and vain the affected song
Of him whose boasted passion is pretense.
The favored few that to his court belong
With noblest gifts the mighty god presents;
Their vigorous accents chain the admiring sense,
And their warm words in torrents stream along.
Oft too—O wondrous excellence of Love!—
Unuttered vows and sighs and accents broken
With far more force the gentle bosom move
Than smoothest phrase with courtly action spoken.
E'en Silence oft has found the power to prove
Both word and prayer, when it is true love's token.

(John Hermann Merivale)

Giordano Bruno

1548-1600

THE PHILOSOPHIC FLIGHT

Now that these wings to speed my wish ascend,
The more I feel vast air beneath my feet,
The more toward boundless air on pinions fleet,
Spurning the earth, soaring to heaven, I tend:
Nor makes them stoop their flight the direful end
Of Dædal's son; but upward still they beat.
What life the while with this death could compete,
If dead to earth at last I must descend?
My own heart's voice in the void air I hear.
Where wilt thou bear me, O rash man! Recall
Thy daring will! This boldness waits on fear!
Dread not, I answer, that tremendous fall:
Strike through the clouds, and smile when death is near,
If death so glorious be our doom at all!

(John Addington Symonds)

Gabriello Chiabrera

1562-1637

EPITAPHS

I

Weep not, beloved friends! nor let the air
For me with sighs be troubled. Not from life
Have I been taken; this is genuine life,
And this alone,—the life which now I live
In peace eternal; where desire and joy
Together move in fellowship without end.—
Francesco Ceni after death enjoined
That thus his tomb should speak for him. And surely
Small cause there is for that fond wish of ours
Long to continue in this world,—a world
That keeps not faith, nor yet can point a hope
To good, whereof itself is destitute.

II

Perhaps some needful service of the state
Drew Titus from the depth of studious bowers,
And doomed him to contend in faithless courts,
Where gold determines between right and wrong.
Yet did at length his loyalty of heart,
And his pure native genius, lead him back
To wait upon the bright and gracious Muses,
Whom he had early loved. And not in vain
Such course he held. Bologna's learned schools
Were gladdened by the sage's voice, and hung
With fondness on those sweet Nestorian strains.
There pleasure crowned his days; and all his thoughts
A roseate fragrance breathed. O human life,
That never art secure from dolorous change!
Behold, a high injunction suddenly
To Arno's side hath brought him, and he charmed
A Tuscan audience: but full soon was called

To the perpetual silence of the grave.
Mourn, Italy, the loss of him who stood
A champion steadfast and invincible,
To quell the rage of literary war!

III

O THOU who movest onward with a mind
Intent upon thy way, pause, though in haste!
'T will be no fruitless moment. I was born
Within Savona's walls, of gentle blood.
On Tiber's banks my youth was dedicate
To sacred studies; and the Roman Shepherd
Gave to my charge Urbino's numerous flock.
Well did I watch, much labored, nor had power
To escape from many and strange indignities;
Was smitten by the great ones of the world,
But did not fall; for Virtue braves all shocks,
Upon herself resting immovably.
Me did a kindlier fortune then invite
To serve the glorious Henry, king of France,
And in his hands I saw a high reward
Stretched out for my acceptance: but Death came.
Now, reader, learn from this my fate, how false,
How treacherous to her promise, is the world,
And trust in God,—to whose eternal doom
Must bend the sceptered potentates of earth.

IV

THERE never breathed a man, who, when his life
Was closing, might not of that life relate
Toils long and hard. The warrior will report
Of wounds, and bright swords flashing in the field,
And blast of trumpets. He who hath been doomed
To bow his forehead in the courts of kings
Will tell of fraud and never-ceasing hate,
Envy and heart-inquietude, derived
From intricate cabals of treacherous friends.
I, who on shipboard lived from earliest youth,

Could represent the countenance horrible
Of the vexed waters, and the indignant rage
Of Auster and Boötes. Fifty years
Over the well steered galleys did I rule.
From huge Pelorus to the Atlantic Pillars,
Rises no mountain to mine eyes unknown;
And the broad gulfs I traversed oft—and—oft.
Of every cloud which in the heavens might stir
I knew the force; and hence the rough sea's pride
Availed not to my vessel's overthrow.
What noble pomp, and frequent, have not I
On regal decks beheld! yet in the end
I learned that one poor moment can suffice
To equalize the lofty and the low.
We sail the sea of life,—a calm one finds,
And one a tempest,—and, the voyage o'er,
Death is the quiet haven of us all.
If more of my condition ye would know,
Savona was my birth-place, and I sprang
Of noble parents: seventy years and three
Lived I,—then yielded to a slow disease.

V

True is it that Ambrosio Salinero,
With an untoward fate, was long involved
In odious litigation; and full long,
Fate harder still! had he to endure assaults
Of racking malady. And true it is
That not the less a frank, courageous heart
And buoyant spirit triumphed over pain;
And he was strong to follow in the steps
Of the fair Muses. Not a covert path
Leads to the dear Parnassian forest's shade,
That might from him be hidden; not a track
Mounts to pellucid Hippocrene, but he
Had traced its windings. This Savona knows,
Yet no sepulchral honors to her son
She paid; for in our age the heart is ruled

Only by gold. And now a simple stone,
Inscribed with this memorial, here is raised
By his bereft, his lonely, Chiabrera.
Think not, O passenger who read'st the lines,
That an exceeding love hath dazzled me:
No,—he was one whose memory ought to spread
Where'er Permessus bears an honored name,
And live as long as its pure stream shall flow.

VI

Destined to war from very infancy
Was I, Roberto Dati, and I took
In Malta the white symbol of the Cross.
Nor in life's vigorous season did I shun
Hazard or toil; among the sands was seen
Of Libya, and not seldom, on the banks
Of wide Hungarian Danube, 't was my lot
To hear the sanguinary trumpet sounded.
So lived I, and repined not at such fate:
This only grieves me, for it seems a wrong,
That stripped of arms I to my end am brought
On the soft down of my paternal home.
Yet haply Arno shall be spared all cause
To blush for me. Thou, loiter not nor halt
In thy appointed way, and bear in mind
How fleeting and how frail is human life!

VII

O flower of all that springs from gentle blood,
And all that generous nurture breeds, to make
Youth amiable! O friend so true of soul
To fair Aglaia! by what envy moved,
Lelius, has Death cut short thy brilliant day
In its sweet opening? and what dire mishap
Has from Savona torn her best delight?
For thee she mourns, nor e'er will cease to mourn;
And, should the outpourings of her eyes suffice not
For her heart's grief, she will entreat Sebeto

Not to withhold his bounteous aid,—Sebeto,
Who saw thee on his margin yield to death,
In the chaste arms of thy beloved love!
What profit riches? what does youth avail?
Dust are our hopes!—I, weeping bitterly,
Penned these sad lines, nor can forbear to pray
That every gentle spirit hither led
May read them not without some bitter tears.

VIII

Not without heavy grief of heart did he
On whom the duty fell (for at that time
The father sojourned in a distant land)
Deposit in the hollow of this tomb
A brother's child, most tenderly beloved!
Francesco was the name the youth had borne,—
Possobonnelli his illustrious house;
And when beneath this stone the corse was laid,
The eyes of all Savona streamed with tears.
Alas! the twentieth April of his life
Had scarcely flowered: and at this early time,
By genuine virtue he inspired a hope
That greatly cheered his country; to his kin
He promised comfort; and the flattering thoughts
His friends had in their fondness entertained
He suffered not to languish or decay.
Now is there not good reason to break forth
Into a passionate lament? O soul!
Short while a pilgrim in our nether world,
Do thou enjoy the calm empyreal air;
And round this earthly tomb let roses rise,—
An everlasting spring!—in memory
Of that delightful fragrance which was once
From thy mild manners quietly exalted.

IX

Pause, courteous spirit!—Balbi supplicates,
That thou, with no reluctant voice, for him
Here laid in mortal darkness, wouldst prefer

A prayer to the Redeemer of the world.
This to the dead by sacred right belongs;
All else is nothing. Did occasion suit
To tell his worth, the marble of this tomb
Would ill suffice: for Plato's lore sublime,
And all the wisdom of the Stagyrite,
Enriched and beautified his studious mind;
With Archimedes, also, he conversed,
As with a chosen friend; nor did he leave
Those laureate wreaths ungathered which the Nymphs
Twine near their beloved Permessus. Finally,
Himself above each lower thought uplifting,
His ears he closed to listen to the songs
Which Sion's kings did consecrate of old;
And his Permessus found on Lebanon.
A blessed man! who of protracted days
Made not, as thousands do, a vulgar sleep;
But truly did he live his life. Urbino,
Take pride in him!—O passenger, farewell!

(*William Wordsworth*)

Tomasso Campanella

1568-1639

THE PEOPLE

The people is a beast of muddy brain
That knows not its own force, and therefore stands
Loaded with wood and stone; the powerless hands
Of a mere child guide it with bit and rein:
One kick would be enough to break the chain;
But the beast fears, and what the child demands,
It does; nor its own terror understands,
Confused and stupefied by bugbears vain.
Most wonderful! with its own hand it ties
And gags itself—gives itself death and war
For pence doled out by kings from its own store.
Its own are all things between earth and heaven;
But this it knows not; and if one arise
To tell this truth, it kills him unforgiven.

(*John Addington Symonds*)

Giambattista Marini

1569-1625

FADING BEAUTY

Beauty—a beam, nay, flame,
Of the great lamp of light—
Shines for a while with fame,
But presently makes night:
Like Winter's short-lived bright,
Or Summer's sudden gleams;
As much more dear, so much less lasting beams.

. . . .

Winged Love away doth fly,
And with him Time doth bear;
And both take suddenly
The sweet, the fair, the dear:
To shining day and clear
Succeeds the obscure night;
And sorrow is the heir of sweet delight.

With what, then, dost thou swell,
O youth of new-born day?
Wherein doth thy pride dwell,
O Beauty, made of clay?
Not with so swift a way
The headlong current flies,
As do the lively rays of two fair eyes.

. . .

That which on Flora's breast,
All fresh and flourishing,
Aurora newly dressed
Saw in her dawning spring;
Quite dry and languishing,
Deprived of honor quite,
Day-closing Hesperus beholds at night.

Fair is the lily; fair
The rose, of flowers the eye!
Both wither in the air,
Their beauteous colors die:
And so at length shall lie,
Deprived of former grace,
The lilies of thy breasts, the roses of thy face.

. . . . .

Do not thyself betray
With shadows; with thy years,
O Beauty (traitors gay!)
This melting life, too, wears,—
Appearing, disappears;
And with thy flying days,
Ends all thy good of price, thy fair of praise.

Trust not, vain creditor,
Thy oft deceived view
In thy false counsellor,
That never tells thee true:
Thy form and flattered hue,
Which shall so soon transpass,
Are far more frail than is thy looking-glass.

Enjoy thy April now,
Whilst it doth freely shine:
This lightning flash and show,
With that clear spirit of thine,
Will suddenly decline;
And those fair murdering eyes
Shall be Love's tomb, where now his cradle lies.

Old trembling age will come,
With wrinkled cheeks and stains,
With motion troublesome,
With void and bloodless veins;
That lively visage wanes,
And, made deformed and old,
Hates sight of glass it loved so to behold.

Thy gold and scarlet shall
   Pale silver-color be;
Thy row of pearls shall fall
   Like withered leaves from tree;
   And thou shalt shortly see
Thy face and hair to grow
All plowed with furrows, over-swollen with snow.

. . . . .

What, then, will it avail,
   O youth advised ill,
In lap of beauty frail
   To nurse a wayward will,
   Like snake in sun-warm hill?
Pluck, pluck betime thy flower,
That springs and parches in the self-same hour.

(*Samuel Daniel*)

Francesco Redi

1626-1698

FROM BACCHUS IN TUSCANY

BACCHUS'S OPINION OF WINE, AND OTHER BEVERAGES

GIVE me, give me Buriano,
Trebbiano, Colombano,—
Give me bumpers, rich and clear!
'T is the true old Aurum Potabile,
Gilding life when it wears shabbily:
Helen's old Nepenthe 't is,
That in the drinking
Swallowed thinking,
And was the receipt for bliss.
Thence it is, that ever and aye,
When he doth philosophize,
Good old glorious Rucellai
Hath it for light unto his eyes;
He lifteth it, and by the shine
Well discerneth things divine:

Atoms with their airy justles,
And all manner of corpuscles;
And, as through a crystal skylight,
How morning differeth from evening twilight;
And further telleth us the reason why go
Some stars with such a lazy light, and some with a
vertigo.

O, how widely wandereth he,
Who in search of verity
Keeps aloof from glorious wine!
Lo, the knowledge it bringeth to me!
For Barbarossa, this wine so bright,
With its rich red look and its strawberry light,
So inviteth me,
So delighteth me,
I should infallibly quench my inside with it,
Had not Hippocrates
And old Andromachus
Strictly forbidden it
And loudly chidden it,
So many stomachs have sickened and died with it.
Yet, discordant as it is,
Two good biggins will not come amiss;
Because I know, while I'm drinking them down,
What is the finish and what is the crown.
A cup of good Corsican
Does it at once;
Or a glass of old Spanish
Is neat for the nonce:
Quackish resources are things for a dunce.

Talk of Chocolate!
Talk of Tea!
Medicines, made—ye gods!—as they are,
Are no medicines made for me.
I would sooner take to poison
Than a single cup set eyes on
Of that bitter and guilty stuff ye

Talk of by the name of Coffee.
Let the Arabs and the Turks
Count it 'mongst their cruel works:
Foe of mankind, black and turbid,
Let the throats of slaves absorb it.
Down in Tartarus,
Down in Erebus,
'Twas the detestable Fifty invented it;
The Furies then took it
To grind and to cook it,
And to Proserpina all three presented it.
If the Mussulman in Asia
Doats on a beverage so unseemly,
I differ with the man extremely.

. . . .

There's a squalid thing, called Beer:
The man whose lips that thing comes near
Swiftly dies; or falling foolish,
Grows, at forty, old and owlish.
She that in the ground would hide her,
Let her take to English Cider:
He who'd have his death come quicker,
Any other Northern liquor.
Those Norwegians and those Laps
Have extraordinary taps:
Those Laps especially have strange fancies;
To see them drink,
I verily think,
Would make me lose my senses.
But a truce to such vile subjects,
With their impious, shocking objects.
Let me purify my mouth
In a holy cup o' th' South;
In a golden pitcher let me
Head and ears for comfort get me,
And drink of the wine of the vine benign
That sparkles warm in Sansovine.

(*Leigh Hunt*)

THE CREATION OF MY LADY

That Love,—whose power and sovranty we own,
And who before all time was did beget
The sun and moon and splendid stars, and set
All lovely things to speak of Him alone,—
Late looking earthward from his supreme throne
Saw that,—although the beauty lingered yet,—
The froward heart of man did quite forget
That all this beauty from His presence shone;
Wherefore, desiring to reclaim his eyes
To heaven by some unequalled new delight,
He gave the world a treasure from the skies,
My Lady's sacred beauty, pure and bright,
Whose body is a robe of woven light,
And fashioned in the looms of Paradise.

(*Sir Edmund Gosse*)

Vincenzo Filicaja

1642-1707

ITALY

Italia! Oh Italia! thou who hast
The fatal gift of beauty, which became
A funeral dower of present woes and past,
On thy sweet brow is sorrow plow'd by shame,
And annals graved in characters of flame.
Oh, God! that thou wert in thy nakedness
Less lovely or more powerful, and couldst claim
Thy right, and awe the robbers back, who press
To shed thy blood, and drink the tears of thy distress;

Then might'st thou more appal, or less desired,
Be homely and be peaceful, undeplored
For thy destructive charms; then, still untired,
Would not be seen the armed torrents pour'd
Down the steep Alps; nor would the hostile horde

Of many-nation'd spoilers from the Po
Quaff blood and water; nor the stranger's sword
Be thy sad weapon of defense, and so
Victor or vanquished, thou the slave of friend or foe.

(*Lord Byron*)

Vittorio Alfieri

1749-1803

TO DANTE

"Great father Alighier, if from the skies
This thy disciple prostrate thou dost see
Before thy gravestone, shaken with deep sighs,
O turn thou not in wrathfulness from me!
O of thy kindness, favoring pure desires,
Illuminate me with a ray of thine;
Must who to pristine, deathless fame aspires
Take arms 'gainst envy and each fell design?"
"I did so, son, to my great sorrow, for
Thereby the names of men too vile to tread
Under my feet are heard for evermore.
If thou dost trust in me, why droop thy head?
Go thunder, triumph, and if thou shouldst chance
To meet with such, pass by nor deign a glance."

(*Lorna De' Lucchi*)

Jacopo Vittorelli

1749-1835

ON A NUN

Of two fair virgins, modest, though admired,
Heaven made us happy; and now, wretched sires,
Heaven for a nobler doom their worth desires,
And gazing upon *either, both* required.
Mine, while the torch of Hymen newly fired
Becomes extinguish'd, soon—too soon—expires:
But thine, within the closing grate retired,

Eternal captive, to her God aspires.
But *thou,* at least, from out the jealous door,
Which shuts between your never-meeting eyes,
May'st hear her sweet and pious voice once more:
I to the marble, where *my* daughter lies,
Rush,—the swoln flood of bitterness I pour,
And knock, and knock, and knock—but none replies.

(*Lord Byron*)

Giacomo Leopardi

1798-1837

TO ITALY

O Italy, I see the lonely towers,
The arches and the columns and the walls
Of bygone days. The glory and the steel
That girt our fathers I behold not. Now
Unarmed, thou show'st a naked breast, a brow
Undiademed. Ah me, what wounds, what blood!
How art thou fallen, O most beautiful!
I cry to heaven, unto earth I cry:
Say, say, who brought her to so dire a pass?
Her arms are bound in chains; with scattered locks
And face unveiled, she sits disconsolate,
Forgotten, and her head between her knees
Hiding, she weeps. Ah, weep, my Italy,
Thou hast good cause, thou who wert born to rule,
Now fallen on so dark a destiny.

Were thy dim eyes two gushing founts of tears
They ne'er could quench thy sorrow and thy shame,
Who wert a queen, and art become a slave.
Who now doth speak of thee, remembering
Thy vaunted past, but saith: She once was great,
She is no more? Why? Why? Where is thy might,
Thine ancient valor, arms, and constancy?
Who hath unclasped thy sword? Who thee betrayed?
What subtle craft, what labor, or what power

Despoiled thee of thy mantle and thy crown?
How, when didst fall from majesty so low?
Will none defend thee, will none fight for thee
Among thy children? Arms, to arms! Alone
I'll fight for thee, I'll fall for thee alone,
And be my blood a brand to fire cold hearts.

Where are thy children? Noise of arms I hear,
Of chariots and of shouting and of drums:
In foreign lands thy sons are combating.
Attend, O Italy. I see afar
A swaying throng of horses and of men,
Whirling of smoke and dust, and in the midst,
As lightning streaks the cloud, a flash of blades.
Art thou not comforted? Thy tear-dimmed eyes
Upon th' uncertain battle canst not bend?
What moves thy youth to fight upon those fields?
Ye gods, for alien lands Italian steel
Is bared. Unhappy he who fighting falls,
Not for his native shores and children dear,
But for the stranger, slain by others' foe,
And dying cannot say: O sacred soil,
I give thee back the life thou gavest me.

Oh fortunate and blest those days of old
When for their country peoples thronged to die.
Be ye for ever honored and most praised,
O Thessalonian passes, where dark fate
To Persian arms allied proved powerless
Against a handful of intrepid souls.
Methinks your waves and plants, your very stones
And watching mountains with incessant voice
Proclaim how all that coast was covered thick
With those undaunted hosts that fell for Greece.
Then, wild with fear, Xerxes o'er Hellespont
Fled, for all time a spectacle and scorn.
Simonides with failing steps did climb
Anthela's mount, where that heroic band
Dying were freed from death, and all about

Gazing with streaming eyes at hills and sea,
Took up his lyre and sang: O blessed ye
Who bared your breasts unto the foe's sharp steel
For love of her who gave you to the light,
Whom Greece hath tested, and the world reveres.
What mighty love your youthful spirits moved
To face 'mid clash of arms such bitter doom?
O children, with what shining countenance
Was Death to you revealed, that smiling thus
Ye ran to him 'mid pain and wounds so sore?
It seemed ye went to dance and feasting gay,
Yet night awaited you, and Tartarus;
Nor child nor spouse stood by when on that shore,
Without a kiss, without a tear, ye died.

But for the Persian 'twas dread chastisement,
Undying anguish. For as 'mid a drove
Of bulls a lion plunging, now on one
Now on another leaps, with claws and teeth
Tearing their flesh, so 'mid the Persian hordes
Raged the horoic fury of the Greeks.
See horses prone and men; see broken tents
And chariots trip the vanquished in their flight.
And see among the foremost, wild-eyed, pale,
The tyrant. See how with barbaric blood
Encrimsoned, the pursuing heroes fall,
One after one, by wounds o'ercome at last.
Live, live, most blessed ones, while yet the world
Hath tongue and hand to blaze your glorious deed!

The stars, uprooted, shall be hurled from heaven
Into the deep, and their majestic fires
'Mid hissing ruin quenched, ere memory
Your image shall unclasp, or spurn your love.
Your tomb an altar is, whereto shall come
Mothers, unto their children showing there
The shining traces of your blood. Behold,
O glorious ones, bowed on this hallowed ground,
I kiss these stones, this sod; may they be blest

And praised eternally from pole to pole.
Ah would that I were buried here with you,
And that this soil were sodden with my blood.
But since fate wills not that my dying eyes
Should close in battle for a land oppressed,
May the gods grant your poet's humble fame
Mingled with yours shall through the ages last.

(Romilda Rendel)

A SÈ STESSO

Now rest for evermore, my weary heart!
Perished the last illusion I believed
Eternal, perished! Truly I can tell
How of our cherished dreams
The hope is quenched and the desire as well.
Now rest for evermore!
Enough of strife!
There's nothing worth one throb of thine; this earth
Deserveth not a sigh! Bitter is life
And wearisome, nought else;
The world's defiled!
Despair for the last time and then be still!
Fate made us at our birth no gift save death;
Scorn nature now, and brutal destiny
Who ruleth hidden for the common ill,
And of all things the infinite vanity!

(Lorna De' Lucchi)

L'INFINITO

I ALWAYS loved this solitary hill,
This hedge as well, which takes so large a share
Of the far-flung horizon from my view;
But seated here, in contemplation lost,
My thought discovers vaster space beyond
Supernal silence and unfathomed peace;
Almost I am afraid; then, since I hear
The murmur of the wind among the leaves,

I match that infinite calm unto this sound
And with my mind embrace eternity,
The vivid, speaking present and dead past;
In such immensity my spirit drowns,
And sweet to me is shipwreck in this sea.

(*Lorna De' Lucchi*)

Giosuè Carducci

1836-1907

SNOWFALL

Silently, slowly falls the snow from an ashen sky,
Cries, and sounds of life from the city rise no more,

No more the hawker's shout and the sound of running
wheels,
No more the joyous song of love and youth arise.

Raucously from the somber spire through the leaden air
The hours moan, like sighs of a world removed from
time.

Wandering birds insistent knock on the glowing panes.
My ghostly friends return, and gaze, and call to me.

Soon, my dear ones, soon—be still, O dauntless heart—
Down to the silence I come, in the shadow I will rest.

(*Romilda Rendel*)

PETRARCH

Master Francesco, I have come to thee
And to thy friend, that gentle, fair-haired dame,
To calm my angry spirit and set free
My grim soul by sweet Sorga's crystal stream.
Look! shade and rest I find beneath this tree!
I sit, and to the lonely shore I call;
Thou comest, and a choir encircles thee
Who greet me with a friendly welcome all.

And that sweet choir—they are those songs of thine,
  Down whose fair sides their golden tresses fall—
Escaping from the rose-wreaths that entwine
  Their gathered folds, in ringlets prodigal;
And one doth shake her locks, and the rebel cry
Breaks from her tuneful lips, "Rome! Italy!"

(William Dudley Foulke)

PRIMO VERE

Behold from sluggish winter's arm
  Spring lifts herself again:
Naked before the steel-cold air
  She shivers as in pain;
Look, Lalage, is that a tear
  In the sun's eye which yet shines clear?

From beds of snow the flowers awake
  Lifting in deep amaze
To heaven their eager eyes: but yet
  More in that wistful gaze
Than wonder lies: sure trembles there,
  O Lalage, some memory fair,

Some dream which 'neath the coverlet white
  Of winter snow they dreamed,
Some sleeping sight of dewy dawns
  And summer suns that gleamed,
And thy bright eyes, O Lalage;
  Was not the dream a prophecy?

To-day my spirit sleeps and dreams;
  Where do my far thoughts fly?
Close to thy beauty's face we stand
  And smile, the spring and I;—
Yet, Lalage, whence come these tears?
  Has spring, too, felt the doom of years?

(John Bailey)

Popular Songs of Tuscany

1

"Sleeping or waking, thou sweet face,
Lift up thy fair and tender brow:
List to thy love in this still place;
He calls thee to thy window now:
But bids thee not the house to quit,
Since in the night this were not meet.
Come to thy window, stay within;
I stand without, and sing and sing:
Come to thy window, stay at home;
I stand without, and make my moan."

2

"I see the dawn e'en now begin to peer:
Therefore I take my leave, and cease to sing.
See how the windows open far and near,
And hear the bells of morning, how they ring!
Through heaven and earth the sounds of ringing swell;
Therefore, bright jasmine flower, sweet maid, farewell!
Through heaven and Rome the sound of ringing goes;
Farewell, bright jasmine flower, sweet maiden rose!"

3

"It was the morning of the first of May,
Into the close I went to pluck a flower;
And there I found a bird of woodland gay,
Who whiled with songs of love the silent hour.
O bird, who fliest from fair Florence, how
Dear love begins, I prithee teach me now!—
Love it begins with music and with song,
And ends with sorrow and with sighs ere long."

4

"Passing across the billowy sea,
I let, alas, my poor heart fall;
I bade the sailors bring it me;
They said they had not seen it fall.

I asked the sailors, one and two;
They said that I had given it you.
I asked the sailors, two and three;
They said that I had given it thee."

5

"What time I see you passing by,
I sit and count the steps you take:
You take the steps; I sit and sigh:
Step after step, my sighs awake.
Tell me, dear love, which more abound,
My sight or your steps on the ground?
Tell me, dear love, which are the most,
Your light steps or the sighs they cost?"

6

"I would I were a bird so free,
That I had wings to fly away:
Unto that window I would flee,
Where stands my love and grinds all day.
Grind, miller, grind; the water's deep!
I cannot grind; love makes me weep.
Grind, miller, grind; the waters flow!
I cannot grind; love wastes me so."

7

"On Sunday morning well I knew
Where gayly dressed you turned your feet;
And there were many saw it too,
And came to tell me through the street:
And when they spoke, I smiled, ah me!
But in my room wept privately;
And when they spoke, I sang for pride,
But in my room alone I sighed."

8

"Strew me with blossoms when I die,
Nor lay me 'neath the earth below;
Beyond those walls, there let me lie,
Where oftentimes we used to go.
There lay me to the wind and rain;
Dying for you, I feel no pain:
There lay me to the sun above;
Dying for you, I die of love."

(John Addington Symonds)

SPANISH

Juan Ruiz de Hita

c. 1343

PRAISE OF LITTLE WOMEN

I WISH to make my sermon brief,—to shorten my
oration,—
For a never-ending sermon is my utter detestation:
I like short women,—suits at law without procrastination,—
And am always most delighted with things of short
duration.

A babbler is a laughing-stock; he's a fool who's always
grinning;
But little women love so much, one falls in love with
sinning.
There are women who are very tall, and yet not worth
the winning,
And in the change of short for long repentance finds
beginning.

To praise the little women Love besought me in my
musing;
To tell their noble qualities is quite beyond refusing:
So I'll praise the little women, and you'll find the thing
amusing;
They are, I know, as cold as snow, whilst flames around
diffusing.

They're cold without, whilst warm within the flame of
Love is raging;
They're gay and pleasant in the street,—soft, cheerful,
and engaging;

They're thrifty and discreet at home,—the cares of life
assuaging:
All this and more;—try, and you'll find how true is
my presaging.

In a little precious stone what splendor meets the eyes!
In a little lump of sugar how much of sweetness lies!
So in a little woman love grows and multiplies:
You recollect the proverb says,—*A word unto the wise.*

A pepper-corn is very small, but seasons every dinner
More than all other condiments, although 'tis sprinkled
thinner:
Just so a little woman is, if Love will let you win her,—
There's not a joy in all the world you will not find
within her.

And as within the little rose you find the richest dyes,
And in a little grain of gold much price and value lies,
As from a little balsam much odor doth arise,
So in a little woman there's a taste of paradise.

Even as the little ruby its secret worth betrays,
Color, and price, and virtue, in the clearness of its
rays,—
Just so a little woman much excellence displays,
Beauty, and grace, and love, and fidelity always.

The skylark and the nightingale, though small and light
of wing,
Yet warble sweeter in the grove than all the birds that
sing:
And so a little woman, though a very little thing,
Is sweeter far than sugar, and flowers that bloom in
spring.

The magpie and the golden thrush have many a thrilling
note,
Each as a gay musician doth strain his little throat,—

A merry little songster in his green and yellow coat:
And such a little woman is, when Love doth make her
dote.

There's naught can be compared to her, throughout the
wide creation;
She is a paradise on earth,—our greatest consolation,—
So cheerful, gay, and happy, so free from all vexation:
In fine, she's better in the proof than in anticipation.

If as her size increases are woman's charms decreased,
Then surely it is good to be from all the great released.
Now of two evils choose the less,—said a wise man of
the East:
By consequence, of woman-kind be sure to choose the
least.

(*H. W. Longfellow*)

Juan II of Castile

1405-1454

CANCION

O LOVE, I never, never thought
Thy power had been so great,
That thou couldst change my fate
By changes in another wrought,
Till now, alas! I know it.

I thought I knew thee well,
For I had known thee long;
But though I felt thee strong,
I felt not all thy spell.

Nor ever, ever had I thought
Thy power had been so great,
That thou couldst change my fate
By changes in another wrought,
Till now, alas! I know it.

(*George Ticknor*)

Diego de Saldaña

15th century

EYES SO TRISTFUL

Eyes so tristful, eyes so tristful,
Heart so full of care and cumber,
I was lapped in rest and slumber,
Ye have made me wakeful, wistful!
In this life of labor endless
Who shall comfort my distresses?
Querulous my soul and friendless
In its sorrow shuns caresses.
Ye have made me, ye have made me
Querulous of you, that care not,
Eyes so tristful, yet I dare not
Say to what ye have betrayed me.

(*H. W. Longfellow*)

Anonymous

15th century

VILLANCICO

Three dark maids,—I loved them when
In Jaën,—
Axa, Fatima, Marien.

Three dark maids who went together
Picking olives in clear weather,
My, but they were in fine feather
In Jaën,—
Axa, Fatima, Marien!—

There the harvests they collected,
Turning home with hearts dejected,
Haggard where the sun reflected
In Jaën,—
Axa, Fatima, Marien—

Three dark Moors so lovely they—
Three dark Moors so lovely, they
Plucked the apples on that day
Near Jaën,—
Axa, Fatima, Marien.

(*Thomas Walsh*)[1]

Cristobal de Castillejo

1490-1550

SOME DAY, SOME DAY

Some day, some day
O troubled breast,
Shalt thou find rest.
If Love in thee
To grief give birth,
Six feet of earth
Can more than he;
There calm and free
And unoppressed
Shalt thou find rest.
The unattained
In life at last,
When life is passed
Shall all be gained;
And no more pained,
No more distressed,
Shalt thou find rest.

(*H. W. Longfellow*)

Anonymous

16th century ?

THE SIESTA

Airs! that wander and murmur round,
Bearing delight where'er ye blow,—
Make in the elms a lulling sound,
While my lady sleeps in the shade below.

[1] Courtesy of the Hispanic Society of America.

Lighten and lengthen her noonday rest,
  Till the heat of the noonday sun is o'er:
Sweet be her slumbers,—though in my breast
  The pain she has waked may slumber no more!
Breathing soft from the blue profound,
  Bearing delight where'er ye blow,
Make in the elms a lulling sound,
  While my lady sleeps in the shade below.

Airs! that over the bending boughs,
  And under the shadows of the leaves,
Murmur soft, like my timid vows,
  Or the secret sighs my bosom heaves,—
Gently sweeping the grassy ground,
  Bearing delight where'er ye blow,
Make in the elms a lulling sound,
  While my lady sleeps in the shade below.

(William Cullen Bryant)

Old Spanish Ballads

16th century

GENTLE RIVER, GENTLE RIVER

Gentle river, gentle river,
Lo, thy streams are stained with gore.
Many a brave and noble captain
Floats along thy willowed shore.

All beside thy limpid waters,
All beside thy sands so bright,
Moorish chiefs and Christian warriors
Joined in fierce and mortal fight.

Lords and dukes and noble princes
On thy fatal banks were slain;
Fatal banks that gave to slaughter
All the pride and flower of Spain.

There the hero, brave Alonso,
Full of wounds and glory died;
There the fearless Urdiales
Fell a victim by his side.

Lo! where yonder, Don Saavedra
Through their squadrons slow retires;
Proud Seville, his native city,
Proud Seville his worth admires.

Close behind a renegado
Loudly shouts with taunting cry:
"Yield thee, yield thee, Don Saavedra.
Dost thou from the battle fly?

"Well I know thy aged parents,
Well thy blooming bride I know;
Seven years I was thy captive,
Seven years of pain and woe.

"May our Prophet grant my wishes,
Haughty chief, thou shalt be mine;
Thou shalt drink that cup of sorrow
Which I drank when I was thine."

Like a lion turns the warrior,
Back he sends an angry glare;
Whizzing came the Moorish javelin,
Vainly whizzing through the air.

Back the hero full of fury
Sent a deep and mortal wound;
Instant sank the renegado
Mute and lifeless on the ground.

With a thousand Moors surrounded,
Brave Saavedra stands at bay;
Wearied out but never daunted,
Cold at length the warrior lay.

Near him, fighting, great Alonso
Stout resists the Paynim bands;
From his slaughtered steed dismounted
Firm entrenched behind him stands.

Furious press the hostile squadrons
Furious he repels their rage;
Loss of blood at length enfeebles;
Who can war with thousands wage?

Where yon rock the plain o'shadows
Close behind its foot retired,
Fainting sank the bleeding hero,
And without a groan expired.

(*Thomas Percy*)

ABENAMAR, ABENAMAR

O THOU Moor of *Morería,*
There were mighty signs and aspects
On the day when thou wert born,
Calm and lovely was the ocean,
Bright and full the moon above.
Moor, the child of such an aspect
Never ought to answer falsely.
Then replied the Moorish captive,
(You shall hear the Moor's reply):

Nor will I untruly answer,
Though I died for saying truth.
I am son of Moorish sire.
My mother was a Christian slave.
In my childhood, in my boyhood,
Often would my mother bid me
Never know the liar's shame.
Ask thou, therefore, King, thy question.
Truly will I answer thee.

Thank thee, thank thee, Abenamar,
For thy gentle answer, thanks.
What are yonder lofty castles,
Those that shine so bright on high?

That, O King, is the Alhambra,
Yonder is the Mosque of God.
There you see the Alixares,
Works of skill and wonder they;
Ten times ten doubloons the builder
Daily for his hire received;
If an idle day he wasted
Ten times ten doubloons he paid.
Farther is the Generalife,
Peerless are its garden groves.
Those are the Vermilion Towers,
Far and wide their fame is known.

Then spake up the King Don Juan
(You shall hear the Monarch's speech):
Wouldst thou marry me Granada,
Gladly would I for thy dowry
Cordoba and Seville give.

I am married, King Don Juan.
King, I am not yet a widow.
Well I love my noble husband.
Well my wedded Lord loves me.

(*Robert Southey*)

THE SONG OF THE GALLEY

Ye mariners of Spain,
  Bend strongly on your oars,
And bring my love again,—
  For he lies among the Moors!

Ye galleys fairly built,
Like castles on the sea,
O, great will be your guilt,
If ye bring him not to me!

The wind is blowing strong,—
The breeze will aid your oars;
O, swiftly fly along,—
For he lies among the Moors!

The sweet breeze of the sea
Cools every cheek but mine;
Hot is its breath to me,
As I gaze upon the brine.

Lift up, lift up your sail,
And bend upon your oars;
O, lose not the fair gale,—
For he lies among the Moors!

It is a narrow strait,—
I see the blue hills over;
Your coming I'll await,
And thank you for my lover.

To Mary I will pray,
While ye bend upon your oars;
'Twill be a blessed day,
If ye fetch him from the Moors!

(*John Gibson Lockhart*)

THE LAMENTATION FOR CELIN

AT the gate of old Granada, when all its bolts are barred,
At twilight, at the Vega-gate, there is a trampling heard;
There is a trampling heard, as of horses treading slow,

And a weeping voice of women, and a heavy sound of
woe!—
"What tower is fallen? what star is set; what chief
come these bewailing?"
"A tower is fallen! a star is set!—Alas! alas for Celin!"

Three times they knock, three times they cry,—and
wide the doors they throw;
Dejectedly they enter, and mournfully they go;
In gloomy lines they mustering stand beneath the hollow
porch,
Each horseman grasping in his hand a black and flam-
ing torch;
Wet is each eye as they go by, and all around is wail-
ing,—
For all have heard the misery,—"Alas! alas for Celin!"

Him yesterday a Moor did slay, of Bencerrage's blood,—
'Twas at the solemn jousting,—around the nobles
stood;
The nobles of the land were by, and ladies bright and
fair
Looked from their latticed windows, the haughty sight
to share:
But now the nobles all lament,—the ladies are bewail-
ing,—
For he was Granada's darling knight,—"Alas! alas for
Celin!"

Before him ride his vassals, in order two by two,
With ashes on their turbans spread, most pitiful to view;
Behind him his four sisters, each wrapped in sable veil,
Between the tambour's dismal strokes take up their
doleful tale;
When stops the muffled drum, ye hear their brotherless
bewailing,
And all the people, far and near, cry,—"Alas! alas for
Celin!"

O, lovely lies he on the bier, above the purple pall,
The flower of all Granada's youth, the loveliest of them
all!
His dark, dark eyes are closed, his rosy lip is pale,
The crust of blood lies black and dim upon his burnished mail;
And evermore the hoarse tambour breaks in upon their
wailing,—
Its sound is like no earthly sound,—"Alas! alas for
Celin!"

The Moorish maid at the lattice stands,—the Moor
stands at his door;
One maid is wringing of her hands, and one is weeping
sore;
Down to the dust men bow their heads, and ashes black
they strew
Upon their broidered garments, of crimson, green, and
blue;
Before each gate the bier stands still,—then bursts the
loud bewailing,
From door and lattice, high and low,—"Alas! alas for
Celin!"

An old, old woman cometh forth, when she hears the
people cry,—
Her hair is white as silver, like horn her glazed eye;
'Twas she that nursed him at her breast,—that nursed
him long ago:
She knows not whom they all lament, but soon she well
shall know!
With one deep shriek, she through doth break, when
her ears receive their wailing,—
"Let me kiss my Celin, ere I die!—Alas! alas for
Celin!"

(*John Gibson Lockhart*)

THE DEATH OF DON PEDRO

HENRY and King Pedro, clasping,
Hold in straining arms each other;
Tugging hard, and closely grasping,
Brother proves his strength with brother.

Harmless pastime, sport fraternal,
Blends not thus their limbs in strife:
Either aims, with rage infernal,
Naked dagger, sharpened knife.

Close Don Henry grapples Pedro,
Pedro holds Don Henry strait,—
Breathing, this, triumphant fury,
That, despair and mortal hate.

Sole spectator of the struggle,
Stands Don Henry's page afar,
In the chase who bore his bugle,
And who bore his sword in war.

Down they go in deadly wrestle,
Down upon the earth they go;
Fierce King Pedro has the vantage,
Stout Don Henry falls below.

Marking then the fatal crisis,
Up the page of Henry ran,
By the waist he caught Don Pedro,
Aiding thus the fallen man.

"King to place, or to depose him,
Dwelleth not in my desire;
But the duty which he owes him
To his master pays the squire."

Now Don Henry has the upmost,
  Now King Pedro lies beneath;
In his heart his brother's poniard
  Instant finds its bloody sheath.

Thus with mortal gasp and quiver,
  While the blood in bubbles welled,
Fled the fiercest soul that ever
  In a Christian bosom dwelled.

(John Gibson Lockhart)

Gil Vicente

16th century

SONG

If thou art sleeping, maiden,
  Awake and open thy door.
'Tis the break of day, and we must away
  O'er meadow, and mount, and moor.

Wait not to find thy slippers,
  But come with thy naked feet;
We shall have to pass through the dewy grass
  And waters wide and fleet.

(H. W. Longfellow)

Sister Marcela de Carpio de San Felix

16th century

AMOR MYSTICUS

Let them say to my lover
That here I lie!
The thing of His pleasure,—
His slave am I.

Say that I seek Him
Only for love,
And welcome are tortures
My passion to prove.

Love giving gifts
Is suspicious and cold;
I have all, my Beloved
When thee I hold.

Hope and devotion
The good may gain;
I am but worthy
Of passion and pain.

So noble a Lord
None serves in vain,
For the pay of my love
Is my love's sweet pain.

I love Thee, to love Thee,—
No more I desire;
By faith is nourished
My love's strong fire.

I kiss Thy hands
When I feel their blows;
In the place of caresses
Thou givest me woes.

But in Thy chastising
Is joy and peace.
O Master and Love
Let Thy blows not cease.

Thy beauty, Beloved,
With scorn is rife,
But I know that Thou lovest me
Better than life.

And because Thou lovest me,
Lover of mine,
Death can but make me
Utterly Thine.

I die with longing
Thy face to see;
Oh! sweet is the anguish
Of death to me!

(John Hay)

Saint Teresa

1515-1582

LINES WRITTEN IN HER BREVIARY

Let nothing disturb thee,
Nothing affright thee;
All things are passing;
God never changeth;
Patient endurance
Attaineth to all things;
Who God possesseth
In nothing is wanting;
Alone God sufficeth.

(H. W. Longfellow)

IF, LORD, THY LOVE FOR ME IS STRONG

If, Lord, Thy love for me is strong
As this which binds me unto Thee,
What holds me from Thee, Lord, so long,
What holds Thee, Lord, so long from me?

O soul, what then desirest thou?
—Lord, I would see Thee, who thus choose Thee.
What fears can yet assail thee now?
—All that I fear is but to lose Thee.

Love's whole possession I entreat,
Lord, make my soul Thine own abode,
And I will build a nest so sweet
It may not be too poor for God.

O soul in God hidden from sin,
What more desires for thee remain,

Save but to love, and love again,
And, all on flame with love within,
Love on, and turn to love again?

(Arthur Symons)

LET MINE EYES SEE THEE

Let mine eyes see Thee,
Sweet Jesus of Nazareth,
Let mine eyes see Thee,
And then see death.

Let them see that care
Roses and jessamine;
Seeing Thy face most fair
All blossoms are therein,
Flower of seraphim,
Sweet Jesus of Nazareth
Let mine eyes see Thee,
And then see death.

Nothing I require
Where my Jesus is;
Anguish all desire,
Saving only this;
All my help is His,
He only succoreth.
Let mine eyes see Thee,
Sweet Jesus of Nazareth,
Let mine eyes see Thee,
And then see death.

(Arthur Symons)

TO-DAY A SHEPHERD

To-day a shepherd and our kin,
O Gil, to random us is sent,
And He is God Omnipotent

For us hath He caſt down the pride
And prison wall of Satanas;
But He is of the kin of Bras,
Of Menga, also of Llorent.
O is not God Omnipotent?

If He is God, how then is He
Come hither and here crucified?
—With His dying sin also died,
Enduring death the innocent.
Gil, how is God Omnipotent!

Why, I have seen him born, pardie
And of a moſt sweet shepherdess.
—If He is God how can He be
With such poor folk as these content?
—Seeſt not He is Omnipotent?

Give over idle parleyings
And let us serve Him, you and I,
And since he came on earth to die,
Let us die with him too, Llorent;
For He is God Omnipotent.

(Arthur Symons)

SHEPHERD, SHEPHERD, HARK

Shepherd, shepherd, hark that calling!
Angels they are, and the day is dawning.
What is this ding-dong,
Or loud singing is it?
Come, Bras, now the day is here,
The shepherdess we'll visit.
Shepherd, shepherd, hark that calling!
Angels they are, and the day is dawning.

Oh, is this the Alcalde's daughter,
Or some lady come from far?
She is the daughter of God the Father,

And she shines like a star.
Shepherd, shepherd, hark that calling!
Angels they are, and the day is dawning.

(*Arthur Symons*)

Luis Vaz de Camoëns

1524-1580

ON THE DEATH OF CATARINA DE ATTAYDA

Those charming eyes within whose starry sphere
Love whilom sat, and smiled the hours away,—
Those braids of light, that shamed the beams of day,—
That hand benignant, and that heart sincere,—
Those virgin cheeks, which did so late appear
Like snow-banks scattered with the blooms of May,
Turned to a little cold and worthless clay,
Are gone, forever gone, and perished here,—

But not unbathed by Memory's warmest tear!
Death thou hast torn, in one unpitying hour,
That fragrant plant, to which, while scarce a flower,
The mellower fruitage of its prime was given;
Love saw the deed,—and as he lingered near
Sighed o'er the ruin, and returned to heaven!

(*R. F. Burton*)

ON REVISITING CINTRA AFTER THE DEATH OF CATARINA

Apparel of green woods and meadows gay;
 Clear and fresh waters innocent of stain,
 Wherein the field and grove are found again,
As from high rocks ye take your downward way;
And shaggy peaks, and ordered disarray
 Of crags abrupt, know that ye strive in vain,
 Till grief consent, to soothe the eye of pain,
Shown the same scene that Pleasure did survey.

Nor as erst seen am I beheld by you,
Rejoiced no more by fields of pleasant green,
Or lively runnels laughing as they dart;
Sown be these fields with seeds of ruth and rue,
And wet with brine of welling tears, till seen
Sere with the herb that suits the broken heart.

(Richard Garnett)

BABYLON AND SION (GOA AND LISBON)

Here, where fecundity of Babel frames
Stuff for all ills wherewith the world doth teem,
Where loyal Love is slurred with disesteem,
For Venus all controls, and all defames;
Where vice's vaunts are counted, virtue's shames;
Where Tyranny o'er Honor lords supreme;
Where blind and erring sovereignty doth deem
That God for deeds will be content with names;

Here in this world where whatso is, is wrong,
Where Birth and Worth and Wisdom begging go
To doors of Avarice and Villainy,—
Trammeled in the foul chaos, I prolong
My days, because I must. Woe to me! Woe!
Sion, had I not memory of thee!

(Richard Garnett)

SONNET

Leave me, all sweet refrains my lip hath made;
Leave me, all instruments attuned for song;
Leave me, all fountains pleasant meads among;
Leave me, all charms of garden and of glade;
Leave me all melodies the pipe hath played;
Leave me, all rural feast and sportive throng;
Leave me, all flocks the reed beguiles along;
Leave me, all shepherds happy in the shade.

Sun, moon and stars, for me no longer glow;
Night would I have, to wail for vanished peace;

Let me from pole to pole no pleasure know;
  Let all that I have loved and cherished cease;
But see that thou forsake me not, my Woe,
  Who wilt, by killing, finally release.

(*Richard Garnett*)

SONNET

Time and the mortal will stand never fast;
  Estrangéd fates man's confidence estrange;
Aye with new quality imbued, the vast
  World seems but victual of voracious change.

New endless growth surrounds on every side,
  Such as we deemed not earth could ever bear,
Only doth sorrow for past woe abide.
And sorrow for past good, if good it were.

Now Time with green hath made the meadows gay,
  Late carpeted with snow by winter frore,
And to lament hath turned my gentle lay;
Yet of all change this chiefly I deplore,
  The human lot, transformed to ill alway,
Not chequered with rare blessing as of yore.

(*Richard Garnett*)

Fra Luis de Leon

1528-1591

THE LIFE OF THE BLESSED

    Region of life and light!
Land of the good whose earthly toils are o'er!
    Nor frost nor heat may blight
    Thy vernal beauty, fertile shore,
Yielding thy blessed fruits for evermore!

    There, without crook or sling,
Walks the Good Shepherd; blossoms white and red
    Round his meek temples cling;
    And, to sweet pastures led,
His own loved flock beneath his eye is fed.

He guides, and near him they
Follow delighted; for he makes them go
Where dwells eternal May,
And heavenly roses blow,
Deathless, and gathered but again to grow.

He leads them to the height
Named of the infinite and long-sought Good,
And fountains of delight;
And where his feet have stood,
Springs up, along the way, their tender food.

And when, in the mid skies,
The climbing sun has reached his highest bound,
Reposing as he lies,
With all his flock around,
He witches the still air with numerous sound.

From his sweet lute flow forth
Immortal harmonies, of power to still
All passions born of earth,
And draw the ardent will
Its destiny of goodness to fulfill.

Might but a little part,
A wandering breath, of that high melody
Descend into my heart,
And change it till it be
Transformed and swallowed up, O love! in thee:

Ah! then my soul should know,
Beloved! where thou liest at noon of day;
And from this place of woe
Released, should take its way
To mingle with thy flock, and never stray.

(William Cullen Bryant)

Miguel de Cervantes

1547-1616

SONNET

When I was marked for suffering, Love forswore
All knowledge of my doom; or else at ease
Love grows a cruel tyrant, hard to please;
Or else a chastisement exceeding sore
A little sin hath brought me. Hush! No more!
Love is a god! All things he knows and sees,
And gods are bland and mild! Who then decrees
The dreadful woe I bear and yet adore?

If I should say, O Chloe, that 'twas thou,
I should speak falsely since, being wholly good
Like Heaven itself, from thee no ill can come.
There is no hope; I must die shortly now,
Not knowing why, since, sure, no witch hath brewed
The drug that might avert my martyrdom.

(Sir Edmund Gosse)

Saint John of the Cross

1549-1591

THE OBSCURE NIGHT OF THE SOUL

Upon an obscure night
Fevered with love in love's anxiety
(O hapless-happy plight!)
I went, none seeing me,
Forth from my house where all things be.

By night, secure from sight,
And by the secret stair, disguisedly,
(O hapless-happy plight!)
By night, and privily,
Forth from my house where all things quiet be.

Blest night of wandering,
In secret, where by none might I be spied,
Nor I see anything;
Without a light or guide,
Save that which in my heart burnt in my side.

That light did lead me on,
More surely than the shining of noontide,
Where well I knew that one
Did for my coming bide;
Where He abode, might none but He abide.

O night that didst lead thus,
O night more lovely than the dawn of light,
O night that broughtest us,
Lover to lover's sight,
Lover with loved in marriage of delight!

Upon my flowery breast
Wholly for Him, and save Himself for none,
There did I give sweet rest
To my belovèd one;
The fanning of the cedars breathed thereon.

When the first moving air
Blew from the tower and waved His locks aside.
His hand, with gentle care,
Did wound me in the side,
And in my body all my senses died.

All things I then forgot,
My cheek on Him who for my coming came;
All ceased, and I was not,
Leaving my cares and shame
Among the lilies, and forgetting them.

(*Arthur Symons*)

O FLAME OF LIVING LOVE

O flame of living love,
That dost eternally
Pierce through my soul with so consuming heat,
Since there's no help above,
Make thou an end of me,
And break the bond of this encounter sweet.

O burn that burns to heal!
O more than pleasant wound!
And O soft hand, O touch most delicate,
That dost new life reveal,
That dost in grace abound,
And, slaying, dost from death to life translate!

O lamps of fire that shined
With so intense a light
That those deep caverns where the senses live,
Which were obscure and blind,
Now with strange glories bright,
Both heat and light to His belovèd give!

With how benign intent
Rememberest thou my breast,
Where thou alone abidest secretly;
And in thy sweet ascent,
With glory and good possessed,
How delicately thou teachest love to me!

(*Arthur Symons*)

Luis de Góngora

1561–1627

THE ROSEMARY SPRAY

The flowers upon the rosemary spray,
Young Maid, may school thy sorrow;
The blue-eyed flower, that blooms to-day,
To honey turns to-morrow.

A tumult stirs thy tender breast,
With jealous pain true-hearted,
That he, whom thy first love hath bless'd
From thee hath coldly parted.

Ungracious boy, who slights thy love,
And overbold disdaining
To ask forgiveness, and remove
The cause of thy complaining.

Hope, come and drive those tears away!
For lovers' jealous sorrow,
Like dewy blue-eyed flower on spray
To honey turns to-morrow.

By thine own joy thou wast undone:
A bliss thou couldst not measure,
Like star at dawn too near the sun,
Eclipsed thee by its pleasure.

Walk forth with eyes serene and fair;
The pearls, that deck the morning,
Are wasted in the day's fierce glare;
With calmness tame his scorning.

Disperse those clouds that but dismay;
Distrust that jealous sorrow:
The blue-eyed flower, that blooms to-day,
To honey turns to-morrow.

(*E. Churton*)

THE ROSE OF LIFE

Blown in the morning, thou shalt fade ere noon:
What boots a life which in such haste forsakes thee?
Th'art wondrous frolick being to die so soon:
And passing proud a little color makes thee.
If thee thy brittle beauty so deceives,
Know then the thing that swells thee is thy bane;
For the same beauty doth in bloody leaves
The sentence of thy early death contain.

Some clown's coarse lungs will poison thy sweet flower
  If by the careless plow thou shalt be torn:
  And many Herods lie in wait each hour
  To murther thee as soon as thou art born,
Nay, force thy bud to blow; their tyrant breath,
Anticipating life, to hasten death.

(*Sir Richard Fanshawe*)

LET ME GO WARM

  LET me go warm and merry still;
  And let the world laugh, an' it will.

Let others muse on earthly things,—
The fall of thrones, the fate of kings,
  And those whose fame the world doth fill;
Whilst muffins sit enthroned in trays,
And orange-punch in winter sways
The merry scepter of my days;—
  And let the world laugh, an' it will.

He that the royal purple wears
From golden plate a thousand cares
  Doth swallow as a gilded pill:
On feasts like these I turn my back,
Whilst puddings in my roasting-jack
Beside the chimney hiss and crack;—
  And let the world laugh, an' it will.

And when the wintry tempest blows,
And January's sleets and snows
  Are spread o'er every vale and hill,
With one to tell a merry tale
O'er roasted nuts and humming ale,
I sit, and care not for the gale;—
  And let the world laugh, an' it will.

Let merchants traverse seas and lands,
For silver mines and golden sands;
  Whilst I beside some shadowy rill,

Just where its bubbling fountain swells,
Do sit and gather stones and shells,
And hear the tale the blackbird tells;—
  And let the world laugh, an' it will.

For Hero's sake the Grecian lover
The stormy Hellespont swam over:
  I cross, without the fear of ill,
The wooden bridge that slow bestrides
The Madrigal's enchanting sides,
Or barefoot wade through Yepes' tides;—
  And let the world laugh, an' it will.

But since the Fates so cruel prove,
That Pyramus should die of love,
  And love should gentle Thisbe kill;
My Thisbe be an apple-tart,
The sword I plunge into her heart
The tooth that bites the crust apart;—
  And let the world laugh, an' it will.

(H. W. Longfellow)

Lope de Vega

1562–1635

A SONG OF THE VIRGIN MOTHER

From Los Pastores de Belen

As ye go through these palm-trees
O holy angels;
Sith sleepeth my child here
Still ye the branches.

O Bethlehem palm-trees
That move to the anger
Of winds in their fury,
Tempestuous voices,
Make ye no clamor,
Run ye less swiftly,
Sith sleepeth the child here
Still ye your branches.

He the divine child
Is here a-wearied
Of weeping the earth-pain,
Here for his rest would he
Cease from his mourning,
Only a little while,
Sith sleepeth this child here
Stay ye the branches.

Cold be the fierce winds,
Treacherous round him.
Ye see that I have not
Wherewith to guard him,
O angels, divine ones
That pass us a-flying,
Sith sleepeth my child here
Stay ye the branches.

(Ezra Pound)

TO-MORROW

Lord, what am I, that, with unceasing care,
Thou didst seek after me,—that thou didst wait,
Wet with unhealthy dews, before my gate,
And pass the gloomy nights of winter there?
O, strange delusion, that I did not greet
Thy blest approach! and, O, to heaven how lost,
If my ingratitude's unkindly frost
Has chilled the bleeding wounds upon thy feet!
How oft my guardian angel gently cried,
"Soul, from thy casement look, and thou shalt see
How he persists to knock and wait for thee!"
And, O, how often to that voice of sorrow,
"To-morrow we will open," I replied!
And when the morrow came, I answered still,
"To-morrow."

(H. W. Longfellow)

Francisco de Quevedo y Villegas

1580–1645

SONNET: DEATH WARNINGS

I SAW the ramparts of my native land,
One time so strong, now dropping in decay,
Their strength destroyed by this new age's way
That has worn out and rotted what was grand.
I went into the fields; there I could see
The sun drink up the waters newly thawed;
And on the hills the moaning cattle pawed,
Their miseries robbed the light of day for me.

I went into my house; I saw how spotted,
Decaying things made that old home their prize;
My withered walking-staff had come to bend.
I felt the age had won; my sword was rotted;
And there was nothing on which to set my eyes
That was not a reminder of the end.

(*John Masefield*)

Pedro Calderon de la Barca

1600–1681

He exceeds all modern dramatists, with the exception of Shakespeare, whom he resembles, however, in the depth of thought and subtlety of imagination of his writings, and in the rare power of interweaving delicate and powerful comic traits with the most tragical situations.—PERCY BYSSHE SHELLEY.

THE DREAM CALLED LIFE

A DREAM it was in which I found myself.
And you that hail me now, then hailed me king,
In a brave palace that was all my own,
Within, and all without it, mine; until,
Drunk with excess of majesty and pride,
Methought I towered so big and swelled so wide
That of myself I burst the glittering bubble

Which my ambition had about me blown
And all again was darkness. Such a dream
As this, in which I may be walking now,
Dispensing solemn justice to you shadows,
Who make believe to listen; but anon
Kings, princes, captains, warriors, plume and steel
Ay, even with all your airy theater,
May flit into the air you seem to rend
With acclamations, leaving me to wake
In the dark tower; or dreaming that I wake
From this that waking is; or this and that,
Both waking and both dreaming; such a doubt
Confounds and clouds our mortal life about.
But whether wake or dreaming, this I know
How dreamwise human glories come and go;
Whose momentary tenure not to break,
Walking as one who knows he soon may wake,
So fairly carry the full cup, so well
Disordered insolence and passion quell,
That there be nothing after to upbraid
Dreamer or doer in the part he played;
Whether to-morrow's dawn shall break the spell,
Or the last trumpet of the Eternal Day,
When dreaming, with the night, shall pass away.

(*Edward FitzGerald*)

FROM "LIFE IS A DREAM"

We live, while we see the sun,
Where life and dreams are as one;
And living has taught me this,
Man dreams the life that is his,
Until his living is done.
The king dreams he is king, and he lives
In the deceit of a king,
Commanding and governing;
And all the praise he receives
Is written in wind, and leaves
A little dust on the way

When death ends all with a breath.
Where then is the gain of a throne,
That shall perish and not be known
In the other dream that is death?
Dreams the rich man of riches and fears,
The fears that his riches breed;
The poor man dreams of his need,
And all his sorrows and tears;
Dreams he that prospers with years
Dreams he that feigns and foregoes,
Dreams he that rails on his foes;
And in all the world, I see,
Man dreams whatever he be,
And his own dream no man knows.
And I too dream and behold,
I dream and I am bound with chains,
And I dreamed that these present pains
Were fortunate ways of old.
What is life? a tale that is told;
What is life? a frenzy extreme,
A shadow of things that seem;
And the greatest good is but small,
That all life is a dream to all,
And that dreams themselves are a dream.

(*Arthur Symons*)

Gustavo Adolfo Becquer

1836–1870

THEY CLOSED HER EYES

They closed her eyes
That were still open;
They hid her face
With a white linen,
And, some sobbing,
Others in silence,
From the sad bedroom
All came away.

The nightlight in a dish
Burned on the floor;
It threw on the wall
The bed's shadow,
And in the shadow
One saw sometime
Drawn in sharp line
The body's shape.

The dawn appeared.
At its first whiteness
With its thousand noises
The town awoke.
Before that contrast
Of light and darkness,
Of life and strangeness
I thought a moment.
My God, how lonely
The dead are!

On the shoulders of men
To church they bore her,
And in a chapel
They left her bier.
There they surrounded
Her pale body
With yellow candles
And black stuffs.

At the last stroke
Of the ringing for the Souls,
An old crone finished
Her last prayers.
She crossed the narrow nave,
The doors moaned,
And the holy place
Remained deserted.

From a clock one heard
The measured ticking,
And from a candle
The guttering.
All things there
Were so dark and mournful,
So cold and rigid,
That I thought a moment;
My God, how lonely
The dead are!

From the high belfry
The tongue of iron
Clanged, giving out
A last farewell.
Crape on their clothes,
Her friends and kindred
Passed in a line
In homage to her.

In the last vault
Dark and narrow,
The pickaxe opened
A niche at one end;
They laid her away there.
Soon they bricked the place up,
And with a gesture
Bade grief farewell.

Pickaxe on shoulder
The gravedigger,
Singing between his teeth,
Passed out of sight.
The night came down,
It was all silent.
Alone in the darkness
I thought a moment,—
My God, how lonely
The dead are!

In the dark nights
Of bitter winter,
When the wind makes
The rafter creak,
When the violent rain
Lashes the windows,
Lonely I remember
That poor girl.

There falls the rain
With its noise eternal,
There the northwind
Fights with the rain.
Stretched in the hollow
Of the damp bricks,
Perhaps her bones
Freeze with the cold.

Does the dust return to dust?
Does the soul fly to heaven?
Or is all vile matter,
Rottenness, filthiness?
I know not, but
There is something—something—
Something which give me
Loathing, terror,—
To leave the dead
So alone, so wretched.

(John Masefield)

Antonio Machado

1879–

POEMS

I

A FRAIL sound of a tunic trailing
across the infertile earth,
and the sonorous weeping
of the old bells.

The dying embers
of the horizon smoke.
White ancestral ghosts
go lighting the stars.

—Open the balcony-window. The hour
of illusion draws near. . . .
The afternoon has gone to sleep
and the bells dream.

2

Figures in the fields against the sky!
Two slow oxen plow
on a hillside early in autumn,
and between the black heads bent down
under the weight of the yoke,
hangs and sways a basket of reeds,
a child's cradle;
And behind the yoke stride
a man who leans towards the earth
and a woman who, into the open furrows,
throws the seed.
Under a cloud of carmine and flame,
in the liquid green gold of the setting,
their shadows grow monstrous.

3

Naked is the earth
and the soul howls to the wan horizon
like a hungry she-wolf.
What do you seek,
poet, in the sunset?
Bitter going, for the path
weighs one down, the frozen wind,
and the coming night and the bitterness
of distance. . . . On the white path
the trunks of frustrate trees show black,

on the distant mountains
there is gold and blood. The sun dies. . . .
What do you seek,
poet, in the sunset?

4

We think to create festivals
of love out of our love,
to burn new incense
on untrodden mountains;
and to keep the secret
of our pale faces,
and why in the bacchanals of life
we carry empty glasses,
while with tinkling echoes and laughing
foams the gold must of the grape. . . .
A hidden bird among the branches
of the solitary park
whistles mockery. . . . We feel
the shadow of a dream in our wine-glass,
and something that is earth in our flesh
feels the dampness of the garden like a caress.

(John Dos Passos)

Spanish Folk Songs

I

Let the rich man fill his belly;
Let him fast that has no bread;
And he may sleep in the moon light
That cannot find a bed.

* * *

If the sea were one great ink-pot
And the sky of paper made,
The evil that's in women
Could not all be said.

* * *

If the sea were one great ink-pot
  And of paper all the sky,
It were not enough for telling
  How deeply men can lie.

* * *

To love with no return
  Is a sad thing to befall;
But a sadder, to come to die
  Before having loved at all.

2

My father was a sailor,
  My brother, a sailor was he,
And the man who would be my lover
  A sailor he must be.

* * *

Oh, a pearl is a thing of much value,
  And a diamond yet more than this;
But I know what to me is most precious,
  And that is a student's kiss.

* * *

Do not look at my face;
  I am brown, I am not fair;
When you look, look below my waist,
  I am sweet altogether there.

* * *

My lover is but a small man,
  So would I have him be;
Fewer leaves and more fruit ever
  We find on the little tree.

(*Havelock Ellis*)

FRENCH

From The Provençal

Dance, and Provençal song, and sun-burnt mirth!—JOHN KEATS.

Guillaume de Poitiers

11th century

BEHOLD THE MEADS

BEHOLD, the meads are green again,
The orchard-bloom is seen again,
Of sky and stream the mien again
    Is mild, is bright!
Now should each heart that loves obtain
    Its own delight.

But I will say no ill of Love,
However slight my guerdon prove:
Repining doth not me behove:
    And yet—to know
How lightly she I fain would move
    Might bliss bestow!

There are who hold my folly great,
Because with little hope I wait;
But one old saw doth animate
    And me assure:
Their hearts are high, their might is great,
    Who will endure.

(*Harriet Waters Preston*)

Marcabrun

12th century

AT THE FOUNTAIN

A FOUNT there is, doth overfling
Green turf and garden walks; in spring

A glory of white blossoming
Shines underneath its guardian tree;
And new-come birds old music sing;
And there, alone and sorrowing,
I found a maid I could not cheer,—

Of beauty meet to be adored,
The daughter of the castle's lord;
Methought the melody outpour'd
By all the birds unceasingly,
The season sweet, the verdant sward,
Might gladden her, and eke my word
Her grief dismiss, would she but hear.

Her tears into the fountain fell;
With sorry sighs her heart did swell;
"O Jesus, King Invisible!"
She cried,—"of thee is my distress!
Through thy deep wrong bereft I dwell:
Earth's best have bidden us farewell,
On thee at thine own shrine to wait.

"And my true Love is also gone,
The free, fair, gentle, valiant One;
So what can I but make my moan,
And how the sad desire suppress
That Louis' name were here unknown,
The prayers, the mandates, all undone
Whereby I am made desolate?"

Soon as I heard this plaintive cry,
Moving the limpid wave anigh,
"Weep not, fair maid! so piteously,
Nor waste thy roses!" thus I cried,—
"Neither despair, for He is by
Who brought this leafy greenery,
And He will give thee joy one day."

"Seigneur! I well believe," she said,—
"Of God I shall be comforted
In yonder world when I am dead;
And many a sinful soul beside;—
But now hath He prohibited
My chief delight. I bow my head,—
But heaven is very far away."

(*Harriet Waters Preston*)

Bernard de Ventadour

12th century

NO MARVEL IS IT

No marvel is it if I sing
Better than other minstrels all:
For more than they I am Love's thrall,
And all myself therein I fling,—
Knowledge and sense, body and soul,
And whatso power I have beside;
The rein that doth my being guide
Impels me to this only goal.

His heart is dead whence did not spring
Love's odor, sweet and magical;
His life doth ever on him pall
Who knoweth not that blessed thing;
Yea! God, who doth my life control,
Were cruel did he bid me bide
A month, or even a day, denied
The love whose rapture I extol.

How keen, how exquisite the sting
Of that sweet odor! At its call
An hundred times a day I fall
And faint, an hundred rise and sing.
So fair the semblance of my dole,
'Tis lovelier than another's pride:
If such the ill doth me betide,
Good hap were more than I could thole.

Yet haste, kind heaven! the sundering
True swains from false, great hearts from small!
The traitor in the dust bid crawl!
The faithless to confession bring!
Ah! if I were the master sole
Of all earth's treasures multiplied,
To see my Lady satisfied
Of my pure faith, I'd give the whole.

(*Harriet Waters Preston*)

Arnaut Daniel

MOT ERAN DOUS MIEI COSSIR

Sweet my musings used to be,
Without shadow of distress,
Till the queen of loveliness,
Lowly, mild, yet frank as day,
Bade me put her love away;
Love so deeply wrought in me.
And because I answered not,
Nay, nor e'en her mercy sought,
All the joy of life is gone,
For it lived in her alone.

O my lady, hearken thee!
For thy wondrous tenderness,
Nor my faltering cry repress;
Bid thy faithful servant stay;
Deign to keep my love, I pray;
Let me not my rival see!
That which never cost thee aught
Were to me with rapture fraught.
Who would grudge the sick man's moan
When his pain is all his own?

Thou art wise as thou art fair,
And thy voice is ever kind;
Thou for all dost welcome find,

With a courtesy so bright,
Praise of all it doth invite.
  Hope and comforting of care
In thy smile are born and live
Wheresoe'er thou dost arrive.
Not my love doth canonize,
But the truth and thine own price.

  Unto one thus everywhere
In the praise of men enshrined,
What's my tribute unrefined?
And yet, lady of delight,
True it is, however trite.
  He shall sway the balance fair
Who a single grain doth give,
Be the poise right sensitive.
So might one poor word suffice
To enhance thy dignities.

(Harriet Waters Preston)

BEL M'ES QUAN LO VENS M'ALENA

Softly sighs the April air,
  Ere the coming of the May;
Of the tranquil night aware,
  Murmur nightingale and jay;
Then, when dewy dawn doth rise,
  Every bird in his own tongue
Wakes his mate with happy cries;
  All their joy abroad is flung.

Gladness, lo! is everywhere
  When the first leaf sees the day;
And shall I alone despair,
  Turning from sweet love away?
Something to my heart replies,
  Thou too wast for rapture strung;
Wherefore else the dreams that rise
  Round thee when the year is young?

One, than Helen yet more fair,
  Loveliest blossom of the May,
Rose-tints hath and sunny hair,
  And a gracious mien and gay;
Heart that scorneth all disguise,
  Lips where pearls of truth are hung,—
God, who gives all sovereignties,
  Knows her like was never sung.

Though she lead through long despair,
  I would never say her nay,
If one kiss—reward how rare!—
  Each new trial might repay.
Swift returns I'd then devise,
  Many labors, but not long.
Following so fair a prize
  I could nevermore go wrong.

(*Harriet Waters Preston*)

Bertran de Born

12th century

SONG OF BATTLE

WELL pleaseth me the sweet time of Easter
That maketh the leaf and the flower come out.
And it pleaseth me when I hear the clamor
Of the birds' bruit about their song through the wood;
And it pleaseth me when I see through the meadows
The tents and pavilions set up, and great joy have I
When I see o'er the campana knights armed and horses
  arrayed.

And it pleaseth me when the scouts set in flight the folk
  with their goods;
And it pleaseth me when I see coming together after
  them an host of armed men.
And it pleaseth me to the heart when I see strong
  castles besieged,

And barriers broken and riven, and I see the host on the
shore all about shut in with ditches,
And closed in with "lisses" of strong piles.

(Ezra Pound)

Peire Vidal

12th century

SONG OF BREATH

Breathing do I draw that air to me
Which I feel coming from Provença,
All that is thence so pleasureth me
That whenever I hear good speech of it
I listen a-laughing and straightway
Demand for each word an hundred more,
So fair to me is the hearing.

No man hath known such sweet repair
'Twixt Rhone's swift stream and Vensa,
From the shut sea to Durensa,
Nor any place with joys so rare
As among the French folk where
I left my heart a-laughing in her care,
Who turns the veriest sullen unto laughter.

(Ezra Pound)

Anonymous

12th century?

ALBA INNOMINATA

In a garden where the whitethorn spreads her leaves
My lady hath her love lain close beside her,
Till the warder cries the dawn—Ah dawn that grieves!
Ah God! Ah God! That dawn should come so soon!

"Please God that night, dear night should never cease,
Nor that my love should parted be from me,
Nor watch cry 'Dawn'—Ah dawn that slayeth peace!
Ah God! Ah God! That dawn should come so soon!

"Fair friend and sweet, thy lips! Our lips again!
Lo, in the meadow there the birds give song!
Ours be the love and Jealousy's the pain!
Ah God! Ah God! That dawn should come so soon!

"Sweet friend and fair take we our joy again
Down in the garden, where the birds are loud,
Till the warder's reed astrain
Cry God! Ah God! That dawn should come so soon!

"Of that sweet wind that comes from Far-Away
Have I drunk deep of my Beloved's breath,
Yea! of my Love's that is so dear and gay.
Ah God! Ah God! That dawn should come so soon!"

ENVOI

Fair is this damsel and right courteous,
And many watch her beauty's gracious way.
Her heart toward love is no wise traitorous.
Ah God! Ah God! That dawn should come so soon!

(*Ezra Pound*)

Marie de France

13th century

SONG FROM CHARTIVEL

HATH any loved you well, down there,
Summer or winter through?
Down there, have you found any fair
Laid in the grave with you?
Is death's long kiss a richer kiss
Than mine was wont to be—
Or have you gone to some far bliss
And quite forgotten me?

What soft enamoring of sleep
Hath you in some soft way?
What charmed death holdeth you with deep
Strange lure by night and day?

A little space below the grass,
  Out of the sun and shade;
But worlds away from me, alas,
  Down there where you are laid.

My brightest waved and wasted gold,
  What is it now to thee—
Whether the rose-red life I hold
  Or white death holdeth me?
Down there you love the grave's own green,
  And evermore you rave
Of some sweet seraph you have seen
  Or dreamt of in the grave.

There you shall lie as you have lain,
  Though in the world above,
Another live your life again,
  Loving again your love:
Is it not sweet beneath the palm?
  Is it not warm day rife
With some long mystic golden calm
  Better than love and life?

The broad quaint odorous leaves like hands
  Weaving the fair day through,
Weave sleep no burnished bird withstands,
  While death weaves sleep for you;
And many a strange rich breathing sound
  Ravishes morn and noon:
And in that place you must have found
  Death a delicious swoon—

Hold me no longer for a word
  I used to say or sing:
Ah, long ago you must have heard
  So many a sweeter thing:
For rich earth must have reached your heart
  And turned the faith to flowers;
And warm wind stolen, part by part,
  Your soul through faithless hours.

And many a soft seed must have won
  Soil of some yielding thought,
To bring a bloom up to the sun
  That else had ne'er been brought;
And, doubtless, many a passionate hue
  Hath made that place more fair,
Making some passionate part of you
  Faithless to me down there.

(*Arthur O'Shaughnessy*)

WOULD I MIGHT GO FAR OVER SEA

Would I might go far over sea,
My Love, or high above the air,
And come to land or heaven with thee,
Where no law is, and none shall be.
Against beholding the most rare
Strange beauty that thou hast for me.

Alas, for, in this bitter land,
Full many a written curse doth stand
Against the kiss thy lips should bear;
Against the sweet gift of thy hands;
Against the knowing that thou art fair,
And too fond loving of thy hair.

(*Arthur O'Shaughnessy*)

The Vidame de Chartres

13th century?

APRIL

When the fields catch flower
  And the underwood is green,
And from bower unto bower
  The songs of the birds begin,
  I sing with sighing between.
When I laugh and sing,
  I am heavy at heart for my sin;
I am sad in the spring
  For my love that I shall not win,
For a foolish thing.

This profit I have of my woe,
  That I know, as I sing,
I know he will needs have it so
  Who is master and king,
  Who is lord of the spirit of spring.
I will serve her and will not spare
  Till her pity awake,
Who is good, who is pure, who is fair,
  Even her for whose sake
Love hath ta'en me and slain unaware.

O my lord, O love,
  I have laid my life at thy feet;
Have thy will thereof,
  Do as it please thee with it,
  For what shall please thee is sweet.
I am come unto thee
  To do thee service, O Love;
Yet cannot I see
  Thou wilt take any pity thereof,
Any mercy on me.

But the grace I have long time sought
  Comes never in sight,
If in her it abideth not,
  Through thy mercy and might,
  Whose heart is the world's delight.
Thou hast sworn without fail I shall die,
  For my heart is set
On what hurts me, I wot not why,
  But cannot forget
What I love, what I sing for and sigh.

She is worthy of praise,
  For this grief of her giving is worth
All the joy of my days
  That lie between death's day and birth,
  All the lordship of things upon earth.

Nay, what have I said?
  I would not be glad if I could;
My dream and my dread
  Are of her, and for her sake I would
That my life were fled.

Lo, sweet, if I durst not pray to you,
  Then were I dead;
If I sang not a little to say to you,
  (Could it be said)
  O my love, how my heart would be fed;
Ah, sweet, who hast hold of my heart,
  For thy love's sake I live,
Do but tell me, ere either depart,
  What a lover may give
For a woman so fair as thou art.

The lovers that disbelieve,
  False rumors shall grieve
And evil-speaking shall part.

(Algernon Charles Swinburne)

Jean Froissart

1337–1404

RONDEL

Love, love, what wilt thou with this heart of mine?
Naught see I fixed or sure in thee!
I do not know thee,—nor what deeds are thine:
Love, love, what wilt thou with this heart of mine?
  Naught see I fixed or sure in thee!

Shall I be mute, or vows with prayers combine?
  Ye who are blessed in loving, tell it me:
Love, love, what wilt thou with this heart of mine?
  Naught see I permanent or sure in thee!

(H. W. Longfellow)

Charles d'Orleans

1391–1465

RONDEL

(To his mistress, to succor his heart that is beleaguered by jealousy)

STRENGTHEN, my Love, this castle of my heart,
And with some store of pleasure give me aid,
For jealousy, with all them of his part,
Strong siege about the weary tower has laid.
Nay, if to break his bands thou art afraid,
Too weak to make his cruel force depart,
Strengthen at least this castle of my heart,
And with some store of pleasure give me aid.
Nay, let not jealousy, for all his art
Be master, and the tower in ruin laid,
That still, ah, Love, thy gracious rule obeyed.
Advance, and give me succor of thy part;
Strengthen, my Love, this castle of my heart.

(*Andrew Lang*)

SPRING

THE year has changed his mantle cold
Of wind, of rain, of bitter air;
And he goes clad in cloth of gold,
Of laughing suns and season fair;
No bird or beast of wood or wold
But doth with cry or song declare
The year lays down his mantle cold.
All founts, all rivers, seaward rolled,
The pleasant summer livery wear,
With silver studs on broidered vair;
The world puts off its raiment old,
The year lays down his mantle cold.

(*Andrew Lang*)

ALONS AU BOIS LE MAY CUEILLIR

We'll to the woods and gather may
Fresh from the footprints of the rain;
We'll to the woods, at every vein
To drink the spirit of the day.
The winds of the spring are out at play,
The needs of spring in heart and brain.
We'll to the woods and gather may
Fresh from the footprints of the rain.

The world's too near her end, you say?—
Hark to the blackbird's mad refrain.
It waits for her, the vast Inane?—
Then, girls, to help her on the way
We'll to the woods and gather may.

(*W. E. Henley*)

DIEU QU'IL LA FAIT

God, that mad'st her well regard her,
How she is so fair and bonny;
For the great charms that are upon her
Ready are all folk to reward her.

Who could part him from her borders
When spells are always renewed on her?
God, that mad'st her well regard her,
How she is so fair and bonny.

From here to there to the sea's border,
Dame nor damsel there's not any
Hath of perfect charms so many.
Thoughts of her are of dream's order:
God, that mad'st her well regard her.

(*Ezra Pound*)

Anonymous

JOHN OF TOURS

John of Tours is back with peace,
But he comes home ill at ease.

"Good-morrow, mother." "Good-morrow, son;
Your wife has borne you a little one."

"Go now, mother, go before,
Make me a bed upon the floor.

"Very low your feet must fall,
That my wife hear not at all."

As it neared the midnight toll,
John of Tours gives up his soul.

"Tell me now, my mother dear,
What's the crying that I hear?"

"Daughter, it's the children wake
Crying with their teeth that ache."

"Tell me, though, my mother dear,
What's the knocking that I hear?"

"Daughter, it's the carpenter
Mending planks upon the stair."

"Tell me, too, my mother dear,
What is the singing that I hear?"

"Daughter, it's the priests in rows
Going round about our house."

"Teli me then, my mother, my dear,
What's the dress that I should wear?"

"Daughter, any reds or blues,
But the black is most in use."

"Nay, but say, my mother, my dear,
Why do you fall weeping here?"

"Oh, the truth must be said,—
It's that John of Tours is dead."

"Mother, let the sexton know
That the grave must be for two;

"Aye, and still have room to spare,
For you must shut the baby there."

(D. G. Rossetti.)

MY FATHER'S CLOSE

INSIDE my father's close,
(Fly away, O my heart, away!)
Sweet apple-blossom blows
So sweet.

Three kings' daughters fair,
(Fly away, O my heart, away!)
They lie below it there
So sweet.

"Ah," says the eldest one,
(Fly away, O my heart, away!)
"I think the day's begun
So sweet."

"Ah," says the second one,
(Fly away, O my heart, away!)
"Far off I hear the drum
So sweet."

"Ah," says the youngest one,
(Fly away, O my heart, away!)
"It's my true love, my own,
So sweet."

"Oh, if he fight and win,
(Fly away, O my heart, away!)
"I keep my love for him,

So sweet:
"Oh, let him lose or win,
He hath it still complete."

(D. G. Rossetti)

BALLADE DE MARGUERITE

I AM weary of lying within the chase
When the knights are meeting in the market-place.

Nay, go not thou to the red-roofed town
Lest the hoofs of the war-horse tread thee down.

But I would not go where the Squires ride,
I would only walk by my Lady's side.

Alack, and alack, thou art overbold,
A Forester's son may not eat of gold.

Will she love me the less that my Father is seen
Each Martinmas day in a doublet green?

Perchance she is sewing at tapestrie;
Spindle and loom are not meet for thee.

Ah, if she is working the arras bright
I might ravel the threads by the fire-light.

Perchance she is hunting of the deer,
How could you follow o'er hill and mere?

Ah, if she is riding with the court,
I might run beside her and wind the morte.

Perchance she is kneeling in St. Denis,
(On her soul may our Lady have gramercy).

Ah, if she is praying in lone chapelle,
I might swing the censer and ring the bell.

Come in, my son, for you look sae pale,
The father shall fill thee a stoup of ale.

But who are these knights in bright array?
Is it a pageant the rich folks play?

'Tis the king of England from over sea,
Who has come unto visit our fair countrie.

But why does the curfew toll sae low?
And why do the mourners walk a-row?

O 'tis Hugh of Amiens, my sister's son,
Who is lying stark, for his day is done.

Nay, nay, for I see white lilies clear:
It is no strong man who lies on the bier.

O 'tis old Dame Jeannette that kept the hall,
I knew she would die at the autumn fall.

Dame Jeannette has not that gold-brown hair,
Old Jeannette was not a maiden fair.

O 'tis none of our kith and none of our kin,
(Her soul may our Lady assoil from sin).

But I hear the boy's voice chaunting sweet,
"Elle est morte, la Marguerite."

Come in, my son, and lie on the bed,
And let the dead folk bury their dead.

O mother, you know I loved her true:
O mother, hath one grave room for two?

(*Oscar Wilde*)

THE DOLE OF THE KING'S DAUGHTER

Seven stars in the still water,
And seven in the sky:
Seven sins on the King's daughter,
Deep in her soul to lie.

Red roses are at her feet,
(Roses are red in her red-gold hair)
And O where her bosom and girdle meet
Red roses are hidden there.

Fair is the knight who lieth slain
Amid the rush and reed,
See the lean fishes that are fain
Upon dead men to feed.

Sweet is the page that lieth there,
(Cloth of gold is goodly prey),
See the black ravens in the air,
Black, O black as the night are they.

What do they there so stark and dead?
(There is blood upon her hand)
Why are the lilies flecked with red?
(There is blood in the river sand).

There are two that ride from the south and east,
And two from the north and west,
For the black raven a goodly feast,
For the King's daughter rest.

There is one man who loves her true,
(Red, O red, is the stain of gore),
He hath duggen a grave by the darksome yew,
(One grave will do for four).

No moon in the still heaven,
In the black water none,
The sins in her soul are seven,
The sin upon his is one.

(*Oscar Wilde*)

MEDIEVAL NORMAN SONGS

I

FAIR is her body, bright her eye,
With smiles her mouth is kind to me;
Then, think no evil, this is she
Whom God hath made my only joy.

Between the earth and heaven high
There is no maid so fair as she;
The beauty of her sweet body
Doth ever fill my heart with joy.

He is a knave, nor do I lie,
Who loveth her not heartily;
The grace that shines from her body
Giveth to lovers all great joy.

II

Sad, lost in thought, and mute I go:
The cause, ah me! you know full well:
But see that nought thereof you tell,
For men will only laugh at woe—
For men will only laugh at woe.

III

Kiss me then, my merry May,
By the soul of love I pray!
Prithee, nay! Tell, tell me why?
If with you I sport and play,
My mother will be vexed to-day.
Tell me why, oh tell me why.

IV

Before my lady's window gay,
The little birds they sing all day,
The lark, the mavis and the dove;

But the sweet nightingale of May,
She whiles the silent hours away,
Chanting of sorrow, joy, and love.

V

I found at daybreak yester morn,
Close by the nest where she was born,
A tender turtle dove:
Oha! ohé! ohesa, hesa, hé!

She fluttered, but she could not fly;
I heard, but would not heed her cry:
She had not learned to love:
Oha! ohé! ohesa, hesa, hé!

Now she is quiet on my breast,
And from her new and living nest
She doth not seek to rove:
Oha! ohé! ohesa, hesa, hé!

VI

This month of May, one pleasant eventide,
I heard a young girl singing on the green;
I came upon her where the ways divide,
And said: "God keep you maiden from all teen.

"Maiden, the God of love you keep and save,
And give you all your heart desires," I cried.
Then she: "Pray tell me, gentle sir and brave,
Whither you wend this pleasant eventide?"

"To you I come, a lover leal and true,
To tell you all my hope and all my care;
Your love alone is what I seek; than you
No woman ever seemed to me more fair."

VII

In this merry morn of May,
When as the year grows young and green,

Into the wood I went my way,
To say farewell unto my queen.

And when we could no longer stay,
Weeping upon my neck she fell,
Oh, send me news from far away,
Farewell, sweet heart of mine, farewell.

VIII

O Love, my love, and perfect bliss!
God in his goodness grant me this—
I see thee soon again.
Nought else I need to take away
The grief that for thy sake alway
Doth keep me in great pain.

Alas, I know not what to do,
Nor how to get good news and true:
Dear God, I pray to Thee;
If else Thou canst not comfort me,
Of Thy great mercy make that he
Send speedy news to me.

Within my father's garden alls
There is a tree—when April falls
It blossometh alway.
There wend I oft in winter drear,
Yes, and in spring, the winds to hear,
The sweet winds at their play.

IX

Alas, poor heart, I pity thee
For all the grief thou hast and care.
My love I see not anywhere;
He is so far away from me.
Until once more his face I see
I shall be sad by night and day;

And if his face I may not see
Then I shall die most certainly:
For other pleasures have I none,
And all my hope is this alone.
No ease I take by night and day:
O Love, my love, to thee I pray
Have pity upon me!

Dear nightingale of woodland gay,
Who singest on the leafy tree,
Go, take a message I thee pray,
A message to my love from me;
Tell, tell him that I waste away
And weaker grow from day to day.

Ah, God! what pain and grief have we
Who are poor lovers, leal and true:
For every week that we pass through,
Five hundred thousand griefs have we:
One cannot think, or count, or tell
The griefs and pains that we know well!

X

Now who is he on earth that lives,
Who knows or with his tongue can say
What grief to poor lovers it gives
To love with loyal heart alway?

So bitter is their portion, yea,
So hard their part!
But this doth more confound my heart;
Unloved to love, and still to pray!
Thinking thereon I swoon away.

XI

Sweet flower, that art so fair and gay,
Come tell me if thou lovest me.
Think well, and tell me presently:
For sore it irks me, by my fay.

For sore it irketh me alway,
  That I know not the mind of thee:
I pray thee, gentle lady gay,
  If so thou wilt, tell truth to me.

For I do love thee so, sweet May,
  That if my heart thou wert to see,
  In sooth I know, of courtesy,
Thou wouldst have pity on me this day.

XII

My love for him shall be
  Fair love and true:
  For he loves me, I know,
And I love him, pardie!

And for I know that he
  Doth love me so,
  I should be all untrue
To love but him, pardie!

XIII

Beneath the branch of the green may
  My merry heart sleeps happily,
  Waiting for him who promised me
To meet me here again this day.

And what is that I would not do
  To please my love so dear to me?
He loves me with leal heart and true,
  And I love him no less, pardie.

Perchance I see him but a day;
  Yet maketh he my heart so free—
  His beauty so rejoiceth me—
That month thereafter I am gay.

XIV

They have said evil of my dear;
Therefore my heart is vexed and drear:
  But what is it to them
If he be fair or foul to see,
Since he is perfect joy to me.

He loves me well: the like do I:
I do not look with half an eye,
  But seek to pleasure him.

From all the rest I choose him here;
I want no other for my dear:
  How then should he displease
Those who may leave him if they please?
  God keep him from all fear.

XV

They lied, those lying traitors all,
Disloyal, hypocritical,
  Who feigned that I spake ill of thee.
  Heed not their words of charity;
For they are flatterers tongued with gall,
    And liars all.

They make the tales that they let fall,
Coining falsehoods, where withal
  They swear that I spake ill of thee:
  Heed not their lies of charity;
For they are flatterers tongued with gall,
    And liars all.

Believe them not, although they call
Themselves thy servants; one and all,
  They lie, or God's course light on me,—
  Whatever oaths they swear to thee,
Or were they thrice as stout and tall,
  They're liars all.

XVI

O nightingale of woodland gay,
Go to my love and to her tell
That I do love her passing well;
And bid her also think of me,
For I to her will bring the may.

The may that I shall bring will be
Nor rose nor any opening flower;
But with my heart I will her dower;
And kisses on her lips I'll lay,
And pray God keep her heartily.

XVII

Maid Marjory sits at the castle gate:
With groans and sighs
She weeps and cries:
Her grief it is great.
Her father asks, "Daughter, what is your woe?
Seek you a husband or lord I trow?"
"Let husbands be.
Give my love to me,
Who pines in the dungeon dark below."

"I' faith, my daughter, thou'll long want him;
For he hangs to-morrow when dawn is dim."

"Then bury my corpse at the gallows' feet;
And men will say they were true lovers sweet."

XVIII

Drink, gossips mine! we drink no wine.
They were three wives that had one heart for
wine;
One to the other said—We drink no wine!
Drink, gossips mine! we drink no wine.

Drink, gossips mine! we drink no wine.
The varlet stood in jerkin tight and fine
To serve the dames with service of good wine.
Drink, gossips mine! we drink no wine.

Drink, gossips mine! we drink no wine.
These wives they cried—Here's service of good wine!
Make we good cheer, nor stint our souls of wine!
Drink, gossips mine! we drink no wine.

Drink, gossips mine! we drink no wine.
The gallant fills, nor seeketh further sign,
But crowns the cups with service of good wine.
Drink, gossips mine! we drink no wine.

Drink, gossips mine! we drink no wine.
Sinning beginneth, and sweet notes combine
With joyance to proclaim the praise of wine!
Drink, gossips mine! we drink no wine.

Drink, gossips mine! we drink no wine.
For fear of husbands will we never pine;
They are not here to mar the taste of wine.
Drink, gossips mine! we drink no wine.

(John Addington Symonds)

BALLADS

The Three Captains

(Collected by Gérard de Nerval)

All beneath the white-rose tree
Walks a lady fair to see,
She is as white as the snows,
She is as fair as the day:
From her father's garden close
Three knights have ta'en her away.

He has ta'en her by the hand,
  The youngest of the three—
"Mount and ride, my bonnie bride,
  On my white horse with me."

And ever they rode, and better they rode,
  Till they came to Senlis town,
The hostess she looked hard at them
  As they were lighting down.

"And are ye here by force," she said,
  "Or are ye here for play?"
"From out my father's garden close
  Three knights me stole away.

"And fain would I win back," she said,
  "The weary way I come:
And fain would see my father dear,
  And fain gc maiden home."

"Oh, weep not, lady fair," said she,
  "You shall win back," she said,
"For you shall take this draught from me
  Will make you lie for dead."

"Come in and sup, fair lady," they said,
  "Come busk ye and be bright;
It is with three bold captains
  That ye must be this night."

When they had eaten well and drunk,
  She fell down like one slain;
"Now, out and alas, for my bonnie may
  Shall live no more again."

"Within her tather's garden stead
  There are three white lilies;
With her body to the lily bed,
  With her soul to Paradise."

They bore her to her father's house,
They bore her all the three,
They laid her in her father's close,
Beneath the white-rose tree.

She had not lain a day, a day,
A day but barely three,
When the may awakes, "Oh, open, father,
Oh, open the door for me.

" 'Tis I have lain for dead, father,
Have lain the long days three,
That I might maiden come again
To my mother and to thee."

(*Andrew Lang*)

The Bridge of Death

"The dance is on the Bridge of Death
And who will dance with me?"
"There's never a man of living men
Will dare to dance with thee."

Now Margaret's gone within her bower,
Put ashes in her hair,
And sackcloth on her bonny breast,
And on her shoulders bare.

There came a knock to her bower door,
And blithe she let him in;
It was her brother from the wars,
The dearest of her kin.

"Set gold within your hair, Margaret,
Set gold within your hair,
And gold upon your girdle band,
And on your breast so fair.

"For we are bidden to dance to-night,
We may not bide away;
This one good night, this one fair night,
Before the red new day."

"Nay, no gold for my head, brother,
Nay, no gold for my hair;
It is the ashes and dust of earth
That you and I must wear.

"No gold for my girdle band,
No gold work on my feet;
But ashes of the fire, my love,
But dust that the serpents eat."

. . . . . .

They danced across the Bridge of Death,
Above the black water,
And the marriage-bell was tolled in hell
For the souls of him and her.

(*Andrew Lang*)

Le Père Sévère

King Louis on his bridge is he,
He holds his daughter on his knee.

She asks a husband at his hand
That is not worth a rood of land.

"Give up your lover speedily,
Or you within the tower must lie."

"Although I must the prison dree,
I will not change my love for thee.

"I will not change my lover fair,
Not for the mother that me bare.

"I will not change my true lover
For friends or for my father dear."

"Now where are all my pages keen,
And where are all my serving men?

"My daughter must lie in the tower alway,
Where she shall never see the day."

. . . .

Seven long years are past and gone
And there has seen her never one.

At ending of the seventh year
Her father goes to visit her.

"My child, my child, how may you be?"
"O father, it fares ill with me.

"My feet are wasted in the mold,
The worms they gnaw my side so cold."

"My child, change your love speedily
Or you must still in prison lie."

" 'Tis better far the cold to dree
Than give my true love up for thee."

(*Andrew Lang*)

The Milk White Doe

It was a mother and a maid
  That walked the woods among,
And still the maid went slow and sad,
  And still the mother sung.

"What ails you, daughter Margaret?
  Why go you pale and wan?
Is it for a cast of bitter love,
  Or for a false leman?"

"It is not for a false lover
  That I go sad to see;
But it is for a weary life
  Beneath the greenwood tree.

"For ever in the good daylight
  A maiden may I go,
But always on the ninth midnight
  I change to a milk white doe.

"They hunt me through the green forest
  With hounds and hunting men;
And ever it is my fair brother
  That is so fierce and keen."

. . . .

"Good-morrow, mother." "Good-morrow, son;
  Where are your hounds so good?"
"Oh, they are hunting a white doe
  Within the glad greenwood.

"And three times have they hunted her,
  And thrice she's won away;
The fourth time that they follow her
  That white doe they shall slay."

. . . .

Then out and spoke the forester,
  As he came from the wood,
"Now never saw I maid's gold hair
  Among the wild deer's blood.

"And I have hunted the wild deer
  In east lands and in west;
And never saw I white doe yet
  That had a maiden's breast."

Then up and spake her fair brother,
  Between the wine and bread,
"Behold, I had but one sister,
  And I have seen her dead."

"But ye must bury my sweet sister
  With a stone at her foot and her head,
And ye must cover her fair body
  With the white roses and red."

And I must out to the greenwood;
The roof shall never shelter me;
And I shall lie for seven long years
On the grass below the hawthorn tree.

(*Andrew Lang*)

A Lady of High Degree

I be pareld most of prise,
I ride after the wild fee.

Will ye that I should sing
Of the love of a goodly thing,
Was no vilein's may?
'Tis sung of a knight so free,
Under the olive tree,
Singing this lay.

Her weed was of samite fine,
Her mantle of white ermine,
Green silk her hose;
Her shoon were silver gray,
Her sandals flowers of May,
Laced small and close.

Her belt was of fresh spring buds,
Set with gold claps and studs,
Fine linen her shift;
Her purse it was of love,
Her chain was the flower thereof,
And Love's gift.

Upon a mule she rode,
The selle was of brent gold,
The bits of silver made;
Three red rose trees there were
That overshadowed her,
For a sun shade.

She riding on a day,
Knights met her by the way,
They did her grace;
"Fair lady, whence be ye?"
"France it is my country,
I come of a high race.

"My sire is the nightingale,
That sings, making his wail,
In the wild wood clear;
The mermaid is mother to me,
That sings in the salt sea,
In the ocean mere."

"Ye come of a right good race,
And are born of a high place,
And of high degree;
Would to God that ye were
Given unto me, being fair,
My lady and love to be."

(*Andrew Lang*)

Lost for a Rose's Sake

I laved my hands,
By the water side;
With the willow leaves
My hands I dried.

The nightingale sung
On the bough of the tree;
Sing, sweet nightingale,
It is well with thee.

Thou hast heart's delight,
I have sad heart's sorrow
For a false, false maid
That will wed to-morrow.

'Tis all for a rose,
That I gave her not,
And I would that it grew
In the garden plot.

And I would the rose-tree
Were still to set,
That my love Marie
Might love me yet.

(*Andrew Lang*)

François Villon

1431–1489

No one has ever more skilfully communicated his own disenchantments; no one ever blown a more ear-piercing note of sadness. It is in death that he finds his truest inspiration; in the swift and sorrowful change that overtakes beauty; in the strange revolution by which great fortunes and renowns are diminished to a handful of churchyard dust; and in the utter passing away of what was once lovable and mighty.—Robert Louis Stevenson.

BALLAD OF THE GIBBET

An Epitaph in the form of a ballad that François Villon wrote of himself and his company, they expecting shortly to be hanged.

Brothers and men that shall after us be,
Let not your hearts be hard to us:
For pitying this our misery
Ye shall find God the more piteous.
Look on us six that are hanging thus,
And for the flesh that so much we cherished
How it is eaten of birds and perished,
And ashes and dust fill our bones' place,
Mock not at us that so feeble be,
But pray God pardon us out of His grace.

Listen we pray you, and look not in scorn,
Though justly, in sooth, we are cast to die;
Ye wot no man so wise is born
That keeps his wisdom constantly.

Be ye then merciful, and cry
To Mary's Son that is piteous,
That his mercy take no stain from us,
Saving us out of the fiery place.
We are but dead, let no soul deny
To pray God succor us of His grace.

The rain out of heaven has washed us clean,
The sun has scorched us black and bare,
Ravens and rooks have pecked at our eyne,
And feathered their nests with our beards and hair.
Round are we tossed, and here and there,
This way and that, at the wild wind's will,
Never a moment my body is still;
Birds they are busy about my face.
Live not as we, not fare as we fare;
Pray God pardon us out of His grace.

L'envoy

Prince Jesus, Master of all, to thee
We pray Hell gain no mastery,
That we come never anear that place;
And ye men, make no mockery,
Pray God, pardon us out of His grace.

(*Andrew Lang*)

RONDEL

Good-by, the tears are in my eyes;
Farewell, farewell, my prettiest;
Farewell, of women born the best;
Good-by, the saddest of good-bys.
Farewell, with many vows and sighs
My sad heart leaves you to your rest;
Farewell, the tears are in my eyes;
Farewell, from you my miseries
Are more than now may be confessed,
And most by thee have I been blessed,

Yea, and for thee have wasted sighs;
Good-by, the last of my good-bys.

(Andrew Lang)

ARBOR AMORIS

I HAVE a tree, a graft of love,
That in my heart has taken root;
Sad are the buds and blooms thereof,
And bitter sorrow is its fruit;
Yet, since it was a tender shoot,
So greatly hath its shadow spread,
That underneath all joy is dead,
And all my pleasant days are flown,
Nor can I slay it, nor instead
Plant any tree, save this alone.

Ah, yet, for long and long enough
My tears were rain about its root,
And though the fruit be harsh thereof,
I scarcely looked for better fruit
Than this, that carefully I put
In garner, for the bitter bread
Whereon my weary life is fed:
Ah, better were the soil unsown
That bears such growths; but Love instead
Will plant no tree, but this alone.

Ah, would that this new spring, whereof
The leaves and flowers flush into shoot,
I might have succor and aid of Love,
To prune these branches at the root,
That long have borne such bitter fruit,
And graft a new bough, comforted
With happy blossoms white and red;
So pleasure should for pain atone,
Nor Love slay this tree, nor instead
Plant any tree, but this alone.

L'envoi

Princess, by whom my hope is fed,
My heart thee prays in lowlihead
To prune the ill boughs overgrown,
Nor slay Love's tree, nor plant instead
Another tree, save this alone.

(*Andrew Lang*)

NO, I AM NOT AS OTHERS ARE

No, I am not, as others are,
Child of the angels, with a wreath
Of planets or of any star.
My father's dead, and lies beneath
The churchyard stone: God rest his breath!
I know that my poor old mother
(And she too knows) must come to death,
And that her son must follow her.

I know that rich and poor and all,
Foolish and wise, and priest and lay,
Mean folk and noble, great and small,
High and low, fair and foul, and they
That wore rich clothing on the way,
Being of whatever stock or stem,
And are coiffed newly every day,
Death shall take every one of them.

Paris and Helen are both dead.
Whoever dies, dies with much pain;
For when his wind and breath are sped
His gall breaks on his heart, and then
He sweats, God knows that sweat of men!
Then shall he pray against his doom
Child, brother, sister, all in vain:
None will be surety in his room.

Death makes him tremble and turn pale,
His veins stretch and his nose fall in,
His flesh grow moist and his neck swell,
Joints and nerves lengthen and wax thin;
Body of woman, that hath been
Soft, tender, precious, smooth and even,
Must thou be spoiled in bone and skin?
Yes, or else go alive to heaven.

(Arthur Symons)

VILLON'S STRAIGHT TIP TO ALL CROSS COVES

Suppose you screeve? or go cheap-jack?
Or fake the broads? or fig a nag?
Or thimble-rig? or knap a yack?
Or pitch a snide? or smash a rag?
Suppose you duff? or nose and lag?
Or get the straight, and land your pot?
How do you melt the multy swag?
Booze and the blowens cop the lot.

Fiddle, or fence, or mace, or mack;
Or moskeneer, or flash the drag;
Dead-lurk a crib, or do a crack;
Pad with a slang, or chuck a fag;
Bonnet, or tout, or mump and gag;
Rattle the tats, or mark the spot;
You can not bank a single stag;
Booze and the blowens cop the lot.

Suppose you try a different tack,
And on the square you flash your flag?
At penny-a-lining make your whack,
Or with the mummers mug and gag?
For nix, for nix the dibbs you bag!
At any graft, no matter what,
Your merry goblins soon stravag:
Booze and the blowens cop the lot.

The Moral

It's up the spout and Charley Wag
With wipes and tickers and what not.
Until the squeezer nips your scrag,
Booze and the blowens cop the lot.

(*W. E. Henley*)

THE BALLAD OF DEAD LADIES

TELL me now in what hidden way is
Lady Flora the lovely Roman?
Where's Hipparchia, and where is Thais,
Neither of them the fairer woman?
Where is Echo, beheld of no man,
Only heard on river and mere,—
She whose beauty was more than human? . . .
But where are the snows of yester-year?

Where's Héloise, the learned nun,
For whose sake Abeillard, I ween,
Lost manhood and put priesthood on?
(From Love he won such dule and teen!)
And where, I pray you, is the Queen
Who willed that Buridan should steer
Sewed in a sack's mouth down the Seine? . . .
But where are the snows of yester-year?

White Queen Blanche, like a queen of lilies,
With a voice like any mermaiden,—
Bertha Broadfoot, Beatrice, Alice,
And Ermengarde the lady of Maine,—
And that good Joan whom Englishmen
At Rouen doomed and burned her there,—
Mother of God, where are they then? . . .
But where are the snows of yester-year?

Nay, never ask this week, fair lord,
Where they are gone, nor yet this year,
Save with this much for an overword,—
But where are the snows of yester-year?

(*D. G. Rossetti*)

TO DEATH, OF HIS LADY

Death, of thee do I make my moan,
Who hadst my lady away from me,
Nor wilt assuage thine enmity
Till with her life thou hast mine own;
For since that hour my strength has flown.
Lo! what wrong was her life to thee,
Death?

Two we were, and the heart was one;
Which now being dead, dead I must be,
Or seem alive as lifelessly
As in the choir the painted stone,
Death!

(*D. G. Rossetti*)

HIS MOTHER'S SERVICE TO OUR LADY

Lady of Heaven and earth, and therewithal
Crowned Empress of the nether clefts of Hell,—
I, thy poor Christian, on thy name do call,
Commending me to thee, with thee to dwell,
Albeit in nought I be commendable.
But all mine undeserving may not mar
Such mercies as thy sovereign mercies are;
Without the which (as true words testify)
No soul can reach thy Heaven so fair and far.
Even in this faith I choose to live and die.

Unto thy Son say thou that I am His,
And to me graceless make Him gracious.
Sad Mary of Egypt lacked not of that bliss,
Nor yet the sorrowful clerk Theophilus,
Whose bitter sins were set aside even thus
Though to the Fiend his bounden service was.
Oh help me, lest in vain for me should pass
(Sweet Virgin that shalt have no loss thereby!)
The blessed Host and sacring of the Mass.
Even in this faith I choose to live and die.

A pitiful poor woman, shrunk and old,
  I am, and nothing learn'd in letter-lore.
Within my parish-cloister I behold
  A painted Heaven where harps and lutes adore,
  And eke an Hell whose damned folk seethe full
    sore:
One bringeth fear, the other joy to me.
That joy, great Goddess, make thou mine to be,—
  Thou of whom all must ask it even as I;
And that which faith desires, that let it see.
  For in this faith I choose to live and die.

O excellent Virgin Princess! thou didst bear
  King Jesus, the most excellent comforter,
Who even of this our weakness craved a share
  And for our sake stooped to us from on high,
Offering to death His young life sweet and fair.
Such as He is, Our Lord, I Him declare,
  And in this faith I choose to live and die.

(*D. G. Rossetti*)

THE COMPLAINT OF THE FAIR ARMORESS

I

Meseemeth I heard cry and groan
  That sweet who was the armorer's maid;
For her young years she made sore moan,
  And right upon this wise she said:
"Ah fierce old age with foul bald head,
To spoil fair things thou art over fain;
  Who holdeth me? who? would God I were dead!
Would God I were well dead and slain!

II

"Lo, thou hast broken the sweet yoke
  That my high beauty held above
All priests and clerks and merchant-folk;
  There was not one but for my love

Would give me gold and gold enough,
Though sorrow his very heart had riven,
To win from me such wage thereof
As now no thief would take if given.

III

"I was right chary of the same,
God wot it was my great folly,
For love of one sly knave of them,
Good store of that same sweet had he;
For all my subtle wiles, perdie,
God wot I loved him well enow;
Right evilly handled me,
But he loved well my gold, I trow.

IV

"Though I gat bruises green and black,
I loved him never the less a jot;
Though he bound burdens on my back,
If he said, 'Kiss me, and heed it not,'
Right little pain I felt, God wot,
When that foul thief's mouth, found so sweet,
Kissed me—Much good thereof I got!
I keep the sin and the shame of it.

V

"And he died thirty year agone.
I am old now, no sweet thing to see;
By God, though, when I think thereon,
And of that good glad time, woe's me,
And stare upon my changed body
Stark naked, that has been so sweet,
Lean, wizen, like a small dry tree,
I am nigh mad with the pain of it.

VI

"Where is my faultless forehead's white,
The lifted eyebrows, soft gold hair,

Eyes wide apart and keen of sight,
  With subtle skill in the amorous air;
  The straight nose, great nor small, but fair,
The small carved ears of shapeliest growth,
  Chin dimpling, color good to wear,
And sweet red splendid kissing mouth?

VII

'The shapely slender shoulders small,
  Long arms, hands wrought in glorious wise,
Round little breasts, the hips withal
  High, full of flesh, not scant of size,
  Fit for all amorous masteries;

. . . .

. . . .

. . . .

VIII

"A writhled forehead, hair gone gray,
  Fallen eyebrows, eyes gone blind and red,
Their laughs and looks all fled away,
  Yea, all that smote men's hearts are fled;
  The bowed nose, fallen from goodlihead;
Foul flapping ears like water-flags;
  Peaked chin, and cheeks all waste and dead,
And lips that are two skinny rags:

IX

"Thus endeth all the beauty of us.
  The arms made short, the hands made lean,
The shoulders bowed and ruinous,
  The breasts, alack! all fallen in;
The flanks too, like the breasts, grown thin;

. . . . .

  For the lank thighs, no thighs but skin,
They are speckled with spots like sausage-meat.

x

"So we make moan for the old sweet days,
  Poor old light women, two or three
Squatting above the straw-fire's blaze,
  The bosom crushed against the knee,
  Like fagots on a heap we be,
Round fires soon lit, soon quenched and done;
  And we were once so sweet, even we!
Thus fareth many and many an one."

(Algernon Charles Swinburne)

A DOUBLE BALLAD OF GOOD COUNSEL

Now take your fill of love and glee,
  And after balls and banquets hie;
In the end ye'll get no good for fee,
  But just heads broken by and by;
  Light loves make beasts of men that sigh;
They changed the faith of Solomon,
  And left not Samson lights to spy;
Good luck has he that deals with none!

Sweet Orpheus, lord of minstrelsy,
  For this with flute and pipe came nigh
The danger of the dog's heads three
  That ravening at hell's door doth lie;
  Fain was Narcissus, fair and shy,
For love's love lightly lost and won,
  In a deep well to drown and die;
Good luck has he that deals with none!

Sardana, flower of chivalry,
  Who conquered Crete with horn and cry,
For this was fain a maid to be
  And learn with girls the thread to ply;
  King David, wise in prophecy,
Forgot the fear of God for one
  Seen washing either shapely thigh:
Good luck has he that deals with none!

For this did Amnon, craftily
  Feigning to eat of cakes of rye,
Deflower his sister fair to see,
  Which was foul incest; and hereby
  Was Herod moved, it is no lie,
To lop the head of Baptist John
  For dance and jig and psaltery;
Good luck has he that deals with none!

Next to myself I tell, poor me,
  How thrashed like clothes at wash was I
Stark naked, I must needs agree;
  Who made me eat so sour a pie
  But Katherine of Vaucelles? thereby
Noé took third part of that fun;
  Such wedding-gloves are ill to buy;
Good luck has he that deals with none!

But for that young man fair and free
  To pass those young maids lightly by,
Nay, would you burn him quick, not he;
  Like broom-horsed witches though he fry,
  They are sweet as civet in his eye;
But trust them, and you're fooled anon;
  For white or brown, and low or high,
Good luck has he that deals with none!

(*Algernon Charles Swinburne*)

FRAGMENT OF DEATH

AND Paris be it or Helen dying,
  Who dies soever, dies with pain.
He that lacks breath and wind for sighing,
  His gall bursts on his heart; and then
  He sweats, God knows what sweat! again,
No man may ease him of his grief;
  Child, brother, sister, none were fain
To bail him thence for his relief.

Death makes him shudder, swoon, wax pale,
  Nose bend, veins stretch, and breath surrender,
Neck swell, flesh soften, joints that fail
  Crack their strained nerves and arteries slender.
  O woman's body found so tender,
Smooth, sweet, so precious in men's eyes,
  Must thou too bear such count to render?
Yes; or pass quick into the skies.

(*Algernon Charles Swinburne*)

BALLAD OF THE LORDS OF OLD TIME

(*After the former argument*)

What more? Where is the third Calixt,
  Last of that name now dead and gone,
Who held four years the Papalist?
  Alfonso king of Aragon,
  The gracious lord, duke of Bourbon,
And Arthur, duke of old Britaine?
  And Charles the Seventh, that worthy one?
Even with the good knight Charlemain.

The Scot too, king of the mount and mist,
  With half his face vermilion,
Men tell us, like an amethyst
  From brow to chin that blazed and shone;
  The Cypriote king of old renown,
Alas! and that good king of Spain,
  Whose name I cannot think upon?
Even with the good knight Charlemain.

No more to say of them I list;
  'Tis all but vain, all dead and done:
For death may no man born resist,
  Nor make appeal when death comes on.
  I make yet one more question;
Where's Lancelot, king of far Bohain?
  Where's he whose grandson called him son?
Even with the good knight Charlemain.

Where is Guesclin, the good Breton?
  The lord of the eastern mountain-chain,
And the good late duke of Alençon?
  Even with the good knight Charlemain.

(*Algernon Charles Swinburne*)

BALLAD OF THE WOMEN OF PARIS

Albeit the Venice girls get praise
  For their sweet speech and tender air,
And though the old women have wise ways
  Of chaffering for amorous ware,
  Yet at my peril dare I swear,
Search Rome, where God's grace mainly tarries,
  Florence and Savoy, everywhere,
There's no good girl's lip out of Paris.

The Naples women, as folk prattle,
  Are sweetly spoken and subtle enough;
German girls are good at tattle,
  And Prussians make their boast thereof;
  Take Egypt for the next remove,
Or that waste land the Tartar harries,
  Spain or Greece, for the matter of love,
There's no good girl's lip out of Paris.

Breton and Swiss know nought of the matter,
  Gascony girls or girls of Toulouse;
Two fishwomen with a half-hour's chatter
  Would shut them up by threes and twos;
  Calais, Lorraine, and all their crews,
(Names enow the mad song marries,)
  England and Picardy, search them and choose,
There's no good girl's lip out of Paris.

Prince, give praise to our French ladies
  For the sweet sound their speaking carries;
'Twixt Rome and Cadiz many a maid is,
  But no good girl's lip out of Paris.

(*Algernon Charles Swinburne*)

BALLAD WRITTEN FOR A BRIDEGROOM

Which Villon gave to a gentleman newly married to send to his wife whom he had won with the sword

At daybreak, when the falcon claps his wings,
  No whit for grief, but noble heart and high
With loud glad noise he stirs himself and springs,
  And takes his meat and toward his lure draws nigh;
  Such good I wish you! Yea, and heartily
I am fired with hope of true love's meed to get;
  Know that Love writes it in his book; for why,
This is the end for which we twain are met.

Mine own heart's lady with no gainsayings
  You shall be always wholly till I die;
And in my right against all bitter things
  Sweet laurel with fresh rose its force shall try;
  Seeing reason wills not that I cast love by
(Nor here with reason shall I chide or fret)
  Nor cease to serve, but serve more constantly;
This is the end for which we twain are met.

And, which is more, when grief about me clings
  Through Fortune's fit or fume of jealousy,
Your sweet kind eye beats down her threatenings
  As wind doth smoke; such power sits in your eye.
  Thus in your field my seed of harvestry
Thrives, for the fruit is like me that I set;
  God bids me tend it with good husbandry;
This is the end for which we twain are met.

Princess, give ear to this my summary;
  That heart of mine your heart's love should forget,
Shall never be: like trust in you put I:
  This is the end for which we twain are met.

(*Algernon Charles Swinburne*)

BALLAD AGAINST THE ENEMIES OF FRANCE

May he fall in with beasts that scatter fire,
  Like Jason, when he sought the fleece of gold,
Or change from man to beast three years entire,
  As King Nebuchadnezzar did of old;
Or else have times as shameful and as bad
As Trojan folk for ravished Helen had;
Or gulfed with Proserpine and Tantalus
Let hell's deep fen devour him dolorous,
  With worse to bear than Job's worst sufferance,
Bound in his prison-maze with Dædalus,
  Who could wish evil to the state of France!

May he four months, like bitterns in the mire,
  Howl with head downmost in the lake-springs cold
Or to bear harness like strong bulls for hire
  To the Great Turk for money down be sold;
Or thirty years like Magdalen live sad,
With neither wool nor web of linen clad;
Drown like Narciss', or swing down pendulous
Like Absalom with locks luxurious
  Or like Judas fallen to reprobance;
Or find such death as Simon sorcerous,
  Who could wish evil to the state of France!

May the old times come of fierce Octavian's ire,
  And in his belly molten coin be told;
May he like Victor in the mill expire,
  Crushed between moving millstones on him rolled,
Or in deep sea drenched breathless, more adrad
Than in the whale's bulk Jonas, when God bade:
From Phœbus' light, from Juno's treasure-house
Driven, and from joys of Venus amorous,
  And cursed of God most high to the utterance,
As was the Syrian king Antiochus,
  Who could wish evil to the state of France!

Envoy

Prince, may the bright-winged brood of Æolus
To sea-king Glaucus' wild wood cavernous
  Bear him bereft of peace and hope's least glance,
For worthless is he to get good of us,
  Who could wish evil to the state of France!

(*Algernon Charles Swinburne*)

THE DISPUTE OF THE HEART AND BODY OF FRANÇOIS VILLON

Who is this I hear?—Lo, this is I, thine heart,
  That holds on merely now by a slender string.
Strength fails me, shape and sense are rent apart,
  The blood in me is turned to a bitter thing,
  Seeing thee skulk here like a dog shivering.—
Yea, and for what?—For that thy sense found sweet.—
What irks it thee?—I feel the sting of it.—
  Leave me at peace.—Why?—Nay now, leave me at peace;
I will repent when I grow ripe in wit.—
  I say no more.—I care not though thou cease.—

What are thou, trow?—A man worth praise perfay.—
  This is thy thirtieth year of wayfaring.—
'Tis a mule's age.—Art thou a boy still?—Nay.—
  Is it hot lust that spurs thee with its sting,
  Grasping thy throat? Know'st thou not anything?—
Yea, black and white, when milk is specked with flies,
I can make out.—No more?—Nay, in no wise.
  Shall I begin again the count of these?—
Thou art undone.—I will make shift to rise.—
  I say no more.—I care not though thou cease.—

I have the sorrow of it, and thou the smart
  Wert thou a poor mad fool or weak of wit,
Then might'st thou plead this pretext with thine heart;
  But if thou know not good from evil a whit,
  Either thy head is hard as stone to hit,

Or shame, not honor, gives thee most content.
What canst thou answer to this argument?—
  When I am dead I shall be well at ease.—
God! what good luck!—Thou art over eloquent.—
  I say no more.—I care not though thou cease.—

Whence is this ill?—From sorrow and not from sin.
  When Saturn packed my wallet up for me
I well believe he put these ills therein.—
  Fool, wilt thou make thy servant lord of thee?
  Hear now the wise king's counsel; thus saith he;
All power upon the stars a wise man hath;
There is no planet that shall do him scathe.—
  Nay, as they made me I grow and I decrease.—
What say'st thou?—Truly this is all my faith.—
  I say no more.—I care not though thou cease.—

Wouldst thou live still?—God help me that I may!—
Then thou must—What? turn penitent and gray?—
Read always—What?—Grave words and good to say;
  Leave off the ways of fools, lest they displease.—
Good; I will do it.—Wilt thou remember?—Yea.—
Abide not till there come an evil day.
  I say no more.—I care not though thou cease.

(Algernon Charles Swinburne)

EPISTLE IN FORM OF A BALLAD TO HIS FRIENDS

Have pity, pity, friends, have pity on me,
  Thus much at least, may it please you, of your grace!
I lie not under hazel or hawthorn-tree
  Down in this dungeon ditch, mine exile's place
  By leave of God and fortune's foul disgrace.
Girls, lovers, glad young folk and newly wed,
Jumpers and jugglers, tumbling heel o'er head,
  Swift as a dart, and sharp as needle-ware,
Throats clear as bells that ring the kine to shed,
  Your poor old friend, what, will you leave him there?

Singers that sing at pleasure, lawlessly,
  Light, laughing, gay of word and deed, that race
And run like folk light-witted as ye be
  And have in hand nor current coin nor base,
  Ye wait too long, for now he's dying apace.
Rhymers of lays and roundels sung and read,
Ye'll brew him broth too late when he lies dead.
  Nor wind nor lightning, sunbeam nor fresh air,
May pierce the thick wall's bound where lies his bed;
Your poor old friend, what, will you leave him there?

O noble folk, from tithes and taxes free,
  Come and behold him in this piteous case,
Ye that nor king nor emperor holds in fee,
  But only God in heaven; behold his face
  Who needs must fast, Sundays and holidays,
Which makes his teeth like rakes; and when he hath fed
With never a cake for banquet but dry bread,
Must drench his bowels with much cold watery fare,
With board nor stool, but low on earth instead;
Your poor old friend, what, will you leave him there?

Princes afore-named, old and young foresaid,
Get me the king's seal and my pardon sped,
  And hoist me in some basket up with care:
So swine will help each other ill bested,
For where one squeaks they run in heaps ahead,
  Your poor old friend, what, will you leave him there?

(*Algernon Charles Swinburne*)

Mellin de Saint-Gelais

1491–1558

THE SONNET OF THE MOUNTAIN

When from afar these mountain tops I view,
I do but mete mine own distress thereby:
High is their head, and my desire is high;
Firm is their foot, my faith is certain, too.

E'en as the winds about their summits blue,
From me, too, breaks betimes the wistful sigh;
And as from them the brooks and streamlets hie,
So from mine eyes the tears run down anew.

A thousand flocks upon them feed and stray;
As many loves within me see the day,
And all my heart for pasture ground divide.

No fruit have they, my lot as fruitless is;
And 'twixt us now nought diverse is but this—
In them the snows, in me the fires abide.

(*Austin Dobson*)

Clement Marot

1495–1544

THE POSY RING

THIS on thy posy-ring I've writ:
"True Love and Faith"
For, failing Love, Faith droops her head,
And lacking faith, why, love is dead
And's but a wraith.
But Death is stingless where they've lit
And stayed, whose names hereon I've writ.

(*Ford Madox Ford*)

A LOVE-LESSON

A SWEET "No! no!" with a sweet smile beneath
Becomes an honest girl,—I'd have you learn it;
As for plain, "Yes!" it may be said, i' faith,
Too plainly and too soft,—pray, well discern it!

Not that I'd have my pleasure incomplete,
Or lose the kiss for which my lips beset you;
But that in suffering me to take it, sweet!
I'd have you say—"No! no! I will not let you!"

(*Leigh Hunt*)

MADAME D'ALBERT'S LAUGH

Yes! that fair neck, too beautiful by half,
Those eyes, that voice, that bloom, all do her honor;
Yet, after all, that little giddy laugh
Is what, in my mind, sits the best upon her.

Good God! 'twould make the very streets and ways,
Through which she passes, burst into a pleasure!
Did melancholy come to mar my days
And kill me in the lap of too much leisure,
No spell were wanting, from the dead to raise me,
But only that sweet laugh wherewith she slays me.

(*Leigh Hunt*)

FRIAR LUBIN

To gallop off to town post-haste,
So oft, the times I cannot tell;
To do vile deed, nor feel disgraced,—
Friar Lubin will do it well.
But a sober life to lead,
To honor virtue, and pursue it,
That's a pious, Christian deed,—
Friar Lubin cannot do it.

To mingle, with a knowing smile,
The goods of others with his own,
And leave you without cross or pile,
Friar Lubin stands alone.
To say 'tis yours is all in vain,
If once he lays his finger to it;
For as to giving back again,
Friar Lubin cannot do it.

With flattering words and gentle tone,
To woo and win some guileless maid,
Cunning pander need you none,—
Friar Lubin knows the trade.

Loud preacheth he sobriety,
But as for water, doth eschew it;
Your dog may drink it,—but not he;
Friar Lubin cannot do it.

Envoy

When an evil deed's to do,
Friar Lubin is stout and true;
Glimmers a ray of goodness through it,
Friar Lubin cannot do it.

(*H. W. Longfellow*)

Jacques Tahureau

1527–1555

SHADOWS OF HIS LADY

WITHIN the sand of what far river lies
The gold that gleams in tresses of my Love?
What highest circle of the Heavens above
Is jeweled with such stars as are her eyes?
And where is the rich sea whose coral vies
With her red lips, that cannot kiss enough?
What dawn-lit garden knew the rose, whereof
The fled soul lives in her cheeks' rosy guise?

What Parian marble that is loveliest,
Can make the whiteness of her brow and breast?
When drew she breath from the Sabæan glade?
Oh, happy rock and river, sky and sea,
Gardens and glades Sabæan, all that be
The far-off splendid semblance of my maid.

(*Andrew Lang*)

MOONLIGHT

THE high Midnight was garlanding her head
With many a shining star in shining skies,
And, of her grace, a slumber on mine eyes,
And, after sorrow, quietness was shed.

Far in dim fields cicalas jargoned
  A thin shrill clamor of complaints and cries;
  And all the woods were pallid, in strange wise,
With pallor of the sad moon overspread.

Then came my lady to that lonely place,
And, from her palfrey stooping, did embrace
  And hang upon my neck, and kissed me over;
Wherefore the day is far less dear than night,
And sweeter is the shadow than the light,
  Since night has made me such a happy lover.

(*Andrew Lang*)

Jean Passerat

1534–1602

LOVE IN MAY

Off with sleep, love, up from bed,
  This fair morn;
See, for our eyes the rosy red
  New dawn is born;
Now that skies are glad and gay
In this gracious month of May,
  Love me, sweet;
Fill my joy in brimming measure;
In this world he hath no pleasure
  That will none of it.

Come, love, through the woods of spring,
  Come walk with me;
Listen, the sweet birds jargoning
  From tree to tree.
List and listen, over all
Nightingale most musical
  That ceases never;
Grief begone, and let us be
For a space as glad as he;
  Time's flitting ever.

Old Time, that loves not lovers, wears
  Wings swift in flight;
All our happy life he bears
  Far in the night.
Old and wrinkled on a day,
Sad and weary shall you say,
  "Ah, fool was I,
That took no pleasure in the grace
Of the flower that from my face
  Time has seen die."

Leave then sorrow, teen, and tears
  Till we be old;
Young we are, and of our years
  Till youth be cold.
Pluck the flower; while Spring is gay
In this happy month of May
  Love me, love;
Fill our joy in brimming measure;
In this world he hath no pleasure
  That will none thereof.

(Andrew Lang)

Pierre de Ronsard

1524–1585

FRAGMENT OF A SONNET

Nature withheld Cassandra in the skies,
For more adornment, a full thousand years;
She took their cream of Beauty, fairest dies,
And shaped and tinted her above all Peers:
Meanwhile Love kept her dearly with his wings,
And underneath their shadow filled her eyes
With such a richness that the cloudy Kings
Of high Olympus uttered slavish sighs.
When from the Heavens I saw her first descend,
My heart took fire, and only burning pains,
They were my pleasures—they my Life's sad end;
Love poured her beauty into my warm veins.

(John Keats)

ROSES

I SEND you here a wreath of blossoms blown,
And woven flowers at sunset gathered,
Another dawn had seen them ruined, and shed
Loose leaves upon the grass at random strown.
By this, their sure example, be it known,
That all your beauties, now in perfect flower,
Shall fade as these, and wither in an hour.
Flowerlike, and brief of days, as the flower sown.

Ah, time is flying, lady,—time is flying;
Nay, 'tis not time that flies but we that go,
Who in short space shall be in churchyard lying,
And of our loving parley none shall know,
Nor any man consider what we were;
Be therefore kind, my love, whilst thou art fair.

(*Andrew Lang*)

THE ROSE

SEE, Mignonne, hath not the Rose,
That this morning did unclose
Her purple mantle to the light,
Lost before the day be dead,
The glory of her raiment red,
Her color, bright as yours is bright?

Ah, Mignonne, in how few hours
The petals of her purple flowers
All have faded, fallen, died;
Sad Nature, mother ruinous,
That seest thy fair child perish thus
'Twixt matin song and even-tide.

Hear me, my darling, speaking sooth,
Gather the fleet flower of your youth,
Take ye your pleasure at the best;
Be merry ere your beauty flit,
For length of days will tarnish it
Like roses that were loveliest.

(*Andrew Lang*)

TO THE MOON

Hide this one night thy crescent, kindly Moon;
So shall Endymion faithful prove, and rest
Loving and unawakened on thy breast;
So shall no foul enchanter importune
Thy quiet course; for now the night is boon,
And through the friendly night unseen I fare,
Who dread the face of foemen unaware,
And watch of hostile spies in the bright noon.
  Thou knowest, Moon, the bitter power of Love;
  'Tis told how shepherd Pan found ways to move,
For little price, thy heart; and of your grace,
  Sweet stars, be kind to this not alien fire,
  Because on earth ye did not scorn desire,
Bethink ye, now ye hold your heavenly place.

(*Andrew Lang*)

TO HIS YOUNG MISTRESS

Fair flower of fifteen springs, that still
  Art scarcely blossomed from the bud,
Yet hast such store of evil will,
  A heart so full of hardihood,
    Seeking to hide in friendly wise
    The mischief of your mocking eyes.

If you have pity, child, give o'er,
  Give back the heart you stole from me,
Pirate, setting so little store
  On this your captive from Love's sea,
    Holding his misery for gain,
    And making pleasure of his pain.

Another, not so fair of face,
  But far more pitiful than you,
Would take my heart, if of his grace,
  My heart would give her of Love's due;
    And she shall have it, since I find
    That you are cruel and unkind.

Nay, I would rather that I died,
Within your white hands prisoning,
Would rather that it still abide
In your ungentle comforting,
Than change its faith, and seek to her
That is more kind, but not so fair.

(*Andrew Lang*)

DEADLY KISSES

Ah, take these lips away; no more,
No more such kisses give to me.
My spirit faints for joy; I see
Through mists of death the dreamy shore,
And meadows by the water-side,
Where all about the Hollow Land
Fare the sweet singers that have died,
With their lost ladies, hand in hand;
Ah, Love, how fireless are their eyes,
How pale their lips that kiss and smile.
So mine must be in little while
If thou wilt kiss me in such wise.

(*Andrew Lang*)

OF HIS LADY'S OLD AGE

When you are very old, at evening
You'll sit and spin beside the fire, and say,
Humming my songs, "Ah well, ah well-a-day.
When I was young, of me did Ronsard sing."
None of your maidens that doth hear the thing,
Albeit with her weary task foredone,
But wakens at my name, and calls you one
Blest, to be held in long remembering.

I shall be low beneath the earth, and laid
On sleep, a phantom in the myrtle shade,
While you beside the fire, a grandame gray,
My love, your pride, remember and regret;
Ah, love me, love, we may be happy yet,
And gather roses, while 'tis called to-day.

(*Andrew Lang*)

ON HIS LADY'S WAKING

My lady woke upon a morning fair,
  What time Apollo's chariot takes the skies,
  And, fain to fill with arrows from her eyes
His empty quiver, Love was standing there:
I saw two apples that her breast doth bear;
  None such the close of the Hesperides
  Yields; nor hath Venus any such as these,
Nor she that had of nursling Mars the care.

Even such a bosom, and so fair it was,
Pure as the perfect work of Phidias,
  That sad Andromeda's discomfiture
Left bare, when Perseus passed her on a day,
And pale as death for fear of death she lay,
  With breast as marble cold, as marble pure.

(*Andrew Lang*)

HIS LADY'S DEATH

Twain that were foes, while Mary lived, are fled;
  One laurel-crowned abides in heaven, and one
  Beneath the earth has fared, a fallen sun,
A light of love among the loveless dead.
The first is chastity, that vanquished
  The archer Love, that held joint empery
  With the sweet beauty that made war on me,
When laughter of lips with laughing eyes was wed.

Their strife the Fates have closed, with stern control,
The earth holds her fair body, and her soul
  An angel with glad angels triumpheth;
Love has no more than he can do; desire
Is buried, and my heart a faded fire,
  And for Death's sake, I am in love with Death.

(*Andrew Lang*)

HIS LADY'S TOMB

As in the gardens, all through May, the rose,
Lovely, and young, and fair appareled,
  Makes sunrise jealous of her rosy red,
When dawn upon the dew of dawning glows;
Graces and Loves within her breast repose,
  The woods are faint with the sweet odor shed,
  Till rains and heavy suns have smitten dead
The languid flower, and the loose leaves unclose,—

So this, the perfect beauty of our days,
When earth and heaven were vocal of her praise,
  The fates have slain, and her sweet soul reposes;
And tears I bring, and sighs, and on her tomb
Pour milk, and scatter buds of many a bloom,
  That dead, as living, she may be with roses.

(*Andrew Lang*)

AND LIGHTLY, LIKE THE FLOWERS

"Ainsi qu'aux fleurs la vieillesse,
Fera ternir votre beauté."—

And lightly, like the flowers,
  Your beauties Age will dim,
  Who makes the song a hymn,
And turns the sweets to sour.

Alas, the chubby Hours
  Grow lank and gray and grim,
And lightly, like the flowers,
  Your beauties Age will dim.

Still rosy are the bowers,
  The walks yet green and trim.
  Among them let your whim
Pass sweetly, like the showers,
And lightly, like the flowers.

(*W. E. Henley*)

THE PARADOX OF TIME

(A variation on Ronsard)

Le temps s'en va, le temps s'en va, madame!
Las! le temps non: mais "NOUS nous en allons!"

TIME goes, you say? Ah, no!
Alas, Time stays, *we* go;
Or else, were this not so,
What need to chain the hours,
For Youth were always ours?
Time goes, you say?—ah, no!

Ours is the eyes' deceit
Of men whose flying feet
Lead through some landscape low;
We pass, and think we see
The earth's fixed surface flee:—
Alas, Time stays,—we go!

Once in the days of old,
Your locks were curling gold,
And mine had shamed the crow.
Now, in the self-same stage,
We've reached the silver age;
Time goes, you say?—ah, no!

Once, when my voice was strong,
I filled the woods with song
To praise your "rose" and "snow";
My bird, that sang, is dead;
Where are your roses fled?
Alas, Time stays,—we go!

See, in what traversed ways,
What backward Fate delays
The hopes we used to know;
Where are your old desires?—
Ah, where those vanished fires?
Time goes, you say?—ah, no!

How far, how far, O Sweet,
The past behind our feet
Lies in the even-glow!
Now on the forward way,
Let us fold hands, and pray;
Alas, Time stays,—*we* go.

(*Austin Dobson*)

THE REVENGE

Fair rebel to thyself and Time,
Who laugh'st at all my tears,
When thou hast lost thy youthful prime,
And age his trophy rears,

Weighing thy inconsiderate pride,
Thou shalt in vain accuse it:
"Why beauty am I now denied,
Or knew not then to use it?"

Then shall I wish, ungentle Fair,
Thou in like flames may'st burn!
Venus, if just, will hear my prayer,
And I shall laugh my turn.

(*Thomas Stanley*)

Joachim du Bellay

1525–1560

FROM THE VISIONS

I

It was the time, when rest, soft sliding downe
From heavens hight into men's heavy eyes,
In the forgetfulness of sleepe doth drowne
The carefull thoughts of mortall miseries;
Then did a ghost before mine eyes appeare,
On that great rivers banck, that runnes by Rome;
Which, calling me by name, bad me to reare
My lookes to heaven, whence all good gifts do come,

And crying lowd, "Lo! now beholde," quoth hee,
"What under this great temple placed is:
Lo, all is nought but flying vanitee!"
So I, that know this world's inconstancies,
Sith onely God surmounts all times decay,
In God alone my confidence do stay.

II

On high hills top I saw a stately frame,
An hundred cubits high by iust assize,
With hundreth pillours fronting faire the same,
All wrought with diamond after Dorick wize:
Nor brick nor marble was the wall in view,
But shining christall, which from top to base
Out of her womb a thousand rayons threw,
One hundred steps of Afrike golds enchase:
Golde was the parget; and the seeling bright
Did shine all scaly with great plates of golde;
The floore of iasp and emeraude was dight.
O, worlds vainesse! Whiles thus I did behold,
An earthquake shooke the hill from lowest seat,
And overthrew this frame with ruine great.

III

Then did a sharped spyre of diamond bright,
Ten feete each way in square, appeare to mee,
Iustly proportion'd up unto his hight,
So far as archer might his level see:
The top thereof a pot did seeme to beare,
Made of the metall which we most do honour;
And in this golden vessel couched weare
The ashes of a mightie emperor:
Upon foure corners of the base were pight,
To beare the frame, foure great lyons of gold;
A worthy tombe for such a worthy wight.
Alas! this world doth nought but grievance hold!
I saw a tempest from the heaven descend,
Which this brave monument with flash did rend.

IV

I saw raysde up on yvorie pillowes tall,
  Whose bases were of richest mettals warke,
The chapters alabaster, the fryses christall,
  The double front of a triumphall arke:
On each side purtraid was a Victorie,
  Clad like a nimph, that winges of silver weares,
And in triumphant chayre was set on hie
  The auncient glory of the Romaine peares.
No worke it seem'd of earthly craftsmans wit,
  But rather wrought by his owne industry,
That thunder-dartes for Iove his syre doth fit.
  Let me no more see faire thing under sky,
Sith that mine eyes have seene so faire a sight
With sodain fall to dust consumed quight.

V

Then was the faire Dodonian tree far seene
  Upon seaven hills to spread his gladsom gleame,
And conquerours bedecked with his greene,
  Along the bancks of the Ausonian streame:
There many an auncient trophee was addrest,
  And many a spoyle, and many a goodly show,
Which that brave races greatnes did attest,
  That whilome from the Troyan blood did flow.
Ravisht I was so rare a thing to vew;
  When, lo! a barbarous troupe of clownish fone
The honour of these noble boughs down threw:
  Under the wedge I heard the tronck to grone;
And, since, I saw the roote in great disdaine
  A twinne of forked trees send forth againe.

VI

I saw a wolfe under a rockie cave
  Noursing two whelps; I saw her little ones
In wanton dalliance the teate to crave,
  While she her neck wreath'd from them for the nones:

I saw her raunge abroad to seeke her food,
  And, roming through the field with greedie rage,
T' embrew her teeth and clawes with lukewarm blood
  Of the small heards, her thirst for to asswage:
I saw a thousand huntsmen, which descended
  Downe from the mountaines bordring Lombardie,
That with an hundred speares her flank wide rended:
  I saw her on the plaine outstretched lie,
Throwing out thousand throbs in her owne soyle;
Soone on a tree uphang'd I saw her spoyle.

(*Edmund Spenser*)

HYMN TO THE WINDS

(*The winds are invoked by the winnowers of corn*)

To you, troop so fleet,
  That with winged wandering feet,
Through the wide world pass,
And with soft murmuring
Toss the green shades of spring
  In woods and grass,
Lily and violet
I give, and blossoms wet,
  Roses and dew;
This branch of blushing roses,
Whose fresh bud uncloses,
  Wind-flowers, too.
Ah, winnow with sweet breath,
Winnow the holt and heath,
  Round this retreat;
Where all the golded morn
We fan the gold o' the corn,
  In the sun's heat.

(*Andrew Lang*)

A VOW TO HEAVENLY VENUS

We that with like hearts love, we lovers twain,
New wedded in the village by thy fane,

Lady of all chaste love, to thee it is
We bring these amaranths, these white lilies,
A sign, and sacrifice; may Love, we pray,
Like amaranthine flowers, feel no decay;
Like these cool lilies may our loves remain,
Perfect and pure, and know not any stain;
And be our hearts, from this thy holy hour,
Bound each to each, like flower to wedded flower.

(*Andrew Lang*)

TO HIS FRIEND IN ELYSIUM

So long you wandered on the dusky plain,
Where flit the shadows with their endless cry,
You reach the shore where all the world goes by,
You leave the strife, the slavery, the pain;
But we, but we, the mortals that remain
  In vain stretch hands; for Charon sullenly
Drives us afar, we may not come anigh
Till that last mystic obolus we gain.
But you are happy in the quiet place,
And with the learned lovers of old days,
  And with your love, you wander evermore
In the dim woods, and drink forgetfulness
Of us your friends, a weary crowd that press
  About the gate, or labor at the oar.

(*Andrew Lang*)

A SONNET TO HEAVENLY BEAUTY

If this our little life is but a day
In the Eternal,—if the years in vain
Toil after hours that never come again,—
If everything that hath been must decay,
Why dreamest thou of joys that pass away,
  My soul, that my sad body doth restrain?
  Why of the moment's pleasure art thou fain?
Nay, thou hast wings,—nay, seek another stay.

There is the joy where to each soul aspires,
And there the rest that all the world desires,
And there is love, and peace, and gracious mirth;
And there in the most highest heavens shalt thou
Behold the Very Beauty, whereof now
Thou worshipest the shadow upon earth.

(*Andrew Lang*)

ROME

O THOU newcomer who seek'st Rome in Rome
And find'st in Rome no thing thou canst call Roman;
Arches worn old and palaces made common,
Rome's name alone within these walls keeps home.

Behold how pride and ruin can befall
One who hath set the whole world 'neath her laws,
All-conquering, now conquered, because
She is Time's prey and Time consumeth all.

Rome that are Rome's one sole last monument,
Rome that alone hast conquered Rome the town,
Tiber alone, transient and seaward bent,
Remains of Rome. O world, thou unconstant mime.
That which stands firm in thee Time batters down,
And that which fleeteth doth outrun swift time.

(*Ezra Pound*)

HEUREUX QUI, COMME ULYSSE, A FAIT UN BEAU VOYAGE

HAPPY who like Ulysses, or that lord
That raped the fleece; returning full and sage,
With usage and the world's wide reason stored,
With his own kin can wait the end of age.
When shall I see, when shall I see, God knows!
My little village smoke; or pass the door,
The old dear door of that unhappy house,
That is to me a kingdom and much more?

Mightier to me the house my fathers made,
 Than your audacious heads, O Halls of Rome;
More than immortal marbles undecayed,
 The thin sad slates that cover up my home;
More than your Tiber is my Loire to me,
 Than Palatine my little Lyré there;
And more than all the winds of all the sea,
 The quiet kindness of the Angevin air.

(*Gilbert K. Chesterton*)

Louise Labé

1526–1566

POVRE AME AMOUREUSE

(*Sapphics*)

When to my lone soft bed at eve returning
Sweet desir'd sleep already stealeth o'er me,
My spirit flieth to the fairy-land of her tyrannous love.

Him then I think fondly to kiss, to hold him
Frankly then to my bosom; I that all day
Have looked for him suffering, repining, yea many long
 days.

O bless'd sleep, with flatteries beguile me;
So, if I n'er may of a surety have him,
Grant to my poor soul amorous the dark gift of this
 illusion.

(*Robert Bridges*)

Remy Belleau

1528–1577

APRIL

April, pride of woodland ways,
 Of glad days,
April, bringing hope and prime,
 To the young flowers that beneath
 Their bud sheath
 Are guarded in their tender time:

April, pride of fields that be
  Green and free,
That in fashion glad and gay,
Stud with flowers red and blue,
  Every hue,
Their jeweled spring array;

April, pride of murmuring
  Winds of spring,
That beneath the winnowed air,
Trap with subtle nets and sweet
  Flora's feet,
Flora's feet, the fleet and fair;

April, by thy hand caressed,
  From her breast
Nature scatters everywhere
Handfuls of all sweet perfumes,
  Buds and blooms,
Making faint the earth and air.

April, joy of the green hours,
  Clothes with flowers
Over all her locks of gold
My sweet lady; and her breast
  With the blest
Buds of summer manifold.

April, with thy gracious wiles,
  Like the smiles,
Smiles of Venus; and thy breath
Like her breath, the gods' delight,
  (From their height
They take the happy air beneath

It is thou that, of thy grace,
  From their place
In the far-off isles dost bring
Swallows over earth and sea,
  Glad to be
Messengers of thee, and Spring.

Daffodil and eglantine,
  And woodbine,
Lily, violet, and rose
Plentiful in April fair,
  To the air,
Their pretty petals do unclose.

Nightingales ye now may hear,
  Piercing clear,
Singing in the deepest shade;
Many and many a babbled note
  Chime and float,
Woodland music through the glade.

April, all to welcome thee,
  Spring sets free
Ancient flames, and with low breath
Wakes the ashes gray and old
  That the cold
Chilled within our hearts to death.

Thou beholdest in the warm
  Hours, the swarm
Of the thievish bees, that flies
Evermore from bloom to bloom
  For perfume,
Hid away in tiny thighs.

Her cool shadows May can boast,
  Fruits almost
Ripe, and gifts of fertile dew,
Manna-sweet and honey-sweet,
  That complete
Her flower garland fresh and new.

Nay, but I will give my praise
  To these days,
Named with the glad name of Her
That from out the form o' the sea
  Came to be
Sudden light on earth and air.

(*Andrew Lang*)

Philippe Desportes

1545–1606

CONQUEST

Those eyes that set my fancy on a fire,
  Those crispéd hairs that hold my heart in chains,
Those dainty hands which conquered my desire,
  That wit which of my thoughts doth hold the reins:
Those eyes for clearness do the stars surpass,
  Those hairs obscure the brightness of the sun,
Those hands more white than ever ivory was,
  That wit even to the skies hath glory won.
O eyes that pierce our hearts without remorse!
  O hairs of right that wear a royal crown!
O hands that conquer more than Cæsar's force!
  O wit that turns huge kingdoms upside down!
Then, Love, be judge, what heart may therewith stand
Such eyes, such hair, such wit, and such a hand?

(*Anonymous: From William Barley's New Book of Tabliture,* 1596)

Theophile de Viau

1591–1626

SLEEP

I've kissed thee, sweetheart, in a dream at least,
And though the core of love is in me still,
This joy, that in my sense did softly thrill,
The ardor of my longing hath appeased
And by this tender strife my spirit, eased,
And half consoled, I soothe myself, until
I find my heart from all its pain released.
My senses, hushed, begin to fall on sleep,
Slumber, for which two weary nights I weep,
Takes thy dear place at last within my eyes,
And though so cold he is, as all men vow,
For me he breaks his natural icy guise,
And shows himself more warm and fond than thou.

(*Sir Edmund Gosse*)

Jean de la Fontaine

1621–1695

La Fontaine is the one French poet who speaks to all the world. No one is more truly and variously human than he. We love him, and laugh with him, even at him sometimes, and should like some day to come across him in the Elysian fields.—John Bailey.

THE COCK AND THE FOX

Upon a tree there mounted guard
A veteran cock, adroit and cunning;
When to the roots a fox up running
Spoke thus, in tones of kind regard:—
"Our quarrel, brother, 's at an end;
Henceforth I hope to live your friend;
For peace now reigns
Throughout the animal domains.
I bear the news. Come down, I pray,
And give me the embrace fraternal;
And please, my brother, don't delay:
So much the tidings do concern all,
That I must spread them far to-day.
Now you and yours can take your walks
Without a fear or thought of hawks;
And should you clash with them or others,
In us you'll find the best of brothers;—
For which you may, this joyful night,
Your merry bonfires light.
But, first, let's seal the bliss
With one fraternal kiss."
"Good friend," the cock replied, "upon my word,
A better thing I never heard;
And doubly I rejoice
To hear it from your voice:
And, really, there must be something in it,
For yonder come two greyhounds, which, I flatter
Myself, are couriers on this very matter:

They come so fast, they'll be here in a minute.
I'll down, and all of us will seal the blessing
With general kissing and caressing."
"Adieu," said Fox, "my errand's pressing;
I'll hurry on my way,
And we'll rejoice some other day."
So off the fellow scampered, quick and light,
To gain the fox-holes of a neighboring height,—
Less happy in his stratagem than flight.
The cock laughed sweetly in his sleeve;—
'Tis doubly sweet deceiver to deceive.

(*Elizur Wright*)

LOVE AND FOLLY

LOVE'S worshipers alone can know
The thousand mysteries that are his;
His blazing torch, his twanging bow,
His blooming age are mysteries.
A charming science—but the day
Were all too short to con it o'er;
So take of me this little lay,
A sample of its boundless lore.

As once, beneath the fragrant shade
Of myrtles fresh in heaven's pure air,
The children, Love and Folly, played,
A quarrel rose betwixt the pair.
Love said the gods should do him right—
But Folly vowed to do it then,
And struck him, o'er the orbs of sight,
So hard he never saw again.

His lovely mother's grief was deep,
She called for vengeance on the deed;
A beauty does not vainly weep,
Nor coldly does a mother plead.
A shade came o'er the eternal bliss
That fills the dwellers of the skies;
Even stony-hearted Nemesis
And Rhadamanthus wiped their eyes.

"Behold," she said, "this lovely boy,"
  While streamed afresh her graceful tears—
"Immortal, yet shut out from joy
  And sunshine, all his future years.
The child can never take, you see,
  A single step without a staff—
The hardest punishment would be
  Too lenient for the crime by half."

All said that Love had suffered wrong,
  And well that wrong should be repaid;
Then weighed the public interest long,
  And long the party's interest weighed.
And thus decreed the court above:
  "Since Love is blind from Folly's blow,
Let Folly be the guide of Love,
  Where'er the boy may choose to go."

(*William Cullen Bryant*)

THE HAG AND THE SLAVIES

THERE was a Hag who kept two Chambermaids,
So well they spun that the Three Sister Spinners,
Compared with them, were bunglers and beginners,
And her sole study was to give them work.
The moment Phœbus left his watery bed,
Up wheel, up distaffs, spin, spin, spin,
Morning out and evening in,
She kept 'em at it like a Turk.
The moment Eos raised her golden head,
A shabby cock would crow his punctual note:
The Hag, still shabbier, from her pallet leaping,
Would huddle on a greasy petticoat,
Light a cracked lamp, and scurry to the bed
Where the poor slaves with all their might
Were fiercely, ravenously sleeping.
One stretched an arm, one opened half an eye,
And both with concentrated spite

Swore through their teeth that the damned cock should
die.

No sooner said than done—that Scrannel crow
Was hushed; but did the assassins profit? No—
The Hag became her own alarum,
And lest the hour should slip her unbeknown,
Began to hustle harum-scarum
Almost before the pair had lain them them.

Thus oft a struggle to escape
But lands us in a still worse scrape:
To exchange the cock for old Sibylla
Was *From Charybdis into Scylla.*

(*Edward Marsh*)

THE CROW AND THE FOX

A Crow sat perched upon an oak,
And in his beak he held a cheese.
A Fox snuffed up the savory breeze,
And thus in honeyed accent spoke:
"O Prince of Crows, such grace of mien
Has never in these parts been seen.
If but your song be half as good,
You are the Phœnix of the wood!"
The Crow, beside himself with pleasure,
And eager to display his voice,
Opened his beak, and dropped his treasure.
The Fox was on it in a trice.
"Learn, sir," said he, "that flatterers live
On those who swallow what they say.
A cheese is not too much to give
For such a piece of sound advice."
The Crow, ashamed to have been such easy prey
Swore, but too late, he shouldn't catch him twice.

(*Edward Marsh*)

Jean-Baptiste Poquelin Molière

1622–1673

TO MONSIEUR DE LA MOTHE LE VAYER

(Upon the death of his son)

Let thy tears, Le Vayer, let them flow;
None of scant cause thy sorrowing can accuse,
Since, losing that which thou for aye dost lose,
E'en the most wise might find a ground for woe.

Vainly we strive with precepts to forego
The drops of pity that are Pity's dues;
And Nature's self, indignant, doth refuse
To count for fortitude that heartless show.

No grief, alas! can now bring back again
The son too dear, by Death untimely ta'en;
Yet, not the less, his loss is hard to bear,
Graced as he was by all the world reveres,
Large heart, keen wit, a lofty soul and rare,
—Surely these claim eternity of tears!

(Austin Dobson)

André Chénier

(1760–1794)

ELEGIES

I

Every man has his sorrows; yet each still
Hides under a calm forehead his own will.
Each pities but himself. Each in his grief
Envies his neighbor: he too seeks relief;
For one man's pain is of no other known:
They hide their sorrows as he hides his own:

And each, with tears and aching heart, can sigh:
All other men are happy, but not I.
They are unhappy all. They, desolate,
Cry against heaven and bid heaven change their fate.
Their fate is changed; they soon, with fresh tears, know
They have but changed one for another woe.

2

A white nymph wandering in the woods by night
Spies a swift satyr, and pretends a flight;
She runs, and, running, feigns to call him back!
The goat-foot, following on her flying track,
Falls down and flounders in the stagnant pool:
Whereat they, while he whimpers, mock the fool.

3

Well, I would have it so. I should have known
How many times I made her will my own.
For once, at least, I should have let her be,
And waited, till I made her come to me.
No. I forget what fretful cries last night
Drove me to bitter silence and to flight;
This morning, O weak heart, I long
To have her back, yet do her pride no wrong.

I fly to her, take all her wrongs, but she
Whom I would pardon will not pardon me.
I it is who am false, unjust, and seek
To show my horrid strength where she is weak.
And floods and tempest come, and tears that flow
Obediently, as she would have them go.
And I, to have some peace, must own defeat,
Kneel down, and take her pardon at her feet.

(*Arthur Symons*)

Pierre Jean de Beranger

1780–1857

THE KING OF YVETOT

THERE flourished once a potentate,
  Whom history doesn't name;
He rose at ten, retired at eight,
  And snored unknown to fame!
A night-cap for his crown he wore,
  A common cotton thing,
Which Jeanette to his bedside bore,
  This jolly little king!
Ho, ho, ho, ho! Ha, ha, ha, ha!
  This jolly little king!

With four diurnal banquets he
  His appetite allayed,
And on a jackass leisurely
  His royal progress made.
No cumbrous state his steps would clog,
  Fear to the winds he'd fling;
His single escort was a dog,
  This jolly little king!
Ho, ho, ho, ho! Ha, ha, ha, ha!
  This jolly little king!

He owned to only one excess,—
  He doted on his glass,—
But when a king gives happiness,
  Why that, you see, will pass!
On every bottle, small or great,
  For which he used to ring,
He laid a tax inordinate,
  This jolly little king!
Ho, ho, ho, ho! Ha, ha, ha, ha!
  This jolly little king!

Such crowds of pretty girls he found
  Occasion to admire,
It gave his subjects double ground
  For greeting him as Sire!
To shoot for cocoanuts he manned
  His army every spring,
But all conscription sternly banned
  This jolly little king!
Ho, ho, ho, ho! Ha, ha, ha, ha!
  This jolly little king!

He eyed no neighboring domain
  With envy or with greed,
And, like a pattern sovereign,
  Took Pleasure for his creed!
Yet, it was not, if aright I ween,
  Until his life took wing,
His subjects saw that he had been
  A jolly little king.
Ho, ho, ho, ho! Ha, ha, ha, ha!
  This jolly little king!

This worthy monarch, readers mine,
  You even now may see,
Embellishing a tavern-sign
  Well known to you and me!
There, when the fête-day bottle flows,
  Their bumpers they will bring,
And toast beneath his very nose
  This jolly little king.
Ho, ho, ho, ho! Ha, ha, ha, ha!
  This jolly little king!

(*William Toynbee*)

Alphonse Marie Louis de Lamartine

1792-1869

THE CEDARS OF LEBANON

Eagles, that wheel above our crests,
Say to the storms that round us blow,
They can not harm our gnarled breasts,
Firm-rooted as we are below.
Their utmost efforts we defy.
They lift the sea-waves to the sky;
But when they wrestle with our arms
Nervous and gaunt, or lift our hair,
Balanced within its cradle fair
The tiniest bird has no alarms.

Sons of the rock, no mortal hand
Here planted us: God-sown we grew.
We are the diadem green and grand
On Eden's summit that He threw.
When waters in a deluge rose,
Our hollow flanks could well enclose
Awhile the whole of Adam's race;
And children of the Patriarch
Within our forest built the Ark
Of Covenant, foreshadowing grace.

We saw the Tribes as captives led.
We saw them back return anon;
As rafters have our branches dead
Cover'd the porch of Solomon;
And later, when the Word, made man,
Came down in God's salvation-plan
To pay for sin the ransom-price,
The beams that form'd the Cross we gave:
These, red in blood of power to save,
Were altars of that Sacrifice.

In memory of such great events,
Men come to worship our remains;
Kneel down in prayer within our tents,
And kiss our old trunks' weather-stains.
The saint, the poet, and the sage,
Hear and shall hear from age to age
Sounds in our foliage like the voice
Of many waters; in these shades
Their burning words are forged like blades,
While their uplifted souls rejoice.

(*Toru Dutt*)

Alfred de Vigny

1797–1863

THE SOUND OF THE HORN

I love the sound of the horn in the deep, dim woodland,
Whether it wail with the doe that is nigh to death,
Or cry the hunter's farewell on the echoes waning,
From leaf to leaf borne on by the north wind's breath.

How often alone, in the shadow at midnight straying,
I have smiled to hear it, how often have wept still more!
For I seemed to hear the rumor of things foreboding
The death of the Paladin knights that lived of yore.

O azure Mountain! O land that my heart is fain of!
Franzona fells, and summits of Marboré,
Fountains that fall with the drifted snows for a burden,
Torrents and brooks of the Pyrenees' chill spray,

Mountains frozen or fertile, throning the seasons,
Who have ice for crown and the meadows about your feet,
'Tis there would I dwell, 'tis there would I wait to hearken
The far-borne sound of the horn blow sad and sweet.

A traveler strayed mayhap when the air is stilly,
Lifts up this brazen voice that the night repeats;
With the sound of his cadenced songs for a while is blending
The tiny bell of the tethered lamb that bleats.

A doe that heareth the sound flies not but rather
Stands still as a stone on the hill-top, while waters chime
In vast uproar with the music for ever calling
From the old romance of the immemorial time.

Souls of the Paladins, say, do your ghosts still haunt us?
Is it you who speak to us still in the blare of the horn?
Roncevaux! Roncevaux! deep in thy somber valley
The shade of the noble Roland is still forlorn!

(*Wilfrid Thorley*)

NATURE

I AM the stage, impassive, mute and cold,
That thrills not where the actor's foot hath trod.
My alabaster halls, my emerald
Stairs, and my tones were sculptured by a god:
Your voice of crying I know not, no, nor see
The passing of the human comedy
That looks to heaven to find its period.

I roll, and to my deep disdain I thrust
The seed of ants and human populations;
Their tenements I know not from their dust,
Their names I know not—I that bear the nations;
Mother in name, in deed a very room
For death; my winter takes its hecatomb,
My spring is careless of your adorations.

Before you, always essenced, always fair,
I shook my locks abroad the winds of heaven,
And trod my customary path in air,
While the divine hands held the balance even

And onward, to that void where all things roll
I shall be carried silently and sole,
And by my breast and brows the airs be riven.

(Margaret Jourdain)

Victor Hugo

1802–1885

A SUNSET

(From "Feuilles d'Automne")

I LOVE the evenings, passionless and fair, I love the evens,
Whether old manor-fronts their ray with golden fulgence leavens,
In numerous leafage bosomed close;
Whether the mist in reefs of fire extend its reaches sheer,
Or a hundred sunbeams splinter in an azure atmosphere
On cloudy archipelagos.

Oh, gaze ye on the firmament! a hundred clouds in motion,
Up-piled in the immense sublime beneath the winds' commotion,
Their unimagined shapes accord:
Under their waves at intervals flame a pale levin through,
As if some giant of the air amid the vapors drew
A sudden elemental sword.

The sun at bay with splendid thrusts still keeps the sullen fold;
And momently at distance sets, as a cupola of gold,
The thatched roof of a cot a-glance;
Or on the blurred horizon joins his battle with the haze;
Or pools the glooming fields about with inter-isolate blaze,
Great moveless meres of radiance.

Then mark you how there hangs athwart the firmament's swept track,

Yonder, a mighty crocodile with vast irradiant back,
A triple row of pointed teeth?
Under its burnished belly slips a ray of eventide,
The flickerings of a hundred glowing clouds its tenebrous side
With scales of golden mail ensheathe.

Then mounts a palace, then the air vibrates—the vision flees.
Confounded to its base, the fearful cloudy edifice
Ruins immense in mounded wrack;
Afar the fragments strew the sky, and each envermeiled cone
Hangeth, peak downward, overhead, like mountains overthrown
When the earthquake heaves its hugy back.

These vapors, with their leaden, golden, iron, bronzèd glows,
Where the hurricane, the waterspout, thunder, and hell repose,
Muttering hoarse dreams of destined harms,—
'Tis God who hangs their multitude amid the skiey deep,
As a warrior that suspendeth from the roof-tree of his keep
His dreadful and resounding arms!

All vanishes! The Sun, from topmost heaven precipitated,
Like a globe of iron which is tossed back fiery red
Into the furnace stirred to fume,
Shocking the cloudy surges, plashed from its impetuous ire,
Even to the zenith spattereth in a flecking scud of fire
The vaporous and inflamèd spaume.

O contemplate the heavens! Whenas the vein-drawn day dies pale,

In every season, every place, gaze through their every
veil?
With love that has not speech for need!
Beneath their solemn beauty is a mystery infinite:
If winter hue them like a pall, or if the summer night
Fantasy them starry brede.

(*Francis Thompson*)

HEARD ON THE MOUNTAIN

(*From "Feuilles d'Automne"*)

Have you sometimes, calm, silent let your tread aspirant
rise
Up to the mountain's summit, in the presence of the
skies?
Was't on the borders of the South? or on the Bretagne
coast?
And at the basis of the mount had you the Ocean
tossed?
And there, learned o'er the wave and o'er the immeas-
urableness,
Calm, silent, have you harkened what it says? Lo, what
it says!
One day at least, whereon my thought, enlicensed to
muse,
Had drooped its wing above the beached margent of
the ooze,
And, plunging from the mountain height into the
immensity,
Beheld upon one side the land, on the other side the sea.
I harkened, comprehended,—never, as from those
abysses,
No, never issued from a mouth, nor moved an ear such
voice as this is!
A sound it was, at outset, immeasurable, confused,
Vaguer than is the wind among the tufted trees effused,
Full of magnificent accords, suave murmurs, sweet as is
The evensong, and mighty as the shock of panoplies
When the hoarse mêlée in its arms the closing squadrons
grips,

And pants, in furious breathings, from the clarions' brazen lips.
Unutterable the harmony, unsearchable its deep,
Whose fluid undulations round the world a girdle keep,
And through the vasty heavens, which by its surges are washed young,
Its infinite volutions roll, enlarging as they throng,
Even to the profound arcane, whose ultimate chasms somber
Its shattered flood englut with time, with space and form and number.
Like to another atmosphere, with thin o'erflowing robe,
The hymn eternal covers all the inundated globe:
And the world, swathed about with this investuring symphony,
Even as it trepidates in the air, so trepidates in the harmony.

And pensive, I attended the ethereal litany,
Lost within this containing voice as if within the sea.

Soon I distinguished, yet as tone which veils confuse and smother,
Amid this voice two voices, one commingled with the other,
Which did from off the land and seas even to the heavens aspire;
Chanting the universal chant in simultaneous quire.
And I distinguished them amid that deep and rumorous sound,
As who beholds two currents thwart amid the fluctuous profound.

The one was of the waters; a be-radiant hymnal speech!
That was the voice of the surges, as they parleyed each with each.
The other, which arose from our abode terranean,
Was sorrowful; and that, alack! the murmur was of man;

And in this mighty quire, whose chantings day and
night resound,
Every wave had its utterance, and every man his sound.

Now, the magnificent Ocean, as I said, unbannering,
A voice of joy, a voice of peace, did never stint to sing,
Most like in Sion's temples to a psaltery psaltering,
And to creation's beauty reared the great lauds of his
song.
Upon the gale, upon the Squall, his clamor borne along
Unpausingly arose to God in more triumphal swell;
And every one among his waves, that God alone can
quell,
When the other of its song made end, into the singing
pressed.
Like that majestic lion whereof Daniel was the guest,
At intervals the Ocean his tremendous murmur awed;
And, toward where the sunset fires fell shaggily and
broad,
Under his golden mane, methought that I saw pass the
hand of God.
Meanwhile, and side by side with that august fanfaron-
nade
The other voice, like the sudden scream of a destrier
affrayed,
Like an infernal door that grates ajar its rusty throat,
Like to a bow of iron that gnarls upon an iron rote,
Grinded; and tears, and shriekings, the anathema, the
lewd taunt,
Refusal of viaticum, refusal of the font,
And clamor, and malediction, and dread blasphemy,
among
That hurtling crowd of rumor from the diverse human
tongue,
Went by as who beholdeth, when the valleys thick
t'ward night,
The long drifts of the birds of dusk pass, blackening
flight on flight.

What was this sound whose thousand echoes vibrated
 unsleeping?
Alas! The sound was earth's and man's, for earth and
 man were weeping.

Brothers! of these two voices strange, most unimaginably,
 Unceasingly regenerated, dying unceasingly,
Harkened of the Eternal throughout His Eternity,
The one voice uttereth NATURE, and the other voice
 HUMANITY.

Then I alit in reverie; for my ministering sprite,
Alack! had never yet deployed a pinion of an ampler
 flight,
Nor ever had my shadow endured so large a day to
 burn:
And long I rested dreaming, contemplating turn by turn
Now that abyss obscure which lurked beneath the
 water's roll,
And now that other untemptable abyss which opened in
 my soul.
And I made question of me, to what issues are we here,
Whither should tend the thwarting threads of all this
 raveled gear;
What doth the soul; to be or live if better worth it is;
And why the Lord, Who, only, reads within that book
 of His,
In fatal hymeneals hath eternally entwined
The vintage-chant of nature with the dirging cry of
 humankind?

(*Francis Thompson*)

THE GRAVE AND THE ROSE

The Grave said to the Rose,
"What of the dews of dawn,
Love's flower, what end is theirs?"
"And what of spirits flown,
The souls whereon doth close
The tomb's mouth unawares?"
The Rose said to the Grave.

The Rose said, "In the shade
From the dawn's tears is made
A perfume faint and strange,
Amber and honey sweet."
"And all the spirits fleet
Do suffer a sky-change,
More strangely than the dew,
To God's own angels new,"
The Grave said to the Rose.

(Andrew Lang)

THE GENESIS OF BUTTERFLIES

The dawn is smiling on the dew that covers
The tearful roses; lo, the little lovers
That kiss the buds, and all the flutterings
In jasmine bloom, and privet, of white wings,
That go and come, and fly, and peep and hide,
With muffled music, murmured far and wide.
Ah, the Spring time, when we think of all the lays
That dreamy lovers send to dreamy mays,
Of the fond hearts within a billet bound,
Of all the soft silk paper that pens wound,
The messages of love that mortals write
Filled with intoxication of delight,
Written in April and before the May time
Shredded and flown, playthings for the wind's playtime,
We dream that all white butterflies above,
Who seek through clouds or waters souls to love,
And leave their lady mistress in despair,
To flit to flowers, as kinder and more fair,
Are but torn love-letters, that through the skies
Flutter, and float, and change to butterflies.

(Andrew Lang)

MORE STRONG THAN TIME

Since I have set my lips to your full cup, my sweet,
Since I my pallid face between your hands have laid,
Since I have known your soul, and all the bloom of it,
And all the perfume rare, now buried in the shade;

Since it was given to me to hear one happy while,
The words wherein your heart spoke all its mysteries,
Since I have seen you weep, and since I have seen you smile,
Your lips upon my lips, and your eyes upon my eyes;

Since I have known above my forehead glance and gleam,
A ray, a single ray, of your star, veiled always,
Since I have felt the fall, upon my lifetime's stream,
Of one rose petal plucked from the roses of your days;

I now am bold to say to the swift changing hours,
Pass, pass upon your way, for I grow never old,
Fleet to the dark abysm with all your fading flowers,
One rose that none may pluck, within my heart I hold.

Your flying wings may smite, but they can never spill
The cup fulfilled of love, from which my lips are wet;
My heart has far more fire than you can frost to chill,
My soul more love than you can make my soul forget.

(*Andrew Lang*)

THE POOR CHILDREN

Take heed of this small child of earth;
He is great; he hath in him God most high.
Children before their fleshly birth
Are lights alive in the blue sky.

In our light bitter world of wrong
They come; God gives us them awhile.
His speech is in their stammering tongue,
And his forgiveness in their smile.

Their sweet light rests upon our eyes.
Alas! their right to joy is plain.
If they are hungry Paradise
Weeps, and, if cold, Heaven thrills with pain.

The want that saps their sinless flower
  Speaks judgment on sin's ministers.
Man holds an angel in his power.
  Ah! deep in Heaven what thunder stirs,

When God seeks out these tender things
  Whom in the shadow where we sleep
He sends us clothed about with wings,
  And finds them ragged babes that weep!

(Algernon Charles Swinburne)

Gérard de Nerval

1808–1855

AN OLD TUNE

THERE is an air for which I would disown
  Mozart's, Rossini's, Weber's melodies,—
A sweet sad air that languishes and sighs,
  And keeps its secret charm for me alone.

Whene'er I hear that music vague and old,
  Two hundred years are mist that rolls away;
The thirteenth Louis reigns, and I behold
  A green land golden in the dying day.

An old red castle, strong with stony towers,
  The windows gay with many colored glass;
Wide plains, and rivers flowing among flowers,
  That bathe the castle basement as they pass.

In antique weed, with dark eyes and gold hair,
  A lady looks forth from her window high;
It may be that I knew and found her fair,
  In some forgotten life, long time gone by.

(Andrew Lang)

Alfred de Musset

1810–1857

SOUVENIR

I WEEP, but with no bitterness I weep,
To look again upon thee, hallowed spot,
O dearest grave, and most of men forgot,
Where buried love doth sleep.

What witchcraft think you that this desert hath,
Dear friends, who take my hand and bid me stay,
Now that the gentle wont of many a day
Would lead me down this path?

Here are the wooded slopes, the flowering heath,
The silver footprints on the silent sand,
The loitering lanes, alive with lovers' breath,
Where first I kissed her hand.

I know these fir-trees, and this mossy stone,
And this deep gorge, and all its winding ways;
These friendly giants, whose primeval moan
Hath rocked my happy days.

My footsteps' echo in this tangled tree
Gives back youth's music, like a singing bird;
Dear haunts, fair wilderness her presence stirred,
Did you not watch for me?

I will not dry these tear-drops: let them flow,
And soothe a bitterness that yet might last,
And o'er my waking-weary eyelids throw
The shadow of the past.

My useless plainings shall not make to cease
The happy echoes of the vows we vowed:
Proud is this forest in its noble peace,
And my heart too is proud.

Give o'er to hopeless grief the bitter hours
You kneel to pray upon a brother's tomb:
Here blows the breath of love, and graveyard flowers
Not in this garden bloom.

See! The moon rides athwart a bank of cloud.
Thy veils, fair Queen of Night, still cling to thee,
But soon thou loosenest thy virgin shroud
And smilest to be free.

As the rich earth, still dank with April rain,
Beneath thy rays exhales day's captive balm,
So from my purged soul, as pure, as calm,
The old love breathes again.

Where are they gone, those ghosts of sorrow pale,
Where fled the passion that my heart defiled?
Once in the bosom of this friendly vale
I am again a child.

O might of time, O changes of the year,
Ye undo sorrow and the tears we shed,
But, touched with pity, on our blossoms were
Your light feet never tread.

Heavenly solace, be for ever blest!
I had not thought a sword could pierce so far
Into the heart, and leave upon the breast
So sweet and dear a scar.

Far from me the sharp word, the thankless mind,
Of vulgar sorrow customary weed,
Shroud that about the corse of love they wind
Who never loved indeed.

Why, Dante, dost thou say the saddest curse
Is joy remembered in unhappy days?
What grief compelled thee to this bitter verse
In sorrow's harsh dispraise?

O'er all the worlds is light bereft of gladness
When sad eclipses cast their blight on us?
Did thy great soul, in its immortal sadness,
Speak to thee, Dante, thus?

No, by this sacred light upon me cast!
Not in thy heart this blasphemy had birth.
It is the truest happiness on earth
To have a happy past.

What! When the soul forlorn finds yet a spark
Mid the hot ashes of her stifled sighs,
And doth that flame, her only treasure, mark
With captivated eyes,

Bathing her wounds in the delicious past
That mirrors brokenly her loves again,
Thy cruel word her feeble joy would blast
And turn to bitter pain?

And couldst thou wrong thine own Francesca so,
Wrong thy bright angel with a word like this,
Her whose lips, parting to rehearse her woe,
Broke an eternal kiss?

What, righteous Heaven, is our human thought,
And to the love of truth who yet will cling,
If every pain or joy e'er shunned or sought
Turns to a doubtful thing?

How can you live, strange souls that nothing awes?
In midst of haste and passion, song and mirth,
Nor all the stars of heaven give you pause,
Nor all the sins of earth;

But when upon your fated way you meet
Some dumb memorial of a passion dead,
That little pebble stops you, and you dread
To bruise your tender feet.

You cry aloud that life is but a dream,
And, to the truth awaking, wring your hands,
And grieve your bubble but a moment stands
 Upon time's foaming stream.

Poor fools! That moment when your soul could shake
The numbing fetters off that it enthrall,
That fleeting moment was your all in all—
 Oh, mourn not for its sake!

But rather mourn your weight of earthly dross,
Your joyless toil, your stains of blood and mire,
Your sunless days, your nights without desire;
 In these was utter loss.

What profit have you of your late lament,
And what from heaven do your murmurs crave,
The plaints you sow upon the barren grave
 Of every pleasure spent?

Life is a dream, and all things pass, I know:
If some fair splendor we be charmed withal,
We pluck the flower, and at the breath we blow
 Its withered petals fall.

Ay, the first kiss and the first virgin vow
That ever mortals upon earth did swear,
That whirlwind caught which strips the frozen bough
 And stones to sand doth wear.

A witness to the lovers' troth was night,
With changeful skies, o'ercast with mystery,
And stars unnumbered, that an inward light
 Devours unceasingly.

They saw death hush the song bird in the glade,
Blast the pale flower, and freeze the torpid worm,
And choke the fountain where the image played
 Of their forgotten form.

Yet they joined hands above the moldering clod,
Blind with love's light that flashed across the sky,
Nor felt the cold eye of the changeless God
Who watches all things die.

Fools! says the sage: thrice blest! the poet says.
What wretched joy is to the faint heart dear
Whom noise of torrents fills with weak amaze
And the wind fills with fear?

I have seen beneath the sun more beauties fail
Than white sea foam or leaves of forest sere;
More than the swallows and the roses frail
Desert the widowed year.

Mine eyes have gazed on sights of deeper woe
Than Juliet dead within the gorged tomb,
And deadlier than the cup that Romeo
Drank to his love and doom.

I have seen my love, when all I loved had perished,
Who to a whited sepulcher is turned;
Seen the thin dust of all I ever cherished
In her cold heart inurned,—

Dust of that faith which, in our bosoms furled,
The gentle night had warded well from doubt.
More than a single life, alas! a world
Was that day blotted out.

Still young I found her, and, men said, more fair;
In heaven's light her eyes could still rejoice,
And her lips opened, and a smile was there,
And sound as of a voice.

But not that gentle voice, that tender grace,
Those eyes I worshiped when they looked their prayer:
My heart, still full of her, searched, searched her face
And could not find her there.

And still I could have gone to her, and cast
My arms about that chill and lifeless stone,
And cried, Where hast thou left it, faithless one,
Where hast thou left the past?

But no: it rather seemed as if by chance
Some unknown woman had that voice and eye;
I looked up into heaven; with cold glance
I passed that statue by.

Not without pangs of shame and bitterness
I watched her smiling shadow glide away;
But what of that? Immortal nature, say,
Have I loved therefore less?

On me the gods may now their lightnings fling,
They cannot undo truth, nor kill the past.
Like a wrecked sailor to a broken mast
To my dead love I cling.

I make no question of what flowers may bloom,
What virtue from the seasons man may borrow,
What heavenly lamp may flood with light to-morrow
The vault of this great tomb.

I only say: Here at this hour, one day,
I loved, and I was loved, and she was fair.
This treasure which no death can filch away
My soul to God shall bear.

(George Santayana)

JUANA

Again I see you, ah my queen,
Of all my old loves that have been,
The first love, and the tenderest;
Do you remember or forget—
Ah me, for I remember yet—
How the last summer days were blest?

Ah lady, when we think of this,
The foolish hours of youth and bliss,
  How fleet, how sweet, how hard to hold.
How old we are, ere spring be green.
You touch the limit of eighteen
  And I am twenty winters old.

My rose, that mid the red roses,
Was brightest, ah, how pale she is.
  Yet keeps the beauty of her prime;
Child, never Spanish lady's face
Was lovely with so wild a grace;
  Remember the dead summertime.

Think of our loves, our feuds of old,
And how you gave your chain of gold
  To me for a peace offering;
And how all night I lay awake
To touch and kiss it for your sake,—
  To touch and kiss the lifeless thing.

Lady, beware for all we say,
This love shall live another day,
  Awakened from his deathly sleep;
The heart that once has been your shrine
For other loves is too divine;
  A home, my dear, too wide and deep.

What did I say,—why do I dream?
Why should I struggle with the stream
  Whose waves return not any day?
Close heart, and eyes, and arms from me;
Farewell, farewell, so must it be,
  So runs, so runs, the world away.

The season bears upon its wing
The swallows and the songs of spring,
  And days that were, and days that flit;
The loved lost hours are far away;

And hope and fame are scattered spray
For me, that gave you love a day
For you that not remember it.

(Andrew Lang)

Théophile Gautier

1811-1872

ART

All things are doubly fair
If patience fashion them
And care—
Verse, enamel, marble, gem.

No idle chains endure:
Yet, Muse, to walk aright
Lace tight
Thy buskin proud and sure.

Fie on facile measure,
A shoe where every lout
At pleasure
Slip his foot in and out!

Sculptor lay by the clay
On which thy nerveless finger
May linger,
Thy thoughts flown far away.

Keep to Carrara rare,
Struggle with Paros cold,
That hold
The subtle line and fair.

Lest haply nature lose
That proud, that perfect line,
Make thine
The bronze of Syracuse.

And with a tender dread
Upon an agate's face
    Retrace
Apollo's golden head.

Despise a watery hue
And tints that soon expire.
    With fire
Burn thine enamel true.

Twine, twine in artful wise
The blue-green mermaid's arms
    Mid charms
Of thousand heraldries.

Show in their triple lobe
Virgin and Child, that hold
    Their globe,
Cross crowned and aureoled.

—All things return to dust
Save beauties fashioned well;
    The bust
Outlasts the citadel.

Oft doth the plowman's heel,
Breaking an ancient clod,
    Reveal
A Cæsar or a god.

The gods, too, die, alas!
But deathless and more strong
    Than brass
Remains the sovereign song.

Chisel and carve and file,
Till thy vague dream imprint
    Its smile
On the unyielding flint.

(*George Santayana*)

POSTHUMOUS COQUETRY

Let there be laid, when I am dead,
Ere 'neath the coffin-lid I lie,
Upon my cheek a little red,
A little black about the eye.

For I in my close bier would fain,
As on the night his vows were made,
Rose-red eternally remain,
With khol beneath my blue eye laid.

Wind me no shroud of linen down
My body to my feet, but fold
The white folds of my muslin gown
With thirteen flounces as of old.

This shall go with me where I go:
I wore it when I won his heart;
His first look hallowed it, and so,
For him, I laid the gown apart.

No immortelles, no broidered grace
Of tears upon my cushions be;
Lay me on my pillow's lace,
My hair across it like a sea.

That pillow, those mad nights of old,
Has seen our slumbering brows unite,
And neath the gondola's black fold
Has counted kisses infinite.

Between my hands of ivory,
Together set for prayer and rest,
Place then the opal rosary
The holy Pope at Rome has blest.

I will lie down then on that bed
And sleep the sleep that shall not cease;
His mouth upon my mouth has said
Pater and *Ave* for my peace.

(*Arthur Symons*)

CLARIMONDE

With elbow buried in the downy pillow
I've lain and read,
All through the night, a volume strangely written
In tongues long dead.

For at my bedside lie no dainty slippers;
And, save my own,
Under the paling lamp I hear no breathing:—
I am alone!

But there are yellow bruises on my body
And violet stains;
Though no white vampire came with lips blood-crimsoned
To suck my veins!

Now I bethink me of a sweet weird story,
That in the dark
Our dead loves thus with seal of chilly kisses
Our bodies mark.

Gliding beneath the coverings of our couches
They share our rest,
And with their dead lips sign their loving visit
On arm and breast.

Darksome and cold the bed where now she slumbers,
I loved in vain,
With sweet eyelids closed, to be reopened
Never again.

Dead sweetheart, can it be that thou hast lifted
With thy frail hand
Thy coffin-lid, to come to me again
From shadowland?

Thou who, one joyous night, didst, pale and speechless,
Pass from us all,
Dropping thy silken mask and gift of flowers
Amidst the ball?

Oh, fondest of my loves, from that far heaven
Where thou must be,
Hast thou returned to pay the debt of kisses
Thou owest to me?

(*Lafcadio Hearn*)

LOVE AT SEA

We are in love's land to-day;
Where shall we go?
Love, shall we start or stay,
Or sail or row?
There's many a wind and way,
And never a May but May;
We are in love's land to-day;
Where shall we go?

Our landwind is the breath
Of sorrows kissed to death
And joys that were;
Our ballast is a rose;
Our way lies where God knows
And love knows where
We are in love's land to-day—

Our seamen are fledged loves,
Our masts are bills of doves,
Our decks fine gold;
Our ropes are dead maids' hair,
Our stores are love-shafts fair
And manifold.
We are in love's land to-day—

Where shall we land you, sweet?
On fields of strange men's feet,
  Or fields near home?
Or where the fire-flowers blow,
Or where the flowers of snow
  Or flowers of foam?
      We are in love's land to-day—

Land me, she says, where love
Shows but one shaft, one dove,
  One heart, one hand.
—A shore like that, my dear,
Lies where no man will steer,
  No maiden land.

(*Algernon Charles Swinburne*)

Leconte de Lisle

1818–1894

HIALMAR SPEAKS TO THE RAVEN

Night in the bloodstained snow: the wind is chill:
And there a thousand tombless warriors lie,
Grasping their swords, wild-featured. All are still.
Above them the black ravens wheel and cry.

A brilliant moon sends her cold light abroad:
Hialmar arises from the reddened slain,
Heavily leaning on his broken sword,
And bleeding from his side the battle-rain.

"Hail to you all: is there one breath still drawn
Among those fierce and fearless lads who played
So merrily, and sang as sweet in the dawn
As thrushes singing in the bramble shade?

"They have no word to say: my helm's unbound,
My breastplate by the ax unriveted:
Blood's on my eyes; I hear a spreading sound,
Like waves or wolves that clamor in my head.

"Eater of men, old raven, come this way,
And with thine iron bill open my breast,
To-morrow find us where we lie to-day,
And bear my heart to her that I love best.

"Through Upsàla, where drink the Jarls and sing,
And clash their golden bowls in company,
Bird of the moor, carry on tireless wing
To Ylmer's daughter there the heart of me.

"And thou shalt see her standing straight and pale,
High pedestaled on some rook-haunted tower:
She has two ear-rings, silver and vermeil,
And eyes like stars that shine in sunset hour.

"Tell her my love, thou dark bird ominous;
Give her my heart, no bloodless heart and vile
But red compact and strong, O raven. Thus
Shall Ylmer's daughter greet thee with a smile.

"Now let my life from twenty deep wounds flow,
And wolves may drink the blood. My time is done.
Young, brave and spotless, I rejoice to go
And sit where all the Gods are, in the sun."

(*James Elroy Flecker*)

Charles Baudelaire

1821–1867

In the poetry of Baudelaire there is a deliberate science of sensual and sexual perversity which has something curious in its accentuation of vice with horror, in its passionate devotion to passions. Baudelaire lived and died solitary, secret, a confessor of sins who had never told the whole truth, an ascetic of passion, a hermit of the Brothel.—Arthur Symons.

LITANY TO SATAN

O grandest of the Angels, and most wise,
O fallen God, fate-driven from the skies,
Satan, at last take pity on our pain.

O first of exiles who endurest wrong,
Yet growest, in thy hatred, still more strong,
Satan, at last take pity on our pain.

O subterranean King, omniscient,
Healer of man's immortal discontent,
Satan, at last take pity on our pain.

To lepers and to outcasts thou dost show
That passion is the paradise below.
Satan, at last take pity on our pain.

Thou by thy mistress Death hast given to man
Hope, the imperishable courtesan.
Satan, at last take pity on our pain.

Thou givest to the Guilty their calm mien
Which damns the crowd around the guillotine.
Satan, at last take pity on our pain.

Thou knowest the corners of the jealous Earth
Where God has hidden jewels of great worth.
Satan, at last take pity on our pain.

Thou dost discover by mysterious signs
Where sleep the buried people of the mines.
Satan, at last take pity on our pain.

Thou stretchest forth a saving hand to keep
Such men as roam upon the roofs in sleep.
Satan, at last take pity on our pain.

Thy power can make the halting Drunkard's feet
Avoid the peril of the surging street.
Satan, at last take pity on our pain.

Thou, to console our helplessness, didst plot
The cunning use of powder and of shot.
Satan, at last take pity on our pain.

In strange and hidden places thou dost move
Where women cry for torture in their love.
Satan, at last take pity on our pain.

Thy awful name is written as with pitch
On the unrelenting foreheads of the rich.
Satan, at last take pity on our pain.

Father of those whom God's tempestuous ire
Has flung from Paradise with sword and fire,
Satan, at last take pity on our pain.

Prayer

Satan, to thee be praise upon the Height
Where thou wast king of old, and in the night
Of Hell, where thou dost dream on silently.
Grant that one day beneath the Knowledge-tree,
When it shoots forth to grace thy royal brow,
My soul may sit, that cries upon thee now.

(*James Elroy Flecker*)

DON JUAN IN HELL

THE night Don Juan came to pay his fees
To Charon, by the caverned water's shore,
A beggar, proud-eyed as Antisthenes,
Stretched out his knotted fingers on the oar.

Mournful, with drooping breasts and robes unsewn
The shapes of women swayed in ebon skies,
Trailing behind him with a restless moan
Like cattle herded for a sacrifice.

Here, grinning for his wage, stood Sganarelle,
And here Don Luis pointed, bent and dim,
To show the dead who lined the holes of hell,
This was that impious son who mocked at him.

The hollow-eyed, the chaste Elvira came,
Trembling and veiled, to view her traitor spouse.
Was it one last bright smile she thought to claim,
Such as made sweet the morning of his vows?

A great stone man rose like a tower on board,
Stood at the helm and cleft the flood profound:
But the calm hero, leaning on his sword,
Gazed back, and would not offer one look round.

(*James Elroy Flecker*)

EPILOGUE

With heart at rest I climbed the citadel's
Steep height, and saw the city as from a tower,
Hospital, brothel, prison, and such hells,

Where evil comes up softly like a flower,
Thou knowest, O Satan, patron of my pain,
Not for vain tears I went up at that hour;

But, like an old sad faithful lecher, fain
To drink delight of that enormous trull
Whose hellish beauty makes me young again.

Whether thou sleep, with heavy vapors full,
Sodden with day, or, new appareled, stand
In gold-laced veils of evening beautiful,

I love thee, infamous city! Harlots and
Hunted have pleasures of their own to give,
The vulgar herd can never understand.

(*Arthur Symons*)

LES HIBOUX

Under the yew-tree's heavy weight
The owls stand in their sullen fashions,
Like Pagan gods of Pagan passions
They dart their eyes and meditate.

Unmoving they stare with living flame
Until the end of the melancholy
Hour sees the oblique sun set in folly,
And darkness falls in shades of shame.
Their aspect to the wise man teaches
All that he needs, all he beseeches,
Tumult and change and discontent;
The man drunk of a shadow that passes
Keeps always the imperishable scent
That makes the wind change and the grasses.

(*Arthur Symons*)

PARFUM EXOTIQUE

When with eyes closed as in an opium dream
I breathe the odor of thy passionate breast,
I see in vision hell's infernal stream
And the sunset fires that have no instant's rest:
An idle island where the unnatural scheme
Of Nature is by savorous fruits oppressed,
And where men's bodies are their women's guest
And women's bodies are not what they seem.

Guided by thine odor towards the heat of veils,
I see a harbor filled with masts and sails,
Wearied by the sea wind that wearies me,

And in the perfume of the tamarind there clings
I know not what of marvelous luxury
Mixed in my soul with the song the mariner sings.

(*Arthur Symons*)

ÉLÉVATION

Above the pools, above the valley of fears,
Above the woods, the clouds, the hills, the trees,
Beyond the sun's and the moon's mad mysteries,
Beyond the confines of the starry spheres,

My spirit, you move with a pure ardency,
And, as one who swoons in the senses of sound,
You furrow furiously the immensity profound
With an indicable and male sensuality.

Fly from those morbid miasmas and their mire;
Purify your own self in the mid air malign,
And there drink, as a delicious and rare wine,
The enormity and the intensity of fire.

Beyond the universe and the vast chagrins
Which load the smoky air with their existence,
Joyous is he who can with a bird's persistence
Rush toward the heavens not fashioned by our sins!

He whose thoughts, like the lark that sings and wings
Its way at dawn toward the sky in a higher flight,
Wandering over the immensity of the night,
Knows the flowers' speech and the speech of silent things!

(*Arthur Symons*)

CORRESPONDENCES

All Nature is a temple where the alive
Pillars breathe often a tremor of mixed words;
Man wanders in a forest of accords
That peer familiarly from each ogive.

Like thinning echoes tumbling to sleep, beyond,
In a unity unbrageous and infinite,
Vast as the night tremendously moonlit,
Perfumes and colors and sounds correspond.

Perfumes blown sweet as infants' naked flesh,
Soft as oboes, green as a studded plain,
—Others, corrupt, rich and triumphant, thresh

Expansions to the infinite of pain:
Amber and myrrh, benzoin and musk condense
To transports in the spirit and the sense!

(*Allen Tate*)

A CARRION

Remember now, my Love, what piteous thing
We saw on a summer's gracious day:
By the roadway a hideous carrion, quivering
On a clean bed of pebbly clay,

With legs flexed in the air like a courtesan,
Burning and sweating venomously,
Calmly disclosed its belly, ironic and wan,
Clamorous with foul ecstasy.

The sun bore down upon this rottenness
As if to roast it with gold fire,
And render back to Nature her own largess
A hundredfold of her desire.

Heaven observed the vaunting carcass there
Blooming with the richness of a flower;
And that almighty stink which corpses wear
Choked you with sleepy power!

The flies swarmed on that putrid vulva; then
A black tumbling rout would seethe
Of maggots, thick like a torrent in a glen,
Over those rags that lived and seemed to breathe.

They darted down and ascended like a wave
Or buzzed impetuously as before;
One would have thought the corpse was held a slave
To living by the life it bore!

This world made music, had its own swift emotion
Like water and the wind running,
Or corn that a winnower, in rhythmic motion,
Fans with fiery cunning.

All forms receded—as in a dream, were still,
Where white visions vaguely start
From the sketch of a painter's long-neglected idyl
Into a perfect art!

Behind the rocks a restless bitch looked on,
  Regarding us with jealous eyes,
Waiting to tear from the livid skeleton
  Her loosed morsel quick with flies.

—And even you will come to this foul shame,
  This horrible infection,
Star of my eyes, my being's inner flame,
  My angel and my passion!

Yes: such you shall be, O queen of heavenly grace,
  Beyond the last sacrament,
When through your bones the sucking flowers and grass
  Weave their rank cerement.

Speak, then, my Beauty, to this dire putrescence,
  To the worm that shall kiss your proud estate,
That I have kept the divine Form and the Essence
  Of my festered loves inviolate!

(*Allen Tate*)

SOIS SAGE O MA DOULEUR

Peace, be at peace, O thou my heaviness,
Thou calledst for the evening, lo! 'tis here,
The City wears a somber atmosphere
That brings repose to some, to some distress.
Now while the heedless throng make haste to press
Where pleasure drives them, ruthless charioteer,
To pluck the fruits of sick remorse and fear,
Come thou with me, and leave their fretfulness.

See how they hang from heaven's high balconies,
The old lost years in faded garments dressed,
And see Regret with faintly smiling mouth;
And while the dying sun sinks in the west,
Hear how, far off, Night walks with velvet tread,
And her long robe trails all about the south.

(*Lord Alfred Douglas*)

LA BEAUTÉ

Fair am I, mortals, as a stone-carved dream,
And all men wound themselves against my breast,
The poet's last desire, the loveliest.
Voiceless, eternal as the world I seem,
In the blue air, strange sphinx, I brood supreme
With heart of snow whiter than swan's white crest,
No movement mars the plastic line—I rest
With lips untaught to laugh or eyes to stream.

Singers who see, in trancèd interludes,
My splendor set with all superb design,
Consume their days, in toilful ecstasy.
To these revealed, the starry amplitudes
Of my great eyes which make all things divine
Are crystal mirrors of eternity.

(*Lord Alfred Douglas*)

LE BALCON

Mother of Memories! O mistress-queen!
Oh! all my joy and all my duty thou!
The beauty of caresses that have been,
The evenings and the hearth remember now,
Mother of Memories! O mistress-queen!

The evenings burning with the glowing fire,
And on the balcony, the rose-stained nights!
How sweet, how kind you were, my soul's desire.
We said things wonderful as chrysolites,
When evening burned beside the glowing fire.

How fair the Sun is in the evening!
How strong the soul, how high the heaven's high tower!
O first and last of every worshiped thing,
Your odorous heart's-blood filled me like a flower.
How fair the sun is in the evening!

The night grew deep between us like a pall,
And in the dark I guessed your shining eyes,
And drank your breath, O sweet, O honey-gall!
Your little feet slept on me sister-wise.
The night grew deep between us like a pall.

I can call back the days desirable,
And live all bliss again between your knees,
For where else can I find that magic spell
Save in your heart and in your Mysteries?
I can call back the days desirable.

These vows, these scents, these kisses infinite,
Will they like young suns climbing up the skies
Rise up from some unfathomable pit,
Washed in the sea from all impurities?
O vows, O scents, O kisses infinite!

(*Lord Alfred Douglas*)

HARMONIE DU SOIR

Now is the hour when, swinging in the breeze,
Each flower, like a censer, sheds its sweet.
The air is full of scents and melodies,
O languorous waltz! O swoon of dancing feet!

Each flower, like a censer, sheds its sweet,
The violins are like sad souls that cry,
O languorous waltz! O swoon of dancing feet!
A shrine of Death and Beauty is the sky.

The violins are like sad souls that cry,
Poor souls that hate the vast black night of Death;
A shrine of Death and Beauty is the sky.
Drowned in red blood, the Sun gives up his breath.

This soul that hates the vast black night of Death
Takes all the luminous past back tenderly,
Drowned in red blood, the Sun gives up his breath.
Thine image like a monstrance shines in me.

(*Lord Alfred Douglas*)

Henri Murger

1822–1861

SPRING IN THE STUDENTS' QUARTER

Winter is passing, and the bells
For ever with their silver lay
Murmur a melody that tells
Of April and of Easter day.
High in sweet air the light vane sets,
The weathercocks all southward twirl;
A sou will buy her violets
And make Nini a happy girl.

The winter to the poor was sore,
Counting the weary winter days,
Watching his little firewood store,
The bitter snowflakes fall always;
And now his last log dimly gleamed,
Lighting the room with feeble glare,
Half cinder and half smoke it seemed
That the wind wafted into air.

Pilgrims from ocean and far isles
See where the east is reddening,
The flocks that fly a thousand miles
From sunsetting to sunsetting;
Look up, look out, behold the swallows,
The throats that twitter, the wings that beat;
And on their song the summer follows,
And in the summer life is sweet.

. . . .

With the green tender buds that know
The shoot and sap of lusty spring
My neighbor of a year ago
Her casement, see, is opening;
Through all the bitter months that were,
Forth from her nest she dared not flee,
She was a study for Boucher,
She now may sit to Gavarni.

(*Andrew Lang*)

OLD LOVES

Louise, have you forgotten yet
The corner of the flowery land,
The ancient garden where we met,
My hand that trembled in your hand?
Our lips found words scarce sweet enough,
As low beneath the willow trees
We sat; have you forgotten, love?
Do you remember, love Louise?

Marie, have you forgotten yet
The loving barter that we made?
The rings we changed, the suns that set,
The woods fulfilled with sun and shade?
The fountains that were musical
By many an ancient trysting tree—
Marie, have you forgotten all?
Do you remember, love Marie?

Christine, do you remember yet
Your room with scents and roses gay?
My garret—near the sky 'twas set—
The April hours, the nights of May?
The clear calm nights—the stars above
That whispered they were fairest seen
Through no cloud-veil? Remember, love.
Do you remember, love Christine?

Louise is dead, and, well-a-day.
Marie a sadder path has ta'en;
And pale Christine has passed away
In southern suns to bloom again.
Alas, for one and all of us—
Marie, Louise, Christine forget;
Our bower of love is ruinous,
And I alone remember yet.

(*Andrew Lang*)

Frédéric Mistral

1830–1914

THE MARES OF THE CAMARGUE

(From the Mirèio)

A HUNDRED mares, all white! their manes
Like mace-reed of the marshy plains
Thick-tufted, wavy, free o' the shears:
And when the fiery squadron rears
Bursting at speed, each mane appears
Even as the white scarf of a fay
Floating upon their necks along the heavens away.

O race of humankind, take shame!
For never yet a hand could tame,
Nor bitter spur that rips the flanks subdue
The mares of the Camargue. I have known,
By treason snared, some captives shown;
Expatriate from their native Rhone,
Led off, their saline pastures far from view;

And on a day, with prompt rebound,
They have flung their riders to the ground,
And at a single gallop, scouring free,
Wide nostril'd to the wind, twice ten
Of long marsh-leagues devour'd, and then,
Back to the Vacarés again,
After ten years of slavery just to breathe salt sea.

For of this savage race unbent
The ocean is the element.
Of old escaped from Neptune's ear, full sure
Still with the white foam fleck'd are they,
And when the sea puffs black from gray,
And ships part cables, loudly neigh
The stallions of Camargue, all joyful in the roar;

And keen as a whip they lash and crack
Their tails that drag the dust, and back
Scratch up the earth, and feel, entering their flesh, where he,
The God, drives deep his trident teeth,
Who in one horror, above, beneath,
Bids storm and watery deluge seethe,
And shatters to their depths the abysses of the sea.

(George Meredith)

THE COCOONING

(From the Mirèio)

When the crop is fair in the olive-yard,
And the earthen jars are ready
For the golden oil from the barrels poured,
And the big cart rocks unsteady
With its tower of gathered sheaves, and strains
And groans on its way through fields and lanes:

When brawny and bare as an old athlete
Comes Bacchus the dance a-leading,
And the laborers all, with juice-dyed feet,
The vintage of Crau are treading,
And the good wine pours from the brimful presses,
And the ruby foam in the vats increases;

When under the leaves of the Spanish broom
The clear silk-worms are holden,
An artist each, in a tiny loom,
Weaving a web of golden,
Fine, frail cells out of sunlight spun,
Where they creep and sleep by the million,—

Glad is Provence on a day like that,
'Tis the time of jest and laughter:
The Ferigoulet and the Baume Muscat
They quaff, and they sing thereafter.
And lads and lasses, their toils between,
Dance to the tinkling tambourine.

(Harriet Waters Preston)

THE LEAF-PICKING

Sing, magnarello, merrily,
As the green leaves you gather!
In their third sleep the silk-worms lie,
And lovely is the weather.
Like brown bees that in open glades
From rosemary gather honey,
The mulberry-trees swarm full of maids,
Glad as the air is sunny!

Sing, magnarello, merrily,
The green leaves are piling!
Two comely children sit on high,
Amid the foliage, smiling.
Sing, magnarello, loud and oft:
Your merry labor hasten.
The guileless pair who laugh aloft
Are learning love's first lesson.

Sing, magnarello, merrily,
As the green leaves you gather!
The sun of May is riding higher,
And ardent is the weather.

Sing, magnarello, heap your leaves,
While sunny is the weather!
He comes to aid her when she grieves:
The two are now together.

(*Harriet Waters Preston*)

Sully Prudhomme

1839–1907

THE STRUGGLE

Nightly tormented by returning doubt,
I dare the sphinx with faith and unbelief;
And through lone hours when no sleep brings relief
The monster rises all my hopes to flout.

In a still agony, the light blown out,
I wrestle with the unknown; nor long nor brief
The night appears, my narrow couch of grief
Grown like the grave with Death walled round about.

Sometimes my mother, coming with her lamp,
Seeing my brow as with a death-sweat damp,
Asks, "Ah, what ails thee, Child? Hast thou no rest?"

And then I answer, touched by her look of yearning,
Holding my beating heart and forehead burning,
"Mother, I strove with God, and was hard prest."

(Arthur O'Shaughnessy)

Catulle Mendès

1841–1909

I GO BY ROAD

I go by road, I go by street—
Lira, la, la!
O white high roads, ye know my feet!
A loaf I carry and, all told,
Three broad bits of lucky gold—
Lira, la, la!
And oh, within my flowering heart,
(Sing, dear nightingale!) is my Sweet.

A poor man met me and begged for bread—
Lira, la, la!
"Brother, take all the loaf," I said,
I shall but go with lighter cheer—
Lira, la, la!
And oh, within my flowering heart
(Sing, sweet nightingale!) is my Dear.

A thief I met on the lonely way—
Lira, la, la!
He took my gold; I cried to him, "Stay!

And take my pocket and make an end."
  Lira, la, la!
And oh, within my flowering heart
(Sing, soft nightingale!) is my Friend.

Now on the plain I have met with death—
  Lira, la, la!
My bread is gone, my gold, my breath.
But oh, this heart is not afraid—
  Lira, la, la!
For oh, within this lonely heart
(Sing, sad nightingale!) is my Maid.

(*Alice Meynell*)

Stéphane Mallarmé

1842–1898

L'APRÈS-MIDI D'UN FAUNE

I WOULD immortalize these nymphs: so bright
Their sunlit coloring, so airy light,
It floats like drowsy down. Loved I a dream?
My doubts, born of oblivious darkness, seem
A subtle tracery of branches grown
The tree's true self—proving that I have known,
Thinking it love, the blushing of a rose.
But think. These nymphs, their loveliness . . . suppose
They bodied forth your senses' fabulous thirst?
Illusion! which the blue eyes of the first,
As cold and chaste as is the weeping spring,
Beget: the other, sighing, passioning,
Is she the wind, warm in your fleece at noon?
No; through this quiet, when a weary swoon
Crushes and chokes the latest faint essay
Of morning, cool against the encroaching day,
There is no murmuring water, save the gush
Of my clear fluted notes; and in the hush
Blows never a wind, save that which through my reed

Puffs out before the rain of notes can speed
Upon the air, with that calm breath of art
That mounts the unwrinkled zenith visibly,
Where inspiration seeks its native sky.
You fringes of a calm Sicilian lake,
The sun's own mirror which I love to take,
Silent beneath your starry flowers, tell
How here I cut the hollow rushes, well
Tamed by my skill, when on the glaucous gold
Of distant lawns about their fountain cold
A living whiteness stirs like a lazy wave;
And at the first slow notes my panpipes gave
These flocking swans, these naiads, rather, fly
Or dive. Noon burns inert and tawny dry,
Nor marks how clean that Hymen slipped away
From me who seek in song the real A.
Wake, then, to the first ardor and the sight,
O lonely faun, of the old fierce white light,
With, lilies, one of you for innocence.
Other than their lips' delicate pretense,
The light caress that quiets treacherous lovers,
My breast, I know not how to tell, discovers
The bitten print of some immortal's kiss.

But hush! a mystery so great as this
I dare not tell, save to my double reed,
Which, sharer of my every joy and need,
Dreams down its cadenced monologues that we
Falsely confuse the beauties that we see
With the bright palpable shapes our song creates:
My flute, as loud as passion modulates,
Purges the common dream of flank and breast
Seen through closed eyes and inwardly caressed,
Of every empty and monotonous line.

Bloom then, O Syrinx, in thy flight malign,
A reed once more beside our trysting-lake.
Proud of my music, let me often make
A song of goddesses and see their rape

Profanely done on many a painted shape.
So when the grape's transparent juice I drain,
I quell regret for pleasures past and feign
A new real grape. For holding towards the sky
The empty skin, I blow it tight and lie
Dream-drunk till evening, eyeing it.
Tell o'er
Remembered joys and plump the grape once more.
Between the reeds I saw their bodies gleam
Who cool no mortal fever in the stream
Crying to the woods the rage of their desires
And their bright hair went down in jeweled fire
Where crystal broke and dazzled shudderingly.
I check my swift pursuit: for see where lie,
Bruised, being twins in love, by languor sweet,
Two sleeping girls, clasped at my very feet.
I seize and run with them, nor part the pair,
Breaking this covert of frail petals, where
Roses drink scent of the sun and our light play
'Mid tumbled flowers shall match the death of day.
I love that virginal fury—ah, the wild
Thrill when a maiden body shrinks, defiled,
Shuddering like arctic light, from lips that sear
Its nakedness . . . the flesh in secret fear!
Contagiously through my linked pair it flies
Where innocence in either, struggling, dies,
Wet with fond tears or some less piteous dew.
Gay in the conquest of these fears, I grew
So rash that I must needs the sheaf divide
Of ruffled kisses heaven itself had tied.
For as I leaned to stifle in the hair
Of one my passionate laughter (taking care
With a stretched finger, that her innocence
Might stain with her companion's kindling sense
To touch the younger little one, who lay
Child-like unblushing) my ungrateful prey
Slips from me, freed by passion's sudden death
Nor heeds the frenzy of my sobbing breath.
Let it pass! others of their hair shall twist

A rope to drag me to those joys I missed.
See how the ripe pomegranates bursting red
To quench the thirst of the mumbling bees have bled;
So too our blood, kindled by some chance fire,
Flows for the swarming legions of desire.
At evening, when the woodland green turns gold
And ashen gray, 'mid the quenched leaves, behold!
Red Etna glows, by Venus visited,
Walking the lava with her snowy tread
Whene'er the flames in thunderous slumber die.
I hold the goddess!
Ah, sure penalty!

But the unthinking soul and body swoon
At last beneath the heavy hush of noon.
Forgetful let me lie where summer's drouth
Sifts fine the sand and then with gaping mouth
Dream planet-struck by the grape's round wine-red star.

Nymphs, I shall see the shade that now you are.

(*Aldous Huxley*)

SIGH

My soul, calm sister, towards thy brow, whereon scarce grieves
An autumn strewn already with its russet leaves,
And towards the wandering sky of thine angelic eyes,
Mounts, as in melancholy gardens may arise
Some faithful fountain sighing whitely towards the blue!
Towards the blue, pale and pure, that sad October knew,
When, in those depths, it mirrored languors infinite,
And agonizing leaves upon the waters white,
Windily drifting, traced a furrow cold and dun,
Where, in one long last ray, lingered the yellow sun.

(*Arthur Symons*)

SEA-WIND

THE flesh is sad, alas! and all the books are read.
Flight, only flight! I feel that birds are wild to tread
The floor of unknown foam, and to attain the skies!
Nought, neither ancient gardens mirrored in the eyes,
Shall hold this heart that bathes in waters its delight,
O nights! nor yet my waking lamp, whose lonely light
Shadows the vacant paper, whiteness profits best,
Nor the young wife who rocks her baby on her breast.
I will depart! O steamer, swaying rope and spar,
Lift anchor for exotic lands that lie afar!
A weariness, outworn by cruel hopes, still clings
To the last farewell handkerchief's last beckonings!
And are not these, the masts inviting storms, not these
That an awakening wind bends over wrecking seas,
Lost, not a sail, a sail, a flowering isle, ere long?
But, O my heart, hear thou, hear thou, the sailors' song!

(*Arthur Symons*)

ANGUISH

TO-NIGHT I do not come to conquer thee,
O Beast that dost the sins of the whole world bear,
Nor with my kisses' weary misery
Wake a sad tempest in thy wanton hair;
It is that heavy and that dreamless sleep
I ask of the close curtains of thy bed,
Which, after all thy treacheries, folds thee deep,
Who knowest oblivion better than the dead.
For Vice, that gnaws with keener tooth than time
Brands me as thee, of barren conquest proud;
But while thou guardest in thy breast of stone
A heart that fears no fang of any crime,
I wander palely, haunted by my shroud,
Fearing to die if I but sleep alone.

(*Arthur Symons*)

José-Maria de Heredia

1842–1905

THE FLUTE: A PASTORAL

Evening! A flight of pigeons in clear sky!
What wants there to allay love's fever now,
  Goatherd! but that thy pipe should overflow,
While through the reeds the river murmurs by?
Here in the plane-tree's shadow where we lie
  Deep grows the grass and cool. Sit and allow
  The wandering goat to scale yon rocky brow
And graze at will, deaf to the weanling's cry.

My flute—a simple thing, seven oaten reeds
Glued with a little wax—sings, plains, or pleads
  In accents deep or shrill as I require;
Come! thou shalt learn Silenus' sacred art,
  And through this channel breath'd will fierce desire
Rise, wing'd with music, from the o'er-labored heart.

(*H. J. C. Grierson*)

THE LABORER

Here is the yoke, with arrow and share near by,
The goad, the scythe that in a day hath mown
Swathes that would make the wide barn-flooring groan,
And here the fork the brown haymakers ply.
Too heavy tools! He hath vowed them utterly
  Unto immortal Rhea, who alone
  Brings seed to blossom from hard tilth. His own
Labor is done and he not loth to die.

Fourscore long years, sun-blistered, poor, he drave
  The coulter, without mirth, through stubborn soil,
Who now goes grimly onward to the grave.
    Yet he bewails the labor too long borne,
  And dreads to find more fallow for his toil
    In sunless fields of Erebus forlorn.

(*Wilfrid Thorley*)

Paul Verlaine

1844–1896

He was the purest lyrical singer that France had ever known. He strikes a discreet and troubling note that leaves its vibrations in the heart and in the nerves forever.—Ludwig Lewisohn.

IL PLEUT DOUCEMENT SUR LA VILLE

Tears fall within mine heart,
As rain upon the town:
Whence does this languor start,
Possessing all mine heart?

O sweet fall of the rain
Upon the earth and roof,
Unto an heart in pain,
O music of the rain.

Tears that have no reason
Fall in my sorry heart:
What, there was no treason?
This grief hath no reason.

Nay, the more desolate,
Because, I know not why,
(Neither for love nor hate)
Mine heart is desolate.

(*Ernest Dowson*)

SPLEEN

Around were all the roses red,
The ivy all around was black.

Dear, so thou only move thine head,
Shall all mine old despairs awake.

Too blue, too tender was the sky,
The air too soft, too green the sea.

Always I fear, I know not why,
Some lamentable flight from thee.

I am so tired of holly-sprays
And weary of the bright box-tree,

Of all the endless country ways;
Of everything, alas, save thee.

(*Ernest Dowson*)

THE SKY IS UP ABOVE THE ROOF

The sky is up above the roof
So blue, so soft.
A tree there, up above the roof,
Swayeth aloft.

A bell within that sky we see,
Chimes low and faint;
A bird upon that tree we see,
Maketh complaint.

Dear God, is not the life up there
Simple and sweet?
How peacefully are borne up there
Sounds of the street.

What hast thou done, who comest here,
To weep alway?
Where hast thou laid, who comest here,
Thy youth away?

(*Ernest Dowson*)

A CLYMENE

Mystical strains unheard,
A song without a word,
Dearest, because thine eyes,
Pale as the skies,

Because thy voice, remote
As the far clouds that float
Veiling for me the whole
Heaven of the soul,

Because the stately scent
Of thy swan's whiteness, blent
With the white lily's bloom
Of thy perfume,

Ah, because thy dear love,
The music breathed above
By angels halo-crowned,
Odor and sound,

Hath, in my subtle heart,
With some mysterious art
Transposed thy harmony,
So let it be.

(*Arthur Symons*)

FANTOCHES

SCARAMOUCHE waves a threatening hand
To Pulcinella, and they stand,
Two shadows, black against the moon.

The old doctor of Bologna pries
For simples with impassive eyes,
And mutters o'er a magic rune.

The while his daughter, scarce half-dressed,
Glides slyly 'neath the trees, in quest
Of her bold pirate lover's sail;

Her pirate from the Spanish main,
Whose passion thrills her in the pain
Of the loud languorous nightingale.

(*Arthur Symons*)

PANTOMIME

Pierrot, no sentimental swain,
Washes a pâté down again
With furtive flagons, white and red.

Cassandre, to chasten his content,
Greets with a tear of sentiment
His nephew disinherited.

That blackguard of a Harlequin
Pirouettes, and plots to win
His Colombine that flits and flies.

Colombine dreams, and starts to find
A sad heart sighing in the wind,
And in her heart a voice that sighs.

(*Arthur Symons*)

CYTHERE

(*Fêtes Galantes*)

By favorable breezes fanned,
A trellised arbor is at hand
To shield us from the summer airs;

The scent of roses, fainting sweet,
Afloat upon the summer heat,
Blends with the perfume that she wears.

True to the promise her eyes gave,
She ventures all, and her mouth rains
A dainty fever through my veins;

And Love, fulfilling all things, save
Hunger, we 'scape, with sweets and ices,
The folly of Love's sacrifices.

(*Arthur Symons*)

DANS L'ALLEE
(*Fêtes Galantes*)

As in the age of shepherd king and queen,
Painted and frail amid her nodding bows,
Under the somber branches, and between
The green and mossy garden-ways she goes,
With little mincing airs one keeps to pet
A darling and provoking perroquet.
Her long-trained robe is blue, the fan she holds
With fluent fingers girt with heavy rings,
So vaguely hints of vague erotic things
That her eye smiles, musing among its folds.
—Blonde too, a tiny nose, a rosy mouth,
Artful as that sly patch that makes more sly,
In her divine unconscious pride of youth,
The slightly simpering sparkle of the eye.

(*Arthur Symons*)

MANDOLINE
(*Fêtes Galantes*)

THE singers of serenades
Whisper their faded vows
Unto fair listening maids
Under the singing boughs.

Tircis, Aminte, are there,
Clitandre has waited long,
And Damis for many a fair
Tyrant makes many a song.

Their short vests, silken and bright,
Their long pale silken trains,
Their elegance of delight,
Twine soft blue silken chains.

And the mandolines and they,
Faintlier breathing, swoon
Into the rose and gray
Ecstasy of the moon.

(*Arthur Symons*)

CLAIR DE LUNE

(*Fêtes Galantes*)

Your soul is a sealed garden, and there go
With masque and bergamasque fair companies
Playing on lutes and dancing and as though
Sad under their fantastic fripperies.

Though they in minor keys go caroling
Of love the conqueror and of live boon
They seem to doubt the happiness they sing
And the song melts into the light of the moon,

The sad light of the moon, so lovely fair
That all the birds dream in the leafy shade
And the slim fountains sob into the air
Among the marble statues in the glade.

(*Arthur Symons*)

A LA PROMENADE

(*Fêtes Galantes*)

The sky so pale, and the trees, such frail things,
Seem as if smiling on our bright array
That flits so light and gray upon the way
With indolent airs and fluttering as of wings.

The fountain wrinkles under a faint wind,
And all the sifted sunlight falling through
The lime-trees of the shadowy avenue
Comes to us blue and shadowy-pale and thinned

Faultlessly fickle, and yet fond enough,
With fond hearts not too tender to be free,
We wander whispering deliciously,
And every lover leads a lady-love,

Whose imperceptible and roguish hand
Darts now and then a dainty tap, the lip
Revenges on an extreme finger-tip,
The tip of the left little finger, and,

The deed being so excessive and uncouth,
A duly freezing look deals punishment,
That in the instant of the act is blent
With a shy pity pouting in the mouth.

(*Arthur Symons*)

CORTEGE

(*Fêtes Galantes*)

A SILVER-VESTED monkey trips
And pirouettes before the face
Of one who twists a kerchief's lace
Between her well-gloved finger-tips.

A little negro, a red elf,
Carries her drooping train, and holds
At arm's-length all the heavy folds,
Watching each fold displace itself.

The monkey never lets his eyes
Wander from the fair woman's breast,
White wonder that to be possessed
Would call a god out of the skies.

Sometimes the little negro seems
To lift his sumptuous burden up
Higher than need be, in the hope
Of seeing what all night he dreams.

She goes by corridor and stair,
Still to the insolent appeals
Of her familiar animals
Indifferent or unaware.

(*Arthur Symons*)

EN BATEAU

(*Fêtes Galantes*)

THE shepherd's star with trembling glint
Drops in black water; at the hint
The pilot fumbles for his flint.

Now is the time, or never, sirs.
No hand that wanders wisely errs:
I touch a hand, and is it hers?

The Knightly Atys strikes the strings,
And to the faithless Chloris flings
A look that speaks of many things.

The Abbé has absolved again
Eglé, the viscount all in vain
Has given his hasty heart the rein.

Meanwhile the moon is up and streams
Upon the skiff that flies and seems
To float upon a tide of dreams.

(Arthur Symons)

CHANSONS D'AUTOMNE

(From Poèmes Saturniens)

When a sighing begins
In the violins
Of the autumn-song,

My heart is drowned
In the slow sound
Languorous and long.

Pale as with pain,
Breath fails me when
The hour tolls deep.
My thoughts recover
The days that are over,
And I weep.

And I go
Where the winds know,
Broken and brief,
To and fro,
As the winds blow
A dead leaf.

(Arthur Symons)

FEMME ET CHATTE

(From Poèmes Saturniens)

THEY were at play, she and her cat,
And it was marvelous to mark
The white paw and the white hand pat
Each other in the deepening dark.

The stealthy little lady hid
Under her mittens' silken sheath
Her deadly agate nails that thrid
The silk-like dagger-points of death.

The cat purred primly and drew in
Her claws that were of steel filed thin:
The devil was in it all the same.
The devil was in it all the same.

And in the boudoir, while a shout
Of laughter in the air rang out,
Four sparks of phosphor shone like flame.

(Arthur Symons)

ART POETIQUE

(From Jadis et Naguère)

MUSIC first and foremost of all!
Choose your measure of odd not even,
Let it melt in the air of heaven,
Pose not, poise not, but rise and fall.

Choose your words, but think not whether
Each to other of old belong:
What so dear as the dim gray song
Where clear and vague are joined together?

'Tis veils of beauty for beautiful eyes,
'Tis the trembling light of the naked noon,
'Tis a medley of blue and gold, the moon
And stars in the cool of autumn skies.

Let every shape of its shade be born;
Color, away! come to me, shade!
Only of shade can the marriage be made
Of dream with dream and of flute with horn.

Shun the Point, lest death with it come,
Unholy laughter and cruel wit
(For the eyes of the angels weep at it)
And all the garbage of scullery-scum.

Take Eloquence, and wring the neck of him!
You had better, by force, from time to time,
Put a little sense in the head of Rhyme:
If you watch him not, you will be at the beck of him

O, who shall tell us the wrongs of Rhyme?
What witless savage or what deaf boy
Has made for us this two-penny toy
Whose bells ring hollow and out of time?

Music always and music still!
Let your verse be the wandering thing
That flutters in the light from a soul on the wing
Towards other skies at a new whim's will.

Let your verse be the luck of the lure
Afloat on the winds that at morning hint
Of the odors of thyme and the savor of mint . . .
And all the rest is literature.

(*Arthur Symons*)

FROM SAGESSE

I

SLUMBER dark and deep
Falls across my life;
I will put to sleep
Hope, desire and strife.

All things pass away,
Good and evil seem
To my soul to-day
Nothing but a dream;

I a cradle laid
In a hollow cave,
By a great hand swayed:
Silence, like the grave.

II

Fairer is the sea
Than the minster high,
Faithful nurse is she,
And last lullaby,
And the Virgin prays
Over the sea's ways.

Gifts or grief and guerdons
From her bounty come,
And I hear her pardons
Chide her angers home;
Nothing in her is
Unforgivingness.

She is piteous,
She the perilous!
Friendly things to us
The wave sings to us:
You whose hope is past,
Here is peace at last.

And beneath the skies,
Brighter-hued than they,
She has azure dyes,
Rose and green and gray.
Better is the sea
Than all fair things or we.

(*Arthur Symons*)

Tristan Corbière

1845–1875

EPITAPH

For Himself

Of many things adulterate:
No penny, yet the friend of fate;
Power enough but naught of will,
Thus free and yet a prisoner still.
Full hearted, yet without full spirit,
A breast for friends—no comrade near it;
Imagination—no ideas.
Love, without the lip that cheers.
Idleness, but no repose.
In him virtue wore vice's clothes.
Blasé although insatiate,
Dead, though not cured of living yet.
Spoiler of life, inopportune;
Parched body, head a tipsy moon.
Hoping, the future he'd deny;
Deceased while waiting life to try
He lived while waiting but to die.

(*Joseph T. Shipley*)

Arthur Rimbaud

1854–1891

SENSATION

On summer evenings blue, pricked by the wheat
On rustic paths the thin grass I shall tread,
And feel its freshness underneath my feet,
And, dreaming, let the wind bathe my bare head.

I shall not speak, nor think, but, walking slow
Through Nature, I shall rove with Love my guide,
As gypsies wander, where, they do not know,
Happy as one walks by a woman's side.

(*Jethro Bithell*)

THE SLEEPER OF THE VALLEY

There's a green hollow where a river sings
Silvering the torn grass in its glittering flight,
And where the sun from the proud mountain flings
Fire—and the little valley brims with light.

A soldier young, with open mouth, bare head,
Sleeps with his neck in dewy water cress,
Under the sky and on the grass his bed,
Pale in the deep green and the light's excess.

He sleeps amid the iris and his smile
Is like a sick child's slumbering for a while.
Nature, in thy warm lap his chilled limbs hide!

The perfume does not thrill him from his rest.
He sleeps in sunshine, hand upon his breast,
Tranquil—with two red holes in his right side.

(*Ludwig Lewisohn*)

HUNGER

If I have any taste, it is hardly
For more than earth and stones.
I always breakfast on air,
Rock, cinders, and iron.

Round, my hungers. Crop, hungers,
  The field of sounds.
Suck the sweet venom
  Of convolvulus.

Eat the stones some one breaks,
The old stones of churches;
The shingle of ancient floods,
Bread sown in gray valleys.

. . . .

The wolf cries under the leaves
Spitting out the gay feathers
Of his meal of poultry:
Like him I consume myself.

Green stuffs and fruits
Await but the gathering,
But the hedge spider
Eats only violets.

May I sleep! May I boil
On the altars of Solomon.
The broth flows over the rust
And mingles with Kedron.

(Edgell Rickword)

SONG OF THE HIGHEST TOWER

May they come, may they come,
The days which enchant us.

I have been so long resigned
That I forget it all.
Fears and sufferings
To the skies are gone,
And the unclean thirst
Darkens my veins.

May they come, may they come,
The days which enchant us.

Like the meadows
Left to ruin,
Spreading and overgrown
With flowers and weeds,
In the angry humming
Of filthy flies.

May they come, may they come
The days which enchant us.

(Edgell Rickword)

LES CHERCHEUSES DE POUX

When, forehead full of torments hot and red,
The child invokes white clouds of hazy dreams,
Two sisters tall and sweet draw near his bed,
Whose fingers frail nails tip with silv'ry gleams.

The child before a window open wide,
Where blue air bathes a maze of flowers, they sit;
And in his heavy hair dew falls, while glide
Their fingers terrible with charm through it.

So hears he sing their breath a dread hush curbs;
How rich with rose and leafy sweets it is!
It sometimes a salival lisp disturbs
On the lip drawn back, or deep desires to kiss.

Through perfumed silences their lashes black
Beat slow; he hears in colorless dim drowse,
Trapped by their soft electric fingers, crack
'Twixt tyrant nails the death of each small louse.

Then wells in him the wine of idleness,
Delirious power, th' harmonica's soft sigh:
The child still feels to their long drawn caress
Ceaselessly heave and swoon a wish to cry.

(*T. Sturge Moore*)

Emile Verhaeren

1855–1916

THE POOR

With hearts of poor men it is so:
That they are full of tears that flow.
That they are pale as head-stones white
In the moon light.

And so with poor men's backs it is—
More bent with heavy miseries
Than sagging roofs of brown huts be
Beside the sea.

And it is so with poor men's hands,
Like leaves along autumnal lands,
Leaves that lie sere and dead and late
Beside the gate.

And it is so with poor men's eyes,
Humble and in all sorrow wise,
And like the cattle's, sad and dumb,
When the storms come.

Oh, it is so with the poor folk
That under misery's iron yoke
Have gestures weary and resigned
On earth's far plains of sun and wind.

(Ludwig Lewisohn)

Albert Samain

1858–1900

PANNYRA OF THE GOLDEN HEEL

The revel pauses and the room is still:
The silver flute invites her with a thrill,
And, buried in her great veils fold and fold,
Rises to dance Pannyra, Heel of Gold.
Her light steps cross; her subtle arm impels
The clinging drapery; it shrinks and swells,
Hollows and floats, and bursts into a whirl:
She is a flower, a moth, a flaming girl.
All lips are silent; eyes are all trance:
She slowly wakes the madness of the dance,
Windy and wild the golden torches burn;
She turns, and swifter yet she tries to turn,
Then stops: a sudden marble stiff she stands.
The veil that round her coiled its spiral bands,
Checked in its course, brings all its folds to rest,
And clinging to bright limb and pointed breast
Shows, as beneath silk waters woven fine,
Pannyra naked in a flash divine!

(James Elroy Flecker)

FROM SUMMER HOURS

Flower petals fall.
  Dull flares the torch's mane;
  Mine eyes to weep were fain,
Mine eyes possess thee all.

Yielded beyond recall,
  Heart, naught shall heal thee again,
  O clay molded into pain . . .
Flower petals fall.

The roses all are dying . . .
I am saying nothing, thou hearest
Under thy motionless hair.

Love is heavy. My soul is sighing . . .
What wing brushes both of us, dearest,
In the sick and soundless air?

(*Jethro Bithell*)

Remy de Gourmont

1858–1915

HAIR

There is great mystery, Simone,
In the forest of your hair.

It smells of hay, and of the stone
Cattle have been lying on;
Of timber, and of new-baked bread
Brought to be one's breakfast fare;
And of the flowers that have grown
Along a wall abandonèd;
Of leather and of winnowed grain;
Of briers and ivy washed by rain;
You smell of rushes and of ferns
Reaped when day to evening turns;

You smell of withering grasses red
Whose seed is under hedges shed;
You smell of nettles and of broom;
Of milk, and fields in clover-bloom;
You smell of nuts, and fruits that one
Gathers in the ripe season;
And of the willow and the lime
Covered in their flowering time;
You smell of honey, of desire,
You smell of air the noon makes shiver;
You smell of earth and of the river;
You smell of love, you smell of fire.

There is great mystery, Simone,
In the forest of your hair.

(*Jethro Bithell*)

Jules Laforgue

1860–1887

FOR THE BOOK OF LOVE

I MAY be dead to-morrow, uncaressed.
 My lips have never touched a woman's, none
 Has given me in a look her soul, not one
Has ever held me swooning at her breast.

I have but suffered, for all nature, trees
 Whipped by the winds, wan flowers, the ashen sky,
 Suffered with all my nerves, minutely, I
Have suffered for my soul's impurities.

And I have spat on love, and, mad with pride,
 Slaughtered my flesh, and life's revenge I brave,
 And, while the whole world else was Instinct's slave,
With bitter laughter Instinct I defied.

In drawing-rooms, the theater, the church,
 Before cold men, the greatest, most refined,
 And women with eyes jealous, proud, or kind,
Whose tender souls no lust would seem to smirch,

I thought: This is the end for which they work.
  Beasts coupling with the groaning beasts they capture.
  And all this dirt for just three minutes' rapture!
Men, be correct! And women, purr and smirk!

(Jethro Bithell)

Maurice Maeterlinck

1862–

SONG

Three little maidens they have slain,
To find out what their hearts contain.

The first of them was brimmed with bliss,
  And everywhere her blood was shed,
For full three years three serpents hiss.

The second full of kindness sweet,
  And everywhere her blood was shed,
Three lambs three years have grass to eat.

The third was full of pain and rue,
  And everywhere her blood was shed,
Three seraphim watch three years through.

(Jethro Bithell)

THE LAST WORDS

And if he ever should come back,
  What am I to say?
—Tell him that I watch'd for him
  All my life away.

And if he should ask me more,
  Nor know my face again?
—Speak gently as a sister speaks,
  He may be in pain.

If he ask me where you are,
  How shall I reply?

—Then give him my golden ring,
Very silently.

And if he should want to know
Why the hall stands bare?
—Then show him the burnt-out lamp
And the door ajar.

And if he should ask me then
How you fell asleep?
—Tell him that I smiled and died.
Do not let him weep.

(Frederick York Powell)

Henri de Regnier

1864–

NIGHT

An odorous shade lingers the fair day's ghost,
And the frail moon now by no wind is tost,
And shadow-laden scents of tree and grass
Build up again a world our eyes have lost.

Now all the wood is but a murmured light
Where leaf on leaf falls softly from the height;
The hidden freshness of the river seems
A breath that mingles with the breath of night.

And time and shade and silence seem to say,
Close now your eyes nor fear to die with day;
For if the daylight win to earth again,
Will not its beauty also find a way?

And flower and stream and forest, will they not
Bring back to-morrow, as to-day they brought,
This shadow-hidden scent—this odorous shade?
Yea, and with more abiding memories fraught.

(Seumas O'Sullivan)

JE NE VEUX DE PERSONNE AUPRES DE MA TRISTESSE

Say, sweet, my grief and I, we may not brook
Even your light footfall, even your shy look,
Even your light hand that touches carelessly
The faded ribbon in the closed-up book.

Let be; my door is closed for this one day,
Nor may morn's freshness through my window stray;
My heart is a guest-chamber, and awaits
Sorrow, a sweet shy guest from far away.

Shyly it comes from its far distant home,
O keep a silence lest its voice be dumb;
For every man that lives and laughs and loves
Must hear that whisper when his hour has come.

(*Seumas O'Sullivan*)

André Spire

1868–

LONELY

They pity me.
"Look at him, see.
Taking his walking stick, and going out. So lonely.
He flees us. Look at his strange eyes.
Not even a book does he take with him. Only
His stick. What does he mean to do?
Is he intent on evil? In revolt? Or fever-sick?"

Alone, O beautiful white road,
Between your ditches full of grass and flowers,
Over your pebbles telling tales of old,
Alone, O forest, with the blue bark of your pines;
And with your wind that parleys with your trees;
And with your ants processioning that drag
Bodies of little beetles on their backs.

Alone, with you, you sun-drenched fields,
All full of cries, and noises, and heads raised alert,
Alone with you, flies, merlins, buzzards, kites,
Rocks, brambles, sources, crevices,
Fogs, clouds, mists, cones, peaks, precipices,
Heat, odor, order, chaos, and disorder,
Among the dialogues your rival mouths
Exchange for ever!
Alone with my stick, alone with my fatigue,
My dust, my throbbing temples, and my dizziness,
And the proud sweat glued to my skin.

(*Jethro Bithell*)

SPRING

Now hand in hand, you little maidens, walk.
Pass in the shadow of the crumbling wall.
Arch your proud bellies under rosy aprons.
And let your eyes so deeply lucid tell
Your joy at feeling flowing into your heart
Another loving heart that blends with yours;
You children faint with being hand in hand.
Walk hand in hand, you languorous maidens, walk.
The boys are turning round, and drinking in
Your sensual petticoats that beat your heels.
And, while you swing your interlacing hands,
Tell, with your warm mouths yearning each to each,
The first books you have read, and your first kisses.
Walk hand in hand, you maidens, friend with friend.

Walk hand in hand, you lovers loving silence.
Walk to the sun that veils itself with willows.
Trail your uneasy limbs by languorous banks,
The stream is full of dusk, your souls are heavy.
You silent lovers, wander hand in hand.

(*Jethro Bithell*)

NUDITIES

The hair is a nudity.—The Talmud.

You said to me: But I will be your comrade;
And visit you, but never chafe your blood;

And we will pass long evenings in your room;
Thinking of our brethren they are murdering;
And through the cruel universe we two
Will seek some country which shall give them rest.
But I shall never see your eye-balls burning,
Nor on your temples purple veins distend,—
I am your equal, I am not your prey.
For see! my clothes are chaste, and almost poor,
You see not even the bottom of my neck.

But I gave answer: Woman, thou art naked.
Fresh as a cup the hair is on thy neck;
Thy chignon, falling down, shakes like a breast;
Thy headbands are as lustful as a herd of goats. . .
Shear thy hair.

Woman, thou art naked.
Thy naked hands rest on our open book;
Thy hands, the subtle ending of thy body,
Thy hands without a ring will touch mine by-and-by. . . .
Mutilate thy hands.

Woman, thou art naked.
Thy singing voice mounts from thy breast;
Thy voice, thy breath, the very warmth of thy flesh,
Spreads itself on my body and penetrates my flesh. . . .
Woman, tear out thy voice.

(*Jethro Bithell*)

Francis Jammes

1868-

AMSTERDAM

The pointed houses lean so you would swear
That they were falling. Tangled vessel masts
Like leafless branches lean against the sky
Amid a mass of green, and red, and rust,
Red herrings, sheepskins, coal along the quays.

Robinson Crusoe passed through Amsterdam,
(At least I think he did), when he returned
From the green isle shaded with cocoa-trees.

What were the feelings of his heart before
These heavy knockers and these mighty doors! . .

Did he look through the window-panes and watch
The clerks who write in ledgers all day long?
Did tears come in his eyes when he remembered
His parrot, and the heavy parasol
Which shaded him in the sad and clement isle?

"Glory to thee, good Lord," he would exclaim,
Looking at chests with tulip-painted lids.
But, saddened by the joy of the return,
He must have mourned his kid left in the vines
Alone, and haply on the island dead.

I have imagined this before the shops
Which make you think of Jews who handle scales,
With bony fingers knotted with green rings.
See! Amsterdam under a shroud of snow
Sleeps in a scent of fog and bitter coal.

Last night the white globes of the lighted inns,
Whence issue heavy women's whistled calls,
Were hanging down like fruits resembling gourds.
Posters blue, red, and green shone on their walls.
The bitter pricking of their sugared beer
Rasped on my tongue and gave my nose the itch.

And in the Jewry where detritus lies,
You smell the raw, cold reek of fresh-caught fish.
The slippery flags are strown with orange-peel.
Some swollen face would open staring eyes,
A wrangling arm moved onions to and fro.

Rebecca, from your little tables you
Were selling sticky sweets, a scanty show. . . .

The sky seemed pouring, like a filthy sea,
A tide of vapor into the canals.
Smoke that one does not see, commercial calm
Rose from the husked roofs and rich table-cloths,
And from the houses' comfort India breathed.

Fain had I been one of those merchant princes,
Who sailed in olden days from Amsterdam
To China, handing over their estate
And home affairs to trusty mandatories.
Like Robinson before a notary
I would have signed my pompous procuration.

Then honesty had piled from day to day
My riches more, and flowered them like a moon-beam
Upon my laden ships' imposing prows.
And in my house the nabobs of Bombay
Would have been tempted by my florid spouse.

The Mogul would have sent a gold-ringed negro
To traffic, with a smiling row of teeth,
Under his spreading parasol. And he
Would have enchanted with his savage tales
My eldest girl, to whom he would have given
A robe of rubies cut by cunning slaves.

I should have had my family portrayed
By some poor wretch whose paintings lived and breathed:
My plump and sumptuous wife with rosy face,
My sons, whose beauty would have charmed the town,
My daughters, with their pure and different grace.

And so to-day, instead of being myself,
I should have been another, visiting
A pompous mansion of old Amsterdam,
Launching my soul before the plain devise,
Under a gable: Here lived Francis Jammes.

(*Jethro Bithell*)

PRAYER TO GO TO PARADISE WITH THE ASSES

O God, when You send for me, let it be
Upon some festal day of dusty roads.
I wish, as I did ever here-below
By any road that pleases me, to go
To Paradise, where stars shine all day long.
Taking my stick out on the great highway,
To my dear friends the asses I shall say:
I am Francis Jammes going to Paradise,
For there is no hell where the Lord God dwells.
Come with me, my sweet friends of azure skies,
You poor, dear beasts who whisk off with your ears
Mosquitoes, peevish blows, and buzzing bees . . .

Let me appear before You with these beasts,
Whom I so love because they bow their head
Sweetly, and halting join their little feet
So gently that it makes you pity them.
Let me come followed by their million ears,
By those that carried panniers on their flanks,
And those that dragged the cars of acrobats,
Those that had battered cans upon their backs,
She-asses limping, full as leather-bottles,
And those too that they breech because of blue
And oozing wounds round which the stubborn flies
Gather in swarms. God, let me come to You
With all these asses into Paradise.
Let angels lead us where your rivers soothe
Their tufted banks, and cherries tremble, smooth
As is the laughing flesh of tender maids.
And let me, where Your perfect peace pervades,
Be like Your asses, bending down above
The heavenly waters through eternity,
To mirror their sweet, humble poverty
In the clear waters of eternal love.

(Jethro Bithell)

LOVE

Lass, when they talk of love, laugh in their face.
They find not love who seek it far and wide.
Man is a cold, hard brute. Your timid grace
Will leave his coarse desires unsatisfied.

He only lies. And he will leave you lone
Upon your hearth with children to look after,
And you will feel so old when he reels home,
To fill the morning hours with obscene laughter.

Do not believe there is any love for the winning.
But go to the garden where the blue skies pour,
And watch, at the greenest rose-tree's dusky core,
The silver spider living alone, and spinning.

(*Jethro Bithell*)

THE CHILD READS AN ALMANAC

The child reads on; her basket of eggs stands by.
She sees the weather signs, the Saints with awe,
And watches the fair houses of the sky:
The *Goat,* the *Bull,* the *Ram,* et cetera.

And so the little peasant maiden knows
That in the constellations we behold,
Are markets like the one to which she goes
Where goats and bulls and rams are bought and sold.

She reads about the market in the sky.
She turns a page and sees the *Scales* and then
Says that in Heaven, as at the grocery,
They weigh salt, coffee and the souls of men.

(*Ludwig Lewisohn*)

Paul Fort

1872–

PAN AND THE CHERRIES

I RECOGNIZED him by his skips and hops,
And by his hair I knew that he was Pan.
Through sunny avenues he ran,
And leapt for cherries to the red tree-tops.
Upon his fleece were pearling water drops
Like little silver stars. How pure he was!

And this was when my spring was arched with blue.

Now, seeing a cherry of a smoother gloss,
He seized it, and bit the kernel from the pulp.
I watched him with great joy. . . . I came anigh. . . .

He spat the kernel straight into my eye.
I ran to kill Pan with my knife!
He stretched his arm out, swirled—
And the whole earth whirled!

Let us adore Pan, god of the world!

(*Jethro Bithell*)

BALLADE

THE pretty maid she died, she died, in love-bed as she lay;
They took her to the churchyard, all at the break of day;
They laid her all alone there, all in her white array;
They laid her all alone there, a-coffined in the clay;
And they came back so merrily, all at the dawn of day;
A-singing, all so merrily, *"The dog must have his day!"*
The pretty maid is dead, is dead, in love-bed as she lay;
And they went off a-field to work, as they do every day.

(*Frederick York Powell*)

Paul Valéry

1872-

NARCISSUS

. . . Perhaps you expected a face that was free from tears,
You calms, you always decked with leaves and flowers,
And haunted depths of the incorruptible,
O nymphs! . . . But yielding to the enchanted slopes
That were my irretrievable roadway to you,
Permit this fair reflection of man's disorder.
Happy your blended forms, you deep and level waters!
I am alone . . . if the gods, the waves, and the echoes
And so many sighs allow! I am alone!
But still I am he who comes unto himself
When he comes near the banks this growth adorns.

On the peaks the light has halted its pure plunder,
The voice of the fountains turns to talk of dusk,
Calm concord hearkens, wherein I hear hope.
I hear the night grass grow in the holy shadows,
And the perfidious moon now elevates her mirror
Even to the secrets of the dying pool.

And I! My body cast upon these reeds,
I languish, Sapphire, in my mournful beauty!
I must henceforth adore the magic waters
Where I have forgotten the olden smile and the rose.
Let me bewail your pure and fatal glory,
Fountain so softly closed around by me,
Where my eyes draw forth from the lethal azure
Those same dark eyes of their astounded soul!
What loss within oneself so calm a place affords!
The soul, even unto destruction, seeks a god
Demanding of the wave, the lonely wave
That gleams inviting soft advent of swan. . . .
Never have thirsty flocks bemired these waters!
Others who have wandered here have found repose,
And in the dark earth a clear, opening tomb;

But it is not calm, alas! that I shall find,
When the opaque delight where the splendor sleeps
Yields to my body the horror of widening leafage
And, driving back the shade and the frightening thickness,
I see! I fall! and come from this tyrant body
Peacefully to share the eternal charms!

There, nude between the arms that spring from the forest,
A tender gleam of daylight doubtfully plays;
And there the glimmer of day becomes a bridegroom,
Pure in the pale place where the sad water lures me,
Delightful spirit, desirable and cold!
I behold in the water my flesh of moon and the dawn-dew,
Obedient form opposed to my desires!
There are the pure stirrings of my silver arms!
My lingering hands in the adorable gold grow weary
Of seeking the captive whom the leaves entwine,
And I cry to echo the names of the hidden gods!

But how fair his mouth in that mute blasphemy!
O likeness! . . . Yet more perfect than myself,
Immortal ephemeron, clear before my eyes,
Pale limbs of pearl and softly silken hair,
Must the shadow darken us who scarce have loved,
Must the night already part us, O Narcissus,
And press between us the blade that halves a fruit!

What is it?
My plaint is baneful? . . .
The mere stir
Of the breath I set upon your lips, my double,
Has coursed a tremor on your limpid wave! . . .
You tremble! But these words I, kneeling, breathe
Are still no more than a hesitant soul between us,
Between that clear brow and my spent memory . . .
I am so near you I can drink you in,
O countenance! . . . My thirst is a naked slave . . .

Till this rapt hour I did not know myself,
Nor how to cherish, how attain my soul! . . .
But watching you, dear slave, obey the least
Of the shadows sadly retreating in my heart,
And on my brow a secret fire and storm,
Watching, O marvel! watching my murmurous mouth
Betray . . . snare on the water a flower of fancy,
And mad events that sparkle in the eye!
I have found a treasure of impotence and pride!
May no sweet virgin whom the satyr stalks,
None! swift in flight, deft in unfeeling fall,
No nymph, no maiden, ever lure me on
As you within the waters, my illimitable soul!

(*Joseph T. Shipley*)

HELEN, THE SAD QUEEN

Azure, I come! from the caves of death withdrawn
To hear the waves break rhythmic on the shores,
To see swift galleys clear, across the dawn,
Lifting from darkness on the blades of golden oars.

My lonely hands now summon forth the kings
Whose salt-gray beards amuse my chaste fingers. . .
I wept. . . . And each his gloomy triumph sings
And behind the stern of his bark the furrow lingers.

I hear sonorous conchs and clarion calls
Marking the lift of the oars and their even falls.
The clear chant of the undulant oarsmen charms
The tumult; and the gods! heroic at the prow,
With their olden smile and the spray hurled at their
brow,
Stretch toward me their indulgent, graven arms.

(*Joseph T. Shipley*)

Charles Guérin

1873–1907

PARTINGS

O TRAGIC hours when lovers leave each other!
Then every mistress feels herself a mother,
And, making of her lap a chair of ease,
Cradles us in the hollow of her knees,
And turns aside her brimful, dreaming eyes,
And with brief voice to our vain vows replies,
And hums a tune, and whispers, and at whiles
Smooths with slow, gliding hand our hair, and smiles
As laughs a babe to angels over him.
In her strange eyes her heart's dark sorrows swim;
Convulsively her arms strain us to her;
She moans and trembles, and, with sudden stir,
Presses her lips upon our eyes, and bids
Silence, and drinks our soul through closed eye-lids.

(*Jethro Bithell*)

Charles Vildrac

1882–

AFTER MIDNIGHT

IT is at morning, twilight they expire;
Death takes in hand, when midnight sounds,
Millions of bodies in their beds,
And scarcely anybody thinks of it. . . .

O men and women, you
About to die at break of day,
I see your hands' uneasy multitude,
Which now the blood deserts for ever!

White people in the throes of death,
Wrestling in all the world to-night,
And whom the weeping dawn will silence,
Fearful I hear your gasping breath!

How many of you there are dying!
How can so many other folks be lying
Asleep upon the shore of your death-rattles!

. . . Here is noise in the house;
I am not the only one who hears you:
Some one has stepped about a room,
Some one has risen to watch over you.

But no! It is a little song I hear.
If some one stepped about a room,
It was to go and rock a little child,
Who has been born this evening in the house.

(Jethro Bithell)

Jules Romains

1885-

ANOTHER SPIRIT ADVANCES

WHAT is it so transforms the boulevard?
The lure of the passersby is not of the flesh;
There are no movements; there are flowing rhythms
And I have no need of eyes to see them there.
The air I breathe is fresh with spirit-savor.
Men are ideas that a mind sends forth.
From them to me all flows, yet is internal;
Cheek to cheek we lie across the distance,
Space in communion binds us in one thought.

(Joseph T. Shipley)

GERMAN

From the Minnesingers

It is a bright, animated, eventful age which we find reflected in the literature of the Minnesingers; not trivial, for the stern premonition of coming struggle is felt; frank, artless, and natural; original, because reaped on fresh fields, by fresh hands; and with a direct impress of Nature, which we find for the first time in any literature.—BAYARD TAYLOR.

Sir Dietmar von Aist

12th century

PARTING AT MORNING

(*Slâfest, dû mîn friedel*)

"DEAR love, dost thou sleep fairly?
Alas, there wakes us early
A pretty bird that flew but now
And perched aloft upon the linden-bough."
"Full softly I was sleeping,
Child, till I heard thee weeping.
Sweet must have its sorrow still;
But all thou bid'st me, sweetheart, I'll fulfill."
The lady fell a-moaning:
"Thou'lt ride and leave me lonely.
And when wilt thou come back to me?
Alas, thou takest all my joy with thee!"

(*Frank C. Nicholson*)

A BIRD WAS SINGING

A BIRD was singing on the linden tree,
Filling the fields with music by the wood;
My heart was lifted, and did long to be
In the old hollow where the rose-bush stood:
Its wilding blossoms I again could see,

Many and fragrant clustered on the brier,
As are my thoughts of her I most admire.
"It seems indeed a thousand years ago,
Since in the arms of my dear love I lay;
And not for any fault of mine I know
He has been strange to me this many a day;
But since I heed not if birds sing or no,
And since the flowers for me have had no sheen,
Short has my pleasure, long my sorrow been."

(Jethro Bithell)

A LADY STOOD

A LADY stood on the turret-stone
Looking away o'er the moorlands lone,
If that her love were riding there.
She saw a falcon in the air:
"O happy falcon flying free,
Flying where thy heart would be!
In all the wood one single tree
Thou choosest to be dear to thee.
And so chose I.
My eyes have singled out a knight;
Now other ladies in their spite
Are envious, and spy.
Why will they plot against my happiness?
I grudge them not the men their arms caress."

(Jethro Bithell)

Sir Heinrich von Rugge

12th century

HE THAT LOVES A ROSY CHEEK

ASK not overmuch for fair
Form and face: let women be
Good: beauty is but a snare:
Gladly woo, if good is she.

After the strewn leaves of roses
Richer the rich mind uncloses.
Boorish is he, and unwise,
Who judges women by the eyes.

(Jethro Bithell)

Sir Reinmar von Hagenau

12th century

AS ON THE HEATHER

I HAVE marked, as on the heather now I strayed,
Fresh-springing sweetly-fashioned violets,
And bolder flowers in flaunting red arrayed;
And this is why the nightingale forgets
The stubborn woe that all the winter long
Weighed on her heart the cheerless trees among.
I have heard her song.

My heart's heaviness, soon as the burgeons burst
Like to a carried burden I laid by:
For the lady for whose love I was athirst
Filled such a chalice for my lips that I,
Revived, the lightsome mood of nature share;
And all that she shall do to me I swear
Is good and fair.

She sundered sorrow from my soul that smiles
Like these pure skies whence all the clouds are flown;
Yet not a thousand women with their wiles
Could have achieved it: my true love alone
Routed the cares that surged by day and night:
So I have chosen her my life's delight
In the world's despite.

My portion shall be rapture without end:
I wot I have no need to nurse alarms;
And, if it come to pass as I intend,
She yet shall lie in secret in my arms.

I shall, when my embraces hold her fast,
Believe that I to Paradise have passed.
If dreams would last!

There are among our friends who love me not
That in my happy face my joy I show:
Their venomed glances are as arrows shot
Beyond the mark: I heed nor friend nor foe.
What profit all the pitfalls they devise?
That love is ripening while they surmise
Escapes their eyes!

(Jethro Bithell)

A CHILDISH GAME

Long as I can call to mind,
Never was so much of ill.
In the world you shall not find
One who does attain his will.
So it was, and is alas!
Grief did ever hearts harass.
Joy and sorrow both shall pass.
He whose passion is misprized
Vainly suffers agony.
Where's the gain, to be despised?—
Only sorrow's usury.
This is all that I have got.
She I loved so well hath not
Deigned assuage my cruel lot.
"Constancy is lovers' aid."—
This is but a juggler's tale.
Since on her my eyes first strayed,
Never did my service fail.
From that service I depart.—
No, I cannot rend my heart.—
Love, a childish game thou art!

(Jethro Bithell)

Sir Hartmann von Aue

12th century

NONE IS HAPPY

None is happy, free from care
In this world, an't be not he
Who in love has ne'er a share,
And who shuns in love to be.
Troubled not with sighs his breath—
Sighs of yearning that to death
Bring full many who have earned,
But receive not, love's caress.
He by passion is not burned,
Such as that which I confess
Is my furnace of distress.

(*Jethro Bithell*)

Sir Walther von der Vogelweide

13th century

THERE IS A LADY

There is a lady conquering with glances:
Happy the hour she was to me revealed!
A hard-embattled legion of my fancies
Against her sent, were forced and fain to yield.
And sure I know that ransom there is none.
Her excellence and beauty have done this,
And her red, laughing mouth that were so sweet to kiss
And so my soul and senses serve and crave her,
Who is so sweet, and pure, and excellent;
And, lest I die of longing for her favor,
I dare to hope that she may yet relent,
And grant the greatest guerdon e'er I won.
Her excellence and beauty have done this,
And her red, laughing mouth that were so sweet to kiss.

(*Jethro Bithell*)

AWAKE!

Awake! The day is coming now
That brings the sweat of anguish to the brow
Of Christians, Jews, and Pagans all!
Many a token in the sky
And on the earth shows it is nigh:
Foretold in Holy Writ withal.
The sun no longer shows
His face; and treason sows
His secret seeds that no man can detect;
Fathers by their children are undone;
The brother would the brother cheat;
And the cowled monk is a deceit,
Who should the way to Heaven direct;
Might is right, and justice there is none.
Arise! we slept, nor of the peril recked.

(*Jethro Bithell*)

WITH A ROD NO MAN ALIVE

With a rod no man alive
Goodness in a child can drive:
Whom you may to honor bring
As a blow a word will sting.
As a blow a word will sting
Whom you may to honor bring:
Goodness in a child can drive
With a rod no man alive.
Have a good care of your tongue,
Guarded speech beseems the young;
Shoot the bolt the door behind,
Lock within the words unkind.
Lock within the words unkind,
Shoot the bolt the door behind;
Guarded speech beseems the young,
Have a good care of your tongue.
Have a good care of your eyes,
They were never meant for spies:

Noble manners let them mind,
Be they to ignoble blind.
Be they to ignoble blind,
Noble manners let them mind:
They were never meant for spies,
Have a good care of your eyes.
  Have a good care of your ears,
Foolish is who all things hears:
Evil speech if they admit,
You will be defiled by it.
You will be defiled by it,
Evil speech if they admit;
Foolish is who all things hears,
Have a good care of your ears.
  Have good care of all the three,
They are often all too free:
Tongue and eyes and ears are bent
On delight and devilment.
On delight and devilment
Tongue and eyes and ears are bent:
They are often all too free,
Have good care of all the three.

(*Jethro Bithell*)

TANDARADEI

UNDER the lindens on the heather,
There was our double resting-place,
Side by side and close together
Garnered blossoms, crushed, and grass
Nigh a shaw in such a vale:
Tandaradei,
Sweetly sang the nightingale.

I came a-walking through the grasses;
Lo! my dear was come before.
Ah! what befell then—listen, listen, lasses—
Makes me glad for evermore.
Kisses?—thousands in good sooth:
Tandaradei,
See how red they've left my mouth.

There had he made ready—featly, fairly—
All of flow'ring herbs a yielding bed,
And that place in secret still smiles rarely.
If by chance your foot that path should tread,
You might see the roses pressed,
Tandaradei,
Where e'enow my head did rest.

How he lay beside me, did a soul discover
(Now may God forfend such shame from me):
Not a soul shall know it save my lover;
Not a soul could see save I and he,
And a certain small brown bird:
Tandaradei,
Trust him not to breathe a word.

(Ford Madox Ford)

Sir Wolfram von Eschenbach

13th century

HIS OWN TRUE WIFE

Hidden lovers' woes
Thou wast wont to sing ere dawn arose:
Bitter parting after raptured meetings.
Whosoever love and lady's greeting
So received that he was torn
From her breast my fear of men,
Thou wouldst sing him counsel, when
Shone the star of morn.
Warder, sing it now no more, lay by thy bugle-horn!
He to whom is given
Not to be from love by morning riven—
Whom the watchers think not to beleaguer,
Hath no need to be alert and eager
To avert the peril rife
In the day: his rest is pure,

Not a warder makes secure
His unhappy life.
Love so sweet bestows in all men's sight his own true
wife!

(*Jethro Bithell*)

Sir Neidhart von Reuental

13th century

ON THE MOUNTAIN

On the mountain, in the valley,
Singing birds again do rally;
Now is seen
Clover green;
Winter, take away thy teen!
Trees that erst were gray to view
Now their verdant robes renew;
In their shade
Nests are made;
Thence the toll of May is paid.
Fought an aged wife for breath
Day and night, and baffled death;
Now she rushes
Like a ram about, and pushes
All the young ones into the bushes.

(*Jethro Bithell*)

Sir Ulrich von Liechtenstein

13th century

LOVE, WHOSE MONTH WAS EVER MAY

When with May the air is sweet,
When the forest fair is clad,
All that have a love to meet
Pair in pleasure, lass and lad.
Merrily arm in arm they go,
For the time will have it so.

Love and love, when linked together,
Love goes with to keep them gay:
All the three, this sunshine weather,
They are making holiday.
Sorrow cannot come between
Hearts where Love and May are seen.
Where to love sweet love is plighted,
Constant and with all the soul,
And the pair are so united
That their love is sound and whole:
God shall make them man and wife
For the bliss of all their life.
He that finds a constant heart,
Constant love, and constant mind,
All his sorrows shall depart.
Love, when constant, is so kind
That it makes a constant breast
Evermore content and blest.
Could I find affection true,
So sincere should be mine own:
We should conquer, being two,
Care I cannot kill alone.
Constant love is all my care:
Love inconstant I forbear.

(Jethro Bithell)

Sir Reinmar von Zweter

13th century

I CAME A-RIDING

I CAME a-riding in a far countrie
On a blue goose, and strange things I did see.
There was a crow and hawk that in a brook
Fished many a swine; a falcon by a bear
Was hunted in the upper realms of air;
Midges were playing chess; and I did look
Upon a stag that span the fine silk thread;
A wolf was shepherd of the lambs that fed

In the willow tops; a cock caught in a trap
Three giants; and a coney trained a hound;
A crab raced with a dove and won a pound.
If this is true, an ass can sew a cap.

(*Jethro Bithell*)

Anonymous

13th century

TRUELOVE

Truelove, come O come to me,
I am waiting here for thee:
I am waiting here for thee,
Truelove, come O come to me!
Sweetest mouth red as the rose,
Come and heal me of my woes:
Come and heal me of my woes,
Sweetest mouth red as the rose.

(*Jethro Bithell*)

Anonymous

14th century ?

SERENADE

Come now, and let us wake them: time
It is that they arise!
But gently to the window climb,
Where love with love together sleeping lies.

I heard a gently flowing river:
Methought it was the Rhine.
And at her window, with his quiver,
Stood Cupid shooting at a love of mine.

I brake three lilies from their stem,
And in at the window threw:
Sleeping or waking, cherish them;
And rise, sweet love, and let me in to you.

"How would it be, were I asleep,
And could not let you in?
For I am lying now so deep
My truelove's arms within."

If you do in your love's arms lie,
Deep in the arms of love,
And if your love should not be I:
On me have mercy God in Heaven above!

And he who made this little song,
And set it to the tune,
He thought it over well and long,
And sang it for "Good-Night" beneath the moon.

(Jethro Bithell)

Anonymous

16th century

WESTPHALIAN SONG

When thou to my true-love com'st
Greet her from me kindly;
When she asks thee how I fare?
Say, folks in Heaven fare finely.

When she asks, "What! Is he sick?"
Say, dead!—and when for sorrow
She begins to sob and cry,
Say, I come to-morrow.

(Samuel Taylor Coleridge)

Anonymous

16th century

A LOVELY ROSE IS SPRUNG

A lovely rose is sprung,
Out of a tender root,
As men of old have sung,

From Jesse's stem a shoot.
And so a flower bright
Has bloomed in coldest winter
E'en in the deepest night.

The little rose I mean
Whereof Isaiah told,
Pure Mary, maid serene
Brought forth alone—behold:
Through God's eternal might
A little child she bore us
E'en in the deepest night.

(*Margarete Münsterberg*)

Martin Luther

1483–1546

A MIGHTY FORTRESS IS OUR GOD

A MIGHTY fortress is our God,
A bulwark never failing,
Our helper He, amid the flood
Of mortal ill prevailing;
For still our ancient foe
Doth seek to work us woe,
His craft and power are great,
And armed with cruel hate,
On earth is not his equal.

Did we in our strength confide,
Our striving would be losing,
Were not the right man on our side,
The man of God's own choosing.
Dost ask who that may be?
Christ Jesus, it is he,
Lord Sabaoth his name,
From age to age the same,
And he must win the battle.

And though this world, with devils filled,
Should threaten to undo us,
We will not fear, for God hath willed
His truth to triumph through us.
The Prince of Darkness grim,
We tremble not at him,
His rage we can endure,
For lo! his doom is sure,
Our little word shall fell him.

That word above all earthly powers—
No thanks for them,—abideth;
The spirit and the gift is ours,
Through him who with us sideth.
Let goods and kindred go,
This mortal life also;
The body they may kill,
God's truth abideth still,
His kingdom is forever.

(F. H. Hedge)

Johann Gottfried von Herder

1744–1803

SIR OLAF

Sir Olaf he rideth west and east
To bid the folk to his bridal feast.

On the wold are dancing an elvish band,
And Erl-king's daughter proffers her hand.

"Now welcome, Sir Olaf: what haste's with thee?
Step into our circle and dance with me."

"To dance I neither will nor may,
To-morrow's dawn is my bridal-day."

"Nay, stay, Sir Olaf, and dance with me,
And golden spurs will I give to thee."

"To dance I neither will nor may,
To-morrow's dawn is my bridal-day."

"Nay, stay, Sir Olaf, and dance with me,
A heap of gold will I give to thee."

"For all thy gold I will not stay,
And dance I neither will nor may."

"If thou wilt not dance, Sir Olaf, with me,
Then Pest and Sickness shall follow thee."

She touched Sir Olaf upon the heart—
Ne'er in his life had he felt such smart.

She lifted him up on his steed that tide,
"Ride home! ride fast to thy troth-plight bride!"

And when he came to his castle-door,
His mother stood there, and trembled sore.

"Now say, sweet son, right speedilie
Why art thou wan, and white of blee?"

"Well may my face be wan and white.
I was in Erl-king's realm last night."

"Now tell me, my son so true and tried,
What thing shall I say to thy plighted bride?"

"Say that I hunt in the good greenwood,
With hound and horse as a good knight should."

When scarce the dawn in heaven shone red,
Came the train with the bride Sir Olaf should wed.

They sat at meat, they sat at wine;
"Now where is Sir Olaf, bridegroom of mine?"

"Sir Olaf rode out to the greenwood free,
With horse and hound to the hunt rode he."

The bride she lifted a cloth of red:
Beneath, Sir Olaf was lying dead.

(Elizabeth Craigmyle)

ESTHONIAN BRIDAL SONG

Deck thyself, maiden,
With the hood of thy mother;
Put on the ribands
Which thy mother once wore:
On thy head the band of duty,
On thy forehead the band of care.
Sit in the seat of thy mother,
And walk in thy mother's footsteps.
And weep not, weep not, maiden:
If thou weepest in thy bridal attire,
Thou wilt weep all thy life.

(W. Taylor)

Ludwig Heinrich Christoph Hölty

1748–1776

HARVEST SONG

Sickles sound;
On the ground
Fast the ripe ears fall;
Every maiden's bonnet
Has blue blossoms on it;
Joy is over all.

Sickles ring,
Maidens sing
To the sickle's sound;
Till the moon is beaming,
And the stubble gleaming,
Harvest songs go round.

All are springing,
All are singing,
Every lisping thing.
Man and master meet;
From one dish they eat;
Each is now a king.

Hans and Michael
Whet the sickle,
Piping merrily.
Now they mow; each maiden
Soon with sheaves is laden,
Busy as a bee.

Now the blisses,
And the kisses!
Now the wit doth flow
Till the beer is out;
Then, with song and shout,
Home they go, yo ho!

(*Charles T. Brooks*)

Johann Wolfgang von Goethe

1749-1832

Perennial, as a possession for ever, Goethe's History and Writings abide there; a thousand-voiced "Melody of Wisdom" which he that has ears may hear.—THOMAS CARLYLE.

THE ERL-KING

O WHO rides by night thro' the woodland so wild?
It is the fond father embracing his child;
And close the boy nestles within his loved arm.
To hold himself fast, and to keep himself warm.

"O father, see yonder! see yonder!" he says;
"My boy, upon what dost thou fearfully gaze?"
"O, 'tis the Erl-King with his crown and his shroud."
"No, my son, it is but a dark wreath of the cloud."

(The Erl-King speaks)
"O come and go with me, thou loveliest child;
By many a gay sport shall thy time be beguiled;
My mother keeps for thee full many a fair toy,
And many a fine flower shall she pluck for my boy."

"O father, my father, and did you not hear
The Erl-King whisper so low in my ear?"
"Be still, my heart's darling—my child, be at ease;
It was but the wild blast as it sung thro' the trees."

Erl-King
"O wilt thou go with me, thou loveliest boy?
My daughter shall tend thee with care and with joy;
She shall bear thee so lightly thro' wet and thro' wild,
And press thee, and kiss thee, and sing to my child."

"O father, my father, and saw you not plain
The Erl-King's pale daughter glide past thro' the rain?"
"O yes, my loved treasure, I knew it full soon;
It was the gray willow that danced to the moon."

Erl-King
"O come and go with me, no longer delay,
Or else, silly child, I will drag thee away."
"O father! O father! now, now, keep your hold,
The Erl-King has seized me—his grasp is so cold!"

Sore trembled the father; he spurr'd thro' the wild,
Clasping close to his bosom his shuddering child;
He reaches his dwelling in doubt and in dread,
But, clasp'd to his bosom, the infant was dead.

(Sir Walter Scott)

WANDERER'S NIGHT-SONGS

I

Thou that from the heavens art,
Every pain and sorrow stillest,
And the doubly wretched heart
Doubly with refreshment fillest,

I am weary with contending!
Why this rapture and unrest?
Peace descending
Come, ah, come into my breast!

II

O'er all the hill-tops
Is quiet now,
In all the tree-tops
Hearest thou
Hardly a breath;
The birds are asleep in the trees:
Wait; soon like these
Thou too shalt rest.

(H. W. Longfellow)

THE LAY OF THE CAPTIVE COUNT

THE COUNT

I KNOW a Flower of beauty rare,
And long with sweetest anguish
To go and cull this Flower so fair;
But here in thrall I languish.
All day I murmur, "Woe is me!"
For, while as yet my steps were free
This lovely flower was in my power.

From these blank walls I gaze in vain
To find my cherished Flower;
The dell is lost, and dim the plain,
So lofty is this tower!
But, be he knave, or be he knight,
Who brings me here my heart's delight,
I'll call him nearest friend and dearest.

THE ROSE

Behold! a Flower divinely bright
Below thy trellis bloweth;
Thou surely meanest me, Sir Knight,
The Rose that richly gloweth:

A princely mind is thine, I ween,
The flower of flowers, the garden-queen,
Methinks must blossom on thy bosom.

THE COUNT

O Rose! we prize thy damask dyes
  Through leafy darkness peering:
As precious thou in maiden's eyes
  As pearl, or gold, or ear-ring.
Thou deckest well her braided hair;
Yet art not thou the wonder fair
Whereon I ponder, ever fonder.

THE LILY

The flaunting Rose is proud of port,
  And proud are they who seek her,
But modest minds will fainer court
  A coyer flower and meeker.
The soft in soul, the pure in heart,
Methinks will chuse the better part,
And love with stilly love the Lily.

THE COUNT

I hold myself unstained and chaste,
  And free from darker failings;
Yet here, a captive wretch, I waste
  My heart in bitter wailings!
Meet emblem of the Undefiled
Art thou, a spotless flower and mild,
But mine is rarer, dearer, fairer.

THE PINK

That rarer, fairer flower am I,
  I bud and bloom so gayly
Here in mine arbor, tended by
  The heedful warden daily;
With clustering petals breathing out
Voluptuous perfume round about,
And thousand glowing colors shewing.

THE COUNT

The brilliant Pink let no man slight,—
The gardener's minion-floweret,
Now must it bask in garish light,
Now shadow must embower it;
But such will never heal my woe;
Mine is a meek-eyed flower, and, though
Serene and tender, hath no splendor.

THE VIOLET

Uneyed and hidden here I bloom,
Wrapped in communings lonely;
Yet will I now, Sir Knight, presume
To speak, though this time only.
If I, the Violet, be thy flower,
It grieves me that I want the power
To lightly clamber tow'rds thy chamber.

THE COUNT

I love the vestal Violet,
Her odor and her color,
But even for her can ne'er forget
My lonely doom of dolor.
Hear, friends, my mournful riddle right:
In vain all round this rocky height
I cast mine eye for what I sigh for.

But far beneath, by streams and groves,
Her bosom overladen
With sorrow for my thraldom, roves
Earth's truest-hearted maiden.
And when she weeps my dreary lot,
And plucks the blue Forget-Me-Not,
It wakes Affection's recollections.

For love like her's hath mystic might,
Which breathes through sundering distance;
And feeds, even in my dungeon's night
My lamp of pale existence.

And, when my heart would break, this thought
Steals over it, Forget-Me-Not!
And I inherit Strength and Spirit.

(James Clarence Mangan)

THE MINSTREL

"WHAT voice, what harp, are those we hear
Beyond the gate in chorus?
Go, page!—the lay delights our ear,
We'll have it sung before us!"
So speaks the king: the stripling flies—
He soon returns; his master cries—
"Bring in the hoary minstrel!"

"Hail, princes mine! Hail, noble knights!
All hail, enchanting dames!
What starry heaven! What blinding lights!
Whose tongue may tell their names?
In this bright hall, amid this blaze,
Close, close, mine eyes! Ye may not gaze
On such stupendous glories!"

The Minnesinger closed his eyes;
He struck his mighty lyre:
Then beauteous bosoms heaved with sighs,
And warriors felt on fire;
The king, enraptured by the strain,
Commanded that a golden chain
Be given the bard in guerdon.

"Not so! Reserve thy chain, thy gold,
For those brave knights whose glances,
Fierce flashing through the battle bold,
Might shiver sharpest lances!
Bestow it on thy Treasurer there—
The golden burden let him bear
With other glittering burdens.

"I sing as in the greenwood bush
The cageless wild-bird carols—
The tones that from the full heart gush
Themselves are gold and laurels!
Yet, might I ask, then thus I ask,
Let one bright cup of wine in flask
Of glowing gold be brought me!"

They set it down: he quaffs it all—
"O! draught of richest flavor!
O! thrice divinely happy hall,
Where that is scarce a favor!
If Heaven shall bless ye, think on me,
And thank your God as I thank ye
For this delicious wine-cup!"

(James Clarence Mangan)

THE ROSE

Once a boy beheld a bright
Rose in dingle growing;
Far, far off it pleased his sight;
Near he viewed it with delight:
Soft it seemed and glowing.
Lo! the rose, the rose so bright,
Rose so brightly blowing!

Spake the boy, "I'll pluck thee, grand
Rose all wildly blowing."
Spake the rose, "I'll wound thy hand,
Thus the scheme thy wit hath planned
Deftly overthrowing."
O! the rose, the rose so grand,
Rose so grandly glowing.

But the stripling plucked the red
Rose in glory growing,
And the thorn his flesh hath bled,

And the rose's pride is fled,
And her beauty's going.
Woe! the rose, the rose once red
Rose once redly glowing.

(*James Clarence Mangan*)

THE KING OF THULÉ

OH! true was his heart while he breathèd,
That King over Thulé of old,
So she that adored him bequeathèd
Him, dying, a beaker of gold.

At banquet and supper for years has
He brimmingly filled it up,
His eyes overflowing with tears as
He drank from that beaker-cup.

When Death came to wither his pleasures
He parceled his cities wide,
His castles, his lands, and his treasures,
But the beaker he laid aside.

They drank the red wine from the chalice.
His barons and marshals brave;
The monarch sat in his rock-palace
Above the white foam of the wave.

And now, growing weaker and weaker
He quaffed his last Welcome to Death,
And hurled the golden beaker
Down into the flood beneath.

He saw it winking and sinking,
And drinking the foam so hoar;
The light from his eyes was shrinking,
Nor drop did he ever drink more.

(*James Clarence Mangan*)

A VOICE FROM THE INVISIBLE WORLD

High o'er his moldering castle walls
  The warrior's phantom glides,
And loudly to the skiff it calls
  That on the billow rides—

"Behold! these arms once vaunted might,
  This heart beat wild and bold—
Behold! these ducal veins ran bright
  With wine-red blood of old.

"The noon in storm, the eve in rest,
  So sped my life's brief day.
What then? *Young bark on Ocean's breast,*
  Cleave thou thy destined way!"

(*James Clarence Mangan*)

AN IRISH LAMENTATION

O! raise the woeful *Pillalu,*
  And let your tears in streams be shed;
Och, orro, orro, ollalu!
  The Master's eldest hope is dead!

Ere broke the morning dim and pale
  The owlet flapped his heavy wing:
We heard the winds at evening wail,
  And now our dirge of death we sing,
    Och, orro, orro, ollalu!

Why wouldst thou go? How couldst thou die?
  Why hast thou left thy parents dear?
Thy friends, thy kindred far and nigh,
  Whose cries, *mo vrone!* thou dost not hear?
    Och, orro, orro, ollalu!

Thy mother, too!—how could she part
  From thee, her darling fair and sweet,

The heart that throbbed within her heart,
The pulse, the blood that bade it beat?
Och, orro, orro, ollalu!

Oh! lost to her and all thy race,
Thou sleepest in the House of Death;
She sees no more thy cherub face,
She drinks no more thy violet breath;
Och, orro, orro, ollalu!

By strand and road, by field and fen,
The sorrowing clans come thronging all;
From camp and dun, from hill and glen,
They crowd around the castle wall.
Och, orro, orro, ollalu!

From East and West, from South and North,
To join the funeral train they hie;
And now the mourners issue forth,
And far they spread the keening cry,
Och, orro, orro, ollalu!

Then raise the woeful *Pillalu,*
And let your tears in streams be shed,
Och, orro, orro, ollalu!
The Chieftain's pride, his heir, is dead.

(*James Clarence Mangan*)

PROMETHEUS

Blacken thy heavens, Jove,
With thunder-clouds,
And exercise thee, like a boy
Who thistles crops,
With smiting oaks and mountain-tops!
Yet must leave me standing
My own firm Earth;
Must leave my cottage, which thou didst not build,
And my warm hearth,
Whose cheerful glow
Thou enviest me.

I know naught more pitiful
Under the sun than you, Gods!
Ye nourish scantily,
With altar-taxes
And with cold lip-service,
This your majesty;—
Would perish, were not
Children and beggars
Credulous fools.

When I was a child,
And knew not whence or whither,
I would turn my wildered eye
To the sun, as if up yonder were
An ear to hear to my complaining,—
A heart, like mine,
On the oppressed to feel compassion.

Who helped me,
When I braved the Titans' insolence?
Who rescued me from death,
From slavery?
Hast thou not all thyself accomplished,
Holy-glowing heart?
And, glowing young and good,
Most ignorantly thanked
The slumberer above there?

I honor thee? For what?
Hast thou the miseries lightened
Of the down-trodden?
Hast thou the tears ever banished
From the afflicted?
Have I not to manhood been molded
By omnipotent Time,
And by Fate everlasting,—
My lords and thine?

Dreamedst thou ever
I should grow weary of living,
And fly to the desert,
Since not all our
Pretty dream-buds ripen?
Here sit I, fashion men
In mine own image,—
A race to be like me,
To weep and to suffer,
To be happy and to enjoy themselves,—
All careless of *thee* too,
As I!

(*John S. Dwight*)

TO THE PARTED ONE

And thou art now no longer near!
  From me, O fairest, thou hast flown!
Nor rings in my accustomed ear
  A single word—a single tone.

As when, at morn, the wanderer's eye
  Pierces the air in vain to see
Where, hidden in the deep-blue sky,
  High up the lark goes singing free,—

So wanders anxiously my gaze
  Piercing the field, the bush, the grove;
On thee still call my frequent lays:
  O, come to me again, dear love.

(*Christopher Pearse Cranch*)

TO A GOLDEN HEART, WORN ROUND HIS NECK

Remembrancer of joys long passed away,
  Relic, from which as yet I cannot part,
O, hast thou power to lengthen love's short day?
  Stronger thy chain than that which bound the heart?

Lili, I fly!—yet still thy fetters press me
  In distant valley, or far lonely wood.
Still with a struggling sigh of pain confess thee
  The mistress of my soul in every mood.

The bird may burst the silken chain that bound him,
  Flying to the green home, which fits him best;
But, ah! he bears the prisoner's badge around him,
  Still by the piece about his neck distressed.
He ne'er can breathe his free wild notes again;
They're stifled by the pressure of his chain.

(Margaret Fuller Ossoli)

MIGNON

KNOWEST thou the land where bloom the lemon trees,
And darkly gleam the golden oranges?
A gentle wind blows down from that blue sky;
Calm stands the myrtle and the laurel high.
Knowest thou the land? So far and fair!
Thou, whom I love, and I will wander there.

Knowest thou the house with all its rooms aglow.
And shining hall and columned portico?
The marble statues stand and look at me.
Alas, poor child, what have they done to thee?
Knowest thou the land? So far and fair.
My Guardian, thou and I will wander there.

Knowest thou the mountain with its bridge of cloud?
The mule plods warily: the white mists crowd.
Coiled in their caves the brood of dragons sleep;
The torrent hurls the rock from steep to steep.
Knowest thou the land? So far and fair.
Father, away! Our road is over there!

(James Elroy Flecker)

THE SHEPHERD'S LAMENT

Up yonder on the mountain
  A thousand times I stand,
Leant on my crook, and gazing
  Down on the valley-land.

I follow the flock to the pasture;
  My little dog watches them still.
I have come below, but I know not
  How I descended the hill.

The beautiful meadow is covered
  With blossoms of every hue;
I pluck them, alas! without knowing
  Whom I shall give them to.

I seek, in the rain and the tempest,
  A refuge under the tree:
Yonder the doors are fastened,
  And all is a dream to me.

Right over the roof of the dwelling
  I see a rainbow stand;
But she has departed forever,
  And gone far out in the land.

Far out in the land, and farther,—
  Perhaps to an alien shore:
Go forward, ye sheep! go forward,—
  The heart of the shepherd is sore.

(*Bayard Taylor*)

FROM FAUST

Prologue in Heaven

Raphæl

The sun makes music as of old
  Amid the rival spheres of Heaven,
On its predestined circle rolled
  With thunder speed: the Angels even

Draw strength from gazing on its glance,
  Though none its meaning fathom may;
The world's unwithered countenance
  Is bright as at creation's day.

GABRIEL

And swift and swift, with rapid lightness,
  The adorned Earth spins silently,
Alternating Elysian brightness
  With deep and dreadful night; the sea
Foams in broad billows from the deep
  Up to the rocks, and rocks and ocean,
Onward, with spheres which never sleep,
  Are hurried in eternal motion.

MICHAEL

And tempests in contention roar
  From land to sea, from sea to land;
And, raging, weave a chain of power,
  Which girds the earth, as with a band.
A flashing desolation there
  Flames before the thunder's way;
But thy servants, Lord, revere
  The gentle changes of thy day.

CHORUS OF THE THREE

The Angels draw strength from thy glance,
  Though no one comprehend thee may;
Thy world's unwithered countenance
  Is bright as on creation's day.

(*Percy Bysshe Shelley*)

SOLDIER'S SONG

CASTLES with lofty
  Ramparts and towers,—
Maidens disdainful
  In Beauty's array,—

All shall be ours!
Bold is the venture,
Splendid the pay!

Lads, let the trumpets
For us be suing,
Calling to pleasure,
Calling to ruin!
Stormy our life is;
Such is its boon:
Maidens and castles
Capitulate soon.
Bold is the venture,
Splendid the pay!
And the soldiers go marching,
Marching away.

(Bayard Taylor)

THE THOUGHT ETERNAL

WHETHER day my spirit's yearning
Unto far, blue hills has led,
Or the night lit all the burning
Constellations at my head—
Hours of light or hours nocturnal
Do I praise our mortal fate:
If man think the thought eternal
He is ever fair and great.

(Ludwig Lewisohn)

Friedrich von Schiller

1759-1805

THEKLA'S SONG

From The Piccolomini

THE cloud doth gather, the green wood roar,
The damsel paces along the shore;
The billows they tumble with might, with might;
And she flings out her voice to the darksome night;
Her bosom is swelling with sorrow;

The world it is empty, the heart will die,
There's nothing to wish for beneath the sky:
Thou Holy One, call thy child away!
I've lived and loved, and that was to-day—
Make ready my grave-clothes to-morrow.

(*Samuel Taylor Coleridge*)

THE MAID OF ORLEANS

At thee *the Mocker* sneers in cold derision,
Through thee he seeks to desecrate and dim
Glory for which he hath no soul or vision,
For "God" and "Angel" are but sounds with him.
He makes the jewels of the heart his booty,
And scoffs at Man's Belief and Woman's Beauty.

Yet thou—a lowly shepherdess!—descended
Not from a kingly but a godly race,
Art crowned by Poësy! Amid the splendid
Of Heaven's high stars she builds thy dwellingplace,
Garlands thy temples with a wreath of glory,
And swathes thy memory in eternal Story.

The Base of this weak world exult at seeing
The Fair defaced, the Lofty in the dust;
Yet grieve not! There are godlike hearts in being
Which worship still the Beautiful and Just.
Let Momus and his mummers please the crowd,
Of nobleness alone a noble mind is proud.

(*James Clarence Mangan*)

THE UNREALITIES

And dost thou faithlessly abandon me?
Must thy cameleon phantasies depart?
Thy griefs, thy gladnesses, take wing and flee
The bower they builded in this lonely heart?
O, Summer of Existence, golden, glowing!
Can nought avail to curb thine onward motion?
In vain! The river of my years is flowing,
And soon shall mingle with the eternal ocean.

Extinguished in dead darkness lies the sun
  That lighted up my shriveled world of wonder;
Those fairy bands Imagination spun
  Around my heart have long been rent asunder.
Gone, gone forever is the fine belief,
  The all-too-generous trust in the Ideal:
All my Divinities have died of grief,
  And left me welded to the Rude and Real.

As clasped the enthusiastic Prince of old
  The lovely statue, stricken by its charms,
Until the marble, late so dead and cold,
  Glowed into throbbing life beneath his arms,
So fondly round enchanting Nature's form,
  I too entwined my passionate arms, till, pressed
In my embraces, she began to warm
  And breathe and revel in my bounding breast.

And, sympathizing with my virgin bliss,
  The speechless things of Earth received a tongue,
They gave me back Affection's burning kiss,
  And loved the Melody my bosom sung:
Then sparkled hues of Life on tree and flower,
  Sweet music from the silver fountain flowed;
All soulless images in that brief hour
  The Echo of my Life divinely glowed!

How struggled all my feelings to extend
  Themselves afar beyond their prisoning bounds!
O, how I longed to enter Life and blend
  Me with its words and deeds, its shapes and sounds.
This human theater, how fair it beamed
  While yet the curtain hung before the scene!
Uprolled, how little then the arena seemed!
  That little how contemptible and mean!

How roamed, imparadised in blest illusion,
  With soul to which the upsoaring Hope lent pinions,
And heart as yet unchilled by Care's intrusion,
  How roamed the stripling-lord through his dominions!

Then Fancy bore him to the palest star
  Pinnacled in the lofty æther dim:
Was nought so elevated, nought so far,
  But thither the Enchantress guided him!

With what rich reveries his brain was rife!
  What adversary might withstand him long?
How glanced and danced before the Car of Life
  The visions of his thought, a dazzling throng!
For there was FORTUNE with her golden crown,
  There flitted LOVE with heart-bewitching boon,
There glittered starry-diademed RENOWN,
  And TRUTH, with radiance like the sun of noon!

But ah! ere half the journey yet was over,
  That gorgeous escort wended separate ways;
All faithlessly forsook the pilgrim-rover,
  And one by one evanished from his gaze.
Away inconstant-handed FORTUNE flew;
  And, while the thirst of Knowledge burned alway
The dreary mists of Doubt arose and threw
  Their shadow over TRUTH's resplendent ray.

I saw the sacred garland-crown of FAME
  Around the common brow its glory shed:
The rapid Summer died, the Autumn came,
  And LOVE, with all his necromancies, fled,
And ever lonelier and silenter
  Grew the dark images of Life's poor dream,
Till scarcely o'er the dusky scenery there
  The lamp of HOPE itself could cast a gleam.

And now, of all, Who, in my day of dolor,
  Alone survives to clasp my willing hand?
Who stands beside me still, my best consoler,
  And lights my pathway to the Phantom-strand?
Thou, FRIENDSHP! stancher of our wounds and sorrows,
  From whom this lifelong pilgrimage of pain
A balsam for its worst afflictions borrows;
  Thou whom I early sought, nor sought in vain!

And thou whose labors by her light are wrought,
  Soother and soberer of the spirit's fever,
Who, shaping all things, ne'er destroyest aught,
  Calm OCCUPATION! thou that weariest never!
Whose efforts rear at last the mighty Mount
  Of Life, though merely grain on grain they lay,
And, slowly toiling, from the vast Account
  Of Time strike minutes, days, and years away.

(*James Clarence Mangan*)

TO MY FRIENDS

BELOVÈD friends! More glorious times than ours
Of old existed: men of loftier powers
  Then we can boast have flourished:—who shall doubt it?
A million stones dug from the depths of Earth
Will bear this witness for the ancient worth,
  If History's chronicles be mute about it.
    But, all are gone—those richly-gifted souls—
      That constellation of illustrious names:
    For Us, for Us, the current moment rolls,
      And We, We live, and have our claims.

My friends! The wanderer tells us—and we own—
That Earth shows many a more luxuriant zone
  Than that whereunder we sedately live;
But, if denied a paradise, our hearts
Are still the home of science and the arts,
  And glow and gladden in the light they give;
    And if beneath our skies the laurel pines,
      And winter desolates our myrtle boughs,
    The curling tendrils of our joyous vines
      Shed freshest greenness round our brows.

May burn more feverish life, more maddening pleasures,
Where four assembled worlds exchange their treasures,
  At London, in the world's Commercial Hall;
A thousand stately vessels come and go,

And costly sights are there, and pomp and show,
And Gold is lord and idolgod of all!
But will the sun be mirrored in the stream
Sullied and darkened by the flooding rains?
No! On the still smooth lake alone his beam
Is brightly imaged, and remains.

The beggar at St. Angelo's might gaze
With scorn upon our North, for he surveys
The one, lone, only, everliving Rome—
All shapes of beauty fascinate his eye;
He sees a brilliant heaven below the sky
Shine in Saint Peter's wonderwaking dome.
But, even while beaming with celestial glory,
Rome is the grave of long-departed years;
It is the green young plant and not the hoary
And time-worn trunk that blooms and cheers.

Prouder achievements may perchance appear
Elsewhere than signalize our humble sphere,
But newer nowhere underneath the sun.
We see in pettier outlines on our stage,
Which miniatures the world of every age,
The storied feats of bypassed eras done.
All things are but redone, reshown, retold,
Fancy alone is ever young and new;
Man and the universe shall both grow old,
But not the forms her pencil drew!

(*James Clarence Mangan*)

Johann Gaudenz von Salis

1762-1834

SONG OF THE SILENT LAND

Into the Silent Land!
Ah! who shall lead us thither?
Clouds in the evening sky more darkly gather,
And shattered wrecks lie thicker on the strand.
Who leads us with a gentle hand
Thither, O, thither,
Into the Silent Land?

Into the Silent Land!
To you, ye boundless regions
Of all perfection! Tender morning-visions
Of beauteous souls! The Future's pledge and band!
Who in Life's battle firm doth stand
Shall bear Hope's tender blossoms
Into the Silent Land!

O Land! O Land!
For all the broken-hearted
The mildest herald by our fate allotted
Beckons, and with inverted torch doth stand
To lead us with a gentle hand
Into the land of the great departed,
Into the Silent Land!

(*H. W. Longfellow*)

Siegfried August Mahlmann

1771-1826

ALLAH

ALLAH gives light in darkness,
Allah gives rest in pain,
Cheeks that are white with weeping
Allah paints red again.

The flowers and the blossoms wither,
Years vanish with flying feet;
But my heart will live on forever,
That here in sadness beat.

Gladly to Allah's dwelling
Yonder would I take flight;
There will the darkness vanish,
There will my eyes have sight.

(*H. W. Longfellow*)

Johann Ludwig Tieck

1773-1853

AUTUMN SONG

A LITTLE bird flew through the dell,
And where the failing sunbeams fell
He warbled thus his wondrous lay.
"Adieu! adieu! I go away:
Far, far,
Must I voyage ere the twilight star!"

It pierced me through, the song he sang,
With many a sweet and bitter pang:
For wounding joy, delicious pain,
My bosom swelled and sank again.
Heart! heart!
Is it drunk with bliss or woe thou art?

Then, when I saw the drifted leaves,
I said, "Already Autumn grieves!
To sunnier skies the swallow hies:
So Love departs and Longing flies,
Far, far,
Where the Radiant and the Beauteous are."

But soon the Sun shone out anew,
And back the little flutterer flew:
He saw my grief, he saw my tears,
And sang, "Love knows no Winter years!
No! no!
While it lives its breath is Summer's glow!"

(*James Clarence Mangan*)

Justinus Kerner

1786-1862

HOME-SICKNESS

THERE calleth me ever a marvelous Horn,
"Come away! Come away!"
Is it earthly music faring astray,
Or is it air-born?
Oh, whether it be a spirit-wile
Or a forest voice,
It biddeth mine ailing heart rejoice,
Yet sorrow the while!

In the greenwood glades—o'er the garlanded bowl—
Night, Noontide, and Morn,
The summoning call of that marvelous Horn
Tones home to my soul!
In vain have I sought for it east and west,
But I darkly feel
That so soon as its music shall cease to peal
I go to my rest!

(*James Clarence Mangan*)

Ludwig Uhland

1787-1862

SPIRITS EVERYWHERE

A MANY a summer is dead and buried
Since over this flood I last was ferried;
And then, as now, the Noon lay bright
On strand, and water, and castled height.

Beside me then in this bark sat nearest
Two companions the best and dearest;
One was a gentle and thoughtful sire,
The other a youth with a soul of fire.

One, outworn by Care and Illness,
Sought the grave of the Just in stillness;
The other's shroud was the bloody rain
And thunder-smoke of the battle plain.

Yet still, when Memory's necromancy
Robes the Past in the hues of Fancy,
Medreameth I hear and see the Twain
With talk and smiles at my side again!

Even the grave is a bond of union;
Spirit and spirit best hold communion!
Seen through Faith, by the Inward Eye,
It is *after* Life they are truly nigh!

Then, ferryman, take this coin, I pray thee,
Thrice thy fare I cheerfully pay thee;
For, though thou seest them not, there stand
Anear me Two from the Phantomland!

(James Clarence Mangan)

ICHABOD! THE GLORY HAS DEPARTED

I RIDE through a dark, dark Land by night,
Where moon is none and no stars lend light,
And rueful winds are blowing,
Yet oft have I trodden this way ere now,
With summer zephyrs a-fanning my brow,
And the gold of the sunshine glowing.

I roam by a gloomy Garden-wall;
The deathstricken leaves around me fall;
And the night-blast wails its dolors;
How oft with my love I have hitherward strayed
When the roses flowered, and all I surveyed
Was radiant with Hope's own colors!

But the gold of the sunshine is shed and gone,
And the once bright roses are dead and wan,
And my love in her low grave molders,
And I ride through a dark, dark Land by night
With never a star to bless me with light,
And the Mantle of Age on my shoulders.

(*James Clarence Mangan*)

DURAND OF BLONDEN

Tow'rds the lofty walls of Balbi, lo! Durand of Blonden hies;
Thousand songs are in his bosom; Love and Pleasure light his eyes.
There, he dreams, his own true maiden, beauteous as the evening-star,
Leaning o'er her turret-lattice, waits to hear her knight's guitar.

In the lindenshaded courtyard soon Durand begins his lay.
But his eyes glance vainly upwards; there they meet no answering ray.
Flowers are blooming in the lattice, rich of odor, fair to see.
But the fairest flower of any, Lady Blanca, where is she?

Ah! while yet he chants the ditty, draws a mourner near and speaks—
"She is dead, is dead forever, whom Durand of Blonden seeks!"
And the knight replies not, breathes not: darkness gathers round his brain:
He is dead, is dead forever, and the mourners weep the twain.

In the darkened castle-chapel burn a many tapers bright:
There the lifeless maiden lies, with whitest wreaths and ribands dight.

There . . . But lo! a mighty marvel! She hath oped her eyes of blue!
All are lost in joy and wonder! Lady Blanca lives anew!

Dreams and visions flit before her, as she asks of those anear,
"Heard I not my lover singing?—Is Durand of Blonden here?"
Yes, O Lady, thou hast heard him; he has died for thy dear sake!
He could wake his trancèd mistress: him shall none for ever wake!

He is in a realm of glory, but as yet he weets not where;
He but seeks the Lady Blanca: dwells she not already there?
Till he finds her must he wander to and fro, as one bereaven,
Ever calling, "Blanca! Blanca!" through the desert halls of Heaven.

(*James Clarence Mangan*)

THE LUCK OF EDENHALL

Of Edenhall the youthful lord
Bids sound the festal trumpet's call;
He rises at the banquet board,
And cries, 'mid the drunken revelers all,
"Now bring me the Luck of Edenhall!"

The butler hears the words with pain,—
The house's oldest seneschal,—
Takes slow from its silken cloth again
The drinking-glass of crystal tall;
They call it *The Luck of Edenhall*.

Then said the lord, "This glass to praise,
Fill with red wine from Portugal!"

The graybeard with trembling hand obeys;
  A purple light shines over all;
  It beams from the Luck of Edenhall.

Then speaks the lord, and waves it light,—
  "This glass of flashing crystal tall
Gave to my sires the Fountain-Sprite;
  She wrote in it, *If this glass doth fall,*
  Farewell then, O Luck of Edenhall!

" 'T was right a goblet the fate should be
  Of the joyous race of Edenhall!
We drink deep draughts right willingly;
  And willingly ring, with merry call,
  Kling! klang! to the Luck of Edenhall!"

First rings it deep, and full, and mild,
  Like to the song of a nightingale;
Then like the roar of a torrent wild;
  Then mutters, at last, like the thunder's fall,
  The glorious Luck of Edenhall.

"For its keeper, takes a race of might
  The fragile goblet of crystal tall;
It has lasted longer than is right;
  Kling! klang!—with a harder blow than all
  Will I try the Luck of Edenhall!"

As the goblet, ringing, flies apart,
  Suddenly cracks the vaulted hall;
And through the rift the flames upstart;
  The guests in dust are scattered all
  With the breaking Luck of Edenhall!

In storms the foe, with fire and sword!
  He in the night had scaled the wall;
Slain by the sword lies the youthful lord,
  But holds in his hand the crystal tall,
  The shattered Luck of Edenhall.

On the morrow the butler gropes alone,
  The graybeard, in the desert hall;
He seeks his lord's burnt skeleton;
  He seeks in the dismal ruin's fall
  The shards of the Luck of Edenhall.

"The stone wall," saith he, "doth fall aside;
  Down must the stately columns fall;
Glass is this earth's Luck and Pride;
  In atoms shall fall this earthly ball,
  One day, like the Luck of Edenhall!"

(*H. W. Longfellow*)

THE CASTLE BY THE SEA

"Hast thou seen that lordly castle,
  That castle by the sea?
Golden and red above it
  The clouds float gorgeously.

"And fain it would stoop downward
  To the mirrored wave below;
And fain it would soar upward
  In the evening's crimson glow."

"Well have I seen that castle,
  That castle by the sea,
And the moon above it standing,
  And the mist rise solemnly."

"The winds and the waves of ocean,
  Had they a merry chime?
Didst thou hear, from those lofty chambers,
  The harp and the minstrel's rhyme?"

"The winds and the waves of ocean,
  They rested quietly;
But I heard on the gale a sound of wail,
  And tears came to mine eye."

"And sawest thou on the turrets
The king and his royal bride,
And the wave of their crimson mantles,
And the golden crown of pride?

"Led they not forth, in rapture,
A beauteous maiden there,
Resplendent as the morning sun,
Beaming with golden hair?"

"Well saw I the ancient parents,
Without the crown of pride;
They were moving slow, in weeds of woe;
No maiden was by her side!"

(H. W. Longfellow)

IN A LOVELY GARDEN WALKING

In a lovely garden walking
Two lovers went hand in hand;
Two wan, worn figures, talking
They sat in the flowery land.

On the cheek they kissed one another,
On the mouth with sweet refrain;
Fast held they each the other.
And were young and well again.

Two little bells rang shrilly—
The dream went with the hour:
She lay in the cloister stilly,
He far in the dungeon-tower!

(George MacDonald)

A LEAF

A leaf falls softly at my feet,
Sated with rain and summer heat;
What time this leaf was green and new,
I still had parents dear and true.

A leaf—how soon it fades away!
Child of the spring, the autumn's prey;
Yet has this leaf outlived, I see,
So much that was most dear to me.

(*John S. Dwight*)

THE HOSTESS' DAUGHTER

Three fellows were marching over the Rhine,
They stopped where they saw the hostess' sign.

"Dear Hostess, have you good beer and wine?
Where have you your daughter so fair and fine?"

"My beer is good, my wine is clear,
My daughter is lying upon the bier."

Now into the chamber she led the way,
There in a black coffin the maiden lay.

The first man drew the veil aside,
And full of sorrow the maid espied.

"Ah, beautiful maiden, if thou couldst live!
To thee alone my love I would give!"

The second laid back the veil again,
And turned away and wept in pain.

"Oh, why must thou lie upon the bier!
Alas, I have loved thee for many a year."

The third man lifted again the veil,
And kissed her upon the lips so pale:

"I loved thee always, I love thee to-day,
And I will love thee forever, and aye."

(*Margarete Münsterberg*)

Friedrich Rueckert

1789-1866

THE RIDE ROUND THE PARAPET

She said, "I was not born to mope at home in loneliness,"—
The Lady Eleanora von Alleyne.
She said, "I was not born to mope at home in loneliness,
When the heart is throbbing sorest there is balsam in the forest,
There is balsam in the forest for its pain,"
Said the Lady Eleanora,
Said the Lady Eleanora von Alleyne.

She doffed her silks and pearls, and donned instead her hunting-gear,
The Lady Eleanora von Alleyne.
She doffed her silks and pearls, and donned instead her hunting-gear,
And, till Summertime was over, as a huntress and a rover
Did she couch upon the mountain and the plain,
She, the Lady Eleanora,
Noble Lady Eleanora von Alleyne.

Returning home agen, she viewed with scorn the tournaments--
The Lady Eleanora von Alleyne.
Returning home agen, she viewed with scorn the tournaments;
She saw the morions cloven and the crowning chaplets woven,
And the sight awakened only the disdain
Of the Lady Eleanora,
Of the Lady Eleanora von Alleyne.

"My feeling towards Man is one of utter scornfulness,"
Said Lady Eleanora von Alleyne.
"My feeling towards Man is one of utter scornfulness,
And he that would o'ercome it, let him ride around the summit
Of my battlemented Castle by the Maine,"
Said the Lady Eleanora,
Said the Lady Eleanora von Alleyne.

So came a knight anon to ride around the parapet,
For Lady Eleanora von Alleyne.
So came a knight anon to ride around the parapet,
Man and horse were hurled together o'er the crags that beetled nether.
Said the Lady, "There, I fancy, they'll remain!"
Said the Lady Eleanora,
Queenly Lady Eleanora von Alleyne!

Then came another knight to ride around the parapet,
For Lady Eleanora von Alleyne.
Then came another knight to ride around the parapet,
Man and horse fell down, asunder, o'er the crags that beetled under.
Said the Lady, "They'll not leap the leap again!"
Said the Lady Eleanora,
Lovely Lady Eleanora von Alleyne!

Came other knights anon to ride around the parapet,
For Lady Eleanora von Alleyne.
Came other knights anon to ride around the parapet,
Till six and thirty corses of both mangled men and horses
Had been sacrificed as victims at the fane
Of the Lady Eleanora,
Stately Lady Eleanora von Alleyne!

That woeful year was by, and Ritter none came afterwards
To Lady Eleanora von Alleyne.
That woeful year was by, and Ritter none came afterwards;
The Castle's lonely basscourt looked a wild o'ergrown-with-grass court.
'Twas abandoned by the Ritters and their train
To the Lady Eleanora,
Haughty Lady Eleanora von Alleyne!

She clomb the silent wall, she gazed around her sovran-like,
The Lady Eleanora von Alleyne!
She clomb the silent wall, she gazed around her sovran-like;
"And wherefore have departed all the Brave, the lion-hearted,
Who have left me here to play the Castellain?"
Said the Lady Eleanora,
Said the Lady Eleanora von Alleyne.

"And is it fled for aye, the palmy time of Chivalry?"
Cried Lady Eleanora von Alleyne.
"And is it fled for aye, the palmy time of Chivalry?
Shame light upon the cravens! May their corpses gorge the ravens,
Since they tremble thus to wear a woman's chain!"
Said the Lady Eleanora,
Said the Lady Eleanora von Alleyne.

The story reached at Gratz the gallant Margrave Gondibert
Of Lady Eleanora von Alleyne.
The story reached at Gratz the gallant Margrave Gondibert.

Quoth he, "I trow the woman must be more or less than
human;
She is worth a little peaceable campaign,
Is the Lady Eleanora,
Is the Lady Eleanora von Alleyne!"

He trained a horse to pace round narrow stones laid
merlonwise,
For Lady Eleanora von Alleyne.
He trained a horse to pace round narrow stones laid
merlonwise,
"Good Gray! do thou thy duty, and this rocky-bosomed
beauty
Shall be taught that all the vauntings are in
vain
Of the Lady Eleanora,
Of the Lady Eleanora von Alleyne!"

He left his castle-halls, he came to Lady Eleanor's,
The Lady Eleanora von Alleyne.
He left his castle-halls, he came to Lady Eleanor's.
"O, lady, best and fairest, here am I,—and, if thou
carest,
I will gallop round the parapet amain,
Noble Lady Eleanora,
Noble Lady Eleanora von Alleyne!"

She saw him spring to horse, that gallant Margrave Gon-
dibert,
The Lady Eleanora von Alleyne.
She saw him spring to horse, that gallant Margrave Gon-
dibert.
"O, bitter, bitter sorrow! I shall weep for this to-morrow!
It were better that in battle he were slain,"
Said the Lady Eleanora,
Said the Lady Eleanora von Alleyne.

Then rode he round and round the battlemented parapet,
For Lady Eleanora von Alleyne.
Then rode he round and round the battlemented parapet:
The Lady wept and trembled, and her paly face resembled,
As she looked away, a lily wet with rain;
Hapless Lady Eleanora!
Hapless Lady Eleanora von Alleyne!

So rode he round and round the battlemented parapet,
For Lady Eleanora von Alleyne!
So rode he round and round the battlemented parapet;
"Accurst be my ambition! He but rideth to perdition,
He but rideth to peridtion without rein!"
Wept the Lady Eleanora,
Wept the Lady Eleanora von Alleyne.

Yet rode he round and round the battlemented parapet,
For Lady Eleanora von Alleyne.
Yet rode he round and round the battlemented parapet.
Meanwhile her terror shook her—yea, her breath well nigh forsook her.
Fire was burning in the bosom and the brain
Of the Lady Eleanora,
Of the Lady Eleanora von Alleyne!

Then rode he round and off the battlemented parapet
To Lady Eleanora von Alleyne.
Then rode he round and off the battlemented parapet.
"Now blest be God for ever! This is marvelous! I never
Cherished hope of laying eyes on thee agayne,"
Cried the Lady Eleanora,
Joyous Lady Eleanora von Alleyne!

"The Man of Men thou art, for thou hast fairly conquered me,
The Lady Eleanora von Alleyne!
The Man of Men thou art, for thou hast fairly conquered me.

I greet thee as my lover, and, ere many days be over,
Thou shalt wed me and be Lord of my domain,"
Said the Lady Eleanora,
Said the Lady Eleanora von Alleyne.

Then bowed the graceful knight, the gallant Margrave Gondibert,
To Lady Eleanora von Alleyne.
Then bowed that graceful knight, the gallant Margrave Gondibert,
And thus he answered coldly, "There be many who as boldly
Will adventure an achievement they disdain,
For the Lady Eleanora,
For the Lady Eleanora von Alleyne.

"Mayest bide until they come, O stately Lady Eleanor!
O, Lady Eleanora von Alleyne!
Mayest bide until they come, O stately Lady Eleanor!
And thou and they may marry, but, for me, I must not tarry,
I have won a wife already out of Spain,
Virgin Lady Eleanora,
Virgin Lady Eleanora von Alleyne!"

Thereon he rode away, the gallant Margrave Gondibert,
From Lady Eleanora von Alleyne.
Thereon he rode away, the gallant Margrave Gondibert.
And long in shame and anguish did that haughty Lady languish,
Did she languish without pity for her pain,
She the Lady Eleanora,
She the Lady Eleanora von Alleyne.

And year went after year, and still in barren maidenhood
Lived Lady Eleanora von Alleyne.

And wrinkled Eld crept on, and still her lot was maidenhood,
And, woe! her end was tragic; she was changed, at length, by magic,
To an ugly wooden image, they maintain;
She, the Lady Eleanora,
She, the Lady Eleanora von Alleyne!

And now, before the gate, in sight of all, transmogrified,
Stands Lady Eleanora von Alleyne.
Before her castle-gate, in sight of all, transmogrified,
And he that won't salute her must be fined in foaming pewter,
If a boor—but, if a burgher, in champagne,
For the Lady Eleanora,
Wooden Lady Eleanora von Alleyne!

(*James Clarence Mangan*)

BARBAROSSA.

THE ancient Barbarossa, the Kaiser Frederick old,
In subterranean castle ensorcelled state doth hold.

Dead was the Kaiser never, he lives in mystic sleep.
Long has he slumbered lonely in that enchanted keep.

The glory of the Empire with him has passed away;
But Emperor and Empire shall have one wakening-day.

The throne is all of ivory where sits the Kaiser dread,
Of porphyry the table whereon he leans his head.

Like fire not flax the beard is, that thick and long has grown
Right through the propping table that is of marble stone.

He nods as if a-dreaming, half-closed his eye of fire.
After long space of silence he beckons to a squire.

To him in sleep he mutters, "Around the castle-hill
See if the ravens flutter, and soar in circles still.

"And if the ancient ravens still circle far and near,
So must I sleep enchanted another hundred year."

(Elizabeth Craigmyle)

Wilhelm Müller

1794-1827

WHITHER?

I HEARD a brooklet gushing
From its rocky fountain near,
Down into the valley rushing,
So fresh and wondrous clear.

I know not what came o'er me,
Nor who the counsel gave;
But I must hasten downward,
All with my pilgrim-stave;

Downward, and ever farther,
And ever the brook beside;
And ever fresher murmured,
And ever clearer, the tide.

Is this the way I was going?
Whither, O brooklet, say!
Thou hast, with thy soft murmur,
Murmured my senses away.

What do I say of a murmur?
That can no murmur be;
'T is the water-nymphs, that are singing
Their roundelays under me.

Let them sing, my friend, let them murmur,
And wander merrily near;
The wheels of a mill are going
In every brooklet clear.

(H. W. Longfellow)

Heinrich Heine

1799-1856

The comfort of coming to a man of genius, who finds in verse his freest and most perfect expression, whose voyage over the deep of poetry destiny makes smooth! The magic of Heine's poetical form is incomparable; he employs this form with the most exquisite lightness and ease, and yet it has at the same time the inborn fulness, pathos, and old-world charm of all true forms of popular poetry. Thus in Heine's poetry, too, one perpetually blends the impression of French modernism and clearness with that of German sentiment and fulness.—MATTHEW ARNOLD.

PROEM

I

OUT of my own great woe
I make my little songs,
Which rustle their feathers in throngs
And beat on her heart even so.

II

They found the way, for their part,
Yet come again, and complain:
Complain, and are not fain
To say what they saw in her heart.

(*Elizabeth Barrett Browning*)

AD FINEM

THE years they come and go,
The races drop in the grave,
Yet never the love doth so
Which here in my heart I have.

Could I see thee but once, one day,
And sink down so on my knee,
And die in thy sight while I say,
"Lady, I love but thee!"

(*Elizabeth Barrett Browning*)

MEIN KIND, WIR WAREN KINDER

My child, we were two children,
Small, merry by childhood's law;
We used to creep to the henhouse,
And hide ourselves in the straw.

We crowed like cocks, and whenever
The passers near us drew—
"Cock-a-doodle!" they thought
'Twas a real cock that crew.

The boxes about our courtyard
We carpeted to our mind,
And lived there both together—
Kept house in a noble kind.

The neighbor's old cat often
Came to pay us a visit;
(We have made the very same speeches
Each with a compliment in it.)

After her health we asked,
Our care and regard to evince—
(We have made the very same speeches
To many an old cat since).

We also sat and wisely
Discoursed, as old folks do,
Complaining how all went better
In those good old times we knew;—

How love, and truth, and believing
Had left the world to itself,
And how so dear was the coffee,
And how so rare was the pelf.

The children's games are over,
The rest is over with youth—
The world, the good games, the good times,
The belief, and the love, and the truth.

(*Elizabeth Barrett Browning*)

ICH WEISS NICHT WAS SOLL ES BEDEUTEN

I canna tell what has come ower me
  That I am sae eerie and wae;
An auld-warld tale comes before me,
    It haunts me by nicht and by day.

From the cool lift the gloamin' draps dimmer,
  And the Rhine slips saftly by;
The taps of the mountains shimmer
    I' the lowe o' the sunset sky.

Up there, in a glamor entrancin',
  Sits a maiden wondrous fair;
Her gowden adornments are glancing,
  She is kaimin' her gowden hair.

As she kaims it the gowd kaim glistens,
  The while she is singin' a song
That hauds the rapt soul that listens,
  With its melody sweet and strong.

The boy, floating by in vague wonder,
  Is seized with a wild weird love;
He sees na the black rocks under,—
  He sees but the vision above.

The waters their waves are flingin'
  Ower boatie and boatman anon;
And this, with her airtful singin',
  The Waterwitch Lurley hath done.

(*Alexander Macmillan*)

THE SEA HATH ITS PEARLS

The sea hath its pearls,
  The heaven hath its stars;
But my heart, my heart,
  My heart hath its love.

Great are the sea, and the heaven;
Yet greater is my heart,
And fairer than pearls or stars
Flashes and beams my love.

Thou little, youthful maiden,
Come unto my great heart;
My heart, and the sea and the heaven
Are melting away with love!

(*H. W. Longfellow*)

SAG' MIR WER EINST DIE UHREN ERFUND

Who was it, tell me, that first of men reckon'd
Time by the hour and the minute and second?
A soulless man, without heart or light,
He sat and he mused in the long winter's night,
And counted the pittering steps of the mouse,
And the pick of the woodworm that gnawed at the house.

Kisses, now tell me, who first did discover?
It was the warm happy mouth of a lover;
He kiss'd without ceasing, he kiss'd without care,
He kiss'd his first kiss in the May-season fair;
The flowers from their emerald cradle upsprang,
The sun brightly beam'd, the birds sweetly sang.

(*Richard Garnett*)

WARUM SIND DENN DIE ROSEN SO BLASS

O dearest, canst thou tell me why
The rose should be so pale?
And why the azure violet
Should wither in the vale?

And why the lark should in the cloud
So sorrowfully sing?
And why from loveliest balsam-buds
A scent of death should spring?

And why the sun upon the mead
  So chillingly should frown?
And why the earth should, like a grave,
  Be moldering and brown?

And why it is that I myself
  So languishing should be?
And why it is, my heart of hearts,
  That thou forsakest me?

(*Richard Garnett*)

ES FÄLLT EIN STERN HERUNTER

See yonder, where a gem of night
Falls helpless from its heavenly height!
It is the brilliant star of Love
That thus forsakes the realms above.

And one by one the wind bereaves
The apple-tree of silvery leaves;
The breezes, in their reckless play,
Spurn them with dancing feet away.

And round and round swims on the pool
The tuneful swan so beautiful,
And ever singing sweet and slow
He sinks into his grave below.

It is so dreary and so dread!
The leaf is wholly witherèd,
The fallen star has flamed away,
The swan has sung his dying lay.

(*Richard Garnett*)

MIR TRAÜMTE VON EINEM KÖNIGSKIND

It was a mighty monarch's child,
Her cheek was pale, her eye was wild;
Beneath a linden's shade I press'd
The maiden to my panting breast.

"I will not have thy father's throne,
I will not have his golden crown,
I will not have his realm so wide,
I will have thee, and nought beside."

"That cannot be," the maiden said,
"Because I am already dead;
And but by night the sods above
I burst for thee, and thy dear love."

(*Richard Garnett*)

DIE ROSE, DIE LILIE, DIE TAUBE, SONNE

The rose and the lily, the moon and the dove,
Once loved I them all with a perfect love.
I love them no longer, I love alone
The Lovely, the Graceful, the Pure, the One
Who twines in one wreath all their beauty and love,
And rose is, and lily, and moon and dove.

(*Richard Garnett*)

AUF MEINER HERZLIEBSTEN ÄUGELEIN

Upon my darling's beaming eyes
I plied my rhyming trade;
Upon my darling's cherry lips
An epigram I made;
My darling has a blooming cheek,
I penn'd a song upon it;
And if she had but had a heart,
Her heart had had a sonnet.

(*Richard Garnett*)

MEIN LIEBCHEN, WIR SASSEN ZUSAMMEN

My darling, we sat together,
We two, in our frail boat;
The night was calm o'er the wide sea
Whereon we were afloat.

The Specter-Island, the lovely,
  Lay dim in the moon's mild glance;
There sounded sweetest music,
  There waved the shadowy dance.

It sounded sweeter and sweeter,
  It waved there to and fro;
But we slid past forlornly
  Upon the great sea-flow.

(*James Thomson*)

ES STEHEN UNBEWEGLICH

For many thousand ages
  The steadfast stars above
Have gazed upon each other
  With ever mournful love.

They speak a certain language,
  So beautiful, so grand,
Which none of the philologians
  Could ever understand.

But I have learned it, learned it,
  For ever, by the grace
Of studying one grammar,
  My heart's own darling's face.

(*James Thomson*)

DIE LOTOSBLUME ÄNGSTIGT

The Lotus-flower doth languish
  Beneath the sun's fierce light;
With drooping head she waiteth
  All dreamily for night.

The Moon is her true lover,
  He wakes her with his glance:
To him she unveils gladly
  Her gentle countenance.

She blooms and glows and brightens,
Intent on him above;
Exhaling, weeping, trembling
With ever-yearning love.

(*James Thomson*)

DIE WELT IST DUMM, DIE WELT IST BLIND

The world is dull, the world is blind,
And daily grows more silly!
It says of you, my lovely child,
You are not quite a lily.

The world is dull, the world is blind,
And judges in stupid fashion;
It knows not how sweet your kisses are,
And how they burn with passion.

(*James Thomson*)

DIE BLAUEN VEILCHEN DER ÄUGELEIN

The violets blue of the eyes divine,
And the rose of the cheeks as red as wine,
And the lilies white of the hands so fine,
They flourish and flourish from year to year,
And only the heart is withered and sere.

(*James Thomson*)

EIN FICHTENBAUM STEHT EINSAM

A pine-tree standeth lonely
In the North on an upland bare;
It standeth whitely shrouded
With snow, and sleepeth there.

It dreameth of a Palm Tree
Which far in the East alone,
In mournful silence standeth
On its ridge of burning stone.

(*James Thomson*)

MIR TRÄUMTE WIEDER DER ALTE TRAUM

The old dream comes again to me:
With May-night stars above,
We two sat under the linden-tree
And swore eternal love.

Again and again we plighted troth,
We chattered, and laughed, and kissed;
To make me well remember my oath
You gave me a bite in the wrist.

O darling with the eyes serene,
And with the teeth so white!
The vows were proper to the scene,
Superfluous was the bite.

(James Thomson)

MEIN HERZ, MEIN HERZ IST TRAURIG

My heart, my heart is mournful,
Yet joyously shines the May;
I stand by the linden leaning,
High on the bastion gray.

The blue town-moat thereunder
Glides peacefully along;
A boy in a boat is angling,
And whistling a careless song.

Beyond, like a well-known picture,
All small and fair, are strewed
Houses and gardens and people,
Oxen and meadows and wood.

The maidens bleach the linen,
And dance in the grass for glee;
The mill-wheel scatters diamonds,
Its far hum reaches me.

Upon the hoary tower
  A sentry-box stands low;
A youth in his coat of scarlet
  There passes to and fro.

He trifles with his musket,
  Which gleams in the sunshine red,
He shoulders and presents it,—
  I would he shot me dead!

(James Thomson)

DER MOND IST AUFGEGANGEN

THE moon is fully risen,
  And shineth o'er the sea;
And I embrace my darling,
  Our hearts are swelling free.

In the arms of the lovely maiden
  I lie alone on the strand;—
"What sounds in the breezes sighing?
  Why trembles your white hand?"

"That is no breeze's sighing,
  That is the mermaiden's song,
The singing of my sisters
  Whom the sea hath drowned so long."

(James Thomson)

SAG', WO IST DEIN SCHÖNES LIEBCHEN

"SAY, where is the maiden sweet,
  Whom you once so sweetly sung,
When the flames of mighty heat
  Filled your heart and fired your tongue?"

Ah, those flames no longer burn,
  Cold and drear the heart that fed;
And this book is but the urn
  Of the ashes of love dead.

(James Thomson)

WIE LANGSAM KRIECHET SIE DAHIN

Old Time is lame and halt,
  The snail can barely crawl:
But how should I find fault,
  Who cannot move at all?

No gleam of cheerful sun!
  No hope my life to save!
I have two rooms, the one
  I die in and the grave.

May be, I've long been dead,
  May be, a giddy train
Of phantoms fills my head,
  And haunts what was my brain.

These dear old gods or devils,
  Who see me stiff and dull,
May like to dance their revels
  In a dead Poet's skull.

Their rage of weird delight
  Is luscious pain to me:
And my bony fingers write
  What daylight must not see.

(*Lord Houghton*)

ENFANT PERDU

In Freedom's War, of "Thirty Years" and more,
  A lonely outpost have I held—in vain!
With no triumphant hope or prize in store,
  Without a thought to see my home again.

I watched both day and night: I could not sleep
  Like my well-tented comrades far behind,
Though near enough to let their snoring keep
  A friend awake, if e'er to doze inclined.

And thus, when solitude my spirits shook,
Or fear—for all but fools know fear sometimes,—
To rouse myself and them, I piped and took
A gay revenge in all my wanton rhymes.

Yes! there I stood, my musket always ready,
And when some sneaking rascal showed his head,
My eye was vigilant, my aim was steady,
And gave his brains an extra dose of lead.

But war and justice have far different laws,
And worthless acts are often done right well;
The rascals' shots were better than their cause,
And I was hit—and hit again, and fell!

That outpost was abandoned: while the one
Lies in the dust, the rest in troops depart;
Unconquered—I have done what could be done,
With sword unbroken, and with broken heart.

(*Lord Houghton*)

ZU FRAGMENTARISCH IST WELT UND LEBEN

This world and this life are so scattered, they try me,
And so to a German professor I'll hie me.
He can well put all the fragments together
Into a system convenient and terse;
While with his night-cap and dressing-robe tatters
He'll stop up the chink of the wide Universe.

(*Charles G. Leland*)

DU BIST WIE EINE BLUME

E'en as a lovely flower,
So fair, so pure thou art;
I gaze on thee, and sadness
Comes stealing o'er my heart.

My hands I fain had folded
Upon thy soft brown hair,
Praying that God may keep thee
So lovely, pure and fair.

(*Kate Freiligrath Kroeker*)

THE MESSAGE

Up, boy! arise, and saddle quick,
And mount your swiftest steed,
And to King Duncan's castle ride
O'er bush and brake with speed.

There slip into the stable soft,
Till one shall see you hide,
Then ask him: Which of Duncan's girls
Is she that is a bride?

And if he say, The dark-haired one,
Then give your mare the spur;
But if he say, The fair-haired one,
You need not hurry here.

You only need, if that's the case,
Buy me a hempen cord,
Ride slowly back and give it me,
But never speak a word.

(*Kate Freiligrath Kroeker*)

TO MY MOTHER

I've kept a haughty heart thro' grief and mirth,
And borne my head perchance a thought too high;
If even a king should look me in the eye
I would not bend it humbly to the earth:
Yet, dearest mother, such the gentle worth
Of thy benignant presence, angel-mild,
It ever hath my proudest moods beguiled,
And given to softer, humbler feelings birth.
Was it thy mind's calm penetrative power,
Thy purer mind, that secretly came o'er me,
And unto Heaven's clearer light upbore me;
Or did remembrance sting me in that hour,
With thought of words and deeds which pierced unkindly
That gentle heart, loving me still so blindly.

(*Matilda Dickson*)

IM TRAUM SAH ICH EIN MÄNNCHEN KLEIN UND PUTZIG

I saw in dream a dapper mannikin
That walked on stilts, each stride an ell or more;
While linen and a dainty dress he wore,
But it was coarse and smirched and stained within.
All inwardly was mean and poor and thin,
Yet with a stately seeming lackered o'er;
His words were full of bluster, and he bore
Himself like one well used to fight and win.
"And know'st thou who he is? Come, look and guess!"
So spake the God of Dreams, and showed me then
Within a glass a billowy multitude.
The mannikin before an altar stood,
My love beside him: both of them said, Yes!
And countless fiends laughed loud and cried
"Amen!"

(Sir Theodore Martin)

MÄDCHEN MIT DEM ROTHEN MÜNDCHEN

Lassie, with the lips sae rosy,
With the eyne sae saft and bricht,
Dear wee lassie, I keep thinkin',
Thinkin' on thee day and nicht.

Winter nichts are lang and eerie;
Oh, gin I were with thee, dear,
Arms about thee, cracking couthly,
With nae mortal by to hear!

With my kisses I would smother
Thy white hand sae jimp and sma',
And my tears for very rapture
On that wee white hand should fa'.

(Sir Theodore Martin)

ANNO 1829

I CRAVE an ampler, worthier sphere:
  I'd liefer bleed at every vein
Than stifle 'mid these hucksters here,
  These lying slaves of paltry gain.

They eat, they drink; they're every whit
  As happy as their type, the mole;
Large are their bounties—as the slit
  Through which they drop the poor man's dole.

With pipe in mouth they go their way,
  With hands in pockets; they are blest
With grand digestions: only *they*
  Are such hard morsels to digest!

The hand that's red with some dark deed,
  Some giant crime, were white as wool
Compared with these sleek saints, whose creed
  Is paying all their debts in full.

Ye clouds that sail to far-off lands,
  O waft me to what clime ye will!
To Lapland's snows, to Lybia's sands,
  To the world's end—but onward still!

Take me, O clouds! They ne'er look down;
  But (proof of a discerning mind)
One moment hung o'er Hamburg town,
  The next they leave it leagues behind.

(*Charles Stuart Calverley*)

THE AZRA

DAILY walked the fair and lovely
Sultan's daughter in the twilight,—
In the twilight by the fountain,
Where the sparkling waters plash.

Daily stood the young slave silent
In the twilight by the fountain,
Where the plashing waters sparkle,
Pale and paler every day.

Once by twilight came the princess
Up to him with rapid questions:
"I would know thy name, thy nation,
Whence thou comest, who thou art."

And the young slave said, "My name is
Mahomet, I come from Yemmen.
I am of the sons of Azra,
Men who perish if they love."

(John Hay)

DEAR MAIDEN

Dear maiden, as each morning
  Thy house I saunter by,
It glads me when at the window
  Thy winsome face I spy.

My face with a silent question
  Thy brown eyes gravely scan:
"Who art thou, and what ails thee,
  Thou strange sick-looking man?"

I am a German Poet,
  In German land well known;
When the best names are spoken,
  They also speak my own.

And what ails me, dear maiden,
  Makes many a German groan;
When the worst woes are spoken,
  They also speak my own.

(John Todhunter)

I MET BY CHANCE

I MET by chance, as I traveled,
  My Darling's whole family,
Small sister, and father, and mother,
  And gladly they greeted me.

They asked how I was most kindly,
  And said, ere I told my tale:
I was not the least bit altered,
  Except that my face was pale.

I asked after aunts and cousins,
  And many a bore of mark,
And after the little puppy
  With his wheezy little bark.

Then after my married Sweetheart
  I asked with polite *sangfroid;*
They beamed on me with the answer
  That she was then in the straw.

With cordial congratulations
  I begged them, stammeringly,
To greet her with heartiest good wishes
  A thousand times from me.

Then out burst the little sister:
  "That small fat puppy of mine
Grew big, went mad, got so horrid,
  We drowned him in the Rhine."

The young one is like her sister,
  In laughing especially;
She has the self-same eyes too
  That wrought me such misery.

(John Todhunter)

I WEPT AS I LAY DREAMING

I wept as I lay dreaming,
I dreamed thou wert laid in thy grave.
I woke, and my cheeks o'erstreaming,
My tears flowed wave on wave.

I wept as I lay sleeping,
I dreamed thou wert false to me.
I woke, and I was weeping,
And long wept bitterly.

I wept as I lay dreaming,
I dreamed thou wert mine again.
I woke, and my tears were streaming,
And ever they stream in vain.

(*John Todhunter*)

I'M BLACK AND BLUE

I'm black and blue from their worrying,
They've tortured me early and late,
Some with their love—God help me!
The others with their hate.

They've poisoned the wine on my table,
They've poisoned the bread on my plate,
Some with their love—God help me!
The others with their hate.

But she who most has worried,
And tortured and troubled—she
Has never either loved me,
Or even hated me.

(*John Todhunter*)

WE CARED FOR EACH OTHER

We cared for each other as boy and maid,
Yet gave Mrs. Grundy no cause for huffing.
At "Man and Wife" we have often played,

Yet never quarreled or came to cuffing.
We have joked together, and shouted for glee,
And kissed and fondled most tenderly.
At last, through the woods in our childish sport
Playing hide-and-seek, like sister and brother,
We hid ourselves in such clever sort
That never again we could find each other.

(*John Todhunter*)

FAREWELL

The linden blossomed, the nightingale sang,
The sun laughed out with a kindly zest,
You kissed me, and round me your arms you flung,
And clasped me close to your heaving breast.

Hoarse croaked the raven, the green leaves fell,
The sun frowned greeting with sullen smile;
Then each of us frostily said: "Farewell!"
You dropped me a curtsy in courtliest style.

(*John Todhunter*)

FRESCO-SONNETS TO CHRISTIAN SETHE

I

I laugh at each dull bore, taste's parasite
Who stares upon me with his goatish eyes;
And those raw freshmen, lean as hungry flies,
Who gape and sniff at me in petty spite.
I laugh, too, at those apes, whose learning trite
Puffs them with pride to pose as critics wise;
And at those dastard rogues, my enemies,
'Gainst poisoned weapons daring me to fight.
Yet when Joy's nosegay of delightful things
Is shattered for us by the hand of Fate,
And at our feet flung withered, without scent,
And when the heart within the breast is rent,
Rent, and stabbed through, sore-wounded, desperate—
What's left us but the laugh that shrilly rings?

2

Give me a mask, I'll join the masquerade,
  Playing the knave that charlatans I see,
  Flaunting in gaudy robes of dignity,
  May count me not a craftsman of their trade.
Come vulgar words and manners to my aid,
  In popular art I'll take my base degree,
  All those rare sparks of genius banned shall be,
  Wherewith stale rogues of late fine tricks have played.
And thus will I dance at the grand masqued-ball,
  'Mid German knights, monks, kings in motley crew,
  Capped to by Harlequin, known to but few,
With their blunt swords of lath cudgelled by all.
  That is their sport. Should I unmask, beware!
  I should dumbfounder every jail-bird there.

(*John Todhunter*)

THE VOYAGE

I STOOD and leant upon the mast
  And counted every wave.
Farewell, my beautiful Fatherland!
  Fast sails my bark so brave!

My fair Love's house, I passed it by,
  The window-panes were glaring;
I gazed my eyes out of my head,
  But none made sign of caring.

O tears, come not into mine eyes,
  Lest ye should dim their seeing!
My sick heart, break not in my breast
  With woe too vast for being!

(*John Todhunter*)

THE WINDOW-GLANCE

PALE Heinrich he came sauntering by,
  Fair Hedwig leaned from her garret.
"God keep me safe!" she said with a sigh,
  "Yon lad looks pale as a spirit!"

The lad his languishing eyes from below
  Uplifted to Hedwig's garret.
They filled fair Hedwig's with lovers' woe,
  She too grew pale as a spirit.

Fair Hedwig, hurt with love's secret harms,
  Looked daily down from her garret.
But soon she lay nightly in Heinrich's arms,
  When wanders each churchyard spirit.

(John Todhunter)

FROM "DIE HEIMKEHR"

1

TELL me where thy lovely love is,
Whom thou once did sing so sweetly,
When the fairy flames enshrouded
Thee, and held thy heart completely.

All the flames are dead and sped now
And my heart is cold and sere;
Behold this book the urn of ashes,
'Tis my true love's sepulchre.

2

The mutilated choir boys
When I begin to sing
Complain about the awful noise
And call my voice too thick a thing.

When light their voices lift them up,
Bright notes against the ear,
Through trills and runs like crystal,
Ring delicate and clear.

They sing of Love that's grown desirous,
Of Love, and joy that is Love's inmost part,
And all the ladies swim through tears
Toward such a work of art.

3

This delightful young man
Should not lack for honorers,
He propitiates me with oysters,
With Rhine wine and liqueurs.

How his coat and pants adorn him!
Yet his ties are more adorning,
In these he daily comes to ask me:
"Are you feeling well this morning?"

He speaks of my extended fame,
My wit, charm, definitions,
And is diligent to serve me,
Is detailed in his provisions.

In evening company he sets his face
In most spiritu*el* positions,
And declaims before the ladies
My *god-like* compositions.

O what comfort is it for me
To find him such, when the days bring
No comfort, at my time of life when
All good things go vanishing.

(*Ezra Pound*)

A MAIDEN LIES IN HER CHAMBER

A MAIDEN lies in her chamber
  Lit by a trembling moon;
Outside there rises and echoes
  A waltz's giddy tune.

"I wonder who breaks my slumber;
  I'll go to the window and see—"
And lo, a skeleton stands there;
  He fiddles and sings with glee:

"A dance you swore to give me,
And you have broken your vow;
To-night there's a ball in the churchyard;
Come out and dance with me now!"

The maid, as though moved by magic,
Obeys, and she leaves the house;
The skeleton, fiddling and singing,
Goes on with its wild carouse.

It fiddles and leaps and dances
And rattles its bones to the tune;
Its skull keeps nodding and nodding
Crazily under the moon.

(Louis Untermeyer)

OH LOVELY FISHERMAIDEN

Oh lovely fishermaiden,
Come, bring your boat to land;
And we will sit together
And whisper, hand in hand.

Oh rest upon my bosom,
And fear no harm from me.
You give your body daily,
Unfearing to the sea. . . .

My heart is like the ocean
With storm and ebb and flow—
And many a pearly treasure
Burns in the depths below.

(Louis Untermeyer)

TWILIGHT

We sat at the hut of the fisher
And idly watched the sea,
While in the hush of evening
The mists rose silently.

The yellow lights in the lighthouse
  Shone like a burnished bell,
And in the hazy distance
  One ship still rose and fell.

We spoke of storm and shipwreck,
  Of sailors and their life.
Pulled between sky and water,
  Fierce joy and lusty strife.

We gossiped of distant places,
  Of North and South we spoke,
Of wild and curious customs,
  And wild and curious folk.

Of how the Ganges sparkles;
  Of great exotic trees;
Of folk who worship the lotus
  Silently, on their knees.

Of Lapland; its slovenly people,
  Flat-headed, broad-featured and small,
That do little else but bake fishes
  And squat by the fire and squall. . . .

The girls all listened breathless;
  Then silence, like a spell . . .
The ship could be seen no longer—
  Swiftly the darkness fell.

(Louis Untermeyer)

THE COFFIN

THE songs, so old and bitter,
  The dreams so wild and drear,
Let's bury them together—
  What ho! A coffin here!

I have so much to bury
  It never will be done,
Unless the coffin's larger
  Than Heidelberg's great Tun.

And bring a bier to match it
Of stoutest oaks and pines;
It must be even longer
Than the long bridge at Mainz.

And also bring twelve giants
Of mightier brawn and bone
Than Christopher, the sainted,
Whose shrine is in Cologne.

And in the great sea sink it
Beneath the proudest wave;
For such a mighty coffin
Should have a mighty grave. . .

You know what makes my coffin
So great, so hard to bear?
It holds my love within it,
And my too heavy care.

(Louis Untermeyer)

THE STORM

A HOWLING storm is brewing,
The wind and rain are wild;
And what can my love be doing,
That pale and frightened child?

There at the window dreaming,
I see her, worn and white;
With eyes no longer beaming,
She stares into the night.

(Louis Untermeyer)

MY SONGS ARE POISONED

MY songs, they say, are poisoned.
How else, love, could it be?
Thou hast, with deadly magic,
Poured poison into me.

My songs, they say, are poisoned.
  How else then could it be?
I carry a thousand serpents
  And, love, among them—thee!

(*Louis Untermeyer*)

WHEN TWO ARE PARTED

When two who love are parted,
  They talk, as friend to friend,
Clasp hands and weep a little,
  And sigh without an end.

We did not weep, my darling,
  Not sigh "Why must this be . . ."
The tears, the sighs, the anguish
  Came later—and to me.

(*Louis Untermeyer*)

I LOVE BUT THEE

Whene'er I look into your eyes
Then all my grief and sorrow flies;
And when I kiss your mouth, oh then
I am made well and strong again.

And when I lean upon your breast
My soul is soothed with godlike rest;
But when you swear, "I love but thee!"
Then I must weep—and bitterly.

(*Louis Untermeyer*)

WHEN YOUNG HEARTS BREAK

When young hearts break with passion
  The stars break into laughter,
They laugh and, in their fashion,
  Gossip a long time after:

"Poor souls, those mortals languish
  With Love; 'tis all they cherish.
It pays them back with anguish
  And pain until they perish.

"We never can discover
  This Love, so brief and breathless,
So fatal to each lover—
  And hence we stars are deathless."

(Louis Untermeyer)

FROM THE NORTH SEA

A Night by the Sea

Starless and chill is the night;
The sea yawns wide,
And stretched on the sea, flat on his paunch
Lies the shapeless form of the North-Wind
Who snivels and groans in stealthy mumblings,
A peevish old grumbler in garrulous humor,
Babbling down to the waves.
And he tells them wild, lawless stories,
Giant tales of gloom and murder,
Ancient sagas from Norway,
And again, with wide-clanging laughter he bellows
The witching spells of the Edda
And crafty rime-runes,
So darkly strong and so potent with magic
That the snowy sea-children
Leap up the waves with shouting,
Hissing in wild joy.

But meanwhile across the flat sea-beach
Over the clinging, spray-soaked sand
Strideth a stranger, whose heart within him
Is far more wild than winds and waters.
Where'er he steps
Sparks are scattered and sea-conches crackle;
And he wraps him close in his gloomy mantle
And presses on through the wind-driven night,
Safely led by the tiny candle,
Enticing and sweet, that glimmers
From a lonely fisher cottage.

Father and brother are out at sea,
And lone as a mother's soul she lives
In the cottage, the fisher-maiden,
The wondrous lovely fisher-maiden.
And by the fireside
Sits harkening to the kettle
Purr in sweet and secret surmise,
And heaps the crackling boughs on the fire,
And blows on it
Till the flapping flames of crimson
Mirrored are in wizard beauty
On her face, set a-glowing,
On her white and tender shoulders
That peer so piteously
From her coarse and faded costume,
And on the heedful little hand
Which more closely binds the under-garment
Round her slender hips.

Then suddenly the door springs wide,
And he enters there, the nocturnal stranger;
Sure of love, his eyes he resteth
On the pale and slender maiden
Who shrinks before his gaze
Like a frail, terrified lily;
And he throws to the ground his mantle
And laughs and speaks:

"Behold, my child, I keep our troth.
I am come, and with me come
The ancient years when the gods from the heavens
To the daughters of mortals descended
And the daughters of mortals embraced them
And with them engendered
Kingly races, the scepter-carriers,
And heroes, wonders o' the world . . .
Don't puzzle, my child, any further
About my divinity,
But I beg of you, mix me some tea with rum;

For outside 'twas cold,—
Before such a night-wind
Even we gods might freeze, though eternal,
And easily catch the godliest sneezings,
A cough like the gods without ending."

(*Howard Mumford Jones*)

Evening Twilight

On the wan sea-strand
Lonely I lay, and in sorrowful brooding.
The sun sank lower and lower, and flung
His red rays, glowing, on the water,
And I watched the far white billows,
In the grip of the flood,
Foaming and roaring, nigher and nigher—
Strange medley of sounds! a whispering and wailing,
A laughing and murmuring, sobbing and sighing,
Low voices, the while, a strange lullaby singing.
Methought I heard long-forgotten legends,
World-old adorable folk-tales,
That long since in boyhood
From neighbors' children I learnt;
When, of a summer evening,
On the steps of stone by the house-door,
We squatted for quiet story-telling,
With small hearts eagerly listening
And young eyes keen for wonders;
While the fair grown-up maidens
Sat, 'mid balm-breathing pots of flowers,
At a window over the way there,
With rosy faces,
Smiling and lit by the moon.

(*John Todhunter*)

Epilog

Like the ears of wheat in a wheat-field growing,
So a thousand thoughts spring and tremble
In the minds of men.

But the tender fancies of love
Are like the happy colors that leap among them;
Red and blue flowers.

Red and blue flowers!
The sullen reaper destroys you as worthless;
Block-headed fools will scornfully thresh you;
Even the penniless wayfarer
Who is charmed and cheered by your faces,
Shakes his poor head,
And calls you pretty weeds!
But the young girl from the village,
Twining her garland,
Honors and gathers you.
And with you she brightens her lovely tresses.
And thus adorned, she hurries to the dancing,
Where fiddles and flutes are sweetly sounding;
Or runs to the sheltering beech-tree,
Where the voice of her lover sounds even sweeter
Than fiddles and flutes.

(*Louis Untermeyer*)

Eduard Möricke

1804-1875

BEAUTY ROHTRAUT

What is the name of King Ringang's daughter?
  Rohtraut, Beauty Rohtraut!
And what does she do the livelong day,
Since she dare not knit and spin alway?
O hunting and fishing is ever her play!
And, heigh! that her huntsman I might be!
I'd hunt and fish right merrily!
    Be silent, heart!

And it chanced that, after this some time,
  Rohtraut, Beauty Rohtraut!
The boy in the Castle has gained access,
And a horse he has got and a huntsman's dress,

To hunt and to fish with the merry Princess;
And, O! that a king's son I might be!
Beauty Rohtraut I love so tenderly.
Hush! hush! my heart.

Under a gray old oak they sat,
Beauty, Beauty Rohtraut!
She laughs: "Why look you so slyly at me?
If you have heart enough, come, kiss me."
Cried the breathless boy, "Kiss thee?"
But he thinks kind fortune has favored my youth;
And thrice he has kissed Beauty Rohtraut's mouth.
Down! down! mad heart.

Then slowly and silently they rode home,—
Rohtraut, Beauty Rohtraut!
The boy was lost in his delight:
"And, wert thou Empress this very night,
I would not heed or feel the blight;
Ye thousand leaves of the wild wood wist
How Beauty Rohtraut's mouth I kiss'd.
Hush! hush! wild heart."

(George Meredith)

Arthur Fitger

1840-1909

EVENING PRAYER

"DAUGHTER, how the door is creaking,
In the dead of night it shakes!"—
Mother o' mine, the wind is shrieking,
Never mind the noise it makes.
On the window beats the rain.
Lie you still,
And I will
Read the evening prayers again.

Ye daughters of Jerusalem, give heed!
Hark to my friend's feet coming o'er the mead.
I hear his feet o'er the dark meadow tripping,
With nightly dew his locks are dripping.

"Daughter, some one's in the house!
  To the stairs I hear him creeping."—
Mother, it's the little mouse
  Nibbling, or the cricket cheeping.
On the window beats the rain.
  Lie you still,
  And I will
Read the evening prayers again.

Ye daughters of Jerusalem, my friend
Comes from the orchard where the blue grapes bend,
From where the brown fig is to purple grown,
He comes, seeks, longs to be with me alone.

"Daughter, are there ghosts that haunt thee?
  Soft feet in thy room I hear."—
Mother, ghosts will never daunt me:
  There will be an angel near.
On the window beats the rain.
  Lie you still,
  And I will
Read the evening prayers again.

O friend, beloved, loveliest and best,
My heart beats loud and louder in my breast;
All eyes now sleep, there shines no candle-ray:
Watchmen of Zion, ye will not betray.

(*Jethro Bithell*)

Friedrich Wilhelm Nietzsche

1844-1900

STAR MORALS

Unto a heavenly course decreed,
Star of the darkness take no heed.

Roll onward through this time and range!
Its woe to thee be far and strange!

To utmost worlds thy light secure:
No pity shall thy soul endure!

But one command is thine: be pure!

(Ludwig Lewisohn)

THE SOLITARY

Harsh cry the crows
And townward take their whirring flight;
Soon comes the snows—
Happy who has a home this night.

With glances dead
Thou gazest backward as of old!
Why hadst thou fled
Unto the world from winter's cold?

The world—a gate
To freezing deserts dumb and bare!
Who lost what late
Thou lost is homeless everywhere.

Pale one, to bleak
And wintry pilgrimages driven,
Smoke-like to seek
The ever colder heights of heaven.

Soar, bird, fling wide
That song of birds in deserts born!
O madman, hide
Thy bleeding heart in ice and scorn.

Harsh cry the crows
And townward take their whirring flight;
Soon comes the snows—
Woe unto him who has no home this night.

(Ludwig Lewisohn)

Detlev von Liliencron

1844-1909

WHO KNOWS WHERE

Battle of Kolin June 18, 1757

On blood, smoke, rain and the dead,
On trampled grass unharvested
The sun poured light.
Dark fell. The battle's rage was o'er,
And many a one came home no more
From Kolin's fight.

A lad, half boy, had shared the fray,
Had first heard bullets whiz that day.
He had to go . . .
And though he swung his flag on high,
Fate touched him, it was his to die,
He had to go . . .

Near him there lay a pious book,
Which still the youngster bore and took
With sword and cup.
A grenadier from Bevern found
The small, stained volume on the ground
And picked it up.

And swiftly to the father brought
This last farewell with silence fraught
And with despair.
Then wrote therein the trembling hand:
"Kolin. My son hid in the sand,
Who knows where!"

And he who here has sung this song,
And he who reads it, both are strong
Of life and fair.
But once art thou and once am I
Hid in the sand eternally,
Who knows where!

(Ludwig Lewisohn)

AFTER THE HUNT

TIRED and thirsty, weary of the way,
I seek the forest-inn that is my own;
Rifle and cap upon a bench I lay,
Beside the water pail my dog lies prone.
The inn's young mistress in the dying day
Stands still as one from whom all joy has flown;
Then she smiles shyly and half turns away—
The guests' departure leaves us soon alone.

(Ludwig Lewisohn)

AUTUMN

A FLOCK of crows high from the Northland flies,
On their dark wings the evening sunshine plays.
Below the Ursulines' calm convent lies
And an old man dreams in its garden ways.
From the cool chapel float the harmonies
Upward in rapture deep of peace and grace
And fall and fade . . . All sound of living dies
While the old man unto Our Lady prays.

(Ludwig Lewisohn)

Gustav Falke

1853-1916

STRAND-THISTLE

THE lady walked by the ocean strand
  O'er the white sand at the fall of day,
  Till a shy red flower stood in her way.
She plucked it, and cast it out of her hand.

She bent down to the gray, forlorn,
  Tall thistle that beside it stood.
  But this was clad in hardihood,
And through her frail hand drove its thorn.

But she brake it, and walked, and sang a lay,
  With tired mouth a tired lay she sang,
  Over the darkening bay it rang,
And on the salt wind died away.

(Jethro Bithell)

GOD'S HARP

THE wind, stirring in the dark foliage, brings
Songs to me of the wakeful nightingale;
At intervals a stranger music rings.
Whence are these voices that now light,
Now deeply echo from the night
And now of their own beauty fail?

The apple bough of white
That at my open window rocks and sways,
Against the pane its dewy blossom lays,
Shines magically in the blanchèd light,
A sabbath radiance covers all the ways;
My vision waxes vast and wide:

Oh, there arises now a solemn tide
For those who live in dreams, the delicate
Souls that to every subtle tone vibrate
Which from God's harp rings forth and prophesies
That he forever
His busy hand in ancient music plies,
And will not end the song of His delight.

Thus ends it never—
Hark, what a tone of love passed through the night.

(*Ludwig Lewisohn*)

Peter Hille

1854-1904

THE MAIDEN

AWKWARD was she yesterday,
Pitiful, and poor, and gray,
Nothing to be seen in her.
Must be on her guard to-day,
As when blossoms snow in May,
Lest they all should blow away.

As there were a Queen in her,
As though God had, unawares,
Planted her in a garden of cares,
Blossoms delicate she bears.
There is courage keen in her,
Though upon the ground she stares

Because she is in blossoms rich,
Because the wind breaks blossoms which
Do not blush for dreams that sinned,
Are not full of innocence,
Caution, shyness, and pretense—
O foolish wind!

(Jethro Bithell)

BEAUTY

Sappho to Chloe

Friend!
Poor, foolish blossom!
How thou shinest for him who
Dishevels thee, and withers thee.

Lo, such a man.
The thrall he is!
His doings loud and running.
Could we be so?
Only a woman walks.
She is, and beauty tarries thence,
Red little ears of curls are opened.

Scents my blood to thee as thine to me?
No, Chloe.
It scenteth not.
Beauty thou knowest not, nor beauty's longing,
The seeking wind of the May of flowers,
Thou knowest it not.

Without a soul through me thou roamest.
Thou glowest hence to other haunts than I.

O fie for shame!
Thou my degenerated one!
How else could I feel thee, thou truant from me!

List: fortunate like to the gods seemeth the man to me,
Who face to face with thee may sit quite near,
And listen into him thy chatter of twittering lips,
That sets the soul on fire.

(*Jethro Bithell*)

Richard Dehmel

1863-1920

MY DRINKING SONG

Yet one more hour, then comes the night;
Drink till the very soul o'erflows.
Glasses, ring!
Look how the sun in wild delight
Drowns in its crimson blood and glows.
Drink and sing:
Sing me the song of living and of dying.
Lo, upon earth the withered vines are lying.
But grapes they gave us ere the fall went flying.
Ho!

Yet one more hour, then comes the night;
In the pale river glints and spins
Somber glow.
'Tis the red moon's awakened light
That peers across the hill and grins;
Sun, oho!
Sing me the song of life, the song of death
Open your lips! Sinful resounds our mood
Cling, clang, sinful as mortal breath—
To drink and laugh one must have flesh and blood.

Yet one more hour, then comes the night;
A bridge grows over the river wide.
Hail! O hail!

It creaks beneath a horseman's might!
Saw ye yon sable horseman ride?
Hail! Thrice hail!
The song of death and life we still are singing!
Crash! A new glass! For upward we go winging
Above this life to which our lives are clinging!
Hail!

(Ludwig Lewisohn)

BEFORE THE STORM

THE sky grew darker with each minute
Outside my room, I felt within it
The clouds, disconsolate and gray.
The ash-tree yonder moved its crown
With heavy creaking up and down,
The dead leaves whirled across the way.

Then ticked, through the close room, unhurried,
As in still vaults where men are buried
The woodworm gnaws, and ticks my watch.
And through the open door close by,
Wailed the piano, thin and shy,
Beneath her touch.

Slate-like upon us weighed the heaven,
Her playing grew more sorrow-riven,
I saw her form.
Sharp gusts upon the ash-tree beat,
The air, aflame with dust and heat,
Sighed for the storm.

Pale through the walls the sounds came sobbing,
Her blind, tear-wasted hands passed throbbing
Across the keys.
Crouching she sang that song of May
That once had sung my heart away,
She panted lest the song should cease.

In the dull clouds no shadow shivered,
The aching music moaned and quivered
Like dull knives in me, stroke on stroke—
And in that song of love was blent
Two children's voices' loud lament—
Then first the lightning broke.

(*Ludwig Lewisohn*)

VIGIL

THE crimson roses burn and glow,
Softly the dark leaves stir and shake,
And I am in the grass awake,
Oh, wert thou here . . .
For soon the mid of night will break!

Into the lake the moonbeams flow,
The garden-gate hides her from view,
The moveless willows stand arow,
My burning forehead seeks the dew;
Oh, I have never loved thee so!

Oh, I have never so deeply known
As often as our close embrace
Made each the other, why thy face
Grew pallid and thy heart made moan
When all my being sought thy grace.

And now—oh, hadst thou seen how there
Two little fire-flies crept alow,
I never more from thee will fare,
Oh, wert thou here,
Or still the crimson roses glow.

(*Ludwig Lewisohn*)

HARVEST SONG

A FIELD of golden wheat there grows,
Even to the world's end it goes.
Grind, O mill, keep grinding!

The wind falters in all the land,
The mills on the horizon stand.
Grind, O mill, keep grinding!

The evening sky turns somber red;
Many poor people cry for bread.
Grind, O mill, keep grinding!

The night's womb holds a storm within;
To-morrow shall the task begin.
Grind, O mill, keep grinding!

The storm shall sweep the fields of earth
Until no man cries out for dearth!
Grind, O mill, keep grinding!

(Ludwig Lewisohn)

THE SILENT TOWN

A TOWN lies in the valley,
A pale day fades and dies;
And it will not be long before
Neither moon nor starlight,
Night only fills the skies.

From all the mountain ridges
Creeps mist, and swathes the town;
No farm, no house, no wet red roof
Can pierce the thickly woven woof,
And scarce even spires and bridges.

But as the wanderer shudders,
Deep down a streak of light rejoices
His heart; and, through the smoke and haze,
Children's voices
Begin a gentle hymn of praise.

(Jethro Bithell)

TO ——?

I HAVE baptized thee Withy, because of thy slender limbs,
And since thou art the rod for God to chastise me withal,
Yea, and because a yearning in thy posture overbrims
Even as in April days sways in the willows tall.

I know thee not—but in the tempest shock,
Some day, I shall hear thee at my door,
And I shall straightway open to thy knock,
Upon thy tameless breasts my tameless breast to lock
To beat with equal beat for evermore.

For I know thee—the eyes like buds are glowing,
And thou wouldst flower, flower, flower!
And thy young ideas scatter like the shower
From shrubs with cataracts bespattered;
And thou wert fain as I do to defy God's tempests
 blowing
Or—be shattered!

(*Jethro Bithell*)

A TRYSTING

So was it even then. So soundlessly
 Over the land the clouded air hung hot,
And underneath the weeping beech's roof
 Were tangled, where is hedged the garden-plot,
The blossom-vapors of the elder-tree;
 My sultry hand she fondled, speaking not,
Voiceless with joy.

There was an odor of graves. . . . No guilt is mine!
 Thou pale light up above there in the sky,
Why stand'st thou like a ghost pent in his shroud!
 Why wilt thou pore upon me like God's eye?
Monitor image of the spirit bowed
 Be quenched! I broke her not! She willed to die
Why should an alien anguish torture me. . . .

The land grows gray. And every willow-trunk
  Like smoke stands in the fog's deep starless sea.
Upon the corn the heavy sky seems sunk.
  Motionless cling the wet leaves to the tree,
As though they all had poison drunk.
  So silent now lies she.
I wish that I were dead.

(Jethro Bithell)

THE LABORER

We have a bed, and a baby too,
My wife!
We have work besides, we have work for two,
And we have the sun, and the wind, and the rain,
And we only need one little thing more,
To be as free as the birds that soar:
Only time.

When we go through the fields on the Sunday morn,
My child,
And far and away o'er the bending corn,
We see the swarming swallows flash,
Then we only need a bit of a dress,
To have the birds' bright loveliness:
Only time.

The storm is gathering black as jet,
Feel the poor.
Only a little eternity yet;
We need nothing else, my wife, my child,
Except all things through us that thrive,
To be bold as the birds through the air that drive:
Only time!

(Jethro Bithell)

VOICE IN DARKNESS

There's moaning somewhere in the dark.
I want to know what it may be.
The wind is angry with the night—

Yet the wind's moan sounds not so near.
The wind will always moan at night.
'Tis in my ear my blood that moans—
My blood, forsooth.

Yet not so strangely moans my blood.
My blood is tranquil like the night.
I think a heart must moan somewhere.

(*Margarete Münsterberg*)

Cäsar Flaischlen

1864-1920

MOST QUIETLY AT TIMES

Most quietly at times and like a dream
In thee re-echoes a far distant song . . .
Thou knowest not whence suddenly it came,
Thou knowest not what it would have of thee . . .
And like a dream most peacefully and still
It dies in distant music, even as it came . . .

As suddenly as in the crowded street,
And in the very winter's frozen heart,
An odor of roses will around thee breathe,
Or as a picture unawares will rise
From far-forgotten happy childhood's days,
And gaze at thee with eyes inquisitive . . .

Most quietly, and lightly as a dream . . .
Thou knowest not whence suddenly it came,
Thou knowest not what it would have of thee,
And like a dream most peacefully and still
It pales and passes, fading when it came.

(*Jethro Bithell*)

Otto Julius Bierbaum

1865-1910

KINDLY VISION

Not in sleep I saw it, but in daylight,
Clear and beautiful by day before me:
Saw a meadow overgrown with daisies,
Round a cottage white in green embowered;
Statues of the gods gleam in the arbor.
And the lady that I walk with loves me,
With a quiet spirit in the coolness
And the peacefulness of this white dwelling,
Full of beauty waiting till we enter.

(Jethro Bithell)

BLACKSMITH PAIN

Pain is a blacksmith,
Hard is his hammer;
With flying flames
His hearth is hot;
A straining storm
Of forces ferocious
Blows his bellows.
He hammers hearts
And tinkers them,
With blows tremendous,
Till hard they hold.—
Well, well forges Pain.—
No storm destroys,
No frost consumes,
No rust corrodes,
What Pain has forged.

(Jethro Bithell)

JEANNETTE

I

What's my sweetheart?—A laundress is she.
Where does she live?—Down by the river.

Where the Isar roars, and the bridge stands high,
And the fluttering shirts hang out to dry:
There lives my pleasure-giver.

In the little cot with the garden plot,
And the shutters green a-showing,
There at the ironing-board she stands,
With the smoothing-iron in her clever hands:
And how her cheeks are glowing!

There she stands in a lily-white blouse
Figured with many a blossom;
Nor corset fastens the soft wavy billows
That bob underneath it, the easiest of pillows,
The swelling rounds of her bosom.

II

A bed, a cupboard, a table, a bench,
And in the midst a strapping wench,
My dolly, my jolly Jeannette.
Her eyes are brown, and so is her hair,
With its curls here, there, and everywhere,
And of cherry-ripe lips she's a swelling pair,
Jeannette! Jeannette!

There's ivy growing right up to the eaves,
And love at the lattice peeps through the leaves,
My dolly, my jolly Jeannette.
Bang goes the door, on my neck she springs,
We are alone, and the old wind sings
The song of a couple of happy things.
Jeannette! Jeannette!

(*Jethro Bithell*)

OFT IN THE SILENT NIGHT

Oft in the silent night
When faint our breathing grows
And sickle-bright the moon
In the dark heaven glows,

When all is quieted
And no desires command,
Then my soul leadeth me
Into my childhood's land.

Then I see how infirm
My little feet did go,
And see my childish eye
And my small hands also,

And hear how then my mouth
Spoke ever pure and plain,
And sink my head and of
My life take thought again:

Didst thou, didst thou always
Tread paths as white and sweet
As thou didst walk upon
With little childish feet?

Hast thou, hast thou always
Spoken as clear and true
As long ago thy voice
Faltering was wont to do?

And hast thou ever looked
So straight into the face
Of the great sun as once
With childhood's fearless grace?

My glance, O Moon, I lift
Unto thy splendor white;
Deep, deep am I made sad
Oft in the silent night.

(*Ludwig Lewisohn*)

Stefan George

1868–1933

STANZAS CONCERNING LOVE

I

A NOVICE when I came beneath thy gaze,
There was no wonder in mine eyes before
And no desire till I beheld thy grace.
Be thou benign to young hands folded where
I pray to be thy servant evermore.
And with long-suffering compassion spare
The feet still faltering on alien ways.

II

Now that my lips are very still and burn
Do I behold whither have gone my feet:
Into a splendid realm for others meet.
Ah, yet perchance it was the hour to turn,
When thro' the lofty gateway seemed to shine
The eyes whose light my bended knees entreat
Seeking my own and giving me a sign.

III

Dead forever is my world of old.
Sense and spirit for thy presence reaches,
Interchange of unimagined speeches,
Grace, withdrawal, service manifold.
Only thee would I in dreams behold,
And I mourn the visions fugitive
With the golden dark wherein they live,
When the cloudless morning rises cold.

(*Ludwig Lewisohn*)

INVOCATION AND PRELUDE

I

GRANT me the great and solemn breath withdrawn,
The glow that with eternal youth is gifted,
Wherewith the wings of childhood once uplifted
Soared in the sacrificial smoke of dawn.

I would not live but in thy breath divine.
Enclose me wholly in thy sanctuary!
One crumb from thy rich table let me carry!
Thus from dark caves rises this prayer of mine.

The Angel spoke: These stormy cries I hear
Speak strange desires among themselves divided.
The granting of such precious gifts unguided
Is not my office, and my grace austere

By zeal or force cannot commanded be!
But I in prayer my arms beside him bending,
Heard all my wakeful yearning's voice ascending:
I loose thee not except thou blessest me.

II

In my life, too, were angry days and evil
And music that rang dissonant and shrill.
Now a kind spirit holds the balance level
And all my deeds are at an Angel's will.

Though often still my faltering soul be broken
Even unto sobbing in a joyless world,
Swift at the anchorage the words are spoken:
To fairer shorelands be thy sails unfurled.

And when storm-driven upon farthest ocean
'Twixt death and madness I am all unmanned,
He grasps the rudder and the wild commotion
Of powers tumultuous hearkens his command.

The embattled waves yield them unto his chiding.
From the pure azure clouds and shadows cease.
On foamless waters soon thy feet are gliding
To blessed islands and a port of peace.

(Ludwig Lewisohn)

RAPTURE

I

I FEEL a breath from other planets blowing
And pallid through the darkness wax the faces
That even now so kind and near were glowing.

Gray and more gray are tree and path and meadow
So that I scarcely know familiar places,
And thou, dear summoner of my pain, bright shadow,

Too far in deeper glow dissolved hast floated
To deem me, after this wild tumult's mazes,
To any earthly love or awe devoted.

Melted I am in music, circling, driven,
In boundless gratitude and nameless praises
Will and desireless to the eternal given.

II

A tempest wafts me and I am elated
In passionate madness of the women grieving
Who deep in dust their prayers have consecrated.

Then I behold the milky mists dislimning,
A noble clearness filled with sunshine leaving
Wherein the farthest mountain peaks are swimming.

The ground beneath me, white and soft, is shaken . . .
By monstrous chasms I mount high and higher
Above the last cloud's silver edge to waken,

In seas of crystal radiance to dip under—
I am a spark of the eternal fire,
And of the eternal voice I am the thunder!

(*Ludwig Lewisohn*)

THE LORD OF THE ISLE

Fishermen will relate that in the South
Upon an island rich in spice and oil
And precious stones that glitter in the sand,
There dwelt a bird who, standing upon earth,
Could tear the crowns of lofty trees asunder
With his strong beak; who, lifting up his wings
Dyed as with ichor of the Tyrian snail,
Unto his low and heavy flight, had been
A shadow in seeming, like a somber cloud.
By day he vanished in the olive groves,
But evening ever brought him to the shore
Where in the coolness of the salt sea-breeze
He raised up his sweet voice and dolphins came,
Who are the friends of song, across the sea
With golden feathers filled and golden sparks.
Thus lived he since the making of the world
And only ship-wrecked sailors saw his form.
But when for the first time the snowy sails
Of man, guided by fortunate winds had turned
Unto his island—to its topmost hill
He rose surveying that beloved place,
And spreading out his mighty pinions
Departed with a muffled cry of pain.

(*Ludwig Lewisohn*)

FROM DAS JAHR DER SEELE

No way too long—no path too steep
Thou by my side my step to keep.
The wide abyss, sepulchral air
Speak of atonement everywhere.

And thus the sober ashen plain
We traverse songless—yet no stain
We know of anger or of rue—
No more we sue—nor I nor you.

I timid spy with tearful eye
If He who richly tunes be nigh
Whom harmony alone doth suit
Who gladly plays our golden lute.

(*Daisy Broicher*)

Peter Baum

1869–1916

HORROR

This is a fearful thing to bear,
That oft to me it seems
I have thine eyes and hair.
Then, helpless, my hands supplicate,
Even as thine own,
And my lips curse me in hate,
And moan.

Thou comest over me so every evening late.

Twin carrion birds
Then o'er the churchyard fly.

(*Jethro Bithell*)

PSALMS OF LOVE

I

Thy nights moan into my days,
Through my dreams courses the blood of thy feet.
O I will drink thy tears away,
I will bear thee up under the crown of my leaves.

The crown of my leaves is cool and full of peace,
Bathed high in waters deep.
Down upon us shall drip the depths of the sky,
From seas eternal through the holy crown of leaves.

Slumber deep in my arms!
My eyes are steel-hard angels watching
Over thy peace.

II

Thy eyes with gloom are gleaming,
And a spinning weeping
Of thy raven hair
Over the linen.

O thy pale face,
And how thy slender fingers
Over the pillows are creeping:—
Touching stammering
Of a sprouting song,
That fain would flower.

My soul with thee is seeking.

III

When the roses' wonder open at morn,
Fain would I come to thee!
Bring cool dew to thy brow,
And laughter to thy lips.

In my nights thy loneliness affrights me;
Nestle deep in the pinions of my soul!
Darkly they rustle over the seas,
To find a way to thee.

IV

When the night goes hence,
Let us from goblets dark
Reach to each other our blood.

And be one eye, one soul,
Shivering over the valleys,
Burning chalices clear.

Seest thou the morning wind? It bears
Hovering life from bush to bush,
Blade of grass to blade.
Be thou mine!

(*Jethro Bithell*)

Alfred Mombert

1872–

SLEEPING THEY BEAR ME

SLEEPING they bear me
Into my homeland.
From far away I come,
Hither over peaks and chasms
Over a dark ocean
Into my homeland.

Now that I have quelled the strongest
of the giants,
Out of the darkest land
Won my way home,
Led by a white fairy hand—

Echo heavy the bells.
And I stagger through the streets
Sleep-bound.

(*Jethro Bithell*)

IDYL

AND my young sweetheart sat at board with me.
I ate and drank and cried most bitterly.
Delicate linen on the board she laid.
And of her own small shift that cloth was made.
She gave to me a little silvern cup.
And it was her own blood that filled it up.
She took a loaf and gave me bread thereof.
And that was her young body warm with love.

Then, as of some strange mystery aware,
She smiled, and put a rose into her hair.

(*Ludwig Lewisohn*)

Carl Busse

1872–

IN THE NIGHT OF THE FULL MOON

All the full-moon night in the coomb
Roars a fallow deer in rut,
Wading through the silvered broom,
With a timid mouse-soft foot.

I am strangely seized, oppressed
By his stifled rage of yearning,
And I feel in my own breast
Tears withholden wildly burning.

(*Jethro Bithell*)

THE QUIET KINGDOM

There is a quiet kingdom's strand,
Like to no other earthly land,
The clouds and winds divide us—
Ah me, and who shall guide us?

It will be found, I say to thee,
By one who yearneth deep as we.

(*Ludwig Lewisohn*)

Richard Schaukal

1874–

IMAGES

I

Over the lids of thine eyes
With soft and light
Gliding of plumage flies
The magical bird of night.

His great, green, lustrous wings
Are heavy with dreamy freight.

Hearken, he sings
Of palm-forests and very strange, sweet things.
Who comes afar and late. . . .

II

And there came mighty birds floating thro' night
With crooked and contemptuous strong beaks,
Who looked upon all life with bitterness
And evil wisdom of their cold, gray eyes
And onward to the dark horizon flew
On their far-shadowing and soundless wings.

(*Ludwig Lewisohn*)

Hugo von Hofmannsthal

1874–1929

THE TWO

Her hand a goblet bore for him—
Her chin and mouth curved like its rim—
So gentle yet so sure her tread,
No drop was from the goblet shed.

So gentle and so firm his hand:
A tameless steed allured his daring
And with a gesture swift, uncaring
He forced its trembling form to stand.

But when at last from her pale hand
He was to take the cup of gold,
Too heavy for them both it was:
For they so trembled like the grass,
That neither hand the other found
And on the ground the dark wine rolled.

(*Ludwig Lewisohn*)

A VENETIAN NIGHT

All thro' the breathing night there seemed to flow,
Thro' the blue night, strange voices to and fro.
There was no sleep in Nature anywhere.
With dewy lips and deep intake of breath

She lay and listened in the vastness darkling
Of all the web of secret things aware.
And streaming, raining, fell the star-light sparkling
Upon the vigil of the garden there.
And ichor of all heavy fruits was swelling
Under the yellow moon and upward welling
Bubbled the glimmering fountains under trees.
And there awakened heavy harmonies.
And where in haste the clouds' dark shadows glided,
A sound of soft and naked steps abided . . .
Softly I rose—by all the magic drawn—
Then floated through the night a sweet intoning
As of the poignant flute's impassioned moaning
Which in his marble hand in thoughtful wise
By the dark laurel holds the dreamy faun,
Yonder where the deep bed of violets lies.
I saw him in his still, marmoreal gleaming,
With rays of blue and silver o'er him streaming;
And where pomegranates open to the night
I heard the murmur of the bees in flight,
And saw them suck, upon the scarlet sunken,
With ripeness and nocturnal passion drunken.
And when the darkness with low breathing now
Brought all the garden fragrance to my brow,
Over the grass I seemed to hear the trailing
Of long and billowy garments thro' the land,
And feel the warm touch of a gentle hand.
In silken whiteness of moonlight were sailing
Impassioned midges in a maddened dance,
And on the lake lay softest radiance
Swaying in silver of its watery path.
I know not whether swans were plashing there
Or the white limbs of Naiads in their bath,
But lovely odor as of woman's hair
Blended with budding aloes everywhere . . .
And all that splendor met in me and I
Was by excess of beauty overcome
That makes words empty and the senses dumb.

(*Ludwig Lewisohn*)

BALLAD OF THE OUTER LIFE

And deep-eyed children cannot long be children,
Knowing of nothing they grow up and die,
And all men go their ways upon the earth.

And bitter fruits are sweetened by and by,
And fall at night like dead birds to the floor,
And in a few days rot even where they lie.

And ever blows the wind, and evermore
A multitude of words we speak and hear,
And now are happy, and now tired and sore.

And roads run through the grass, and towns uprear
Their torch-filled toils, some menacingly live,
And some cadaverously dry and drear.

Why are these built aloft? And ever strive,
So countless many, not to be the same?
And tears drive laughter out till death arrive?

What profits man this ever-changing game?
Full-grown are we, yet still like chartless ships,
And wandering never follow any aim.

What profit hath he who the furthest roams?
And yet he sayeth much who "evening" saith,
A word from which deep melancholy drips

Like heavy honey out of hollow combs.

(*Jethro Bithell*)

MANY INDEED MUST PERISH IN THE KEEL

Many indeed must perish in the keel,
Chained where the heavy oars of vessels smite,
Others direct the rudder on the bridge,
And know the flight of birds and charted stars.

Others with weary limbs lie evermore
By the inextricable roots of life,
For others chairs are with the sibyls set,
The Queens, in whose abode they dwell at home,
With brain untaxed and soft unhampered hands.

But from those lives a shadow falls athwart
On these the lighter, and as to earth and air
The light is with the hard life bound in one.

I cannot free my eyelids from fatigues
Of nations long-forgotten, no, nor guard
My soul in terror from the soundless fall
Of stars remote in deeps of cosmic dark.

Existence plies her shuttle through the woof
Of many fates indissolubly one,
And my own portion of this common life
Is more than taper flame or slender lyre.

(*Jethro Bithell*)

STANZAS ON MUTABILITY

I

Still on my cheeks I feel their fondling breath:
  How can it be that days so very nigh
Are gone, for ever gone, and merged in death!

This is a thing that no man fathoms quite,
  And far too cruel for complaint or cry,
That all things slip and drip out of men's sight.

And that my own untrammeled I hath found
  Out of a little child its gradual stair,
To me unearthly, dumb, strange as a hound.

Then: that I was a hundred summers ere
  My birth, and that my forebears underground
Are closely kin to me as my own hair.

As much at one with me as my own hair.

II

The hours! when we are gazing at the peerless
  Blue of the sea, and read Death's riddle stark
So easily and solemnly and fearless.

As little pale-faced maidens stand and hark,
  Cold always, with their great eyes opened wide,
Hearken in silence looking into the dark,

Out of their sleep-drunk limbs they feel life glide
  Noiselessly into grass, and trees of the wood,
And smiling tiredly know some little pride,

Even as a holy martyr sheds her blood.

(Jethro Bithell)

Arno Holz

1863–

A LEAVE-TAKING

His friend the watchman was still awake,
The Town-hall roof one silver flake,
And the moon hung over it.

He scarcely knew what grief he bore,
At every step his heart beat sore,
And his knapsack weighed him down.

The street it was so long, so long,
And he heard a voice singing a song:
When the breeze of the May is blowing!

Now elder boughs o'er the hedgerow nod,
And he sees the marble Mother of God
Standing white at the Minster door.

Here he stood for a moment still,
And heard what the jackdaw whistled shrill
Up above on the steeple cross.

Then the landlord of the Lion Hotel
Put out his lights, and slowly the bell
Of the Minster clock pealed ten.

Everything was, as it used to be,
The nightingale sang on the linden-tree,
And the fountain dreamily ran.

Out of his coat the rose he dashed,
The flower with his stick on the flags he thrashed,
Till the sparks flew, then he went.

The lamp o'er the gateway flickered red,
And the wood into which his pathway led
Stood black in the moonlight there . . .

And where the path the Saints' Stone reaches,
Just where it bends around the beeches,
It all came back to him.

The leaves rustled, he stood and stood:
He stared down where, beneath the wood,
The roofs were glistening.

He saw the house in the garden gleaming,
And this was the end, was the end of the dream-
ing,
And—the roofs were glistening!

His heart beat wild with piteous pain!
When I come, when I come, when I come back
again!

But he never came back any more.

(Jethro Bithell)

ROSES RED

Roses red
Wind themselves around my lance severe.

Through white woods of lilies
Snorts my stallion.

Out of emerald lakes,
Reeds in hair,
Slender, veilless virgins rise.

I ride as I were bronze.

Ever,
Hard before me,
Flies the Phœnix bird,
Singing.

(*Jethro Bithell*)

BUDDHA

By night around my temple grove
watch seventy brazen cows.
A thousand mottled stone lampions flicker.

Upon a red throne of lac
I sit in the Holy of Holies.

Over me
thro' the beams of sandle-wood,
in the ceiling's open square,
stand the stars.

I blink.

Were I now to rise up
my ivory shoulders would splinter the roof;
and the oval diamond upon my brow
would stave in the moon.

The chubby priests may snore away.
I rise not up.
I sit with legs crossed under
and observe my navel.

It is a blood red ruby
in a naked belly of gold.

(*William Ellery Leonard*)

PHANTASUS

Its roof among the stars projected,
The courtyard throbbed with factory roar,
The common human hive erected,
With hurdy-gurdies at the door.
The dark rat scurried in the basement,
A shop served brandy, grog, and beer,
And to the top-floor's broken casement
Man's wretchedness was native here.

There by his lamp he sat in fever—
Wild scorn of men, speak not at all!
And wrote his songs to last forever,
A dreamer and a prodigal.
Into his garret could be taken
Table and bed—just room for breath;
He was as poor and as forsaken,
As once that God from Nazareth.

And tho' the world, a venal harlot,
Her old taunt: "Crazed and useless!" hissed
A radiant spirit girth with scarlet
His forehead and his eyes had kissed.
And when in lonely awe he wondered
The verse beneath his hand to see,
Forever more from him were sundered
The world in its banality.

His only coat was ripped and tattered,
Dry bread a neighbor's hand would share,
He sighed: O Muse! and nothing mattered,
Of want and misery unaware.
Thus by his lamp he sat in fever,
When day had fled and night would fall,
And wrote his songs to last forever,
A dreamer and a prodigal.

(*Ludwig Lewisohn*)

Karl Bulcke

1875-

THERE IS AN OLD CITY

An old town lies afar
From where the great towns be;
The storm roars over the town;
Beside it thunders the sea.

There is an ancient house
Long locked the gate has been.
On its gray walls the trembling
Blades of the grass are green.

There is a lonely heart,
Strange, full of fears,
That town and that house and that heart
Shut in my boyhood's years. . . .

(*Ludwig Lewisohn*)

Rainer Maria Rilke

1875-1926

PRAYER OF THE MAIDENS TO MARY

I

O see how narrow are our days,
  How full of fear our bed;
We reach out awkward arms always
  To gather the roses red.

Thou must be mild to us, Mary,
  Out of Thy blood we blow;
And what a pain is yearning
  Thou alone canst know;

For Thou hast known this maiden's woe
  In Thine own soul's desire;
It feels as cold as Christmas snow,
  And yet is all on fire . . .

II

AFTER THE PRAYER

But I feel how my heart is glowing
  Warmer and warmer in my breast,
And every evening poorer growing,
  Nor any night can bring me rest.

I tear at the white silken tissue,
And my shy dreams cry out to Thee:
    Let me be sorrow of Thy sorrow,
    O let us both
By the same wonder wounded be.

(Jethro Bithell)

ABISHAG

I

She lay, and serving-men her lithe arms took,
And bound them round the withering old man,
And on him through the long sweet hours she lay,
A little fearful of his many years.

And many times she turned amidst his beard
Her face, as often as the night-owl screeched,
And all that was the night around them reached
Its feelers manifold of longing fears.

As they had been the sisters of the child
The stars trembled, and fragrance searched the room,
The curtain stirring sounded with a sign
Which drew her gentle glances after it.

But she clung close upon the dim old man,
And, by the night of nights not over-taken,
Upon the cooling of the King she lay
Maidenly, and lightly as a soul.

II

The King sate thinking out the empty day
Of deeds accomplished and untasted joys,
And of his favorite bitch that he had bred—
But with the evening Abishag was arched
Above him. His disheveled life lay bare,
Abandoned as diffamèd coasts, beneath
The quiet constellation of her breasts.

But many times, as one in women skilled,
He through his eyebrows recognized the mouth
Unmoved, unkissed; and saw: the comet green
Of her desires reached not to where he lay.
He shivered. And he listened like a hound,
And sought himself in his remaining blood.

(*Jethro Bithell*)

FOR, LORD, THE CROWDED CITIES BE . . .

For, Lord, the crowded cities be
Desolate and divided places,
Flight as from flames upon their ways is,
And comfortless of any graces
Their little time fades utterly.
And men who dwell there heavy and humbly move
About dark rooms with dread in all their bearing,
Less than the spring-time flocks in fire and daring;
And somewhere breathes and watches earth for faring,
But they are here and do not know thereof.
And children grow up where the shadows falling
From wall and window have the light exiled,
And know not that without the flowers are calling
Unto a day of distance, wind and wild—
And every child must be a saddened child.
There blossom virgins to the unknown turning
And for their childhood's faded rest are fain
And do not find for what their soul is burning,
And trembling, close their timid buds again.

And bear in chambers shadowed and unsleeping
The days of disappointed motherhood,
And the long night's involuntary weeping,
And the cold years devoid of glow or good.
In utter darkness stand their deathbeds lowly,
For which thro' gradual years the gray heart pants;
And die as tho' in chains, and dying slowly
Go forth from life in guise of mendicants.

(*Ludwig Lewisohn*)

THE YOUTH DREAMS

Oh, I should love to be like one of those
Who thro' the night on tameless horses ride,
With torches like disheveled tresses wide
Which the great wind of gallop streaming blows.
And I would stand as on a shallop's prow,
Slender and tall and like a banner rolled.
Dark but for helmeting of ruddy gold
That glints and gleams. Behind me in a row
Ten men who from the equal darkness glow
With helmets of the changeful gold designed,
Now clear as glass, now dark and old and blind.
And one by me blows me a vision of space
Upon a trumpet glittering that cries,
Or makes a solitary blackness rise
Thro' which as in a rapid dream we race:
The houses slant behind us to their knees,
The crooked streets to meet us bend and strain,
The squares flee from us: but we grapple these,
And still our horses rustle like the rain.

(*Ludwig Lewisohn*)

THE SONG OF LOVE

How shall I guard my soul so that it be
Touched not by thine? And how shall it be brought,
Lifted above thee, unto other things?
Ah, gladly would I hide it utterly
Lost in the dark where are no murmurings,

In strange and silent places that do not
Vibrate when thy deep soul quivers and sings.
But all that touches us two makes us twin,
Even as the bow crossing the violin
Draws but one voice from the two strings that meet.
Upon what instrument are we two spanned?
And what great player has us in his hand?
O song most sweet.

(Ludwig Lewisohn)

SILENT HOUR

Whoever weeps somewhere out in the world
Weeps without cause in the world
Weeps over me.

Whoever laughs somewhere out in the night
Laughs without cause in the night
Laughs at me.

Whoever wanders somewhere in the world
Wanders in vain in the world
Wanders to me.

Whoever dies somewhere in the world
Dies without cause in the world
Looks at me.

(Jessie Lemont)

PRESAGING

I am like a flag unfurled in space,
I scent the oncoming winds and must bend with them,
While the things beneath are not yet stirring,
While the doors close gently and there is silence in the chimneys
And the windows do not yet tremble and the dust is still heavy—
Then I feel the storm and am vibrant like the sea
And expand and withdraw into myself
And thrust myself forth and am alone in the great storm.

(Jessie Lemont)

Ernst Hardt

1876–

THE SPECTER

The ashen feelers of the frigid morrow
Were groping at my forehead pale with sorrow,
And colder than these walls that round me stand.

Sleep fled from me, and ciphers half and whole
In phalanx upon phalanx chased my soul;
I raised my head and, horribly unmanned,

I glared upon a curling, crooked thing
A griffin shape down by thee cowering,
That held thy loved heart in a cruel hand,

And gnawed at it with teeth most steep and hard,
Until the cock's crow sounded from the yard,
Then fled it—and the young day scaled the land.

I pressed my fevered head and wept, undone,
I knew that also this made us as one,
The torture that is low and like a brand,

Which eats up nights and days and all our life.

(*Jethro Bithell*)

Hermann Hesse

1877–

SPRING SONG

The storm cries every night,
Its great, moist wing falters and sweeps,
In dreamy flight the plover falls;
Now nothing sleeps
And through the land stirs new delight,
For the Spring calls.

Oh in these nights I cannot sleep
Youth stirs my heart!
From the blue wells of memory start
The ardent glories of that dawn
And look at me with eyes so deep,
And tremble, and are gone.

Be still, my heart, give o'er!
Though in the heavy blood holds sway
The passionate sweet pain
And lead thee the old paths again—
Unto youth's land no more
Forever goes thy way.

(*Ludwig Lewisohn*)

NIGHT

Often this thought wakens me unawares,
That through the chill of night a vessel fares
Seeking an ocean, touching on a shore
For which my soul must yearn forevermore;
That in still places which no sailor knows
A crimson, undiscovered Northlight glows,
That an unknown and lovely lady's arm
Pulses amid the pillows white and warm;
That one long destined to become my friend
Finds in an alien sea a somber end,
And that my mother, strange and far apart,
Speaks at this hour my name within her heart.

(*Ludwig Lewisohn*)

Karl Gustave Vollmoeller

1878–1922

NOCTURNE IN G MINOR

The nightwind sings and rustles through the reeds.
The pallid lilacs by the lake are sweet.
"I wait for thee! Ah, when will come thy feet
Down the chill steps. . . . Hush. . . 'tis the gate.
. . . none heeds. . . ."

The nightwind sings and rustles through the reeds.
The nightwind sweeps and whispers by the boat.
The lake is calm. "Ah, hide me in thine arm,
Against that bosom, young and white and warm. . . .
How scarlet are thy lips, how wild thy throat."

The nightwind sweeps and whispers by the boat.

The frosty nightwind trembles through the reeds.
"Hark! Birds of dawn!" "If ever this rapture die!"
"Thou weepest?" "Sweet and bitter is my cry."
The gate is closed. The harsh moon upward speeds.

The nightwind storms and shivers through the reeds.

(*Ludwig Lewisohn*)

SCANDINAVIAN

OLD NORSE

From the Elder Edda

c. 1000

The Poetic Edda is the original storehouse of Germanic mythology. It is, indeed, in many ways the greatest literary monument preserved to us out of the antiquity of the kindred races which we call Germanic. The mythological poems include, in the Voluspo, one of the vastest conceptions of the creation and ultimate destruction of the world ever crystallized in literary form.—Henry Adams Bellows.

VOLUSPO

The Wise-Woman's Prophecy

1. Hearing I ask from the holy races,
From Heimdall's sons, both high and low;
Thou wilt, Valfather, that well I relate
Old tales I remember of men long ago.

2. I remember yet the giants of yore,
Who gave me bread in the days gone by;
Nine worlds I knew, the nine in the tree
With mighty roots beneath the mold.

3. Of old was the age when Ymir lived;
Sea nor cool waves nor sand there were;
Earth had not been, nor heaven above,
But a yawning gap, and grass nowhere.

4. Then Bur's sons lifted the level land,
Mithgarth the mighty there they made;
The sun from the south warmed the stones of earth,
And green was the ground with growing leeks.

5. The sun, the sister of the moon, from the south
Her right hand cast over heaven's rim;
No knowledge she had where her home should be,
The moon knew not what might was his,
The stars knew not where their stations were.

6. Then sought the gods their assembly-seats,
The holy ones, and council held;
Names then gave they to noon and twilight,
Morning they named, and the waning moon,
Night and evening, the years to number.

7. At Ithavoll met the mighty gods,
Shrines and temples they timbered high;
Forges they set, and they smithied ore,
Tongs they wrought, and tools they fashioned.

8. In their dwellings at peace they played at tables,
Of gold no lack did the gods then know,—
Till thither came up giant-maids three,
Huge of might, out of Jotunheim.

9. Then sought the gods their assembly-seats,
The holy ones, and council held,
To find who should raise the race of dwarfs
Out of Brimir's blood and the legs of Blain.

10. There was Motsognir the mightiest made
Of all the dwarfs, and Durin next;
Many a likeness of men they made,
The dwarfs in the earth, as Durin said.

11. Nyi and Nithi, Northri and Suthri,
Austri and Vestri, Althjof, Dvalin,
Nar and Nain, Niping, Dain,
Bifur, Bofur, Bombur, Nori,
An and Onar, Ai, Mjothvitnir.

12. Vigg and Gandalf, Vindalf, Thrain,
Thekk and Thorin, Thror, Vit and Lit,
Nyr and Myrath,—now have I told—
Regin and Rathsvith—the list aright.

13. Fili, Kili, Fundin, Nali,
Heptifili, Hannar, Sviur,
Frar, Hornbori, Fraeg and Loni,
Aurvang, Jari, Eikinskjaldi.

14. The race of the dwarfs in Dvalin's throng
Down to Lofar the list must I tell;
The rocks they left, and through wet lands
They sought a home in the fields of sand.

15. There were Draupnir and Dolgthrasir,
Hor, Haugspori, Hlevang, Gloin,
Dori, Ori, Duf, Andvari,
Skirfir, Virfir, Skafith, Ai.

16. Alf and Yngvi, Eikinskjaldi,
Fjalar and Frosti, Fith and Ginnar;
So for all time shall the tale be known,
The list of all the forbears of Lofar.

17. Then from the throng did three come forth,
From the home of the gods, the mighty and gracious;
Two without fate on the land they found,
Ask and Embla, empty of might.

18. Soul they had not, sense they had not,
Heat nor motion, nor goodly hue;
Soul gave Othin, sense gave Hönir,
Heat gave Lothur and goodly hue.

19. An ash I know, Yggdrasil its name,
With water white is the great tree wet;
Thence come the dews that fall in the dales,
Green by Urth's well does it ever grow.

20. Thence come the maidens mighty in wisdom,
Three from the dwelling down 'neath the tree;
Urth is one named, Verthandi the next,—
On the wood they scored,—and Skuld the third.
Laws they made there, and life allotted
To the sons of men, and set their fates.

21. The war I remember, the first in the world,
When the gods with spears had smitten Gollveig,
And in the hall of Hor had burned her,—
Three times burned, and three times born,
Oft and again, yet ever she lives.

22. Heith they named her who sought their home,
The wide-seeing witch, in magic wise;
Minds she bewitched that were moved by her magic,
To evil women a joy she was.

23. On the host his spear did Othin hurl,
Then in the world did war first come;
The wall that girdled the gods was broken,
And the field by the warlike Wanes was trodden.

24. Then sought the gods their assembly-seats,
The holy ones, and council held,
Whether the gods should tribute give,
Or to all alike should worship belong.

25. Then sought the gods their assembly-seats,
The holy ones, and council held,
To find who with venom the air had filled,
Or had given Oth's bride to the giants' brood.

26. In swelling rage then rose up Thor,—
Seldom he sits when he such things hears,—
And the oaths were broken, the words and bonds,
The mighty pledges between them made.

27. I know of the horn of Heimdall, hidden
Under the high-reaching holy tree;
On it there pours from Valfather's pledge
A mighty stream: would you know yet more?

28. Alone I sat when the Old One sought me,
The terror of gods, and gazed in mine eyes:
"What hast thou to ask? why comest thou hither?
Othin, I know where thine eye is hidden."

29. I know where Othin's eye is hidden,
Deep in the wide-famed well of Mimir;
Mead from the pledge of Othin each morn
Does Mimir drink: would you know yet more?

30. Necklaces had I and rings from Heerfather,
Wise was my speech and my magic wisdom;
. . . .
Widely I saw over all the worlds.

31. On all sides saw I Valkyries assemble,
Ready to ride to the ranks of the gods;
Skuld bore the shield, and Skogul rode next,
Guth, Hild, Gondul, and Geirskogul.
Of Herjan's maidens the list have ye heard,
Valkyries ready to ride o'er the earth.

32. I saw for Baldr, the bleeding god,
The son of Othin, his destiny set:
Famous and fair in the lofty fields,
Full grown in strength the mistletoe stood.

33. From the branch which seemed so slender and fair
Came a harmful shaft that Hoth should hurl;
But the brother of Baldr was born ere long,
And one night old fought Othin's son.

34. His hands he washed not, his hair he combed not,
Till he bore to the bale-blaze Baldr's foe,
But in Fensalir did Frigg weep sore
For Valhall's need: would you know yet more?

35. One did I see in the wet woods bound,
A lover of ill, and to Loki like;
By his side does Sigyn sit, nor is glad
To see her mate: would you know yet more?

36. From the east there pours through poisoned vales
With swords and daggers the river Slith.
. . . . . .
. . . . . .

37. Northward a hall in Nithavellir
Of gold there rose for Sindri's race;
And in Okolnir another stood,
Where the giant Brimir his beer-hall had.

38. A hall I saw, far from the sun,
On Nastrond it stands, and the doors face north;
Venom drops through the smoke-vent down,
For around the walls do serpents wind.

39. I saw there wading through rivers wild
Treacherous men and murderers too,
And workers of ill with wives of men;
There Nithogg sucked the blood of the slain,
And the wolf tore men; would you know yet more?

40. The giantess old in Ironwood sat,
In the east, and bore the brood of Fenrir;
Among these one in monster's guise
Was soon to steal the sun from the sky.

41. There feeds he full on the flesh of the dead,
And the home of the gods he reddens with gore;
Dark grows the sun, and in summer soon
Come mighty storms: would you know yet more?

42. On a hill there sat, and smote on his harp,
Eggther the joyous, the giants' warder;
Above him the cock in the bird-wood crowed,
Fair and red did Fjalar stand.

43. Then to the gods crowed Gollinkambi,
He wakes the heroes in Other's hall;
And beneath the earth does another crow,
The rust-red bird at the bars of Hel.

44. Now Garm howls loud before Gnipahellir,
The fetters will burst, and the wolf run free;
Much do I know, and more can see
Of the fate of the gods, the mighty in fight.

45. Brothers shall fight and fell each other,
And sisters' sons shall kinship stain;
Hard is it on earth, with mighty whoredom;
Ax-time, sword-time, shields are sundered,
Wind-time, wolf-time, ere the world falls;
Nor ever shall men each other spare.

46. Fast move the sons of Mim, and fate
Is hard in the note of the Ghallarhorn;
Loud blows Heimdall, the horn is aloft,
In fear quake all who on Hel-roads are.

47. Yggdrasil shakes, and shiver on high
The ancient limbs, and the giant is loose;
To the head of Mim does Othin give heed,
But the kinsman of Surt shall slay him soon.

48. How fare the gods? how fare the elves?
All Jotunheim groans, the gods are at council;
Loud roar the dwarfs by the doors of stone,
The masters of the rocks: would you know yet more?

49. Now Garm howls loud before Gnipahellir,
The fetters will burst, and the wolf run free;
Much do I know, and more can see
Of the fate of the gods, the mighty in fight.

50. From the east comes Hrym with shield held high;
In giant-wrath does the serpent writhe;
O'er the waves he twists, and the tawny eagle
Gnaws corpses screaming; Naglfar is loose.

51. O'er the sea from the north there sails a ship
With the people of Hel, at the helm stands Loki;
After the wolf do wild men follow,
And with them the brother of Byleist goes.

52. Surt fares from the south with the scourge of branches,
The sun of the battle-gods shone from his sword;
The crags are sundered, the giant-women sink,
The dead throng Hel-way, and heaven is cloven.

53. Now comes to Hlin yet another hurt,
When Othin fares to fight with the wolf,
And Beli's fair slayer seeks out Surt,
For there must fall the joy of Frigg.

54. Then comes Sigfather's mighty son,
Vithar, to fight with the foaming wolf;
In the giant's son does he thrust his sword
Full to the heart: his father is avenged.

55. Hither there comes the son of Hlothyn,
The bright snake gapes to heaven above;
. . . . . .
Against the serpent goes Othin's son.

56. In anger smites the warder of earth,—
Forth from their homes must all men flee;—
Nine paces fares the son of Fjorgyn,
And, slain by the serpent, fearless he sinks.

57. The sun turns black, earth sinks in the sea,
The hot stars down from heaven are whirled;
Fierce grows the steam and the life-feeding flame,
Till fire leaps high about heaven itself.

58. Now Garm howls loud before Gnipahellir,
The fetters will burst, and the wolf run free;
Much do I know, and more can see
Of the fate of the gods, the mighty in fight.

59. Now do I see the earth anew
Rise all green from the waves again;
The cataracts fall, and the eagle flies,
And fish he catches beneath the cliffs.

60. The gods in Ithavoll meet together,
Of the terrible girdler of earth they talk,
And the mighty past they call to mind,
And the ancient runes of the Ruler of Gods.

61. In wondrous beauty once again
Shall the golden tables stand mid the grass,
Which the gods had owned in the days of old,
. . . . .

62. Then fields unsowed bear ripened fruit,
All ills grow better, and Baldr comes back;
Baldr and Hoth dwell in Hropt's battle-hall,
And the mighty gods: would you know yet more?

63. Then Hönir wins the prophetic wand,
. . . . .
And the sons of the brothers of Tveggi abide
In Vindheim now: would you know yet more?

64. More fair than the sun, a hall I see,
Roofed with gold, on Gimle it stands;
There shall the righteous rulers dwell,
And happiness ever there shall they have.

65. There comes on high, all power to hold,
A mighty lord, all lands he rules.
. . . . . .
. . . . . .

66. From below the dragon dark comes forth,
Nithhogg flying from Nithalfjoll;
The bodies of men on his wings he bears,
The serpent bright: but now must I sink.

(Henry Adams Bellows)[2]

THE FIRST LAY OF GUDRUN

For this is the Great Story of the North, which should be to all our race what the Tale of Troy was to the Greeks.—WILLIAM MORRIS.

GUDRUN of old days
Drew near to dying
As she sat in sorrow
Over Sigurd;
Yet she sighed not
Nor smote hand on hand,
Nor wailed she aught
As other women.

Then went earls to her,
Full of all wisdom,
Fain help to deal
To her dreadful heart:
Hushed was Gudrun
Of wail, or greeting,
But with a heavy woe
Was her heart a-breaking.

Bright and fair
Sat the great earls' brides,
Gold arrayed
Before Gudrun;
Each told the tale
Of her great trouble,
The bitterest bale
She erst abode.

[2] Courtesy of the American-Scandinavian Foundation.

Then spake Giaflaug,
Giuki's sister:
"Lo upon earth
I live most loveless
Who of five mates
Must see the ending,
Of daughters twain
And three sisters,
Of brethren eight,
And abide behind lonely."

Naught gat Gudrun
Of wail and greeting,
So heavy was she
For her dead husband,
So dreadful-hearted
For the King laid dead there.

Then spake Herborg
Queen of Hunland—
"Crueler tale
Have I to tell of,
Of my seven sons
Down in the Southlands,
And the eighth man, my mate,
Felled in the death-mead.

"Father and mother,
And four brothers,
On the wide sea
The winds and death played with;
The billows beat
On the bulwark boards.

"Alone must I sing o'er them,
Alone must I array them,
Alone must my hands deal with
Their departing;

And all this was
In one season's wearing,
And none was left
For love or solace.

"Then was I bound
A prey of the battle,
When that same season
Wore to its ending;
As a tiring may
Must I bind the shoon
Of the duke's high dame,
Every day at dawning.

"From her jealous hate
Gat I heavy mocking,
Cruel lashes
She laid upon me,
Never met I
Better master
Or mistress worser
In all the wide world."

Naught gat Gudrun
Of wail or greeting,
So heavy was she
For her dead husband,
So dreadful-hearted
For the King laid dead there.

Then spake Gullrond,
Giuki's daughter—
"O foster-mother,
Wise as thou mayst be,
Naught canst thou better
The young wife's bale."
And she bade uncover
The dead King's corpse.

She swept the sheet
Away from Sigurd,
And turned his cheek
Towards his wife's knees—
"Look on thy loved one,
Lay lips to his lips,
E'en as thou wert clinging
To thy king alive yet!"

Once looked Gudrun—
One look only,
And saw her lord's locks
Lying all bloody,
The great man's eyes
Glazed and deadly,
And his heart's bulwark
Broken by sword-edge.

Back then sank Gudrun,
Back on the bolster,
Loosed was her head array,
Red did her cheeks grow,
And the rain-drops ran
Down over her knees.

Then wept Gudrun,
Giuki's daughter,
So that the tears flowed
Through the pillow;
As the geese withal
That were in the homefield,
The fair fowls the may owned,
Fell a-screaming.

Then spake Gullrond,
Giuki's daughter—
"Surely knew I
No love like your love
Among all men,

On the mold abiding;
Naught wouldst thou joy in
Without or within doors,
O my sister,
Save beside Sigurd."

Then spake Gudrun,
Giuki's daughter—
"Such was my Sigurd
Among the sons of Giuki,
As is the king leek
O'er the low grass waxing,
Or a bright stone
Strung on band,
Or a pearl of price
On a prince's brow.
"Once was I counted
By the king's warriors
Higher than any
Of Herjan's mays;
Now am I as little
As the leaf may be,
Amid wind-swept wood
Now when dead he lieth.

"I miss from my seat,
I miss from my bed,
My darling of sweet speech.
Wrought the sons of Giuki,
Wrought the sons of Giuki,
This sore sorrow,
Yea, for their sister,
Most sore sorrow.

"So may your lands
Lie waste on all sides,
As ye have broken
Your bounden oaths!
Ne'er shalt thou, Gunnar,

The gold have joy of,
The dear-bought rings
Shall drag thee to death,
Whereon thou swarest
Oath unto Sigurd.

"Ah, in the days by-gone
Greath mirth in the homefield
When my Sigurd
Set saddle on Grani,
And they went their ways
For the wooing of Brynhild!
An ill day, an ill woman,
And most ill hap!"

Then spake Brynhild,
Budli's daughter—
"May the woman lack
Both love and children,
Who gained greeting
For thee, O Gudrun!
Who gave thee this morning
Many words!"

Then spake Gullrond,
Giuki's daughter—
"Hold peace of such words
Thou hated of all folk!
The bane of brave men
Hast thou been ever,
All waves of ill
Wash over thy mind,
To seven great kings
Hast thou been a sore sorrow,
And the death of good will
To wives and women."

Then spake Brynhild,
Budli's daughter—

"None but Atli
Brought bale upon us,
My very brother
Born of Budli.

"When we saw in the hall
Of the Hunnish people
The gold a-gleaming
On the kingly Giukings;
I have paid for that faring
Oft and full,
And for the sight
That then I saw."

By a pillar she stood
And strained its wood to her;
From the eyes of Brynhild,
Budli's daughter,
Flashed out fire,
And she snorted forth venom,
As the sore wounds she gazed on
Of the dead-slain Sigurd.

(William Morris and Eiríkr Magnusson)

THE LAY OF SIGURD

Sigurd of yore
Sought the dwelling of Giuki,
As he fared, the young Volsung,
After fight won;
Troth he took
From the two brethren;
Oath swore they betwixt them,
Those bold ones of deed.

A may they gave to him
And wealth manifold,
Gudrun the young,
Giuki's daughter:

They drank and gave doom
Many days together,
Sigurd the young,
And the sons of Giuki.

Until they wended
For Brynhild's wooing,
Sigurd a-riding
Amidst their rout;
The wise young Volsung
Who know of all ways—
Ah! he had wed her,
Had fate so willed it.

Southlander Sigurd
A naked sword,
Bright, well grinded,
Laid betwixt them;
No kiss he won
From the fair woman,
Nor in arms of his
Did the Hun King hold her,
Since he gat the young maid
For the son of Giuki.

No lack in her life
She wotted of now,
And at her death-day
No dreadful thing
For a shame indeed
Or a shame in seeming;
But about and betwixt
Went baleful fate.

Alone, abroad,
She sat of an evening,
Of full many things
She fell a-talking:

"O for my Sigurd!
I shall have death,
Or my fair, my lovely,
Laid in mine arms.

"For the word once spoken,
I sorrow sorely—
His queen is Gudrun,
I am wed to Gunnar;
The dread Norns wrought for us
A long while of woe."

Oft with heart deep
In dreadful thoughts
O'er ice-fields and ice-hills
She fared a-night time
When he and Gudrun
Were gone to their fair bed,
And Sigurd wrapped
The bed-gear round her.

"Ah! now the Hun King
His queen in arms holdeth,
While love I go lacking,
And all things longed for
With no delight
But in dreadful thought."

These dreadful things
Thrust her toward murder:
—"Listen, Gunnar,
For thou shalt lose
My wide lands,
Yea, me myself!
Never love I my life,
With thee for my lord—

"I will fare back thither
From whence I came,

To my nighest kin
And those that know me
There shall I sit
Sleeping my life away,
Unless thou slayest
Sigurd the Hun King,
Making thy might more
E'en than his might was!

"Yea, let the son fare
After the father,
And no young wolf
A long while nourish!
For on each man lieth
Vengeance lighter,
And peace shall be surer
If the son live not."

Adrad was Gunnar,
Heavy-hearted was he,
And in doubtful mood
Day-long he sat.
For naught he wotted,
Nor might see clearly
What was the seemliest
Of deeds to set hand to;
What of all deeds
Was best to be done:
For he minded the vows
Sworn to the Volsung,
And the sore wrong
To be wrought against Sigurd.

Wavered his mind
A weary while,
No wont it was
Of those days worn by,
That queens should flee
From the realms of their kings.

"Brynhild to me
Is better than all,
The child of Budli
Is the best of women.
Yea, and my life
Will I lay down,
Ere I am twinned
From that woman's treasure."

He bade call Hogni
To the place where he bided;
With all the trust that might be,
Trowed he in him.

"Wilt thou bewray Sigurd
For his wealth's sake?
Good it is to rule
O'er the Rhine's metal;
And well content
Great wealth to wield,
Biding in peace
And blissful days."

One thing alone Hogni
Had for an answer:
"Such doings for us
Are naught seemly to do;
To rend with sword
Oaths once sworn,
Oaths once sworn,
And troth once plighted.

"Nor know we on mold,
Men of happier days,
The while we four
Rule over the folk;
While the bold in battle,
The Hun king, bides living.

"And no nobler kin
Shall be known afield,
If our five sons
We long may foster;
Yea, a goodly stem
Shall surely wax.
—But I clearly see
In what wise it standeth,
Brynhild's sore urging
O'ermuch on thee beareth.

"Guttorm shall we
Get for the slaying,
Our younger brother
Bare of wisdom;
For he was out of
All the oaths sworn,
All the oaths sworn,
And the plighted troth."

Easy to rouse him
Who of naught recketh!
—Deep stood the sword
In the heart of Sigurd.

There, in the hall,
Gat the high-hearted vengeance;
For he cast his sword
At the reckless slayer:
Out at Guttorm
Flew Gram the mighty,
The gleaming steel
From Sigurd's hand.

Down fell the slayer
Smitten asunder;
The heavy head
And the hands fell one way,
But the feet and such like
Aback where they stood.

Gudrun was sleeping
Soft in the bed,
Empty of sorrow
By the side of Sigurd:
When she awoke
With all pleasure gone,
Swimming in blood
Of Frey's beloved.

So sore her hands
She smote together,
That the great-hearted
Gat raised in bed;
—"O Gudrun, weep not
So woefully,
Sweet lovely bride,
For thy brethren live for thee!

"A young child have I
For heritor;
Too young to win forth
From the house of his foes.—
Black deeds and ill
Have they been a-doing,
Evil rede
Have they wrought at last.

Late, late, rideth with them
Unto the Thing,
Such sister's son,
Though seven thou bear,—
—But well I wot
Which way all goeth;
Alone wrought Brynhild
This bale against us.

"That maiden loved me
Far before all men,
Yet wrong to Gunnar
I never wrought;

Brotherhood I heeded
And all bounden oaths,
That none should deem me
His queen's darling."

Weary sighed Gudrun,
As the king gat ending,
And so sore her hands
She smote together,
That the cups arow
Rang out therewith,
And the geese cried on high
That were in the homefield.

Then laughed Brynhild,
Budli's daughter,
Once, once only,
From out her heart;
When to her bed
Was borne the sound
Of the sore greeting
Of Giuki's daughter.

Then, quoth Gunnar,
The king, the hawk-bearer,
"Whereas, thou laughest,
O hateful woman,
Glad on thy bed,
No good it betokeneth:
Why lackest thou else
Thy lovely hue?
Feeder of foul deeds,
Fey do I deem thee,

"Well worthy art thou
Before all women,
That thine eyes should see
Atli slain of us;

That thy brother's wounds
Thou shouldst see a-bleeding,
That his bloody hurts
Thine hands should bind."

"No man blameth thee, Gunnar,
Thou hast fulfilled death's measure
But naught Atli feareth
All thine ill will;
Life shall he lay down
Later than ye,
And still bear more might
Aloft than thy might.

"I shall tell thee, Gunnar,
Though well the tale thou knowest,
In what early days
Ye dealt abroad your wrong:
Young was I then,
Worn with no woe,
Good wealth I had
In the house of my brother!

"No mind had I
That a man should have me,
Or ever ye Giukings,
Rode into our garth;
There ye sat on your steeds
Three kings of the people—
—Ah! that that faring
Had never befallen!

"Then spake Atli
To me apart,
And said that no wealth
He would give unto me,
Neither gold nor lands
If I would not be wedded;

Nay, and no part
Of the wealth apportioned,
Which in my first days
He gave me duly;
Which in my first days
He counted down.

"Wavered the mind
Within me then,
If to fight I should fall
And the felling of folk,
Bold in myrny
Because of my brother;
A deed of fame
Had that been to all folk,
But to many a man
Sorrow of mind.

"So I let all sink
Into peace at the last:
More grew I minded
For the mighty treasure,
The red-shining rings
Of Sigmund's son;
For no man's wealth else
Would I take unto me.

"For myself had I given
To that great king
Who sat amid gold
On the back of Grani:
Nought were his eyen
Like to your eyen,
Nor in any wise
Went his visage with yours;
Though ye might deem you
Due kings of men.

"One I loved,
One, and none other,
The gold-decked may
Had no doubtful mind;
Thereof shall Atli
Wot full surely,
When he getteth to know
I am gone to the dead.

"Far be it from me,
Feeble and wavering,
Ever to love
Another's love—
—Yet shall my woe
Be well avenged."

Up rose Gunnar,
The great men's leader,
And cast his arms
About the queen's neck
And all went nigh
One after other,
With their whole hearts
Her heart to turn.

But then all these
From her neck she thrust
Of her long journey
No man should let her.

Then called he Hogni
To have talk with him:
"Let all folk go
Forth into the hall,
Thine with mine—
—O need sore and mighty!—
To wot if we yet
My wife's parting may stay.
Till with time's wearing
Some hindrance wax."

One answer Hogni
Had for all;
"Nay, let hard need
Have rule thereover,
And no man let her
Of her long journey!
Never born again,
May she come back thence!

"Luckless she came
To the lap of her mother,
Born into the world
For utter woe,
To many a man
For heart-whole mourning."

Upraised he turned
From the talk and the trouble,
To where the gem-field
Dealt out goodly treasure;
As she looked and beheld
All the wealth that she had,
And the hungry bondmaids,
And maids of the hall.

With no good in her heart
She donned her gold byrny,
Ere she thrust the sword-point
Through the midst of her body:
On the bolster's far side
Sank she adown,
And, smitten with sword,
Still bethought her of redes.

"Let all come forth
Who are fain the red gold,
Or things less worthy
To win from my hands;

To each one I give
A necklace gilt over,
Wrought hangings and bed-gear
And bright woven weed."

All they kept silence,
And thought what to speak,
Then all at once
Answer gave:
"Full enow are death-doomed,
Fain are we to live yet,
Maids of the hall
All meet work winning."

From her wise heart at last
The linen-clad damsel,
The one of few years
Gave forth the word:
"I will that none driven
By hand or by word,
For our sake should lose
Well-loved life.

"Thou on the bones of you
Surely shall burn,
Less dear treasure
At your departing
Nor with Menia's Meal
Shall ye come to see me."

"Sit thee down, Gunnar,
A word must I say to thee
Of the life's ruin
Of thy lightsome bride—
—Nor shall thy ship
Swim soft and sweetly
For all that I
Lay life adown.

"Sooner than ye might deem
Shall ye make peace with Gudrun,
For the wise woman
Shall lull in the young wife
The hard memory
Of her dead husband.

"There is a may born
Reared by her mother,
Whiter and brighter
Than is the bright day;
She shall be Swanhild,
She shall be Sunbeam.

"Thou shalt give Gudrun
Unto a great one,
Noble, well-praised
Of the world's folk;
Not with her goodwill,
Or love shalt thou give her;
Yet will Atli
Come to win her,
My very brother,
Born of Budli.

—"Ah! many a memory
Of how ye dealt with me,
How sorely, how evilly
Ye ever beguiled me,
How all pleasure left me
The while my life lasted!—

"Fain wilt thou be
Oddrun to win,
But thy good liking
Shall Atli let;
But in secret wise
Shall ye win together,

And she shall love thee
As I had loved thee,
If in such wise
Fate had willed it.

"But with all ill
Shall Atli sting thee,
Into the strait worm-close
Shall he cast thee.

"But no long space
Shall slip away
Ere Atli too
All life shall lose.
Yea, all his weal
With the life of his sons,
For a dreadful bed
Dights Gudrun for him,
From a heart sore laden,
With the sword's sharp edge.

"More seemly for Gudrun,
Your very sister,
In death to wend after
Her love first wed;
Had but good rede
To her been given,
Or if her heart
Had been like to my heart.

—"Faint my speech groweth—
But for our sake
Ne'er shall she lose
Her life beloved;
The sea shall have her,
High billows bear her
Forth unto Jonakr's
Fair land of his fathers.

"There shall she bear sons,
Stays of a heritage,
Stays of a heritage,
Jonakr's sons;
And Swanhild shall she
Send from the land,
That may born of her,
The may born of Sigurd.

"Her shall bite
The rede of Bikki,
Whereas for no good
Wins Jormunrek life;
And so is clean perished
All the kin of Sigurd,
Yea, and more greeting,
And more for Gudrun.

"And now one prayer
Yet pray I of thee—
The last word of mine
Here in the world—
So broad on the field
Be the burg of the dead
That fair space may be left
For us all to lie down,
All those that died
At Sigurd's death!

"Hang round that burg
Fair hangings and shields,
Web by Gauls woven,
And folk of the Gauls:
There burn the Hun King
Lying beside me.

"But on the other side
Burn by the Hun King
Those who served me

Strewn with treasure;
Two at the head,
And two at the feet,
Two hounds therewith,
And two hawks moreover:
Then is all dealt
With even dealing.

"Lay there amidst us
The ring-dight metal,
The sharp-edged steel,
That so lay erst;
When we both together
Into one bed went,
And were called by the name
Of man and wife.

"Never, then, belike
Shall clash behind him
Valhall's bright door
With rings bedight:
And if my fellowship
Followeth after,
In no wretched wise
Then shall we wend.

"For him shall follow
My five bondmaids,
My eight bondsmen,
No borel folk:
Yea, and my fosterer,
And my father's dower
That Budli of old days
Gave to his dear child.

"Much have I spoken,
More would I speak,
If the sword would give me
Space for speech;

But my words are waning,
My wounds are swelling—
Naught but truth have I told—
—And now make I ending."

(*William Morris and Eirikr Magnusson*)

COUNSELS OF SIGRDRIFA

Now this is my first counsel:
That thou with thy kin
Be guiltless, guileless ever;
Nor hasty of wrath
Despite of wrong done,—
Unto the Dead good that doeth.
—Lo! the second counsel:
That oath thou swearest never
But trusty oath and true;
Grim tormenting
Gripes troth-breakers,
Cursèd wretch is the wolf of vows.
—This is my third rede:
That thou at the Thing
Deal not with the fools of folk;
For unwise man
From mouth lets fall
Worser word than well he wotteth.
Yet hard it is
That holding of peace
When men shall deem thee dastard,
Or deem the lie said soothly;
But woeful is home witness
Unless right good thou gettest it:
Ah! on another day
Drive the life from out him
And pay the liar back for his lying!
—Now behold the fourth rede:
If ill witch thee bideth,
Woe-begetting by the way,
Good going farther
Rather than guesting,

Though thick night be on thee!
    Far-seeing eyes
    Need all sons of men
Who wend in wrath to war;
    For baleful women
    Bide oft by the highway,
Swords and hearts to soften.
    —And now the fifth rede:
    As fair as thou seest
Brides on the bench abiding,
    Let not love's silver
    Rule over thy sleeping;
Draw no woman to kind kissing!
    —For the sixth thing I rede:
    When men sit a-drinking
Amid ale-words and ill words,
    Deal thou nought
    With the drunken fight-staves!
For wine stealeth wit from many.
    Brawling and drink
    Have brought unto men
Sorrow sore oft enow;
    Yea! bane unto some,
    And to some weary bale;
Many are the griefs of mankind.
    —For the seventh I rede thee:
    If strife thou raisest
With a man right high of heart,
    Better fight a-field
    Than burn in the fire
Within thine hall fair to behold.
    —The eighth rede that I give thee:
    Unto all ill look thou,
And hold thy heart from all beguiling!
    Draw to thee no maiden!
    No man's wife bewray thou!
Urge them not to unmeet pleasure!
    —This is the ninth counsel:
    That thou have heed of dead folk

Whereso thou findest them a-field;
Be they sick-dead,
Be they sea-dead,
Or come to ending by war-weapons.
Let bath be made
For such men foredone!
Wash thou hands and feet thereof,
Comb their hair and dry them
Ere the coffin has them;
Then bid them sleep full sweetly!
—This for the tenth counsel:
That thou give trust never
Unto oaths of foeman's kin,
Beest thou bane of his brother,
Or hast thou fell'd his father;
Wolf in young son waxes,
Though he with gold be gladden'd.
For wrong and hatred
Shall rest them never,
Nay! nor sore sorrow;
Both wit and weapons
Must the king have
Who is fain to be the foremost.
—The last rede and eleventh:
Unto all ill look thou,
And watch thy friends' ways ever!

(*William Morris and Eiríkr Magnusson*)

DANISH

Anonymous

14th-16th centuries

BALLADS

The Elected Knight

Sir Oluf he rideth over the plain,
Full seven miles broad and seven miles wide;
But never, ah! never, can meet with the man
A tilt with him dare ride.

He saw under the hill-side
  A knight full well equipped;
His steel was black, his helm was barred;
  He was riding at full speed.

He wore upon his spurs
  Twelve little golden birds;
Anon in eddies the wild wind blew,
  And there sat all the birds and sang.

He wore upon his mail
  Twelve little golden wheels;
Anon in eddies the wild wind blew,
  And round and round the wheels they flew.

He wore before his breast
  A lance that was poised in rest,
And it was sharper than diamond-stone;
  It made Sir Oluf's heart to groan.

He wore upon his helm
  A wreath of ruddy gold;
And that gave him the Maidens Three,
  The youngest was fair to behold.

Sir Oluf questioned the knight eftsoon
  If he were come from heaven down;
"Art thou Christ of Heaven?" quoth he,
  "So will I yield me unto thee."

"I am not Christ the Great,
  Thou shalt not yield thee yet;
I am an Unknown Knight,
  Three modest Maidens have me bedight."

"Art thou a knight elected?
  And have three maidens thee bedight?
So shalt thou ride a tilt this day,
  For all the maidens' honor!"

The first tilt they together rode,
They put their steeds to the test;
The second tilt they together rode,
They proved their manhood best.

The third tilt they together rode,
Neither of them would yield;
The fourth tilt they together rode,
They both fell on the field.

Now lie the lords upon the plain,
And their blood runs unto death;
Now sit the Maidens in the high tower,
The youngest sorrows till death.

(*H. W. Longfellow*)

The Mer-Man, and Marstig's Daughter

"Now rede me, dear mither, a sonsy rede;
A sonsy rede swythe rede to me,
How Marstig's daughter I may fa',
My love and lemman gay to be."

She's made him a steed o' the clear water;
A saddle and bridle o' sand made she;
She's shap'd him into a knight sae fair,
Syne into Mary's kirk-yard rade he.

He's tied his steed to the kirk-stile,
Syne wrang-gates round the kirk gaed he;
When the Mer-man entered the kirk-door,
Awa the sma' images turned their ee'.

The priest afore the altar stood:
"O, what for a gude knight may this be?"
The may leugh till hersell, and said,
"God gif that gude knight were for me!"

The Mer-man he stept o'er ae deas,
And he has steppit over three:
"O maiden, pledge me faith and troth!
O Marstig's daughter, gang wi' me!"

And she raught out her lily hand,
  And pledg'd it to the knight sae free:
"Hae; there's my faith and troth, Sir Knight,
  And willingly I'll gang wi' thee."

Out frae the kirk gaed the bridal train,
  And on they danc'd wi' fearless glee;
And down they danc'd unto the strand,
  Till twasome now alane they be:
"O Marstig's daughter, haud my steed,
  And the bonniest ship I'll bigg for thee!"

And whan they came to the white sand,
  To shore the sma' boats turning came;
And whan they came to the deep water,
  The maiden sank in the saut sea faem.

The shriek she shriek'd amang the waves
  Was heard far up upo' the land:
"I rede gude ladies, ane and a',
  They dance wi' nae sic unco man."

(Robert Jamieson)

Elfer Hill

I laid my haffet on Elfer Hill;
  Saft slooming clos'd my ee';
And there twa selcouth ladies came,
  Sae fain to speak to me.

Ane clappit me then, wi' cheek sae white,
  And rown'd intill mine ear:
"Rise up, fair youth, and join our dance;
  Rise up, but doubt or fear!

"Wake up, fair youth, and join the dance,
  And we will tread the ring,
While mair nor eardly melody
  My ladies for thee sing."

Syne ane, the fairest may on mold,
  Sae sweet a sang began;
The hurling stream was still'd herewi',
  Sae fast afore that ran.

The striving stream was still'd herewi',
  Sae fast that wont to rin;
The sma' fish, in the flood that swam,
  Amo' their faes now blin'.

The fishes a', in flood that were,
  Lay still, baith fin and tail;
The sma' fowls in the shaw began
  To whitter in the dale.

"O, hear, thou fair, thou young swain!
  And thou wi' us will dwell,
Then will we teach thee book and rune,
  To read and write sae well.

"I'll lear thee how the bear to bind,
  And fasten to the aik tree;
The dragon, that liggs on mickle goud,
  Afore thee fast shall flee."

They danced out, and they danced in,
  In the Elfer ring sae green;
All silent sat the fair young swain,
  And on his sword did lean.

"Now hear, thou fair, thou young swain,
  But and thou till us speak,
Then shall on sword and sharp knife
  Thy dearest heart-blood reek."

Had God nae made my luck sae gude,
  That the cock did wap his wing,
I boot hae bidden on Elfer Hill,
  In the Elf-ladies' ring.

I rede the Danish young swains,
That to the court will ride,
That they ne'er ride to Elfer Hill,
Nor sleep upon its side.

(*Robert Jamieson*)

Johannes Evald

1743-1781

KING CHRISTIAN

King Christian stood by the lofty mast
In mist and smoke;
His sword was hammering so fast
Through Gothic helm and brain it passed;
Then sank each hostile hulk and mast
In mist and smoke.
"Fly!" shouted they, "fly, he who can!
Who braves of Denmark's Christian
The stroke?"

Nils Juel gave heed to the tempest's roar;
Now is the hour!
He hoisted his blood-red flag once more,
And smote upon the foe full sore,
And shouted loud, through the tempest's roar,
"Now is the hour!"
"Fly!" shouted they, "for shelter fly!
Of Denmark's Juel who can defy
The power?"

North Sea! a glimpse of Wessel rent
Thy murky sky!
Then champions to thine arms were sent;
Terror and Death glared where he went;
From the waves was heard a wail that rent
Thy murky sky!
From Denmark thunders Tordenskiol';
Let each to Heaven commend his soul,
And fly!

Path of the Dane to fame and might!
    Dark-rolling wave!
Receive thy friend, who, scorning flight,
Goes to meet danger with despite,
Proudly as thou the tempest's might,
    Dark-rolling wave!
And, amid pleasures and alarms,
And war and victory, be thine arms
    My grave!

(*H. W. Longfellow*)

Jens Baggesen

1764-1826

CHILDHOOD

There was a time when I was very small,
  When my whole frame was but an ell in height;
Sweetly, as I recall it, tears do fall,
  And therefore I recall it with delight.

I sported in my tender mother's arms,
  And rode a-horse-back on best father's knee;
Alike were sorrows, passions, and alarms,
  And gold, and Greek, and love, unknown to me.

Then seemed to me this world far less in size,
  Likewise it seemed to me less wicked far;
Like points in heaven, I saw the stars arise,
  And longed for wings that I might catch a star.

I saw the moon behind the island fade,
  And thought, "O, were I on that island there,
I could find out of what the moon is made,
  Find out how large it is, how round, how fair!"

Wondering, I saw God's sun, through western skies,
  Sink in the ocean's golden lap at night,
And yet upon the morrow early rise,
  And paint the eastern heaven with crimson light;

And thought of God, the gracious Heavenly Father,
Who made me, and that lovely sun on high,
And all those pearls of heaven thick-strung together,
Dropped, clustering, from his hand o'er all the sky.

With childish reverence, my young lips did say
The prayer my pious mother taught to me:
"O gentle God! O, let me strive alway
Still to be wise, and good, and follow thee!"

So prayed I for my father and my mother,
And for my sister, and for all the town;
The king I knew not, and the beggar-brother,
Who, bent with age, went, sighing, up and down.

They perished, the blithe days of boyhood perished,
And all the gladness, all the peace I knew!
Now have I but their memory, fondly cherished;—
God! may I never, never lose that too!

(*H. W. Longfellow*)

Adam Oehlenschlager

1779-1850

THERE IS A CHARMING LAND

THERE is a charming land
Where grow the wide-armed beeches
By the salt eastern Strand.
Old Denmark, so we call
These rolling hills and valleys,
And this is Freia's Hall.

Here sat in days of yore
The warriors in armor,
Well rested from the war.
They scattered all their foes,
And now beneath great barrows
Their weary bones repose.

The land is lovely still,
With blue engirdling ocean
And verdant vale and hill,
Fair women, comely maids,
Strong men and lads are dwelling
In Denmark's island glades.

(Robert Hillyer) [1]

NORWEGIAN

Henrik Arnold Thaulov Wergeland

1808-1845

THE WALL-FLOWER

O Wall-flower! or ever thy bright leaves fade,
My limbs will be that of which all are made;
Before ever thou losest thy crown of gold,
My flesh will be mold.

And yet open the casement! till I am dead
Let my last look rest on thy golden head!
My soul would kiss thee before it flies
To the open skies.

Twice I am kissing thy fragrant mouth,
And the first kiss wholly is thine, in truth;
But the second remember, dear Love! to close
On my fair white Rose.

I shall not be living its Spring to see;
But bring it my greeting when that shall be,
And say that I wish'd that upon my grave
It should bloom and wave.

Yes! say that I wish'd that against my breast
The Rose should lie that thy lips caress'd;
And, Wall-flower! do thou into Death's dark porch
Be its bridal torch!

(Sir Edmund Gosse)

[1] Courtesy of the American-Scandinavian Foundation.

Henrik Ibsen

1828-1906

IN THE ORCHARD

In the sunny orchard closes,
  While the warblers sing and swing,
Care not whether blustering Autumn
  Break the promises of Spring!
Rose and white, the apple blossom
  Hides you from the sultry sky—
Let it flutter, blown and scatter'd,
  On the meadows by-and-by!

Will you ask about the fruitage
  In the season of the flowers?
Will you murmur, will you question,
  Count the run of weary hours?
Will you let the scarecrow clapping
  Drown all happy sounds and words?
Brothers! there is better music
  In the singing of the birds.

From your heavy-laden garden
  Will you hunt the mellow thrush;
He will play you for protection
  With his crown-song's liquid rush.
O but you will win the bargain,
  Though your fruit be spare and late,
For remember Time is flying
  And will shut the garden gate.

With my living, with my singing,
  I will tear the hedges down.
Sweep the grass and heap the blossom!
  Let it shrivel, pale and brown!
Swing the wicket! Sheep and cattle,
  Let them graze among the best!
I broke oft the flowers; what matter
  Who may revel with the rest?

(Sir Edmund Gosse)

Björnsterne Björnson

1832-1910

FATHERLAND SONG
(Norwegian National Hymn)

Yes, we love this land together,
Where the wild sea foams,
Furrowed, beat by wind and weather,
With the thousand homes.
Yes, we love her; with her blending
Father, mother, birth,
And that saga-twilight sending
Dreams upon our earth.

This the land that Harold savèd
With his warriors young;
All for this land Haakon bravèd,
Whilst that Oevin sung.
Olaf with his blood hath printed
Cross upon her loam;
From her highlands Swerre stinted
Not to talk to Rome.

Peasants ground their axes' edges
At the call to go;
Tordenskjold along the ledges
Homeward lit the foe.
Women too stood up that day,
Smote as they were men;
Others could but weep and pray,
Nor was that in vain.

Evil times could not undo us,
We outstood the same;
But when straits were sorest, tó us
Blue-eyed Freedom came.
That gave strength of olden story
Hunger, war, to face;
That gave even death its glory,
Gave new ties of race.

Foe its weapon cast, and slew them—
Up our visors then!
We in wonder hastened tó them,
For they were our kin.
Southward, sped by shame, we thither
Fared into their land;
Now we stand three sons together
And shall ever stand.

Norsemen, ye in hut and hall,
Thank the Lord of Hosts!
Guard he will the land and all,
Howso dark the coasts.
All for which the fathers perished,
And the mothers wept,
Hath the Lord in stillness cherished—
So we won and kept.

Yes, we love this land together,
Where the wild sea foams,
Furrowed, beat by wind and weather,
With the thousand homes.
As our fathers' battles freed us
Out of old distress,
We'll to war, if once she need us,
For her peace no less.

(*William Ellery Leonard*)

THE BOY AND THE FLUTE

Through the forest the boy wends all day long:
For there he has heard such a wonderful song.
He carved him a flute of the willow-tree,
And tried what the tune within it might be.
The tune came out of it sad and gay;
But while he listen'd it pass'd away.
He fell asleep, and once more it sung,
And over his forehead it lovingly hung.

He thought he would catch it, and wildly woke;
And the tune in the pale night faded and broke.
"O God! my God! take me up to Thee!
For the tune Thou hast made is consuming me."
And the Lord God said: " 'Tis a friend divine,
Though never one hour shalt thou hold it thine.
Yet all other music is poor and thin
By the side of this which thou never shalt win!"

(Sir Edmund Gosse)

SWEDISH

Gustav Rosenhane

1619-1684

Sonnets

I

Deep in a vale where rocks on every side
  Shut out the winds, and scarcely let the sun
  Between them dart his rays down one by one,
Where all was still and cool in summer-tide,
And softly, with her whispering waves that sighed,
  A little river, that had scarce begun
  Her silver course, made bold to fleet and run
Down leafy falls to woodlands dense and wide,
There stood a tiny plain, just large enow
  To give small mountain-folk right room to dance,
  With oaks and limes and maples ringed around;
Hither I came, and viewed its turf askance,
  Its solitude with beauty seemed a-glow,—
  My Love had walked there and 'twas holy ground!

II

And then I sat me down, and gave the rein
  To my wild thoughts, till many a song that rang
  From boughs around where hidden warblers sang

Recalled me from myself; then "Oh! in vain"
I said, "do these outpour the tender strain?
  Can these sweet birds that with such airs harangue
  Their feathered loves, like me, feel sorrow's pang?
Ah! would that I, like them, had pinions twain!
Straight would I fly to her whom I love best,
  Nor vainly warbling in the woodland sing,
But chirp my prayer, and preen my plumèd crest,
  And to this spot once more her beauty bring,
  And flutter round her flight with supple wing,
And lead her to my secret leafy nest."

(*Sir Edmund Gosse*)

Olof Wexionius

1656-1690?

ON THE DEATH OF A PIOUS LADY

The earthly roses at God's call have made
  Way, lady, for a dress of heavenly white,
  In which thou walk'st with other figures bright,
Once loved on earth, who now, like thee arrayed,
Feast on two-fold ambrosia, wine and bread;
  They lead thee up by sinuous paths of light
  Through lilied fields that sparkle in God's sight,
And crown thee with delights that never fade.
O thou thrice-sainted mother, in that bliss,
Forget not thy two daughters, whom a kiss
  At parting left as sad as thou art glad;
In thy deep joy think how for thee they weep,
Or conjure through the shifting glass of sleep
  The saint heaven hath, the mother once they had.

(*Sir Edmund Gosse*)

Erik Johann Stagnelius

1793-1823

MEMORY

O camp of flowers, with poplars girdled round,
  Gray guardians of life's soft and purple bud!
  O silver spring, beside whose brimming flood

My pensive childhood its Elysium found!
O happy hours by love and fancy crowned,
  Whose horn of plenty flatteringly subdued
  My heart into a trance, whence, with a rude
And horrid blast, fate came my soul to hound!
Who was the goddess that empowered you all
  Thus to bewitch me? Out of wasting snow
  And lily-leaves her head-dress should be made!
Weep, my poor lute! nor on Astræa call,
  She will not smile, nor I, who mourn below,
  Till I, a shade in heaven, clasp her, a shade.

(*Sir Edmund Gosse*)

Esaias Tegner

1782-1846

From FRITHIOF'S SAGA

Frithiof's Homestead

Three miles extended around the fields of the homestead; on three sides
Valleys and mountains and hills, but on the fourth side was the ocean.
Birch-woods crowned the summits, but over the downsloping hill-sides
Flourished the golden corn, and man-high was waving the rye-field.
Lakes, full many in number, their mirror held up for the mountains,
Held for the forest up, in whose depths the high-antlered reindeers
Had their kingly walk, and drank of a hundred brooklets.
But in the valleys, full widely around, there fed on the green-sward
Herds with sleek, shining sides, and udders that longed for the milk-pail.
'Mid these were scattered, now here and now there, a vast countless number

Of white-woolled sheep, as thou seest the white-looking
stray clouds,
Flock-wise, spread o'er the heavenly vault, when it
bloweth in spring-time.
Twice twelve swift-footed coursers, mettlesome, fast-
fettered storm-winds,
Stamping stood in the line of stalls, all champing their
fodder,
Knotted with red their manes, and their hoofs all
whitened with steel shoes.
The banquet-hall, a house by itself, was timbered of
hard fir.
Not five hundred men (at ten times twelve to the
hundred)
Filled up the roomy hall, when assembled for drinking
at Yule-tide.
Thorough the hall, as long as it was, went a table of
holm-oak,
Polished and white, as of steel; the columns twain of the
high-seat
Stood at the end thereof, two gods carved out of an elm-
tree;
Odin with lordly look, and Frey with the sun on his
frontlet.
Lately between the two, on a bear-skin (the skin, it was
coal-black,
Scarlet-red was the throat, but the paws were shodden
with silver),
Thorsten sat with his friends, Hospitality sitting with
Gladness.
Oft, when the moon among the night clouds flew, related
the old man
Wonders from far distant lands he had seen, and cruises
of Vikings
Far on the Baltic and Sea of the West, and the North
Sea.
Hushed sat the listening bench, and their glances hung
on the graybeard's

Lips, as a bee on the rose; but the Skald was thinking of Bragé,
Where, with silver beard, and runes on his tongue, he is seated
Under the leafy beach, and tells a tradition by Mimer's
Ever-murmuring wave, himself a living tradition.
Mid-way the floor (with thatch was it strewn), burned forever the fire-flame
Glad on its stone-built hearth; and through the wide-mouthed smoke-flue
Looked the stars, those heavenly friends, down into the great hall.
But round the walls, upon nails of steel, were hanging in order
Breastplate and helm with each other, and here and there in among them
Downward lightened a sword, as in winter evening a star shoots.
More than helmets and swords, the shields in the banquet-hall glistened,
White as the orb of the sun, or white as the moon's disk of silver.
Ever and anon went a maid round the board and filled up the drink-horns;
Ever she cast down her eyes and blushed; in the shield her reflection
Blushed too, even as she;—this gladdened the hard-drinking champions.

(*H. W. Longfellow*)

Frithiof's Farewell

"No more shall I see
In its upward motion
The smoke of the Northland. Man is a slave;
The Fates decree.
On the waste of the ocean,
There is my fatherland, there is my grave.

"Go not to the strand,
Ring, with thy bride,
After the stars spread their light through the sky.
Perhaps in the sand,
Washed up by the tide,
The bones of the outlawed Viking may lie.

"Then quoth the king,
' 'T is mournful to hear
A man like a whimpering maiden cry,
The death-song they sing
Even now in mine ear.
What avails it? He who is born must die.' "

(H. W. Longfellow)

RUSSIAN

Folk Songs

THE PLAINT OF THE WIFE

THE WIFE

Fain would I be sleeping, dreaming:
Heavy lies my head upon the pillow.
Up and down the passage goes my husband's father,
Angrily about it keeps he pacing.

CHORUS

Thumping, scolding, thumping, scolding,—
Never lets his daughter sleep.

FATHER-IN-LAW

Up, up, up, thou sloven there!
Up, up, up, thou sluggard there!
Slovenly, slatternly, sluggardish slut!

THE WIFE

Fain would I be sleeping, dreaming:
Heavy lies my head upon the pillow.
Up and down the passage goes my husband's mother,
Angrily about it keeps she pacing.

CHORUS

Thumping, scolding, thumping, scolding,—
Never lets her daughter sleep.

MOTHER-IN-LAW

Up, up, up! thou sloven there!
Up, up, up! thou sluggard there!
Slovenly, slatternly, sluggardish slut!

THE WIFE

Fain would I be sleeping, dreaming:
Heavy lies my head upon the pillow.
Up and down the passage steals my well-beloved One,—
All so lightly, softly, keeps he whispering.

THE LOVER

Sleep, sleep, sleep, my darling One!
Sleep, sleep, sleep, my precious One!
Driven out, thrown away, married too soon!

(W. R. S. Ralston)

SORROW

Whither shall I, the fair maiden, flee from Sorrow?
If I fly from Sorrow into the dark forest,—
After me runs Sorrow with an ax:
"I will fell, I will fell the green oaks;
I will seek, I will find the fair maiden."
If I fly from Sorrow into the open field,—
After me runs Sorrow with a scythe:
"I will mow, I will mow the open field;
I will seek, I will find the fair maiden."
Whither then shall I flee from Sorrow?
If I rush from Sorrow into the blue sea,—
After me comes Sorrow as a huge fish;
"I will drink, I will swallow the blue sea;
I will seek, I will find the fair maiden."
If I seek refuge from Sorrow in marriage,—
Sorrow follows me as my dowry;
If I take to my bed to escape from Sorrow,—
Sorrow sits beside my pillow;
And when I shall have fled from Sorrow into the damp
earth,—
Sorrow will come after me with a spade.
Then will Sorrow stand over me, and cry triumphantly,
"I have driven, I have driven, the maiden into the damp
earth!"

(W. R. S. Ralston)

LOVE-SONG

The little wild birds have come flying
From beyond the sea, the blue sea;
The little birds go fluttering
About the bushes, over the open field:
All have their mates and rejoice in love.
Only the good youth, Alexàndrushka,
A homeless orphan in the wide world,
Grieves like a pining cuckoo,
And melts away in burning tears.
The poor lad has no one,
No one in the wide world to fondle him,—
No one ever brings joy to the orphan,
Uttering words of kind endearment.
Should he go out into the open field,
There to trample under foot his cares,
His misery and his bitter longing,
His longing and his misery not to be shaken off,—
Or should he go out into the dark forest,
His sorrow will not fly away.
The heart of the good youth
Is eaten up with care;
He fades, he withers in his loneliness,
Like a blade of grass in the midst of a wild plain.
To the youth not even God's light is dear.
But Dunya dear has taken pity
On the poor fellow, on the orphan;
She has caress'd the homeless One,
She has spoken to him terms of endearment,—
The beautiful maiden has fallen in love
With the lad Alexàndrushka.
She has cover'd him with her silken veil,
She has call'd him her darling, her Belovèd One:
And his sorrow and sighing have pass'd away.

(*W. R. S. Ralston*)

Ivan Andreevich Kriloff

1768-1844

THE PEASANT AND THE SHEEP

A PEASANT haled a sheep to court,
And pressed against her there a serious objection.
A fox, as judge, is ready for a fault's detection,
Hears plaintiff first and, then, defendant in retort;
Taking in turn each point, and cool, though others stammer,
He seeks the cause of all the clamor.
The peasant says:—"My lord! when visiting my yard,
I found two chickens missing; 'twas in early morning;
Only their bones and feathers served me as a warning;
This sheep alone was there on guard!"
The sheep replies:—"No strange event my slumbers marred;
Prithee, the evidence of neighbors don't discard;
Against me ne'er was brought a charge of thieving
Or other crime
At any time;
As to my tasting flesh, 'tis notion past conceiving."
Here are the fox's judgments from their earliest weaving:—
"I noway can accept the pleadings of this sheep,
Because all rogues are skilled to keep
Their wicked purposes from others.
'Tis clear from plaintiff's words that, on the given night,
Defendant held the fowl-house well in sight;
Now, who can think she smothers
An inborn wish for viands choice?
So I decide, by conscience' sacred voice,
She cannot have admitted
Hens were for her unfitted!
Her guilt is clear and lets the peasant win;
The carcase comes to me, and he will get the skin."

(*C. Fillingham Coxwell*)

Alexander Sergeyevich Pushkin

1799-1837

He is placed in the company of Dante, Shakespeare, and Goethe by his compatriots. The intensity of his passionate nature was governed by a wide intelligence, a capacity for detachment, and above all by a sense of measure and harmony.—Babette Deutsch and Avraham Yarmolinsky.

AUTUMN

October at last has come! The thicket has shaken
The last leaf lingering down from the naked branch.
Autumn is breathing cold, the road is frozen—
The brook still runs with a murmur behind the mill,
But the pond is still; my neighbor is up and away
With a hunt, away to the farthest dreaming field,
Where the winter wheat will suffer from his mad sport,
And the bark of dogs will startle the forest oaks.

It is my time now! I never could love the spring,
The dragging thaw, the mud, the stench—I am sick
In spring: my blood's astray, my mind is oppressed
With a yearning pain. Winter is better for me.
I love the serious snow-fields under the moon!
How the light run of the sled is swift and free,
And the hand of a love down under the sables
warm! . . .

And Oh the fun, to be shod with the sharpened steel,
And glide on the glassy face of the standing river!
The shining alarm of a winter holiday!
But still there's a limit in things!—A half year's snow—
Even at last to the old cave-dweller, the bear,
It is long enough! You can not forever and ever
Slide in a sled with the beautiful young Armida,
Or sulk behind double glass by a friendly stove. . . .

They commonly scold the last days of autumn: to me,
My reader and friend, they are dear; their beauty is quiet,

Their modesty brilliant; they draw me to them like a
child
Whom the family does not love. I will tell you frankly:
Of all the seasons of time I can love but one;
I find in her—I am not a vainglorious lover,
Though willful of fancy—I find in my love much good.

How shall I tell you? She ravishes me
As a dying virgin, perhaps, might ravish you.
Condemned, and bending meekly, and murmuring not.
Not angry—a smile on the fading lips—
She does not perceive the abysmal opening mouth
Of the tomb—the purplish light on her features, plays—
To-day she is here—she lives—and to-morrow not.

Sweet mournful days, charm of the dreaming eyes,
Your beauty is dear to me that says farewell!
I love the sumptuous decline of nature's life,
The tents of the forest adorned with purple and gold,
And loud with the sound of the faster breath of the
wind,
A billowy curtain of fog concealing the sky,
And the sun's rare beam, and the early frost,
And the threat of the gray-head winter standing off!

With every autumn that comes I bloom again;
It is good for my health, it is good, this Russian cold;
I fall afresh in love with the habit of being;
Sleep flies early, and hunger is in its place,
The blood romps joyfully through my heart,
Desire seethes up—I laugh again, I am young,
I am living life—such is my organism
(If you will excuse me, please, the prosaism).

So saddle my horse; and into the plentiful open
With fluttering mane he will carry me flying, and under
His body his glittering hoofs will ring like a tune
Through the frozen valley, will crackle and crash on the
ice—

Till the brief day dies! And then the chimney, forgotten,
Will waken again with fire—will pour sharp light,
Or dimly glow, while I sit reading long,
And nourishing the long thoughts in my soul. . . .

(*Max Eastman*)

MESSAGE TO SIBERIA

Deep in the Siberian mine,
Keep your patience proud;
The bitter toil shall not be lost,
The rebel thought unbowed.

The sister of misfortune, Hope,
In the under-darkness dumb
Speaks joyful courage to your heart:
The day desired will come.

And love and friendship pour to you
Across the darkened doors,
Even as round your galley-beds
My free music pours.

The heavy-hanging chains will fall,
The walls will crumble at a word;
And Freedom greet you in the light,
And brothers give you back the sword.

(*Max Eastman*)

WORK

Here is the long-bided hour: the labor of years is accomplished.
Why should this sadness unplumbed secretly weigh on my heart?
Is it, my work being done, I stand like a laborer, useless,
One who has taken his pay, a stranger to tasks that are new?

Is it the work I regret, the silent companion of midnight,
Friend of the golden-haired Dawn, friend of the gods of the hearth?

(Babette Deutsch and Avrahm Yarmolinsky)

THE PROPHET

Athirst in spirit, through the gloom
Of an unpeopled waste I blundered,
And saw a six-winged Seraph loom
Where the two pathways met and sundered.
He laid his fingers on my eyes:
His touch lay soft as slumber lies,—
And like an eagle's, his crag shaken,
Did my prophetic eyes awaken.
Upon my ears his fingers fell
And sound rose,—stormy swell on swell:
I heard the spheres revolving, chiming,
The angels in their soaring sweep,
The monsters moving in the deep,
The green vine in the valley climbing.
And from my mouth the Seraph wrung
Forth by its roots my sinful tongue;
The evil things and vain it babbled
His hand drew forth and so effaced,
And the wise serpent's tongue he placed
Between my lips with hand blood-dabbled;
And with a sword he clove my breast,
Plucked out the heart he made beat higher,
And in my stricken bosom pressed
Instead a coal of living fire.
Upon the wastes, a lifeless clod,
I lay, and heard the voice of God:
"Arise, oh, prophet, watch and hearken,
And with my Will thy soul engird,
Roam the gray seas, the roads that darken,
And burn men's hearts with this, my Word."

(Babette Deutsch and Avrahm Yarmolinsky)

Fyodor Tyutchev

1803-1873

AS OCEAN'S STREAM

As ocean's stream girdles the ball of earth,
From circling seas of dream man's life emerges,
And as night moves in silence up the firth
The secret tide around our mainland surges.

The voice of urgent waters softly sounds;
The magic skiff uplifts white wings of wonder.
The tide swells swiftly and the white sail rounds,
Where the blind waves in shoreless darkness thunder.

And the wide heavens, starred and luminous,
Out of the deep in mystery aspire.
The strange abyss is burning under us;
And we sail onward, and our wake is fire.

(*Babette Deutsch and Avrahm Yarmolinsky*)

Nikolay Platonovich Ogarev

1813-1879

THE ROAD

FAINT shines the far moon
  Through misty night,
Sad lies the dead field
  In the moon's light.
White with frost along
  The road without end,
Bare-branched their long line
  Birches extend.
Bells tinkle, the team
  Swiftly whirls along,
My drowsy driver hums
  Softly his song.
Onward I travel
  In my crazy cart,
Sadly, pitying
  The land of my heart.

(*P. E. Matheson*)

Mikhail Yuryevich Lermontov

1814-1841

This brilliant bully and egotistic rake was, after his own fashion, a knight of the Grail and a poetic genius such as rarely graces any language.—Babette Deutsch and Avraham Yarmolinsky.

DAGGER

I love you well, my steel-white dagger,
Comrade luminous and cold;
Forged by a Georgian dreaming vengeance,
Whetted by Circassians bold.

A tender hand, in grace of parting,
Gave you to mark a meeting brief;
For blood there glimmered on your metal
A shining tear—the pearl of grief.

And black eyes, clinging to my glances,
Filled deep with liquid sorrow seemed;
Like your clear blade where flame is trembling,
They darkened quickly and they gleamed.

You were to be my long companion.
Give me your counsel to the end!
I will be hard of soul and faithful,
Like you, my iron-hearted friend!

(*Max Eastman*)

A SAIL

White is the sail and lonely
On the misty infinite blue;
Flying from what in the homeland?
Seeking for what in the new?

The waves romp, and the winds whistle,
And the mast leans and creaks;
Alas! He flies not from fortune,
And no good fortune he seeks.

Beneath him the stream, luminous, azure,
Above him the sun's golden breast;
But he, a rebel, invites the storms,
As though in the storms were rest.

(*Max Eastman*)

COMPOSED WHILE UNDER ARREST

When waves invade the yellowing wheat,
And the saplings sway with a wind-song brief;
When the raspberry plum in the garden sweet
Hides him under the cool green leaf;

When sprinkled with lights of limpid dew,
At rose of evening or gold of morn,
The lilies-of-the-valley strew
Their silver nodding under the thorn;

When the brook in the valley with cooling breast,
Plunging my soul in a cloudy dream,
Murmurs a legend of lands of rest
At the rise of his happy and rapid stream;

Then humbled is my heart's distress,
And lulled the anguish of my blood;
Then in the earth my happiness,
Then in the heaven my God.

(*Max Eastman*)

A THOUGHT

I gaze with grief upon our generation.
Its future black or vacant—and to-day,
Bent with a load of doubt and understanding,
In sloth and cold stagnation it grows old.
When scarcely from the cradle we were rich
In follies, in our fathers' tardy wits.
Life wearied us—a road without a goal,
A feast upon a foreign holiday.

Toward good and evil shamefully impassive,
In mid-career we fade without a fight.
Before a danger pusillanimous,
Before a power that scorns us we are slaves.
Precocious fruit, untimely ripe, we hang,
Rejoicing neither sight nor touch nor tongue,
A wrinkled orphan runt among the blossoms,
Their beauty's hour the hour of its decay.

The hues of poetry, the shapes of art,
Wake in our minds no lovely ecstasy.
We hoard the dregs of feelings that are dead,
Misers, we dig and hide a debased coin.
We hate by chance, we love by accident;
We make no sacrifice to hate or love.
Within our minds presides a secret chill
Even while the flame is burning in our blood.
A bore to us our fathers' gorgeous sporting,
Their conscientious childish vast debauch.
We hasten tomb-wards without joy or glory,
With but a glance of ridicule thrown back.
A surly-hearted crowd and soon forgotten,
We pass in silence, trackless from the world,
Tossing no fruit of dreaming to the ages,
No deed of genius even half begun.
Our dust the justice of the citizen
In future time will judge in songs of venom. . . .
Will celebrate the weak and squandering father
In bitter mockery the cheated son.

(*Max Eastman*)

THE MOUNTAIN

A GOLDEN cloud slept for her pleasure
All night on the gaunt hill's breast;
Light-heart to her play-ground of azure,
How early she sped from the nest.

But the soft moist trace of her sleeping
Lay in the folds of the hill.
He pondered; his tears are creeping
Down to the desert still.

(Max Eastman)

THE REED

There sat a happy fisherman
Upon a river bank.
Before him on the wind's wings
Tall reeds swayed rank on rank.

He cut him down a dry reed,
He pierced it through and through,
Then pinched one end together,
And in the other blew.

As if to life awaking,
The reed to speak began.
Was it the wind's voice calling
Or was it voice of man?

The reed sang slow and sadly—
"Oh let me, let me be,
Oh happy, happy fisherman,
For you are killing me.

"I was a comely maiden
With life and joy aglow.
In my step-mother's house
I flowered long ago.

"And many tears and bitter
I innocently shed,
And often in the darkness
I wished that I was dead.

"She had a son beloved
Of her and none besides,
Who frightened honest people
And ravished girlish brides.

"And once we went at evening
Upon the steep high shore
To look upon the sunset
And hear the waters roar.

"He gave me gold and silver—
I would not take his gold.
He asked me for my true love—
My heart grew sad and cold.

"Then in my soft young bosom
His heavy knife-blade sank,
And here my corpse he buried
Upon the river bank.

"Out of my stricken bosom
A great dry reed uprose,
And in it live my dolor,
My pain and all my woes.

"Oh happy, happy fisherman,
Pray let me, let me be,
Or have you never suffered
And tasted misery?"

(*J. J. Robbins*)

FROM "THE DÆMON" (Part I, xv)

On the sightless seas of ether,
Rudderless, without a sail,
Choirs of stars uplift their voices,
Where the mist waves rise and fail.

Through the hemless fields of heaven
Wander wide and tracelessly
Clouds, unshepherded, unnumbered,
Pale, ephemeral and free.

Hour of parting, hour of meeting,
Neither gladden them nor fret;
Theirs no yearning toward the future,
Theirs no haunting of regret.

On the grim day of disaster
These remember, worlds away:
Be beyond earth's reach as they are,
And indifferent as they.

(*Babette Deutsch and Avrahm Yarmolinsky*)

Afanasy Afanasyevich Foeth (Shenshin)

1820-1892

MORNING SONG

I CAME to you with a greeting,
To tell you the sun has arisen,
With his hot happy light
He is trembling among the leaves;

To tell you the forest is waking,
Every twig is awaking,
And every bird is shaking his wings,
Is full of the thirst of spring;

With all of the midnight's passion
Again in the morning I come,
And my spirit is still as eager
To wait upon joy and you;

And all of the winds of the heaven
Blow happiness to me,
And I know not the theme of the singing,
But a song is lifting its wings.

(*Max Eastman*)

Nikolai Nekrasov

1821-1877

THE CAPITALS ARE ROCKED

THE capitals are rocked with thunder
Of orators in wordy feuds.
But in the depths of Russia, yonder
An age-old awful silence broods.

Only the wind in wayside willows,
Coming and going, does not cease;
And corn-stalks touch in curving billows
The earth that cherishes and pillows,
Through endless fields of changeless peace.

(*Babette Deutsch and Avrahm Yarmolinsky*)

Ivan Savvich Nikitin

1824-1861

A NIGHT IN A VILLAGE

Sultry air, the smoke of shavings,
  Dirt spread over all,
Feet and benches dirty; cobwebs
  To adorn the wall:
Smoke-begrimed each cottage chamber;
  Bread and water stale;
Spinners coughing, children crying—
  Want and woe prevail.
Hand to mouth lifelong they labor,
  Then a pauper's grave—
Ah! what need to learn the lesson—
  "Trust, my soul, be brave!"

(*P. E. Matheson*)

Fyodor Sologub

1863–1927

THE AMPHORA

In a gay jar upon his shoulder
The slave morosely carries wine.
His road is rough with bog and bowlder,
And in the sky no planets shine.
Into the dark with stabbing glances
He peers, his careful steps are slow,
Lest on his breast as he advances
The staining wine should overflow.
I bear my amphora of sorrow,
Long brimming with the wine it hides;

There poison for each waiting morrow
Ferments within the painted sides.
I follow secret ways and hidden
To guard the evil vessel, lest
A careless touch should pour unbidden
Its bitterness upon my breast.

(*Babette Deutsch and Avrahm Yarmolinsky*)

AUSTERE THE MUSIC OF MY SONGS

Austere the music of my songs:
The echo of sad utterance fills them,
A bitter breath, far-wafted, chills them;
And is my back not bent to thongs?

The mists of day on darkness fall;
To reach my promised land I follow
A vain road that the shadows swallow;
The world rears round me like a wall.

At times from that far land the vain
Faint voice will sound like distant thunder.
Can the long waiting on a wonder
Obliterate the long bleak pain?

(*Babette Deutsch and Avrahm Yarmolinsky*)

Vyacheslav Ivanov

1866–

THE HOLY ROSE

The holy Rose her leaves will soon unfold.
The tender bud of dawn already lies
Reddening on the wide, transparent skies.
Love's star is a white sail the still seas hold.
Here in the light-soaked space above the wold,
Through the descending dew the arches rise
Of the unseen cathedral, filled with cries
From the winged weavers threading it with gold.

Here on the hill, the cypress, in accord
With me, stands praying: a cowled eremite.
And on the rose's cheeks the tears fall light.
Upon my cell the patterned rays are poured.
And in the East, the purple vines bleed bright,
And seething overflow. . . . Hosanna, Lord!

(Babette Deutsch and Avrahm Yarmolinsky)

Ivan Bunin

1870–

FLAX

She sits on tumulus Savoor, and stares,
Old woman Death, upon the crowded road.
Like a blue flame the small flax-flower flares
Thick through the meadows sowed.

And says old woman Death: "Hey, traveler!
Does any one want linen, linen fit
For funeral wear? A shroud, madam or sir,
I'll take cheap coin for it!"

And says serene Savoor: "Don't crow so loud!
Even the winding-sheet is dust, and cracks
And crumbles into earth, that from the shroud
May spring the sky-blue flax."

(Babette Deutsch and Avrahm Yarmolinsky)

Valery Bryusov

1873-1924

RADIANT RANKS OF SERAPHIM

Radiant ranks of seraphim
Stir the air about our bed.
With their windy wings and dim
Our hot cheeks are comforted.

Low the circling seraphs bend,
And we tremble and rejoice
At hosannas that ascend,
Winged with their unearthly voice.

Cloudy luminous faces hover,
And the wing-swept candles wane.
And our fiery breasts they cover
As with hidden holy rain.

(Babette Deutsch and Avrahm Yarmolinsky)

Alexander Blok

1880-1921

RUSSIA

To sin, unshamed, to lose, unthinking,
The count of careless nights and days,
And then, while the head aches with drinking,
Steal to God's house, with eyes that glaze;

Thrice to bow down to earth, and seven
Times cross oneself beside the door,
With the hot brow, in hope of heaven,
Touching the spittle-covered floor;

With a brass farthing's gift dismissing
The offering, the holy Name
To mutter with loose lips, in kissing
The ancient, kiss-worn icon-frame;

And coming home, then, to be tricking
Some wretch out of the same small coin,
And with an angry hiccup, kicking
A lean cur in his trembling groin;

And where the icon's flame is quaking
Drink tea, and reckon loss and gain,
From the fat chest of drawers taking
The coupons wet with spittle-stain;

And sunk in feather-beds to smother
In slumber, such as bears may know,—
Dearer to me than every other
Are you, my Russia, even so.

(Babette Deutsch and Avrahm Yarmolinsky)

From THE TWELVE

It was given to this delicate and remote lyricist to produce the outstanding poem of the Proletarian Revolution. He wrote his brief, crowded epic, "The Twelve," in January, 1918, with, as he said, the tumult of a falling world assailing his ears, and it is told that the composition took him a single night. The piece is known far beyond the confines of Russia and is accessible in many languages.—Babette Deutsch and Avrahm Yarmolinsky.

I

Black night.
White snow.
The wind, the wind!
It will not let you go.
The wind, the wind!
Through God's whole world it blows.

The wind is weaving
The white snow.
Brother ice peeps from below.
Stumbling and tumbling,
Folk slip and fall.
God pity all! . . .

The wind lashes at the cross-roads
And the frost stings to the bone.
With his nose stuck in his collar
A bourgeois stands alone.

And who's this fellow tosses his long hair
And mutters with a mournful air:
"Renegades!
Russia is dead"?
One of those pen-pushing blades—
Gently bred.

Here's a frocked one, black and bulky,
Sidling like a beast.
Why so sulky,
Comrade priest?

You used to strut,
Do you recall,
Your belly with its pendent cross
Shining on one and all? . . .

It is late.
One flickering lamp
In the street. A stooping tramp
Goes past with shuffling gait.
The shrill winds hiss.

"Come here,
Poor dear,
Give us a kiss."
"Bread!"
"Oh, get ahead!"

Pitchy sky; no stars, no chart.
Hate, sorrowful hate,
Bursts the heart.
Black, holy hate.
Comrade,
Watch your gait.

2

The wind is a whirl, the snow is a dance.
In the night twelve men advance.

Black, narrow rifle-straps,
Cigarettes, tilted caps.

A convict's stripes would fit their backs.
Fires mark their nightly tracks.

Freedom, ekh, freedom—
Unhallowed, unblessed!
Trah-tah-tah! . . .

Fires blaze upon their track.
Their rifle-straps are gleaming black.

March to the revolution's pace;
We've a fierce enemy to face.

More daring, friends, take aim, the lot!
At Holy Russia let's fire a shot.

At hutted Russia,
Fat-rumped and solid,
Russia, the stolid!

Ekh, ekh, unhallowed, unblessed. . . .

9

The city's roar is far away,
Black silence broods on Neva's brink.
No more police! We can be gay,
Comrades, without a drop to drink.

A bourgeois, a lonely mourner,
His nose tucked in his ragged fur,
Stands lost and idle on the corner,
Tagged by a cringing, mangy cur.

The bourgeois like a hungry mongrel,—
A silent question,—stands and begs;
The old world like a kinless mongrel
Stands there, its tail between its legs. . . .

11

And the twelve, unblessed, uncaring,
Still go marching on,
Ripe for death and daring,
Pitying none.

On, with rifles lifted
At the hidden enemy.
Through deaf alleys where the snow is sifted,
Where the lonely tempest tosses free.
Onward, where the snow has drifted
Clutching at the marcher's knee.

The red flag
Flaunts in their faces.

Steady beat
Their sounding paces.

Grimly followed
Are their traces.

Ruthlessly the storm-wind smites
Days and nights.

Forward, forward, the thundering beat
Of the workers' marching feet!

12

Onward as a haughty host they march.
Ho! Who else is there? Come out!
Only wind, wind bellying the flag,
Tossing the red flag about.

On ahead a snowdrift towers sheer.
Who is hiding in the drift? Come out!
A starving mongrel shambles in the rear,
Limping off as though he feared a clout.

"Skip! Or I'll prick your mangy fur
With this tickling bayonet!
The old world is a mongrel cur. . . .
Beatings are the best you'll get."

Teeth keen-gleaming in a hungry grin,
Furtively he follows on behind.
The mongrel has nor kith nor kin . . .
"Hey! Who goes there? Answer quickly, mind!

Who's waving the red flag? You cannot see
In the darkness, through the blinding snow.
There is some one stirring stealthily
In the shadows, secretly and slow.

We will get you and your comrades too!
Best surrender while you're breathing still,
Comrade . . . it will be the worse for you.
Come! or else we'll shoot to kill."

Crrack-crack-crack! But solitary
Echo answers, from the houses thrown,
While the storm-wind, wild and merry,
Laughs among the snows alone.

Crrack-crack-crack!
Crrrack-crack-crack!

Forward as a haughty host they tread.
A hungry mongrel shambles in the rear.
Bearing forth the banner's windy red,
Where the vagrant snow-veils veer,
In dim hands no bullets sear,
On the tempest gently thrown,
Like a snow of diamonds blown
In mist-white roses garlanded—
Christ marches on. And twelve are led.

(*Babette Deutsch and Avrahm Yarmolinsky*)

THE SCYTHIANS

You are the millions, we are multitude
And multitude and multitude.
Come, fight! Yea, we are Scythians,
Yea, Asians, a squint-eyed, greedy brood.

For you—the centuries, for us—one hour.
Like slaves, obeying and abhorred,
We were the shield between the breeds
Of Europe and the raging Mongol horde.

For centuries the hammers on your forge
Drowned out the avalanche's boom;
You heard like wild, fantastic tales
Old Lisbon's and Messina's sudden doom.

Yea, you have long since ceased to love
As our hot blood can love; the taste
You have forgotten, of a love
That burns like fire and like fire lays waste.

All things we love: cold numbers' burning chill,
The ecstasies that secret bloom.
All things we know: the Gallic light
And the parturient Germanic gloom.

And we remember all: Parisian hells,
The breath of Venice's lagoons,
Far fragrance of green lemon groves,
And dim Cologne's cathedral-splintered moons.

And flesh we love, its color and its taste,
Its deathly odor, heavy, raw.
And is it our guilt if your bones
May crack beneath our powerful supple paw?

It is our wont to seize wild colts at play:
They rear and impotently shake
Wild manes—we crush their mighty croups.
And shrewish women slaves we tame—or break.

Come unto us, from the black ways of war,
Come to our peaceful arms and rest.
Comrades, while it is not too late,
Sheathe the old sword. May brotherhood be blest.

If not, we have not anything to lose.
We also know old perfidies.
By sick descendants you will be
Accursed for centuries and centuries.

To welcome pretty Europe, we shall spread
And scatter in the tangled space
Of our wide thickets. We shall turn
To you our alien Asiatic face.

For centuries your eyes were toward the East.
Our pearls you hoarded in your chests,
And mockingly you bode the day
When you could aim your cannon at our breasts.

The time has come. Disaster beats its wings.
With every day the insults grow.
The hour will strike, and without ruth
Your proud and powerless Pæstums be laid low.

Oh, pause, old world, while life still beats in you,
Oh, weary one, oh, worn, oh, wise!
Halt here, as once did Œdipus
Before the Sphinx's enigmatic eyes.

Yea, Russia is a Sphinx. Exulting, grieving,
And sweating blood, she cannot sate
Her eyes that gaze and gaze and gaze
At you with stone-lipped love for you, and hate.

Go, all of you, to Ural fastnesses.
We clear the ground for the appalling scenes
Of war between the savage Mongol hordes
And pitiless science with its massed machines.

But we, we shall no longer be your shield.
But, careless of the battle-cries,
Will watch the deadly duel seethe,
Aloof, with indurate and narrow eyes.

We will not move when the ferocious Hun
Despoils the corpse and leaves it bare,
Burns towns, herds cattle in the church,
And smell of white flesh roasting fills the air.

For the last time, old world, we bid you come,
Feast brotherly within our walls.
To share our peace and glowing toil
Once only the barbarian lyre calls.

(*Babette Deutsch and Avrahm Yarmolinsky*)

Vladimir Mayakovsky

1894-

OUR MARCH

Slog brute streets with rebel tramping!
Higher, the crags of haughty heads!
We will wash all the planets' cities
In the surge of a second flood.

Pied days, these.
Slow drags the dray of years.
Our god's Speed.
Our hearts are drums.

Who can match the glow of our golds?
Will the waspy bullets bite?
We strike back with songs for weapons.
Massive gold—our thundering voices.

Lacquer the lawn, green,
Carpet the days, grass;
Harness the quick years, sky,
Under a rainbow yoke.

Look at heaven, gaping with boredom:
We have shut it out from our songs.
Hey, Great Dipper, demand
That they hoist us to heaven alive.

Drink to joy! Shout!
Spring has flooded our blood.
Heart, exult, beat!
Our breasts are as crashing brass.

(*Babette Deutsch and Avrahm Yarmolinsky*)

ENGLISH

Anonymous

c. 1250

SUMER IS ICUMEN IN

SUMER is icumen in,
   Lhude sing cuccu;
Groweth sed and bloweth med
   And springth the wude nu.
      Sing cuccu!

Awe bleteth after lomb,
   Lhouth after calve cu;
Bulluc sterteth, bucke verteth,
   Murie sing cuccu.

Cuccu, cuccu, wel
   Singes thu, cuccu:
   Na swike thu naver nu;
Sing cuccu, nu,
   Sing cuccu,
   Sing cuccu, sing cuccu, nu.

Geoffrey Chaucer

1340?–1400

BALADE

From THE PROLOGUE TO THE LEGEND OF GOOD WOMEN

HYD, Absolon, they gilte tresses clere;
Ester, ley thou thy meknesse al a-doun;
Hyd, Jonathas, al thy frendly manere;
Penalopee, and Marcia Catoun,
Mak of your wyfhod no comparisoun;
Hyde ye your beautes, Isoude and Eleyne,
Alceste is here, that al that may desteyne.

Thy faire bodye, lat hit nat appere,
Lavyne; and thou, Lucresse of Rome toun,
And Polixene, that boghte love so dere,
Eek Cleopatre, with al thy passioun,
Hyde ye your trouthe in love and your renoun;
And thou, Tisbe, that hast for love swich peyne:
Alceste is here, that al that may desteyne.

Herro, Dido, Laudomia, alle in-fere,
Eek Phyllis, hanging for thy Demophoun,
And Canace, espyed by thy chere,
Ysiphile, betrayed with Jasoun,
Mak of your trouthe in love no bost ne soun;
Nor Ypermistre or Adriane, ne pleyne;
Alceste is here, that al that may desteyne.

TRUTH

FLEE fro the prees, and dwelle with sothfastnesse,
Suffyce unto thy good, though hit be smal;
For hord hath hate, and climbing tikelnesse,
Press hath envye, and wele blent overal;
Savour no more than thee bihove shal;
Werk wel thy-self, that other folk canst rede;
Alceste is here, that al that may desteyne.

Tempest thee noght al croked to redresse,
In trust of hir that turneth as a bal:
Gret reste stant in litel besinesse;
And eek be war to sporne ageyn an al;
Stryve noght, as doth the crokke with the wal.
Daunte thy-self, that dauntest otheres dede;
And trouthe shal delivere, hit is no drede.

That thee is sent, receyve in buxumnesse,
The wrastling for this worlde axeth a fal.
Her nis non hoom, her nis but wildernesse:

Forth, pilgrim, forth! Forth, beste, out of they stal!
Know thy contree, look up, thank God of al;
Hold the hye wey, and lat thy gost thee lede:
And trouthe shall delivere, hit is no drede.

Therfore, thou vache, leve thyn old wrecchednesse
Unto the worlde; leve now to be thral;
Crye him mercy, that of his hy goodnesse
Made thee of noght, and in especial
Draw unto him, and pray in general
For thee, and eek for other, hevenlich mede;
And trouthe shal delivere, hit is no drede.

GENTILESSE

The firste stok, fader of gentilesse—
What man that claymeth gentil for to be,
Must folowe his trace, and alle his wittes dresse
Vertu to sewe, and vyces for to flee.
For unto vertu longeth dignitee,
And noght the revers, saufly dar I deme,
Al were he mytre, croune, or diademe.

This firste stok was ful of rightwisnesse,
Trewe of his word, sobre, pitous, and free,
Clene of his goste, and loved besinesse,
Ageinst the vyce of slouthe, in honestee;
And, but his heir love vertu, as dide he,
He is noght gentil, thogh he riche seme,
Al were he mytre, croune, or diademe.

Vyce may wel be heir to old richesse;
But ther nay no man, as men may wel see,
Bequethe his heir his vertuous noblesse
That is appropred unto no degree,
But to the firste fader in magestee,
That maketh him his heir, that can him queme,
Al were he mytre, croune, or diademe.

LAK OF STEDFASTNESSE

Som tyme this world was so stedfast and stable,
That mannes word was obligacioun,
And now hit is so fals and deceivable,
That word and deed, as in conclusioun,
Ben no-thing lyk, for turned up so doun
Is al this world for mede and wilfulnesse,
That al is lost for lak of stedfastnesse.

What maketh this world to be so variable,
But lust that folk have in dissensioun?
Among us now a man is holde unable,
But-if he can, by som collusioun,
Don his neighbour wrong or oppressioun.
What causeth this, but wilful wrechhednesse,
That all is lost, for lak of stedfastnesse?

Trouthe is put doun, resoun is holden fable;
Vertu hath now no dominacioun,
Pitee exyled, no man is merciable.
Through covetyse is blent discrecioun;
The world hath mad a permutacioun
Fro right to wrong, fro trouthe to fikelnesse,
That al is lost, for lak of stedfastness.

O prince, desyre to be honourable,
Cherish they folk and hate extorcioun!
Suffre no thing, that may be reprevable
To thyn estate, don in thy regioun.
Shew forth they swerd of castigacioun,
Dred God, do law, love trouthe and worthinesse,
And wed thy folk agein to stedfastnesse.

Anonymous

16th-17th centuries

BALLADS

Sir Patrick Spens

The king sits in Dumferling toune,
  Drinking the blude-reid wine:
"O whar will I get guid sailor,
  To sail this schip of mine?"

Up and spak an eldern knicht,
  Sat at the kings richt kne:
"Sir Patrick Spence is the best sailor,
  That sails upon the se."

The king has written a braid letter,
  And signd it wi his hand,
And sent it to Sir Patrick Spence,
  Was walking on the sand.

The first line that Sir Patrick red,
  A loud lauch lauched he;
The next line that Sir Patrick red,
  The teir blinded his ee.

"O wha is this has don this deid,
  This ill deid don to me,
To send me out this time o' the yeir,
  To sail upon the se!

"Mak hast, mak haste, my mirry men all,
  Our guid schip sails the morne:"
"O say na sae, my master deir,
  For I feir a deadlie storme.

"Late late yestreen I saw the new moone,
  Wi the auld moone in hir arme,
And I feir, I feir, my deir master,
  That we will cum to harme."

O our Scots nobles wer richt laith
  To weet their cork-heild schoone;
Bot lang owre a' the play wer playd,
  Thair hats they swam aboone.

O lang, lang may their ladies sit,
  Wi thair fans into their hand,
Or eir they se Sir Patrick Spence
  Cum sailing to the land.

O lang, lang may the ladies stand,
  Wi thair gold kems in their hairs,
Waiting for thair ain deir lords,
  For they'll se thame na mair.

Haf owre, haf owre to Aberdour,
  It's fiftie fadom deip,
And thair lies guid Sir Patrick Spence,
  Wi the Scots lords at his feit.

The Wife of Usher's Well

There lived a wife at Usher's Well,
  And a wealthy wife was she;
She had three stout and stalwart sons,
  And sent them oer the sea.

They hadna been a week from her,
  A week but barely ane,
Whan word came to the carline wife
  That her three sons were gane.

They hadna been a week from her,
  A week but barely three,
Whan word came to the carlin wife
  That her sons she'd never see.

"I wish the wind may never cease,
  Nor fashes in the flood,
Till my three sons come hame to me,
  In earthly flesh and blood."

It fell about the Martinmass,
When nights are lang and mirk,
The carlin wife's three sons came hame,
And their hats were o the birk.

It neither grew in syke nor ditch,
Nor yet in ony sheugh;
But at the gates o Paradise,
That birk grew fair eneugh.

"Blow up the fire, my maidens,
Bring water from the well;
For a' my house shall feast this night,
Since my three sons are well."

And she has made to them a bed,
She's made it large and wide,
And she's taen her mantle her about,
Sat down at the bed-side.

Up then crew the red, red cock,
And up and crew the gray;
The eldest to the youngest said,
"'Tis time we were away."

The cock he hadna crawd but once,
And clappd his wings at a',
When the youngest to the eldest said,
"Brother, we must awa.

"The cock doth craw, the day doth daw,
The channerin worm doth chide;
Gin we be mist out o our place,
A sair pain we maun bide.

"Fare ye weel, my mother dear!
Fareweel to barn and byre!
And fare ye weel, the bonny lass
That kindles my mother's fire!"

Bonny Barbara Allan

It was in and about the Martinmas time,
When the green leaves were a falling,
That Sir John Græme, in the West Country,
Fell in love with Barbara Allan.

He sent his man down through the town,
To the place where she was dwelling:
"O haste and come to my master dear,
Gin ye be Barbara Allan."

O hooly, hooly rose she up,
To the place where he was lying,
And when she drew the curtain by,
"Young man, I think you're dying."

"O it's I'm sick, and very, very sick,
And 'tis a' for Barbara Allan:"
"O the better for me ye's never be,
Tho your heart's blood were a spilling.

"O dinna ye mind, young man," said she,
"When ye was in the tavern a drinking,
That ye made the healths gae round and round,
And slighted Barbara Allan?"

He turnd his face unto the wall,
And death was with him dealing:
"Adieu, adieu, my dear friends all,
And be kind to Barbara Allan."

And slowly, slowly raise she up,
And slowly, slowly left him,
And sighing said, she coud not stay,
Since death of life had reft him.

She had not gane a mile but twa,
When she heard the dead-bell ringing,
And every jow that the dead-bell geid,
It cry'd, Woe to Barbara Allan!

"O mother, mother, make my bed!
O make it saft and narrow!
Since my love died for me to-day,
I'll die for him to-morrow."

Lord Randal

"O where hae ye been, Lord Randal, my son?
O where hae ye been, my handsome young man?"
"I hae been to the wild wood; mother, make my bed soon,
For I'm weary wi hunting, and fain wald lie down."

"Where gat ye your dinner, Lord Randal, my son?
Where gat ye your dinner, my handsome, young man?"
"I din'd wi my true-love; mother, make my bed soon,
For I'm weary wi hunting, and fain wald lie down."

"What gat ye to your dinner, Lord Randal, my son?
What gat ye to your dinner, my handsome young man?"
"I gat eels boiled in broo; mother, make my bed soon,
For I'm weary wi hunting, and fain wald lie down."

"What became of your bloodhounds, Lord Randal, my son?
What became of your bloodhounds, my handsome young man?"
"O they swelld and they died; mother, make my bed soon,
For I'm weary wi hunting, and fain wald lie down."

"O I fear ye are poison'd, Lord Randal, my son!
O I fear ye are poisond, my handsome young man!"
"O yes! I am poisond; mother, make my bed soon,
For I'm sick at the heart, and I fain wald lie down."

Bonnie George Campbell

Hie upon Hielands,
And low upon Tay,
Bonnie George Campbell
Rade out on a day.

Saddled and bridled
  And gallant rade he;
Hame cam his gude horse,
  But never cam he!

Out cam his auld mither
  Greeting fu' sair,
And out cam his bonnie bride
  Rivin' her hair.

Saddled and bridled
  And booted rade he;
Toom hame cam the saddle,
  But never cam he!

"My meadow lies green,
  And my corn is unshorn;
My barn is to big,
  And my babie's unborn."

Saddled and bridled
  And booted rade he;
Toom hame cam the saddle,
  But never cam he.

The Twa Corbies

As I was walking all alane,
I heard twa corbies making a mane;
The tane unto the t'other say,
"Where sall we gang and dine today?"

"In behint yon auld fail dyke,
I wot there lies a new slain knight;
And naebody kens that he lies there
But his hawk, his hound, and lady fair.

"His hound is to the hunting gane,
His hawk to fetch the wild-fowl hame,
His lady's ta'en another mate,
So we may mak our dinner sweet.

"Ye'll sit on his white hause-bane,
And I'll pike out his bonny blue een;
Wi ae lock o his gowden hair,
We'll theek our nest when it grows bare.

"Mony a one for him makes mane,
But nane sall ken where he is gane;
Oer his white banes, when they are bare,
The wind sall blaw for evermair."

The Maid Freed From the Gallows

"O good Lord Judge, and sweet Lord Judge,
  Peace for a little while!
Methinks I see my own father,
  Come riding by the stile.

"O father, O father, a little of your gold,
  And likewise of your fee!
To keep my body from yonder grave,
  And my neck from the gallows-tree."

"None of my gold now you shall have,
  Nor likewise of my fee;
For I am come to see you hangd,
  And hangéd you shall be."

"O good Lord Judge, and sweet Lord Judge,
  Peace for a little while!
Methinks I see my own mother,
  Come riding by the stile.

"O mother, O mother, a little of your gold.
  And likewise of your fee,
To keep my body from yonder grave,
  And my neck from the gallows-tree!"

"None of my gold now shall you have,
  Nor likewise of my fee;
For I am come to see you hangd,
  And hangéd you shall be."

"O good Lord Judge, and sweet Lord Judge,
  Peace for a little while!
Methinks I see my own brother,
  Come riding by the stile.

"O brother, O brother, a little of your gold,
  And likewise of your fee,
To keep my body from yonder grave,
  And my neck from the gallows-tree!"

"None of my gold now shall you have,
  Nor likewise of my fee;
For I am come to see you hangd,
  And hangéd you shall be."

"O good Lord Judge, and sweet Lord Judge,
  Peace for a little while!
Methinks I see my own sister,
  Come riding by the stile.

"O sister, O sister, a little of your gold,
  And likewise of your fee,
To keep my body from yonder grave,
  And my neck from the gallows-tree!"

"None of my gold now shall you have,
  Nor likewise of my fee;
For I am come to see you hangd,
  And hangéd you shall be."

"O good Lord Judge, and sweet Lord Judge,
  Peace for a little while!
Methinks I see my own true-love,
  Come riding by the stile.

"O true-love, O true-love, a little of your gold,
  And likewise of your fee,
To save my body from yonder grave,
  And my neck from the gallows-tree."

"Some of my gold now you shall have,
  And likewise of my fee,
For I am come to see you saved,
  And savéd you shall be."

Sweet William's Ghost

There came a ghost to Margret's door,
  With many a grievous groan,
And ay he tirléd at the pin,
  But answer made she none.

"Is that my father Philip,
  Or is't my brother John?
Or is't my true-love Willy,
  From Scotland new come home?"

" 'Tis not thy father Philip,
  Nor yet thy brother John;
But 'tis thy true-love Willy,
  From Scotland new come home.

"O sweet Margret, O dear Margret,
  I pray thee speak to me;
Give me my faith and troth, Margret,
  As I gave it to thee."

"Thy faith and troth thou's never get,
  Nor yet will I thee lend,
Till that thou come within my bower,
  And kiss my cheek and chin."

"If I should come within thy bower,
  I am no earthly man;
And should I kiss thy rosy lips,
  Thy days will not be lang.

"O sweet Margret, O dear Margret,
  I pray thee speak to me;
Give me my faith and troth, Margret,
  As I gave it to thee."

"Thy faith and troth thou's never get,
  Nor yet will I thee lend,
Till you take me to yon kirk,
  And wed me with a ring."

"My bones are buried in yon kirkyard,
  Afar beyond the sea,
And it is but my spirit, Margret,
  That's now speaking to thee."

She stretchd out her lilly-white hand,
  And, for to do her best,
"Hae, there's your faith and troth, Willy;
  God send your soul good rest."

Now she has kilted her robes of green
  A piece below her knee,
And a' the live-lang winter night
  The dead corp followed she.

"Is there any room at your head, Willy?
  Or any room at your feet?
Or any room at your side, Willy,
  Wherein that I may creep?"

"There's no room at my head, Margret,
  There's no room at my feet;
There's no room at my side, Margret,
  My coffin's made so meet."

Then up and crew the red, red cock,
  And up then crew the gray:
" 'Tis time, 'tis time, my dear Margret,
  That you were going away."

No more the ghost to Margret said,
  But, with a grievous groan,
Evanishd in a cloud of mist,
  And left her all alone.

"O stay, my only true-love, stay,"
  The constant Margret cry'd;
Wan grew her cheeks, she closd her een,
  Stretchd her soft limbs, and dy'd.

Helen of Kirconnell

I wish I were where Helen lies,
Night and day on me she cries;
O that I were where Helen lies,
  On fair Kirconnell lea!

Curst be the heart that thought the thought,
And curst the hand that fired the shot,
When in my arms burd Helen dropt,
  And died to succour me!

O think na ye my heart was sair,
When my Love dropp'd and spak nae mair!
There did she swoon wi' meikle care,
  On fair Kirconnell lea.

As I went down the water side,
None but my foe to be my guide,
None but my foe to be my guide,
  On fair Kirconnell lea;

I lighted down my sword to draw,
I hackéd him in pieces sma',
I hackéd him in pieces sma',
  For her sake that died for me.

O Helen fair, beyond compare!
I'll mak a garland o' thy hair,
Shall bind my heart for evermair,
  Until the day I die!

O that I were where Helen lies!
Night and day on me she cries;
Out of my bed she bids me rise,
  Says, "Haste, and come to me!"

O Helen fair! O Helen chaste!
If I were with thee, I'd be blest,
Where thou lies low and taks thy rest,
On fair Kirconnell lea.

I wish my grave were growing green,
A winding-sheet drawn owre my e'en,
And I in Helen's arms lying,
On fair Kirconnell lea.

I wish I were where Helen lies!
Night and day on me she cries;
And I am weary of the skies,
For her sake that died for me.

Edmund Spenser

1552–1599

AMORETTI

LXX

Fresh Spring, the herald of loves mighty king,
In whose cote-armor richly are displayd
All sorts of flowers the which on earth do spring,
In goodly colors gloriously arrayd,
Goe to my love, where she is carelesse layd,
Yet in her winters bowre, not well awake;
Tell her the joyous time wil not be staid,
Unlesse she doe him by the forelock take:
Bid her therefore her selfe soone ready make,
To wayt on Love amongst his lovely crew,
Where every one that misseth then her make
Shall be by him amearst with penance dew.
Make hast therefore, sweet love, whilest it is prime;
For none can call againe the passèd time.

LXXV

One day I wrote her name upon the strand,
But came the waves and washed it away:
Agayne I wrote it with a second hand,
But came the tyde, and made my paynes his pray.

Vayne man, sayd she, that doest in vaine assay,
A mortall thing so to immortalize,
For I my selve shall lyke to this decay,
And eek my name bee wyped out lykewize.
Not so, (quod I) let baser things devize
To dy in dust, but you shall live by fame:
My verse your vertues rare shall eternize,
And in the hevens wryte your glorious name.
Where whenas death shall al the world subdew,
Our love shall live, and later life renew.

LXXIX

Men call you fayre, and you doe credit it,
For that your selfe ye dayly such doe see:
But the trew fayre, that is the gentle wit,
And vertuous mind, is much more praysd of me.
For all the rest, how ever fayre it be,
Shall turne to nought and loose that glorious hew:
But onely that is permanent and free
From frayle corruption, that doth flesh ensew.
That is true beautie: that doth argue you
To be divine and borne of heavenly seed:
Deriv'd from that fayre Spirit, from whom al true
And perfect beauty did at first proceed.
He onely fayre, and what he fayre hath made,
All other fayre lyke flowres untymely fade.

PROTHALAMION

Calm was the day, and through the trembling air
Sweet, breathing Zephyrus did softly play
A gentle spirit, that lightly did delay
Hot Titan's beams, which then did glister fair;
When I (whom sullen care,
Through discontent of my long fruitless stay
In princes' court, and expectation vain
Of idle hopes, which still do fly away,
Like empty shadows, did afflict my brain)
Walked forth to ease my pain

Along the shore of silver streaming Thames;
Whose rutty bank, the which his river hems,
Was painted all with variable flowers,
And all the meads adorned with dainty gems
Fit to deck maidens' bowers,
And crown their paramours
Against the bridal day, which is not long—
  Sweet Thames! run softly, till I end my song.

There, in a meadow, by the river's side,
A flock of nymphs I chancéd to espy,
All lovely daughters of the flood thereby,
With goodly greenish locks, all loose untied,
As each had been a bride.
And each one had a little wicker basket,
Made of fine twigs, entrailéd curiously,
In which they gathered flowers to fill their flasket,
And with fine fingers cropt full feateously
The tender stalks on high.
Of every sort, which in that meadow grew,
They gathered some: the violet, pallid blue,
The little daisy, that at evening closes,
The virgin lily, and the primrose true,
With store of vermeil roses,
To deck their bridegroom's posies
Against the bridal day, which was not long—
  Sweet Thames! run softly, till I end my song.

With that I saw two swans of goodly hue
Come softly swimming down along the Lee;
Two fairer birds I yet did never see.
The snow, which doth the top of Pindus strew,
Did never whiter shew,
Nor Jove himself, when he a swan would be
For love of Leda, whiter did appear;
Yet Leda was, they say, as white as he,
Yet not so white as these, nor nothing near;

So purely white they were,
That even the gentle stream, the which them bare,
Seemed foul to them, and bade his billows spare
To wet their silken feathers, lest they might
Soil their fair plumes with water not so fair,
And mar their beauties bright,
That shone as heaven's light,
Against their bridal day, which was not long—
  Sweet Thames! run softly, till I end my song.

Eftsoons the nymphs, which now had flowers their fill,
Ran all in haste to see that silver brood,
As they came floating on the crystal flood;
Whom when they saw, they stood amazéd still,
Their wondering eyes to fill;
Them seemed they never saw a sight so fair
Of fowls so lovely, that they sure did deem
Them heavenly born, or to be that same pair
Which through the sky draw Venus' silver team;
For sure they did not seem
To be begot of any earthly seed,
But rather angels, or of angel's breed;
Yet were they bred of summer's heat, they say,
In sweetest season, when each flower and weed
The earth did fresh array;
So fresh they seemed as day,
Even as their bridal day, which was not long—
  Sweet Thames! run softly, till I end my song.

Then forth they all out of their baskets drew
Great store of flowers, the honor of the field,
That to the sense did fragrant odors yield,
All which upon those goodly birds they threw
And all the waves did strew,
That like old Peneus' waters they did seem,
When down along by pleasant Tempe's shore,
Scattered with flowers, through Thessaly they stream,
That they appear, through lilies' plenteous store,
Like a bride's chamber floor.

Two of those nymphs meanwhile, two garlands bound
Of freshest flowers which in that mead they found,
The which presenting all in trim array,
Their snowy foreheads there withal they crowned,
Whilst one did sing this lay,
Prepared against that day,
Against their bridal day, which was not long—
Sweet Thames! run softly till I end my song.

"Ye gentle birds! the world's fair ornament,
And heaven's glory, whom this happy hour
Doth lead unto your lover's blissful bower,
Joy may you have, and gentle hearts' content
Of your love's couplement;
And let fair Venus, that is queen of love,
With her heart-quelling son upon you smile,
Whose smile, they say, hath virtue to remove
All love's dislike, and friendship's faulty guile
Forever to assoil;
Let endless peace your steadfast hearts accord,
And blessed plenty wait upon your board;
And let your bed with pleasures chaste abound,
That fruitful issue may to you afford,
Which may your foes confound,
And make your joys redound
Upon your bridal day, which is not long—"
Sweet Thames! run softly, till I end my song.

So ended she; and all the rest around
To her redoubled that her undersong,
Which said their bridal day should not be long.
And gentle Echo from the neighbor ground
Their accents did resound.
So forth those joyous birds did pass along,
Adown the Lee, that to them murmured low,
As he would speak, but that he lacked a tongue,
Yet did by signs his glad affection show,
Making his stream run slow.

And all the fowl which in his flood did dwell
'Gan flock about these twain, that did excel
The rest, so far as Cynthia doth shend
The lesser stars. So they, enrangéd well,
Did on those who attend,
And their best service lend
Against their wedding day, which was not long—
Sweet Thames! run softly, till I end my song.

At length they all to merry London came,
To merry London, my most kindly nurse,
That to me gave this life's first native source,
Though from another place I take my name,
An house of ancient fame.
There when they came, whereas those bricky towers
The which on Thames' broad, aged back do ride,
Where now the studious lawyers have their bowers,
There whilom wont the Templar Knights to bide
Till they decayed through pride.
Next whereunto there stands a stately place,
Where oft I gainéd gifts and goodly grace
Of that great lord, which therein wont to dwell,
Whose want too well now feels my friendless case;
But ah! here fits not well
Old woes, but joys, to tell
Against the bridal day, which is not long—
Sweet Thames! run softly, till I end my song.

Yet therein now doth lodge a noble peer,
Great England's glory, and the world's wide wonder,
Whose dreadful name late through all Spain did thunder,
And Hercules' two pillars standing near
Did make to quake and fear:
Fair branch of honor, flower of chivalry!
That fillest England with thy triumph's fame,
Joy have thou of thy noble victory,
And endless happiness of thine own name,
That promiseth the same;

That through thy prowess, and victorious arms,
Thy country may be freed from foreign harms;
And great Elisa's glorious name may ring
Through all the world, filled with thy wide alarms,
Which some brave muse may sing
To ages following,
Upon the bridal day, which is not long—
Sweet Thames! run softly, till I end my song.

From those high towers this noble lord issuing,
Like radiant Hesper, when his golden hair
In th' ocean billows he hath bathéd fair,
Descended to the river's open viewing,
With a great train ensuing.
Above the rest were goodly to be seen
Two gentle knights of lovely face and feature
Beseeming well the bower of any queen,
With gifts of wit, and ornaments of nature,
Fit for so goodly stature,
That like the twins of Jove they seemed in sight,
Which deck the baldrick of the heavens bright;
They two, forth pacing to the river's side,
Received those two fair brides, their love's delight;
Which, at th' appointed tide,
Each one did make his bride
Against their bridal day, which is not long—
Sweet Thames! run softly, till I end my song.

Sir Philip Sidney

1554–1586

A DITTY

My true-love hath my heart, and I have his,
By just exchange one for another given:
I hold his dear, and mine he cannot miss,
There never was a better bargain driven:
My true-love hath my heart, and I have his.

His heart in me keeps him and me in one,
My heart in him his thoughts and senses guides:
He loves my heart, for once it was his own,
I cherish his because in me it bides:
My true-love hath my heart, and I have his.

ASTROPHEL AND STELLA

I

Loving in truth, and fain in verse my love to show,
That she, dear she, might take some pleasure of my pain,—
Pleasure might cause her read, reading might make her know,
Knowledge might pity win, and pity grace obtain,—
I sought fit words to paint the blackest face of woe,
Studying inventions fine, her wits to entertain,
Oft turning others' leaves, to see if thence would flow
Some fresh and fruitful showers upon my sunburnt brain.
But words came halting forth, wanting Invention's stay;
Invention, Nature's child, fled step-dame Study's blows;
And others' feet still seemed but strangers' in my way.
Thus, great with child to speak, and helpless in my throes,
Biting my truant pen, beating myself for spite;
"Fool," said my Muse to me, "look in thy heart, and write."

XXXI

With how sad steps, O Moon, thou climb'st the skies!
How silently, and with how wan a face!
What, may it be that even in heavenly place
That busy archer his sharp arrows tries?
Sure, if that long-with-love-acquainted eyes
Can judge of love, thou feel'st a lover's case,
I read it in thy looks; thy languished grace,
To me, that feel the like, thy state descries.
Then, even of fellowship, O Moon, tell me,
Is constant love deemed there but want of wit?

Are beauties there as proud as here they be?
Do they above love to be loved, and yet
Those lovers scorn whom that love doth possess?
Do they call virtue there ungratefulness?

Michael Drayton

1563–1631

From IDEA

Since there's no help, come, let us kiss and part!
Nay, I have done, you get no more of me;
And I am glad, yea, glad with all my heart,
That thus so cleanly I myself can free.
Shake hands for ever, cancel all our vows;
And when me meet at any time again,
Be it not seen in either of our brows,
That we one jot of former love retain.
Now at the last gasp of Love's latest breath,
When, his pulse failing, Passion speechless lies,
When Faith is kneeling by his bed of death,
And Innocence is closing up his eyes,—
Now, if thou wouldst, when all have given him over,
From death to life thou might'st him yet recover.

Christopher Marlowe

1564–1593

THE PASSIONATE SHEPHERD TO HIS LOVE

Come live with me and be my love,
And we will all the pleasures prove,
That valleys, groves, hills and fields,
Woods or steepy mountains yields.

And we will sit upon the rocks,
Seeing the shepherds feed their flocks
By shallow rivers, to whose falls
Melodious birds sing madrigals.

And I will make thee beds of roses,
And a thousand fragrant posies,
A cap of flowers and a kirtle
Embroidered all with leaves of myrtle;

A gown made of the finest wool,
Which from our pretty lambs we pull;
Fair-linèd slippers for the cold,
With buckles of the purest gold;

A belt of straw and ivy buds,
With coral clasps and amber studs;
And if these pleasures may thee move,
Come live with me and be my love.

The shepherd swains shall dance and sing
For thy delight each May morning;
If these delights thy mind may move,
Then live with me and be my love.

William Shakespeare

1564–1616

SONNETS

XII

When I do count the clock that tells the time,
And see the brave day sunk in hideous night;
When I behold the violet past prime,
And sable curls all silvered o'er with white;
When lofty trees I see barren of leaves,
Which erst from heat did canopy the herd,
And summer's green all girded up in sheaves
Borne on the bier with white and bristly beard,
Then of thy beauty do I question make,
That thou among the wastes of time must go,
Since sweets and beauties do themselves forsake
And die as fast as they see others grow;
And nothing 'gainst Time's scythe can make defense
Save breed, to brave him when he takes thee hence.

XV

When I consider everything that grows
Holds in perfection but a little moment,
That this huge stage presenteth nought but shows
Whereon the stars in secret influence comment;
When I perceive that men as plants increase,
Cheeréd and checked even by the self-same sky,
Vaunt in their youthful sap, at height decrease,
And wear their brave state out of memory—
Then the conceit of this inconstant stay
Sets you most rich in youth before my sight,
Where wasteful Time debateth with Decay,
To change your day of youth to sullied night;
And all in war with Time for love of you,
As he takes from you, I engraft you new.

XVIII

Shall I compare thee to a summer's day?
Thou art more lovely and more temperate;
Rough winds do shake the darling buds of May,
And summer's lease hath all too short a date.
Sometime too hot the eye of heaven shines,
And often is his gold complexion dimmed;
And every fair from fair sometime declines,
By chance, or nature's changing course untrimmed.
But thy eternal summer shall not fade
Nor lose possession of that fair thou owest;
Nor shall Death brag thou wander'st in his shade,
When in eternal lines to time thou growest.
So long as men can breathe or eyes can see,
So long lives this and this gives life to thee.

XIX

Devouring Time, blunt thou the lion's paws,
And make the earth devour her own sweet brood;
Pluck the keen teeth from the fierce tiger's jaws,
And burn the long-liv'd phœnix in her blood;

Make glad and sorry seasons as thou fleets,
And do whate'er thou wilt, swift-footed Time,
To the wide world and all her fading sweets;
But I forbid thee one most heinous crime:
O! carve not with thy hours my love's fair brow,
Nor draw no lines there with thine antique pen;
Him in thy course untainted do allow
For beauty's pattern to succeeding men.
Yet, do thy worst, old Time: despite thy wrong,
My love shall in my verse ever live young.

XXIX

When, in disgrace with fortune and men's eyes,
I all alone beweep my outcast state
And trouble deaf heaven with my bootless cries
And look upon myself and curse my fate,
Wishing me like to one more rich in hope,
Featured like him, like him with friends possessed,
Desiring this man's art and that man's scope,
With what I most enjoy contented least;
Yet in these thoughts myself almost despising,
Haply I think on thee, and then my state,
Like to the lark at break of day arising
From sullen earth, sings hymns at heaven's gate;
For thy sweet love remembered such wealth brings
That then I scorn to change my state with kings.

XXX

When to the sessions of sweet silent thought
I summon up remembrance of things past,
I sigh the lack of many a thing I sought,
And with old woes new wail my dear time's waste:
Then can I drown an eye, unused to flow,
For precious friends hid in death's dateless night,
And weep afresh love's long since canceled woe,
And moan the expense of many a vanished sight:
Then can I grieve at grievances foregone,

And heavily from woe to woe tell o'er
The sad account of fore-bemoanèd moan,
Which I new pay as if not paid before.
But if the while I think on thee, dear friend,
All losses are restored and sorrows end.

XXXIII

Full many a glorious morning have I seen
Flatter the mountain-tops with sovereign eye,
Kissing with golden face the meadows green,
Gilding pale streams with heavenly alchemy;
Anon permit the basest clouds to ride
With ugly rack on his celestial face,
And from the forlorn world his visage hide,
Stealing unseen to west with this disgrace:
Even so my sun one early morn did shine
With all-triumphant splendor on my brow;
But out, alack! he was but one hour mine;
The region cloud hath maskèd him from me now.
Yet him for this my love no wit disdaineth;
Suns of the world may stain when heaven's sun staineth.

LIV

O, how much more doth beauty beauteous seem
By that sweet ornament which truth doth give!
The rose looks fair, but fairer we it deem
For that sweet odor which doth in it live.
The canker-blooms have full as deep a dye
As the perfumèd tincture of the roses,
Hang on such thorns, and play as wantonly
When summer's breath their maskèd buds discloses:
But, for their virtue only is their show,
They live unwooed and unrespected fade,
Die to themselves. Sweet roses do not so;
Of their sweet deaths are sweetest odors made:
And so of you, beauteous and lovely youth,
When that shall fade, my verse distills your truth.

LV

Not marble, nor the gilded monuments
Of princes, shall outlive this powerful rhyme;
But you shall shine more bright in these contents
Than unswept stone besmeared with sluttish time.
When wastful war shall statues overturn,
And broils root out the work of masonry,
Nor Mars his sword nor war's quick fire shall burn
The living record of your memory.
'Gainst death and all-oblivious enmity
Shall you pace forth; your praise shall still find room
Even in the eyes of all posterity
That wear this world out to the ending doom.
So, till the judgment that yourself arise,
You live in this, and dwell in lovers' eyes.

LXIV

When I have seen by Time's fell hand defaced
The rich proud cost of outworn buried age;
When sometime lofty towers I see down-razed
And brass eternal slave to mortal rage;
When I have seen the hungry ocean gain
Advantage on the kingdom of the shore,
And the firm soil win of the watery main,
Increasing store with loss and loss with store;
When I have seen such interchange of state,
Or state itself confounded to decay;
Ruin hath taught me thus to ruminate,
That Time will come and take my love away.
This thought is as a death, which cannot choose
But weep to have that which it fears to lose.

LXV

Since brass, nor stone, nor earth, nor boundless sea,
But sad mortality o'er-sways their power,
How with this rage shall beauty hold a plea,
Whose action is no stronger than a flower?

O, how shall summer's honey breath hold out
Against the wreckful siege of battering days,
When rocks impregnable are not so stout,
Nor gates of steel so strong, but Time decays?
O fearful meditation! where, alack,
Shall Time's best jewel from Time's chest lie hid?
Or what strong hand can hold his swift foot back?
Or who his spoil of beauty can forbid?
O, none, unless this miracle have might,
That in black ink my love may still shine bright.

LXVI

Tired with all these, for restful death I cry,
As, to behold desert a beggar born,
And needy nothing trimmed in jollity,
And purest faith unhappily forsworn,
And gilded honor shamefully misplaced,
And maiden virtue rudely strumpeted,
And right perfection wrongfully disgraced,
And strength by limping sway disablèd,
And art made tongue-tied by authority,
And folly doctor-like controlling skill,
And simple truth miscalled simplicity,
And captive good attending captain ill:
Tired with all these, from these would I be gone,
Save that, to die, I leave my love alone.

LXXI

No longer mourn for me when I am dead
Than you shall hear the surly sullen bell
Give warning to the world that I am fled
From this vile world, with vilest worms to dwell:
Nay, if you read this line, remember not
The hand that writ it; for I love you so
That I in your sweet thoughts would be forgot
If thinking on me then should make you woe.
O, if, I say, you look upon this verse

When I perhaps compounded am with clay,
Do not so much as my poor name rehearse,
But let your love even with my life decay,
Lest the wise world should look into your moan
And mock you with me after I am gone.

LXXIII

That time of year thou mayst in me behold
When yellow leaves, or none, or few, do hang
Upon those boughs which shake against the cold,
Bare ruined choirs, where late the sweet birds sang.
In me thou see'st the twilight of such day
As after sunset fadeth in the west,
Which by and by black night doth take away,
Death's second self, that seals up all in rest.
In me thou see'st the glowing of such fire
That on the ashes of his youth doth lie,
As the death-bed whereon it must expire
Consumed with that which it was nourished by.
This thou perceivest, which makes thy love more strong,
To love that well which thou must leave ere long.

XC

Then hate me when thou wilt; if ever, now;
Now, while the world is bent my deeds to cross,
Join with the spite of fortune, make me bow,
And do not drop in for an after-loss:
Ah, do not, when my heart hath 'scaped this sorrow,
Come in the rearward of a conquered woe;
Give not a windy night a rainy morrow,
To linger out a purposed overthrow.
If thou wilt leave me, do not leave me last,
When other petty griefs have done their spite,
But in the onset come: so shall I taste
At first the very worst of fortune's might,
And other strains of woe, which now seem woe,
Compared with loss of thee will not seem so.

XCVII

How like a winter hath my absence been
From thee, the pleasure of the fleeting year!
What freezings have I felt, what dark days seen!
What old December's bareness everywhere!
And yet this time removed was summer's time,
The teeming autumn, big with rich increase,
Bearing the wanton burden of the prime,
Like widowed wombs after their lords' decease:
Yet this abundant issue seemed to me
But hope of orphans and unfathered fruit;
For summer and his pleasures wait on thee,
And, thou away, the very birds are mute;
Or, if they sing, 'tis with so dull a cheer
That leaves look pale, dreading the winter's near.

XCVIII

From you have I been absent in the spring,
When proud-pied April dressed in all his trim
Hath put a spirit of youth in every thing,
That heavy Saturn laughed and leaped with him.
Yet nor the lays of birds nor the sweet smell
Of different flowers in odor and in hue
Could make me any summer's story tell,
Or from their proud lap pluck them where they grew;
Nor did I wonder at the lily's white,
Nor praise the deep vermilion in the rose;
They were but sweet, but figures of delight,
Drawn after you, you pattern of all those.
Yet seemed it winter still, and, you away,
As with your shadow I with these did play.

CII

My love is strengthen'd, though more weak in seeming;
I love not less, though less the show appear:
That love is merchandiz'd whose rich esteeming
The owner's tongue doth publish everywhere.

Our love was new, and then but in the spring,
When I was wont to greet it with my lays;
As Philomel in summer's front doth sing,
And stops her pipe in growth of riper days:
Not that the summer is less pleasant now
Than when her mournful hymns did hush the night,
But that wild music burthens every bough,
And sweets grown common lose their dear delight.
Therefore, like her, I sometime hold my tongue,
Because I would not dull you with my song.

CVI

When in the chronicle of wasted time
I see descriptions of the fairest wights,
And beauty making beautiful old rhyme
In praise of ladies dead and lovely knights,
Then, in the blazon of sweet beauty's best,
Of hand, of foot, of lip, of eye, of brow,
I see their antique pen would have expressed
Even such a beauty as you master now.
So all their praises are but prophecies
Of this our time, all you prefiguring;
And, for they looked but with divining eyes,
They had not skill enough your worth to sing:
For we, which now behold these present days,
Have eyes to wonder, but lack tongues to praise.

CVII

Not mine own fears, nor the prophetic soul
Of the wide world dreaming on things to come,
Can yet the lease of my true love control,
Supposed as forfeit to a confined doom.
The mortal moon hath her eclipse endured
And the sad augurs mock their own presage;
Incertainties now crown themselves assured
And peace proclaims olives of endless age.
Now with the drops of this most balmy time

My love looks fresh, and Death to me subscribes,
Since, spite of him, I'll live in this poor rhyme,
While he insults o'er dull and speechless tribes:
And thou in this shalt find thy monument,
When tyrants' crests and tombs of brass are spent.

CXVI

Let me not to the marriage of true minds
Admit impediments. Love is not love
Which alters when it alteration finds,
Or bends with the remover to remove:
O, no! it is an ever-fixèd mark
That looks on tempests and is never shaken;
It is the star to every wandering bark,
Whose worth's unknown, although his height be taken.
Love's not Time's fool, though rosy lips and cheeks
Within his bending sickle's compass come;
Love alters not with his brief hours and weeks,
But bears it out even to the edge of doom.
If this be error and upon me proved,
I never writ, nor no man ever loved.

CXXIX

The expense of spirit in a waste of shame
Is lust in action; and till action, lust
Is perjured, murderous, bloody, full of blame,
Savage, extreme, rude, cruel, not to trust,
Enjoyed no sooner but despisèd straight;
Past reason hunted, and no sooner had
Past reason hated, as a swallowed bait
On purpose laid to make the taker mad;
Mad in pursuit and in possession so;
Had, having, and in quest to have, extreme;
A bliss in proof, and proved, a very woe;
Before, a joy proposed; behind, a dream.
All this the world well knows; yet none knows well
To shun the heaven that leads men to this hell.

CXXX

My mistress' eyes are nothing like the sun;
Coral is far more red than her lips' red:
If snow be white, why then her breasts are dun;
If hairs be wires, black wires grow on her head.
I have seen roses damasked, red and white,
But no such roses see I in her cheeks;
And in some perfumes is there more delight
Than in the breath that from my mistress reeks.
I love to hear her speak, yet well I know
That music hath a far more pleasing sound;
I grant I never saw a goddess go;
My mistress, when she walks, treads on the ground:
And yet, by heaven, I think my love as rare
As any she belied with false compare.

CXXXVIII

When my love swears that she is made of truth,
I do believe her, though I know she lies,
That she might think me some untutor'd youth,
Unlearned in the world's false subtleties.
Thus vainly thinking that she thinks me young,
Although she knows my days are past the best,
Simply I credit her false-speaking tongue:
On both sides thus is simple truth supprest.
But wherefore says she not she is unjust?
And wherefore say not I that I am old?
O! love's best habit is in seeming trust,
And age in love loves not to have years told:
Therefore I lie with her, and she with me,
And in our faults by lies we flatter'd be.

CXLVI

Poor soul, the center of my sinful earth,
Thrall to these rebel powers that thee array,
Why dost thou pine within and suffer dearth,
Painting thy outward walls so costly gay?

Why so large cost, having so short a lease,
Dost thou upon thy fading mansion spend?
Shall worms, inheritors of this excess,
Eat up thy charge? Is this thy body's end?
Then, soul, live thou upon thy servant's loss,
And let that pine to aggravate thy store;
Buy terms divine in selling hours of dross;
Within be fed, without be rich no more:
So shalt thou feed on Death, that feeds on men,
And Death once dead, there's no more dying then.

SONGS FROM THE PLAYS

From Love's Labor's Lost

When icicles hang by the wall,
  And Dick the shepherd blows his nail,
And Tom bears logs into the hall,
  And milk comes frozen home in pail,
When blood is nipped and ways be foul,
Then nightly sings the staring owl,
"Tu-whit, tu-who!" a merry note,
While greasy Joan doth keel the pot.

When all aloud the wind doth blow,
  And coughing drowns the parson's saw,
And birds sit brooding in the snow,
  And Marian's nose looks red and raw,
When roasted crabs hiss in the bowl,
Then nightly sings the staring owl,
"Tu-whit, tu-who!" a merry note,
While greasy Joan doth keel the pot.

From Much Ado About Nothing

Sigh no more, ladies, sigh no more,
  Men were deceivers ever,
One foot in sea and one on shore,
  To one thing constant never:

Then sigh not so, but let them go,
  And be you blithe and bonny,
Converting all your sounds of woe
  Into Hey nonny, nonny.

Sing no more ditties, sing no moe,
  Of dumps so dull and heavy!
The fraud of men was ever so,
  Since summer first was leavy:
Then sigh not so, but let them go,
  And be you blithe and bonny,
Converting all your sounds of woe
  Into Hey nonny, nonny.

From As You Like It

  Under the greenwood tree
  Who loves to lie with me,
  And turn his merry note
  Unto the sweet birds' throat,
Come hither, come hither, come hither:
  Here shall he see
  No enemy
But winter and rough weather.

  Who doth ambition shun
  And loves to live i' the sun,
  Seeking the food he eats
  And pleased with what he gets,
Come hither, come hither, come hither:
  Here shall he see
  No enemy
But winter and rough weather.

Blow, blow, thou winter wind,
Thou art not so unkind
  As man's ingratitude;
Thy tooth is not so keen,
Because thou art not seen,
  Although thy breath be rude.

Heigh ho! sing, heigh ho! unto the green holly:
Most friendship is feigning, most loving mere folly:
Then, heigh ho, the holly!
This life is most jolly.

Freeze, freeze, thou bitter sky,
That dost not bite so nigh
As benefits forgot:
Though thou the waters warp,
Thy sting is not so sharp
As friend remembered not.
Heigh ho! sing, heigh ho! etc.

It was a lover and his lass,
With a hey, and a ho, and a hey nonino,
That o'er the green corn-field did pass
In the spring time, the only pretty ring time
When birds do sing, hey ding a ding, ding;
Sweet lovers love the spring.

Between the acres of the rye,
With a hey, and a ho, and a hey nonino,
These pretty country folks would lie,
In spring time, etc.

This carol they began that hour,
With a hey, and a ho, and a hey nonino,
How that a life was but a flower
In spring time, etc.

And therefore take the present time,
With a hey, and a ho, and a hey nonino;
For love is crownèd with the prime
In spring time, etc.

From Twelfth Night

O mistress mine, where are you roaming?
O, stay and hear, your true love's coming,
That can sing both high and low:

Trip no further, pretty sweeting,
Journeys end in lovers meeting,
  Every wise man's son doth know.

What is love? 'Tis not hereafter;
Present mirth hath present laughter;
  What's to come is still unsure:
In delay there lies no plenty;
Then come kiss me, sweet and twenty,
  Youth's a stuff will not endure.

From Measure for Measure

Take, O, take those lips away,
  That so sweetly were forsworn;
And those eyes, the break of day,
  Lights that do mislead the morn:
But my kisses bring again,
                    Bring again;
Seals of love, but sealed in vain,
                    Sealed in vain.

From Cymbeline

Hark, hark! the lark at heaven's gate sings,
  And Phœbus 'gins arise,
His steeds to water at those springs
  On chaliced flowers that lies;
And winking Mary-buds begin
  To ope their golden eyes:
With every thing that pretty is,
  My lady sweet, arise;
    Arise, arise.

Fear no more the heat o' the sun,
  Nor the furious winter's rages;
Thou thy wordly task hast done,
  Home art gone, and ta'en thy wages:
Golden lads and girls all must,
As chimney-sweepers, come to dust.

Fear no more the frowns o' the great;
  Thou art paſt the tyrant's ſtroke;
Care no more to clothe and eat;
  To thee the reed is as the oak:
The scepter, learning, physic, muſt
All follow this, and come to duſt.

Fear no more the lightning-flash,
  Nor the all-dreaded thunder-ſtone;
Fear not slander, censure rash;
  Thou haſt finished joy and moan:
All lovers young, all lovers muſt
Consign to thee, and come to duſt.

No exorciser harm thee!
  Nor no witchcraft charm thee!
Ghoſt unlaid forbear thee!
  Nothing ill come near thee!
Quiet consummation have;
And renownèd be thy grave!

From The Tempest

Full fathom five thy father lies;
    Of his bones are coral made;
Those are pearls that were his eyes:
    Nothing of him that doth fade
But doth suffer a sea-change
Into something rich and ſtrange.
Sea-nymphs hourly ring his knell:
                                        Ding-dong.
Hark! now I hear them,—ding-dong, bell.

Where the bee sucks, there suck I;
In a cowslip's bell I lie;
There I couch when owls do cry.
On the bat's back I do fly
After summer merrily.
Merrily, merrily shall I live now
Under the blossom that hangs on the bough.

Ben Jonson

1573–1637

HYMN TO DIANA

From Cynthia's Revels

Queen and huntress, chaste and fair,
Now the sun is laid to sleep,
Seated in thy silver chair,
State in wonted manner keep:
Hesperus entreats thy light,
Goddess excellently bright.

Earth, let not thy envious shade
Dare itself to interpose;
Cynthia's shining orb was made
Heaven to clear when day did close:
Bless us then with wished sight,
Goddess excellently bright.

Lay thy bow of pearl apart
And thy crystal-shining quiver;
Give unto the flying hart
Space to breathe, how short soever:
Thou that mak'st a day of night—
Goddess excellently bright!

SONG TO CELIA

Drink to me only with thine eyes,
And I will pledge with mine;
Or leave a kiss but in the cup,
And I'll not look for wine.
The thirst that from the soul doth rise
Doth ask a drink divine;
But might I of Jove's nectar sup,
I would not change for thine.

I sent thee late a rosy wreath,
  Not so much honoring thee
As giving it a hope that there
  It could not withered be.
But thou thereon didst only breathe,
  And sent'st it back to me;
Since when it grows, and smells, I swear,
  Not of itself but thee.

SIMPLEX MUNDITIIS

From EPICŒNE; OR, THE SILENT WOMAN

STILL to be neat, still to be dressed,
As you were going to a feast;
Still to be powdered, still perfumed:
Lady, it is to be presumed,
Though art's hid causes are not found,
All is not sweet, all is not sound.

Give me a look, give me a face
That makes simplicity a grace;
Robes loosely flowing, hair as free:
Such sweet neglect more taketh me
Than all the adulteries of art;
They strike mine eyes, but not my heart.

ON MY FIRST SON

FAREWELL, thou child of my right hand, and joy;
My sin was too much hope of thee, loved boy.
Seven years thou wert lent to me, and I thee pay,
Exacted by thy fate, on the just day.
O, could I lose all father now! for why
Will man lament the state he should envy—
To have so soon 'scaped world's and flesh's rage,
And, if no other misery, yet age?
Rest in soft peace; and, asked, say, "Here doth lie
Ben Jonson his best piece of poetry;
For whose sake henceforth all his vows be such
As what he loves may never like too much."

TO PENSHURST

Thou art not, Penshurst, built, to envious show,
Of touch or marble; nor canst boast a row
Of polished pillars, or a roof of gold:
Thou hast no lantern, whereof tales are told;
Or stair, or courts; but stand'st an ancient pile,
And, these grudged at, art reverenced the while.
Thou joy'st in better marks, of soil, of air,
Of wood, of water; therein thou art fair.
Thou hast thy walks for health, as well as sport;
Thy mount, to which the dryads do resort,
Where Pan and Bacchus their high feasts have made,
Beneath the broad beech and the chestnut shade;
That taller tree, which of a nut was set
At his great birth where all the Muses met.
There in the writhèd bark are cut the names
Of many a sylvan, taken with his flames;
And thence the ruddy satyrs oft provoke
The lighter fauns to reach thy Lady's Oak.
Thy copse, too, named of Gamage, thou hast there,
That never fails to serve thee seasoned deer
When thou wouldst feast or exercise thy friends.
The lower land, that to the river bends,
Thy sheep, thy bullocks, kine, and calves do feed;
The middle grounds thy mares and horses breed.
Each bank doth yield thee conies; and the tops,
Fertile of wood, Ashore and Sidney's copse,
To crown thy open table, doth provide
The purpled pheasant with the speckled side;
The painted partridge lies in every field,
And for thy mess is willing to be killed.
And if the high-swollen Medway fail thy dish,
Thou hast thy ponds, that pay thee tribute fish,
Fat, agèd carps that run into thy net,
And pikes, now weary their own kind to eat,
As loath the second draught or cast to stay,
Officiously at first themselves betray,
Bright eels that emulate them, and leap on land,

Before the fisher or into his hand.
Then hath thy orchard fruit, thy garden flowers,
Fresh as the air, and new as are the hours.
The early cherry, with the later plum,
Fig, grape, and quince, each in his time doth come;
The blushing apricot and wooly peach
Hang on thy walls that every child may reach.
And though thy walls be of the country stone,
They are reared with no man's ruin, no man's groan;
There's none that dwell about them wish them down;
But all come in, the farmer and the clown,
And no one empty handed, to salute
Thy lord and lady, though they have no suit;
Some bring a capon, some a rural cake,
Some nuts, some apples; some that think they make
The better cheeses bring them; or else send
By their ripe daughters, whom they would commend
This way to husbands, and whose baskets bear
An emblem of themselves in plum or pear.
But what can this (more than express their love)
Add to thy free provisions, far above
The need of such? whose liberal board doth flow
With all that hospitality doth know;
Where comes no guest but is allowed to eat
Without his fear, and of thy lord's own meat;
Where the same beer and bread, and selfsame wine,
That is his lordship's shall be also mine,
And I not fain to sit, as some this day,
At great men's tables, and yet dine away.
Here no man tells my cups, nor, standing by,
A waiter, doth my gluttony envy,
But gives me what I call, and lets me eat;
He knows below he shall find plenty of meat;
Thy tables hoard not up for the next day;
Nor, when I take my lodging, need I pray
For fire, or lights, or livery; all is there;
As if thou then wert mine, or I reigned here:
There's nothing I can wish for which I stay.
That found King James when, hunting late this way

With his brave son, the Prince, they saw thy fires
Shine bright on every hearth, as the desires
Of thy Penates had been set on flame,
To entertain them; or the country came,
With all their zeal, to warm their welcome here.
What—great I will not say, but sudden—cheer
Didst thou then make 'em! and what praise was heaped
On thy good lady then, who therein reaped
The just reward of her high housewifery;
To have her linen, plate, and all things nigh,
When she was far; and not a room but dressed
As if it had expected such a guest!
These, Penshurst, are thy praise, and yet not all.
Thy lady's noble, fruitful, chaste withal.
His children thy great lord may call his own,
A fortune in this age but rarely known.
They are, and have been, taught religion; thence
Their gentler spirits have sucked innocence.
Each morn and even they are taught to pray,
With the whole household, and may, every day,
Read in their virtuous parents' noble parts
The mysteries of manners, arms, and arts.
Now, Penshurst, they that will proportion thee
With other edifices, when they see
Those proud, ambitious heaps, and nothing else,
May say their lords have built, but thy lord dwells.

TO WILLIAM CAMDEN

Camden, most reverend head, to whom I owe
All that I am in arts, all that I know
(How nothing's that!), to whom my country owes
The great renown and name wherewith she goes;
Than thee the age sees not that thing more grave,
More high, more holy, that she more would crave.
What name, what skill, what faith hast thou in things!
What sight in searching the most antique springs!
What weight and what authority in thy speech!
Man scarce can make that doubt but thou canst teach.

Pardon free truth, and let thy modesty,
Which conquers all, be once overcome by thee.
Many of thine this better could than I;
But for their powers, accept my piety.

John Donne

1573–1631

SONG

Go and catch a falling star,
  Get with child a mandrake root,
Tell me where all past years are,
  Or who cleft the devil's foot,
Teach me to hear mermaids' singing,
  Or to keep off envy's stinging,
    And find
    What wind
Serves to advance an honest mind.

If thou be'st born to strange sights,
  Things invisible go see,
Ride ten thousand days and nights,
  Till Age snow white hairs on thee;
Thou, when thou return'st, wilt tell me
All strange wonders that befell thee,
    And swear
    No where
Lives a woman true and fair.

If thou find'st one, let me know;
  Such a pilgrimage were sweet.
Yet do not; I would not go,
  Though at next door we might meet.
Though she were true when you met her,
And last till you write your letter,
    Yet she
    Will be
False, ere I come, to two or three.

LOVE'S DEITY

I LONG to talk with some old lover's ghost
  Who died before the god of love was born.
I cannot think that he who then loved most,
  Sunk so low as to love one which did scorn.
But since this god produced a destiny
And that vice-nature, custom, lets it be,
  I must love her that loves not me.

Sure, they which made him god, meant not so much,
  Nor he in his young godhead practiced it.
But when an even flame two hearts did touch,
  His office was indulgently to fit
Actives to passives. Correspondency
Only his subject was; it cannot be
  Love, till I love her who loves me.

But every modern god will not extend
  His vast prerogative as far as Jove.
To rage, to lust, to write to, to commend,
  All is the purlieu of the god of love.
O! were we wakened by this tyranny
To ungod this child again, it could not be
  I should love her who loves not me.

Rebel and atheist too, why murmur I,
As though I felt the worst that love could do?
Love may make me leave loving, or might try
  A deeper plague, to make her love me too;
Which, since she loves before, I'm loth to see.
Falsehood is worse than hate; and that must be,
  If she whom I love, should love me.

THE FUNERAL

WHOEVER comes to shroud me, do not harm
    Nor question much
That subtle wreath of hair about mine arm;

The mystery, the sign you must not touch,
For 'tis my outward soul,
Viceroy to that which, unto heav'n being gone,
Will leave this to control
And keep these limbs, her provinces, from dissolution.

For if the sinewy thread my brain lets fall
Through every part
Can tie those parts, and make me one of all;
Those hairs, which upward grew, and strength and art
Have from a better brain,
Can better do 't: except she meant that I
By this should know my pain,
As prisoners then are manacled, when they're condemned to die.

Whate'er she meant by 't, bury it with me,
For since I am
Love's martyr, it might breed idolatry
If into other hands these reliques came.
As 't was humility
To afford to it all that a soul can do,
So 't is some bravery
That, since you would have none of me, I bury some of you.

THE GOOD MORROW

I WONDER, by my troth, what thou and I
Did till we loved? were we not weaned till then,
But sucked on country pleasures, childishly?
Or snorted we in the Seven Sleepers' den?
'Twas so; but this, all pleasures fancies be.
If ever any beauty I did see
Which I desired, and got, 'twas but a dream of thee.

And now good morrow to our waking souls,
Which watch not one another out of fear;
For love all love of other sights controls,
And makes one little room an everywhere.

Let sea-discoverers to new worlds have gone;
Let maps to other, worlds on worlds have shown;
Let us possess one world; each hath one, and is one.

My face in thine eye, thine in mine appears,
And true, plain hearts do in the faces rest;
Where can we find two better hemispheres
Without sharp north, without declining west?
Whatever dies, was not mixed equally;
If our two loves be one, or thou and I
Love so alike that none do slacken, none can die.

SONG

Sweetest love, I do not go
For weariness of thee,
Nor in hope the world can show
A fitter love for me;
But since that I
Must die at last, 'tis best,
To use myself in jest,
Thus by feigned deaths to die.

Yesternight the sun went hence,
And yet is here to-day;
He hath no desire nor sense,
Nor half so short a way:
Then fear not me,
But believe that I shall make
Speedier journeys, since I take
More wings and spurs than he.

O how feeble is man's power,
That, if good fortune fall,
Cannot add another hour,
Nor a lost hour recall!
But come bad chance,
And we join to it our strength,
And we teach it art and length,
Itself o'er us to advance.

When thou sigh'st, thou sigh'st not wind,
But sigh'st my soul away;
When thou weep'st, unkindly kind,
My life's blood doth decay.
It cannot be
That thou lov'st me as thou say'st,
If in thine my life thou waste;
Thou art the best of me.

Let not thy divining heart
Forethink me any ill;
Destiny may take thy part,
And may thy fears fulfil.
But think that we
Are but turned aside to sleep;
They who one another keep
Alive, ne'er parted be.

THE BLOSSOM

Little think'st thou, poor flower,
Whom I have watched six or seven days,
And seen thy birth, and seen what every hour
Gave to thy growth, thee to this height to raise,
And now dost laugh and triumph on this bough,
Little think'st thou
That it will freeze anon, and that I shall
Tomorrow find thee fallen, or not at all.

Little think'st thou, poor heart
That labour'st yet to nestle thee,
And think'st by hovering here to get a part
In a forbidden or forbidding tree,
And hop'st her stiffness by long siege to bow;
Little think'st thou,
That thou tomorrow, ere that sun doth wake,
Must with this sun and me a journey take.

But thou which lov'st to be
Subtle to plague thyself, wilt say,
Alas, if you must go, what's that to me?

Here lies my business, and here I will stay:
You go to friends, whose love and means present
Various content
To your eyes, ears, and tongue, and every part.
If then your body go, what need you a heart?

Well then, stay here; but know,
When thou hast stayed and done thy most;
A naked thinking heart, that makes no show,
Is to a woman but a kind of ghost;
How shall she know my heart; or having none,
Know thee for one?
Practice may make her know some other part,
But take my word, she doth not know a heart.

Meet me at London, then,
Twenty days hence, and thou shalt see
Me fresher, and more fat, by being with men,
Than if I had stayed still with her and thee.
For God's sake, if you can, be you so too:
I would give you
There to another friend, whom we shall find
As glad to have my body as my mind.

A LECTURE UPON THE SHADOW

Stand still, and I will read to thee
A lecture, love, in Love's philosophy.
These three hours that we have spent,
Walking here, two shadows went
Along with us, which we ourselves produced;
But, now the sun is just above our head,
We do those shadows tread,
And to brave clearness all things are reduced.
So whilst our infant loves did grow,
Disguises did, and shadows, flow,
From us, and our cares; but, now 'tis not so.

That love hath not attained the highest degree
Which is still diligent lest others see.

Except our loves at this noon stay,
We shall new shadows make the other way.
As the first were made to blind
Others, these which come behind
Will work upon our selves, and blind our eyes.
If our loves faint, and westwardly decline,
To me thou, falsely, thine,
And I to thee mine actions shall disguise.
The morning shadows wear away,
But these grow longer all the day.
But oh, love's day is short if love decay.

Love is a growing, or full constant light;
And his first minute after noon is night.

A HYMN TO GOD THE FATHER

Wilt thou forgive that sin where I begun,
Which was my sin, though it were done before?
Wilt thou forgive that sin through which I run,
And do run still, though still I do deplore?
When thou hast done, thou hast not done;
For I have more.

Wilt thou forgive that sin which I have won
Others to sin, and made my sins their door?
Wilt thou forgive that sin which I did shun
A year or two, but wallowed in a score?
When thou hast done, thou hast not done;
For I have more.

I have a sin of fear, that when I've spun
My last thread, I shall perish on the shore;
But swear by thyself that at my death thy Son
Shall shine as he shines now and heretofore;
And having done that, thou hast done;
I fear no more.

Richard Barnefield

1574–1627

THE NIGHTINGALE

As it fell upon a day
In the merry month of May,
Sitting in a pleasant shade
Which a grove of myrtles made,
Beasts did leap and birds did sing,
Trees did grow and plants did spring;
Every thing did banish moan
Save the Nightingale alone:
She, poor bird, as all forlorn,
Leaned her breast up-till a thorn,
And there sung the dolefull'st ditty
That to hear it was great pity.
Fie, fie, fie, now would she cry;
Teru, teru, by and by;
That to hear her so complain
Scarce I could from tears refrain;
For her griefs so lively shown
Made me think upon mine own.
Ah! thought I, thou mourn'st in vain,
None takes pity on thy pain:
Senseless trees they cannot hear thee,
Ruthless beasts they will not cheer thee:
King Pandion he is dead,
All thy friends are lapped in lead;
All thy fellow birds do sing
Careless of thy sorrowing:
Even so, poor bird, like thee
None alive will pity me.

John Fletcher

1579–1625

ASPATIA'S SONG

From The Maid's Tragedy

Lay a garland on my hearse
  Of the dismal yew;
Maidens, willow branches bear;
  Say I dièd true.

My love was false, but I was firm
  From my hour of birth;
Upon my buried body lie
  Lightly, gentle earth!

George Wither

1588–1667

THE LOVER'S RESOLUTION

Shall I, wasting in despair,
Die, because a woman's fair?
Or make pale my cheeks with care
'Cause another's rosy are?
Be she fairer than the day,
Or the flowery meads in May,
    If she think not well of me,
    What care I how fair she be?

Shall my silly heart be pined,
'Cause I see a woman kind?
Or a well disposèd nature
Joinèd with a lovely feature?
Be she meeker, kinder, than
Turtle-dove or pelican,
    If she be not so to me,
    What care I how kind she be?

Shall a woman's virtues move
Me to perish for her love?
Or her well deserving known
Make me quite forget my own?
Be she with that goodness blest
Which may merit name of Best
  If she be not such to me,
  What care I how good she be?

'Cause her fortune seems too high,
Shall I play the fool and die?
She that bears a noble mind,
If not outward helps she find,
Thinks what with them he would do
That without them dares her woo;
  And unless that mind I see,
  What care I how great she be?

Great, or good, or kind, or fair,
I will ne'er the more despair;
If she love me, this believe,
I will die ere she shall grieve;
If she slight me when I woo,
I can scorn, and let her go;
  For if she be not for me,
  What care I for whom she be?

William Browne

1590?–1645?

ON THE COUNTESS OF PEMBROKE

Underneath this sable hearse
Lies the subject of all verse:
Sidney's sister, Pembroke's mother:
Death, ere thou hast slain another
Fair, and learned, and good as she,
Time shall throw a dart at thee.

Marble piles let no man raise
To her name: in after days,
Some kind woman, born as she,
Reading this, like Niobe
Shall turn marble, and become
Both her mourner and her tomb.

Robert Herrick

1591–1674

THE ARGUMENT OF HIS BOOK

I SING of brooks, of blossoms, birds, and bowers,
Of April, May, of June and July flowers.
I sing of Maypoles, hock-carts, wassails, wakes,
Of bridegrooms, brides, and of their bridal-cakes.
I write of youth, of love, and have access
By these to sing of cleanly wantonness.
I sing of dews, of rains, and, piece by piece,
Of balm, of oil, of spice, and ambergris.
I sing of times trans-shifting, and I write
How roses first came red and lilies white.
I write of groves, of twilights, and I sing
The court of Mab and of the fairy king.
I write of hell; I sing (and ever shall)
Of heaven, and hope to have it after all.

AN ODE FOR BEN JONSON

AH, Ben!
Say how, or when
Shall we, thy guests,
Meet at those lyric feasts
Made at the Sun,
The Dog, the Triple Tun?
Where we such clusters had,
As made us nobly wild, not mad;
And yet each verse of thine
Out-did the meat, out-did the frolic wine.

My Ben!
Or come again,
Or send to us
Thy wit's great overplus;
But teach us yet
Wisely to husband it,
Lest we that talent spend;
And having once brought to an end
That precious stock, the store
Of such a wit the world should have no more.

TO LIVE MERRILY AND TO TRUST TO GOOD VERSES

Now is the time for mirth;
  Nor cheek or tongue be dumb;
For with the flowery earth
  The golden pomp is come.

The golden pomp is come;
  For now each tree does wear,
Made of her pap and gum,
  Rich beads of amber here.

Now reigns the rose, and now
  The Arabian dew besmears
My uncontrollèd brow
  And my retorted hairs.

Homer, this health to thee,
  In sack of such a kind
That it would make thee see
  Though thou wert ne'er so blind.

Next, Virgil I'll call forth,
  To pledge this second health
In wine whose each cup's worth
  An Indian commonwealth.

A goblet next I'll drink
  To Ovid; and suppose,
Made he the pledge, he'd think
  The world had all one nose.

Then this immensive cup
  Of aromatic wine,
Catullus, I quaff up
  To that terse Muse of thine.

Wild I am now with heat;
  O Bacchus! cool thy rays!
Or frantic, I shall eat
  Thy thyrse and bite the bays.

Round, round, the roof does run;
  And, being ravished thus,
Come, I will drink a tun
  To my Propertius.

Now, to Tibullus next,
  This flood I drink to thee.
But stay; I see a text
  That this presents to me:

Behold, Tibullus lies
  Here burnt, whose small return
Of ashes scarce suffice
  To fill a little urn.

Trust to good verses, then;
  They only will aspire,
When pyramids, as men,
  Are lost i' the funeral fire.

And when all bodies meet,
  In Lethe to be drowned,
Then only numbers sweet
  With endless life are crowned.

TO DAFFODILS

Fair daffodils, we weep to see
You haste away so soon;
As yet the early rising sun
Has not attained his noon.
Stay, stay,
Until the hasting day
Has run
But to the even-song;
And, having prayed together, we
Will go with you along.

We have short time to stay as you,
We have as short a spring;
As quick a growth to meet decay,
As you, or anything.
We die,
As your hours do, and dry
Away,
Like to the summer's rain,
Or as the pearls of morning's dew,
Ne'er to be found again.

UPON JULIA'S CLOTHES

Whenas in silks my Julia goes,
Then, then, methinks, how sweetly flows
That liquefaction of her clothes.

Next, when I cast mine eyes, and see
That brave vibration, each way free,
O, how that glittering taketh me!

SWEET DISORDER

A sweet disorder in the dress
Kindles in clothes a wantonness:
A lawn about the shoulders thrown
Into a fine distraction—

An erring lace, which here and there
Enthrals the crimson stomacher—
A cuff neglectful, and thereby
Ribbands to flow confusedly—
A winning wave, deserving note,
In the tempestuous petticoat—
A careless shoe-string, in whose tie
I see a wild civility—
Do more bewitch me than when art
Is too precise in every part.

GRACE FOR A CHILD

Here a little child I stand,
Heaving up my either hand;
Cold as paddocks though they be,
Here I lift them up to Thee,
For a benison to fall
On our meat and on us all. Amen.

TO THE VIRGINS TO MAKE MUCH OF TIME

Gather ye rosebuds while ye may,
  Old Time is still a-flying;
And this same flower that smiles to-day,
  To-morrow will be dying.

The glorious lamp of heaven, the sun,
  The higher he's a-getting,
The sooner will his race be run,
  And nearer he's to setting.

That age is best which is the first,
  When youth and blood are warmer;
But being spent, the worse and worst
  Times still succeed the former.

Then be not coy, but use your time,
  And while ye may, go marry;
For, having lost but once your prime,
  You may forever tarry.

THE MAD MAID'S SONG

Good morrow to the day so fair;
Good morning, sir, to you;
Good morrow to mine own torn hair,
Bedabbled with the dew.

Good morning to this primrose too;
Good morrow to each maid
That will with flowers the tomb bestrew
Wherein my love is laid.

Ah, woe is me, woe, woe is me,
Alack, and well-a-day!
For pity, sir, find out that bee
Which bore my love away.

I'll seek him in your bonnet brave;
I'll seek him in your eyes;
Nay, now I think they've made his grave
I' the bed of strawberries.

I'll seek him there; I know, ere this,
The cold, cold earth doth shake him;
But I will go, or send a kiss
By you, sir, to awake him.

Pray hurt him not; though he be dead,
He knows well who do love him,
And who with green turfs rear his head,
And who do rudely move him.

He's soft and tender: pray take heed;
With bands of cowslips bind him,
And bring him home. But 'tis decreed
That I shall never find him.

TO MEADOWS

Ye have been fresh and green,
Ye have been filled with flowers;
And ye the walks have been
Where maids have spent their hours.

You have beheld how they
With wicker arks did come,
To kiss and bear away
The richer cowslips home.

Ye've heard them sweetly sing,
And seen them in a round;
Each virgin, like a spring,
With honeysuckles crowned.

But now, we see none here
Whose silvery feet did tread,
And with dishevelled hair
Adorned this smoother mead.

Like unthrifts, having spent
Your stock, and needy grown,
Ye're left here to lament
You poor estates, alone.

George Herbert

1593–1633

VIRTUE

Sweet day, so cool, so calm, so bright,
The bridal of the earth and sky;
The dew shall weep thy fall to-night,
For thou must die.

Sweet rose, whose hue, angry and brave,
Bids the rash gazer wipe his eye,
Thy root is ever in its grave,
And thou must die.

Sweet spring, full of sweet days and roses,
A box where sweets compacted lie,
My music shows ye have your closes,
And all must die.

Only a sweet and virtuous soul,
Like seasoned timber, never gives;
But though the whole world turn to coal,
Then chiefly lives.

PEACE

SWEET Peace, where dost thou dwell? I humbly crave,
Let me once know.
I sought thee in a secret cave,
And ask'd, if Peace were there.
A hollow wind did seem to answer, No:
Go seek elsewhere.

I did; and going did a rainbow note:
Surely, thought I,
This is the lace of Peace's coat:
I will search out the matter.
But while I lookt the clouds immediately
Did break and scatter.

Then went I to a garden and did spy
A gallant flower,
The crown Imperiall: Sure, said I,
Peace at the root must dwell.
But when I digg'd, I saw a worm devoure
What show'd so well.

At length I met a rev'rend good old man;
Whom when for Peace
I did demand, he thus began:
There was a Prince of old
At Salem dwelt, who liv'd with good increase
Of flock and fold.

He sweetly liv'd; yet sweetnesse did not save
His life from foes.
But after death out of his grave
There sprang twelve stalks of wheat;
Which many wondring at, got some of those
To plant and set.

It prosper'd strangely, and did soon disperse
Through all the earth:
For they that taste it do rehearse,
That vertue lies therein;
A secret vertue, bringing peace and mirth
By flight of sinne.

Take of this grain, which in my garden grows,
And grows for you;
Make bread of it: and that repose
And peace, which ev'ry where
With so much earnestness you do pursue
Is onely there.

THE COLLAR

I STRUCK the board, and cried, "No more;
I will abroad!
What, shall I ever sigh and pine?
My lines and life are free; free as the road,
Loose as the wind, as large as store.
Shall I be still in suit?
Have I no harvest but a thorn
To let me blood, and not restore
What I have lost with cordial fruit?
Sure there was wine
Before my sighs did dry it; there was corn
Before my tears did drown it;
Is the year only lost to me?
Have I no bays to crown it,

No flowers, no garlands gay? all blasted,
All wasted?
Not so, my heart; but there is fruit,
And thou hast hands.
Recover all thy sigh-blown age
On double pleasures; leave thy cold dispute
Of what is fit and not; forsake thy cage,
Thy rope of sands
Which petty thoughts have made; and made to thee
Good cable, to enforce and draw,
And be thy law,
While thou didst wink and wouldst not see.
Away! take heed;
I will abroad.
Call in thy death's head there, tie up thy fears:
He that forbears
To suit and serve his need
Deserves his load."
But as I raved, and grew more fierce and wild
At every word,
Methought I heard one calling, "Child";
And I replied, "My Lord."

LOVE

Love bade me welcome; yet my soul drew back,
Guilty of dust and sin.
But quick-eyed Love, observing me grow slack
From my first entrance in,
Drew nearer to me, sweetly questioning
If I lacked anything.

"A guest," I answered, "worthy to be here."
Love said, "You shall be he."
"I, the unkind, ungrateful? Ah, my Dear,
I cannot look on Thee."
Love took my hand, and, smiling, did reply,
"Who made the eyes but I?"

"Truth, Lord, but I have marred them; let my shame
Go where it doth deserve."
"And know you not," says Love, "who bore the blame?"
"My Dear, then I will serve."
"You must sit down," says Love, "and taste my meat."
So I did sit and eat.

THE PULLEY

When God at first made man,
Having a glass of blessings standing by,
"Let us," said He, "pour on him all we can:
Let the world's riches, which dispersèd lie,
Contract into a span."

So strength first made a way;
Then beauty flowed, then wisdom, honor, pleasure
When almost all was out, God made a stay,
Perceiving that, alone of all His treasure,
Rest in the bottom lay.

"For if I should," said He,
"Bestow this jewel also on My creature,
He would adore My gifts instead of Me,
And rest in nature, not the God of nature;
So both should losers be.

"Yet let him keep the rest,
But keep them with repining restlessness:
Let him be rich and weary, that at least,
If goodness lead him not, yet weariness
May toss him to My breast."

THE FLOWER

How fresh, O Lord, how sweet and clean
Are Thy returns! Even as the flowers in spring,
To which, besides their own demean,

The late-past frosts tributes of pleasure bring.
Grief melts away
Like snow in May,
As if there were no such cold thing.

Who would have thought my shrivelled heart
Could have recovered greenness? It was gone
Quite underground, as flowers depart
To see their mother-root when they have blown;
Where they together
All the hard weather,
Dead to the world, keep house unknown.

These are Thy wonders, Lord of power,
Killing and quickening, bringing down to hell
And up to heaven in an hour;
Making a chiming of a passing-bell.
We say amiss
This or that is;
Thy word is all, if we could spell.

O that I once past changing were,
Fast in Thy paradise, where no flower can wither!
Many a spring I shoot up fair,
Offering at heaven, growing and groaning thither;
Nor doth my flower
Want a spring shower,
My sins and I joining together.

But while I grow in a straight line,
Still upwards bent, as if heaven were mine own,
Thy anger comes, and I decline.
What frost to that? What pole is not the zone
Where all things burn,
When Thou dost turn,
And the least frown of Thine is shown?

And now in age I bud again:
After so many deaths I live and write;
I once more smell the dew and rain,

And relish versing. O my only Light,
It cannot be
That I am he
On whom Thy tempests fell all night.

These are Thy wonders, Lord of love,
To make us see we are but flowers that glide;
Which when we once can find and prove,
Thou hast a garden for us where to bide.
Who would be more,
Swelling through store,
Forfeit their paradise by their pride.

Thomas Carew

1594?–1639

DISDAIN RETURNED

He that loves a rosy cheek,
Or a coral lip admires,
Or from star-like eyes doth seek
Fuel to maintain his fires;
As old Time makes these decay,
So his flames must waste away.

But a smooth and steadfast mind,
Gentle thoughts, and calm desires,
Hearts with equal love combined,
Kindle never-dying fires.
Where these are not, I despise
Lovely cheeks or lips or eyes.

No tears, Celia, now shall win
My resolved heart to return;
I have searched that soul within,
And find nought but pride and scorn:
I have learned thy arts, and now
Can disdain as much as thou.
Some power in my revenge convey
That love to her I cast away.

ASK ME NO MORE

Ask me no more where Jove bestows,
When June is past, the fading rose;
For in your beauty's orient deep
These flowers, as in their causes, sleep.

Ask me no more whither do stray
The golden atoms of the day,
For, in pure love, heaven did prepare
Those powders to enrich your hair.

Ask me no more whither doth haste
The nightingale when May is past;
For in your sweet dividing throat
She winters, and keeps warm her note.

Ask me no more where those stars light
That downwards fall in dead of night,
For in your eyes they sit, and there
Fixèd become as in their sphere.

Ask me no more if east or west
The phœnix builds her spicy nest;
For unto you at last she flies,
And in your fragrant bosom dies.

James Shirley

1596–1666

A DIRGE

From The Contention of Ajax and Ulysses

The glories of our blood and state
  Are shadows, not substantial things;
There is no armor against fate;
Death lays his icy hand on kings:
      Scepter and crown
      Must tumble down,

And in the dust be equal made
With the poor crooked scythe and spade.

Some men with swords may reap the field,
  And plant fresh laurels where they kill;
But their strong nerves at last must yield;
  They tame but one another still:
    Early or late
    They stoop to fate,
And must give up their murmuring breath
When they, pale captives, creep to death.

The garlands wither on your brow;
  Then boast no more your mighty deeds;
Upon Death's purple altar now
  See where the victor-victim bleeds:
    Your heads must come
    To the cold tomb;
Only the actions of the just
Smell sweet, and blossom in their dust.

William Davenant

1606–1668

SONG

The lark now leaves his watery nest,
  And climbing shakes his dewy wings.
He takes this window for the East,
  And to implore your light he sings—
Awake, awake! the morn will never rise
Till she can dress her beauty at your eyes.

The merchant bows unto the seaman's star,
  The plowman from the sun his season takes;
But still the lover wonders what they are
  Who look for day before his mistress wakes.
Awake, awake! break through your veils of lawn!
Then draw your curtains, and begin the dawn!

Edmund Waller

1606–1687

GO LOVELY ROSE!

Go, lovely Rose!
Tell her that wastes her time and me
That now she knows,
When I resemble her to thee,
How sweet and fair she seems to be.

Tell her that's young,
And shuns to have her graces spied,
That hadst thou sprung
In deserts, where no men abide,
Thou must have uncommended died.

Small is the worth
Of beauty from the light retired;
Bid her come forth,
Suffer herself to be desired,
And not blush so to be admired.

Then die! that she
The common fate of all things rare
May read in thee;
How small a part of time they share
That are so wondrous sweet and fair!

ON A GIRDLE

That which her slender waist confined,
Shall now my joyful temples bind;
No monarch but would give his crown,
His arms might do what this has done.

It was my heaven's extremest sphere,
The pale which held that lovely deer,
My joy, my grief, my hope, my love,
Did all within this circle move!

A narrow compass! and yet there
Dwelt all that's good, and all that's fair!
Give me but what this ribband bound,
Take all the rest the sun goes round!

John Milton

1608-1674

L'ALLEGRO

Hence, loathèd Melancholy,
Of Cerberus and blackest Midnight born
In Stygian cave forlorn,
'Mongst horrid shapes, and shrieks, and sights unholy!
Find out some uncouth cell,
Where brooding darkness spreads his jealous wings,
And the night-raven sings;
There, under ebon shades and low-browed rocks,
As ragged as thy locks,
In dark Cimmerian desert ever dwell.
But come, thou goddess fair and free,
In heaven yclept Euphrosyne,
And by men heart-easing Mirth;
Whom lovely Venus, at a birth,
With two sister Graces more,
To ivy-crownèd Bacchus bore;
Or whether (as some sager sing)
The frolic wind that breathes the spring,
Zephyr, with Aurora playing,
As he met her once a-Maying,
There, on beds of violets blue,
And fresh-blown roses washed in dew,
Filled her with thee, a daughter fair,
So buxom, blithe, and debonair.
Haste thee, nymph, and bring with thee
Jest and youthful Jollity,
Quips and Cranks and wanton Wiles,
Nods and Becks and wreathèd Smiles,
Such as hang on Hebe's cheek,

And love to live in dimple sleek;
Sport, that wrinkled Care derides,
And Laughter holding both his sides.
Come, and trip it, as ye go,
On the light, fantastic toe;
And in thy right hand lead with thee
The mountain-nymph, sweet Liberty.
And if I give thee honor due,
Mirth, admit me of thy crew,
To live with her, and live with thee,
In unreprovèd pleasures free:
To hear the lark begin his flight,
And, singing, startle the dull night,
From his watch-tower in the skies,
Till the dappled dawn doth rise;
Then to come in spite of sorrow,
And at my window bid good morrow,
Through the sweetbriar or the vine
Or the twisted eglantine,
While the cock, with lively din,
Scatters the rear of darkness thin,
And to the stack or the barn door
Stoutly struts his dames before;
Oft listening how the hounds and horn
Cheerly rouse the slumbering morn,
From the side of some hoar hill,
Through the high wood echoing shrill;
Sometime walking, not unseen,
By hedgerow elms, on hillocks green,
Right against the eastern gate,
Where the great sun begins his state,
Robed in flames and amber light,
The clouds in thousand liveries dight;
While the ploughman, near at hand,
Whistles o'er the furrowed land,
And the milkmaid singeth blithe,
And the mower whets his scythe,
And every shepherd tells his tale
Under the hawthorn in the dale.

Straight mine eye hath caught new pleasures,
Whilst the landskip round it measures:
Russet lawns and fallows gray,
Where the nibbling flocks do stray;
Mountains on whose barren breast
The laboring clouds do often rest;
Meadows trim, with daisies pied;
Shallow brooks and rivers wide.
Towers and battlements it sees
Bosomed high in tufted trees,
Where perhaps some beauty lies,
The cynosure of neighboring eyes.
Hard by a cottage chimney smokes
From betwixt two agèd oaks,
Where Corydon and Thyrsis, met,
Are at their savory dinner set
Of herbs and other country messes,
Which the neat-handed Phillis dresses;
And then in haste her bower she leaves,
With Thestylis to bind the sheaves,
Or, if the earlier season lead,
To the tanned haycock in the mead.
Sometimes, with secure delight,
The upland hamlets will invite,
When the merry bells ring round,
And the jocund rebecks sound
To many a youth and many a maid
Dancing in the checkered shade;
And young and old come forth to play
On a sunshine holiday,
Till the livelong daylight fail.
Then to the spicy, nut-brown ale,
With stories told of many a feat:
How faery Mab the junkets eat;
She was pinched and pulled, she said;
And he, by friar's lanthorn led,
Tells how the drudging goblin sweat
To earn his cream-bowl duly set,
When in one night, ere glimpse of morn,

His shadowy flail hath threshed the corn
That ten day-laborers could not end;
Then lies him down the lubber fiend,
And, stretched out all the chimney's length,
Basks at the fire his hairy strength,
And, crop-full, out of doors he flings
Ere the first cock his matin rings.
Thus done the tales, to bed they creep,
By whispering winds soon lulled asleep.
Towered cities please us then,
And the busy hum of men,
Where throngs of knights and barons bold,
In weeds of peace, high triumphs hold,
With store of ladies, whose bright eyes
Rain influence, and judge the prize
Of wit or arms, while both contend
To win her grace whom all commend.
There let Hymen oft appear
In saffron robe, with taper clear,
And pomp and feast and revelry,
With mask and antique pageantry;
Such sights as youthful poets dream
On summer eves by haunted stream.
Then to the well-trod stage anon,
If Jonson's learnèd sock be on,
Or sweetest Shakespeare, Fancy's child,
Warble his native wood-notes wild.
And ever, against eating cares,
Lap me in soft Lydian airs,
Married to immortal verse,
Such as the meeting soul may pierce,
In notes with many a winding bout
Of linkèd sweetness long drawn out
With wanton heed and giddy cunning,
The melting voice through mazes running,
Untwisting all the chains that tie
The hidden soul of harmony;
That Orpheus' self may heave his head
From golden slumber on a bed

Of heaped Elysian flowers, and hear
Such strains as would have won the ear
Of Pluto to have quite set free
His half-regained Eurydice.
These delights if thou canst give,
Mirth, with thee I mean to live.

IL PENSEROSO

Hence, vain, deluding joys,
  The brood of Folly without father bred!
How little you bested,
  Or fill the fixèd mind with all your toys!
Dwell in some idle brain,
  And fancies fond with gaudy shapes possess,
As thick and numberless
  As the gay motes that people the sunbeams,
Or likest hovering dreams,
  The fickle pensioners of Morpheus' train.
But hail, thou goddess sage and holy!
Hail, divinest Melancholy!
Whose saintly visage is too bright
To hit the sense of human sight,
And therefore to our weaker view
O'erlaid with black, staid Wisdom's hue;
Black, but such as in esteem
Prince Memnon's sister might beseem,
Or that starred Ethiop queen that strove
To set her beauty's praise above
The sea-nymphs, and their powers offended.
Yet thou art higher far descended:
Thee bright-haired Vesta long of yore
To solitary Saturn bore;
His daughter she (in Saturn's reign
Such mixture was not held a stain).
Oft in glimmering bowers and glades
He met her, and in secret shades
Of woody Ida's inmost grove,
Whilst yet there was no fear of Jove.

Come, pensive nun, devout and pure,
Sober, steadfast, and demure,
All in a robe of darkest grain,
Flowing with majestic train,
And sable stole of cypress lawn
Over thy decent shoulders drawn.
Come, but keep thy wonted state,
With even step and musing gait
And looks commercing with the skies,
Thy rapt soul sitting in thine eyes;
There, held in holy passion still,
Forget thyself to marble, till
With a sad, leaden, downward cast
Thou fix them on the earth as fast.
And join with thee calm Peace and Quiet,
Spare Fast, that oft with gods doth diet,
And hears the Muses in a ring
Aye round about Jove's altar sing;
And add to these retirèd Leisure,
That in trim gardens takes his pleasure;
But, first and chiefest, with thee bring
Him that yon soars on golden wing,
Guiding the fiery-wheelèd throne,
The cherub Contemplation;
And the mute Silence hist along,
'Less Philomel will deign a song,
In her sweetest, saddest plight,
Smoothing the rugged brow of night,
While Cynthia checks her dragon yoke
Gently o'er the accustomed oak.
Sweet bird, that shunn'st the noise of folly,
Most musical, most melancholy!
Thee, chauntress, oft the woods among
I woo, to hear thy even-song;
And, missing thee, I walk unseen
On the dry, smooth-shaven green,
To behold the wandering moon,
Riding near her highest noon,
Like one that had been led astray

Through the heaven's wide, pathless way,
And oft, as if her head she bowed,
Stooping through a fleecy cloud.
Oft, on a plat of rising ground,
I hear the far-off curfew sound,
Over some wide-watered shore,
Swinging slow with sullen roar;
Or, if the air will not permit,
Some still, removèd place will fit,
Where glowing embers through the room
Teach light to counterfeit a gloom,
Far from all resort of mirth,
Save the cricket on the hearth,
Or the bellman's drowsy charm
To bless the doors from nightly harm.
Or let my lamp at midnight hour
Be seen in some high, lonely tower,
Where I may oft outwatch the Bear,
With thrice-great Hermes, or unsphere
The spirit of Plato to unfold
What worlds or what vast regions hold
The immortal mind that hath forsook
Her mansion in this fleshly nook;
And of those demons that are found
In fire, air, flood, or under ground,
Whose power hath a true consent
With planet or with element.
Sometime let gorgeous Tragedy
In sceptered pall come sweeping by,
Presenting Thebes, or Pelops' line,
Or the tale of Troy divine,
Or what (though rare) of later age
Ennobled hath the buskined stage.
But, O sad virgin, that thy power
Might raise Musaeus from his bower;
Or bid the soul of Orpheus sing
Such notes as, warbled to the string,
Drew iron tears down Pluto's cheek,
And made hell grant what love did seek;

Or call up him that left half told
The story of Cambuscan bold,
Of Camball, and of Algarsife,
And who had Canace to wife,
That owned the virtuous ring and glass,
And of the wondrous horse of brass
On which the Tartar king did ride;
And if aught else great bards beside
In sage and solemn tunes have sung,
Of tourneys, and of trophies hung,
Of forests, and enchantments drear,
Where more is meant than meets the ear.
Thus, Night, oft see me in thy pale career,
Till civil-suited Morn appear,
Not tricked and frounced, as she was wont
With the Attic boy to hunt,
But kerchiefed in a comely cloud,
While rocking winds are piping loud,
Or ushered with a shower still,
When the gust hath blown his fill,
Ending on the rustling leaves,
With minute-drops from off the eaves.
And when the sun begins to fling
His flaring beams, me, goddess, bring
To archèd walks of twilight groves,
And shadows brown, that Sylvan loves,
Of pine or monumental oak,
Where the rude axe with heavèd stroke
Was never heard the nymphs to daunt,
Or fright them from their hallowed haunt.
There in close covert by some brook,
Where no profaner eye may look,
Hide me from day's garish eye,
While the bee with honied thigh,
That at her flowery work doth sing,
And the waters murmuring,
With such consort as they keep,
Entice the dewy-feathered sleep:
And let some strange, mysterious dream

Wave at his wings, in airy stream
Of lively portraiture displayed,
Softly on my eyelids laid;
And, as I wake, sweet music breathe
Above, about, or underneath,
Sent by some spirit to mortals good,
Or the unseen genius of the wood.
But let my due feet never fail
To walk the studious cloister's pale,
And love the high embowèd roof,
With antique pillars massy proof,
And storied windows richly dight,
Casting a dim, religious light.
There let the pealing organ blow
To the full-voiced quire below,
In service high and anthems clear,
As may with sweetness, through mine ear,
Dissolve me into ecstasies,
And bring all heaven before mine eyes.
And may at last my weary age
Find out the peaceful hermitage,
The hairy gown and mossy cell,
Where I may sit and rightly spell
Of every star that heaven doth shew,
And every herb that sips the dew,
Till old experience do attain
To something like prophetic strain.
These pleasures, Melancholy, give,
And I with thee will choose to live.

LYCIDAS

In this Monody the Author bewails a learned Friend, unfortunately drowned in his passage from Chester on the Irish Seas, 1637; and, by occasion, foretells the ruin of our corrupted Clergy, then in their height.

Yet once more, O ye laurels, and once more,
Ye myrtles brown, with ivy never sere,
I come to pluck your berries harsh and crude,
And with forced fingers rude

Shatter your leaves before the mellowing year.
Bitter constraint and sad occasion dear
Compels me to disturb your season due;
For Lycidas is dead, dead ere his prime,
Young Lycidas, and hath not left his peer.
Who would not sing for Lycidas? he knew
Himself to sing, and build the lofty rhyme.
He must not float upon his watery bier
Unwept, and welter to the parching wind,
Without the meed of some melodious tear.
  Begin, then, Sisters of the sacred well
That from beneath the seat of Jove doth spring;
Begin, and somewhat loudly sweep the string.
Hence with denial vain and coy excuse:
So may some gentle Muse
With lucky words favor *my* destined urn,
And as he passes turn,
And bid fair peace be to my sable shroud!
  For we were nursed upon the self-same hill,
Fed the same flock, by fountain, shade, and rill;
Together both, ere the high lawns appeared
Under the opening eyelids of the Morn,
We drove a-field, and both together heard
What time the gray-fly winds her sultry horn,
Battening our flocks with the fresh dews of night,
Oft till the star that rose at evening bright
Toward heaven's descent had sloped his westering wheel.
Meanwhile the rural ditties were not mute;
Tempered to the oaten flute
Rough Satyrs danced, and Fauns with cloven heel
From the glad sound would not be absent long;
And old Damœtas loved to hear our song.
  But, oh! the heavy change, now thou art gone,
Now thou art gone and never must return!
Thee, Shepherd, thee the woods and desert caves,
With wild thyme and the gadding vine o'ergrown,
And all their echoes, mourn.
The willows, and the hazel copses green,
Shall now no more be seen

Fanning their joyous leaves to thy soft lays.
As killing as the canker to the rose,
Or taint-worm to the weanling herds that graze,
Or frost to flowers that their gay wardrobe wear,
When first the white-thorn blows;
Such, Lycidas, thy loss to shepherd's ear.
 Where were ye, Nymphs, when the remorseless deep
Closed o'er the head of your loved Lycidas?
For neither were ye playing on the steep
Where your old bards, the famous Druids, lie,
Nor on the shaggy top of Mona high,
Nor yet where Deva spreads her wizard stream.
Ay me! I fondly dream,
"Had ye been there," . . . for what could that have done?
What could the Muse herself that Orpheus bore,
The Muse herself, for her enchanting son,
Whom universal nature did lament,
When, by the rout that made the hideous roar,
His gory visage down the stream was sent,
Down the swift Hebrus to the Lesbian shore?
 Alas! what boots it with uncessant care
To tend the homely, slighted, shepherd's trade,
And strictly meditate the thankless Muse?
Were it not better done, as others use,
To sport with Amaryllis in the shade,
Or with the tangles of Neæra's hair?
Fame is the spur that the clear spirit doth raise
(That last infirmity of noble mind)
To scorn delights and live laborious days;
But the fair guerdon when we hope to find,
And think to burst out into sudden blaze,
Comes the blind Fury with the abhorrèd shears
And slits the thin-spun life. "But not the praise,"
Phœbus replied, and touched my trembling ears:
"Fame is no plant that grows on mortal soil,
Nor in the glistering foil
Set off to the world, nor in broad rumor lies,
But lives and spreads aloft by those pure eyes
And perfect witness of all-judging Jove;

As he pronounces lastly on each deed,
Of so much fame in heaven expect thy meed."
O fountain Arethuse, and thou honored flood,
Smooth-sliding Mincius, crowned with vocal reeds,
That strain I heard was of a higher mood.
But now my oat proceeds,
And listens to the Herald of the Sea
That came in Neptune's plea.
He asked the waves, and asked the felon winds,
What hard mishap hath doomed this gentle swain?
And questioned every gust of rugged wings,
That blows from off each beakèd promontory.
They knew not of his story;
And sage Hippotades their answer brings,
That not a blast was from his dungeon strayed:
The air was calm, and on the level brine
Sleek Panopé with all her sisters played.
It was that fatal and perfidious bark,
Built in the eclipse, and rigged with curses dark,
That sunk so low that sacred head of thine.
Next, Camus, reverend sire, went footing slow,
His mantle hairy, and his bonnet sedge,
Inwrought with figures dim, and on the edge
Like to that sanguine flower inscribed with woe.
"Ah! who hath reft," quoth he, "my dearest pledge?"
Last came, and last did go,
The Pilot of the Galilean Lake;
Two massy keys he bore of metals twain
(The golden opes, the iron shuts amain).
He shook his mitred locks, and stern bespake:—
"How well could I have spared for thee, young swain,
Enow of such as, for their bellies' sake,
Creep, and intrude, and climb into the fold!
Of other care they little reckoning make
Than how to scramble at the shearers' feast
And shove away the worthy bidden guest.
Blind mouths! that scarce themselves know how to hold
A sheep-hook, or have learned ought else the least
That to the faithful herdman's art belongs!

What recks it them? What need they? They are sped;
And, when they list, their lean and flashy songs
Grate on their scrannel pipes of wretched straw;
The hungry sheep look up, and are not fed,
But, swoln with wind and the rank mist they draw,
Rot inwardly, and foul contagion spread;
Besides what the grim wolf with privy paw
Daily devours apace, and nothing said.
But that two-handed engine at the door
Stands ready to smite once, and smite no more."
Return, Alphëus; the dread voice is past
That shrunk thy streams; return, Sicilian Muse,
And call the vales, and bid them hither cast
Their bells and flowerets of a thousand hues.
Ye valleys low, where the mild whispers use
Of shades, and wanton winds, and gushing brooks,
On whose fresh lap the swart star sparely looks,
Throw hither all your quaint enameled eyes
That on the green turf suck the honeyed showers,
And purple all the ground with vernal flowers.
Bring the rathe primrose that forsaken dies,
The tufted crow-toe, and pale jessamine,
The white pink, and the pansy freaked with jet,
The glowing violet,
The musk-rose, and the well-attired woodbine,
With cowslips wan that hang the pensive head,
And every flower that sad embroidery wears;
Bid amaranthus all his beauty shed,
And daffadillies fill their cups with tears,
To strew the laureate hearse where Lycid lies.
For so, to interpose a little ease,
Let our frail thoughts dally with false surmise.
Ay me! whilst thee the shores and sounding seas
Wash far away, where'er thy bones are hurled;
Whether beyond the stormy Hebrides,
Where thou perhaps under the whelming tide,
Visit'st the bottom of the monstrous world;
Or whether thou, to our moist vows denied,
Sleep'st by the fable of Bellerus old,
Where the great Vision of the guarded mount

Looks toward Namancos and Bayona's hold.
Look homeward, Angel, now, and melt with ruth:
And, O ye dolphins, waft the hapless youth.
  Weep no more, woeful shepherds, weep no more,
For Lycidas, your sorrow, is not dead,
Sunk though he be beneath the watery floor.
So sinks the day-star in the ocean bed,
And yet anon repairs his drooping head,
And tricks his beams, and with new-spangled ore
Flames in the forehead of the morning sky:
So Lycidas sunk low, but mounted high,
Through the dear might of Him that walked the waves,
Where, other groves and other streams along,
With nectar pure his oozy locks he laves,
And hears the unexpressive nuptial song,
In the blest kingdoms meek of joy and love.
There entertain him all the Saints above,
In solemn troops, and sweet societies,
That sing, and singing in their glory move,
And wipe the tears for ever from his eyes.
Now, Lycidas, the shepherds weep no more;
Henceforth thou art the Genius of the shore,
In thy large recompense, and shalt be good
To all that wander in that perilous flood.

  Thus sang the uncouth swain to the oaks and rills,
While the still morn went out with sandals gray;
He touched the tender stops of various quills,
With eager thought warbling his Doric lay:
And now the sun had stretched out all the hills,
And now was dropped into the western bay.
At last he rose, and twitched his mantle blue:
To-morrow to fresh woods, and pastures new.

ON HIS HAVING ARRIVED AT THE AGE OF TWENTY-THREE

How soon hath Time, the subtle thief of youth,
Stolen on his wing my three-and-twentieth year!
My hasting days fly on with full career,

But my late spring no bud or blossom shew'th.
Perhaps my semblance might deceive the truth
That I to manhood am arrived so near;
And inward ripeness doth much less appear,
That some more timely-happy spirits endu'th.
Yet, be it less or more, or soon or slow,
It shall be still in strictest measure even
To that same lot, however mean or high,
Toward which Time leads me, and the will of Heaven.
All is, if I have grace to use it so,
As ever in my great Task-Master's eye.

TO MR. H. LAWES ON HIS AIRS

Harry, whose tuneful and well-measured song
  First taught our English music how to span
  Words with just note and accent, not to scan
  With Midas' ears, committing short and long,
Thy worth and skill exempts thee from the throng,
  With praise enough for Envy to look wan;
  To after age thou shalt be writ the man
  That with smooth air couldst humor best our tongue.
Thou honor'st Verse, and Verse must lend her wing
  To honor thee, the priest of Phœbus' quire,
  That tunest their happiest lines in hymn or story.
Dante shall give Fame leave to set thee higher
  Than his Casella, whom he wooed to sing,
  Met in the milder shades of Purgatory.

TO MR. LAWRENCE

Lawrence, of virtuous father virtuous son,
  Now that the fields are dank, and ways are mire,
  Where shall we sometimes meet, and by the fire
  Help waste a sullen day, what may be won
From the hard season gaining? Time will run
  On smoother, till Favonius reinspire
  The frozen earth, and clothe in fresh attire
  The lily and rose, that neither sowed nor spun.

What neat repast shall feast us, light and choice,
 Of Attic taste, with wine, whence we may rise
 To hear the lute well touched or artful voice
Warble immortal notes and Tuscan air?
 He who of those delights can judge, and spare
 To interpose them oft, is not unwise.

ON HIS BLINDNESS

When I consider how my light is spent
Ere half my days in this dark world and wide,
And that one talent which is death to hide
Lodged with me useless, though my soul more bent
To serve therewith my Maker, and present
My true account, lest He returning chide,
"Doth God exact day-labor, light denied?"
I fondly ask. But Patience, to prevent
That murmur, soon replies, "God doth not need
Either man's work or his own gifts. Who best
Bear his mild yoke, they serve him best. His state
Is kingly: thousands at his bidding speed,
And post o'er land and ocean without rest;
They also serve who only stand and wait."

ON THE LATE MASSACRE IN PIEDMONT

Avenge, O Lord, thy slaughtered saints, whose bones
Lie scattered on the Alpine mountains cold;
Even them who kept thy truth so pure of old,
When all our fathers worshiped stocks and stones,
Forget not: in thy book record their groans
Who were thy sheep, and in their ancient fold
Slain by the bloody Piedmontese, that rolled
Mother with infant down the rocks. Their moans
The vales redoubled to the hills, and they
To heaven. Their martyred blood and ashes sow
O'er all the Italian fields, where still doth sway
The triple Tyrant; that from these may grow
A hundredfold, who, having learnt thy way,
Early may fly the Babylonian woe.

Sir John Suckling

1609–1642

WHY SO PALE AND WAN?

From Aglaura

Why so pale and wan, fond lover?
  Prithee, why so pale?
Will, when looking well can't move her,
  Looking ill prevail?
  Prithee, why so pale?

Why so dull and mute, young sinner?
  Prithee, why so mute?
Will, when speaking well can't win her,
  Saying nothing do 't?
  Prithee, why so mute?

Quit, quit for shame! This will not move;
  This cannot take her.
If of herself she will not love,
  Nothing can make her:
  The devil take her!

THE CONSTANT LOVER

Out upon it, I have loved
  Three whole days together!
And am like to love three more,
  If it prove fair weather.

Time shall moult away his wings,
  Ere he shall discover
In the whole wide world again
  Such a constant lover.

But the spite on 't is, no praise
  Is due at all to me:
Love with me had made no stays,
  Had it any been but she.

Had it any been but she,
And that very face,
There had been at least ere this
A dozen dozen in her place.

Richard Lovelace

1618–1658

TO LUCASTA, ON GOING TO THE WARS

Tell me not, sweet, I am unkind,
That from the nunnery
Of thy chaste breast and quiet mind
To war and arms I fly.

True, a new mistress now I chase,
The first foe in the field;
And with a stronger faith embrace
A sword, a horse, a shield.

Yet this inconstancy is such
As thou too shalt adore;
I could not love thee, dear, so much,
Loved I not honor more.

TO ALTHEA, FROM PRISON

When Love with unconfinèd wings
Hovers within my gates,
And my divine Althea brings
To whisper at the grates;
When I lie tangled in her hair
And fettered to her eye,
The birds that wanton in the air
Know no such liberty.

When flowing cups run swiftly round
With no allaying Thames,
Our careless heads with roses bound,
Our hearts with loyal flames;

When thirsty grief in wine we steep,
When healths and draughts go free,
Fishes that tipple in the deep
Know no such liberty.

When, like committed linnets, I
With shriller throat shall sing
The sweetness, mercy, majesty,
And glories of my king;
When I shall voice aloud how good
He is, how great should be,
Enlargèd winds, that curl the flood,
Know no such liberty.

Stone walls do not a prison make,
Nor iron bars a cage;
Minds innocent and quiet take
That for an hermitage;
If I have freedom in my love,
And in my soul am free,
Angels alone, that soar above,
Enjoy such liberty.

Andrew Marvell

1621–1678

THE GARDEN

How vainly men themselves amaze,
To win the palm, the oak, or bays,
And their incessant labors see
Crowned from some single herb or tree
Whose short and narrow-vergèd shade
Does prudently their toils upbraid,
While all the flowers and trees do close
To weave the garlands of repose!

Fair quiet, have I found thee here,
And Innocence, thy sister dear?
Mistaken long, I sought you then
In busy companies of men.

Your sacred plants, if here below,
Only among the plants will grow;
Society is all but rude
To this delicious solitude.

No white nor red was ever seen
So amorous as this lovely green.
Fond lovers, cruel as their flame,
Cut in these trees their mistress' name.
Little, alas! they know or heed,
How far these beauties hers exceed!
Fair trees! wheres'e'er your bark I wound,
No name shall but your own be found.

When we have run our passion's heat,
Love hither makes his best retreat.
The gods, that mortal beauty chase,
Still in a tree did end their race;
Apollo hunted Daphne so,
Only that she might laurel grow;
And Pan did after Syrinx speed,
Not as a nymph, but for a reed.

What wondrous life is this I lead!
Ripe apples drop about my head;
The luscious clusters of the vine
Upon my mouth do crush their wine;
The nectarine, and curious peach,
Into my hands themselves do reach;
Stumbling on melons, as I pass,
Insnared with flowers, I fall on grass.

Meanwhile the mind, from pleasure less,
Withdraws into its happiness;—
The mind, that ocean where each kind
Does straight its own resemblance find;
Yet it creates, transcending these,
Far other worlds, and other seas,
Annihilating all that's made
To a green thought in a green shade.

Here at the fountain's sliding foot,
Or at some fruit-tree's mossy root,
Casting the body's vest aside,
My soul into the boughs does glide:
There, like a bird, it sits and sings,
Then whets and combs its silver wings,
And, till prepared for longer flight,
Waves in its plumes the various light.

Such was that happy garden-state,
While man there walked without a mate:
After a place so pure and sweet,
What other help could yet be meet!
But 'twas beyond a mortal's share
To wander solitary there:
Two paradises 'twere in one,
To live in paradise alone.

How well the skillful gardener drew
Of flowers, and herbs, this dial new;
Where, from above, the milder sun
Does through a fragrant zodiac run,
And, as it works, the industrious bee
Computes its time as well as we!
How could such sweet and wholesome hours
Be reckoned but with herbs and flowers?

TO HIS COY MISTRESS

Had we but world enough, and time,
This coyness, lady, were no crime.
We would sit down, and think which way
To walk, and pass our long love's day.
Thou by the Indian Ganges' side
Shouldst rubies find: I by the tide
Of Humber would complain. I would
Love you ten years before the flood,
And you should, if you please, refuse
Till the conversion of the Jews;

My vegetable love should grow
Vaster than empires and more slow;
An hundred years should go to praise
Thine eyes, and on thy forehead gaze;
Two hundred to adore each breast,
But thirty thousand to the rest;
An age at least to every part,
And the last age should show your heart.
For, lady, you deserve this state,
Nor would I love at lower rate.
  But at my back I always hear
Time's wingèd chariot hurrying near,
And yonder all before us lie
Deserts of vast eternity.
Thy beauty shall no more be found,
Nor, in thy marble vault, shall sound
My echoing song; then worms shall try
That long-preserved virginity,
And your quaint honor turn to dust,
And into ashes all my lust:
The grave's a fine and private place,
But none, I think, do there embrace.
  Now, therefore, while the youthful hue
Sits on thy skin like morning dew,
And while thy willing soul transpires
At every pore with instant fires,
Now let us sport us while we may,
And now, like amorous birds of prey,
Rather at once our time devour,
Than languish in his slow-chapped power.
Let us roll all our strength and all
Our sweetness up into one ball,
And tear our pleasures with rough strife
Thorough the iron gates of life;
Thus, though we cannot make our sun
Stand still, yet we will make him run.

THE MOWER TO THE GLOWWORMS

Ye living lamps, by whose dear light
The nightingale does sit so late,
And studying all the summer night,
Her matchless songs does meditate;

Ye country comets, that portend
No war nor prince's funeral,
Shining unto no higher end
Than to presage the grass's fall;

Ye glowworms, whose officious flame
To wandering mowers shows the way
That in the night have lost their aim,
And after foolish fires do stray;

Your courteous lights in vain you waste,
Since Juliana here is come,
For she my mind hath so displaced
That I shall never find my home.

BERMUDAS

Where the remote Bermudas ride
In the ocean's bosom unespied,
From a small boat that rowed along,
The listening winds received this song:

"What should we do but sing His praise,
That led us through the watery maze,
Unto an isle so long unknown,
And yet far kinder than our own?
Where He the huge sea-monsters wracks,
That lift the deep upon their backs,
He lands us on a grassy stage,
Safe from the storms, and prelate's rage.
He gave us this eternal spring,
Which here enamels everything,
And sends the fowls to us in care,

On daily visits through the air;
He hangs in shades the orange bright,
Like golden lamps in a green night,
And does in the pomegranates close
Jewels more rich than Ormus shows;
He makes the figs our mouths to meet,
And throws the melons at our feet;
But apples plants of such a price,
No tree could ever bear them twice;
With cedars chosen by His hand,
From Lebanon, He stores the land,
And makes the hollow seas, that roar,
Proclaim the ambergris on shore.
He cast (of which we rather boast)
The gospel's pearl upon our coast,
And in these rocks for us did frame
A temple where to sound His name.
Oh! let our voice His praise exalt,
Till it arrive at heaven's vault,
Which, thence perhaps rebounding, may
Echo beyond the Mexique Bay."

Thus sung they, in the English boat,
An holy and a cheerful note;
And all the way, to guide their chime,
With falling oars they kept the time.

Henry Vaughan

1622–1695

THE RETREAT

Happy those early days, when I
Shined in my angel-infancy!
Before I understood this place
Appointed for my second race,
Or taught my soul to fancy aught
But a white, celestial thought;

When yet I had not walked above
A mile or two from my first love,
And looking back—at that short space—
Could see a glimpse of his bright face;
When on some gilded cloud or flower
My gazing soul would dwell an hour,
And in those weaker glories spy
Some shadows of eternity;
Before I taught my tongue to wound
My conscience with a sinful sound,
Or had the black art to dispense
A several sin to every sense,
But felt through all this fleshly dress
Bright shoots of everlastingness.
O, how I long to travel back,
And tread again that ancient track!
That I might once more reach that plain,
Where first I left my glorious train;
From whence the enlightened spirit sees
That shady city of palm trees.
But ah! my soul with too much stay
Is drunk, and staggers in the way!
Some men a forward motion love,
But I by backward steps would move;
And when this dust falls to the urn,
In that state I came, return.

PEACE

My soul, there is a country
Far beyond the stars,
Where stands a wingèd sentry
All skilful in the wars.
There, above noise and danger,
Sweet Peace sits crowned with smiles,
And One born in a manger
Commands the beauteous files.
He is thy gracious friend,
And—O my soul, awake!—

Did in pure love descend
  To die here for thy sake.
If thou canst get but thither,
  There grows the flower of peace,
The rose that cannot wither,
  Thy fortress and thy ease.
Leave, then, thy foolish ranges;
  For none can thee secure
But One who never changes,
  Thy God, thy life, thy cure.

THE WORLD

I SAW eternity, the other night,
Like a great ring of pure and endless light,
    All calm as it was bright;
And round beneath it time in hours, days, years,
    Driven by the spheres,
Like a vast shadow moved, in which the world
    And all her train were hurled.
The doting lover in his quaintest strain
    Did there complain;
Near him, his lute, his fancy, and his flights,
    Wit's sour delights,
With gloves and knots, the silly snares of pleasure,
    Yet his dear treasure,
All scattered lay, while he his eyes did pour
    Upon a flower.

The darksome statesman, hung with weights and woe,
Like a thick midnight-fog, moved there so slow
    He did nor stay nor go;
Condemning thoughts, like sad eclipses, scowl
    Upon his soul,
And clouds of crying witnesses without
    Pursued him with one shout.
Yet digged the mole, and, lest his ways be found,
    Worked under ground,

Where he did clutch his prey. But one did see
That policy:
Churches and altars fed him; perjuries
Were gnats and flies;
It rained about him blood and tears; but he
Drank them as free.

The fearful miser on a heap of rust
Sat pining all his life there, did scarce trust
His own hands with the dust;
Yet would not place one piece above, but lives
In fear of thieves.
Thousands there were as frantic as himself,
And hugged each one his pelf:
The downright epicure placed heaven in sense,
And scorned pretense;
While others, slipped into a wide excess,
Said little less;
The weaker sort slight, trivial wares enslave,
Who think them brave;
And poor, despisèd Truth sat counting by
Their victory.

Yet some, who all this while did weep and sing,
And sing and weep, soared up into the ring.
But most would use no wing.
"O fools!" said I, "thus to prefer dark night
Before true light!
To live in grots and caves, and hate the day
Because it shows the way,
The way which from this dead and dark abode
Leads up to God;
A way where you might tread the sun and be
More bright than he!"
But as I did their madness so discuss,
One whispered thus:
"This ring the Bridegroom did for none provide
But for His bride."

DEPARTED FRIENDS

THEY are all gone into the world of light!
  And I alone sit lingering here;
Their very memory is fair and bright,
    And my sad thoughts doth clear.

It glows and glitters in my cloudy breast
  Like stars upon some gloomy grove,
Or those faint beams in which this hill is dressed
    After the sun's remove.

I see them walking in an air of glory,
  Whose light doth trample on my days;
My days, which are at best but dull and hoary,
    Mere glimmering and decays.

O holy hope and high humility,
  High as the heavens above!
These are your walks, and you have showed them me
    To kindle my cold love.

Dear, beauteous death! the jewel of the just,
  Shining nowhere but in the dark,
What mysteries do lie beyond thy dust,
    Could man outlook that mark!

He that hath found some fledged bird's nest may know
  At first sight if the bird be flown;
But what fair well or grove he sings in now,
    That is to him unknown.

And yet, as angels in some brighter dreams
  Call to the soul when man doth sleep,
So some strange thoughts transcend our wonted themes,
    And into glory peep.

If a star were confined into a tomb,
  Her captive flames must needs burn there;
But when the hand that locked her up gives room,
    She'll shine through all the sphere.

O Father of eternal life, and all
Created glories under Thee!
Resume Thy spirit from this world of thrall
Into true liberty.

Either disperse these mists, which blot and fill
My perspective still as they pass,
Or else remove me hence unto that hill
Where I shall need no glass.

John Dryden

1631–1700

TO THE MEMORY OF MR. OLDHAM

Farewell, too little, and too lately known,
Whom I began to think and call my own:
For sure our souls were near allied, and thine
Cast in the same poetic mold with mine.
One common note on either lyre did strike,
And knaves and fools we both abhorr'd alike.
To the same goal did both our studies drive;
The last set out the soonest did arrive.
Thus Nisus fell upon the slippery place,
While his young friend perform'd and won the race.
O early ripe! to thy abundant store
What could advancing age have added more?
It might (what nature never gives the young)
Have taught the numbers of thy native tongue.
But satire needs not those, and wit will shine
Thro' the harsh cadence of a rugged line:
A noble error, and but seldom made,
When poets are by too much force betray'd.
Thy generous fruits, tho' gather'd ere their prime,
Still shew'd a quickness; and maturing time
But mellows what we write to the dull sweets of rhyme.

Once more, hail and farewell; farewell, thou young,
But ah too short, Marcellus of our tongue;
Thy brows with ivy, and with laurels bound;
But fate and gloomy night encompass thee around.

SONG

From Marriage a la Mode

Why should a foolish marriage vow,
  Which long ago was made,
Oblige us to each other now,
  When passion is decay'd?
We lov'd, and we lov'd, as long as we could,
  Till our love was lov'd out in us both;
But our marriage is dead, when the pleasure is fled:
  'Twas pleasure first made it an oath.

If I have pleasures for a friend,
  And farther love in store,
What wrong has he whose joys did end,
  And who could give no more?
'Tis a madness that he should be jealous of me,
  Or that I should bar him of another:
For all we can gain is to give ourselves pain,
  When neither can hinder the other.

SONG

From Amphitryon

Fair Iris I love, and hourly I die,
But not for a lip, nor a languishing eye:
She's fickle and false, and there we agree,
For I am as false and as fickle as she.
We neither believe what either can say;
And, neither believing, we neither betray.
'Tis civil to swear, and say things of course;
We mean not the taking for better or worse.

When present, we love; when absent, agree:
I think not of Iris, nor Iris of me.
The legend of love no couple can find,
So easy to part, or so equally join'd.

SONG

From Secret Love

I feed a flame within, which so torments me,
That it both pains my heart, and yet contents me:
'Tis such a pleasing smart, and I so love it,
That I had rather die than once remove it.

Yet he for whom I grieve shall never know it;
My tongue does not betray, nor my eyes show it:
Not a sigh, nor a tear, my pain discloses,
But they fall silently, like dew on roses.

Thus to prevent my love from being cruel,
My heart's the sacrifice, as 't is the fuel:
And while I suffer this, to give him quiet,
My faith rewards my love, tho' he deny it.

On his eyes will I gaze, and there delight me;
Where I conceal my love, no frown can fright me:
To be more happy, I dare not aspire;
Nor can I fall more low, mounting no higher.

A SONG FOR ST. CECILIA'S DAY

1687

From harmony, from heavenly harmony
This universal frame began:
When Nature underneath a heap
Of jarring atoms lay
And could not heave her head,
The tuneful voice was heard from high,
"Arise, ye more than dead!"

Then cold and hot and moist and dry
In order to their stations leap,
    And Music's power obey.
From harmony, from heavenly harmony
    This universal frame began:
    From harmony to harmony
Through all the compass of the notes it ran,
The diapason closing full in man.

What passion cannot Music raise and quell?
    When Jubal struck the chorded shell,
  His listening brethren stood around,
  And, wondering, on their faces fell
  To worship that celestial sound:
Less than a god they thought there could not dwell
    Within the hollow of that shell
    That spoke so sweetly and so well.
What passion cannot Music raise and quell?

  The trumpet's loud clangor
    Excites us to arms,
  With shrill notes of anger
    And mortal alarms.
  The double double double beat
    Of the thundering drum
    Cries "Hark! the foes come;
Charge, charge! 'tis too late to retreat!"

  The soft complaining flute
    In dying notes discovers
    The woes of hopeless lovers,
Whose dirge is whispered by the warbling lute.

    Sharp violins proclaim
  Their jealous pangs and desperation,
  Fury, frantic indignation,
  Depth of pain, and height of passion
    For the fair disdainful dame.

But oh! what art can teach,
What human voice can reach
The sacred organ's praise?
Notes inspiring holy love,
Notes that wing their heavenly ways
To mend the choirs above.

Orpheus could lead the savage race,
And trees unrooted left their place,
Sequacious of the lyre:
But bright Cecilia raised the wonder higher:
When to her organ vocal breath was given,
An angel heard, and straight appeared—
Mistaking earth for heaven.

Grand Chorus

As from the power of sacred lays
The spheres began to move,
And sung the great Creator's praise
To all the blest above;
So when the last and dreadful hour
This crumbling pageant shall devour,
The trumpet shall be heard on high,
The dead shall live, the living die,
And Music shall untune the sky.

CHARACTERS FROM THE SATIRES

Achitophel

Of these the false Achitophel was first,
A name to all succeeding ages curst:
For close designs and crooked counsels fit,
Sagacious, bold, and turbulent of wit,
Restless, unfixed in principles and place,
In power unpleased, impatient of disgrace;
A fiery soul, which working out its way,
Fretted the pigmy body to decay
And o'er-informed the tenement of clay.

A daring pilot in extremity,
Pleased with the danger, when the waves went high,
He sought the storms; but, for a calm unfit,
Would steer too nigh the sands to boast his wit.
Great wits are sure to madness near allied
And thin partitions do their bounds divide;
Else, why should he, with wealth and honor blest,
Refuse his age the needful hours of rest?
Punish a body which he could not please,
Bankrupt of life, yet prodigal of ease?
And all to leave what with his toil he won
To that unfeathered two-legged thing, a son,
Got, while his soul did huddled notions try,
And born a shapeless lump, like anarchy.
In friendship false, implacable in hate,
Resolved to ruin or to rule the state;
To compass this the triple bond he broke,
The pillars of the public safety shook,
And fitted Israel for a foreign yoke;
Then, seized with fear, yet still affecting fame,
Usurped a patriot's all-atoning name.
So easy still it proves in factious times
With public zeal to cancel private crimes.

Zimri

Some of their chiefs were princes of the land;
In the first rank of these did Zimri stand,
A man so various that he seemed to be
Not one, but all mankind's epitome:
Stiff in opinions, always in the wrong,
Was everything by starts and nothing long;
But in the course of one revolving moon
Was chymist, fiddler, statesman, and buffoon;
Then all for women, painting, rhyming, drinking,
Besides ten thousand freaks that died in thinking.
Blest madman, who could every hour employ
With something new to wish or to enjoy!

Railing and praising were his usual themes,
And both, to show his judgment, in extremes:
So over violent or over civil
That every man with him was God or Devil.
In squandering wealth was his peculiar art;
Nothing went unrewarded but desert.
Beggared by fools whom still he found too late,
He had his jest, and they had his estate.
He laughed himself from Court; then sought relief
By forming parties, but could ne'er be chief:
For spite of him, the weight of business fell
On Absalom and wise Achitophel;
Thus wicked but in will, of means bereft,
He left not faction, but of that was left.

Og and Doeg

And hasten Og and Doeg to rehearse,
Two fools that crutch their feeble sense on verse,
Who by my Muse to all succeeding times
Shall live in spite of their own dogrel rhymes.
Doeg, though without knowing how or why,
Made still a blundering kind of melody;
Spurred boldly on, and dashed through thick and thin.
Through sense and nonsense, never out nor in;
Free from all meaning, whether good or bad,
And, in one word, heroically mad,
He was too warm on picking-work to dwell,
But faggoted his notions as they fell,
And, if they rhymed and rattled, all was well.
Spiteful he is not, though he wrote a satire,
For still there goes some thinking to ill-nature;
He needs no more than birds and beasts to think,
All his occasions are to eat and drink.
If he call rogue and rascal from a garret,
He means you no more mischief than a parrot;
The words for friend and foe alike were made,
To fetter them in verse is all his trade. . . .
Railing in other men may be a crime,

But ought to pass for mere instinct in him;
Instinct he follows and no farther knows,
For to write verse with him is to *transprose;*
'Twere pity treason at his door to lay
Who *makes heaven's gate a lock to its own key;*
Let him rail on, let his invective Muse
Have four and twenty letters to abuse,
Which if he jumbles to one line of sense,
Indict him of a capital offence.
In fire-works give him leave to vent his spite,
Those are the only serpents he can write;
The height of his ambition is, we know,
But to be master of a puppet-show;
On that one stage his works may yet appear,
And a month's harvest keeps him all the year.

Now stop your noses, readers, all and some,
For here's a tun of midnight work to come,
Og from a treason-tavern rolling home.
Round as a globe, and liquored every chink,
Goodly and great he sails behind his link.
With all this bulk there's nothing lost in Og,
For every inch that is not fool is rogue: . . .
When wine has given him courage to blaspheme,
He curses God, but God before cursed him;
And if man could have reason, none has more,
That made his paunch so rich and him so poor.
With wealth he was not trusted, for Heaven knew
What 'twas of old to pamper up a Jew;
To what would he on quail and pheasant swell
That even on tripe and carrion could rebel?
But though Heaven made him poor, with reverence speaking,
He never was a poet of God's making;
The midwife laid her hand on his thick skull,
With this prophetic blessing—*Be thou dull;*
Drink, swear, and roar, forbear no lewd delight
Fit for thy bulk, do anything but write.
Thou art of lasting make, like thoughtless men,

A strong nativity—but for the pen;
Eat opium, mingle arsenic in thy drink,
Still thou mayest live, avoiding pen and ink.
I see, I see, 'tis counsel given in vain,
For treason, botched in rhyme, will be thy bane;
Rhyme is the rock on which thou art to wreck,
'Tis fatal to thy fame and to thy neck.
Why should thy meter good king David blast?
A psalm of his will surely be thy last.
Darest thou presume in verse to meet thy foes.
Thou whom the penny pamphlet foiled in prose?
Doeg, whom God for mankind's mirth has made,
O'ertops thy talent in thy very trade;
Doeg to thee, thy paintings are so coarse,
A poet is, though he's the poet's horse.
A double noose thou on thy neck dost pull
For writing treason and for writing dull;
To die for faction is a common evil,
But to be hanged for nonsense is the devil.
Hadst thou the glories of thy King exprest,
Thy praises had been satires at the best;
But thou in clumsy verse, unlicked, unpointed,
Hast shamefully defiled the Lord's anointed:
I will not rake the dunghill of thy crimes,
For who would read thy life that reads thy rhymes?
But of king David's foes be this the doom,
May all be like the young man Absalom;
And for my foes may this their blessing be,
To talk like Doeg and to write like thee.

Sir Charles Sedley

1639?–1701

TO CELIA

Not, Celia, that I juster am,
Or better than the rest!
For I would change each hour like them,
Were not my heart at rest.

But I am tied to very thee
By every thought I have;
Thy face I only care to see,
Thy heart I only crave.

All that in woman is adored
In thy dear self I find;
For the whole sex can but afford
The handsome and the kind.

Why then should I seek further store
And still make love anew?
When change itself can give no more,
'Tis easy to be true.

Matthew Prior

1664–1721

A BETTER ANSWER

Dear Chloe, how blubbered is that pretty face!
Thy cheek all on fire, and thy hair all uncurled!
Prithee quit this caprice, and (as old Falstaff says)
Let us e'en talk a little like folks of this world.

How canst thou presume thou hast leave to destroy
The beauties which Venus but lent to thy keeping?
Those looks were designed to inspire love and joy;
More ordinary eyes may serve people for weeping.

To be vexed at a trifle or two that I writ,
Your judgment at once and my passion you wrong;
You take that for fact which will scarce be found wit:
Od's life! must one swear to the truth of a song?

What I speak, my fair Chloe, and what I write, shows
The difference there is betwixt nature and art:
I court others in verse, but I love thee in prose;
And they have my whimsies, but thou hast my heart.

The god of us verse-men (you know, child), the sun,
  How after his journeys he sets up his rest;
If at morning o'er earth 'tis his fancy to run,
  At night he reclines on his Thetis's breast.

So when I am wearied with wandering all day,
  To thee, my delight, in the evening I come:
No matter what beauties I saw in my way;
  They were but my visits, but thou art my home.

Then finish, dear Chloe, this pastoral war,
  And let us like Horace and Lydia agree;
For thou art a girl as much brighter than her
  As he was a poet sublimer than me.

AN ODE

The merchant, to secure his treasure,
  Conveys it in a borrowed name:
Euphelia serves to grace my measure,
  But Chloe is my real flame.

My softest verse, my darling lyre
  Upon Euphelia's toilet lay,
When Chloe noted her desire
  That I should sing, that I should play.

My lyre I tune, my voice I raise;
  But with my numbers mix my sighs;
And whilst I sing Euphelia's praise,
  I fix my soul on Chloe's eyes.

Fair Chloe blushed, Euphelia frowned,
  I sung and gazed, I played and trembled:
And Venus to the Loves around
  Remarked how ill we all dissembled.

Joseph Addison

1672–1719

HYMN

THE spacious firmament on high,
With all the blue ethereal sky,
And spangled heavens, a shining frame,
Their great Original proclaim.
The unwearied Sun from day to day
Does his Creator's power display;
And publishes to every land
The work of an Almighty hand.

Soon as the evening shades prevail,
The Moon takes up the wondrous tale;
And nightly to the listening Earth
Repeats the story of her birth:
Whilst all the stars that round her burn,
And all the planets in their turn,
Confirm the tidings as they roll,
And spread the truth from pole to pole.

What though in solemn silence all
Move round the dark terrestrial ball;
What though nor real voice nor sound
Amidst their radiant orbs be found?
In Reason's ear they all rejoice,
And utter forth a glorious voice;
Forever singing as they shine,
"The Hand that made us is divine."

Alexander Pope

1688–1744

ODE ON SOLITUDE

HAPPY the man whose wish and care
 A few paternal acres bound,
Content to breathe his native air
  In his own ground.

Whose herds with milk, whose fields with bread,
Whose flocks supply him with attire,
Whose trees in summer yield him shade,
In winter fire.

Bless'd who can unconcern'dly find
Hours, days, and years slide soft away,
In health of body, peace of mind,
Quiet by day;

Sound sleep by night: study and ease
Together mix'd; sweet recreation;
And innocence, which most does please,
With Meditation.

Thus let me live, unseen, unknown,
Thus unlamented let me die;
Steal from the world, and not a stone
Tell where I lie.

CHARACTERS FROM THE SATIRES

Atticus

Peace to all such! but were there one whose fires
True genius kindles, and fair fame inspires;
Blest with each talent, and each art to please,
And born to write, converse, and live with ease,
Should such a man, too fond to rule alone,
Bear, like the Turk, no brother near the throne,
View him with scornful, yet with jealous eyes,
And hate for arts that caused himself to rise;
Damn with faint praise, assent with civil leer,
And, without sneering, teach the rest to sneer;
Willing to wound, and yet afraid to strike,
Just hint a fault, and hesitate dislike;
Alike reserved to blame, or to commend,
A timorous foe, and a suspicious friend;
Dreading e'en fools, by flatterers besieged,
And so obliging, that he ne'er obliged;

Like Cato, give his little senate laws,
And sit attentive to his own applause:
While wits and Templars every sentence raise,
And wonder with a foolish face of praise—
Who but must laugh, if such a man there be?
Who would not weep, if Atticus were he?

Sporus

Let Sporus tremble—— What? that thing of silk,
Sporus, that mere white curd of ass's milk?
Satire or sense, alas! can Sporus feel,
Who breaks a butterfly upon a wheel?
Yet let me flap this bug with gilded wings,
This painted child of dirt, that stinks and stings;
Whose buzz the witty and the fair annoys,
Yet wit ne'er tastes, and beauty ne'er enjoys:
So well-bred spaniels civilly delight
In mumbling of the game they dare not bite.
Eternal smiles his emptiness betray,
As shallow streams run dimpling all the way.
Whether in florid impotence he speaks,
And, as the prompter breathes, the puppet squeaks;
Or at the ear of Eve, familiar toad!
Half froth, half venom, spits himself abroad,
In puns, or politics, or tales, or lies,
Or spite, or smut, or rhymes, or blasphemies.
His wit all see-saw, between that and this,
Now high, now low, now master up, now miss,
And he himself one vile antithesis.
Amphibious thing! that acting either part,
The trifling head, or the corrupted heart;
Fop at the toilet, flatterer at the board,
Now trips a lady, and now struts a lord.
Eve's tempter thus the Rabbins have express'd,
A cherub's face, a reptile all the rest.
Beauty that shocks you, parts that none will trust,
Wit that can creep, and pride that licks the dust.

Wharton

Wharton! the scorn and wonder of our days,
Whose ruling passion was the lust of praise:
Born with whate'er could win it from the wise,
Women and fools must like him, or he dies:
Though wondering senates hung on all he spoke,
The club must hail him master of the joke.
Shall parts so various aim at nothing new?
He'll shine a Tully and a Wilmot too.
Then turns repentant, and his God adores
With the same spirit that he drinks and whores;
Enough if all around him but admire,
And now the punk applaud, and now the friar.
Thus with each gift of Nature and of art,
And wanting nothing but an honest heart;
Grown all to all, from no one vice exempt,
And most contemptible, to shun contempt;
His passion still, to covet general praise,
His life, to forfeit it a thousand ways;
A constant bounty which no friend has made;
An angel tongue, which no man can persuade;
A fool, with more of wit than half mankind,
Too rash for thought, for action too refined;
A tyrant to the wife his heart approves;
A rebel to the very king he loves;
He dies, sad outcast of each Church and State,
And, harder still! flagitious, yet not great.
Ask you why Wharton broke through every rule?
'Twas all for fear the knaves should call him fool.

Chloe

"Yet Chloe sure was form'd without a spot."—
Nature in her then err'd not, but forgot.
"With every pleasing, every prudent part,
Say, what can Chloe want?"—She wants a heart.
She speaks, behaves, and acts, just as she ought,
But never, never reached one generous thought.

Virtue she finds too painful an endeavor,
Content to dwell in decencies for ever.
So very reasonable, so unmoved,
As never yet to love, or to be loved.
She, while her lover pants upon her breast,
Can mark the figures on an Indian chest;
And when she sees her friend in deep despair,
Observes how much a chintz exceeds mohair!
Forbid it, Heaven, a favor or a debt
She e'er should cancel—but she may forget.
Safe is your secret still in Chloe's ear;
But none of Chloe's shall you ever hear.
Of all her dears she never slander'd one,
But cares not if a thousand are undone.
Would Chloe know if you're alive or dead?
She bids her footman put it in her head.
Chloe is prudent—would you too be wise?
Then never break your heart when Chloe dies.

Henry Carey

1693?–1743

SALLY IN OUR ALLEY

Of all the girls that are so smart
  There's none like pretty Sally;
She is the darling of my heart,
  And she lives in our alley.
There is no lady in the land
  Is half so sweet as Sally;
She is the darling of my heart,
  And she lives in our alley.

Her father he makes cabbage-nets
  And through the streets does cry 'em;
Her mother she sells laces long
  To such as please to buy 'em:

But sure such folks could ne'er beget
  So sweet a girl as Sally!
She is the darling of my heart,
  And she lives in our alley.

When she is by, I leave my work,
  I love her so sincerely;
My master comes like any Turk,
  And bangs me most severely:
But let him bang his bellyful,
  I'll bear it all for Sally;
She is the darling of my heart,
  And she lives in our alley.

Of all the days that's in the week
  I dearly love but one day—
And that's the day that comes betwixt
  A Saturday and Monday;
For then I'm drest all in my best
  To walk abroad with Sally;
She is the darling of my heart,
  And she lives in our alley.

My master carries me to church,
  And often am I blamèd
Because I leave him in the lurch
  As soon as text is namèd;
I leave the church in sermon-time
  And slink away to Sally;
She is the darling of my heart,
  And she lives in our alley.

When Christmas comes about again,
  O then I shall have money;
I'll board it up, and, box and all,
  I'll give it to my honey:
I would it were ten thousand pound,
  I'd give it all to Sally;
She is the darling of my heart,
  And she lives in our alley.

My master and the neighbors all
  Make game of me and Sally,
And, but for her, I'd better be
  A slave and row a galley;
But when my seven long years are out
  O then I'll marry Sally,—
O then we'll wed, and then we'll bed.
  But not in our alley!

William Shenstone

1714–1763

WRITTEN AT AN INN AT HENLEY

To thee, fair freedom! I retire
  From flattery, cards, and dice, and din;
Nor art thou found in mansions higher
  Than the low cot or humble inn.

'Tis here with boundless power I reign;
  And every health which I begin
Converts dull port to bright champagne;
  Such freedom crowns it, at an inn.

I fly from pomp, I fly from plate!
  I fly from falsehood's specious grin!
Freedom I love, and form I hate,
  And choose my lodgings at an inn.

Here, waiter! take my sordid ore,
  Which lacqueys else might hope to win;
It buys, what courts have not in store,
  It buys me freedom at an inn.

Whoe'er has traveled life's dull round,
  Where'er his stages may have been,
May sigh to think he still has found
  The warmest welcome at an inn.

Thomas Gray

1716–1771

ELEGY

WRITTEN IN A COUNTRY CHURCH-YARD

THE Curfew tolls the knell of parting day,
The lowing herd wind slowly o'er the lea,
The plowman homeward plods his weary way,
And leaves the world to darkness and to me.

Now fades the glimmering landscape on the sight,
And all the air a solemn stillness holds,
Save where the beetle wheels his droning flight,
And drowsy tinklings lull the distant folds;

Save that from yonder ivy-mantled tower
The moping owl does to the moon complain
Of such as, wandering near her secret bower,
Molest her ancient solitary reign.

Beneath those rugged elms, that yew-tree's shade,
Where heaves the turf in many a moldering heap,
Each in his narrow cell for ever laid,
The rude Forefathers of the hamlet sleep.

The breezy call of incense-breathing Morn,
The swallow twittering from the straw-built shed,
The cock's shrill clarion, or the echoing horn,
No more shall rouse them from their lowly bed.

For them no more the blazing hearth shall burn,
Or busy housewife ply her evening care:
No children run to lisp their sire's return,
Or climb his knees the envied kiss to share.

Oft did the harvest to their sickle yield,
Their furrow oft the stubborn glebe has broke;
How jocund did they drive their team afield!
How bowed the woods beneath their sturdy stroke.

Let not Ambition mock their useful toil,
  Their homely joys, and destiny obscure;
Nor Grandeur hear with a disdainful smile
  The short and simple annals of the poor.

The boast of heraldry, the pomp of power,
  And all that beauty, all that wealth e'er gave,
Await alike the inevitable hour.
  The paths of glory lead but to the grave.

Nor you, ye Proud, impute to These the fault,
  If Memory o'er their Tomb no Trophies raise,
Where through the long-drawn isle and fretted vault
  The pealing anthem swells the note of praise.

Can storied urn or animated bust
  Back to its mansion call the fleeting breath?
Can Honor's voice provoke the silent dust,
  Or Flattery soothe the dull cold ear of Death?

Perhaps in this neglected spot is laid
  Some heart once pregnant with celestial fire;
Hands, that the rod of empire might have swayed,
  Or waked to ecstasy the living lyre.

But Knowledge to their eyes her ample page
  Rich with the spoils of time did ne'er unroll;
Chill Penury repressed their noble rage,
  And froze the genial current of the soul.

Full many a gem of purest ray serene,
  The dark unfathomed caves of ocean bear:
Full many a flower is born to blush unseen,
  And waste its sweetness on the desert air.

Some village Hampden, that with dauntless breast
  The little tyrant of his fields withstood,
Some mute inglorious Milton here may rest,
  Some Cromwell guiltless of his country's blood.

The applause of listening senates to command,
  The threats of pain and ruin to despise,
To scatter plenty o'er a smiling land,
  And read their history in a nation's eyes,

Their lot forbade: nor circumscribed alone
  Their growing virtues, but their crimes confined;
Forbade to wade through slaughter to a throne,
  And shut the gates of mercy on mankind,

The struggling pangs of conscious truth to hide,
  To quench the blushes of ingenuous shame,
Or heap the shrine of Luxury and Pride
  With incense kindled at the Muse's flame.

Far from the madding crowd's ignoble strife,
  Their sober wishes never learned to stray;
Along the cool sequestered vale of life
  They kept the noiseless tenor of their way.

Yet even these bones from insult to protect,
  Some frail memorial still erected nigh,
With uncouth rhymes and shapeless sculpture decked,
  Implores the passing tribute of a sigh.

Their name, their years, spelt by the unlettered muse,
  The place of fame and elegy supply;
And many a holy text around she strews,
  That teach the rustic moralist to die.

For who, to dumb Forgetfulness a prey,
  This pleasing anxious being e'er resigned,
Left the warm precincts of the cheerful day,
  Nor cast one longing lingering look behind?

On some fond breast the parting soul relies,
  Some pious drops the closing eye requires;
Even from the tomb the voice of Nature cries,
  Even in our ashes live their wonted fires.

For thee, who mindful of the unhonored dead
  Dost in these lines their artless tale relate;
If chance, by lonely contemplation led,
  Some kindred spirit shall inquire thy fate,—

Haply some hoary-headed swain may say,
  "Oft have we seen him at the peep of dawn
Brushing with hasty steps the dews away
  To meet the sun upon the upland lawn.

"There at the foot of yonder nodding beech
  That wreathes its old fantastic roots so high,
His listless length at noontide would he stretch,
  And pore upon the brook that babbles by.

"Hard by yon wood, now smiling as in scorn,
  Muttering his wayward fancies he would rove,
Now drooping, woeful-wan, like one forlorn,
  Or crazed with care, or crossed in hopeless love.

"One morn I missed him on the customed hill,
  Along the heath, and near his favorite tree;
Another came; nor yet beside the rill,
  Nor up the lawn, nor at the wood was he;

"The next, with dirges due in sad array
  Slow through the church-way path we saw him borne.—
Approach and read (for thou canst read) the lay,
  Graved on the stone beneath yon aged thorn."

THE EPITAPH

Here rests his head upon the lap of Earth
  A Youth to Fortune and to Fame unknown.
Fair Science frowned not on his humble birth,
  And Melancholy marked him for her own.

Large was his bounty, and his soul sincere,
  Heaven did a recompense as largely send:

He gave to Misery all he had, a tear,
He gained from Heaven ('twas all he wished) a friend.

No farther seek his merits to disclose,
Or draw his frailties from their dread abode
(There they alike in trembling hope repose),
The bosom of his Father and his God.

THE PROGRESS OF POESY

I. 1

Awake, Æolian lyre, awake,
And give to rapture all thy trembling strings!
From Helicon's harmonious springs
A thousand rills their mazy progress take;
The laughing flowers that round them blow
Drink life and fragrance as they flow.
Now the rich stream of music winds along
Deep, majestic, smooth, and strong,
Through verdant vales and Ceres' golden reign:
Now rolling down the steep amain,
Headlong, impetuous, see it pour;
The rocks and nodding groves rebellow to the roar.

I. 2

Oh sovereign of the willing soul,
Parent of sweet and solemn-breathing airs,
Enchanting shell! the sullen Cares
And frantic Passions hear thy soft control.
On Thracia's hills the Lord of War
Has curbed the fury of his car
And dropped his thirsty lance at thy command.
Perching on the sceptred hand
Of Jove, thy magic lulls the feathered king
With ruffled plumes and flagging wing;
Quenched in dark clouds of slumber lie
The terror of his beak and lightnings of his eye.

I. 3

Thee the voice, the dance, obey,
Tempered to thy warbled lay.
O'er Idalia's velvet-green
The rosy-crownèd Loves are seen,
On Cytherea's day,
With antic Sports and blue-eyed Pleasures
Frisking light in frolic measures:
Now pursuing, now retreating,
Now in circling troops they meet;
To brisk notes in cadence beating
Glance their many-twinkling feet.
Slow melting strains their Queen's approach declare:
Where'er she turns the Graces homage pay;
With arms sublime, that float upon the air,
In gliding state she wins her easy way;
O'er her warm cheek and rising bosom move
The bloom of young Desire and purple light of Love.

II. 1

Man's feeble race what ills await:
Labour, and Penury, the racks of Pain,
Disease, and Sorrow's weeping train,
And Death, sad refuge from the storms of Fate!
The fond complaint, my song, disprove,
And justify the laws of Jove.
Say, has he given in vain the heavenly Muse?
Night, and all her sickly dews,
Her spectres wan, and birds of boding cry,
He gives to range the dreary sky;
Till down the eastern cliffs afar
Hyperion's march they spy, and glittering shafts of war.

II. 2

In climes beyond the solar road,
Where shaggy forms o'er ice-built mountains roam,
The Muse has broke the twilight-gloom
To cheer the shivering native's dull abode.

And oft, beneath the odorous shade
Of Chili's boundless forests laid,
She deigns to hear the savage youth repeat,
In loose numbers wildly sweet,
Their feather-cinctured chiefs and dusky loves.
Her track, where'er the goddess roves,
Glory pursue, and generous Shame,
Th' unconquerable Mind, and Freedom's holy flame.

II. 3

Woods that wave o'er Delphi's steep,
Isles that crown th' Ægean deep,
Fields that cool Ilissus laves,
Or where Mæander's amber waves
In lingering labyrinths creep,
How do your tuneful echoes languish,
Mute but to the voice of Anguish?
Where each old poetic mountain
Inspiration breathed around,
Every shade and hallowed fountain
Murmured deep a solemn sound;
Till the sad Nine in Greece's evil hour
Left their Parnassus for the Latian plains:
Alike they scorn the pomp of tyrant Power,
And coward Vice that revels in her chains.
When Latium had her lofty spirit lost,
They sought, O Albion! next, thy sea-encircled coast.

III. 1

Far from the sun and summer-gale,
In thy green lap was Nature's darling laid,
What time, where lucid Avon strayed,
To him the mighty mother did unveil
Her awful face: the dauntless child
Stretched forth his little arms, and smiled.
'This pencil take,' she said, 'whose colours clear
Richly paint the vernal year.

Thine too these golden keys, immortal boy!
This can unlock the gates of Joy;
Of Horror that, and thrilling Fears,
Or ope the sacred source of sympathetic tears.'

III. 2

Nor second he that rode sublime
Upon the seraph-wings of Ecstasy,
The secrets of th' abyss to spy.
He passed the flaming bounds of Place and Time:
The living throne, the sapphire blaze,
Where angels tremble while they gaze,
He saw; but, blasted with excess of light,
Closed his eyes in endless night.
Behold where Dryden's less presumptuous car
Wide o'er the fields of glory bear
Two coursers of ethereal race,
With necks in thunder clothed, and long-resounding pace!

III. 3

Hark! his hands the lyre explore:
Bright-eyed Fancy, hovering o'er,
Scatters from her pictured urn
Thoughts that breathe and words that burn.
But, ah, 'tis heard no more!
O lyre divine, what daring spirit
Wakes thee now? Though he inherit
Nor the pride nor ample pinion
That the Theban Eagle bear,
Sailing with supreme dominion
Through the azure deep of air,
Yet oft before his infant eyes would run
Such forms as glitter in the Muse's ray,
With orient hues unborrowed of the sun:
Yet shall he mount, and keep his distant way
Beyond the limits of a vulgar fate,
Beneath the good how far—but far above the great.

William Collins

1721–1759

ODE TO EVENING

If aught of oaten stop, or pastoral song,
May hope, chaste Eve, to soothe thy modest ear,
  Like thy own solemn springs,
  Thy springs and dying gales,

O nymph reserved, while now the bright-haired sun
Sits in yon western tent, whose cloudy skirts,
  With brede ethereal wove,
  O'erhang his wavy bed:

Now air is hushed, save where the weak-eyed bat,
With short shrill shriek, flits by on leathern wing,
  Or where the beetle winds
  His small but sullen horn,

As oft he rises 'midst the twilight path,
Against the pilgrim borne in heedless hum:
  Now teach me, maid composed,
  To breathe some softened strain,

Whose numbers, stealing through thy darkening vale
May not unseemly with its stillness suit,
  As, musing slow, I hail
  Thy genial loved return!

For when thy folding-star arising shows
His paly circlet, at his warning lamp
  The fragrant Hours, the elves
  Who slept in buds the day,

And many a nymph who wreathes her brows with sedge,
And sheds the freshening dew, and, lovelier still
  The pensive Pleasures sweet,
  Prepare thy shadowy ear:

Then lead, calm votaress, where some sheety lake
Cheers the lone heath, or some time-hallowed pile
  Or upland fallows gray
  Reflect its last cool gleam.

Or if chill blustering winds, or driving rain,
Forbid my willing feet, be mine the hut
  That from the mountain's side
  Views wilds, and swelling floods,

And hamlets brown, and dim-discovered spires,
And hears their simple bell, and marks o'er all
  Thy dewy fingers draw
  The gradual dusky veil.

While Spring shall pour his showers, as oft he wont,
And bathe thy breathing tresses, meekest Eve!
  While Summer loves to sport
  Beneath thy lingering light;

While sallow Autumn fills thy lap with leaves;
Or Winter, yelling through the troublous air,
  Affrights thy shrinking train,
  And rudely rends thy robes;

So long, regardful of thy quiet rule,
Shall Fancy, Friendship, Science, rose-lipped Health,
  Thy gentlest influence own,
  And hymn thy favorite name!

ODE

WRITTEN IN THE BEGINNING OF THE YEAR 1746

How sleep the brave, who sink to rest
By all their country's wishes blest!
When Spring, with dewy fingers cold,
Returns to deck their hallowed mold,
She there shall dress a sweeter sod
Than Fancy's feet have ever trod.

By fairy hands their knell is rung;
By forms unseen their dirge is sung;
There Honor comes, a pilgrim gray,
To bless the turf that wraps their clay;
And Freedom shall awhile repair,
To dwell, a weeping hermit, there!

Oliver Goldsmith

1728–1774

SONG

From THE VICAR OF WAKEFIELD

WHEN lovely woman stoops to folly,
And finds too late that men betray,
What charm can soothe her melancholy?
What art can wash her guilt away?

The only art her guilt to cover,
To hide her shame from every eye,
To give repentance to her lover,
And wring his bosom, is—to die.

William Blake

1757–1827

THE PIPER

PIPING down the valleys wild,
Piping songs of pleasant glee,
On a cloud I saw a child,
And he laughing said to me:

"Pipe a song about a Lamb!"
So I piped with merry cheer.
"Piper, pipe that song again;"
So I piped: he wept to hear.

"Drop thy pipe, thy happy pipe;
Sing thy songs of happy cheer:"

So I sang the same again,
While he wept with joy to hear.

"Piper, sit thee down and write
In a book, that all may read."
So he vanished from my sight,
And I plucked a hollow reed,

And I made a rural pen,
And I stained the water clear,
And I wrote my happy songs
Every child may joy to hear.

NURSE'S SONG

When the voices of children are heard on the green
And laughing is heard on the hill,
My heart is at rest within my breast
And everything else is still.

"Then come home, my children, the sun is gone down
And the dews of night arise;
Come, come, leave off play, and let us away
Till the morning appears in the skies."

"No, no, let us play, for it is yet day
And we cannot go to sleep;
Besides, in the sky the little birds fly
And the hills are all covered with sheep."

"Well, well, go and play till the light fades away
And then go home to bed."
The little ones leapèd and shoutèd and laughed
And all the hills echoèd.

ON ANOTHER'S SORROW

Can I see another's woe,
And not be in sorrow too?
Can I see another's grief,
And not seek for kind relief?

Can I see a falling tear,
And not feel my sorrow's share?
Can a father see his child
Weep, nor be with sorrow filled?

Can a mother sit and hear
An infant groan, an infant fear?
No, no! never can it be!
Never, never can it be!

And can He who smiles on all
Hear the wren with sorrows small,
Hear the small bird's grief and care,
Hear the woes that infants bear,

And not sit beside the nest,
Pouring pity in their breast;
And not sit the cradle near,
Weeping tear on infant's tear;

And not sit both night and day,
Wiping all our tears away?
O, no! never can it be!
Never, never can it be!

He doth give His joy to all;
He becomes an infant small;
He becomes a man of woe;
He doth feel the sorrow too.

Think not thou canst sigh a sigh,
And thy Maker is not by;
Think not thou canst weep a tear,
And thy Maker is not near.

O! He gives to us His joy
That our grief He may destroy;
Till our grief is fled and gone
He doth sit by us and moan.

THE LITTLE BLACK BOY

My mother bore me in the southern wild,
And I am black, but O! my soul is white;
White as an angel is the English child,
But I am black, as if bereaved of light.

My mother taught me underneath a tree,
And, sitting down before the heat of day,
She took me on her lap and kissèd me,
And, pointing to the east, began to say:

'Look on the rising sun,—there God does live,
And gives His light, and gives His heat away;
And flowers and trees and beasts and men receive
Comfort in morning, joy in the noonday.

'And we are put on earth a little space,
That we may learn to bear the beams of love;
And these black bodies and this sunburnt face
Is but a cloud, and like a shady grove.

'For when our souls have learned the heat to bear,
The cloud will vanish; we shall hear His voice,
Saying: "Come out from the grove, my love and care,
And round my golden tent like lambs rejoice." '

Thus did my mother say, and kissèd me;
And thus I say to little English boy.
When I from black and he from white cloud free,
And round the tent of God like lambs we joy,

I'll shade him from the heat, till he can bear
To lean in joy upon our Father's knee;
And then I'll stand and stroke his silver hair,
And be like him, and he will then love me.

THE CLOD AND THE PEBBLE

"Love seeketh not itself to please,
Nor for itself hath any care,
But for another gives its ease,
And builds a Heaven in Hell's despair."

So sung a little Clod of Clay,
Trodden with the cattle's feet,
But a Pebble of the brook
Warbled out these meters meet:

"Love seeketh only Self to please,
To bind another to Its delight,
Joys in another's loss of ease,
And builds a Hell in Heaven's despite."

THE SICK ROSE

O Rose, thou art sick!
The invisible worm,
That flies in the night,
In the howling storm,

Has found out thy bed
Of crimson joy;
And his dark secret love
Does thy life destroy.

THE TIGER

Tyger, tyger: burning bright
In the forests of the night,
What immortal hand or eye
Could frame thy fearful symmetry?

In what distant deeps or skies
Burnt the fire of thine eyes?
On what wings dare he aspire?
What the hand dare seize the fire?

And what shoulder, and what art,
Could twist the sinews of thy heart?
And, when thy heart began to beat,
What dread hand, and what dread feet?

What the hammer? what the chain?
In what furnace was thy brain?
What the anvil? what dread grasp
Dare its deadly terrors clasp?

When the stars threw down their spears,
And watered heaven with their tears,
Did he smile his work to see?
Did he who made the Lamb make thee?

Tyger, tyger: burning bright
In the forests of the night,
What immortal hand or eye,
Dare frame thy fearful symmetry?

AH, SUNFLOWER

Ah, Sunflower! weary of time,
Who countest the steps of the Sun;
Seeking after that sweet golden clime,
Where the traveler's journey is done;

Where the Youth pined away with desire,
And the pale Virgin shrouded in snow,
Arise from their graves, and aspire
Where my Sun-flower wishes to go!

THE GARDEN OF LOVE

I went to the Garden of Love,
And saw what I never had seen:
A Chapel was built in the midst,
Where I used to play on the green.

And the gates of this chapel were shut,
And "Thou shalt not" writ over the door;
So I turned to the Garden of Love,
That so many sweet flowers bore;

And I saw it was fillèd with graves,
And tombstones where flowers should be;
And priests in black gowns were walking their rounds,
And binding with briars my joys and desires.

A POISON TREE

I WAS angry with my friend:
I told my wrath, my wrath did end.
I was angry with my foe:
I told it not, my wrath did grow.

And I watered it in fears,
Night and morning with my tears;
And I sunnèd it with smiles,
And with soft deceitful wiles.

And it grew both day and night
Till it bore an apple bright;
And my foe beheld it shine,
And he knew that it was mine,

And into my garden stole
When the night had veiled the pole:
In the morning glad I see
My foe outstretched beneath the tree.

LONDON

I WANDER through each chartered street,
Near where the chartered Thames does flow,
And mark in every face I meet
Marks of weakness, marks of woe.

In every cry of every man,
In every infant's cry of fear,

In every voice, in every ban,
The mind-forged manacles I hear.

How the chimney-sweeper's cry
Every blackening church appals;
And the hapless soldier's sigh
Runs in blood down palace walls

But most through midnight streets I hear
How the youthful harlot's curse
Blasts the new-born infant's tear,
And blights with plagues the marriage hearse.

From MILTON

And did those feet in ancient time
  Walk upon England's mountains green?
And was the holy Lamb of God
On England's pleasant pastures seen?

And did the Countenance Divine
  Shine forth upon our clouded hills?
And was Jerusalem builded here
Among these dark Satanic Mills?

Bring me my Bow of burning gold!
Bring me my Arrows of desire!
Bring me my Spear! O clouds, unfold!
  Bring me my Chariot of fire!

I will not cease from Mental Fight,
  Nor shall my Sword sleep in my hand,
Till we have built Jerusalem
  In England's green and pleasant Land.

ETERNITY

He who bends to himself a joy
Does the winged life destroy;
But he who kisses the joy as it flies
Lives in eternity's sunrise.

Robert Burns

1759–1796

HIGHLAND MARY

Ye banks and braes, and streams around
  The castle o' Montgomery,
Green be your woods and fair your flowers,
  Your waters never drumlie!
There Summer first unfald her robes,
  And there the langest tarry;
For there I took the last fareweel,
  O' my sweet Highland Mary.

How sweetly bloomed the gay, green birk,
  How rich the hawthorn's blossom,
As underneath their fragrant shade
  I clasped her to my bosom!
The golden hours on angel wings
  Flew o'er me and my dearie;
For dear to me as light and life
  Was my sweet Highland Mary.

Wi' monie a vow and locked embrace
  Our parting was fu' tender;
And, pledging aft to meet again,
  We tore oursels asunder.
But O, fell Death's untimely frost,
  That nipt my flower sae early!
Now green's the sod, and cauld's the clay,
  That wraps my Highland Mary!

O pale, pale now, those rosy lips,
  I aft hae kissed sae fondly;
And closed for ay, the sparkling glance
  That dwalt on me sae kindly;
And moldering now in silent dust
  That heart that lo'ed me dearly!
But still within my bosom's core
  Shall live my Highland Mary.

SONG: MARY MORISON

O Mary, at thy window be!
  It is the wished, the trysted hour.
Those smiles and glances let me see,
  That make the miser's treasure poor.
How blythely wad I bide the stoure,
  A weary slave frae sun to sun,
Could I the rich reward secure—
  The lovely Mary Morison!

Yestreen, when to the trembling string
  The dance gaed through the lighted ha',
To thee my fancy took its wing,
  I sat, but neither heard nor saw:
Though this was fair, and that was braw,
  And yon the toast of a' the town,
I sighed, and said amang them a':
  "Ye are na Mary Morison!"

O Mary, canst thou wreck his peace
  Wha for thy sake wad gladly die?
Or canst thou break that heart of his
  Whase only faut is loving thee?
If love for love thou wilt na gie,
At least be pity to me shown:
A thought ungentle canna be
  The thought o' Mary Morison.

YE FLOWERY BANKS

Ye flowery banks o' bonie Doon,
  How can ye blume sae fair?
How can ye chant, ye little birds,
  And I sae fu' o' care?

Thou'll break my heart, thou bonie bird,
  That sings upon the bough:
Thou minds me o' the happy days
  When my fause luve was true!

Thou'll break my heart, thou bonie bird,
That sings beside thy mate:
For sae I sat, and sae I sang,
And wist na o' my fate!

Aft hae I rov'd by bonie Doon
To see the woodbine twine,
And ilka bird sang o' its luve,
And sae did I o' mine.

Wi' lightsome heart I pu'd a rose
Frae aff its thorny tree,
And my fause luver staw my rose,
But left the thorn wi' me.

OF A' THE AIRTS

Of a' the airts the wind can blaw
I dearly like the west,
For there the bonie lassie lives,
The lassie I lo'e best.
There wild woods grow, and rivers row,
And monie a hill between,
But day and night, my fancy's flight
Is ever wi' my Jean.

I see her in the dewy flowers—
I see her sweet an' fair.
I hear her in the tunefu' birds—
I hear her charm the air.
There's not a bonie flower that springs
By fountain, shaw, or green;
There's not a bonie bird that sings,
But minds me o' my Jean.

A RED, RED ROSE

O, my luve is like a red, red rose,
That's newly sprung in June.
O my luve is like the melodie,
That's sweetly played in tune.

As fair art thou, my bonie lass,
  So deep in luve am I,
And I will luve thee still, my dear,
  Till a' the seas gang dry.

Till a' the seas gang dry, my dear,
  And the rocks melt wi' the sun!
And I will luve thee still, my dear,
  While the sands o' life shall run.

And fare thee weel, my only luve,
  And fare thee weel awhile!
And I will come again, my luve,
  Though it were ten thousand mile!

FLOW GENTLY, SWEET AFTON

Flow gently, sweet Afton, among thy green braes!
Flow gently, I'll sing thee a song in thy praise!
My Mary's asleep by thy murmuring stream—
Flow gently, sweet Afton, disturb not her dream!

Thou stock dove whose echo resounds through the glen,
Ye wild whistling blackbirds in yon thorny den,
Thou green-crested lapwing, thy screaming forbear—
I charge you, disturb not my slumbering fair!

How lofty, sweet Afton, thy neighboring hills,
Far marked with the courses of clear winding rills!
There daily I wander, as noon rises high,
My flocks and my Mary's sweet cot in my eye.

How pleasant thy banks and green valleys below,
Where wild in the woodlands the primroses blow;
There oft, as mild Evening weeps over the lea,
The sweet-scented birk shades my Mary and me.

Thy crystal stream, Afton, how lovely it glides,
And winds by the cot where my Mary resides!
How wanton thy waters her snowy feet lave,
As, gathering sweet flowerets, she stems thy clear wave!

Flow gently, sweet Afton, among thy green braes!
Flow gently, sweet river, the theme of my lays!
My Mary's asleep by thy murmuring stream—
Flow gently, sweet Afton, disturb not her dream!

MY HEART'S IN THE HIGHLANDS

FAREWELL to the Highlands, farewell to the North,
The birth-place of valor, the country of worth!
Wherever I wander, wherever I rove,
The hills of the Highlands for ever I love.

My heart's in the Highlands, my heart is not here,
My heart's in the Highlands a-chasing the deer,
A-chasing the wild deer and following the roe—
My heart's in the Highlands, wherever I go.

Farewell to the mountains high-covered with snow,
Farewell to the straths and green valleys below,
Farewell to the forests and wild-hanging woods,
Farewell to the torrents and loud-pouring floods!

My heart's in the Highlands, my heart is not here;
My heart's in the Highlands a-chasing the deer,
A-chasing the wild deer and following the roe—
My heart's in the Highlands, wherever I go!

JOHN ANDERSON MY JO

JOHN ANDERSON my jo, John,
When we were first acquent,
Your locks were like the raven,
Your bonie brow was brent;
But now your brow is beld, John,
Your locks are like the snaw,
But blessings on your frosty pow,
John Anderson my jo!

John Anderson my jo, John,
We clamb the hill thegither,
And monie a cantie day, John,
We've had wi' ane anither;
Now we maun totter down, John,
And hand in hand we'll go,
And sleep thegither at the foot,
John Anderson my jo!

SONG: GREEN GROW THE RASHES

GREEN grow the rashes, O;
Green grow the rashes, O;
The sweetest hours that e'er I spend,
Are spent amang the lasses, O.

There's nought but care on every han',
In every hour that passes, O:
What signifies the life o' man,
An 'twere na for the lasses, O.

The war'ly race may riches chase,
An' riches still may fly them, O;
An' though at last they catch them fast,
Their hearts can ne'er enjoy them, O.

But gie me a cannie hour at e'en,
My arms about my dearie, O,
An' war'ly cares, an' war'ly men
May a' gae tapsalteerie, O!

For you sae douce, ye sneer at this;
Ye're nought but senseless asses, O;
The wisest man the warl' e'er saw,
He dearly loved the lasses, O.

Auld Nature swears, the lovely dears
Her noblest work she classes, O:
Her 'prentice han' she tried on man,
An' then she made the lasses, O.

TAM GLEN

My heart is a-breaking, dear tittie,
  Some counsel unto me come len'.
To anger them a' is a pity,
  But what will I do wi' Tam Glen?

I'm thinking, wi' sic a braw fellow
  In poortith I might wak a fen'.
What care I in riches to wallow,
  If I mauna marry Tam Glen?

There's Lowrie, the laird o' Dumeller:
  "Guid-day to you," brute! he comes ben.
He brags and he blaws o' his siller,
  But when will he dance like Tam Glen?

My minnie does constantly deave me,
  And bids me beware o' young men.
They flatter, she says, to deceive me—
  But wha can think sae o' Tam Glen?

My daddie says, gin I'll forsake him,
  He'll gie me guid hunder marks ten.
But if it's ordained I maun tak him,
  O, wha will I get but Tam Glen?

Yestreen at the valentines' dealing,
  My heart to my mou gied a sten,
For thrice I drew ane without failing,
  And thrice it was written, "Tam Glen"!

The last Halloween I was waukin
  My droukit sark-sleeve, as ye ken—
His likeness came up the house staukin,
  And the very gray breeks o' Tam Glen!

Come, counsel, dear tittie, don't tarry!
  I'll gie ye my bonie black hen,
Gif ye will advise me to marry
  The lad I lo'e dearly, Tam Glen.

AULD LANG SYNE

Should auld acquaintance be forgot,
And never brought to mind?
Should auld acquaintance be forgot,
And auld lang syne?

Cho.—For auld lang syne, my dear,
For auld lang syne,
We'll tak a cup o' kindness yet
For auld lang syne!

And surely ye'll be your pint-stowp,
And surely I'll be mine,
And we'll tak a cup o' kindness yet
For auld lang syne!

We twa hae run about the braes
And pou'd the gowans fine,
But we've wandered monie a weary fit
Sin' auld lang syne.

We two hae paidl'd in the burn
Frae morning sun till dine,
But seas between us braid hae roared
Sin' auld lang syne.

And there's a hand, my trusty fiere,
And gie's a hand o' thine,
And we'll tak a right guid-willie waught
For auld lang syne!

WILLIE BREWED A PECK O' MAUT

O, Willie brew'd a peck o' maut,
An' Rob an' Allan cam to see.
Three blyther hearts that lee-lang night
Ye wad na found in Christendie.

Cho.—We are na fou, we're nae that fou,
But just a drappie in our e'e!
The cock may craw, the day may daw,
And ay we'll taste the barley bree!

Here are we met, three merry boys,
Three merry boys, I trow, are we;
An' mony a night we've merry been,
And mony mae we hope to be!

It is the moon, I ken her horn,
That's blinkin' in the lift sae hie:
She shines sae bright to wyle us hame,
But, by my sooth, she'll wait a wee!

Wha first shall rise to gang awa,
A cuckold, coward loun is he!
Wha first beside his chair shall fa',
He is the King amang us three!

William Wordsworth

1770–1850

INFLUENCE OF NATURAL OBJECTS

Wisdom and Spirit of the universe!
Thou Soul, that art the Eternity of thought!
And giv'st to forms and images a breath
And everlasting motion! not in vain,
By day or star-light, thus from my first dawn
Of childhood didst thou intertwine for me
The passions that build up our human soul;
Not with the mean and vulgar works of Man;
But with high objects, with enduring things,
With life and nature; purifying thus
The elements of feeling and of thought,
And sanctifying by such discipline
Both pain and fear,—until we recognize
A grandeur in the beatings of the heart.

Nor was this fellowship vouchsafed to me
With stinted kindness. In November days,
When vapors rolling down the valleys made
A lonely scene more lonesome; among woods
At noon; and 'mid the calm of summer nights,
When, by the margin of the trembling lake,
Beneath the gloomy hills, homeward I went
In solitude, such intercourse was mine:
Mine was it in the fields both day and night,
And by the water, all the summer long.
And in the frosty season, when the sun
Was set, and, visible for many a mile,
The cottage-windows through the twilight blazed,
I heeded not the summons: happy time
It was indeed for all of us; for me
It was a time of rapture! Clear and loud
The village-clock tolled six—I wheeled about,
Proud and exulting like an untired horse
That cares not for his home.—All shod with steel
We hissed along the polished ice, in games
Confederate, imitative of the chase
And woodland pleasures,—the resounding horn,
The pack loud-chiming, and the hunted hare.
So through the darkness and the cold we flew,
And not a voice was idle: with the din
Smitten, the precipices rang aloud;
The leafless trees and every icy crag
Tinkled like iron; while far-distant hills
Into the tumult sent an alien sound
Of melancholy, not unnoticed while the stars,
Eastward, were sparkling clear, and in the west
The orange sky of evening died away.
Not seldom from the uproar I retired
Into a silent bay, or sportively
Glanced sideway, leaving the tumultuous throng,
To cut across the reflex of a star;
Image, that, flying still before me, gleamed
Upon the glassy plain: and oftentimes,
When we had given our bodies to the wind,

And all the shadowy banks on either side
Came sweeping through the darkness, spinning still
The rapid line of motion, then at once
Have I, reclining back upon my heels,
Stopped short; yet still the solitary cliffs
Wheeled by me—even as if the earth had rolled
With visible motion her diurnal round!
Behind me did they stretch in solemn train,
Feebler and feebler, and I stood and watched
Till all was tranquil as a summer sea.

SHE DWELT AMONG THE UNTRODDEN WAYS

She dwelt among the untrodden ways
Beside the springs of Dove,
A Maid whom there were none to praise
And very few to love:

A violet by a mossy stone
Half hidden from the eye!
—Fair as a star, when only one
Is shining in the sky.

She lived unknown, and few could know
When Lucy ceased to be;
But she is in her grave, and, oh,
The difference to me!

I TRAVELED AMONG UNKNOWN MEN

I traveled among unknown men,
In lands beyond the sea;
Nor, England! did I know till then
What love I bore to thee.

'Tis past, that melancholy dream!
Nor will I quit thy shore
A second time; for still I seem
To love thee more and more.

Among thy mountains did I feel
  The joy of my desire;
And she I cherished turned her wheel
  Beside an English fire.

Thy mornings showed, thy nights concealed
  The bowers where Lucy played;
And thine too is the last green field
  That Lucy's eyes surveyed.

A SLUMBER DID MY SPIRIT SEAL

A SLUMBER did my spirit seal;
  I had no human fears;
She seemed a thing that could not feel
  The touch of earthly years.

No motion has she now, no force;
  She neither hears nor sees;
Rolled round in earth's diurnal course,
  With rocks, and stones, and trees.

THE SOLITARY REAPER

BEHOLD her, single in the field,
Yon solitary Highland Lass!
Reaping and singing by herself;
Stop here, or gently pass!
Alone she cuts and binds the grain,
And sings a melancholy strain;
O listen! for the Vale profound
Is overflowing with the sound.

No Nightingale did ever chaunt
More welcome notes to weary bands
Of travelers in some shady haunt,
Among Arabian sands:

A voice so thrilling ne'er was heard
In spring-time from the Cuckoo-bird,
Breaking the silence of the seas
Among the farthest Hebrides.

Will no one tell me what she sings?—
Perhaps the plaintive numbers flow
For old, unhappy, far-off things,
And battles long ago:
Or is it some more humble lay,
Familiar matter of to-day?
Some natural sorrow, loss, or pain,
That has been, and may be again?

Whate'er the theme, the Maiden sang
As if her song could have no ending;
I saw her singing at her work,
And o'er the sickle bending;—
I listened, motionless and still;
And, as I mounted up the hill,
The music in my heart I bore,
Long after it was heard no more.

LONDON 1802

Milton! thou shouldst be living at this hour:
England hath need of thee: she is a fen
Of stagnant waters: altar, sword, and pen,
Fireside, the heroic wealth of hall and bower,
Have forfeited their ancient English dower
Of inward happiness. We are selfish men;
Oh! raise us up, return to us again;
And give us manners, virtue, freedom, power.
Thy soul was like a Star, and dwelt apart;
Thou hadst a voice whose sound was like the sea:
Pure as the naked heavens, majestic, free,
So didst thou travel on life's common way,
In cheerful godliness; and yet thy heart
The lowliest duties on herself did lay.

COMPOSED UPON WESTMINSTER BRIDGE
SEPT. 3, 1802

Earth has not anything to show more fair:
Dull would he be of soul who could pass by
A sight so touching in its majesty:
This city now doth like a garment wear
The beauty of the morning; silent, bare,
Ships, towers, domes, theaters, and temples lie
Open unto the fields, and to the sky;
All bright and glittering in the smokeless air.
Never did sun more beautifully steep
In his first splendor, valley, rock, or hill;
Ne'er saw I, never felt, a calm so deep!
The river glideth at his own sweet will:
Dear God! the very houses seem asleep;
And all that mighty heart is lying still!

IT IS A BEAUTEOUS EVENING, CALM AND FREE

It is a beauteous evening, calm and free,
The holy time is quiet as a Nun
Breathless with adoration: the broad sun
Is sinking down in its tranquillity;
The gentleness of heaven broods o'er the Sea:
Listen! the mighty Being is awake,
And doth with his eternal motion make
A sound like thunder—everlastingly.
Dear Child! dear Girl! that walkest with me here,
If thou appear untouched by solemn thought,
Thy nature is not therefore less divine:
Thou liest in Abraham's bosom all the year,
And worship'st at the Temple's inner shrine,
God being with thee when we know it not.

THE WORLD IS TOO MUCH WITH US

The world is too much with us: late and soon,
Getting and spending, we lay waste our powers:
Little we see in Nature that is ours;
We have given our hearts away, a sordid boon!
This Sea that bares her bosom to the moon;
The winds that will be howling at all hours,
And are up-gathered now like sleeping flowers;
For this, for everything, we are out of tune;
It moves us not.—Great God! I'd rather be
A Pagan suckled in a creed outworn;
So might I, standing on this pleasant lea,
Have glimpses that would make me less forlorn;
Have sight of Proteus rising from the sea;
Or hear old Triton blow his wreathèd horn.

ODE TO DUTY

Stern Daughter of the Voice of God!
O Duty! if that name thou love,
Who art a light to guide, a rod
To check the erring, and reprove;
Thou, who art victory and law
When empty terrors overawe;
From vain temptations dost set free;
And calm'st the weary strife of frail humanity!

There are who ask not if thine eye
Be on them; who, in love and truth,
Where no misgiving is, rely
Upon the genial sense of youth:
Glad Hearts! without reproach or blot;
Who do thy work, and know it not:
O if through confidence misplaced
They fail, thy saving arms, dread Power, around
them cast.

Serene will be our days and bright,
And happy will our nature be,
When love is an unerring light,
And joy its own security.
And they a blissful course may hold
Even now, who, not unwisely bold,
Live in the spirit of this creed;
Yet seek thy firm support, according to their need.

I, loving freedom, and untried;
No sport of every random gust,
Yet being to myself a guide,
Too blindly have reposed my trust:
And oft, when in my heart was heard
Thy timely mandate, I deferred
The task, in smoother walks to stray;
But thee I now would serve more strictly, if I may.

Through no disturbance of my soul,
Or strong compunction in me wrought,
I supplicate for thy control;
But in the quietness of thought:
Me this unchartered freedom tires;
I feel the weight of chance-desires:
My hopes no more must change their name,
I long for a repose that ever is the same.

Stern Lawgiver! yet thou dost wear
The Godhead's most benignant grace;
Nor know we anything so fair
As is the smile upon thy face:
Flowers laugh before thee on their beds
And fragrance in thy footing treads;
Thou dost preserve the stars from wrong;
And the most ancient heavens, through Thee, are fresh
and strong.

To humbler functions, awful Power!
I call thee: I myself commend

Unto thy guidance from this hour;
Oh, let my weakness have an end!
Give unto me, made lowly wise,
The spirit of self-sacrifice;
The confidence of reason give;
And in the light of truth thy Bondman let me live!

ODE

Intimations of Immortality from Recollections of Early Childhood

I

There was a time when meadow, grove and stream,
The earth, and every common sight,
To me did seem
Appareled in celestial light,
The glory and the freshness of a dream.
It is not now as it hath been of yore;—
Turn wheresoe'er I may,
By night or day,
The things which I have seen I now can see no more.

II

The Rainbow comes and goes,
And lovely is the Rose;
The Moon doth with delight
Look round her when the heavens are bare;
Waters on a starry night
Are beautiful and fair;
The sunshine is a glorious birth;
But yet I know, where'er I go,
That there hath passed away a glory from the earth.

III

Now, while the birds thus sing a joyous song,
And while the young lambs bound
As to the tabor's sound,
To me alone there came a thought of grief:

A timely utterance gave that thought relief,
        And I again am strong.
The cataracts blow their trumpets from the steep;
No more shall grief of mine the season wrong;
I hear the Echoes through the mountains throng,
The Winds come to me from the fields of sleep,
        And all the earth is gay;
          Land and sea
      Give themselves up to jollity,
        And with the heart of May
        Doth every Beast keep holiday;—
          Thou Child of Joy,
Shout round me, let me hear thy shouts, thou happy
          Shepherd-boy!

IV

Ye blessèd Creatures, I have heard the call
        Ye to each other make; I see
The heavens laugh with you in your jubilee;
        My heart is at your festival,
        My head hath its coronal,
The fullness of your bliss, I feel—I feel it all.
        Oh evil day! if I were sullen
        While Earth herself is adorning,
          This sweet May-morning,
        And the Children are culling
          On every side,
        In a thousand valleys far and wide,
        Fresh flowers; while the sun shines warm,
And the Babe leaps up on his Mother's arm:—
        I hear, I hear, with joy I hear!
        —But there's a Tree, of many, one,
A single Field which I have looked upon,
Both of them speak of something that is gone:
        The Pansy at my feet
        Doth the same tale repeat:
Whither is fled the visionary gleam?
Where is it now, the glory and the dream?

V

Our birth is but a sleep and a forgetting:
The Soul that rises with us, our life's Star,
Hath had elsewhere its setting,
And cometh from afar:
Not in entire forgetfulness,
And not in utter nakedness,
But trailing clouds of glory do we come
From God, who is our home:
Heaven lies about us in our infancy!
Shades of the prison-house begin to close
Upon the growing Boy,
But he beholds the light, and whence it flows,
He sees it in his joy;
The Youth, who daily farther from the east
Must travel, still is Nature's Priest,
And by the vision splendid
Is on his way attended;
At length the Man perceives it die away,
And fade into the light of common day.

VI

Earth fills her lap with pleasures of her own;
Yearnings she hath in her own natural kind.
And, even with something of a Mother's mind,
And no unworthy aim,
The homely Nurse doth all she can
To make her Foster-child, her Inmate Man,
Forget the glories he hath known,
And that imperial palace whence he came.

VII

Behold the Child among his new-born blisses,
A six years' Darling of a pigmy size!
See, where 'mid work of his own hand he lies,
Fretted by sallies of his mother's kisses,
With light upon him from his father's eyes!

See, at his feet, some little plan or chart,
Some fragment from his dream of human life,
Shaped by himself with newly-learnèd art;
A wedding or a festival,
A mourning or a funeral;
And this hath now his heart,
And unto this he frames his song:
Then will he fit his tongue
To dialogues of business, love, or strife;
But it will not be long
Ere this be thrown aside,
And with new joy and pride
The little Actor cons another part;
Filling from time to time his "humorous stage"
With all the Persons, down to palsied Age,
That Life brings with her in her equipage;
As if his whole vocation
Were endless imitation.

VIII

Thou, whose exterior semblance doth belie
Thy Soul's immensity;
Thou best Philosopher, who yet dost keep
Thy heritage, thou Eye among the blind,
That, deaf and silent, read'st the eternal deep,
Haunted for ever by the eternal mind,—
Mighty Prophet! Seer blest!
On whom those truths do rest,
Which we are toiling all our lives to find,
In darkness lost, the darkness of the grave;
Thou, over whom thy Immortality
Broods like the Day, a Master o'er a Slave,
A Presence which is not to be put by;
Thou little Child, yet glorious in the might
Of heaven-born freedom on thy being's height,
Why with such earnest pains dost thou provoke
The years to bring the inevitable yoke,
Thus blindly with thy blessedness at strife?
Full soon thy Soul shall have her earthly freight,

And custom lie upon thee with a weight,
Heavy as frost, and deep almost as life!

IX

O joy! that in our embers
Is something that doth live,
That nature yet remembers
What was so fugitive!
The thought of our past years in me doth breed
Perpetual benediction: not indeed
For that which is most worthy to be blest—
Delight and liberty, the simple creed
Of Childhood, whether busy or at rest,
With new-fledged hope still fluttering in his breast:—
Not for these I raise
The song of thanks and praise;
But for those obstinate questionings
Of sense and outward things,
Fallings from us, vanishings;
Blank misgivings of a Creature
Moving about in worlds not realized,
High instincts before which our mortal nature
Did tremble like a guilty Thing surprised:
But for those first affections,
Those shadowy recollections,
Which, be they what they may,
Are yet the fountain-light of all our day,
Are yet a master-light of all our seeing;
Uphold us, cherish, and have power to make
Our noisy years seem moments in the being
Of the eternal Silence: truths that wake,
To perish never:
Which neither listlessness, nor mad endeavor,
Nor Man nor Boy,
Nor all that is at enmity with joy,
Can utterly abolish or destroy!
Hence in a season of calm weather
Though inland far we be,

Our Souls have sight of that immortal sea
Which brought us hither,
Can in a moment travel thither,
And see the Children sport upon the shore,
And hear the mighty waters rolling evermore.

X

Then sing, ye Birds, sing, sing a joyous song!
And let the young Lambs bound
As to the tabor's sound!
We in thought will join your throng,
Ye that pipe and ye that play,
Ye that through your hearts to-day
Feel the gladness of the May!
What though the radiance which was once so bright
Be now for ever taken from my sight,
Though nothing can bring back the hour
Of splendor in the grass, of glory in the flower;
We will grieve not, rather find
Strength in what remains behind;
In the primal sympathy
Which having been must ever be;
In the soothing thoughts that spring
Out of human suffering;
In the faith that looks through death,
In years that bring the philosophic mind.

XI

And O, ye Fountains, Meadows, Hills, and Groves,
Forebode not any severing of our loves!
Yet in my heart of hearts I feel your might;
I only have relinquished one delight
To live beneath your more habitual sway.
I love the Brooks which down their channels fret,
Even more than when I tripped lightly as they;
The innocent brightness of a new-born Day
Is lovely yet;
The Clouds that gather round the setting sun

Do take a sober coloring from an eye
That hath kept watch o'er man's mortality;
Another race hath been, and other palms are won.
Thanks to the human heart by which we live,
Thanks to its tenderness, its joys, and fears,
To me the meanest flower that blows can give
Thoughts that do often lie too deep for tears.

Sir Walter Scott

1771–1832

SOLDIER, REST! THY WARFARE O'ER

From The Lady of the Lake

Soldier, rest! thy warfare o'er,
  Sleep the sleep that knows not breaking;
Dream of battled fields no more,
  Days of danger, nights of waking.
In our isle's enchanted hall,
  Hands unseen thy couch are strewing,
Fairy strains of music fall,
  Every sense in slumber dewing.
Soldier, rest! thy warfare o'er,
Dream of fighting fields no more:
Sleep the sleep that knows not breaking,
Morn of toil, nor night of waking.

No rude sound shall reach thine ear,
  Armor's clang, or war-steed champing,
Trump nor pibroch summon here
  Mustering clan, or squadron tramping.
Yet the lark's shrill fife may come
  At the daybreak from the fallow,
And the bittern sound his drum,
  Booming from the sedgy shallow.
Ruder sounds shall none be near,
Guards nor warders challenge here,
Here's no war-steed's neigh and champing,
Shouting clans or squadrons stamping.

Huntsman, rest! thy chase is done;
  While our slumbrous spells assail ye,
Dream not, with the rising sun,
  Bugles here shall sound reveillé.
Sleep! the deer is in his den;
  Sleep! thy hounds are by thee lying;
Sleep! nor dream in yonder glen
How thy gallant steed lay dying.
Huntsman, rest! thy chase is done;
Think not of the rising sun,
For at dawning to assail ye,
Here no bugles sound reveillé.

Samuel Taylor Coleridge

1772–1834

KUBLA KHAN

In Xanadu did Kubla Khan
A stately pleasure-dome decree:
Where Alph, the sacred river, ran
Through caverns measureless to man
  Down to a sunless sea.
So twice five miles of fertile ground
With walls and towers were girdled round:
And here were gardens bright with sinuous rills
Where blossomed many an incense-bearing tree;
And here were forests ancient as the hills,
Enfolding sunny spots of greenery.

But oh! that deep romantic chasm which slanted
Down the green hill athwart a cedarn cover!
A savage place! as holy and enchanted
As e'er beneath a waning moon was haunted
By woman wailing for her demon-lover!
And from this chasm, with ceaseless turmoil seething,
As if this earth in fast thick pants were breathing,

A mighty fountain momently was forced;
Amid whose swift half-intermitted burst
Huge fragments vaulted like rebounding hail,
Or chaffy grain beneath the thresher's flail:
And 'mid these dancing rocks at once and ever
It flung up momently the sacred river.
Five miles meandering with a mazy motion
Through wood and dale the sacred river ran,
Then reached the caverns measureless to man,
And sank in tumult to a lifeless ocean:
And 'mid this tumult Kubla heard from far
Ancestral voices prophesying war!
The shadow of the dome of pleasure
Floated midway on the waves;
Where was heard the mingled measure
From the fountain and the caves.
It was a miracle of rare device,
A sunny pleasure-dome with caves of ice!

A damsel with a dulcimer
In a vision once I saw:
It was an Abyssinian maid,
And on her dulcimer she played,
Singing of Mount Abora.
Could I revive within me
Her symphony and song.
To such a deep delight 't would win me,
That with music loud and long,
I would build that dome in air,
That sunny dome! those caves of ice!
And all who heard should see them there,
And all should cry, Beware! Beware!
His flashing eyes, his floating hair!
Weave a circle round him thrice,
And close your eyes with holy dread,
For he on honey-dew hath fed,
And drunk the milk of Paradise.

Charles Lamb

1775–1834

THE OLD FAMILIAR FACES

I HAVE had playmates, I have had companions,
In my days of childhood, in my joyful school-days;
All, all are gone, the old familiar faces.

I have been laughing, I have been carousing,
Drinking late, sitting late, with my bosom cronies;
All, all are gone, the old familiar faces.

I loved a love once, fairest among women;
Closed are her doors on me, I must not see her—
All, all are gone, the old familiar faces.

I have a friend, a kinder friend has no man;
Like an ingrate, I left my friend abruptly;
Left him, to muse on the old familiar faces.

Ghost-like I paced round the haunts of my childhood.
Earth seemed a desert I was bound to traverse,
Seeking to find the old familiar faces.

Friend of my bosom, thou more than a brother,
Why wert not thou born in my father's dwelling?
So might we talk of the old familiar faces—

How some they have died, and some they have left me,
And some are taken from me; all are departed;
All, all are gone, the old familiar faces.

Walter Savage Landor

1775–1864

ROSE AYLMER

AH what avails the sceptered race,
  Ah what the form divine!
What every virtue, every grace!
  Rose Aylmer, all were thine.

Rose Aylmer, whom these wakeful eyes
May weep, but never see,
A night of memories and of sighs
I consecrate to thee.

PAST RUINED ILION

Past ruined Ilion Helen lives,
Alcestis rises from the shades;
Verse calls them forth; 'tis verse that gives
Immortal youth to mortal maids.

Soon shall Oblivion's deepening veil
Hide all the peopled hills you see,
The gay, the proud, while lovers hail
These many summers you and me.

ON HIS SEVENTY-FIFTH BIRTHDAY

I strove with none, for none was worth my strife;
Nature I loved, and next to Nature, Art;
I warmed both hands before the fire of life,
It sinks, and I am ready to depart.

DIRCE

From Pericles and Aspasia

Stand close around, ye Stygian set,
With Dirce in one boat conveyed,
Or Charon, seeing, may forget
That he is old, and she a shade.

Thomas Love Peacock

1785–1866

THE WAR-SONG OF DINAS VAWR

From The Misfortunes of Elphin

The mountain sheep are sweeter,
But the valley sheep are fatter;

We therefore deemed it meeter
To carry off the latter.
We made an expedition;
We met a host, and quelled it;
We forced a strong position,
And killed the men who held it.

On Dyfed's richest valley,
Where herds of kine were brousing,
We made a mighty sally,
To furnish our carousing.
Fierce warriors rushed to meet us;
We met them, and o'erthrew them:
They struggled hard to beat us;
But we conquered them, and slew them.

As we drove our prize at leisure,
The king marched forth to catch us:
His rage surpassed all measure,
But his people could not match us.
He fled to his hall-pillars;
And, ere our force we led off,
Some sacked his house and cellars,
While others cut his head off.

We there, in strife bewild'ring,
Spilt blood enough to swim in:
We orphaned many children,
And widowed many women.
The eagles and the ravens
We glutted with our foemen;
The heroes and the cravens,
The spearmen and the bowmen.

We brought away from battle,
And much their land bemoaned them,
Two thousand head of cattle,
And the head of him who owned them:

Ednyfed, King of Dyfed,
His head was borne before us;
His wine and beasts supplied our feasts,
And his overthrow, our chorus.

George Gordon, Lord Byron

1788–1824

SHE WALKS IN BEAUTY

She walks in beauty, like the night
  Of cloudless climes and starry skies;
And all that's best of dark and bright
  Meet in her aspect and her eyes:
Thus mellowed to that tender light
  Which heaven to gaudy day denies.

One shade the more, one ray the less,
  Had half impaired the nameless grace
Which waves in every raven tress,
  Or softly lightens o'er her face;
Where thoughts serenely sweet express
  How pure, how dear their dwelling-place.

And on that cheek, and o'er that brow,
  So soft, so calm, yet eloquent,
The smiles that win, the tints that glow,
  But tell of days in goodness spent,
A mind at peace with all below,
  A heart whose love is innocent!

STANZAS FOR MUSIC

There be none of Beauty's daughters
  With a magic like thee;
And like music on the waters
  Is thy sweet voice to me;
When, as if its sound were causing
The charméd ocean's pausing,
The waves lie still and gleaming,
And the lulled winds seem dreaming;

And the midnight moon is weaving
  Her bright chain o'er the deep;
Whose breast is gently heaving,
  As an infant's asleep.
So the spirit bows before thee,
To listen and adore thee;
With a full but soft emotion,
Like the swell of summer's ocean.

SO, WE'LL GO NO MORE A-ROVING

So, we'll go no more a-roving
  So late into the night,
Though the heart be still as loving,
  And the moon be still as bright.

For the sword outwears its sheath,
  And the soul wears out the breast,
And the heart must pause to breathe,
  And Love itself have rest.

Though the night was made for loving,
  And the day returns too soon,
Yet we'll go no more a-roving
  By the light of the moon.

THE ISLES OF GREECE

The isles of Greece! the isles of Greece
  Where burning Sappho loved and sung,
Where grew the arts of war and peace,
  Where Delos rose, and Phœbus sprung!
Eternal summer gilds them yet,
But all, except their sun, is set.

The Scian and the Teian muse,
  The hero's harp, the lover's lute,
Have found the fame your shores refuse;
  Their place of birth alone is mute
To sounds which echo further west
Than your sires' "Islands of the Blest."

The mountains look on Marathon—
  And Marathon looks on the sea;
And musing there an hour alone,
  I dreamed that Greece might still be free;
For standing on the Persians' grave,
I could not deem myself a slave.

A king sate on the rocky brow
  Which looks o'er sea-born Salamis;
And ships, by thousands, lay below,
  And men in nations—all were his!
He counted them at break of day—
And when the sun set, where were they?

And where are they? and where art thou,
  My country? On thy voiceless shore
The heroic lay is tuneless now—
  The heroic bosom beats no more!
And must thy lyre, so long divine,
Degenerate into hands like mine?

'Tis something in the dearth of fame,
  Though linked among a fettered race,
To feel at least a patriot's shame,
  Even as I sing, suffuse my face;
For what is left the poet here?
For Greeks a blush—for Greece a tear.

Must *we* but weep o'er days more blest?
  Must *we* but blush?—Our fathers bled.
Earth! render back from out thy breast
  A remnant of our Spartan dead!
Of the three hundred grant but three,
To make a new Thermopylae!

What, silent still? and silent all?
  Ah! no—the voices of the dead
Sound like a distant torrent's fall,
  And answer, "Let one living head,
But one, arise—we come, we come!"
'Tis but the living who are dumb.

In vain—in vain; strike other chords;
  Fill high the cup with Samian wine!
Leave battles to the Turkish hordes,
  And shed the blood of Scio's vine!
Hark! rising to the ignoble call—
How answers each bold Bacchanal!

You have the Pyrrhic dance as yet;
  Where is the Pyrrhic phalanx gone?
Of two such lessons, why forget
  The nobler and the manlier one?
You have the letters Cadmus gave—
Think ye he meant them for a slave?

Fill high the bowl with Samian wine!
  We will not think of themes like these!
It made Anacreon's song divine.
  He served—but served Polycrates—
A tyrant; but our masters then
Were still, at least, our countrymen.

The tyrant of the Chersonese
  Was freedom's best and bravest friend;
That tyrant was Miltiades!
  O that the present hour would lend
Another despot of the kind!
Such chains as his were sure to bind.

Fill high the bowl with Samian wine!
  On Suli's rock, and Parga's shore,
Exists the remnant of a line
  Such as the Doric mothers bore;
And there, perhaps, some seed is sown,
The Heracleidan blood might own.

Trust not for freedom to the Franks—
  They have a king who buys and sells;
In native swords and native ranks
  The only hope of courage dwells.
But Turkish force and Latin fraud
Would break your shield, however broad.

Fill high the bowl with Samian wine!
  Our virgins dance beneath the shade—
I see their glorious black eyes shine;
  But gazing on each glowing maid,
My own the burning teardrop laves,
To think such breasts must suckle slaves.

Place me on Sunium's marbled steep,
  Where nothing, save the waves and I,
May hear our mutual murmurs sweep;
  There, swan-like, let me sing and die.
A land of slaves shall ne'er be mine—
Dash down yon cup of Samian wine!

Percy Bysshe Shelley

1792–1822

TO ——

Music, when soft voices die,
Vibrates in the memory—
Odors, when sweet violets sicken,
Live within the sense they quicken.

Rose leaves, when the rose is dead,
Are heaped for the belovèd's bed;
And so thy thoughts, when thou art gone,
Love itself shall slumber on.

THE INDIAN SERENADE

I arise from dreams of thee
In the first sweet sleep of night,
When the winds are breathing low,
And the stars are shining bright:
I arise from dreams of thee,
And a spirit in my feet
Hath led me—who knows how?
To thy chamber window, Sweet!

The wandering airs they faint
On the dark, the silent stream—

The Champak odors fail
Like sweet thoughts in a dream;
The nightingale's complaint,
It dies upon her heart;—
As I must on thine,
Oh, belovèd as thou art!

Oh lift me from the grass!
I die! I faint! I fail!
Let thy love in kisses rain
On my lips and eyelids pale.
My cheek is cold and white, alas!
My heart beats loud and fast;—
Oh! press it to thine own again,
Where it will break at last.

TO NIGHT

Swiftly walk over the western wave,
Spirit of Night!
Out of the misty eastern cave,
Where, all the long and lone daylight,
Thou wovest dreams of joy and fear,
Which make thee terrible and dear,—
Swift be thy flight!

Wrap thy form in a mantle gray,
Star-inwrought!
Blind with thine hair the eyes of Day;
Kiss her until she be wearied out;
Then wander o'er city, and sea, and land,
Touching all with thine opiate wand—
Come, long-sought!

When I arose and saw the dawn,
I sighed for thee;
When light rode high, and the dew was gone,
And noon lay heavy on flower and tree,
And the weary Day turned to his rest,
Lingering like an unloved guest,
I sighed for thee.

Thy brother Death came, and cried,
    Wouldst thou me?
Thy sweet child Sleep, the filmy-eyed,
Murmured like a noon-tide bee,
Shall I nestle near thy side?
Wouldst thou me?—And I replied,
    No, not thee!

Death will come when thou art dead,
    Soon, too soon—
Sleep will come when thou art fled;
Of neither would I ask the boon
I ask of thee, belovèd Night—
Swift be thine approaching flight,
    Come soon, soon!

CHORUS FROM HELLAS

The world's great age begins anew,
  The golden years return,
The earth doth like a snake renew
  Her winter weeds outworn:
Heaven smiles, and faiths and empires gleam,
Like wrecks of a dissolving dream.

A brighter Hellas rears its mountains
  From waves serener far;
A new Peneus rolls his fountains
  Against the morning star.
Where fairer Tempes bloom, there sleep
Young Cyclads on a sunnier deep.

A loftier Argo cleaves the main,
  Fraught with a later prize;
Another Orpheus sings again,
  And loves, and weeps, and dies.
A new Ulysses leaves once more
Calypso for his native shore.

Oh, write no more the tale of Troy,
If earth Death's scroll must be!
Nor mix with Laian rage the joy
Which dawns upon the free:
Although a subtler Sphinx renew
Riddles of death Thebes never knew.

Another Athens shall arise,
And to remoter time
Bequeath, like sunset to the skies,
The splendor of its prime;
And leave, if naught so bright may live,
All earth can take or Heaven can give.

Saturn and Love their long repose
Shall burst, more bright and good
Than all who fell, than One who rose,
Than many unsubdued:
Not gold, not blood, their altar dowers,
But votive tears and symbol flowers.

Oh, cease! must hate and death return?
Cease! must men kill and die?
Cease! drain not to its dregs the urn
Of bitter prophecy.
The world is weary of the past,
Oh, might it die or rest at last!

OZYMANDIAS

I MET a traveler from an antique land
Who said: Two vast and trunkless legs of stone
Stand in the desert. Near them, on the sand,
Half sunk, a shattered visage lies, whose frown,
And wrinkled lip, and sneer of cold command,
Tell that its sculptor well those passions read
Which yet survive, stamped on these lifeless things,
The hand that mocked them and the heart that fed;
And on the pedestal these words appear:
"My name is Ozymandias, king of kings:

Look on my works, ye Mighty, and despair!"
Nothing beside remains. Round the decay
Of that colossal wreck, boundless and bare
The lone and level sands stretch far away.

ODE TO THE WEST WIND

I

O WILD West Wind, thou breath of Autumn's being,
Thou, from whose unseen presence the leaves dead
Are driven, like ghosts from an enchanter fleeing,

Yellow, and black, and pale, and hectic red,
Pestilence-stricken multitudes: O thou,
Who chariotest to their dark wintry bed

The wingèd seeds, where they lie cold and low,
Each like a corpse within its grave, until
Thine azure sister of the Spring shall blow

Her clarion o'er the dreaming earth, and fill
(Driving sweet buds like flocks to feed in air)
With living hues and odors plain and hill:

Wild Spirit, which art moving everywhere;
Destroyer and preserver; hear, oh, hear!

II

Thou on whose stream, 'mid the steep sky's commotion,
Loose clouds like earth's decaying leaves are shed,
Shook from the tangled boughs of Heaven and Ocean,

Angels of rain and lightning: there are spread
On the blue surface of thine airy surge,
Like the bright hair uplifted from the head

Of some fierce Mænad, even from the dim verge
Of the horizon to the zenith's height,
The locks of the approaching storm. Thou dirge

Of the dying year, to which this closing night
Will be the dome of a vast sepulcher,
Vaulted with all thy congregated might

Of vapors, from whose solid atmosphere
Black rain, and fire, and hail will burst: oh, hear!

III

Thou who didst waken from his summer dreams
The blue Mediterranean, where he lay
Lulled by the coil of his crystàlline streams,

Beside a pumice isle in Baiæ's bay,
And saw in sleep old palaces and towers
Quivering within the wave's intenser day,

All overgrown with azure moss and flowers
So sweet, the sense faints picturing them! Thou
For whose path the Atlantic's level powers

Cleave themselves into chasms, while far below
The sea-blooms and the oozy woods which wear
The sapless foliage of the ocean, know

Thy voice, and suddenly grow gray with fear,
And tremble and despoil themselves: oh, hear!

IV

If I were a dead leaf thou mightest bear;
If I were a swift cloud to fly with thee;
A wave to pant beneath thy power, and share

The impulse of thy strength, only less free
Than thou, O uncontrollable! If even
I were as in my boyhood, and could be

The comrade of thy wanderings over Heaven,
As then, when to outstrip thy skiey speed
Scarce seemed a vision; I would ne'er have striven

As thus with thee in prayer in my sore need.
Oh, lift me as a wave, a leaf, a cloud!
I fall upon the thorns of life! I bleed!

A heavy weight of hours has chained and bowed
One too like thee: tameless, and swift, and proud.

V

Make me thy lyre, even as the forest is:
What if my leaves are falling like its own!
The tumult of thy mighty harmonies

Will take from both a deep, autumnal tone,
Sweet though in sadness. Be thou, Spirit fierce,
My spirit! Be thou me, impetuous one!

Drive my dead thoughts over the universe
Like withered leaves to quicken a new birth!
And, by the incantation of this verse,

Scatter, as from an unextinguished hearth
Ashes and sparks, my words among mankind!
Be through my lips to unawakened earth

The trumpet of a prophecy! O wind,
If Winter comes, can Spring be far behind?

John Keats

1795–1821

ODE TO A NIGHTINGALE

My heart aches, and a drowsy numbness pains
  My sense, as though of hemlock I had drunk,
Or emptied some dull opiate to the drains
  One minute past, and Lethe-wards had sunk:
'Tis not through envy of thy happy lot,
  But being too happy in thine happiness,—

That thou, light-wingèd Dryad of the trees,
In some melodious plot
Of beechen green, and shadows numberless,
Singest of summer in full-throated ease.

O for a draught of vintage! that hath been
Cooled a long age in the deep delvèd earth,
Tasting of Flora and the country green,
Dance, and Provençal song, and sunburnt mirth!
O for a beaker full of the warm South,
Full of the true, the blushful Hippocrene,
With beaded bubbles winking at the brim,
And purple-stainèd mouth;
That I might drink, and leave the world unseen,
And with thee fade away into the forest dim:

Fade far away, dissolve, and quite forget
What thou among the leaves hast never known,
The weariness, the fever, and the fret
Here, where men sit and hear each other groan;
Where palsy shakes a few, sad, last gray hairs,
Where youth grows pale, and specter-thin, and dies;
Where but to think is to be full of sorrow
And leaden-eyed despairs,
Where Beauty cannot keep her lustrous eyes,
Or new Love pine at them beyond to-morrow.

Away! away! for I will fly to thee,
Not charioted by Bacchus and his pards,
But on the viewless wings of Poesy,
Though the dull brain perplexes and retards:
Already with thee! tender is the night,
And haply the Queen-Moon is on her throne,
Clustered around by all her starry Fays;
But here there is no light,
Save what from heaven is with the breezes blown
Through verdurous glooms and winding mossy ways.

I cannot see what flowers are at my feet,
  Nor what soft incense hangs upon the boughs,
But, in embalmèd darkness, guess each sweet
  Wherewith the seasonable month endows
The grass, the thicket, and the fruit-tree wild;
  White hawthorn, and the pastoral eglantine;
    Fast-fading violets covered up in leaves;
      And mid-May's eldest child,
  The coming musk-rose, full of dewy wine,
    The murmurous haunt of flies on summer eves.

Darkling I listen; and for many a time
  I have been half in love with easeful Death,
Called him soft names in many a musèd rhyme,
  To take into the air my quiet breath;
Now more than ever seems it rich to die,
  To cease upon the midnight with no pain,
    While thou art pouring forth thy soul abroad
      In such an ecstasy!
  Still wouldst thou sing, and I have ears in vain—
    To thy high requiem become a sod.

Thou wast not born for death, immortal Bird!
  No hungry generations tread thee down;
The voice I hear this passing night was heard
  In ancient days by emperor and clown:
Perhaps the self-same song that found a path
  Through the sad heart of Ruth, when, sick for home,
    She stood in tears amid the alien corn;
      The same that oft-times hath
  Charmed magic casements, opening on the foam
    Of perilous seas, in faery lands forlorn.

Forlorn! the very word is like a bell
  To toll me back from thee to my sole self!
Adieu! the fancy cannot cheat so well
  As she is famed to do, deceiving elf.
Adieu! adieu! thy plaintive anthem fades
  Past the near meadows, over the still stream,

Up the hill-side; and now 'tis buried deep
In the next valley-glades:
Was it a vision, or a waking dream?
Fled is that music:—Do I wake or sleep?

ODE ON A GRECIAN URN

Thou still unravished bride of quietness,
Thou foster-child of silence and slow time,
Sylvan historian, who canst thus express
A flowery tale more sweetly than our rhyme:
What leaf-fringed legend haunts about thy shape
Of deities or mortals, or of both,
In Tempe or the dales of Arcady?
What men or gods are these? What maidens loth?
What mad pursuit? What struggle to escape?
What pipes and timbrels? What wild ecstasy?

Heard melodies are sweet, but those unheard
Are sweeter; therefore, ye soft pipes, play on;
Not to the sensual ear, but, more endeared,
Pipe to the spirit ditties of no tone:
Fair youth, beneath the trees, thou canst not leave
Thy song, nor ever can those trees be bare;
Bold Lover, never, never canst thou kiss,
Though winning near the goal—yet, do not grieve;
She cannot fade, though thou hast not thy bliss,
For ever wilt thou love, and she be fair!

Ah, happy, happy boughs! that cannot shed
Your leaves, nor ever bid the Spring adieu;
And, happy melodist, unwearièd,
For ever piping songs for ever new;
More happy love! more happy, happy love!
For ever warm and still to be enjoyed,
For ever panting, and for ever young;
All breathing human passion far above,
That leaves a heart high-sorrowful and cloyed,
A burning forehead, and a parching tongue.

Who are these coming to the sacrifice?
  To what green altar, O mysterious priest,
Lead'st thou that heifer lowing at the skies,
  And all her silken flanks with garlands dressed?
What little town by river or sea shore,
  Or mountain-built with peaceful citadel,
    Is emptied of its folk, this pious morn?
And, little town, thy streets for evermore
  Will silent be; and not a soul to tell
    Why thou art desolate, can e'er return.

O Attic shape! Fair attitude! with brede
  Of marble men and maidens overwrought,
With forest branches and the trodden weed;
  Thou, silent form, dost tease us out of thought
As doth eternity: Cold Pastoral!
  When old age shall this generation waste,
    Thou shalt remain, in midst of other woe
Than ours, a friend to man, to whom thou say'st,
  "Beauty is truth, truth beauty,"—that is all
    Ye know on earth, and all ye need to know.

TO AUTUMN

Season of mists and mellow fruitfulness,
  Close bosom-friend of the maturing sun:
Conspiring with him how to load and bless
  With fruit the vines that round the thatch-eves run;
To bend with apples the mossed cottage-trees,
  And fill all fruit with ripeness to the core;
    To swell the gourd, and plump the hazel shells
With a sweet kernel; to set budding more,
  And still more, later flowers for the bees,
  Until they think warm days will never cease,
    For Summer has o'er-brimmed their clammy cells.

Who hath not seen thee oft amid thy store?
  Sometimes whoever seeks abroad may find

Thee sitting careless on a granary floor,
  Thy hair soft-lifted by the winnowing wind;
Or on a half-reaped furrow sound asleep,
  Drowsed with the fume of poppies, while thy hook
    Spares the next swath and all its twinèd flowers:
And sometimes like a gleaner thou dost keep
  Steady thy laden head across a brook;
  Or by a cider-press, with patient look,
    Thou watchest the last oozings hours by hours.

Where are the songs of Spring? Ay, where are they?
  Think not of them, thou hast thy music too,—
While barrèd clouds bloom the soft-dying day,
And touch the stubble-plains with rosy hue;
Then in a wailful choir the small gnats mourn
  Among the river sallows, borne aloft
    Or sinking as the light wind lives or dies;
And full-grown lambs loud bleat from hilly bourn;
  Hedge-crickets sing; and now with treble soft
  The red-breast whistles from a garden-croft;
  And gathering swallows twitter in the skies.

ROBIN HOOD

No! those days are gone away,
And their hours are old and gray,
And their minutes buried all
Under the down-trodden pall
Of the leaves of many years.
Many times have winter's shears,
Frozen north, and chilling east,
Sounded tempests to the feast
Of the forest's whispering fleeces,
Since men knew nor rent nor leases.

  No, the bugle sounds no more,
And the twanging bow no more;
Silent is the ivory shrill
Past the heath and up the hill;

There is no mid-forest laugh,
Where lone Echo gives the half
To some wight, amazed to hear
Jesting, deep in forest drear.

On the fairest time of June
You may go, with sun or moon,
Or the seven stars to light you,
Or the polar ray to right you;
But you never may behold
Little John, or Robin bold;
Never one, of all the clan,
Thrumming on an empty can
Some old hunting ditty, while
He doth his green way beguile
To fair hostess Merriment,
Down beside the pasture Trent;
For he left the merry tale
Messenger for spicy ale.

Gone, the merry morris din;
Gone, the song of Gamelyn;
Gone, the tough-belted outlaw
Idling in the "grené shawe";
All are gone away and past!
And if Robin should be cast
Sudden from his turfed grave,
And if Marian should have
Once again her forest days,
She would weep, and he would craze:
He would swear, for all his oaks,
Fall'n beneath the dockyard strokes,
Have rotted on the briny seas;
She would weep that her wild bees
Sang not to her—strange! that honey
Can't be got without hard money!

So it is; yet let us sing,
Honor to the old bowstring!

Honor to the bugle-horn!
Honor to the woods unshorn!
Honor to the Lincoln green!
Honor to the archer keen!
Honor to tight Little John
And the horse be rode upon!
Honor to bold Robin Hood,
Sleeping in the underwood!
Honor to Maid Marian,
And to all the Sherwood-clan!
Though their days have hurried by,
Let us two a burden try.

LINES ON THE MERMAID TAVERN

Souls of Poets dead and gone,
What Elysium have ye known,
Happy field or mossy cavern,
Choicer than the Mermaid Tavern?
Have ye tippled drink more fine
Than mine host's Canary wine?
Or are fruits of Paradise
Sweeter than those dainty pies
Of venison? O generous food!
Dressed as though bold Robin Hood
Would, with his maid Marian,
Sup and bowse from horn and can.

I have heard that on a day
Mine host's signboard flew away,
Nobody knew whither, till
An astrologer's old quill
To a sheepskin gave the story—
Said he saw you in your glory,
Underneath a new old sign
Sipping beverage divine,
And pledging with contented smack
The Mermaid in the Zodiac.

Souls of Poets dead and gone,
What Elysium have ye known,
Happy field or mossy cavern,
Choicer than the Mermaid Tavern?

LA BELLE DAME SANS MERCI

O WHAT can ail thee, knight-at-arms,
Alone and palely loitering?
The sedge has withered from the lake,
And no birds sing.

O what can ail thee, knight-at-arms,
So haggard and so woe-begone?
The squirrel's granary is full,
And the harvest's done.

I see a lily on thy brow
With anguish moist and fever dew,
And on thy cheek a fading rose
Fast withereth too.

I met a lady in the meads,
Full beautiful—a faery's child;
Her hair was long, her foot was light,
And her eyes were wild.

I made a garland for her head,
And bracelets too, and fragrant zone;
She looked at me as she did love,
And made sweet moan.

I set her on my pacing steed,
And nothing else saw all day long,
For sidelong would she bend, and sing
A faery's song.

She found me roots of relish sweet,
And honey wild, and manna dew,
And sure in language strange she said—
"I love thee true!"

She took me to her elfin grot,
  And there she wept and sighed full sore,
And there I shut her wild wild eyes
  With kisses four.

And there she lullèd me asleep,
  And there I dreamed—ah! woe betide!
The latest dream I ever dreamed
  On the cold hill's side.

I saw pale kings and princes too,
  Pale warriors, death-pale were they all;
They cried—"La Belle Dame sans Merci
  Thee hath in thrall!"

I saw their starved lips in the gloam,
  With horrid warning gapèd wide,
And I awoke and found me here,
  On the cold hill's side.

And this is why I sojourn here,
  Alone and palely loitering,
Though the sedge is withered from the lake
  And no birds sing.

WHEN I HAVE FEARS THAT I MAY CEASE TO BE

When I have fears that I may cease to be
Before my pen has gleaned my teeming brain,
Before high-pilèd books, in charact'ry,
Hold like rich garners the full-ripened grain;
When I behold, upon the night's starred face,
Huge cloudy symbols of a high romance,
And think that I may never live to trace
Their shadows, with the magic hand of chance;
And when I feel, fair creature of an hour!
That I shall never look upon thee more,

Never have relish in the faery power
Of unreflecting love;—then on the shore
Of the wide world I stand alone, and think,
Till Love and Fame to nothingness do sink.

John Henry, Cardinal Newman

1801–1890

THE PILLAR OF THE CLOUD

Lead, Kindly Light, amid the encircling gloom,
Lead Thou me on!
The night is dark, and I am far from home!
Lead Thou me on.
Keep Thou my feet; I do not ask to see
The distant scene—one step enough for me.

I was not ever thus, nor prayed that Thou
Shouldst lead me on.
I loved to choose and see my path, but now
Lead Thou me on!
I loved the garish day, and spite of fears,
Pride ruled my will: remember not past years.

So long Thy power hath blest me, sure it still
Will lead me on,
O'er moor and fen, o'er crag and torrent till
The night is gone,
And with the morn those angel faces smile
Which I have loved long since, and lost awhile.

Alfred, Lord Tennyson

1809–1892

MARIANA

With blackest moss the flower-plots
Were thickly crusted, one and all:
The rusted nails fell from the knots
That held the pear to the gable-wall.

The broken sheds looked sad and strange:
  Unlifted was the clinking latch;
  Weeded and worn the ancient thatch
Upon the lonely moated grange.
    She only said, "My life is dreary,
      He cometh not," she said;
    She said, "I am aweary, aweary,
      I would that I were dead!"

Her tears fell with the dews at even;
  Her tears fell ere the dews were dried;
She could not look on the sweet heaven,
  Either at morn or eventide.
After the flitting of the bats,
  When thickest dark did trance the sky,
  She drew her casement-curtain by,
And glanced athwart the glooming flats.
    She only said, "The night is dreary,
      He cometh not," she said;
    She said, "I am aweary, aweary,
      I would that I were dead!"

Upon the middle of the night,
  Waking she heard the night-fowl crow:
The cock sung out an hour ere light;
  From the dark fen the oxen's low
Came to her: without hope of change,
  In sleep she seemed to walk forlorn,
  Till cold winds woke the gray-eyed morn
About the lonely moated grange.
    She only said, "My life is dreary,
      He cometh not," she said;
    She said, "I am aweary, aweary,
      I would that I were dead!"

About a stone-cast from the wall
  A sluice with blackened waters slept,
And o'er it many, round and small,
  The clustered marish-mosses crept.

Hard by a poplar shook alway,
All silver-green with gnarlèd bark:
For leagues no other tree did mark
The level waste, the rounding gray.
She only said, "The night is dreary,
He cometh not," she said;
She said, "I am aweary, aweary,
I would that I were dead!"

And ever when the moon was low,
And the shrill winds were up and away,
In the white curtain, to and fro,
She saw the gusty shadow sway.
But when the moon was very low,
And wild winds bound within their cell,
The shadow of the poplar fell
Upon her bed, across her brow.
She only said, "My life is dreary,
He cometh not," she said;
She said, "I am aweary, aweary,
I would that I were dead!"

All day within the dreamy house,
The doors upon their hinges creaked;
The blue fly sung in the pane; the mouse
Behind the moldering wainscot shrieked,
Or from the crevice peered about.
Old faces glimmered through the doors,
Old footsteps trod the upper floors,
Old voices called her from without.
She only said, "My life is dreary,
He cometh not," she said;
She said, "I am aweary, aweary,
I would that I were dead!"

The sparrow's chirrup on the roof,
The slow clock ticking, and the sound
Which to the wooing wind aloof
The poplar made, did all confound

Her sense; but most she loathed the hour
When the thick-moted sunbeam lay
Athwart the chambers, and the day
Was sloping toward his western bower.
Then said she, "I am very dreary,
He will not come," she said;
She wept, "I am aweary, aweary,
O God, that I were dead!"

ULYSSES

It little profits that an idle king,
By this still hearth, among these barren crags,
Matched with an aged wife, I mete and dole
Unequal laws unto a savage race,
That hoard, and sleep, and feed, and know not me.
I cannot rest from travel. I will drink
Life to the lees. All times I have enjoyed
Greatly, have suffered greatly, both with those
That loved me, and alone; on shore, and when
Through scudding drifts the rainy Hyades
Vexed the dim sea. I am become a name;
For always roaming with a hungry heart
Much have I seen and known; cities of men,
And manners, climates, councils, governments,
Myself not least, but honored of them all;
And drunk delight of battle with my peers,
Far on the ringing plains of windy Troy.
I am a part of all that I have met.
Yet all experience is an arch where-through
Gleams that untraveled world, whose margin fades
Forever and forever when I move.
How dull it is to pause, to make an end,
To rust unburnished, not to shine in use!
As though to breathe were life. Life piled on life
Were all too little, and of one to me
Little remains. But every hour is saved
From that eternal silence, something more,

A bringer of new things; and vile it were
For some three suns to store and hoard myself,
And this gray spirit yearning in desire
To follow knowledge like a sinking star,
Beyond the utmost bound of human thought.
  This is my son, mine own Telemachus,
To whom I leave the scepter and the isle—
Well-loved of me, discerning to fulfill
This labor, by slow prudence to make mild
A rugged people, and through soft degrees
Subdue them to the useful and the good.
Most blameless is he, centered in the sphere
Of common duties, decent not to fail
In offices of tenderness, and pay
Meet adoration to my household gods,
When I am gone. He works his work, I mine.
  There lies the port; the vessel puffs her sail;
There gloom the dark broad seas. My mariners,
Souls that have toiled, and wrought, and thought with me—
That ever with a frolic welcome took
The thunder and the sunshine, and opposed
Free hearts, free foreheads—you and I are old;
Old age hath yet his honor and his toil;
Death closes all. But something ere the end,
Some work of noble note, may yet be done,
Not unbecoming men that strove with gods.
The lights begin to twinkle from the rocks;
The long day wanes; the slow moon climbs; the deep
Moans round with many voices. Come, my friends,
'Tis not too late to seek a newer world.
Push off, and sitting well in order smite
The sounding furrows; for my purpose holds
To sail beyond the sunset, and the baths
Of all the western stars, until I die.
It may be that the gulfs will wash us down
It may be we shall touch the Happy Isles,
And see the great Achilles, whom we knew.

Though much is taken, much abides; and though
We are not now that strength which in old days
Moved earth and heaven, that which we are, we are;
One equal temper of heroic hearts,
Made weak by time and fate, but strong in will
To strive, to seek, to find, and not to yield.

SONG FROM MAUD

Come into the garden, Maud,
  For the black bat, night, has flown,
Come into the garden, Maud,
  I am here at the gate alone;
And the woodbine spices are wafted abroad,
  And the musk of the rose is blown.

For a breeze of morning moves,
  And the planet of love is on high,
Beginning to faint in the light that she loves
  On a bed of daffodil sky,
To faint in the light of the sun she loves,
  To faint in his light, and to die.

All night have the roses heard
  The flute, violin, bassoon;
All night has the casement jessamine stirred
  To the dancers dancing in tune;
Till a silence fell with the waking bird,
  And a hush with the setting moon.

I said to the lily, "There is but one,
  With whom she has heart to be gay.
When will the dancers leave her alone?
  She is weary of dance and play."
Now half to the setting moon are gone,
  And half to the rising day;
Low on the sand and loud on the stone
  The last wheel echoes away.

I said to the rose, "The brief night goes
In babble and revel and wine.
O young lord-lover, what sighs are those,
For one that will never be thine?
But mine, but mine," so I sware to the rose,
"Forever and ever, mine."

And the soul of the rose went into my blood,
As the music clashed in the Hall;
And long by the garden lake I stood,
For I heard your rivulet fall
From the lake to the meadow and on to the wood,
Our wood, that is dearer than all;

From the meadow your walks have left so sweet
That whenever a March-wind sighs
He sets the jewel-print of your feet
In violets blue as your eyes,
To the woody hollows in which we meet
And the valleys of Paradise.

The slender acacia would not shake
One long milk-bloom on the tree;
The white lake-blossom fell into the lake
As the pimpernel dozed on the lea;
But the rose was awake all night for your sake,
Knowing your promise to me;
The lilies and roses were all awake,
They sighed for the dawn and thee.

Queen rose of the rosebud garden of girls,
Come hither, the dances are done,
In gloss of satin and glimmer of pearls,
Queen lily and rose in one;
Shine out, little head, sunning over with curls,
To the flowers, and be their sun.

There has fallen a splendid tear
  From the passion-flower at the gate.
She is coming, my dove, my dear;
  She is coming, my life, my fate.
The red rose cries, "She is near, she is near;"
  And the white rose weeps, "She is late;"
The larkspur listens, "I hear, I hear;"
  And the lily whispers, "I wait."

She is coming, my own, my sweet;
  Were it ever so airy a tread,
My heart would hear her and beat,
  Were it earth in an earthy bed;
My dust would hear her and beat,
  Had I lain for a century dead,
Would start and tremble under her feet,
  And blossom in purple and red.

BREAK, BREAK, BREAK

Break, break, break,
  On thy cold gray stones, O Sea!
And I would that my tongue could utter
  The thoughts that arise in me.

O well for the fisherman's boy,
  That he shouts with his sister at play!
O well for the sailor lad,
  That he sings in his boat on the bay!

And the stately ships go on
  To their haven under the hill;
But O for the touch of a vanished hand,
  And the sound of a voice that is still!

Break, break, break,
  At the foot of thy crags, O Sea!
But the tender grace of a day that is dead
  Will never come back to me.

SONGS FROM THE PRINCESS

1

Tears, idle tears, I know not what they mean,
Tears from the depth of some divine despair
Rise in the heart, and gather to the eyes,
In looking on the happy autumn-fields,
And thinking of the days that are no more.

Fresh as the first beam glittering on a sail,
That brings our friends up from the underworld,
Sad as the last which reddens over one
That sinks with all we love below the verge;
So sad, so fresh, the days that are no more.

Ah, sad and strange as in dark summer dawns
The earliest pipe of half-awakened birds
To dying ears, when unto dying eyes
The casement slowly grows a glimmering square;
So sad, so strange, the days that are no more.

Dear as remembered kisses after death,
And sweet as those by hopeless fancy feigned
On lips that are for others; deep as love,
Deep as first love, and wild with all regret;
O Death in Life, the days that are no more!

2

The splendor falls on castle walls
And snowy summits old in story;
The long light shakes across the lakes,
And the wild cataract leaps in glory.
Blow, bugle, blow, set the wild echoes flying,
Blow, bugle; answer, echoes, dying, dying, dying.

O, hark, O, hear! how thin and clear,
And thinner, clearer, farther going!
O, sweet and far from cliff and scar
The horns of Elfland faintly blowing!

Blow, let us hear the purple glens replying,
Blow, bugle; answer, echoes, dying, dying, dying.

O love, they die in yon rich sky,
They faint on hill or field or river;
Our echoes roll from soul to soul,
And grow for ever and for ever.
Blow, bugle, blow, set the wild echoes flying,
And answer, echoes, answer, dying, dying, dying.

TO VERGIL

WRITTEN AT THE REQUEST OF THE MANTUANS FOR THE NINETEENTH CENTURY OF VERGIL'S DEATH

ROMAN Vergil, thou that singest Ilion's lofty temples robed in fire,
Ilion falling, Rome arising, wars, and filial faith, and Dido's pyre;

Landscape-lover, lord of language more than he that sang the "Works and Days,"
All the chosen coin of fancy flashing out from many a golden phrase;

Thou that singest wheat and woodland, tilth and vine-yard, hive and horse and herd;
All the charm of all the Muses often flowering in a lonely word;

Poet of the happy Tityrus piping underneath his beechen bowers;
Poet of the poet-satyr whom the laughing shepherd bound with flowers;

Chanter of the Pollio, glorying in the blissful years again to be,
Summers of the snakeless meadow, unlaborious earth and oarless sea;

Thou that seest Universal Nature moved by Universal Mind;
Thou majestic in thy sadness at the doubtful doom of human kind;

Light among the vanished ages; star that gildest yet this phantom shore;
Golden branch amid the shadows, kings and realms that pass to rise no more;

Now thy Forum roars no longer, fallen every purple Cæsar's dome—
Though thine ocean-roll of rhythm sound forever of Imperial Rome—

Now the Rome of slaves hath perished, and the Rome of freemen holds her place,
I, from out the northern island sundered once from all the human race,

I salute thee, Mantovano, I that loved thee since my day began,
Wielder of the stateliest measure ever molded by the lips of man.

Robert Browning

1812–1889

HOME-THOUGHTS, FROM ABROAD

Oh, to be in England
Now that April's there,
And whoever wakes in England
Sees, some morning, unaware,
That the lowest boughs and the brushwood sheaf
Round the elm-tree bole are in tiny leaf,
While the chaffinch sings on the orchard bough
In England—now!

And after April, when May follows,
And the whitethroat builds, and all the swallows?
Hark, where my blossomed pear-tree in the hedge
Leans to the field and scatters on the clover
Blossoms and dewdrops—at the bent spray's edge—
That's the wise thrush; he sings each song twice over,
Lest you should think he never could recapture
The first fine careless rapture!
And though the fields look rough with hoary dew,
All will be gay when noontide wakes anew
The buttercups, the little children's dower
—Far brighter than this gaudy melon-flower!

HOME-THOUGHTS, FROM THE SEA

Nobly, nobly Cape Saint Vincent to the Northwest died away;
Sunset ran, one glorious blood-red, reeking into Cadiz Bay;
Bluish 'mid the burning water, full in face Trafalgar lay;
In the dimmest Northeast distance dawned Gibraltar grand and gray;
"Here and here did England help me: how can I help England?"—say
Whoso turns as I, this evening, turn to God to praise and pray,
While Jove's planet rises yonder, silent over Africa.

MEETING AT NIGHT

The gray sea and the long black land;
And the yellow half-moon large and low;
And the startled little waves that leap
In fiery ringlets from their sleep,
As I gain the cove with pushing prow,
And quench its speed i' the slushy sand.

Then a mile of warm sea-scented beach;
Three fields to cross till a farm appears;

A tap at the pane, the quick sharp scratch
And blue spurt of a lighted match,
And a voice less loud, through its joys and fears,
Than the two hearts beating each to each!

PARTING AT MORNING

Round the cape of a sudden came the sea,
And the sun looked over the mountain's rim:
And straight was a path of gold for him,
And the need of a world of men for me.

PORPHYRIA'S LOVER

The rain set early in to-night,
  The sullen wind was soon awake,
It tore the elm-tops down for spite,
  And did its worst to vex the lake:
I listened with heart fit to break.
When glided in Porphyria; straight
  She shut the cold out and the storm,
And kneeled and made the cheerless grate
  Blaze up, and all the cottage warm;
Which done, she rose, and from her form
Withdrew the dripping cloak and shawl,
  And laid her soiled gloves by, untied
Her hat and let the damp hair fall,
  And, last, she sat down by my side
And called me. When no voice replied,
She put my arm about her waist,
  And made her smooth white shoulder bare
And all her yellow hair displaced,
  And, stooping, made my cheek lie there,
And spread, o'er all, her yellow hair,
Murmuring how she loved me—she
  Too weak, for all her heart's endeavor,
To set its struggling passion free
  From pride, and vainer ties dissever,

And give herself to me forever.
But passion sometimes would prevail,
  Nor could to-night's gay feast restrain
A sudden thought of one so pale
  For love of her, and all in vain:
So, she was come through wind and rain.
Be sure I looked up at her eyes
  Happy and proud; at last I knew
Porphyria worshiped me; surprise
  Made my heart swell, and still it grew
While I debated what to do.
That moment she was mine, mine, fair,
  Perfectly pure and good: I found
A thing to do, and all her hair
  In one long yellow string I wound
Three times her little throat around,
And strangled her. No pain felt she;
  I am quite sure she felt no pain.
As a shut bud that holds a bee,
  I warily oped her lids: again
Laughed the blue eyes without a stain.
And I untightened next the tress
  About her neck; her cheek once more
Blushed bright beneath my burning kiss:
  I propped her head up as before,
Only, this time my shoulder bore
Her head, which droops upon it still:
  The smiling rosy little head,
So glad it has its utmost will,
  That all it scorned at once is fled,
And I, its love, am gained unstead!
Porphyria's love: she guessed not how
  Her darling one wish would be heard.
And thus we sit together now,
  And all night long we have not stirred,
And yet God has not said a word!

MY LAST DUCHESS

FERRARA

THAT'S my last Duchess painted on the wall,
Looking as if she were alive. I call
That piece a wonder, now: Frà Pandolf's hands
Worked busily a day, and there she stands.
Will 't please you sit and look at her? I said
"Frà Pandolf" by design, for never read
Strangers like you that pictured countenance,
The depth and passion of its earnest glance,
But to myself they turned (since none puts by
The curtain I have drawn for you, but I)
And seemed as they would ask me, if they durst,
How such a glance came there; so not the first
Are you to turn and ask thus. Sir, 't was not
Her husband's presence only, called that spot
Of joy into the Duchess' cheek: perhaps
Frà Pandolf chanced to say, "Her mantle laps
Over my lady's wrist too much," or "Paint
Must never hope to reproduce the faint
Half-flush that dies along her throat:" such stuff
Was courtesy, she thought, and cause enough
For calling up that spot of joy. She had
A heart—how shall I say?—too soon made glad,
Too easily impressed; she liked whate'er
She looked on, and her looks went everywhere.
Sir, 't was all one! My favor at her breast,
The dropping of the daylight in the West,
The bough of cherries some officious fool
Broke in the orchard for her, the white mule
She rode with round the terrace—all and each
Would draw from her alike the approving speech,
Or blush, at least. She thanked men,—good! but thanked
Somehow—I know not how—as if she ranked
My gift of a nine-hundred-years-old name
With anybody's gift. Who'd stoop to blame
This sort of trifling? Even had you skill

In speech—(which I have not)—to make your will
Quite clear to such an one, and say, "Just this
Or that in you disgusts me; here you miss,
Or there exceed the mark"—and if she let
Herself be lessoned so, nor plainly set
Her wits to yours, forsooth, and made excuse,
—E'en then would be some stooping; and I choose
Never to stoop. Oh, sir, she smiled, no doubt,
Whene'er I passed her; but who passed without
Much the same smile? This grew; I gave commands;
Then all smiles stopped together. There she stands
As if alive. Will 't please you rise? We'll meet
The company below, then. I repeat,
The Count your master's known munificence
Is ample warrant that no just pretense
Of mine for dowry will be disallowed;
Though his fair daughter's self, as I avowed
At starting, is my object. Nay, we'll go
Together down, sir. Notice Neptune, though,
Taming a sea-horse, thought a rarity,
Which Claus of Innsbruck cast in bronze for me!

THE BISHOP ORDERS HIS TOMB AT ST. PRAXED'S CHURCH

ROME, 15—

Vanity, saith the preacher, vanity!
Draw round my bed; is Anselm keeping back?
Nephews—sons mine . . . ah God, I know not!
Well—
She, men would have to be your mother once,
Old Gandolf envied me, so fair she was!
What's done is done, and she is dead beside,
Dead long ago, and I am Bishop since,
And as she died so must we die ourselves,
And thence ye may perceive the world's a dream.
Life, how and what is it? As here I lie
In this state-chamber, dying by degrees,

Hours and long hours in the dead night, I ask,
"Do I live; am I dead?" Peace, peace seems all.
St. Praxed's ever was the church for peace;
And so, about this tomb of mine. I fought
With tooth and nail to save my niche, ye know.
—Old Gandolf cozened me, despite my care;
Shrewd was that snatch from out the corner south
He graced his carrion with, God curse the same!
Yet still my niche is not so cramped but thence
One sees the pulpit o' the epistle-side,
And somewhat of the choir, those silent seats,
And up into the aëry dome where live
The angels, and a sunbeam's sure to lurk.
And I shall fill my slab of basalt there,
And 'neath my tabernacle take my rest,
With those nine columns round me, two and two,
The odd one at my feet where Anselm stands,
Peach-blossom marble all, the rare, the ripe,
As fresh-poured red wine of a mighty pulse.
—Old Gandolf with his paltry onion-stone,
Put me where I may look at him! True peach,
Rosy and flawless; how I earned the prize!
Draw close. That conflagration of my church
—What then? So much was saved if aught were missed!
My sons, ye would not be my death? Go dig
The white-grape vineyard where the oil-press stood,
Drop water gently till the surface sinks,
And if ye find . . . ah God, I know not, I! . . .
Bedded in store of rotten fig-leaves soft,
And corded up in a tight olive-frail,
Some lump, ah God, of *lapis lazuli,*
Big as a Jew's head cut off at the nape,
Blue as a vein o'er the Madonna's breast—
Sons, all have I bequeathed you, villas, all,
That brave Frascati villa with its bath—
So, let the blue lump poise between my knees,
Like the God the Father's globe on both his hands
Ye worship in the Jesu Church so gay,

For Gandolf shall not choose but see and burst!
Swift as a weaver's shuttle fleet our years;
Man goeth to the grave, and where is he?
Did I say basalt for my slab, sons? Black—
'Twas ever antique-black I meant! How else
Shall ye contrast my frieze to come beneath?
The bas-relief in bronze ye promised me,
Those Pans and Nymphs ye wot of, and perchance
Some tripod, thyrsus, with a vase or so,
The Savior at his sermon on the mount,
St. Praxed in a glory, and one Pan
Ready to twitch the Nymph's last garment off,
And Moses with the tables . . . but I know
Ye mark me not! What do they whisper thee,
Child of my bowels, Anselm? Ah, ye hope
To revel down my villas while I gasp
Bricked o'er with beggar's moldy travertine
Which Gandolf from his tomb-top chuckles at!
Nay, boys, ye love me—all of jasper, then!
'Tis jasper ye stand pledged to, lest I grieve
My bath must needs be left behind, alas!
One block, pure green as a pistachio-nut,
There's plenty jasper somewhere in the world—
And have I not St. Praxed's ear to pray
Horses for ye, and brown Greek manuscripts,
And mistresses with great smooth marbly limbs?
—That's if ye carve my epitaph aright,
Choice Latin, picked phrase, Tully's every word,
No gaudy ware like Gandolf's second line—
Tully, my masters? Ulpian serves his need!
And then how I shall lie through centuries,
And hear the blessed mutter of the Mass,
And see God made and eaten all day long,
And feel the steady candle-flame, and taste
Good strong, thick, stupefying incense-smoke!
For as I lie here, hours of the dead night,
Dying in state and by such slow degrees,
I fold my arms as if they clasped a crook,

And stretch my feet forth straight as stone can point,
And let the bedclothes for a mort-cloth drop
Into great laps and folds of sculptor's-work.
And as yon tapers dwindle, and strange thoughts
Grow, with a certain humming in my ears,
About the life before I lived this life,
And this life too, popes, cardinals, and priests,
St. Praxed at his sermon on the mount,
Your tall pale mother with her talking eyes,
And new-found agate urns as fresh as day,
And marble's language, Latin pure, discreet,
—Aha, ELUCESCEBAT quoth our friend?
No Tully, said I, Ulpian at the best!
Evil and brief hath been my pilgrimage.
All *lapis,* all, sons! Else I give the Pope
My villas. Will ye ever eat my heart?
Ever your eyes were as a lizard's quick;
They glitter like your mother's for my soul,
Or ye would heighten my impoverished frieze,
Piece out its starved design, and fill my vase
With grapes, and add a vizor and a Term,
And to the tripod ye would tie a lynx
That in his struggle throws the thyrsus down,
To comfort me on my entablature
Whereon I am to lie till I must ask
"Do I live, am I dead?" There, leave me, there!
For ye have stabbed me with ingratitude
To death—ye wish it—God, ye wish it! Stone—
Gritstone, a-crumble! Clammy squares which sweat
As if the corpse they keep were oozing through—
And no more *lapis* to delight the world!
Well, go! I bless ye. Fewer tapers there,
But in a row. And, going, turn your backs
—Aye, like departing altar-ministrants,
And leave me in my church, the church for peace,
That I may watch at leisure if he leers—
Old Gandolf—at me, from his onion-stone,
As still he envied me, so fair she was!

CALIBAN UPON SETEBOS

OR, NATURAL THEOLOGY IN THE ISLAND

"Thou thoughtest that I was altogether such an one as thyself."

['Will sprawl, now that the heat of day is best,
Flat on his belly in the pit's much mire,
With elbows wide, fists clenched to prop his chin.
And, while he kicks both feet in the cool slush,
And feels about his spine small eft-things course,
Run in and out each arm, and make him laugh;
And while above his head a pompion-plant,
Coating the cave-top as a brow its eye,
Creeps down to touch and tickle hair and beard,
And now a flower drops with a bee inside,
And now a fruit to snap at, catch and crunch—
He looks out o'er yon sea which sunbeams cross
And recross till they weave a spider-web
(Meshes of fire, some great fish breaks at times),
And talks to his own self, howe'er he please,
Touching that other, whom his dam called God.
Because to talk about Him, vexes—ha,
Could He but know! and time to vex is now,
When talk is safer than in winter-time.
Moreover Prosper and Miranda sleep;
In confidence he drudges at their task,
And it is good to cheat the pair, and gibe,
Letting the rank tongue blossom into speech.]
Setebos, Setebos, and Setebos!
'Thinketh, He dwelleth i' the cold o' the moon.
'Thinketh He made it, with the sun to match,
But not the stars; the stars came otherwise;
Only made clouds, winds, meteors, such as that;
Also this isle, what lives and grows thereon,
And snaky sea which rounds and ends the same.

'Thinketh, it came of being ill at ease.
He hated that He cannot change His cold,
Nor cure its ache. 'Hath spied an icy fish

That longed to 'scape the rock-stream where she lived,
And thaw herself within the lukewarm brine
O' the lazy sea her stream thrusts far amid,
A crystal spike 'twixt two warm walls of wave;
Only, she ever sickened, found repulse
At the other kind of water, not her life.
(Green-dense and dim-delicious, bred o' the sun),
Flounced back from bliss she was not born to breathe,
And in her old bounds buried her despair,
Hating and loving warmth alike; so He.

'Thinketh, He made thereat the sun, this isle,
Trees and the fowls here, beast and creeping thing.
Yon otter, sleek-wet, black, lithe as a leech;
Yon auk, one fire-eye in a ball of foam,
That floats and feeds; a certain badger brown
He hath watched hunt with that slant white-wedge eye
By moonlight; and the pie with the long tongue
That pricks deep into oakwarts for a worm,
And says a plain word when she finds her prize,
But will not eat the ants; the ants themselves
That build a wall of seeds and settled stalks
About their hole—He made all these and more,
Made all we see, and us, in spite; how else?
He could not, Himself, make a second self
To be His mate; as well have made Himself.
He would not make what He mislikes or slights,
An eyesore to Him, or not worth His pains;
But did, in envy, listlessness or sport,
Make what Himself would fain, in a manner, be—
Weaker in most points, stronger in a few,
Worthy, and yet mere playthings all the while,
Things He admires and mocks, too—that is it.
Because, so brave, so better though they be,
It nothing skills if He begin to plague.
Look now, I melt a gourd-fruit into mash,
Add honeycomb and pods, I have perceived,
Which bite like finches when they bill and kiss—
Then, when froth rises bladdery, drink up all,

Quick, quick, till maggots scamper through my brain;
Last, throw me on my back i' the seeded thyme,
And wanton, wishing I were born a bird.
Put case, unable to be what I wish,
I yet could make a live bird out of clay.
Would not I take clay, pinch my Caliban
Able to fly?—for, there, see, he hath wings,
And great comb like the hoopoe's to admire,
And there, a sting to do his foes offense,
There, and I will that he begin to live,
Fly to yon rock-top, nip me off the horns
Of grigs high up that make the merry din
Saucy through their veined wings, and mind me not.
In which feat, if his leg snapped, brittle clay,
And he lay stupid-like—why I should laugh;
And if he, spying me should fall to weep,
Beseech me to be good, repair his wrong,
Bid his poor leg smart less or grow again—
Well, as the chance were this might take or else
Not take my fancy, I might hear his cry
And give the manikin three sound legs for one,
Or pluck the other off, leave him like an egg,
And lessoned he was mine and merely clay.
Were this no pleasure lying in the thyme,
Drinking the mash, with brain become alive
Making and marring clay at will? So He.

'Thinketh such shows nor right no wrong in Him,
Nor kind nor cruel; He is strong and Lord.
'Am strong myself compared to yonder crabs
That march now from the mountain to the sea;
'Let twenty pass and stone the twenty-first,
Loving not, hating not, just choosing so.
'Say, the first straggler that boasts purple spots
Shall join the file, one pincer twisted off;
'Say this bruised fellow shall receive a worm,
And two worms he whose nippers end in red;
As it likes me each time I do: so He.

Well then, 'supposeth He is good i' the main,
Placable if His mind and ways were guessed,
But rougher than His handiwork, be sure!
Oh, He hath made things worthier than Himself,
And envieth that, so helped, such things do more
Than He who made them! What consoles but this?
That they, unless through Him, do naught at all,
And must submit; what other use in things?
'Hath cut a pipe of pithless elder-joint
That, blown through, gives exact the scream o' the jay
When from her wing you twitch the feathers blue.
Sound this, and little birds that hate the jay
Flock within stone's throw, glad their foe is hurt.
Put case such pipe could prattle and boast forsooth,
"I catch the birds, I am the crafty thing,
I make the cry my maker cannot make
With his great round mouth; he must blow through mine!"
Would not I smash it with my foot? So He.

But wherefore rough, why cold and ill at ease?
Aha, that is a question! Ask, for that,
What knows—the something over Setebos
That made Him, or He maybe, found and fought,
Worsted, drove off and did to nothing, perchance.
There may be something quiet o'er His head,
Out of His reach, that feels nor joy nor grief,
Since both derive from weakness in some way.
I joy because the quails come; would not joy
Could I bring quails here when I have a mind.
This Quiet, all it hath a mind to, doth.
'Esteemeth stars the outposts of its couch,
But never spends much thought nor care that way.
It may look up, work up—the worse for those
It works on! 'Careth but for Setebos
The many-handed as a cuttle-fish,
Who, making Himself feared through what He does,
Looks up, first, and perceives he cannot soar
To what is quiet and hath happy life;

Next looks down here, and out of very spite
Makes this a bauble-world to ape yon real,
These good things to match those as hips do grapes.
'Tis solace making baubles, aye, and sport.
Himself peeped late, eyed Prosper at his books
Careless and lofty, lord now of the isle;
Vexed, 'stitched a book of broad leaves, arrow-shaped,
Wrote thereon, he knows what, prodigious words;
Has peeled a wand and called it by a name;
Weareth at whiles for an enchanter's robe
The eyed skin of a supple oncelot;
And hath an ounce sleeker than youngling mole,
A four-legged serpent he makes cower and couch,
Now snarl, now hold its breath and mind his eye,
And saith she is Miranda and my wife.
'Keeps for his Ariel a tall pouch-bill crane
He bids go wade for fish and straight disgorge;
Also a sea-beast, lumpish, which he snared,
Blinded the eyes of, and brought somewhat tame,
And split its toe-webs, and now pens the drudge
In a hole o' the rock, and calls him Caliban;
A bitter heart that bides its time and bites.
'Plays thus at being Prosper in a way.
Taketh his mirth with make-believes; so He.

His dam held that the Quiet made all things
Which Setebos vexed only; 'holds not so.
Who made them weak, meant weakness He might vex.
Had He meant other, while His hand was in,
Why not make horny eyes no thorn could prick,
Or plate my scalp with bone against the snow,
Or overscale my flesh 'neath joint and joint
Like an orc's armor? Aye—so spoil His sport!
He is the One now; only He doth all.

'Saith, He may like, perchance, what profits him.
Aye, himself loves what does him good; but why?
'Gets good no otherwise. This blinded beast
Loves whoso places flesh-meat on his nose.

But, had he eyes, would want no help, but hate
Or love, just as it liked him; he hath eyes.
Also it pleaseth Setebos to work,
Use all His hands, and exercise much craft,
By no means for the love of what is worked.

'Tasteth himself, no finer good i' the world
When all goes right, in this safe summertime,
And he wants little, hungers, aches not much,
Than trying what to do with wit and strength.
'Falls to make something; 'piled yon pile of turfs,
And squared and stuck there squares of soft white chalk,
And, with a fish-tooth, scratched a moon on each,
And set up endwise certain spikes of tree,
And crowned the whole with a sloth's skull atop,
Found dead i' the woods, too hard for one to kill.
No use at all i' the work, for work's sole sake;
'Shall some day knock it down again: so He.

'Saith He is terrible; watch His feats in proof!
One hurricane will spoil six good months' hope.
He hath a spite against me, that I know,
Just as He favors Prosper, who knows why?
So it is, all the same, as well I find.
'Wove wattles half the winter, fenced them firm
With stone and stake to stop she-tortoises
Crawling to lay their eggs here. Well, one wave,
Feeling the foot of Him upon its neck,
Gaped as a snake does, lolled out its large tongue,
And licked the whole labor flat; so much for spite.

'Saw a ball flame down late (yonder it lies)
Where half an hour before, I slept i' the shade.
Often they scatter sparkles; there is force!
'Dug up a newt He may have envied once
And turned to stone, shut up inside a stone.
Please Him and hinder this?—What Prosper does?
Aha, if He would tell me how! Not He!
There is the sport; discover how or die!

All need not die, for of the things o' the isle
Some flee afar, some dive, some run up trees;
Those at His mercy—why they please Him most
When . . . when . . . well, never try the same way twice!
Repeat what act has pleased, He may grow wroth.
You must not know His ways, and play Him off,
Sure of the issue. Doth the like himself:
'Spareth a squirrel that it nothing fears
But steals the nut from underneath my thumb,
And when I threat, bites stoutly in defense.
'Spareth an urchin that contrariwise,
Curls up into a ball, pretending death
For fright at my approach; the two ways please.
But what would move my choler more than this,
That either creature counted on its life
Tomorrow and next day and all days to come
Saying, forsooth, in the inmost of its heart,
"Because he did so yesterday with me,
And otherwise with such another brute,
So must he do henceforth and always."—Aye?
Would teach the reasoning couple what "must" means!
'Doth as he likes, or wherefore Lord? So He.

'Conceiveth all things will continue thus,
And we shall have to live in fear of Him
So long as He lives, keeps his strength; no change,
If He have done His best, make no new world
To please Him more, so leave off watching this—
If He surprise not even the Quiet's self
Some strange day—or, suppose, grow into it
As grubs grow butterflies. Else, here we are,
And there is He, and nowhere help at all.

'Believeth with the life, the pain shall stop.
His dam held different, that after death
He both plagued enemies and feasted friends:
Idly! He doth His worst in this our life.
Giving just respite lest we die through pain,
Saving last pain for worst—with which, an end.

Meanwhile, the beſt way to escape His ire
Is, not to seem too happy. 'Sees, himself,
Yonder two flies, with purple films and pink,
Bask on the pompion-bell above; kills both.
'Sees two black painful beetles roll their ball
On head and tail as if to save their lives;
Moves them the ſtick away they ſtrive to clear.

Even so, 'would have him misconceive, suppose
This Caliban ſtrives hard and ails no less,
And always, above all else, envies Him;
Wherefore he mainly dances on dark nights,
Moans in the sun, gets under holes to laugh,
And never speaks his mind save housed as now.
Outside, 'groans, curses. If He caught me here,
O'erheard this speech, and asked "What chuckleſt at?"
'Would, to appease Him, cut a finger off,
Or of my three kid yearlings burn the beſt,
Or let the toothsome apples rot on tree,
Or push my tame beaſt for the orc to taſte;
While myself lit a fire, and made a song,
And sung it, *"What I hate, be consecrate,*
To celebrate Thee and Thy ſtate, no mate
For Thee; what see for envy in poor me?"
Hoping the while, since evils sometimes mend,
Warts rub away and sores are cured with slime,
That some ſtrange day, will either the Quiet catch
And conquer Setebos, or likelier He
Decrepit may doze, doze, as good as die.

[What, what? A curtain o'er the world at once!
Crickets ſtop hissing; not a bird—or, yes,
There scuds His raven that has told Him all!
It was fool's play, this prattling! Ha! The wind
Shoulders the pillared duſt, death's house o' the move,
And faſt invading fires begin! White blaze—
A tree's head snaps—and there, there, there, there, there,
His thunder follows! Fool to gibe at Him!

Lo! 'Lieth flat and loveth Setebos!
'Maketh his teeth meet through his upper lip,
Will let those quails fly, will not eat this month
One little mess of whelks, so he may 'scape!]

Arthur Hugh Clough

1819–1861

WHERE LIES THE LAND?

WHERE lies the land to which the ship would go?
Far, far ahead, is all her seamen know.
And where the land she travels from? Away,
Far, far behind, is all that they can say.

On sunny noons upon the deck's smooth face,
Linked arm in arm, how pleasant here to pace;
Or, o'er the stern reclining, watch below
The foaming wake far widening as we go.

On stormy nights when wild northwesters rave,
How proud a thing to fight with wind and wave!
The dripping sailor on the reeling mast
Exults to bear, and scorns to wish it past.

Where lies the land to which the ship would go?
Far, far ahead, is all her seamen know.
And where the land she travels from? Away,
Far, far behind, is all that they can say.

SAY NOT THE STRUGGLE NOUGHT AVAILETH

SAY not the struggle nought availeth,
  The labor and the wounds are vain,
The enemy faints not, nor faileth,
  And as things have been they remain.

If hopes were dupes, fears may be liars;
  It may be, in yon smoke concealed,
Your comrades chase e'en now the fliers,
  And, but for you, possess the field.

For while the tired waves, vainly breaking,
Seem here no painful inch to gain,
Far back, through creeks and inlets making,
Comes silent, flooding in, the main.

And not by eastern windows only,
When daylight comes, comes in the light,
In front, the sun climbs slow, how slowly;
But westward, look, the land is bright.

Matthew Arnold

1822–1888

REQUIESCAT

Strew on her roses, roses,
And never a spray of yew!
In quiet she reposes;
Ah, would that I did too!

Her mirth the world required;
She bathed it in smiles of glee.
But her heart was tired, tired,
And now they let her be.

Her life was turning, turning,
In mazes of heat and sound.
But for peace her soul was yearning,
And now peace laps her round.

Her cabined, ample spirit,
It fluttered and failed for breath.
To-night it doth inherit
The vasty hall of death.

DOVER BEACH

The sea is calm to-night,
The tide is full, the moon lies fair
Upon the straits;—on the French coast the light
Gleams and is gone; the cliffs of England stand,

Glimmering and vast, out in the tranquil bay.
Come to the window, sweet is the night-air!
Only, from the long line of spray
Where the sea meets the moon-blanched land,
Listen! you hear the grating roar
Of pebbles which the waves draw back, and fling,
At their return, up the high strand,
Begin, and cease, and then again begin,
With tremulous cadence slow, and bring
The eternal note of sadness in.

Sophocles long ago
Heard it on the Ægean, and it brought
Into his mind the turbid ebb and flow
Of human misery; we
Find also in the sound a thought,
Hearing it by this distant northern sea.

The sea of faith
Was once, too, at the full, and round earth's shore
Lay like the folds of a bright girdle furled.
But now I only hear
Its melancholy, long, withdrawing roar,
Retreating, to the breath
Of the night-wind, down the vast edges drear
And naked shingles of the world.

Ah, love, let us be true
To one another! for the world, which seems
To lie before us like a land of dreams,
So various, so beautiful, so new,
Hath really neither joy, nor love, nor light,
Nor certitude, nor peace, nor help for pain;
And we are here as on a darkling plain
Swept with confused alarms of struggle and flight,
Where ignorant armies clash by night.

George Meredith

1828–1909

LOVE IN THE VALLEY

Under yonder beech-tree single on the greensward,
  Couched with her arms behind her golden head,
Knees and tresses folded to slip and ripple idly,
  Lies my young love sleeping in the shade.
Had I the heart to slide an arm beneath her,
  Press her parting lips as her waist I gather slow,
Waking in amazement she could not but embrace me—
  Then would she hold me and never let me go?

Shy as the squirrel and wayward as the swallow,
  Swift as the swallow along the river's light
Circleting the surface to meet his mirrored winglets,
  Fleeter she seems in her stay than in her flight.
Shy as the squirrel that leaps among the pine-tops,
  Wayward as the swallow overhead at set of sun,
She whom I love is hard to catch and conquer,
  Hard, but O the glory of the winning were she won!

When her mother tends her before the laughing mirror,
  Tying up her laces, looping up her hair,
Often she thinks, were this wild thing wedded,
  More love should I have, and much less care.
When her mother tends her before the lighted mirror,
  Loosening her laces, combing down her curls,
Often she thinks, were this wild thing wedded,
  I should miss but one for many boys and girls.

Heartless she is as the shadow in the meadows
  Flying to the hills on a blue and breezy noon.
No, she is athirst and drinking up her wonder;
  Earth to her is young as the slip of the new moon.
Deals she an unkindness, 'tis but her rapid measure,
  Even as in a dance; and her smile can heal no less:

Like the swinging May-cloud that pelts the flowers with
hailstones
Off a sunny border, she was made to bruise and bless.

Lovely are the curves of the white owl sweeping
Wavy in the dusk lit by one large star.
Lone on the fir-branch, his rattle-note unvaried,
Brooding o'er the gloom, spins the brown evejar.
Darker grows the valley, more and more forgetting;
So were it with me if forgetting could be willed.
Tell the grassy hollow that holds the bubbling wellspring,
Tell it to forget the source that keeps it filled.

Stepping down the hill with her fair companions,
Arm in arm, all against the raying west,
Boldly she sings, to the merry tune she marches,
Brave is her shape, and sweeter unpossessed.
Sweeter, for she is what my heart first awaking
Whispered the world was; morning light is she.
Love that so desires would fain keep her changeless;
Fain would fling the net, and fain have her free.

Happy, happy time, when the white star hovers
Low over dim fields fresh with bloomy dew,
Near the face of dawn, that draws athwart the darkness,
Threading it with color, like yewberries the yew.
Thicker crowd the shades as the grave east deepens
Glowing, and with crimson a long cloud swells.
Maiden still the morn is; and strange she is, and secret;
Strange her eyes; her cheeks are cold as cold sea-shells.

Sunrays, leaning on our southern hills and lighting
Wild cloud-mountains that drag the hills along,
Oft ends the day of your shifting brilliant laughter
Chill as a dull face frowning on a song.
Aye, but shows the southwest a ripple-feathered bosom
Blown to silver while the clouds are shaken and ascend
Scaling the mid-heavens as they stream, there comes a
sunset
Rich, deep like love in beauty without end.

When at dawn she sighs, and like an infant to the window
  Turns grave eyes craving light, released from dreams,
Beautiful she looks, like a white waterlily
  Bursting out of bud in havens of the streams.
When from bed she rises clothed from neck to ankle
  In her long nightgown sweet as boughs of May,
Beautiful she looks, like a tall garden-lily
  Pure from the night, and splendid for the day.

Mother of the dews, dark-eyelashed twilight,
  Low-lidded twilight, o'er the valley's brim,
Rounding on thy breast sings the dew-delighted skylark,
  Clear as though the dewdrops had their voice in him.
Hidden where the rose-flush drinks the rayless planet,
  Fountain-full he pours the spraying fountain-showers.
Let me hear her laughter, I would have her ever
  Cool as dew in twilight, the lark above the flowers.

All the girls are out with their baskets for the primrose;
  Up lanes, woods through, they troop in joyful bands.
My sweet leads. She knows not why, but now she loiters,
  Eyes the bent anemones, and hangs her hands.
Such a look will tell that the violets are peeping,
  Coming the rose; and unaware a cry
Springs in her bosom for odors and for color,
  Covert and the nightingale; she knows not why.

Kerchiefed head and chin she darts between her tulips,
  Streaming like a willow gray in arrowy rain.
Some bend beaten cheek to gravel, and their angel
  She will be; she lifts them, and on she speeds again.
Black the driving rain-cloud breasts the iron gateway;
  She is forth to cheer a neighbor lacking mirth.
So when sky and grass met rolling dumb for thunder
  Saw I once a white dove, sole light of earth.

Prim little scholars are the flowers of her garden,
  Trained to stand in rows, and asking if they please.

I might love them well but for loving more the wild ones.
  O my wild ones! they tell me more than these.
You, my wild one, you tell of honeyed field-rose,
  Violet, blushing eglantine in life; and even as they,
They by the wayside are earnest of your goodness,
  You are of life's, on the banks that line the way.

Peering at her chamber the white crowns the red rose,
  Jasmine winds the porch with stars two and three.
Parted is the window; she sleeps; the starry jasmine
  Breathes a falling breath that carries thoughts of me.
Sweeter unpossessed, have I said of her my sweetest?
  Not while she sleeps. While she sleeps the jasmine breathes,
Luring her to love; she sleeps; the starry jasmine
  Bears me to her pillow under white rose-wreaths.

Yellow with birdfoot-trefoil are the grass-glades;
  Yellow with cinquefoil of the dew-gray leaf;
Yellow with stonecrop; the moss-mounds are yellow;
  Blue-necked the wheat sways, yellowing to the sheaf.
Green-yellow, bursts from the copse the laughing yaffle;
  Sharp as a sickle is the edge of shade and shine.
Earth in her heart laughs looking at the heavens,
  Thinking of the harvest. I look and think of mine.

This I may know: her dressing and undressing
  Such a change of light shows as when the skies in sport
Shift from cloud to moonlight; or edging over thunder
  Slips a ray of sun; or sweeping into port
White sails furl; or on the ocean borders
  White sails lean along the waves leaping green.
Visions of her shower before me, but from eyesight
  Guarded she would be like the sun were she seen.

Front door and back of the mossed old farmhouse
  Open with the morn, and in a breezy link
Freshly sparkles garden to stripe-shadowed orchard,
  Green across a rill where on sand the minnows wink.

Busy in the grass the early sun of summer
  Swarms, and the blackbird's mellow fluting notes
Call my darling up with round and roguish challenge;
  Quaintest, richest carol of all the singing throats!

Cool was the woodside; cool as her white dairy
  Keeping sweet the cream-pan; and there the boys from school,
Cricketing below, rushed brown and red with sunshine;
  O the dark translucence of the deep-eyed cool!
Spying from the farm, herself she fetched a pitcher
  Full of milk, and tilted for each in turn the beak.
Then a little fellow, mouth up and on tiptoe,
  Said, "I will kiss you"; she laughed and leaned her cheek.

Doves of the firwood walling high our red roof
  Through the long noon coo, crooning through the coo.
Loose droop the leaves, and down the sleepy roadway
  Sometimes pipes a chaffinch; loose droops the blue.
Cows flap a slow tail knee-deep in the river,
  Breathless, given up to sun and gnat and fly.
Nowhere is she seen; and if I see her nowhere,
  Lightning may come, straight rains and tiger sky.

O the golden sheaf, the rustling treasure-armful!
  O the nutbrown tresses nodding interlaced!
O the treasure-tresses one another over
  Nodding! O the girdle slack about the waist!
Slain are the poppies that shot their random scarlet
  Quick amid the wheat-ears. Wound about the waist,
Gathered, see these brides of Earth one blush of ripeness!
  O the nutbrown tresses nodding interlaced!

Large and smoky red the sun's cold disk drops,
  Clipped by naked hills, on violet-shaded snow.
Eastward large and still lights up a bower of moonrise,
  Whence at her leisure steps the moon aglow.
Nightlong on black print-branches our beech-tree
  Gazes in this whiteness; nightlong could I.

Here may life on death or death on life be painted.
  Let me clasp her soul to know she cannot die!

Gossips count her faults; they scour a narrow chamber
  Where there is no window, read not heaven or her.
"When she was a tiny," one aged woman quavers,
  Plucks at my heart and leads me by the ear.
Faults she had once as she learned to run and tumbled;
  Faults of feature some see, beauty not complete.
Yet, good gossips, beauty that makes holy
  Earth and air, may have faults from head to feet.

Hither she comes; she comes to me; she lingers,
  Deepens her brown eyebrows, while in new surprise
High rise the lashes in wonder of a stranger;
  Yet am I the light and living of her eyes.
Something friends have told her fills her heart to
    brimming,
  Nets her in her blushes, and wounds her, and tames.—
Sure of her haven, O like a dove alighting,
  Arms up, she dropped; our souls were in our names.

Soon will she lie like a white frost sunrise.
  Yellow oats and brown wheat, barley pale as rye,
Long since your sheaves have yielded to the thresher,
  Felt the girdle loosened, seen the tresses fly.
Soon will she lie like a blood-red sunset,
  Swift with the tomorrow, green-winged spring!
Sing from the southwest, bring her back the truants,
  Nightingale and swallow, song and dipping wing.

Soft new beech-leaves, up to beamy April
  Spreading bough on bough a primrose mountain, you
Lucid in the moon, raise lilies to the sky-fields,
  Youngest green transfused in silver shining through;
Fairer than the lily, than the wild white cherry;
  Fair as in image my seraph love appears
Borne to me by dreams when dawn is at my eyelids—
  Fair as in the flesh she swims to me on tears.

Could I find a place to be alone with heaven,
  I would speak my heart out; heaven is my need.
Every woodland tree is flushing like the dogwood,
  Flashing like the whitebeam, swaying like the reed.
Flushing like the dogwood crimson in October;
  Streaming like the flag-reed southwest blown;
Flashing as in gusts the sudden-lighted whitebeam:
  All seem to know what is for heaven alone.

LUCIFER IN STARLIGHT

On a starred night Prince Lucifer uprose.
  Tired of his dark dominion swung the fiend
  Above the rolling ball in cloud part screened,
Where sinners hugged their specter of repose.
Poor prey to his hot fit of pride were those.
  And now upon his western wing he leaned,
  Now his huge bulk o'er Afric's sands careened,
Now the black planet shadowed Arctic snows.
Soaring through wider zones that pricked his scars
  With memory of the old revolt from Awe,
He reached a middle height, and at the stars,
Which are the brain of heaven, he looked, and sank.
Around the ancient track marched, rank on rank,
  The army of unalterable law.

Dante Gabriel Rossetti

1828–1882

THE BLESSED DAMOZEL

The blessed damozel leaned out
  From the golden bar of heaven;
Her eyes were deeper than the depth
  Of waters stilled at even;
She had three lilies in her hand,
  And the stars in her hair were seven.

Her robe, ungirt from clasp to hem,
  No wrought flowers did adorn,
But a white rose of Mary's gift,
  For service meetly worn;
Her hair that lay along her back
  Was yellow like ripe corn.

Her seemed she scarce had been a day
  One of God's choristers;
The wonder was not yet quite gone
  From that still look of hers;
Albeit, to them she left, her day
  Had counted as ten years.

(To one, it is ten years of years.
  . . . Yet now, and in this place,
Surely she leaned o'er me—her hair
  Fell all about my face . . .
Nothing; the autumn fall of leaves.
  The whole year sets apace.)

It was the rampart of God's house
  That she was standing on;
By God built over the sheer depth
  The which is space begun;
So high, that looking downward thence
  She scarce could see the sun.

It lies in heaven, across the flood
  Of ether, as a bridge.
Beneath, the tides of day and night
  With flame and darkness ridge
The void, as low as where this earth
  Spins like a fretful midge.

Around her, lovers, newly met
  'Mid deathless love's acclaims,
Spoke evermore among themselves
  Their heart-remembered names;
And the souls mounting up to God
  Went by her like thin flames.

And still she bowed herself and stooped
  Out of the circling charm;
Until her bosom must have made
  The bar she leaned on warm,
And the lilies lay as if asleep
  Along her bended arm.

From the fixed place of heaven she saw
  Time like a pulse shake fierce
Through all the worlds. Her gaze still strove
  Within the gulf to pierce
Its path; and now she spoke as when
  The stars sang in their spheres.

The sun was gone now; the curled moon
  Was like a little feather
Fluttering far down the gulf; and now
  She spoke through the still weather.
Her voice was like the voice the stars
  Had when they sang together.

(Ah sweet! Even now, in that bird's song,
  Strove not her accents there,
Fain to be harkened? When those bells
  Possessed the mid-day air,
Strove not her steps to reach my side
  Down all the echoing stair?)

"I wish that he were come to me,
  For he will come," she said.
"Have I not prayed in heaven?—on earth,
  Lord, Lord, has he not prayed?
Are not two prayers a perfect strength?
  And shall I feel afraid?

"When round his head the aureole clings,
  And he is clothed in white,
I'll take his hand and go with him
  To the deep wells of light;

As unto a stream we will step down,
And bathe there in God's sight.

"We two will stand beside that shrine,
Occult, withheld, untrod,
Whose lamps are stirred continually
With prayers sent up to God;
And see our old prayers, granted, melt
Each like a little cloud.

"We two will lie i' the shadow of
That living, mystic tree
Within whose secret growth the Dove
Is sometimes felt to be,
While every leaf that His plumes touch
Saith His Name audibly.

"And I myself will teach to him,
I myself, lying so,
The songs I sing here; which his voice
Shall pause in, hushed and slow,
And find some knowledge at each pause,
Or some new thing to know."

(Alas! We two, we two, thou say'st!
Yea, one wast thou with me
That once of old. But shall God lift
To endless unity
The soul whose likeness with thy soul
Was but its love for thee?)

"We two," she said, "will seek the groves
Where the lady Mary is,
With her five handmaidens, whose names
Are five sweet symphonies,
Cecily, Gertrude, Magdalen,
Margaret, and Rosalys.

"Circlewise sit they, with bound locks
And foreheads garlanded;

Into the fine cloth, white like flame,
  Weaving the golden thread,
To fashion the birth-robes for them
  Who are just born, being dead.

"He shall fear, haply, and be dumb;
  Then will I lay my cheek
To his, and tell about our love,
  Not once abashed or weak;
And the dear Mother will approve
  My pride, and let me speak.

"Herself shall bring us, hand in hand,
  To Him round whom all souls
Kneel, the clear-ranged unnumbered heads
  Bowed with their aureoles;
And angels meeting us shall sing,
  To their citherns and citoles.

"There will I ask of Christ the Lord
  Thus much for him and me—
Only to live as once on earth
  With Love, only to be,
As then awhile, forever now
  Together, I and he."

She gazed and listened and then said,
  Less sad of speech than mild—
"All this is when he comes." She ceased.
  The light thrilled toward her, filled
With angels in strong, level flight.
  Her eyes prayed, and she smiled.

(I saw her smile.) But soon their path
  Was vague in distant spheres;
And then she cast her arms along
  The golden barriers,
And laid her face between her hands,
  And wept. (I heard her tears.)

Christina Rossetti

1830–1894

SONG

When I am dead, my dearest,
Sing no sad songs for me;
Plant thou no roses at my head,
Nor shady cypress-tree:
Be the green grass above me
With showers and dewdrops wet;
And if thou wilt, remember,
And if thou wilt, forget.

I shall not see the shadows,
I shall not feel the rain;
I shall not hear the nightingale
Sing on, as if in pain;
And dreaming through the twilight
That doth not rise nor set,
Haply I may remember,
And haply may forget.

A BIRTHDAY

My heart is like a singing bird
Whose nest is in a watered shoot;
My heart is like an apple-tree
Whose boughs are bent with thick-set fruit;
My heart is like a rainbow shell
That paddles in a halcyon sea;
My heart is gladder than all these,
Because my love is come to me.

Raise me a dais of silk and down;
Hang it with vair and purple dyes;
Carve it in doves and pomegranates,
And peacocks with a hundred eyes;

Work it in gold and silver grapes,
  In leaves and silver fleur-de-lys;
Because the birthday of my life
  Is come, my love is come to me.

REMEMBER

Remember me when I am gone away,
Gone far away into the silent land;
When you can no more hold me by the hand,
Nor I half turn to go, yet turning stay.
Remember me when no more, day by day,
You tell me of our future that you planned:
Only remember me; you understand
It will be late to counsel then or pray.
Yet if you should forget me for a while
And afterwards remember, do not grieve:
For if the darkness and corruption leave
A vestige of the thoughts that once I had,
Better by far you should forget and smile
Than that you should remember and be sad.

William Morris

1834–1896

AN APOLOGY

Of Heaven or Hell I have no power to sing,
I cannot ease the burden of your fears,
Or make quick-coming death a little thing,
Or bring again the pleasures of past years,
Nor for my words shall ye forget your tears,
Or hope again for aught that I can say,
The idle singer of an empty day.

But rather, when aweary of your mirth,
From full hearts still unsatisfied ye sigh,
And, feeling kindly unto all the earth,
Grudge every minute as it passes by,

Made the more mindful that the sweet days die—
Remember me a little then, I pray,
The idle singer of an empty day.

The heavy trouble, the bewildering care
That weighs us down who live and earn our bread,
These idle verses have no power to bear;
So let me sing of names rememberéd,
Because they, living not, can ne'er be dead,
Or long time take their memory quite away
From us poor singers of an empty day.

Dreamer of dreams, born out of my due time,
Why should I strive to set the crooked straight?
Let it suffice me that my murmuring rime
Beats with light wing against the ivory gate,
Telling a tale not too importunate
To those who in the sleepy region stay,
Lulled by the singer of an empty day.

Folk say a wizard to a northern king
At Christmas-tide such wondrous things did show
That through one window men beheld the spring,
And through another saw the summer glow,
And through a third the fruited vines arow,
While still, unheard, but in its wonted way,
Piped the drear wind of that December day.

So with this Earthly Paradise it is,
If ye will read aright and pardon me,
Who strive to build a shadowy isle of bliss
Midmost the beating of the steely sea,
Where tossed about all hearts of men must be;
Whose ravening monsters mighty men shall slay,
Not the poor singer of an empty day.

Algernon Charles Swinburne

1837–1909

THE GARDEN OF PROSERPINE

Here, where the world is quiet,
  Here, where all trouble seems
Dead winds' and spent waves' riot
  In doubtful dreams of dreams;
I watch the green field growing
For reaping folk and sowing,
For harvest-time and mowing,
  A sleepy world of streams.

I am tired of tears and laughter,
  And men that laugh and weep;
Of what may come hereafter
  For men that sow to reap:
I am weary of days and hours,
Blown buds of barren flowers,
Desires and dreams and powers,
  And everything but sleep.

Here life has death for neighbor,
  And far from eye or ear
Wan waves and wet winds labor,
  Weak ships and spirits steer;
They drive adrift, and whither
They wot not who make thither;
But no such winds blow hither,
  And no such things grow here.

No growth of moor or coppice,
  No heather-flower or vine,
But bloomless buds of poppies,
  Green grapes of Proserpine,
Pale beds of blowing rushes,
Where no leaf blooms or blushes
Save this whereout she crushes
  For dead men deadly wine.

Pale, without name or number,
  In fruitless fields of corn,
They bow themselves and slumber
  All night till light is born;
And like a soul belated,
In hell and heaven unmated,
By cloud and mist abated
  Comes out of darkness morn.

Though one were strong as seven,
  He too with death shall dwell,
Nor wake with wings in heaven,
  Nor weep for pains in hell;
Though one were fair as roses,
His beauty clouds and closes;
And well though love reposes,
  In the end it is not well.

Pale, beyond porch and portal,
  Crowned with calm leaves, she stands
Who gathers all things mortal
  With cold immortal hands;
Her languid lips are sweeter
Than love's who fears to greet her
To men that mix and meet her
  From many times and lands.

She waits for each and other,
  She waits for all men born;
Forgets the earth her mother,
  The life of fruits and corn;
And spring and seed and swallow
Take wing for her and follow
Where summer song rings hollow
  And flowers are put to scorn.

There go the loves that wither,
  The old loves with wearier wings;
And all dead years draw thither,
  And all disastrous things;

Dead dreams of days forsaken,
Blind buds that snows have shaken,
Wild leaves that winds have taken,
  Red strays of ruined springs.

We are not sure of sorrow,
  And joy was never sure;
To-day will die to-morrow;
  Time stoops to no man's lure;
And love, grown faint and fretful,
With lips but half regretful
Sighs, and with eyes forgetful
  Weeps that no loves endure.

From too much love of living,
  From hope and fear set free,
We thank with brief thanksgiving
  Whatever gods may be
That no life lives for ever;
That dead men rise up never;
That even the weariest river
  Winds somewhere safe to sea.

Then star nor sun shall waken,
  Nor any change of light:
Nor sound of waters shaken,
  Nor any sound or sight:
Nor wintry leaves nor vernal,
Nor days nor things diurnal:
Only the sleep eternal
  In an eternal night.

CHORUS

From Atalanta in Calydon

When the hounds of spring are on winter's traces,
  The mother of months in meadow or plain
Fills the shadows and windy places
  With lisp of leaves and ripple of rain;

And the brown bright nightingale amorous
Is half assuaged for Itylus,
For the Thracian ships and the foreign faces,
  The tongueless vigil, and all the pain.

Come with bows bent and with emptying of quivers,
  Maiden most perfect, lady of light,
With a noise of winds and many rivers,
  With a clamor of waters, and with might;
Bind on thy sandals, O thou most fleet,
Over the splendor and speed of thy feet;
For the faint east quickens, the wan west shivers,
  Round the feet of the day and the feet of the night.

Where shall we find her, how shall we sing to her,
  Fold our hands round her knees, and cling?
O that man's heart were as fire and could spring to her,
  Fire, or the strength of the streams that spring!
For the stars and the winds are unto her
As raiment, as songs of the harp-player;
For the risen stars and the fallen cling to her,
  And the southwest-wind, and the west-wind sing.

For winter's rains and ruins are over,
  And all the season of snows and sins;
The days dividing lover and lover,
  The light that loses, the night that wins;
And time remembered is grief forgotten,
And frosts are slain and flowers begotten,
And in green underwood and cover
  Blossom by blossom the spring begins.

The full streams feed on flower of rushes,
  Ripe grasses trammel a traveling foot,
The faint fresh flame of the young year flushes
  From leaf to flower and flower to fruit;
And fruit and leaf are as gold and fire,
And the oat is heard above the lyre,
And the hoofèd heel of a satyr crushes
  The chestnut-husk at the chestnut-root.

And Pan by noon and Bacchus by night,
  Fleeter of foot than the fleet-foot kid,
Follows with dancing and fills with delight
  The Mænad and the Bassarid;
And soft as lips that laugh and hide
The laughing leaves of the trees divide,
And screen from seeing and leave in sight
  The god pursuing, the maiden hid.

The ivy falls with the Bacchanal's hair
  Over her eyebrows hiding her eyes;
The wild vine slipping down leaves bare
  Her bright breast shortening into sighs;
The wild vine slips with the weight of its leaves,
But the berried ivy catches and cleaves
To the limbs that glitter, the feet that scare
  The wolf that follows, the fawn that flies.

Thomas Hardy

1840–1928

DRUMMER HODGE

They throw in Drummer Hodge, to rest
  Uncoffined—just as found:
His landmark is a kopje-crest
  That breaks the veldt around;
And foreign constellations west
  Each night above his mound.

Young Hodge the Drummer never knew—
  Fresh from his Wessex home—
The meaning of the broad Karoo,
  The Bush, the dusty loam,
And why uprose to nightly view
  Strange stars amid the gloam.

Yet portion of that unknown plain
  Will Hodge for ever be;

His homely Northern breast and brain
Grow to some Southern tree,
And strange-eyed constellations reign
His stars eternally.

HAP

If but some vengeful god would call to me
From up the sky, and laugh: "Thou suffering thing,
Know that thy sorrow is my ecstasy,
That thy love's loss is my hate's profiting!"

Then would I bear it, clench myself, and die,
Steeled by the sense of ire unmerited;
Half-eased in that a Powerfuller than I
Had willed and meted me the tears I shed.

But not so. How arrives it joy lies slain,
And why unblooms the best hope ever sown?
—Crass Casualty obstructs the sun and rain,
And dicing Time for gladness casts a moan. . . .
These purblind Doomsters had as readily strown
Blisses about my pilgrimage as pain.

LET ME ENJOY

(Minor Key)

Let me enjoy the earth no less
Because the all-enacting Might
That fashioned forth its loveliness
Had other aims than my delight.

About my path there flits a Fair,
Who throws me not a word or sign;
I'll charm me with her ignoring air,
And laud the lips not meant for mine.

From manuscripts of moving song
Inspired by scenes and dreams unknown,

I'll pour out raptures that belong
To other, as they were my own.

And some day hence, towards Paradise
And all its blest—if such should be—
I will lift glad, afar-off eyes,
Though it contain no place for me.

ON AN INVITATION TO THE UNITED STATES

My ardors for emprize nigh lost
Since Life has bared its bones to me,
I shrink to seek a modern coast
Whose riper times have yet to be;
Where the new regions claim them free
From that long drip of human tears
Which peoples old in tragedy
Have left upon the centuried years.
For, wonning in these ancient lands,
Enchased and lettered as a tomb,
And scored with prints of perished hands,
And chronicled with dates of doom,
Though my own Being bear no bloom
I trace the lives such scenes enshrine,
Give past exemplars present room,
And their experience count as mine.

THE ROMAN ROAD

The Roman Road runs straight and bare
As the pale parting-line in hair
Across the heath. And thoughtful men
Contrast its days of Now and Then,
And delve, and measure, and compare;

Visioning on the vacant air
Helmed legionaries, who proudly rear
The Eagle, as they pace again
The Roman Road.

But no tall brass-helmed legionnaire
Haunts it for me. Uprises there
A mother's form upon my ken,
Guiding my infant steps, as when
We walked that ancient thoroughfare,
The Roman Road.

NEAR LANIVET, 1872

There was a stunted handpost just on the crest,
Only a few feet high;
She was tired, and we stopped in the twilight-time
for rest,
At the crossways close thereby.

She leant back, being so weary, against its stem,
And laid her arms on its own,
Each open palm stretched out to each end of them,
Her sad face sideways thrown.

Her white-clothed form at this dim-lit cease of day
Made her look as one crucified
In my gaze at her from the midst of the dusty way,
And hurriedly "Don't," I cried.

I do not think she heard. Loosing thence she said,
As she stepped forth ready to go,
"I am rested now. —Something strange came into
my head;
I wish I had not leant so!"

And wordless we moved onward down from the hill
In the west cloud's murked obscure,
And looking back we could see the handpost still
In the solitude of the moor.

"It struck her too," I thought, for as if afraid
She heavily breathed as we trailed;
Till she said, "I did not think how 'twould look in
the shade,
When I leant there like one nailed."

I, lightly: "There's nothing in it. For *you,* anyhow!"
—"O I know there is not," said she . . .
"Yet I wonder . . . If no one is bodily crucified now,
In spirit one may be!"

And we dragged on and on, while we seemed to see
In the running of Time's far glass
Her crucified, as she had wondered if she might be
Some day. —Alas, alas!

THE FALLOW DEER AT THE LONELY HOUSE

One without looks in tonight
Through the curtain-chink
From the sheet of glistening white;
One without looks in tonight
As we sit and think
By the fender-brink.

We do not discern those eyes
Watching in the snow;
Lit by lamps of rosy dyes
We do not discern those eyes
Wondering, aglow,
Fourfooted, tiptoe.

Gerard Manley Hopkins

1844-1898

GOD'S GRANDEUR

The world is charged with the grandeur of God.
It will flame out, like shining from shook foil;
It gathers to a greatness, like the ooze of oil
Crushed. Why do men then now not reck his rod?
Generations have trod, have trod, have trod;
And all is seared with trade; bleared, smeared with toil;
And wears man's smudge and shares man's smell; the soil
Is bare now, nor can foot feel, being shod.

And for all this, nature is never spent;
  There lives the dearest freshness deep down things;
And though the last lights off the black West went
  Oh, morning, at the brown brink eastward, springs—
Because the Holy Ghost over the bent
  World broods with warm breast and with ah! bright wings.

PIED BEAUTY

Glory be to God for dappled things—
  For skies of couple-color as a brindled cow;
    For rose-moles all in stipple upon trout that swim;
Fresh-firecoal chestnut-falls; finches' wings;
  Landscape plotted and pieced—fold, fallow, and plough;
    And all trades, their gear and tackle and trim.

All things counter, original, spare, strange;
  Whatever is fickle, freckled (who knows how?)
    With swift, slow; sweet, sour; adazzle, dim;
He fathers-forth whose beauty is past change:
          Praise him.

THOU ART INDEED JUST, LORD

Thou art indeed just, Lord, if I contend
With thee; but, sir, so what I plead is just.
Who do sinners' ways prosper? and why must
Disappointment all I endeavor end?
  Wert thou my enemy, O thou my friend,
How wouldst thou worse, I wonder, than thou dost
Defeat, thwart me? Oh, the sots and thralls of lust
Do in spare hours more thrive than I that spend,
Sir, life upon thy cause. See, banks and brakes
Now, leavèd how thick! lacèd they are again
With fretty chervil, look, and fresh wind shakes
Them; birds build—but not I build; no, but strain,
Time's eunuch, and not breed one work that wakes.
Mine, O thou lord of life, send my roots rain.

Alice Meynell

1850–1923

THE SHEPHERDESS

She walks—the lady of my delight—
A shepherdess of sheep.
Her flocks are thoughts. She keeps them white;
She guards them from the steep;
She feeds them on the fragrant height,
And folds them in for sleep.

She roams maternal hills and bright,
Dark valleys safe and deep.
Into that tender breast at night
The chastest stars may peep.
She walks—the lady of my delight—
A shepherdess of sheep.

She holds her little thoughts in sight,
Though gay they run and leap.
She is so circumspect and right;
She has her soul to keep.
She walks—the lady of my delight—
A shepherdess of sheep.

Francis Thompson

1857–1907

ARAB LOVE-SONG

The hunchèd camels of the night
Trouble the bright
And silver waters of the moon.
The maiden of the moon will soon
Through Heaven stray and sing,
Star gathering.
Now while the dark about our love is strewn,
Light of my dark, blood of my heart, O come!
And night will catch her breath up, and be dumb.

Leave thy father, leave thy mother
And thy brother;
Leave the black tents of thy tribe apart!
Am I not thy father and thy brother,
And thy mother?
And thou—what needest with thy tribe's black tents
Who hast the red pavilion of my heart?

DAISY

Where the thistle lifts a purple crown
Six foot out of the turf,
And the harebell shakes on the windy hill—
O the breath of the distant surf!—

The hills look over on the South,
And southward dreams the sea,
And with the sea-breeze hand in hand
Came innocence and she.

Where 'mid the gorse the raspberry
Red for the gatherer springs,
Two children did we stray and talk
Wise, idle, childish things.

She listened with big-lipped surprise,
Breast-deep 'mid flower and spine:
Her skin was like a grape, whose veins
Run snow instead of wine.

She knew not those sweet words she spake,
Nor knew her own sweet way;
But there's never a bird, so sweet a song
Thronged in whose throat that day.

Oh, there were flowers in Storrington
On the turf and on the spray;
But the sweetest flower on Sussex hills
Was the daisy-flower that day!

Her beauty smoothed earth's furrowed face
  She gave me tokens three:—
A look, a word of her winsome mouth,
  And a wild raspberry.

A berry red, a guileless look,
  A still word,—strings of sand!
And yet they made my wild, wild heart
  Fly down to her little hand.

For standing artless as the air,
  And candid as the skies,
She took the berries with her hand,
  And the love with her sweet eyes.

The fairest things have fleetest end,
  Their scent survives their close:
But the rose's scent is bitterness
  To him that loved the rose.

She looked a little wistfully,
  Then went her sunshine way:—
The sea's eye had a mist on it,
  And the leaves fell from the day.

She went her unremembering way,
  She went and left in me
The pang of all the partings gone
  And partings yet to be.

She left me marvelling why my soul
  Was sad that she was glad;
At all the sadness in the sweet,
  The sweetness in the sad.

Still, still I seemed to see her, still
  Look up with soft replies,
And take the berries with her hand,
  And the love with her lovely eyes.

Nothing begins, and nothing ends,
That is not paid with moan;
For we are born in others' pain,
And perish in our own.

Alfred Edward Housman

1859–1936

WITH RUE MY HEART IS LADEN

With rue my heart is laden
For golden friends I had.
For many a rose-lipt maiden
And many a lightfoot lad.

By brooks too broad for leaping
The lightfoot boys are laid;
The rose-lipt girls are sleeping
In fields where roses fade.

WHITE IN THE MOON

White in the moon the long road lies,
The moon stands blank above;
White in the moon the long road lies
That leads me from my love.

Still hangs the hedge without a gust,
Still, still the shadows stay:
My feet upon the moonlit dust
Pursue the ceaseless way.

The world is round, so travelers tell,
And straight though reach the track,
Trudge on, trudge on, 'twill all be well,
The way will guide one back.

But ere the circle homeward hies
Far, far it must remove:
White in the moon the long road lies
That leads me from my love.

LOVELIEST OF TREES

Loveliest of trees, the cherry now
Is hung with bloom along the bough,
And stands about the woodland ride
Wearing white for Eastertide.

Now, of my threescore years and ten,
Twenty will not come again,
And take from seventy springs a score,
It only leaves me fifty more.

And since to look at things in bloom
Fifty springs are little room,
About the woodlands I will go
To see the cherry hung with snow.

FAR IN A WESTERN BROOKLAND

Far in a western brookland
  That bred me long ago
The poplars stand and tremble
  By pools I used to know.

There, in the windless night-time,
  The wanderer, marveling why,
Halts on the bridge to hearken
  How soft the poplars sigh.

He hears: long since forgotten
  In fields where I was known,
Here I lie down in London
  And turn to rest alone.

There, by the starlit fences,
  The wanderer halts and hears
My soul that lingers sighing
  About the glimmering weirs.

Rudyard Kipling

1865–1936

RECESSIONAL

God of our fathers, known of old,
  Lord of our far-flung battle-line,
Beneath whose awful Hand we hold
  Dominion over palm and pine—
Lord God of Hosts, be with us yet,
Lest we forget—lest we forget!

The tumult and the shouting dies;
  The captains and the kings depart:
Still stands Thine ancient sacrifice,
  An humble and a contrite heart.
Lord God of Hosts, be with us yet,
Lest we forget—lest we forget!

Far-called, our navies melt away;
  On dune and headland sinks the fire:
Lo, all our pomp of yesterday
  Is one with Nineveh and Tyre!
Judge of the Nations, spare us yet,
Lest we forget—lest we forget!

If, drunk with sight of power, we loose
  Wild tongues that have not Thee in awe,
Such boastings as the Gentiles use,
  Or lesser breeds without the Law—
Lord God of Hosts, be with us yet,
Lest we forget—lest we forget!

For heathen heart that puts her trust
  In reeking tube and iron shard,
All valiant dust that builds on dust,
  And guarding, calls not Thee to guard,
For frantic boast and foolish word—
Thy Mercy on Thy People, Lord!

Amen.

Ernest Dowson

1867–1900

VITAE SUMMA BREVIS SPEM NOS VETAT INCOHARE LONGAM

They are not long, the weeping and the laughter,
  Love and desire and hate:
I think they have no portion in us after
  We pass the gate.

They are not long, the days of wine and roses:
  Out of a misty dream
Our path emerges for a while, then closes
  Within a dream.

NON SUM QUALIS ERAM BONAE SUB REGNO CYNARAE

Last night ah, yesternight, betwixt her lips and mine
There fell thy shadow, Cynara! thy breath was shed
Upon my soul between the kisses and the wine;
And I was desolate and sick of an old passion,
  Yea, I was desolate and bowed my head:
I have been faithful to thee, Cynara! in my fashion.

All night upon mine heart I felt her warm heart beat,
Night-long within mine arms in love and sleep she lay;
Surely the kisses of her bought red mouth were sweet;
But I was desolate and sick of an old passion,
  When I awoke and found the dawn was gray:
I have been faithful to thee, Cynara! in my fashion.

I have forgot much, Cynara! gone with the wind,
Flung roses, roses riotously with the throng,
Dancing, to put thy pale, lost lilies out of mind;
But I was desolate and sick of an old passion,
  Yea, all the time, because the dance was long:
I have been faithful to thee, Cynara! in my fashion.

I cried for madder music and for stronger wine,
But when the feast is finished and the lamps expire,
Then falls thy shadow, Cynara! the night is thine;
And I am desolate and sick of an old passion,
  Yea hungry for the lips of my desire:
I have been faithful to thee, Cynara! in my fashion.

William Henry Davies

1870–

LEISURE

WHAT is this life if, full of care,
We have no time to stand and stare.

No time to stand beneath the boughs
And stare as long as sheep or cows.

No time to see, when woods we pass,
Where squirrels hide their nuts in grass.

No time to see, in broad daylight,
Streams full of stars, like stars at night.

No time to turn at Beauty's glance,
And watch her feet, how they can dance.

No time to wait till her mouth can
Enrich that smile her eyes began.

A poor life this if, full of care,
We have no time to stand and stare.

Walter de la Mare

1873–

THE LISTENERS

"Is there anybody there?" said the Traveler,
  Knocking on the moonlit door;
And his horse in the silence champed the grasses
  Of the forest's ferny floor:

And a bird flew up out of the turret,
  Above the Traveler's head:
And he smote upon the door again a second time;
  "Is there anybody here?" he said.
But no one descended to the Traveler;
  No head from the leaf-fringed sill
Leaned over and looked into his gray eyes,
  Where he stood perplexed and still.
But only a host of phantom listeners
  That dwelt in the lone house then
Stood listening in the quiet of the moonlight
  To that voice from the world of men:
Stood thronging the faint moonbeams on the dark stair,
  That goes down to the empty hall,
Hearkening in the air stirred and shaken
  By the lonely Traveler's call.
And he felt in his heart their strangeness,
  Their stillness answering his cry,
While his horse moved, cropping the dark turf,
  'Neath the starred and leafy sky;
For he suddenly smote on the door, even
  Louder, and lifted his head:—
"Tell them I came, and no one answered,
  That I kept my word," he said.
Never the least stir made the listeners,
  Though every word he spake
Fell echoing through the shadowiness of the still house
  From the one man left awake:
Ay, they heard his foot upon the stirrup,
  And the sound of iron on stone,
And how the silence surged softly backward,
  When the plunging hoofs were gone.

John Masefield

1878–

SONNET

From Lollingdon Downs

Here in the self is all that man can know
Of Beauty, all the wonder, all the power,
All the unearthly color, all the glow,
Here in the self which withers like a flower;
Here in the self which fades as hours pass,
And droops and dies and rots and is forgotten
Sooner, by ages, than the mirroring glass
In which it sees its glory still unrotten.
Here in the flesh, within the flesh, behind,
Swift in the blood and throbbing on the bone,
Beauty herself, the universal mind,
Eternal April wandering alone;
The God, the holy Ghost, the atoning Lord,
Here in the flesh, the never yet explored.

Aldous Huxley

1894–

FIRST PHILOSOPHER'S SONG

A poor degenerate from the ape
Whose hands are four, whose tail's a limb,
I contemplate my flaccid shape
And know I may not rival him,

Save with my mind—a nimbler beast
Possessing a thousand sinewy tails,
A thousand hands, with which it scales,
Greedy of luscious truth, the greased

Poles and the coco palms of thought,
Thrids easily through the mangrove maze
Of metaphysics, walks the taut
Frail dangerous liana ways

That link across wide gulfs remote
Analogies between tree and tree;
Outruns the hare, outhops the goat;
Mind fabulous, mind sublime and free!

But oh, the sound of simian mirth!
Mind, issued from the monkey's womb,
Is still umbilical to earth,
Earth its home and earth its tomb.

Robert Graves

1895–

LOST LOVE

His eyes are quickened so with grief,
He can watch a grass or leaf
Every instant grow; he can
Clearly through a flint wall see,
Or watch the startled spirit flee
From the throat of a dead man.
Across two counties he can hear,
And catch your words before you speak.
The woodlouse or the maggot's weak
Clamor rings in his sad ear;
And noise so slight it would surpass
Credence:—drinking sound of grass,
Worm talk, clashing jaws of moth
Chumbling holes in cloth:
The groan of ants who undertake
Gigantic loads for honor's sake,
Their sinews creak, their breath comes thin;
Whir of spiders when they spin.
And minute whispering, mumbling, sighs
Of idle grubs and flies.
This man is quickened so with grief,
He wanders god-like or like thief
Inside and out, below, above,
Without relief seeking lost love.

PURE DEATH

This I admit, Death is terrible to me,
To no man more so, naturally,
And I have disenthralled my natural terror
Of every comfortable philosopher
Or tall dark doctor of divinity:
Death stands again in his true rank and order.

Therefore it was, when between you and me
Giving presents became a malady,
The exchange increasing surplus on each side
Till there was nothing but ungivable pride
That was not over-given, and this degree
Called a conclusion not to be denied,

That we at last bethought ourselves, made shift
And simultaneously this final gift
Gave. Each with shaking hands unlocks
The sinister, long, brass-bound coffin-box,
Unwraps pure Death, with such bewilderment
As greeted our love's first accomplishment.

THE COOL WEB

Children are dumb to say how hot the day is,
How hot the scent is of the summer rose,
How dreadful the black wastes of evening sky,
How dreadful the tall soldiers drumming by.

But we have speech, that cools the hottest sun,
And speech that dulls the hottest rose's scent.
We spell away the overhanging night,
We spell away the soldiers and the fright.

There's a cool web of language winds us in,
Retreat from too much gladness, too much fear:

We grow sea-green at last and coldly die
In brininess and volubility.

But if we let our tongues lose self-possession,
Throwing off language and its wateriness
Before our death, instead of when death comes,
Facing the brightness of the children's day,
Facing the rose, the dark sky and the drums,
We shall go mad no doubt and die that way.

Stephen Spender

1909–

THE PYLONS

The secret of these hills was stone, and cottages
Of that stone made,
And crumbling roads
That turned on sudden hidden villages.

Now over these small hills they have built the concrete
That trails black wire:
Pylons, those pillars
Bare like nude, giant girls that have no secret.

The valley with its gilt and evening look
And the green chestnut
Of customary root
Are mocked dry like the parched bed of a brook.

But far above and far as sight endures
Like whips of anger
With lightning's danger
There runs the quick perspective of the future.

This dwarfs our emerald country by its trek
So tall with prophecy:
Dreaming of cities
Where often clouds shall lean their swan-white neck.

NEW YEAR

Here at the center of the turning year,
The turning Polar North,
The frozen streets, and the black fiery joy
Of the Child launched again forth,
I ask that all the years and years
Of future disappointment, like a snow
Chide me at one fall now.

I leave him who burns endlessly
In the brandy pudding crowned with holly,
And I ask that Time should freeze my skin
And all my fellow travellers harden
Who are not flattered by this town
Nor up its twenty storeys whirled
To prostitutes without infection.

Cloak us in accidents and in the failure
Of the high altar and marital adventure;
In family disgrace, denunciation
Of bankers, a premier's assassination.
From the government windows
Let heads of headlines watch depart,
Strangely depart by staying, those

Who build a new world in their heart.
Where scythe shall curve but not upon our neck
And lovers proceed to their forgetting work,
Answering the harvests of obliteration.
After the frozen years and streets
Our tempered will shall plough across the nations.
The engine hurrying through the lucky valley
The hand that moves to guide the silent lines
Effect their beauty without robbery.

IRISH

From the Gaelic

Colum-Cille

6th century

(Attributed)

FAREWELL TO IRELAND

Alas for the voyage, O High King of Heaven,
Enjoined upon me,
For that I on the red plain of bloody Cooldrevin
Was present to see.

How happy the son is of Dima; no sorrow
For him is designed,
He is having, this hour, round his own hill in Durrow,
The wish of his mind.

The sounds of the winds in the elms, like strings of
A harp being played,
The note of a blackbird that claps with the wings of
Delight in the shade.

With him in Ros-Grencha the cattle are lowing
At earliest dawn,
On the brink of the summer the pigeons are cooing
And doves in the lawn.

Three things am I leaving behind me, the very
Most dear that I know,
Tir-Leedach I'm leaving, and Durrow and Derry;
Alas, I must go!

Yet my visit and feasting with Comgall have eased me
At Cainneach's right hand,
And all but thy government, Eiré, have pleased me,
Thou waterful land.

(Douglas Hyde)

Hugh O'Donnell

16th century

(Attributed)

DARK ROSALEEN

O my dark Rosaleen,
  Do not sigh, do not weep!
The priests are on the ocean green,
  They march along the deep.
There's wine from the royal Pope,
  Upon the ocean green;
And Spanish ale shall give you hope,
  My dark Rosaleen!
  My own Rosaleen!
Shall glad your heart, shall give you hope,
Shall give you health and help, and hope,
  My Dark Rosaleen.

Over hills, and through dales,
  Have I roamed for your sake;
All yesterday I sailed with sails
  On river and on lake.
The Erne, at its highest flood,
  I dashed across unseen,
For there was lightning in my blood,
  My dark Rosaleen!
  My own Rosaleen!
Oh! there was lightning in my blood,
Red lightning lightened through my blood,
  My Dark Rosaleen!

All day long in unrest,
  To and fro do I move,
The very soul within my breast
  Is wasted for you, love!
The heart in my bosom faints
  To think of you, my Queen,

My life of life, my saint of saints,
  My dark Rosaleen!
  My own Rosaleen!
To hear your sweet and sad complaints,
My life, my love, my saint of saints,
  My Dark Rosaleen!

Woe and pain, pain and woe,
  Are my lot, night and noon,
To see your bright face clouded so,
  Like to the mournful moon.
But yet will I rear your throne
  Again in golden sheen;
'Tis you shall reign, shall reign alone,
  My dark Rosaleen!
  My own Rosaleen!
'Tis you shall have the golden throne,
'Tis you shall reign, shall reign alone,
  My Dark Rosaleen!

Over dews, over sands,
  Will I fly for your weal:
Your holy, delicate white hands
  Shall girdle me with steel.
At home in your emerald bowers,
  From morning's dawn till e'en,
You'll pray for me, my flower of flowers,
  My dark Rosaleen!
  My fond Rosaleen!
You'll think of me through daylight's hours,
My virgin flower, my flower of flowers,
  My Dark Rosaleen!

I could scale the blue air,
  I could plow the high hills,
Oh, I could kneel all night in prayer,
  To heal your many ills!
And one beamy smile from you
  Would float like light between

My toils and me, my own, my true,
  My dark Rosaleen!
  My fond Rosaleen!
Would give me life and soul anew,
A second life, a soul anew,
  My Dark Rosaleen!

O! the Erne shall run red
  With redundance of blood,
The earth shall rock beneath our tread,
  And flames wrap hill and wood,
And gun-peal, and slogan cry
  Wake many a glen serene,
Ere you shall fade, ere you shall die,
  My dark Rosaleen!
  My own Rosaleen!
The Judgment Hour must first be nigh
Ere you can fade, ere you can die,
  My Dark Rosaleen!

(James Clarence Mangan)

O'Gnive

16th century

THE DOWNFALL OF THE GAEL

My heart is in woe,
And my soul deep in trouble,—
For the mighty are low,
And abased are the noble:

The Sons of the Gael
Are in exile and mourning,
Worn, weary, and pale
As spent pilgrims returning;

Or men who, in flight
From the field of disaster,
Beseech the black night
On their flight to fall faster;

Or seamen aghast
When their planks gape asunder,
And the waves fierce and fast
Tumble through in hoarse thunder;

Or men whom we see
That have got their death-omen,—
Such wretches are we
In the chains of our foemen!

Our courage is fear,
Our nobility vileness,
Our hope is despair,
And our comeliness foulness.

There is mist on our heads,
And a cloud chill and hoary
Of black sorrow, sheds
An eclipse on our glory.

From Boyne to the Linn
Has the mandate been given,
That the children of Finn
From their country be driven.

That the sons of the king—
Oh, the treason and malice!—
Shall no more ride the ring
In their own native valleys;

No more shall repair
Where the hill foxes tarry,
Nor forth to the air
Fling the hawk at her quarry:

For the plain shall be broke
By the share of the stranger,
And the stone-mason's stroke
Tell the woods of their danger;

The green hills and shore
Be with white keeps disfigured,
And the Mote of Rathmore
Be the Saxon churl's haggard!

The land of the lakes
Shall no more know the prospect
Of valleys and brakes—
So transformed is her aspect!

The Gael cannot tell,
In the uprooted wildwood
And the red ridgy dell,
The old nurse of his childhood:

The nurse of his youth
Is in doubt as she views him,
If the wan wretch, in truth,
Be the child of her bosom.

We starve by the board,
And we thirst amid wassail—
For the guest is the lord,
And the host is the vassal.

Through the woods let us roam,
Through the wastes wild and barren;
We are strangers at home!
We are exiles in Erin!

And Erin's a bark
O'er the wide waters driven!
And the tempest howls dark,
And her side planks are riven!

And in billows of might
Swell the Saxon before her,—
Unite, oh, unite!
Or the billows burst o'er her!

(Sir Samuel Ferguson)

Egan O'Rahilly

18th century

LAMENT FOR BANBA

O MY land! O my love!
What a woe, and how deep,
Is thy death to my long mourning soul!
God alone, God above,
Can awake thee from sleep,
Can release thee from bondage and dole!
Alas, alas, and alas!
For the once proud people of Banba!

As a tree in its prime,
Which the ax layeth low,
Didst thou fall, O unfortunate land!
Not by time, nor thy crime,
Came the shock and the blow.
They were given by a false felon hand!
Alas, alas, and alas!
For the once proud people of Banba!

O, my grief of all griefs
Is to see how thy throne
Is usurped, whilst thyself art in thrall!
Other lands have their chiefs,
Have their kings, thou alone
Art a wife, yet a widow withal!
Alas, alas, and alas!
For the once proud people of Banba!

The high house of O'Neill
Is gone down to the dust,
The O'Brien is clanless and banned;
And the steel, the red steel
May no more be the trust
Of the Faithful and Brave in the land!
Alas, alas, and alas!
For the once proud people of Banba!

True, alas! Wrong and Wrath
Were of old all too rife.
Deeds were done which no good man admires
And perchance Heaven hath
Chastened us for the strife
And the blood-shedding ways of our sires!
Alas, alas, and alas!
For the once proud people of Banba!

But, no more! This our doom,
While our hearts yet are warm,
Let us not over weakly deplore!
For the hour soon may loom
When the Lord's mighty hand
Shall be raised for our rescue once more!
And all our grief shall be turned into joy
For the still proud people of Banba!

(James Clarence Mangan)

Raferty

d. 1835

I AM RAFERTY

I AM Raferty the Poet
Full of hope and love,
With eyes that have no light,
With gentleness that has no misery.

Going west upon my pilgrimage
By the light of my heart,
Feeble and tired
To the end of my road.

Behold me now,
And my face to the wall,
A-playing music
Unto empty pockets.

(Douglas Hyde)

Anonymous

A POEM TO BE SAID ON HEARING THE BIRDS SING

A FRAGRANT prayer upon the air
My child taught me,
Awaken there, the morn is fair,
The birds sing free;
Now dawns the day, awake and pray,
And bend the knee;
The Lamb who lay beneath the clay
Was slain for thee.

(Douglas Hyde)

Thomas Moore

1779–1852

HOW OFT HAS THE BANSHEE CRIED

How oft has the Banshee cried!
How oft has death untied
Bright links that Glory wove.
Sweet bonds entwined by Love!
Peace to each manly soul that sleepeth;
Rest to each faithful eye that weepeth;
Long may the fair and brave
Sigh o'er the hero's grave!

We're fallen on evil days!
Star after star decays,
Every bright name that shed
Light o'er the land is fled.
Dark falls the tear of him that mourneth
Lost joy, or hope that ne'er returneth:
But brightly flows the tear
Wept o'er a hero's bier.

Quenched are our beacon lights—
Thou, of the Hundred Fights!
Thou, on whose burning tongue
Truth, peace and freedom hung!
Both mute—but long as valor shineth,
Or mercy's soul at war repineth,
So long shall Erin's pride
Tell how they lived and died.

Anonymous

THE WEARIN' O' THE GREEN

Oh, Paddy dear! and did ye hear the news that's goin' round?
The shamrock is forbid by law to grow on Irish ground!
No more St. Patrick's day we'll keep; his color can't be seen,
For there's a cruel law ag'in' the Wearin' o' the Green!

I met with Napper Tandy, and he took me by the hand,
And he said, "How's poor ould Ireland, and how does she stand?"
"She's the most distressful country that ever yet was seen,
For they're hanging men and women there for the Wearin' o' the Green."

An' if the color we must wear is England's cruel red,
Let it remind us of the blood that Ireland has shed;
Then pull the shamrock from your hat, and throw it on the sod,
An' never fear, 'twill take root there, though under foot 'tis trod.

When law can stop the blades of grass from growin' as they grow,
An' when the leaves in summer time their color dare not show,

Then I will change the color, too, I wear in my caubeen;
But till that day, plaise God, I'll stick to the Wearin' o' the Green.

Katherine Tynan

1861–1931

THE DOVES

The house where I was born,
Where I was young and gay,
Grows old amid its corn,
Amid its scented hay.

Moan of the cushat dove,
In silence rich and deep;
The old head I love
Nods to its quiet sleep.

Where once were nine and ten
Now two keep house together;
The doves moan and complain
All day in the still weather.

What wind, bitter and great,
Has swept the country's face,
Altered, made desolate
The heart-remembered place?

What wind, bitter and wild,
Has swept the towering trees
Beneath whose shade a child
Long since gathered heartease?

Under the golden eaves
The house is still and sad,
As though it grieves and grieves
For many a lass and lad.

The cushat doves complain
All day in the still weather;
Where once were nine or ten
But two keep house together.

William Butler Yeats

1865–

TO AN ISLE IN THE WATER

Shy one, shy one,
Shy one of my heart,
She moves in the firelight
Pensively apart.

She carries in the dishes,
And lays them in a row.
To an isle in the water
With her would I go.

She carries in the candles,
And lights the curtained room,
Shy in the doorway
And shy in the gloom;

And shy as a rabbit,
Helpful and shy.
To an isle in the water
With her would I fly.

WHEN YOU ARE OLD

When you are old and gray and full of sleep,
And nodding by the fire, take down this book,
And slowly read, and dream of the soft look
Your eyes had once, and of their shadows deep;

How many loved your moments of glad grace,
And loved your beauty with love false or true;

But one man loved the pilgrim soul in you,
And loved the sorrows of your changing face.

And bending down beside the glowing bars
Murmur, a little sadly, how love fled
And paced upon the mountains overhead
And hid his face amid a crowd of stars.

THE EVERLASTING VOICES

O sweet everlasting Voices be still;
Go to the guards of the heavenly fold
And bid them wander obeying your will
Flame under flame, till Time be no more;
Have you not heard that our hearts are old,
That you call in birds, in wind on the hill,
In shaken boughs, in tide on the shore?
O sweet everlasting Voices be still.

THE COLD HEAVEN

Suddenly I saw the cold and rook-delighting Heaven
That seemed as though ice burned and was but the more ice,
And thereupon imagination and heart were driven
So wild that every casual thought of that and this
Vanished, and left but memories, that should be out of season
With the hot blood of youth, of love crossed long ago;
And I took all the blame out of all sense and reason,
Until I cried and trembled and rocked to and fro,
Riddled with light. Ah! when the ghost begins to quicken,
Confusion of the death-bed over, is it sent
Out naked on the roads, as the books say, and stricken
By the injustice of the skies for punishment?

TO A FRIEND WHOSE WORK HAS COME TO NOTHING

Now all the truth is out,
Be secret and take defeat
From any brazen throat,
For how can you compete,
Being honor bred, with one
Who, were it proved he lies
Were neither shamed in his own
Nor in his neighbors' eyes?
Bred to a harder thing
Than Triumph, turn away
And like a laughing string
Whereon mad fingers play
Amid a place of stone,
Be secret and exult,
Because of all things known
That is most difficult.

George William Russell ("A. E.")

1867–1935

A MOUNTAIN WIND

The cold limbs of the air
Brush by me on the hill,
Climb to the utmost crag,
Leap out, then all is still.

Ah, but what high intent
In the cold will of wind;
What scepter would it grasp
To leave these dreams behind!

Trail of celestial things:
White centaurs, winged in flight,
Through the fired heart sweep on,
A hurricane of light.

I have no plumes for air:
Earth hugs to it my bones.
Leave me, O sky-born powers,
Brother to grass and stones.

A HOLY HILL

Be still: be still: nor dare
Unpack what you have brought,
Nor loosen on this air
Red gnomes of your thought.

Uncover: bend the head
And let the feet be bare;
This air that thou breathest
Is holy air.

Sin not against the Breath,
Using ethereal fire
To make seem as faery
A wanton desire.

Know that this granite height
May be a judgment throne,
Dread thou the unmovable will,
The wrath of stone.

THE LONELY

Lone and forgotten
Through a long sleeping,
In the heart of age
A child woke weeping.

No invisible mother
Was nigh him there
Laughing and nodding
From earth and air.

No elfin comrades
Came at his call,
And the earth and the air
Were blank as a wall.

The darkness thickened
Upon him creeping,
In the heart of age
A child lay weeping.

IMMORTALITY

We must pass like smoke or live within the spirit's fire;
For we can no more than smoke unto the flame return
If our thought has changed to dream, our will unto desire,
As smoke we vanish though the fire may burn.

Lights of infinite pity star the gray dusk of our days:
Surely here is soul: with it we have eternal breath:
In the fire of love we live, or pass by many ways,
By unnumbered ways of dream to death.

John Millington Synge

1871–1909

PRELUDE

Still south I went and west and south again,
Through Wicklow from the morning till the night,
And far from cities, and the sights of men,
Lived with the sunshine and the moon's delight.

I knew the stars, the flowers, and the birds,
The gray and wintry sides of many glens,
And did but half remember human words,
In converse with the mountains, moors, and fens.

IN KERRY

We heard the thrushes by the shore and sea,
And saw the golden stars' nativity,
Then round we went the lane by Thomas Flynn,
Across the church where bones lie out and in;
And there I asked beneath a lonely cloud
Of strange delight, with one bird singing loud,
What change you'd wrought in graveyard, rock and sea,
This new wild paradise to wake for me. . . .
Yet knew no more than knew those merry sins
Had built this stack of thigh-bones, jaws and shins.

Moira O'Neill

CORRYMEELA

Over here in England I'm helpin' wi' the hay,
And I wisht I was in Ireland the livelong day;
Weary on the English hay, an' sorra take the wheat!
Och! Corrymeela, an' the blue sky over it.

There's a deep dumb river flowin' by beyont the heavy trees,
This livin' air is moithered wi' the hummin' o' the bees;
I wisht I'd hear the Claddagh burn go runnin' through the heat,
Past Corrymeela, wi' the blue sky over it.

The people that's in England is richer nor the Jews,
There's not the smallest young gossoon but thravels in his shoes!
I'd give the pipe between me teeth to see a barefut child,
Och! Corrymeela, an' the low south wind.

Here's hands so full o' money an' hearts so full o' care,
By the luck o' love! I'd still go light for all I did go bare.
"God save ye, colleen dhas," I said; the girl she thought me wild!
Fair Corrymeela, an' the low south wind.

D'ye mind me now, the song at night is mortal hard to raise,
The girls are heavy goin' here, the boys are ill to plase;
When ones't I'm out this workin' hive, 'tis I'll be back again—
Aye, Corrymeela, in the same soft rain.

The puff o' smoke from one ould roof before an English town!
For a *shaugh* wid Andy Feelan here I'd give a silver crown,
For a curl o' hair like Mollie's ye'll ask the like in vain,
Sweet Corrymeela, an' the same soft rain.

Thomas MacDonagh

1878–1916

JOHN-JOHN

I DREAMT last night of you, John-John,
And thought you called to me;
And when I woke this morni
Yourself I hoped to see
But I was all alone,
Though still I hea
I put my boots an
And took my S
And went full s
At Nen

The fair wa
Five years
When firs
And cam
For the
And s
And
Of
B

I turned my face to home again,
And called myself a fool
To think you'd leave the thimble-men
And live again by rule,
To go to mass and keep the fast
And till the little patch;
My wish to have you home was past
Before I raised the latch
And pushed the door and saw you, John,
Sitting down there.

How cool you came in here, begad,
As if you owned the place!
But rest yourself there now, my lad,
'Tis good to see your face;
My dream is out, and now by it
I think I know my mind:
At six o'clock this house you'll quit,
And leave no grief behind;—
But until six o'clock, John-John,
My bit you'll share.

The neighbors' shame of me began
When first I brought you in;
To wed and keep a tinker man
They thought a kind of sin;
But now this three years since you've gone
'Tis pity me they do,
And that I'd rather have, John-John,
Than that they'd pity you,
Pity for me and you, John-John,
I could not bear.

Oh, you're my husband right enough,
ut what's the good of that?
u know you never were the stuff
e the cottage cat,
tch the fire and hear me lock
r and put out Shep—

But there, now, it is six o'clock
And time for you to step.
God bless and keep you far, John-John!
And that's my prayer.

Seumas O'Sullivan

1878–

THE STARLING LAKE

My sorrow that I am not by the little dún
By the lake of the starlings at Rosses under the hill,
And the larks there, singing over the fields of dew,
Or evening there and the sedges still.
For plain I see now the length of the yellow sand,
And Lissadell far off and its leafy ways,
And the holy mountain whose mighty heart
Gathers into it all the colored days.
My sorrow that I am not by the little dún
By the lake of the starlings at evening when all is still,
And still in whispering sedges the herons stand.
'Tis there I would nestle at rest till the quivering moon
Uprose in the golden quiet over the hill.

Padraic Pearse

1880–1916

IDEAL

Naked I saw thee,
O beauty of beauty!
And I blinded my eyes
For fear I should flinch.

I heard thy music,
O sweetness of sweetness!
And I shut my ears
For fear I should fail.

I kissed thy lips
O sweetness of sweetness!
And I hardened my heart
For fear of my ruin.

I blinded my eyes
And my ears I shut,
I hardened my heart
And my love I quenched.

I turned my back
On the dream I had shaped,
And to this road before me
My face I turned.

I set my face
To the road here before me,
To the work that I see,
To the death that I shall meet.

(Translated from the Gaelic by Thomas MacDonagh)

Padraic Colum

1881–

RIVER-MATES

I'll be an otter, and I'll let you swim
A mate beside me; we will venture down
A deep, dark river, when the sky above
Is shut of the sun; spoilers are we,
Thick-coated; no dog's tooth can bite at our veins,
With eyes and ears of poachers; deep-earthed ones
Turned hunters; let him slip past
The little vole; my teeth are on an edge
For the King-fish of the River!

I hold him up
The glittering salmon that smells of the sea;
I hold him high and whistle!

Now we go
Back to our earths; we will tear and eat
Sea-smelling salmon; you will tell the cubs
I am the Booty-bringer, I am the Lord
Of the River; the deep, dark, full and flowing River!

A DROVER

To Meath of the pastures,
From wet hills by the sea,
Through Leitrim and Longford
Go my cattle and me.

I hear in the darkness
Their slipping and breathing.
I name them the bye-ways
They're to pass without heeding.

Then the wet, winding roads,
Brown bogs with black water;
And my thoughts on white ships
And the King o' Spain's daughter.

O! farmer, strong farmer!
You can spend at the fair
But your face you must turn
To your crops and your care.

And soldiers—red soldiers!
You've seen many lands;
But you walk two by two,
And by captain's commands.

O! the smell of the beasts,
The wet wind in the morn;
And the proud and hard earth
Never broken for corn;

And the crowds at the fair,
The herds loosened and blind,
Loud words and dark faces
And the wild blood behind.

(O! strong men with your best
I would strive breast to breast
I could quiet your herds
With my words, with my words.)

I will bring you, my kine,
Where there's grass to the knee;
But you'll think of scant croppings
Harsh with salt of the sea.

Joseph Campbell

1881–

THE BLIND MAN AT THE FAIR

O to be blind!
To know the darkness that I know.
The stir I hear is empty wind,
The people idly come and go.

The sun is black, tho' warm and kind,
The horsemen ride, the streamers blow
Vainly in the fluky wind,
For all is darkness where I go.

The cattle bellow to their kind,
The mummers dance, the jugglers throw,
The thimble-rigger speaks his mind—
But all is darkness where I go.

I feel the touch of womankind,
Their dresses flow as white as snow;
But beauty is a withered rind
For all is darkness where I go.

Last night the moon of Lammas shined,
Rising high and setting low;

But light is nothing to the blind—
All, all is darkness where they go.

White roads I walk with vacant mind,
White cloud-shapes round me drifting slow,
White lilies waving in the wind—
And darkness everywhere I go.

THE OLD WOMAN

As a white candle
  In a holy place,
So is the beauty
  Of an aged face.

As the spent radiance
  Of the winter sun,
So is a woman
  With her travail done.

Her brood gone from her,
  And her thoughts as still
As the waters
  Under a ruined mill.

James Stephens

1882–

DEIRDRE

Do not let any woman read this verse;
It is for men, and after them their sons
And their sons' sons.

The time comes when our hearts sink utterly;
When we remember Deirdre and her tale,
And that her lips are dust.

Once she did tread the earth; men took her
    hand;
They looked into her eyes and said their say,
And she replied to them.

More than a thousand years it is since she
Was beautiful: she trod the living grass;
She saw the clouds.

A thousand years! The grass is still the same,
The clouds as lovely as they were that time
When Deirdre was alive.

But there has never been a woman born
Who was so beautiful, not one so beautiful
Of all the women born.

Let all men go apart and mourn together;
No man can ever love her; not a man
Can ever be her lover.

No man can bend before her; no man say—
What could one say to her? There are no words
That one could say to her!

Now she is but a story that is told
Beside the fire! No man can ever be
The friend of that poor queen.

THE DAISIES

In the scented bud of the morning—O,
  When the windy grass went rippling far,
I saw my dear one walking slow,
  In the field where the daisies are.

We did not laugh and we did not speak
  As we wandered happily to and fro;
I kissed my dear on either cheek,
  In the bud of the morning—O.

A lark sang up from the breezy land,
  A lark sang down from a cloud afar,
And she and I went hand in hand
  In the field where the daisies are.

THE GOAT PATHS

THE crooked paths go every way
Upon the hill—they wind about
Through the heather in and out
Of the quiet sunniness.
And there the goats, day after day,
Stray in sunny quietness,
Cropping here and cropping there,
As they pause and turn and pass,
Now a bit of heather spray,
Now a mouthful of the grass.

In the deeper sunniness,
In the place where nothing stirs,
Quietly in quietness,
In the quiet of the furze,
For a time they come and lie
Staring on the roving sky.

If you approach they run away,
They leap and stare, away they bound,
With a sudden angry sound,
To the sunny quietude;
Crouching down where nothing stirs
In the silence of the furze,
Crouching down again to brood
In the sunny solitude.

If I were as wise as they,
I would stray apart and brood,
I would beat a hidden way
Through the quiet heather spray
To a sunny solitude;

And should you come I'd run away,
I would make an angry sound,
I would stare and turn and bound
To the deeper quietude,
To the place where nothing stirs
In the silence of the furze.

In that airy quietness
I would think as long as they;
Through the quiet sunniness
I would stray away to brood
By a hidden, beaten way
In the sunny solitude,

I would think until I found
Something I can never find,
Something lying on the ground,
In the bottom of my mind.

James Joyce

1882–

I HEAR AN ARMY

I hear an army charging upon the land,
And the thunder of horses plunging, foam about their knees:
Arrogant, in black armor, behind them stand,
Disdaining the reins, with fluttering whips, the charioteers.

They cry unto the night their battle-name:
I moan in sleep when I hear afar their whirling laughter.
They cleave the gloom of dreams, a blinding flame,
Clanging, clanging upon my heart as upon an anvil.

They come shaking in triumph their long, green hair:
They come out of the sea and run shouting by the shore.
My heart, have you no wisdom thus to despair?
My love, my love, my love, why have you left me alone?

Joseph Plunkett

1887–1916

THE SPARK

Because I used to shun
Death and the mouth of hell

And count my battles won
If I should see the sun
The blood and smoke dispel,

Because I used to pray
That living I might see
The dawning light of day
Set me upon my way
And from my fetters free,

Because I used to seek
Your answer to my prayer
And that your soul should speak
For strengthening of the weak
To struggle with despair,

Now I have seen my shame
That I should thus deny
My soul's divinest flame,
Now shall I shout your name,
Now shall I seek to die

By any hands but these
In battle or in flood,
On any lands or seas,
No more shall I spare ease,
No more shall I spare blood

When I have need to fight
For heaven or for your heart,
Against the powers of light
Or darkness I shall smite
Until their might depart,

Because I know the spark
Of God has no eclipse,
Now Death and I embark
And sail into the dark
With laughter on our lips.

Francis Ledwidge

1891–1917

LAMENT FOR THE POETS: 1916

I HEARD the Poor Old Woman say:
"At break of day the fowler came,
And took my blackbirds from their songs
Who loved me well thro' shame and blame.

No more from lovely distances
Their songs shall bless me mile by mile,
Nor to white Ashbourne call me down
To wear my crown another while.

With bended flowers the angels mark
For the skylark the place they lie,
From there its little family
Shall dip their wings first in the sky.

And when the first surprise of flight
Sweet songs excite, from the far dawn
Shall there come blackbirds loud with love,
Sweet echoes of the singers gone.

But in the lonely hush of eve
Weeping I grieve the silent bills."
I heard the Poor Old Woman say
In Derry of the little hills.

ARDAN MÓR

As I was climbing Ardan Mór
From the shore of Sheelin lake,
I met the herons coming down
Before the water's wake.

And they were talking in their flight
Of dreamy ways the herons go
When all the hills are withered up
Nor any waters flow.

AMERICAN

From the American Indian

LOVE SONG (Papago)

Early I rose
In the blue morning;
My love was up before me,
It came running up to me from the doorways of the Dawn.

On Papago Mountain
The dying quarry
Looked at me with my love's eyes.

(Mary Austin)

NEITHER SPIRIT NOR BIRD (Shoshone)

Neither spirit nor bird;
That was my flute you heard
Last night by the river.
When you came with your wicker jar
Where the river drags the willows,
That was my flute you heard,
Wacoba, Wacoba,
Calling, Come to the willows!

Neither the wind nor a bird
Rustled the lupine blooms.
That was my blood you heard
Answer your garment's hem
Whispering through the grasses;
That was my blood you heard
By the wild rose under the willows.

That was no beast that stirred,
That was my heart you heard,
Pacing to and fro
In the ambush of my desire,
To the music my flute let fall.
Wacoba, Wacoba,
That was my heart you heard
Leaping under the willows.

(Mary Austin)

COME NOT NEAR MY SONGS (Shoshone)

Come not near my songs,
You who are not my lover,
Lest from out that ambush
Leaps my heart upon you!

When my songs are glowing
As an almond thicket
With the bloom upon it,
Lies my heart in ambush
All amid my singing;
Come not near my songs,
You who are not my lover!

Do not hear my songs,
You who are not my lover!
Over-sweet the heart is,
Where my love has bruised it,
Breathe you not that fragrance,
You who are not my lover.
Do not stoop above my song,
With its languor on you,
Lest from out my singing
Leaps my heart upon you!

(Mary Austin)

LAMENT OF A MAN FOR HIS SON (Paiute)

Son, my son!
I will go up to the mountain
And there I will light a fire

To the feet of my son's spirit,
And there will I lament him;
Saying,
O my son,
What is my life to me, now you are departed?

Son, my son,
In the deep earth
We softly laid thee
In a chief's robe,
In a warrior's gear.
Surely there,
In the spirit land
Thy deeds attend thee!
Surely,
The corn comes to the ear again!
But I, here,
I am the stalk that the seed-gatherers
Descrying empty, afar, left standing.
Son, my son!
What is my life to me, now you are departed?

(Mary Austin)

THE GRASS ON THE MOUNTAIN (Paiute)

Oh, long, long
The snow has possessed the mountains.

The deer have come down and the big-horn,
They have followed the Sun to the south
To feed on the mesquite pods and the bunch grass.
Loud are the thunder drums
In the tents of the mountains.
Oh, long, long
Have we eaten chia seeds
And dried deer's flesh of the summer killing.
We are wearied of our huts
And the smoky smell of our garments.

We are sick with desire of the sun
And the grass on the mountain.

(Mary Austin)

HUNTING-SONG (Navaho)

COMES the deer to my singing,
Comes the deer to my song,
Comes the deer to my singing.

He, the blackbird, he am I,
Bird beloved of the wild deer,
Comes the deer to my singing.

From the Mountain Black,
From the summit,
Down the trail, coming, coming now,
Comes the deer to my singing.

Through the blossoms,
Through the flowers, coming, coming now,
Comes the deer to my singing.

Through the flower dew-drops,
Coming, coming now,
Comes the deer to my singing.

Through the pollen, flower pollen,
Coming, coming now,
Comes the deer to my singing.

Starting with his left fore-foot,
Stamping, turns the frightened deer.
Comes the deer to my singing.

Quarry mine, blessed am I
In the luck of the chase.
Comes the deer to my singing.

Comes the deer to my singing,
Comes the deer to my song,
Comes the deer to my singing.

(Natalie Curtis)

SONG OF THE HORSE (Navaho)

How joyous his neigh!
Lo, the Turquoise Horse of Johano-ai,
How joyous his neigh!
There on precious hides outspread standeth he;
How joyous his neigh!
There on tips of fair fresh flowers feedeth he;
How joyous his neigh!
There of mingled waters holy drinketh he;
How joyous his neigh!
There he spurneth dust of glittering grains;
How joyous his neigh!
There in mist of sacred pollen hidden, all hidden he;
How joyous his neigh!
There his offspring may grow and thrive for evermore;
How joyous his neigh!

(Natalie Curtis)

SONG OF THE RAIN CHANT (Navaho)

Far as man can see,
Comes the rain,
Comes the rain with me.

From the Rain-Mount,
Rain-Mount far away,
Comes the rain,
Comes the rain with me.

'Mid the lightnings,
'Mid the lightning zigzag,
'Mid the lightning flashing,
Comes the rain,
Comes the rain with me.

'Mid the swallows,
'Mid the swallows blue,
Chirping glad together,
Comes the rain,
Comes the rain with me.

Through the pollen,
Through the pollen blest,
All in pollen hidden
Comes the rain,
Comes the rain with me.

Far as man can see,
Comes the rain,
Comes the rain with me.

(Natalie Curtis)

KOROSTA KATZINA SONG (Hopi)

1

YELLOW butterflies
Over the blossoming virgin corn,
With pollen-painted faces
Chase one another in brilliant throng.

2

Blue butterflies
Over the blossoming virgin beans,
With pollen-painted faces
Chase one another in brilliant streams.

3

Over the blossoming corn,
Over the virgin corn
Wild bees hum;
Over the blossoming corn,
Over the virgin beans
Wild bees hum.

4

Over your field of growing corn
All day shall hang the thunder-cloud;
Over your field of growing corn
All day shall come the rushing rain.

(Natalie Curtis)

CORN-GRINDING SONG (Laguna)

Butterflies, butterflies,
Now fly away to the blossoms,
Fly, blue-wing,
Fly, yellow-wing,
Now fly away to the blossoms,
Fly, red-wing,
Fly, white-wing,
Now fly away to the blossoms,
Butterflies, away!
Butterflies, butterflies,
Now fly away to the blossoms.
Butterflies, away!

(Natalie Curtis)

THE VOICE THAT BEAUTIFIES THE LAND (Navaho)

1

The voice that beautifies the land!
The voice above,
The voice of the thunder,
Among the dark clouds
Again and again it sounds,
The voice that beautifies the land.

2

The voice that beautifies the land!
The voice below,
The voice of the grasshopper,
Among the flowers and grasses
Again and again it sounds,
The voice that beautifies the land.

(Washington Matthews)

SONG TO THE MOUNTAINS (Pawnee)

1

Mountains loom upon the path we take;
Yonder peak now rises sharp and clear;
Behold! It stands with its head uplifted,
Thither we go, since our way lies there.

2

Mountains loom upon the path we take;
Yonder peak now rises sharp and clear;
Behold! We climb, drawing near its summit;
Steeper grows the way and slow our steps.

3

Mountains loom upon the path we take;
Yonder peak that rises sharp and clear,
Behold us now on its head uplifted;
Planting there our feet, we stand secure.

4

Mountains loom upon the path we take;
Yonder peak that rose so sharp and clear,
Behold us now on its head uplifted;
Resting there at last we sing our song.

(Alice C. Fletcher)

A LOVER'S LAMENT (Tewa)

My little breath, under the willows by the water-side we used to sit,
And there the yellow cottonwood bird came and sang.
That I remember and therefore I weep.
Under the growing corn we used to sit,
And there the little leaf bird came and sang.
That I remember and therefore I weep.
There on the meadow of yellow flowers we used to walk.
Alas! how long ago that we two walked in that pleasant way.

Then everything was happy, but alas! how long ago.
There on the meadow of crimson flowers we used to walk.
Oh, my little breath, now I go there alone in sorrow.

(H. J. Spinden)

THE COYOTE AND THE LOCUST (Zuñi)

LOCUST, locust, playing a flute,
Locust, locust, playing a flute!
Away up on the pine-tree bough,
Closely clinging,
Playing a flute,
Playing a flute!

(Frank Cushing)

OJIBWA WAR SONGS

1

HEAR my voice, Birds of War!
I prepare a feast for you to feed on;
I see you cross the enemy's lines;
Like you I shall go.
I wish the swiftness of your wings;
I wish the vengeance of your claws;
I muster my friends;
I follow your flight.
Ho, you young men warriors,
Bear your angers to the place of fighting!

2

From the south they came, Birds of War—
Hark! to their passing scream.
I wish the body of the fiercest,
As swift, as cruel, as strong.
I cast my body to the chance of fighting.
Happy I shall be to lie in that place,
In that place where the fight was,
Beyond the enemy's line.

3

Here on my breast have I bled!
See—see! these are fighting-scars!
Mountains tremble at my yell!
I strike for life.

(H. H. Schoolcraft)

THREE SONGS FROM THE HAIDA

(Queen Charlotte's Island, British Columbia)

LOVE SONG

Beautiful is she, this woman,
As the mountain flower;
But cold, cold, is she,
Like the snowbank
Behind which it blooms.

THE BEAR'S SONG

(Whoever can sing this song is admitted forever to the friendship of the bears)

I have taken the woman of beauty
For my wife;
I have taken her from her friends.
I hope her kinsmen will not come
And take her away from me.
I will be kind to her.
Berries, berries I will give her from the hill
And roots from the ground.
I will do everything to please her.
For her I made this song and for her I sing it.

SONG FOR FINE WEATHER

O good Sun,
Look thou down upon us:
Shine, shine on us, O Sun,
Gather up the clouds, wet, black, under thy arms—

That the rains may cease to fall.
Because thy friends are all here on the beach
Ready to go fishing—
Ready for the hunt.
Therefore look kindly on us, O Good Sun!
Give us peace within our tribe
And with all our enemies.
Again, again we call—
Hear us, hear us, O Good Sun!

(Constance Lindsay Skinner)

William Cullen Bryant

1794–1878

THANATOPSIS

To him who in the love of Nature holds
Communion with her visible forms, she speaks
A various language; for his gayer hours
She has a voice of gladness, and a smile
And eloquence of beauty, and she glides
Into his darker musings, with a mild
And healing sympathy, that steals away
Their sharpness, ere he is aware. When thoughts
Of the last bitter hour come like a blight
Over thy spirit, and sad images
Of the stern agony, and shroud, and pall,
And breathless darkness, and the narrow house,
Make thee to shudder, and grow sick at heart;—
Go forth, under the open sky, and list
To Nature's teachings, while from all around—
Earth and her waters, and the depths of air—
Comes a still voice—Yet a few days, and thee
The all-beholding sun shall see no more
In all his course; nor yet in the cold ground,
Where thy pale form was laid, with many tears,
Nor in the embrace of ocean, shall exist
Thy image. Earth, that nourished thee, shall claim
Thy growth, to be resolved to earth again,

And, lost each human trace, surrendering up
Thine individual being, shalt thou go
To mix forever with the elements,
To be a brother to the insensible rock
And to the sluggish clod, which the rude swain
Turns with his share, and treads upon. The oak
Shall send his roots abroad, and pierce thy mould.

Yet not to thine eternal resting-place
Shalt thou retire alone, nor couldst thou wish
Couch more magnificent. Thou shalt lie down
With patriarchs of the infant world—with kings,
The powerful of the earth—the wise, the good,
Fair forms, and hoary seers of ages past,
All in one mighty sepulchre. The hills
Rock-ribbed and ancient as the sun,—the vales
Stretching in pensive quietness between;
The venerable woods—rivers that move
In majesty, and the complaining brooks
That make the meadows green; and, poured round all,
Old Ocean's gray and melancholy waste,—
Are but the solemn decorations all
Of the great tomb of man. The golden sun,
The planets, all the infinite host of heaven,
Are shining on the sad abodes of death,
Through the still lapse of ages. All that tread
The globe are but a handful to the tribes
That slumber in its bosom.—Take the wings
Of morning, pierce the Barcan wilderness,
Or lose thyself in the continuous woods
Where rolls the Oregon, and hears no sound,
Save his own dashings—yet the dead are there:
And millions in those solitudes, since first
The flight of years began, have laid them down
In their last sleep—the dead reign there alone.
So shalt thou rest, and what if thou withdraw
In silence from the living, and no friend
Take note of thy departure? All that breathe
Will share thy destiny. The gay will laugh

When thou art gone, the solemn brood of care
Plod on, and each one as before will chase
His favorite phantom; yet all these shall leave
Their mirth and their employments, and shall come
And make their bed with thee. As the long train
Of ages glide away, the sons of men,
The youth in life's green spring, and he who goes
In the full strength of years, matron and maid,
The speechless babe, and the gray-headed man—
Shall one by one be gathered to thy side,
By those, who in their turn shall follow them.

So live, that when thy summons comes to join
The innumerable caravan, which moves
To that mysterious realm, where each shall take
His chamber in the silent halls of death,
Thou go not, like the quarry-slave at night,
Scourged to his dungeon, but, sustained and soothed
By an unfaltering trust, approach thy grave,
Like one who wraps the drapery of his couch
About him, and lies down to pleasant dreams.

TO A WATER FOWL

Whither, midst falling dew,
While glow the heavens with the last steps of day,
Far, through their rosy depths, dost thou pursue
Thy solitary way?

Vainly the fowler's eye
Might mark thy distant flight to do thee wrong,
As, darkly seen against the crimson sky,
Thy figure floats along.

Seek'st thou the plashy brink
Of weedy lake, or marge of river wide,
Or where the rocking billows rise and sink
On the chafed ocean-side?

There is a Power whose care
Teaches thy way along that pathless coast—
The desert and illimitable air—
Lone wandering, but not lost.

All day thy wings have fanned,
At that far height, the cold, thin atmosphere,
Yet stoop not, weary, to the welcome land,
Though the dark night is near.

And soon that toil shall end;
Soon shalt thou find a summer home, and rest,
And scream among thy fellows; reeds shall bend,
Soon, o'er thy sheltered nest.

Thou'rt gone, the abyss of heaven
Hath swallowed up thy form; yet, on my heart
Deeply has sunk the lesson thou hast given,
And shall not soon depart.

He who, from zone to zone,
Guides through the boundless sky thy certain flight,
In the long way that I must tread alone,
Will lead my steps aright.

TO THE FRINGED GENTIAN

Thou blossom bright with autumn dew,
And colored with the heaven's own blue,
That openest when the quiet light
Succeeds the keen and frosty night,

Thou comest not when violets lean
O'er wandering brooks and springs unseen,
Or columbines, in purple dressed,
Nod o'er the ground-bird's hidden nest.

Thou waitest late and com'st alone,
When woods are bare and birds are flown,
And frosts and shortening days portend
The aged year is near his end.

Then doth thy sweet and quiet eye
Look through its fringes to the sky,
Blue—blue—as if that sky let fall
A flower from its cerulean wall.

I would that thus, when I shall see
The hour of death draw near to me,
Hope, blossoming within my heart,
May look to heaven as I depart.

Ralph Waldo Emerson

1803–1882

THE RHODORA

On Being Asked, Whence Is the Flower?

In May, when sea-winds pierced our solitudes,
I found the fresh Rhodora in the woods,
Spreading its leafless blooms in a damp nook,
To please the desert and the sluggish brook.
The purple petals, fallen in the pool,
Made the black water with their beauty gay;
Here might the red-bird come his plumes to cool,
And court the flower that cheapens his array.
Rhodora! if the sages ask thee why
This charm is wasted on the earth and sky,
Tell them, dear, that if eyes were made for seeing,
Then Beauty is its own excuse for being:
Why thou wert there, O rival of the rose!
I never thought to ask, I never knew:
But, in my simple ignorance, suppose
The self-same Power that brought me there brought you.

BRAHMA

If the red slayer think he slays,
Or if the slain think he is slain,
They know not well the subtle ways
I keep, and pass, and turn again.

Far or forgot to me is near;
  Shadow and sunlight are the same;
The vanished gods to me appear;
  And one to me are shame and fame.

They reckon ill who leave me out;
  When me they fly, I am the wings;
I am the doubter and the doubt,
  And I the hymn the Brahmin sings.

The strong gods pine for my abode,
  And pine in vain the sacred Seven;
But thou, meek lover of the good!
  Find me, and turn thy back on heaven.

CONCORD HYMN

SUNG AT THE COMPLETION OF THE BATTLE MONUMENT, JULY 4, 1837

By the rude bridge that arched the flood,
  Their flag to April's breeze unfurled,
Here once the embattled farmers stood,
  And fired the shot heard round the world.

The foe long since in silence slept;
  Alike the conqueror silent sleeps;
And Time the ruined bridge has swept
  Down the dark stream which seaward creeps.

On this green bank, by this soft stream,
  We set to-day a votive stone;
That memory may their dead redeem,
  When, like our sires, our sons are gone.

Spirit, that made those heroes dare
  To die, and leave their children free,
Bid Time and Nature gently spare
  The shaft we raise to them and thee.

THE PROBLEM

I LIKE a church; I like a cowl;
I love a prophet of the soul;
And on my heart monastic aisles
Fall like sweet strains, or pensive smiles:
Yet not for all his faith can see
Would I that cowlèd churchman be.

Why should the vest on him allure,
Which I could not on me endure?

Not from a vain or shallow thought
His awful Jove young Phidias brought;
Never from lips of cunning fell
The thrilling Delphic oracle;
Out from the heart of nature rolled
The burdens of the Bible old;
The litanies of nations came,
Like the volcano's tongue of flame,
Up from the burning core below,—
The canticles of love and woe:
The hand that rounded Peter's dome
And groined the aisles of Christian Rome
Wrought in a sad sincerity;
Himself from God he could not free;
He builded better than he knew;—
The conscious stone to beauty grew.

Know'st thou what wove yon woodbird's nest
Of leaves, and feathers from her breast?
Or how the fish outbuilt her shell,
Painting with morn each annual cell?
Or how the sacred pine-tree adds
To her old leaves new myriads?
Such and so grew these holy piles,
Whilst love and terror laid the tiles.
Earth proudly wears the Parthenon,
As the best gem upon her zone,

And Morning opes with haste her lids
To gaze upon the Pyramids;
O'er England's abbeys bends the sky,
As on its friends, with kindred eye;
For out of Thought's interior sphere
These wonders rose to upper air;
And Nature gladly gave them place,
Adopted them into her race,
And granted them an equal date
With Andes and with Ararat.

These temples grew as grows the grass;
Art might obey, but not surpass.
The passive Master lent his hand
To the vast soul that o'er him planned;
And the same power that reared the shrine
Bestrode the tribes that knelt within.
Ever the fiery Pentecost
Girds with one flame the countless host,
Trances the heart through chanting choirs,
And through the priest the mind inspires.
The word unto the prophet spoken
Was writ on tables yet unbroken;
The word by seers or sibyls told,
In groves of oak, or fanes of gold,
Still floats upon the morning wind,
Still whispers to the willing mind.
One accent of the Holy Ghost
The heedless world hath never lost.
I know what say the fathers wise,—
The Book itself before me lies,
Old *Chrysostom,* best Augustine,
And he who blent both in his line,
The younger *Golden Lips* or mines,
Taylor, the Shakespeare of divines.
His words are music in my ear,
I see his cowlèd portrait dear;
And yet, for all his faith could see,
I would not the good bishop be.

GIVE ALL TO LOVE

Give all to love;
Obey thy heart;
Friends, kindred, days,
Estate, good-fame,
Plans, credit and the Muse,—
Nothing refuse.

'Tis a brave master;
Let it have scope:
Follow it utterly,
Hope beyond hope:
High and more high
It dives into noon,
With wing unspent,
Untold intent;
But it is a god,
Knows its own path
And the outlets of the sky.

It was never for the mean;
It requireth courage stout.
Souls above doubt,
Valor unbending,
It will reward,—
They shall return
More than they were,
And ever ascending.

Leave all for love;
Yet, hear me, yet,
One word more thy heart behoved,
One pulse more of firm endeavor,—
Keep thee to-day,
To-morrow, forever,
Free as an Arab
Of thy beloved.

Cling with life to the maid;
But when the surprise,
First vague shadow of surmise
Flits across her bosom young,
Of a joy apart from thee,
Free be she, fancy-free;
Nor thou detain her vesture's hem,
Nor the palest rose she flung
From her summer diadem.

Though thou loved her as thyself,
As a self of purer clay,
Though her parting dims the day,
Stealing grace from all alive;
Heartily know,
When half-gods go,
The gods arrive.

EACH AND ALL

LITTLE thinks, in the field, yon red-cloaked clown
Of thee from the hill-top looking down;
The heifer that lows in the upland farm,
Far-heard, lows not thine ear to charm;
The sexton, tolling his bell at noon,
Deems not that great Napoleon
Stops his horse, and lists with delight,
Whilst his files sweep round yon Alpine height;
Nor knowest thou what argument
Thy life to thy neighbor's creed has lent.
All are needed by each one;
Nothing is fair or good alone.
I thought the sparrow's note from heaven,
Singing at dawn on the alder bough;
I brought him home, in his nest, at even;
He sings the song, but it cheers not now,
For I did not bring home the river and sky;—
He sang to my ear,—they sang to my eye.
The delicate shells lay on the shore;
The bubbles of the latest wave

Fresh pearls to their enamel gave,
And the bellowing of the savage sea
Greeted their safe escape to me.
I wiped away the weeds and foam,
I fetched my sea-born treasures home;
But the poor, unsightly, noisome things
Had left their beauty on the shore
With the sun and the sand and the wild uproar.
The lover watched his graceful maid,
As 'mid the virgin train she strayed,
Nor knew her beauty's best attire
Was woven still by the snow-white choir.
At last she came to his hermitage,
Like the bird from the woodlands to the cage;—
The gay enchantment was undone,
A gentle wife, but fairy none.
Then I said, 'I covet truth;
Beauty is unripe childhood's cheat;
I leave it behind with the games of youth:'—
As I spoke, beneath my feet
The ground-pine curled its pretty wreath,
Running over the club-moss burrs;
I inhaled the violet's breath;
Around me stood the oaks and firs;
Pine-cones and acorns lay on the ground;
Over me soared the eternal sky,
Full of light and of deity;
Again I saw, again I heard,
The rolling river, the morning bird;—
Beauty through my senses stole;
I yielded myself to the perfect whole.

THE INFORMING SPIRIT

I

There is no great and no small
To the Soul that maketh all:
And where it cometh, all things are;
And it cometh everywhere.

II

I am owner of the sphere,
Of the seven stars and the solar year,
Of Cæsar's hand, and Plato's brain,
Of Lord Christ's heart, and Shakespeare's strain.

BACCHUS

Bring me wine, but wine which never grew
In the belly of the grape,
Or grew on vine whose tap-roots, reaching through,
Under the Andes to the Cape,
Suffer no savor of the earth to 'scape.
Let its grapes the morn salute
From a nocturnal root,
Which feels the acrid juice
Of Styx and Erebus;
And turns the woe of Night,
By its own craft, to a more rich delight.

We buy ashes for bread;
We buy diluted wine;
Give me of the true,—
Whose ample leaves and tendrils curled
Among the silver hills of heaven
Draw everlasting dew;
Wine of wine,
Blood of the world,
Form of forms, and mould of statures,
That I intoxicated,
And by the draught assimilated,
May float at pleasure through all natures;
The bird-language rightly spell,
And that which roses say so well.

Wine that is shed
Like the torrents of the sun
Up the horizon walls,
Or like the Atlantic streams, which run
When the South Sea calls.

Water and bread,
Food which needs no transmuting,
Rainbow-flowering, wisdom-fruiting,
Wine which is already man,
Food which teach and reason can.

Wine which Music is,—
Music and wine are one,—
That I, drinking this,
Shall hear far Chaos talk with me;
Kings unborn shall walk with me;
And the poor grass shall plot and plan
What it will do when it is man.
Quickened so, will I unlock
Every crypt of every rock.

I thank the joyful juice
For all I know;—
Winds of remembering
Of the ancient being blow,
And seeming-solid walls of use
Open and flow.

Pour, Bacchus! the remembering wine;
Retrieve the loss of me and mine!
Vine for vine be antidote,
And the grape requite the lote!
Haste to cure the old despair,—
Reason in Nature's lotus drenched,
The memory of ages quenched;
Give them again to shine;
Let wine repair what this undid;
And where the infection slid,
A dazzling memory revive;
Refresh the faded tints,
Recut the aged prints,
And write my old adventures with the pen
Which on the first day drew,
Upon the tablets blue,
The dancing Pleiads and eternal men.

NATURE

A SUBTLE chain of countless rings
The next unto the farthest brings;
The eye reads omens where it goes,
And speaks all languages the rose;
And, striving to be man, the worm
Mounts through all the spires of form.

TERMINUS

IT is time to be old,
To take in sail:—
The god of bounds,
Who sets to seas a shore,
Came to me in his fatal rounds,
And said: 'No more!
No farther shoot
Thy broad ambitious branches, and thy root.
Fancy departs: no more invent;
Contract thy firmament
To compass of a tent.
There's not enough for this and that,
Make thy option which of two;
Economize the failing river,
Not the less revere the Giver,
Leave the many and hold the few.
Timely wise accept the terms,
Soften the fall with wary foot;
A little while
Still plan and smile,
And,—fault of novel germs,—
Mature the unfallen fruit.
Curse, if thou wilt, thy sires,
Bad husbands of their fires,
Who, when they gave thee breath,
Failed to bequeath
The needful sinew stark as once,

The Baresark marrow to thy bones,
But left a legacy of ebbing veins,
Inconstant heat and nerveless reins,—
Amid the Muses, left thee deaf and dumb,
Amid the gladiators, halt and numb.'

As the bird trims her to the gale,
I trim myself to the storm of time,
I man the rudder, reef the sail,
Obey the voice at eve obeyed at prime:
'Lowly faithful, banish fear,
Right onward drive unharmed;
The port, well worth the cruise, is near,
And every wave is charmed.'

Henry Wadsworth Longfellow

1807–1882

MY LOST YOUTH

Often I think of the beautiful town
That is seated by the sea;
Often in thought go up and down
The pleasant streets of that dear old town,
And my youth comes back to me.
And a verse of a Lapland song
Is haunting my memory still:
"A boy's will is the wind's will,
And the thoughts of youth are long, long thoughts."

I can see the shadowy lines of its trees,
And catch, in sudden gleams,
The sheen of the far-surrounding seas,
And islands that were the Hesperides
Of all my boyish dreams.
And the burden of that old song,
It murmurs and whispers still:
"A boy's will is the wind's will,
And the thoughts of youth are long, long thoughts."

I remember the black wharves and the slips,
  And the sea-tides tossing free;
And Spanish sailors with bearded lips,
And the beauty and mystery of the ships,
  And the magic of the sea.
    And the voice of that wayward song
    Is singing and saying still:
    "A boy's will is the wind's will,
And the thoughts of youth are long, long thoughts."

I remember the bulwarks by the shore,
  And the fort upon the hill;
The sunrise gun, with its hollow roar,
The drum-beat repeated o'er and o'er,
  And the bugle wild and shrill.
    And the music of that old song
    Throbs in my memory still:
    "A boy's will is the wind's will,
And the thoughts of youth are long, long thoughts."

I remember the sea-fight far away,
  How it thundered o'er the tide!
And the dead captains, as they lay
In their graves, o'erlooking the tranquil bay
  Where they in battle died.
    And the sound of that mournful song
    Goes through me with a thrill:
    "A boy's will is the wind's will,
And the thoughts of youth are long, long thoughts."

I can see the breezy dome of groves,
  The shadows of Deering's Woods;
And the friendships old and the early loves
Come back with a Sabbath sound, as of doves
  In quiet neighborhoods.
    And the verse of that sweet old song,
    It flutters and murmurs still:
    "A boy's will is the wind's will,
And the thoughts of youth are long, long thoughts."

I remember the gleams and glooms that dart
  Across the school-boy's brain;
The song and the silence in the heart,
That in part are prophecies, and in part
  Are longings wild and vain.
    And the voice of that fitful song
    Sings on, and is never still:
    "A boy's will is the wind's will,
And the thoughts of youth are long, long thoughts."

There are things of which I may not speak;
  There are dreams that cannot die;
There are thoughts that make the strong heart weak,
And bring a pallor into the cheek,
  And a mist before the eye.
    And the words of that fatal song
    Come over me like a chill:
    "A boy's will is the wind's will,
And the thoughts of youth are long, long thoughts."

Strange to me now are the forms I meet
  When I visit the dear old town;
But the native air is pure and sweet,
And the trees that o'ershadow each well-known street,
  As they balance up and down,
    Are singing the beautiful song,
    Are sighing and whispering still:
    "A boy's will is the wind's will,
And the thoughts of youth are long, long thoughts."

And Deering's Woods are fresh and fair,
  And with joy that is almost pain
My heart goes back to wander there,
And among the dreams of the days that were,
  I find my lost youth again.
    And the strange and beautiful song,
    The groves are repeating it still:
    "A boy's will is the wind's will,
And the thoughts of youth are long, long thoughts."

THE SKELETON IN ARMOR

SPEAK! speak! thou fearful guest!
Who, with thy hollow breast
Still in rude armor drest,
  Comest to daunt me!
Wrapt not in Eastern balms,
But with thy fleshless palms
Stretched, as if asking alms,
  Why dost thou haunt me?

Then, from those cavernous eyes
Pale flashes seemed to rise,
As when the Northern skies
  Gleam in December;
And, like the water's flow
Under December's snow,
Came a dull voice of woe
  From the heart's chamber.

'I was a Viking old!
My deeds, though manifold,
No Skald in song has told,
  No Saga taught thee!
Take heed, that in thy verse
Thou dost the tale rehearse,
Else dread a dead man's curse;
  For this I sought thee.

'Far in the Northern Land,
By the wild Baltic's strand,
I, with my childish hand,
  Tamed the gerfalcon;
And, with my skates fast-bound
Skimmed the half-frozen Sound,
That the poor whimpering hound
  Trembled to walk on.

'Oft to his frozen lair
Tracked I the grisly bear,
While from my path the hare
Fled like a shadow;
Oft through the forest dark
Followed the were-wolf's bark,
Until the soaring lark
Sang from the meadow.

'But when I older grew,
Joining a corsair's crew,
O'er the dark sea I flew
With the marauders.
Wild was the life we led;
Many the souls that sped,
Many the hearts that bled,
By our stern orders.

'Many a wassail-bout
Wore the long Winter out;
Often our midnight shout
Set the cocks crowing,
As we the Berserk's tale
Measured in cups of ale,
Draining the oaken pail,
Filled to o'erflowing.

'Once as I told in glee
Tales of the stormy sea,
Soft eyes did gaze on me,
Burning yet tender:
And as the white stars shine
On the dark Norway pine,
On that dark heart of mine
Fell their soft splendor.

'I wooed the blue-eyed maid,
Yielding, yet half afraid,
And in the forest's shade
Our vows were plighted.

Under its loosened vest
Fluttered her little breast,
Like birds within their nest
By the hawk frighted.

'Bright in her father's hall
Shields gleamed upon the wall,
Loud sang the minstrels all,
Chanting his glory;
When of old Hildebrand
I asked his daughter's hand,
Mute did the minstrels stand
To hear my story.

'While the brown ale he quaffed,
Loud then the champion laughed,
And as the wind-gusts waft
The sea-foam brightly,
So the loud laugh of scorn,
Out of those lips unshorn,
From the deep drinking-horn
Blew the foam lightly.

'She was a Prince's child,
I but a Viking wild,
And though she blushed and smiled,
I was discarded!
Should not the dove so white
Follow the sea-mew's flight,
Why did they leave that night
Her nest unguarded?

'Scarce had I put to sea,
Bearing the maid with me,
Fairest of all was she
Among the Norsemen!
When on the white sea-strand,
Waving his armed hand,
Saw we old Hildebrand,
With twenty horsemen.

'Then launched they to the blast,
Bent like a reed each mast,
Yet we were gaining fast,
  When the wind failed us;
And with a sudden flaw
Came round the gusty Skaw,
So that our foe we saw
  Laugh as he hailed us.

'And as to catch the gale
Round veered the flapping sail,
"Death!" was the helmsman's hail,
  "Death without quarter!"
Mid-ships with iron keel
Struck we her ribs of steel;
Down her black hulk did reel
  Through the black water!

'As with his wings aslant,
Sails the fierce cormorant,
Seeking some rocky haunt,
  With his prey laden,—
So toward the open main,
Beating to sea again,
Through the wild hurricane,
  Bore I the maiden.

'Three weeks we westward bore,
And when the storm was o'er,
Cloud-like we saw the shore
  Stretching to leeward;
There for my lady's bower
Built I the lofty tower,
Which, to this very hour,
  Stands looking seaward.

'There lived we many years;
Time dried the maiden's tears;

She had forgot her fears,
  She was a mother;
Death closed her mild blue eyes,
Under that tower she lies;
Ne'er shall the sun arise
  On such another!

'Still grew my bosom then,
Still as a stagnant fen!
Hateful to me were men,
  The sunlight hateful!
In the vast forest here,
Clad in my warlike gear,
Fell I upon my spear,
  Oh, death was grateful!

'Thus, seamed with many scars,
Bursting these prison bars,
Up to its native stars
  My soul ascended!
There from the flowing bowl
Deep drinks the warrior's soul,
Skoal! to the Northland! *skoal!*'
  Thus the tale ended.

THE RAINY DAY

The day is cold, and dark, and dreary;
It rains, and the wind is never weary;
The vine still clings to the mouldering wall,
But at every gust the dead leaves fall,
  And the day is dark and dreary.

My life is cold, and dark, and dreary;
It rains, and the wind is never weary;
My thoughts still cling to the mouldering Past,
But the hopes of youth fall thick in the blast,
  And the days are dark and dreary.

Be still, sad heart! and cease repining;
Behind the clouds is the sun still shining;
Thy fate is the common fate of all,
Into each life some rain must fall,
Some days must be dark and dreary.

CHAUCER

An old man in a lodge within a park;
The chamber walls depicted all around
With portraitures of huntsman, hawk, and hound,
And the hurt deer. He listeneth to the lark,
Whose song comes with the sunshine through the dark
Of painted glass in leaden lattice bound;
He listeneth and he laugheth at the sound,
Then writeth in a book like any clerk.
He is the poet of the dawn, who wrote
The Canterbury Tales, and his old age
Made beautiful with song; and as I read
I hear the crowing cock, I hear the note
Of lark and linnet, and from every page
Rise odors of ploughed field or flowery mead.

SHAKESPEARE

A vision as of crowded city streets,
With human life in endless overflow;
Thunder of thoroughfares; trumpets that blow
To battle; clamor, in obscure retreats,
Of sailors landed from their anchored fleets;
Tolling of bells in turrets, and below
Voices of children, and bright flowers that throw
O'er garden walls their intermingled sweets!
This vision comes to me when I unfold
The volume of the Poet paramount,
Whom all the Muses loved, not one alone;—
Into his hands they put the lyre of gold,
And, crowned with sacred laurel at their font,
Placed him as Musagetes on their throne.

MILTON

I PACE the sounding sea-beach and behold
How the voluminous billows roll and run,
Upheaving and subsiding, while the sun
Shines through their sheeted emerald far unrolled,
And the ninth wave, slow gathering fold by fold
All its loose-flowing garments into one,
Plunges upon the shore, and floods the dun
Pale reach of sands, and changes them to gold.
So in majestic cadence rise and fall
The mighty undulations of thy song,
O sightless bard, England's Mæonides!
And ever and anon, high over all
Uplifted, a ninth wave superb and strong,
Floods all the soul with its melodious seas.

John Greenleaf Whittier

1807–1892

THE FAREWELL

OF A VIRGINIA SLAVE MOTHER TO HER DAUGHTERS SOLD INTO SOUTHERN BONDAGE

Gone, gone,—sold and gone,
To the rice-swamp dank and lone.
Where the slave-whip ceaseless swings,
Where the noisome insect stings,
Where the fever demon strews
Poison with the falling dews,
Where the sickly sunbeams glare
Through the hot and misty air;
Gone, gone—sold and gone,
To the rice-swamp dank and lone,
From Virginia's hills and waters;
Woe is me, my stolen daughters!

Gone, gone,—sold and gone,
To the rice-swamp dank and lone.
There no mother's eye is near them,
There no mother's ear can hear them;
Never, when the torturing lash
Seams their back with many a gash,
Shall a mother's kindness bless them,
Or a mother's arms caress them.
Gone, gone,—sold and gone,
To the rice-swamp dank and lone,
From Virginia's hills and waters;
Woe is me, my stolen daughters!

Gone, gone,—sold and gone,
To the rice-swamp dank and lone.
Oh, when weary, sad, and slow,
From the fields at night they go,
Faint with toil, and racked with pain,
To their cheerless homes again,
There no brother's voice shall greet them,
There no father's welcome meet them.
Gone, gone,—sold and gone,
To the rice-swamp dank and lone,
From Virginia's hills and waters;
Woe is me, my stolen daughters!

Gone, gone,—sold and gone,
To the rice-swamp dank and lone.
From the tree whose shadow lay
On their childhood's place of play;
From the cool spring where they drank;
Rock, and hill, and rivulet bank;
From the solemn house of prayer,
And the holy counsels there;
Gone, gone,—sold and gone,
To the rice-swamp dank and lone,
From Virginia's hills and waters;
Woe is me, my stolen daughters!

Gone, gone,—sold and gone,
To the rice-swamp dank and lone;
Toiling through the weary day,
And at night the spoiler's prey.
Oh, that they had earlier died,
Sleeping calmly, side by side,
Where the tyrant's power is o'er,
And the fetter galls no more!
Gone, gone,—sold and gone,
To the rice-swamp dank and lone,
From Virginia's hills and waters;
Woe is me, my stolen daughters!

Gone, gone,—sold and gone,
To the rice-swamp dank and lone.
By the holy love He beareth;
By the bruisèd reed He spareth;
Oh, may He, to whom alone
All their cruel wrongs are known,
Still their hope and refuge prove,
With a more than mother's love.
Gone, gone,—sold and gone,
To the rice-swamp dank and lone,
From Virginia's hills and waters;
Woe is me, my stolen daughters!

TELLING THE BEES

Here is the place; right over the hill
Runs the path I took;
You can see the gap in the old wall still,
And the stepping-stones in the shallow brook.

There is the house, with the gate red-barred,
And the poplars tall;
And the barn's brown length, and the cattleyard,
And the white horns tossing above the wall.

There are the beehives ranged in the sun;
And down by the brink

Of the brook are her poor flowers, weed-o'errun,
  Pansy and daffodil, rose and pink.

A year has gone, as the tortoise goes,
  Heavy and slow;
And the same rose blows, and the same sun glows,
  And the same brook sings of a year ago.

There's the same sweet clover-smell in the breeze;
  And the June sun warm
Tangles his wings of fire in the trees,
  Setting, as then, over Fernside farm.

I mind me how with a lover's care
  From my Sunday coat
I brushed off the burrs, and smoothed my hair,
  And cooled at the brookside my brow and throat.

Since we parted, a month had passed,—
  To love, a year;
Down through the beeches I looked at last
  On the little red gate and the well-sweep near.

I can see it all now,—the slantwise rain
  Of light through the leaves,
The sundown's blaze on her window-pane,
  The bloom of her roses under the eaves.

Just the same as a month before,—
  The house and the trees,
The barn's brown gable, the vine by the door,—
  Nothing changed but the hives of bees.

Before them, under the garden wall,
  Forward and back,
Went drearily singing the chore-girl small,
  Draping each hive with a shred of black.

Trembling, I listened: the summer sun
  Had the chill of snow;
For I knew she was telling the bees of one
  Gone on the journey we all must go!

Then I said to myself, 'My Mary weeps
  For the dead to-day:
Haply her blind old grandsire sleeps
  The fret and the pain of his age away.'

But her dog whined low; on the doorway sill,
  With his cane to his chin,
The old man sat; and the chore-girl still
  Sung to the bees stealing out and in.

And the song she was singing ever since
  In my ear sounds on:—
'Stay at home, pretty bees, fly not hence!
  Mistress Mary is dead and gone!'

THE SISTERS

Annie and Rhoda, sisters twain,
Woke in the night to the sound of rain,

The rush of wind, the ramp and roar
Of great waves climbing a rocky shore.

Annie rose up in her bed-gown white,
And looked out into the storm and night.

'Hush, and hearken!' she cried in fear,
'Hearest thou nothing, sister dear?'

'I hear the sea, and the plash of rain,
And roar of the northeast hurricane.

'Get thee back to the bed so warm,
No good comes of watching a storm.

'What is it to thee, I fain would know,
That waves are roaring and wild winds blow?

'No lover of thine 's afloat to miss
The harbor-lights on a night like this.'

'But I heard a voice cry out my name,
Up from the sea on the wind it came!

'Twice and thrice have I heard it call,
And the voice is the voice of Estwick Hall!'

On her pillow the sister tossed her head.
'Hall of the Heron is safe,' she said.

'In the tautest schooner that ever swam
He rides at anchor in Annisquam.

'And, if in peril from swamping sea
Or lee shore rocks, would he call on thee?'

But the girl heard only the wind and tide,
And wringing her small white hands she cried:

'O sister Rhoda, there's something wrong;
I hear it again, so loud and long.

' "Annie! Annie!" I hear it call,
And the voice is the voice of Estwick Hall!'

Up sprang the elder, with eyes aflame,
'Thou liest! He never would call thy name!

'If he did, I would pray the wind and sea
To keep him forever from thee and me!'

Then out of the sea blew a dreadful blast;
Like the cry of a dying man it passed.

The young girl hushed on her lips a groan,
But through her tears a strange light shone,—

The solemn joy of her heart's release
To own and cherish its love in peace.

'Dearest!' she whispered, under breath,
'Life was a lie, but true is death.

'The love I hid from myself away
Shall crown me now in the light of day.

'My ears shall never to wooer list,
Never by lover my lips be kissed.

'Sacred to thee am I henceforth,
Thou in heaven and I on earth!'

She came and stood by her sister's bed:
'Hall of the Heron is dead!' she said.

'The wind and the waves their work have done,
We shall see him no more beneath the sun.

'Little will reck that heart of thine;
It loved him not with a love like mine.

'I, for his sake, were he but here,
Could hem and 'broider thy bridal gear,

'Though hands should tremble and eyes be wet,
And stitch for stitch in my heart be set.

'But now my soul with his soul I wed;
Thine the living, and mine the dead!'

Edgar Allan Poe

1809–1849

TO HELEN

Helen, thy beauty is to me
  Like those Nicæan barks of yore,
That gently, o'er a perfumed sea,
  The weary, wayworn wanderer bore
  To his own native shore.

On desperate seas long wont to roam,
  Thy hyacinth hair, thy classic face,
Thy Naiad airs have brought me home
  To the glory that was Greece
  And the grandeur that was Rome.

Lo! in yon brilliant window-niche
  How statue-like I see thee stand,
The agate lamp within thy hand!
  Ah, Psyche, from the regions which
  Are Holy Land!

ULALUME

THE skies they were ashen and sober;
The leaves they were crispèd and sere—
The leaves they were withering and sere:
It was night, in the lonesome October
Of my most immemorial year;
It was hard by the dim lake of Auber,
In the misty mid region of Weir—
It was down by the dank tarn of Auber,
In the ghoul-haunted woodland of Weir.

Here once, through an alley Titanic,
Of cypress, I roamed with my Soul—
Of cypress, with Psyche, my Soul.
These were days when my heart was volcanic
As the scoriac rivers that roll—
As the lavas that restlessly roll
Their sulphurous currents down Yaanek
In the ultimate climes of the Pole—
That groan as they roll down Mount Yaanek
In the realms of the Boreal Pole.

Our talk had been serious and sober,
But our thoughts they were palsied and sere—
Our memories were treacherous and sere—
For we knew not the month was October,
And we marked not the night of the year—
(Ah, night of all nights in the year!)
We noted not the dim lake of Auber,
(Though once we had journeyed down here)
Remembered not the dank tarn of Auber,
Nor the ghoul-haunted woodland of Weir.

And now, as the night was senescent
And star-dials pointed to morn—
As the star-dials hinted of morn—
At the end of our path a liquescent
And nebulous luster was born.

Out of which a miraculous crescent
  Arose with a duplicate horn—
Astarte's bediamonded crescent
  Distinct with its duplicate horn.

And I said—"She is warmer than Dian;
  She rolls through an ether of sighs—
  She revels in a region of sighs:
She has seen that the tears are not dry on
  These cheeks, where the worm never dies,
And has come past the stars of the Lion
  To point us the path to the skies—
  To the Lethean peace of the skies—
Come up, in despite of the Lion,
  To shine on us with her bright eyes—
Come up through the lair of the Lion,
  With love in her luminous eyes."

But Psyche, uplifting her finger,
  Said—"Sadly this star I mistrust—
  Her pallor I strangely mistrust—
Oh, hasten!—oh, let us not linger!
  Oh, fly!—let us fly!—for we must."
In terror she spoke, letting sink her
  Wings till they trailed in the dust—
In agony sobbed, letting sink her
  Plumes till they trailed in the dust—
  Till they sorrowfully trailed in the dust.

I replied—"This is nothing but dreaming:
  Let us on by this tremulous light!
  Let us bathe in this crystalline light!
Its sybillic splendor is beaming
  With Hope and in Beauty to-night:—
  See! it flickers up the sky through the night!
Ah, we safely may trust to its gleaming,
  And be sure it will lead us aright:
We safely may trust to a gleaming
  That cannot but guide us aright,
  Since it flickers up to Heaven through the night."

Thus I pacified Psyche and kissed her,
  And tempted her out of her gloom—
  And conquered her scruples and gloom;
And we passed to the end of a vista,
  But were stopped by the door of a tomb—
  By the door of a legended tomb;
And I said—"What is written, sweet sister,
  On the door of this legended tomb?"
  She replied—"Ulalume—Ulalume!—
  'Tis the vault of thy lost Ulalume!"

Then my heart it grew ashen and sober
  As the leaves that were crispèd and sere—
  As the leaves that were withering and sere;
And I cried—"It was surely October
  On *this* very night of last year
  That I journeyed—I journeyed down here—
  That I brought a dread burden down here!
  On this night of all nights in the year,
  Ah, what demon has tempted me here?
Well I know, now, this dim lake of Auber—
  This misty mid region of Weir—
Well I know, now, this dank tarn of Auber—
  This ghoul-haunted woodland of Weir."

ANNABEL LEE

It was many and many a year ago,
  In a kingdom by the sea
That a maiden there lived whom you may know
  By the name of Annabel Lee;—
And this maiden she lived with no other thought
  Than to love and be loved by me.

I was a child and *she* was a child,
  In this kingdom by the sea,
But we loved with a love that was more than love—
  I and my Annabel Lee—
With a love that the wingèd seraphs in Heaven
  Coveted her and me.

And this was the reason that, long ago,
  In this kingdom by the sea,
A wind blew out of a cloud, chilling
  My beautiful Annabel Lee;
So that her high-born kinsmen came
  And bore her away from me,
To shut her up in a sepulcher
  In this kingdom by the sea.

The angels, not half so happy in Heaven,
  Went envying her and me:—
Yes!—that was the reason (as all men know,
  In this kingdom by the sea)
That the wind came out of the cloud, by night,
  Chilling and killing my Annabel Lee.

But our love it was stronger by far than the love
  Of those who were older than we—
  Of many far wiser than we—
And neither the angels in Heaven above,
  Nor the demons down under the sea,
Can ever dissever my soul from the soul
  Of the beautiful Annabel Lee:—

For the moon never beams without bringing me dreams
  Of the beautiful Annabel Lee;
And the stars never rise but I feel the bright eyes
  Of the beautiful Annabel Lee;
And so, all the night-tide, I lie down by the side
Of my darling,—my darling,—my life and my bride,
  In the sepulcher there by the sea—
  In her tomb by the sounding sea.

ISRAFEL

In Heaven a spirit doth dwell
  'Whose heart-strings are a lute;'
None sing so wildly well
As the angel Israfel,

And the giddy stars (so legends tell)
Ceasing their hymns, attend the spell
Of his voice, all mute.

Tottering above
In her highest noon,
The enamored moon
Blushes with love,
While, to listen, the red levin
(With the rapid Pleiads, even,
Which were seven,)
Pauses in Heaven.

And they say (the starry choir
And the other listening things)
That Israfeli's fire
Is owing to that lyre
By which he sits and sings—
The trembling living wire
Of those unusual strings.

But the skies that angel trod,
Where deep thoughts are a duty—
Where Love's a grown-up God—
Where the Houri glances are
Imbued with all the beauty
Which we worship in a star.

Therefore, thou art not wrong,
Israfeli, who despisest
An unimpassioned song;
To thee the laurels belong,
Best bard, because the wisest!
Merrily live, and long!

The ecstasies above
With thy burning measures suit—
Thy grief, thy joy, thy hate, thy love,
With the fervor of thy lute—
Well may the stars be mute!

Yes, Heaven is thine; but this
  Is a world of sweets and sours;
  Our flowers are merely—flowers,
And the shadow of thy perfect bliss
  Is the sunshine of ours.

If I could dwell
Where Israfel
  Hath dwelt, and he where I,
He might not sing so wildly well
  A mortal melody,
While a bolder note than this might swell
  From my lyre within the sky.

THE CONQUEROR WORM

Lo! 't is a gala night
  Within the lonesome latter years!
An angel throng, bewinged, bedight
  In veils, and drowned in tears,
Sit in a theatre, to see
  A play of hopes and fears,
While the orchestra breathes fitfully
  The music of the spheres.

Mimes, in the form of God on high,
  Mutter and mumble low,
And hither and thither fly—
  Mere puppets they, who come and go
At bidding of vast formless things
  That shift the scenery to and fro,
Flapping from out their Condor wings
  Invisible Woe!

That motley drama—oh, be sure
  It shall not be forgot!
With its Phantom chased for evermore,
  By a crowd that seize it not,

Through a circle that ever returneth in
To the self-same spot,
And much of Madness, and more of Sin,
And Horror the soul of the plot.

But see, amid the mimic rout
A crawling shape intrude!
A blood-red thing that writhes from out
The scenic solitude!
It writhes!—it writhes!—with mortal pangs
The mimes become its food,
And seraphs sob at vermin fangs
In human gore imbued.

Out—out are the lights—out all!
And, over each quivering form,
The curtain, a funeral pall,
Comes down with the rush of a storm,
While the angels, all pallid and wan,
Uprising, unveiling, affirm
That the play is the tragedy, 'Man,'
And its hero the Conqueror Worm.

ELDORADO

Gaily bedight,
A gallant knight,
In sunshine and in shadow,
Had journeyed long,
Singing a song,
In search of Eldorado.

But he grew old—
This knight so bold—
And o'er his heart a shadow
Fell as he found
No spot of ground
That looked like Eldorado.

And, as his strength
Failed him at length,
He met a pilgrim shadow—
'Shadow,' said he,
'Where can it be—
This land of Eldorado?'

'Over the Mountains
Of the Moon,
Down the Valley of the Shadow,
Ride, boldly ride,'
The shade replied,—
'If you seek for Eldorado.'

Henry David Thoreau

1817–1862

SMOKE

Light-winged Smoke, Icarian bird,
Melting thy pinions in thy upward flight;
Lark without song, and messenger of dawn,
Circling above the hamlets as thy nest;
Or else, departing dream, and shadowy form
Of midnight vision, gathering up thy skirts;
By night star-veiling, and by day
Darkening the light and blotting out the sun;
Go thou, my incense, upward from this hearth,
And ask the gods to pardon this clear flame.

MIST

Low-anchored cloud,
Newfoundland air,
Fountain-head and source of rivers,
Dew-cloth, dream-drapery,
And napkin spread by fays;
Drifting meadow of the air,
Where bloom the daisied banks and violets,

And in whose fenny labyrinth
The bittern booms and heron wades;
Spirit of lakes and seas and rivers,
Bear only perfumes and the scent
Of healing herbs to just men's fields.

Walt Whitman

1819–1892

THERE WAS A CHILD WENT FORTH

THERE was a child went forth every day,
And the first object he look'd upon, that object he became,
And that object became part of him for the day or a
certain part of the day,
Or for many years or stretching cycles of years.

The early lilacs became part of this child,
And grass and white and red morning-glories, and white
and red clover, and the song of the phœbe-bird,
And the Third-month lambs and the sow's pink-faint
litter, and the mare's foal and cow's calf,
And the noisy brood of the barnyard or by the mire of the
pond-side,
And the fish suspending themselves so curiously below
there, and the beautiful curious liquid,
And the water-plants with their graceful flat heads, all
became part of him.

The field-sprouts of Fourth-month and Fifth-month be
came part of him,
Winter-grain sprouts and those of the light-yellow corn,
and the esculent roots of the garden,
And the apple-trees cover'd with blossoms and the fruit
afterward, and wood-berries, and the commonest
weeds by the road,
And the old drunkard staggering home from the out-
house of the tavern whence he had lately risen,

And the schoolmistress that pass'd on her way to the
 school,
And the friendly boys that pass'd, and the quarrelsome
 boys,
And the tidy and fresh-cheek'd girls, and the barefoot
 negro boy and girl,
And all the changes of city and country wherever he
 went.
His own parents, he that had father'd him and she that
 had conceiv'd him in her womb and birth'd him,
They gave this child more of themselves than that,
They gave him afterward every day, they became part of
 him.

The mother at home quietly placing the dishes on the
 supper-table,
The mother with mild words, clean her cap and gown, a
 wholesome odor falling off her person and clothes as
 she walks by,
The father, strong, self-sufficient, manly, mean, anger'd,
 unjust,
The blow, the quick loud word, the tight bargain, the
 crafty lure,
The family usages, the language, the company, the furni-
 ture, the yearning and swelling heart,
Affection that will not be gainsay'd, the sense of what is
 real, the thought if after all it should prove unreal,
The doubts of day-time and the doubts of night-time, the
 curious whether and how,
Whether that which appears so is so, or is it all flashes
 and specks?
Men and women crowding fast in the streets, if they are
 not flashes and specks what are they?
The streets themselves and the façades of houses, and
 goods in the windows,
Vehicles, teams, the heavy-plank'd wharves, the huge
 crossing at the ferries,
The village on the highland seen from afar at sunset, the
 river between,

Shadows, aureola and mist, the light falling on roofs and
gables of white or brown two miles off,
The schooner near by sleepily dropping down the tide,
the little boat slack-tow'd astern,
The hurrying tumbling waves, quick-broken crests,
slapping,
The strata of color'd clouds, the long bar of maroon-tint
away solitary by itself, the spread of purity it lies
motionless in,
The horizon's edge, the flying sea-crow, the fragrance of
salt marsh and shore mud,
These became part of that child who went forth every
day, and who now goes, and will always go forth
every day.

THIS COMPOST

I

SOMETHING startles me where I thought I was safest;
I withdraw from the still woods I loved;
I will not go now on the pastures to walk;
I will not strip the clothes from my body to meet my
lover the sea;
I will not touch my flesh to the earth, as to other flesh, to
renew me.

O how can it be that the ground does not sicken?
How can you be alive, you growths of spring?
How can you furnish health, you blood of herbs, roots,
orchards, grain?
Are they not continually putting distemper'd corpses
within you?
Is not every continent work'd over and over with sour
dead?

Where have you disposed of their carcasses?
Those drunkards and gluttons of so many generations;
Where have you drawn off all the foul liquid and meat?

I do not see any of it upon you to-day—or perhaps I am
deceiv'd;
I will run a furrow with my plough—I will press my
spade through the sod, and turn it up underneath;
I am sure I shall expose some of the foul meat.

II

Behold this compost! behold it well!
Perhaps every mite has once form'd part of a sick person
—Yet behold!
The grass of spring covers the prairies,
The bean bursts noiselessly through the mould in the
garden,
The delicate spear of the onion pierces upward,
The apple-buds cluster together on the apple-branches,
The resurrection of the wheat appears with pale visage
out of its graves,
The tinge awakes over the willow-tree and the mulberry-
tree,
The he-birds carol mornings and evenings, while the she-
birds sit on their nests,
The young of poultry break through the hatch'd eggs,
The new-born of animals appear—the calf is dropt from
the cow, the colt from the mare,
Out of its little hill faithfully rise the potato's dark green
leaves,
Out of its hill rises the yellow maize-stalk—the lilacs
bloom in the door-yards;
The summer growth is innocent and disdainful above all
those strata of sour dead.
What chemistry!
That the winds are really not infectious,
That this is no cheat, this transparent green-wash of the
sea, which is so amorous after me,
That it is safe to allow it to lick my naked body all over
with its tongues,
That it will not endanger me with the fevers that have de-
posited themselves in it,
That all is clean, forever and forever.

That the cool drink from the well tastes so good,
That blackberries are so flavorous and juicy,
That the fruits of the apple-orchard, and of the orange-orchard—that melons, grapes, peaches, plums, will none of them poison me,
That when I recline on the grass I do not catch any disease,
Though probably every spear of grass rises out of what was once a catching disease.

III

Now I am terrified at the Earth! it is that calm and patient,
It grows such sweet things out of such corruptions,
It turns harmless and stainless on its axis, with such endless successions of diseas'd corpses,
It distils such exquisite winds out of such infused fetor,
It renews with such unwitting looks, its prodigal, annual, sumptuous crops,
It gives such divine materials to men, and accepts such leavings from them at last.

I SAW IN LOUISIANA A LIVE-OAK GROWING

I SAW in Louisiana a live-oak growing,
All alone stood it, and the moss hung down from the branches;
Without any companion it grew there, uttering joyous leaves of dark green,
And its look, rude, unbending, lusty, made me think of myself;
But I wonder'd how it could utter joyous leaves, standing alone there, without its friend, its lover near—for I knew I could not;
And I broke off a twig with a certain number of leaves upon it, and twined around it a little moss,
And brought it away—and I have placed it in sight in my room;

It is not needed to remind me as of my own dear friends,
(For I believe lately I think of little else than of them:)
Yet it remains to me a curious token—it makes me think of manly love;
For all that, and though the live-oak glistens there in Louisiana, solitary, in a wide flat space,
Uttering joyous leaves all its life, without a friend, a lover, near,
I know very well I could not.

A NOISELESS, PATIENT SPIDER

A NOISELESS, patient spider,
I mark'd, where, on a little promontory, it stood, isolated;
Mark'd how, to explore the vacant, vast surrounding,
It launch'd forth filament, filament, filament, out of itself;
Ever unreeling them—ever tirelessly speeding them.

And you, O my Soul, where you stand,
Surrounded, surrounded, in measureless oceans of space,
Ceaselessly musing, venturing, throwing,—seeking the spheres, to connect them;
Till the bridge you will need, be form'd—till the ductile anchor hold;
Till the gossamer thread you fling, catch somewhere, O my Soul.

OUT OF THE CRADLE ENDLESSLY ROCKING

OUT of the cradle endlessly rocking,
Out of the mocking-bird's throat, the musical shuttle,
Out of the Ninth-month midnight,
Over the sterile sands and the fields beyond, where the child leaving his bed wandered alone, bareheaded, barefoot,
Down from the showered halo,
Up from the mystic play of shadows twining and twisting as if they were alive,

Out from the patches of briers and blackberries,
From the memories of the bird that chanted to me,
From your memories, sad brother, from the fitful risings
and fallings I heard,
From under that yellow half-moon late-risen and swollen
as if with tears,
From those beginning notes of yearning and love there
in the mist,
From the thousand responses of my heart never to cease,
From the myriad thence-aroused words,
From the word stronger and more delicious than any,
From such as now they start the scene revisiting,
As a flock, twittering, rising, or overhead passing,
Borne hither, ere all eludes me, hurriedly,
A man, yet by these tears a little boy again,
Throwing myself on the sand, confronting the waves,
I, chanter of pains and joys, uniter of here and hereafter,
Taking all hints to use them, but swiftly leaping beyond
them,
A reminiscence sing.

Once Paumanok,
When the lilac-scent was in the air and Fifth-month grass
was growing,
Up this seashore in some briers,
Two feathered guests from Alabama, two together,
And their nest, and four light-green eggs spotted with
brown,
And every day the he-bird to and fro near at hand,
And every day the she-bird crouched on her nest, silent,
with bright eyes,
And every day I, a curious boy, never too close, never
disturbing them,
Cautiously peering, absorbing, translating.

Shine! shine! shine!
Pour down your warmth, great sun!
While we bask, we two together.

Two together!
Winds blow south, or winds blow north,
Day come white, or night come black,
Home, or rivers and mountains from home,
Singing all time, minding no time,
While we two keep together.

Till of a sudden,
Maybe killed, unknown to her mate,
One forenoon the she-bird crouched not on the nest,
Nor returned that afternoon, nor the next,
Nor ever appeared again.

And thenceforward all summer in the sound of the sea,
And at night under the full of the moon in calmer weather,
Over the hoarse surging of the sea,
Or flitting from brier to brier by day,
I saw, I heard at intervals the remaining one, the he-bird,
The solitary guest from Alabama.

Blow! blow! blow!
Blow up sea-winds along Paumanok's shore;
I wait and I wait till you blow my mate to me.

Yes, when the stars glistened,
All night long on the prong of a moss-scalloped stake,
Down almost amid the slapping waves,
Sat the lone singer wonderful causing tears.

He called on his mate,
He poured forth the meanings which I of all men know,
Yes, my brother, I know,—
The rest might not, but I have treasured every note,
For more than once dimly down to the beach gliding,
Silent, avoiding the moonbeams, blending myself with the shadows,
Recalling now the obscure shapes, the echoes, the sounds and sights after their sorts,
The white arms out in the breakers tirelessly tossing,

I, with bare feet, a child, the wind wafting my hair,
Listened long and long.
Listened to keep, to sing, now translating the notes,
Following you, my brother.

Soothe! soothe! soothe!
Close on its wave soothes the wave behind,
And again another behind embracing and lapping, every one close,
But my love soothes not me, not me.

Low hangs the moon, it rose late,
It is lagging—O I think it is heavy with love, with love.

O madly the sea pushes upon the land,
With love, with love.

O night! do I not see my love fluttering out among the breakers?
What is that little black thing I see there in the white?

Loud! loud! loud!
Loud I call to you, my love!

High and clear I shoot my voice over the waves,
Surely you must know who is here, is here,
You must know who I am, my love.

Low-hanging moon!
What is that dusky spot in your brown yellow?
O it is the shape, the shape of my mate!
O moon, do not keep her from me any longer.

Land! land! O land!
Whichever way I turn, O I think you could give me my mate back again if you only would,
For I am almost sure I see her dimly whichever way I look.

O rising stars!
Perhaps the one I want so much will rise, will rise with some of you.

O throat! O trembling throat!
Sound clearer through the atmosphere!
Pierce the woods, the earth,
Somewhere listening to catch you must be the one I want.

Shake out carols!
Solitary here, the night's carols!
Carols of lonesome love! death's carols!
Carols under that lagging, yellow, waning moon!
O under that moon where she droops almost down into the sea!
O reckless despairing carols!

But soft! sink low!
Soft! let me just murmur,
And do you wait a moment, you husky-noised sea,
For somewhere I believe I heard my mate responding to me,
So faint, I must be still, be still to listen,
But not altogether still, for then she might not come immediately to me.

Hither, my love!
Here I am! here!
With this just-sustained note I announce myself to you,
This gentle call is for you my love, for you.

Do not be decoyed elsewhere:
That is the whistle of the wind, it is not my voice,
That is the fluttering, the fluttering of the spray,
Those are the shadows of leaves.

O darkness! O in vain!
O I am very sick and sorrowful.

O brown halo in the sky near the moon, drooping upon the sea!
O troubled reflection in the sea!

O throat! O throbbing heart!
And I singing uselessly, uselessly all the night.

O past! O happy life! O songs of joy!
In the air, in the woods, over fields,
Loved! loved! loved! loved! loved!
But my mate no more, no more with me!
We two together no more.

The aria sinking.
All else continuing, the stars shining,
The winds blowing, the notes of the bird continuous echoing,
With angry moans the fierce old mother incessantly moaning,
On the sands of Paumanok's shore gray and rustling,
The yellow half-moon enlarged, sagging down, drooping, the face of the sea almost touching,
The boy ecstatic, with his bare feet the waves, with his hair the atmosphere dallying,
The love in the heart long pent, now loose, now at last tumultuously bursting,
The aria's meaning, the ears, the soul, swiftly depositing,
The strange tears down the cheeks coursing,
The colloquy there, the trio, each uttering,
The undertone, the savage old mother incessantly crying,
To the boy's soul's questions sullenly timing, some drowned secret hissing,
To the outsetting bard.

Demon or bird (said the boy's soul)
Is it indeed toward your mate you sing? or is it really to me?
For I, that was a child, my tongue's use sleeping, now I have heard you,
Now in a moment I know what I am for, I awake,
And already a thousand singers, a thousand songs, clearer, louder and more sorrowful than yours,
A thousand warbling echoes have started to life within me, never to die.

O you singer solitary, singing by yourself, projecting me,
O solitary me listening, never more shall I cease perpetuating you,
Never more shall I escape, never more the reverberations,
Never more the cries of unsatisfied love be absent from me,
Never again leave me to be the peaceful child I was before what there in the night,
By the sea under the yellow and sagging moon,
The messenger there aroused, the fire, the sweet hell within,
The unknown want, the destiny of me.

O give me the clew! (It lurks in the night here somewhere)
O if I am to have so much, let me have more!

A word then, (for I will conquer it)
The word final, superior to all,
Subtle, sent up—what is it?—I listen;
Are you whispering it, and have been all the time, you sea-waves?
Is that it from your liquid rims and wet sands?

Whereto answering, the sea,
Delaying not, hurrying not,
Whispered me through the night, and very plainly before daybreak,
Lisped to me the low and delicious word death,
And again death, death, death, death,
Hissing melodious, neither like the bird nor like my aroused child's heart,
But edging near as privately for me, rustling at my feet,
Creeping thence steadily up to my ears and laving me softly all over,
Death, death, death, death, death.

Which I do not forget,
But fuse the song of my dusky demon and brother,
That he sang to me in the moonlight on Paumanok's gray beach,

With the thousand responsive songs at random,
My own songs awaked from that hour,
And with them the key, the word up from the waves,
The word of the sweetest song and all songs,
That strong and delicious word which, creeping to my feet,
(Or like some old crone rocking the cradle, swathed in sweet garments, bending aside)
The sea whispered me.

WHEN LILACS LAST IN THE DOORYARD BLOOMED

I

When lilacs last in the dooryard bloomed,
And the great star early drooped in the western sky at night,
I mourned, and yet shall mourn with ever-returning spring.

Ever-returning spring, trinity sure to me you bring,
Lilac blooming perennial and drooping star in the west,
And thought of him I love.

II

O powerful western fallen star!
O shades of night—O moody, tearful night!
O great star disappeared—O the black murk that hides the star!
O cruel hands that hold me powerless—O helpless soul of me!
O harsh surrounding cloud that will not free my soul.

III

In the dooryard fronting an old farmhouse near the white-washed palings,
Stands the lilac-bush tall-growing with heart-shaped leaves of rich green,

With many a pointed blossom rising delicate, with the perfume strong I love,
With every leaf a miracle—and from this bush in the dooryard,
With delicate-colored blossoms and heart-shaped leaves of rich green,
A sprig with its flower I break.

IV

In the swamp in secluded recesses,
A shy and hidden bird is warbling a song.
Solitary the thrush,
The hermit withdrawn to himself, avoiding the settlements,
Sings by himself a song.

Song of the bleeding throat,
Death's outlet song of life (for well dear brother I know,
If thou wast not granted to sing thou wouldst surely die.)

V

Over the breast of the spring, the land, amid cities,
Amid lanes and through old woods, where lately the violets peeped from the ground, spotting the gray débris,
Amid the grass in the fields each side of the lanes, passing the endless grass,
Passing the yellow-speared wheat, every grain from its shroud in the dark-brown fields uprisen,
Passing the apple-tree blows of white and pink in the orchards,
Carrying a corpse to where it shall rest in the grave,
Night and day journeys a coffin.

VI

Coffin that passes through lanes and streets,
Through day and night with the great cloud darkening the land,

With the pomp of the inlooped flags with the cities
draped in black,
With the show of the States themselves as of crape-veiled
women standing,
With processions long and winding and the flambeaus
of the night,
With the countless torches lit, with the silent sea of faces
and the unbared heads,
With the waiting depot, the arriving coffin, and the
somber faces,
With dirges through the night, with the thousand voices
rising strong and solemn,
With all the mournful voices of the dirges poured around
the coffin,
The dim-lit churches and the shuddering organs—where
amid these you journey,
With the tolling tolling bells' perpetual clang,
Here, coffin that slowly passes,
I give you my sprig of lilac.

VII

(Nor for you, for one alone,
Blossoms and branches green to coffins all I bring,
For fresh as the morning, thus would I chant a song for
you, O sane and sacred death.
All over bouquets of roses,
O death, I cover you over with roses and early lilies,
But mostly and now the lilac that blooms the first,
Copious I break, I break the sprigs from the bushes,
With loaded arms I come, pouring for you,
For you, and the coffins all of you, O death.)

VIII

O western orb sailing the heaven,
Now I know what you must have meant as a month
since I walked,
As I walked in silence the transparent shadowy night,
As I saw you had something to tell as you bent to me
night after night,

As you drooped from the sky low down as if to my side (while the other stars all looked on),
As we wandered together the solemn night (for something, I know not what, kept me from sleep),
As the night advanced, and I saw on the rim of the west how full you were of woe,
As I stood on the rising ground in the breeze in the cool transparent night,
As I watched where you passed and was lost in the netherward black of the night,
As my soul in its trouble dissatisfied sank, as where you, sad orb,
Concluded, dropped in the night, and was gone.

IX

Sing on, there in the swamp,
O singer bashful and tender! I hear your notes, I hear your call,
I hear, I come presently, I understand you;
But a moment I linger, for the lustrous star has detained me,
The star, my departing comrade, holds and detains me.
O how shall I warble myself for the dead one there I loved?
And how shall I deck my song for the large sweet soul that has gone?
And what shall my perfume be for the grave of him I love?

Sea-winds blown from east and west,
Blown from the Eastern sea and blown from the Western sea, till there on the prairies meeting,
These, and with these, and the breath of my chant,
I'll perfume the grave of him I love.

XI

O what shall I hang on the chamber walls?
And what shall the pictures be that I hang on the walls,
To adorn the burial-house of him I love?

Pictures of growing spring and farms and homes,
With the Fourth-month eve at sundown, and the gray smoke lucid and bright,
With floods of the yellow gold of the gorgeous, indolent, sinking sun, burning, expanding the air,
With the fresh sweet herbage under foot, and the pale green leaves of the trees prolific,
In the distance the flowing glaze, the breast of the river, with a wind-dapple here and there,
With ranging hills on the banks, with many a line against the sky, and shadows,
And the city at hand with dwellings so dense, and stacks of chimneys,
And all the scenes of life and the workshops, and the workmen homeward returning.

XII

Lo, body and soul—this land,
My own Manhattan with spires, and the sparkling and hurrying tides, and the ships,
The varied and ample land, the South and the North in the light, Ohio's shores and flashing Missouri,
And ever the far-spreading prairies covered with grass and corn.

Lo, the most excellent sun so calm and haughty,
The violet and purple morn with just-felt breezes,
The gentle soft-born measureless light,
The miracle spreading, bathing all, the fulfilled noon,
The coming eve delicious, the welcome night and the stars,
Over my cities shining all, enveloping man and land.

XIII

Sing on, sing on you gray-brown bird,
Sing from the swamps, the recesses, pour your chant from the bushes,
Limitless out of the dusk, out of the cedars and pines.

Sing on dearest brother, warble your reedy song,
Loud human song, with voice of uttermost woe.

O liquid and free and tender!
O wild and loose to my soul—O wondrous singer!
You only I hear—yet the star holds me (but will soon depart),
Yet the lilac with mastering odor holds me.

XIV

Now while I sat in the day and looked forth,
In the close of the day with its light and the fields of spring, and the farmers preparing their crops,
In the large unconscious scenery of my land with its lakes and forests,
In the heavenly aerial beauty (after the perturbed winds and the storms),
Under the arching heavens of the afternoon swift passing, and the voices of children and women,
The many-moving sea-tides, and I saw the ships how they sailed,

And the summer approaching with richness, and the fields all busy with labor,
And the infinite separate houses, how they all went on, each with its meals and minutia of daily usages,
And the streets how their throbbings throbbed, and the cities pent—lo, then and there,
Falling upon them all and among them all, enveloping me with the rest,
Appeared the cloud, appeared the long black trail,
And I knew death, its thought, and the sacred knowledge of death.

Then with the knowledge of death as walking one side of me,
And the thought of death close-walking the other side of me,
And I in the middle as with companions, and as holding the hands of companions,

I fled forth to the hiding, receiving night that talks not,
Down to the shores of the water, the path by the swamp
in the dimness.
To the solemn shadowy cedars and ghostly pines so still.
And the singer so shy to the rest received me,
The gray-brown bird I know received us comrades three,
And he sang the carol of death, and a verse for him
I love.

From deep secluded recesses,
From the fragrant cedars and the ghostly pines so still,
Came the carol of the bird.

And the charm of the carol rapt me,
As I held as if by their hands my comrades in the night,
And the voice of my spirit tallied the song of the bird.

Come lovely and soothing death,
Undulate round the world, serenely arriving, arriving,
In the day, in the night, to all, to each,
Sooner or later delicate death.

Praised be the fathomless universe,
For life and joy, and for objects and knowledge curious,
And for love, sweet love—but praise! praise! praise!
For the sure-enwinding arms of cool-enfolding death.

Dark mother always gliding near with soft feet,
Have none chanted for thee a chant of fullest welcome?
Then I chant it for thee, I glorify thee above all,
I bring thee a song that when thou must indeed come,
come unfalteringly.

Approach, strong deliveress!
When it is so, when thou hast taken them, I joyously sing
the dead,
Lost in the loving floating ocean of thee,
Laved in the flood of thy bliss, O death.

From me to thee glad serenades,
Dances for thee I propose, saluting thee, adornments and
feastings for thee,

And the sights of the open landscapes and the high-spread sky are fitting,
And life and the fields, and the huge and thoughtful night.
The night in silence under many a star,
The ocean shore and the husky whispering wave whose voice I know,
And the soul turning to thee, O vast and well-veiled death,
And the body gratefully nestling close to thee.

Over the tree-tops I float thee a song,
Over the rising and sinking waves, over the myriad fields and the prairies wide,
Over the dense-packed cities all and the teeming wharves and ways,
I float this carol with joy, with joy to thee O death.

XV

To the tally of my soul,
Loud and strong kept up the gray-brown bird,
With pure deliberate notes, spreading, filling the night.

Loud in the pines and cedars dim,
Clear in the freshness moist and the swamp-perfume,
And I with my comrades there in the night.

While my sight that was bound in my eyes unclosed,
As to long panoramas of visions.

And I saw askant the armies,
I saw as in noiseless dreams hundreds of battle-flags,
Borne through the smoke of the battles and pierced with missiles I saw them,
And carried hither and yon through the smoke, and torn and bloody,
And at last but a few shreds left on the staffs (and all in silence),
And the staffs all splintered and broken.

I saw battle-corpses, myriads of them,
And the white skeletons of young men, I saw them,
I saw the débris and débris of all the slain soldiers of the war,
But I saw they were not as was thought,
They themselves were fully at rest, they suffered not,
The living remained and suffered, the mother suffered,
And the wife and the child and the musing comrade suffered,
And the armies that remained suffered.

XVI

Passing the visions, passing the night,
Passing, unloosing the hold of my comrades' hands,
Passing the song of the hermit bird and the tallying song of my soul,
Victorious song, death's outlet song, yet varying, ever-altering song,
As low and wailing, yet clear the notes, rising and falling, flooding the night,
Sadly sinking and fainting, as warning and warning, and yet again bursting with joy,
Covering the earth and filling the spread of the heaven,
As that powerful psalm in the night I heard from recesses,
Passing, I leave thee lilac with heart-shaped leaves,
I leave thee there is the door-yard, blooming, returning with spring.

I cease from my song for thee,
From my gaze on thee in the west, fronting the west, communing with thee,
O comrade lustrous with silver face in the night.

Yet each to keep and all, retrievements out of the night,
The song, the wondrous chant of the gray-brown bird,
And the tallying chant, the echo aroused in my soul,
With the lustrous and drooping star with the countenance full of woe,

With the holders holding my hand nearing the call of
 the bird,
Comrades mine, and I in the midst, and their memory
 ever to keep, for the dead I loved so well,
For the sweetest, wisest soul of all my days and lands—
 and this for his dear sake,
Lilac and star and bird twined with the chant of my soul,
There in the fragrant pines and the cedars dusk and dim.

I HEAR AMERICA SINGING

I HEAR America singing, the varied carols I hear,
Those of mechanics, each one singing his as it should be
 blithe and strong,
The carpenter singing his as he measures his plank or
 beam,
The mason singing his as he makes ready for work, or
 leaves off work,
The boatman singing what belongs to him in his boat,
 the deckhand singing on the steamboat deck,
The shoemaker singing as he sits on his bench, the hatter
 singing as he stands,
The wood-cutter's song, the ploughboy's on his way in
 the morning, or at noon intermission or at sundown,
The delicious singing of the mother, or of the young wife
 at work, or of the girl sewing or washing,
Each singing what belongs to him or her and to none else,
The day what belongs to the day—at night the party of
 young fellows, robust, friendly,
Singing with open mouths their strong melodious songs.

ON THE BEACH AT NIGHT

On the beach at night,
Stands a child with her father,
Watching the east, the autumn sky.
Up through the darkness,
While ravening clouds, the burial clouds, in black masses
 spreading,

Lower sullen and fast athwart and down the sky,
Amid a transparent clear belt of ether yet left in the east,
Ascends large and calm the lord-star Jupiter,
And nigh at hand, only a very little above,
Swim the delicate sisters the Pleiades.

From the beach the child holding the hand of her father,
Those burial-clouds that lower victorious soon to devour all,
Watching, silently weeps.

Weep not, child,
Weep not, my darling,
With these kisses let me remove your tears,
The ravening clouds shall not long be victorious,
They shall not long possess the sky, they devour the stars only in apparition,
Jupiter shall emerge, be patient, watch again another night, the Pleiades shall emerge,
They are immortal, all those stars both silvery and golden shall shine out again,
The great stars and the little ones shall shine out again, they endure,
The vast immortal suns and the long-enduring pensive moons shall again shine.

Then dearest child mournest thou only for Jupiter?
Considerest thou alone the burial of the stars?
Something there is,
(With my lips soothing thee, adding I whisper,
I give thee the first suggestion, the problem and indirection,)
Something there is more immortal even than the stars,
(Many the burials, many the days and nights, passing away,)
Something that shall endure longer even than lustrous Jupiter,
Longer than sun or any revolving satellite,
Or the radiant sisters the Pleiades.

Emily Dickinson

1830–1886

SUCCESS

SUCCESS is counted sweetest
By those who ne'er succeed.
To comprehend a nectar
Requires sorest need.

Not one of all the purple host
Who took the flag to-day
Can tell the definition,
So clear, of victory,

As he, defeated, dying,
On whose forbidden ear
The distant strains of triumph
Break, agonized and clear.

A WOUNDED DEER LEAPS HIGHEST

A WOUNDED deer leaps highest,
I've heard the hunter tell;
'Tis but the ecstasy of death,
And then the brake is still.

The smitten rock that gushes,
The trampled steel that springs:
A cheek is always redder
Just where the hectic stings!

Mirth is the mail of anguish,
In which it cautious arm,
Lest anybody spy the blood
And "You're hurt" exclaim!

EXCLUSION

THE soul selects her own society,
Then shuts the door;
On her divine majority
Obtrude no more.

Unmoved, she notes the chariot's pausing
At her low gate;
Unmoved, an emperor is kneeling
Upon her mat.

I've known her from an ample nation
Choose one;
Then close the valves of her attention
Like stone.

SUSPENSE

ELYSIUM is as far as to
The very nearest room,
If in that room a friend await
Felicity or doom.

What fortitude the soul contains,
That it can so endure
The accent of a coming foot,
The opening of a door!

I DIED FOR BEAUTY

I died for beauty, but was scarce
Adjusted in the tomb,
When one who died for truth was lain
In an adjoining room.

He questioned softly why I failed?
"For beauty," I replied.
"And I for truth,—the two are one;
We brethren are," he said.

And so, as kinsmen met a night,
We talked between the rooms,
Until the moss had reached our lips,
And covered up our names.

BECAUSE I COULD NOT STOP FOR DEATH

Because I could not stop for Death,
He kindly stopped for me;
The carriage held but just ourselves
And Immortality.

We slowly drove, he knew no haste,
And I had put away
My labor, and my leisure too,
For his civility.

We passed the school where children played
At wrestling in a ring;
We passed the fields of gazing grain,
We passed the setting sun.

We paused before a house that seemed
A swelling of the ground;
The roof was scarcely visible,
The cornice but a mound.

Since then 't is centuries; but each
Feels shorter than the day
I first surmised the horses' heads
Were toward eternity.

AFTER A HUNDRED YEARS

After a hundred years
Nobody knows the place,—
Agony, that enacted there,
Motionless as peace.

Weeds triumphant ranged,
Strangers strolled and spelled

At the lone orthography
Of the elder dead.

Winds of summer fields
Recollect the way,—
Instinct picking up the key
Dropped by memory.

I HAD NOT MINDED WALLS

I HAD not minded walls
Were Universe one rock,
And far I heard his silver call
The other side the block.

I'd tunnel until my groove
Pushed sudden through to his,
Then my face take recompense—
The looking in his eyes.

But 't is a single hair,
A filament, a law—
A cobweb wove in adamant,
A battlement of straw—

A limit like the veil
Unto the lady's face,
But every mesh a citadel
And dragons in the crease!

George Santayana

1863–

I WOULD I MIGHT FORGET THAT I AM I

I WOULD I might forget that I am I,
And break the heavy chain that binds me fast,
Whose links about myself my deeds have cast.
What in the body's tomb doth buried lie
Is boundless; 'tis the spirit of the sky,
Lord of the future, guardian of the past,

And soon must forth, to know his own at last.
In his large life to live, I fain would die.
Happy the dumb beast, hungering for food,
But calling not his suffering his own;
Blessèd the angel, gazing on all good,
But knowing not he sits upon a throne;
Wretched the mortal, pondering his mood,
And doomed to know his aching heart alone.

AS IN THE MIDST OF BATTLE THERE IS ROOM

As in the midst of battle there is room
For thoughts of love, and in foul sin for mirth;
As gossips whisper of a trinket's worth
Spied by the death-bed's flickering candle-gloom;
As in the crevices of Cæsar's tomb
The sweet herbs flourish on a little earth:
So in this great disaster of our birth
We can be happy, and forget our doom.
For morning, with a ray of tenderest joy
Gilding the iron heaven, hides the truth,
And evening gently woos us to employ
Our grief in idle catches. Such is youth;
Till from that summer's trance we wake, to find
Despair before us, vanity behind.

Edwin Arlington Robinson

1869–1935

LUKE HAVERGAL

Go to the western gate, Luke Havergal,
There where the vines cling crimson on the wall,
And in the twilight wait for what will come.
The leaves will whisper there of her, and some,
Like flying words, will strike you as they fall;
But go, and if you listen she will call.
Go to the western gate, Luke Havergal—
Luke Havergal.

No, there is not a dawn in eastern skies
To rift the fiery night that's in your eyes;
But there, where western glooms are gathering,
The dark will end the dark, if anything:
God slays Himself with every leaf that flies,
And hell is more than half of paradise.
No, there is not a dawn in eastern skies—
In eastern skies.

Out of a grave I come to tell you this,
Out of a grave I come to quench the kiss
That flames upon your forehead with a glow
That blinds you to the way that you must go.
Yes, there is yet one way to where she is,
Bitter, but one that faith may never miss.
Out of a grave I come to tell you this—
To tell you this.

There is the western gate, Luke Havergal,
There are the crimson leaves upon the wall.
Go, for the winds are tearing them away,—
Nor think to riddle the dead words they say,
Nor any more to feel them as they fall;
But go, and if you trust her she will call.
There is the western gate, Luke Havergal—
Luke Havergal.

MINIVER CHEEVY

Miniver Cheevy, child of scorn,
  Grew lean while he assailed the seasons;
He wept that he was ever born,
  And he had reasons.

Miniver loved the days of old
  When swords were bright and steeds were prancing;
The vision of a warrior bold
  Would set him dancing.

Miniver sighed for what was not,
  And dreamed, and rested from his labors;
He dreamed of Thebes and Camelot,
  And Priam's neighbors.

Miniver mourned the ripe renown
  That made so many a name so fragrant;
He mourned Romance, now on the town,
  And Art, a vagrant.

Miniver loved the Medici,
  Albeit he had never seen one;
He would have sinned incessantly
  Could he have been one.

Miniver cursed the commonplace
  And eyed a khaki suit with loathing;
He missed the mediæval grace
  Of iron clothing.

Miniver scorned the gold he sought,
  But sore annoyed was he without it;
Miniver thought, and thought, and thought,
  And thought about it.

Miniver Cheevy, born too late,
  Scratched his head and kept on thinking;
Miniver coughed, and called it fate,
  And kept on drinking.

MR. FLOOD'S PARTY

Old Eben Flood, climbing alone one night
Over the hill between the town below
And the forsaken upland hermitage
That held as much as he should ever know
On earth again of home, paused warily.
The road was his with not a native near;
And Eben, having leisure, said aloud,
For no man else in Tilbury Town to hear:

"Well, Mr. Flood, we have the harvest moon
Again, and we may not have many more;
The bird is on the wing, the poet says,
And you and I have said it here before.
Drink to the bird." He raised up to the light
The jug that he had gone so far to fill,
And answered huskily: "Well, Mr. Flood,
Since you propose it, I believe I will."

Alone, as if enduring to the end
A valiant armor of scarred hopes outworn,
He stood there in the middle of the road
Like Roland's ghost winding a silent horn.
Below him, in the town among the trees,
Where friends of other days had honored him,
A phantom salutation of the dead
Rang thinly till old Eben's eyes were dim.

Then, as a mother lays her sleeping child
Down tenderly, fearing it may awake,
He set the jug down slowly at his feet
With trembling care, knowing that most things break;
And only when assured that on firm earth
It stood, as the uncertain lives of men
Assuredly did not, he paced away,
And with his hand extended paused again:

"Well, Mr. Flood, we have not met like this
In a long time; and many a change has come
To both of us, I fear, since last it was
We had a drop together. Welcome home!"
Convivially returning with himself,
Again he raised the jug up to the light;
And with an acquiescent quaver said:
"Well, Mr. Flood, if you insist, I might.

"Only a very little, Mr. Flood——
For auld lang syne. No more, sir; that will do."
So, for the time, apparently it did,
And Eben evidently thought so too;

For soon amid the silver loneliness
Of night he lifted up his voice and sang,
Secure, with only two moons listening,
Until the whole harmonious landscape rang—

"For auld lang syne." The weary throat gave out,
The last word wavered; and the song being done,
He raised again the jug regretfully
And shook his head, and was again alone.
There was not much that was ahead of him,
And there was nothing in the town below—
Where strangers would have shut the many doors
That many friends had opened long ago.

THE SHEAVES

Where long the shadows of the wind had rolled,
Green wheat was yielding to the change assigned;
And as by some vast magic undivined
The world was turning slowly into gold.
Like nothing that was ever bought or sold
It waited there, the body and the mind;
And with a mighty meaning of a kind
That tells the more the more it is not told.
So in a land where all days are not fair,
Fair days went on till on another day
A thousand golden sheaves were lying there,
Shining and still, but not for long to stay—
As if a thousand girls with golden hair
Might rise from where they slept and go away.

Amy Lowell

1874–1925

PATTERNS

I walk down the garden paths,
And all the daffodils
Are blowing, and the bright blue squills.

I walk down the patterned garden paths
In my stiff, brocaded gown.
With my powdered hair and jeweled fan,
I too am a rare
Pattern. As I wander down
The garden paths.

My dress is richly figured,
And the train
Makes a pink and silver stain
On the gravel, and the thrift
Of the borders.
Just a plate of current fashion,
Tripping by in high-heeled, ribboned shoes.
Not a softness anywhere about me,
Only whale-bone and brocade.
And I sink on a seat in the shade
Of a lime tree. For my passion
Wars against the stiff brocade.
The daffodils and squills
Flutter in the breeze
As they please.
And I weep;
For the lime tree is in blossom
And one small flower has dropped upon my bosom.

And the plashing of waterdrops
In the marble fountain
Comes down the garden paths.
The dripping never stops.
Underneath my stiffened gown
Is the softness of a woman bathing in a marble basin,
A basin in the midst of hedges grown
So thick, she cannot see her lover hiding,
But she guesses he is near,
And the sliding of the water
Seems the stroking of a dear
Hand upon her.
What is Summer in a fine brocaded gown!

I should like to see it lying in a heap upon the ground,
All the pink and silver crumpled up on the ground.

I would be the pink and silver as I ran along the paths,
And he would stumble after,
Bewildered by my laughter.
I should see the sun flashing from his sword hilt and the buckles on his shoes.
I would choose
To lead him in a maze along the patterned paths,
A bright and laughing maze for my heavy-booted lover,
Till he caught me in the shade,
And the buttons of his waistcoat bruised my body as he clasped me,
Aching, melting, unafraid.
With the shadows of the leaves and the sundrops,
And the plopping of the waterdrops,
All about us in the open afternoon—
I am very like to swoon
With the weight of this brocade,
For the sun sifts through the shade.

Underneath the fallen blossom
In my bosom,
Is a letter I have hid.
It was brought to me this morning by a rider from the Duke.
"Madam, we regret to inform you that Lord Hartwell
Died in action Thursday se'n night."
As I read it in the white, morning sunlight,
The letters squirmed like snakes.
"Any answer, Madam," said my footman.
"No," I told him.
"See that the messenger takes some refreshment.
No, no answer."
And I walked into the garden,
Up and down the patterned paths,
In my stiff, correct brocade.
The blue and yellow flowers stood up proudly in the sun,

Each one.
I stood upright too,
Held rigid to the pattern
By the stiffness of my gown.
Up and down I walked,
Up and down.

In a month he would have been my husband.
In a month, here, underneath this lime,
We would have broke the pattern;
He for me, and I for him,
He as Colonel, I as Lady,
On this shady seat.
He had a whim
That sunlight carried blessing.
And I answered, "It shall be as you have said."
Now he is dead.
In Summer and in Winter I shall walk
Up and down
The patterned garden paths
In my stiff, brocaded gown.
The squills and daffodils
Will give place to pillared roses, and to asters, and to snow.
I shall go
Up and down,
In my gown.
Gorgeously arrayed,
Boned and stayed.
And the softness of my body will be guarded from embrace
By each button, hook, and lace.
For the man who should loose me is dead,
Fighting with the Duke in Flanders,
In a pattern called a war.
Christ! What are patterns for?

Robert Frost

1875–

THE RUNAWAY

Once when the snow of the year was beginning to fall,
We stopped by a mountain pasture to say "Whose colt?"
A little Morgan had one forefoot on the wall,
The other curled at his breast. He dipped his head
And snorted at us. And then he had to bolt.
We heard the miniature thunder where he fled,
And we saw him, or thought we saw him, dim and gray,
Like a shadow against the curtain of falling flakes.
"I think the little fellow's afraid of the snow.
He isn't winter-broken. It isn't play
With the little fellow at all. He's running away.
I doubt if even his mother could tell him, 'Sakes,
It's only weather.' He'd think she didn't know!
Where is his mother? He can't be out alone."
And now he comes again with a clatter of stone
And mounts the wall again with whited eyes
And all his tail that isn't hair up straight.
He shudders his coat as if to throw off flies.
"Whoever it is that leaves him out so late,
When other creatures have gone to stall and bin,
Ought to be told to come and take him in."

AN OLD MAN'S WINTER NIGHT

All out of doors looked darkly in at him
Through the thin frost, almost in separate stars,
That gathers on the pane in empty rooms.
What kept his eyes from giving back the gaze
Was the lamp tilted near them in his hand.
What kept him from remembering what it was
That brought him to that creaking room was age.
He stood with barrels round him—at a loss.
And having scared the cellar under him
In clomping there, he scared it once again
In clomping off;—and scared the outer night,

Which has its sounds, familiar, like the roar
Of trees and crack of branches, common things,
But nothing so like beating on a box.
A light he was to no one but himself
Where now he sat, concerned with he knew what,
A quiet light, and then not even that.
He consigned to the moon, such as she was,
So late-arising, to the broken moon
As better than the sun in any case
For such a charge, his snow upon the roof,
His icicles along the wall to keep;
And slept. The log that shifted with a jolt
Once in the stove, disturbed him and he shifted,
And eased his heavy breathing, but still slept.
One aged man—one man—can't keep a house,
A farm, a countryside, or if he can,
It's thus he does it of a winter night.

THE OVEN BIRD

There is a singer everyone has heard,
Loud, a mid-summer and a mid-wood bird,
Who makes the solid tree trunks sound again.
He says that leaves are old and that for flowers
Mid-summer is to spring as one to ten.
He says the early petal-fall is past
When pear and cherry bloom went down in showers
On sunny days a moment overcast;
And comes that other fall we name the fall.
He says the highway dust is over all.
The bird would cease and be as other birds
But that he knows in singing not to sing.
The question that he frames in all but words
Is what to make of a diminished thing.

THE TUFT OF FLOWERS

I went to turn the grass once after one
Who mowed it in the dew before the sun.

The dew was gone that made his blade so keen
Before I came to view the leveled scene.

I looked for him behind an isle of trees;
I listened for his whetstone on the breeze.

But he had gone his way, the grass all mown,
And I must be, as he had been—alone,

"As all must be," I said within my heart,
"Whether they work together or apart."

But as I said it, swift there passed me by
On noiseless wing a bewildered butterfly,

Seeking with memories grown dim o'er night
Some resting flower of yesterday's delight.

And once I marked his flight go round and round,
As where some flower lay withering on the ground.

And then he flew as far as eye could see,
And then on tremulous wing came back to me.

I thought of questions that have no reply,
And would have turned to toss the grass to dry;

But he turned first, and led my eye to look
At a tall tuft of flowers beside a brook,

A leaping tongue of bloom the scythe had spared
Beside a reedy brook the scythe had bared.

I left my place to know them by their name,
Finding them butterfly weed when I came.

The mower in the dew had loved them thus,
By leaving them to flourish, not for us,

Nor yet to draw one thought of ours to him.
But from sheer morning gladness at the brim.

The butterfly and I had lit upon,
Nevertheless, a message from the dawn,

That made me hear the wakening birds around,
And hear his long scythe whispering to the ground,

And feel a spirit kindred to my own;
So that henceforth I worked no more alone;

But glad with him, I worked as with his aid,
And weary, sought at noon with him the shade;

And dreaming, as it were, held brotherly speech
With one whose thought I had not hoped to reach.

"Men work together," I told him from the heart,
"Whether they work together or apart."

Carl Sandburg

1878–

GRASS

PILE the bodies high at Austerlitz and Waterloo.
Shovel them under and let me work—
I am the grass; I cover all.

And pile them high at Gettysburg
And pile them high at Ypres and Verdun.
Shovel them under and let me work.
Two years, ten years, and the passengers ask the conductor:
What place is this?
Where are we now?

I am the grass.
Let me work.

THREE SPRING NOTATIONS ON BIPEDS

1

THE down drop of the blackbird,
The wing catch of arrested flight,
The stop midway and then off:
off for triangles, circles, loops
of new hieroglyphs—
This is April's way: a woman:
"O yes, I'm here again and your heart
knows I was coming."

2

White pigeons rush at the sun,
A marathon of wing feats is on:
"Who most loves danger? Who most loves
wings? Who somersaults for God's sake
in the name of wing power
in the sun and blue
on an April Thursday."
So ten winged heads, ten winged feet,
race their white forms over Elmhurst.
They go fast: once the ten together were
a feather of foam bubble, a chrysanthemum
whirl speaking to silver and azure.

3

The child is on my shoulders.
In the prairie moonlight the child's legs
hang over my shoulders.
She sits on my neck and I hear her calling
me a good horse.
She slides down—and into the moon silver of a
prairie stream
She throws a stone and laughs at the clug-clug.

Nicholas Vachel Lindsay

1879–1931

THE EAGLE THAT IS FORGOTTEN

(JOHN P. ALTGELD)

SLEEP softly . . . eagle forgotten . . . under the stone.
Time has its way with you there, and the clay has its own.

"We have buried him now," thought your foes, and in secret rejoiced.
They made a brave show of their mourning, their hatred unvoiced.
They had snarled at you, barked at you, foamed at you, day after day.
Now you were ended. They praised you . . . and laid you away.

The others, that mourned you in silence and terror and truth,
The widow bereft of her crust, and the boy without youth,
The mocked and the scorned and the wounded, the lame and the poor,
That should have remembered forever, . . . Remember no more.

Where are those lovers of yours, on what name do they call,
The lost, that in armies wept over your funeral pall?
They call on the names of a hundred high-valiant ones,
A hundred white eagles have risen, the sons of your sons.
The zeal in their wings is a zeal that your dreaming began.
The valor that wore out your soul in the service of man.

Sleep softly . . . eagle forgotten . . . under the stone.
Time has its way with you there, and the clay has its own.
Sleep on, O brave-hearted, O wise man that kindled the flame—

To live in mankind is far more than to live in a name,
To live in mankind, far, far more than . . . to live in a name.

Ezra Pound

1885–

THE GARDEN

En robe de parade.
Samain

Like a skein of loose silk blown against a wall
She walks by the railing of a path in Kensington Gardens,
And she is dying piece-meal of a sort of emotional anæmia.

And round about there is a rabble
Of the filthy, sturdy, unkillable infants of the very poor.
They shall inherit the earth.

In her is the end of breeding.
Her boredom is exquisite and excessive.
She would like some one to speak to her,
And is almost afraid that I will commit that indiscretion.

John Gould Fletcher

1886–

SONG OF THE MODERNS

We more than others have the perfect right
To see the cities like flambeaux flare along the night.

We more than others have the right to cast away
Thought like a withered leaf, since it has served its day;

Since for this transient joy which not for long can burn
Within our hearts, we gave up in return

Ten thousand years of holy magic power
Drawn from the darkness to transcend death's hour.

For every witch that died an electric lamp shall flare,
For every wizard drowned, the clear blue air

Shall roar with jazz-bands into listening ears;
For every alchemist who spent in vain his years

Seeking the stone of truth, a motor-horn
Shall scare the sheep that wander among the corn.

And there shall be no more the spirits of the deep,
Nor holy satyrs slumbering upon the steep,

Nor angels at a manger or a cross.
Life shall go on; to ugly gain or loss;

Yet vaster and more tragic, till at last
This present too shall make part of the past:—

Till all the joy and tragedy that man knows
To-day, become stiff gravestones in long rows:

Till none dare look on the mountains ranked afar,
And think 'These are the cast-off leavings of some star.'

LAST JUDGMENT

THERE fell red rain of spears athwart the sky,
Flame flapped upon a heather-covered moor,
Green waves tossed high the ships that steamed near
shore
And dashed their keels to wreck. Aloof and high

The evening star like a gold plummet fell
Into the shadowy horror of a sea
Frozen to glass. The sky split. Vacantly
Across the void there trailed the Snake of Hell.

Now out of every graveyard on the earth
There suddenly writhed in flame and stood up new as
man
A being whose girth no human eye could span;
Two heads it had—one like a babe at birth,

The other like a skull. It hollowly spoke
Like wind that roars in echoes huge and vast,
Against the unconceived, unfathomed past:—
'Now ended is God's high and pitiless joke.'

"H. D."

1886–

ADONIS

I

Each of us like you
has died once,
each of us like you
has passed through drift of wood-leaves
cracked and bent
and tortured and unbent
in the winter frost—
then burnt into gold points,
lighted afresh,
crisp amber, scales of gold-leaf,
gold turned and re-welded
in the sun-heat.

Each of us like you
has died once,
each of us has crossed an old wood-path
and found the winter leaves
so golden in the sun-fire
that even the live wood-flowers
were dark.

II

Not the gold on the temple-front
where you stand
is as gold as this,
not the gold that fastens your sandal,
nor the gold reft
through your chiseled locks

is as gold as this last year's leaf,
not all the gold hammered and wrought
and beaten
on your lover's face,
brow and bare breast
is as golden at this.

Each of us like you
has died once,
each of us like you
stands apart, like you
fit to be worshiped.

OREAD

WHIRL up, sea—
Whirl your pointed pines,
Splash your great pines
On our rocks,
Hurl your green over us,
Cover us with your pools of fir.

William Rose Benét

1886–

ETERNAL MASCULINE

NEITHER will I put myself forward as others may do,
Neither, if you wish me to flatter, will I flatter you;
I will look at you grimly, and so you will know I am true.

Neither when all do agree and lout low and salute,
And you are beguiled by the tree and devout for the fruit,
Will I seem to be aught but the following eyes of a brute.

I will stand to one side and sip of my hellebore wine,
I will snarl and deride the antics and airs of the swine;
You will glance in your pride, but I will deny you a sign.

I will squint at the moon and be peaceful because I am
dead,
I will whistle a tune and be glad of the harshness I said.
O you will come soon, when the stars are a mist overhead!

You will come, with eyes fierce; you will act a defiant
surprise.
Quick lightnings will pierce to our hearts from the pain
in our eyes,
Standing strained and averse, with the trembling of love
that defies.

And then I will know, by the heartbreaking turn of your
head,
My madness brought low in a hell that is spared to the
dead.
The upas will grow from the poisonous words that I said;

From under its shade out to where like a statue you stand,
Without wish to evade, I will reach, I will cry with my
hand,
With my spirit dismayed, with my eyes and my mouth
full of sand. . . .

THE WOODCUTTER'S WIFE

Times she'll sit quiet by the hearth, and times
She'll ripple with a fit of twinkling rhymes
And rise and pirouette and flirt her hand,
Strut jackdaw-like, or stamp a curt command
Or, from behind my chair, suddenly blind me;
Then, when I turn, be vanished from behind me.

Times she'll be docile as the gentlest thing
That ever blinked in fur or folded wing,
And then, like lightning in the dead of night,
Fill with wild, crackling, intermitting light
My mind and soul and senses,—and next be
Aloof, askance as a dryad in a tree.

Then she'll be gone for days; when next I turn,
There, coaxing yellow butter from the churn,
Rubbing to silver every pan of tin,
Or conjuring color from the rooms within
Through innocent flowers, she'll hum about the house
Bright-eyed and secret as a velvet mouse.

'T is not your will They do,—no, nor the Will
That hushes Anselm's chapel overhill.
Something that drifts in clouds, that sings in rain,
That laughs in sunlight, shudders in the pain
Of desolate seas, or broods in basking earth
Governs Their melancholy and Their mirth.

Elusive still! Elusive as my reason
For trudging woodward in or out of season
To swing the ringing ax, as year by year
The inexplicable end draws slowly near,
And, in between, to think and think about it,—
Life's puzzling dream,—deride, believe, and doubt it.

But if I leave her seriously alone
She comes quite near, preëmpts some woodland stone,
Spreads out her kirtle like a shimmering dress
And fills my mind's remorseful emptiness
With marvelous jewels made of words and wit
Till all my being sings because of it,

Sings of the way her bronze hair waves about
And her amber-lighted eyes peer out;
Sings of her sudden laughter floating wild,
Of all her antics of a fairy child,
Of her uplifted head and swift, demure
Silence and awe, than purity more pure.

So I must scratch my head and drop my ax,
While in her hands my will is twisted wax;
So when she goes, deaf, dumb and blind I sit
Watching her empty arm-chair opposite,
Witched by evasive brightness in the brain
That grows full glory when she comes again.

Robinson Jeffers

1887–

NIGHT

The ebb slips from the rock, the sunken
Tide-rocks lift streaming shoulders
Out of the slack, the slow west
Sombering its torch; a ship's light
Shows faintly, far out,
Over the weight of the prone ocean
On the low cloud.

Over the dark mountain, over the dark pinewood,
Down the long dark valley along the shrunken river,
Returns the splendor without rays, the shining of shadow,
Peace-bringer, the matrix of all shining and quieter of
    shining.
Where the shore widens on the bay she opens dark wings
And the ocean accepts her glory. O soul worshipful of
    her
You like the ocean have grave depths where she dwells
    always,
And the film of waves above that takes the sun takes also
Her, with more love. The sun-lovers have a blond favorite,
A father of lights and noises, wars, weeping and laughter,
Hot labor, lust and delight and the other blemishes.
    Quietness
Flows from her deeper fountain; and he will die; and she
    is immortal.

Far off from here the slender
Flocks of the mountain forest
Move among stems like towers
Of the old redwoods to the stream,
No twig crackling; dip shy
Wild muzzles into the mountain water
Among the dark ferns.

O passionately at peace you being secure will pardon
The blasphemies of glowworms, the lamp in my tower, the fretfulness
Of cities, the crescents of the planets, the pride of the stars.
This August night in a rift of cloud Antares reddens,
The great one, the ancient torch, a lord among lost children,
The earth's orbit doubled would not girdle his greatness, one fire
Globed, out of grasp of the mind enormous; but to you O Night
What? Not a spark? What flicker of a spark in the faint far glimmer
Of a lost fire dying in the desert, dim coals of a sandpit the Bedouins
Wandered from at dawn. . . . Ah singing prayer to what gulfs tempted
Suddenly are you more lost? To us the near-hand mountain
Be a measure of height, the tide-worn cliff at the sea-gate a measure of continuance.

The tide, moving the night's
Vastness with lonely voices,
Turns, the deep dark-shining
Pacific leans on the land,
Feeling his cold strength
To the outmost margins: you Night will resume
The stars in your time.

O passionately at peace when will that tide draw shoreward?
Truly the spouting fountains of light, Antares, Arcturus,
Tire of their flow, they sing one song but they think silence.
The striding winter giant Orion shines, and dreams darkness.

And life, the flicker of men and moths and wolf on the
hill,
Though furious for continuance, passionately feeding,
passionately
Remaking itself upon its mates, remembers deep inward
The calm mother, the quietness of the womb and the egg,
The primal and the latter silences: dear Night it is
memory
Prophesies, prophecy that remembers, the charm of the
dark.
And I and my people, we are willing to love the four-
score years
Heartily; but as a sailor loves the sea, when the helm is
for harbor.

Have men's minds changed,
Or the rock hidden in the deep of the waters of the soul
Broken the surface? A few centuries
Gone by, was none dared not to people
The darkness beyond the stars with harps and habitations.
But now, dear is the truth. Life is grown sweeter and
lonelier,
And death is no evil.

CONTINENT'S END

At the equinox when the earth was veiled in a late rain,
wreathed with wet poppies, waiting spring,
The ocean swelled for a far storm and beat its boundary,
the ground-swell shook the beds of granite.

I gazing at the boundaries of granite and spray, the
established sea-marks, felt behind me
Mountain and plain, the immense breadth of the conti-
nent, before me the mass and doubled stretch of
water.

I said: You yoke the Aleutian seal-rocks with the lava
and coral sowings that flower the south,

Over your flood the life that sought the sunrise faces ours that has followed the evening star.

The long migrations meet across you and it is nothing to you, you have forgotten us, mother.
You were much younger when we crawled out of the womb and lay in the sun's eye on the tideline.

It was long and long ago; we have grown proud since then and you have grown bitter; life retains
Your mobile soft unquiet strength; and envies hardness, the insolent quietness of stone.

The tides are in our veins, we still mirror the stars, life is your child, but there is in me
Older and harder than life and more impartial, the eye that watched before there was an ocean.

That watched you fill your beds out of the condensation of thin vapor and watched you change them,
That saw you soft and violent wear your boundaries down, eat rock, shift places with the continents.

Mother, though my song's measure is like your surf-beat's ancient rhythm I never learned it of you.
Before there was any water there were tides of fire, both our tones flow from the older fountain.

Elinor Wylie

1887–1928

THE EAGLE AND THE MOLE

Avoid the reeking herd,
Shun the polluted flock,
Live like that stoic bird,
The eagle of the rock.

The huddled warmth of crowds
Begets and fosters hate;
He keeps, above the clouds,
His cliff inviolate.

When flocks are folded warm,
And herds to shelter run,
He sails above the storm,
He stares into the sun.

If in the eagle's track
Your sinews cannot leap,
Avoid the lathered pack,
Turn from the steaming sheep.

If you would keep your soul
From spotted sight or sound,
Live like the velvet mole;
Go burrow underground.

And there hold intercourse
With roots of trees and stones,
With rivers at their source,
And disembodied bones.

ADDRESS TO MY SOUL

My soul, be not disturbed
By planetary war;
Remain securely orbed
In this contracted star.

Fear not, pathetic flame;
Your sustenance is doubt:
Glassed in translucent dream
They cannot snuff you out.

Wear water, or a mask
Of unapparent cloud;
Be brave and never ask
A more defunctive shroud.

The universal points
Are shrunk into a flower;
Between its delicate joints
Chaos keeps no power.

The pure integral form,
Austere and silver-dark,
Is balanced on the storm
In its predestined arc.

Small as a sphere of rain
It slides along the groove
Whose path is furrowed plain
Among the suns that move.

The shapes of April buds
Outlive the phantom year:
Upon the void at odds
The dewdrop falls severe.

Five-petalled flame, be cold:
Be firm, dissolving star:
Accept the stricter mould
That makes you singular.

Thomas Stearns Eliot

1888–

THE LOVE SONG OF J. ALFRED PRUFROCK

S'io credesse che mia risposta fosse
A persona che mai tornasse al mondo,
Questa fiamma staria senza piu scosse.
Ma perciocche giammai di questo fondo
Non torno vivo alcun, s'i'odo il vero,
Senza tema d'infamia ti rispondo.

Let us go then, you and I,
When the evening is spread out against the sky
Like a patient etherized upon a table;
Let us go, through certain half-deserted streets,
The muttering retreats
Of restless nights in one-night cheap hotels
And sawdust restaurants with oyster-shells:

Streets that follow like a tedious argument
Of insidious intent
To lead you to an overwhelming question. . . .
Oh, do not ask, "What is it?"
Let us go and make our visit.

In the room the women come and go
Talking of Michelangelo.
The yellow fog that rubs its back upon the window-panes,
The yellow smoke that rubs its muzzle on the window-panes
Licked its tongue into the corners of the evening,
Lingered upon the pools that stand in drains,
Let fall upon its back the soot that falls from chimneys,
Slipped by the terrace, made a sudden leap,
And seeing that it was a soft October night,
Curled once about the house, and fell asleep.

And indeed there will be time
For the yellow smoke that slides along the street,
Rubbing its back upon the window-panes;
There will be time, there will be time
To prepare a face to meet the faces that you meet;
There will be time to murder and create,
And time for all the works and days of hands
That lift and drop a question on your plate;
Time for you and time for me,
And time yet for a hundred indecisions,
And for a hundred visions and revisions,
Before the taking of a toast and tea.

In the room the women come and go
Talking of Michelangelo.

And indeed there will be time
To wonder, "Do I dare?" and, "Do I dare?"
Time to turn back and descend the stair,
With a bald spot in the middle of my hair—
(They will say: "How his hair is growing thin!")
My morning coat, my collar mounting firmly to the chin,

My necktie rich and modest, but asserted by a simple pin—
(They will say: "But how his arms and legs are thin!")
Do I dare
Disturb the universe?
In a minute there is time
For decisions and revisions which a minute will reverse.
For I have known them all already, known them all:
Have known the evenings, mornings, afternoons,
I have measured out my life with coffee spoons;
I know the voices dying with a dying fall
Beneath the music from a farther room.
So how should I presume?

And I have known the eyes already, known them all—
The eyes that fix you in a formulated phrase,
And when I am formulated, sprawling on a pin,
When I am pinned and wriggling on the wall,
Then how should I begin
To spit out all the butt-ends of my days and ways?
And how should I presume?

And I have known the arms already, known them all—
Arms that are braceleted and white and bare
(But in the lamplight, downed with light brown hair!)
Is it perfume from a dress
That makes me so digress?
Arms that lie along a table, or wrap about a shawl.
And should I then presume?
And how should I begin?

. . . .

Shall I say, I have gone at dusk through narrow streets
And watched the smoke that rises from the pipes
Of lonely men in shirt-sleeves, leaning out of windows? . . .

I should have been a pair of ragged claws
Scuttling across the floors of silent seas.

. . . .

And the afternoon, the evening, sleeps so peacefully!
Smoothed by long fingers,
Asleep . . . tired . . . or it malingers,
Stretched on the floor, here beside you and me.
Should I, after tea and cakes and ices,
Have the strength to force the moment to its crisis?
But though I have wept and fasted, wept and prayed,
Though I have seen my head (grown slightly bald) brought in upon a platter,
I am no prophet—and here's no great matter;
I have seen the moment of my greatness flicker,
And I have seen the eternal Footman hold my coat, and snicker,
And in short, I was afraid.

And would it have been worth it, after all,
After the cups, the marmalade, the tea,
Among the porcelain, among some talk of you and me,
Would it have been worth while,
To have bitten off the matter with a smile,
To have squeezed the universe into a ball
To roll it toward some overwhelming question,
To say: "I am Lazarus, come from the dead,
Come back to tell you all, I shall tell you all"—
If one, settling a pillow by her head,
 Should say: "That is not what I meant at all;
 That is not it, at all."

And would it have been worth it, after all,
Would it have been worth while,
After the sunsets and the dooryards and the sprinkled streets,
After the novels, after the teacups, after the skirts that trail along the floor—
And this, and so much more?—
It is impossible to say just what I mean!
But as if a magic lantern threw the nerves in patterns on a screen:

Would it have been worth while
If one, settling a pillow or throwing off a shawl,
And turning toward the window, should say:
  "That is not it at all,
  That is not what I meant, at all."

No! I am not Prince Hamlet, nor was meant to be;
Am an attendant lord, one that will do
To swell a progress, start a scene or two,
Advise the prince; no doubt, an easy tool,
Deferential, glad to be of use,
Politic, cautious, and meticulous;
Full of high sentence, but a bit obtuse;
At times, indeed, almost ridiculous—
Almost, at times, the Fool.

I grow old . . . I grow old . . .
I shall wear the bottoms of my trousers rolled.

Shall I part my hair behind? Do I dare to eat a peach?
I shall wear white flannel trousers, and walk upon the beach.
I have heard the mermaids singing, each to each.

I do not think that they will sing to me.

I have seen them riding seaward on the waves
Combing the white hair of the waves blown back
When the wind blows the water white and black.

We have lingered in the chambers of the sea
By sea-girls wreathed with seaweed red and brown
Till human voices wake us, and we drown.

MORNING AT THE WINDOW

They are rattling breakfast plates in basement kitchens
And along the trampled edges of the street
I am aware of the damp souls of housemaids
Sprouting despondently at area gates.

The brown waves of fog toss up to me
Twisted faces from the bottom of the street,
And tear from a passer-by with muddy skirts
An aimless smile that hovers in the air
And vanishes along the level of the roofs.

THE HIPPOPOTAMUS

The broad-backed hippopotamus
Rests on his belly in the mud;
Although he seems so firm to us
He is merely flesh and blood.

Flesh and blood is weak and frail,
Susceptible to nervous shock;
While the True Church can never fail
For it is based upon a rock.

The hippo's feeble steps may err
In compassing material ends,
While the True Church need never stir
To gather in its dividends.

The 'potamus can never reach
The mango on the mango-tree;
But fruits of pomegranate and peach
Refresh the church from over sea.

At mating time the hippo's voice
Betrays inflexions hoarse and odd,
But every week we hear rejoice
The Church, at being one with God.

The hippopotamus's day
Is passed in sleep; at night he hunts;
God works in a mysterious way—
The Church can sleep and feed at once.

I saw the 'potamus take wing
Ascending from the damp savannas,

And quiring angels round him sing
The praise of God, in loud hosannas.

Blood of the Lamb shall wash him clean
And him shall heavenly arms enfold,
Among the saints he shall be seen
Performing on a harp of gold.

He shall be washed as white as snow,
By all the martyr'd virgins kist,
While the True Church remains below
Wrapt in the old miasmal mist.

John Crowe Ransom

1888–

HERE LIES A LADY

Here lies a lady of beauty and high degree.
Of chills and fever she died, of fever and chills,
The delight of her husband, her aunts, an infant of three,
And of medicos marvelling sweetly on her ills.

For either she burned, and her confident eyes would blaze,
And her fingers fly in a manner to puzzle their heads—
What was she making? Why, nothing; she sat in a maze
Of old scraps of laces, snipped into curious shreds—

Or this would pass, and the light of her fire decline
Till she lay discouraged and cold as a thin stalk white and blown,
And would not open her eyes, to kisses, to wine;
The sixth of these states was her last; the cold settled down.

Sweet ladies, long may ye bloom, and toughly I hope ye may thole,
But was she not lucky? In flowers and lace and mourning,
In love and great honour we bade God rest her soul
After six little spaces of chill, and six of burning.

TWO IN AUGUST

Two that could not have lived their single lives
As can some husbands and wives
Did something strange: they tensed their vocal chords
And attacked each other with silences and words
Like catapulted stones and arrowed knives.

Dawn was not yet; night is for loving or sleeping,
Sweet dreams or safekeeping;
Yet he of the wide brows that were used to laurel
And she, the famed for gentleness, must quarrel,
Furious both of them, and scared, and weeping.

How sleepers groan, twitch, wake to such a mood
Is not well understood,
Nor why two entities grown almost one
Should rend and murder trying to get undone,
With individual tigers in their blood.

In spring's luxuriant weather had the bridal
Transpired, nor had the growing parts been idle,
Nor was it easily dissolved;
Therefore they tugged but were still intervolved,
With pain prodigious. The exploit was suicidal.

She in terror fled from the marriage chamber
Circuiting the dark room like a string of amber
Round and round and back,
And would not light one lamp against the black,
And heard the clock that clanged: Remember, Remember.

And he must tread barefooted the dim lawn,
Soon he was up and gone;
High in the trees the night-mastered birds were crying
With fear upon their tongues, no singing nor flying
Which are their lovely attitudes by dawn.

Whether those bird-cries were of heaven or hell
There is no way to tell;
In the long ditch of darkness the man walked
Under the hackberry trees where the birds talked
With words too sad and strange to syllable.

Conrad Aiken

1889–

DISCORDANTS

Music I heard with you was more than music,
And bread I broke with you was more than bread;
Now that I am without you, all is desolate;
All that was once so beautiful is dead.

Your hands once touched this table and this silver,
And I have seen your fingers hold this glass.
These things do not remember you, belovèd,—
And yet your touch upon them will not pass.

For it was in my heart you moved among them,
And blessed them with your hands and with your eyes;
And in my heart they will remember always,—
They knew you once, O beautiful and wise.

SOUND OF BREAKING

Why do you cry out, why do I like to hear you
Cry out, here in the dewless evening, sitting
Close, close together, so close that the heart stops beating
And the brain its thought? Wordless, worthless mortals
Stumbling, exhausted, in this wilderness
Of our conjoint destruction! Hear the grass
Raging about us! Hear the worms applaud!
Hear how the ripples make a sound of chaos!
Hear now, in these and the other sounds of evening,
The first brute step of God!

About your elbow,
Making a ring of thumb and finger, I
Slide the walled blood against the less-walled blood,
Move down your arm, surmount the wrist-bone, shut
Your long slim hand in mine. Each finger-tip
Is then saluted by a finger-tip;
The hands meet back to back, then face to face;
Then lock together. And we, with eyes averted,
Smile at the evening sky of alabaster,
See nothing, lose our souls in the maelstrom, turning
Downward in rapid circles.

Bitter woman,
Bitter of heart and brain and blood, bitter as I
Who drink your bitterness—can this be beauty?
Do you cry out because the beauty is cruel?
Terror, because we downward sweep so swiftly?
Terror of darkness?

It is a sound of breaking,
The world is breaking, the world is a sound of breaking,
Many-harmonied, diverse, profound,
A shattering beauty. See, how together we break,
Hear what a crashing of disordered chords and discords
Fills the world with falling, when we thus lean
Our two mad bodies together!

It is a sound
Of everlasting grief, the sound of weeping,
The sound of disaster and misery, the sound
Of passionate heartbreak at the centre of the world.

Archibald MacLeish

1892-

ARS POETICA

A POEM should be palpable and mute
As a globed fruit

Dumb
As old medallions to the thumb

Silent as the sleeve-worn stone
Of casement where the moss has grown—

A poem should be wordless
As the flight of birds

. . . . . .

A poem should be motionless in time
As the moon climbs

Leaving, as the moon releases
Twig by twig the night-entangled trees,

Leaving, as the moon behind the winter leaves,
Memory by memory the mind—

A poem should be motionless in time
As the moon climbs

. . . . . .

A poem should be equal to:
Not true

For all the history of grief
An empty doorway and a maple leaf

For love
The leaning grasses and two lights above the sea—

A poem should not mean
But be.

YOU, ANDREW MARVELL

And here face down beneath the sun,
And here upon earth's noonward height,
To feel the always coming on,
The always rising of the night.

To feel creep up the curving east
The earthly chill of dusk and slow
Upon those under lands the vast
And ever-climbing shadow grow,

And strange at Ecbatan the trees
Take leaf by leaf the evening, strange,
The flooding dark about their knees,
The mountains over Persia change,

And now at Kermanshah the gate,
Dark, empty, and the withered grass,
And through the twilight now the late
Few travelers in the westward pass.

And Baghdad darken and the bridge
Across the silent river gone,
And through Arabia the edge
Of evening widen and steal on,

And deepen on Palmyra's street
The wheel rut in the ruined stone,
And Lebanon fade out and Crete
High through the clouds and overblown,

And over Sicily the air
Still flashing with the landward gulls,
And loom and slowly disappear
The sails above the shadowy hulls,

And Spain go under and the shore
Of Africa, the gilded sand,
And evening vanish and no more
The low pale light across that land,

Nor now the long light on the sea—
And here face downward in the sun
To feel how swift, how secretly,
The shadow of the night comes on. . . .

Edna St. Vincent Millay

1892-

SONNET

Euclid alone has looked on Beauty bare.
Let all who prate of Beauty hold their peace,
And lay them prone upon the earth and cease

To ponder on themselves, the while they stare
At nothing, intricately drawn nowhere
In shapes of shifting lineage; let geese
Gabble and hiss, but heroes seek release
From dusty bondage into luminous air.
O blinding hour, O holy, terrible day,
When first the shaft into his vision shone
Of light anatomized! Euclid alone
Has looked on Beauty bare. Fortunate they
Who, though once only and then but far away,
Have heard her massive sandal set on stone.

Louise Bogan

1897–

MEDUSA

I HAD come to the house, in a cave of trees,
Facing a sheer sky.
Everything moved,—a bell hung ready to strike,
Sun and reflection wheeled by.

When the bare eyes were before me
And the hissing hair,
Held up at a window, seen through a door.
The stiff bald eyes, the serpents on the forehead
Formed in the air.

This is a dead scene forever now.
Nothing will ever stir.
The end will never brighten it more than this,
Nor the rain blur.

The water will always fall, and will not fall,
And the tipped bell make no sound.
The grass will always be growing for hay
Deep on the ground.

And I shall stand here like a shadow
Under the great balanced day,
My eyes on the yellow dust that was lifting in the wind,
And does not drift away.

THE ALCHEMIST

I BURNED my life that I might find
A passion wholly of the mind,
Thought divorced from eye and bone,
Ecstasy come to breath alone.
I broke my life to seek relief
From the flawed light of love and grief.

With mounting beat the utter fire
Charred existence and desire.
It died low, ceased its sudden thresh.
I had found unmysterious flesh—
Not the mind's avid substance—still
Passionate beyond the will.

Allen Tate

1899–

THE CROSS

THERE is a place that some men know,
I cannot see the whole of it
Nor how I came there. Long ago
Flame burst out of a secret pit
Crushing the world with such a light
The day sky fell to moonless black,
The kingly sun to hateful night
For those, once seeing, turning back:
For love so hates mortality,
Which is the providence of life,
She will not let it blessèd be
But curses it with mortal strife,
Until beside the blinding rood
Within that world-destroying pit
—Like young wolves that have tasted blood,
Of death, men taste no more of it;
So blind, in so severe a place,
(All life before in the black grave)

The last alternatives the face
Of life, without life to save,
Being from all salvation weaned—
A stag charged both at heel and head;
Who would come back is turned a fiend
Instructed by the fiery dead.

EMBLEMS

I

MARYLAND Virginia Caroline
Pent images in sleep
Clay valleys rocky hills old-fields of pine
Unspeakable, and deep

Out of that source of time my farthest blood
Runs strangely to this day
Unkempt the fathers waste in solitude
Under the hills of clay

Far from their woe fled to its thither side
To a river in Tennessee
In an alien house I will stay
Yet find their breath to be
All that my stars betide—
There some time to abide
Took wife and child with me.

II

When it is all over and the blood
Runs out, do not bury this man
By the far river (where never stood
His fathers) flowing to the west
But take him east where life began,
O my brothers there is rest
In the depths of an eastward river
That I can understand; only
Do not think the truth we hold
I hold the slighter for this lonely

Reservation of the heart,
Men cannot live forever
But they must die forever
So take this body, at sunset,
To the great stream whose pulses start
In the blue hills, and let
These ashes drift from the Long Bridge
Where only a late gull breaks
That deep and populous grave
Whose heart with memory shakes.

III

By the great river the forefathers to beguile
Them, being inconceivably young, carved out
Deep hollows of memory on a river isle
Now lost, their murmurs the ghost of a shout

In the hollows where the forefathers
Without beards their eyes bright and long
Lay down at sunset by the green river
In the tall willows amid bird-song

And the long sleep by the cool river
They've slept full and long, till now the air
Waits twilit for their echo—the burning shiver
Of August strikes like a hawk the crouching hare.

Hart Crane

1899-1932

PRAISE FOR AN URN

IN MEMORIAM: ERNEST NELSON

It was a kind and northern face
That mingled in such exile guise
The everlasting eyes of Pierrot
And, of Gargantua, the laughter.

His thoughts, delivered to me
From the white coverlet and pillow,
I see now, were inheritances—
Delicate riders of the storm.

The slant moon on the slanting hill
Once moved us toward presentiments
Of what the dead keep, living still,
And such assessments of the soul

As, perched in the crematory lobby,
The insistent clock commented on,
Touching as well upon our praise
Of glories proper to the time.

Still, having in mind gold hair,
I cannot see that broken brow
And miss the dry sound of bees
Stretching across a lucid space.

Scatter these well-meant idioms
Into the smoky spring that fills
The suburbs, where they will be lost.
They are no trophies of the sun.

REPOSE OF RIVERS

The willows carried a slow sound,
A sarabande the wind mowed on the mead.
I could never remember
That seething, steady leveling of the marshes
Till age had brought me to the sea.

Flags, weeds. And remembrance of steep alcoves
Where cypresses shared the noon's
Tyranny; they drew me into hades almost.
And mammoth turtles climbing sulphur dreams
Yielded, while sun-silt ripples them
Asunder . . .

How much I would have bartered! the black gorge
And all the singular nestings in the hills
Where beavers learn stitch and tooth.
The pond I entered once and quickly fled—
I remember now its singing willow rim.

And finally, in that memory all things nurse;
After the city that I finally passed
With scalding unguents spread and smoking darts
The monsoon cut across the delta
At gulf gates . . . There, beyond the dykes

I heard wind flaking sapphire, like this summer,
And willows could not hold more steady sound.

INDEX OF FIRST LINES

A band is buried here, not strong, but sweet; 310
A beautiful place is the town of Lo-yang, 20
A beauty that all night long teaches love-tricks to Venus and the moon, 143
A beggar to the graveyard hied, 59
A Bird was singing on the linden tree, 816
A certain youthful lady in Thoulouse, 502
A clever man builds a city, 4
A Crow sat perched upon an oak, 731
A dream it was in which I found myself, 645
A field of golden wheat there grows, 910
A flock of crows high from the Northland flies, 905
A flower of all that springs from gentle blood, 597
A fount there is, doth overfling, 654
A Fragrant prayer upon the air, 1280
A frail sound of a tunic trailing, 650
A gentle wind fans the calm night: 17
A Goat was nibbling on a Vine, 326
A golden cloud slept for her pleasure, 1005
A grievous folly shames my sixtieth year—, 153
A howling storm is brewing, 895
A Hundred mares, all white; their manes, 773
A lady stood on the turret-stone, 817
A leaf falls softly at my feet, 861
A little bird flew through the dell, 854
A little wild bird sometimes at my ear, 572
A lonely pond in age-old stillness sleeps . . . 50
A lovely rose is sprung, 827
A maiden lies in her chamber, 892
A many a summer is dead and buried, 855
A mighty fortress is our God, 828
A mountain was in great distress and loud, 327
A noiseless, patient spider, 1354
A novice when I came beneath thy gaze, 918
A peasant haled a sheep to court, 997
A pine-tree standeth lonely, 878
A poem should be palpable and mute, 1410
A plague is Love, a plague! but yet, 344
A poor degenerate from the ape, 1267
A pot of wine among flowers, 21
A rich man bought a Swan and Goose—, 328
A Shepherd-boy beside a stream, 327
A silver-vested monkey trips, 789
A slumber did my spirit seal; 1167
A subtle chain of countless rings, 1324
A sweet disorder in the dress, 1079
A sweet "No! no!" with a sweet smile beneath, 707
A thing which fades, 44
A town lies in the valley, 911
A tumult in a Syrian town had place: 147
A vision as of crowded city streets, 1333
A weasel, by a person caught, 432
A white nymph wandering in the woods by night, 733
A wounded deer leaps highest, 1372

Above the pools, above the valley of fears, 765
After a hundred years, 1374
Again I see you, ah my queen, 753
Ah, Ben!, 1076
Ah! fair and lovely bloom the flowers of youth, 255
Ah for the throes of a heart sorely wounded!, 94
Ah! Love, my Master, hear me swear, 342
Ah, Sunflower! weary of time, 1153
Ah, take these lips away; no more, 714
Ah what avails the sceptered race, 1181
Ah Woe is me, of passion naught I knew, 416
Ainsi qu'aux fleurs la viellesse, 716
Airs! that wander and murmur round, 620
Alas! alas! thou turn'st in vain, 589
Alas for me, who loved a falcon well!, 571
Alas for the voyage, O High King of Heaven, 1272
Alas, poor heart, I pity thee, 675
Alas, so all things now do hold their peace!, 558
Albeit the Venice girls get praise, 701
All beneath the white-rose tree, 680
All Nature is a temple where the alive, 766
All out of doors looked darkly in at him, 1384
All the full moon night in the coomb, 925
All the whole world is living without war, 470
All things are doubly fair, 755
All thro' the breathing night there seemed to flow, 926
Allah gives light in darkness, 853
Along the road all shapes must travel by, 552
Although I do not know, 48
Although it is not plainly visible to the eye, 45
An Ass put on a Lion's skin and went, 327
An early dew woos the half-opened flowers, 104
An odorous shade lingers the fair day's ghost, 802
An old man in a lodge within a park, 1333
An old town lies afar, 934
And deep-eyed children cannot long be children, 928
And did those feet in ancient time, 1155
And dost thou faithlessly abandon me?, 848
And hasten Og and Doeg to rehearse, 1126
And here face down beneath the sun, 1411
And if he ever should come back, 801
And my young sweetheart sat at board with me, 924
And Paris be it or Helen dying, 699
And, Pergamos, 284
And so an easier life our Cyclops drew, 312
And there shall come forth a rod out of the stem of Jesse, 20::
And thou art now no longer near!, 843
Annie and Rhoda, sisters twain, 1338
April, pride of woodland ways, 724
Apparel of green woods and meadows gay, 634
Arise up on thy feet, O Quiet Heart!, 240
Around my garden the little wall is low, 27
Around were all the roses red, 783
Art thou not hungry for thy children, Zion, 210
As a white candle, 1295
As Aesop was with boys at play, 431
As I walk'd thinking through a little grove, 570
As I was climbing Ardan Mór, 1300
As I was walking all alane, 1030
As in the age of shepherd king and queen, 792
As in the gardens, all through May, the rose, 716

As in the midst of battle there is room, 1376
As it fell upon a day, 1073
As ocean's stream girdles the ball of earth, 1002
As the heart panteth after the water brooks, so panteth, 169
As the war-trumpet drowns the rustic flute, 332
As ye go through these palm-trees, 643
Ask me no more where Jove bestows, 1089
Ask not overmuch for fair, 817
At daybreak, when the falcon claps his wings, 702
At the equinox when the earth was veiled in a late rain, 1398
At the gate of old Granada, when all its bolts are barred, 627
At thee *the Mocker* sneers in cold derision, 848
Athirst in spirit, through the gloom, 1001
Austere the music of my songs, 1010
Avenge, O Lord, thy slaughtered saints, whose bones, 1107
Avoid the reeking herd, 1399
Awake, Æolian lyre, awake, 1142
Awake! The day is coming now, 821
Aweary am I of living in town and village, 96
Awkward was she yesterday, 906
Ay me, alas! the beautiful bright hair, 543
Azure, I come! from the eaves of death withdrawn, 813

Be life what it has been, and let us hold; 451
Be still; be still: nor dare, 1286
Beautiful is she, this woman, 1310
Beauty— a beam, nay, flame, 600
Beauty in woman; the high will's decree, 500
Because he is young, 36
Because I could not stop for Death, 1374
Because I think not ever to return, 508
Because I used to shun, 1298
Because mine eyes can never have their fill, 533
Because river-fog, 47
Before thy door too long of late, 405
Behold, a virgin shall conceive, and bear a son, and, 200
Behold from sluggish winter's arm, 612
Behold her, single in the field, 1167
Behold, how good and how pleasant it is for brethren to dwell, 178
Before my lady's window gay, 673
Behold, the meads are green again, 654
Behold, thou art fair, my love; behold, thou art fair, 194
Behold yon mountain's hoary height, 387
Being in thought of love, I chanced to see, 502
Being one day at my window all alone, 553
Belovèd friends! More glorious times than ours, 851
Beneath the branch of the green may, 677
Between thirty and forty, one is distracted by the Five Lusts, 28
Black night, 1013
Blacken thy heavens, Jove, 841
Bless the Lord, O my soul: and all that is within me, 176
Blessed is the man that walketh not in the counsel of the ungodly, 166
Blow, blow, thou winter wind, 1057
Blown in the morning, thou shalt fade ere noon:, 641
Boy, I hate their empty shows, 400
Break, break, break, 1211
Breathing do I draw that air to me, 660
Bring me wine, but wine which never grew, 1322
Brothers and men that shall after us be, 688
But I feel how my heart is glowing, 935
But twelve short years you lived, my son, 334

But who art thou, with curious beauty graced, 578
Butterflies, butterflies, 1307
By favorable breezes fanned, 786
By night around my temple grove, 932
By night on my bed I sought him whom my soul loveth:, 193
By the rivers of Babylon, there we sat down yea, we, 180
By the rude bridge that arched the flood, 1316
By ways remote and distant waters sped, 367

Calm was the day, and through the trembling air, 1037
Camden, most reverend head, to whom I owe, 1065
Can I see another's woe, 1149
Cast thy bread upon the waters: for thou shalt find it, 190
Chaeronean Plutarch, to thy deathless praise, 329
Chattering swallow! what shall we, 269
Children are dumb to say how hot the day is, 1269
Child, who went gathering the flowers of death, 106
Choice soul, in whom, as in a glass, we see, 579
Cliffs that rise a thousand feet, 18
Cloud-Maidens that float on forever, 287
Cold blows the winter wind: 't is Love, 343
Cold, cold the year draws to its end, 12
Come into the garden, Maud, 1209
Come live with me and be my love, 1044
Come not near my songs, 1302
Come now, and let us wake them; time, 826
Come on then, ye dwellers by Nature in darkness and like to the leaves' generations, 285
Comes the deer to my singing, 1304
Comrades, the morning breaks, the sun is up, 151
Could I take me to some cavern for mine hiding, 282
Courage, my Soul! now to the silent wood, 66
Covered with snow, the herd, with none to guide, 337
Crushed by the waves upon the crag was I, 333
Creator Spirit, by whose aid, 457
Cupid, as he lay among, 263

Daily walked the fair and lovely, 885
Dante, a sigh that rose from the heart's core, 503
Dante Alighieri, Cecco, your good friend, 544
Dante Alighieri, if I jest and lie, 551
Dante Alighieri in Becchina's praise, 548
Dante, whenever this thing happeneth, 540
Dark to me is the earth. Dark to me are the heavens, 115
Daughter, how the door is creaking, 901
Daughters of love, whose voice is melody, 253
Dead forever is my world of old, 918
Dear Chloe, how blubbered is that pretty face!, 1129
Dear father and dear mother: Let me crave, 440
Dear Fronto, famed alike in peace and war, 441
Dear Love, dost thou sleep fairly?, 816
Dear maiden, as each morning, 886
Dear youth, too early lost, who now art laid, 440
Death, of thee do I make my moan, 694
Death, since I find not one with whom to grieve, 534
Death, why hast thou made life so hard to bear, 482
Deathless Aphrodite, throned in flowers, 257
Deck thyself, maiden, 831
Deep in a distant bay, and deeply hidden, 452
Deep in a vale where rocks on every side, 988
Deep in the grass there lies a dead gazelle, 3

Deep in the Siberian mine, 1000
Descended of an ancient line, 389
Destined to war from very infancy, 597
Devouring Time, blunt thou the lion's paws, 1046
Diana guardeth our estate, 366
Did I ever think, 43
Dion of Tarsus, here I lie, who sixty years have seen, 330
Do not conceive that I shall here recount, 509
Do not let any woman read this verse, 1295
Dreams that delude with flying shade men's minds, 433
Drink, gossips mine! we drink no wine, 679
Drink to me only with thine eyes, 1061

Each lover's longing leads him naturally, 539
Each of us like you, 1392
Eagle! why soarest thou above that tomb?, 330
Eagles, that wheel above our crests, 736
Early I rose, 1301
Earth has not anything to show more fair, 1169
E'en as a lovely flower, 882
Elysium is as far as to, 1373
Enjoy your time, my soul! another race, 261
Enter and learn the story of the rulers, 109
Euclid alone has looked on Beauty bare, 1412
Even as a young man, 19
Even as the day when it is yet at dawning, 496
Even now, 66
Evening! a flight of pigeons in clear sky! 782
Every man has his sorrows; yet each still, 732
Eyes so tristful, eyes so tristful, 619

Fain would I be sleeping, dreaming, 994
Faint shines the far moon, 1002
Fair am I, mortals, as a stone-carved dream, 769
Fair daffodils, we weep to see, 1079
Fair flower of fifteen springs, that still, 713
"Fair is Alexis" I no sooner said, 349
Fair Iris I love, and hourly I die, 1121
Fair is her body, bright her eye, 673
Fair rebel to thyself and Time, 718
Fair Salamis, the billow's roar, 277
Families, when a child is born, 33
Far as man can see, 1305
Far in a western brookland, 1262
Far from the deep roar of the Aegean main, 349
Far from thy dearest self, the scope, 592
Farewell, thou child of my right hand, and joy, 1062
Farewell to the Highlands, farewell to the North, 1160
Farewell, too little, and too lately known, 1120
Fate to beauty still must give, 452
Fear no more the heat o' the sun, 1059
Figures in the fields against the sky!, 651
Fishermen will relate that in the South, 921
Five oxen, grazing in a flowery mead, 349
Flap, flap, the captive bird in the cage, 16
Flee fro the prees, and dwelle with sothfastnesse, 1022
Flow gently, sweet Afton, among thy green braes!, 1159
Flower petals fall, 799
Flowers hast thou in thyself, and foliage, 500
For a thing done, repentance is no good, 549
For Crethis' store of tales and pleasant chat, 335

For Human nature Hope remains alone, 262
For, Lord, the crowded cities be, 936
For many thousand ages, 877
For noble minds, the worst of miseries, 262
Fortune has brought me down—her wonted way—, 95
Fresh Spring, the herald of loves mighty king, 1036
Friend!, 907
Friend, if the mute and shrouded dead, 368
Friend sparrow, do not eat, I pray, 50
From harmony, from heavenly harmony, 1122
From you have I been absent in the spring, 1052
Fruitful earth drinks up the rain, 269
Full fathom five thy father lies; 1060
Full many a glorious morning have I seen, 1048
Full oft of old the islands changed their name, 336

Gaily bedight, 1347
Gather ye rosebuds while ye may, 1080
Gem of all isthmuses and isles that lie, 367
Gentle river, gentle river, 621
Gently I stir a white feather fan, 23
Give all to love; 1319
Give ear to my prayer, O God; and hide not thyself from my supplication, 171
Give me a mask, I'll join the masquerade, 890
Give me, give me Buriano, 602
Glory be to God for dappled things—, 1257
Glory to God and to God's Mother chaste, 553
Glory to Osiris, the Prince of Everlastingness, 236
Go and catch a falling star, 1066
Go, lovely Rose!, 1091
Go tell the Spartans, thou that passeth by, 274
Go to the western gate, Luke Havergal, 1376
God is our refuge and strength, a very present help in trouble, 170
God of our fathers, known of old, 1263
God, that mad'st her well regard her, 667
Gone, gone,—sold and gone, 1334
Gone is Youth, gone with praise—Youth full of marvelous things!, 90
Good-by, the tears are in my eyes; 689
Good morrow to the day so fair, 1081
Gramercy, Death, as you've my love to win, 551
Grant me the great and solemn breath withdrawn, 918
Great father Alighier, if from the skies, 606
Great Fortune is an hungry thing, 275
Great Venus, Queene of Beautie and of grace, 352
Green grow the rashes, O; 1161
Green Spring receiveth, 5
Gudrun of old days, 951
Guido, I would that Lapo, thou, and I, 531

Had we but world enough, and time, 1112
Hail, aged God who lookest on thy Father, 248
Hail, thou Great God in thy Boat, 244
Hail, thou who shinest from the Moon, 244
Happy insect! what can be, 265
Happy the man, who his whole time doth bound, 451
Happy the man whose wish and care, 1131
Happy those early days, when I, 1115
Happy who like Ulysses, or that lord, 723
Hark, hark! the lark at heaven's gate sings, 1059
Harry, whose tuneful and well-measured song, 1106

Harsh cry the crows, 903
Has not the night been as a drunken rose, 59
Hast thou seen that lordly castle, 860
Hath any loved you well, down there, 661
Have pity, pity, friends, have pity on me, 705
Have you sometimes, calm silent let your tread aspirant rise, 741
He calleth to me out of Seir, Watchman, what of the night?, 202
He is coming, my long-desired lord, whom I have, 39
He is no friend who in thine hour of pride, 144
He that dwelleth in the secret place of the most High, 175
He that has grown to wisdom hurries not, 472
He that loves a rosy cheek, 1088
He that owns wealth, in mountain, wold, or waste, 146
He unto whom thou art so partial, 438
He who bends to himself a joy, 1155
Health from the lover of the country, me, 395
Hear my little voice, Birds of War!, 1309
Hearing I ask from the holy races, 942
Hear'st thou, my soul, what serious things, 460
Helen, thy beauty is to me, 1340
Hence, loathèd Melancholy, 1092
Hence, vain, deluding joys, 1096
Hence, ye profane! I hate you all; 397
Henry and King Pedro, clasping, 628
Her face has made my life most proud and glad, 477
Her hand a goblet bore for him, 926
Here a little child I stand, 1080
Here are cakes for thy body, 249
Here at the center of the turning year, 1271
Here Cleita sleeps. You ask her life and race?, 311
Here in the self is all that man can know, 1267
Here is the long-bided hour:, 1000
Here is the place; right over the hill, 1336
Here is the yoke, with arrow and share near by, 782
Here lapped in hallowed slumber Saon lies, 335
Here lie I, Timon; who, alive, all living men did hate: 334
Here lies a lady of beauty and high degree, 1407
Here, where fecundity of Babel frames, 635
Here, where the world is quiet, 1248
Hidden lovers' woes, 823
Hide this one night thy crescent, kindly Moon; 713
Hie upon Hielands, 1029
High o'er his moldering castle walls, 840
High on the Mountain of Sunrise where standeth the Temple of Sebek, 245
Highest of Immortals bright, 52
His eyes are quickened so with grief, 1268
His friend the watchman was still awake, 930
His lamp, his bow, and quiver laid aside, 326
Ho, Moeris! whether on thy way so fast?, 381
Homage to thee, O Ra, at thy tremendous rising!, 235
Hoping all the time, 45
Horns to bulls wise Nature lends; 267
How beautiful are thy feet with shoes, O Prince's daughter, 198
How can one e'er be sure, 49
How delightful, at sunset, to loosen the boat!, 24
How doth the city sit solitary, that was full of people!, 202
How fresh, O Lord, how sweet and clean, 1086
How goes the night?, 1
How happy in his low degree, 392
How I forsook, 587

How joyous his neigh!, 1305
How like a winter hath my absence been, 1052
How long must we two hide the burning gaze, 348
How oft has the Banshee cried!, 1280
How shall I guard my soul, so that it be, 937
How sleep the brave, who sink to rest, 1147
How soon hath Time, the subtle thief of youth, 1105
How will you manage, 35
How vainly men themselves amaze, 1110
Hyd, Absolon, they gilte tresses clere; 1021

I always loved this solitary hill, 610
I am all bent to glean the golden ore, 540
I am come into my garden, my sister, my spouse: 195
I am enamored, and yet not so much, 545
I am here, I have traversed the Tomb, I behold thee, 240
I am like a flag unfurled in space, 938
I am Raferty the Poet, 1279
I am so out of love through poverty, 550
I am so passing rich in poverty, 484
I am the flute of Daphnis. On this wall, 308
I am the Lord of Light, the self-begotten Youth, 241
I am the Prince in the Field, 241
I am the pure lotus, 247
I am the Pure, the True of Word, Triumphant, 243
I am the pure traveler, 244
I am the rose of Sharon, and the lily of the valleys, 192
I am the Serpent, fat with years, 247
I am the stage, impassive, mute and cold, 738
I am the tomb of Crethon; here you read, 339
I am weary of lying within the chase, 670
I am Yesterday, To-day and To-morrow, 243
I arise from dreams of thee, 1188
I built my hut in a zone of human habitation, 18
I burned my life that I might find, 1414
I came a-riding in a far countrie, 825
I came to you with a greeting, 1008
I canna tell what has come ower me, 873
I cease not from desire till my desire, 157
I, Chang P'ing-Tzu, had traversed the Nine Wilds and seen their wonders, 14
I could resign that eye of blue, 439
I crave an ampler, worthier sphere; 885
I cried unto God with my voice, even unto God with my voice; 172
I died for beauty, but was scarce, 1373
I do not ask—for you are fair, 423
I do not love thee, Doctor Fell, 435
I dreamt I climbed to a high, high plain; 29
I dreamt I saw great Venus by me stand, 320
I dreamt last night of you, John—John, 1289
I even I know the Eastern Gate of Heaven, 246
I feed a flame within, which so torments me, 1122
I feel a breath from other planets blowing, 920
I find no peace, and all my war is done; 559
I fly to her, take all her wrongs, but she, 733
I found at daybreak yester morn, 674
I found myself one day all, all alone, 573
I gaze with grief upon our generation, 1004
I go by road, I go by street, 776
I had come to the house, in a cave of trees, 1413
I had not minded walls, 1375

I have borne the anguish of love, which ask me not to describe: 159
I have a tree, a graft of love, 690
I have baptized thee Withy, because of thy slender limbs, 912
I have had playmates, I have had companions, 1181
I have it in my heart to serve God so, 477
I have marked, as on the heather now I strayed, 818
I have taken the woman of beauty, 1310
I hear America singing, the varied carols I hear, 1370
I hear an army charging upon the land, 1298
I heard a brooklet gushing, 870
I heard how, to the beat of some quick tune, 146
I heard the Poor Old Woman say, 1300
I hold him, verily, of mean emprise, 473
I know a Flower of beauty rare, 834
I know a spot where Love delights to dream, 308
I know not if from uncreated spheres, 586
I know that this my crying, like the crying, 220
I laid my haffet on Elfer Hill; 979
I laugh at each dull bore, taste's parasite, 889
I laved my hands, 687
I like a church; I like a cowl; 1317
I long to talk with some old lover's ghost, 1067
I look at the crisp, golden-threaded hair, 564
I love the evenings, passionless and fair, I love the evens, 739
I love the sound of the horn in the deep dim woodland, 737
I love you well, my steel-white dagger, 1003
I may be dead to-morrow, uncaressed, 800
I met a traveler from an antique land, 1191
I met by chance, as I traveled, 887
I never did on cleft Parnassus dream, 434
I pace the sounding sea-beach and behold, 1334
I passed a tomb among green shades, 106
I pray thee, Dante, shouldst thou meet with Love, 503
I recognized him by his skips and hops, 810
I ride through a dark, dark Land by night, 856
I said to heaven that glowed above, 160
I saw eternity, the other night, 1117
I saw in dream a dapper mannikin, 884
I saw in Louisiana a live-oak growing, 1353
I saw the ramparts of my native land, 645
I see the dawn e'en now begin to peer; 613
I send a garland to my love, 350
I send thee myrrh, not that thou mayest be, 331
I sing of brooks, of blossoms, birds, and bowers, 1076
I sing the glorious Power with azure eyes, 254
I strove with none; for none was worth my strife, 1182
I struck the board, and cried, "No more; 1084
I stood and leant upon the mast, 890
I traveled among unknown men, 1166
I traveled with them, 99
I walk down the garden paths, 1380
I wander through each chartered street, 1154
I was a joke at dinners; aye, any would-be wit, 419
I was angry with my friend: 1154
I was upon the high and blessed mound, 542
I weep, but with no bitterness I weep, 748
I went to the Garden of Love, 1153
I went to turn the grass once after one, 1385
I wept as I lay dreaming, 888
I will lift up mine eyes unto the hills, from whence cometh my help, 178

I wish I could lend a coat, 37
I wish I were where Helen lies, 1035
I wish to make my sermon brief,—to shorten my oration, 616
I wonder, by my troth, what thou and I, 1068
I would I might forget that I am I, 1375
I would I were a bird so free, 614
I would immortalize these nymphs so bright, 777
I would that even now, 49
If amorous faith, a heart of guileless ways, 560
If any man would know the very cause, 476
If aught of oaten stop, or pastoral song, 1146
If but some vengeful god would call to me, 1253
If Dante mourns, there wheresoe'er he be, 561
If I did come of set intent, 335
If I entreat this lady that all grace, 505
If I have any taste, it is hardly, 795
If I were fire, I'd burn the world away, 549
If it were not for the voice, 46
If it be destined that my Life, from thine, 560
If livelihood by knowledge were endowed, 145
If, Lord, Thy love for me is strong, 631
If no love is, O God, what feel I so?, 556
If now thou seest me a wreck, worn out and minished of, 89
If only, when one heard, 45
If parting be decreed for the two of us, 211
If the red slayer thinks he slays, 1315
If this our little life is but a day, 722
If thou art sleeping, maiden, 629
If you could see, fair brother, how dead beat, 498
I'll be an otter, and I'll let you swim, 1292
I'll frame, my Heliodora! a garland for thy hair, 346
I'll sing of heroes and of kings, 265
I'm black and blue from their worrying, 888
I'm full of everything I do not want, 547
In a garden where the whitethorn spreads her leaves, 66c
In a gay jar upon his shoulder, 1009
In a lovely garden walking, 861
In all thy humors, whether grave or mellow, 439
In Freedom's War, of "Thirty Years" and more, 881
In Heaven a spirit doth dwell, 1344
In heaven-high musings and many, 279
In May, when sea-winds pierced our solitudes, 1315
In my boat that goes, 47
In my life, too, were angry days and evil, 919
In sensuous coil, 57
In the blossom-land Japan, 234
In the Great House, and in the House of Fire, 238
In the midst of my garden, 94
In the scented bud of the morning—O, 1296
In the southern land many birds sing; 30
In the summer of the first year of Chia-yu, 30
In the sunny orchard closes, 985
In this merry morn of May, 674
In Xanadu did Kubla Khan, 1179
Incense, and flesh of swine, and this year's grain, 407
Inside my father's close, 669
Into a little close of mine I went, 576
Into the Silent Land!, 852
"Is there anybody there?" said the Traveler, 1265
It is a beauteous evening, calm and free, 1169
It is at morning, twilight they expire; 814

It is not right for you to know, so do not ask, Leuconoe, 408
It is time to be old, 1324
It little profits that an idle king, 1207
It was a kind and northern face, 1416
It was a lover and his lass, 1058
It was a mighty monarch's child, 875
It was a mother and a maid, 684
It was in and about the Martinmas time, 1028
It was many and many a year ago, 1343
It was the morning of the first of May, 613
It was the time, when rest, soft sliding downe, 718
Italia! Oh Italia! thou who hast, 605
Its roof among the stars projected, 933
It's up the spout and Charley Wag, 693
I've kept a haughty heart thro' grief and mirth, 883
I've kissed thee, sweetheart, in a dream at least, 727

John Anderson my Jo, John, 1160
John of Tours is back with peace, 668
Jove descends in sleet and snow, 256
Just look, Manetto, at that wry-mouthed minx; 508

King Christian stood by the lofty mast, 981
King Louis on his bridge is he, 683
Kiss me then, my merry May, 673
Kiss me, sweet; the wary lover, 363
Knowest thou the land where bloom the lemon trees, 844

Lady of Heaven and earth, and therewithal, 694
Lady that hast my heart within thy hand, 156
Lass, when they talk of love, laugh in their face, 809
Lassie, with thy lips sae rosy, 884
Last All Saints' holy-day, even now gone by, 532
Last night ah, yesternight, betwixt her lips and mine, 1264
Lawrence, of virtuous father virtuous son, 1106
Lay a garland on my hearse, 1074
Lead, Kindly Light, amid the encircling gloom, 1204
Leave me, all sweet refrains my lip hath made; 635
Leave thine own home, O youth, seek distant shores!, 432
Lesbia forever on me rails, 364
Lest you should think that verse shall die, 394
Let him kiss me with the kisses of his mouth: for thy love is better than wine, 191
Let me enjoy the earth no less, 1253
Let me go warm and merry still; 642
Let me not to the marriage of true minds, 1064
Let mine eyes see Thee, 632
Let nothing disturb thee, 631
Let others pile their yellow ingots high, 413
Let sailors watch the waning Pleiades, 310
Let Sporus tremble—What? that thing of silk, 1133
Let the day perish wherein I was born, and the night, 180
Let the rich man fill his belly; 652
Let them say to my lover, 629
Let thy tears, Le Vayer, let them flow; 732
Let us go then, you and I, 1401
Light-winged Smoke, Icarian bird, 1348
Like a great rock, far out at sea, 50
Like a skein of loose silk blown against a wall, 1390
Like many a one, when you had gold, 341
Like the ears of wheat in a wheat-field growing, 899

Like the sweet apple which reddens upon the topmost bough, 259
Like the wild hyacinth flower which on the hills is found, 260
Like those boats which are returning, 48
Like to a god he seems to me, 366
Little thinks, in the field, yon red-cloaked clown, 1320
Little think'st thou, poor flower, 1070
Lo! 'tis a gala night, 1346
Locust, locust, playing a flute, 1309
Lone and forgotten, 1286
Long as I can call to mind, 819
Long Nature travailed, till at last she bore, 331
Lord, thou hast been our dwelling place in all generations, 174
Lord, what am I, that, with unceasing care, 644
Louise, have you forgotten yet, 772
Love, and the Lady Lagia, Guido and I, 504
Love bade me welcome; yet my soul drew back, 1085
Love has its secrets, joy has its revealings, 119
Love, I am sick for thee, sick with an absolute grief, 118
Love, like a mountain-wind, upon an oak, 261
Love, love, what wilt thou with this heart of mine?, 665
Love mocks us all, Then cast aside, 406
Love seeketh not itself to please, 1152
Love, that liveth and reigneth in my thought, 558
Love, the great master of true eloquence, 593
Love was before the light began, 104
Love will not have me cry, 479
Loveliest of trees, the cherry now, 1262
Lovely courier of the sky, 273
Love's worshippers alone can know, 729
Loving in truth, and fain in verse my love to show, 1043
Low-anchored cloud, 1348

Maid Marjory sits at the castle gate; 679
Maidens young and virgins tender, 410
Make me a bowl, a mighty bowl, 272
Many indeed must perish in the keel, 928
Maryland Virginia Caroline, 1415
Master Brunetto, this my little maid, 531
Master Francesco, I have come to thee, 611
May he fall in with beasts that scatter fire, 703
May they come, may they come, 796
Men call you fayre, and you doe credit it, 1037
Menodotis's portrait here is kept, 338
Men's hearts love gold and jade; 26
Meliboeus, stretched in the shadow of the broad beech, 373
Meseemeth I heard cry and groan, 695
Milton! thou shouldst be living at this hour, 1168
Mingling my prayer, 47
Miniver Cheevy, child of scorn, 1377
Morning and evening, sleep she drove away, 339
Most quietly at time and like a dream, 914
Mother, I cannot mind my wheel; 260
Mother of Memories! O mistress-queen!, 769
Mountains loom upon the path we take; 1308
Much have I labored, much read o'er, 125
Music first and foremost of all!, 791
Music I heard with you was more than music, 1409
Music, when soft voices die, 1188
Must hapless man, in ignorance sedate, 442
My ardors for emprize nigh lost, 1254
My beauty is not wine to me, 102

My child, we were two children, 872
My curse be on the day when first I saw, 538
My darling, we sat together, 876
My father was a sailor, 653
My friend is lodging high in the Eastern Range, 23
My funeral-shaft, and marble shapes that dwell, 337
My heart aches, and a drowsy numbness pains, 1194
My heart is a-breaking, dear tittie, 1162
My heart is in woe, 1275
My heart is like a singing bird, 1245
My heart, my heart is mournful, 879
My heart rejoiceth in the Lord, mine horn is exalted in, 164
My heart, thinking, 38
My heart's so heavy with a hundred things, 548
My Lady mine, I send, 478
My lady woke upon a morning fair, 715
My little breath, under the willows by the water-side we used to sit, 1308
My love, 44
My love for him shall be, 677
My love is strengthen'd, though more weak in seeming; 1052
My mistress' eyes are nothing like the sun; 1055
My mother bore me in the southern wild, 1151
My name, my country, what are they to thee, 348
My neighbor Hunks's house and mine, 435
My precious life I spent considering, 145
My songs, they say, are poisoned, 895
My sorrow that I am not by the little dún, 1291
My soul, be not disturbed, 1400
My soul, calm sister, towards thy brow, whereon scarce grieves, 780
My soul, there is a country, 1116
My sweetest Lesbia, let us live and love, 363
My thoughts are as a garden-plot, that knows, 98
My true-love hath my heart, and I have his, 1042
Mycilla dyes her locks, 'tis said, 341
Mystical strains unheard, 784

Naked I saw thee, 1291
Naked is the earth, 651
Nature withheld Cassandra in the skies, 711
Nay, prithee tell me, Love, when I behold, 582
Nay, Xanthias, feel ashamed, 409
Neither spirit nor bird:, 1301
Neither will I put myself forward as others may do, 1393
Never the tramp of foot or horse, 258
Night in the bloodstained snow; the wind is chill; 760
Nightly tormented by returning doubt, 775
Night's first sweet silence fell, and on my bed, 433
Niobe on Phrygian sands, 271
No dust have I to cover me, 337
No, I am not, as others are, 691
No longer mourn for me when I am dead, 1050
No marvel is it if I sing, 656
No more, O my spirit, 283
No mortal thing enthralled these longing eyes, 580
No single thing abides; but all things flow, 354
No! those days are gone away, 1199
No way too long—no path too steep, 921
Nobly, nobly Cape Saint Vincent to the Northwest died away; 1215
None could ever say that she, 365
None is happy, free from care, 820

Nor exults he nor complains he; silent bears whate'er befalls him, 93
Not, Celia, that I juster am, 1128
Not in sleep I saw it, but in daylight, 915
Not marble, nor the gilded monuments, 1049
Not mine own fears, nor the prophetic soul, 1053
Not such your burden, happy youths, as ours, 329
Not without heavy grief of heart did he, 599
Now all the truth is out, 1285
Now do our eyes behold, 275
Now get thee back, retreat, depart, O Serpent, 246
Now hand in hand, you little maidens, walk, 804
Now hath my life across a stormy sea, 581
Now is the hour when, swinging in the breeze, 770
Now is the time for mirth, 1077
Now rede me, dear mither, a sonsy rede; 978
Now take your fill of love and glee, 698
Now that my lips are very still and burn, 918
Now that these wings to speed my wish ascend, 593
Now the bright crocus flames, and now, 343
Now this is my first counsel, 974
Now to Great Britain we must make our way, 567
Now will I a lover be; 268
Now Winter's winds are banished from the sky, 345
Now, while thou hast the wondrous power of word, 144
Now who is he on earth that lives, 676
Now would to God swift ships had ne'er been made!, 335

O boy cutting grass, 36
O camp of flowers, with poplars girdled round, 989
O come let us sing unto the Lord: let us make a joyful, 176
O cricket, from your cheery cry, 51
O cuckoo, 45
O Dearest, canst thou tell me why, 874
O everlasting Kingdom of the Sceptre, 242
O flame of living love, 640
O Fountain of Bandusia!, 407
O Gentle ships that skim the seas, 342
O give thanks unto the Lord; for he is good; for his, 178
O God, when You send for me, let it be, 808
"O good Lord Judge, and sweet Lord Judge," 1031
O good Sun, 1310
O Grandest of the Angels, and most wise, 761
O Hesperus, thou bringest all good things—, 259
O, how much more doth beauty beauteous seem, 1048
O Italy, I see the lonely towers, 607
O Lady amorous, 494
O Lord our Lord, how excellent is thy name in all the earth!, 166
O Love, I never, never thought, 618
O love, my love, and perfect bliss!, 675
O Love, O thou, that, for my fealty, 541
O Love, who all this while hast urged me on, 492
O lovely age of gold!, 590
O many things adulterate; 794
O Mary, at thy window be!, 1157
O mistress mine, where are you roaming?, 1058
O my dark Rosaleen, 1273
O my Heart, my Mother, my Heart, my Mother, 238
O my land! O my love!, 1278
O, my luv is like a red, red rose, 1158
O nightingale of woodland gay, 679
O pine-tree standing, 37

O! raise the woeful *Phillalu,* 840
O Rose, thou art sick!, 1152
O see how narrow are our days, 934
O sleep, O tranquil son of noiseless Night, 587
O Spring, thou youthful beauty of the year, 590
O sweet everlasting Voices be still; 1284
O Sylvan prophet, whose eternal fame, 459
O that thou wert as my brother, that sucked the breasts, 199
O Thou Moor of Morería, 623
O thou newcomer who seek'st Rome in Rome, 723
O thou that held'st the blessed Veda dry, 77
O Thou that often hast within thine eyes, 504
O Thou who movest onward with a mind, 595
O Thou who speedest Time's advancing wing, 237
O to be blind!, 1294
O Tragic hours when lovers leave each other!, 814
O universal Mother, who dost keep, 252
O Wall-flower! or ever thy bright leaves fade, 984
O what can ail thee knight-at-arms, 1202
O where hae ye been, Lord Randal, my son?, 1029
O who rides by night thro' the woodland so wild?, 832
O wild West Wind, thou breath of Autumn's being, 1192
O, Willie brew'd a peck o' maut, 1163
October at last has come! The thicket has shaken, 998
O'er all the hill-tops, 834
Of a' the airts the wind can blaw, 1158
Of all the girls that are so smart, 1135
Of beasts am I, of men was he most brave, 331
Of Edenhall the youthful lord, 858
Of Heaven or Hell I have no power to sing, 1246
Of that wherein thou art a questioner, 543
Of these the false Achitophel was first, 1124
Of two fair virgins, modest, though admired, 606
Off in the twilight hung the low full moon, 261
Off with sleep, love up from bed, 710
Oft am I by the women told, 266
Oft have I said, I say it once more, 160
Oft in the silent night, 916
Often I think of the beautiful town, 1325
Often this thought wakens me unawares, 940
Oh, I should love to be like one of those, 937
Oh, long, long, 1303
Oh lovely fishermaiden, 893
Oh, Paddy dear! and did ye hear the news that's goin' round?, 1281
Oh Ship! new billows sweep thee out, 405
Oh, to be in England, 1214
Oh! true was his heart while he breathed, 839
Oh virgin queen of mountain-side and woodland, 412
Old battle field, fresh with Spring flowers again—, 50
Old Eben Flood, climbing alone one night, 1378
Old I am, yet can (I think), 271
Old men, white-haired, beside the ancestral graves, 51
Old time is lame and halt, 881
Omit, omit, my simple friend, 403
On a hill there blooms a palm, 218
On a starred night Prince Lucifer uprose, 1240
On a throne of new gold the Son of the Sky, 25
On blood, smoke, rain and the dead, 904
On summer evenings blue, pricked by the wheat, 794
On Sunday morning well I knew, 614
On the beach at night, 1370

On the mountain, in the valley, 824
On the shore of Nawa, 35
On the sightless seas of ether, 1007
On the wan sea-strand, 899
Once a boy beheld a bright, 838
Once he will miss, twice he will miss, 105
Once on a time did Eucritus and I, 301
Once when the snow of the year was beginning to fall, 1384
One day I wrote her name upon the strand, 1036
One heifer and one fleecy sheep, 332
One silent night of late, 263
One with eyes the fairest, 280
One without looks in tonight, 1256
Open thy doors, O Lebanon, that the fire may devour thy cedars, 204
Open to me!, 245
Or a crystal spring, wherein, 272
Out of my own great woe, 871
Out of the cradle endlessly rocking, 1354
Out upon it, I have loved, 1108
Over here in England I'm helpin' with the hay, 1288
Over the lids of thine eyes, 925

Pain is a blacksmith, 915
Painter, by unmatch'd desert, 269
Pale Heinrich he came sauntering by, 890
Pan loved his neighbor Echo; Echo loved, 325
Passing across the billowy sea, 613
Past ruined Ilion Helen lives, 1182
Pause, courteous spirit! Balbi supplicates, 598
Peace, be at peace, O thou my heaviness, 768
Peace to all such! but were there one whose fires, 1132
Peer of the golden gods is he to Sappho, 258
Perchance that I might learn what pity is, 582
Perhaps some needful service of the state, 594
Perhaps you expected a face that was free from tears, 811
Pile the bodies high at Austerlitz and Waterloo, 1387
Piping down the valleys wild, 1148
Pitiless heat from heaven pours, 60
Pity! mourn in plaintive tone, 364
Poor in my youth, and in life's later scenes, 330
Poor soul, the center of my sinful earth, 1055
Praise ye the Lord for the avenging of Israel, when the, 162
Prince, may the bright-winged brood of Aeolus, 704
Pure is the body on the Earth, 248
Pushan, God of golden day, 55

Queen and huntress, chaste and fair, 1061
Quick-falling dew, 50

Radiant ranks of seraphim, 1011
Ravished by all that to the eyes is fair, 586
Receive, dear friend, the truths I teach, 399
Region of life and light!, 636
Remember me when I am gone away, 1246
Remember now, my Love, what piteous thing, 767
Remembrancer of joys long passed away, 843
Remembering what passed, 49
Returning from its daily quest, my Spirit, 506
Rise and hold up the curved glass, 87
Roman Vergil, thou that singest Ilion's lofty temples robed in fire, 1213

Roses (Love's delight) let's join, 268
Round about me hum the winds of autumn, 260
Round the cape of a sudden came the sea, 1216
Ruined and ill,—a man of two score; 28

Saki, for God's love, come and fill my glass; 150
Sad, lost in thought, and mute I go; 673
Say not the struggle nought availeth, 1231
Say, sweet my grief and I, we may not brook, 803
Sad Thyrsis weeps till his blue eyes are dim, 309
Say, where is the maiden sweet, 880
Say, wouldst thou guard thy son, 510
Scaramouche waves a threatening hand, 785
Season of mists and mellow fruitfulness, 1198
See, here's the grand approach, 436
See, Mignonne, hath not the Rose, 712
See the Spring herself discloses, 270
See yonder, where a gem of night, 875
Set Love in order, thou that lovest Me, 471
Set me whereas the sun doth parch the green, 559
Seven stars in the still water, 672
Shady, shady the wood in front of the Hall, 19
Shall I compare thee to a summer's day?, 1046
Shall I, wasting in despair, 1074
Shall we make love, 39
She dwelt among the untrodden ways, 1166
She lay, and serving men her lithe arms took, 935
She said, "I was not born to mope at home in loneliness"—, 863
She sits on a tumulus Savoor, and stares, 1011
She walks in beauty, like the night, 1184
She walks—the lady of my delight—, 1258
She went up the mountain to pluck wild herbs; 11
She, who could neither rest nor sleep, 145
Shepherd, shepherd, hark that calling!, 633
Shepherds that on this mountain ridge abide, 339
Should any ask me on His form to dwell, 144
Should auld acquaintance be forgot, 1163
Shy one, shy one, 1283
Sickles sound; 831
Sigh no more, ladies, sigh no more, 1056
Sigurd of Yore, 957
Silently, slowly falls the snow from an ashen sky, 611
Since brass, nor stone, nor earth, nor boundless sea, 1049
Since earth has put you away, O sons of Barmak, 105
Since I am convinced, 48
Since I have set my lips to your full cup, my sweet, 745
Since I heard, 44
Since nought avails, let me arise and leave, 145
Since there's no help, come, let us kiss and part!, 1044
Sing, magnarello, merrily, 775
Sir Olaf he rideth west and east, 829
Sir Oluf he rideth over the plain, 976
Sleep softly . . . eagle forgotten . . . under the stone, 1389
Sleeper, the palm-trees drink the breathless noon, 104
Sleeping or waking, thou sweet face, 613
Sleeping they bear me, 924
Slog brute streets with rebel tramping!, 1020
Slumber dark and deep, 792
So leave her, and cast care from thy heart with a sturdy, 88
So long you wandered on the dusky plain, 722
So may the auspicious Queen of Love, 386

So now the very bones of you are gone, 350
So was it even then. So soundlessly, 912
So, we'll go no more a-roving, 1185
Softly sighs the April air, 658
Soldier, rest! thy warfare o'er, 1178
Some day, some day, 620
Some of their chiefs were princes of the land; 1125
Something startles me where I thought I was safest, 1351
Som tyme this world was so stedfast and stable, 1024
Son, my son!, 1302
Souls of Poets dead and gone, 1201
Speak! speak! thou fearful guest!, 1328
Spread the board with linen snow, 453
Stand close around, ye Stygian set, 1182
Stand still, and I will read to thee, 1071
Starless and chill is the night; 897
Startled, 48
Stay weary traveler, stay!, 347
Stern daughter of the voice of God!, 1170
Still on my cheeks I feel their fondling breath; 929
Still round thy towers descend the fertile rain!, 97
Still south I went and west and south again, 1287
Still to be neat, still to be dressed, 1062
Stranger, the bark you see before you says, 370
Strengthen, my Love, this castle of my heart, 666
Strew me with blossoms when I die, 615
Strew on her roses, roses, 1232
Success is counted sweetest, 1372
Suddenly I saw the cold and rook-delighting Heaven, 1284
Suffenus, whom so well you know, 368
Sultry air, the smoke of shavings, 1009
Sumer is icumen in, 1021
Suppose you screeve? or go cheap-jack?, 692
Sweet are the whispers of yon pine that makes, 288
Sweet day, so cool, so calm, so bright, 1082
Sweet flower, that art so fair and gay, 676
Sweet in goodly fellowship, 456
Sweet maid, if thou wouldst charm my sight, 148
Sweet my musings used to be, 657
Sweet Peace, where dost thou dwell? I humbly crave, 1083
Sweetest love, I do not go, 1069
Swiftly walk over the western wave, 1189

Take heed of this small child of earth; 746
Take, O, take those lips away, 1059
Tears, ere thy death, for many a one I shed, 93
Tears fall within mine heart, 783
Tears, idle tears, I know not what they mean, 1212
Tell him, O night, 105
Tell me, good dog, whose tomb you guard so well, 331
Tell me not, sweet, I am unkind, 1109
Tell me now in what hidden way is, 693
Tell me where thy lovely love is, 891
That love—whose power and sovranty we own, 605
That morn which saw me made a bride, 342
That time of year thou mayst in me behold, 1051
That which her slender waist confined, 1091
That's my last Duchess painted on the wall, 1218
The ancient Barbarossa, the Kaiser Frederick old, 869
The ashen feelers of the frigid morrow, 939
The beauty of Israel is slain upon thy high places: 165

The beloved person must I think, 44
The blessed damozel leaned out, 1240
The broad-backed hippopotamus, 1406
The capitals are rocked with thunder, 1008
The child reads on; her basket of eggs stands by, 809
The churl that wants another's fare, 431
The cloud doth gather, the green wood roar, 847
The cold limbs of the air, 1285
The crimson roses burn and glow, 910
The crooked paths go every way, 1297
The Curfew tolls the knell of parting day, 1138
The dance is on the Bridge of Death, 682
The day is cold, and dark, and dreary, 1332
The day will soon be gone, 49
The dawn is smiling on the dew that covers, 745
The days of Spring are here! the eglantine, 159
The deer which lives, 46
The down drop of the blackbird, 1388
The dress that my Brother has put on is thin, 38
The earth is the Lord's, and the fullness thereof; 168
The earthly roses at God's call have made, 989
The ebb slips from the rock, the sunken, 1396
The expense of spirit in a waste of shame, 1054
The fields are chill; the sparse rain has stopped; 23
The firste stok, fader of gentilesse, 1023
The flesh is sad, alas! and all the books are read, 781
The flower of Virtue is the heart's content; 491
The flowers upon the rosemary spray, 640
The fruit-tree's branch by very wealth, 57
The gloom of death is on the raven's wing, 347
The glories of our blood and state, 1089
The gods have heard me, Lyce, 411
The golden hair that Gulla wears, 438
The gourd has still its bitter leaves, 2
The Grave said to the Rose, 744
The gray sea and the long black land, 1215
The haven and last refuge of my pain, 586
The heavens declare the glory of God; and the firmament, 168
The high Midnight was garlanding her head, 709
The holy Rose her leaves will soon unfold, 1010
The hours! when we are gazing at the peerless, 930
The house where I was born, 1282
The hunchèd camels of the night, 1258
The isles of Greece! the isles of Greece, 1185
The jewel of the secret treasury, 154
The king sits in Dumferling toune, 1025
The lady walked by the ocean strand, 905
The lark now leaves his watery nest, 1090
The linden blossomed, the nightingale sang, 889
The little wild birds have come flying, 996
The Lord is my shepherd; I shall not want, 168
The Lotus-flower doth languish, 877
The man in righteousness arrayed, 402
The man that never will declare his thought, 144
The man who feels not, more or less, somewhat, 545
The merchant, to secure his treasure, 1130
The moon and seven Pleiades have set; 261
The moon is fully risen, 880
The morning glory climbs above my head, 1
The mountain sheep are sweeter, 1182
The mountain summits sleep, glens, cliffs, and caves, 255

The mutilated choir boys, 891
The night Don Juan came to pay his fees, 763
The nightwind sings and rustles through the reeds, 940
The old dream comes again to me: 879
The old man's fair-haired consort, whose dewy axle-tree, 422
The people is a beast of muddy brain, 599
The poets have muddied all the little fountains, 86
The pointed houses lean so you would swear, 805
The prayers I make will then be sweet indeed, 584
The pretty maid she died, she died, in love-bed as she lay, 810
The province I govern is humble and remote; 26
The rain is due to fall, 33
The rain set early in to-night, 1216
The readers and the hearers like my books, 438
The revel pauses and the room is still; 798
The roadside thistle, eager, 50
The Roman Road runs straight and bare, 1254
The rose and the lily, the moon and the dove, 876
The rose is not the rose unless thou see; 152
The sea hath its pearls, 873
The sea hath tempered it; the mighty sun, 98
The Sea is calm to-night, 1232
The secret of these hills was stone, and cottages, 1270
The shepherd's star with trembling glint, 789
The Shining Eye of Horus cometh, 248
The singers of serenades, 787
The skies they were ashen and sober, 1341
The sky grew darker with each minute, 909
The sky is up above the roof, 784
The sky so pale, and the trees, such frail things, 788
The snow lies deep: nor sun nor melting shower, 424
The songs, so old and bitter, 894
The soote season, that bud and bloom forth brings, 557
The soul selects her own society, 1373
The spacious firmament on high, 1131
The storm cries every night, 939
The sun has risen on the eastern brim of the world, 12
The sun makes music as of old, 845
The sweetly-favored face, 481
The time I went to see my Sister, 46
The violets blue of the eyes divine, 878
The voice that beautifies the land!, 1307
The willows carried a slow sound, 1417
The wind, stirring in the dark foliage, brings, 906
The wing of separation, 96
The world is charged with the grandeur of God, 1256
The world is dull, the world is blind, 878
The world is too much with us; late and soon, 1170
The world's great age begins anew, 1190
The year has changed his mantle cold, 666
The years they come and go, 871
Thee, Sovereign God, our grateful accents praise; 458
Then hate me when thou wilt; if ever, now; 1051
Then Lelex rose, an old experienced man, 425
There are abandoned corners of our Exile, 213
There be none of Beauty's daughters, 1184
There calleth me ever a marvelous Horn, 855
There came a ghost to Margret's door, 1033
There fell red rain of spears athwart the sky, 1391
There flourished once a potentate, 734
There is a charming land, 983

There is a lady conquering with glances, 820
There is a place that some men know, 1414
There is a quiet kingdom's strand, 925
There is a singer that everyone has heard, 1385
There is an air for which I would disown, 747
There is great mystery, Simone, 799
There is no great and no small, 1321
There is no thing in all the world but love, 112
There lived a wife at Usher's Well, 1026
There never breathed a man, who, when his life, 595
There sat a happy fisherman, 1006
There was a child went forth every day, 1349
There was a Hag who kept two Chambermaids, 730
There was a stunted handpost just on the crest, 1255
There was a time when I was very small, 982
There was a time when meadow, grove and stream, 1172
There went out in the dawning light, 456
There's a green hollow where a river sings, 795
There's moaning somewhere in the dark, 913
Theris the old, the waves that harvested, 338
These are the days of our youth, our days of glory and honor, 121
They are all gone into the world of light!, 1119
They are not long, the weeping and the laughter, 1264
They are rattling breakfast plates in basement kitchens, 1405
They called my love a poor blind maid: 100
They call thee rich; I deem thee poor; 341
They closed her eyes, 647
They fought south of the Castle, 10
They have said evil of my dear; 678
They lied, those lying traitors all, 678
They pity me, 803
They throw in Drummer Hodge, to rest, 1252
They told me, Heraclitus, they told me you were dead, 334
They were at play, she and her cat, 791
This delightful young man, 892
This dust was Timas; and they say, 260
This earth Pythonax and his brother hides, 351
This fairest lady, who, as well I wot, 541
This fairest one of all the stars, whose flame, 572
This I admit, Death is terrible to me, 1269
This I ask Thee—tell it to me truly, Lord!, 125
This is a fearful thing to bear, 922
This month of May, one pleasant eventide, 674
This morn a young squire shall be made a knight; 491
This mound the Achaens reared—Achilles' tomb—, 330
This noiseless ball and top so round, 340
This on thy posy-ring I've writ; 707
This rudely sculptured porter-pot, 333
This shade-bestowing pear-tree, thou, 3
This stone, beloved Sabinus, on thy grave, 330
This warning, Gallus, for thy love I send, 418
This world and this life are so scattered, they try me, 882
Those charming eyes within whose starry sphere, 634
Those eyes that set my fancy on a fire, 727
Those ships which left, 48
Thou art God, and all things formed are Thy servants, 208
Thou art great, and compared with Thy greatness, all, 207
Thou art indeed just, Lord, if I contend, 1257
Thou art Light celestial, and the eyes of the pure shall behold Thee, 208
Thou art not dead, my Prote! thou art flown, 351

Thou art not, Penshurst, built, to envious show, 1063
Thou art One, the first of every number, and the, 206
Thou art wise. And wisdom is the fount of life and, 209
Thou blossom bright with autumn dew, 1314
Thou existest, but hearing of ear cannot reach Thee, 207
Thou green and blooming, cool and shaded hill, 559
Thou knowest, love, I know that thou dost know, 581
Thou livest, but not from any restricted season nor from any known period, 207
Thou still unravished bride of quietness, 1197
Thou sweetly smelling fresh red rose, 463
Thou that art wise, let wisdom minister, 544
Thou that from the heavens art, 833
Thou wert the morning star among the living, 348
Though short her strain, nor sung with mighty boast; 332
Though thou, indeed, hast quite forgotten ruth, 505
Three dark maids,—I loved them when, 619
Three fellows were marching over the Rhine, 862
Three little maidens they have slain, 801
Three miles extended around the fields of the homestead; on three sides, 990
Through the forest the boy wends all day long: 987
Thus saith the great god Thoth, 239
Thy dawn, O Ra, opens the new horizon, 250
Thy eyes with gloom are gleaming, 923
Thy nights moan into my days, 922
Time and the mortal will stand never fast; 636
Time goes, you say? Ah, No!, 717
Time is the root of all this earth; 65
Times she'll sit quiet by the hearth, and times, 1394
Tired and thirsty, weary of the way, 905
Tired with all these, for restful death I cry, 1050
'Tis hard to find in life, 58
To Archæanassa, on whose furrow'd brow, 349
To every heart which the sweet pain doth move, 511
To gallop off to town post-haste, 708
To him who in the love of Nature holds, 1311
To John I owed great obligation; 438
To lighten my darkness, 103
To Meath of the pastures, 1293
To mortal men Peace giveth these good things; 274
To read my book, the virgin shy, 438
To shaggy Pan, and all the Wood-Nymphs fair, 333
To sin, unshamed, to lose, unthinking, 1012
To the dim light and the large circle of shade, 537
To thee, fair freedom! I retire, 1137
To you, troop so fleet, 721
To-day a shepherd and our kin, 632
To-morrow you will live, you always cry:, 436
To-night, grave sir, both my poor house and I, 436
To-night I do not come to conquer thee, 781
Too much good luck no less than misery, 583
Tow'rds the lofty walls of Balbi, lo! Durand of Blonden hies, 857
True is it that Ambroisio Salinero, 596
Truelove, come O come to me, 826
Tumultuous sea, whose wrath and foam are spent, 334
Twain that were foes, while Mary lived, are fled, 715
'Twas spring, and dawn returning breathed new-born, 449
Two ladies to the summit of my mind, 537
Two steps from my garden rail, 217

Two that could not have lived their single lives, 1408
Tyger, tyger: burning bright, 1152
Tyre brought me up, who born in thee has been, 345

Under the greenwood tree, 1057
Under the lindens on the heather, 822
Under the pondweed do the great fish go, 2
Under the yew-tree's heavy weight, 764
Under yonder beech-tree single on the greensward, 1234
Underneath this myrtle shade, 267
Underneath this sable hearse, 1075
Unknown love, 39
Until thine hands clasp girdlewise the waist of the Belov'd, 147
Unto a heavenly course decreed, 902
Unto my thinking, thou beheld'st all worth, 499
Unto the blithe and lordly Fellowship, 485
Up, boy! arise, and saddle quick, 883
Up yonder on the mountain, 845
Upon a day, came Sorrow in to me, 536
Upon a tree there mounted guard, 728
Upon an obscure night, 638
Upon my darling's beaming eyes, 876

Vanity, saith the preacher, vanity!, 1219
Vanquished and weary, was my soul in me, 542
Venus, again thou mov'st a war, 400
Venus, take my votive glass, 348
Vex no man's secret soul—if that can be—, 146
Vital spark of heavenly flame!, 443

Wail, wail, Ah for Adonis! He is lost to us, lovely Adonis!, 315
Wake! For the Sun, who scattered into flight, 126
Want quickens wit: Want's pupils needs must work, 306
We are in love's land to-day; 759
We cared for each other as boy and maid, 888
We grow to the sound of the wind, 101
We have a bed, and a baby too, 913
We heard the thrushes by the shore and sea, 1288
We in our wandering, 454
We live, while we see the sun, 646
We more than others have the perfect right, 1390
We must pass like smoke or live within the spirit's fire, 1287
We sat at the hut of the fisher, 893
We that with like hearts love, we lovers twain, 721
We think to create festivals, 652
Weep, ah weep love's losing, love's with its dwellingplace, 80
Weep for me, friends, for now that I am hence, 98
Weep not, beloved friends! nor let the air, 594
Weep! Weep! Weep!, 106
Weeping and wakeful all the night I lie, 329
Well, I would have it so, I should have known, 733
Well pleaseth me the sweet time of Easter, 659
Wharton! the scorn and wonder of our days, 1134
What am I to do with my Sister?, 35
What celebration should there be?, 410
What could he know of sky and stars, or heavens all-hidden like, 146
What from the founder Aesop fell, 430
What has this bugbear Death to frighten man, 361
What ho! my shepherds, sweet it were, 309
What is it so transforms the boulevard?, 815
What is the name of King Ringang's daughter?, 900

What is this life if, full of care, 1265
What makes a happy life, dear friend, 439
What makes my bed seem hard, seeing it is soft, 420
What man is he that yearneth, 276
What more? Where is the third Calixt, 700
What should be said of him cannot be said; 585
What sin was mine, sweet, silent boy-god, Sleep, 443
What slender youth, bedew'd with liquid odors, 402
What time I see you passing by, 614
What voice, what harp, are those we hear, 837
Whatever good is naturally done, 546
What's my sweetheart?—A laundress is she, 915
When, 46
When a sighing begins, 790
When evening comes, 38
When, forehead full of torments hot and red, 797
When from afar these mountain tops I view, 706
When God at first made man, 1086
When God had finished Master Messerin, 498
When I am dead, my dearest, 1245
When I behold Becchina in a rage, 547
When I consider everything that grows, 1046
When I consider how my light is spent, 1107
When I do count the clock that tells the time, 1045
When I have fears that I may cease to be, 1203
When I have seen by Time's fell hand defaced, 1049
When I was marked for suffering, Love forswore, 638
When icicles hang by the wall, 1056
When, in disgrace with fortune and men's eyes, 1047
When in the chronicle of wasted time, 1053
When lilacs last in the dooryard bloomed, 1361
When Love with unconfined wings, 1109
When lovely woman stoops to folly, 1148
When my love swears that she is made of truth, 1055
When storms blow loud, 't is sweet to watch at ease, 358
When the crop is fair in the olive-yard, 774
When the dawn comes, 45
When the fields catch flower, 663
When the hounds of spring are on winter's traces, 1250
When the night goes hence, 923
When the prime mover of my many sighs, 585
When the roses wonder open at morn, 923
When the voices of children are heard on the green, 1149
When the yellow bird's note was almost stopped, 27
When these graven lines you see, 336
When thou must home to shades of underground, 416
When thou to my true-love com'st, 827
When to my lone soft bed at eve returning, 724
When to the sessions of sweet silent thought, 1047
When two who love are parted, 896
When waves invade the yellowing wheat, 1004
When winds that move not its calm surface sweep, 325
When with eyes closed as in an opium dream, 765
When with May the air is sweet, 824
When you are old and gray and full of sleep, 1283
When you are very old, at evening, 714
When young hearts break with passion, 896
Whenas in silks my Julia goes, 1079
Whence come you, all of you so sorrowful?, 532
Whene'er I look into your eyes, 896
Whenever he observes me purchasing, 441

Where are the bay-leaves, Thestylis, and the charms?, 293
Where is my ruined life, and where the fame, 153
Where is the home for me?, 281
Where lies the land to which the ship would go?, 1231
Where long the shadows of the wind had rolled, 1380
Where the bee sucks, there suck I; 1060
Where the remote Bermudas ride, 1114
Where the thistle lifts a purple crown, 1259
Whether day my spirit's yearning, 847
While my hair was still but straight across my forehead, 22
While yet the grapes were green, thou didst refuse me, 331
Whilst human kind, 353
Whirl up, sea—, 1393
White in the moon the long road lies, 1261
White is the sail and lonely, 1003
Whither is thy beloved gone, O thou fairest among women?, 197
Whither, midst falling dew, 1313
Whither shall I, the fair maiden, flee from Sorrow?, 995
Who can support the anguish of love?, 99
Who is she coming, whom all gaze upon, 501
Who is this I hear? Lo, this is I, thine heart, 704
Who owns these cattle, Corydon? Philondas? Prythee say, 298
Who shall understand the mysteries of Thy creations? 209
Who was it, tell me, that first of men reckon'd, 874
Whoever comes to shroud me, do not harm, 1067
Whoever hath washed his hands of living, 145
Whoever weeps somewhere out in the world, 938
Whoever without money is in love, 550
Why do you cry out, why do I like to hear you, 1409
Why from the danger did mine eyes not start, 506
Why, if Becchina's heart were diamond, 546
Why should a foolish marriage vow, 1121
Why so pale and wan, fond lover?, 1108
Why wait we for the torches' lights?, 256
Wild pigeon of the leaves, 101
'Will sprawl, now that the heat of day is best, 1223
Will ye that I should sing, 686
Wilt thou forgive that sin where I begun, 1072
Wind from the east, oh Lapwing of the day, 155
Wind themselves around my lance severe, 931
Winter has at last come, 47
Winter is passing, and the bells, 771
Wisdom and Spirit of the universe!, 1164
Wise to have gone so early to reward, 105
With a rod no man alive, 821
With blackest moss the flower-plots, 1204
With courage seek the kingdom of the dead; 340
With elbow buried in the downy pillow, 758
With heart at rest I climbed the citadel's, 764
With hearts of poor men it is so; 797
With how sad steps, O Moon, thou climb'st the skies!, 1043
With other women I beheld my love; 501
With reeds and bird-lime from the desert air, 338
With rue my heart is laden, 1261
With the shrewd and upright man, 59
With your fair eyes a charming light I see, 580
Within a copse I met a shepherd-maid, 507
Within the covert of a shady grove, 349
Within the gentle heart Love shelters him, 474
Within the sand of what far river lies, 709
Wonderful are thy works, as my soul overwhelmingly knoweth, 206

Woo not the world too rashly, for behold, 99
Would I might go far over sea, 663
Would that my father had taught me the craft of a keeper of sheep, 325
Wretched Catullus, play the fool no more: 365

Ye banks and braes, and streams around, 1156
Ye elves of hills, brooks, standing lakes and groves, 425
Ye flowery banks o' bonnie Doon, 1157
Ye graceful peasant-girls and mountain-maids, 569
Ye have been fresh and green, 1082
Ye ladies, walking past me piteous-eyed, 533
Ye living lamps, by whose dear light, 1114
Ye mariners of Spain, 624
Ye mountain valleys, pitifully groan!, 321
Ye wild-eyed Muses, sing the Twins of Jove, 254
Yea, let me praise my lady, whom I love; 472
Yellow butterflies, 1306
Yes! hope may with my strong desire keep pace, 584
Yes! that fair neck, too beautiful by half, 708
Yes, we love this land together, 986
Yet Chloe sure was form'd without a spot, 1134
Yet once more, O ye laurels, and once more, 1100
Yet one more hour, then comes the night; 908
Yonder great shadow—that blot on the passionate glare, 222
You are the millions, we are the multitude, 1017
You give your cheeks a rosy stain, 340
You have coats and robes, 3
You said to me; But I will be your comrade, 804
You shun me, Chloe, wild and shy, 406
You told me, Maro, whilst you live, 439
Young men dancing, and the old, 271
Your soul is a sealed garden, and there go, 788

INDEX OF TITLES

A Beauty That All Night Long, 143
A Better Answer, 1129
A Bird Was Singing, 816
A Birthday, 1245
A Captive of Love, 420
A Carrion, 767
A Childish Game, 819
A Clymene, 784
A Complaint by Night of the Lover Not Beloved, 558
A Dirge, 1089
A Ditty, 1042
A Double Ballad of Good Counsel, 698
A Dream of Venus, 320
A Drover, 1293
A Farewell, 348
A Fib Detected, 369
A Garland for Heliodora, 346
A Gentle Wind, 17
A Happy Man, 336
A Hinted Wish, 439
A Holy Hill, 1286
A Hymn to God the Father, 1072
A La Promenade, 788
A Lady of High Degree, 686
A Lady Stood, 817
A Leaf, 861
A Leave-Taking, 930
A Lecture Upon the Shadow, 1071
A Love-Lesson, 707
A Lovely Rose Is Sprung, 827
A Lover's Lament (Tewa), 1305
A Maiden Lies in Her Chamber, 892
A Mighty Fortress Is Our God, 828
A Mountain Wind, 1285
A Night by the Sea, 897
A Night in a Village, 1009
A Noiseless, Patient Spider, 1354
A Pastoral, 456
A Pastoral Elegy, 413
A Persian Song of Hafiz, 148
A Poem To Be Said on Hearing the Birds Sing, 1280
A Poet Thinks, 33
A Poison Tree, 1154
A Prayer for Purification, 582
A Red, Red Rose, 1158
A Sacred Grove, 308
A Sail, 1003
A Shepherd's Gift, 333
A Slumber Did My Spirit Seal, 1167
A Song of the Open Road, 454
A Song of the Virgin Mother, 643
A Sonnet to Heavenly Beauty, 722
A Sunset, 739
A Sylvan Revel, 309
A Thought, 1004
A Trysting, 912
A Venetian Night, 926
A Virgin Declares Her Beauties, 509
A Voice from the Invisible World, 840
A Vow to Heavenly Venus, 721
A Wounded Deer Leaps Highest, 1372
Abenamar, Abenamar, 623
Abishag, 935
Abla, 86
Abu Nowas for the Barmacides, 105
Achitophel, 1124
Acme and Septimius, 371
Ad Finem, 871
Ad Leuconoen, 408
Ad Xanthiam Phoceum, 409
Address to My Soul, 1400
Address to Venus, 352
Adonis, 1392
Adoration of the Disk by King Akhnaten and Princess Nefer Neferiu Aten, 250
Aesop at Play, 431
Aesop's Fables, 326-328
After a Hundred Years, 1374
After Midnight, 814
After the Hunt, 905
Against the Fear of Death, 361
Agamemnon, Chorus from, 275
Age, 266
Aglaura, From, 1108
Ah, Sunflower, 1153
Ah Woe Is Me, 416
Ajax, Chorus from, 277
Alas!, 145
Alas for Youth, 125
Alba Innominata, 660
Albi, Ne Doreas, 406
Alcestis, Chorus from, 279
All Things Drink, 269

Allah, 853
Alone, 261
Alons Au Bois Le May Cueillir, 667
Aminta, From, 590
Amor Mysticus, 629
Amoretti, 1036
Amphitryon, 1121
Amsterdam, 805
An Apology, 1246
An Inscription by the Sea, 337
An Irish Lamentation, 840
An Ode, 1130
An Ode for Ben Jonson, 1076
An Old Man's Winter Night, 1384
An Old Song, 234
An Old Tune, 747
Anacreon's Dove, 273
Anacreontics, 263-273
And, Lightly, Like the Flowers, 716
Anguish, 781
Annabel Lee, 1343
Anno, 1829, 885
Another Spirit Advances, 815
April, 663
April, 724
Arab Love-Song, 1258
Arbor Amoris, 690
Ardan Mór, 1300
Aristeides, 332
Ars Poetica, 1410
Art, 755
Art Poetique, 791
Artificial Beauty, 340
As in the Midst of Battle There Is Room, 1376
As Ocean's Stream, 1002
As On the Heather, 818
As You Like It, 1057
Ask Me No More, 1089
Aspatia's Song, 1074
Astrophel and Stella, 1043
At the Fountain, 654
Atalanta in Calydon; Chorus, 1250
Atticus, 1132
Auf Meiner Herzliebsten Äugelein, 876
Auld Lang Syne, 1163
Austere the Music of My Songs, 1010
Autumn, 905
Autumn, 998
Autumn Song, 854
Awake!, 821
Aweary Am I, 96

Babylon and Sion (Goa and Lisbon), 6..
Bacchai, Chorus from the, 281
Bacchus, 1322
Bacchus in Tuscany, From, 602
Bacchus's Opinion of Wine, and Other Beverages, 602
Balade, 1021
Ballad Against the Enemies of France, 703
Ballad of the Gibbet, 688
Ballad of the Lords of Old Time, 700
Ballad of the Outer Life, 928
Ballad of the Women of Paris, 701
Ballad Written for a Bridegroom, 702
Ballade, 810
Ballade de Marguerite, 670
Ballads, 680
Ballads, 976
Ballads, 1025
Ballads, Old Spanish, 621-628
Ballata: Concerning a Shepherd Maid, 507
Ballata: He reveals, in a Dialogue, his increasing love for Mandetta, 502
Ballata: He will gaze upon Beatrice, 533
Ballata: His Talk with Certain Peasant-girls, 569
Ballata: In Exile at Sarzana, 508
Ballata: Of a continual Death in Love, 505
Ballata: Of his Lady among other Ladies, 501
Ballata: Of True and False Singing, 572
Ballata: One speaks of the Beginning of his Love, 572
Barbarossa, 869
Baucis, 337
Baucis and Philemon, 425
Beauty, 267
Beauty, 907
Beauty Rohtraut, 900
Because I Could Not Stop for Death, 1374
Before the Storm, 909
Behold the Meads, 654
Bel M'es Quan Lo Vens M'alena, 658
Bermudas, 1114
Beyond Religion, 353
Birds, 101
Black Marigolds, 66
Blacksmith Pain, 915
Bonnie George Campbell, 1029
Bonny Barbara Allan, 1028
Book of Odes, 1-4

Book of the Dead, 235-251
Bought Locks, 438
Brahma, 1315
Break, Break, Break, 1211
Buddha, 932
Bustan, The, 146

Caliban Upon Setebos, 1223
Cancion, 618
Cantica, 471
Canzone, 470
Canzone, 473
Canzone: He beseeches Death for the Life of Beatrice, 534
Canzone: His Lament for Selvaggia, 543
Canzone: His Portrait of his Lady, 564
Canzone: Of His Dead Lady, 482
Canzone: Of his Love, with the Figure of a sudden Storm, 496
Canzone: Of the Gentle Heart, 474
Canzone: To Love and To His Lady, 492
Canzonetta: A Bitter Song to His Lady, 494
Canzonetta: He will Neither Boast nor Lament to his Lady, 479
Canzonetta: Of His Lady and Of His Making her Likeness, 478
Canzonetta: Of His Lady in Absence, 481
Catch, 570
Celestial Love, 580
Celestial Wisdom, 442
Chansons D'Automne, 790
Characters from the Satires, 1124
Characters from the Satires, 1132
Chaucer, 1333
Childhood, 982
Chloe, 1134
Chorus from Atalanta in Calydon, 1250
Chorus from Hellas, 1190
Chorus of Birds, 285
Chorus of Satyrs, Driving Their Goats, 280
Claim To Love, 589
Clair De Lune, 788
Clarimonde, 758
Clearing at Dawn, 23
Cleitagoras, 339
Cleonicos, 310
Come Not Near My Songs (Shoshone), 1302
Complaint of a Lover Rebuked, 558
Composed Upon Westminster Bridge, Sept. 3, 1802, 1169
Composed While Under Arrest, 1004
Concord Hymn, 1316
Conquest, 727
Continent's End, 1398
Cordova, 97
Corn-grinding Song (Laguna), 1307
Correspondences, 766
Corrymeela, 1288
Cortege, 789
Corydon and Thyrsis, 378
Counsels of Sigrdrifa, 974
Country Life, 392
Country Pleasures, 441
Courage, 145
Crethis, 335
Critics, 438
Cupid Turned Plowman, 326
Cyclops, Choruses from the, 280
Cymbeline, 1059
Cynthia's Revels, 1061
Cythere, 786

Dagger, 1003
Daisy, 1259
Dans l'Allee, 787
Dante, 585
Dark Rosaleen, 1273
Das Jahr Der Seele, From, 921
Dates, 101
David's Lament for Saul and Jonathan, 165
Deadly Kisses, 714
Dear Maiden, 886
Death, 105
Death of Daphnis, The, 288
Deirdre, 1295
Departed Friends, 1119
Der Mond Ist Aufgegangen, 880
Dialogue: Lover and Lady, 463
Die Blauen Veilchen Der Äugelein, 878
"Die Heimkehr," From, 891-896
Die Lotosblume Ängstigt, 877
Die Rose, Die Lilie, Die Taube, Die Sonne, 876
Die Welt Ist Dumm, Die Welt Ist Blind, 878
Dies Irae, 460
Dieu Qu'il La Fait, 667
Dion of Tarsus, 330
Dirce, 1182
Discordants, 1409
Disdain Returned, 1088
Don Juan in Hell, 763
Doricha, 350
Dover Beach, 1232

Drinking Alone in the Moonlight, 21
Drummer Hodge, 1252
Du Bist Wie Eine Blume, 882
Durand of Blonden, 857

Each and All, 1320
Ecclesiastes, 190
Eclogues, 373-381
Ein Fichtenbaum Steht Einsam, 878
Elder Edda, From the, 942
Eldorado, 1347
Elegies, 732
Elegy, 1138
Elevation, 765
Elfer Hill, 979
Emblems, 1415
En Bateau, 789
Encouragement to Exile, 432
Enfant Perdu, 881
Enjoyment, 261
Envoy, 704
Epicœne; or, The Silent Woman, From, 1062
Epilog, 899
Epilogue, 764
Epistle in Form of a Ballad to His Friends, 705
Epitaph, 452
Epitaph, 794
Epitaph of Achilles, 330
Epitaph of an Infant, 336
Epitaphs, 594
Erinna, 332
Erotion, 440
Es Fallt Ein Stern Herunter, 875
Es Stehen Unbeweglich, 877
Esthonian Bridal Song, 831
Eternal Masculine, 1393
Eternity, 1155
Eumares, 334
Evening Prayer, 901
Evening Twilight, 899
Ever Watchful, 93
Exclusion, 1373
Extremum Tanain, 405
Eyes So Tristful, 619

Fading Beauty, 600
Fantoches, 784
Far in a Western Brookland, 1262
Farewell, 349
Farewell, 889
Farewell to Anactoria, 258
Farewell to Ireland, 1272
Fatherland Song, 986
Faust, From, 845
Femme Et Chatte, 791
Ferrara, 1218
Fighting South of the Castle, 10
First Philosopher's Song, 1267
Flax, 1011
Flow Gently, Sweet Afton, 1159
Fool and False, 59
Folk Songs, 994
For, Lord, the Crowded Cities Be, 936
For the Book of Love, 800
Forever Dead, 261
Fragment, 255
Fragment of a Sonnet, 711
Fragment of Death, 699
Fragments, 259
Fresco-Sonnets to Christian Sethe, 889
Friar Lubin, 708
Friendship, 144
Frithiofs Saga, 990
From Sagesse, 792
From the Arabic, 112
From The Visions, 718
Full Moon, 261

Gentilesse, 1023
Gentle River, Gentle River, 621
Georgics, The, 384
Gītā Gōvinda, 77
Give All to Love, 1319
Go Lovely Rose!, 1091
God's Grandeur, 1256
God's Harp, 906
Gone Is Youth, 90
Grace for a Child, 1080
Grapes, 331
Grass, 1387
Greek Anthology, The, 328
Gulistan, The, 144

Hair, 799
Hamâsah, 95
Hannah's Song of Thanksgiving, 164
Hap, 1253
Harmonie Du Soir, 770
Haroun Al-Rachid for Heart's-Life, 106
Haroun's Favorite Song, 104
Harvest-Home, 301
Harvest Song, 831
Harvest Song, 910
He Approacheth the Hall of Judgment, 238
He Asketh Absolution of God, 237
He Biddeth Osiris To Arise from the Dead, 240
He Cometh Forth Into the Day, 240

He Commandeth a Fair Wind, 245
He Defendeth His Heart Against the Destroyer, 243
He Embarketh in the Boat of Ra, 244
He Entereth the House of the Goddess Hathor, 244
He Establisheth His Triumph, 244
He Hath No Parallel, 144
He Holdeth Fast to the Memory of His Identity, 238
He Is Declared True of Word, 239
He Is Like the Serpent Saka, 247
He Is Like the Lotus, 247
He Kindleth a Fire, 248
He Knoweth the Souls of the East, 246
He Knoweth the Souls of the West, 245
He Maketh Himself One With Osiris, 241
He Maketh Himself One With the God Ra, 241
He Maketh Himself One With the Only God, Whose Limbs Are the Many Gods, 242
He Overcometh the Serpent of Evil in the Name of Ra, 246
He Prayeth for Ink and Palette That He May Write, 248
He Singeth a Hymn to Osiris, the Lord of Eternity, 236
He Singeth in the Underworld, 248
He That Loves a Rosy Cheek, 817
He Walketh by Day, 243
Heard on the Mountain, 741
Helen of Kirconnell, 1035
Helen, the Sad Queen, 813
Help, 146
Heraclitus, 334
Here Lies a Lady, 1407
Her Rival for Aziza, 106
Herdsmen, The, 298
Hesperus the Bringer, 259
Heureux Qui, Comme Ulysse, A Fait Un Beau Voyage, 723
Hialmar Speaks to the Raven, 760
Highland Mary, 1156
Hippolytus, Choruses from, 282
His Camel, 88
His Children, 95
His Lady's Death, 715
His Lady's Tomb, 716
His Mother's Service to Our Lady, 694
His Own True Wife, 823
His Son, 334
Holiday, 410
Home-Sickness, 855
Home-Thoughts, from Abroad, 1214
Home-Thoughts, from the Sea, 1215
Homeric Hymns, 252
Hope, 262
Horror, 922
How Goes the Night?, 1
How Oft Has the Banshee Cried, 1280
Hunger, 795
Hunting-Song (Navaho), 1304
Hyaku-Nin-Isshu, 49
Hylas, 418
Hymn, 1131
Hymn for St. John's Eve, 459
Hymn to Athena, 254
Hymn to Castor and Pollux, 254
Hymn to Diana, 366
Hymn to Diana, 1061
Hymn to Earth the Mother of All, 252
Hymn to Selene, 253
Hymn to the Winds, 721
Hymn to Vishnu, 77

I Am Raferty, 1279
I Built My Hut, 18
I Came A-Riding, 825
I Died for Beauty, 1373
I Go by Road, 776
I Had Not Minded Walls, 1375
I Hear America Singing, 1370
I Hear an Army, 1298
I Love But Thee, 896
I Met by Chance, 887
I Saw in Louisiana a Live-Oak Growing, 1358
I Traveled Among Unknown Men, 1166
I Traveled With Them, 99
I Wait My Lord, 2
I Wept as I Lay Dreaming, 888
I Would I Might Forget That I Am I, 1375
Ich Weiss Nicht Was Soll Es Bedeuten, 873
Ichabod! The Glory Has Departed, 856
Idea, 1044
Ideal, 1291
Idyl, 924
Idyll of the Rose, 449
If It Be Destined, 560

If, Lord, Thy Love for Me Is Strong, 631
Il Pastor Fido, From, 587
Il Penseroso, 1096
Il Pleut Doucement Sur La Ville, 783
I'm Black and Blue, 888
Im Traum Sah Ich Ein Männchen Klein Und Putzig, 884
Images, 925
Immortality, 1287
In a Lovely Garden Walking, 861
In Kerry, 1288
In the Mountains on a Summer Day, 23
In the Night of the Full Moon, 925
In the Orchard, 985
In the Spring, 343
Incantation, The, 293
Indra, The Supreme God, 52
Influence of Natural Objects, 1164
Inscriptions at the City of Brass, 109
Intimations of Immortality from Recollections of Early Childhood, 1172
Invitation to the Dance, 453
Inviting a Friend to Supper, 436
Invocation, 420
Invocation and Prelude, 918
Iphigeneia in Aulis, Chorus from, 284
Isaiah, 200-202
Israfel, 1344
It Is a Beauteous Evening, Calm and Free, 1160
Italy, 605

Je Ne Veux De Personne Aupres De Ma Tristesse, 803
Jeannette, 915
Jeremiah, 202
Job, The Book of, 180
John Anderson My Jo, 1160
John-John, 1289
John of Tours, 668
Joy May Kill, 583
Juana, 753

Kindly Vision, 915
King Christian, 981
Kings, 57
Kokin Shu, 43
Korosta Katzina Song (Hopi), 1306
Kubla Kahn, 1179

La Beaute, 769
La Belle Dame Sans Merci, 1202
Lady of the Lake, 1178
Lak of Stedfastnesse, 1024
L'Allegro, 1092
Lament of a Man for His Son (Paiute), 1302
Lament for Adonis, 315
Lament for Banba, 1278
Lament for Bion, 321
Lament for the Poets: 1916, 1300
Lament for the Two Brothers Slain by Each Other's Hand, 275
Laments, 105
L'Apres-Midi D'Un Faune, 777
Last Judgment, 1391
Latin Hymns, 457
Le Balcon, 769
Les Hiboux, 764
Les Chercheuses De Poux, 797
Lesbia Railing, 364
Leisure, 1265
Lente, Lente, 422
Let Me Enjoy, 1253
Let Me Go Warm, 642
Let Mine Eyes See Thee, 632
Let Us Drink, 256
"Life is a Dream", From, 646
Lines on the Mermaid Tavern, 1201
Lines Written in Her Breviary, 631
L'Infinito, 610
Litany to Satan, 761
Lo-Yang, 20
Lodging with the Old Man of the Stream, 26
London, 1154
London, 1802, 1168
Lonely, 803
Lord Randal, 1029
Losing a Slave-Girl, 27
Lost Desire, 345
Lost for a Rose's Sake, 687
Lost Love, 1268
Love, 104
Love, 261
Love, 265
Love, 593
Love, 808
Love, 1085
Love and Death, 368
Love and Folly, 729
Love at Sea, 759
Love at the Door, 343
Love in May, 710
Love in the Valley, 1234
Love Sleeping, 349
Love Song, 280
Love-Song, 996
Love Song (Papago), 1301
Love Song, 1310

Love, The Light-Giver, 580
Love, Whose Month Was Ever May, 824
Loveliest of Trees, 1262
Love's Deity, 1067
Love's Entreaty, 581
Love's Fidelity, 559
Love's Inconsistency, 559
Love's Justification, 584
Love's Labor's Lost, 1056
Love's Last Resource, 145
Love's Lesson, 325
Lucifer in Starlight, 1240
Luke Havergal, 1376
Lycidas, 1100
Lycidas and Moeris, 381

Madame D'Albert's Laugh, 708
Mädchen Mit Den Rothen Mündchen, 884
Magic, 425
Madrigal, 540
Mandoline, 787
Many Indeed Must Perish in the Keel, 928
Manyo Shu, 35
Mariana, 1204
Marriage à la mode, 1121
Maytime, 3
Measure for Measure, 1059
Medieval Norman Songs, 673
Medusa, 1413
Meeting at Night, 1215
Mein Herz, Mein Herz Ist Traurig, 879
Mein Kind Wir Waren Kinder, 872
Mein Liebchen, Wir Sassen Zusammen, 876
Memory, 989
Menodotis, 338
Mesnevi, 145
Message to Siberia, 1000
Metamorphoses, From the, 425
Mignon, 844
Milton, 1155
Milton, 1334
Miniver Cheevy, 1377
Mir Traümte Von Einem Königskind, 875
Mir Träumte Wieder Der Alte Traum, 879
Mist, 1348
Mr. Flood's Party, 1378
Moonlight, 709
More Strong Than Time, 745
Morning and Evening Star, 348
Morning at the Window, 1405
Morning Song, 1008
Most Quietly at Times, 914
Mot Eran Dous Miei Cossir, 657
Mother, I Cannot Mind My Wheel, 260
Mu'allaqat, 80
Much Ado About Nothing, 1056
Mufaddaliyat, 88
My Drinking Song, 908
My Father's Close, 669
My Heart's in the Highlands, 1160
My Last Duchess, 1218
My Lost Youth, 1325
My Songs are Poisoned, 895
My Sweetest Lesbia, 363

Narcissus, 811
Nature, 738
Nature, 1324
Nature's Travail, 331
Near Lanivet, 1872, 1255
Near Neighbors, 435
Neither Spirit Nor Bird (Shoshone), 1301
New Year, 1271
Night, 220
Night, 802
Night, 940
Night, 1396
No, I Am Not As Others Are, 691
No Marvel Is It, 656
No Matter, 348
No More, O My Spirits, 283
No Single Thing Abides, 354
Nocturne in G Minor, 940
Non Amo Te, 435
Non Sum Qualis Eram Bonae Sub Regno Cynarae, 1264
None is Happy, 820
Norman Songs, Medieval, 673-679
Not of Itself But Thee, 331
Not Such Your Burden, 329
Nudities, 804
Nurse's Song, 1149

O Gentle Ships, 342
O Flame of Living Love, 640
O For the Wings of a Dove, 282
O Sè Stesso, 610
Ode, 80
Ode, 99
Ode, 100
Ode, 147
Ode, 1147
Ode, 1172
Ode on a Grecian Urn, 1197
Ode on Solitude, 1131
Ode to a Nightingale, 1194
Ode to Anactoria, 258
Ode to Aphrodite, 257
Ode to Duty, 1170
Ode to Evening, 1146

Ode to the West Wind, 1192
Odes, 150
Oedipus Coloneus, Chorus from, 276
Of a' the Airts, 1158
Of Caution, 510
Of England, and of Its Marvels, 567
Of Himself, 345
Of His Death, 342
Of His Lady's Old Age, 714
Of the Months, 485
Oft in the Silent Night, 916
Og and Doeg, 1126
Oh Lovely Fishermaiden, 893
Ojibwa War Songs, 1309
Old Age, 89
Old and New, 11
Old I Am, 271
Old Loves, 772
Old Poem, 12
Old Scent of the Plum Tree, 49
Old Testament, 162
On a Blind Girl, 100
On a Fowler, 338
On a Girdle, 1091
On a Nun, 606
On a Seal, 349
On Alexis, 349
On an Invitation to the United States, 1254
On an Old Woman, 341
On Another's Sorrow, 1149
On Archaeanassa, 349
On Being Sixty, 28
On His Blindness, 1107
On His Having Arrived at the Age of Twenty-Three, 1105
On His Lady's Waking, 715
On His Seventy-fifth Birthday, 1182
On Knighthood, 491
On My First Son, 1062
On Revisiting Cintra After the Death of Catarina, 634
On the Beach at Night, 1370
On the Birth of His Son, 33
On the Brink of Death, 581
On the Burial of His Brother, 367
On the Countess of Pembroke, 1075
On the Death of a Pious Lady, 989
On the Death of a Young and Favorite Slave, 440
On the Death of Catarina de Attayda, 634
On the Deception of Appearances, 144
On the Late Massacre in Piedmont, 1107
On the Mountain, 824
On Two Brothers, 351
Once More Fields and Gardens, 19
One Girl, 259
Open Thy Doors, O Lebanon, 204
Opportunity, 578
Oread, 1393
Our March, 1020
Out of the Cradle Endlessly Rocking, 1354
Ozymandias, 1191
Pan and the Cherries, 810
Panchatantra, 57
Pannyra of the Golden Heel, 798
Parfum Exotique, 765
Parting, 211
Parting at Morning, 816
Parting at Morning, 1216
Partings, 814
Past Ruined Ilion, 1182
Patterns, 1380
Peace, 66
Peace, 1083
Peace, 1116
Peace on Earth, 274
Pericles and Aspasia, From, 1182
Persian Fopperies, 400
Petrarch, 611
Phantasus, 933
Philocles, 340
Pied Beauty, 1257
Pindar, 332
Plutarch, 329
Poems, 650
Popular Songs of Tuscany, 613
Porphyria's Lover, 1216
Post-Obits and the Poets, 438
Pour Us Wine, 87
Poverty, 59
Poverty, 262
Povre Ame Amoureuse, 724
Praise for an Urn, 1416
Praise of Little Women, 616
Prayer of the Maidens to Mary, 934
Prayer to go to Paradise With the Asses, 808
Prelude, 1287
Prelude, The Georgics, 384
Presaging, 938
Primo Vere, 612
Proem, 871
Procrastination, 436
Prologue in Heaven: Faust, 845
Prologue to the First Satire, 434
Prolonged Sonnet, 498

Prolonged Sonnet, 552
Prometheus, 841
Prothalamion, 1037
Provençal, From the, 654-672
Psalms, 166
Psalms of Love, 922
Pure Death, 1269
Pushan, God of Pasture, 55

Quits, 438

Radiant Ranks of Seraphim, 1011
Remembering Golden Bells, 28
Rapture, 920
Recessional, 1263
Rejoicing at the Arrival of Ch'en Hsiung, 26
Remember, 1246
Repose of Rivers, 1417
Requiescat, 1232
Revenge!, 411
Revenge to Come, 419
Rhodanthe, 329
Riches, 330
Rigveda, 52
River-mates, 1292
Robin Hood, 1199
Rome, 723
Rondel, 666
Rondel, 689
Rose Aylmer, 1181
Roses, 268
Roses Red, 931
Round About Me, 260
Rubaiyat, 126
Russia, 1012

Sacred Book, The, 125
Sag! Wo Ist Dein Schönes Liebchen, 880
Sag' Mir Wer Einst Die Uhren Erfund, 874
Sailing Homeward, 18
Sally in Our Alley, 1135
Saon of Acanthus, 335
Sappho, 366
Say Not the Struggle Nought Availeth, 1231
Sea Dirge, 333
Sea-Wind, 781
Secret Love, 1122
Sensation, 794
Serenade, 826
Sestina, 537
Seven Against Thebes, Chorus from, 275
Seven Poems, 47
Seven Poems, 50
Sextus the Usurer, 441
Shady, Shady, 19
Shadows of His Lady, 709
Shakespeare, 1333
She Dwelt Among the Untrodden Ways, 1166
She Walks in Beauty, 1184
Shepherd, Shepherd, Hark, 633
Shi King, 1-4
Shui Shu, 46
Sigh, 780
Signs of Love, 560
Silent Hour, 938
Simplex Munditiis, 1062
Sir Olaf, 829
Sir Patrick Spens, 1025
Sirmio, 367
Sleep, 443
Sleep, 727
Sleeping They Bear Me, 924
Smoke, 1348
Snowfall, 611
So, We'll Go No More A-Roving, 1185
Sois Sage O Ma Douleur, 768
Soldier, Rest! Thy Warfare O'er, 1178
Some Day, Some Day, 620
Song, 629
Song, 801
Song, 1066
Song, 1069
Song, 1090
Song, 1121
Song, 1121
Song, 1122
Song, 1148
Song, 1245
Song for Fine Weather, 1310
Song for St. Cecilia's Day, 1122
Song from Chartivel, 661
Song from Maud, 1209
Song: Green Grow the Rashes, 1161
Song: Mary Morison, 1157
Song of Battle, 659
Song of Breath, 660
Song of Deborah and Barak, The, 162
Song of Songs, The, 191-199
Song of the Clouds, 287
Song of the Highest Tower, 796
Song of the Horse (Navaho), 1305
Song of the Moderns, 1390
Song of the Rain Chant (Navaho), 1305
Song of the Silent Land, 852
Song to Celia, 1061
Song to the Mountains (Pawnee), 1308
Songs of the People, 217
Songs from the Princess, 1212
Songs from the Plays, 1056

Sonnet, 635
Sonnet, 636
Sonnet, 638
Sonnet, 1267
Sonnet, 1412
Sonnet: A Lady Laments for Her Lost Lover, 571
Sonnet: A Rapture Concerning His Lady, 501
Sonnet: A Trance of Love, 542
Sonnet: Death is not without but within him, 541
Sonnet: Death Warnings, 645
Sonnet: In absence from Becchina, 548
Sonnet: He argues his case with Death, 551
Sonnet: He compares all Things with his Lady and finds them Wanting, 500
Sonnet: He craves interpreting of a Dream of his, 544
Sonnet: He is out of Heart with his Time, 476
Sonnet: He is past all Help, 549
Sonnet: He jests concerning his Poverty, 484
Sonnet: He rails against Dante, 548
Sonnet: He speaks of a third Love of his, 504
Sonnet: He will not be too Deeply in Love, 545
Sonnet: He will Praise His Lady, 472
Sonnet: Of all he would do, 549
Sonnet: Of an Ill-favored Lady, 508
Sonnet: Of Beatrice de' Portinari, 532
Sonnet: Of Beauty and Duty, 537
Sonnet: Of Becchina, 546
Sonnet: Of Becchina in a Rage, 547
Sonnet: Of His Lady in Heaven, 477
Sonnet: Of His Lady's Face, 477
Sonnet: Of His Pain from a new Love, 506
Sonnet: Of Love, in honor of his Mistress Becchina, 546
Sonnet: Of Love in Men and Devils, 545
Sonnet: Of Moderation and Tolerance, 472
Sonnet: Of the Eyes of a Certain Mandetta, 502
Sonnet: Of the Making of a Master Messerin, 498
Sonnet: Of Virtue, 491
Sonnet: Of Why he would be a Scullion, 550
Sonnet: On the Detection of a False Friend, 504
Sonnet: On the Grave of Selvaggia, 542
Sonnet: On the 9th of June, 1290, 536
Sonnet: On the 20th June, 1291, 547
Sonnet: On why he is unhanged, 550
Sonnet: To a Friend who does not pity his Love, 505
Sonnet: To certain Ladies, 532
Sonnet: To Dante Alighieri, 499
Sonnet: To Dante Alighieri, 503
Sonnet: To Dante Alighieri, 539
Sonnet: To Dante Alighieri, 540
Sonnet: To Dante Alighieri, 543
Sonnet: To Dante Alighieri, 551
Sonnet: To his Lady Joan, of Florence, 500
Sonnet: To Love in great Bitterness, 541
Sonnet: To the Lady Pietra degli Scrovigni, 538
Sonnet: To the same Ladies, 533
Sonnets, 561
Sonnets, 988
Sonnets, 1045
Sorrow, 995
Sopolis, 335
Sound of Breaking, 1409
Souvenir, 748
Spanish Folk Songs, 652-653
Spirit of Plato, 330
Spirits Everywhere, 855
Spleen, 783
Sporus, 1133
Spring, 270
Spring, 345
Spring, 590
Spring, 666
Spring, 804
Spring in the Students' Quarter, 771
Spring Song, 939
Stanzas for Music, 1184
Students' Songs, Medieval Latin, 454
Star Morals, 902
Stanzas Concerning Love, 918
Stanzas on Mutability, 929
Strand-Thistle, 905
Suave Mari Magno, 358
Success, 1372
Sumer Is Icumen In, 1021
Summer Hours, From, 799
Summer Is Come, 557
Suspense, 1373

Sweet Disorder, 1079
Sweet William's Ghost, 1033

Take the Crust, 145
Tam Glen, 1162
Tandaradei, 822
Te Deum, The, 458
Tears, 93
Tears of the World, 98
Tell Him, O Night, 105
Telling the Bees, 1336
Temperament, 439
Terminus, 1324
Thanatopsis, 1311
The Alchemist, 1414
The Amphora, 1009
The Argument of His Book, 1076
The Ass in the Lion's Skin, 327
The Azra, 885
The Ballad of Dead Ladies, 693
The Bear's Song, 1310
The Bishop Orders his Tomb at St. Praxed's Church, 1219
The Blessed Damozel, 1240
The Blind Man at the Fair, 1294
The Blossom, 1070
The Bones of Chuang Tzu, 14
The Boy and the Flute, 987
The Bridge of Death, 682
The Camel-Rider, 112
The Capitals are Rocked, 1008
The Castle by the Sea, 860
The Cedars of Lebanon, 736
The Cheat of Cupid, or The Ungentle Guest, 263
The Child Reads an Almanac, 809
The Cicada, 30
The Clod and the Pebble, 1152
The Cocooning, 774
The Cock and the Fox, 728
The Coffin, 894
The Cold Heaven, 1284
The Collar, 1084
The Combat, 268
The Complaint of The Fair Armoress, 695
The Complaisant Swain, 423
The Conqueror Worm, 1346
The Constant Lover, 1108
The Contention of Ajax and Ulysses, From, 1089
The Cool Web, 1269
The Coyote and the Locust (Zuñi), 1309
The Craft of a Keeper of Sheep, 325
The Creation of My Lady, 605
The Cross, 1414
The Crow and the Fox, 731
The Cup, 272
The Cyclops, 312
The Daemon, from, 1007
The Daisies, 1296
The Damsel, 94
The Dancer, 146
The Days of Our Youth, 121
The Dead Man Ariseth and Singeth a Hymn to the Sun, 235
The Dead of the Wilderness, 222
The Death of Don Pedro, 628
The Death of Lesbia's Bird, 364
The Desolate City, 115
The Dispute of the Heart and Body of Francois Villon, 704
The Dog in the River, 431
The Dole of the King's Daughter, 672
The Doom of Beauty, 579
The Doves, 1282
The Downfall of the Gael, 1275
The Dream Called Life, 645
The Drunken Rose, 59
The Dust of Timas, 260
The Dying Christian to His Soul, 443
The Eagle and the Mole, 1399
The Eagle that is Forgotten, 1389
The Elected Knight, 976
The Emperor, 25
The Epicure, 267
The Epitaph of Eusthenes, 310
The Erl-King, 832
The Everlasting Voices, 1284
The Excursion, 24
The Fallow Deer at the Lonely House, 1256
The Farewell of a Virginia Slave Mother, 1334
The First Lay of Gudrun, 951
The Fisherman, 338
The Fishermen, 306
The Flower, 1086
The Flute; A Pastoral, 782
The Flute of Daphnis, 308
The Fountain, 98
The Fountain at the Tomb, 347
The Funeral, 1067
The Garden, 1110
The Garden, 1390
The Garden of Love, 1153
The Garden of Proserpine, 1248
The Garland and the Girdle, 583
The Genesis of Butterflies, 745
The Gift of Speech, 44
The Goat Paths, 1297
The Golden Age, 590
The Good Morrow, 1068
The Grass on the Mountain (Paiute), 1303
The Grasshopper, 265
The Grave and the Rose, 744

The Grave of Hipponax, 311
The Great Physician, 147
The Great Summons, 5
The Grief of Love, 118
The Hag and the Slavies, 730
The Heart on the Hill, 559
The Hippopotamus, 1406
The Holy Rose, 1010
The Home of Aphrodite, 281
The Hostess' Daughter, 862
The Immortality of Verse, 394
The Indian Serenade, 1188
The Informing Spirit, 1321
The Isles of Greece, 1185
The King of Thulé, 839
The King of Yvetot, 734
The Laborer, 782
The Laborer, 913
The Lamentation for Celin, 627
The Last Journey, 340
The Last Words, 801
The Lay of the Captive Count, 834
The Lay of Sigurd, 957
The Leaf-Picking, 775
The Life of the Blessed, 636
The Lion Over the Tomb of Leonidas, 331
The Listeners, 1265
The Little Black Boy, 1151
The Little Love-God, 344
The Lonely, 1286
The Lonely Isle, 452
The Lord of the Isle, 921
The Love Secret, 119
The Lover's Posy, 350
The Lover's Resolution, 1074
The Love Song of J. Alfred Prufrock, 1401
The Luck of Edenhall, 858
The Mad Maid's Song, 1081
The Maid Freed from the Gallows, 1031
The Maid of Orleans, 848
The Maiden, 906
The Maid's Tragedy, 1074
The Malady of Love is Nerves, 433
The Man and the Weasel, 432
The Mares of the Camargue, 773
The Mathmid, 213
The Mer-man and Marstig's Daughter, 978
The Message, 883
The Messiah, 200
The Messiah, 376
The Milk White Doe, 684
The Minstrel, 837
The Misery of Jerusalem, 202
The Misfortunes of Elphin, From, 1182
The Monument of Cleita, 311
The Moral, 693
The Morning Glory, 1
The Mountain, 1005
The Mountain in Labor, 327
The Mower to the Glowworms, 1114
The Nightingale, 1073
The North Sea, From, 897-899
The Obscure Night of the Soul, 638
The Ocean, 325
The Old Familiar Faces, 1181
The Old Man of Verona, 451
The Old Story, 341
The Old Woman, 1295
The Other World, 249
The Oven Bird, 1385
The Palm Tree, 94
The Paradox of Time, 717
The Passionate Shepherd to His Love, 1044
The Pear-Tree, 3
The Peasant and the Sheep, 997
The Penalty of Virtue, 57
The People, 599
The Philosophic Flight, 593
The Picture, 269
The Pillar of the Cloud, 1204
The Pine Tree for Diana, 412
The Piper, 1148
The Pitcher, 29
The Plaint of the Wife, 994
The Poor, 797
The Poor Children, 746
The Posy Ring, 707
The Problem, 1317
The Profane, 397
The Progress of Poesy, 1142
The Prophet, 1001
The Pulley, 1086
The Purpose of Fable-Writing, 430
The Pylons, 1270
The Quiet Kingdom, 925
The Rainy Day, 1332
The Raven, 347
The Reed, 1006
The Retreat, 1115
The Revenge, 718
The Rhodora, 1315
The Ride Round the Parapet, 863
The River of Heaven, 39
The River-Merchant's Wife: A Letter, 22
The Road, 1002
The Rod of Jesse, 201
The Roman Road, 1254
The Rose, 712
The Rose, 838

The Rose of Life, 641
The Rosemary Spray, 540
The Royal Crown, 206
The Runaway, 1384
The Scholar in the Narrow Street, 16
The Scythians, 1017
The Sea Hath Its Pearls, 873
The Seasons, 60
The Sheaves, 1380
The Shepherd-Boy and the Wolf, 327
The Shepherdess, 1258
The Shepherd's Gratitude, 373
The Shepherd's Lament, 845
The Ship of State, 405
The Sick Rose, 1152
The Siesta, 620
The Silent Town, 911
The Silent Woman, 1062
The Sisters, 1338
The Skeleton in Armor, 1328
The Sky is Up Above the Roof, 784
The Sleeper, 104
The Sleeper of the Valley, 795
The Solitary, 903
The Solitary Reaper, 1167
The Song of Lo-Fu, 12
The Song of Love, 937
The Song of the Galley, 624
The Song of the Narcissus, 102
The Song of Troylus, 556
The Sonnet of the Mountain, 706
The Sooth-Sayer, 146
The Sound of the Horn, 737
The South, 30
The Spark, 1298
The Specter, 939
The Spinning Woman, 339
The Starling Lake, 1291
The Stone, 330
The Storm, 256
The Storm, 895
The Strength of Fate, 279
The Struggle, 775
The Swallow, 269
The Swan and the Goose, 328
The Tempest, 1060
The Thought Eternal, 847
The Three Captains, 680
The Tiger, 1152
The Tomb of Crethon, 339
The Tomb of Diogenes, 331
The Transfiguration of Beauty, 582
The Tuft of Flowers, 1385
The Twa Corbies, 1030
The Twelve, from, 1013
The Two, 926
The Unrealities, 848
The Vicar of Wakefield, From, 1148
The Vine and the Goat, 326
The Voice That Beautifies the Land (Navaho), 1307
The Voyage, 890
The Wall-Flower, 984
The War-Song of Dinas Vawr, 1182
The Wazir Dandan for Prince Sharkan, 105
The Wearin' O' the Green, 1281
The Wife of Usher's Well, 1026
The Window-Glance, 890
The Wing of Separation, 96
The Wish, 271
The Woodcutter's Wife, 1394
The World, 1117
The World is Too Much With Us, 1170
The Wounded Cupid, 263
The Yacht, 370
The Youth Dreams, 937
Thekla's Song, 847
There is a Charming Land, 983
There is A Lady, 820
There is An Old City, 934
There's No Lust Like To Poetry, 456
There was a Child Went Forth, 1349
Thermoplyae, 274
They Closed Her Eyes, 647
This Compost, 1351
Thou Art Indeed Just, Lord, 1257
Thousand and One Nights, 100-112
Three Ballate, 573
Three Poems, 586
Three Songs from the Haida, 1310
Three Spring Notations on Bipeds, 1388
Thy Garden, 98
Thyrsis, 309
Time, 65
Timon's Epitaph, 334
To—? 912
To—, 1188
To a Friend Whose Work Has Come to Nothing, 1285
To a Golden Heart, Worn Round his Neck, 843
To Althea, from Prison, 1109
To an Ambitious Friend, 403
To an Isle in the Water, 1283
To Archinus, 335
To Autumn, 1198
To a Waterfowl, 1313
To Brunetto Latini, 531
To Celia, 363

To Celia, 1128
To Chloe, 406
To Cloe, 439
To Daffodils, 1079
To Dante, 506
To Dante, 606
To Dante Alighieri, 544
To Dante Alighieri, 553
To Death, of His Lady, 694
To Fuscus Aristus, 395
To Guido Cavalcanti, 531
To Helen, 1340
To Himself, 365
To his Book, 438
To his Coy Mistress, 1112
To his Friend In Elysium, 722
To his Mistress In Absence, 592
To his Wife, 451
To His Young Mistress, 713
To Italy, 607
To Li Chien, 26
To Licinius, 399
To Lighten My Darkness, 103
To Live Merrily and to Trust to Good Verses, 1077
To Lucasta, On Going to the Wars, 1109
To Maecenas, 389
To Meadows, 1082
To Monsieur De La Mothe Le Vayer, 732
To Mr. H. Lawes on His Airs, 1106
To Mr. Lawrence, 1106
To My Friends, 851
To My Mother, 883
To Night, 1189
To Penshurst, 1063
To Phidyle, 4-7
To Prote, 351
To Pyrrha, 402
To Sally, 402
To Sleep, 587
To Tan Ch'iu, 23
To Thaliarchus, 387
To the Fountain of Bandusia, 407
To the Fringed Gentian, 1314
To the Memory of Mr. Oldham, 1120
To the Moon, 713
To the Parted One, 843
To the Ship in Which Virgil Sailed to Athens, 386
To the Supreme Being, 584
To the Virgins to Make Much of Time, 1080
To Varus, 368
To Venus, 400
To Vergil, 1213
To Vittoria Colonna, 585
To William Camden, 1065
To Zion, 210
To-day a Shepherd, 632
To-morrow, 644
Treasure, 341
Tristia, 424
True Friendship, 58
True Or False, 365
True Love, 826
Truth, 1022
Tumadir Al-Khansa for Her Brother, 106
Twelfth Night, 1058
Twilight, 893
Two in August, 1408
Two Lyrics, 576

Ulalume, 1341
Ulysses, 1207
Under the Pondweed, 2
Undying Thirst, 333
United, 348
Upon a Maid that Died the Day She was Married, 342
Upon Julia's Clothes, 1079

Vanity of Vanities, 347
Veni Creator Spiritus, 457
Verses on Blenheim, 436
Vigil, 910
Vigil of Venus, The, 444
Villancico, 619
Villon's Straight Tip to all Cross Coves, 692
Virtue, 1082
Visions, 553
Vita Nuova, from La, 511
Vitae Summa Brevis Spem Nos Vetat Incohare Longam, 1264
Voice In Darkness, 913
Voluspo, 942

Wanderer's Night-Songs, 833
Warum Sind Denn Die Rosen So Blass, 874
Watchman, What of the Night? 202
We are Such Stuff as Dreams, 433
We Cared for Each Other, 888
Wealth, 146
Westphalian Song, 827
Wharton, 1134
What Makes A Happy Life, 439
When I Have Fears that I May Cease to Be, 1203
When Lilacs Last in the Door-yard Bloomed, 1361
When Thou must Home, 416
When Two are Parted, 896
When You are Old, 1283
When Young Hearts Break, 896

Where Lies the Land? 1231
White in the Moon, 1261
Whither? 870
Who knows Where, 904
Why so Pale And Wan? 1108
Wie Langsam Kriechet Sie Dahin, 881
Willie Brewed A Peck O' Maut, 1163
Winter At Tomi, 424
With a Rod No Man Alive, 821
With Rue my Heart is Laden, 1261
Without the Herdsman, 337
Woman, 4
Woo Not the World, 99
Work, 1000
Would I might go Far over Sea, 663
Written at an Inn at Henley, 1137

Ye Flowery Banks, 1157
You, Andrew Marvell, 1411
You Will Die, 4
Youth and Age, 255
Youthful Age, 271

Zechariah, 204
Zimri, 1125
Zu Fragmentarisch Ist Welt Und Leben, 882

INDEX OF AUTHORS

"A. E.", 1285-1287
Abd-ar-Rahman, I., 94
Abu 'L-'Alá Al-Ma' Arrí, 96
Addison, Joseph, 1131
Aeschylus, 275
Agathias, 329
Aiken, Conrad, 1409-1410
Akahito, 37
Al-Aswad Son of Ya'fur, 89
Alcaeus, 256
Alcman, 255
Alfieri, Vittorio, 606
Alqamah, 88
Amarou, 59
American Indian, 1301-1311
Anacreon, 263-273
Antara, 86
Antella, Simone dall', 552
Antipater, 332-333
Anytes, 333
Archias of Byzantium, 333
Aristophanes, 285-287
Arnold, Matthew, 1232-1233
Asclepiades, 334
Ausonius, 449-451

Bacchylides, 274
Baggesen, Jens, 982-983
Bahā Ad-dīn Zuhayr, 100
Barberino, Francesco da, 509-511
Barnefield, Richard, 1073
Basho, 50-51
Baudelaire, Charles, 761-770
Baum, Peter, 922
Becquer, Gustavo Adolfo, 657
Bellay, Joachim du, 718-723
Belleau, Remy, 724-726
Benét, William Rose, 1393-1395
Beranger, Pierre Jean de, 734-735
Bernard de Ventadour, 656
Bertran de Born, 659
Bhartrihari, 65
Bialik, Chaim Nachman, 213
Bierbaum, Otto Julius, 915-916
Bilhana, 66
Bion, 315-320
Björnson, Björnsterne, 986-988
Blake, William, 1148-1155
Blok, Alexander, 1012-1020
Bloomgarden, Solomon, 234
Boccaccio, Giovanni, 561-564
Bogan, Louise, 1413-1414
Browne, William, 1075-1076
Browning, Robert, 1214-1231
Bruno, Giordano, 593
Bryant, William Cullen, 1311-1315
Bryusov, Valery, 1011
Bulcke, Karl, 934
Bunin, Ivan, 1011
Burns, Robert, 1156-1164
Busse, Carl, 925
Byron, George Gordon Lord, 1184-1188

Calderon de la Barca Pedro, 645-646
Callimachus, 334-335
Camoens, Luis Vaz de, 634-636
Campanella, Tomasso, 599
Campbell, Joseph, 1294-1295
Carducci, Giosuè, 611-612
Carew, Thomas, 1088-1089
Carey, Henry, 1135-1137
Carphyllides, 336
Casa, Giovanni della, 587
Castillejo, Cristobal de, 620
Catullus, 363-373
Cavalcanti, Guido, 499-509
Cecco Angiolieri da Siena, 544-552
Cervantes, Miguel de, 638
Chan Fang-sheng, 18
Chang Hēng, 14
Charles d'Orleans, 666-667
Chaucer, Geoffrey, 1021-1024
Chenier, Andre, 732-733
Chiabrera, Gabriello, 594-599
Ch'ien Wēn-ti, Emperor, 20
Ch'ü Yüan, 5
Ciullo d'Alcamo, 463-469
Claudian, 451-452
Clough, Arthur Hugh, 1231-1232
Coleridge, Samuel Taylor, 1179-1180
Collins, William, 1146-1148
Colonne, Guido delle, 492-494
Colum-Cille, 1272
Colum, Padraic, 1292-1294
Corbiere, Tristan, 794
Crane, Hart, 1416-1418
Crinagoras, 336

Daihaku, Princess, 35
Daniel, Arnaut, 657
Dante Alighieri, 511-539
Davenant, William, 1090

Davies, William Henry, 1265
de la Mare, Walter, 1265-1266
Dehmel, Richard, 908-913
Desportes, Philippe, 727
Dickinson, Emily, 1372-1375
Dietmar von Aist, Sir, 816
Diotimus, 337
Donne, John, 1066-1072
Dowson, Ernest, 1264-1265
Drayton, Michael, 1044
Dryden, John, 1120-1128

Eliot, Thomas Stearns, 1401-1407
Emerson, Ralph Waldo, 1315-1325
Emperor Hadrian, 443
Erinna, 337
Euripides, 279-284
Evald, Johannes, 981-982

Falke, Gustav, 905-906
Filicaja, Vincenzo, 605
Firdawsí, 125
Fitger, Arthur, 901
Flaischlen, Cäsar, 914
Fletcher, John, 1074
Fletcher, John Gould, 1390-1392
Foeth, Afanasy Afanasyevich, 1008
Folcachiero de' Folcachieri, 470-471
Fort, Paul, 810
Froissart, Jean, 665
Frost, Robert, 1384-1387
Fu Hsüan, 17
Fujiwara Ietaka, 49
Fujiwara No Michinobu, 49
Fujiwara No Toshiyuki, 45

Gabriello Chiabrera, 594-599
Gautier, Theophile, 755-759
George, Stefan, 918-921
Glaucus, 337
Goethe, Johann Wolfgang von, 832-847
Goldsmith, Oliver, 1148
Gongóra, Luis de, 640
Gourmont, Remy de, 799-800
Graves, Robert, 1268-1270
Gray, Thomas, 1138-1145
Guarini, Giovanni Battista, 587-590
Guérin, Charles, 814
Guerzo di Montecanti, 476
Guillaume de Poitiers, 654
Guinicelli, Guido, 472-476

"H. D.", 1392-1393
Ha-Levi, Judah, 210
Hadrian, The Emperor, 443
Hafiz, 148-161
Hakutsu, The Priest, 37
Hardt, Ernst, 939
Hardy, Thomas, 1252-1256
Hartmann von Aue, Sir, 820
Heine, Heinrich, 871-900
Heinrich von Rugge, Sir, 817
Herbert, George, 1082-1088
Herder, Johann Gottfried von, 829-831
Heredia, José-Maria de, 782
Herrick, Robert, 1076-1082
Hesse, Hermann, 939-940
Hille, Peter, 906-907
Hioki no Ko-Okima, 35
Hitomaro, 36, 46
Hittân, son of Al-Mu' Allà of Tayyi, 95
Hofmannsthal, Hugo von, 926-929
Hölty, Ludwig Heinrich Christoph, 831
Holz, Arno, 930-933
Hopkins, Gerard Manley, 1256-1257
Horace, 386
Horikawa, Lady, 49
Housman, Alfred Edward, 1261-1262
Hugo, Victor, 739-746
Huxley, Aldous, 1267-1268

Ibn Al-Arabi, 99-100
Ibn Darrâj Al-Andalûsi, 96
Ibn Gabirol, Solomon, 206-209
Ibn Kolthúm, 87
Ibn Zaydún, 97
Ibsen, Henrik, 985
Imr El Kais, 80
Isidorus, 338
Ivanov, Vyacheslav, 1010

Jacopo da Lentino, 477-481
Jalalu'ddin Rumi, 143
Jammes, Francis, 805-809
Jayadeva, 77
Jeffers, Robinson, 1396-1399
John of the Cross, Saint, 638-640
Jonson, Ben, 1061-1066
Joyce, James, 1298
Juan Ruiz de Hita, 616
Juan II of Castile, 618
Juvenal, 442

Kalidasa, 60
Keats, John, 1194-1204
Kerner, Justinus, 885
Khansá, 93
Ki No Akimine, 44
Kipling, Rudyard, 1263
Kiyowara Fukuyabu, 47
Kriloff, Ivan Andreevich, 997

La Fontaine, Jean de, 728-731
Labe, Louise, 724
Laforgue, Jules, 800
Lamartine, Alphonse Marie Louis de, 736-737
Lamb, Charles, 1181
Landor, Walter Savage, 1181-1182
Leconte, de Lisle, 760
Ledwidge, Francis, 1300
Leon, Fra Luis de, 636
Leonidas of Alexandria, 338
Leonidas of Tarentum, 338
Leopardi, Giacomo, 607
Lermontov, Mikhail Yuryevich, 1003-1008
Liliencron, Detlev von, 904-905
Lindsay, Nicholas Vachel, 1389-1390
Li T'ai-po, 21-24
Longfellow, Henry Wadsworth, 1325-1334
Lovelace, Richard, 1109-1110
Lowell, Amy, 1380-1383
Lucianus, 340
Lucretius, 352-362
Lui Chi, 33
Lucillius, 341
Luther, Martin, 828

MacDonagh, Thomas, 1289-1291
Machado, Antonio, 650-652
Machiavelli, Niccolo, 578
MacLeish, Archibald, 1410-1412
Maeterlinck, Maurice, 801
Mahlmann, Siegfried August, 853
Maiano, Dante da, 543-544
Mallarmé, Stephane, 777-781
Marcabrun, 654
Marcela de Carpio de San Felis, Sister, 629
Marcus Argentarius, 341
Marie de France, 661
Marini, Giambattista, 600
Marlowe, Christopher, 1044
Marot, Clement, 707-708
Martial, 435-441
Marvell, Andrew, 1110-1115
Masefield, John, 1267
Mayakovsky, Vladimir, 1020
Medici, Lorenzo de', 576
Meleager, 342
Mendes, Catulle, 776
Meredith, George, 1234-1240
Meynell, Alice, 1258
Michelangelo, Buonarroti, 579
Millay, Edna St. Vincent, 1412-1413
Milton, John, 1092-1107
Mimnermus, 255
Minamoto No Shigeyuki, 47
Minnesingers, From the, 816
Mistral, Frederic, 773-775
Mitsune, 44
Molière, Jean-Baptiste Poquelin, 732
Mombert, Alfred, 924
Moore, Thomas, 1280-1281
Möricke, Eduard, 900
Moronelli di Fiorenza, Pier, 494-496
Morris, William, 1246-1247
Moschus, 321-326
Müller, Wilhelm, 870
Murger, Henri, 771-772
Musset, Alfred de, 748-753
Mu'tamid, King of Seville, 98-99

Nakatsukasa, 46
Neidhart von Reuental, Sir, 824
Nekrasov, Nikolai, 1008
Nerval, Gerard de, 747
Newman, John Henry, Cardinal, 1204
Nicarchus, 347
Niccolo degli Albizzi, 498
Nicias, 347
Nietzsche, Friedrich Wilhelm, 902-903
Nikitin, Ivan Savvich, 1009

O'Donnell, Hugh, 1273-1275
Oehlenschlager, Adam, 983
Ogarev, Nikolay Platonovich, 1002
O'Gnive, 1275-1277
Okura, 36
Omar b. Abi Rabi'a, 94
Omar Khayyám, 126-143
O'Neill, Moira, 1288-1289
Onakatomi Yoshinobu, 46
Ono No Komachi, 44
Ono No Takamura, 43
Ono No Yoshiki, 44
O'Rahilly, Egan, 1278-1279
O'Sullivan, Seumas, 1291
Ou-yang Hsiu, 30-33
Ovid, 420-430

Palladas, 347
Passerat, Jean, 710
Paulus Silentiarius, 348
Peacock, Thomas Love, 1182-1184
Pearse, Padraic, 1291-1292
Persius, 434
Petrarca, Francesco, 553-561
Petronius Arbiter, 432-433
Phaedrus, 430-432
Pistoia, Cino da, 539-543
Plato, 348
Plunkett, Joseph, 1298-1299
Po Chü-I, 26-28

Poe, Edgar Allan, 1340-1348
Poliziano, Angelo, 573
Pope, Alexander, 1131-1135
Posidippus, 350
Pound, Ezra, 1390
Princess Shoku, 49
Prinzivalle, Doria, 496-498
Prior, Matthew, 1129-1130
Propertius, 416-419
Prudhomme, Sully, 775
Pugliesi, Giacomino, 481-484
Pushkin, Alexander Sergeyevich, 998-1001

Quevedo y Villegas, Francisco de, 645
Quirino, Giovanni, 553

Raferty, 1279
Ransom, John Crowe, 1407-1409
Redi, Francesco, 602-605
Regnier, Henri de, 802-803
Reinmar von Hagenau, Sir, 818-819
Reinmar von Zweter, Sir, 825
Rilke, Rainer Maria, 934-938
Rimbaud, Arthur, 794-797
Robinson, Edwin Arlington, 1376-1380
Romains, Jules, 815
Ronsard, Pierre de, 711-718
Rosenhane, Gustav, 988-989
Rossetti, Christina, 1245-1246
Rossetti, Dante Gabriel, 1240-1244
Rueckert, Friedrich, 863-869
Rufinus, 350
Russell, George William ("A. E."), 1285-1287
Rustico di Filippo, 498

Sacchetti, Franco, 569-571
Sa'di, 144-148
Saigyo Hoshi, 47
Salis, Johann Gaudenz von, 852
Samain, Albert, 798-799
Saint Francis of Assisi, 471-472
Saint Gelais, Mellin de, 706
Sakanoye, The Lady of, 38
Salamah Son of Jandal, 90
Saldaña, Diego de, 619
San Geminiano, Folgore da, 485-492
Sandburg, Carl, 1387-1388
Sant' Angelo, Bartolomeo di, 484
Santayana, George, 1375-1376
Sanuki, Lady, 50
Sappho, 257-261
Schaukal, Richard, 925
Schiller, Friedrich von, 847-851
Scott, Sir Walter, 1178-1179
Sedley, Sir Charles, 1128-1129
Shakespeare, William, 1045-1060
Shelley, Percy Bysshe, 1188-1194
Shenstone, William, 1137
Shirley, James, 1089-1090
Sidney, Sir Philip, 1042
Sidonius Apollinaris, 453
Simmias of Thebes, 351
Simonides, 351
Simonides of Ceos, 274
Sologub, Fyodor, 1009
Sophocles, 276-277
Spender, Stephen, 1270-1271
Spenser, Edmund, 1036-1042
Spire, André, 803-804
Stagnelius, Erik Johann, 989-990
Statius, 443
Stephens, James, 1295-1298
Suckling, Sir John, 1108-1109
Su Tung-P'o, 33
Swinburne, Algernon Charles, 1248-1252
Synge, John Millington, 1287-1288

Ta' Abbata Sharra, 93
Tahureau, Jacques, 709
T'ao Ch'ien, 18, 19, 20
Tasso, Torquato, 590-593
Tate, Allen, 1414-1416
Tegner, Esaias, 990-993
Tennyson, Alfred, Lord, 1204-1214
Theocritus, 288-314
Theognis, 261-263
Teresa, Saint, 631-633
Thompson, Francis, 1258-1261
Thoreau, Henry David, 1348-1349
Tibullus, 413
Tieck, Johann Ludwig, 854
Tso Ssŭ, 16
Tsurayuki, 46
Tu Fu, 24-25
Tynan, Katherine, 1282-1283
Tyutchev, Fyodor, 1002

Uberti, Fazio degli, 564-569
Uhland, Ludwig, 855-862
Ulrich von Liechtenstein, Sir, 824

Valéry, Paul, 811-813
Vaughan, Henry, 1115-1120
Vega, Lope de, 643
Verhaeren, Emile, 797-798
Verlaine, Paul, 783-792
Viau, Theophile de, 727
Vicente, Gil, 629
Vidal, Peire, 660
Vidame de Chartres, The, 663

Vigny, Alfred de, 737-739
Vildrac, Charles, 814
Villon, François, 688-705
Virgil, 373-384
Vittorelli, Jacopo, 606
Vollmoeller, Karl Gustave, 940

Waller, Edmund, 1091-1092
Walther von der Vogelweide, Sir, 820-822
Wang Chien, 30
Wergeland, Henrik Arnold Thaulov, 984
Wexionius, Olof, 989
Whitman, Walt, 1349-1371
Whittier, John Greenleaf, 1334-1340
Wither, George, 1074-1075
Wolfram von Eschenbach, Sir, 823
Wordsworth, William, 1164-1178
Wylie, Eleanor, 1399-1401

Yakamochi, 38
Yeats, William Butler, 1283-1285
Yehoash, 234
Yüan Chēn, 29
Yuhara, Prince, 35

Zoroaster, 125